MyVirtualChild

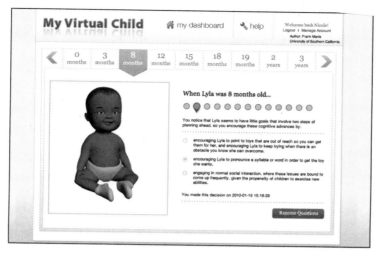

My Virtual Child   🏠 my dashboard   🔧 help   Welcome back Nicole!
Logout | Manage Account
Author: Frank Manis
University of Southern California

0 months | 3 months | **8 months** | 12 months | 15 months | 18 months | 19 months | 2 years | 3 years

When Lyla was 8 months old...

You notice that Lyla seems to have little goals that involve two steps of planning ahead, so you encourage these cognitive advances by:

- ○ encouraging Lyla to point to toys that are out of reach so you can get them for her, and encouraging Lyla to keep trying when there is an obstacle you know she can overcome.
- ◉ encouraging Lyla to pronounce a syllable or word in order to get the toy she wants.
- ○ engaging in normal social interaction, where these issues are bound to come up frequently, given the propensity of children to exercise new abilities.

You made this decision on 2010-01-15 15:18:29

Resume Questions

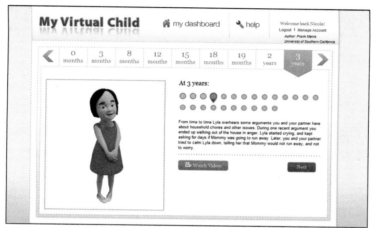

My Virtual Child   🏠 my dashboard   🔧 help   Welcome back Nicole!
Logout | Manage Account
Author: Frank Manis
University of Southern California

0 months | 3 months | 8 months | 12 months | 15 months | 18 months | 19 months | 2 years | **3 years**

At 3 years:

From time to time Lyla overhears some arguments you and your partner have about household chores and other issues. During one recent argument you ended up walking out of the house in anger. Lyla started crying, and kept asking for days if Mommy was going to run away. Later, you and your partner tried to calm Lyla down, telling her that Mommy would not run away, and not to worry.

📹 Watch Videos   Next

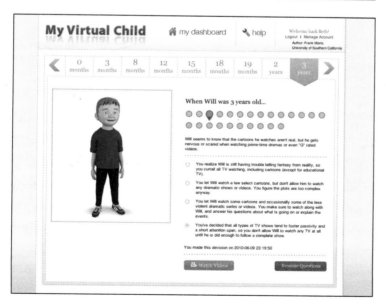

My Virtual Child   🏠 my dashboard   🔧 help   Welcome back Beth!
Logout | Manage Account
Author: Frank Manis
University of Southern California

0 months | 3 months | 8 months | 12 months | 15 months | 18 months | 19 months | 2 years | **3 years**

When Will was 3 years old...

Will seems to know that the cartoons he watches aren't real, but he gets nervous or scared when watching prime-time dramas or even "G" rated videos.

- ○ You realize Will is still having trouble telling fantasy from reality, so you curtail all TV watching, including cartoons (except for educational TV).
- ○ You let Will watch a few select cartoons, but don't allow him to watch any dramatic shows or videos. You figure the plots are too complex anyway.
- ○ You let Will watch some cartoons and occasionally some of the less violent dramatic series or videos. You make sure to watch along with Will, and answer his questions about what is going on or explain the events.
- ◉ You've decided that all types of TV shows tend to foster passivity and a short attention span, so you don't allow Will to watch any TV at all until he is old enough to follow a complete show.

You made this decision on 2010-06-09 23:19:50

📹 Watch Videos   Resume Questions

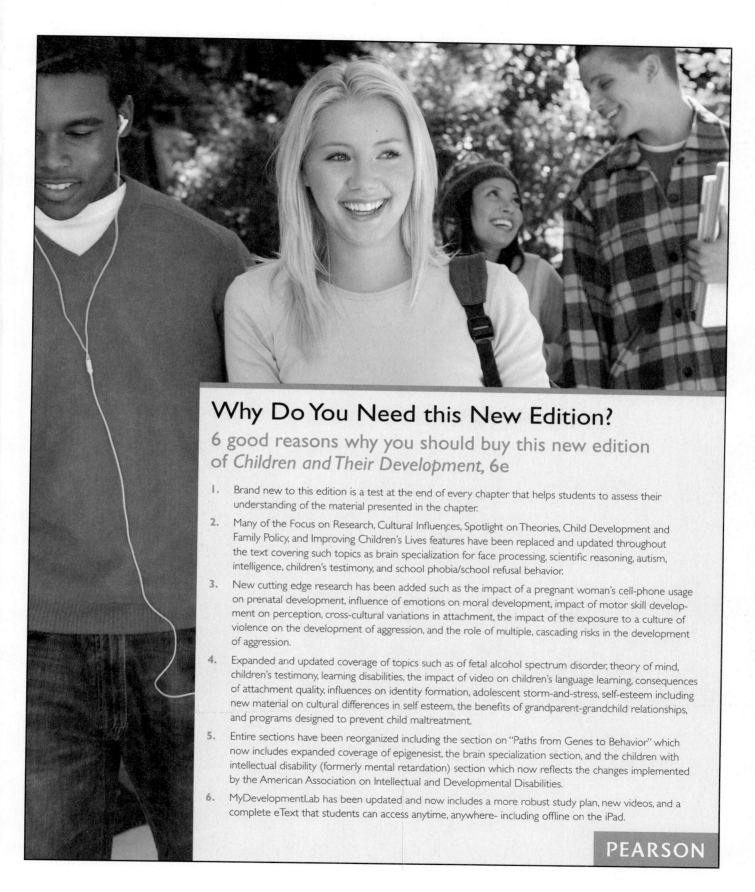

Why Do You Need this New Edition?

6 good reasons why you should buy this new edition of *Children and Their Development,* 6e

1. Brand new to this edition is a test at the end of every chapter that helps students to assess their understanding of the material presented in the chapter.

2. Many of the Focus on Research, Cultural Influences, Spotlight on Theories, Child Development and Family Policy, and Improving Children's Lives features have been replaced and updated throughout the text covering such topics as brain specialization for face processing, scientific reasoning, autism, intelligence, children's testimony, and school phobia/school refusal behavior.

3. New cutting edge research has been added such as the impact of a pregnant woman's cell-phone usage on prenatal development, influence of emotions on moral development, impact of motor skill development on perception, cross-cultural variations in attachment, the impact of the exposure to a culture of violence on the development of aggression, and the role of multiple, cascading risks in the development of aggression.

4. Expanded and updated coverage of topics such as of fetal alcohol spectrum disorder, theory of mind, children's testimony, learning disabilities, the impact of video on children's language learning, consequences of attachment quality, influences on identity formation, adolescent storm-and-stress, self-esteem including new material on cultural differences in self esteem, the benefits of grandparent-grandchild relationships, and programs designed to prevent child maltreatment.

5. Entire sections have been reorganized including the section on "Paths from Genes to Behavior" which now includes expanded coverage of epigenesist, the brain specialization section, and the children with intellectual disability (formerly mental retardation) section which now reflects the changes implemented by the American Association on Intellectual and Developmental Disabilities.

6. MyDevelopmentLab has been updated and now includes a more robust study plan, new videos, and a complete eText that students can access anytime, anywhere- including offline on the iPad.

PEARSON

Sixth Edition

Children and Their Development

Robert V. Kail
Purdue University

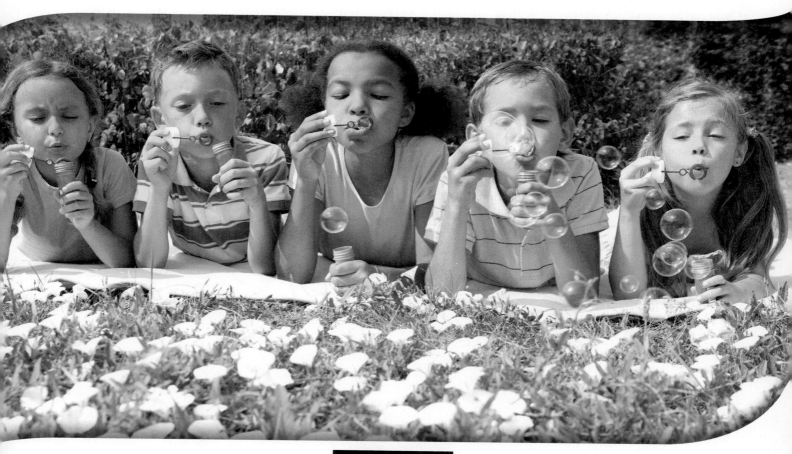

PEARSON

Boston   Columbus   Indianapolis   New York   San Francisco   Upper Saddle River   Amsterdam
Cape Town   Dubai   London   Madrid   Milan   Munich   Paris   Montreal   Toronto   Delhi
Mexico City   Sao Paulo   Sydney   Hong Kong   Seoul   Singapore   Taipei   Tokyo

Editorial Director: Craig Campanella
Editor in Chief: Jessica Mosher
Executive Editor: Jeff Marshall
Project Manager (Editorial): LeeAnn Doherty
Editorial Assistant: Michael Rosen
VP, Director of Marketing: Brandy Dawson
Executive Marketing Manager: Jeanette Koskinas
Marketing Manager: Nicole Kunzmann
Senior Managing Editor, Production: Maureen Richardson
Project Manager (Production): Annemarie Franklin
Operations Supervisor: Mary Fischer
Senior Operations Specialist: Sherry Lewis
Art Director: Leslie Osher
Interior and Cover Design: Wanda España
Cover Photo: Dmitriy Shironosov/Shutterstock
Media Project Manager: Beth Stoner
Composition/Full-Service Project Management: S4Carlisle Publishing Services/Shyam
  Ramasubramony
Printer/Binder: QuadGraphics
Cover Printer: Lehigh-Phoenix Color/Hagerstown

Credits and acknowledgments borrowed from other sources and reproduced, with permission, in this textbook appear on appropriate page within text or on page 546–547.

Library of Congress Cataloging-in-Publication Data

Kail, Robert V.
    Children and their development / Robert V. Kail.—6th ed.
        p. cm.
    Includes bibliographical references and index.
    ISBN-13: 978-0-205-03494-9 (alk. paper)
    ISBN-10: 0-205-03494-2 (alk. paper)
     1. Child development.   I. Title.
    HQ767.9.K345 2012
    305.231—dc23

                        2011019902

10 9 8 7 6 5 4 3 2 1

Student Edition: ISBN 13: 978-0-205-03494-9
                ISBN 10:   0-205-03494-2
Exam Copy: ISBN 13: 978-0-205-03528-1
                ISBN 10:   0-205-03528-0
A la Carté: ISBN 13: 978-0-205-19333-2
                ISBN 10:   0-205-19333-1

PEARSON

To Laura, Matt, and Ben

Brief Contents

Contents

Preface

Like many professors-turned-textbook-authors, I wrote this book because none of the texts available met the aims of the child-development classes that I teach. In the next few paragraphs, I want to describe those aims and how this book is designed to achieve them.

Goal 1: Use effective pedagogy to promote students' learning. The focus on a student-friendly book begins with the structure of the chapters. Each chapter consists of three or four modules that provide a clear and well-defined organization to the chapter. Each module begins with a set of learning objectives and a vignette that introduces the topic to be covered. Special topics that are set off in other textbooks as feature boxes are fully integrated with the main text and identified by a distinctive icon. Each module ends with several questions intended to help students check their understanding of the major ideas in the module.

The end of each chapter includes several additional study aids. "Unifying Themes" links the ideas in the chapter to a major developmental theme. "See for Yourself" suggests activities that allow students to observe topics in child development firsthand. "Test Yourself" questions further confirm and cement students' understanding of the chapter material. The "Key Terms" section lists all of the important boldfaced terms appearing in the chapter. The "Summary" is a concise, one-page review of the chapter.

These different pedagogical elements *do* work; students using previous editions frequently comment that the book is easy to read and presents complex topics in an understandable way.

Goal 2: Use fundamental developmental issues as a foundation for students' learning of research and theory in child development. The child-development course sometimes overwhelms students because of the sheer number of topics and studies. Of course, today's child-development science is really propelled by a concern with a handful of fundamental developmental issues, such as the continuity of development and the roles of nature and nurture in development. In *Children and Their Development,* four of these foundational issues are introduced in Chapter 1, then reappear in subsequent chapters to scaffold students' understanding. As I mentioned already, the end of the chapter includes the "Unifying Themes" feature, in which the ideas from the chapter are used to illustrate one of the foundational themes. By occurring repeatedly throughout the text, the themes remind students of the core issues that drive child-development science.

Goal 3: Teach students that child-development science draws on many complementary research methods, each of which contributes uniquely to scientific progress. In Module 1.4, I portray child-development research as a dynamic process in which scientists make a series of decisions as they plan their work. In the process, they create a study that has both strengths and weaknesses. Each of the remaining chapters of the book contains a "Focus on Research" feature that illustrates this process by showing—in an easy-to-read, question-and-answer format—the different decisions that investigators made in designing a particular study. The results are shown, usually with an annotated figure, so that students can learn how to interpret graphs. The investigators' conclusions are described, and I end each "Focus on Research" feature by mentioning the kind of converging evidence that would strengthen the authors' conclusions. Thus, the research methods introduced in Chapter 1 reappear in every chapter, depicting research as a collaborative enterprise that depends on the contributions of many scientists using different methods.

Goal 4: Show students how the findings from child-development research can improve children's lives. Child-development scientists and students alike want to know how the findings of research can be used to promote children's development. In Chapter 1 of *Children and Their Development,* I describe the different means by which researchers can use their work to improve children's lives. In the chapters that follow, these ideas come alive in two special features: "Improving Children's Lives" provides research-based solutions to common problems in children's lives; "Child Development and Family Policy" demonstrates how research has inspired change in social policies that affect children and families. From these features, students realize that child-development research really matters—parents, teachers, and policymakers can use research to foster children's development.

New to the Sixth Edition

In updating the coverage of research, I have added hundreds of new citations to research published since 2000. I have also added significant new content to every chapter. Of particular note:

Chapter 1 includes new examples of research (including an example of a field experiment) and now covers quasi-experiments as well.

Chapter 2 includes a new "Focus on Research" feature and a reorganized section on "Paths from Genes to Behavior," with expanded coverage of epigenesis.

Chapter 3 has an updated "Focus on Research" feature, expanded coverage of fetal alcohol spectrum disorder, and new material on the impact of cell-phone usage on prenatal development.

Chapter 4 has new coverage of the National Bone Health campaign, an updated "Spotlight on Theory" feature, and a much reorganized section on brain specialization that includes a new "Focus on Research" feature.

Chapter 5 has an updated "Child Development and Family Policy" feature, a new "Focus on Research" feature, and a new section on the impact of motor-skill development on perception.

Chapter 6 includes a new "Focus on Research" feature and updated coverage on theory of mind, including a new "Influencing Children's Lives" feature devoted to autism.

Chapter 7 has a much-revised section on children's eyewitness testimony, including a revised and expanded "Child Development and Family Policy" feature, along with a new "Focus on Research" feature on scientific reasoning.

Chapter 8 contains an updated "Spotlight on Theory" feature on intelligence; a completely rewritten section on children with intellectual disability (formerly, mental retardation), reflecting changes implemented by the American Association on Intellectual Development and Developmental Disabilities; and significantly revised coverage of learning disabilities.

Chapter 9 describes work on the impact of video on children's language learning and includes a new "Focus on Research" feature on the influence of "baby media."

Chapter 10 has new material on the origins of disgust, a completely revised "Improving Children's Lives" feature on school phobia (now called *school refusal behavior*), a new section on cross-cultural variants in attachment, and

much-revised coverage on the consequences of attachment quality.

Chapter 11 includes expanded coverage of influences on identity formation, expanded coverage of adolescent storm-and-stress, and much-revised coverage of self-esteem, including new material on cultural differences in self-esteem.

Chapter 12 has new "Focus on Research" and "Cultural Influences" features, new material on the influences of emotions on moral development, coverage of the role of a culture of violence on the development of aggression, and new material on the role of multiple, cascading risks in the development of aggression.

Chapter 13 includes a new "Focus on Research" feature, completely revised coverage of gender-related differences in math (with a new "Cultural Influences" feature), and an updated "Spotlight on Theories" feature.

Chapter 14 has a new "Focus on Research" feature concerning programs that help parents and children adjust to divorce, as well as expanded coverage of the benefits of grandparent–grandchild relationships and new material on programs designed to prevent child maltreatment.

Chapter 15 has expanded coverage on new technologies (video game play, social networking), along with new material on mutual antipathies and on the impact of disasters on children's development.

Support Materials

Children and Their Development, Sixth Edition, is accompanied by a superb set of ancillary materials.

PRINT AND MEDIA SUPPLEMENTS FOR THE INSTRUCTOR

Download Instructor Resources at the Instructor's Resource Center

Register or log in to the Instructor Resource Center to download textbook supplements from our online catalog or to request premium content for your school's course management system. Go to **http://www.pearsonhighered.com/educator**.

This time-saving resource provides you with electronic versions of a variety of teaching resources all in one place, allowing you to customize your lecture notes, PowerPoint slides, and media presentations.

For technical support for any of your Pearson products, you and your students can contact **http://247 .pearsoned.com**.

Save Time and Improve Results with Mydevelopmentlab

MyDevelopmentLab (**www.mydevelopmentlab.com**) is a learning and assessment tool that enables instructors to assess student performance and adapt course content without investing additional time or resources. Students benefit from an easy-to-use site through which they can test themselves on key content, track their progress, and utilize individually tailored study plans. MyDevelopmentLab is designed with instructor flexibility in mind: you decide the extent of integration into your course, from independent self-assessment for students to total course management. By transferring faculty members' most time-consuming tasks—content delivery, student assessment, and grading—to automated tools, MyDevelopmentLab enables faculty to spend more quality time with students. In addition to the activities students access through their customized study plans, instructors are provided with extra lecture notes, video clips, and activities that reflect the content areas their class may be struggling with. Instructors can bring these resources into class, or easily post them online for students to access. An access code is required and can be obtained at **www.mydevelopmentlab.com**.

My Virtual Child (ISBN 0136049346)

My Virtual Child is an interactive, Web-based simulation that allows students to act as a parent and raise their own "child." By making decisions about specific scenarios, students can raise their children from birth to age 18 and learn firsthand how their own decisions and other parenting actions affect their child over time. At each age, students are given feedback about the various milestones their child has attained; key stages of the child's development will include personalized feedback. As in real life, certain "unplanned" events may occur randomly. The just-released 2.0 version includes a complete redesign; a student personality test at the beginning of the program, the results of which will have an impact on the temperament of their child; observations video throughout the program to help illustrate key concepts; and a wider range of ethnicities for students to select from. Access codes are needed for My Virtual Child, and instructors can obtain a code at no cost via the Pearson Web site (**www.pearsonhighered .com**) or at **www.myvirtualchild.com**.

Pearson Teaching Films Lifespan Development Video (ISBN 0-205-65602-1)

These videos bring to life many key concepts discussed in the text. Each video has two parts: one with an introduction to the concept being illustrated and again with commentary describing what is taking place at crucial points in the video. These videos are also available on MyDevelopmentLab (**www.mydevelopmentlab.com**).

Instructor's Resource Manual (ISBN 0205035353)

Each chapter in the manual includes the following resources: Chapter Learning Objectives; Key Terms; Lecture Suggestions and Discussion Topics; Classroom Activities, Demonstrations, and Exercises; Out-of-Class Assignments and Projects; Lecture Notes; Multimedia Resources; Video Resources; and Handouts. Designed to make your lectures more effective and to save you preparation time, this extensive resource gathers together the most effective activities and strategies for teaching your developmental psychology course. Available for download on the Instructor's Resource Center at **www.pearsonhighered.com**.

Test Item File (ISBN 0205035345)

The test bank contains multiple-choice, true/false, short-answer, and essay questions. An additional feature for the test bank is the identification of each question as factual, conceptual, or applied. This allows professors to customize their tests and to ensure a balance of question types. Each chapter of the test-item file begins with the Total Assessment Guide, an easy-to-reference grid that makes creating tests easier by organizing the test questions by text section, question type, and nature of the question as factual, conceptual, or applied. Available for download on the Instructor's Resource Center at **www.pearsonhighered.com**.

MyTest Testing Software (ISBN 0205035329)

A powerful assessment-generation program that helps instructors easily create and print quizzes and exams. Questions and tests can be authored online, allowing instructors ultimate flexibility and the ability to efficiently manage assessments anytime, anywhere! Instructors can easily access existing questions, and can edit, create, and store tests using simple drag-and-drop techniques and Word-like controls. Metadata for each question provides information on difficulty level and page number of the corresponding text discussion. In addition, each question maps to the text's major sections and learning objectives. For more information, go to **www.PearsonMyTest.com**.

Powerpoint Slides (ISBN 0205035310)

These PowerPoint slides provide an active format for presenting concepts from each chapter and feature relevant figures and tables from the text. Available for download from the Instructor's Resource Center at **www.pearsonhighered.com**.

Video-Enhanced Powerpoint Slides (ISBN 0205226930)

These slides, available on the Instructor's Resource DVD (ISBN 0205226930), bring the book's design right into the classroom, drawing students into the lecture and providing wonderful interactive activities, visuals, and videos.

CRS Questions (ISBN 0205216277)

The Classroom Response System (CRS) facilitates class participation in lectures as well as acting as a method of measuring student comprehension. CRS also enables student polling and in-class quizzes. CRS is highly effective in engaging students with class lectures, in addition to adding an element of excitement to the classroom. Simply, CRS is a technology that allows professors to pose questions to their students through text-specific PowerPoints provided by Pearson. Student reply using handheld transmitters called "clickers," which capture and immediately display student responses. These responses are saved in the system gradebook and/or can later be downloaded to either a Blackboard or WebCT gradebook for assessment purposes. Available for download from the Instructor's Resource Center at **www.pearsonhighered.com**.

ClassPrep

Available for instructors within MyDevelopmentLab, this exciting new instructor resource makes lecture preparation easier and less time consuming. ClassPrep collects the very best class preparation resources—art and figures from our leading texts, videos, lecture activities, classroom activities, demonstrations, and much more—in one convenient online destination. You can select resources appropriate for your lecture, many of which can be downloaded directly, or you can build your own folder of resources and present them from within ClassPrep.

PRINT AND MEDIA SUPPLEMENTS FOR THE STUDENT

Coursesmart Ebook

CourseSmart Textbooks Online is an exciting choice for students looking to save money. As an alternative to purchasing the print textbook, students can subscribe to the same content online and save up to 60% off the suggested list price of the print text. With a CourseSmart eTextbook, students can search the text, make notes online, print out reading assignments that incorporate lecture notes, and bookmark important passages for later review. For more information, or to subscribe to the CourseSmart eTextbook, visit **www.coursesmart.com**.

MYDEVELOPMENTLAB

The new MyDevelopmentLab delivers **proven results** in helping students succeed. It provides **engaging experiences** that personalize, stimulate, and measure learning for each student. And, it comes from a **trusted partner** with educational expertise and an eye on the future. MyDevelopmentLab can be used by itself or linked to any learning management system.

MyDevelopmentLab delivers **proven results** in helping individual students succeed.

- Pearson MyLabs are used by millions of students each year across a variety of disciplines.
- MyDevelopmentLab works—but don't take our word for it. Visit **www.pearsonhighered.com/elearning** to read white papers, case studies, and testimonials from instructors and students that consistently demonstrate the success of our MyLabs.

MyDevelopmentLab provides **engaging experiences** that personalize, stimulate, and measure learning for each student.

- **MyVirtualChild.** This interactive simulation allows students to raise a child from birth to age 18 and monitor the effects of their parenting decisions over time.
- **Media assignments** for each chapter—including videos with assignable questions—feed directly into the gradebook, enabling instructors to track student progress automatically.
- A **personalized study plan** for each student, based on Bloom's Taxonomy, arranges content from less complex thinking (like remembering and understanding) to more complex critical thinking (like applying and analyzing). This layered approach promotes better critical thinking skills, and helps students succeed in the course and beyond.
- An **assignment calendar** allows instructors to assign graded activities, with specific deadlines, and measure student progress.
- **Pearson eText** lets students access their textbook anytime, anywhere, and any way they want—including listening online or downloading to an iPad.
- **Class Prep** collects the very best class presentation resources in one convenient online destination, so instructors can keep students engaged throughout every class.

MyDevelopmentLab comes from a **trusted partner** with educational expertise and an eye on the future.

- Pearson supports instructors with workshops, training, and assistance from Pearson Faculty Advisors—so you get the help you need to make MyDevelopmentLab work for your course.

Pearson gathers feedback from instructors and students during the development of content and the feature enhancements of each release to ensure that our products meet your needs.

MYVIRTUALCHILD

MyVirtualChild, included within MyDevelopmentLab or sold as a standalone product, is an interactive simulation that allows students to raise a child from birth to age 18 and monitor the effects of their parenting decisions over time. By incorporating physical, social, emotional, and cognitive development at several age levels, MyVirtualChild helps students think critically as they apply their coursework to the practical experiences of raising a virtual child. Throughout the program, students are given feedback about the various milestones their child has attained; key stages of the child's development will include personalized feedback. As in real life, certain "unplanned" events may occur randomly. Observational videos are included throughout the program to help illustrate key concepts. Critical thinking questions within the program help students to apply what they are learning about in class and in their textbook to their own virtual child. These questions can be assigned or used as the basis for in-class discussion.

SUPPLEMENTARY TEXTS

Contact your Pearson Education representative to package this supplementary text with *Children and Their Development, Sixth Edition:*

Current Directions in Developmental Psychology: Readings from the Association for Psychological Science, edited by Lynn S. Liben (ISBN 0-205-59750-5). This updated and exciting reader includes 30 articles that have been carefully selected for the undergraduate audience, and taken from the very accessible *Current Directions in Psychological Science* journal. These timely, cutting-edge articles allow instructors to bring their students real-world perspective—from a reliable source—about today's most current and pressing issues in developmental psychology. For details or to find out how to get these readers at no additional cost when purchased with Pearson psychology texts, please contact your local Pearson sales representative.

Acknowledgments

Textbook authors do not produce books on their own. I want to thank the many reviewers who generously gave their time and effort to help sharpen my thinking about child development and shape the development of this text. I am especially grateful to the following people who reviewed various aspects of the manuscript:

Barbara Carr, Wayland Baptist University
Sharon Carter, Davidson County Community College
Wanda Clark, South Plains College
Tara Dekkers, Northwestern College
Janet Gebelt, Westfield State University
Sara Goldstein, Montclair State University
Susan Harris, Southern Methodist University
Myra Harville, Holmes Community College
Alisha Janowsky, University of Central Florida
Jyotsna Kalavar, Penn State University-New Kensington Campus
Jennifer Kampmann, South Dakota State University
William Kimberlin, Lorain County Community College
Brenda Lohman, Iowa State University
Michael Meehan, Maryville University–St. Louis
Terri Mortensen, Nova Southeastern University
Lois Muir, University of Montana
Linda Petroff, Central Community College
Brady Phelps, South Dakota State University
Laura Pirazzi, San Jose State University
Ariane Schratter, Maryville College
Russell Searight, Lake Superior State University
Dawn Strongin, California State University–Stanislaus
Jennifer Vu, University of Delaware
Jared Warren, Brigham Young University
Gaston Weisz, Adelphi University/University of Phoenix Online
Joan Zook, SUNY Geneseo

Thanks, as well, to those who reviewed the previous editions of this book: Mark B. Alcorn, University of Northern Colorado; John Bates, Indiana University; R. M. J. Bennett, University of Dundee; Rebecca Bigler, University of Texas–Austin; Matiko Bivins, University of Houston–Downtown; James Black, University of Illinois; Tanya Boone, California State University, Bakersfield; Ty W. Boyer, University of Maryland; Renate Brenneke, Kellogg Community College; K. Robert Bridges, Pennsylvania State University; Maureen |Callanan, University of California–Santa Cruz; Li Cao, University of West Georgia; Jessica Carpenter, Elgin Community College; Andrew L. Carrano, Southern Connecticut State

University; Grace E. Cho, University of Illinois at Urbana-Champaign; Jane E. Clark, University of Maryland; Malinda Colwell, Texas Tech University; Joan Cook, County College of Morris; Sandra Crosser, Ohio Northern University; E. Mark Cummings, University of Notre Dame; Jim Dannemiller, University of Wisconsin–Madison; Lisabeth DiLalla, Southern University School of Medicine; Janet DiPietro, Johns Hopkins University; Linda Dunlap, Marist College; Kathleen Fox, Salisbury State University; Vernon C. Hall, Syracuse University; Beth Hentges, University of Houston–Clear Lake; Laura Hess, Purdue University; Erika Hoff, Florida Atlantic University; George Hollich, Purdue University; William Holt, UMASS Dartmouth; Carol S. Huntsinger, College of Lake County; Anastasia Kitsantas, George Mason University; Suzanne Koprowski, Waukesha County Technical College; Gary E. Krolikowski, SUNY Geneseo; Gary Ladd, University of Illinois; Marta Laupa, University of Nevada; Elizabeth Lemerise, Western Kentucky University; Dennis A. Lichty, Wayne State College; Frank Manis, University of Southern California; Kirsten Matthews, Harper College; Susan McClure, Westmoreland County Community College; Monica L. McCoy, Converse College; Michael S. McGee, Radford University; Jack Meacham, University of Buffalo; Rick Medlin, Stetson University; Jacquelyn Mice, Auburn University; Lonna M. Murphy, Iowa State University; Lisa Oakes, University of Iowa; Robert Pasnak, George Mason University; Brad Pillow, Northern Illinois University; Christopher Radi, University of New Mexico; Arlene Rider, Marist College; Glenn I. Roisman, University of Illinois at Urbana-Champaign; Lori Rosenthal, Lasell College; Karen Rudolph, University of Illinois; Alice C. Schermerhorn, University of Notre Dame; Tony Simon, Furman University; Cynthia Stifter, Pennsylvania State University; Marianne Taylor, University of Puget Sound; Lee Ann Thompson, Case Western Reserve University; Lesa Rae Vartanian, Indiana University–Purdue University Fort Wayne; May X. Wang, Metropolitan State College of Denver; Everett Waters, SUNY Stony Brook; Amy Weiss, University of Iowa; Adam Winsler, George Mason University; Ric Wynn, County College of Morris; Barbara Zimmerman, Dana College.

Without their thoughtful comments, this book would be less complete, less accurate, and less interesting.

I also owe a debt of thanks to many people who helped take this project from a first draft to a bound book. Wanda España designed a book that is both beautiful and functional. LeeAnn Doherty skillfully orchestrated the many activities that were involved in actually producing the book.

I am particularly grateful to three people for their special contributions to *Children and Their Development*. Jeff Marshall supported the book enthusiastically and guided its revision. Over the years, Harriett Prentiss and Susan Moss labored long to make my writing clear and inviting. To all these individuals, many, many thanks.

—*Robert V. Kail*

To the Student

In this book, we'll trace children's development from conception through adolescence. Given this goal, you may expect to find chapters devoted to early childhood, middle childhood, and the like. But this book is organized differently—around topics. Chapters 2 through 5 are devoted to the genetic and biological bases of human development, and the growth of perceptual and motor skills. Chapters 6 through 9 cover intellectual development—how children learn, think, reason, and solve problems. Chapters 10 through 15 concern social and emotional development—how children acquire the customs of their society and learn to play the social roles expected of them.

This organization reflects the fact that when scientists conduct research on children's development, they usually study how some specific aspect of how a child develops. For example, a researcher might study how memory changes as children grow or how friendship in childhood differs from that in adolescence. Thus, the organization of this book reflects the way researchers actually study child development.

ORGANIZATION OF CHAPTERS AND LEARNING AIDS

Each of the 15 chapters in the book includes two to four modules that are listed at the beginning of each chapter. Each module begins with a set of learning objectives phrased as questions, a mini-outline listing the major subheadings of the module, and a brief vignette that introduces the topic to be covered in the module. The learning objectives, mini-outline, and vignette tell you what to expect in the module.

Each module in Chapters 2 through 15 includes at least one special feature that expands upon or highlights a topic. There are five different kinds of features:

Focus on Research provides details on the design and methods used in a particular research study. Closely examining specific studies demystifies research and shows that scientific work is a series of logical steps conducted by real people.

Cultural Influences shows how culture influences children and illustrates that developmental journeys are diverse. All children share the biological aspects of development, but their cultural contexts differ. This feature celebrates the developmental experiences of children from different backgrounds.

Improving Children's Lives shows how research and theory can be applied to improve children's development. These practical solutions to everyday problems show the relevance of research and theory to real life.

Child Development and Family Policy shows how results from research are used to create social policy that is designed to improve the lives of children and their families.

Spotlight on Theories examines an influential theory of development and shows how it has been tested in research.

Three other elements of the book are designed to help you focus on the main points of the text. First, whenever a key term is introduced in the text, it appears in *blue bold italic* like this and the definition appears in **black boldface type.** This format should make key terms easier for you to find and learn. Second, about half the pages in the book include a sentence in large type that extends into the margin. This sentence summarizes a key point that is made in the surrounding text. Third, Summary Tables throughout the book review key ideas and provide a capsule account of each.

Each module concludes with "Check Your Learning" questions to help you review the major ideas in that module. There are three kinds of questions: recall, interpret, and apply. If you can answer the questions in "Check Your Learning" correctly, you are on your way to mastering the material in the module. However, do not rely exclusively on "Check Your Learning" as you study for exams. The questions are designed to give you a quick check of your understanding, not a comprehensive assessment of your knowledge of the entire module.

At the very end of each chapter are several additional study aids. "Unifying Themes" links the contents of the chapter to the developmental themes introduced in Module 1.3. "See for Yourself" suggests some simple activities for exploring issues in child development on your own. "Test Yourself" questions further confirm and cement your understanding of the chapter material. The "Key Terms" section lists all of the important terms that appear in the chapter, along with the page where each term is defined. Finally, the "Summary" provides a concise review of the entire chapter, organized by module and the primary headings within the module.

TERMINOLOGY

Every field has its own terminology, and child development is no exception. I use several terms to refer to different periods of infancy, childhood, and adolescence.

Although these terms are familiar, I use each to refer to a specific range of ages:

Newborn	Birth to 1 month
Infant	1 month to 1 year
Toddler	1 to 2 years
Preschooler	2 to 6 years
School-age child	6 to 12 years
Adolescent	12 to 18 years
Adult	18 years and older

Sometimes, for the sake of variety, I use other terms that are less tied to specific ages, such as *babies, youngsters,* and *elementary-school children.* When I do, you will be able to tell from the context what groups are being described.

I also use very specific terminology in describing research findings from different cultural and ethnic groups. The appropriate terms to describe different cultural, racial, and ethnic groups change over time. For example, the terms *colored people, Negroes, Black Americans,* and *African Americans* have all been used to describe Americans who trace their ancestry to individuals who emigrated from Africa. In this book, I use the term *African American* because it emphasizes the unique cultural heritage of this group of people. Following this same line of reasoning, I use the terms *European American* (instead of *Caucasian* or *White*), *Native American* (instead of *Indian* or *American Indian*), *Asian American,* and *Hispanic American.*

These labels are not perfect. Sometimes they blur distinctions within ethnic groups. For example, the term *Hispanic American* ignores differences between individuals who came to the United States from Puerto Rico, Mexico, and Guatemala; the term *Asian American* blurs variations among people whose heritage is Japanese, Chinese, or Korean. Whenever researchers identified the subgroups in their research sample, I use the more specific terms in describing results. When you see the more general terms, remember that conclusions may not apply to all subgroups within the ethnic group.

A FINAL WORD

I wrote this book to make child development come alive for my students at Purdue. Although I can't teach you directly, I hope this book sparks your interest in children and their development. Please let me know what you like and dislike about the book so that I can improve it in later editions. You can send email to me at **rkail@purdue .edu**—I'd love to hear from you.

About the Author

Robert V. Kail is Professor of Psychological Sciences at Purdue University. His undergraduate degree is from Ohio Wesleyan University, and his PhD is from the University of Michigan. Kail is editor of *Psychological Science* and the incoming editor *of Child Development Perspectives.* He received the McCandless Young Scientist Award from the American Psychological Association, was named the Distinguished Sesquicentennial Alumnus in Psychology by Ohio Wesleyan University, and is a fellow of the Association for Psychological Science. His research focuses on cognitive development during childhood and adolescence. Away from the office, he enjoys photography and working out. His Web site is: **http://www2 .psych.purdue.edu/~rk/home.html**

Children and Their Development

1

The Science of Child Development

1.1

Setting the Stage

1.2

Foundational Theories of Child Development

1.3

Themes in Child-Development Research

1.4

Doing Child-Development Research

Beginning as a microscopic cell, every person takes a fascinating journey designed to lead to adulthood. This trip is filled with remarkably interesting and challenging events. In this book, we'll trace this journey as we learn about the science of child development, a multidisciplinary study of all aspects of growth from conception to young adulthood. As an adult, you've already lived the years that are the heart of this book. I hope you enjoy reviewing your own developmental path from the perspective of child-development research, and that this perspective leads you to new insights into the developmental forces that have made you the person you are today.

Chapter 1 sets the stage for our study of child development. We begin, in **Module 1.1**, by looking at the philosophical foundations for child development and the events that led to the creation of child development as a new science. In **Module 1.2**, we examine theories that are central to the science of child development. In **Module 1.3**, we explore themes that guide much research in child development. Finally, in **Module 1.4**, we learn about the methods scientists use to study children and their development.

1.1 Setting the Stage

OUTLINE

Historical Views of Children and Childhood

Origins of a New Science

LEARNING OBJECTIVES

- What ideas did philosophers have about children and childhood?
- How did the modern science of child development emerge?
- How do child-development scientists use research findings to improve children's lives?

Kendra loves her 12-month-old son Joshua, but she's also eager to return to her job as a loan officer at a local bank. Kendra knows a woman in her neighborhood who has cared for some of her friends' children, and they all think she is wonderful. But down deep Kendra wishes she knew more about whether this type of care is really best for Joshua. She also wishes that her neighbor's day-care center had a "stamp of approval" from someone who knows how to evaluate these facilities.

Kendra's concern about the best way to care for her infant son is just the most recent in a long line of questions that she's had about Joshua since he was born. When Joshua was just a few days old, Kendra wondered if he could recognize her face and her voice. As her son grows, she'll continue to have questions: Why is he so shy at preschool? Should he take classes for gifted children, or would he be better off in regular classes? What can she do to be sure that he doesn't use drugs?

These questions—and hundreds more like them—touch issues and concerns that parents such as Kendra confront regularly as they do their best to rear their children. And parents aren't the only ones asking these questions. Many professionals who deal with children—teachers, health care providers, and social workers, for example—often wonder what's best for children's development. Does children's self-esteem affect their success in school? Should we believe young children when they claim they've been abused? And ultimately, government officials must decide what programs and laws provide the greatest benefit for children and their families. How does welfare reform affect families? Are teenagers less likely to have sex when they participate in abstinence-only programs?

So many questions, and all of them important! Fortunately, the field of child development, which traces physical, mental, social, and emotional development from conception to maturity, provides answers to many of them. To begin, let's look at the origins of child development as a science.

Historical Views of Children and Childhood

For thousands of years, philosophers have speculated on the fundamental nature of childhood and the conditions that foster children's well-being. Plato (428–347 BC) and Aristotle (384–322 BC), the famous Greek philosophers, believed that schools and parents had the responsibility for teaching children the self-control that would make them effective citizens. But both philosophers, particularly Aristotle, also worried that too much discipline would stifle children's initiative and individuality, making them unfit to be leaders.

Plato and Aristotle also had ideas about knowledge and how it was acquired. Plato argued that children are born with innate knowledge of many concrete objects, such as animals and people, as well as with knowledge of abstractions such as courage, love, and goodness. In Plato's view, children's sensory experiences simply trigger knowledge they've had since birth. The first time a child sees a dog, her innate knowledge allows her to recognize it as such; no learning is necessary. In contrast, Aristotle denied the existence of innate knowledge; instead, he theorized that knowledge is rooted in perceptual experience. Children acquire knowledge piece by piece, based on the information provided by their senses.

These contrasting views resurfaced during the Age of Enlightenment. The English philosopher John Locke (1632–1704), portrayed the human infant as a *tabula rasa* or "blank slate" and claimed that experience molds the infant, child, adolescent, and adult into a unique individual. According to Locke, parents should instruct, reward, and discipline young children, gradually relaxing their authority as children grow. In our opening vignette, Locke would advise Kendra that Joshua's experiences in child care will surely affect his development (though Locke would not specify how).

During the following century, Locke's view was challenged by the French philosopher Jean Jacques Rousseau (1712–1778), who believed that newborns are endowed with an innate sense of justice and morality that unfolds naturally as children grow. During this unfolding, children move through the developmental stages that we recognize today—infancy, childhood, and adolescence. Instead of emphasizing parental discipline, Rousseau argued that parents should be responsive and receptive to their children's needs. Rousseau would downplay the impact of child-care experiences per se on Joshua's development, insisting instead that the key is having caregivers who are responsive to Joshua's needs.

Rousseau shared Plato's view that children begin their developmental journeys well prepared with a stockpile of knowledge. Locke, like Aristotle 2,000 years before him, believed that children begin these journeys packed lightly, but pick up necessary knowledge along the way, through experience. These philosophical debates might have continued for millennia except for a landmark event: the emergence of child development as a science.

Origins of a New Science

The push toward child development as a science came from two unexpected events in England in the 19th century. One was the Industrial Revolution. Beginning in the mid-1700s, England was transformed from a largely rural

Q&A **QUESTION 1.1**
Morgan is an 18-month-old and her father believes that she should have a very structured day, one that includes some physical activity, time spent reading and doing puzzles, and, finally, lots of reassuring hugs and kisses. Is Morgan's dad a believer in the Rousseau or Locke view of childhood?
(Answer is on page 6.)

nation relying on agriculture to an urban-oriented society organized around factories, including textile mills that produced cotton cloth. Children moved with their families to cities and worked long hours in factories, under horrendous conditions, for little pay. Accidents were common and many children were maimed or killed. In the textile mills, for example, the youngest children often had the job of picking up loose cotton from beneath huge power looms as the machines were running.

Reformers were appalled at these conditions and worked to enact laws that would limit child labor and put more children in schools. These initiatives were the subject of prominent political debates throughout much of the 1800s; after all, the factory owners were among the most powerful people in Britain, and they actively opposed efforts to limit their access to plentiful, cheap labor. But the reformers ultimately carried the day and in the process made the well-being of children a national concern.

Also setting the stage for a new science of child development was Charles Darwin's groundbreaking work on evolution. He argued that individuals within a species differ: some individuals are better adapted to a particular environment, making them more likely to survive and to pass along their characteristics to future generations. Some scientists of the day noted similarities between Darwin's description of evolutionary change in species and age-related changes in human behavior. **This prompted many scientists—including Darwin himself—to write what became known as** *baby biographies,* **detailed, systematic observations of individual children.** The observations in the biographies were often subjective and conclusions were sometimes reached based on minimal evidence. Nevertheless, the systematic and extensive records in baby biographies paved the way for objective, analytic research.

Philosophers have long asked questions about children but only since the 19th century have scientists studied child development.

Taking the lead in the new science at the dawn of the 20th century was G. Stanley Hall (1844–1924), who generated theories of child development based on evolutionary theory and conducted many studies to determine age trends in children's beliefs about a range of topics. More importantly, Hall founded the first scientific journal in English where scientists could publish findings from child-development research. Hall also founded a child-study institute at Clark University and was the first president of the American Psychological Association.

Meanwhile, in France Alfred Binet (1857–1911) had begun to devise the first mental tests, which we'll examine in Module 8.2. In Austria, Sigmund Freud (1856–1939) had startled the world with his suggestion that the experiences of early childhood seemed to account for patterns of behavior in adulthood; and in the United States John B. Watson (1878–1958), the founder of behaviorism, had begun to write and lecture on the importance of reward and punishment for child-rearing practices. (You'll learn more about Freud's and Watson's contributions in Module 1.2.)

In 1933, these emerging scientific forces came together in a new interdisciplinary organization, the Society for Research in Child Development (SRCD). Among its members were psychologists, physicians, educators, anthropologists, and biologists, all linked by a common interest in discovering the conditions that would promote children's welfare and foster their development (Parke, 2004). In the ensuing years, SRCD has grown to a membership of more than 5,000 scientists and is now the main professional organization for child-development researchers. It continues to promote multidisciplinary research and to encourage application of research findings to improve children's lives.

> Researchers influence policy by providing needed knowledge, acting as advocates for children, by evaluating programs, and by devising model programs.

Progress in the field was halted by World War II, when most child-development scientists in the United States abandoned their research to assist the war effort (Sears, 1975). By the 1950s and 1960s, though, the field was thriving, marking the beginning of the modern era of child-development research. Most of the research described in this book has its origins in work done during these years.

Child-development researchers have learned much during these 50 years. Because of this success, a new branch of child-development research has emerged. *Applied developmental science* **uses developmental research to promote healthy development, particularly for vulnerable children and families** (Lerner, Fisher, & Giannino, 2006). Scientists with this research interest contribute to sound family policy through a number of distinct pathways (Shonkoff, 2010). Some ensure that consideration of policy issues and options is based on factual knowledge derived from child-development research: When government officials need to address problems affecting children, child-development experts can provide useful information about children and their development (Fasig, 2002). Others contribute by serving as advocates for children. Working with a child-advocacy group, child-development researchers can alert policymakers to children's needs and can argue for family policy that addresses those needs. Still other child-development experts evaluate the impact of government policies (e.g., the No Child Left Behind Act) on children and families. Finally, a particularly good way to sway policymakers is to create a working program. When researchers create a program that effectively combats problems affecting children or adolescents (e.g., sudden infant death syndrome or teenage pregnancy), this can become powerful ammunition for influencing policy (Huston, 2008).

 ANSWER 1.1
His emphasis on structure suggests that he believes in the importance of children's experiences, which is a basic concept in Locke's view of childhood.

Thus, from its origins more than 100 years ago, modern child-development science has become a mature discipline. It has generated a vast catalog of knowledge of children from which exciting discoveries continue to emanate. Scientists actively use this knowledge to improve children's lives, as we'll see in the "Child Development and Family Policy" features that appear in many chapters throughout the book. The research that you'll encounter throughout this book is rooted in a set of developmental theories that provide the foundation of modern child-development research; they are the focus of the next module.

 ## Check Your Learning

RECALL What two events set the stage for the creation of child-development science?

Who were the leaders of the new field of child development before the formation of the Society for Research in Child Development?

INTERPRET Explain the similarities between Rousseau's and Plato's views of child development; how did their views differ from those shared by Locke and Aristotle?

APPLY Suppose a child-development researcher was an expert on the impact of nutrition on children's physical and emotional development. Describe several different ways in which the researcher might help to inform public policy concerning children's nutrition.

1.2 Foundational Theories of Child Development

OUTLINE	LEARNING OBJECTIVES
The Biological Perspective	• What are the major tenets of the biological perspective?
The Psychodynamic Perspective	• How do psychodynamic theories account for development?
The Learning Perspective	• What is the focus of learning theories?
The Cognitive-Developmental Perspective	• How do cognitive-developmental theories explain changes in children's thinking?
The Contextual Perspective	• What are the main points of the contextual approach?

Will has just graduated from high school, first in his class. For his proud mother, Betty, this is a time to reflect on Will's past and ponder his future. Will has always been a happy, easygoing child—a joy to rear—and he's always been interested in learning. Betty wonders why he is so perpetually good-natured and so curious. If she knew the secret, she laughed, she could write a best-selling book and be a guest on The Colbert Report!

Before you read on, stop for a moment and think about Betty's question. How would you explain Will's interest in learning, his good nature, and his curiosity? Perhaps Betty has been a fantastic mother, doing all the right things at just the right time? Perhaps year after year his teachers quickly recognized Will's curiosity and encouraged it? Or was it simply Will's destiny to be this way? Each of these explanations is a very simple theory: Each tries to explain Will's curiosity and good nature. In child-development research, theories are much more complicated, but the purpose is the same: to explain behavior and development. **In child development, a** *theory* **is an organized set of ideas that is designed to explain and make predictions about development.**

A theory leads to hypotheses that we can test in research; in the process, each hypothesis is confirmed or rejected. Think about the different explanations for Will's behavior. Each one leads to unique hypotheses. If, for example, teachers' encouragement has caused Will to be curious, we hypothesize that he should no longer be curious if teachers stop encouraging that curiosity. When the outcomes of research are as hypothesized, the theory gains support. When results run counter to the hypothesis, the theory is incorrect and is revised. These revised theories then provide the basis for new hypotheses, which lead to new research, and the cycle continues. With each step along the way, the theory comes closer to becoming a complete account. Throughout the book, in "Spotlight on Theories" features, we'll look at specific theories, the hypotheses derived from them, and the outcomes of research testing those hypotheses.

Over the history of child development as a science, many theories have guided research and thinking about children's development. The earliest developmental theories paved the way for newer, improved theories. In this module, I describe the earlier theories that provide the scientific foundation for modern ones, because the newer theories that I describe later in the book are best understood in terms of their historical roots.

Five major theoretical perspectives have guided most research on children and their development.

Many early theories shared assumptions and ideas about children and development. Grouped together, they form five major theoretical perspectives in child-development research: the biological, psychodynamic, learning, cognitive-developmental, and contextual perspectives. As you read about each perspective in the next few pages, think about how it differs from the others in its view of development.

The Biological Perspective

According to the biological perspective, intellectual and personality development, as well as physical and motor development, are rooted in biology. One of the first biological theories, maturational theory, was proposed by Arnold Gesell (1880–1961). **According to** *maturational theory,* **child development reflects a specific and pre-arranged scheme or plan within the body.** In Gesell's view, development is simply a natural unfolding of a biological plan; experience matters little. Like Jean Jacques Rousseau 200 years before him, Gesell encouraged parents to let their children develop naturally. Without interference from adults, Gesell claimed, such behaviors as speech, play, and reasoning would emerge spontaneously according to a predetermined developmental timetable.

Maturational theory was discarded because it had little to say about the impact of the environment on children's development. However, other biological theories give greater weight to experience. *Ethological theory* **views development from an evolutionary perspective.** In this theory, many behaviors are adaptive; that is, they have survival value. For example, clinging, grasping, and crying are adaptive for infants because they elicit caregiving from adults. Ethological theorists assume that people inherit many of these adaptive behaviors.

So far, ethological theory seems like maturational theory, with a dash of evolution for taste. How does experience fit in? Ethologists believe that all animals are biologically programmed so that some kinds of learning occur only at certain ages. **A** *critical period* **is the time in development when a specific type of learning can take place; before or after the critical period, the same learning is difficult or even impossible.**

One well-known example of a critical period comes from the work of Konrad Lorenz (1903–1989), a zoologist who noticed that newly hatched chicks follow their mother about. He theorized that chicks are biologically programmed to follow the first moving object that they see. **Usually this was the mother, so following her was the first step in** *imprinting,* **creating an emotional bond with the mother.** Lorenz tested his theory by showing that if he removed the mother immediately after chicks hatched and replaced her with another moving object, the chicks would follow that object and treat it as "Mother." As the photo shows, this included Lorenz himself! But the chick had to see the moving object within about a day of hatching. Otherwise, the chick would not imprint on the moving object. In other words, the critical period for imprinting lasts about a day; when chicks experience the moving object outside of the critical period, imprinting does not take place. Even though the underlying mechanism is biological, experience is essential for triggering programmed, adaptive behaviors.

Newly hatched chicks follow the first moving object they see, treating it as "mother" even when it's a human.

Ethological theory and maturational theory both highlight the biological bases of child development. Biological theorists remind us that children's behavior is the product of a long evolutionary history. Consequently, a biological theorist would tell Betty that Will's good nature and his outstanding academic record are both largely products of his biological endowment—his heredity.

The Psychodynamic Perspective

The psychodynamic perspective is the oldest scientific perspective on child development, originating in the work of Sigmund Freud (1856–1939) in the late 19th and early 20th centuries. Freud was a physician who specialized in diseases of the nervous system. Many of his patients were adults whose disorders seemed to have no obvious biological causes. As Freud listened to his patients describe their problems and their lives, he became convinced that early experiences establish patterns that endure throughout a person's life. **Using his patients' case histories, Freud created the first** *psychodynamic theory,* **which holds that development is largely determined by how well people resolve conflicts they face at different ages.**

The role of conflict is evident in Freud's description of the three primary components of personality. **The** *id* **is a reservoir of primitive instincts and drives.** From birth, the id presses for immediate gratification of bodily needs and wants. A hungry baby crying illustrates the id in action. **The** *ego* **is the practical, rational component of personality.** The ego begins to emerge during the first year of life, as infants learn that they cannot always have what they want. The ego tries to resolve conflicts that occur when the instinctive desires of the id encounter the obstacles of the real world. The ego often tries to channel the id's impulsive demands into socially more acceptable channels. For example, in the photo, the child without the toy is obviously envious of the child who has the toy. According to Freud, the id would urge the child to grab the toy, but the ego would encourage the child to play with the peer and, in the process, the attractive toy.

The third component of personality, the *superego,* **is the "moral agent" in the child's personality.** It emerges during the preschool years as children begin to internalize adult standards of right and wrong. If the peer in the previous example left the attractive toy unattended, the id might tell the child to grab the toy and run; the superego would remind the child that taking another's toy would be wrong.

Today, scientists recognize many shortcomings that undermine Freud's theory as a whole (e.g., some key ideas are too vague to be tested in research). Nevertheless, two of Freud's insights have had lasting impact on child-development research and theory. First, he noted that early experiences can have enduring effects on children's development. Second, he suggested that children often experience conflict between what they want to do and what they know they should do.

ERIKSON'S PSYCHOSOCIAL THEORY. Erik Erikson (1902–1994), Freud's student, embraced Freud's idea of conflict, but he emphasized the psychological and

Q&A **QUESTION 1.2**
Keunho and Young-shin are sisters who moved to Toronto from Korea when they were 15 and 10 years old, respectively. Although both of them have spoken English almost exclusively since their arrival in Canada, Keunho still speaks with a bit of an accent and occasionally makes grammatical errors; Young-shin's English is flawless—she speaks like a native. How could you explain Young-shin's greater skill in terms of a critical period?
(Answer is on page 15.)

According to Freud's theory, the id would encourage the child on the right to grab the toy away from the other child, but the superego would remind her that this would be wrong.

TABLE 1-1

ERIKSON'S EIGHT STAGES OF PSYCHOSOCIAL DEVELOPMENT

Psychosocial Stage	Age	Challenge
Basic trust versus mistrust	Birth to 1 year	To develop a sense that the world is safe, a "good place"
Autonomy versus shame and doubt	1 to 3 years	To realize that one is an independent person who can make decisions
Initiative versus guilt	3 to 6 years	To develop a willingness to try new things and to handle failure
Industry versus inferiority	6 years to adolescence	To learn basic skills and to work with others
Identity versus identity confusion	Adolescence	To develop a lasting, integrated sense of self
Intimacy versus isolation	Young adulthood	To commit to another in a loving relationship
Generativity versus stagnation	Middle adulthood	To contribute to younger people, through child rearing, child care, or other productive work
Integrity versus despair	Late life	To view one's life as satisfactory and worth living

social aspects of conflict rather than the biological and physical aspects. **In Erikson's** *psychosocial theory*, **development consists of a sequence of stages, each defined by a unique crisis or challenge.** The complete theory includes the eight stages shown in Table 1-1. The name of each stage reflects the challenge that individuals face at a particular age. For example, the challenge for young adults is to become involved in a loving relationship. Adults who establish this relationship experience intimacy; those who don't experience isolation.

Erikson also argued that the earlier stages of psychosocial development provide the foundation for the later stages. For example, adolescents who do not meet the challenge of developing an identity will not establish truly intimate relationships. Instead, they will become overly dependent on their partners as a source of identity.

Whether we call them conflicts, challenges, or crises, the psychodynamic perspective emphasizes that the trek to adulthood is difficult because the path is strewn with obstacles. Outcomes of development reflect the manner and ease with which children surmount life's barriers. When children overcome early obstacles easily, they are better able to handle the later ones. Returning to this module's opening vignette, a psychodynamic theorist would tell Betty that Will's cheerful disposition and his academic record suggest that he handled life's early obstacles well, which is a good sign for his future development.

The Learning Perspective

Learning theorists endorse John Locke's view that the infant's mind is a blank slate on which experience writes. John Watson (1878–1958) was the first theorist to apply this approach to child development. He argued that learning determines what children will be. For Watson, experience was all that mattered in determining the course of development.

The learning perspective emphasizes the role of experience in children's development.

EARLY LEARNING THEORIES. Watson did little research to support his claims, but B. F. Skinner (1904–1990) filled this gap. **Skinner studied** *operant conditioning,* **in which the consequences of a behavior determine whether a behavior is repeated in the**

future. Skinner showed that two kinds of consequences were especially influential. **A *reinforcement* is a consequence that increases the future likelihood of the behavior that it follows.** Positive reinforcement consists of giving a reward—such as chocolate, gold stars, or paychecks—to increase the likelihood of repeating a previous behavior. When parents want to encourage their daughter to clean her room, they could use positive reinforcement by rewarding her with praise, food, or money whenever she completed the chore. Negative reinforcement consists of rewarding people by taking away unpleasant things. The same parents could use negative reinforcement by saying that whenever their daughter cleaned her room, she wouldn't have to wash the dishes or fold laundry.

A *punishment* is a consequence that decreases the future likelihood of the behavior that it follows. Punishment suppresses a behavior by either adding something aversive or by withholding a pleasant event. When the child failed to clean her room, the parents could punish her by making her do extra chores (adding something aversive) or by not allowing her to watch television (withholding a pleasant event).

Applied properly, reinforcement and punishment are indeed powerful influences on children. However, researchers discovered that children sometimes learn without reinforcement or punishment. **Children learn much simply by watching those around them, which is known as *imitation* or *observational learning.*** For example, imitation occurs when one toddler throws a toy after seeing a peer do so, or when a school-age child offers to help an older adult carry groceries because she's seen her parents do the same, or, as in the photo, when a son tries to shave like his father.

Throughout development, children learn much from imitating the actions of others.

SOCIAL COGNITIVE THEORY.   Perhaps imitation makes you think of "monkey-see, monkey-do," or simple mimicking. Early investigators had this view, too, but research quickly showed that this was wrong. Children do not always imitate what they see around them. Instead, children are more likely to imitate when the person they see is popular, smart, or talented. They're also more likely to imitate when the behavior they see is rewarded than when it is punished. Findings like these imply that imitation is more complex than sheer mimicry. Children do not mechanically copy what they see and hear; instead, they look to others for information about appropriate behavior. When popular, smart peers are reinforced for behaving in a particular way, it makes sense to imitate them.

Albert Bandura (1925–) based his *social cognitive theory* on this more complex view of reward, punishment, and imitation. Bandura calls his theory "cognitive" because he believes that children are actively trying to understand what goes on in their world; the theory is "social" because, along with reinforcement and punishment, what other people do is an important source of information about the world (Bandura, 2000, 2006).

Bandura also argues that experience gives children a sense of *self-efficacy,* beliefs about their own abilities and talents. Self-efficacy beliefs help determine when children will imitate others. A child who sees himself as athletically untalented, for example, will not try to imitate LeBron James dunking a basketball, despite the fact that LeBron is obviously talented and popular. But the youngster in the photo is likely to imitate LeBron, because he believes he's talented and thus it makes sense to try to imitate LeBron. Thus, whether children imitate others depends on who the other person is,

When someone is as talented as LeBron James, it makes sense for others to try to imitate him—and young children often do just that (mimic LeBron and other talented people).

whether that person's behavior is rewarded, and the children's beliefs about their own talents.

Bandura's social cognitive theory is a far cry from Skinner's operant conditioning. The social cognitive child, who actively interprets events, has replaced the operant conditioning child, who responds mechanically to reinforcement and punishment. Nevertheless, Skinner, Bandura, and all learning theorists share the view that experience propels children along their developmental journeys. Returning to this module's opening scenario, they would tell Betty that she can thank experience for making Will both happy and successful academically.

The Cognitive-Developmental Perspective

The *cognitive-developmental perspective* **focuses on how children think and on how their thinking changes as they grow.** Jean Piaget (1896–1980) proposed the best known of these theories. He believed that children naturally try to make sense of their world. That is, throughout infancy, childhood, and adolescence, youngsters want to understand the workings of both the physical and the social world. For example, infants want to know about objects: "What happens when I push this toy off the table?" And babies want to know about people: "Who is this person who feeds and cares for me?"

Piaget argued that as children try to comprehend their world, they act like scientists in creating theories about the physical and social worlds. They try to weave all that they know about objects and people into a complete theory. Children's theories are tested daily by experience because their theories lead them to expect certain things to happen. As with real scientific theories, when the predicted events occur, a child's belief in her theory grows stronger. When the predicted events do not occur, the child must revise her theory. For example, think about the baby in the photo and her theory of objects like the rattle she's holding. Her theory of objects might include the idea that "If I let go, the rattle will fall to the floor." If the infant drops some other object—a plate or an article of clothing—she will find that it, too, falls to the floor and she can make the theory more general: Objects that are dropped fall to the floor.

Piaget also believed that at a few critical points in development, children realize their theories have basic flaws. When this happens, they revise their theories radically. These changes are so fundamental that the revised theory is, in many respects, a brand-new theory. Piaget claimed that radical revisions occur three times in development: once at about age 2, a second time at about age 7, and a third time just before adolescence. These radical changes mean that children go through four distinct stages in cognitive development. Each stage represents a fundamental change in how children understand and organize their environment, and each stage is characterized by more sophisticated types of reasoning. For example, the sensorimotor stage begins at birth and lasts until about age 2. As the name implies, sensorimotor thinking is closely linked to the infant's sensory and motor skills. This stage and the three later stages are shown in Table 1-2.

According to Piaget, children's thinking becomes more sophisticated as they develop, reflecting the more sophisticated theories that children create. Returning to our opening scenario, Piaget would have little to say about Will's good nature. As for his academic success, Piaget would explain that all children naturally want to understand their worlds; Will is simply unusually

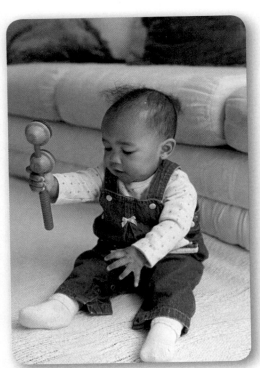

In Piaget's theory, even infants have rudimentary theories about objects and their properties.

TABLE 1-2

PIAGET'S FOUR STAGES OF COGNITIVE DEVELOPMENT

Stage	Approximate Age	Characteristics
Sensorimotor	Birth to 2 years	Infant's knowledge of the world is based on senses and motor skills. By the end of the period, infant uses mental representations.
Preoperational	2 to 6 years	Child learns how to use symbols such as words and numbers to represent aspects of the world, but relates to the world only through his or her perspective.
Concrete operational	7 to 11 years	Child understands and applies logical operations to experiences, provided they are focused on the here and now.
Formal operational	Adolescence and beyond	Adolescent or adult thinks abstractly, speculates on hypothetical situations, and reasons deductively about what may be possible.

---

skilled in this regard. In Module 6.1, we will further explore Piaget's contribution to our understanding of cognitive development, as well as more modern theories.

The Contextual Perspective

Most developmentalists agree that the environment is an important force in development. Traditionally, however, most theories of child development have emphasized environmental forces that affect children directly. Examples of direct environmental influences would be a parent praising a child, an older sibling teasing a younger one, and a nursery-school teacher discouraging girls from playing with trucks. These direct influences are important in children's lives, but in the contextual perspective they are simply one part of a much larger system, in which each element of the system influences all other elements. This larger system includes one's parents and siblings as well as important individuals outside of the family, such as extended family, friends, and teachers. The system also includes institutions that influence development, such as schools, television, the workplace, and a church, temple, or mosque.

All these people and institutions fit together to form a person's *culture*—**the knowledge, attitudes, and behavior associated with a group of people.** *Culture* can refer to a particular country or people (e.g., French culture); to a specific point in time (e.g., popular culture of the 1990s); or to groups of individuals who maintain specific, identifiable cultural traditions, such as African American families that celebrate Kwanzaa. A culture provides the context in which a child develops and thus is a source of many important influences on development throughout childhood and adolescence.

One of the first theorists to emphasize cultural context in children's development was Lev Vygotsky (1896–1934). A Russian psychologist, Vygotsky focused on ways that adults convey to children the beliefs, customs, and skills of their culture. Vygotsky believed that because a fundamental aim of all societies is to enable children to acquire essential cultural values and skills, every aspect of a child's development must be considered against this backdrop. For example, most parents in the United States want their children to work hard in school and to go to college. In the same way, Efe parents living in Africa want their children to learn to gather food, build houses, and, as you can see in the photo, to hunt; these skills are fundamental to the Efe because

According to the contextual view, parents help children master the essential values and skills of their culture, such as learning how to hunt.

The contextual approach emphasizes the many different elements of culture that affect children's development.

they are critical for survival in their environment. Vygotsky viewed development as an apprenticeship in which children develop when they work with skilled adults, including teachers and parents. In Module 6.2, we'll learn more about Vygotsky's distinctive contributions to our understanding of cognitive development.

Returning to our opening vignette, Vygotsky would agree with learning theorists in telling Betty that the environment has been pivotal in her son's amiable disposition and his academic achievements. However, the contextual theorist would insist that "environment" means much more than the reinforcements, punishments, and observations that are central to learning theory. The contextual theorist would emphasize the manner in which Betty had conveyed the value of curiosity and academic success to her son; also contributing to Will's development was Betty's membership in a cultural group that values doing well in school.

THE BIG PICTURE. Comparing the basics of five major perspectives in six pages is like trying to see all the major sights of a large city in a day: It can be done, but it's demanding and, after a while, everything blurs together. Relax. The Summary Table gives a capsule account of all five perspectives and their important theories.

These perspectives are the basis for contemporary theories that I introduce throughout this book. For example, Piaget's theory is the forerunner of modern explanations of infants' understanding of objects and of preschoolers' theory of mind (both described in Module 6.3). Similarly, Erikson's theory has contributed to work on mother–infant attachment (see Module 10.3) and formation of identity during adolescence (see Module 11.1).

The modern theories described throughout the book are derived from all five perspectives listed in the Summary Table. Why? Because no single perspective provides

SUMMARY TABLE

CHARACTERISTICS OF DEVELOPMENTAL PERSPECTIVES

Perspective	Key Assumptions	Illustrative Theories
Biological	Development is determined primarily by biological forces.	*Maturational theory:* emphasizes development as a natural unfolding of a biological plan
		Ethological theory: emphasizes that children's and parents' behavior has adapted to meet specific environmental challenges
Psychodynamic	Development is determined primarily by how a child resolves conflicts at different ages.	*Freud's theory:* emphasizes the conflict between primitive biological forces and societal standards for right and wrong
		Erikson's theory: emphasizes the challenges posed by the formation of trust, autonomy, initiative, industry, and identity
Learning	Development is determined primarily by a child's environment.	*Skinner's operant conditioning:* emphasizes the role of reinforcement and punishment
		Bandura's social cognitive theory: emphasizes children's efforts to understand their world, using reinforcement, punishment, and others' behavior
Cognitive-Developmental	Development reflects children's efforts to understand the world.	*Piaget's theory:* emphasizes the different stages of thinking that result from children's changing theories of the world
Contextual	Development is influenced by immediate and more distant environments, which typically influence each other.	*Vygotsky's theory:* emphasizes the role of parents (and other adults) in conveying culture to the next generation

a truly complete explanation of all aspects of children's development. Theories from the cognitive-developmental perspective are useful for understanding how children's thinking changes as they grow older. By contrast, theories from the contextual and learning perspectives are particularly valuable in explaining how environmental forces such as parents, peers, schools, and culture influence children's development. By drawing on all the perspectives, we'll be better able to understand the different forces that contribute to children's development. Just as you can better appreciate a beautiful painting by examining it from different vantage points, child-development researchers often rely on multiple perspectives to understand why children develop as they do.

Another way to understand the forces that shape development is to consider several themes of development—themes that cut across different theoretical perspectives and specific research topics. We'll look at these themes in Module 1.3.

 ANSWER 1.2

Perhaps there is a critical period for language learning that ends at the beginning of adolescence. That is, children learn to speak a language like a native if exposed to that language extensively in childhood but not if most of their exposure takes place later, in adolescence and young adulthood. (We'll learn more about such a critical period in Chapter 9.)

 Check Your Learning

RECALL Describe different theories that typify the biological perspective on child development.

What are the main features of the contextual perspective on child development?

INTERPRET Explain the similarities and the differences in Erikson's and Piaget's stage theories of children's development.

APPLY A friend complains that his 1-year-old seems to cry a lot compared to other 1-year-olds. How would theorists from each of the five perspectives listed in the Summary Table is on previous page explain his son's excessive crying?

 1.3 **Themes in Child-Development Research**

OUTLINE	LEARNING OBJECTIVES
Early Development Is Related to Later Development but Not Perfectly	• How well can developmental outcomes be predicted from early life?
Development Is Always Jointly Influenced by Heredity and Environment	• How do heredity and environment influence development?
Children Influence Their Own Development	• What role do children have in their own development?
Development in Different Domains Is Connected	• Is development in different domains connected?

Javier Suarez smiled broadly as he held his newborn grandson for the first time. So many thoughts rushed into his mind: What would Ricardo experience growing up? Would the poor neighborhood they live in prevent him from reaching his potential? Would the family genes for good health be passed on? How would Ricardo's life growing up as a Chicano in the United States differ from Javier's own experiences growing up in Mexico?

Like many grandparents, Javier wonders what the future holds for his grandson. His questions actually reflect four basic themes in development that are the focus of this module. These themes will provide you with a foundation for understanding and organizing the many specific facts about child development that fill the rest of this book. To help you do this, at the end of Chapters 2 through 15, the "Unifying Themes" feature links the contents of the chapter to one of the themes.

Early Development Is Related to Later Development but Not Perfectly

This theme concerns the predictability of development. Do you believe that happy, cheerful 5-year-olds remain outgoing and friendly throughout their lives? If you do, this shows that you believe development is a continuous process: According to this view, once a child begins down a particular developmental path, he or she stays on that path throughout life. In other words, if Ricardo is friendly and smart as a 5-year-old, he should be friendly and smart as a 15- and 25-year-old. The other view, that development is not continuous, is shown in the cartoon. Sweet, cooperative Trixie has become a demanding, assertive child. According to this view, Ricardo might be friendly and smart as a 5-year-old but obnoxious and foolish at 15 and quiet but wise at 25! **Thus, the** *continuity–discontinuity* **issue is really about the "relatedness" of development: Are early aspects of development consistently related to later aspects?**

In reality, neither of these views is accurate. Development is not perfectly predictable. A friendly, smart 5-year-old does not guarantee a friendly, smart 15- or 25-year-old, but the chances of a friendly, smart adult are greater than if the child were obnoxious and foolish. There are many ways to become a friendly and smart 15-year-old; being a friendly and smart 5-year-old is not a required step, but it is probably the most direct route!

Development Is Always Jointly Influenced by Heredity and Environment

I want to introduce this theme with a story about my sons. Ben, my first son, was a delightful baby and toddler. He awoke each morning with a smile on his face, eager to start another fun-filled day. Ben was rarely upset; when he was, he was quickly consoled by being held or rocked. I presumed that his cheerful disposition must

 QUESTION 1.3

As a child, Heather was painfully shy and withdrawn, but as an adult she was very outgoing, the life of many a party. What does Heather's life tell us about the continuity or discontinuity of shyness? *(Answer is on page 18.)*

Trixie's transition from a cooperative child to a demanding one illustrates discontinuity in development.

reflect fabulous parenting. Consequently, I was stunned when my second son, Matt, spent much of the first year of his life being fussy and cranky. He was easily irritated and hard to soothe. Why wasn't the all-star parenting that had been so effective with Ben working with Matt? The answer, of course, is that Ben's parenting wasn't the sole cause of his happiness. I thought environmental influences accounted for his amiable disposition, but in fact, biological influences also played an important role.

Virtually all aspects of development are determined by the combined forces of heredity and environment.

    This anecdote illustrates the *nature–nurture* **issue: What roles do biology (nature) and environment (nurture) play in child development?** If Ricardo is outgoing and friendly, is it due to his heredity or his experiences? Scientists once hoped to answer questions like this by identifying either heredity or environment as *the* cause. Their goal was to be able to say, for example, that intelligence was due to heredity or that personality was due to experience. Today, we know that virtually no aspects of child development are due exclusively to either heredity or environment. Instead, development is always shaped by both—nature and nurture interact (Sameroff, 2010). In fact, a major goal of child-development research is to understand how heredity and environment jointly determine children's development.

Children Influence Their Own Development

I often ask students in my child-development classes about their plans for when they have children. How will they rear them? What do they want their children to grow up to be? It's interesting to hear students' responses. Many have big plans for their future children. It's just as interesting, though, to watch students who already have children roll their eyes in a "You don't have a clue" way at what the others say. The parent-students in class admit that they, too, once had grand designs about child rearing. What they quickly learned, however, was that their children shaped the way in which they parented.

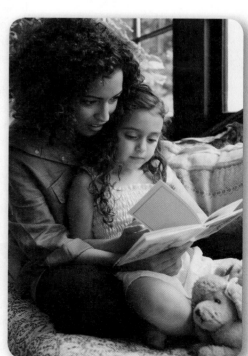

    These two points of view illustrate the *active–passive child* **issue: Are children simply at the mercy of the environment (passive child), or do children actively influence their own development through their own unique individual characteristics (active child)?** The passive view corresponds to Locke's description of the child as a blank slate on which experience writes; the active view corresponds to Rousseau's view of development as a natural unfolding that takes place within the child. Today, we know that experiences are indeed crucial, but not always in the way Locke envisioned. Often, it's a child's interpretation of experiences that shapes his or her development. From birth, children like Ricardo are trying to make sense of their world, and in the process they help shape their own destinies.

    Also, a child's unique characteristics may cause him or her to have some experiences but not others. Think about the child in the photo, who loves having parents read picture books. Her excitement is contagious and makes her parents eager to read to her night after night. In contrast, if a child squirms or seems bored during reading, parents may not take the time to read to the child. In both cases, children's behavior during reading influences whether parents read to them in the future.

This youngster's obvious enjoyment makes it more likely that her parents will read to her more in the future, showing that children can influence their own development.

Development in Different Domains is Connected

Child-development researchers usually examine different domains or areas of development, such as physical growth, cognition, language, personality, and social relationships. One researcher might study how children learn to speak grammatically; another might explore children's reasoning about moral issues. Of course, you should *not* think of each aspect of development as an independent entity, completely separate from the others. To the contrary, development in different domains is always intertwined. Cognitive and social development, for example, are not independent; advances in one area affect advances in the other. Ricardo's cognitive growth (e.g., he becomes an excellent student) will influence his social development (e.g., he becomes friends with peers who share his enthusiasm for school).

Having introduced the themes, let's see them together once before we move on.

- *Continuity:* Early development is related to later development but not perfectly.
- *Nature and nurture:* Development is always jointly influenced by heredity and environment.
- *Active children:* Children influence their own development.
- *Connections:* Development in different domains is connected.

Most child-development scientists would agree that these are important general themes in children's development. However, just as lumber, bricks, pipe, and wiring can be used to assemble an incredible assortment of houses, these themes show up in different ways in the major theories of child development. Think, for example, about the nature–nurture issue. Of the five perspectives, the biological perspective is at one extreme in emphasizing the impact of nature; at the other extreme are the learning and contextual perspectives, which emphasize nurture.

The perspectives also see different degrees of connectedness across different domains of development. Piaget's cognitive-developmental theory takes the hardest line: Because children strive to have a single integrated theory to explain the world, cognitive and social growth are closely interconnected. That is, because children interpret all aspects of their lives with the same unified view of the world, everything is linked. The learning perspective, in contrast, holds that the degree of connectedness depends entirely on the nature of environmental influences. Similar environmental influences in different domains of children's lives produce many connections; dissimilar environmental influences would produce few connections.

 ANSWER 1.3
In Heather's life, shyness was definitely discontinuous. Even though Heather was shy early in life, she was not shy later.

 Check Your Learning

RECALL Describe the difference between continuous development and discontinuous development.

Cite examples showing that development in different domains is connected.

INTERPRET Explain the difference between nature and nurture and how these forces are thought to affect children's development.

APPLY How might parents respond differently to a very active child compared to a very quiet child?

Doing Child-Development Research

OUTLINE	LEARNING OBJECTIVES
Measurement in Child-Development Research	• How do scientists measure topics of interest in children's development?
General Designs for Research	• What general research designs are used in child-development research?
Designs for Studying Age-Related Change	• What designs are unique to the study of age-related change?
Ethical Responsibilities	• What ethical procedures must researchers follow?
Communicating Research Results	• How do researchers communicate results to other scientists?

Leah and Joan are both mothers of 10-year-old boys. Their sons have many friends, but the basis for the friendships is not obvious to the mothers. Leah believes that opposites attract: children form friendships with peers who have complementary interests and abilities. Joan doubts this; her son seems to seek out other boys who are near-clones of himself in their interests and abilities.

Suppose Leah and Joan know you're taking a course in child development, so they ask you to settle their argument. You know, from Module 1.2, that Leah and Joan each have simple theories about children's friendships. Leah's theory is that complementary children are more often friends, whereas Joan's theory is that similar children are more often friends. You know that these theories should be tested with research. But how? In fact, like all scientists, child-development researchers follow the scientific method, which involves several steps:

- Identify a question to be answered or a phenomenon to be understood.
- Form a hypothesis that is a tentative answer to the question or a tentative explanation of the phenomenon.
- Select a method for collecting data that can be used to evaluate the hypothesis.

In our vignette, Leah and Joan have already taken the first two steps: They want to know why children become friends and each has a simple theory of this phenomenon, a theory that can be used to generate hypotheses. What remains is to find a method for collecting data, which is our focus for the rest of this module. How do child-development scientists select methods for gathering evidence that's useful for testing hypotheses about child development?

In fact, in devising methods, child-development scientists must make several important decisions. They need to decide how to measure the phenomenon of interest; they must design their study; they must be sure their proposed research respects the rights of the individuals participating; and, after the study is complete, they must communicate their results to other researchers.

Child-development researchers do not always stick to this sequence of steps. For example, researchers usually consider the rights of research participants as they make each of the other decisions, perhaps rejecting a procedure because it violates those rights. Nevertheless, for simplicity, I will use this sequence to describe the steps in doing developmental research.

> Child-development researchers use the scientific method in which they formulate hypotheses, then collect data to evaluate those hypotheses.

Measurement in Child-Development Research

Research usually begins by deciding how to measure the topic or behavior of interest. For example, the first step toward answering Leah's and Joan's question about friendships would be to decide how to measure friendships. Child-development researchers typically use one of four approaches: observing systematically, using tasks to sample behavior, asking children for self reports, and measuring physiological responses.

In naturalistic observation, researchers record children's spontaneous behavior in natural environments, such as this school cafeteria.

SYSTEMATIC OBSERVATION. **As the name implies,** *systematic observation* **involves watching children and carefully recording what they do or say.** Two forms of systematic observation are common. **In** *naturalistic observation,* **children are observed as they behave spontaneously in some real-life situation.** Of course, researchers can't keep track of everything that a child does. **Beforehand they must decide which** *variables*—**factors that can take on different values— to record.** Researchers studying friendship, for example, might decide to observe children in a school lunchroom like the one in the photo. They would record where each child sits and who talks to whom. They might also decide to observe children at the start of the first year in a middle school, because many children make new friends at this time.

Naturalistic observation is illustrated in research by Ensor and Hughes (2008), who studied conversations between mothers and their 2-year-olds. They used video cameras to record mother–child conversations before or during a meal. From these videotapes, the researchers measured the number of times that conversations referred to thoughts, desires, and feelings. They also scored the manner in which mothers and children took turns as they conversed (e.g., whether a mother's comment related to her child's prior comment).

In *structured observation,* **the researcher creates a setting likely to elicit the behavior of interest.** Structured observations are particularly useful for studying behaviors that are difficult to observe naturally. Some phenomena occur rarely, such as emergencies. An investigator using naturalistic observation to study children's responses to emergencies wouldn't make much progress, because emergencies don't occur at predetermined times and locations. However, using structured observation, an investigator might stage an emergency, perhaps by having a nearby adult cry for help and then observing children's responses.

Other behaviors are difficult for researchers to observe because they occur in private settings, not public ones. For example, much interaction between friends takes place at home, where investigators cannot observe unobtrusively. However, children who are friends could be asked to come to the researcher's laboratory, which might be furnished with chairs and tables. They would be asked to perform some activity typical of friends, such as playing a game or deciding what movie to see. By observing friends' interactions in a setting like the one in the photo on page 21 (perhaps through a one-way mirror), researchers could learn more about how friends interact.

A good example of structured observation comes from a study by Sturge-Apple, Davies, and Cummings (2010) of parenting strategies. These researchers asked a mother to join her 6-year-old child in a room that included many attractive toys. Mother and child were encouraged to play with the toys for five minutes, then mothers were told to encourage the child to help clean up the toys. The play and cleanup sessions were videotaped and later the researchers used the tapes to measure parental behavior, including, for example, the extent to which mothers used praise and approval to encourage their children to clean up. By creating a situation that would be moderately challenging for mothers—most 6-year-olds would rather continue playing, not clean up!—Sturge-Apple et al. hoped to gain insights into parental behavior.

Although structured observations allow researchers to observe behaviors that would otherwise be difficult to study, investigators must be careful that the settings they create do not disturb the behavior of interest. For instance, observing friends as they play a game in a mock family room has many artificial aspects to it: The friends are not in their own homes, they were told (in general terms) what to do, and they know they're being observed. Similarly, the moms in the study by Sturge-Apple et al. study knew that they were being videotaped and may have wanted to show their very best parenting behavior. Any or all of these factors may cause children and parents to behave differently than they would in the real world. Researchers must be careful that their method does not distort the behavior they are observing.

Structured observation involves creating a situation—asking children to play a game—that is likely to lead to behaviors of interest, such as competition.

SAMPLING BEHAVIOR WITH TASKS. When investigators can't observe a behavior directly, an alternative is to create tasks that are thought to sample the behavior of interest. For example, to measure memory, investigators sometimes use a digit span task: Children listen as a sequence of numbers is presented aloud. After the last digit is presented, children try to repeat the digits in the exact order in which they heard them. To measure children's ability to recognize different emotions, investigators sometimes use the task shown in Figure 1-1. The child has been asked to look at the facial expressions and point to the person who is happy.

Sampling behavior with tasks is popular with child-development researchers because it is so convenient. A major problem with this approach, however, is determining whether the task really samples the behavior of interest. For example, asking children to judge emotions from photographs may not be valid, because it underestimates what children do in real life. Can you think of reasons why this might be the case? I mention several reasons on page 35, just before "Check Your Learning."

SELF REPORTS. The third approach to measurement, using self reports, is actually a special case of using tasks to measure children's behavior. *Self reports* **are simply children's answers to questions about the topic of interest.** When questions are posed in written form, the report is a questionnaire; when questions are posed orally, the report is an interview. In either format, questions are created that probe different aspects of the topic of interest. For example, if you believe that children more often become friends

FIGURE 1-1

when they have interests in common, then research participants might be told the following:

> Jacob and Dave just met each other at school. Jacob likes to read and plays the clarinet in the school orchestra; Dave likes to play games on his Xbox 360 and is a star on the basketball team. Do you think Jacob and Dave will become friends?

Child participants would decide, perhaps using a rating scale, whether the boys are likely to become friends.

A typical questionnaire comes from a study by Yip, Seaton, and Sellers (2010), who were interested in measuring the extent to which African American adolescents' racial identity was affected by the racial diversity within their school. To measure adolescents' racial identity, they created a 6-item questionnaire that included statements such as "I think a lot about what being Black means for my life" and "I understand pretty well what being Black means to me." Adolescents indicated how much each statement was true of them, using a 4-point scale that ranged from "strongly disagree" to "strongly agree."

Child-development scientists study children with systematic observation, sampling behavior with tasks, self reports, and physiological responses.

Self reports are useful because they can lead directly to information on the topic of interest. They are also relatively convenient, particularly when they can be administered to groups of children or adolescents. However, self reports are not always valid measures of children's behavior, because children's answers are sometimes inaccurate. Why? When asked about past events, children may not remember them accurately. For example, an adolescent asked about childhood friends may not remember those friendships well. **Also, children sometimes answer incorrectly due to** *response bias*—**some responses may be more socially acceptable than others, and children are more likely to select those than socially unacceptable answers.** For example, some adolescents in the Yip et al. (2010) study may have been reluctant to admit that they had little sense of a Black identity. But, as long as investigators keep these weaknesses in mind, self reports are a valuable tool for child-development research.

PHYSIOLOGICAL MEASURES. A final approach is less common but can be very powerful: measuring children's physiological responses. Heart rate, for example, often slows down when children are paying close attention to something interesting. Consequently, researchers often measure heart rate to determine a child's degree of attention. As another example, the hormone cortisol is often secreted in response to stress. By measuring cortisol levels in children's saliva, scientists can determine when children are experiencing stress (Cutuli et al., 2010).

As both of these examples suggest, physiological measures are usually specialized, in that they focus on a particular aspect of a child's behavior (attention and stress in the two examples). What's more, they're often used alongside other behaviorally oriented methods. A researcher studying stress might observe children, looking for overt signs of stress; ask parents to rate their children's stress; and also measure cortisol in children's saliva. If all three measures lead to the same conclusions about stress, then the researcher can be much more confident about the conclusions.

Another important group of physiological measures includes those used to study brain activity. Techniques developed during the past 25 years allow modern scientists to record many facets of brain functioning in real time, as children are performing specific tasks. I describe these methods in Module 4.3. For now, the important point is that child-development scientists are making great strides in identifying the brain regions associated with reasoning, memory, emotions, and other psychological functions.

The four approaches to measurement are presented in the Summary Table.

SUMMARY TABLE

WAYS OF MEASURING BEHAVIOR IN CHILD-DEVELOPMENT RESEARCH

Method	Strength	Weakness
Systematic observation		
Naturalistic observation	Captures children's behavior in its natural setting	Difficult to use with behaviors that are rare or that typically occur in private settings
Structured observation	Can be used to study behaviors that are rare or that typically occur in private settings	May be invalid if the structured setting distorts the behavior
Sampling behavior with tasks	Convenient; can be used to study most behaviors	May be invalid if the task does not sample behavior as it occurs naturally
Self reports (questionnaires and interviews)	Convenient; can be used to study most behaviors	May be invalid because children answer incorrectly due to forgetting or response bias
Physiological measures	Can provide independent, converging evidence that can confirm behavioral measures	Are often specific to particular types of behaviors and, consequently, may not be available for all topics

EVALUATING MEASURES. After researchers choose a method of measurement, they must show that it is both reliable and valid. **A measure is** *reliable* **if the results are consistent over time.** A measure of friendship, for example, would be reliable if it yields the same results about friendship each time it is administered. **A measure is** *valid* **if it really measures what researchers think it measures.** For example, a measure of friendship is valid only if it can be shown to actually measure friendship (and not, for example, popularity). Validity is often established by showing that the measure is closely related to another measure known to be valid. We could show the validity of a questionnaire that claims to measure friendship by showing that scores on the questionnaire are related to peers' and parents' ratings of friendship.

Throughout this book, you'll come across many studies using these different methods. You'll also see that studies of the same topic or behavior often use different methods. This is very desirable: Because the approaches to measurement have different strengths and weaknesses, finding the same results regardless of the approach leads to particularly strong conclusions. Suppose, for example, that a researcher using self reports claims that arguments, like the one shown in the photo, are more common in boys' friendships than in girls' friendships. It would be reassuring that other investigators have found the same result from systematic observation and from sampling behavior with tasks.

If arguments like this one are more common among boys than girls, then that difference should be evident in observations of children's behavior as well as in other measures, such as self reports.

REPRESENTATIVE SAMPLING. Valid measures depend not only on the method of measurement, but also on the children who are tested. **Researchers are usually interested in broad groups of children called** *populations.* Examples of populations would be all American 7-year-olds or all African American adolescents. However, it would be extremely difficult for researchers to study every member of such large groups. **Virtually all studies include only a** *sample* **of children, a subset of the population.** Researchers must take care that their sample really represents the population of interest. An unrepresentative sample can lead to invalid research. For example, what would you think of a study of children's friendship if you learned that

Much research is based on samples of children living in developed countries in North America and other parts of the world; those results may not generalize to children living in developing nations.

the sample consisted entirely of 8-year-olds whose friends were primarily preschool children? This sample of 8-year-olds would seem to be very unusual, and you would hesitate to generalize the results from this sample back to the population at large.

As you read on, you'll discover that much of the research I describe was conducted with samples of middle-class European American youngsters. Are these samples representative of all children in the United States? Of children like those in the photo who grow up in developing countries? Sometimes, but not always. Be careful not to assume that findings from this group necessarily apply to people in other groups.

General Designs for Research

Having formulated a hypothesis, identified variables, and selected a method to collect data on the topic or behavior of interest, researchers must then choose and implement an overall conceptual approach called a *research design.* Child-development researchers usually use one of two designs: correlational or experimental studies.

CORRELATIONAL STUDIES. **In a** *correlational study,* **investigators look at relations between variables as they exist naturally in the world.** In the simplest possible correlational study, a researcher measures two variables, then sees how they are related. Imagine a researcher who wants to test the idea that smarter children have more friends. To test this claim, the researcher would measure two variables for each child: the number of friends the child has and the child's intelligence.

The results of a correlational study are usually expressed as a *correlation coefficient,* **abbreviated** *r,* **which stands for the direction and strength of a relation between two variables.** Correlations can range from −1.0 to +1.0:

- *When* **r** *equals 0, two variables are completely unrelated:* Children's intelligence is unrelated to the number of friends they have.
- *When* **r** *is greater than 0, scores are related positively:* Children who are smart tend to have more friends than children who are not as smart. That is, greater intelligence is associated with having more friends.
- *When* **r** *is less than 0, scores are related, but inversely:* Children who are smart tend to have fewer friends than children who are not as smart. That is, greater intelligence is associated with having fewer friends.

In interpreting a correlation coefficient, you need to consider both the sign *and* the size of the correlation. The sign indicates the *direction* of the relation between variables. **A** *positive correlation* **means that larger values on one variable are associated with larger values on the second variable; a** *negative correlation* **means that larger values on one variable are associated with smaller values on a second variable.** For example, Belsky, Houts, and Pasco Fearon (2010) wondered whether the age at which girls entered puberty was related to the security of their emotional attachment to their mother during infancy (a topic that we'll examine in detail in Module 10.3). The investigators assessed security of mother–infant attachment when girls were 15 months old and used data from physical exams to determine when girls entered puberty. The correlation was .47, indicating that, in general, daughters with more secure attachment as infants tended to enter puberty at an older age.

> Correlational studies allow scientists to examine naturally-occuring relations between variables.

The *strength* of a relation is measured by how much the correlation differs from 0, either positively or negatively. If the correlation between intelligence and number of friends were .75, the relation between these variables would be very strong: Knowing a child's intelligence, you could accurately predict how many friends the child has. If, instead, the correlation were .25, the link between intelligence and number of friends would be relatively weak: Although more intelligent children would have more friends on the average, there would be many exceptions to this rule. Similarly, a correlation of −.75 would indicate a strong negative relation between intelligence and number of friends, but a correlation of −.25 would indicate a weak negative relation. Thus, in the study by Belsky et al. (2010) on links between attachment and onset of puberty, the correlation of .47 indicates a medium-sized relation between attachment security and age of onset of puberty. Many girls with secure attachment to their mother as infants entered puberty at a relatively older age, but not all of them; some girls with secure attachment started puberty at a relatively younger age.

The results of a correlational study tell whether variables are related, but this design doesn't address the question of cause and effect between the variables. In other words, finding a correlation between variables does not necessarily imply a causal relation between them. Suppose a researcher finds that the correlation between intelligence and number of friends is .7. This means that children who are smarter have more friends than children who are not as smart. How would you interpret this correlation? Figure 1-2 shows that three interpretations are possible. Maybe being smart causes children to have more friends. Another interpretation is that having more friends causes children to be smarter. A third interpretation is that neither variable causes the other; instead, intelligence and number of friends are caused by a third variable that was not measured in the study. Perhaps parents who are warm and supportive tend to have children who are smart and who also have many friends. Any of these interpretations could be true. Cause and effect cannot

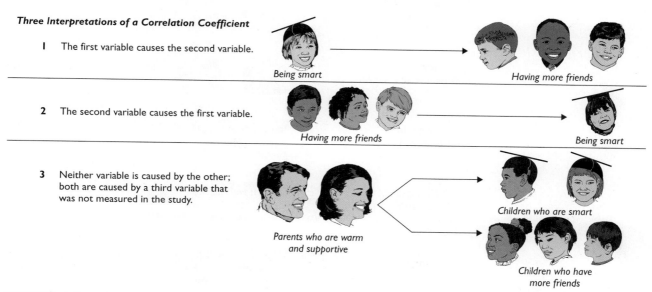

Three Interpretations of a Correlation Coefficient

1   The first variable causes the second variable.

Being smart → *Having more friends*

2   The second variable causes the first variable.

Having more friends → *Being smart*

3   Neither variable is caused by the other; both are caused by a third variable that was not measured in the study.

Parents who are warm and supportive → *Children who are smart* / *Children who have more friends*

FIGURE 1-2

be distinguished in a correlational study. Consequently, when investigators want to track down causes, they must use a different design, an experimental study.

EXPERIMENTAL STUDIES.   In an *experiment*, **an investigator systematically varies the factors thought to cause a particular behavior. The factor that is varied is called the** *independent variable;* **the behavior that is measured is called the** *dependent variable.* In an experiment, the investigator randomly assigns children to different groups or conditions that are treated exactly alike except for the single factor that varies across groups (i.e., the independent variable). The dependent variable is then measured in all groups. Because children have been assigned to groups randomly, differences between the groups must reflect the different treatment the children received in the experiment.

Suppose, for example, that an investigator hypothesizes that children share more with friends than with children they do not know. Figure 1-3 shows how the investigator might test this hypothesis. Based on random assignment, some fifth-grade children are asked to come to the investigator's laboratory with a good friend. Other fifth-graders come to the laboratory site without a friend and are paired with a child they don't know. The laboratory itself is decorated to look like a comfortable room in a house. The investigator creates a task in which one child is given an interesting object to play with—perhaps a Wii video game console—but the other child receives nothing. The experimenter explains the task to the children and then claims that she needs to leave the room briefly. Actually, the experimenter goes to a room with a one-way mirror and observes whether the child with the Wii offers to let the other child play with it.

This same scenario is used with all pairs of children: The room and Wii are the same and the experimenter is always away for the same amount of time. The

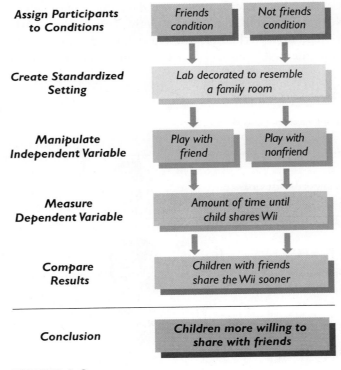

FIGURE 1-3

circumstances are held as constant as possible for all children, except that some children participate with friends but others do not. If children who participated with friends shared the Wii more quickly or more readily with the other child, the investigator could say with confidence that children are more likely to share with their friends than with children they don't know. Conclusions about cause and effect are possible because there was a direct manipulation of an independent variable (participating with a friend or with an unknown child) under controlled conditions.

You can see the use of an experiment in a study by Zmyj and colleagues (2010). Infants readily imitate other's actions. However, are infants selective in their imitation? As I mentioned earlier, older children readily imitate those whose actions indicate that they are competent, but don't imitate those who seem incompetent. Would infants do the same? To answer this question, Zmyj and colleagues randomly assigned 14-month-olds to observe either a reliable adult or an unreliable adult. For example, the reliable adult announced that he was going to put on his shoes and did so, with a confident look on his face. In contrast, the unreliable adult, after saying that he was going to put on his shoes, looked puzzled and put a shoe on his hand. Later, the same adult was shown turning on an unfamiliar lamp-in-a-box by touching the side of the box with his head. Finally, infants were shown the same lamp-in-a-box and encouraged to play with it.

> Experimental studies allow scientists to reach conclusions about cause and effect.

In this experiment, the presence or absence of a reliable adult was the independent variable and the dependent variable was the extent to which infants imitated the adult by touching the box with their forehead. In fact, infants were far more likely to imitate the adult who was reliable: 59% of the infants imitated the adult when he was reliable but only 30% did so when he was unreliable. Because infants were randomly assigned to conditions, Zmyj et al. (2010) could conclude that the adult's apparent reliability *caused* infants to be more likely to imitate.

Child-development researchers usually conduct experiments such as this one in laboratory-like settings to control all the variables that might influence the outcome of the research. A shortcoming of laboratory work is that behavior is sometimes not studied in its natural setting. Consequently, the results may be invalid because they are artificial—specific to the laboratory setting and not representative of the behavior in the natural environment.

To avoid this limit, researchers sometimes rely on a special type of experiment. **In a** *field experiment,* **the researcher manipulates independent variables in a natural setting so that the results are more likely to be representative of behavior in real-world settings.** To illustrate a field experiment, let's return to the hypothesis that children share more with friends. We might conduct the research in a classroom where students must complete a group assignment. In collaboration with teachers, we place the children in groups of three: in some groups, all three children are good friends; in others, the three children are acquaintances but not friends. When the assignment is complete, the teacher gives each group leader many stickers and tells the leader to distribute them to group members based on how much each child contributed. We predict that leaders will share more (i.e., distribute the stickers more evenly) when group members are friends than when they are not.

A good example of a field experiment is a study by DeLoache and colleagues (2010), who wondered whether videos designed to promote vocabulary learning actually help babies to learn words. They assigned 1-year-olds randomly to one of three conditions: in one, several times each week infant and parent watched a commercial

DVD designed to increase an infant's vocabulary; in a second condition, parents were simply told the 25 words featured in the DVD and encouraged to help their infants master them; in a third, control condition, infants saw no videos and parents weren't told the words. After four weeks, experimenters tested infants' knowledge of the 25 words in the DVD. Infants were shown two objects, one depicting a word shown in the video. The experiment said the word and asked infants to point to the corresponding object.

In this experiment, the independent variable was the type of exposure to the words (via DVD, from parents, none) and the dependent variable was the number of times that infants pointed to the correct object upon hearing the word. Was the video useful? No. Infants who had watched the video knew the same number of words as infants in the control condition. And infants in both of these groups knew *fewer* words than infants whose parents had been encouraged to teach words. Because infants were randomly assigned to conditions, DeLoache and colleagues (2010) could conclude that the type of exposure to words *caused* differences in the number of words that infants learned.

> In a quasi-experiment, scientists take advantage of naturally occurring events to create different experimental groups.

Field experiments allow investigators to draw strong conclusions about cause and effect because they embed manipulation of an independent variable in a natural setting. However, field experiments are often impractical because of logistical problems. In most natural settings, children are supervised by adults (e.g., parents and teachers) who must be willing to become allies in the proposed research. Adults may not want to change their routines to fit a researcher's needs. In addition, researchers usually sacrifice some control in field experiments. In the study by DeLoache of baby videos, for example, the investigators relied upon parents to show the videos as instructed and to provide honest reports of how often they watched the videos with their children. No doubt some parents complied with instructions better than others and some parents were more truthful in their reports of how often they watched videos.

Another important variation is the *quasi-experiment,* **which typically involves examining the impact of an independent variable by using groups that were not created with random assignment.** Think, for example, about how child-development researchers could study the consequences for children's development of (a) a mother's smoking, (b) exposure to natural disasters such as Hurricane Katrina, or (c) growing up in a rural area instead of a city. In these instances, conducting a true experiment is either impossible or unethical—children can't be randomly assigned to a mother who smokes or to grow up on a farm. However, children living in these conditions can be compared with children living in contrasting situations (e.g., with children whose mothers don't smoke or with children living in cities). The tricky part is that, because children weren't assigned to groups randomly, the groups may differ along other dimensions as well. For example, less educated people are more likely to smoke; consequently, a difference favoring children of women who don't smoke might reflect the tendency for these women to be better educated. This problem can be addressed, somewhat, by using statistical analyses that hold these other variables constant (i.e., that can control for the fact that groups differ along other variables, such as education).

Like most designs, quasi-experiments have strengths and weaknesses. Consequently, no single investigation can definitely answer a question, and researchers rarely rely on one study or even one method to reach conclusions. Instead, they prefer to find converging evidence from studies using as many different kinds of methods as possible. Suppose, for example, that our hypothetical laboratory and field experiments show that children do indeed share more readily with their friends. One way to be more confident of this conclusion would be to do correlational research, perhaps by observing children during lunch and measuring how often they share food with different people.

Designs for Studying Age-Related Change

Sometimes child-development research is directed at a single age group, such as fifth-grade children (as in the experiment on sharing between friends and nonfriends), memory in preschool-age children, or mother–infant relationships in 1-year-olds. When this is the case, after deciding how to measure the behavior of interest and whether the study will be correlational or experimental, the investigator could skip directly to the last step and determine whether the study is ethical.

However, much research in child development concerns changes that occur as children develop. Consequently, in conjunction with the chosen general research design, investigators must also select a strategy for assessing age-related change. Three strategies are used to incorporate different age groups into experimental and correlational research: the longitudinal approach, the cross-sectional approach, and the longitudinal-sequential approach.

LONGITUDINAL DESIGN. In a *longitudinal design,* **the same individuals are observed or tested repeatedly at different points in their lives.** As the name implies, the longitudinal approach takes a lengthwise view of development and is the most direct way to watch growth occur. As Figure 1-4 shows, in a longitudinal study, children might be tested first at age 6 and then again at ages 9 and 12. The longitudinal approach is well suited to studying almost any aspect of development. More important, it is the only way to answer questions about the continuity or discontinuity of behavior: Will characteristics such as aggression, dependency, or mistrust observed in infancy or early childhood persist into adulthood? Will a traumatic event, such as being abandoned by one's parents, influence later social

Longitudinal Study

FIGURE 1-4

and intellectual development? Such questions can be explored only by testing children early in development and then retesting them later. For example, the study of parenting by Belsky et al. (2010) (described on page 24) was part of an ongoing longitudinal study of more than 1,000 children born in the United States in 1991, in which children were tested repeatedly during childhood, adolescence, and young adulthood. Consequently, investigators can see how children's experiences during the preschool years affect them as adolescents and young adults.

Usually the repeated testing of longitudinal studies extends over years, but not always. **In a *microgenetic study,* a special type of longitudinal design, children are tested repeatedly over a span of days or weeks, typically with the aim of observing change directly as it occurs.** For example, researchers might test children every week, starting when they are 12 months old and continuing until 18 months. Microgenetic studies are particularly useful when investigators have hypotheses about a specific period when developmental change should occur. In this case, researchers arrange to test children frequently before, during, and after this period, hoping to see change as it happens (e.g., Opfer & Siegler, 2007).

The longitudinal approach, however, has disadvantages that frequently offset its strengths. An obvious one is cost: The expense of keeping up with a large sample of people can be staggering. Other problems are not so obvious:

- *Practice effects:* When children are given the same test many times, they may become "test-wise." Improvement over time that is attributed to development may actually stem from practice with a particular test. Changing the test from one session to the next solves the practice problem but can make it difficult to compare responses to different tests.

- *Selective attrition:* Another problem is the constancy of the sample over the course of research. Some children may drop out because they move away. Others may simply lose interest and choose not to continue. These dropouts often differ significantly from their peers, which can distort the outcome. For example, a study might find that memory improves between 8 and 11 years. What has actually happened, however, is that 8-year-olds who found the testing too difficult quit the study, thereby raising the group average when children were tested as 11-year-olds.

- *Cohort effects:* **When children in a longitudinal study are observed over a period of several years, the developmental change may be specific to a specific generation of people known as a *cohort.*** For example, the longitudinal study that I described earlier includes babies born in 1991 in the United States. The results of this study may be general (i.e., apply to infants born in 1950 as well as infants born in 2000), but they may reflect experiences that were unique to infants born in the early 1990s.

Because of these and other problems with the longitudinal method, child-development researchers often use cross-sectional studies instead.

> Cross-sectional designs are convenient but only longitudinal designs can answer questions about the continuity of development.

CROSS-SECTIONAL DESIGN. In a *cross-sectional design,* **developmental changes are identified by testing children of different ages at one point in their development.** In other words, as shown in Figure 1-5, a researcher might chart the differences in some attribute between, say, 6-, 9-, and 12-year-olds. For example, when Verkuyten and De Wolf (2007) studied age-related change in

Cross-Sectional Study

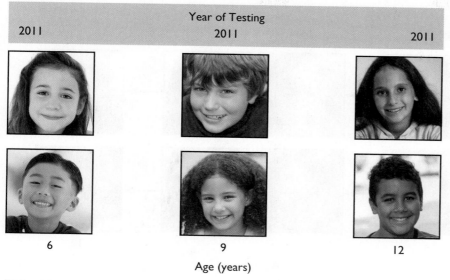

FIGURE 1-5

children's preference for their own group, they tested 6-, 8-, and 10-year-olds. This was much faster than waiting the four years for the 6-year-olds to become 10-year-olds, and avoided many of the problems associated with longitudinal studies, including practice effects and selective attrition. But cohort effects are still a problem: The results may apply to children who are 6, 9, and 12 years old at the time of testing (in the example in the figure, 2011) and not generalize to previous or future generations. Cross-sectional studies also have a unique shortcoming: Because children are tested at only one point in their development, we learn nothing about the continuity of development. Consequently, we cannot tell whether an aggressive 6-year-old remains aggressive at ages 9 and 12, because an individual child would be tested at age 6, 9, or 12, but not at all three ages.

LONGITUDINAL-SEQUENTIAL STUDIES. Neither longitudinal nor cross-sectional studies are foolproof; each has weaknesses. Consequently, sometimes investigators use a design that is a hybrid of the traditional designs. A longitudinal-sequential study includes sequences of samples, each studied longitudinally. For example, researchers might start with 6- and 9-year-olds. As shown in Figure 1-6, each group is tested twice—at the beginning of the study and again three years later. As in a pure longitudinal study, the longitudinal-sequential design provides some information about continuity of development: Researchers can determine whether aggressive 6-year-olds become aggressive 9-year-olds and whether aggressive 9-year-olds become aggressive 12-year-olds. Of course, to determine whether aggressive 6-year-olds become aggressive 12-year-olds would require a full-blown longitudinal study.

Another advantage of the longitudinal-sequential study is that researchers can determine whether their study is plagued by practice effects or cohort effects: The key is to compare the results for the age common to both sequences (in the example in the figure, 9-year-olds). Practice and cohort effects tend to make scores different

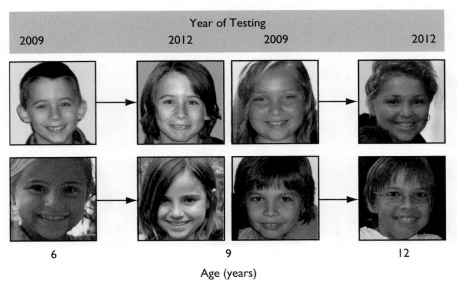

FIGURE 1-6

for the two groups of 9-year-olds, so if scores are the same, a researcher can be confident that practice and cohort effects are not a problem in the study.

Each of the three designs for studying development (longitudinal, cross-sectional, longitudinal-sequential) can be combined with the two general research

SUMMARY TABLE

DESIGNS USED IN CHILD-DEVELOPMENT RESEARCH

Type of Design	Definition	Strengths	Weaknesses
GENERAL DESIGNS			
Correlational	Observe variables as they exist in the world and determine their relations	Behavior is measured as it occurs naturally	Cannot determine cause and effect
Experimental	Manipulate independent and dependent variables	Control of variables allows conclusions about cause and effect	Work is often laboratory based, which can be artificial
DEVELOPMENTAL DESIGNS			
Longitudinal	One group of children is tested repeatedly as they develop	Only way to chart an individual's development and look at the continuity of behavior over time	Expensive; participants drop out; repeated testing can distort performance
Cross-sectional	Children of different ages are tested at the same time	Convenient; solves most problems associated with longitudinal studies	Cannot study continuity of behavior; cohort effects complicate interpretation of differences between groups
Longitudinal-sequential	Different sequences of children are tested longitudinally	Provides information about continuity; researchers can determine the presence of practice and cohort effects	Provides less information about continuity than a full longitudinal study and is more time consuming than a cross-sectional study

designs (observational, experimental), resulting in six prototypic designs. To illustrate the different possibilities, think back to our hypothetical laboratory experiment on children's sharing with friends and nonfriends (described on page 26). If we tested 7- and 11-year-olds with either friends or nonfriends, this would be a cross-sectional experimental study. If instead we observed 7-year-olds' spontaneous sharing at lunch, then observed the same children four years later, this would be a longitudinal correlational study.

The different designs are summarized in the Summary Table. In this book, you'll read about studies using these various designs, although the two cross-sectional designs will show up more frequently than the other designs. Why? For most developmentalists, the ease of cross-sectional studies compared to longitudinal studies more than compensates for the limitations of cross-sectional studies.

INTEGRATING FINDINGS FROM DIFFERENT STUDIES. Several times in this module, I've emphasized the value of conducting multiple studies on a topic using different methods. The advantage of this approach, of course, is that conclusions are most convincing when the results are the same regardless of method.

In reality, though, findings are often inconsistent. Suppose, for example, that many researchers find that children often share with friends, some researchers find that children share occasionally with friends, and a few researchers find that children never share with friends. What results should we believe? What should we conclude? *Meta-analysis* **is a tool that allows researchers to synthesize the results of many studies to estimate relations between variables** (Cooper, Hedges, & Valentine, 2009). In conducting a meta-analysis, investigators find all studies published on a topic over a substantial period of time (e.g., 10 to 20 years), then record and analyze the results and important methodological variables.

> Meta-analysis allows researchers to integrate the findings from many similar studies, making it possible to determine the generality and consistency of research results.

The usefulness of meta-analysis is illustrated in a study by Juffer and van IJzendoorn (2007), who asked whether adopted children differ from nonadopted children in terms of self-esteem. They found 88 studies, published between 1970 and 2007, that included nearly 11,000 adopted persons. In each of the 88 studies, self-esteem was measured, often by asking participants to rate themselves on scales containing items such as "I am a worthwhile person." Analyzing across the results of all 88 studies, Juffer and van IJzendoorn found that self-esteem did not differ in adopted and nonadopted individuals. This was true regardless of the age of the child when adopted and was true for international versus domestic adoptions as well as for children adopted by parents of their own race versus parents of another race. Evidently, adoption has no impact on self-esteem; Juffer and van IJzendoorn argued that this outcome shows "adopted children's resilience to recover from severe deprivation within the context of the adoptive family" (2007, p. 1079).

Thus, meta-analysis is a particularly powerful tool because it allows scientists to determine whether a finding generalizes across many studies that used different methods. In addition, meta-analysis can reveal the impact of those different methods on results (e.g., whether self reports suggests more sharing between friends than observational studies).

Ethical Responsibilities

Having selected a way of measuring the behavior of interest and having chosen appropriate general and developmental designs, researchers must confront one

Before children can participate in research, a parent or legal guardian must provide written consent.

very important remaining step: They must determine whether their research is ethical, that it does not violate the rights of the children who participate in it. Of course, scientists must always consider the ethics of research with humans, but especially for children, who are vulnerable and sensitive. Professional organizations and government agencies have codes of conduct that specify the rights of research participants and procedures to protect those participants. The following guidelines are included in all those codes:

- *Minimize risks to research participants:* Use methods that have the least potential for harm to or stress on research participants. During the research, monitor the procedures to be sure to avoid any unforeseen stress or harm.

- *Describe the research to potential participants so they can determine whether they wish to participate:* **Prospective research participants should understand the research so they can make an educated decision about participating, which is known as obtaining** *informed consent.* Children are minors and are not legally capable of giving consent; consequently, as shown in the photograph, researchers must describe the study to parents and ask them for permission for their children to participate.

- *Avoid deception; if participants must be deceived, provide a thorough explanation of the true nature of the research as soon as possible:* Providing complete information about a study in advance can sometimes bias or distort participants' responses. Consequently, investigators sometimes provide only partial information or even mislead participants about the true purpose of the study. As soon as it is feasible—typically just after the experiment—any false information must be corrected and the reasons for the deception must be provided.

- *Keep results anonymous or confidential:* Research results should be anonymous, which means that participants' data cannot be linked to their names. When anonymity is not possible, research results should be confidential, which means that only the investigator conducting the study knows the identities of the individuals. 👁️ Watch the **Video** on **mydevelopmentlab.com**

👁️ Watch the **Video** *Importance of Informed Consent* on **mydevelopmentlab .com** This video describes the Tuskegee Syphilis Study, which is one of the most infamous research projects ever; it resulted in many of the modern safe-guards for research participants.

QUESTION 1.4

Ethan, a 10-year-old, was at school when a researcher asked if he wanted to earn $10 doing an experiment. The money sounded good to Ethan, so he participated. Despite the pay, Ethan left the experiment upset because he overheard the experimenter telling his teacher how poorly Ethan had done. What are three ethical problems with this research?

(Answer is on page 35.)

Before researchers can conduct a study, they must convince review boards consisting of scientists from many disciplines that they have carefully addressed each of these ethical points. If the review board objects to some aspects of the proposed study, the researcher must revise those aspects and present the study anew for the review board's approval.

Much child-development research does not raise ethical red flags because the methods are harmless and avoid deception. Some methods, however, involve risk or deception; in these cases, review boards must balance the rights of children against the value of the research for contributing to knowledge and thereby improving children's lives. For example, in Module 10.3 we'll see that one tool for studying mother–infant relationships involves separating mothers and infants briefly, then watching infants' responses. Many infants are upset when the mother leaves and some are difficult to console when she returns. Obviously, this method is not pleasant for infants. But scientists have determined that it produces no lasting harm and therefore is suitable as long as parents receive a thorough description of the study beforehand and they consent to participate.

Communicating Research Results

When the study is complete and the data have been analyzed, researchers write a report of their work. This report uses a standard format that usually includes four main sections: an introduction that describes the topic or question that was studied and the authors' hypotheses; a method section that describes the research design and the procedures used; a results section that presents the study's findings, verified with statistical analyses; and a discussion section in which the authors explain the links between their results and their hypotheses.

Researchers submit the report to one of several scientific journals that specialize in child-development research. Some of these are *Child Development*, *Developmental Psychology*, and *Developmental Science*. The editor of the journal asks other scientists to evaluate the report, to decide whether the work was well done and the findings represent a substantial advance in scientific understanding of a topic. If the reviewing scientists recommend that the report be published, it will appear in the journal, where other child-development researchers can learn of the results.

> Researchers communicate the results of their research by publishing them in scientific journals.

These reports of research are the basis for virtually all the information I present in this book. As you read, you'll see names in parentheses, followed by a date, like this:

(Levine, Waite, & Bowman, 2007).

This indicates the person(s) who did the research and the year report describing the research was published. By looking in the References section, which begins on page 514 and is organized alphabetically, you can find the title of the article and the journal in which it was published.

Maybe all these different steps in research seem tedious and involved to you. For a child-development researcher, however, much of the fun of doing research is planning a novel study that will provide useful information to other specialists. This is one of the most creative and challenging parts of child-development research.

The "Focus on Research" features that appear in the remaining chapters of this book are designed to convey both the creativity and the challenge of doing child-development research. Each feature focuses on a specific study. Some are studies that have just recently been published; others are classics that defined a new area of investigation or provided definitive results in some area. In each "Focus" feature, I trace the decisions that researchers made as they planned their study. In the process, you'll see the ingenuity of researchers as they pursue questions of child development. You'll also see that any individual study has limitations. Only when converging evidence from many studies—each using a unique combination of measurement methods and designs—points to the same conclusion can we feel confident about research results.

Responses to question on page 22 about using photographs to measure children's understanding of emotions: Children's understanding of emotions depicted in photographs may be less accurate than in real life because (1) in

 ANSWER 1.4
First, the experimenter apparently did not describe the study in detail to Ethan, only mentioning the pay. Second, children can participate only with the written consent of a parent or legal guardian. Third, results are anonymous and not to be shared with others.

real life, facial features are usually moving—not still, as in the photographs—and movement may be one of the clues that children naturally use to judge emotions; (2) in real life, facial expressions are often accompanied by sounds, and children may use both sight and sound to understand emotion; and (3) in real life, children often judge facial expressions of people they know (parents, siblings, peers, teachers), and knowing the "usual" appearance of a face may help children determine emotions accurately.

 Check Your Learning

RECALL List the ethical responsibilities of scientists who do research with children.

What steps are involved in reporting the results of research to the scientific community?

INTERPRET Compare the strengths and weaknesses of different approaches to measurement in child-development research.

APPLY Suppose you wanted to determine the impact of divorce on children's academic achievement. What would be the merits of correlational versus experimental research on this topic? How would a longitudinal study differ from a cross-sectional study?

See for Yourself

One good way to see how children influence their own development is to interview parents who have more than one child. Ask them if they used the same child-rearing methods with each child or if they used different techniques with each. If they used different techniques, find out why.

You should see that, although parents try to be consistent in a general philosophy for rearing their children, many of the specific parenting techniques will vary from one child to the next, reflecting the children's influence on the parents. See for yourself!

Summary

1.1 Setting the Stage

Historical Views of Children and Childhood

Plato and Aristotle provided the first philosophical views of childhood. Their ideas were picked up in the 17th century. Locke emphasized the role of experience in children's lives, but Rousseau viewed development as a natural unfolding.

Origins of a New Science

Child development emerged as a science in the 19th century, reflecting reformers' concern for children's well-being and enthusiasm for Darwin's theory of evolution. Leaders in the new field were G. Stanley Hall (theories of child development), Binet (mental tests), Freud (early experience), and Watson (behaviorism). Child-development researchers help shape family policy by providing knowledge about children so that policies can be based on accurate information. They also contribute by serving as advocates for children, by evaluating the impact of social programs, and by developing effective programs that can be implemented elsewhere.

1.2 Foundational Theories of Child Development

Theories provide explanations for development and hypotheses for research. Traditionally, five broad perspectives have guided researchers.

The Biological Perspective
According to this perspective, biological factors are critical for development. In maturational theory, child development reflects a natural unfolding of a prearranged biological plan. Ethological theory states that children's and parents' behavior is often adaptive.

The Psychodynamic Perspective
Freud emphasized the roles of early experience and conflict in children's development. Erikson proposed that psychosocial development consists of eight stages, each characterized by a particular struggle.

The Learning Perspective
Operant conditioning is based on reinforcement, punishment, and environmental control of behavior. Social learning theory proposes that people learn by observing others. Social cognitive theory emphasizes that children actively interpret what they see.

The Cognitive-Developmental Perspective
The cognitive-developmental perspective focuses on thought processes. Piaget proposed that children's thinking progresses through four stages.

The Contextual Perspective
Vygotsky emphasized the role of culture in children's development. He argued that skilled adults help children acquire the beliefs, customs, and skills of their culture.

1.3 Themes in Child-Development Research

Four themes help unify the findings from child-development research that are presented throughout this book.

Early Development Is Related to Later Development but Not Perfectly
Development is not perfectly predictable; early development sets the stage for later development but does not fix it.

Development Is Always Jointly Influenced by Heredity and Environment
Heredity and environment are interactive forces that work together to chart the course of development.

Children Influence Their Own Development
Children constantly interpret their experiences and, by their individual characteristics, often influence the experiences they have.

Development in Different Domains Is Connected
Development in different domains of children's lives is always connected. Cognitive development affects social development and vice versa.

1.4 Doing Child-Development Research

Measurement in Child-Development Research
Research typically begins by determining how to measure the phenomenon. Systematic observation involves recording children's behavior as it takes place, in either a natural environment or a structured setting. Researchers sometimes create tasks to obtain samples of children's behavior. In self reports, children answer questions posed by the experimenter. Sometimes researchers also measure physiological responses (e.g., heart rate). Researchers must also obtain a sample that is representative of a larger population.

General Designs for Research
In correlational studies, investigators examine relations between variables as they occur naturally. In experimental studies, they manipulate an independent variable to determine the impact on a dependent variable. Field studies involve manipulation of independent variables in a natural setting. Quasi-experiments take advantage of natural assignments of children to groups or conditions. The best approach is to use both experimental and correlational studies to provide converging evidence.

Designs for Studying Age-Related Change
To study developmental change, some researchers use a longitudinal design in which the same children are

observed repeatedly as they grow. A cross-sectional de-sign involves testing children in different age groups. Meta-analysis synthesizes the results of different studies on the same topic.

Ethical Responsibilities

Experimenters must minimize the risks to potential research participants, describe the research so that potential participants can decide whether they want to participate, avoid deception, and keep results anonymous or confidential.

Communicating Research Results

Once research data are analyzed, investigators publish the results in scientific journals. These publications form the foundation of scientific knowledge about child development.

Test Yourself

✓●—[Study and **Review** on mydevelopmentlab.com

1. The view of a child's mind as a *tabula rasa* emphasizes the role of _____ in shaping a child's development.

2. _____ are detailed, systematic observations of individual children.

3. In maturational theory, development consists of _____.

4. Ethologists show that some behaviors can only be learned during a _____ when organisms are biologically prepared for that learning.

5. Freud's psychodynamic theory emphasized the role of _____ in shaping later development.

6. In Erikson's psychosocial theory, development is driven by the need to resolve conflict between _____.

7. Operant conditioning + _____ = social cognitive theory.

8. According to Jean Piaget, children of all ages create _____.

9. Finding that early development is related to later development is evidence for _____ in development.

10. According to the _____ of children, they are masters of their own destinies.

11. A potential shortcoming of structured observations is that _____.

12. In a _____, high scores on one variable are associated with high scores on a second variable.

13. A measure is _____ when it actually measures what it's supposed to measure.

14. In a(n) _____, a researcher manipulates an independent variable and measures its effect on a dependent variable.

15. The biggest advantage of longitudinal studies is that a researcher can _____.

Answers: (1) experience; (2) Baby biographies; (3) the unfolding of a specific and pre-arranged scheme or plan within the body; (4) critical period; (5) early experiences; (6) a person's biological drives and society's standards of right; (7) observational learning; (8) theories that help them understand their worlds; (9) continuity; (10) active view; (11) the artificial nature of the setting may distort the behavior of interest; (12) positive correlation; (13) valid; (14) experimental study; (15) determine the extent to which behaviors at a younger age are related to behaviors at an older age

Key Terms

active–passive child   17
applied developmental science   6
baby biographies   5
cognitive-developmental perspective   12
cohort   30
continuity–discontinuity   16

correlation coefficient   24
correlational study   24
critical period   8
cross-sectional design   30
culture   13
dependent variable   26
ego   9

ethological theory   8
experiment   26
field experiment   27
id   9
imitation   11
imprinting   8
independent variable   26

informed consent   34
longitudinal design   29
maturational theory   8
meta-analysis   33
microgenetic study   30
naturalistic observation   20
nature–nurture   17
negative correlation   24
observational learning   11
operant conditioning   10

populations   23
positive correlation   24
psychodynamic theory   9
psychosocial theory   10
punishment   11
quasi-experiment   28
reinforcement   11
reliable   23
research design   24
response bias   22

sample   23
self-efficacy   11
self reports   21
social cognitive theory   11
structured observation   20
superego   9
systematic observation   20
theory   7
valid   23
variables   20

2

Genetic Bases of Child Development

2.1

Mechanisms of Heredity

2.2

Heredity, Environment, and Development

I wish I had a dollar for every time my parents or in-laws said about one of my children, "He (or she) comes by that naturally." The usual prompt for their comment is that the child has just done something exactly as I or my wife did at that same age. By their remarks, grandparents remind us that many behavioral characteristics are inherited from parents just as physical characteristics like height and hair color are inherited.

In this chapter, we'll see how heredity influences children and their development. We'll start, in **Module 2.1**, by examining the basic mechanisms of heredity. Then, in **Module 2.2**, we'll see how heredity and environment work together to shape children's development.

 2.1 ## Mechanisms of Heredity

OUTLINE

The Biology of Heredity

Single Gene Inheritance

Genetic Disorders

LEARNING OBJECTIVES

- **What are chromosomes and genes?**
- **What are dominant and recessive traits? How are they inherited?**
- **What disorders are inherited? Which are caused by too many or too few chromosomes?**

Leslie and Glenn have decided to try to have a baby. They are thrilled at the thought of starting their own family but also worried because Leslie's grandfather had sickle-cell disease and died when he was just 20 years old. Leslie is terrified that their baby could inherit the disease that killed her grandfather. Leslie and Glenn wish someone could reassure them that their baby will be okay.

How could we reassure Leslie and Glenn? For starters, we need to know more about sickle-cell disease. Red blood cells like the ones in the photo carry oxygen and carbon dioxide to and from body tissues. When a person has sickle-cell disease, the red blood cells look like those in the photo at the top of page 42: long and curved like a sickle. These stiff, misshapen cells can't pass through small capillaries, so oxygen can't reach all parts of the body. The trapped sickle cells also block the way of white blood cells that are the body's natural defense against bacteria. As a result, people with sickle-cell disease—including Leslie's grandfather and many other African Americans, who are more prone to this painful disease than other groups—often die from infections before the age of 20.

Sickle-cell disease is inherited. Because Leslie's grandfather had the disorder, it apparently runs in her family. Would Leslie's baby inherit the disease? To answer this question, we need to examine the mechanisms of heredity.

Red blood cells carry oxygen throughout the body.

The Biology of Heredity

The teaspoon of semen released into the vagina during an ejaculation contains from 200 million to 500 million sperm. Only a few hundred of these actually complete the 6- or 7-inch journey to the fallopian tubes. If an egg is present, many sperm

Sickle-shaped blood cells associated with sickle-cell disease cannot pass through the body's smallest blood vessels.

Fertilization takes place when a sperm penetrates an egg cell.

A dropper is being used to place sperm in the dish that contains egg cells.

simultaneously begin to burrow their way through the cluster of nurturing cells that surround the egg. When a sperm like the one in the middle photo penetrates the cellular wall of the egg, chemical changes that occur immediately block out all other sperm. **Each egg and sperm cell contains 23** *chromosomes,* **tiny structures in the nucleus that contain genetic material.** When a sperm penetrates an egg, their chromosomes combine to produce 23 pairs of chromosomes. The development of a new human being is under way.

For most of history, the merging of sperm and egg took place only after sexual intercourse. No longer. In 1978, Louise Brown captured the world's attention as the first test-tube baby conceived in a laboratory dish instead of in her mother's body. Today, assisted reproductive technology is no longer experimental; it is used more than 140,000 times annually with American women, producing more than 55,000 babies (Centers for Disease Control and Prevention, 2007). Many new techniques are available to couples who cannot conceive a child through sexual intercourse. **The best known,** *in vitro fertilization,* **involves mixing sperm and egg together in a laboratory dish and then placing several fertilized eggs in a woman's uterus.** The bottom photo shows this laboratory version of conception, with the sperm in the dropper being placed in the dish containing the eggs. If the eggs are fertilized, in about 24 hours they are placed in a woman's uterus, with the hope that they will become implanted in the wall of her uterus.

The sperm and egg usually come from the prospective parents, but sometimes they are provided by donors. Occasionally the fertilized egg is placed in the uterus of a surrogate mother who carries the baby throughout pregnancy. Thus, a baby could have as many as five "parents": the man and woman who provide the sperm and egg, the surrogate mother who carries the baby, and the couple who rears the child.

New reproductive techniques offer hope for couples who have long wanted a child but have been unable to conceive, and studies of the first generation of children conceived via these techniques indicates that their social and emotional development is perfectly normal (Golombok, et al., 2006; MacCallum, Golombok, & Brinsden, 2007). But there are difficulties as well. Only about one-third of the attempts at in vitro fertilization succeed. What's more, when a woman becomes pregnant, she is more likely to have twins or triplets because multiple eggs are transferred to increase the odds that at least one fertilized egg will implant in her uterus. She is also at greater risk for giving birth to a baby with low birth weight or birth defects. Finally, the procedure is expensive—the typical cost in the United States of a single cycle of treatment is between $10,000 and $15,000—and often is not covered by health insurance. These problems emphasize that, although technology has increased the alternatives for infertile couples, pregnancy on demand is still in the realm of science fiction.

Whatever the source of the egg and sperm, and wherever they meet, their merger is a momentous event: The resulting 23 pairs of chromosomes define a child's heredity—what he or she "will do naturally." For Leslie and Glenn, this moment also determines whether their child inherits sickle-cell disease.

To understand how heredity influences child development, let's begin by taking a closer look at chromosomes. The photo shows all 46 chromosomes, organized in pairs ranging from the largest to the smallest. **The first 22 pairs of chromosomes are called** *autosomes;* **and the chromosomes in each pair are about the same size.** In the 23rd pair, however, the chromosome labeled X is much larger than the chromosome labeled Y. **The 23rd pair determines the sex of the child; hence, these two are known as the** *sex chromosomes.* An egg always contains an X 23rd chromosome, but a sperm contains either an X or a Y. When an X-carrying sperm fertilizes the egg, the 23rd pair is XX and the result is a girl. When a Y-carrying sperm fertilizes the egg, the 23rd pair is XY and the result is a boy.

Humans have 23 pairs of chromosomes: 22 pairs of autosomes, and one pair of sex chromosomes.

Each chromosome actually consists of one molecule of *deoxyribonucleic acid—DNA* **for short.** The DNA molecule resembles a spiral staircase. As you can see in Figure 2-1, the rungs of the staircase carry the genetic code, which consists of pairs of nucleotide bases: Adenine is paired with thymine, and guanine is paired with cytosine. The order of the nucleotide pairs is the code that causes the cell to create specific amino acids, proteins, and enzymes—important biological building blocks. **Each group of nucleotide bases that provides a specific set of biochemical instructions is a** *gene.* For example, three consecutive thymine nucleotides is the instruction to create the amino acid phenylalanine.

Figure 2-2 on page 44 summarizes these links between chromosomes, genes, and DNA. The figure shows that each cell contains chromosomes that carry genes made up of DNA.

A child's 46 chromosomes include about 25,000 genes. Chromosome 1 has the most genes (nearly 3,000) and the Y chromosome has the fewest (just over 200). Most of these genes are the same in all people—fewer than 1% of genes cause differences between people (Human Genome Project, 2003). **The complete set of genes makes up a person's heredity and is known as the person's** *genotype.* Through biochemical instructions that are coded in DNA, genes regulate the development of all human characteristics and abilities. **Genetic instructions, in conjunction with environmental influences, produce a** *phenotype,* **an individual's physical, behavioral, and psychological features.**

In the rest of this module, we'll see the different ways that instructions contained in genes produce different phenotypes.

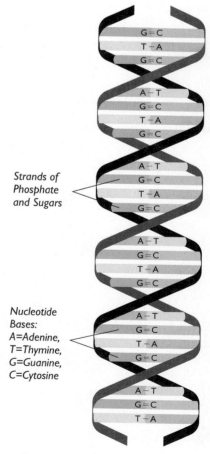

Strands of Phosphate and Sugars

Nucleotide Bases: A=Adenine, T=Thymine, G=Guanine, C=Cytosine

Single Gene Inheritance

How do genetic instructions produce the misshapen red blood cells of sickle-cell disease? **Genes come in different forms that are known as** *alleles.* In the case of red blood cells, for example, one of two alleles can be present on chromosome 11. One allele has instructions for normal red blood cells; the other allele has instructions

FIGURE 2-1

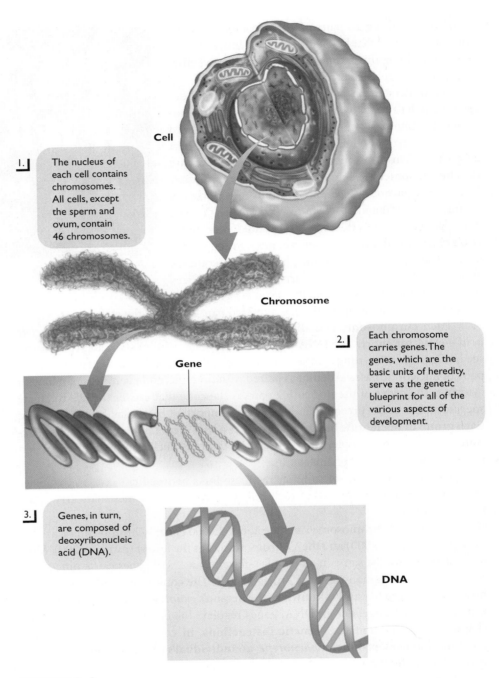

Cell

1. The nucleus of each cell contains chromosomes. All cells, except the sperm and ovum, contain 46 chromosomes.

Chromosome

2. Each chromosome carries genes. The genes, which are the basic units of heredity, serve as the genetic blueprint for all of the various aspects of development.

Gene

3. Genes, in turn, are composed of deoxyribonucleic acid (DNA).

DNA

FIGURE 2-2

for sickle-shaped red blood cells. **Sometimes the alleles in a pair of chromosomes are the same, which makes them** *homozygous.* **Sometimes the alleles differ, which makes them** *heterozygous.* In Leslie's case, her baby could be homozygous, in which case it would have two alleles for normal cells or two alleles for sickle-shaped cells. Leslie's baby might also be heterozygous, which means that it would have one allele for normal cells and one for sickle-shaped cells.

How does a genotype produce a phenotype? The answer is simple when a person is homozygous. When both alleles are the same and therefore have chemical instructions for the same phenotype, that phenotype usually results. (We'll see some exceptions in Module 2.2.) If Leslie's baby had alleles for normal red blood cells on both of the chromosomes in its 11th pair, the baby would be almost guaranteed to have normal cells. If, instead, the baby had two alleles for sickle-shaped cells, her baby would almost certainly suffer from the disease.

When a person is heterozygous, the process is more complex. **Often one allele is *dominant*, which means that its chemical instructions are followed whereas instructions of the other, the *recessive* allele, are ignored.** In the case of sickle-cell disease, the allele for normal cells is dominant and the allele for sickle-shaped cells is recessive. This is good news for Leslie: As long as either she or Glenn contributes the allele for normal red blood cells, her baby will not develop sickle-cell disease.

Figure 2-3 summarizes what we've learned about sickle-cell disease. The letter *A* denotes the allele for normal blood cells, and *a* denotes the allele for sickle-shaped cells. In the diagram, Glenn's genotype is homozygous dominant because he's positive that no one in his family has had sickle-cell disease. From Leslie's family history, she could be homozygous dominant or heterozygous; in the diagram, I've assumed the latter. You can see that Leslie and Glenn cannot have a baby with sickle-cell disease. However, their baby might be affected in another way. **Sometimes one allele does not dominate another completely, a situation known as *incomplete dominance.*** In incomplete dominance, the phenotype that results often falls between the phenotype associated with either allele. This is the case for the genes that control red blood cells. **Individuals with one dominant and one recessive allele have *sickle-cell trait*: In most situations they have no problems, but when they are seriously short of oxygen they suffer a temporary, relatively mild form of the disease.** Thus, sickle-cell trait is likely to appear when the person exercises vigorously or is at high altitudes (Sullivan, 1987). Leslie and Glenn's baby would have sickle-cell trait if it inherited a recessive gene from Leslie and a dominant gene from Glenn, as shown in Figure 2-3.

One aspect of sickle-cell disease that we haven't considered so far is why this disorder primarily affects African American children. The "Cultural Influences" feature addresses this point and, in the process, tells more about how heredity operates.

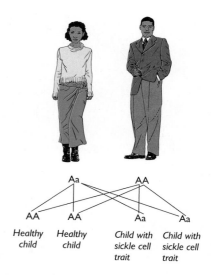

Aa   AA

AA   AA   Aa   Aa

Healthy   Healthy   Child with   Child with
child   child   sickle cell sickle cell
                    trait   trait

FIGURE 2-3

 QUESTION 2.1
If Glenn learned that he was heterozygous dominant for sickle-cell disease instead of homozygous dominant, how would this affect the chance that he and Leslie would have a child with sickle-cell disease? *(Answer is on page 49.)*

Cultural Influences

Why Do African Americans Inherit Sickle-Cell Disease?

Sickle-cell disease affects about 1 in 400 African American children. In contrast, virtually no European American children have the disorder. Why? Surprisingly, because the sickle-cell allele has a benefit: Individuals with this allele are more resistant to malaria, an infectious disease that is one of the leading causes of childhood death worldwide. Malaria is transmitted by mosquitoes, so it is most common in warm climates, including many parts of Africa. Compared to Africans who have alleles for normal blood cells, Africans with the sickle-cell allele are less likely to die from malaria, which means that the sickle-cell allele is passed along to the next generation.

This explanation of sickle-cell disease has two implications. First, sickle-cell disease should be found in any group of people living where malaria is common. In fact, sickle-cell disease affects Hispanic Americans who trace their roots to malaria-prone regions of the Caribbean, Central America, and South America. Second, malaria is rare in the United States, which means that the sickle-cell allele has no survival value to African Americans. Accordingly, the sickle-cell allele should become less common in successive generations of African Americans, and research indicates that this is happening.

There is an important lesson here. An allele may have survival value in one environment but not in others. In more general terms, the impact of heredity depends on the environment. We'll explore this lesson in more detail in Module 2.2.

The simple genetic mechanism responsible for sickle-cell disease, involving a single gene pair with one dominant allele and one recessive allele, is also responsible for many other common traits, as shown in Table 2-1. In each case, individuals with the recessive phenotype have two recessive alleles, one from each parent. Individuals with the dominant phenotype have at least one dominant allele.

TABLE 2-1

SOME COMMON PHENOTYPES ASSOCIATED WITH SINGLE PAIRS OF GENES

Dominant Phenotype	Recessive Phenotype
Curly hair	Straight hair
Normal hair	Pattern baldness (men)
Dark hair	Blond hair
Thick lips	Thin lips
Cheek dimples	No dimples
Normal hearing	Some types of deafness
Normal vision	Nearsightedness
Farsightedness	Normal vision
Normal color vision	Red-green color blindness
Type A blood	Type O blood
Type B blood	Type O blood
Rh-positive blood	Rh-negative blood

Source: McKusick, 1995.

Most of the traits listed in Table 2-1 are biological and medical phenotypes. These same patterns of inheritance can cause serious disorders, as we'll see in the next section.

Genetic Disorders

Genetics can harm development in two ways. First, some disorders are inherited. Sickle-cell disease is an example of an inherited disorder. Second, sometimes eggs or sperm have more or fewer than the usual 23 chromosomes. In the next few pages, we'll see how inherited disorders and abnormal numbers of chromosomes can alter a child's development.

INHERITED DISORDERS. Sickle-cell disease is one of many disorders that are homozygous recessive—triggered when a child inherits recessive alleles from both parents. Table 2-2 lists four more disorders that are commonly inherited in this manner.

TABLE 2-2

COMMON DISORDERS ASSOCIATED WITH RECESSIVE ALLELES

Disorder	Frequency	Characteristics
Albinism	1 in 15,000 births	Skin lacks melanin, which causes visual problems and extreme sensitivity to light.
Cystic fibrosis	1 in 3,000 births among European Americans; less common in African and Asian Americans	Excess mucus clogs respiratory and digestive tracts. Lung infections are common.
Phenylketonuria (PKU)	1 in 10,000 births	Phenylalanine, an amino acid, accumulates in the body and damages the nervous system, causing mental retardation.
Tay–Sachs disease	1 in 2,500 births among Jews of European descent	The nervous system degenerates in infancy, causing deafness, blindness, mental retardation, and, during the preschool years, death.

Source: Based on American Lung Association, 2007; Committee on Genetics, 1996; Hellekson, 2001; Thompson, 2007.

Relatively few serious disorders are caused by dominant alleles. Why? If the allele for the disorder is dominant, every person with at least one of these alleles will have the disorder. But individuals affected with these disorders typically do not live long enough to reproduce, so dominant alleles that produce fatal disorders soon vanish from the species. **An exception is** *Huntington's disease,* **a fatal disease characterized by progressive degeneration of the nervous system.** Huntington's disease is caused by a dominant allele found on chromosome 4. Individuals who inherit this disorder develop normally through childhood, adolescence, and young adulthood. However, during middle age, nerve cells begin to deteriorate, causing muscle spasms, depression, and significant changes in personality. By the time symptoms of Huntington's disease appear, adults who are affected may have already produced children, many of whom go on to develop the disease themselves.

Fortunately, most inherited disorders are rare. PKU, for example, occurs once in every 10,000 births, and Huntington's disease occurs even less frequently. Nevertheless, adults who believe that these disorders run in their family often want to know whether their children will inherit the disorder. The "Improving Children's Lives" feature shows how these couples can get help in deciding whether to have children.

Improving Children's Lives

Genetic Counseling

Family planning is not easy for couples who fear that their children may inherit serious or even fatal diseases. The best advice is to seek the help of a genetic counselor before a woman becomes pregnant. With the couple's help, a genetic counselor constructs a detailed family history that can be used to decide whether it's likely that either the man or the woman has the allele for the disorder that concerns them.

A family tree for Leslie and Glenn, the couple from the opening vignette, would confirm that Leslie is likely to carry the recessive allele for sickle-cell disease. The genetic counselor would then take the next step, obtaining a sample of Leslie's cells (probably from a blood test). The cells would be analyzed to determine whether the 11th chromosome carries the recessive allele for sickle-cell disease. If Leslie learns that she is homozygous—has two dominant alleles for healthy blood cells—then she and Glenn can be assured their children will not have sickle-cell disease. If Leslie learns that she has one recessive allele, then she and Glenn will know they have a 50% risk of having a baby with sickle-cell trait. Tests can also be administered after a woman is pregnant to determine whether the child she is carrying has an inherited disorder. We'll learn about these tests in Chapter 3.

Children with Down syndrome typically have upward-slanting eyes, with a fold over the eyelid; a flattened facial profile; and a smaller-than-average nose and mouth.

More common than inherited diseases are disorders caused by the wrong number of chromosomes, as we'll see next.

ABNORMAL NUMBER OF CHROMOSOMES. Sometimes individuals do not receive the normal complement of 46 chromosomes. If they are born with extra, missing, or damaged chromosomes, development is always disturbed. **The best example is** *Down syndrome,* **a genetic disorder that is caused by an extra 21st chromosome and that results in intellectual disability.*** Like the child in the photo, persons with Down syndrome have almond-shaped eyes and a fold over the eyelid. The head, neck, and nose of a child with this disorder are usually smaller than normal. During the first several months, babies with Down syndrome seem to develop normally. Thereafter, though, their mental and behavioral development begins to lag behind the average child's. For example, a child with Down syndrome might not sit up without help until about 1 year, not walk until 2, or not talk until 3—months or even years behind children without Down syndrome. By childhood, motor and mental development is substantially delayed.

*The scientific name is trisomy 21 because a person with the disorder has three 21st chromosomes instead of two. But the common name is Down syndrome, reflecting the name of the English physician, John Langdon Down, who identified the disorder in the 1860s.

Rearing a child with Down syndrome presents special challenges. During the preschool years, children with Down syndrome need special programs to prepare them for school. Educational achievements of children with Down syndrome are likely to be limited and their life expectancy ranges from 25 to 60 years (Yang, Rasmussen, & Friedman, 2002). Nevertheless, as we'll see in Chapter 8, many persons with Down syndrome lead fulfilling lives.

What causes Down syndrome? Individuals with Down syndrome typically have an extra 21st chromosome that is usually provided by the egg (Machatkova et al., 2005). Why the mother provides two 21st chromosomes is unknown. However, the odds that a woman will bear a child with Down syndrome increase markedly as she gets older. For a woman in her late 20s, the risk of giving birth to a baby with Down syndrome is about 1 in 1,000; for a woman in her early 40s, the risk is about 1 in 50. The increased risk may be because a woman's eggs have been in her ovaries since her own prenatal development. Eggs may deteriorate over time as part of aging, or eggs may become damaged because an older woman has a longer history of exposure to hazards in the environment, such as X-rays.

An extra autosome (as in Down syndrome), a missing autosome, or a damaged autosome always has far-reaching consequences for development because the autosomes contain huge amounts of genetic material. In fact, nearly half of all fertilized eggs abort spontaneously within two weeks, primarily because of abnormal autosomes. Thus, most eggs that could not develop normally are removed naturally (Moore & Persaud, 1993).

Abnormal sex chromosomes can also disrupt development. Table 2-3 lists four of the more frequent disorders associated with atypical numbers of X and Y chromosomes. Keep in mind that *frequent* is a relative term; although these disorders occur more frequently than PKU or Huntington's disease, the table shows that most are rare. Notice that no disorders consist solely of Y chromosomes. The presence of an X chromosome appears to be necessary for life.

 ANSWER 2.1
Glenn and Leslie would have a 25% chance of having a child with sickle-cell disease, a 50% chance of a child with sickle-cell trait, and a 25% chance of having a child with neither sickle-cell disease nor sickle-cell trait.

TABLE 2-3

COMMON DISORDERS ASSOCIATED WITH THE SEX CHROMOSOMES

Disorder	Sex Chromosomes	Frequency	Characteristics
Klinefelter's syndrome	XXY	1 in 500 to 1,000 male births	Tall, small testicles, sterile, below-normal intelligence, passive
XYY complement	XYY	1 in 1,000 male births	Tall, some cases apparently have below-normal intelligence
Turner's syndrome	X	1 in 2,500 to 5,000 female births	Short, limited development of secondary sex characteristics, problems perceiving spatial relations
XXX syndrome	XXX	1 in 500 to 1,200 female births	Normal stature but delayed motor and language development

Source: Based on Milunsky, 2002.

These genetic disorders demonstrate the remarkable power of heredity. Nevertheless, to fully understand how heredity influences development, we need to consider the environment, which we'll do in Module 2.2.

Check Your Learning

RECALL Describe the difference between dominant and recessive alleles.

Distinguish genetic disorders that are inherited from those that involve abnormal numbers of chromosomes.

INTERPRET Why do relatively few genetic disorders involve dominant alleles?

APPLY Suppose that a friend of yours discovers that she may have the recessive allele for the disease cystic fibrosis. What advice would you give her?

2.2 Heredity, Environment, and Development

OUTLINE	LEARNING OBJECTIVES
Behavioral Genetics	• What methods do scientists use to study the impact of heredity and environment on children's development?
Paths from Genes to Behavior	• How do heredity and environment work together to influence child development?

Sadie and Molly are fraternal twins. As babies, Sadie was calm and easily comforted, but Molly was fussy and hard to soothe. When they entered school, Sadie relished contact with other people and preferred play that involved others. Meanwhile, Molly was more withdrawn and was quite happy to play alone. Their grandparents wonder why these twins seem so different.

Why are Sadie and Molly so different despite having similar genes? To answer this question, we'll first look at the methods that child-development scientists use to study hereditary and environmental influences on children's development. Then we'll examine some basic principles that govern hereditary and environmental influences.

Behavioral Genetics

Behavioral genetics **is the branch of genetics that deals with inheritance of behavioral and psychological traits.** Behavioral genetics is complex, in part because behavioral and psychological phenotypes are complex. The traits controlled by single genes—like those shown in Table 2-1—usually represent "either–or" phenotypes. That is, the genotypes are usually associated with two (or sometimes three) well-defined phenotypes. For example, a person either has normal color vision or has red-green color blindness; a person has blood that clots normally, has sickle-cell trait, or has sickle-cell disease.

Most important behavioral and psychological characteristics are not either–or cases but represent an entire range of different outcomes. Take extroversion as an example. You probably know a few extremely outgoing individuals and a few intensely shy persons, but most of your friends and acquaintances are somewhere in between. Classifying your friends would produce a distribution of individuals across a continuum, from extreme extroversion at one end to extreme introversion at the other.

Many behavioral and psychological characteristics, including intelligence and aspects of personality, are distributed in this fashion, with a few individuals at the ends of the continuum and most near the middle. **Phenotypes distributed like this often reflect the combined activity of many separate genes, a pattern known as** *polygenic inheritance.* To see how many genes work together to produce a behavioral phenotype that spans a continuum, let's consider a hypothetical example. Suppose that four pairs of genes contribute to extroversion, that the allele for extroversion is dominant, and that the total amount of extroversion is simply the total of the dominant alleles. If uppercase letters represent dominant alleles and lowercase letters represent the recessive allele, the four gene pairs would be *Aa*, *Bb*, *Cc*, and *Dd*.

These four pairs of genes produce 81 different genotypes and 9 distinct phenotypes. For example, a person with the genotype *AABBCCDD* has 8 alleles for extroversion (a party animal). A person with the genotype *aabbccdd* has no alleles for extroversion (a wallflower). All other genotypes involve some combinations of dominant and recessive alleles, so these are associated with phenotypes representing intermediate levels of extroversion. In fact, Figure 2-4 shows that the most common outcome is for people to inherit exactly 4 dominant and 4 recessive alleles: 19 of the 81 genotypes produce this pattern (e.g., *AABbccDd*, *AaBbcCDd*). A few extreme

> Behavioral characteristics often reflect polygenic inheritance in which a phenotype depends on the combined actions of many genes.

FIGURE 2-4

Identical twins are called *monozygotic* twins because they came from a single fertilized egg that split in two; consequently, they have identical genes.

cases (very outgoing or very shy), when coupled with many intermediate cases, produce the familiar bell-shaped distribution that characterizes many behavioral and psychological traits.

Remember, this example is completely hypothetical. Extroversion is *not* based on the combined influence of four pairs of genes. But this example shows how several genes working together could produce a continuum of phenotypes. Something like our example is probably involved in the inheritance of numerous human behavioral traits, except that many more pairs of genes are involved and the environment also influences the phenotype (Plomin et al., 2001).

METHODS OF BEHAVIORAL GENETICS. If many behavioral phenotypes involve countless genes, how can we hope to unravel the influence of heredity? Traditionally, behavior geneticists have relied on statistical methods in which they compare groups of people known to differ in their genetic similarity. Twins, for example, provide important clues about the influence of heredity. **Identical twins are called** *monozygotic twins* **because they come from a single fertilized egg that splits in two.** Because identical twins come from the same fertilized egg, they have the same genes that control body structure, height, and facial features, which explains why identical twins like those in the photo look alike. **In contrast, fraternal or** *dizygotic twins* **come from two separate eggs fertilized by two separate sperm.** Genetically, fraternal twins are just like any other siblings; on average, about half their genes are the same. In twin studies, scientists compare identical and fraternal twins to measure the influence of heredity. If identical twins are more alike than fraternal twins, this implicates heredity.

An example will help illustrate the logic underlying comparisons of identical and fraternal twins. Suppose we want to determine whether extroversion is inherited. We would first measure extroversion in a large number of identical and fraternal twins. We might use a questionnaire with scores ranging from 0 to 100 (100 indicating maximal extroversion). Some of the hypothetical results are shown in Table 2-4.

TABLE 2-4

TWINS' HYPOTHETICAL SCORES ON A MEASURE OF EXTROVERSION

	Fraternal Twins				Identical Twins		
Family	One Twin	Other Twin	Difference Between Twins	Family	One Twin	Other Twin	Difference Between Twins
Burress	80	95	15	Brady	100	95	5
Jacobs	70	50	20	Moss	32	30	2
Manning	10	35	25	Seau	18	15	3
Strahan	25	5	20	Vrabel	55	60	5
Toomer	40	65	25	Welker	70	62	8

Look first at the results for the fraternal twins. Most have similar scores: The Burress twins both have high scores but the Manning twins have low scores. Looking at the identical twins, their scores are even more alike, typically differing by no more than five points. This greater similarity among identical twins than among fraternal twins would be evidence that extroversion is inherited, just as the fact that identical twins look more alike than fraternal twins is evidence that facial appearance is inherited.

You can see the distinctive features of this approach in the "Focus on Research" feature, which describes a twin study that examined the influence of heredity on learning a second language.

Focus on Research

Hereditary and Environmental Bases of Second-Language Learning

Who were the investigators, and what was the aim of the study? Children and adolescents differ in the ease with which they learn a second language. For some, a second language comes easily; new words and grammar are mastered quickly and with relatively little effort. For others, though, second-language learning can be frustratingly slow and difficult. Philip Dale and his colleagues—Nicole Harlaar, Claire Haworth, and Robert Plomin (2010)—wondered whether heredity contributed to the ease of second-language learning; to find out, they conducted a twin study.

How did the investigators measure the topic of interest? Foreign-language teachers were asked to rate their students' proficiency in four domains of foreign-language learning: listening, speaking, reading, and writing. These were combined to create an overall measure of skill in foreign-language learning.

Who were the children in the study? The sample included 231 pairs of identical twins and 373 pairs of fraternal twins. They were approximately 14 years old when teachers rated their foreign-language proficiency.

What was the design of the study? This study was correlational because Dale and his colleagues examined similarity of second-language proficiency in identical and fraternal twins. The study was actually part of a much larger longitudinal project tracing the development of twins in the United Kingdom. But the present study simply looked at 14-year-olds, so it's neither cross-sectional nor longitudinal.

Were there ethical concerns with the study? No. Teachers' ratings resembled the evaluations they made of students regularly in class and the ratings were kept confidential. Parents provided consent for their children's participation in the longitudinal project.

What were the results? The primary results are correlations for foreign-language proficiency for twins. For fraternal twins, the correlation was .48, indicating that when one fraternal twin excelled in language learning, the other often did as well. However, the correlation for identical twins was greater, .78, indicating a much closer match in foreign-language skill for identical twins.

What did the investigators conclude? Because skill in a foreign language was much more similar among identical twins than among fraternal twins, this suggests an important role for heredity in the ease with which adolescents learn a second language.

Heredity is implicated when identical twins are more alike than fraternal twins and when adopted children resemble their biological parents more than their adoptive parents.

What converging evidence would strengthen these conclusions? The adolescents in the study were studying different languages, but the sample was too small for Dale and his colleagues to determine if the impact of heredity on learning ability would vary depending upon the second language (e.g., German versus Korean). It would be important to know whether these results hold generally or, instead, depend upon the similarity of the second language to an adolescent's native language.

Adopted children are another important source of information about heredity. In this case, adopted children are compared with their biological parents, who provide the child's genes, and their adoptive parents, who provide the child's environment. If a behavior has genetic roots, then adopted children's behavior should resemble that of their biological parents even though they have never met them. But if the adopted children resemble their adoptive parents, we know that family environment affects behavior.

If we wanted to use an adoption study to determine whether extroversion is inherited, we would measure extroversion in a large sample of adopted children, their biological mothers, and their adoptive mothers. (Why just mothers? Obtaining data from biological fathers of adopted children is often difficult.) The results of this hypothetical study are shown in Table 2-5.

TABLE 2-5

HYPOTHETICAL SCORES FROM AN ADOPTION STUDY ON A MEASURE OF EXTROVERSION

Child's Name	Child's Score	Biological Mother's Score	Adoptive Mother's Score
Anila	60	70	35
Jerome	45	50	25
Kerri	40	30	80
Michael	90	80	50
Troy	25	5	55

Overall, children's scores are similar to their biological mothers' scores: Extroverted children like Michael tend to have extroverted biological mothers. Introverted children like Troy tend to have introverted biological mothers. In contrast, children's scores don't show any clear relation to their adoptive mothers' scores. For example, although Michael has the highest score and Troy has the lowest, their adoptive mothers have very similar scores. Children's greater similarity to biological than to adoptive parents is evidence indicating that extroversion is inherited, or at least that it has a strong genetic component.

The key features of an adoption study are evident in work reported by Plomin and colleagues (Plomin et al., 1997). They wanted to determine hereditary and environmental contributions to intelligence. Consequently, they administered intelligence tests to biological mothers in the last few months of pregnancy and to adoptive mothers in the year following adoption. Every few years, the children took an intelligence test. At every age, children's intelligence was correlated more strongly with the biological mother's intelligence than with the adoptive mother's intelligence, which suggests that heredity plays an important role in determining intelligence (see Figure 2-5).

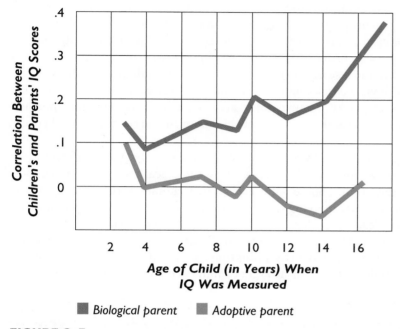

FIGURE 2-5

    Twin studies and adoption studies, which are described in the Summary Table, are powerful tools. They are not foolproof, however. Maybe you noticed a potential flaw in twin studies: Parents and other people may treat identical twins more similarly than they treat fraternal twins. This would make identical twins more similar than fraternal twins in their experiences as well as in their genes. Adoption studies have their own Achilles' heel. Adoption agencies sometimes try to place youngsters in homes like those of their biological parents. For example, if an agency believes that the biological parents are bright, the agency may try harder to have the child adopted by parents that the agency believes are bright. This can bias adoption studies because biological and adoptive parents end up being similar.

SUMMARY TABLE

PRIMARY RESEARCH METHODS FOR BEHAVIORAL GENETICS

Method	Defined	Evidence for Heredity	Main Weakness
Twin study	Compares monozygotic and dizygotic twins	Monozygotic twins more alike than dizygotic twins	Others may treat monozygotic twins more similarly than they treat dizygotic twins
Adoption study	Compares children with their biological and adoptive parents	Children more like biological parents than adoptive parents	Selective placement: Children's adoptive parents may resemble their biological parents

The problems associated with twin and adoption studies are not insurmountable. Because twin and adoption studies have different faults, if the two kinds of studies produce similar results on the influence of heredity, we can be confident of those results. In addition, behavioral geneticists are moving beyond traditional methods such as twin and adoption studies to connect behavior to molecular genetics (Dick & Rose, 2002; Plomin & Crabbe, 2000). Today, researchers are able to isolate particular segments of DNA in human chromosomes. These segments then serve as markers for identifying specific alleles. The procedure is complicated, but the basic approach often begins by identifying people who differ in the behavior or psychological trait of interest. For example, researchers might identify children who are outgoing and children who are shy, or they might identify children who read well and children who read poorly. The researchers rub the inside of the children's mouths with cotton swabs, which yield cheek cells that contain DNA. The cells are analyzed in a lab, and the DNA markers for the two groups are compared. If the markers differ consistently, then alleles near the marker probably contribute to the differences between the groups.

Techniques like these have the potential to identify the many different genes that contribute to complex behavioral and psychological traits. Of course, these new methods have limits. Some require very large samples of children, which can be hard to obtain when studying rare disorders. Also, some require that an investigator have an idea, even before beginning the study, about which chromosomes to search and where. These can be major hurdles. But, when used with traditional methods of behavioral genetics (e.g., adoption studies), the new methods promise much greater understanding of how genes influence behavior and development (Plomin & Crabbe, 2000).

WHICH PSYCHOLOGICAL CHARACTERISTICS ARE AFFECTED BY HEREDITY?   Research reveals consistent genetic influence in many psychological areas, including personality, mental ability, psychological disorders, and attitudes and interests. One expert summarized this work by saying, "Nearly every . . . psychological phenotype (normal and abnormal) is significantly influenced by genetic factors" (Bouchard, 2004, p. 151). In the examples of twin and adoption studies, we've already seen the impact of heredity on foreign-language learning and intelligence. You can see the range of genetic influence from a trio of twin studies, each involving young children:

- The number of letter sounds that children knew (e.g., "kuh" for k, which is an important prerequisite for learning to read) was correlated .68 for identical twins but .53 for fraternal twins (Taylor & Schatschneider, 2010).
- Scores on a measure of the ability to resist temptation—that is, obeying an instruction to not eat a tempting snack or touch an attractive gift—were correlated .38 for identical twins but .16 for fraternal twins (Gagne & Saudino, 2010).
- Scores on a measure of aggressive play with peers were correlated .64 for male identical twins but .34 for male fraternal twins and .54 for female identical twins but .36 for female fraternal twins (Van Hulle, Lemery-Chalfant, & Goldsmith, 2007).

Each of these studies shows the familiar signature of genetic influence: Be it knowing letter sounds, resisting temptation, or aggressing against peers, identical twins were more alike than were fraternal twins (i.e., larger correlations for identical twins than for fraternal twins).

We will look at the contributions of heredity (and environment) to children's development throughout this book. For now, keep in mind two conclusions from twin studies and adoption studies like those I've described so far. On the one hand, the impact of heredity on behavioral development is substantial and widespread. Heredity has a sizable influence on such different aspects of development as intelligence and personality. In understanding children and their development, we must always think about how heredity may contribute. On the other hand, heredity is never the sole determinant of behavioral development. If genes alone were responsible, then identical twins should have identical behavioral and psychological phenotypes. But we've seen that the correlations for identical twins fall short of 1, which would indicate identical scores of identical twins. Correlations of .5 and .6 mean that identical twins' scores are not perfectly consistent. One twin may, for example, play very aggressively with peers but the other does not. These differences reflect the influence of the environment. In fact, as we saw in Chapter 1, scientists agree that virtually all psychological and behavioral phenotypes involve nature and nurture working together to shape development (Diamond, 2009).

Paths from Genes to Behavior

How do genes work together to make, for example, some children brighter than others and some children more outgoing than others? That is, how does the information in strands of DNA influence a child's behavioral and psychological development? The specific paths from genes to behavior are largely uncharted (Meaney, 2010), but in the next few pages we'll discover some of their general properties.

HEREDITY AND ENVIRONMENT INTERACT DYNAMICALLY THROUGHOUT DEVELOPMENT. A traditional but simple-minded view of heredity and environment is that heredity provides the clay of life and experience does the sculpting. In fact, genes and environments constantly interact to produce phenotypes throughout a child's development (Meaney, 2010; Rutter, 2007). To illustrate, we often think there is a direct link between a genotype and a phenotype—given a certain genotype, a specific phenotype occurs, necessarily and automatically. In fact, the path from genotype to phenotype is massively more complicated and less direct than this. A more accurate description would be that a genotype leads to a phenotype but only if the environment "cooperates" in the usual manner.

A good example of this is the disease phenylketonuria (PKU for short), which can be expressed only when children inherit a recessive gene on the long arm of chromosome 12 from both parents (i.e., the child is homozygous recessive). Children with this genotype lack an enzyme that breaks down phenylalanine, an amino acid. Consequently, phenylalanine accumulates in the child's body, damaging the nervous system and leading to retarded mental development. Phenylalanine is abundant in many foods that most children eat regularly—meat, chicken, eggs, cheese—so the environment usually provides the input (phenylalanine) necessary for the phenotype (PKU) to emerge. However, in the middle of the 20th century, the biochemical basis for PKU was discovered and now newborns are tested for the disorder. Infants who have the genotype for the disease are immediately placed on a diet that limits phenylalanine and the disease does not appear; the nervous system of such a child develops normally. In more general terms, a genotype is expressed differently (no disease) when it is exposed to a different environment (one lacking phenylalanine).

The effect can work in the other direction, too, with the environment triggering genetic expression. That is, children's experiences can help to determine how and when genes are activated. For instance, teenage girls begin to menstruate at a younger age if they've had a stressful childhood (Belsky, Houts, & Fearon, 2010). The exact pathway of influence is unknown (though it probably involves the hormones that are triggered by stress and those that initiate ovulation), but this is a clear case in which the environment advances the genes that regulate the developmental clock (Ellis, 2004). ◉ Watch the Video on mydevelopmentlab.com

I've used a rare disease (PKU) and a once-in-a-lifetime event (onset of menstruation) to show intimate connections between nature and nurture in children's development. These examples may make it seem as if such connections are relatively rare, but nothing could be further from the truth. At a biological level, genes always operate in a cellular environment. There is constant interaction between genetic instructions and the nature of the immediate cellular environment, which can be influenced by a host of much broader environmental factors (e.g., hormones triggered by a child's experiences). **This continuous interplay between genes and multiple levels of the environment (from cells to culture) that drives development is known as** *epigenesis.* Returning to the analogy of sculpting clay, an epigenetic view of molding would be that new and different forms of genetic clay are constantly being added to the sculpture, leading to resculpting by the environment, which causes more clay to be added, and the cycle continues. Hereditary clay and environmental sculpting are continuously interweaving and influencing each other.

Because of the epigenetic principle, you need to be wary when you read statements like "X percent of a trait is due to heredity." **In fact, behavioral geneticists often use correlations from twin and adoption studies to calculate a** *heritability coefficient,* **which estimates the extent to which differences between people reflect heredity.** For example, intelligence has a heritability coefficient of about .5, which means that about 50% of the differences in intelligence between people is due to heredity (Bouchard, 2004).

Why be cautious? One reason is that many people mistakenly interpret heritability coefficients to mean that 50% of *an individual's* intelligence is due to heredity; this is incorrect because heritability coefficients apply to groups of people, not to a single person.

A second reason for caution is that heritability coefficients apply only to a specific group of people living in a specific environment. They cannot be applied to other groups of people living in the same environment or to the same people living elsewhere. For example, a child's height is certainly influenced by heredity, but the value of a heritability coefficient depends on the environment. When children grow in an environment that has ample nutrition—allowing all children to grow to their full genetic potential—heritability coefficients will be large. But when some children receive inadequate nutrition, this aspect of their environment will limit their height and, in the process, reduce the heritability coefficient.

◉ **Watch** the **Video** *Down Syndrome—Enhancing Development* on **mydevelopmentlab.com** to learn more about reaction range. Think about how developmental paths may differ for children with genetic disorders such as Down Syndrome (described on pages 48-49), depending on the environment in which they develop.

> The influence of genes on behavior always depends on the environment in which genetic instructions are carried out.

Similarly, the heritability coefficient for reading disability is larger for parents who are well educated than for parents who aren't (Friend, DeFries, & Olson, 2008). Why? Well-educated parents more often provide the academically stimulating environment that fosters a child's reading; consequently, reading disability in this group usually reflects heredity. In contrast, less educated parents less often provide the needed stimulation, and thus reading disability reflects a mixture of genetic and environmental influences.

This brings us back to the principle that began this section: "Heredity and environment interact dynamically throughout development." Both genes and environments are powerful influences on development, but we can only understand one by considering the other, too. This is another reason why it is essential to expand research beyond the middle-class, European American youngster that has been the favorite of child-development scientists. Only by studying diverse groups of children can we really understand the many ways in which genes and environments propel children along their developmental journeys.

GENES CAN INFLUENCE THE KIND OF ENVIRONMENT TO WHICH A CHILD IS EXPOSED.   In other words, "nature" can help determine the kind of "nurturing" that a child receives (Scarr, 1992; Scarr & McCartney, 1983). A child's genotype can lead people to respond to the child in a specific way. For example, imagine a child who is bright and outgoing (both due, in part, to the child's genes). That child may receive plenty of attention and encouragement from teachers. In contrast, a child who is not as bright and more withdrawn (again, due in part to heredity) may easily be overlooked by teachers. In addition, as children grow and become more independent, they actively seek environments related to their genetic makeup. Children who are bright (due in part to heredity) may actively seek peers, adults, and activities that strengthen their intellectual development. Similarly, children like the one in the photo, who are outgoing (due in part to heredity), seek the company of other people, particularly extroverts like themselves. **This process of deliberately seeking environments that fit one's heredity is called** *niche-picking.* Niche-picking is first seen in childhood and becomes more common as children get older and can control their environments.

Children who are outgoing often like to be with other people and deliberately seek them out, a phenomenon known as *niche-picking.*

Niche-picking is a prime example of the interaction between nature, nurture, and development. Experiences determine which phenotypes emerge, and genotypes influence the nature of children's experiences. The story of Sadie and Molly also makes it clear that, to understand how genes influence development, we need to look carefully at how environments work, our next topic.

ENVIRONMENTAL INFLUENCES TYPICALLY MAKE CHILDREN WITHIN A FAMILY DIFFERENT.   One of the fruits of behavioral genetic research is greater understanding of the manner in which environments influence children. Traditionally, scientists considered some environments beneficial for children and others detrimental. This view has been especially strong with regard to family environments. Some parenting practices are thought to be more effective than

 QUESTION 2.2
Erik, 19, and Jason, 16, are brothers. Erik excels in school: he gets straight A's, is president of the math club, and enjoys tutoring younger children. Jason hates school and his grades show it. How can nonshared environmental influences explain these differences? *(Answer is on page 60.)*

FIGURE 2-6

 ANSWER 2.2

Here are three examples of nonshared environmental influences. First, Erik's parents may have had higher academic standards for him, as the older child, and insisted that he do well in school; perhaps they relaxed their standards for Jason. Second, perhaps Erik found a circle of friends who enjoyed school and encouraged one another to do well in school; Jason may have found a group of friends who enjoyed hanging out at the mall instead of studying. Third, by the luck of the draw, Erik may have had a string of outstanding teachers who made school exciting; Jason may have had an equal number of not-so-talented teachers who made school boring.

others, and parents who use these effective practices are believed to have children who are, on average, better off than children of parents who don't use these practices. This view leads to a simple prediction: Children within a family should be similar because they all receive the same type of effective (or ineffective) parenting. However, dozens of behavioral genetic studies show that, in reality, siblings are not very much alike in their cognitive and social development (Plomin & Spinath, 2004).

Does this mean that family environment is not important? No. **These findings point to the importance of** *nonshared environmental influences,* **the environmental forces that make siblings different from one another.** Although environmental forces are important, they usually affect each child in a unique way, which makes siblings differ. For example, parents may be more affectionate with one child than another, they may use more physical punishment with one child than another, or they may have higher expectations for school achievement for one child than another. One teenager may have friends who like to drink while a sibling has friends who discourage drinking. All of these contrasting environmental influences tend to make siblings different, not alike (Liang & Eley, 2005). Environments are important, but, as I describe their influence throughout this book, you should remember that each child in a family experiences a unique environment.

Much of what I have said about genes, environment, and development is summarized in Figure 2-6. Parents are the source of children's genes and, at least for young children, the primary source of children's experiences. Children's genes also influence the experiences they have and the impact of those experiences on them. However, to capture the idea of nonshared environmental influences, we would need a separate diagram for each child, reflecting the fact that parents provide unique genes and a unique family environment for each of their offspring. And to capture the idea that genes are expressed across a child's lifetime, we would need to repeat the diagram for each child many times, emphasizing that heredity–environment influences at any given point are affected by prior heredity–environment exchanges.

Using this framework, we can speculate about why Sadie and Molly, the fraternal twins from this module's opening vignette, are so different. Perhaps their parents passed along more genes for sociability to Sadie than to Molly. During infancy, their parents included both girls in play groups with other babies. Sadie found this exciting, but Molly found it annoying and a bit stressful. Over time, their parents unwittingly worked hard to foster Sadie's relationships with her peers. They worried less about Molly's peer relationships because she seemed to be perfectly content to look at books, to color, or to play alone with puzzles. Apparently heredity gave Sadie a slighter larger dose of sociability, but experience ended up accentuating the difference between the sisters.

In a similar manner, throughout the rest of this book we'll examine links between nature, nurture, and development. One of the best places to see the interaction of nature and nurture is during prenatal development, which is the topic of Chapter 3.

Check Your Learning

RECALL What is polygenic inheritance and how does it explain behavioral phenotypes?

Describe the basic features, logic, and weaknesses of twin and adoption studies.

INTERPRET Explain how niche-picking shows the interaction between heredity and environment.

APPLY Leslie and Glenn, the couple from Module 2.1 who were concerned that their baby could have sickle-cell disease, are already charting their baby's life course. Leslie, who has always loved to sing, is confident that her baby will be a fantastic musician and easily imagines a regular routine of music lessons, rehearsals, and concerts. Glenn, a pilot, is just as confident that his child will share his love of flying; he is already planning trips the two of them can take together. Are Leslie's and Glenn's ideas more consistent with the active or passive views of children? What advice might you give to Leslie and Glenn about factors they are ignoring?

UNIFYING THEMES   Nature and Nurture

This entire chapter is devoted to a single theme: *Development is always jointly influenced by heredity and environment.* We have seen, again and again, how heredity and environment are essential ingredients in all developmental recipes, though not always in equal parts. In sickle-cell disease, an allele has survival value in malaria-prone environments but not in environments where malaria has been eradicated. Children with genes for normal intelligence develop below-average, average, or above-average intelligence, depending on the environment in which they grow. Nature and nurture . . . development always depends on both.

See for Yourself

The Human Genome Project, completed in 2003, was designed to identify the exact location of all 25,000 human genes in human DNA and to determine the sequence of roughly 3 billion pairs of nucleotides like those shown in the diagram on page 43. The project has produced maps of each chromosome showing the location of known genes. You can see these maps at a Web site maintained by the Human Genome Project, **www.genome.gov/10001772**.

At this site, you can select a "favorite" chromosome and see which genes have been located on it. See for yourself!

Summary

2.1 Mechanisms of Heredity

The Biology of Heredity
At conception, the 23 chromosomes in the sperm merge with the 23 chromosomes in the egg. The 46 chromosomes that result include 22 pairs of autosomes plus 2 sex chromosomes. Each chromosome is one molecule of DNA, which consists of nucleotides organized in a structure that resembles a spiral staircase. A section of DNA that provides specific biochemical instructions is called a *gene*. All of a person's genes make up a genotype; *phenotype* refers

to the physical, behavioral, and psychological characteristics that develop when the genotype is exposed to a specific environment.

Single Gene Inheritance

Different forms of the same gene are called *alleles*. A person who inherits the same allele on a pair of chromosomes is homozygous; in this case, the biochemical instructions on the allele are followed. A person who inherits different alleles is heterozygous; in this case, the instructions of the dominant allele are followed, whereas those of the recessive allele are ignored. In incomplete dominance, the person is heterozygous but the phenotype is midway between the dominant and recessive phenotypes.

Genetic Disorders

Most inherited disorders are carried by recessive alleles. Examples include sickle-cell disease, albinism, cystic fibrosis, phenylketonuria, and Tay–Sachs disease. Inherited disorders are rarely carried by dominant alleles because individuals with such a disorder usually don't live long enough to have children. An exception is Huntington's disease, which doesn't become symptomatic until middle age.

Most fertilized eggs that do not have 46 chromosomes are aborted spontaneously soon after conception. One exception is Down syndrome, caused by an extra 21st chromosome. Down-syndrome individuals have a distinctive appearance and are intellectually disabled. Disorders of the sex chromosomes, such as Klinefelter's syndrome, are more common because these chromosomes contain less genetic material.

2.2 Heredity, Environment, and Development

Behavioral Genetics

Behavioral and psychological phenotypes that reflect an underlying continuum (such as intelligence) often involve polygenic inheritance. In polygenic inheritance, the phenotype reflects the combined activity of many distinct genes. Polygenic inheritance has been examined traditionally by studying twins and adopted children, and more recently, by identifying DNA markers. These studies indicate substantial influence of heredity in many areas, including intelligence, psychological disorders, and personality.

Paths from Genes to Behavior

The impact of heredity on a child's development depends on the environment in which the genetic instructions are carried out; these heredity–environment interactions occur throughout a child's life. A child's genotype can affect the kinds of experiences he or she has; children and adolescents often actively seek environments related to their genetic makeup. Environments affect siblings differently (nonshared environmental influence): Each child in a family experiences a unique environment.

Test Yourself

✓•–[Study and **Review** on **mydevelopmentlab.com**

1. The human genotype consists of 22 pairs of _____ and one pair of sex chromosomes.

2. Each chromosome actually consists of one molecule of _____.

3. Inherited disorders are usually caused by _____ alleles.

4. Genetic counseling usually involves obtaining a detailed family history as well as _____.

5. When a child has extra, missing, or damaged chromosomes, the usual result is that _____.

6. Many fertilized eggs are aborted spontaneously soon after conception, typically due to _____.

7. _____ is the branch of genetics concerned with the inheritance of behavioral and psychological traits.

8. In _____, the phenotype reflects the combined influence of many pairs of genes.

9. When a fertilized egg splits in two, _____ result.

10. Twin studies are based on the assumption that _____.

11. In an adoption study, an inherited trait will cause adopted children to resemble their _____.

12. The main drawback to adoption studies is that _____.

13. _____ refers to the constant interaction across development between genes and multiple levels of the environment.

14. Niche-picking refers to the fact that children and adolescents _____.

15. _____ make children within a family different from each other.

Key Terms

alleles   43
autosomes   43
behavioral genetics   50
chromosomes   42
deoxyribonucleic acid—DNA   43
dizygotic twins   52
dominant   45
Down syndrome   48
epigenesis   58

gene   43
genotype   43
heritability coefficient   58
heterozygous   43
homozygous   43
Huntington's disease   47
in vitro fertilization   42
incomplete dominance   45
monozygotic twins   52

niche-picking   59
nonshared environmental
influences   60
phenotype   43
polygenic inheritance   51
recessive   45
sex chromosomes   43
sickle-cell trait   45

3 Prenatal Development, Birth, and the Newborn

3.1

From Conception to Birth

3.2

Influences on Prenatal Development

3.3

Happy Birthday!

3.4

The Newborn

If you ask parents to name some of the most memorable experiences of their lives, many mention events associated with pregnancy and childbirth. From the exciting news that a woman is pregnant through birth nine months later, the entire experience evokes awe and wonder. The events of pregnancy and birth provide the foundation on which all child development is built. In **Module 3.1**, we'll trace the events of prenatal development that transform sperm and egg into a living, breathing human being. In **Module 3.2**, we'll learn about some developmental problems that can occur before birth. In **Module 3.3**, we'll turn to birth. We'll see what happens during labor and delivery, and we'll consider some problems that can arise. In **Module 3.4**, we'll discover what newborn babies are like.

3.1 From Conception to Birth

OUTLINE

Period of the Zygote
(Weeks 1–2)

Period of the Embryo
(Weeks 3–8)

Period of the Fetus
(Weeks 9–38)

LEARNING OBJECTIVES

- What happens to a fertilized egg in the first 2 weeks after conception?

- When do body structures and internal organs emerge in prenatal development?
- When do body systems begin to function well enough to support life?

Eun Jung has just learned that she is pregnant with her first child. Like many other parents-to-be, she and her husband, Kinam, are ecstatic. But they also soon realize how little they know about "what happens when" during pregnancy. Eun Jung is eager to visit her obstetrician to learn more about the normal timetable of events during pregnancy.

The changes that transform a fertilized egg into a newborn human make up *prenatal development*. Prenatal development takes an average of 38 weeks, which are divided into three stages: the period of the zygote, the period of the embryo, and the period of the fetus. Each period gets its name from the term used to describe the baby-to-be at that point in prenatal development.

In this module, we'll trace the major developments during each period. As we go, you'll learn the answer to the "what happens when" question that intrigues Eun Jung.

Period of the Zygote (Weeks 1–2)

The diagram in Figure 3-1 on page 66 traces the major events of the first period of prenatal development, which begins with fertilization and lasts about 2 weeks. **It ends when the fertilized egg, called a** *zygote,* **implants itself in the wall of the uterus.** During these 2 weeks, the zygote grows rapidly through cell division and travels down the fallopian tube toward the uterus. Within hours, the zygote divides for the first time; then division occurs every 12 hours. Occasionally, the zygote separates into two clusters that develop into identical twins. Fraternal twins, which are more common, are created when two eggs are released and each is fertilized by a different sperm

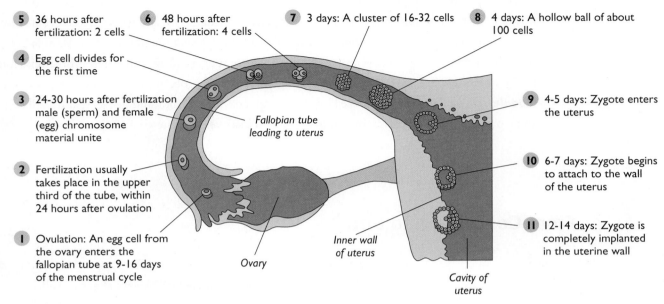

5 36 hours after fertilization: 2 cells

6 48 hours after fertilization: 4 cells

7 3 days: A cluster of 16-32 cells

8 4 days: A hollow ball of about 100 cells

4 Egg cell divides for the first time

3 24-30 hours after fertilization male (sperm) and female (egg) chromosome material unite

Fallopian tube leading to uterus

9 4-5 days: Zygote enters the uterus

2 Fertilization usually takes place in the upper third of the tube, within 24 hours after ovulation

10 6-7 days: Zygote begins to attach to the wall of the uterus

1 Ovulation: An egg cell from the ovary enters the fallopian tube at 9-16 days of the menstrual cycle

Inner wall of uterus

Ovary

11 12-14 days: Zygote is completely implanted in the uterine wall

Cavity of uterus

FIGURE 3-1

By the end of the period of the zygote, the fertilized egg has been implanted in the wall of the uterus and has begun to make connections with the mother's blood vessels.

cell. **After about 4 days, the zygote consists of about 100 cells, resembles a hollow ball, and is called a** *blastocyst.*

By the end of the first week, the zygote reaches the uterus. **The next step is** *implantation:* **The blastocyst burrows into the uterine wall and establishes connections with the mother's blood vessels.** Implantation takes about a week to complete and triggers hormonal changes that prevent menstruation, letting the woman know she has conceived.

As shown in the photograph, the implanted blastocyst is less than a millimeter in diameter, yet its cells have already begun to differentiate. In Figure 3-2, which shows a cross-section of the blastocyst and the wall of the uterus, you can see different layers of cells. **A small cluster of cells near the center of the blastocyst, the** *germ disc,* **eventually develops into the baby.** The other cells are destined to become structures that support, nourish, and protect the developing organism. **The layer of cells closest to the uterus becomes the** *placenta,* **a structure for exchanging nutrients and wastes between the mother and the developing organism.**

Implantation and differentiation of cells mark the end of the period of the zygote. Comfortably sheltered in the uterus, the blastocyst is well prepared for the remaining 36 weeks of the marvelous journey to birth.

Period of the Embryo (Weeks 3–8)

After the blastocyst is completely embedded in the uterine wall, it is called an *embryo.* This new period typically begins the third week after conception and lasts until the end of the eighth week. During the period of the embryo, body structures

Mother's blood vessels

Germ disc, which develops into the fetus

Cavity of the uterus

Cells that will form the placenta, the structure that will link the fetus to the mother

FIGURE 3-2

At 3 weeks after conception, the fertilized egg is about 2 millimeters long and resembles a salamander.

and internal organs develop. At the beginning of the period, three layers form in the embryo. **The outer layer or** *ectoderm* **will become hair, the outer layer of skin, and the nervous system; the middle layer or** *mesoderm* **will form muscles, bones, and the circulatory system; the inner layer or** *endoderm* **will form the digestive system and the lungs.**

One dramatic way to see the changes that occur during the embryonic period is to compare a 3-week-old embryo with an 8-week-old embryo. The 3-week-old embryo shown in the top photo is about 2 millimeters long. Cell specialization is under way, but the organism looks more like a salamander than a human being. But growth and specialization proceed so rapidly that the 8-week-old embryo shown in the bottom photo looks very different: You can see an eye, the jaw, an arm, and a leg. The brain and the nervous system are also developing rapidly, and the heart has been beating for nearly a month. Most of the organs found in a mature human are in place, in some form. (The sex organs are a notable exception.) Yet, being only an inch long and weighing a fraction of an ounce, the embryo is much too small for the mother to feel its presence.

The embryo's environment is shown in Figure 3-3 on page 68. **The embryo rests in an** *amniotic sac,* **which is filled with** *amniotic fluid* **that cushions the embryo and maintains a constant temperature.** The embryo is linked to the mother by two structures. **The** *umbilical cord* **houses blood vessels that join the embryo to the placenta.** In the placenta, the blood vessels from the umbilical cord run close to the mother's blood vessels but aren't actually connected to them. **Instead, the blood flows through** *villi,* **finger-like projections from the umbilical blood vessels that are shown in Figure 3-3.** As you can see, villi lie in close proximity to the mother's blood vessels and thus allow nutrients, oxygen, vitamins, and waste products to be exchanged between mother and embryo.

At 8 weeks after conception, near the end of the period of the embryo, the fertilized egg is obviously recognizable as a baby-to-be.

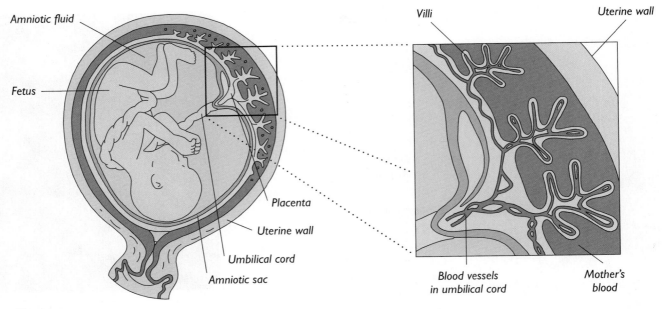

FIGURE 3-3

With body structures and internal organs in place, another major milestone passes in prenatal development. What's left is for these structures and organs to begin working properly. This is accomplished in the final period of prenatal development, as we'll see in the next section.

Period of the Fetus (Weeks 9–38)

The final and longest phase of prenatal development, the *period of the fetus,* **extends from the ninth week after conception until birth.** During this period, the baby-to-be becomes much larger and its bodily systems begin to work. The increase in size is remarkable. At the beginning of this period, the fetus weighs less than an ounce. At about 4 months, the fetus weighs roughly 4 to 8 ounces, enough for the mother to feel it move: Pregnant women often describe these fluttering movements as feeling like popcorn popping or a gold-fish swimming inside them! During the last 5 months of pregnancy, the fetus gains an average of an additional 7 or 8 pounds before birth. Figure 3-4, which depicts the fetus at one-eighth of its actual size, shows these incredible increases in size.

During the fetal period, the finishing touches are put on the body systems that are essential to human life, such as the nervous, respiratory, and digestive systems. Some high-lights of this period include the following: ◉ Watch the **Video** on **mydevelopmentlab.com**

Body parts and systems begin to function in the period of the fetus.

◉ Watch the **Video** *Fetal Development* on **mydevelopmentlab.com** to learn more about prenatal development. This animation traces prenatal development from the 4th month of pregnancy to birth and shows the many physical and behavioral changes that take place in these months.

• At 4 weeks after conception, a flat set of cells curls to form a tube. One end of the tube swells to form the brain; the rest forms the spinal cord. By the start of the fetal period, the brain has distinct structures and has begun to regulate body functions. **During the period of the fetus, all regions of the brain grow, par-ticularly the** *cerebral cortex,* **the wrinkled surface of the brain that regulates many important human behaviors.**

• Near the end of the embryonic period, male embryos develop testes and female embryos develop ovaries. In the third month, the testes in a male fetus secrete

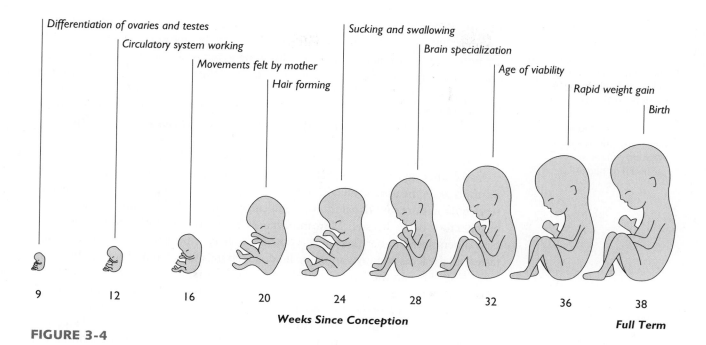

Differentiation of ovaries and testes

Circulatory system working

Movements felt by mother

Hair forming

Sucking and swallowing

Brain specialization

Age of viability

Rapid weight gain

Birth

9   12   16   20   24   28   32   36   38

Weeks Since Conception

Full Term

FIGURE 3-4

a hormone that causes a set of cells to become a penis and scrotum; in a female fetus, this hormone is absent, so the same cells become a vagina and labia.

- During the fifth and sixth months after conception, eyebrows, eyelashes, and scalp hair emerge. **The skin thickens and becomes covered with a thick greasy substance,** *vernix,* **that protects the fetus during its long bath in amniotic fluid.**

- By about 6 months after conception, fetuses differ in their usual heart rates and in how much their heart rate changes in response to physiological stress. In one study (DiPietro et al., 2007), fetuses with greater heart rate variability were, as 2-month-olds, more advanced in their motor, mental, and language development. Greater heart rate variability may be a sign that the nervous system is responding efficiently to environmental change (as long as the variability is not extreme).

With these and other rapid changes, by 22 to 28 weeks most systems function well enough that a fetus born at this time has a chance to survive, which is why this age range is called the *age of viability.* By this age, the fetus has a distinctly baby-like look, as you can see in the photo. However, babies born this early have trouble breathing because their lungs are not yet mature. Also, they cannot regulate their body temperature very well because they lack the insulating layer of fat that appears in the eighth month after conception. With modern neonatal intensive care, infants born this early can survive, but they face other challenges, as I'll describe in Module 3.3.

At 22 to 28 weeks after conception, the fetus has achieved the age of viability, meaning that it has a chance of surviving if born prematurely.

QUESTION 3.1

Rachel is 8 months pregnant and spends hours each day talking to her baby-to-be. Rachel's husband considers this a waste of time, but Rachel's convinced that her baby-to-be must benefit. What do you think?

(Answer is on page 72.)

FETAL BEHAVIOR.   During the fetal period, the fetus actually starts to behave (Joseph, 2000). The delicate movements that were barely noticeable at 4 months are now obvious. In fact, the fetus is a budding gymnast and kick-boxer rolled into one. It will punch or kick and turn somersaults. When active, the fetus will move about once a minute (DiPietro et al, 2004). However, these bursts of activity are followed by times when the fetus is still, as regular activity cycles emerge. Although movement is common in a healthy pregnancy, some fetuses are more active than others, and these differences predict infants' behavior: An active fetus is more likely than an inactive fetus to be an unhappy, difficult baby (DiPietro et al., 1996).

Another sign of growing behavioral maturity is that the senses work. There's not much to see in the uterus (imagine being in a cave with a flashlight that has a weak battery), but there are sounds galore. The fetus can hear the mother's heart beating and can hear her food being digested. More importantly, the fetus can hear its mother speak and hear others speak to her (Lecanuet, Granier-Deferre, & Busnel, 1995). And there are tastes: As the fetus swallows amniotic fluid, it responds to different flavors in the fluid.

Not only can the fetus detect sounds and flavors, it can also remember these sensory experiences later. For example, when sounds are played through a loud-speaker placed on a pregnant woman's abdomen, the fetus usually responds to the sound and vibrations by moving. However, if the sound is repeated every 30 seconds, the fetus gradually stops responding, indicating that it recognizes the stimulation as familiar. What's more, if the sounds are played at 8 months after conception, the fetus can remember them a month later (Dirix et al., 2009).

With these memory skills operating late in pregnancy, there's an obvious question: After birth, does a baby remember events experienced in the uterus? Yes. In one study (Mennella, Jagnow, & Beauchamp, 2001), women drank carrot juice several days a week during the last month of pregnancy. When their infants were 5 and 6 months old, they preferred cereal flavored with carrot juice. In another study, pregnant women read aloud *The Cat in the Hat* daily for the last several weeks of pregnancy (DeCasper & Spence, 1986). After birth, the newborns were allowed to suck on a special pacifier that controlled a tape recorder. The newborns would suck to hear a tape of their mother reading *The Cat in the Hat* but not to hear her reading other stories. Evidently, newborns recognized the familiar, rhythmic quality of *The Cat in the Hat* from their prenatal story times. The ability of the fetuses in these studies to learn from experience shows that prenatal development leaves babies well prepared for life outside the uterus.

The fetus moves, perceives, and remembers.

After reading about findings like these, you may be tempted to buy products that claim to "teach" the fetus, by providing auditory stimulation (e.g., rhythmic sounds, speech, music). Makers of these products claim that a fetus exposed to this stimulation will reach developmental milestones earlier and be better prepared for school. However, I suggest that you save your money. The learning shown in the studies described in the previous paragraph—such as recognizing voices—occurs quite rapidly after birth without prenatal "education." Also, some of the more sophisticated forms of learning that are claimed to occur are probably impossible in utero, either because they require simultaneous visual stimulation (e.g., to pair voices with faces) or because they depend on brain development that takes place after birth.

The prenatal changes described in this module are summarized in the Summary Table. The milestones listed in the table make it clear that prenatal development does a remarkable job of preparing the fetus for independent living as a newborn baby. But these astonishing prenatal changes can take place only when a woman provides a healthy environment for her baby-to-be. The "Improving Children's Lives" feature describes what pregnant women should do to provide the best foundation for prenatal development.

SUMMARY TABLE

CHANGES DURING PRENATAL DEVELOPMENT

Trimester	Period	Weeks	Size	Highlights
First	Zygote	1–2		Fertilized egg becomes a blastocyst that is implanted in the uterine wall
	Embryo	3–4	1/4 inch	Period of rapid growth; most body parts, including nervous system (brain and spinal cord), heart, and limbs are formed
	Embryo	5–8	1 inch, fraction of an ounce	
	Fetus	9–12	3 inches, about an ounce	Rapid growth continues, most body systems begin to function
Second	Fetus	13–24	12–15 inches, about 2 pounds	Continued growth; fetus is now large enough for the mother to feel its movements, fetus is covered with vernix
Third	Fetus	25–38	20 inches, 7–8 pounds	Continued growth; body systems become mature in preparation for birth, layer of fat is acquired, reaches the age of viability

Improving Children's Lives

Five Steps Toward a Healthy Baby

1. Visit a health care provider for regular prenatal checkups. You should have monthly visits until you get close to your due date, when you will have a checkup every other week or maybe even weekly.

2. Eat healthy foods. Be sure your diet includes foods from each of the five major food groups (cereals, fruits, vegetables, dairy products, and meats and beans). Your health care provider may recommend that you supplement your diet with vitamins, minerals, and iron to be sure you are providing your baby with all the nutrients it needs.

3. Stop drinking alcohol and caffeinated beverages. Stop smoking. Consult your health care provider before taking any over-the-counter medications or prescription drugs.

4. Exercise throughout pregnancy. If you are physically fit, your body is better equipped to handle the needs of the baby.

5. Get enough rest, especially during the last 2 months of pregnancy. Also, attend childbirth education classes so that you'll be prepared for labor, delivery, and your new baby.

As critically important as these steps are, they unfortunately do not guarantee a healthy baby. In Module 3.2, we'll see how prenatal development can sometimes go awry.

 Check Your Learning

 ANSWER 3.1
The fetus can hear Rachel speaking, and these one-sided conversations probably help the fetus to become familiar with Rachel's voice. There aren't other obvious benefits, however, because the fetus can't understand *what* she's saying.

RECALL Describe the three stages of prenatal development. What are the highlights of each?

What findings show that the fetus behaves?

INTERPRET Compare the events of prenatal development that precede the age of viability with those that follow it.

APPLY In the last few months before birth, the fetus has some basic perceptual and motor skills; a fetus can hear, see, taste, and move. What are the advantages of having these skills in place months before they're really needed?

 3.2 Influences on Prenatal Development

OUTLINE

General Risk Factors

Teratogens: Diseases, Drugs, and Environmental Hazards

How Teratogens Influence Prenatal Development

Prenatal Diagnosis and Treatment

LEARNING OBJECTIVES

• How is prenatal development influenced by a pregnant woman's nutrition, the stress she experiences while pregnant, and her age?

• What is a teratogen, and what specific diseases, drugs, and environmental hazards can be teratogens?

• How do teratogens affect prenatal development?

• How can prenatal development be monitored? Can abnormal prenatal development be corrected?

Chloe was barely 2 months pregnant at her first prenatal checkup. As she waited for her appointment, she looked at the list of questions that she wanted to ask her obstetrician. "I spend much of my workday talking on my cell phone. Is radiation from the phone harmful to my baby?" "When my husband and I get home from work, we'll have a glass of wine to help unwind from the stress of the day. Is moderate drinking like this okay?" "I'm 38. I know older women more often give birth to babies with disabilities. Is there any way I can know if my baby will have disabilities?"

A ll of Chloe's questions concern potential harm to her baby-to-be. She worries about the safety of her cell phone, about her nightly glass of wine, and about her age. Chloe's concerns are well-founded. Beginning with conception, environmental factors influence the course of prenatal development, and they are the focus of this module. If you're sure you can answer all of Chloe's questions, skip this module and go directly to Module 3.3 on page 86. Otherwise, read on to learn about problems that sometimes arise in pregnancy.

General Risk Factors

As the name implies, general risk factors can have widespread effects on prenatal development. Scientists have identified three general risk factors: nutrition, stress, and a mother's age.

NUTRITION.   The mother is the developing child's sole source of nutrition, so a balanced diet that includes foods from each of the five major food groups is vital. Most pregnant women need to increase their intake of calories by about 10% to 20% to meet the needs of prenatal development. A woman should expect to gain between 25 and 35 pounds during pregnancy, assuming that her weight was normal before pregnancy. A woman who was underweight before becoming pregnant may gain as much as 40 pounds; a woman who was overweight should gain at least 15 pounds (Institute of Medicine, 1990). Of this gain, about one-third reflects the weight of the baby, the placenta, and the fluid in the amniotic sac; another third comes from increases in a woman's fat stores; yet another third comes from the increased volume of blood and increases in the size of her breasts and uterus (Whitney & Hamilton, 1987).

Sheer amount of food is only part of the equation for a healthy pregnancy. *What* a pregnant woman eats is also very important. Proteins, vitamins, and minerals are essential for normal prenatal development. For example, folic acid, one of the B vitamins, is important for the nervous system to develop properly (Shaw et al., 1995). **When mothers do not consume adequate amounts of folic acid, their babies are at risk for** *spina bifida,* **a disorder in which the embryo's neural tube does not close properly during the first month of pregnancy.** Because the neural tube develops into the brain and spinal cord, improper closing results in permanent damage to the spinal cord and the nervous system. Many children with spina bifida need to use crutches, braces, or wheelchairs. Other prenatal problems have also been traced to inadequate proteins, vitamins, or minerals, so health care providers typically recommend that pregnant women supplement their diet with additional proteins, vitamins, and minerals.

> Adequate nutrition in terms of calories as well as proteins, vitamins, and minerals is essential for healthy prenatal development.

When a pregnant woman does not provide adequate nourishment, the infant is likely to be born prematurely and to be underweight. Inadequate nourishment during the last few months of pregnancy can particularly affect the nervous system, because this is a time of rapid brain growth. Finally, babies who do not receive adequate nourishment are vulnerable to illness (Morgane et al., 1993).

STRESS.   Does a pregnant woman's mood affect the zygote, embryo, or fetus in her uterus? Is a woman who is happy during pregnancy more likely to give birth to a happy baby? Is a pregnant woman like the harried office worker in the photo on page 74 more likely to give birth to an irritable baby? **These questions address the impact on prenatal development of chronic** *stress,* **which refers to a person's physical and psychological responses to threatening or**

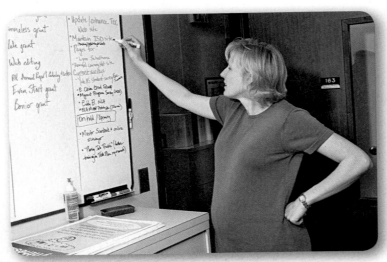

When pregnant women experience chronic stress, they're more likely to give birth early or have smaller babies, but this may be because women who are stressed are more likely to smoke or drink and less likely to rest, exercise, and eat properly.

challenging situations. We can answer these questions with some certainty for nonhumans. When pregnant female animals experience constant stress, such as repeated electric shock or intense overcrowding, their offspring are often smaller than average and prone to other physical and behavioral problems (DiPietro, 2004).

Determining the impact of stress on human pregnancy is more difficult because, for ethical reasons, we must rely largely on correlational studies. Studies typically show that women who report greater anxiety during pregnancy more often give birth early or have babies who weigh less than average (Copper et al., 1996; Tegethoff et al., 2010). What's more, when women are anxious throughout pregnancy, their children are less able to pay attention as infants and more prone to behavioral problems as preschoolers (Huizink et al., 2002; O'Conner et al., 2002). Similar results emerged from studies of pregnant women exposed to disasters, such as the September 11 attacks on the World Trade Center: their children's physical and behavioral development was affected (Engel et al., 2005; Laplante et al., 2004). Finally, the harmful effects of stress are not linked to anxiety in general but are specific to worries about pregnancy, particularly in the first few months (Davis & Sandman, 2010; DiPietro et al., 2006).

Increased stress can harm prenatal development in several ways. First, when a pregnant woman experiences stress, her body secretes hormones that reduce the flow of oxygen to the fetus while increasing its heart rate and activity level (Monk et al., 2000). Second, stress can weaken a pregnant woman's immune system, making her more susceptible to illness (Cohen & Williamson, 1991), which can, in turn, damage fetal development. Third, pregnant women under stress are more likely to smoke or drink alcohol and less likely to rest, exercise, and eat properly (DiPietro, 2004). All these behaviors endanger prenatal development.

I want to emphasize that the results described here apply to women who experience *chronic* stress. Virtually all women are sometimes anxious or upset while pregnant. But occasional, relatively mild anxiety is not thought to have harmful consequences for prenatal development.

> Problems during pregnancy are more common when a woman experiences chronic stress and when she is 35 or older.

MOTHER'S AGE. Traditionally, the 20s were thought to be the prime childbearing years. Teenage women as well as women who were 30 or older were considered less fit for the rigors of pregnancy. Is being a 20-something really important for a successful pregnancy? Let's answer this question separately for teenage and older women. Compared to women in their 20s, teenage women are more likely to have problems during pregnancy, labor, and delivery. This is largely because pregnant teenagers are more likely to be economically disadvantaged and to not get good prenatal care, because they are unaware of the need and wouldn't be able to afford it if they did. For example, in one study (Turley, 2003), children of teenage moms were compared with their cousins, whose mothers were the older sisters of the teenage moms but had given birth when they were in their 20s. The two groups of children were very similar in academic skills and behavioral problems, indicating that it's probably the typical family background of teenage moms that is the obstacle, not their age. Similarly, research done on African American adolescents indicates that when differences in prenatal care are taken into account, teenagers are just as likely as women in their 20s to have problem-free pregnancies and give birth to healthy babies (Goldenberg & Klerman, 1995).

Nevertheless, even when a teenager receives adequate prenatal care and gives birth to a healthy baby, all is not rosy. Children of teenage mothers generally do less well in school and more often have behavioral problems (D'Onofrio et al., 2009; Fergusson & Woodward, 2000). The problems of teenage motherhood—incomplete education, poverty, and marital difficulties—affect the child's later development (Moore & Brooks-Gunn, 2002). In the "Spotlight on Theories" feature, we'll see one explanation that child-development researchers have proposed for why these problems occur.

Spotlight on Theories

A Theory of the Risks Associated with Teenage Motherhood

BACKGROUND Children born to teenage mothers typically don't fare very well. During childhood and adolescence, these children usually have lower scores on mental-ability tests, they get lower grades in school, and they more often have behavioral problems (e.g., they're too aggressive). However, why teen motherhood leads to these outcomes remains poorly understood.

THE THEORY Sara Jaffee (2003) believes that teenage motherhood leads to harmful consequences through two distinct mechanisms. **One mechanism, called** *social influence,* **refers to events set in motion when a teenage girl gives birth— events that make it harder for her to provide a positive environment for her child's development.** For example, she may drop out of school, limiting her employment opportunities. Or she may try to finish school but become a neglectful parent because she spends so much time studying.

According to the second mechanism, called *social selection,* **some teenage girls are more likely than others to become pregnant, and those same factors that cause girls to become pregnant may put their children at risk.** Take conduct disorder as an example. Teenage girls with conduct disorder—who often lie, break rules, and are aggressive physically and verbally—are more likely to get pregnant than girls who don't have conduct disorder. The behaviors that define conduct disorder don't bode well for effective parenting. In addition, conduct disorder has a genetic component, which teenage mothers could pass along to their children.

According to social selection, the mother's age at birth is not really critical; these girls would have difficulty parenting effectively even if they delayed motherhood into their 20s or 30s. Instead, the factors that put girls at risk for becoming pregnant as teenagers also put children from those pregnancies at risk.

Hypothesis: According to the social influence mechanism, measures of the child-rearing environment should predict outcomes for children born to teenage moms. For example, if teenage motherhood results in less education and less income, then these variables should predict children's outcomes. According to the social selection mechanism, the same characteristics that are associated with a teenage girl's becoming pregnant should predict outcomes for her children. For example, if teenage girls are more likely to get pregnant when they're not as smart and have conduct disorder, then these same variables should predict outcomes for the children of these teenage moms.

Test: Jaffee (2003) evaluated both hypotheses in a 20-year longitudinal study conducted in New Zealand in which about 20% of the mothers had given birth while teenagers. She measured mothers' antisocial behavior as well as their education and income. She also assessed children's outcomes. For simplicity, we'll consider just one outcome: whether the children had, as adolescents or young adults, committed any criminal offenses.

Jaffee found that, compared to children born to older mothers, children born to teenage mothers were nearly three times more likely to have committed a criminal offense. This was due to both social influence and social selection mechanisms. Consistent with the social influence mechanism, teenage moms were less educated and had lower incomes, and these variables predicted their children's criminal activity. Consistent with the social selection mechanism, teenage moms were more likely to have a history of antisocial behavior, and this history predicted their children's criminal activity.

Conclusion: The adverse outcomes associated with teenage motherhood don't have a single explanation. Some of the adversity can be traced to cascading events brought on by giving birth as a teenager: Early motherhood limits education and income, hindering a mother's efforts to provide an environment that's conducive to a child's development. But some of the adversity does not reflect early motherhood per se; instead, girls who become pregnant teenagers often have characteristics that lead to adverse outcomes regardless of the age at which they gave birth.

Application: Policymakers have created many social programs designed to encourage teenagers to delay childbearing. Jaffee's work suggests two additional needs. First, policies are needed to limit the cascading harmful effects of childbearing for those teens who do get pregnant (e.g., programs to allow them to complete their education without neglecting their children). Second, many of the problems associated with teenage pregnancy are only coincidentally related to the fact that the mother is a teenager; programs are needed to help these girls learn effective parenting methods.

Of course, not all teenage mothers and their infants follow this dismal life course. Some teenage mothers finish school, find good jobs, and have happy marriages; their children do well in school, academically and socially. These successes are more likely when teenage moms live with a relative—typically the child's grandmother (Gordon, Chase-Lansdale, & Brooks-Gunn, 2004). However, teenage pregnancies with "happy endings" are definitely the exception; for many teenage mothers and their children, life is a struggle. Educating teenagers about the true consequences of teen pregnancy is crucial. Fortunately, the pregnancy rate among U.S. teenagers has declined steadily from its peak in the early 1990s (Hamilton, Martin, & Ventura, 2010).

Are older women better suited for pregnancy? This is an important question because present-day American women typically are waiting longer than ever to become pregnant. Completing an education and beginning a career often delay childbearing. In fact, the birthrate in the early 2000s among 40- to 44-year-olds is at its highest since the 1960s (Hamilton et al., 2010).

Today we know that older women like the one in the photo have more difficulty getting pregnant and are less likely to have successful pregnancies. Women in their 20s are twice as fertile as women in their 30s (Dunson, Colombo, & Baird, 2002), and past 35 years of age, the risks of miscarriage and stillbirth increase rapidly. Among

40- to 45-year-olds, for example, nearly half of all pregnancies result in miscarriage (Andersen et al., 2000). What's more, women in their 40s are more liable to give birth to babies with Down syndrome. However, as mothers, older women are quite effective. For example, they are just as able to provide the sort of sensitive, responsive caregiving that promotes a child's development (Bornstein et al., 2006).

In general, then, prenatal development is most likely to proceed normally when women are between the ages of 20 and 35, are healthy and eat right, get good health care, and lead lives that are free of chronic stress. But even in these optimal cases, prenatal development can be disrupted, as we'll see in the next section.

Teratogens: Diseases, Drugs, and Environmental Hazards

In the late 1950s, many pregnant women in Germany took thalidomide, a drug to help them sleep. Soon, however, came reports that many of these women were giving birth to babies with deformed arms, legs, hands, or fingers. **Thalidomide was a powerful** *teratogen,* **an agent that causes abnormal prenatal development.** Ultimately, more than 10,000 babies worldwide were harmed before thalidomide was withdrawn from the market (Kolberg, 1999).

Prompted by the thalidomide disaster, scientists began to study teratogens extensively. Today, we know a great deal about the three primary types of teratogens: diseases, drugs, and environmental hazards. Let's look at each.

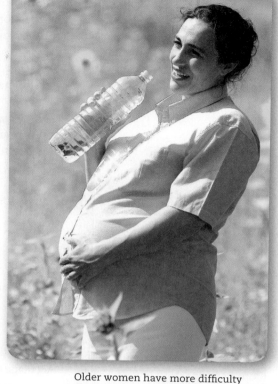

Older women have more difficulty getting pregnant and are more likely to have miscarriages, but they are quite effective mothers.

DISEASES. Sometimes women become ill while pregnant. Most diseases, such as colds and many strains of flu, do not affect the developing organism. However, several bacterial and viral infections can be very harmful and, in some cases, fatal to the embryo or fetus; five of the most common of these are listed in Table 3-1.

TABLE 3-1

TERATOGENIC DISEASES AND THEIR CONSEQUENCES

Disease	Potential Consequences
AIDS	Frequent infections, neurological disorders, death
Cytomegalovirus	Deafness, blindness, abnormally small head, developmental disabilities
Genital herpes	Encephalitis, enlarged spleen, improper blood clotting
Rubella (German measles)	Developmental disabilities; damage to eyes, ears, and heart
Syphilis	Damage to the central nervous system, teeth, and bones

Some of these diseases pass from the mother through the placenta to attack the embryo or fetus directly. They include cytomegalovirus (a type of herpes), rubella, and syphilis. Other diseases attack at birth: The virus is present in the lining of the birth canal, and the baby is infected during the birth process. Genital herpes is transmitted this way. AIDS is transmitted both ways—through the placenta and during passage through the birth canal.

The only way to guarantee that these diseases do not harm prenatal development is for a woman to not contract the disease before or during her pregnancy. Medication may help the woman, but does not prevent the disease from damaging the developing baby.

DRUGS. Thalidomide illustrates the harm that drugs can cause during prenatal development. Table 3-2 lists other drugs that are known teratogens.

When pregnant women drink large amounts of alcohol, their children often have fetal alcohol syndrome. Children with fetal alcohol syndrome tend to have a small head and a thin upper lip as well as developmental disabilities.

TABLE 3-2	
TERATOGENIC DRUGS AND THEIR CONSEQUENCES	
Drug	**Potential Consequences**
Accutane	Abnormalities of the central nervous system, eyes, and ears
Alcohol	Fetal alcohol spectrum disorder, cognitive deficits, retarded growth
Aspirin	Deficits in intelligence, attention, and motor skills
Caffeine	Lower birth weight, decreased muscle tone
Cocaine and heroin	Retarded growth, irritability in newborns
Marijuana	Lower birth weight, less motor control
Nicotine	Retarded growth, possible cognitive impairments

Notice that most of the drugs in the list are substances that you may use routinely: Accutane (used to treat acne), alcohol, aspirin, caffeine, and nicotine. Nevertheless, when consumed by pregnant women, they present special dangers (Behnke & Eyler, 1993).

Cigarette smoking is typical of the potential harm from teratogenic drugs (Cornelius et al., 1995; Espy et al., 2011). The nicotine in cigarette smoke constricts blood vessels and thus reduces the oxygen and nutrients that can reach the fetus through the placenta. Therefore, pregnant women who smoke are more likely to miscarry (abort the fetus spontaneously) and to bear children who are smaller than average at birth (Cnattingius, 2004). Furthermore, as children develop, they are more likely to show signs of impaired attention, language, and cognitive skills, along with behavioral problems (Brennan et al., 2002; Wakschlag et al., 2006). Finally, even secondhand smoke harms the fetus: When pregnant women don't smoke but fathers do, babies tend to be smaller at birth (Friedman & Polifka, 1996). Most of these harmful effects depend on degree of exposure—heavy smoking is more harmful than moderate smoking—and on the fetal genotype: Some children inherit genes that are more effective in defending, in utero, against the toxins in cigarette smoke (Price et al., 2010).

Alcohol also carries serious risk. **Pregnant women who regularly consume quantities of alcoholic beverages may give birth to babies with** *fetal alcohol spectrum disorder (FASD).* The most extreme form, fetal alcohol syndrome (FAS), is most likely among pregnant women who are heavy recreational drinkers—that is, women who drink 5 or more ounces of alcohol a few times each week (Jacobson & Jacobson, 2000; Lee, Mattson, & Riley, 2004). Children with FAS usually grow more slowly than normal and have heart problems and misshapen faces. Like the child in the photo, youngsters with FAS often have a small head, a thin upper lip, a short nose, and widely spaced eyes. FAS is the leading cause of developmental disabilities in the United States, and children with FAS have serious attentional, cognitive, and behavioral problems (e.g., Howell et al., 2006; Sokol, Delaney-Black, & Nordstrom, 2003). ◉—⬛Watch the Video on **mydevelopmentlab.com**

◉—⬛Watch the **Video** *Fetal Alcohol Syndrome: Sidney* on **mydevelopmentlab .com** to learn more about the impact of teratogens. This video shows how prenatal development can be disrupted when a pregnant woman drinks alcohol.

Does this mean that moderate drinking is safe? No. When women drink moderately throughout pregnancy, their children are often afflicted with partial fetal alcohol syndrome (p-FAS), which refers to children whose physical growth is normal but who have some facial abnormalities and impaired cognitive skills. Another less-severe variant is alcohol-related neurodevelopmental disorder (ARND). Children with ARND are normal in appearance but have deficits in attention, memory, and intelligence (Loock et al., 2005).

Is there any amount of drinking that's safe during pregnancy? Maybe, but that amount has yet to be determined. Gathering definitive data is complicated by two factors: First, researchers usually determine the amount a woman drinks by her responses to interviews or questionnaires. If for some reason she does not accurately report her consumption, it is impossible to accurately estimate the amount of harm associated with drinking. Second, any safe level of consumption is probably not the same for all women. Based on their health and heredity, some women may be able to consume more alcohol more safely than others.

These factors make it impossible to guarantee safe levels of alcohol or any of the other drugs listed in Table 3-2. The best policy, therefore, is for a pregnant woman to avoid drugs if at all possible (including over-the-counter, prescription, and illegal drugs) and to consult a health care professional before using essential drugs.

ENVIRONMENTAL HAZARDS. As a by-product of life in an industrialized world, people are often exposed to toxins in food they eat, fluids they drink, and air they breathe. Chemicals associated with industrial waste are the most common environmental teratogens, and the quantities involved are usually minute. However, as is true for drugs, amounts that go unnoticed by an adult can cause serious damage to a developing fetus (Moore, 2003). Table 3-3 lists four well-documented environmental teratogens.

QUESTION 3.2
Sarah is 22 and pregnant for the first time. She smokes half a pack of cigarettes each day and has one bottle of light beer with dinner. Sarah can't believe that the relatively small amounts she smokes and drinks could hurt the baby she's carrying. What would you say?
(Answer is on page 86.)

TABLE 3-3

ENVIRONMENTAL TERATOGENS AND THEIR CONSEQUENCES

Hazard	Potential Consequences
Lead	Developmental disabilities
Mercury	Retarded growth, developmental disabilities, cerebral palsy
PCBs	Impaired memory and verbal skills
X-rays	Retarded growth, leukemia, developmental disabilities

Polychlorinated biphenyls (PCBs) illustrate the danger of environmental teratogens. These chemicals were used in electrical transformers and paints, until the U.S. government banned them in the 1970s. However, like many industrial by-products, they seeped into the waterways, where they contaminated fish and wildlife. The amount of PCBs in a typical contaminated fish does not affect adults, but when pregnant women ate large numbers of PCB-contaminated fish, their children's cognitive skills and reading achievement were impaired (Jacobson & Jacobson, 1996).

You may be wondering about one ubiquitous feature of modern environments that doesn't appear in Table 3-3: cell phones. Is a pregnant woman's cell-phone usage hazardous to the health of her fetus? At this point, there's no definitive answer to that question. The radiofrequency radiation that cell phones generate has sometimes been linked to health risks in adults (e.g., cancer), but the findings are very inconsistent

(National Radiological Protection Board, 2004; Verschaeve, 2009). There are few scientific studies of the impact of cell phones on prenatal development. In a study conducted in Denmark, cell-phone use during *and after* pregnancy was associated with increased risk for behavior problems in childhood (Divan et al., 2008). In another study, conducted in Spain, cell-phone use late in pregnancy was associated with lower motor development but greater mental development in 14-month-olds (Vrijheid et al., 2010). At this point, more research is needed to know if radiofrequency radiation from a pregnant woman's cell phone is a health risk. We do know, of course, another way in which cell phones represent a huge health risk for pregnant women: Talking while driving is incredibly distracting and reduces a driver's performance to the level seen by people driving under the influence of alcohol (Strayer, Drews, & Crouch, 2006). So, while we wait for research to provide more information, the best advice for a pregnant woman would be to keep a cell phone at a distance when it's not being used and *never* use it while driving.

> Environmental teratogens are particularly dangerous because pregnant women may not realize they are present.

Environmental teratogens like those shown in Table 3-3 are treacherous because people are often unaware of their presence in the environment. The women in the Jacobson and Jacobson (1996) study, for example, did not realize they were eating PCB-laden fish. This invisibility makes it more difficult for a pregnant woman to protect herself from environmental teratogens. Pregnant women need to be particularly careful of the foods they eat and the air they breathe. Be sure all foods are cleaned thoroughly to rid them of insecticides. Try to avoid convenience foods, which often contain many chemical additives. Stay away from air that's been contaminated by household products such as cleansers, paint strippers, and fertilizers. Women in jobs that require contact with potential teratogens (e.g., housecleaners, hairdressers) should switch to less potent chemicals. For example, they should use baking soda instead of more chemically laden cleansers. They should also wear protective gloves, aprons, and masks to reduce their contact with potential teratogens. Finally, because environmental teratogens continue to increase, check with a health care provider to learn if other materials should be avoided.

How Teratogens Influence Prenatal Development

By assembling all the evidence of harm caused by diseases, drugs, and environmental hazards, scientists have identified five important general principles about how teratogens usually work (Hogge, 1990; Jacobson & Jacobson, 2000; Vorhees & Mollnow, 1987):

1. **The impact of a teratogen depends on the genotype of the organism.** A substance may be harmful to one species but not to another. To determine the safety of thalidomide, researchers had tested thalidomide in pregnant rats and rabbits, whose offspring developed normal limbs. Yet, when pregnant women took the same drug in comparable doses, many produced children with deformed limbs. Thalidomide was harmless to rats and rabbits but not to people. Moreover, some women who took thalidomide gave birth to babies with normal limbs, yet others who took comparable doses at the same time in their pregnancies gave birth to babies with deformities. Apparently, heredity makes some individuals more susceptible than others to a teratogen.

2. **The impact of teratogens changes over the course of prenatal development.** The timing of exposure to a teratogen is critical. Figure 3-5 shows how the

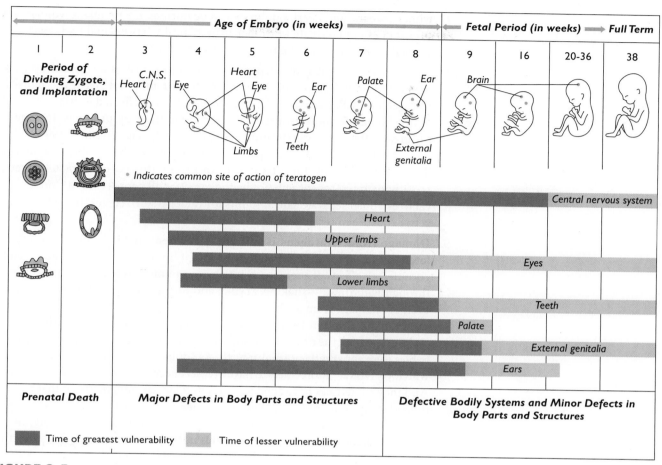

FIGURE 3-5

consequences of teratogens differ for the periods of the zygote, embryo, and fetus. During the period of the zygote, exposure to teratogens usually results in spontaneous abortion of the fertilized egg. During the embryonic period, exposure produces major defects in body structure. For example, women who took thalidomide during the embryonic period had babies with ill-formed or missing limbs. Women who contract rubella during the embryonic period have babies with heart defects. During the fetal period, exposure to teratogens either produces minor defects in body structure or causes body systems to function improperly. For example, when women drink large quantities of alcohol during the fetal period, the fetus develops fewer brain cells.

Even within the different periods of prenatal development, developing body parts and systems are more vulnerable at certain times. The blue shading in Figure 3-5 indicates a time of maximum vulnerability; orange shading indicates a time when the developing organism is less vulnerable. The heart, for example, is most sensitive to teratogens during the first two-thirds of the embryonic period. Exposure to teratogens before this time rarely produces heart damage; exposure after this time results in milder damage.

3. **Each teratogen affects a specific aspect (or aspects) of prenatal development.** Said another way, teratogens do not harm all body systems; instead, damage is selective. If a pregnant woman contracts rubella, her baby may have problems

with eyes, ears, and heart, but limbs will be normal. If a pregnant woman consumes PCB-contaminated fish, her baby typically has normal body parts and normal motor skills, but below-average cognitive skills.

4. **The impact of teratogens depends on the dose.** Just as a single drop of oil won't pollute a lake, small doses of teratogens may not harm the fetus. In research on PCBs, for example, cognitive skills were affected only among children who had the greatest prenatal exposure to these by-products. In general, the greater the exposure, the greater the risk for damage (Adams, 1999).

    An implication of this principle is that researchers should be able to determine safe levels for a teratogen. In reality, this is very difficult because sensitivity to teratogens will not be the same for all people (and it's not practical to establish separate safe amounts for each person). Hence, the safest rule is zero exposure to teratogens.

5. **Damage from teratogens is not always evident at birth, but may appear later in life.** In the case of malformed infant limbs or babies born addicted to cocaine, the effects of a teratogen are obvious immediately. A cocaine baby goes through withdrawal—shaking, crying, and inability to sleep. Sometimes, however, the damage from a teratogen becomes evident only as the child develops. For example, between 1947 and 1971 many pregnant women in North America and Europe took the drug diethylstilbestrol (DES) to prevent miscarriages. Their babies were apparently normal at birth. As adults, however, daughters of women who took DES are more likely to have breast cancer or a rare cancer of the vagina. And they sometimes have abnormalities in their reproductive tract that make it difficult to become pregnant. Sons of women who took DES are at risk for testicular abnormalities and for testicular cancer (National Cancer Institute, 2006). In this case, the impact of the teratogen is not evident until decades after birth.

THE REAL WORLD OF PRENATAL RISK. I have discussed risk factors individually, as if each were the only potential threat to prenatal development. In reality, many infants are exposed to multiple general risks and multiple teratogens. Pregnant women who drink alcohol often smoke and drink coffee as well (Haslam & Lawrence, 2004). Pregnant women who are under stress often drink alcohol, and may self-medicate with aspirin or other over-the-counter drugs. Many of these same women live in poverty, which means they may have inadequate nutrition and receive minimal medical care during pregnancy. When all the risks are combined, prenatal development is rarely optimal (Yumoto, Jacobson, & Jacobson, 2008).

> The impact of teratogens depends on the genotype of the organism as well as the timing and amount of exposure to the teratogen.

This pattern explains why it's often challenging for child-development researchers to determine the harm associated with individual teratogens. Cocaine is a perfect example. You may remember stories in newspapers and magazines about "crack babies" and their developmental problems. In fact, the jury is still out on the issue of cocaine as a teratogen (Jones, 2006). Some investigators (e.g., Bennett, Bendersky, & Lewis, 2008; Dennis et al., 2006) find the harmful effects that made headlines in the 1990s, whereas others (e.g., Brown et al., 2004; Frank et al., 2001) argue that most of the effects attributed to cocaine also reflect the impact of concurrent smoking and drinking and the inadequate parenting that these children receive. Similarly, harmful effects attributed to smoking during pregnancy may also stem from the fact that pregnant women who smoke are more likely to be less educated and to have a history of psychological problems, including antisocial behavior (D'Onofrio et al., 2010).

Of course, findings like these don't mean that pregnant women should feel free to light up (or, for that matter, to shoot up). Instead, they highlight the difficulties involved in determining the harm associated with a single risk factor (e.g., smoking) when it usually occurs alongside many other risk factors (e.g., inadequate parenting, continued exposure to smoke after birth).

From what you've read in the past few pages, you might think that the developing fetus has little chance of escaping harm. But most babies are born in good health. Of course, a good policy for pregnant women is to avoid diseases, drugs, and environmental hazards that are known teratogens. This, coupled with thorough prenatal medical care and adequate nutrition, is the best recipe for normal prenatal development.

Prenatal Diagnosis and Treatment

"I really don't care whether I have a boy or girl, just as long as my baby's healthy." Legions of parents worldwide have felt this way, but until recently all they could do was hope for the best. Today, however, advances in technology give parents a much better idea of whether their baby is developing normally.

Even before a woman becomes pregnant, a couple may go for genetic counseling, which I described in Module 2.1. A counselor constructs a family tree for each prospective parent to check for heritable disorders. If it turns out that one (or both) carries a disorder, further tests can determine the person's genotype. With this more detailed information, a genetic counselor can discuss choices with the prospective parents. They may choose to go ahead and conceive "naturally," taking their chances that the child will be healthy. Or they could decide to use sperm or eggs from other people. Yet another choice would be to adopt a child.

A standard part of prenatal care is ultrasound, in which sound waves are used to generate an image of the fetus.

After a woman is pregnant, how can we know if prenatal development is progressing normally? Traditionally, obstetricians gauged development by feeling the size and position of the fetus through a woman's abdomen. This technique was not very precise and, of course, couldn't be done at all until the fetus was large enough to feel. Today, however, new techniques have revolutionized our ability to monitor prenatal growth and development. **A standard part of prenatal care in North America is** *ultrasound,* **a procedure that uses sound waves to generate a picture of the fetus.** As the photo shows, an instrument about the size of a hair dryer is rubbed over the woman's abdomen; the image is shown on a nearby TV monitor. The pictures that are generated are hardly portrait quality; they are grainy and it takes an expert's eye to distinguish what's what. Nevertheless, the procedure is painless and parents are thrilled to be able to see their babies and watch them move.

Ultrasound can be used as early as 4 or 5 weeks after conception; before this time the fetus is not large enough to generate an interpretable image. Ultrasound pictures are useful for determining the date of conception, which

Ultrasound images can reveal the position of the fetus in the uterus and reveal the presence of multiple pregnancies.

enables the physician to predict the due date more accurately. Ultrasound pictures are also valuable in showing the position of the fetus and placenta in the uterus, and they can be used to identify gross physical deformities, such as abnormal growth of the head. As shown in the photo on page 83, ultrasound can also help in detecting twins or other multiple pregnancies. Finally, beginning at about 20 weeks after conception, ultrasound images can reveal the child's sex.

When a genetic disorder is suspected, two other techniques are particularly valuable because they provide a sample of fetal cells that can be analyzed. **In** *amniocentesis,* **a needle is inserted through the mother's abdomen to obtain a sample of the amniotic fluid that surrounds the fetus.** Amniocentesis is typically performed at approximately 16 weeks after conception. As you can see in Figure 3-6, ultrasound is used to guide the needle into the uterus. The fluid contains skin cells that can be grown in a laboratory dish and then analyzed to determine the genotype of the fetus.

In *chorionic villus sampling (CVS),* **a sample of tissue is obtained from the chorion (a part of the placenta) and analyzed.** Figure 3-7 shows that a small tube, inserted through the vagina and into the uterus, is used to collect a small plug of cells from the placenta. CVS is often preferred over amniocentesis because it can be done about 9 to 12 weeks after conception, nearly 4 to 6 weeks earlier than amniocentesis. (Amniocentesis can't be performed until the amniotic sac is large enough to provide easy access to amniotic fluid.)

Results are returned from the lab in about 2 weeks following amniocentesis and in 7 to 10 days following CVS. (The wait is longer for amniocentesis because genetic material can't be evaluated until enough cells have reproduced for analysis.) With samples obtained from either amniocentesis or CVS, about 200 different genetic disorders can be detected. For example, for pregnant women in their late 30s or 40s, either amniocentesis or CVS is often used to determine whether the fetus has Down syndrome. These procedures are virtually error-free, but they have a price: Miscarriages are slightly more likely after amniocentesis or CVS (Wilson, 2000). A woman must decide if the beneficial information gained from amniocentesis or CVS justifies the slightly increased risk of a miscarriage. These procedures are summarized in the Summary Table.

Ultrasound, amniocentesis, and chorionic villus sampling have made it much easier to determine if prenatal development is progressing normally. But what happens when it is not? Until recently a woman's options were limited: She could

FIGURE 3-6   **FIGURE 3-7**

SUMMARY TABLE

METHODS OF PRENATAL DIAGNOSIS

Procedure	Description	Primary Uses
Ultrasound	Sound waves used to generate an image of the fetus	Determine due date and position of fetus in uterus; check for physical deformities, multiple births, and child's sex
Amniocentesis	Sample of fetal cells is obtained from amniotic fluid	Screen for genetic disorders
Chorionic villus sampling (CVS)	Sample of tissue is obtained from the chorion (part of the placenta)	Screen for genetic disorders

continue the pregnancy or end it. But options are expanding. **A whole new field called** *fetal medicine* **is concerned with treating prenatal problems before birth.** Many tools are now available to solve problems that are detected during pregnancy (Rodeck & Whittle, 2009). One approach is to treat disorders medically, by administering drugs or hormones to the fetus. For example, in fetal hypothyroidism, the fetal thyroid gland does not produce enough hormones, leading to retarded physical and mental development. This disorder can be treated by injecting the necessary hormones directly into the amniotic cavity, resulting in normal growth. Another example is congenital adrenal hyperplasia, an inherited disorder in which the fetal adrenal glands produce too much androgen, causing early maturation of boys or masculinization of girls. In this case, treatment consists of injecting hormones into the mother that reduce the amount of androgen secreted by the fetal adrenal glands (Evans, Platt, & De La Cruz, 2001).

Another way to correct prenatal problems is fetal surgery (Warner, Altimier, & Crombleholme, 2007). For example, spina bifida has been corrected with fetal surgery in the seventh or eighth month of pregnancy. Surgeons cut through the mother's abdominal wall to expose the fetus, then cut through the fetal abdominal wall; the spinal cord is repaired and the fetus is returned to the uterus. When treated with prenatal surgery, infants with spina bifida are less likely to need a shunt to drain fluid from the brain and, as preschoolers, are more likely to be able to walk without support (Adzick, et al. 2011).

> Fetal medicine treats prenatal problems medically, with surgery, and with genetic engineering.

Fetal surgery has also been used to treat a disorder affecting identical twins in which one twin—the "donor"—pumps blood through its own and the other twin's circulatory system. The donor twin usually fails to grow; surgery corrects the problem by sealing off the unnecessary blood vessels between the twins (Baschat, 2007). Fetal surgery holds great promise, but it is still highly experimental and therefore considered as a last resort.

Another potential approach to treating prenatal problems is *genetic engineering*—**replacing defective genes with synthetic normal genes.** Take sickle-cell disease as an example. Remember, from Module 2.1, that if a baby inherits the recessive allele for sickle-cell disease from both parents, the child will produce misshapen red blood cells that can't pass through capillaries. In theory, it should be possible to take a sample of cells from the fetus, remove the recessive genes from the 11th pair of chromosomes, and replace them with the dominant genes. These "repaired" cells could then be injected into the fetus, where they would multiply and cause normal red blood cells to be produced (David & Rodeck, 2009). As with fetal surgery, however, translating idea into practice is challenging. Researchers are still studying these techniques with mice and sheep and there have been some successful applications with older children (Coutelle et al., 2005; Maguire et al., 2009). However, routine use of this method in fetal medicine is still years away.

Answers to Chloe's questions: Return to Chloe's questions in the module-opening vignette (page 72) and answer them for her. If you're not certain, I'll help by giving you the pages in this module where the answers appear:

⊠ **Question about her cell phone—page 79**

⊠ **Question about her nightly glass of wine—page 78**

⊠ **Question about giving birth to a baby with developmental disabilities—page 77**

ANSWER 3.2

She's probably wrong. There are no known "safe" amounts of cigarette smoking and drinking. For example, her drinking might be enough to cause alcohol-related neuro-developmental disorder.

 Check Your Learning

RECALL What are the important general factors that pose risks for prenatal development?

Describe the main techniques for prenatal diagnosis that are available today.

INTERPRET Explain how the impact of a teratogen changes over the course of prenatal development.

APPLY What would you say to a 45-year-old woman who is eager to become pregnant but is unsure about the possible risks associated with pregnancy at this age?

 Happy Birthday!

OUTLINE	LEARNING OBJECTIVES
Labor and Delivery	● What are the stages in labor and delivery?
Approaches to Childbirth	● What are "natural" ways of coping with the pain of childbirth? Is childbirth at home safe?
Adjusting to Parenthood	● What are the effects of postpartum depression?
Birth Complications	● What are some complications that can occur during birth?

Dominique is six months pregnant; soon she and her partner will begin childbirth classes at the local hospital. She is relieved that the classes are finally starting because this means that pregnancy is nearly over. But all the talk she has heard about "breathing exercises" and "coaching" sounds mysterious to her. Dominique wonders what's involved and how the classes will help her during labor and delivery.

As women near the end of pregnancy, they find that sleeping and breathing become more difficult, they tire more rapidly, they become constipated, and their legs and feet swell. Women look forward to birth, both to relieve their discomfort and, of course, to see their baby. In this module, we'll see the different stages involved in birth, review various approaches to childbirth, and look at problems that can arise. We'll also look at childbirth classes like the one Dominique will be taking.

Labor and Delivery

In a typical pregnancy, a woman goes into labor about 38 weeks after conception. The timing of labor depends on the flow of hormonal signals between the placenta and the brain and adrenal glands of the fetus. When estrogen and other hormones reach critical levels, the muscles in the uterus begin to contract, the first sign of labor (Mastorakos & Ilias, 2003).

Labor is named appropriately, for it is the most intense, prolonged physical effort that humans experience. Labor is usually divided into the three stages shown in Figure 3-8. The first stage begins when the muscles of the uterus start to contract. These contractions force amniotic fluid up against the cervix, the opening at the bottom of the uterus that is the entryway to the birth canal. The wavelike motion of the amniotic fluid with each contraction causes the cervix to enlarge gradually.

The Three Stages of Labor

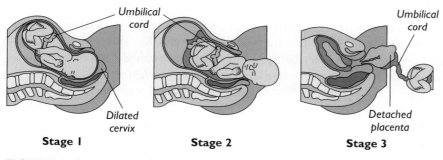

Umbilical cord

Umbilical cord

Dilated cervix

Detached placenta

Stage 1 **Stage 2** **Stage 3**

FIGURE 3-8

At the beginning of this stage, contractions are weak and spaced irregularly. They gradually become stronger and more frequent. At the end of Stage 1, in the transition phase, contractions are intense and sometimes occur without interruption. Women report that the transition phase is the most painful part of labor. By the end of transition, the cervix is about 10 centimeters (4 inches) in diameter.

Stage 1 lasts from 12 to 24 hours for the birth of a first child, and most of the time is spent in the relative tranquility of the early phase. Stage 1 is usually shorter for subsequent births, with 3 to 8 hours being common. However, as the wide ranges suggest, these times are only rough approximations; the actual times vary greatly among women and are virtually impossible to predict.

When the cervix is fully enlarged, the second stage of labor begins. Most women feel a strong urge to push the baby out, using their abdominal muscles. This pushing, along with uterine contractions, propels the baby down the birth canal. **Soon the top of the baby's head appears, an event known as** *crowning.* In about an hour for first births and less for later births, the baby passes through the birth canal and emerges from the mother's body. **Most babies arrive head first, but a small percentage come out feet or bottom first, which is known as a** *breech presentation.*

Watch the **Video** on **mydevelopmentlab.com**

Watch the **Video** *Labor* on **mydevelopmentlab.com** to learn more about labor and delivery. This video compresses an entire labor and delivery into 10 minutes; it is graphic, showing delivery of the infant and of the placenta.

(I was one of these rare bottom-first babies and have been the butt of bad jokes ever since.) The baby's birth marks the end of the second stage of labor.

With the baby born, you might think that labor is over, but it's not. There is a third stage, in which the placenta (also called, appropriately, the *afterbirth*) is expelled from the uterus. The placenta becomes detached from the wall of the uterus and contractions force it out through the birth canal. This stage is quite brief, typically lasting 10 to 15 minutes.

The three stages of labor are summarized in the following table.

SUMMARY TABLE		
STAGES OF LABOR		
Stage	**Duration**	**Primary Milestone**
1	12–24 hours	Cervix enlarges to 10 cm
2	1 hour	Baby moves down the birth canal
3	10–15 minutes	Placenta is expelled

Approaches to Childbirth

When my mother went into labor (with me), she was admitted to a nearby hospital, where she soon was administered a general anesthetic. My father went to a waiting room, where he and other fathers-to-be anxiously awaited news of their babies. Sometime later my mother recovered from anesthesia and learned that she had given birth to a healthy baby boy. My father had grown tired of waiting and gone back to work, so he got the good news in a phone call.

These were standard hospital procedures in 1950, and virtually all American babies were born this way. No longer. In the middle of the 20th century, two European physicians—Grantly Dick-Read (1959) and Ferdinand Lamaze (1958)—criticized the traditional view in which labor and delivery had come to involve elaborate medical procedures that were often unnecessary and that often left women afraid of giving birth. A pregnant woman's fear led her to be tense, thereby increasing the pain she experienced during labor. These physicians argued for a more "natural" or prepared approach to childbirth, viewing labor and delivery as life events to be celebrated rather than medical procedures to be endured.

> Prepared childbirth emphasizes education, relaxation, and the presence of a supportive coach.

Today many varieties of prepared childbirth are available to pregnant women. However, most share some fundamental beliefs. One is that birth is more likely to be problem free and rewarding when mothers and fathers understand what's happening during pregnancy, labor, and delivery. Consequently, *prepared childbirth* means going to classes to learn basic facts about pregnancy and childbirth (like the material presented in this chapter).

A second common element is that natural methods of dealing with pain are emphasized over medication. Why? When a woman is anesthetized, either with general anesthesia or regional anesthesia (in which only the lower body is numbed), she can't use her abdominal muscles to help push the baby through the birth canal. Without this pushing, the obstetrician may have to use mechanical devices to pull the baby through the birth canal, which involves some risk (Johanson et al., 1993). Also, drugs that reduce the pain of childbirth cross the placenta and can affect the baby. Consequently, when a woman receives large doses of pain-relieving medication, her baby is often withdrawn or irritable for days or even weeks (Brazelton, Nugent, & Lester, 1987; Ransjoe-Arvidson et al., 2001). These effects are temporary, but they may give the new mother the impression that she has a difficult baby. It is best, therefore, to minimize the use of pain-relieving drugs during birth.

Relaxation is the key to reducing birth pain without drugs. Because pain often feels greater when a person is tense, pregnant women learn to relax during labor, through deep breathing or by visualizing a reassuring, pleasant scene or experience. Whenever they begin to experience pain during labor, they use these methods to relax.

A third common element of prepared childbirth is the involvement of a supportive "coach." The father-to-be, a relative, or close friend attends childbirth classes with the mother-to-be. The coach learns the techniques for coping with pain and, like the men in the photo, practices them with the pregnant woman. During labor and delivery, the coach is present to help the woman use the techniques she has learned and to offer support and encouragement. This preparation and support are effective in reducing the amount of medication that women like Dominique from the vignette take during labor (Maimburg et al., 2010).

Another basic premise of the trend toward natural childbirth is that birth need not always take place in a hospital. Nearly all babies in the United States are born in hospitals; only 1% are born at home (Studelska, 2006). Yet around the world—in Europe, South America, and Asia—many children are born at home, reflecting a cultural view that the best place to welcome a new family member is at home, surrounded by family members.

During childbirth preparation classes, pregnant women learn exercises that help them to relax and reduce the pain associated with childbirth.

For Americans accustomed to hospital delivery, home delivery can seem like a risky proposition. And, in fact, in the least developed countries of the world, where hospital delivery is far less common, the neonatal mortality rate (number of infants who live less than a month) is nine times higher than in the United States. In India alone, more than a million babies die before they are a month old; many parents do not name their newborns so that they will not become attached to a child who is likely to die (UNICEF, 2008).

The statistics are shocking, but you should not take them as an argument for the necessity of hospital births. In many of the least developed countries of the world, traditionally no trained health care professionals are present at birth. When such professionals—typically a midwife—are present, labor and delivery become much safer for mother and infant alike, even when delivery takes place at home, as in the photo. Of course, sometimes problems emerge during pregnancy and labor, and in these instances ready access to a medical facility is essential. Combining these two elements—a health care professional present at every birth and specialized facilities available for problems—substantially reduces neonatal mortality (World Health Organization, 2005).

This combination also works well in developed countries. Birth at home is safe if a woman is healthy, her pregnancy has been problem free, labor and

In many countries around the world, a midwife is present to deliver the baby.

delivery are expected to be problem free, a trained health care professional is there to assist, and comprehensive medical care is available should the need arise (Wax, Pinette, & Cartin, 2010). Most women are more relaxed during labor in their homes, and they enjoy the greater control they have over labor and birth in a home delivery. But if there is any reason to believe that problems requiring medical assistance might occur, labor and delivery should take place in the hospital rather than at home.

Adjusting to Parenthood

For parents, the time immediately after a trouble-free birth is full of excitement, pride, and joy—the much-anticipated baby is finally here! But it is also a time of adjustments for parents (and for siblings, as we'll see in Module 14.3). A woman experiences many physical changes after birth. Her breasts begin to produce milk and her uterus gradually becomes smaller, returning to its normal size in 5 or 6 weeks. Meanwhile, levels of female hormones (e.g., estrogen) drop.

> Some mothers experience postpartum depression in which they are constantly irritable and apathetic.

Parents must also adjust psychologically. They reorganize old routines, particularly for first-born children, to fit the young baby's sleep–wake cycle (which is described in Module 3.4). In the process, fathers sometimes feel left out as mothers devote most of their attention to the baby.

Researchers once believed that an important part of parents' adjustment involved forming an emotional bond with the infant. That is, the first few days of life were thought to be a critical period for close physical contact between parents and babies; without such contact, parents and babies would find it difficult to bond emotionally (Klaus & Kennell, 1976). Today, however, we know that such contact in the first few days after birth—although beneficial for babies and pleasurable for babies and parents alike—is not essential for normal development (Eyer, 1992). In Module 10.3, we'll learn what steps are essential to forge these emotional bonds and when they typically take place.

Becoming a parent can be a huge adjustment, so it's not surprising that roughly half of all new mothers find that their initial excitement gives way to irritation, resentment, and crying spells—the so-called "baby blues." These feelings usually last a week or two and probably reflect both the stress of caring for a new baby and the physiological changes that take place as a woman's body returns to a nonpregnant state (Brockington, 1996).

 QUESTION 3.3

Rosa gave birth a week ago. Once or twice a day she has crying spells and usually gets angry at her husband, even though he's been quite helpful to her and the baby. Do you think Rosa has postpartum depression?

(Answer is on page 94.)

For 10% to 15% of new mothers, however, irritability continues for months and is often accompanied by feelings of low self-worth, disturbed sleep, poor appetite, and apathy—a condition known as *postpartum depression.* Postpartum depression does not strike randomly. Biology contributes: Particularly high levels of hormones during the later phases of pregnancy place women at risk for postpartum depression (Harris et al., 1994). Experience also contributes: Women are more likely to experience postpartum depression when they were depressed before pregnancy, are coping with other life stresses (e.g., death of a loved one or moving to a new residence), did not plan to become pregnant, and/or lack other adults (e.g., the father) to support their adjustment to motherhood (O'Hara, 2009).

Women who are lethargic and emotionless do not mother warmly and enthusiastically. They don't touch and cuddle their new babies much or talk to them. And depressed moms are less effective in the common but essential tasks of feeding and sleep routines (Field, 2010). When postpartum depression persists over years, children's development is affected (Wachs, Black, & Engle, 2009). For example, antisocial behavior is more common (Hay et al., 2010), and such effects are stronger when children have few opportunities to interact with nondepressed adults.

Thus, postpartum depression should not be taken lightly: If a mother's depression doesn't lift after a few weeks, she should seek help. Home visits by trained health care professionals can be valuable (van Doesum et al., 2008). During these visits, these visitors show moms better ways to cope with the many changes that accompany the new baby; they also provide emotional support by being a caring, sensitive listener; and, if necessary, they can refer the mother to other needed resources in the community. Finally, it's worth mentioning one simple way to reduce the risk of postpartum depression: breast-feeding. Moms who breast-feed are less likely to become depressed, perhaps because breast-feeding releases hormones that are antidepressants (Gagliardi, 2005).

Birth Complications

Women who are healthy when they become pregnant usually have a normal pregnancy, labor, and delivery. When women are not healthy or don't receive adequate prenatal care, problems can surface during labor and delivery. (Of course, even healthy women can have problems, but not as often.) The more common birth complications are listed in Table 3-4.

TABLE 3-4

COMMON BIRTH COMPLICATIONS

Complication	Features
Cephalopelvic disproportion	The infant's head is larger than the pelvis, making it impossible for the baby to pass through the birth canal.
Irregular position	In shoulder presentation, the baby is lying crosswise in the uterus and the shoulder appears first; in breech presentation, the buttocks appear first.
Preeclampsia	A pregnant woman has high blood pressure, protein in her urine, and swelling in her extremities (due to fluid retention).
Prolapsed umbilical cord	The umbilical cord precedes the baby through the birth canal and is squeezed shut, cutting off oxygen to the baby.

Some of these complications, such as a prolapsed umbilical cord, are dangerous because they can disrupt the flow of blood through the umbilical cord. **If this flow of blood is disrupted, infants do not receive adequate oxygen, a condition known as** *hypoxia.* Hypoxia sometimes occurs during labor and delivery because the umbilical cord is pinched or squeezed shut, cutting off the flow of blood. Hypoxia is very serious because it can lead to developmental disabilities or death (Hogan et al., 2006).

To guard against hypoxia, fetal heart rate is monitored during labor, either by ultrasound or with a tiny electrode that is passed through the vagina and attached to the scalp of the fetus. An abrupt change in heart rate can be a sign that the fetus is not receiving enough oxygen. If the heart rate does change suddenly, a health care professional will try to determine whether the fetus is in distress, perhaps by measuring fetal heart rate with a stethoscope on the mother's abdomen.

When a fetus is in distress or when the fetus is in an irregular position or is too large to pass through the birth canal, a physician may decide to remove it from the mother's uterus surgically (Guillemin, 1993). **In a** *cesarean section (C-section),* **an incision is made in the abdomen to remove the baby from the uterus.** A C-section is riskier for mothers than a vaginal delivery because of increased bleeding and greater danger of infection. A C-section poses little risk for babies, although they are often briefly lethargic from the anesthesia that the mother receives before the operation. Mother–infant interactions are much the same for babies delivered vaginally or by planned or unplanned C-sections (Durik, Hyde, & Clark, 2000).

Birth complications not only are hazardous for a newborn's health, but also have long-term effects. When babies experience many birth complications, they are at risk for becoming aggressive or violent and for developing schizophrenia (e.g., Cannon et al., 2000; de Haan et al., 2006). This is particularly true for newborns with birth complications who later experience family adversity, such as living in poverty. In one study (Arseneault et al., 2002), boys who had life-threatening birth complications such as umbilical cord prolapse or preeclampsia were more aggressive as 6-year-olds and more violent as 17-year-olds (e.g., they participated in gang fights or carried weapons). But this was only true when boys had also experienced family adversity, such as limited income or the absence of a parent. This outcome underscores the importance of receiving excellent health care throughout pregnancy and labor and a supportive environment throughout childhood.

PREMATURITY AND LOW BIRTH WEIGHT. Normally, gestation takes 38 weeks from conception to birth. *Premature infants* **are born at 35 weeks after conception (or earlier).** *Small-for-date infants* **are substantially smaller than would be expected based on the length of time since conception.** Sometimes these two complications coincide, but not necessarily. Some, but not all, small-for-date infants are premature; conversely, some, but not all, premature infants are small-for-date. In other words, an infant can go the full 9-month term and be under the average 7- to 8-pound birth weight of newborns; the child is therefore small-for-date but not premature. Similarly, an infant born at 7 months that weighs 3 pounds (the average weight of a 7-month fetus) is only premature. But if the baby born after 7 months weighs less than the average, it is both premature and small-for-date.

Of the two complications, prematurity is the less serious. In the first year or so, premature infants often lag behind full-term infants in many facets of development, but by age 2 or 3 years, differences vanish and most premature infants develop normally thereafter (Greenberg & Crnic, 1988).

Prospects are usually not so optimistic for small-for-date babies such as the one shown in the photo. These infants are most often born to women who smoke or drink alcohol frequently during pregnancy or who do not eat enough nutritious food (Chomitz, Cheung, & Lieberman, 1995). Babies who weigh less than 1,500 grams (3.3 pounds) at birth often do not survive; when they do, their cognitive and motor development are usually delayed (Kavsek & Bornstein, 2010). The "Focus on Research" feature describes a study showing the nature of impaired cognitive processes in low-birth-weight babies.

Small-for-date babies often survive, but their cognitive and motor development typically is delayed.

Focus on Research

Impaired Memory Functions in Low-Birth-Weight Babies

Who were the investigators, and what was the aim of the study? Cognitive development is often delayed in low-birth-weight babies. Susan Rose and her colleagues (Rose, Feldman, & Jankowski, 2009) hoped to understand whether memory developed normally in low-birth-weight babies.

How did the investigators measure the topic of interest? Memory is an essential skill, for it allows us to benefit from past experiences. Without memory, everything would be experienced as brand new, à la Drew Barrymore's character in *50 First Dates*. Psychologists have devised many tasks to study different facets of memory; we'll see some of these in Module 7.2. Rose and her colleagues used several memory tasks, including an imitation task in which an experimenter demonstrated a brief sequence of novel events, such as making a gong from two posts, a base, and a metal plate. After a brief delay, children were given the parts and encouraged to reproduce what they'd seen.

Who were the children in the study? The sample originally included 144 full-term babies who weighed at least 2,500 grams at birth and 59 babies born prematurely who weighed, on average, about 1,100 grams at birth. The two groups of babies were matched by gender (about even numbers of boys and girls), by race (about 90% of the infants were African American or Hispanic), and by mother's education (an average of just over 13 years of education). The memory tasks were administered when children were 2-year-olds and again as 3-year-olds.

What was the design of the study? The study was correlational because the investigators were interested in the relation that existed naturally between two variables: birth weight and memory skill. The study was longitudinal because children were tested twice: at 2 and 3 years of age. (Actually, they were tested at younger and older ages as well, but for simplicity I'm focusing on these two ages.)

Were there ethical concerns with the study? No. The tasks were ones commonly used with toddlers; they posed no known risks to the children. The investigators obtained permission from the parents for the children to participate.

What were the results? The graph in Figure 3-9 shows the percentage of actions in each event that children successfully imitated. Memory obviously improves substantially between 2 and 3 years. Nevertheless, at each age, children who had been born prematurely imitated a smaller percentage of events than did children born after a full term.

What did the investigators conclude? Low birth weight impairs a basic cognitive skill—in this case, memory—and during the toddler years there's no evidence that children born prematurely "catch up": They're just as far behind at age 3 as at age 2.

What converging evidence would strengthen these conclusions? The results show that low birth weight affects children's memory. More convincing would be additional longitudinal results showing that impaired basic skills in low-birth-weight children makes them more likely to be diagnosed with a learning disability, more likely to repeat a grade, or less likely to graduate from high school.

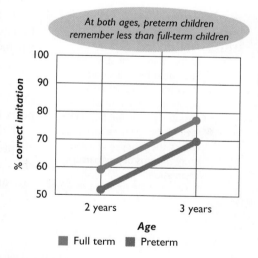

FIGURE 3-9

Small-for-date babies who weigh more than 1,500 grams have better prospects if they receive appropriate care. Like the infant in the photo on page 92, small-for-date babies are placed in special, sealed beds where temperature and air quality are regulated carefully. These beds effectively isolate infants, depriving them of environmental stimulation. Consequently, they often receive auditory stimulation, such as a tape recording of soothing music or their mother's voice, or visual stimulation provided from a mobile placed over the bed. Infants also receive tactile stimulation—they are "massaged" several times daily. These forms of stimulation foster physical and cognitive development in small-for-date babies (Field & Diego, 2010).

This special care should continue when infants leave the hospital for home. Consequently, interventions for small-for-date babies typically include training programs designed for parents of infants and young children. In these programs, parents learn how to respond appropriately to their child's behaviors. For example, they are taught the signs that a baby is in distress, overstimulated, or ready to interact. Parents also learn games and activities to use to foster their child's development. In addition, children are enrolled in high-quality child-care centers where the curriculum is coordinated with the parent training. This sensitive care promotes development in low-birth-weight babies; for example, sometimes they catch up to full-term infants in terms of cognitive development (Hill, Brooks-Gunn, & Waldfogel, 2003).

Long-term positive outcomes for these infants depend critically on providing a supportive and stimulating home environment. Unfortunately, not all at-risk babies have these optimal experiences. Many experience stress or disorder in their family lives. In these cases, development is usually affected (Poehlmann et al., 2011). The importance of a supportive environment for at-risk babies was dramatically demonstrated in a longitudinal study of all children born in 1955 on the Hawaiian island of Kauai (Werner, 1995). At-risk newborns who grew up in stable homes were indistinguishable from children born without birth complications. ("Stable family environment" was defined as two supportive, mentally healthy parents present throughout childhood.) When at-risk newborns had an unstable family environment because of divorce, parental alcoholism, or mental illness, for example, they lagged behind their peers in intellectual and social development.

The Hawaiian study underscores a point I have made several times in this chapter: Development is best when pregnant women receive good prenatal care and children live in a supportive environment. The "Cultural Influences" feature makes the same point in a different way, by looking at infant mortality around the world.

Q&A ANSWER 3.3
At this point, probably not. Soon after birth, it's normal for women to experience occasionally feelings of sadness and anger. But if Rosa's feelings persist for a few more weeks, then they're likely to be symptoms of postpartum depression.

Cultural Influences

Infant Mortality

If you were the proud parent of a newborn and a citizen of Afghanistan, the odds are 1 in 6 that your baby would die before his or her first birthday—worldwide, Afghanistan has the highest infant mortality rate, defined as the percentage of infants who die before their first birthday. In contrast, if you were a parent and a citizen of the Czech Republic, Iceland, Finland, or Japan, the odds are less than 1 in 300 that your baby would die in his or her first year, because these countries have among the lowest infant mortality rates.

The graph in Figure 3-10 puts these numbers in a broader, global context, depicting infant mortality rates for 15 developed nations as well as for 15 least-developed countries.

Not surprisingly, risks to infants are far greater—about 20 times, on average—in the least-developed nations compared to developed nations (UNICEF, 2007). In fact, the differences are so great that the graphs for the two groups of nations must be drawn on different scales.

If you're an American, you may be surprised to see that the United States ranks near the bottom of the list of developed nations. The difference is small, but if the United States were to reduce its infant mortality rate to the 4% that's common in European countries, this would mean that 8,000 American babies who now die annually before their first birthday would live.

What explains these differences in infant mortality rates? For American infants, low birth weight is critical. The United States has more babies with low birth weight than virtually all other developed countries, and we've already seen that low birth weight places an infant at risk. Low birth weight can usually be prevented when a pregnant woman gets regular prenatal care, but many pregnant women in the United States receive inadequate or no prenatal care because they have no health insurance (Cohen, Martinez, & Ward, 2010). Virtually all the countries that rank ahead of the United States provide complete prenatal care at little or no cost. Many of these countries also provide paid leaves of absence for pregnant women (OECD, 2006).

In the least-developed countries, inadequate prenatal care is common and mothers often have inadequate nutrition. After birth, infants in these countries face the twin challenges of receiving adequate nutrition and avoiding disease. However, with improved prenatal care and improved health care and nutrition for infants, the global infant mortality rate has been cut in half since 1990 (UNICEF, 2007). With continued improvements in such care, the main challenges for infants worldwide will be walking, talking, and bonding with parents, not sheer survival.

FIGURE 3-10

 ## Check Your Learning

RECALL What are the three stages of labor? What are the highlights of each?

Describe the main features of prepared approaches to childbirth.

INTERPRET Explain why some at-risk newborns develop normally but others do not.

APPLY Lynn is pregnant with her first child and would like to give birth at home. Her husband is totally against the idea and claims that it's much too risky. What advice would you give them?

3.4   The Newborn

OUTLINE

Assessing the Newborn

The Newborn's Reflexes

Newborn States

Perception and Learning in the Newborn

LEARNING OBJECTIVES

- How do we determine if a baby is healthy and adjusting to life outside the uterus?
- How do reflexes help newborns interact with the world?
- What behavioral states are observable in newborns?
- How well do newborns experience the world? Can they learn from experience?

Lisa and Matt, the proud but exhausted parents, were astonished at how their lives revolved around 10-day-old Hannah's eating and sleeping. Lisa felt as if she were feeding Hannah around the clock. When Hannah napped, Lisa would think of many things she should do but usually napped herself because she was so tired. Matt wondered when Hannah would start sleeping through the night so that he and Lisa could get a good night's sleep themselves.

This newborn baby—my son, Ben—is covered with vernix and is bow-legged; his head is distorted from the journey down the birth canal.

The newborn baby that thrills parents like Lisa and Matt is actually rather homely, as this photo of my son Ben shows. I took it when he was 20 seconds old. Like other newborns, Ben is covered with blood and vernix, the white-colored "grease" that protects the fetus's skin during the many months of prenatal development. His head is temporarily distorted from coming through the birth canal, he has a potbelly, and he is bow-legged. Still, to us he was beautiful, and we were glad he'd finally arrived.

What can newborns like Hannah and Ben do? We'll answer that question in this module and, as we do, learn when Lisa and Matt can expect to resume a full night's sleep.

Assessing the Newborn

Imagine that a mother has just asked you if her newborn baby is healthy. How would you decide? **The** *Apgar score,* **a measure devised by Virginia Apgar, is used to evaluate the newborn baby's condition.** Health professionals look for five vital signs, including breathing, heartbeat, muscle tone, presence of reflexes (e.g., coughing), and skin tone. As you can see in Table 3-5, each of the five vital signs receives a score of 0, 1, or 2, with 2 being optimal.

The five scores are added together, with a score of 7 or more indicating a baby in good physical condition. A score of 4 to 6 means that the newborn will need special attention and care. A score of 3 or less signals a life-threatening situation that requires emergency medical care (Apgar, 1953).

The Apgar score provides a quick, approximate assessment of the newborn's status by focusing on the body systems needed to sustain life. For a comprehensive evaluation of the newborn's well-being, pediatricians and child-development specialists use the Neonatal Behavioral Assessment Scale, or NBAS (Brazelton & Nugent, 1995). The NBAS is used with newborns to 2-month-olds to provide a

TABLE 3-5

FIVE SIGNS EVALUATED IN THE APGAR SCORE

Points	Activity	Pulse	Grimace (response to irritating stimulus)	Appearance (skin color)	Respiration
2	Baby moves limbs actively	100 beats per minute or more	Baby cries intensely	Normal color all over	Strong breathing and crying
1	Baby moves limbs slightly	Fewer than 100 beats per minute	Baby grimaces or cries	Normal color except for extremities	Slow, irregular breathing
0	No movement; muscles flaccid	Not detectable	Baby does not respond	Baby is blue-gray, pale all over	No breathing

detailed portrait of the baby's behavioral repertoire. The scale includes 28 behavioral items along with 18 items that test reflexes. The baby's performance is used to evaluate functioning of four systems:

- *Autonomic.* The newborn's ability to control body functions such as breathing and temperature regulation
- *Motor.* The newborn's ability to control body movements and activity level
- *State.* The newborn's ability to maintain a state (e.g., staying alert or staying asleep)
- *Social.* The newborn's ability to interact with people

The NBAS is based on the view that newborns are remarkably competent individuals who are well prepared to interact with the environment. Reflecting this view, examiners go to great lengths to bring out a baby's best performance. They do everything possible to make a baby feel comfortable and secure during testing. Also, if the infant does not first succeed on an item, the examiner provides some assistance (Alberts, 2005).

Not only is the NBAS useful to clinicians in evaluating the well-being of individual babies, researchers have found it a valuable tool as well. Sometimes performance on the NBAS is used as a dependent variable. For example, harm associated with teratogens has been shown by lower scores on the NBAS (e.g., Engel et al., 2009). Researchers also use scores on the NBAS to predict later development (e.g., Stjernqvist, 2009).

The Newborn's Reflexes

As we've just seen, the NBAS was based on a view—shared widely by child-development researchers—that newborns are well prepared to begin interacting with their world. **An important part of this preparation is a rich set of** *reflexes,* **unlearned responses that are triggered by a specific form of stimulation.** Table 3-6 on page 98 lists the many reflexes commonly found in newborn babies. ⊙—Watch the Video on **mydevelopmentlab.com**

Some reflexes pave the way for newborns to get the nutrients they need to grow: Rooting and sucking ensure that the newborn is well prepared to begin a new diet of life-sustaining milk. Other reflexes protect the newborn from danger in the environment. The blink and withdrawal reflexes, for example, help newborns avoid unpleasant

⊙—Watch the Video *Reflexes* on **mydevelopmentlab.com** to learn more about a newborn baby's reflexes. This video describes a few reflexes that I haven't described (e.g., breathing) as well as the rooting and sucking reflexes and, at the very end of the video, a few of the reflexes listed in Table 3-6.

TABLE 3-6

SOME MAJOR REFLEXES FOUND IN NEWBORNS

Name	Response	Significance
Babinski	A baby's toes fan out when the sole of the foot is stroked from heel to toe.	Unknown
Blink	A baby's eyes close in response to bright light or loud noise.	Protects the eyes
Moro	A baby throws its arms out and then inward (as if embracing) in response to a loud noise or when its head falls.	May help a baby cling to its mother
Palmar	A baby grasps an object placed in the palm of its hand.	Precursor to voluntary grasping
Rooting	When a baby's cheek is stroked, it turns its head toward the stroking and opens its mouth.	Helps a baby find the nipple
Stepping	A baby who is held upright by an adult and is then moved forward begins to step rhythmically.	Precursor to voluntary walking
Sucking	A baby sucks when an object is placed in its mouth.	Permits feeding
Withdrawal	A baby withdraws its foot when the sole is pricked with a pin.	Protects a baby from unpleasant stimulation

stimulation. Yet other reflexes serve as the foundation for larger, voluntary patterns of motor activity. For example, the stepping reflex looks like a precursor to walking.

Reflexes indicate whether the newborn's nervous system is working properly. For example, infants with damage to their sciatic nerve, which is found in the spinal cord, do not show the withdrawal reflex; infants who have problems with the lower part of the spine do not show the Babinski reflex. If these or other reflexes are weak or missing altogether, a thorough physical and behavioral assessment is called for (Falk & Bornstein, 2005).

Newborn States

Newborns spend most of their day alternating among four states (St. James-Roberts & Plewis, 1996; Wolff, 1987):

> Newborns alternate between four behavioral states: alert inactivity, waking activity, crying, and sleeping.

- *Alert inactivity.* The baby is calm, with eyes open and attentive; the baby looks as if he is deliberately inspecting his environment.
- *Waking activity.* The baby's eyes are open, but they seem unfocused; the baby moves her arms or legs in bursts of uncoordinated motion.
- *Crying.* The baby cries vigorously, usually accompanying this with agitated but uncoordinated motion.
- *Sleeping.* The baby's eyes are closed and the baby drifts back and forth from periods of regular breathing and stillness to periods of irregular breathing and gentle arm and leg motion.

Researchers have been particularly interested in crying, because parents want to know why babies cry and how to calm them; and sleeping, because babies spend so much time asleep!

CRYING.   Newborns spend 2 to 3 hours each day crying or on the verge of crying. If you haven't spent much time around newborns, you might think that all crying is pretty much alike. In fact, babies cry for different reasons and cry differently for each one. In fact, scientists and parents can identify three distinctive types of cries (Snow, 1998). **A** *basic cry* **starts softly, then gradually becomes more intense and usually occurs when a baby is hungry or tired; a** *mad cry* **is a more intense version of a basic cry; and a** *pain cry* **begins with a sudden, long burst of crying, followed by a long pause and gasping.**

Parents are naturally concerned when their baby cries, and if they can't quiet a crying baby, their concern mounts and can easily give way to frustration and annoyance. It's no surprise, then, that parents develop little tricks for soothing their babies. Many Western parents will lift a baby to the shoulder and walk or gently rock the baby. Sometimes they will also sing lullabies, pat the baby's back, or give the baby a

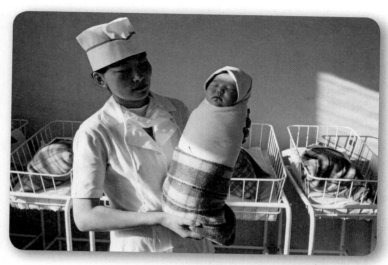

Swaddling is an effective way to soothe a baby who's upset.

pacifier. Yet another method is to put a newborn into a car seat and go for a drive; I remember doing this, as a last resort, at 2:00 AM with my son Ben when he was 10 days old. After about the 12th time around the block, he finally stopped crying and fell asleep!

Another useful technique is *swaddling,* **in which an infant is wrapped tightly in a blanket.** Swaddling, shown in the photo, is used in many cultures around the world, including Turkey and Peru as well as countries in Asia. Swaddling provides warmth and tactile stimulation that usually works well to soothe a baby (Delaney, 2000).

Parents are sometimes reluctant to respond to their crying infant for fear of producing a baby who cries constantly. Yet they hear their baby's cry as a call for help that they shouldn't ignore. What to do? Should parents respond? "Yes, usually" is probably the best answer (Hubbard & van IJzendoorn, 1991). If parents respond *immediately, every time* their infant cries, the result may well be a fussy, whiny baby. Instead, parents need to consider why their infant is crying and the intensity of the crying. On the one hand, when a baby wakes during the night and cries quietly, a parent might wait before responding, giving the baby a chance to calm herself. On the other hand, when parents hear a loud noise from an infant's bedroom followed by a mad cry, they should respond immediately. Parents need to remember that crying is actually the newborn's first attempt to communicate with others. They need to decide what the infant is trying to tell them and whether that warrants a quick response or whether they should let the baby soothe herself.

 QUESTION 3.4
When Mary's 4-month-old son cries, she rushes to him immediately and does everything possible to console him. Is this a good idea? *(Answer is on page 102.)*

SLEEPING. Crying may get parents' attention, but sleep is what newborns do more than anything else. They sleep 16 to 18 hours daily. The problem for tired parents like Lisa and Matt from the vignette is that newborns sleep in naps taken round the clock. Newborns typically go through a cycle of wakefulness and sleep about every 4 hours. That is, they will be awake for about an hour, sleep for 3 hours, then start the cycle anew. During the hour when newborns are awake, they regularly move between the different waking states several times. Cycles of alert inactivity, waking activity, and crying are common.

As babies grow older, the sleep–wake cycle gradually begins to correspond to the day–night cycle (St. James-Roberts & Plewis, 1996). Most babies begin sleeping through the night when they are about 3 or 4 months old, a major milestone for bleary-eyed parents like Lisa and Matt.

Co-sleeping, in which infants and young children sleep with their parents, is common in many countries around the world.

By 6 months, most North American infants are sleeping in a crib in their own rooms. Although this practice seems "natural" to North American parents, in much of the rest of the world, children sleep with their parents throughout infancy and the preschool years. Such parent–child "co-sleeping" is commonly found in cultures where people define themselves less as independent individuals and more as part of a group. For parents in cultures that value such interdependence—including Egypt, Italy, Japan, Korea, and Malaysia as well as the Maya in Guatemala and the Inuit in Canada—co-sleeping is an important step in forging parent–child bonds, just as sleeping alone is an important step toward independence in cultures that value self-reliance (Nelson, Schiefenhoevel, & Haimerl, 2000; Tan, 2009; Worthman & Brown, 2007).

How does co-sleeping work? Infants may sleep in a cradle placed next to their parents' bed or in a basket that's in their parents' bed. When they outgrow this arrangement, they sleep in the bed with their mother; depending on the culture, the father may sleep in the same bed (as shown in the photo), in another bed in the same room, in another room, or in another house altogether!

You might think that co-sleeping would make children more dependent on their parents, but research provides no evidence of this (Cortesi et al., 2004; Okami, Weisner, & Olmstead, 2002). Plus, co-sleeping has the benefit of avoiding the lengthy, elaborate rituals that are often involved in getting youngsters to sleep in their own rooms, alone. With co-sleeping, children and parents simply go to bed together, with few struggles.

While asleep, babies alternate between two types of sleep. **In** *rapid-eye-movement (REM) sleep,* **newborns move their arms and legs, they may grimace, and their eyes may dart beneath their eyelids.** Brain waves register fast activity, the heart beats more rapidly, and breathing is more rapid. **In regular or** *non-REM sleep,* **breathing, heart rate, and brain activity are steady and newborns lie quietly without the twitching associated with REM sleep.** REM sleep becomes less frequent as infants grow. By 4 months, only 40% of sleep is REM sleep. By the first birthday, REM sleep drops to 25%, not far from the adult average of 20% (Halpern, MacLean, & Baumeister, 1995).

The function of REM sleep is still debated. Older children and adults dream during REM sleep, and brain waves during REM sleep resemble those of an alert, awake person. Consequently, many scientists believe that REM sleep stimulates the brain in some way that helps foster growth in the nervous system (Halpern et al., 1995; Roffwarg, Muzio, & Dement, 1966).

SUDDEN INFANT DEATH SYNDROME.   For many parents of young babies, sleep is sometimes a cause of concern. **In** *sudden infant death syndrome (SIDS),* **a healthy baby dies suddenly, for no apparent reason.** Approximately 1 to 3 of every 1,000 American babies dies from SIDS. Most of them are between 2 and 4 months old.

Scientists don't know the exact causes of SIDS, but one idea is that 2- to 4-month-old infants are particularly vulnerable to SIDS because many newborn reflexes are waning during these months and thus infants may not respond effectively when breathing becomes difficult. They may not reflexively move the head away from a blanket or pillow that is smothering them (Lipsitt, 2003).

Researchers have also identified several risk factors associated with SIDS (Sahni, Fifer, & Myers, 2007). Babies are more vulnerable if they were born prematurely or with low birth weight. They are also more vulnerable when their parents smoke. SIDS is more likely when a baby sleeps on its stomach (face down) than when it sleeps on its back (face up). Finally, SIDS is more likely during winter, when babies sometimes become overheated from too many blankets and too-heavy sleepwear (Carroll & Loughlin, 1994). Evidently, SIDS infants, many of whom were born prematurely or with low birth weight, are less able to withstand physiological stresses and imbalances that are brought on by cigarette smoke, breathing that is temporarily interrupted, or overheating (Simpson, 2001).

As evidence about causes of SIDS accumulated, child advocates called for action. The result is described in the "Child Development and Family Policy" feature.

> Infants are at greater risk for SIDS when they are born prematurely or with low birth weight, and when they are exposed to physiological stresses such as overheating.

Child Development and Family Policy

Back to Sleep!

In 1992, based on mounting evidence that SIDS more often occurred when infants slept on their stomachs, the American Academy of Pediatrics (AAP) began advising parents to put babies to sleep on their backs or sides. In 1994, the AAP joined forces with the U.S. Public Health Service to launch a national program to educate parents about the dangers of SIDS and the importance of putting babies to sleep on their backs. The "Back to Sleep" campaign was widely publicized through brochures, posters like the one shown in Figure 3-11, and videos. Since the "Back to Sleep" campaign began, research shows that far more infants are now sleeping on their backs and that the incidence of SIDS has dropped (Dwyer & Ponsonby, 2009). However, it became clear that African American infants were still twice as likely to die from SIDS, apparently because they were much more likely to be placed on their stomachs to sleep. Consequently, in the 21st century the National Institutes of Health partnered with groups such as the Women in the NAACP and the National Council of 100 Black Women to train thousands of people to convey the "Back to Sleep" message in a culturally appropriate manner to African American communities (NICHD, 2004). The goal is for African American infants to benefit from the life-saving benefits of the "Back to Sleep" program. The message for all parents—particularly if their babies were premature or small-for-date—is to keep their babies away from smoke, to put them on their backs to sleep, and to not overdress them or wrap them too tightly in blankets.

FIGURE 3-11

Perception and Learning in the Newborn

Do you believe it is important to talk to newborns and give them fuzzy little toys? Should their rooms be bright and colorful? If you do, you really believe two things about newborns. First, you believe that newborns can have perceptual experiences—they can see, smell, hear, taste, and feel. Second, you believe that sensory experiences are somehow registered in the newborn through learning and memory, because unless experiences are registered, they can't influence later behavior. You'll be happy to know that research confirms your beliefs. All the basic perceptual systems are operating at some level at birth. The world outside the uterus can be seen, smelled, heard, tasted, and felt (Cohen & Cashon, 2003; Slater et al., 2010). Moreover, newborns show the capacity to learn and remember. They change their behavior based on their experiences (Rovee-Collier & Barr, 2010).

We'll discuss these perceptual changes in more detail in Chapter 5, and we'll discuss learning and memory in Chapter 7. For now, the important point is that newborns are remarkably prepared to interact with the world. Adaptive reflexes coupled with perceptual and learning skills provide a solid foundation for the rest of child development.

 ANSWER 3.4

Probably not. Mary needs to relax a bit. If her son is in danger, she'll recognize a pain cry or a mad cry. Otherwise, Mary should wait a moment before going to her son, to try to decide why he's crying and to give him a chance to calm himself.

 ## Check Your Learning

RECALL What are the different functions of reflexes?

Describe the four primary states of infant behavior.

INTERPRET Compare the Apgar and the NBAS as measures of a newborn baby's well-being.

APPLY What would you recommend to parents of a 2-month-old who are very worried about SIDS?

UNIFYING THEMES Continuity

This chapter is a good opportunity to highlight the theme that *early development is related to later development but not perfectly.* Remember the Hawaiian study? This study showed that outcomes for at-risk infants are not uniform. When at-risk infants grow up in a stable, supportive environment, they become quite normal children. But when they grow up in stressful environments, they lag intellectually and socially. Similarly, SIDS is more likely to affect babies born prematurely and with low birth weight, yet not all of these babies die of SIDS. When premature and low-birth-weight babies sleep on their backs, are not overheated, and do not inhale smoke, they're unlikely to die from SIDS. Traumatic events early in development, such as being born early or underweight, do not predetermine the rest of a child's life, but they do make some developmental paths easier to follow than others.

See for Yourself

Words can hardly capture the miracle of a newborn baby. If you have never seen a newborn, you need to see one, or even better, a roomful. Arrange to visit the maternity ward of a local hospital, which will include a nursery for newborns. Through a large viewing window, you will be able to observe a few or as many as 15 to 20 newborns. These babies will no longer be covered with blood or vernix, but you will be able to see how the newborn's head is often distorted by its journey through the birth canal. As you watch the babies, look for reflexive behavior and changes in states. Watch while a baby sucks its fingers. Find a baby who seems to be awake and alert, then note how long the baby stays this way. When alertness wanes, watch for the behaviors that replace it. Finally, observe how different the newborns look and act from each other. The wonderful variety and diversity found among human beings is already evident in those who are hours or days old. See for yourself!

Summary

3.1 From Conception to Birth

Period of the Zygote (Weeks 1–2)
The first period of prenatal development lasts 2 weeks. This period begins when the egg is fertilized.

Period of the Embryo (Weeks 3–8)
The second period of prenatal development is when most major body structures are formed.

Period of the Fetus (Weeks 9–38)
In the third period of prenatal development, the fetus becomes much larger and body systems begin to function.

3.2 Influences on Prenatal Development

General Risk Factors
Prenatal development can be harmed if a pregnant woman does not provide adequate nutrition for the developing organism or experiences considerable stress. Teenagers often have problem pregnancies because they rarely receive adequate prenatal care. After age 35, women are less fertile and more likely to have problem pregnancies, but they are effective mothers.

Teratogens: Diseases, Drugs, and Environmental Hazards
Teratogens are agents that can cause abnormal prenatal development. Several diseases and drugs are teratogens. Environmental teratogens are particularly dangerous because a pregnant woman may not know when these substances are present.

How Teratogens Influence Prenatal Development
The effect of teratogens depends on the genotype of the organism as well as the timing and amount of exposure. The impact of a teratogen may not be evident until later in life.

Prenatal Diagnosis and Treatment
Ultrasound uses sound waves to generate a picture of the fetus that reveals the position of the fetus, its sex, and any gross physical deformities. When genetic disorders are suspected, amniocentesis or chorionic villus sampling is used to determine the genotype of the fetus. Fetal medicine corrects problems of prenatal development medically, surgically, or through genetic engineering.

3.3 Happy Birthday!

Labor and Delivery
Labor consists of three stages. In Stage 1, the muscles of the uterus contract, causing the cervix to enlarge. In Stage 2, the baby moves through the birth canal. In Stage 3, the placenta is delivered.

Approaches to Childbirth
In prepared childbirth, mothers-to-be come to understand what takes place during birth and learn to cope with pain through relaxation and the help of a supportive coach.

Although most American babies are born in hospitals, home birth is safe when the mother is healthy, the delivery is expected to be trouble free, and a health care professional is present.

Adjusting to Parenthood
Following the birth of a child, a woman's body changes physically. Both parents also adjust psychologically and sometimes fathers feel left out. After giving birth, some women experience postpartum depression: They are irritable, have poor appetite and disturbed sleep, and are apathetic.

Birth Complications
During labor and delivery, the flow of blood to the fetus can be disrupted, causing hypoxia, a lack of oxygen to the fetus.

If the fetus is endangered, the doctor may do a cesarean section, removing it from the uterus surgically. Babies with many birth complications are at risk for becoming aggressive and developing schizophrenia.

Premature babies develop more slowly at first but catch up in a few years. Small-for-date babies who weigh less than 1,500 grams often do not develop normally; larger small-for-date babies fare well when their environment is stimulating and stress-free.

Infant mortality is relatively high in many countries around the world, primarily because of inadequate care before birth and inadequate nutrition and disease after birth.

3.4 The Newborn

Assessing the Newborn
The Apgar score measures five vital signs to determine a newborn's physical well-being. The Neonatal Behavioral Assessment Scale evaluates a baby's behavioral and physical status.

The Newborn's Reflexes
Some reflexes help infants to adjust to life outside the uterus, some protect them, and some are the basis for later motor behavior.

Newborn States
Newborns spend their day in one of four states: alert inactivity, waking activity, crying, and sleeping. A newborn's crying includes a basic cry, a mad cry, and a pain cry.

Newborns spend approximately two-thirds of every day asleep and go through a complete sleep–wake cycle once every 4 hours or so. Newborns spend about half their time in REM sleep, characterized by active brain waves and frequent movements of the eyes and limbs. REM sleep may stimulate nervous system growth.

Some healthy babies die from sudden infant death syndrome (SIDS). Babies are vulnerable to SIDS when they are premature, have low birth weight, sleep on their stomachs, are overheated, and/or are exposed to cigarette smoke. Encouraging parents to place babies on their backs for sleeping has reduced the number of SIDS cases.

Perception and Learning in the Newborn
Newborns' perceptual and learning skills function reasonably well, which allows them to experience the world.

Test Yourself

✓• Study and Review on **mydevelopmentlab.com**

1. The fertilized egg implants in the wall of the uterus during the period of the _____.

2. Differentiation of cells begins in the period of the _____.

3. The developing organism becomes much larger and its bodily systems begin to work during the period of the _____.

4. General risk factors during prenatal development include inadequate nutrition, stress, and _____.

5. Diseases, drugs, and _____ are common categories of teratogens.

6. Exposure to teratogens during the period of the fetus usually results in _____.

7. _____ is a procedure that generates an image of the fetus, which can be used to determine its sex and the existence of multiple pregnancies.

8. One way to check for genetic disorders in a fetus is amniocentesis; another is _____.

9. The first stage of labor is usually the longest, but the baby is born in the _____ stage.

10. Prepared childbirth emphasizes education, _____, and the presence of a supportive coach.

11. A woman who, following childbirth, experiences prolonged irritation, feelings of low-self worth, and disturbed sleep is probably suffering from _____.

12. At-risk infants often develop normally if _____.

13. _____ uses five vital signs to provide a quick, rough evaluation of a newborn's status.

14. Infants spend their day alternating between sleeping, crying, alert inactivity, and _____.

15. The national program to eliminate sudden infant death syndrome (SIDS) encouraged _____.

Answers: (1) zygote; (2) embryo; (3) fetus; (4) maternal age; (5) environmental hazards; (6) minor defects in bodily structure or improperly functioning body systems; (7) Ultrasound; (8) chorionic villus sampling (CVS); (9) second; (10) relaxation; (11) postpartum depression; (12) they are exposed to a stable, supportive environment; (13) The Apgar score; (14) waking activity; (15) parents to place infants on their backs for sleeping

Key Terms

age of viability   69
amniocentesis   84
amniotic fluid   67
amniotic sac   67
Apgar score   96
basic cry   99
blastocyst   66
breech presentation   87
cerebral cortex   68
cesarean section (C-section)   92
chorionic villus sampling (CVS)   84
crowning   87
ectoderm   67
endoderm   67
embryo   66
fetal alcohol spectrum disorder
(FASD)   78

fetal medicine   85
genetic engineering   85
germ disc   66
hypoxia   91
implantation   66
mad cry   99
mesoderm   67
non-REM sleep   100
pain cry   99
period of the fetus   68
placenta   66
postpartum depression   90
premature infants   92
prenatal development   65
rapid-eye-movement (REM)
sleep   100
reflexes   97

small-for-date infants   92
social influence   75
social selection   75
spina bifida   73
stress   73
sudden infant death syndrome
(SIDS)   100
swaddling   99
teratogen   77
ultrasound   83
umbilical cord   67
vernix   69
villi   67
zygote   65

4

Growth and Health

 4.1

Physical Growth

 4.2

Challenges to Healthy Growth

 4.3

The Developing Nervous System

Humans take longer to become physically mature than any other animal. We spend about 20% of our lives—all of childhood and adolescence—growing physically. This slow journey to physical maturity is an interesting story in itself. But physical growth is just as important for its impact on other aspects of children's development, including cognition, social behavior, and personality. As children grow physically, they become less dependent on others for care, they're treated differently by adults, and they come to view themselves as older and more mature. By knowing more about children's physical growth, you'll be better prepared to understand other aspects of development that we'll study in the rest of this book.

In this chapter, we'll learn how children grow physically. In **Module 4.1**, we'll look at different facets of physical growth and some of the reasons why people differ in their physical growth and stature. Then, in **Module 4.2**, we'll explore problems that can disrupt physical growth. In **Module 4.3**, we'll look at physical growth that's not so obvious—the development of the brain.

 4.1 **Physical Growth**

OUTLINE

Features of Human Growth

Mechanisms of Physical Growth

The Adolescent Growth Spurt and Puberty

LEARNING OBJECTIVES

- What are the important features of physical growth during childhood? How do they vary from child to child?
- How do sleep and nutrition contribute to healthy growth?
- What are the physical changes associated with puberty, and what are their consequences?

Pete has just had his 15th birthday, but, as far as he is concerned, there is no reason to celebrate. Although most of his friends have grown about 6 inches in the past year or so, have a much larger penis and larger testicles, and have mounds of pubic hair, Pete looks just as he did when he was 10 years old. He is embarrassed by his appearance, particularly in the locker room, where he looks like a little boy among men. "Won't I ever change?" he wonders.

For parents and children alike, physical growth is a topic of great interest. Parents marvel at how quickly babies add pounds and inches; 2-year-olds proudly proclaim, "I bigger now!" Many adolescents take great satisfaction in finally becoming taller than a parent; others, like Pete, suffer through their teenage years as they wait for the physical signs of maturity.

In this module, we'll examine some of the basic features of physical growth and variations in growth patterns. We'll also consider the mechanisms responsible for growth. Finally, we'll end the module by studying puberty, a phase of physical growth so special that it should be considered separately.

Features of Human Growth

DESCRIBING GROWTH. Probably the most obvious way to measure physical growth is in terms of sheer size—height and weight. The growth charts in Figure 4-1 show the average changes in height and weight that take place as children grow from birth to age 20. Between birth and 2 years, for example, average height increases from 19 to 32 inches; average weight increases from 7 to 22 pounds. (An interesting rule of thumb is that boys achieve half their adult height by 2 years, and girls by 18 months.)

What is not so obvious from growth charts is that increases in height and weight are not steady. Looking at the average increase in weight and height annually—as opposed to the average total weight and height for each year—gives quite a different picture of the pattern of physical growth. Figure 4-2 shows that growth is extraordinarily rapid during the first year, when the average baby gains about 10 inches and 15 pounds. Growth is fairly steady through the preschool and elementary-school years: about 3 inches and 7 to 8 pounds each year. In early adolescence, growth is rapid again. During this growth spurt, which corresponds to the peaks in the middle of the charts in Figure 4-2, teenagers typically grow 4 inches and gain 16 to 17 pounds each year. After this spurt, which begins 1 to 2 years earlier in girls, growth again slows as children reach adulthood.

As children grow, their body parts develop at different rates, which means that infants and young children are not simply scaled-down versions of adults. The head and trunk grow faster than the legs. As you can see in Figure 4-3, infants and toddlers have disproportionately large heads and trunks, making them look top-heavy compared to older children and adolescents. As growth of the hips, legs, and feet catches up later in childhood, bodies take on proportions that are more adultlike.

> Growth is particularly rapid in infancy and adolescence.

MUSCLE, FAT, AND BONES. Other important features of physical growth take place inside the body, with the development of muscle, fat, and bones. Virtually all of the body's muscle fibers are present at birth. During childhood,

FIGURE 4-1

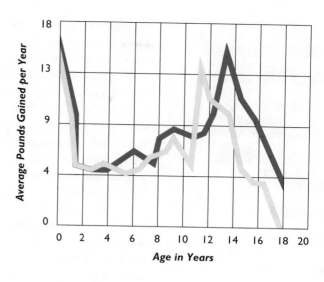

■ *Boys* ▨ *Girls*

FIGURE 4-2

muscles become longer and thicker as individual fibers fuse together. This process accelerates during adolescence, particularly for boys.

A layer of fat appears under the skin near the end of the fetal period of prenatal development; just as insulation in walls stabilizes the temperature inside a house, fat helps the fetus and infant regulate body temperature. Fat continues to accumulate rapidly during the first year after birth, producing the familiar look we call *baby fat*. During the preschool years, children actually become leaner, but in the early elementary-school years they begin to acquire more fat again. This happens gradually at first, then more rapidly during adolescence. The increase in fat in adolescence is more pronounced in girls than in boys.

Bone begins to form during prenatal development. What will become bone starts as *cartilage*, a soft, flexible tissue. During the embryonic period, the center of the tissue turns to bone. **Then, shortly before birth, the ends of the cartilage structures, known as** *epiphyses,* **turn to bone.** Now the structure is hard at each end and in the center. Working from the center, cartilage turns to bone until finally the enlarging center section reaches the epiphyses, ending skeletal growth.

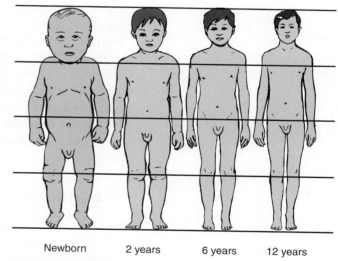

Newborn   2 years   6 years   12 years

FIGURE 4-3

If you combine the changes in muscle, fat, and bone with changes in body size and shape, you have a fairly complete picture of physical growth during childhood. What's missing? The central nervous system, which we cover separately in Module 4.3.

VARIATIONS ON THE AVERAGE PROFILE.   The picture of children's physical growth that I have described so far is a typical profile; there are important variations on this prototype. For example, when the University of Oregon Ducks won

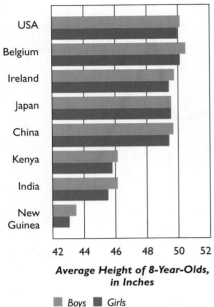

Average Height of 8-Year-Olds, in Inches

■ *Boys* ■ *Girls*

FIGURE 4-4

the first NCAA men's basketball tournament in 1939, the average height of their starting lineup was 6 feet, 2 inches. When the University of Connecticut Huskies won the tournament in 2011, the average height of their starting lineup was 6 feet, 6 inches, a difference of 4 inches. Of course, the changing heights of basketball players simply correspond to changes in the U.S. population at large. Today, adults and children are taller and heavier than previous generations, due largely to improved health and nutrition. **Changes in physical development from one generation to the next are known as** *secular growth trends*. Secular trends have been quite large. A medieval knight's armor would fit today's 10- to 12-year-old boy; the average height of American sailors in the War of 1812 was 5 feet 2 inches!

"Average" physical growth varies not only from one generation to the next, but also from one country to another. Figure 4-4 shows the average height of 8-year-old boys and girls in several countries around the world. Youngsters from the United States, Western European countries, Japan, and China are about the same height, approximately 49 inches. Children in Africa and India are shorter, averaging just under 46 inches; and 8-year-olds in Polynesia are shorter still, averaging 43 inches.

We also need to remember that "average" and "normal" are not the same. Many children are much taller or shorter than average and perfectly normal, of course. For example, among American 8-year-old boys, normal weights range from approximately 44 pounds to 76 pounds. In other words, an extremely light but normal 8-year-old boy would weigh only slightly more than half as much as his extremely heavy but normal peer. What is normal can vary greatly, and this applies not only to height and other aspects of physical growth, but also to all aspects of development. Whenever a "typical" or average age is given for a developmental milestone, you should remember that the normal range for passing the milestone is much wider. Some children pass the milestone sooner than the stated age and some later, but all are normal.

We've seen that children's heights vary within a culture, across time, and between cultures. What accounts for these differences? To answer this question, we need to look at the mechanisms responsible for human growth.

Mechanisms of Physical Growth

Physical growth is easily taken for granted. Compared to other milestones of child development, such as learning to read, physical growth seems to come so easily. Children, like weeds, seem to sprout without any effort at all. In reality, physical growth is complicated. Of course, heredity is involved: As a general rule, two tall parents will have tall children; two short parents will have short children; and one tall parent and one short parent will have average-height offspring.

How are genetic instructions translated into actual growth? Sleep and nutrition are both involved.

SLEEP. In Module 3.4, we saw that infants spend more time asleep than awake. The amount of time that children spend asleep drops gradually, from roughly 11 hours at age 3 to 10 hours at age 7 and 9 hours at age 12 (Snell, Adam, & Duncan, 2007). **Sleep is essential for normal growth because about 80% of the hormone that stimulates growth—named, appropriately,** *growth hormone*—**is secreted while children and adolescents sleep** (Smock, 1998). Growth hormone is secreted during sleep by the pituitary gland in the brain; from the brain, growth hormone travels to the liver, where it triggers the release of another hormone, somatomedin, which causes muscles and bones to grow (Tanner, 1990).

Sleep also affects children's development in a less direct but no less important manner. Children's sleep affects their cognitive processes and their adjustment to school. When children do not sleep well—they wake frequently during the night or they do not sleep a consistent amount each night—they often are less successful in school (Buckhalt et al., 2009) and they are more likely to be anxious, depressed, or have low self-esteem (El-Sheikh et al., 2010).

One way to avoid sleep-related problems in younger children is a bedtime routine that helps them wind down from busy daytime activities. This routine should start at about the same time every night ("It's time to get ready for bed") and end at about the same time (when the parent leaves the child and the child tries to fall asleep). When children follow a routine consistently, they find it easier to fall asleep and are more likely to get a restful night's sleep. Also, children tend to sleep longer and better (i.e., without constant tossing and turning) when they share a bedroom with few other people (Buckhalt, El-Sheikh, & Keller, 2007).

> Sleep is essential because most growth hormone is secreted when children are asleep and because children do poorly in school when they don't sleep well.

Sleep loss can be a particular problem for adolescents. On the one hand, adolescents often stay up later at night, finishing ever-larger amounts of homework, spending time with friends, or working at a part-time job. On the other hand, adolescents often start school earlier than younger elementary-school students. The result is often a sleepy adolescent who struggles to stay awake during the school day (Carskadon, 2002). Over time, being "sleepless in school" is clearly harmful. In one longitudinal study (Fredriksen et al., 2004), children who gradually slept less between sixth and eighth grade had the most symptoms of depression and the largest drop in self-esteem. Thus, for adolescents and children, a good night's sleep is an important part of healthy academic and physical development.

NUTRITION. The fuel for growth comes from the foods children eat and the liquids they drink. Nutrition is particularly important during infancy, when physical growth is so rapid. In a 2-month-old, roughly 40% of the body's energy is devoted to growth. Most of the remaining energy fuels basic bodily functions, such as digestion and respiration.

Because growth requires so much high energy, young babies must consume an enormous number of calories in relation to their body weight. An adult needs to consume only 15 to 20 calories per pound, depending on level of activity, but a 12-pound 3-month-old should eat about 50 calories per pound of body weight, or 600 calories. What's the best way for babies to receive the calories they need? The "Improving Children's Lives" feature has some answers.

Improving Children's Lives

What's the Best Food for Babies?

Breast-feeding is the best way to ensure that babies get the nourishment they need. Human milk contains the proper amounts of carbohydrates, fats, protein, vitamins, and minerals for babies. Breast-feeding also has several other advantages compared to bottle-feeding (Dewey, 2001). First, when babies like the one in the photo are

Breast-feeding provides babies with all the nutrients they need, protects babies from disease, and makes for an easier transition to solid foods.

Q&A QUESTION 4.1
Tameka is pregnant with her first child and wonders whether breast-feeding is really worthwhile. What advantages of breast-feeding would you mention to her? (*Answer is on page 121.*)

breast-fed, they are ill less often because a mother's breast milk contains antibodies that kill bacteria and viruses. Second, breast-fed babies are less prone to diarrhea and constipation. Third, breast-fed babies typically make the transition to solid foods more easily, apparently because they are accustomed to changes in the taste of breast milk that reflect a mother's diet. Fourth, breast milk cannot be contaminated (as long as a nursing mother avoids certain drugs, such as cocaine); in contrast, contamination is often a significant problem when formula is used in developing countries to bottle-feed babies.

The many benefits of breast-feeding do not mean that bottle-feeding is harmful. Formula, when prepared in sanitary conditions, provides generally the same nutrients as human milk, but infants are more prone to develop allergies from formula, and formula does not protect infants from disease. However, bottle-feeding does have advantages. A mother who cannot readily breast-feed can still enjoy the intimacy of feeding her baby, and other family members can participate in feeding. In fact, breast- and bottle-fed babies forge comparable emotional bonds with their mothers (Jansen, de Weerth, & Riksen-Walraven, 2008), so women in industrialized countries can choose either method and know that their babies' dietary and psychological needs will be met.

In the United States and Canada, newborns and very young babies are often breast-fed exclusively. Beginning at about 4 to 6 months, breast-feeding is supplemented by cereal and strained fruits and vegetables. Strained meats are introduced at 7 to 9 months and finely chopped table foods are introduced at 10 to 12 months (International Food Information Council Foundation [IFICF], 2000).

A good rule is to introduce only one new food at a time. For instance, a 7-month-old having cheese for the first time should have no other new foods for a few days. In this way, allergies that may develop—manifested as skin rash or diarrhea—can be linked to a particular food, making it easier to prevent recurrences.

Preschoolers grow more slowly than infants and toddlers, so they need to eat less per pound than before. One rule of thumb is that preschoolers should consume about 40 calories per pound of body weight, which works out to be roughly 1,500 to 1,700 calories daily for many children in this age group.

More important than the sheer number of calories, however, is a balanced diet that includes all five major food groups (grains, vegetables, fruits, milk, and meat and beans). A healthy diet also avoids too much sugar and, especially, too much fat. For preschool children, no more than approximately 30% of the daily caloric intake should come from fat, which works out to be roughly 500 calories from fat. Unfortunately, too many preschool children like the ones in the photo become hooked on fast-food meals, which are notoriously high in fat. A Whopper˚, fries, and shake have nearly 600 calories from fat, 100 more than children should consume all day! Excessive fat intake is the first step toward obesity (which I'll discuss later in this chapter), so parents need to limit their preschool children's fat intake (Whitaker et al., 1997).

Encouraging preschool children to eat healthy foods is tough for parents because some preschoolers become notoriously picky eaters. Like the little girl in the photo at the bottom of page 113, toddlers and preschool children find foods that they once ate willingly "yucky." As a toddler, my daughter loved green beans. When she reached 2, she decided that green beans were awful and refused to eat them. Though such finickiness can be annoying, it may actually be adaptive for increasingly independent preschoolers. Because preschoolers don't know what is safe to eat and what isn't, eating only familiar foods protects them from potential harm (Aldridge, Dovey, & Halford, 2009).

Parents should not be overly concerned about this finicky period. Although some children eat less than before (in terms of calories per pound), virtually all picky eaters get adequate food for growth. Nevertheless, picky-eating children can make mealtime miserable for all. What's a parent to do? Experts (Aldridge et al., 2009; American Academy of Pediatrics, 2008) recommend several guidelines for encouraging children to be more open-minded about foods and for dealing with them when they aren't:

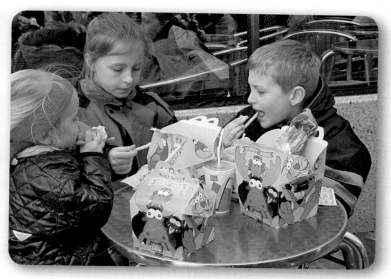

Many American children eat far too many fast-food meals, which are notoriously high in calories.

- When possible, allow children to pick among different healthy foods (e.g., milk versus yogurt).

- Allow children to eat foods in any order they want.

- Offer children new foods one at a time and in small amounts; encourage but don't force children to eat new foods.

- When children reject a new food, continue to offer it over several meals so that it will become familiar (which lowers children's resistance to a new food).

- Don't force children to "clean their plates."

- Don't spend mealtimes talking about what the child is or is not eating; instead, talk about other topics that interest the child.

- Never use food to reward or punish children.

By following these guidelines, mealtimes can be pleasant and children can receive the nutrition they need to grow.

The Adolescent Growth Spurt and Puberty

The biological start of adolescence is *puberty,* **which refers to the adolescent growth spurt and sexual maturation.** The adolescent growth spurt is easy to see in the graphs in Figure 4-1. Physical growth is slow during the elementary-school years: In an average year, a 6- to 10-year-old girl or boy gains about 5 to 7 pounds and grows 2 to 3 inches. During the peak of the adolescent growth spurt, though, a girl may gain as many as 20 pounds in a year and a boy, 25 (Tanner, 1970). This growth spurt lasts a few years.

The figure also shows that girls typically begin their growth spurt about 2 years before boys do. That is, girls typically start the growth spurt at about age 11, reach their peak rate of growth at about 12, and achieve their mature stature at about age 15. In contrast, boys start the growth spurt at 13, hit peak growth at 14, and reach mature stature at 17. This 2-year difference in the growth spurt can lead to awkward social interactions between 11- and 12-year-old boys and girls because during those years, as the photo on page 114 shows, girls are often taller and much more mature looking than boys.

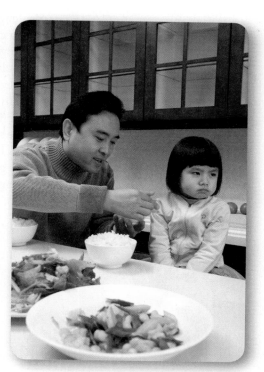

Beginning at about 2 years of age, many youngsters become very picky eaters; they reject foods that they once ate willingly.

During the growth spurt, girls are often much taller than boys of the same age.

During the growth spurt, bones become longer (which, of course, is why adolescents grow taller) and become more dense. Bone growth is accompanied by several other changes that differ for boys and girls. Muscle fibers become thicker and denser during adolescence, producing substantial increases in strength. However, muscle growth is much more pronounced in boys than in girls (Smoll & Schutz, 1990). Body fat also increases during adolescence, but much more rapidly in girls than in boys. Finally, heart and lung capacities increase more in adolescent boys than in adolescent girls. Together, these changes help to explain why the typical adolescent boy has more strength, is quicker, and has greater endurance than the typical adolescent girl.

In the "Child Development and Family Policy" feature, you'll see how healthy bone growth in adolescence is also an essential defense against a disease that strikes during middle age.

Child Development and Family Policy

Preventing Osteoporosis

Osteoporosis **is a disease in which a person's bones become thin and brittle, and, as a consequence, sometimes break.** Although osteoporosis can strike at any age, people over 50 are at greatest risk because at that age bone tissue starts to break down more rapidly than new bone can be formed. About 10 million Americans have osteoporosis. Approximately 80% are women, because after menopause the ovaries no longer produce as much estrogen, which guards against bone deterioration.

Osteoporosis often has its roots in childhood and adolescence, because this is when bones acquire nearly all their mass. For bones to develop properly, children and adolescents need to consume approximately 1,300 milligrams of calcium daily. This is the equivalent of about 3 cups of milk, half an ounce of cheese, and a cup of spinach. In addition, children and adolescents should engage in weight-bearing exercise for 30 minutes daily, on at least 5 days a week. Weight-bearing exercises cause bones to carry the body weight, thus strengthening them. Walking briskly, running, playing tennis, climbing stairs, aerobic dancing, and cross-country skiing are all good forms of weight-bearing exercise. Swimming, cycling, and rowing do not require the bones to support body weight, so they are not good weight-bearing exercises (although, of course, they do benefit the heart, lungs, and muscles).

Unfortunately, many adolescents do not get enough calcium or exercise for healthy bone growth. Consequently, in 1998 the U.S. Centers for Disease Control and Prevention, the U.S. Department of Health and Human Services' Office of Women's Health, and the National Osteoporosis Foundation collaborated to create a national bone health campaign. Originally called "Powerful Girls. Powerful Bones™," the program was designed to encourage 9- to 12-year-old girls to consume more calcium and to exercise more often. Ads appeared in magazines and newspapers and on radio and TV to emphasize the importance of healthy bone growth. A Web site was created that includes information about bone health along with games that allow adolescents to learn more about how diet and exercise contribute to healthy growth. In addition, the program establishes links with local communities, such as providing lesson plans and activities on bone health for teachers and school nurses. In 2008, the program was renamed "Best Bones Forever™" and was extended to include 12- to 18-year-olds.

This campaign is too new for us to know its effectiveness. (After all, the real test won't come for another 35 to 40 years when the girls in the target audience reach the age when they'll be at risk for osteoporosis.) However, the hope is that by communicating effectively with adolescents and their parents (emphasizing that healthy bones are an essential part of overall healthy, positive growth), adolescents will get more calcium and become more active physically, thereby forging the strong bones that are the best defense against osteoporosis.

Adolescents not only become taller and heavier, but also become mature sexually. **Sexual maturation includes change in** *primary sex characteristics,* **which refer to organs that are directly involved in reproduction.** These include the ovaries, uterus, and vagina in girls and the scrotum, testes, and penis in boys. **Sexual maturation also includes change in** *secondary sex characteristics,* **which are physical signs of maturity that are not linked directly to the reproductive organs.** These include the growth of breasts and the widening of the pelvis in girls, the appearance of facial hair and the broadening of shoulders in boys, and the appearance of body hair and changes in voice and skin in both boys and girls.

Changes in primary and secondary sexual characteristics occur in a predictable sequence for boys and for girls. Figure 4-5 shows these changes and the ages when they typically occur for boys and girls. For girls, puberty begins

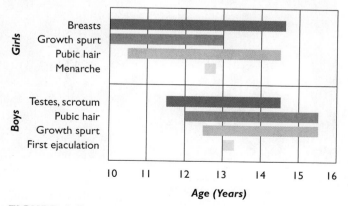

Average Timing of Pubertal Changes in North American Youth
(The beginning of the bar marks the start of change and the end of the bar marks its completion.)

FIGURE 4-5

with growth of the breasts and the growth spurt, followed by the appearance of pubic hair. *Menarche,* **the onset of menstruation, typically occurs at about age 13.** Early menstrual cycles are usually irregular and without ovulation.

For boys, puberty usually commences with the growth of the testes and scrotum, followed by the appearance of pubic hair, the start of the growth spurt, and growth of the penis. **At about age 13, most boys reach** *spermarche,* **the first spontaneous ejaculation of sperm-laden fluid.** Initial ejaculations often contain relatively few sperm; only months or sometimes years later are there sufficient sperm to fertilize an egg (Chilman, 1983).

The onset of sexual maturity is one of the first signs that an adolescent is on the threshold of adulthood. As we'll see in the "Cultural Influences" feature, many cultures celebrate this transition.

Cultural Influences

Adolescent Rites of Passage

Throughout much of history, many cultures have had special rituals or rites of passage that recognized adolescence as a unique phase in an individual's life. In ancient Japan, for example, a ceremony was performed for 12- and 14-year-old boys and girls in which they received adult clothing and adult hairstyles. Traditionally, as adolescents, indigenous Australian males walked alone in the wilderness, retracing their ancestors' paths.

Modern variants of these ceremonies include bar and bat mitzvah, which recognize that young Jewish adolescents are now responsible for their own actions, and Quinceañera (shown in the photo), which celebrates coming of age in 15-year-old girls in many Spanish-speaking regions in North, Central, and South America.

The Western Apache, who live in the southwest portion of the United States, are unusual in having a traditional ceremony to celebrate a girl's menarche (Basso, 1970). After a girl's first menstrual period, a group of older adults decide when the ceremony will be held and select a sponsor—a woman of good character and wealth (she helps to pay for the ceremony) who is unrelated to the initiate. On the day before the ceremony, the sponsor serves a large feast for the girl and her family; at the end of the ceremony, the family reciprocates, symbolizing that the sponsor is now a member of their family.

The ceremony itself begins at sunrise and lasts a few hours. As shown in the photo, the initiate dresses in ceremonial attire. The ceremony includes eight distinct phases in which the initiate dances or chants, sometimes accompanied by her sponsor or a medicine man. The intent of these actions is to transform the girl into

Quinceañera is a ritual practiced among Spanish-speaking cultures in the Americas; it honors a girl's 15th birthday.

"Changing Woman," a heroic figure in Apache myth. With this transformation comes longevity and perpetual strength.

Whenever and wherever ceremonies like this are performed, they serve many of the same functions. On the one hand, they are a sign to everyone in the community that the initiate is now an adult. On the other hand, these rituals tell the initiates themselves that their community now has adultlike expectations for them.

MECHANISMS OF MATURATION. What causes the many physical changes that occur during puberty? The pituitary gland in the brain is the key player. As I mentioned on pages 110–111, the pituitary helps to regulate physical development by releasing growth hormone. In addition, the pituitary regulates pubertal changes by signaling other glands to secrete hormones. During the early elementary-school years— long before there are any outward signs of puberty— the pituitary signals the adrenal glands to release androgens, initiating the biochemical changes that will produce body hair. A few years later, in girls the pituitary signals the ovaries to release estrogen, which causes the breasts to enlarge, the female genitals to mature, and fat to accumulate. In boys the pituitary signals the testes to release the androgen testosterone, which causes the male genitals to mature and muscle mass to increase.

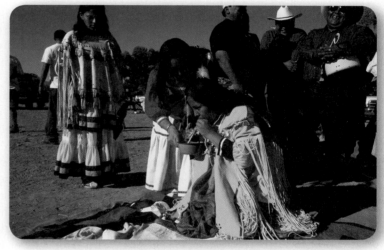

The Apache celebrate menarche with a special ceremony in which a girl is said to become a legendary hero.

The timing of pubertal events is regulated, in part, by genetics. This is shown by the closer synchrony of pubertal events in identical twins than in fraternal twins: If one identical twin has body hair, the odds are that the other twin will, too (Mustanski et al., 2004). Genetic influence is also shown by the fact that a mother's age at menarche is related to her daughter's age at menarche (Belsky, Bakermans-Kranenburg, & van IJzendoorn, 2007). However, these genetic forces are strongly influenced by the environment, particularly an adolescent's nutrition and health. In general, puberty occurs earlier in adolescents who are well nourished and healthy than in adolescents who are not. For example, puberty occurs earlier in girls who are heavier and taller but later in girls who are afflicted with chronic illnesses or who receive inadequate nutrition (St. George, Williams, & Silva, 1994).

Three other findings underscore the importance of nutrition and health for the onset of puberty. Cross-cultural comparisons reveal that menarche occurs earlier in areas of the world where nutrition and health care are adequate. For example, menarche occurs an average of 2 to 3 years earlier in Western European and North American countries than in African countries. Also, within regions, socioeconomic status matters: Girls from affluent homes are more likely to receive adequate nutrition and health care and, consequently, they reach menarche earlier (Steinberg, 1999). Finally, girls from developing countries who are adopted into affluent homes experience puberty earlier than peers in their home countries (Teilmann et al., 2006).

Historical data point to the same conclusion concerning the importance of nutrition and health care. In many industrialized countries around the world, the average age of menarche has declined steadily over the past 150 years. For example, in Europe the average age of menarche was 17 in 1840, compared to about 13 years today. This drop reflects improvements in general health and better health care over this period. In these countries, age of menarche is no longer dropping, which suggests that with adequate nutrition the biological lower limit for menarche is, on average, about 13 years.

You may remember, from Chapter 1, that the social environment also influences the onset of puberty, at least for girls. Menarche occurs at younger ages in girls who experience chronic stress or who are depressed (Belsky, Steinberg, & Draper, 1991; Moffitt et al., 1992). For example, Ellis and Garber (2000) found that girls entered puberty at a younger age when their mothers' romantic relationships were stressful and when their mothers had remarried or had a boyfriend. And Belsky et al. (2007) discovered that girls have their first menstrual period at a younger age when their mothers used harsh punishment with them as preschoolers and young children.

The timing of menarche is determined by genetics, nutrition, health, and social environment.

The exact nature of these links is not known, but many explanations focus on the circumstances that would trigger the release of hormones that regulate menarche. One proposal is that when young girls experience chronic socioemotional stress—their family life is harsh and they lack warm, supportive parents—the hormones elicited by this stress may help to activate the hormones that trigger menarche. This mechanism would even have an evolutionary advantage: If events of a girl's life suggest that her future reproductive success is uncertain—as indicated by chronic socioemotional stress—then it may be adaptive to reproduce as soon as possible instead of waiting until later when she would be more mature and better able to care for her offspring. That is, the evolutionary gamble in this case might favor "lower-quality" offspring early over "higher-quality" offspring later (Ellis, 2004).

A different account, one that emphasizes the role of fathers, is described in the "Spotlight on Theories" feature.

Spotlight on Theories

A Paternal Investment Theory of Girls' Pubertal Timing

BACKGROUND Environmental factors can cause adolescent girls to enter puberty earlier. Some scientists believe that stress is the main factor in an adolescent girl's life that may cause her to mature early, but other scientists have continued to look for other factors that influence the onset of puberty in girls.

THE THEORY Bruce J. Ellis (Ellis & Essex, 2007; Ellis et al., 2003) has proposed a paternal investment theory that emphasizes the role of fathers in determining the timing of puberty. This theory is rooted in an evolutionary perspective that links timing of puberty—and, in the process, timing of reproduction—to the resources (defined broadly) in the child's environment. When an environment is predictable and rich in resources, it is adaptive to delay reproduction, because this allows an adolescent girl to complete her own physical, cognitive, and socioemotional development, with the end result that she is a better parent. In contrast, when an environment is unstable and has few resources, it may be adaptive to mature and reproduce early rather than risk the possibility that reproduction may be impossible later.

According to Ellis, when a girl's childhood experiences indicate that paternal investment is common and of high quality, this may delay timing of maturation. But when those experiences indicate that paternal investment is uncommon and often of low quality, this may trigger early maturation. Delaying puberty is adaptive when high-quality fathers are plentiful, because it allows the girl to mature herself; but accelerating puberty is adaptive when high-quality fathers are rare, because it allows a girl to be mature sexually should a high-quality father become available and because it means that her mother is likely to be available to help with child care.[1]

Hypothesis: If a girl's childhood experiences with paternal investment influence the timing of maturation, then the quantity and quality of a girl's experiences with her own father should predict the age when she enters puberty. Girls who have infrequent or negative interactions with their fathers should enter puberty earlier than girls who have frequent or positive interactions with their fathers, because infrequent or negative experiences would indicate that the environment has few high-quality fathers.

Test: Tither and Ellis (2008) studied two groups of biological sisters. In one group the father was absent due to divorce or separation; in the other, families were intact. Tither and Ellis measured the quality of the father's parenting and the age when daughters experienced menarche.

Two main findings support the theory. First, younger sisters had experienced a longer absence of the father—greater disruption—than older sisters and thus they should have experienced menarche earlier. They did, beginning to menstruate at an earlier age than both their older sisters and younger sisters from intact families. Second, this effect was most pronounced in daughters whose fathers were psychologically distant or had mental health problems. These girls experienced a double dose of ineffective fathering: He was usually absent and did more harm than good when he was present.

Conclusion: As predicted, pubertal timing was influenced by the quantity and quality of father–daughter interactions. Puberty was earlier when father–daughter interactions were uncommon or negative, which, according to Ellis, indicates that the environment contains relatively few high-quality fathers.

Application: We saw in Module 3.2 that teenage moms and their children usually travel a rocky road; it's always best if adolescent girls delay childbearing until they're older. Paternal investment theory suggests that one way to reduce teen pregnancy is to encourage fathers to have more and more positive interactions with their daughters. This will help delay the onset of puberty, reducing the odds that she'll become pregnant as a teenager and helping in other ways as well, as we'll see on page 332. Of course, a father's investment in his daughters (as well as his sons) has benefits that extend far beyond physical maturation, as we'll see throughout the book.

---

[1]These are not conscious mechanisms: young girls are not saying to themselves, "The men around here are losers; I need to be ready in case a good one comes along." Instead, neural pathways that are sensitive to the presence of caring men may act to suppress the paths that trigger puberty.

These and other theories are being actively studied today. Where scientists agree, however, is that onset of menarche is *not* just under genetic and biological control; social and emotional factors also contribute.

As teenagers enter puberty, they become very concerned with their appearance.

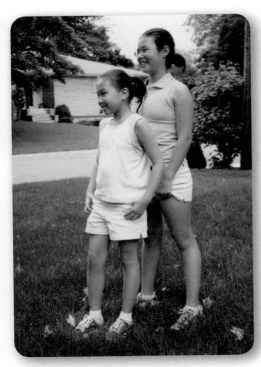

Because children enter puberty at different ages, early-maturing children often tower over their late-maturing agemates.

PSYCHOLOGICAL IMPACT OF PUBERTY. Of course, teenagers are well aware of the changes taking place in their bodies. Not surprisingly, some of these changes affect adolescents' psychological development. For example, compared to children and adults, adolescents are much more concerned about their overall appearance. Like the girl in the top photo, many teenagers look in the mirror regularly, checking for signs of additional physical change. Generally, girls worry more than boys about appearance and are more likely to be dissatisfied with their appearance (Vander Wal & Thelen, 2000). Girls are particularly likely to be unhappy with their appearance when appearance is a frequent topic of conversation with friends, leading girls to spend more time comparing their own appearance with that of their peers. Peers have relatively little influence on boys' satisfaction with their appearance; instead, boys are unhappy with their appearance when they expect to have an idealized strong, muscular body but don't (Jones, 2004).

In addition, adolescents are affected by the timing of maturation: Many children begin puberty years before or after these norms. An early-maturing boy might begin puberty at age 11, whereas a late-maturing boy might start at age 15 or 16. An early-maturing girl might start puberty at 9; a late-maturing girl may start at 14 or 15. For example, the girls shown in the bottom photo are the same age, but only one has reached puberty.

Maturing early or late has psychological consequences that differ for boys and girls. Several longitudinal studies show that early maturation can be harmful for girls. Girls who mature early often lack self-confidence, are less popular, are more likely to be depressed and have behavior problems, and are more likely to smoke and drink (Ge, Conger, & Elder, 2001; Mendle, Turkheimer, & Emery, 2007). Early maturation can also have life-changing effects on early-maturing girls who are pressured into sex and become mothers while still teenagers: as adults they typically have less prestigious, lower-paying jobs (Mendle et al., 2007). These harmful outcomes are more likely when girls enter puberty early and their family life is marked by poverty or conflict with parents (Lynne-Landsman, Graber, & Andrews, 2010; Rudolph & Troop-Gordon, 2010).

These negative effects of early maturation are not necessarily the same for all groups of U.S. adolescents. In one study that included a nationally representative sample of American adolescents (Cavanagh, 2004), European American and Latina girls who matured early were twice as likely to be sexually active, but maturing early had no impact on sexual activity in African American girls. What's more, although the peer group influenced whether early-maturing girls were sexually active, the nature of that peer-group influence differed for European American and Latina girls. For early-maturing European American girls, sexual activity was associated with having friends who did poorly in school and who engaged in problem behavior (e.g., drinking, fighting, skipping school). In contrast, for early-maturing Latinas, sexual activity was associated with having older boys in the peer group, who apparently encourage them to engage in activities, such as drinking, smoking, and sex, for which they are ill prepared.

The good news here is that the harmful effects of early maturation can be offset by other factors: When early-maturing girls have warm, supportive parents, for example, they are less likely to suffer the harmful consequences of early maturation (Ge et al., 2002).

The findings for boys are much more confusing. Some early studies suggested that early maturation benefits boys. For example, in an extensive longitudinal study of adolescents growing up in Milwaukee during the 1970s (Simmons & Blyth, 1987), the early-maturing boys dated more often and had more positive feelings about their physical development and their athletic abilities. But other studies have supported the "off-time hypothesis" for boys. In this view, being early *or* late is stressful for boys, who strongly prefer to be "on time" in their physical development (Natsuaki, Biehl, & Ge, 2009). Yet another view is that puberty per se is stressful for boys, but the timing is not (Ge et al., 2003).

Scientists cannot yet explain this bewildering pattern of results. But it's clear that the transition to puberty seems to have few long-lasting effects for boys. In contrast to what happens with girls, by young adulthood, for boys the effects associated with puberty and its timing vanish. When Pete, the late-maturing boy in the opening vignette, finally matures, others will treat him like an adult and the few extra years of being treated like a child will not be harmful (Weichold & Silbereisen, 2005).

 ANSWER 4.1
You could tell her that breast-fed babies tend to be healthier, get diarrhea less often, and make the transition to solid foods more easily. You could also mention that it's impossible to contaminate breast milk.

 ## Check Your Learning

RECALL Summarize the mechanisms of physical growth.

What is puberty and how does it differ for boys and girls?

INTERPRET Why is sleep important for healthy growth and development?

APPLY At first blush, the onset of puberty would seem to be due entirely to biology. In fact, the child's environment influences the onset of puberty. Summarize the ways in which biology and experience interact to trigger the onset of puberty.

 ## 4.2 Challenges to Healthy Growth

OUTLINE	LEARNING OBJECTIVES
Malnutrition	• What is malnutrition? What are its consequences? What is the solution to malnutrition?
Eating Disorders: Anorexia and Bulimia	• How do nature and nurture lead some adolescent girls to diet excessively?
Obesity	• Why do some children become obese? How can they lose weight permanently?
Disease	• How do diseases and accidents threaten children's development?
Accidents	

Ricardo, 12, has been overweight for most of his life. He dislikes the playground games that entertain most of his classmates during recess, preferring to stay indoors. He has relatively few friends and is not particularly happy with his lot in life. Many times Ricardo has lost weight from dieting, but he's always regained it quickly. His parents know that being overweight is a health hazard, and they wonder if there is anything that will help their son.

Compared to many childhood tasks, physical growth seems easy. To paraphrase a famous line from the movie *Field of Dreams,* "If you feed them, they will grow." Of course, it's not this simple, in part because many children face obstacles on the path of healthy physical growth. Some obstacles concern nutrition. Growth requires enormous reserves of energy, and many children do not eat enough food to provide this energy. Other children and adolescents eat too much. Other problems are diseases and accidents, which affect millions of children worldwide. We'll look at these problems in this module, and as we do, we'll understand some of the reasons why Ricardo is overweight and what he can do about it.

Malnutrition

An adequate diet is only a dream to many of the world's children. **Worldwide, about one in four children under age 5 suffers from** *malnutrition,* **as indicated by being small for their age** (UNICEF, 2006). Many, like the children in the photo, are from third-world countries. In fact, nearly half of the world's undernourished children live in India, Bangladesh, and Pakistan (UNICEF, 2006). But malnutrition is regrettably common in industrialized countries, too. Many American children growing up homeless and in poverty are malnourished. Approximately 10% of American households do not have adequate food (Nord, Andrews, & Carlson, 2007).

Malnutrition is acute in third-world countries, where one child in three is malnourished.

Malnourishment is especially damaging during infancy because growth is so rapid during these years. By the school-age years, children with a history of infant malnutrition often have difficulty maintaining attention in school; they are easily distracted. Malnutrition during rapid periods of growth apparently damages the brain, affecting a child's abilities to pay attention and learn (Benton, 2010; Morgane et al., 1993).

Malnutrition would seem to have a simple cure: an adequate diet. But the solution is more complex than that. Malnourished children are frequently listless and inactive, behaviors that are useful because they conserve energy. At the same time, when children are routinely unresponsive and lethargic, parents may provide fewer and fewer experiences that foster their children's development. For example, parents who start out reading to their children at night may stop because their malnourished children seem uninterested and inattentive. The result is a self-perpetuating cycle in which malnourished children are forsaken by parents, who feel that nothing they do gets a response, so they quit trying. A biological influence—lethargy stemming from insufficient nourishment—causes a profound change in the experiences—parental teaching—that shape a child's development (Worobey, 2005).

To break the vicious cycle, children need more than an improved diet. Their parents must also be taught how to foster their children's development. Programs that combine dietary supplements with parent training offer promise in treating malnutrition (Engle & Huffman, 2010). Children in these programs often catch up with their peers in physical and intellectual growth, showing that the best way to treat malnutrition is by addressing both biological and sociocultural factors (Super, Herrera, & Mora, 1990).

SHORT-TERM HUNGER. Breakfast should provide about one-fourth of a child's daily calories. Yet, many children—in developed and developing countries—do not eat breakfast (Grantham-McGregor, Ani, & Gernald, 2001). When children don't eat breakfast, they often have difficulty paying attention or remembering in school (Pollitt, 1994).

One strategy to attack this problem is to provide free and reduced-price meals for children at school. Lunch programs are the most common, but breakfast and dinner are sometimes available, too. These programs have a tremendous positive impact on children. Because they are better fed, they are absent from school less often and their achievement scores improve (Grantham-McGregor et al., 2001).

Eating Disorders: Anorexia and Bulimia

In 2006, Brazilian supermodel Ana Carolina Reston died of kidney failure, just months after turning 21. At her death she weighed less than 90 pounds and had a body mass index of about 13—much lower than the 16 that is the benchmark for starvation. Reston suffered from an eating disorder: *Anorexia nervosa* **is a disorder marked by a persistent refusal to eat and an irrational fear of being overweight.** Individuals with anorexia nervosa have a grossly distorted image of their own body. Like the girl in the photo, they claim to be overweight despite being painfully thin (Wilson, Heffernan, & Black, 1996). Anorexia is a very serious disorder, often leading to heart damage. Without treatment, as many as 15% of adolescents with anorexia die (Wang & Brownell, 2005). A related eating disorder is bulimia nervosa. **Individuals with** *bulimia nervosa* **alternate between binge eating periods when they eat uncontrollably and purging through self-induced vomiting or with laxatives.** The frequency of binge eating varies remarkably among people with bulimia nervosa, from a few times a week to more than 30 times. What's common to all is the feeling that they cannot stop eating (Mizes, Scott, & Tonya, 1995).

Anorexia and bulimia are alike in many respects. Both disorders primarily affect females and emerge in adolescence (Wang & Brownell, 2005). What's more, many of the same factors put teenage girls at risk for both eating disorders. Jacobi and colleagues (2004) conducted a meta-analysis of more than 300 longitudinal and cross-sectional studies of individuals with eating disorders. They concluded that heredity puts some girls at risk, and molecular genetic studies have implicated genes that regulate both anxiety and food intake (Klump & Culbert, 2007). Several psychosocial factors also put people at risk for eating disorders. When children have a history of eating problems, such as being a picky eater or being diagnosed with pica (i.e., eating nonfood objects such as chalk, paper, or dirt), they're at greater risk for anorexia and bulimia during adolescence. Teenagers who experience negative self-esteem or mood or anxiety disorders are at risk (Hutchinson, Rapee, & Taylor, 2010). However, the most important risk factor for adolescents is being overly concerned about one's body and weight and having a history of dieting (George & Franko, 2010). And why do some teens become concerned about being thin? From the influence of peers and the media. Teenage girls worry about being overweight when they have friends who diet to stay thin and when they frequently watch TV shows that emphasize attractive, thin characters (Grabe, Hyde, & Ward, 2008; Paxton, Eisenberg, & Neumark-Sztainer, 2006).

The meta-analysis also identified some risk factors that are unique to anorexia and bulimia. For example, overprotective parenting is associated with anorexia but not bulimia. In contrast, obesity in childhood is associated with bulimia but not anorexia.

Adolescent girls with anorexia nervosa believe that they are overweight and refuse to eat.

👁—Watch the **Video** *Body Image and Eating Disorders* on **mydevelopmentlab** **.com** to learn more about eating disorders. As you watch the video, think about how parents can encourage their children to strike a balance between eating healthy foods but without overreacting and becoming too concerned with weight and appearance.

Although eating disorders are more common in girls, boys make up about 10% of diagnosed cases of eating disorders. Because boys with eating disorders are far less common, researchers have conducted much less research with males. However, some of the known risk factors are childhood obesity, low self-esteem, pressure from parents and peers to lose weight, and participating in sports that emphasize being lean (Ricciardelli & McCabe, 2004; Shoemaker & Furman, 2009). 👁—Watch the **Video** on **mydevelopmentlab.com**

Fortunately, there are programs that can help protect teens from eating disorders (Stice & Shaw, 2004). The most effective programs are designed for at-risk youth—for example, for those who already say they are unhappy with their body. The best programs are interactive—they encourage youth to become involved and to learn new skills, such as ways to resist social pressure to be thin. They also work to change critical attitudes (e.g., ideals regarding thinness) and critical behaviors (e.g., dieting and overeating). At-risk adolescents who participate in these programs are helped; they are more satisfied with their appearance and less likely to diet or overeat. For those teens affected by eating disorders, treatment is available: Like prevention programs, treatment typically focuses on modifying key attitudes and behaviors (Puhl & Brownell, 2005).

Obesity

Ricardo, the boy in this module's opening vignette, is overweight; he is very heavy for his height. **The technical definition for overweight is based on the** *body mass index (BMI),* **which is an adjusted ratio of weight to height.** Children and adolescents who are in the upper 5% (very heavy for their height) are defined as being overweight. Using these standards, in 2001 the U.S. Surgeon General announced that childhood obesity had reached epidemic proportions. In the past 25 to 30 years, the number of overweight children has doubled and the number of overweight adolescents has tripled, so that today roughly one child or adolescent out of six is overweight (U.S. Department of Health and Human Services, 2010).

Like the boy in the photo, overweight youngsters are often unpopular, have low self-esteem, and do poorly in school (Puhl & Latner, 2007). Furthermore, throughout life they are at risk for many medical problems, including high blood pressure and diabetes, because the vast majority of overweight children and adolescents become overweight adults (U.S. Department of Health and Human Services, 2010).

Heredity plays an important role in juvenile obesity. Adoption studies have found that children and adolescents' weight is related to the weight of their biological parents, rather than the weight of their adoptive parents (Stunkard et al., 1986). Genes may influence obesity by influencing a person's activity level. In other words, being genetically more prone to inactivity makes it more difficult to burn off calories and easier to gain weight. **Heredity may also help set** *basal metabolic rate,* **the speed at which the body consumes calories.** Children and adolescents with a slower basal metabolic rate burn off calories less rapidly, making it easier for them to gain weight (Epstein & Cluss, 1986).

The environment is also influential. Television advertising, for example, encourages youth to eat tasty but fattening foods. Parents play a role, too. They may inadvertently encourage obesity by emphasizing external rather than internal eating signals. Infants eat primarily because of internal signals: They eat when they experience hunger and stop eating when they feel full. During the

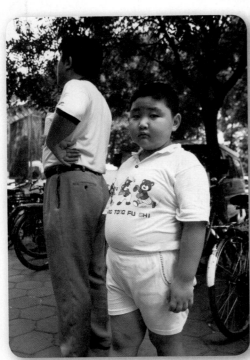

Childhood obesity has reached epidemic proportions in the United States.

preschool years, this internal control of eating is often gradually replaced by external signals. Parents who urge children to "clean their plates" even when the children are no longer hungry are teaching their children to ignore internal cues to eating. Thus, obese children and adolescents may overeat because they rely on external cues and disregard internal cues to stop (Coelho et al., 2009; Wansink & Sobal, 2007).

Obese youth can lose weight. The most effective weight-loss programs have several features in common (Epstein et al., 2007; Foreyt & Goodrick, 1995; Israel et al., 1994):

In programs that treat obesity, children and parents set goals for eating and exercise, then monitor progress toward those goals.

- The focus of the program is to change obese children's eating habits, encourage them to become more active, and discourage sedentary behavior.

- As part of the treatment, children learn to monitor their eating, exercise, and sedentary behavior. Goals are established in each area, and rewards are earned when the goals are met.

- Parents are trained to help children set realistic goals and to use behavioral principles to help children meet these goals. Parents also monitor their own lifestyles to be sure they aren't accidentally fostering their child's obesity.

When programs incorporate these features, obese children do lose weight. However, even after losing weight, many of these children remain overweight. Consequently, it is best to avoid overweight and obesity in the first place; the *Surgeon General's Call for Action* emphasizes the role of increased physical activity and good eating habits in warding off overweight and obesity (U.S. Department of Health and Human Services, 2001). For example, children and adolescents can be encouraged to eat healthier foods by making such foods more available and by reducing their price (Faith et al., 2007). Frankly, however, we know relatively little about how to prevent obesity: many obesity prevention programs simply don't work (Stice, Shaw, & Marti, 2006). Those that do seem to target a broad range of healthy behaviors (e.g., not smoking, encouraging physical activity) rather than focusing on obesity per se.

 QUESTION 4.2
Joshua is a 10-year-old who is 25 pounds overweight. What can he and his parents do to help him lose weight?
(Answer is on page 127.)

Disease

Around the world, nearly 10 million children die before their fifth birthday; countries in Africa account for more than half of these childhood deaths (UNICEF, 2008). These are staggering numbers—roughly the equivalent of *all* U.S. 1-, 2-, and 3-year-olds dying in a single year. The leading killers of young children worldwide are five conditions: pneumonia, diarrhea, measles, malaria, and malnutrition (World Health Organization, 2005). The majority of these deaths can be prevented with proven, cost-effective treatments. For example, measles kills nearly half a million children annually but can be prevented with vaccinations. Similarly, diarrhea kills by dehydrating youngsters, yet children can avert death by promptly drinking water that contains salt and potassium.

As part of a vigorous effort to prevent childhood illness, for the past two decades the World Health Organization (WHO) has worked to vaccinate children worldwide. Due to these efforts, vaccination rates have skyrocketed in many developing countries. More recently, WHO has joined with the United Nations Children's Fund (UNICEF) to create Integrated Management of Childhood Illness (IMCI), a program to combat pneumonia, diarrhea, measles, malaria, and malnutrition (World Health Organization, 1997). Because many children who are ill have symptoms related to

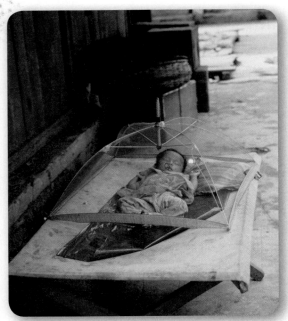

One way to protect young children from disease is to adopt practices that foster healthy growth, such as having them sleep in netting that protects them from mosquitoes that carry malaria.

two or more of these five conditions, IMCI uses an integrated strategy that focuses on the overall health of the child. One component of IMCI is training health care professionals to become more skilled in dealing with childhood illnesses. A second component is improving health care systems so that they are better able to respond to childhood illness (e.g., ensuring that required medicines are available). A third component involves changing family and community practices to make them more conducive to healthy growth. For example, to protect children from mosquitoes that carry malaria, children are encouraged to sleep in netting, as the baby in the photo is doing. IMCI has been adopted in more than 60 countries and is playing a pivotal role in improving children's health worldwide (Bhutta et al., 2010; Victora et al., 2006).

Accidents

In the United States, most infant deaths are due to medical conditions associated with birth defects or low birth weight. From age 1 on, however, children are far more likely to die from accidents than from any other single cause (National Center for Health Statistics, 2007). Motor vehicle accidents are the most common cause of accidental death in children. Regrettably, many of these deaths could have been prevented had children and adolescents been wearing seat belts, or had infants and children been restrained properly in an approved infant car seat like the one shown in the photo. Without such restraint, children and adolescents typically suffer massive head injuries when thrown through the windshield or onto the road.

Many infants and toddlers also drown, die from burns, or suffocate. Often these deaths result because young children are supervised inadequately. All too common, for example, are reports of young children who wander away, jump or fall into an unfenced swimming pool, then drown. Parents need to remember that children are often eager to explore their environs, but are unable to recognize many hazards. Parents must constantly keep a protective eye on their young children. With older children, parents must be careful that they don't overestimate their children's skills. Some accidents happen because parents have too much confidence in their children's cognitive and motor skills. They may allow a child like the boy in the photo on page 127 to ride to school in a bike lane adjacent to a street filled with commuters, even though many children may not consistently pay attention while biking or sometimes attempt to cross busy streets when there's not enough time to do so safely (Morrongiello, Klemencic, & Corbett, 2008; Plumert, Kearney, & Cremer, 2007).[2]

For adolescents, motor vehicle accidents remain the leading cause of death. The difference, of course, is that adolescents are no longer passengers but are driving. Sadly, far too many adolescents are killed because they drive too fast, drive while drunk, or drive without wearing a seat belt (U.S. Department of Health and Human Services, 2004). Among teenage boys,

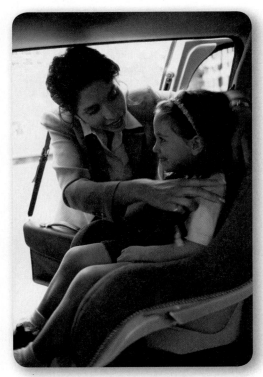

One simple way to protect infants, toddlers, and young children is to insist that they be restrained in an approved seat when riding in a car.

[2]As a 10-year-old, my son Matt crashed his new bike right into the back of a parked car because he was too busy watching the gears shift. Fortunately, he escaped with just a few scrapes, but this illustrates how easily a childhood lapse in concentration can lead to a cycling accident.

firearms represent a leading cause of death. In fact, firearms kill more 15- to 19-year-old African American youth than any other single cause (Federal Interagency Forum on Child and Family Statistics, 2007).

Although the term *accident* implies that the event happened by chance and no one was to blame, in reality most accidents involving children and adolescents can be foreseen and either prevented or steps taken to reduce injury. In the case of automobile accidents, for example, the simple step of wearing a seat belt enhances safety immensely. Accidents involving firearms can be reduced by making guns less accessible to children and adolescents (e.g., locking away guns and ammunition separately). School- and community-based safety programs represent a cost-effective way to reduce childhood accidents (Hotz et al., 2009; Spinks et al., 2004). Children can learn safe ways of walking or riding their bikes to school, then be allowed to practice these skills while supervised by an adult. With programs like these, children readily learn behaviors that foster safety.

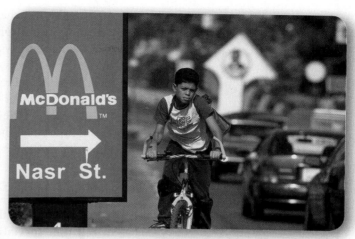

Children sometimes have accidents because parents overestimate their children's abilities and thus allow them to engage in dangerous activities, such as riding bikes on unsafe streets.

 Check Your Learning

RECALL Summarize the factors that put adolescent girls at risk for anorexia nervosa and for bulimia nervosa.

What are the leading causes of death for toddlers and preschool children? For adolescents?

INTERPRET Distinguish the biological factors that contribute to obesity from the environmental factors.

APPLY How does malnutrition show the impact that children can have on their own development?

 ANSWER 4.2

Joshua and his parents need to work together to create a healthier lifestyle, one that changes his eating habits and encourages him to be more active. They need to agree upon realistic goals (e.g., losing 6 pounds in a month; 20 minutes of outdoor play each day) and use rewards to help Joshua achieve those goals. Also, Joshua needs to learn how to record what and how much he eats, along with recording his exercise.

 4.3 **The Developing Nervous System**

OUTLINE
Organization of the Mature Brain

The Developing Brain

LEARNING OBJECTIVES
• **What are the parts of a nerve cell? How is the brain organized?**

• **When is the brain formed in prenatal development? When do different regions of the brain begin to function?**

While crossing the street, 10-year-old Martin was struck by a passing car. He was in a coma for a week, but then gradually became more alert, and now he seems to be aware of his surroundings. Needless to say, Martin's mother is grateful that he survived the accident, but she wonders what the future holds for her son.

Neurons come in many shapes, but they all have the same function of transmitting information.

The physical changes that we see as children grow are impressive, but even more awe-inspiring are the changes we cannot see, those involving the brain and the nervous system. An infant's feelings of hunger, a child's laugh, and an adolescent's efforts to learn algebra all reflect the functioning of the brain and the rest of the nervous system. All the information that children learn, including language and other cognitive skills, is stored in the brain.

How does the brain accomplish these many tasks? How is the brain affected by an injury like the one that Martin suffered? To begin to answer these questions, let's look at how the brain is organized in adults.

Organization of the Mature Brain

The basic unit of the brain and the rest of the nervous system is the *neuron,* **a cell that specializes in receiving and transmitting information.** Neurons come in many different shapes, as you can see in the three photos. Figure 4-6 makes it easier to understand the basic parts found in all neurons. **The** *cell body* **at the center of the neuron contains the basic biological machinery that keeps the neuron alive. The receiving end of the neuron, the** *dendrite,* **looks like a tree with many branches.** The highly branched dendrite allows one neuron to receive input from many thousands of other neurons (Morgan & Gibson, 1991). **The tubelike structure at the other end of the cell body is the** *axon,* **which sends information to other neurons. The axon is wrapped in** *myelin,* **a fatty sheath that allows it to transmit information more rapidly.** The boost in neural speed from myelin is like the difference between driving and flying: from about 6 feet per second to 50 feet per second. **At the end of the axon are small knobs called** *terminal buttons,* **which release** *neurotransmitters,* **chemicals that carry information to nearby neurons.** Finally, you'll see that the terminal buttons of one axon don't actually touch the dendrites of other neurons. **The gap between one neuron and the next is a** *synapse.* Neurotransmitters cross synapses to carry information between neurons.

Take 50 to 100 billion neurons like these and you have the beginnings of a human brain. An adult's brain weighs a little less than 3 pounds, and it easily fits into your hands. **The wrinkled surface of the brain is the** *cerebral cortex;* **made up of about 10 billion neurons, the cortex regulates many of the functions that we think of as distinctly human. The cortex consists of left and right halves, called** *hemispheres,* **that are linked by millions of axons in a thick bundle called the** *corpus callosum.* The characteristics that you value most—your engaging personality, your "way with words," your uncanny knack for reading others—are all controlled by specific regions of the cortex, many of which are shown in Figure 4-7.

Personality and your ability to make and carry out plans are largely functions of an area at the front of the cortex that is called, appropriately, the *frontal cortex.* For most people, the ability to produce and understand language, to reason, and to compute is largely due to neurons in the cortex of the left hemisphere. Also for most people, artistic and musical abilities, perception of spatial relations, and the ability to recognize faces and emotions come from neurons in the right hemisphere.

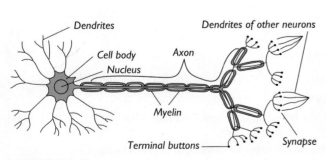

Dendrites

Dendrites of other neurons

Cell body

Axon

Nucleus

Myelin

Terminal buttons

Synapse

FIGURE 4-6

Now that we know a bit of the organization of the mature brain, let's look at how the brain develops and begins to function.

The Developing Brain

Scientists who study brain development are guided by several key questions: How and when do brain structures develop? When do different brain regions begin to function? Why do brain regions take on different functions? In this section, we'll see how research has answered each question.

EMERGING BRAIN STRUCTURES.   We know from Module 3.1 that the beginnings of the brain can be traced to the period of the zygote. **At roughly 3 weeks after conception, a group of cells forms a flat structure known as the** *neural plate.* At 4 weeks, the neural plate folds to form a tube that ultimately becomes the brain and spinal cord. When the ends of the tube fuse shut, neurons are produced in one small region of the neural tube. Production of neurons begins about 10 weeks after conception, and by 28 weeks the developing brain has virtually all the neurons it will ever have. During these weeks, neurons form at the incredible rate of more than 4,000 per second (Kolb, 1989).

From the neuron-manufacturing site in the neural tube, neurons migrate to their final positions in the brain. The brain is built in stages, beginning with the innermost layers. Neurons in the deepest layer are positioned first, followed by neurons in the second layer, and so on. This layering process continues until all six layers of the mature brain are in place, which occurs about 7 months after conception (Rakic, 1995). As you can see in Figure 4-8, the nerve cells move to the top by wrapping themselves around supporting cells, just as a snake might climb a pole.

In the fourth month of prenatal development, axons begin to acquire myelin—the fatty wrap that speeds neural transmission. This process continues through infancy and into childhood and adolescence (Paus, 2010). Neurons that carry sensory information are the first to acquire myelin; neurons in the cortex are among the last. You can see the effect of more myelin in improved coordination and reaction times. The older the infant and, later, the child, the more rapid and coordinated are his or her reactions. (We'll talk more about this phenomenon when we discuss fine-motor skills in Module 5.3.)

In the months after birth, the brain grows rapidly. Axons and dendrites grow longer, and, like a maturing tree, dendrites quickly sprout new limbs. As the number of dendrites increases, so does the number of synapses, reaching a peak at about the first birthday. This rapid neural growth is shown in Figure 4-9 on page 130. **Soon after, synapses begin to disappear gradually, a phenomenon**

FIGURE 4-7

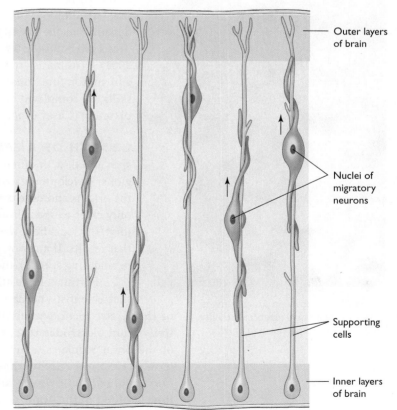

Just like a snake might climb a pole, neurons migrate to their final location in the brain by wrapping themselves around supporting cells.

FIGURE 4-8

| At birth | I month | 3 months | 15 months | 24 months |

FIGURE 4-9

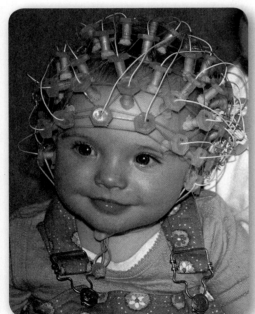

One way to study brain functioning is to record the brain's electrical activity using electrodes placed on a child's scalp.

known as *synaptic pruning.* Thus, beginning in infancy and continuing into early adolescence, the brain goes through its own version of "downsizing," weeding out unnecessary connections between neurons. This pruning depends on the activity of the neural circuits: synapses that are active are preserved but those that aren't active are eliminated (Webb, Monk, & Nelson, 2001). Pruning is completed first for brain regions associated with sensory and motor functions. Regions associated with basic language and spatial skills are completed next, followed by regions associated with attention and planning (Casey et al., 2005).

GROWTH OF A SPECIALIZED BRAIN. Because the mature brain is specialized, with different psychological functions localized in particular regions, developmental researchers have had a keen interest in determining the origins and time course of the brain's specialization. For many years, the only clues to specialization came from children who had suffered brain injury. The logic here was to link the location of the injury to the impairment that results: If a region of the brain regulates a particular function (e.g., understanding speech), then damage to that region should impair the function.

Fortunately, relatively few children suffer brain injury. But this meant that scientists needed other methods to study brain development. **One of them,** *electroencephalography,* **involves measuring the brain's electrical activity from electrodes placed on the scalp, as shown in the photo.** If a region of the brain regulates a function, then the region should show distinctive patterns of electrical activity while a child is using that function. **A newer technique,** *functional magnetic resonance imaging (fMRI),* **uses magnetic fields to track the flow of blood in the brain.** With this method, shown in the photo on page 131, the research participant's brain is literally wrapped in an incredibly powerful magnet that can track blood flow in the brain as participants perform different cognitive tasks (Casey et al., 2005). The logic here is that active brain regions need more oxygen, which increases blood flow to those regions.

None of these methods is perfect; each has draw-backs. In cases of brain injury, for example, multiple areas of the brain may be damaged, making it hard to link impaired functioning to a particular brain region. fMRI is used sparingly because it's very expensive and participants must lie still for several minutes at a time. Despite these limitations, the combined outcome of research using these different approaches has identified some general principles that describe the brain's specialization as children develop.

1. Specialization occurs early in development. Maybe you expect the brain to be completely unspecialized? In fact, many regions are already specialized very early in infancy. For example, early specialization of the frontal cortex is shown by the finding that damage to this region in infancy results in impaired decision making and abnormal emotional responses (Anderson et al., 2001). Similarly, studies using electroencephalography show that a newborn infant's left hemisphere generates more electrical activity in response to speech than the right hemisphere (Molfese & Burger-Judisch, 1991). Thus, by the time a child is born, the cortex of the left hemisphere is already specialized for language processing. As we'll see in Chapter 9, this specialization allows language to develop rapidly during infancy. Finally, studies of children with prenatal brain damage indicate that by infancy the right hemisphere is specialized for understanding certain kinds of spatial relations (Stiles et al., 2005).

2. Specialization takes two specific forms. First, with development the brain regions active during processing become more focused and less diffuse—an analogy would be to a thunderstorm that covers a huge region versus one that packs the same power in a much smaller region (Durston et al., 2006). Second, the kinds of stimuli that trigger brain activity shift from being general to being specific (Johnson, Grossman, & Cohen Kadosh, 2009). Both forms of specialization are evident in the "Focus on Research" feature.

In functional magnetic resonance imaging (fMRI), a powerful magnet tracks the flow of blood to different brain regions, which shows parts of the brain that are active as children perform different tasks.

Focus on Research

Brain Specialization for Face Processing

Who were the investigators, and what was the aim of the study? In the mature brain, a region on the underside of the temporal cortex known as the fusiform gyrus seems to play a special role in recognizing faces. For example, imaging studies show that this region is particularly active when individuals detect the presence of a face or must distinguish one face from another (Kanwisher & Yovel, in press). Suzanne Scherf and her colleagues—Marlene Berhmann, Kate Humphreys, and Beatriz Luna (2007)—wanted to know whether this brain region was equally involved in processing faces by children, adolescents, and adults.

How did the investigators measure the topic of interest? Scherf and her colleagues showed brief hmovies depicting faces, buildings, open fields, and objects.

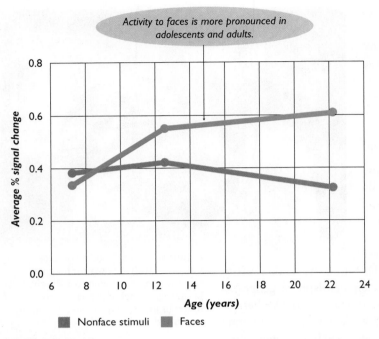

FIGURE 4-10

Participants simply watched the movies—32 of them in all—while lying in an fMRI scanner like the one shown on page 131.

Who were the participants in the study? The researchers tested 5- to 8-year-olds, 11- to 14-year-olds, and 20- to 23-year-olds.

What was the design of the study? This study was experimental because Scherf and her colleagues were interested in the impact of the type of stimulus—faces versus other types of stimuli—on brain activity. The study was cross-sectional because it included three groups (children, adolescents, and adults), each tested once.

Were there ethical concerns with the study? No. The behavioral task was harmless—simply watching short movies. Generally fMRI is very safe. However, researchers routinely check to see whether prospective participants might have metal in their bodies (e.g., a pacemaker or hearing aid or an object from an accident, such as a bullet), which is a hazard because of the powerful magnets that are built into scanners. The researchers described these potential risks to participants (and, for children and adolescents, their parents), then obtained written consent.

What were the results? Figure 4-10 shows the magnitude of activation in the fusiform region for all three age groups, separately for faces and nonface stimuli. Notice that children show no specialization in this brain region; activation is equally large for faces and nonfaces. With adolescents, there is some specialization—more activity for faces—and specialization is even greater in adults.

What did the investigators conclude? By early adolescence, face processing is well established in the fusiform gyrus. As Scherf and her colleagues put it, "Our results suggest that the transition from childhood to early adolescence appears to represent an important transition in the development of face-specificity in the [brain]" (p. F28).

What converging evidence would strengthen these conclusions? An obvious way to provide converging evidence would be to use electroencephalography (described on page 130) to record electrical activity in the brain as children, adolescents, and adults watched these same movies. The Scherf et al. findings would be supported if a differentiated pattern of electrical activity—greater activity in response to faces—emerged in adolescence and became stronger in adulthood.

Thus, the study by Scherf et al. shows both forms of specificity: face processing becomes focused in a particular area (shown by the increased activity to faces) and becomes tuned narrowly to faces (more activity to faces compared to other stimuli).

3. Different brain systems specialize at different rates. Think of a new housing development involving construction of many multistory homes. In each house, the first floor is completed before higher floors, but some houses are finished before others are even started. In this same way, brain regions involving basic sensory and perceptual processes specialize well before those regions necessary for higher-order processes (Fox, Levitt, & Nelson, 2010). Similarly, some brain systems that are sensitive to reward reach maturity in adolescence, but the systems responsible for self-control aren't fully specialized until adulthood (Somerville & Casey, 2010).[3]

4. **Successful specialization requires stimulation from the environment.** To return to the analogy of the brain as a house, the newborn's brain is perhaps best conceived as a partially finished, partially furnished house: A general organizational framework is there, with preliminary neural pathways designed to perform certain functions. The left hemisphere no doubt has some language pathways and the frontal cortex has some emotion-related pathways. However, completing the typical organization of the mature brain requires input from the environment (Greenough & Black, 1992). **In this case, environmental input influences** *experience-expectant growth:* **Over the course of evolution, human infants have typically been exposed to some forms of stimulation that are used to adjust brain wiring, strengthening some circuits and eliminating others.** For example, under normal conditions, healthy human infants experience moving visual patterns (e.g., faces) and varied sounds (e.g., voices). Just as a newly planted seed depends on a water-filled environment for growth, a developing brain depends on environmental stimulation to fine-tune circuits for vision, hearing, and other systems (Black, 2003).

The region of the brain that controls the fingers of the left hand is probably well developed in this skilled cellist.

Of course, experiences later in life also sculpt the brain (and we'll see this in several chapters later in this book). *Experience-dependent growth* **denotes changes in the brain that are not linked to specific points in development and that vary across individuals and across cultures.** Experience-dependent growth is illustrated by a preschool child's learning of a classmate's name, an elementary-school child's discovery of a shortcut home from school, and an adolescent's mastery of the functions of a new cell phone. In each case, brain circuits are modified in response to an individual's experiences. With today's technology, we can't see these daily changes in the brain. But when they accumulate over many years—as when individuals acquire expertise in a skill—brain changes can be detected. For example, skilled cellists like the one in the photo have extensive brain regions devoted to controlling the fingers of the left hand as they are positioned on the strings (Elbert et al., 1995). Similarly, years of driving a taxicab produces changes in the hippocampus, a region of the brain implicated in navigation and way-finding (Maguire, Woollett, & Spiers, 2006). ◉ **Watch** the **Video** on **mydevelopmentlab.com**

> **Experience fine tunes circuits in the developing brain.**

5. **The immature brain's lack of specialization confers a benefit: greater plasticity.** Just as the structures in a housing development follow a plan that specifies the location of each house and its design, brain development usually follows a predictable course that reflects epigenetic interactions (page 57) between the genetic code and required environmental input. Sometimes, however, the normal course is disrupted. A person may experience events harmful to the brain (e.g., injured in an

◉ **Watch** the **Video** *Brain Building* on **mydevelopmentlab.com** to learn more about the impact of experience on brain development. As you see the different experiences that parents provide their babies, decide which ones represent experience-expectant growth and which represent experience-dependent growth.

---

[3]This may be one reason why adolescents engage in such risky behavior (e.g., drinking while driving, unprotected sex): The brain centers associated with self-control are immature relative to those associated with reward (Somerville & Casey, 2010).

accident) or may be deprived of some essential ingredients of successful "brain building" (e.g., necessary experiences).

Research that examines the consequences of these atypical experiences shows that the brain has some flexibility: it is plastic. Remember Martin, the child in the vignette whose brain was damaged when he was struck by a car? His language skills were impaired after the accident. This was not surprising, because the left hemisphere of Martin's brain had absorbed most of the force of the collision. But within several months, Martin had completely recovered his language skills. Apparently other neurons took over language-related processing from the damaged neurons. This recovery of function is not uncommon, particularly for young children, and shows that the brain is plastic. In other words, young children often recover more skills after brain injury than older children and adults, apparently because functions are more easily reassigned in the young brain (Stiles et al., 2005; Demir, Levine, & Goldin-Meadow, 2010).

There are, however, limits to plasticity. These are shown by studies of Romanian children who were abandoned soon after birth and lived for months—sometimes years—in orphanages where care was appalling: infants and toddlers were provided food and shelter but few toys, minimal speech with caregivers, and no personal relationships with caregivers. Following adoption by families in the United Kingdom, these children progressed rapidly in their cognitive development but did not catch up to the normal course of development; what's more, cognitive deficits were greater for children who had stayed longer in the orphanages (Rutter et al., 2010). Experiences later in these children's development could not compensate for the extreme deprivation in infancy, showing that the brain is not completely plastic.

BRAIN-BASED EDUCATION?   Greater understanding of brain development and the impact of experience has, quite naturally, led many scientists, educators, and parents to hope that this knowledge could lead to improved education. After all, if the brain is the organ of learning and the goal of school is to promote students' learning, then knowledge of brain development should yield better ways to teach. Many have jumped on the "brain-based education" bandwagon, and it is true that research on brain development is providing valuable insights into some very specific academic skills, such as the nature of children's reading problems (Szücks & Goswami, 2007). However, there is reason to be cautious about redesigning an entire curriculum based on our current understanding of brain development. Many critics point out that although our current understanding of brain development may lead to a handful of very general statements about the conditions that foster children's learning, we know too little to devise full-fledged curricula that are "brain-friendly" (McCandless, 2003). As Kurt Fischer, Director of Harvard's Mind, Brain, and Education Program, and his colleague Mary Helen Immordino-Yang (2008, p. xviii) put it,

> Unfortunately, most of what is called "brain-based education" has no grounding at all in brain or cognitive science. . . . In typical claims for brain-based education, beliefs about learning and schooling are restated in the language of brain science, but there is no brain research on which those restatements are based.

Still, there is reason to be optimistic that coming decades will provide the foundation needed for a curriculum based on solid understanding of the emerging brain (Fischer & Immordino-Yang, 2008).

QUESTION 4.3

Ashley was distraught when her 2-year-old daughter fell down a full flight of steps and hit her head against a concrete wall, which led to a trip to the emergency room. What could you say to reassure Ashley about her daughter's prognosis?

(Answer is on page 134.)

ANSWER 4.3

You could explain that young children recover from brain injury more often than older children and adults do. So, unless her daughter has suffered extensive damage to the brain, she should be okay.

Check Your Learning

RECALL List the major parts of a nerve cell and the major regions of the cerebral cortex.

Describe evidence that shows the brain's plasticity.

INTERPRET Compare growth of the brain before birth with growth of the brain after birth.

APPLY How does the development of the brain, as described in this module, compare to the general pattern of physical growth described in Module 4.1?

UNIFYING THEMES   Connections

This chapter is an excellent opportunity to highlight the theme that *development in different domains is connected.* Consider the impact of the timing of puberty. Whether a child matures early or late affects social development (early-maturing girls are often less popular) and academic performance (early-maturing girls often do poorly in school). Or consider the impact of malnutrition. Malnourished youngsters are often listless, which affects how their parents interact with them (they're less likely to provide stimulating experiences). Less stimulation, in turn, slows the children's intellectual development. Physical, cognitive, social, and personality development are linked: Change in one area generally leads to change of some kind in the others.

See for Yourself

Children love playgrounds. Unfortunately, hundreds of thousands of American children are injured on playgrounds annually. Some of these accidents could have been prevented had parents (or other adults) been present, or if parents who were physically present had been paying closer attention to the children at play. Go to a local playground and watch children as they play. Notice how many children unknowingly put themselves at risk as they play. Also notice how well the children's play is monitored by adults. See for yourself!

Summary

4.1 Physical Growth

Features of Human Growth

Physical growth is particularly rapid during infancy, slows during the elementary-school years, and then accelerates again during adolescence. Physical growth refers not only to increases in height and weight, but also to development of muscle, fat, and bones.

Children are taller today than in previous generations. Average heights vary around the world, and within any culture there is considerable variation in the normal range of height.

Mechanisms of Physical Growth

Physical growth depends on sleep, in part because most growth hormone is secreted while children sleep. Nutrition is also important, particularly during periods of rapid growth, such as infancy and adolescence. Breast-feeding provides babies with all the nutrients they need and has other advantages. Many children and adolescents do not get adequate nutrients because of poor diets.

The Adolescent Growth Spurt and Puberty

Puberty includes the adolescent growth spurt as well as sexual maturation. Girls typically begin the growth spurt earlier than boys, who acquire more muscle, less fat, and greater heart and lung capacities. Sexual maturation, which includes primary and secondary sex characteristics, occurs in predictable sequences for boys and girls.

Pubertal changes occur when the pituitary gland signals the adrenal gland, ovaries, and testes to secrete hormones that initiate physical changes. The timing of puberty is influenced strongly by health, nutrition, and social environment.

Pubertal change affects adolescents' psychological functioning. Teens become concerned about their appearance. Early maturation tends to be harmful for girls because it may cause them to engage in age-inappropriate behavior. Timing of maturation seems to be less of an issue for boys.

4.2 Challenges to Healthy Growth

Malnutrition

Malnutrition is a global problem—including in the United States—that is particularly harmful during infancy, when growth is so rapid. Malnutrition can cause brain damage, affecting children's intelligence and ability to pay attention. Treating malnutrition requires improving children's diet and training their parents to provide stimulating environments.

Eating Disorders: Anorexia and Bulimia

Anorexia and bulimia are eating disorders that typically affect adolescent girls. They are characterized by an irrational fear of being overweight. Several factors contribute to these disorders, including heredity, a childhood history of eating problems, and, during adolescence, negative self-esteem and a preoccupation with one's body and weight. Eating disorders are far less common in boys; risk factors include childhood obesity, low self-esteem, social pressure to lose weight, and participation in certain sports. Treatment and prevention programs emphasize changing adolescents' views of thinness and their eating-related behaviors.

Obesity

Many obese children and adolescents are unpopular, have low self-esteem, and are at risk for medical disorders. Obesity reflects both heredity and acquired eating habits. In the most effective programs for treating obesity in youth, both children and their parents set eating and exercise goals and monitor their daily progress.

Disease

Millions of children around the world die annually from pneumonia, diarrhea, measles, malaria, and malnutrition. Integrated Management of Childhood Illness is a new, integrated approach designed to promote children's health.

Accidents

In the United States, children and adolescents are more likely to die from accidents than any other single cause. Many of these fatalities involve motor vehicles and could be prevented if passengers were restrained properly. Older children and adolescents are sometimes involved in accidents because parents overestimate their abilities.

4.3 The Developing Nervous System

Organization of the Mature Brain

Nerve cells, called *neurons*, are composed of a cell body, a dendrite, and an axon. The mature brain consists of billions of neurons organized into nearly identical left and right hemispheres connected by the corpus callosum. The frontal cortex is associated with personality and goal-directed behavior; the cortex in the left hemisphere, with language; and the cortex in the right hemisphere, with nonverbal processes.

The Developing Brain

Brain structure begins in prenatal development, when neurons form at an incredible rate. After birth, neurons in the central nervous system become wrapped in myelin, allowing them to transmit information more rapidly. Throughout childhood, unused synapses disappear gradually through a process of pruning.

Brain specialization is evident in infancy; further specialization involves more focused brain areas and narrowing of stimuli that trigger brain activity. Different systems specialize at different rates. Specialization depends upon stimulation from the environment. The relative lack of specialization in the immature brain makes it better able to recover from injury.

Test Yourself

✓● Study and Review on mydevelopmentlab.com

1. Physical growth is particularly rapid during infancy and _____.

2. Sleep is essential for normal growth because this is when most _____ is secreted.

3. Breast-feeding has many advantages for infants, including protecting from disease (through the mother's antibodies), reducing cases of diarrhea and constipation, easing the transition to solid foods, and _____.

4. The role of the environment in triggering puberty is shown by cross-national comparisons, by historical data, and by the impact of _____ on the onset of puberty in girls.

5. Maturing early often has harmful consequences for _____.

6. To break the vicious cycle of malnutrition, children need an improved diet and _____.

7. Adolescents afflicted with _____ alternate between binge eating and purging themselves.

8. One reason why obese children overeat is that they pay attention to _____ cues to eating.

9. Integrated Management of Childhood Illness attempts to combat childhood diseases by improving skills of health care professionals, improving health care systems so that they're more responsive to childhood diseases, and _____.

10. _____ are the leading cause of death for U.S. adolescents.

11. The _____ is the part of the neuron that contains the biological machinery that keeps it alive.

12. During prenatal development and continuing into childhood and adolescence, axons of nerve cells acquire myelin, a fatty wrap that allows neurons to _____.

13. With development, brain systems become more specialized, in that the smaller brain regions become activated and _____.

14. In _____ growth, a developing brain depends upon environmental stimulation to fine-tune neural circuits.

15. A developing brain is more plastic than a mature brain, which means that following injury a developing brain _____.

Answers: (1) adolescence; (2) growth hormone; (3) avoiding contamination, which can be a significant problem with bottle-feeding in developing countries; (4) the social environment (in particular, a stressful environment); (5) girls; (6) parental education that teaches parents how to foster their children's development; (7) bulimia; (8) external; (9) changing family and community practices to prevent illness (e.g., having children sleep with mosquito netting); (10) Motor-vehicle accidents; (11) cell body; (12) transmit information more rapidly; (13) more specific stimuli trigger brain activity; (14) experience-expectant; (15) is more likely to recover

Key Terms

anorexia nervosa   123
axon   128
basal metabolic rate   124
body mass index (BMI)   124
bulimia nervosa   123
cell body   128
cerebral cortex   128
corpus callosum   128
dendrite   128
electroencephalography   130
epiphyses   109

experience-dependent growth   133
experience-expectant growth   133
frontal cortex   128
functional magnetic resonance imaging (fMRI)   130
growth hormone   110
hemispheres   128
malnutrition   122
menarche   116
myelin   128
neural plate   129

neuron   128
neurotransmitters   128
osteoporosis   114
primary sex characteristics   115
puberty   113
secondary sex characteristics   115
secular growth trends   110
spermarche   116
synapse   128
synaptic pruning   129
terminal buttons   128

5 Perceptual and Motor Development

5.1

**Basic Sensory
and Perceptual
Processes**

5.2

**Complex Perceptual
and Attentional
Processes**

5.3

Motor Development

When my daughter was a toddler, her afternoon naps often came at a time when her older brother needed to practice his drums. We closed her bedroom door, of course, but the thumping of the drums was still plenty loud! The first few times this happened, she would startle when the drumming began, then soon fall back to sleep. After a few days, though, she hardly stirred at all when the drumming began. My daughter's behavior illustrates perception in action: Our senses are assaulted with stimulation, but much of it is ignored. *Sensory and perceptual processes* **are the means by which people receive, select, modify, and organize stimulation from the world.** Sensory and perceptual processes are the first step in the complex process that eventually results in "knowing." We'll begin studying perceptual development, in **Module 5.1**, by looking at the origins of sensory processes in infancy. In **Module 5.2** we'll see how more complex perceptual and attentional processes develop in childhood.

Perceptual processes are closely linked to *motor skills*—**coordinated movements of the muscles and limbs.** Perception often guides a child's movement: A child uses vision to avoid obstacles. In turn, a child's movement in the environment provides enormous variety in perceptual stimulation. In **Module 5.3**, we'll see how improvements in motor skill enhance children's ability to explore, understand, and enjoy the world.

5.1 Basic Sensory and Perceptual Processes

OUTLINE	LEARNING OBJECTIVES
Smell, Taste, and Touch	• Are newborn babies able to smell and taste? Do they respond to touch and experience pain?
Hearing	• How well do infants hear? How do they use sounds to understand their world?
Seeing	• How accurate is infants' vision? Do infants perceive color?
Integrating Sensory Information	• How do infants integrate information from different senses?

Darla adores her 3-day-old daughter, Olivia. She loves holding her, talking to her, and simply watching her. Darla is certain that Olivia is already getting to know her, coming to recognize her face and the sound of her voice. Darla's husband, Steve, thinks Darla is crazy. He tells her, "Everyone knows that babies are born blind. And they probably can't hear much either." Darla doubts that Steve is right, but she wishes someone would tell her about babies' vision and hearing.

Darla's questions are really about her newborn daughter's sensory and perceptual skills. To help her understand, we need to remember that humans have different kinds of sense organs, each receptive to a unique kind of physical energy. The retina at the back of the eye, for example, is sensitive to some types of electromagnetic energy, and sight is the result. The eardrum detects changes in air pressure, and hearing is the result. Cells at the top of the nasal passage detect airborne molecules, and smell is the result. In each case, the sense organ translates the physical stimulation into nerve impulses that are sent to the brain.

The senses begin to function early in life, which is why this module is devoted entirely to infancy. How can we know what an infant senses? Because infants can't tell us what they smell, hear, or see, researchers have had to devise other ways to

Infants' perception is studied by determining whether they respond differently when stimuli are changed.

find out. In many studies, an investigator presents two stimuli to a baby, such as a high-pitched tone and a low-pitched tone or a sweet-tasting substance and a sour-tasting substance. Then the investigator records the baby's responses, such as heart rate, facial expression, or eye movements. If the baby consistently responds differently to the two stimuli (e.g., she looks in the direction of one tone, but not the other), the baby must be distinguishing between them.

Another approach is based on the fact that infants usually prefer novel stimuli over familiar stimuli. **When a novel stimulus is presented, babies pay much attention, but they pay less attention as it becomes more familiar, a phenomenon known as** *habituation.* Researchers use habituation to study perception by repeatedly presenting a stimulus such as a low-pitched tone until an infant barely responds. Then they present a second stimulus, such as a high-pitched tone. If the infant responds strongly, then researchers conclude that he can distinguish the two stimuli.

In this module, you'll learn what these techniques have revealed about infants' sensory and perceptual processes. These processes are interesting in their own right—you'll see that an infant's senses are astonishingly powerful. But they are also important to study as a basis for understanding a child's complicated thoughts and feelings; before we can delve into these issues, we first need to know how skillfully infants take in information from the world around them.

Smell, Taste, and Touch

Watch the **Video** *Perception* on **mydevelopmentlab.com** to learn more about some perceptual skills in young babies. Be sure to notice the baby's response to a bitter-tasting liquid!

Newborns have a keen sense of smell; they respond positively to pleasant smells and negatively to unpleasant smells (Mennella & Beauchamp, 1997). They have a relaxed, contented-looking facial expression when they smell honey or chocolate, but they frown, grimace, or turn away when they smell rotten eggs or ammonia. Young babies can also recognize familiar odors. Newborns will look in the direction of a pad that is saturated with their own amniotic fluid. They will also turn toward a pad saturated with the odor of their mother's breast milk or her perfume (Porter & Winburg, 1999; Schaal, Soussignan, & Marlier, 2002). Watch the **Video** on **mydevelopmentlab.com**

Newborns also have a highly developed sense of taste. They readily differentiate salty, sour, bitter, and sweet tastes (Rosenstein & Oster, 1997). Most infants seem to have a "sweet tooth." They react to sweet substances by smiling, sucking, and licking their lips (e.g., Steiner et al., 2001). In contrast, you can probably guess what the infant in the photo has tasted! This grimace is typical when infants are fed bitter- or sour-tasting substances (Kaijura, Cowart, & Beauchamp, 1992). Infants are also sensitive to changes in the taste of breast milk that reflect a mother's diet. Infants will nurse more after their mother has consumed a sweet-tasting substance such as vanilla (Mennella & Beauchamp, 1997).

Newborns are sensitive to touch. As I described in Module 3.4, many areas of the newborn's body respond reflexively when touched. Touching an infant's cheek, mouth, hand, or foot produces reflexive movements, documenting that infants perceive touch. What's more, babies' behavior in response to apparent pain-provoking stimuli suggests that they experience pain (Warnock & Sandrin, 2004). Look, for example, at the baby in the photo who is receiving an inoculation. He's opened his mouth to cry and, although we can't hear him, the sound of his cry is probably the unique pattern

Infants and toddlers do *not* like bitter and sour tastes!

associated with pain. The pain cry begins suddenly, is high-pitched, and is not easily soothed. This baby is agitated, his heart rate has jumped, and he's trying to move his hands, arms, and legs (Craig et al., 1993; Goubet, Clifton, & Shah, 2001). All together, these signs strongly suggest that babies experience pain.

Perceptual skills are extraordinarily useful to newborns and young babies. Smell and touch help them recognize their mothers and make it much easier for them to learn to eat. Early development of smell, taste, and touch prepares newborns and young babies to learn about the world.

Hearing

We know, from Module 3.1, that a fetus can hear at 7 or 8 months after conception. As you would expect from these results, newborns typically respond to sounds in their surroundings. If a parent is quiet but then coughs, an infant may startle, blink his eyes, and move his arms or legs. These responses may seem natural, but they do indeed indicate that infants are sensitive to sound.

An infant's response to an inoculation—a distinctive facial expression coupled with a distinctive cry—clearly suggests that the baby feels pain.

Not surprisingly, infants do not hear as well as adults. *Auditory threshold* **refers to the quietest sound that a person can hear.** An adult's auditory threshold is fairly easy to measure: A tone is presented, and the adult simply tells when he or she hears it. To test auditory thresholds in infants, who obviously cannot report what they hear, researchers have devised a number of clever techniques (Saffran, Werker, & Werner, 2006). For example, in one simple method, the infant is seated on a parent's lap. Both parent and baby wear headphones, as does an observer seated in another room who watches the baby through an observation window. When the observer believes the baby is attentive, he signals the experimenter, who sometimes presents a tone over the baby's headphones and at other times does nothing. Neither the observer nor the parent knows when tones are going to be presented, and they can't hear the tones through their headphones. On each trial, the observer simply judges if the baby responds in any fashion, such as by turning her head or changing her facial expression or activity level. Afterward, the experimenter determines how well the observer's judgments match the trials: If a baby can hear the tone, the observer should have noted a response only when a tone was presented.

This type of testing reveals that, overall, adults can hear better than infants; adults can hear some very quiet sounds that infants can't (Saffran et al., 2006). More important, this testing shows that infants hear sounds best that have pitches in the range of human speech—neither very high- nor very low-pitched. Infants can differentiate vowels from consonant sounds, and by 4½ months they can recognize their own names (Jusczyk, 1995; Mandel, Jusczyk, & Pisoni, 1995). In Module 9.1, we'll learn more about infants' remarkable skill at hearing language sounds.

Infants also can distinguish different musical sounds. They can distinguish different melodies and prefer melodies that are pleasant sounding over those that are unpleasant sounding or dissonant (Trainor & Heinmiller, 1998). And infants are sensitive to the rhythmic structure of music. After infants have heard a simple sequence of notes, they can tell the difference between a new sequence that fits the original versus one that doesn't (Hannon & Trehub, 2005). This early sensitivity to music is remarkable but perhaps not so surprising when you consider that music is (and has been) central in all cultures.

Thus, by the middle of the first year, most infants respond to much of the information provided by sound. However, not all infants are able to do so, which is the topic of the "Improving Children's Lives" feature.

QUESTION 5.1

Tiffany is worried that her 12-month-old daughter may be hearing impaired. What symptoms would suggest that she has cause for concern? If these symptoms are present, what should she do?

(Answer is on page 146.)

 # Improving Children's Lives

Hearing Impairment in Infancy

Some infants are born with limited hearing. Others are born deaf. (Exact figures are hard to determine, because infants' hearing is rarely tested precisely.) African, Asian, European, and Hispanic American babies are equally susceptible. Heredity is the leading cause of hearing impairment in newborns. After birth, the leading cause is meningitis, an inflammation of the membranes surrounding the brain and spinal cord.

What are signs of hearing impairment that a parent should watch for? Obviously, parents should be concerned if a young baby never responds to sudden, loud sounds. They should also be concerned if their baby has repeated ear infections, if he does not turn his head in the direction of sounds by the age of 4 or 5 months, does not respond to his own name by 8 or 9 months, and does not begin to imitate speech sounds and simple words by 12 months.

If parents notice these problems, their baby should be examined by a physician, who will check for ear problems, and an audiologist, who will measure the infant's hearing. Parents should never delay checking for possible hearing impairment. The earlier the problem is detected, the more the baby can be helped.

Many children with hearing impairments benefit from a cochlear implant, a device that converts speech signals into electrical impulses that can stimulate nerve cells.

If testing reveals that a baby has impaired hearing, several treatments are possible, depending on the degree of hearing loss. Some children with partial hearing benefit from mechanical devices. Hearing aids help some children, but others—like the child in the photo—benefit from a cochlear implant, an electronic device placed in the ear that converts speech into electric signals that stimulate nerve cells in the inner ear. Training in lipreading helps others. Children with profound hearing loss can learn to communicate with sign language. By mastering language (either oral language or sign language) and communicating effectively, a child's cognitive and social development will be normal. The key is to recognize impairment promptly.

Seeing

When babies are awake, they spend a lot of time looking around. Sometimes they seem to be scanning their environment broadly, and sometimes they seem to be focusing on nearby objects. But what do they actually see? Is their visual world a sea of gray blobs? Or do they see the world essentially as adults do? Actually, neither is the case, but, as you'll see, the second is closer to the truth.

From birth, babies respond to light and can track moving objects with their eyes. But what is the clarity of their vision, and how can we measure it?

Visual acuity **is defined as the smallest pattern that can be distinguished dependably.** You've undoubtedly had your visual acuity measured by trying to read rows of progressively smaller letters on a chart. The same basic logic is used in tests of infants' acuity, which are based on two premises. First, most infants will look at patterned stimuli instead of plain, nonpatterned stimuli. For example, if we were to show the two stimuli in Figure 5-1 to infants, most would look longer at the striped pattern than at the gray pattern. Second, as we make the lines narrower (along with the spaces between them), there comes a point at which the black and white stripes become so fine that they simply blend together and appear gray, just like the all-gray pattern.

FIGURE 5-1

FIGURE 5-2

To estimate an infant's acuity, then, we pair the gray square with squares that have different widths of stripes, like those in Figure 5-2: When infants look at the two stimuli equally, it indicates that they are no longer able to distinguish the stripes of the patterned stimulus. By measuring the width of the stripes and their distance from an infant's eye, we can estimate acuity (detecting thinner stripes indicates better acuity). Measurements of this sort indicate that newborns and 1-month-olds see at 20 feet what normal adults see at 200 to 400 feet. Infants' acuity improves rapidly and, by the first birthday, is essentially the same as that of a normal adult (Kellman & Arterberry, 2006).

Infants begin to see the world not only with greater acuity during the first year, but also in color! How do we perceive color? The wavelength of light is the source of color perception. Figure 5-3 shows that lights we see as red have a relatively long wavelength, whereas violet, at the other end of the color spectrum, has a much shorter wavelength. **We detect wavelength—and therefore color—with specialized neurons called** *cones* **that are in the retina of the eye.** Some cones are particularly sensitive to short-wavelength light (blues and violets), others are sensitive to medium-wavelength light (greens and yellows), and still others are sensitive to long-wavelength light (reds and oranges). These different kinds of cones are linked in complex circuits of neurons in the eye and in the brain, and this neural circuitry allows us to see the world in color.

These circuits gradually begin to function in the first few months after birth. Newborns and young babies can perceive few colors, but by 3 months the three kinds of cones and their associated circuits are working and infants are able to see the full range of colors (Kellman & Arterberry, 2006). In fact, by 3 to 4 months, infants' color perception seems similar to that of adults (Adams & Courage, 1995; Franklin, Pilling, & Davies, 2005). In particular, infants, like adults, tend to see categories of

Wavelength of Light in Nanometers (billionths of a meter)

A mother who breast-feeds provides her baby with a multimedia event: The baby sees, smells, hears, feels, and tastes her!

color. For example, if a yellow light's wavelength is gradually increased, the infant will suddenly perceive it as a shade of red rather than a shade of yellow (Dannemiller, 1998).

The ability to perceive color, along with rapidly improving visual acuity, gives infants great skill in making sense out of their visual experiences. What makes this growing visual skill even more powerful is that, as we'll see in the next section, infants are also starting to connect information obtained from different senses.

Integrating Sensory Information

So far, we have discussed infants' sensory systems separately. In reality, of course, most infant experiences are better described as "multimedia events." A nursing mother like the one in the photo provides visual and taste cues to her baby. A rattle stimulates vision, hearing, and touch. In fact, much stimulation is not specific to one sense but spans multiple senses. Temporal information, such as duration or tempo, can be conveyed by sight or sound. For example, you can detect the rhythm of a person clapping by seeing the hands meet or by hearing the sound of hands striking. Similarly, the texture of a surface—whether it's rough or smooth, for example—can be detected by sight or by feel.

Infants readily perceive many of these relations. For example, infants can recognize visually an object that they have only touched previously (Sann & Streri, 2007). Similarly, they can detect relations between information presented visually and auditorily. For example, babies look longer when an object's motion matches its sound (it makes higher-pitched sounds while rising but lower-pitched sounds while falling) than when it doesn't (Walker et al., 2010). They can also link the temporal properties of visual and auditory stimulation, such as duration and rhythm (Lewkowicz, 2000). Finally, they link their own body movement to their perceptions of musical rhythm, giving new meaning to the phrase "feel the beat, baby!" (Gerry, Faux, & Trainor, 2010).

Traditionally, coordinating information from different senses (e.g., vision with hearing, vision with touch) was thought to be a demanding task for infants. However, recent thinking challenges this view. One idea is that cross-modal perception is actually easier for infants, because in infancy regions in the brain devoted to sensory processing are not yet specialized. For example, some regions in an adult's brain respond only to visual stimuli; those same regions in an infant's brain respond to visual *and* auditory input (Spector & Maurer, 2009).

Another explanation of infants' ability to integrate information from different senses is described in the "Spotlight on Theories" feature.

Spotlight on Theories

The Theory of Intersensory Redundancy

BACKGROUND Traditionally, linking information from different senses (e.g., vision with hearing, vision with touch) was said to be a challenging task for infants and, consequently, one that should emerge later, only after infants first master perceptual processes in each sense separately. In this view, a baby might perceive a favorite teddy bear's appearance, feel, and smell but would only gradually integrate these perceptions.

THE THEORY   However, Lorraine Bahrick and Robert Lickliter (2002; Bahrick, Lickliter, & Flom, 2004) have proposed a different view. **They note that certain information, such as duration, rate, and intensity, is** *amodal,* **in that it can be presented in different senses.** For example, when a mother claps her hands in time to music, the sounds of the claps as well as the appearance of the hands coming together and moving apart provide clues to the tempo of the music.

In Bahrick and Lickliter's *intersensory redundancy theory,* **the infant's perceptual system is particularly attuned to amodal information that is presented to multiple sensory modes.** That is, perception is best—particularly for young infants—when information is presented redundantly to multiple senses. When an infant sees and hears the mother clapping (visual, auditory information), he focuses on the information conveyed to both senses and pays less attention to information that's only available in one sense, such as the color of the mother's nail polish or the sounds of her humming along with the tune. Or the infant can learn that the mom's lips are chapped from seeing the flaking skin and by feeling the roughness as the mother kisses him. According to intersensory redundancy theory, it's as if infants follow the rule: "Any information that's presented in multiple senses must be important, so pay attention to it!"

> Infants readily integrate information that is presented redundantly to different senses.

Hypothesis: If infants are particularly attentive to information presented redundantly to multiple senses, then they should notice changes in amodal information *at a younger age* when the information is presented to multiple senses than when it's presented to a single sense. In other words, if the mom claps slowly at first but then quickly, infants should detect this change at a younger age when they see and hear the clapping than when they only see her or only hear her.

Test: Flom and Bahrick (2007) studied infants' ability to detect differences in an adult's emotional expression—whether she was happy, angry, or sad. In the multimodal condition, infants saw a video depicting a woman who appeared to be talking directly to them. Her facial expression and tone of voice conveyed one of the three emotions. After several trials, infants saw a new video depicting the same woman expressing a different emotion. At 4 months of age, infants looked longer at the new video, showing that they detected the change in the woman's emotional expression. However, when the experiment was repeated but with the soundtrack turned off—so that emotional information was conveyed by vision alone—infants did not detect the difference in emotional expression until they were 7 months old.

Conclusion: This result supports the hypothesis. Infants detected a change in emotional expression at a younger age (4 months) when it was presented in multiple sensory modes than when it was presented in a single mode (7 months).

Application: The theory of intersensory redundancy says that infants learn best when information is simultaneously presented to multiple senses. Parents can use this principle to help babies learn. Language learning is a good example. Of course, talking to babies is beneficial (a topic we explore in depth in Chapter 9). But talking face-to-face with babies is best because then they see the visual cues that distinguish language sounds. When Mom says "oooh," her lips form a tight circle; when she says "ahhhh," her mouth is open wide. By talking face-to-face, Mom is presenting information about sounds redundantly—auditorily and visually—making it easier for her infants to distinguish these sounds (Burnham & Dodd, 2004).

ANSWER 5.1
By 12 months, Tiffany's daughter should be looking in the direction of sounds (and should have been doing so for several months), should respond to her name, and should make some speech-like sounds of her own. If she doesn't do these things, Tiffany should take her daughter to see a pediatrician and to an audiologist, right away!

Integrating information from different senses is yet another variation on the theme that has dominated this module: Infants' sensory and perceptual skills are impressive. Olivia, Darla's newborn daughter from the opening vignette, can definitely smell, taste, and feel pain. She can distinguish sounds; her vision is a little blurry but will improve rapidly, and she'll soon see the full range of colors; and she makes connections between sights and sounds and between other senses. Of course, over the coming year her perceptual skills will become more finely tuned: Olivia will become particularly adept at identifying stimuli that are common in her environment (Scott, Pascalis, & Nelson, 2007). But for now, Olivia, like most infants, is well prepared to make sense out of her environment.

 ## Check Your Learning

RECALL Summarize what is known about infants' ability to smell, taste, and touch.

Describe the important developmental milestones in vision during infancy.

INTERPRET Compare the impact of nature and nurture on the development of infants' sensory and perceptual skills.

APPLY Perceptual skills are quite refined at birth and become mature very rapidly. What evolutionary purposes are served by this rapid development?

 ## Complex Perceptual and Attentional Processes

OUTLINE
Perceiving Objects
Attention
Attention Deficit Hyperactivity Disorder

LEARNING OBJECTIVES
• How do infants perceive objects?
• How does attention improve as children grow older?
• What is attention deficit hyperactivity disorder?

Soon after Stephen entered first grade, his teacher remarked that he sometimes seemed out of control. He was easily distracted, often moving aimlessly from one activity to another. He also seemed to be impulsive and had difficulty waiting his turn. This behavior continued in second grade and he began to fall behind in reading and arithmetic. His classmates were annoyed by his behavior and began to avoid him. His parents wonder whether Stephen just has lots of boyish energy or whether he has a problem.

Where we draw the dividing line between "basic" and "complex" perceptual processes is rather arbitrary. As you'll see, Module 5.2 is a logical extension of the information presented in Module 5.1. We'll begin by looking at how we perceive objects. We'll also look at the processes of attention and some children who have attentional problems. By the end of the module, you'll understand why Stephen behaves as he does.

Perceiving Objects

When you look at the top photo, you easily recognize it as "eyeball," even though all that's physically present in the photograph are many different-colored dots. In this case, perception actually creates an object from sensory stimulation, determining that certain features go together to form objects. This is often challenging because we see several objects together, with some partially hidden. Nevertheless, in the bottom photo, we recognize that the orange is a distinct object, not just an orange-colored bulge in the apple.

A newborn's perception of objects is limited, but develops rapidly in the first few months after birth (Johnson, 2001). By 4 months, infants use a number of cues to determine which elements go together to form objects. One important cue is motion: Elements that move together are usually part of the same object (Kellman & Banks, 1998). For example, at the left of Figure 5-4, a pencil appears to be moving back and forth behind a colored square. If the square were removed, you would be surprised to see a pair of pencil stubs, as shown on the right side of the diagram. The common movement of the pencil's eraser and point lead us to believe that they're part of the same pencil.

Young infants, too, are surprised by demonstrations like this. If they see a display like the moving pencils, they will then look very briefly at a whole pencil, apparently because they expected it. In contrast, if after seeing the moving pencil they're shown the two pencil stubs, they look much longer, as if trying to figure out what happened (Amso & Johnson, 2006; Aslin, 1987; Eizenman & Bertenthal, 1998). Evidently, even very young babies use common motion to create objects from different parts.

Motion is one clue to object unity, but infants use others, too, including color, texture, and aligned edges. As you can see in Figure 5-5 on page 148, infants more often group features together (i.e., believe they're part of the same object) when they're the same color, have the same texture, and when their edges are aligned (Johnson, 2001).

PERCEPTUAL CONSTANCIES. A challenge for infants is recognizing that an object is the same even though it may look different. For example, when a mother moves away from her baby, the image that she casts on the retinas of her baby's eyes gets smaller. Do babies have a nightmare that their mother's head is

Perceptual processes allow us to interpret this pattern of lines, textures, and colors as an eyeball.

Many cues tell us that these are four objects, not one unusually shaped object: The objects differ in color; the apples have a slightly different texture than the oranges, and the apples in the foreground partially block the oranges in the background.

FIGURE 5-4

 QUESTION 5.2
When 6-month-old Sebastian watches his mother type on a keyboard, how does he know that her fingers and the keyboard are not simply one big unusual object?
(Answer is on page 157.)

Infants believe that this display has one pencil.

Infants believe that this display has two pencils.

Cue

Color

Texture

Aligned edges

FIGURE 5-5

shrinking as she moves away? No. **Early on, infants master** *size constancy,* **the realization that an object's actual size remains the same despite changes in the size of its retinal image.**

How do we know that infants have a rudimentary sense of size constancy? Suppose we let an infant look at an unfamiliar teddy bear. Then we show the infant the same bear, at a different distance, paired with a larger replica of the bear. If infants lack size constancy, the two bears will be equally novel and babies should respond to each similarly. If, instead, babies have size constancy, they will recognize the first bear as familiar, the larger bear as novel, and be more likely to respond to the novel bear. In fact, by 4 or 5 months, babies treat the bear that they've seen twice at different distances— and, therefore, with different retinal images—as familiar (Granrud, 1986). This outcome is possible only if infants have size constancy. Thus, infants do not believe that mothers (and other people or objects) constantly change size as they move closer or farther away (Kellman & Arterberry, 2006).

Size is just one of several perceptual constancies. Others are brightness and color constancy as well as shape constancy, shown in Figure 5-6. All these constancies are achieved, at least in rudimentary form, by 4 months (Aslin, 1987; Dannemiller, 1998). Consequently, even young infants are not confused, thinking that the world is filled with many very similar-looking but different objects. Instead, they can tell that an object is the same, even though it may look different. Mom is still Mom, whether she's nearby or far away and whether she's clearly visible outdoors or barely visible in a dimly lit room.

DEPTH. In addition to knowing *what* an object is, babies need to know *where* it is. Determining left and right as well as high and low is relatively easy because these dimensions—horizontal, vertical—can be represented directly on the retina's flat surface. Distance or depth is more complicated because this dimension is not represented directly on the retina. Instead, many different cues are used to estimate distance or depth.

At what age can infants perceive depth? Eleanor Gibson and Richard Walk (1960) addressed this question in a classic experiment that used a specially designed apparatus. **The** *visual cliff* **is a glass-covered platform; on one side a pattern appears directly under the glass, but on the other it appears several feet below the glass.** Consequently, one side looks shallow but the other appears to have a steep drop-off, like a cliff. As you can see in the photo, in the experiment the baby is placed on the platform and the mother coaxes her infant to come to her. Most babies willingly crawl to their mothers when she stands on the shallow side. But virtually all babies refuse to cross the deep side, even when the mother calls the infant by name and tries to lure him or her with an attractive toy. Clearly, infants can perceive depth by the time they are old enough to crawl.

What about babies who cannot yet crawl? When babies as young as 1½ months are simply placed on the deep side of the platform, their heartbeat slows down. Heart rate often decelerates when

Shape Constancy: Even though the door appears to change shape as it opens, we know that it really remains a rectangle.

FIGURE 5-6

people notice something interesting, so this would suggest that 1½-month-olds notice that the deep side is different. At 7 months, infants' heart rate accelerates, a sign of fear. Thus, although young babies can detect a difference between the shallow and deep sides of the visual cliff, only older, crawling babies are actually afraid of the deep side (Campos et al., 1978).

How do infants infer depth, on the visual cliff or anywhere? They use several kinds of cues. **Among the first are** *kinetic cues,* **in which motion is used to estimate depth.** *Visual expansion* **refers to the fact that as an object moves closer, it fills an ever-greater proportion of the retina.** Visual expansion is why we flinch when someone unexpectedly tosses a soda can toward us and it's what allows a batter to estimate when a baseball will arrive over the plate. **Another cue,** *motion parallax,* **refers to the fact that nearby moving objects move across our visual field faster than those at a distance.** Motion parallax is in action when you look out the side window in a moving car: Trees next to the road move rapidly across the visual field but mountains in the distance move much more slowly. Babies use these cues in the first weeks after birth; for example, 1-month-olds blink if a moving object looks as if it's going to hit them in the face (Nánez & Yonas, 1994).

Another cue becomes important at about 4 months. *Retinal disparity* **is based on the fact that the left and right eyes often see slightly different versions of the same scene.** When objects are distant, the images appear in very similar positions on the retina; when objects are near, the images appear in much different positions. Thus, greater disparity in positions of the image on the retina signals that an object is close. At about 4 months, infants use retinal disparity as a depth cue, correctly inferring that objects are nearby when disparity is great (Kellman & Arterberry, 2006).

By 7 months, infants use several cues for depth that depend on the arrangement of objects in the environment (e.g., Hemker et al., 2010). **These are sometimes called** *pictorial cues* **because they're the same cues that artists use to convey depth in drawings and paintings.**

Infants avoid the "deep side" of the visual cliff, indicating that they perceive depth.

Texture gradient: ***The texture of objects changes from coarse but distinct for nearby objects to finer and less distinct for distant objects.*** In the photo, we judge the distinct flowers to be close and the blurred ones, distant.

Interposition: **Nearby objects partially obscure more distant objects.** The glasses obscure the bottle, so we decide that the glasses are closer (and use this same cue to decide that the right glass is closer than the left glass).

Linear perspective: **Parallel lines come together at a single point in the distance.** Thus, we use the space between the lines as a cue to distance and, consequently, decide that the train in the photo is far away because the parallel tracks grow close together.

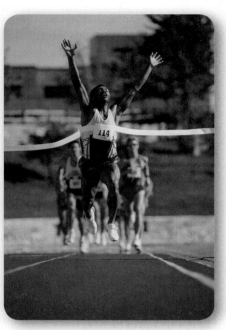

Relative size: **Nearby objects look substantially larger than objects in the distance.** Knowing that the runners are really about the same size, we judge the ones that look smaller to be farther away.

THE IMPACT OF MOTOR-SKILL DEVELOPMENT. A common theme in the past few pages is that infants develop powerful perceptual skills over their first year. This change reflects an epigenetic plan in which genetic instructions unfold in the context of a stimulating environment—and essential to this plan are the infant's own emerging motor skills. That is, as I mentioned at the beginning of this chapter, as infants' motor skills improve, they experience their environment differently and literally see their world in new and more sophisticated ways.

One example of the impact of motor skills comes from infants' growing ability to hold and manipulate objects. As we'll see in Module 5.3, 4-month-olds can hold a toy with their fingers but not until a few months later do infants become skilled at holding a toy, turning it to see its appearance on different sides, and stroking it with a finger to discover its texture. These improved motor skills allow children to learn more about the properties of objects and literally change how they perceive objects: Infants who can explore objects are more likely to understand the three-dimensional nature of objects and to notice the details of an object's appearance, such as its color (Perone et al., 2008; Soska, Adolph, & Johnson, 2010).

Another example makes use of a familiar phenomenon: When you drive down a tree-lined road, the trees rapidly move from ahead of you to behind you.

Having spent many hours in a car, you interpret the changing appearance of the trees as a cue that you are moving. For this same reason, if you're sitting in an airliner parked at the gate and an airliner at an adjacent gate backs out, you feel as if you're moving forward. This experience can be simulated by placing people in rooms like the one shown in Figure 5-7, where the side walls and ceiling can move forward or backward (as shown by the arrows). If the walls move from front to back, adults seated in the middle of the room feel as if they're moving forward and they often lean back to compensate. Infants who can move themselves by creeping or crawling do, too, but infants who can't move themselves do not (Uchiyama et al., 2008). Only after gaining the experience of propelling themselves through the environment do infants interpret front-to-back movement to mean that they are moving. Thus, just as an art-appreciation course allows you to see the *Mona Lisa* from a different perspective, infants' emerging abilities to move themselves and to manipulate objects create bold new perceptual experiences.

> Advances in infants' motor skills allow them to perceive the environment in more sophisticated ways.

FIGURE 5-7

These same themes—rapidly changing perceptual skills that are influenced by experience—are apparent in the next section, which focuses on how infants perceive faces.

PERCEIVING FACES. The human face is a particularly important object to infants. Young babies readily look at faces. One-month-olds look mostly at the outer edges of the face. However, by 3 months of age, infants focus almost entirely on the interior of the face, particularly the eyes and lips.

Some theorists argue that babies are innately attracted to stimuli that are face-like. The claim here is that some aspect of the face—perhaps three high-contrast blobs close together—constitutes a distinctive stimulus that is readily recognized, even by newborns. For example, newborns turn their eyes to follow a moving face more than they turn their eyes for nonface stimuli (Johnson, Grossman, & Farroni, 2008). This preference for faces over face-like stimuli supports the view that infants are innately attracted to faces. However, preference for tracking a moving face changes abruptly at about 4 weeks of age: infants now track all moving stimuli. One idea is that newborns' face-tracking is a reflex, based on primitive circuits in the brain, that is designed to enhance attention to face-like stimuli. Starting at about 4 weeks, circuits in the brain's cortex begin to control infants' looking at faces and other stimuli (Morton & Johnson, 1991).

> Older infants perceive faces as a unique configuration of distinctive elements.

By 7 or 8 months, infants process faces in much the same way that adults do—as a configuration in which the internal elements (e.g., eyes, nose, mouth) are arranged and spaced in a unique way. Younger infants, in contrast, often perceive faces as an independent collection of facial features, as if they have not yet learned that the arrangement and spacing of features is critical (Bhatt et al., 2005; Schwarzer, Zauner, & Jovanic, 2007).

Through the first six months after birth, infants have a very general prototype for a face—one that includes human and nonhuman faces (Pascalis, de Haan, & Nelson, 2002). However, between 6 and 12 months of age, infants fine-tune their prototype of a face so that it reflects those kinds of faces that are familiar in their environments. In the "Focus on Research" feature, we'll see that this age-related refinement of facial configurations results in a highly unusual outcome: 3-month-olds outperform 9-month-olds!

Focus on Research

Specialized Face Processing During Infancy

Who were the investigators, and what was the aim of the study? All human faces have the same basic features—eyes, nose, and mouth in the familiar configuration. But faces of different groups differ in their details. For example, people of African descent often have a relatively broad nose and people of Asian descent often have a fold of skin in the upper eyelid that covers the inner corner of the eye. As infants are exposed to faces in their environments and fine-tune their face-recognition processes, they might *lose* the ability to recognize some kinds of faces. For example, a young infant's broadly tuned face-recognition processes might work well for faces of Asian, African, and European individuals, but an older infant's more finely tuned processes might only recognize faces from familiar groups. Testing this hypothesis was the aim of a study by David Kelly, Shaoying Liu, Kang Lee, Paul Quinn, Olivier Pascalis, Alan Slater, and Liezhong Ge (2009).

How did the investigators measure the topic of interest? Kelly and colleagues wanted to determine whether infants could recognize faces from different groups equally well. Consequently, they had infants view a photo of an adult's face (e.g., an Asian man). Then that face was paired with a novel face of the same group (e.g., a different Asian man). Experimenters recorded participants' looking at the two faces.

The expectation was that if the participants recognized the familiar face, they would look longer at the novel face.

Who were the participants in the study? The study included 46 3-month-olds and 41 9-month-olds from Hangzhou, China. (The researchers also tested 6-month-olds but for simplicity I'm not describing their results.) One-third of the infants at each age saw Asian faces, another third saw African faces, and another third saw European faces.

What was the design of the study? This study was experimental. The independent variables included the type of face (African, Asian, European) and the familiarity of the face on the test trial (novel, familiar). The dependent variable was the participants' looking at the two faces on the test trial. The study was cross-sectional because it included 3-, 6-, and 9-month-olds, each tested once.

Were there ethical concerns with the study? No. There was no obvious harm associated with looking at pictures of faces.

What were the results? If infants recognized the familiar face, they should look more at the novel face; if they did not recognize the familiar face, they should look equally at the novel and familiar faces. The graph in Figure 5-8 shows the percentage of time that participants looked at the novel face. The 3-month-olds looked longer at novel faces from all three groups (more than 50% preference for the novel face). In contrast, 9-month-olds looked longer at the novel Asian faces but not the novel African or European faces.

What did the investigators conclude? Kelly and colleagues concluded that during the first year, "the ability to recognize own-race faces was retained, whereas the capacity to individuate other-race faces was simultaneously reduced, demonstrating a pattern of perceptual narrowing" (2009, p. 111). That is, from experience infants finely tune their face-processing systems to include only faces from familiar groups.

What converging evidence would strengthen these conclusions? These findings show that 3-month-olds' face-processing systems work equally well on faces from different racial groups. The investigators could determine how broadly the system is tuned by studying infants' recognition of faces of young children and comparing the responses of infants who have older siblings with those who do not.

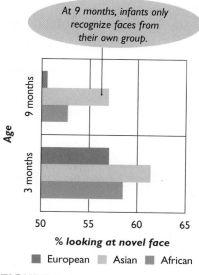

FIGURE 5-8

The findings from the "Focus on Research" study suggest a crucial role for experience: Older infants' greater familiarity with faces leads to a more precise configuration of faces, one that includes faces of familiar racial and ethnic groups. This interpretation is supported by the finding that individuals born in Asia but adopted as infants by European parents recognize European faces better than Asian faces (Sangrigoli et al., 2005).

These changes in face-recognition skill show the role of experience in fine-tuning infants' perception, a theme that will emerge again in the early phases of language learning (Module 9.1). And these improved face-recognition skills are adaptive, for they provide the basis for social relationships that infants form during the rest of the first year, which we'll examine in Module 10.3.

Attention

Have you ever been in a class where you knew you should be listening and taking notes, but the lecture was just so boring that you started noticing other things—the construction going on outside or an attractive person seated nearby? After a while, maybe you reminded yourself to "pay attention!" We get distracted because our perceptual systems are marvelously powerful. They provide us with far more information at any one time than we could possible interpret. *Attention* **is the process by which we select information that will be processed further.** In a class, for example, where the task is to direct your attention to the lecture, it is easy to ignore other stimuli if the lecture is interesting. But if the lecture is not interesting, other stimuli intrude and capture your attention.

> Infants typically respond to an unfamiliar stimulus but pay less attention as it becomes more familiar.

The roots of attention can be seen in infancy. Remember how my daughter would startle when she first heard her brother drumming? Her response was normal not only for infants but also for children and adults. **When presented with a strong or unfamiliar stimulus, an** *orienting response* **usually occurs: A person startles, fixes the eyes on the stimulus, and shows changes in heart rate and brain-wave patterns.** Collectively, these responses indicate that the infant is attending to this stimulus. Remember, too, that my daughter quickly began to ignore the sound of drumming. After repeated presentations of a stimulus, people become accustomed to it, so their orienting response diminishes and eventually disappears. These are signs of habituation, which we discussed on page 140. Habituation indicates that attention is selective: A stimulus that once garnered attention no longer does.

The orienting response and habituation can both be demonstrated easily in the laboratory. For example, in one study (Zelazo et al., 1989), speech was played through one of two loudspeakers placed on either side of an infant. At first, most newborns turned their heads toward the source of the speech, but after several trials they no longer responded. Thus, newborns oriented to the novel sound but then gradually habituated to the sound as it became more familiar.

The orienting response and habituation are both useful to infants. On the one hand, orienting makes the infant aware of potentially important or dangerous events in the environment. On the other hand, constantly responding to insignificant stimuli is wasteful, so habituation keeps infants like the one in the photo from wasting too much energy on biologically nonsignificant stimuli (Rovee-Collier, 1987). Given the biological significance of being able to habituate, it's not too surprising that infants who habituate more rapidly tend to grow up to be more intelligent children (Rose et al., 1997).

During the preschool years, children gradually become better able to regulate their attention. You can see these changes in the way that youngsters play with novel toys. When 3½-year-old Michael got a new truck, he looked at it carefully, bringing it close to his face for careful inspection. Then he spent minutes rolling it back and forth on the floor, making "Rrr-rrr" sounds. When Michael plays like this, he often ignores nearby distractions such as the start of a TV show. In contrast, when 1-year-old Michele got a new "busy box," she looked at it and played, but without the intensity and focus that marked Michael's play with the truck. She was also easily distracted, readily turning her head when her sister entered the room (Ruff & Capozzoli, 2003). Similar age differences are evident when children watch TV: Older children stay engaged longer and are less easily distracted (Richards & Anderson, 2004). Maintaining focused attention is a demanding skill, one that emerges gradually during the preschool years and beyond (Hatania & Smith, 2010).

An equally important part of "paying attention" is inhibiting unwanted or interfering thoughts and behaviors. In other words, returning to the example of the boring lecture, paying attention is often difficult because other stimuli, such as the

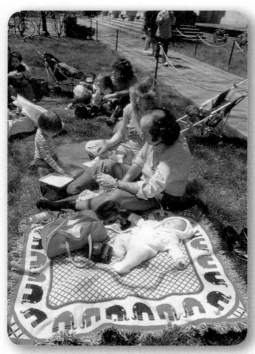

Attentional processes allow infants (and older children) to ignore stimuli that aren't important.

pleasant scent of a nearby classmate, or other thoughts, such as wondering about an upcoming exam, often intrude and direct attention elsewhere. Actively inhibiting these stimuli and thoughts is often difficult for adults, so it's not surprising that effective inhibitory skills develop gradually during the preschool and elementary-school years (Diamond, 2006). For example, when children are asked to sort pictures according to one rule (e.g., sort by color) and then asked to sort them again using a different rule (e.g., now sort by shape), young children often return to sorting by the old rule, even though they can describe the new rule perfectly! While sorting, young children are less able to inhibit the old rule, which causes them to sort some cards by color even when they know the new rule says to sort by shape (Davidson et al., 2006; Zelazo et al., 2003).

In the meantime, parents and teachers *can* help young children pay attention better. Of course, periodically reminding children to pay attention helps them to stay focused. But that's not enough. We can make relevant information more salient than irrelevant information. For example, closing a classroom door may not eliminate competing sounds and smells entirely, but it will make them less salient. Or, when preschoolers are working at a table or desk, we can remove all objects that are not necessary for the task. And when we change rules or procedures for children, we should expect that some children will revert back to the old way of doing things. They're not being difficult; the "old way" simply can't be inhibited and children follow it, often without realizing what they're doing.

Techniques like these improve some but not all children's attention, as we'll see in the next section.

Attention Deficit Hyperactivity Disorder

Children with attention deficit hyperactivity disorder—ADHD for short—have special problems when it comes to paying attention. Roughly 3% to 5% of all school-age children are diagnosed with ADHD; boys outnumber girls by a 3:1 ratio (Wicks-Nelson & Israel, 2006). Stephen, the child in the module-opening vignette, exhibits three symptoms at the heart of ADHD (American Psychiatric Association, 2004):

- *Hyperactivity:* Like the boy in the photo, children with ADHD are unusually energetic, fidgety, and unable to keep still, especially in situations like school classrooms where they need to limit their activity.

- *Inattention:* Youngsters with ADHD skip from one task to another. They do not pay attention in class and seem unable to concentrate on schoolwork.

- *Impulsivity:* Children with ADHD often act before thinking; they may run into a street before looking for traffic or interrupt others who are speaking.

Hyperactivity is one of three main symptoms of ADHD; the others are inattention and impulsivity.

Not all children with ADHD show all these symptoms to the same degree. Most children with ADHD are hyperactive and either impulsive or inattentive (Barkley, 2003). Children with ADHD often have problems with academic performance, conduct, and getting along with their peers (Murray-Close et al., 2010; Stevens & Ward-Estes, 2006).

Many myths surround ADHD. Some concern causes. At one time or another, TV, food allergies, sugar, and poor home life have all been proposed as causes of ADHD, but research does not consistently support any of these (e.g., Wolraich et al., 1994). Instead, heredity is an important factor (Saudino & Plomin, 2007). Twin studies show that identical twins are often both diagnosed with ADHD, but this is uncommon for fraternal twins (Pennington, Willcutt, & Rhee, 2005). In addition, prenatal exposure to alcohol and other drugs can place children at risk for ADHD (Milberger et al., 1997).

Another myth is that most children "grow out of" ADHD in adolescence or young adulthood. More than half the children who are diagnosed with ADHD will have problems related to overactivity, inattention, and impulsivity as adolescents and young adults (Biederman et al., 2010). Few of these young adults complete college, and some will have work- and family-related problems (Biederman et al., 2006; Murphy, Barkley, & Bush, 2002). One final myth is that many healthy children are wrongly diagnosed with ADHD. The number of children diagnosed with ADHD *did* increase substantially toward the end of the 20th century, but not because children are being routinely misdiagnosed; rather, the increased numbers reflect growing awareness of ADHD and more frequent diagnoses of ADHD in girls and adolescents (Goldman et al., 1998).

> The best treatment for ADHD combines stimulant drugs with training in cognitive and social skills.

Because ADHD affects academic and social success throughout childhood and adolescence, researchers have worked hard to find effective treatments. The "Child Development and Family Policy" feature describes these efforts.

Child Development and Family Policy

What's the Best Treatment for ADHD?

By the mid-1980s, it was clear that ADHD could be treated. For example, children with ADHD often respond well to stimulant drugs such as Ritalin. It may seem odd that stimulants are given to children who are already overactive, but these drugs stimulate the parts of the brain that normally inhibit hyperactive and impulsive behavior. Thus, stimulants actually have a calming influence for many youngsters with ADHD, allowing them to focus their attention (Barkley, 2004).

Drug therapy was not the only approach: Psychosocial treatments designed to improve children's cognitive and social skills also worked, and often included home-based intervention and intensive summer programs. For example, children can be taught to remind themselves to read instructions before starting assignments. And they can be reinforced by others for inhibiting impulsive and hyperactive behavior (Barkley, 2004).

These treatments were well known by the late 1980s, yet many researchers were troubled by large gaps in our understanding. One gap concerned the long-term success of treatment. Most studies had measured the impact of weeks or months of treatment; virtually nothing was known about the effectiveness of treatment over longer periods. Another gap concerned the most effective combination of treatments and whether this was the same for all children. That is, is medication plus psychosocial treatment the best for all children and for all facets of children's development (i.e., academic and social)?

Prompted by these concerns, scientific advisory groups met in the late 1980s and early 1990s to identify the gaps in understanding and the research needed to fill the gaps. In 1992, the National Institute of Mental Health used reports of these groups to request proposals for research. After intensive review, the top six applications were selected and synthesized to create the Multimodal Treatment Study of Children with ADHD—the MTA for short (Richters et al., 1995). The MTA involves 18 scientists who are experts on ADHD and nearly 600 elementary-school children with ADHD. The children were assigned to different treatment modes and received treatment for 14 months. The impact of treatment has been measured every few years for several different domains of children's development.

The initial results—obtained at the end of the 14 months of treatment—showed that medication alone was the best way to treat hyperactivity per se. However, for a variety of other measures, including academic and social skills as well as parent–child relations, medication plus psychosocial treatment was somewhat more effective than medication alone (The MTA Cooperative Group, 1999). In contrast, in follow-up studies conducted 6 and 8 years after the 14-month treatment period ended, the treatment groups no longer differed and all groups fared worse than children without ADHD: Children with ADHD were more likely to be inattentive, hyperactive, and impulsive; they were more aggressive; and they were less likely to succeed in school (Molina et al., 2009).

For researchers, parents, and children with ADHD, these are disappointing results. Yet they point to an important conclusion, one with implications for policy: Several months of intensive treatment will not "cure" ADHD; instead, ADHD is perhaps better considered a chronic condition, like diabetes or asthma, that requires ongoing monitoring and treatment (Hazell, 2009).

 ANSWER 5.2
Her hands and fingers move together, independently of the keyboard, and her hands and fingers have a common color and texture that differs from those of the keyboard.

Tragically, many children who need these treatments do not receive them. African American and Hispanic American children are far less likely than European American youngsters to be diagnosed with and treated for ADHD, even when they have the same symptoms (Miller, Nigg, & Miller, 2009; Stevens, Harman, & Kelleher, 2005). Why? Income plays a role. African American and Hispanic American families are more often economically disadvantaged and consequently they are less able to pay for diagnosis and treatment. Racial bias also contributes. Parents and professionals often attribute the symptoms of ADHD in European American children to a biological problem that can be treated medically; in African American or Hispanic American children, they more often attribute these symptoms to poor parenting, life stresses, or other sources that can't be treated (Kendall & Hatton, 2002).

Obviously, all children with ADHD deserve appropriate treatment. Teachers and other professionals dealing with children must be sure that poverty and racial bias do not prevent children from receiving the care they need.

 ## Check Your Learning

RECALL Describe the cues that babies use to infer depth.

What are the main symptoms of ADHD?

INTERPRET Describe evidence showing that early experience with faces fine-tunes the infant's perception of faces.

APPLY What happens to children with ADHD when they become adolescents and young adults? How does this address the issue of continuity of development?

5.3 Motor Development

OUTLINE	LEARNING OBJECTIVES
Locomotion	• What are the component skills involved in learning to walk, and at what age do infants typically master them?
Fine-Motor Skills	• How do infants learn to coordinate the use of their hands? When and why do most children begin to prefer to use one hand?
Physical Fitness	• Are children physically fit? Do they benefit from participating in sports?

Nancy is 14 months old and a world-class crawler. Using hands and knees, she gets nearly anywhere she wants to go. Nancy does not walk and seems to have no interest in learning how. Her dad wonders whether he should be doing something to help Nancy progress beyond crawling. And down deep, he worries that perhaps he should have provided more exercise or training for Nancy when she was younger.

The photos on this page have a common theme. Each depicts an activity involving *motor skills*—coordinated movements of the muscles and limbs. In each activity, success demands that each movement be done in a precise way and in a specific sequence. For example, to use a stick shift properly, you need to move the clutch pedal, gas pedal, and the stick shift in specific ways and in exactly the right sequence. If you don't give the car enough gas as you let out the clutch, you'll kill the engine. If you give it too much gas, the engine races and the car lurches forward.

If new activities are demanding for adults, think about the challenges infants face. **Infants must learn** *locomotion,* **that is, to move about in the world.** Newborns are relatively immobile, but infants soon learn to crawl, stand, and walk. Learning to move through the environment upright leaves the arms and hands free. Taking full advantage of this arrangement, the human hand has fully independent fingers

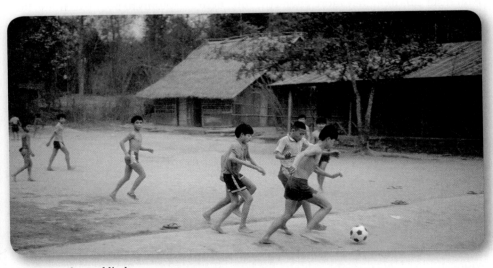

Motor skills involve coordinating movements of muscles and limbs.

(instead of a paw), with the thumb opposing the remaining four fingers. An opposable thumb makes it possible for humans to grasp and manipulate objects. **Infants must learn the** *fine-motor skills* **associated with grasping, holding, and manipulating objects.** In the case of feeding, for example, infants progress from being fed by others to holding a bottle, to feeding themselves with their fingers, to eating with a spoon. Each new skill requires incredibly complex physical movements.

Although demanding, locomotion and fine-motor skills are well worth mastering because of their benefits. Being able to locomote and to grasp gives children access to an enormous amount of information about their environment. They can explore objects that look interesting, and they can keep themselves close to parents. Improved motor skills promote children's cognitive and social development, not to mention make a child's life more interesting!

In this module, we'll see how children acquire locomotor and fine-motor skills. As we do, we'll find out if Nancy's dad should be worrying about her lack of interest in walking.

Locomotion

In little more than a year, advances in posture and locomotion change the newborn from an almost motionless being into an upright, standing individual who walks through the environment. Figure 5-9 shows some of the important milestones in motor development and the age by which most infants achieve them. By about 4 months, most babies can sit upright with support. By 6 or 7 months, they can sit without support, and by 7 or 8 months, they can stand if they hold on to an object for support. A typical 11-month-old can stand alone briefly and walk with assistance. **Youngsters at this age are called** *toddlers,* **after the toddling manner of early walking.** Of course, not all children walk at exactly the same age. Some walk before their first birthday;

FIGURE 5-9

others, like Nancy, the world-class crawler in the module-opening vignette, take their first steps as late as 17 or 18 months of age. By 24 months, most children can climb steps, walk backwards, and kick a ball.

Researchers once thought that these developmental milestones reflected maturation (e.g., McGraw, 1935). Walking, for example, was thought to emerge naturally when the necessary muscles and neural circuits matured. Today, however, locomotion—and, in fact, all motor development—is viewed from a new perspective. **According to** *dynamic systems theory,* **motor development involves many distinct skills that are organized and reorganized over time to meet the demands of specific tasks.** For example, walking includes maintaining balance, moving limbs, perceiving the environment, and having a reason to move. Only by understanding each of these skills and how they are combined to allow movement in a specific situation can we understand walking (Thelen & Smith, 1998).

In the remainder of this section, we'll see how learning to walk reflects the maturity and coalescence of many component skills.

POSTURE AND BALANCE. The ability to maintain an upright posture is fundamental to walking. But upright posture is virtually impossible for young infants because the shape of their body makes them top-heavy. Consequently, as soon as a young infant starts to lose her balance, she tumbles over. Only with growth of the legs and muscles can infants maintain an upright posture (Thelen, Ulrich, & Jensen, 1989).

> To walk, infants must master and coordinate many distinct skills, such as maintaining posture and balance.

Once infants can stand upright, they must continuously adjust their posture to avoid falling down (Metcalfe et al., 2005). By a few months after birth, infants begin to use visual cues and an inner-ear mechanism to adjust their posture. To show the use of visual cues for balance, researchers had babies sit in a room with striped walls that moved. When adults sit in such a room, they perceive themselves as moving (not the walls) and adjust their posture accordingly; so do infants, which shows that they use vision to maintain upright posture (Bertenthal & Clifton, 1998). In addition, when 4-month-olds who are propped in a sitting position lose their balance, they try to keep their head upright. They do this even when blindfolded, which means they are using cues from their inner ear to maintain balance (Woollacott, Shumway-Cook, & Williams, 1989).

Balance is not, however, something that infants master just once. Instead, infants must relearn balancing for sitting, crawling, walking, and other postures. Why? The body rotates around different points in each posture (e.g., the wrists for crawling versus the ankles for walking), and different muscle groups are used to generate compensating motions when infants begin to lose their balance. Consequently, it's hardly surprising that infants who easily maintain their balance while sitting topple over time after time when crawling. Once they walk, infants must adjust their posture further when they carry objects because these affect balance (Garciaguirre, Adolph, & Shrout, 2007). Infants must recalibrate the balance system as they take on each new posture, just as basketball players recalibrate their muscle movements when they move from dunking to shooting a three-pointer (Adolph, 2000, 2002).

STEPPING. Another essential element of walking is moving the legs alternately, repeatedly transferring the weight of the body from one foot to the other. Children don't step spontaneously until approximately 10 months, because they must be able to stand upright to step.

Can younger children step if they are held upright? Thelen and Ulrich (1991) devised a clever procedure to answer this question. Infants were placed on a treadmill and held upright by an adult. When the belt on the treadmill started to move, infants could respond in one of several ways. They might simply let both legs be dragged rearward by the belt. Or they might let their legs be dragged briefly, then move them forward together in a hopping motion. Many 6- and 7-month-olds demonstrated the mature pattern of alternating steps on each leg that is shown in the photo. Even more amazing is that when the treadmill was equipped with separate belts for each leg that moved at different speeds, babies adjusted, stepping more rapidly on the faster belt. Apparently, the alternate stepping motion that is essential for walking is evident long before infants walk independently. Walking unassisted is not possible, though, until other component skills are mastered.

ENVIRONMENTAL CUES. Many infants learn to walk in the relative security of flat, uncluttered floors at home. But they soon discover that the environment offers a variety of surfaces, some more conducive to walking than others. Infants use cues in the environment to judge whether a surface is suitable for walking. For example, they are more likely to cross a bridge when it's wide and has a rigid handrail than when it is narrow and has a wobbly handrail (Berger, Adolph, & Lobo, 2005). If they can't decide whether a surface is safe, they depend on an adult's advice (Tamis-LeMonda et al., 2008). Results like these show that infants use perceptual cues to decide whether a surface is safe for walking.

COORDINATING SKILLS. Dynamic systems theory emphasizes that learning to walk demands orchestration of many individual skills. Each component skill must first be mastered alone and then integrated with the other skills (Werner, 1948). **That is, mastery of intricate motions requires both** *differentiation*—**mastery of component skills—and their** *integration*—**combining them in proper sequence into a coherent, working whole.** In the case of walking, not until 9 to 15 months of age has the child mastered the component skills so that they can be coordinated to allow independent, unsupported walking.

Mastering individual skills and coordinating them well does not happen overnight. Instead, each takes time and repeated practice. For example, with concentrated practice, toddlers learn to change their stride to walk more slowly down steep slopes (Gill, Adolph, & Vereijken, 2009). However, improvements are limited to the movements that were trained. For example, when infants practice crawling on steep slopes, there is no transfer to walking on steep slopes, because the motions differ (Adolph, 1997). Thus, just as daily practice in kicking a soccer ball won't improve your golf game, infants who receive much practice in one motor skill don't usually improve in others.

These findings from laboratory research are not the only evidence that practice promotes motor development. As you'll see in the "Cultural Influences" feature, cross-cultural research points to the same conclusion.

Young babies step reflexively when they are held upright and moved forward.

Cultural Influences

Cultural Practices That Influence Motor Development

In Europe and North America, most infants typically walk alone near their first birthday. But infants in other cultures often begin to walk (and reach other milestones listed on page 159) at an earlier age because child-care customs allow children to

In many African cultures, infants are routinely carried piggyback style, which strengthens the infants' legs, allowing them to walk at a younger age.

practice their emerging motor skills. For example, in some traditional African cultures, infants sit and walk at younger ages. Why? Infants are commonly carried by their parents in the "piggyback" style shown in the photo, which helps develop muscles in the infants' trunk and legs.

Some cultures even take a further step. They believe that practice is essential for motor skills to develop normally and so parents (or siblings) provide daily training sessions. For example, the Kipsigis of Kenya help children learn to sit by having them sit while propped up (Super, 1981). Among the West Indians of Jamaica, mothers have an elaborate exercise routine that allows babies to practice walking (Hopkins & Westra, 1988). This training provides additional opportunities for children to learn the elements of different motor skills, and, not surprisingly, infants with these opportunities learn to sit and walk earlier.

You may be surprised that some cultures do just the opposite: They have practices that discourage motor development. The Ache, an indigenous group in Paraguay, protect infants and toddlers from harm by carrying them constantly (Kaplan & Dove, 1987). In Chinese cities, parents often allow their children to crawl only on a bed surrounded by pillows, in part because they don't want their children crawling on a dirty floor (Campos et al., 2000). In both cases, infants reach motor milestones a few months later than the ages listed on page 159.

Even European and North American infants are crawling at older ages today than they did in previous generations (Dewey et al., 1998). This generational difference reflects the effectiveness of the "Back to Sleep" campaign described on page 101. Because today's babies spend less time on their tummies, they have fewer opportunities to discover that they can propel themselves by creeping, which would otherwise prepare them for crawling.

Thus, cultural practices can accelerate or delay the early stages of motor development, depending on the nature of practice that infants and toddlers receive. In the long run, however, the age of mastering various motor milestones is not critical for children's development. All healthy children learn to walk, and whether this happens a few months before or after the "typical" ages shown on page 159 has no bearing on children's later development.

BEYOND WALKING. If you can recall the feeling of freedom that accompanied your first driver's license, you can imagine how the world expands for infants and toddlers as they learn to move independently. The first tentative steps soon are followed by others that are more skilled. With more experience, infants take longer, straighter steps. Like adults, they begin to swing their arms, rotating the left arm forward as the right leg moves, then repeating with the right arm and left leg (Ledebt, 2000; Ledebt, van Wieringen, & Savelsbergh, 2004). Children's growing skill is evident in their running and hopping. Most 2-year-olds have a hurried walk instead of a true run; they move their legs stiffly (rather than bending them at the knees) and are not airborne as is the case when running. By 5 or 6 years, children run easily, quickly changing directions or speed. Similarly, an average 2- or 3-year-old will hop a few times on one foot, typically keeping the upper body very stiff; by age 5 or 6, children can hop long distances on one foot or alternate hopping first on one foot a few times, then on the other.

Fine-Motor Skills

A major accomplishment in infancy is skilled use of the hands (Bertenthal & Clifton, 1998). Newborns have little apparent control of their hands, but 1-year-olds are extraordinarily talented.

REACHING AND GRASPING. At about 4 months, infants can successfully reach for objects (Bertenthal & Clifton, 1998). These early reaches often look clumsy, and for a good reason. When infants reach, their arms and hands don't move directly and smoothly to the desired object (as is true for older children and adults). Instead, the infant's hand moves like a ship under the direction of an unskilled navigator. It moves a short distance, slows, then moves again in a slightly different direction, a process that's repeated until the hand finally contacts the object (McCarty & Ashmead, 1999). As infants grow, their reaches have fewer movements, though they are still not as continuous and smooth as older children's and adults' reaches (Berthier, 1996).

A typical 4-month-old grasps an object with fingers alone.

Reaching requires that an infant move the hand to the location of a desired object. Grasping poses a different challenge: Now the infant must coordinate movements of individual fingers in order to grab an object. Grasping, too, becomes more efficient during infancy. Most 4-month-olds just use their fingers to hold objects. Like the baby in the photo, they wrap an object tightly with their fingers alone. Not until 7 or 8 months do most infants use their thumbs to hold objects (Siddiqui, 1995). At about this age, infants begin to position their hands to make it easier to grasp an object. In trying to grasp a long, thin rod, for example, infants place their fingers perpendicular to the rod, which is the best position for grasping (Wentworth, Benson, & Haith, 2000). And they reach more slowly for smaller objects that require a more precise grip (Zaal & Thelen, 2005). Infants need not see their hand to position it correctly: They position the hand just as accurately in reaching for a lighted object in a darkened room as when reaching in a lighted room (McCarty et al., 2001).

Infants' growing control of each hand is accompanied by greater coordination of the two hands. Although 4-month-olds use both hands, their motions are not coordinated; rather, each hand seems to have a mind of its own. Infants may hold a toy motionless in one hand while shaking a rattle in the other. At roughly 5 to 6 months of age, infants can coordinate the motions of their hands so that each hand performs different actions that serve a common goal. So a child might, for example, hold a toy animal in one hand and pet it with the other (Karniol, 1989). These skills continue to improve after children's first birthday: 1-year-olds reach for most objects with one hand; by 2 years, they reach with one or two hands, as appropriate, depending on the size of the object (van Hof, van der Kamp, & Savelsbergh, 2002).

By age 5, fine-motor skills are developed to the point that most youngsters can dress themselves.

These many changes in reaching and grasping are well illustrated as infants learn to feed themselves. At about 6 months, they are often given "finger foods" such as sliced bananas and green beans. Infants can easily pick up such foods, but getting them into the mouth is another story. The hand grasping the food may be raised to the cheek, then moved to the edge of the lips, and finally shoved into the mouth. Mission accomplished—but only with many detours along the way! Eye–hand coordination improves rapidly, so before long foods that vary in size, shape, and texture reach the mouth directly.

At about the first birthday, youngsters are usually ready to try eating with a spoon. At first, they simply play with the spoon, dipping it in and out of a dish filled with food or sucking on an empty spoon. With a little help, they learn to fill the spoon with food and place it in the mouth, though the motion is awkward because they don't rotate the wrist. Instead, most 1-year-olds fill a spoon by placing it directly over a dish and lowering it until the bowl of the spoon is full. Then, they raise the spoon to the mouth, all the while keeping the wrist rigid. In contrast, 2-year-olds rotate the hand at the wrist while scooping food from a dish and placing the spoon in the mouth—the same motion that adults use.

After infancy, fine-motor skills progress rapidly. Preschool children become much more dexterous, able to make many precise and delicate movements with their hands and fingers. Greater fine-motor skill means that preschool children can begin to care for themselves. No longer must they rely primarily on parents to feed and clothe them; instead, they become increasingly skilled at feeding and dressing themselves. A 2- or 3-year-old, for example, can put on some simple clothing and use zippers but not buttons; by 3 or 4 years, children can fasten buttons and take off their clothes when going to the bathroom; like the child in the top photo, most 5-year-olds can dress and undress themselves, except for tying shoes, which children typically master at about age 6.

In each of these actions, the same principles of dynamic systems theory apply as seen in our earlier discussion about locomotion. Complex acts involve many component movements. Each must be performed correctly and in the proper sequence. Development involves first mastering the separate elements and then assembling them to form a smoothly functioning whole. Eating finger food, for example, requires grasping food, moving the hand to the mouth, then releasing the food.

As the demands of tasks change and as children develop, the same skills are often reassembled to form a different sequence of movements.

Most toddlers use the left hand to hold an object steady and the right hand to explore the object.

HANDEDNESS. When young babies reach for objects, they don't seem to prefer one hand over the other; they use their left and right hands interchangeably. They may shake a rattle with their left hand and moments later pick up blocks with their right. By the first birthday, most youngsters are emergent right-handers. Like the toddler in the bottom photo, they use the left hand to steady the toy while the right hand manipulates the object. This early preference for one hand becomes stronger and more consistent during the preschool years and is well established by kindergarten (Marschik et al., 2008; Rönnqvist & Domellöff, 2006).

What determines whether children become left- or right-handed? Some scientists believe that a gene biases children toward right-handedness (Annett,

2008). Consistent with this idea, identical twins are more likely than fraternal twins to have the same handedness—both are right-handed or both are left-handed (Sicotte, Woods, & Mazziotta, 1999). But experience also contributes to handedness. Modern industrial cultures favor right-handedness. School desks, scissors, and can openers, for example, are designed for right-handed people and can be used by left-handers only with difficulty. In the United States, elementary-school teachers used to urge left-handed children to use their right hands. As this practice has diminished, the percentage of left-handed children has risen steadily (Levy, 1976). Thus, handedness seems to have both hereditary and environmental influences.

Physical Fitness

Using one's motor skills—that is, being active physically—has many benefits for children. It promotes growth of muscles and bone, cardiovascular health, and cognitive processes (Best, 2010; Hillman et al., 2009; National High Blood Pressure Education Program Working Group, 1996), and can help to establish a lifelong pattern of exercise (Perkins et al., 2004). Individuals who exercise regularly—30 minutes, at least 3 times a week—reduce their risk for obesity, cancer, heart disease, diabetes, and psychological disorders, including depression and anxiety (Tomson et al., 2003). Running, vigorous walking, swimming, aerobic dancing, biking, and cross-country skiing are all examples of activities that can provide this level of intensity.

Unfortunately, when children are tested with a full battery of fitness tests, such as the mile run, pull-ups, and sit-ups, fewer than half usually meet standards for fitness on all tasks (Morrow, 2005). No doubt you'll remember, from Module 4.2, the U.S. Surgeon General's pronouncement that obesity has reached epidemic proportions among American children and adolescents (U.S. Department of Health and Human Services, 2001).

Many factors contribute to low levels of fitness. In most schools, physical education classes meet only once or twice a week and are usually not required of high-school students (Johnston, Delva, & O'Malley, 2007). Even when students are in these classes, they spend a surprisingly large proportion of time—nearly half—standing around instead of exercising (Lowry et al., 2001; Parcel et al., 1989). Television and other sedentary leisure-time activities may contribute, too. Youth who spend much time online or watching TV often tend to be less fit physically (Lobelo et al., 2009), but the nature of this relation remains poorly understood: Children glued to a TV or computer screen likely have fewer opportunities to exercise, but it might be that children in poor physical condition chose sedentary activities over exercise.

Many experts believe that U.S. schools should offer physical education more frequently each week. And many suggest that physical education classes should offer a range of activities in which all children can participate and that can be the foundation for a lifelong program of fitness (National Association for Sport and Physical Fitness, 2004). Thus, instead of emphasizing team sports such as touch football, physical education classes should emphasize activities like running, walking, racquet sports, and swimming; these can be done throughout adolescence and adulthood, either alone or with another person. Families can encourage fitness, too. Instead of spending an afternoon watching TV and eating popcorn, they can, go biking together.

 QUESTION 5.3
Jenny and Ian are both left-handed and they fully expected their son, Tyler, to prefer his left hand, too. But he's 8 months old already and seems to use both hands to grasp toys and other objects. Should Jenny and Ian give up their dream of being the three left-handed musketeers?
(Answer is on page 167.)

Participating in sports can enhance children's physical, motor, cognitive, and social development.

When adult coaches emphasize winning or frequently criticize players, many children lose interest and quit.

PARTICIPATING IN SPORTS. Many children and adolescents get exercise by participating in team sports, including baseball, softball, basketball, and soccer. Obviously, when children such as the girls in the top photo play sports, they get exercise and improve their motor skills. But there are other benefits, too. Sports can enhance participants' self-esteem and can help them to learn initiative (Bowker, 2006; Donaldson & Ronan, 2006). Sports can also give children a chance to learn important social skills, such as how to work effectively as part of a group, often in complementary roles. Finally, playing sports allows children to use their emerging cognitive skills as they devise new playing strategies or modify the rules of a game.

These benefits of participating in sports are balanced by potential hazards. Several studies have linked youth participation in sports to delinquent and antisocial behavior (e.g., Gardner, Roth, & Brooks-Gunn, 2009). However, outcomes are usually positive when sports participation is combined with participation in activities that involve adults, such as school, religious, or youth groups (Linver, Roth, & Brooks-Gunn, 2009; Zarrett et al., 2009). Still, these potential benefits hinge on the adults who are involved. When adult coaches encourage their players and emphasize skill development, children usually enjoy playing, often improve their skills, and increase their self-esteem (Coatsworth & Conroy, 2009). In contrast, when coaches—like the man in the bottom photo—emphasize winning over skill development and criticize or punish players for bad plays, children lose interest and stop playing. When adolescents find sports too stressful, they often get "burned out": they lose interest and quit (Raedeke & Smith, 2004).

To encourage youth to participate, adults (and parents) need to have realistic expectations for children and coach positively, praising children instead of criticizing them. They need to remember that children play games for recreation, which means they should have fun!

Check Your Learning

RECALL Describe the skills that infants must master to be able to walk.

How do fine-motor skills improve with age?

INTERPRET What are the pros and cons of children and adolescents participating in organized sports?

APPLY Describe how participation in sports illustrates connections between motor, cognitive, and social development.

 ANSWER 5.3
No. At 8 months it's too early for Tyler to show a consistent preference for one hand. They need to wait; by 13 to 15 months of age they should have a much better idea of whether Tyler will be left-handed.

UNIFYING THEMES   Active Children

Each module in this chapter touched on the theme that *children influence their own development*. That is, repeatedly we saw that infants are extremely well equipped to interpret and explore their environments. In Module 5.1, we saw that most sensory systems function quite well in the first year, providing infants with accurate raw data to interpret. In Module 5.2, we learned that attentional skills originate in infancy; through habituation, infants ignore some stimuli and attend to others. Finally, in Module 5.3, we discovered that locomotor and fine-motor skills improve rapidly in infancy; by the first birthday, infants can move independently and handle objects skillfully. Collectively, these accomplishments make the infants extraordinarily well prepared to explore their world and make sense of it.

See for Yourself

To see the origins of attention, you need a baby and a small bell. A 1- to 5-month-old is probably best because babies at this age can't locomote, so they won't wander away. While the infant is awake, place it on its back. Then move behind the baby's head (out of sight) and ring the bell a few times. You don't need to ring the bell loudly—an "average" volume will do. You should see the orienting response described on page 154: The baby will open its eyes wide and perhaps try to turn in the direction of the sound. Every two or three minutes, ring the bell again. You should see the baby respond less intensely each time until, finally, it ignores the bell completely. Attention in action! See for yourself!

Summary

5.1 Basic Sensory and Perceptual Processes

Smell, Taste, and Touch
Newborns are able to smell and can recognize their mother's odor; they also taste, preferring sweet substances and responding negatively to bitter and sour tastes. Infants respond to touch. Judging from their responses to painful stimuli, which are similar to older children's, we can say they experience pain.

Hearing

Babies can hear, although they are less sensitive to high- and low-pitched sounds than are adults. Babies can distinguish different sounds (both from language and music).

Seeing

A newborn's visual acuity is relatively poor, but 1-year-olds can see as well as adults with normal vision. Color vision develops as different sets of cones begin to function; by 3 or 4 months, children can see color as well as adults can.

Integrating Sensory Information

Infants begin to integrate information from different senses (e.g., sight and sound, sight and touch). Infants are often particularly attentive to information presented redundantly to multiple senses.

5.2 Complex Perceptual and Attentional Processes

Perceiving Objects

Infants use motion, color, texture, and edges to distinguish objects. By about 4 months, infants have begun to master size, brightness, shape, and color constancy. Infants first perceive depth by means of kinetic cues, including visual expansion and motion parallax. Later, they use retinal disparity and pictorial cues (linear perspective, texture gradient, relative size, interposition) to judge depth. Infants perceive faces early in the first year. Experience leads infants to fine-tune their facial template so that it resembles the faces they see most often.

Attention

Attention helps select information for further processing. Infants orient to a novel stimulus, but as it becomes more familiar, they habituate, meaning that they respond less. Compared to older children, preschoolers are less able to pay attention to a task. Younger children's attention can be improved by getting rid of irrelevant stimuli.

Attention Deficit Hyperactivity Disorder

Children with ADHD are typically inattentive, hyperactive, and impulsive. They sometimes have conduct problems and do poorly in school. According to the Multimodal Treatment Study of Children with ADHD, in the short term the most effective approach to ADHD combines medication with psychosocial treatment.

5.3 Motor Development

Locomotion

Infants progress through a sequence of motor milestones during the first year, culminating in walking a few months after the first birthday. Like most motor skills, learning to walk involves differentiation of individual skills, such as maintaining balance and stepping on alternate legs, and then integrating these skills into a coherent whole. This differentiation and integration of skills is central to the dynamic systems theory of motor development. Experience can accelerate specific motor skills.

Fine-Motor Skills

Infants first use only one hand at a time, then both hands independently, then both hands in common actions, and, finally, both hands in different actions with a common purpose.

Most people are right-handed, a preference that emerges after the first birthday and that becomes well established during the preschool years. Handedness is determined by heredity but can be influenced by experience and cultural values.

Physical Fitness

Although children report spending much time being physically active, in fact, fewer than half of American school children meet all standards for physical fitness. Part of the explanation for the lack of fitness is inadequate physical education in school. Television may also contribute. Experts recommend that physical education in the schools be more frequent and more oriented toward developing patterns of lifetime exercise. Families can become more active, thereby encouraging children's fitness.

Participating in sports can promote motor, cognitive, and social development. But participation in sports sometimes leads to antisocial behavior, and children sometimes quit playing when coaches emphasize winning over skill development.

Test Yourself

✓—[Study and **Review** on mydevelopmentlab.com

1. Newborns prefer _____-tasting substances.

2. Infants can best hear sounds pitched _____.

3. If an infant does not respond to his or her name by _____ months, this may be a sign of hearing impairment.

4. By three or four months of age, infants' color perception is similar to that of adults, including the

fact that infants see the spectrum as representing different _____ of color.

5. According to _____, infants are particularly sensitive to amodal information that is presented in more than one sensory system simultaneously.

6. Infants use many cues to object unity, including common motion, color, _____, and aligned edges.

7. Infants use kinetic cues to judge depth, including visual expansion and _____.

8. Between 3 and 9 months of age, face processing becomes more finely tuned, which explains why 3-month-olds have better recognition of _____.

9. When infants encounter an unfamiliar stimulus, they often show a(n) _____ in which they startle, they stare at the stimulus, and their heart rate changes.

10. The three defining symptoms of attention deficit hyperactivity disorder include hyperactivity, inattention, and _____.

11. Maintaining an upright posture is particularly challenging for infants because their body _____.

12. _____ refers to breaking down a complex motor skill into its component parts.

13. Four-month-olds use both hands to explore an object, but the two hands _____.

14. By their _____ birthday, most children show a preference for one hand over the other (and for most of them, it's the right hand).

15. Children and adolescents often drop out of organized sports when _____.

Answers: (1) sweet; (2) in the range of human voices; (3) 8 or 9; (4) categories; (5) intersensory redundancy theory; (6) texture; (7) motion parallax; (8) faces of nonhuman mammals and faces from other races; (9) orienting response; (10) impulsivity; (11) shape makes them top-heavy; (12) Differentiation; (13) aren't well coordinated; each acts as if it has a mind of its own; (14) first; (15) coaches emphasize winning over skill development and participation.

Key Terms

amodal 145
attention 154
auditory threshold 141
cones 143
differentiation 161
dynamic systems theory 160
fine-motor skills 159
habituation 140
integration 161
interposition 150

intersensory redundancy theory 145
kinetic cues 149
linear perspective 150
locomotion 158
motion parallax 149
motor skills 139
orienting response 154
pictorial cues 149
relative size 150
retinal disparity 149

sensory and perceptual processes 139
size constancy 148
texture gradient 149
toddlers 159
visual acuity 143
visual cliff 148
visual expansion 149

6

Theories of Cognitive Development

Setting the Stage: Piaget's Theory

Modern Theories of Cognitive Development

Understanding in Core Domains

On the TV show *Family Guy*, Stewie is a 1-year-old who can't stand his mother (Stewie: "Hey, mother, I come bearing a gift. I'll give you a hint: It's in my diaper and it's not a toaster.") and hopes to dominate the world. Much of the humor, of course, turns on the idea that babies are capable of sophisticated thinking—they just can't express it. Of course, few adults would really attribute such advanced thinking skills to a baby. But what thoughts *do* lurk in the mind of an infant who is not yet speaking? And how do an infant's fledgling thoughts blossom into the powerful reasoning skills that older children, adolescents, and adults use daily? In other words, how does thinking change as children develop; and why do these changes take place?

For many years, the best answers to these questions came from the theory proposed by Jean Piaget that was mentioned in Module 1.2. We'll look at this theory in more detail in **Module 6.1**. In **Module 6.2**, we'll examine some of the modern theories that guide today's research on children's thinking. Finally, in **Module 6.3**, we'll see how children acquire knowledge of objects, living things, and people.

6.1 Setting the Stage: Piaget's Theory

OUTLINE

Basic Principles of Piaget's Theory

Stages of Cognitive Development

Piaget's Contributions to Child Development

LEARNING OBJECTIVES

- What are the basic principles of Piaget's theory of cognitive development?
- How does thinking change as children move through Piaget's four stages of development?
- What are the lasting contributions of Piaget's theory? What are some of its shortcomings?

When Ethan, an energetic 2½-year-old, saw a monarch butterfly for the first time, his mother, Kat, told him, "Butterfly, butterfly; that's a butterfly, Ethan." A few minutes later, a zebra swallowtail landed on a nearby bush and Ethan shouted in excitement, "Butterfly, Mama, butterfly!" A bit later, a moth flew out of another bush; with even greater excitement in his voice, Ethan shouted, "Butterfly, Mama, more butterfly!" Even as Kat was telling Ethan, "No, honey, that's a moth, not a butterfly," she marveled at how rapidly Ethan seemed to grasp new concepts with so little direction from her. How was this possible?

For much of the 20th century, scientists would have answered Kat's question by referring to Jean Piaget's theory. Piaget was trained as a biologist, but he developed a keen interest in the branch of philosophy dealing with the nature and origins of knowledge (epistemology). He decided to investigate the origins of knowledge not as philosophers had—through discussion and debate—but by doing experiments with children.

Because Piaget's theory led the way to all modern theories of cognitive development, it's a good introduction to the study of children's thinking. We'll first consider some basic principles of the theory, where we will discover why Ethan understands as quickly as he does. Then we'll look at Piaget's stages of development and end the module by examining the enduring contributions of Piaget's work to child-development science.

Basic Principles of Piaget's Theory

Piaget believed that children are naturally curious. They always want to make sense out of their experience and, in the process, construct their understanding of the world. For Piaget, children at all ages are like scientists in that they create theories about how the world works. Of course, children's theories are often incomplete, and sometimes incorrect. Nevertheless, theories are valuable to the child because they make the world seem more predictable.

In using their theories to make sense of what's going on around them, children often have new experiences that are readily understood within the context of these theories. **According to Piaget,** *assimilation* **occurs when new experiences are readily incorporated into a child's existing theories.** Imagine an infant like the one in the photo who knows that the family dog barks and often licks her in the face. When she has the same experience at a relative's house, this makes sense because it fits her simple theory of dogs. Thus, understanding the novel dog's behavior represents assimilation. But sometimes theories are incomplete or incorrect, causing children to have unexpected experiences. **For Piaget,** *accommodation* **occurs when a child's theories are modified based on experience.** The baby with a theory of dogs is surprised the first time she encounters a cat—it resembles a dog but meows instead of barks and rubs up against her instead of licking. Revising her theory to include this new kind of animal illustrates accommodation.

This infant's "theory of dogs" includes the facts that dogs are friendly and like licking people's faces.

Assimilation and accommodation are illustrated in the vignette at the beginning of the module. Piaget would say that when Kat named the monarch butterfly for Ethan, he formed a simple theory, something like "butterflies are bugs with big wings." The second butterfly differed in color but was still a bug with big wings, so it was readily assimilated into Ethan's new theory of butterflies. However, when Ethan referred to the moth as a butterfly, Kat corrected him. Presumably, Ethan was then forced to accommodate to this new experience. The result was that he changed his theory of butterflies to make it more precise; the new theory might be something like "butterflies are bugs with thin bodies and big, colorful wings." He also created a new theory, something like "a moth is a bug with a bigger body and plain wings."

In this example, assimilation and accommodation involve ideas, but they begin much earlier, in a young baby's actions. For example, a baby who can grasp a ball soon discovers that she can grasp blocks, rattles, and other small objects; extending grasping to new objects illustrates assimilation. When she discovers that some objects can't be grasped unless she uses two hands, this illustrates accommodation: Her revised "theory of grasping" now distinguishes objects that can be grasped with one hand from those that require two hands.

Assimilation and accommodation are usually in balance, or equilibrium. That is, children find they can readily assimilate most experiences into their existing theories, but occasionally they need to accommodate their theories to adjust to new experiences. This balance between assimilation and accommodation is illustrated both by the baby's theories of small animals and by Ethan's understanding of butterflies.

Periodically, however, the balance is upset and a state of disequilibrium results. Children discover that their current theories are not adequate because they are spending much more time accommodating than assimilating. **When disequilibrium occurs, children reorganize their theories to return to a state of equilibrium, a process that Piaget called** *equilibration.* To restore the balance, current but now-outmoded ways of thinking are replaced by a qualitatively different, more advanced theory.

Returning to the metaphor of the child as a scientist, sometimes scientists find that a theory contains critical flaws. When this occurs, they can't simply revise; they must create a new theory that draws upon the older theory but is fundamentally different. For example, when the astronomer Copernicus realized that the Earth-centered theory of the solar system was wrong, he retained the concept of a central object but proposed that it was the Sun, a fundamental change in the theory. In much the same way, children periodically reach a point when their current theories seem to be wrong much of the time, so they abandon these theories in favor of more advanced ways of thinking about their physical and social worlds.

> All children were said to pass through all four of Piaget's stages, but some children were thought to do so more rapidly than others.

According to Piaget, these revolutionary changes in thought occur three times over the life span, at approximately 2, 7, and 11 years of age. This divides cognitive development into four stages: the *sensorimotor stage* (birth to age 2, encompassing infancy); the *preoperational stage* (ages 2 to 6, encompassing preschool and early elementary school); the *concrete operational stage* (ages 7 to 11, encompassing middle and late elementary school); and the *formal operational stage* (ages 11 and up, encompassing adolescence and adulthood).

Piaget held that all children go through these four stages and in exactly this sequence. For example, sensorimotor thinking should always lead to preoperational thinking; a child cannot "skip" preoperational thinking and move directly from sensorimotor to concrete operational thought. However, the ages listed are only approximate: Some youngsters were thought to move through the stages more rapidly than others, depending on their ability and their experience. In the next section, we'll look more closely at each stage.

Stages of Cognitive Development

Just as you can recognize a McDonald's restaurant by the golden arches and Nike products by the swoosh, each of Piaget's stages is marked by a distinctive way of thinking about and understanding the world. In the next few pages, we'll learn about these unique trademarks or characteristics of Piaget's stages.

THE SENSORIMOTOR STAGE. We know from Chapter 5 that infants' perceptual and motor skills improve quickly during the first year. Piaget proposed that these rapidly changing perceptual and motor skills in the first two years of life form a distinct phase in human development: **The** *sensorimotor stage* **spans birth to 2 years, a period during which the infant progresses from simple reflex actions to symbolic processing.** In the 24 months of this stage, infants' thinking progresses remarkably along three important fronts. ◉─Watch the **Video** on **mydevelopmentlab.com**

ADAPTING TO AND EXPLORING THE ENVIRONMENT. Newborns respond reflexively to many stimuli, but between 1 and 4 months, reflexes are first modified by experience. An infant may inadvertently touch his lips with his thumb, which leads to sucking and the pleasing sensations associated with sucking. Later, the infant tries to recreate these sensations by guiding his thumb to his mouth. Sucking no

◉─Watch the **Video** *Sensorimotor Development* on **mydevelopmentlab .com** to learn more about Piaget's landmarks of cognitive development from birth to 2 years. After you finish Module 6.2, watch this video a second time; as you do, think about how the changes described by Piaget would be explained by modern theories of cognitive development.

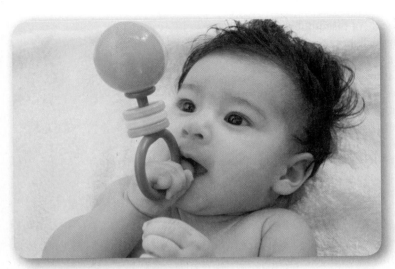

Between 4 and 8 months, infants eagerly explore new objects.

longer occurs only reflexively when a mother places a nipple at the infant's mouth; instead, the infant can initiate sucking by himself.

Between 4 and 8 months, the infant shows greater interest in the world, paying far more attention to objects. For example, the infant shown in the top photo accidentally shook a new rattle. Hearing the interesting noise, the infant grasped the rattle again, tried to shake it, and expressed great pleasure at the sound that resulted. This sequence was repeated several times.

At about 8 months of age, infants reach a watershed: the onset of deliberate, intentional behavior. For the first time, the "means" and "end" of activities are distinct. If, for example, a father places his hand in front of a toy, an infant will move his hand to be able to play with the toy. "Moving the hand" is the means to achieve the goal of "grasping the toy." Using one action as a means to achieve another end is the first indication of purposeful, goal-directed behavior during infancy.

Beginning at about 12 months, infants become active experimenters. An infant may deliberately shake a number of different objects trying to discover which produce sounds and which do not. Or an infant may decide to drop different objects to see what happens. An infant will discover that stuffed animals land quietly, whereas bigger toys often make a more satisfying "clunk" when they hit the ground. These actions represent a significant extension of intentional behavior: Now babies repeat actions with different objects solely for the purpose of seeing what will happen.

UNDERSTANDING OBJECTS. The world is filled with animate objects such as dogs, spiders, and college students, as well as inanimate objects such as cheeseburgers, socks, and this book. But they all share a fundamental property: They exist independently of our actions and thoughts concerning them. Much as we may dislike spiders, they still exist when we close our eyes or wish they would go away. **Understanding that objects exist independently is called** *object permanence.* Piaget made the astonishing claim that infants lack this understanding for much of the first year. That is, he proposed that an infant's understanding of objects could be summarized as "out of sight, out of mind." For infants, objects are fleeting, existing when in sight and no longer existing when out of sight.

According to Piaget, 8-month-olds have limited understanding of objects: They believe that when objects are out of sight, they no longer exist.

The bottom photo illustrates the sort of research that led Piaget to conclude that infants lack object permanence. If a tempting object such as an attractive toy is placed in front of a 4- to 8-month-old, the infant will probably reach for and grasp the object. If, however, the object is then hidden by a barrier, or, as in the photo, covered with a cloth, the infant will neither reach nor search. Instead, like the baby in the photo, the infant seems to lose all interest in the object, as if the now-hidden object no longer exists. Paraphrasing the familiar phrase, "out of sight, out of existence!"

Beginning at about 8 months, infants search for an object that an experimenter has covered with a cloth. In fact, many 8- to 12-month-olds love to play this game—an adult covers the object and the infant sweeps away the cover, laughing and smiling all the while! But, despite this accomplishment, Piaget believed that their understanding of object permanence is incomplete. At this age, when infants see an object hidden under one container several times, then see it hidden under a second container, they usually look for the toy under the first container. This fascinating phenomenon is known as the "A not B error" (because babies reach for an object at the first location, A, not the second location, B), and Piaget claimed that it shows infants' limited understanding of objects: Infants do not distinguish the object from the actions they use to locate it, such as reaching for a particular container. In fact, according to Piaget, infants do not have full understanding of object permanence until about 18 months of age.

USING SYMBOLS. By 18 months, most infants have begun to talk and gesture, evidence of the emerging capacity to use symbols. Words and gestures are symbols that stand for something else. When the baby in the photo waves, this is just as effective and symbolic as saying "goodbye" to bid farewell. Children also begin to engage in pretend play, another use of symbols. A 20-month-old may move her hand back and forth in front of her mouth, pretending to brush her teeth.

Once infants can use symbols, they begin to anticipate the consequences of actions mentally instead of having to perform them. Imagine that an infant and parent construct a tower of blocks next to an open door. Leaving the room, a 12- to 18-month-old might close the door, knocking over the tower, because he cannot foresee the outcome of closing the door. But an 18- to 24-month-old can anticipate the consequence of closing the door and move the tower beforehand.

In just 2 years, the infant progresses from reflexive responding to actively exploring the world, understanding objects, and using symbols. These achievements are remarkable and set the stage for preoperational thinking, which we'll examine next.

By 18 months of age, most toddlers will use simple gestures, which is evidence of their emerging ability to use symbols.

THE PREOPERATIONAL STAGE. With the magic power of symbols, the child crosses the hurdle into preoperational thinking. The *preoperational stage,* **which spans ages 2 to 7, is marked by the child's use of symbols to represent objects and events.** Throughout this period, preschool children gradually become proficient at using common symbols, such as words, gestures, graphs, maps, and models. Although preschool children's ability to use symbols represents a huge advance over sensorimotor thinking, their thinking remains quite limited compared to that of school-age children. Why? To answer this question, we need to look at some important characteristics of thought during the preoperational stage.

Preoperational children typically believe that others see the world—both literally and figuratively—exactly as they do. *Egocentrism* **refers to young children's difficulty in seeing the world from another's viewpoint.** When youngsters stubbornly cling to their own way, they are not simply being contrary. Instead, preoperational children do not comprehend that other people have different ideas and feelings. ◉─Watch the Video on **mydevelopmentlab.com**

Suppose, for example, you ask the preschooler in Figure 6-1 on page 176 to select the image that shows how the objects on the table look to you. Most will select the drawing on the far left, which shows how the objects look to the child, rather than the drawing on the far right—the correct choice. Preoperational youngsters evidently suppose that the mountains are seen the same way by all; they presume that theirs is the only view, rather than one of many conceivable views (Piaget & Inhelder, 1956).

Preoperational children are egocentric—they have difficult seeing another person's viewpoint.

◉─Watch the Video *Egocentrism Task* on **mydevelopmentlab.com** to learn more about a preschool child's egocentrism; the child believes that others see the objects on a table just as he sees them. In contrast, an older, concrete operational child knows that others see the objects from their own perspective.

FIGURE 6-1

Egocentrism sometimes leads preoperational youngsters to attribute their own thoughts and feelings to others. **Preoperational children sometimes credit inanimate objects with life and lifelike properties, a phenomenon known as** *animism* (Piaget, 1929). A rainy-day conversation that I had with Christine, a 3½-year-old, illustrates preoperational animism.

> CHRISTINE: The sun is sad today.
>
> RK: Why?
>
> CHRISTINE: Because it's cloudy. He can't shine. And he can't see me!
>
> RK: What about your trike? Is it happy?
>
> CHRISTINE: No. He's sad, too.
>
> RK: Why is that?
>
> CHRISTINE: 'Cause I can't ride him. And because he's all alone in the garage.

Caught up in her egocentrism, Christine believes that objects like the sun and her tricycle think and feel as she does.

Children in the preoperational stage also have the psychological equivalent of tunnel vision: They often concentrate on one aspect of a problem but totally ignore other, equally relevant aspects. *Centration* **is Piaget's term for this narrowly focused thought that characterizes preoperational youngsters.** Piaget demonstrated centration in his experiments involving conservation, which tested when children realize that important properties of objects (or sets of objects) stay the same despite changes in their physical appearance.

A typical conservation problem, involving conservation of liquid quantity, is shown in the photos. Children are shown identical glasses filled with the same amount of juice. After children agree that the two glasses have the same amount, juice is poured from one glass into a taller, thinner glass. The juice looks different in the tall, thin glass—it rises higher—but of course the amount is unchanged.

In the conservation task, preoperational children believe that the tall, thin glass has more liquid, an error reflecting the centered thought that is common in children at this stage.

Nevertheless, preoperational children claim that the tall, thin glass has more juice than the original glass. (And, if the juice is poured into a wider glass, they believe it has less.)

What is happening here? According to Piaget, preoperational children center on the level of the juice in the glass. If the juice is higher after it is poured, preoperational children believe that there must be more juice now than before. Because preoperational thinking is centered, these youngsters ignore the fact that the change in the level of the juice is always accompanied by a change in the diameter of the glass.

Centration and egocentrism are major limits to preoperational children's thinking, but these are overcome in the next stage, the concrete operational stage.

THE CONCRETE OPERATIONAL STAGE. During the early elementary-school years, children enter a new stage of cognitive development that is distinctly more adultlike and much less childlike. **In the** *concrete operational stage,* **which spans ages 7 to 11, children first use mental operations to solve problems and to reason.** What are the mental operations that are so essential to concrete operational thinking? *Mental operations* **are strategies and rules that make thinking more systematic and more powerful.** Some mental operations apply to numbers. For example, addition, subtraction, multiplication, and division are familiar arithmetic operations that concrete operational children use. Other mental operations apply to categories of objects. For example, classes can be added (mothers + fathers = parents) and subtracted (parents − mothers = fathers). Still other mental operations apply to spatial relations among objects. For example, if point A is near points B and C, then points B and C must be close to each other.

Another important property of mental operations is that they can be reversed. Each operation has an inverse that can "undo" or reverse the effect of an operation. If you start with 5 and add 3, you get 8; by subtracting 3 from 8, you reverse your steps and return to 5. For Piaget, reversibility of this sort applied to all mental operations. Concrete operational children are able to reverse their thinking in a way that preoperational youngsters cannot. In fact, reversible mental operations explain why concrete operational children pass the conservation task shown on page 176: Concrete operational thinkers understand that if the transformation were reversed (for example, the juice was poured back into the original container), the quantities would be identical. **Watch** the **Video** on **mydevelopmentlab.com**

Concrete operational thinking is much more powerful than preoperational thinking. Remember that preoperational children are egocentric (believing that others see the world as they do) and centered in their thinking; neither of these limitations applies to children in the concrete operational stage. But concrete operational thinking has its own limits. As the name implies, concrete operational thinking is limited to the tangible and real, to the here and now. The concrete operational youngster takes "an earth-bound, concrete, practical-minded sort of problem-solving approach, one that persistently fixates on the perceptible and inferable reality right there in front of him" (Flavell, 1985, p. 98). That is, thinking abstractly and hypothetically is beyond the ability of concrete operational thinkers.

THE FORMAL OPERATIONAL STAGE. In the *formal operational stage,* **which extends from roughly age 11 into adulthood, children and adolescents apply mental operations to abstract entities; they think hypothetically and reason deductively.** Freed from the concrete and the real, adolescents explore the possible—what might be and what could be.

Q&A QUESTION 6.1
When 3-year-old Jamila talks on the phone, she often answers questions by nodding her head. Jamila's dad has explained that her listeners can't see her—that she needs to say "yes" or "no." But Jamila invariably returns to head-nodding. How would Jean Piaget explain this behavior to Jamila's dad? *(Answer is on page 181.)*

(Answer is on page 181.)

Watch the **Video** *Conservation Tasks* on **mydevelopmentlab.com** to learn more about conservation. Be sure to listen to children's explanations for their answers, because these reveal the nature of their understanding. (By the way, this video is taken from a film that I used when I first taught child development in 1975. The video looks dated, but today's children respond to conservation problems in the same way that children did 35 years ago!)

Concrete-operational thinking is limited to the tangible and real, to the here and now.

Unlike reality-oriented concrete operational children, formal operational thinkers understand that reality is not the only possibility. They can envision alternative realities and examine the consequences of those propositions. For example, ask a concrete operational child, "What would happen if gravity meant that objects floated up?" or "What would happen if men gave birth?" and you're likely to get a confused or even irritated look and comments like "It doesn't—they fall" or "They don't—women have babies." Reality is the foundation of concrete operational thinking. In contrast, formal operational adolescents use hypothetical reasoning to probe the implications of fundamental change in physical or biological laws.

Formal operations also allow adolescents to take a different, more sophisticated approach to problem solving. Formal operational thinkers can solve problems by creating hypotheses (sets of possibilities) and testing them. Piaget (Inhelder & Piaget, 1958) showed this aspect of adolescent thinking by presenting children and adolescents with several flasks, each containing what appeared to be the same clear liquid. They were told that one combination of the clear liquids would produce a blue liquid and were asked to determine the necessary combination.

Children in the concrete operational stage often solve problems by "plunging right in" instead of thinking hypothetically to come up with a well-defined set of solutions to a problem.

A typical concrete operational youngster, like the ones in the photo, plunges right in, mixing liquids from different flasks haphazardly. In contrast, formal operational adolescents understand that the key is setting up the problem in abstract, hypothetical terms. The problem is not really about pouring liquids but about systematically forming hypotheses about different combinations of liquids and testing them systematically. A teenager might mix liquid from the first flask with liquids from each of the other flasks. If none of these combinations produces a blue liquid, he or she would mix the liquid in the second flask with each of the remaining liquids. A formal operational thinker would continue in this manner until he or she found the critical pair that produced the blue liquid.

Because adolescents' thinking is not concerned solely with reality, they are also better able to reason logically from premises and draw appropriate conclusions. **The ability to draw appropriate conclusions from facts is known as** *deductive reasoning.* Suppose we tell a person the following two facts:

1. If you hit a glass with a hammer, the glass will break.
2. Don hit a glass with a hammer.

The correct conclusion is that "the glass broke," a conclusion that formal operational adolescents will reach. Concrete operational youngsters, too, will sometimes reach this conclusion, but based on their experience and not because the conclusion is logically necessary. To see the difference, imagine that the two facts are now:

1. If you hit a glass with a feather, the glass will break.
2. Don hit a glass with a feather.

The conclusion "the glass broke" follows from these two statements just as logically as it did from the first pair. In this instance, however, the conclusion is counterfactual—it goes against what experience tells us is really true. Concrete operational 10-year-olds resist reaching conclusions that are counter to known facts; they reach conclusions based on their knowledge of the world. In contrast, formal operational 15-year-olds often reach counterfactual conclusions. They understand that these problems are about abstract entities that need not correspond to real-world relations.

Hypothetical reasoning and deductive reasoning are powerful tools for formal operational thinkers. In fact, we can characterize this power by paraphrasing the quotation about concrete operational thinking that appears on page 177: "Formal operational youth take an abstract, hypothetical approach to problem solving; they are not constrained by the reality that is staring them in the face but are open to different possibilities and alternatives." The ability to ponder different alternatives makes possible the experimentation with lifestyles and values that occurs in adolescence, topics we'll encounter on several occasions later in this book. ⊙—|Watch the **Video** on **mydevelopmentlab.com**

With the achievement of formal operations, cognitive development is over in Piaget's theory. Adolescents and adults acquire more knowledge as they grow older, but their fundamental way of thinking remains unchanged, in Piaget's view. Table 6-1 summarizes Piaget's description of cognitive changes between birth and adulthood.

⊙—|**Watch** the **Video** *Deductive Reasoning* on **mydevelopmentlab.com**. The video shows a concrete operational child and a formal operational adolescent solving the "if a feather hits a glass" problem. As you watch the video, notice how the concrete operational child clings to reality; in contrast, the formal operational adolescent follows the rule, even knowing that it does not match her knowledge of feathers and glass.

TABLE 6-1

PIAGET'S FOUR STAGES OF COGNITIVE DEVELOPMENT

Stage	Approximate Age	Characteristics
Sensorimotor	Birth to 2 years	Infant's knowledge of the world is based on senses and motor skills. By the end of the period, infant uses mental representations and understands object permanence.
Preoperational	2 to 6 years	Child learns how to use symbols such as words and numbers to represent aspects of the world, but relates to the world only through his or her own perspective. Thinking is centered.
Concrete operational	7 to 11 years	Child understands and applies logical operations to experiences, provided they are focused on the here and now.
Formal operational	Adolescence and beyond	Adolescent or adult thinks abstractly, speculates on hypothetical situations, and reasons deductively about what may be possible.

Piaget's Contributions to Child Development

Piaget's theory dominated child-development research and theory for much of the 20th century. As one expert phrased it, "many of Piaget's contributions have become so much a part of the way we view cognitive development nowadays that they are virtually invisible" (Flavell, 1996, p. 202). Three of these contributions are worth emphasizing (Brainerd, 1996; Siegler & Ellis, 1996):

- *The study of cognitive development itself.* Before Piaget, cognition was not part of the research agenda for child-development scientists. Piaget showed why cognitive processes are central to development and offered some methods that could be used to study them.

- *A new view of children.* Piaget emphasized *constructivism,* **the view that children are active participants in their own development who systematically construct ever-more sophisticated understandings of their worlds.** This view now pervades thinking about children (so much so that it's one of the themes in this book), but it began with Piaget.

- *Fascinating, often counterintuitive discoveries.* One reason why Piaget's work attracted so much attention is that many of the findings were completely unexpected and became puzzles that child-development researchers couldn't resist trying to solve. For example, researchers have tested thousands of youngsters trying to understand the "A not B" error (page 175) and why children fail the conservation task (page 176). In the words of one expert, "Piaget had the greenest thumb ever for unearthing fascinating and significant developmental progressions" (Flavell, 1996, p. 202).

TEACHING PRACTICES THAT FOSTER COGNITIVE GROWTH: EDUCATIONAL APPLICATIONS OF PIAGET'S THEORY. Piaget's contributions extend beyond research. In fact, his view of cognitive development helps to identify teaching practices that promote cognitive growth:

- *Facilitate rather than direct children's learning.* Cognitive growth occurs as children construct their own understanding of the world, so the teacher's role is to create environments where children can discover for themselves how the world works. A teacher shouldn't simply tell children that addition and subtraction are complementary, but instead should provide children with materials that allow them to discover the complementarity themselves.
- *Recognize individual differences when teaching.* Cognitive skills develop at different rates in different children. Consequently, instruction geared to an entire class is often boring for some students and much too challenging for others. *Instruction is most effective when it is tailored to individual students.* For some students in a classroom, the goal of addition instruction may be to master basic facts; for others, it may be to learn about properties such as commutativity and associativity.
- *Be sensitive to children's readiness to learn.* Children profit from experience only when they can interpret this experience with their current cognitive structures. It follows, then, that *the best teaching experiences are slightly ahead of children's current level of thinking.* As a youngster begins to master basic addition, don't jump right to subtraction, but first go to slightly more difficult addition problems.
- *Emphasize exploration and interaction.* Cognitive growth can be particularly rapid when children discover inconsistencies and errors in their own thinking (Legare, Gelman, & Wellman, 2010). *Teachers should therefore encourage children to look at the consistency of their thinking but then let children take the lead in sorting out the inconsistencies.* If a child is making mistakes in borrowing on subtraction problems, a teacher shouldn't correct the error directly; rather, the teacher should encourage the child to look at a large number of these errors to discover what he or she is doing wrong.

WEAKNESSES OF PIAGET'S THEORY. Although Piaget's contributions to child development are legendary, some elements of his theory have held up better than others (Miller, 2011; Siegler & Alibali, 2005).

- *Piaget's theory underestimates cognitive competence in infants and young children and overestimates cognitive competence in adolescents.* In Piaget's theory, cognitive development is steady in early childhood but not particularly rapid. In contrast, a main theme of modern child-development science is that of the extraordinarily competent infant and toddler. By using more sensitive tasks than Piaget's, modern investigators have shown that infants and toddlers are vastly more capable than expected based on Piaget's theory. For example, we'll see in Module 6.3 that infants have much greater understanding of objects than Piaget believed. Paradoxically, however, Piaget *overestimated* cognitive skill in adolescents, who often fail to reason according to formal operational principles and revert to less sophisticated reasoning. For example, we'll see in Module 7.2 that adolescents often let their beliefs bias their reasoning.

Piaget's theory underestimated infants' competence and overestimated adolescents' competence.

- *Piaget's theory is vague concerning mechanisms of change.* Many of the key components of the theory, such as accommodation and assimilation, turned out to be too vague to test scientifically. Consequently, scientists abandoned them in favor of other cognitive processes that could be evaluated more readily and provide more convincing accounts of children's thinking.

- *Piaget's stage model does not account for variability in children's performance.* In Piaget's view, each stage of intellectual development has unique characteristics that leave their mark on everything a child does. Preoperational thinking is defined by egocentrism and centration; formal operational thinking is defined by abstract and hypothetical reasoning. Consequently, children's performance on different tasks should be very consistent. In fact, children's thinking falls far short of this consistency. A child's thinking may be sophisticated in some domains but naïve in others (Siegler, 1981). This inconsistency does not support Piaget's view that children's thinking should always reflect the distinctive imprint of their current stage of cognitive development. In other words, cognitive development is not as stage-like as Piaget believed.

- *Piaget's theory undervalues the influence of the sociocultural environment on cognitive development.* Returning to the metaphor of the child as scientist, Piaget describes the child as a lone scientist, constantly trying to figure out by herself how her theory coordinates with data and experience. In reality, a child's effort to understand her world is a far more social enterprise than Piaget described. Her growing understanding of the world is profoundly influenced by interactions with family members, peers, and teachers and takes place against the backdrop of cultural values. Piaget's theory did not neglect these social and cultural forces entirely, but they are not prominent in the theory.

Because of the criticisms of Piaget's theory, many researchers have taken several different paths in studying cognitive development. In the next module, we'll look at three different approaches that are linked to Piaget's work.

 ANSWER 6.1
Piaget would reassure Jamila's dad that her behavior is perfectly normal. Preschoolers usually believe that others see the world as they do, a phenomenon that Piaget called *egocentrism*. In this case, Jamila knows that she's nodding her head, so she believes that others must know it, too.

 Check Your Learning

RECALL What are the stages of cognitive development in Piaget's theory? What are the defining characteristics of each?

Summarize the main shortcomings of Piaget's account of cognitive development.

INTERPRET Piaget championed the view that children participate actively in their own development. How do the sensorimotor child's contributions differ from the formal operational child's contributions?

APPLY Based on what you know about Piaget's theory, what would his position have been on the continuity–discontinuity issue discussed in Module 1.3?

6.2 Modern Theories of Cognitive Development

OUTLINE

The Sociocultural Perspective: Vygotsky's Theory

Information Processing

Core-Knowledge Theories

LEARNING OBJECTIVES

- In Vygotsky's sociocultural theory, how do adults and other people contribute to children's cognitive development?
- According to information-processing psychologists, how does thinking change with development?
- What naïve theories do children hold about physics, psychology, and biology?

Victoria, a 4-year-old, loves solving jigsaw puzzles with her dad. She does the easy ones by herself. But she often has trouble with the harder ones, so her dad helps—he orients pieces correctly and reminds Victoria to look for edge pieces. Victoria may do 10 to 12 puzzles before she loses interest, then delights in telling her mom, in great detail, about all the puzzles she solved. After these marathon puzzle sessions, Victoria's dad is often surprised that a child who is sophisticated in her language skills struggles with the harder puzzles.

Many theories have built on the foundation of Piaget's pioneering work. In this module, we'll look at three different theoretical approaches, each designed to take research in cognitive development beyond Piaget's theory. As we do, you'll learn more about Victoria's cognitive and language skills.

The Sociocultural Perspective: Vygotsky's Theory

Child-development scientists often refer to child development as a journey that can proceed along many different paths. As we've seen, in Piaget's theory, children make the journey alone as they interact with the physical world. Other people (and culture in general) certainly influence the direction that children take, but the child is seen as a solitary adventurer–explorer boldly forging ahead.

In contrast, according to the *sociocultural perspective,* **children are products of their culture: Children's cognitive development is not only brought about by social interaction, it is inseparable from the cultural contexts in which children live.** To illustrate, Gauvain (1998) argues that cultural contexts organize cognitive development in several ways. First, culture often defines which cognitive activities are valued: American youngsters are expected to learn to read but not to navigate using the stars. Second, culture provides tools that shape the way children think (Gauvain & Munroe, 2009). The cognitive skills that children use to solve arithmetic problems, for example, depend on whether their culture provides an abacus like the one in the photograph, or paper and pencil, or a handheld calculator. Third, higher-level cultural practices help children to organize their knowledge and communicate it to others. For instance, in most American schools, students are expected to think and work alone rather than to collaborate (Matusov, Bell, & Rogoff, 2002). Thus,

Sociocultural theories emphasize that cultures influence cognitive development by the tools that are available to support children's thinking, such as an abacus.

as Gauvain emphasizes, "Culture penetrates human intellectual functioning and its development at many levels, and it does so through many organized individual and social practices" (1998, p. 189).

One of the original—and still quite influential—sociocultural theories was proposed by Lev Vygotsky (1896–1934), the Russian psychologist described in Chapter 1. Vygotsky saw development as an apprenticeship in which children advance when they collaborate with others who are more skilled. That is, according to Vygotsky (1978), child development is never a solitary journey. Instead, children always travel with others and usually progress most rapidly when they walk hand-in-hand with an expert partner. **For Vygotsky and other sociocultural theorists, the social nature of cognitive development is captured in the concept of** *intersubjectivity,* **which refers to mutual, shared understanding among participants in an activity.** When Victoria and her father solve puzzles together, they share an understanding of the goals of their activity and of their roles in solving the puzzles. **Such shared understanding allows Victoria and her dad to work together in complementary fashion on the puzzles.** **Such interactions typify** *guided participation,* **in which cognitive growth results from children's involvement in structured activities with others who are more skilled than they.** Through guided participation, children learn from others how to connect new experiences and new skills with what they already know (Rogoff, 2003). Guided participation is shown when a child learns a new video game from a peer or an adolescent learns a new karate move from a partner.

> Vygotsky viewed development as an apprenticeship in which children progress by collaborating with skilled partners.

Vygotsky died of tuberculosis when he was only 37 years old, so he never had the opportunity to formulate a complete theory of cognitive development like that of Piaget. Nevertheless, his ideas are influential because they fill some gaps in Piaget's account of cognitive development. Three of Vygotsky's most important contributions are the concepts of zone of proximal development, scaffolding, and private speech.

THE ZONE OF PROXIMAL DEVELOPMENT. Angela likes helping her 11-year-old son with his math homework, particularly when it includes word problems. Her son does most of the work but Angela often gives him hints. For example, she might help him decide what arithmetic operations are required. When Angela's son tries to solve these problems by himself, he rarely succeeds. **The difference between what Angela's son can do with assistance and what he can do alone defines the** *zone of proximal development.* That is, the zone refers to the difference between the level of performance a child can achieve when working independently and the higher level of performance that is possible when working under the guidance of more skilled adults or peers (Daniels, 2011; Wertsch & Tulviste, 1992).

Think, for example, about a preschooler who is asked to clean her bedroom. She doesn't know where to begin. By structuring the task for the child—"start by putting away your books, then your toys, then your dirty clothes"—an adult can help the child accomplish what she cannot do by herself. Similarly, the zone of proximal development explains why Victoria, in the module-opening vignette, solves difficult jigsaw puzzles with a bit of help from her dad. Just as training wheels help children learn to ride a bike by allowing them to concentrate on other aspects of bicycling, collaborators help children perform effectively by providing structure, hints, and reminders.

The idea of a zone of proximal development follows naturally from Vygotsky's basic premise that cognition develops first in a social setting and only gradually comes under the child's independent control. Understanding how the shift from social to individual learning occurs brings us to the second of Vygotsky's key contributions.

Experienced teachers often provide much direct instruction as children first encounter a task, then provide less instruction as children "catch on."

SCAFFOLDING. Have you ever had the good fortune to work with a master teacher, one who seemed to know exactly when to say the right thing to help you over an obstacle but otherwise let you work uninterrupted? *Scaffolding* **refers to a teaching style that matches the amount of assistance to the learner's needs.** Early in learning a new task, when a child knows little, teachers such as the one in the photo provide a lot of direct instruction. But, as the child begins to catch on to the task, the teacher provides less instruction and only occasional reminders (Gauvain, 2001).

We saw earlier how a parent helping a preschooler clean her room must provide detailed structure. As the child does the task more often, the parent needs to provide less structure. Similarly, when high-school students first try to do proofs in geometry, the teacher must lead them through each step; as the students begin to understand how proofs are done and can do more on their own, the teacher gradually provides less help.

Do parents worldwide scaffold their children's learning? If so, do they use similar methods? The "Cultural Influences" feature answers these questions.

Cultural Influences

How Do Parents in Different Cultures Scaffold Their Children's Learning?

Cross-cultural research by Barbara Rogoff and her colleagues (1993) suggests that parents and other adults in many cultures scaffold learning, but they do it in different ways. These researchers studied parents and 1- to 2-year-olds in four different settings: a medium-sized U.S. city, a small tribal village in India, a large city in Turkey, and a town in the highlands of Guatemala. In one part of the study, parents tried to get their toddlers to operate a novel toy (for example, a wooden doll that danced when a string was pulled). No ground rules or guidelines concerning teaching were given; parents were free to be as direct or uninvolved as they cared.

What did parents do? In all four cultural settings, the vast majority attempted to scaffold their children's learning, either by dividing a difficult task into easier subtasks or by doing parts of the task themselves, particularly the more complicated parts. However, as the graphs in Figure 6-2 show, parents in different cultures scaffold in different ways. Turkish parents give the most verbal instruction and use some gestures (pointing, nodding, and shrugging). U.S. parents also use these methods, but to slightly lesser degrees. Turkish and U.S. parents almost never touch (such as nudging a child's elbow) or gaze (use eye contact, such as winking or staring). Indian parents seem to use roughly equal amounts of speech, gesture, and touch or gaze to scaffold. Guatemalan parents also use all three techniques, and, overall, Guatemalan parents give the most scaffolding of the four cultures. Evidently, parents worldwide try to simplify learning tasks for their children, but the methods that they use to scaffold learning vary across cultures.

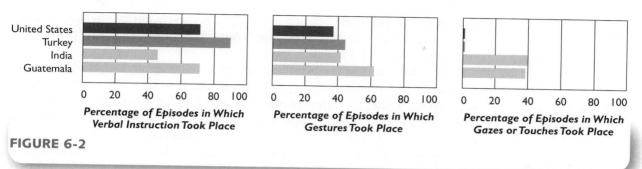

FIGURE 6-2

The defining characteristic of scaffolding—giving help but not more than is needed—clearly promotes learning (Cole, 2006). Youngsters do not learn readily when they are constantly told what to do or when they are simply left to struggle through a problem unaided. However, when teachers collaborate with them—allowing children to take on more and more of a task as they master its different elements—they learn more effectively (Murphy & Messer, 2000). Scaffolding is an important technique for transferring skills from others to the child, both in formal settings like schools and in informal settings like the home or playground.

PRIVATE SPEECH.   The little boy in the photo is talking to himself as he plays. **This behavior demonstrates** *private speech,* **comments not directed to others but intended to help children regulate their own behavior.** Vygotsky viewed private speech as an intermediate step toward self-regulation of cognitive skills (Fernyhough, 2010). At first, children's behavior is regulated by speech from other people that is directed toward them. When youngsters first try to control their own behavior and thoughts without others present, they instruct themselves by speaking aloud. **Finally, as children gain ever-greater skill, private speech becomes** *inner speech,* **Vygotsky's term for thought.**

If children use private speech to help control their behavior, then we should see children using it more often on difficult tasks than on easy tasks, and more often after a mistake than after a correct response. These predictions are generally supported in research (Berk, 2003), which documents the power of language in helping children learn to control their own behavior and thinking.

Vygotsky's view of cognitive development as an apprenticeship, a collaboration between expert and novice, complements the Piagetian view of cognitive development described in Module 6.1. Also like Piaget's theory, Vygotsky's perspective has several implications for helping children to learn. We've already seen that a teacher's main mission is to scaffold student's learning, not direct it. In other words, teachers should provide an environment that will allow students to learn on their own. This involves finding a middle ground: Students learn little when teachers provide too much instruction (e.g., "Here's how you do it and here's the right answer") or too little instruction ("Try to figure it out yourself"). Instead, a teacher needs to determine a child's current knowledge and provide the experience—in the form of a suggestion, question, or activity—that propels the child to more sophisticated understanding (Polman, 2004; Scrimsher & Tudge, 2003).

Young children often talk to themselves as they're performing difficult tasks; this helps them control their own behavior.

Perhaps even more important is Vygotsky's emphasis on learning as a cooperative activity in which students work together. Sometimes this collaboration takes the form of peer tutoring, in which students teach each other. Tutors often acquire a richer and deeper understanding of the topic they teach; tutees benefit, too, in part because teaching is one-on-one but also because tutees are more willing to tell a peer when an explanation is not clear.

Another form of cooperative learning involves groups of students working together on projects (e.g., a group presentation) or to achieve common goals (e.g., deciding rules for a classroom). These activities help students to take responsibility for a project and to become good "team players." Students also learn how to consider different viewpoints and how to resolve conflicts.

Cooperative learning does pay off for students. They do learn—achievement scores increase (Rohrbeck et al., 2003). What's more, cooperative learning improves students' self-concepts—students feel more competent—and they learn social skills, such as how to negotiate, build consensus, and resolve conflicts (Ginsburg-Block, Rohrbeck, & Fantuzzo, 2006).

Information Processing

In Module 6.1, we saw that a criticism of Piaget's theory is that the mechanisms of change—accommodation, assimilation, and equilibration—were vague and difficult to study scientifically. Consequently, identifying mechanisms of growth has been a priority of child-development scientists, and in the 1960s researchers first began to use computer systems to explain how thinking develops. **Just as computers consist of both hardware and software that the computer runs,** *information-processing theory* **proposes that human cognition consists of mental hardware and mental software.** Figure 6-3 shows how information-processing psychologists use the computer analogy to examine human cognition. The mental hardware has three components: sensory memory, working memory, and long-term memory.

In the information-processing approach, cognition relies upon mental hardware and mental software.

Sensory memory **is where information is held in raw, unanalyzed form very briefly (no longer than a few seconds).** For example, look at your hand as you clench your fist, rapidly open your hand (to extend your fingers), and then rapidly reclench your fist. If you watch carefully, you'll see an image of your fingers that lasts momentarily after you reclench your hand. What you're seeing is an image stored in sensory memory.

Working memory **is the site of ongoing cognitive activity.** In a personal computer, RAM (random-access memory) holds the software that we're using and stores data used by the software. In much the same way, working memory includes both ongoing cognitive processes and the information that they require (Baddeley, 1996). For example, as you read these sentences, part of working memory is allocated to the cognitive processes responsible for determining the meanings of individual words; working memory also briefly stores the results of these analyses while they are used by other cognitive processes to give meaning to sentences.

Long-term memory **is a limitless, permanent storehouse of knowledge of the world.** Long-term memory is like a computer's hard drive, a fairly permanent storehouse of programs and data. It includes facts (e.g., Charles Lindbergh flew the Atlantic in the *Spirit of St. Louis*), personal events (e.g., "I moved to Maryland in July 1999"), and skills (e.g., how to play the cello).

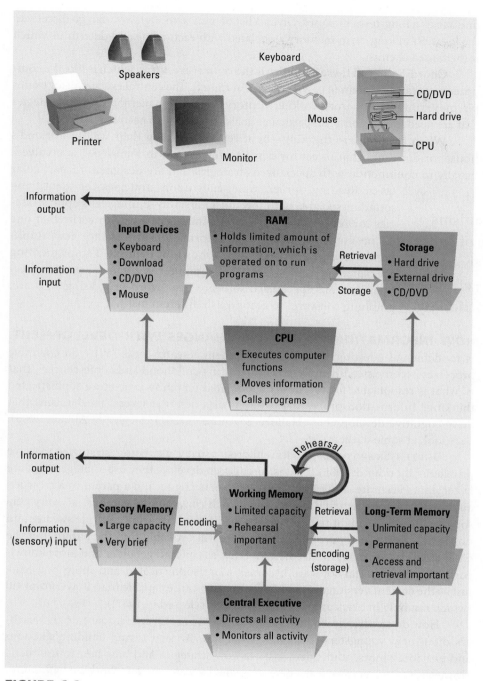

FIGURE 6-3

Information in long-term memory is rarely forgotten, though it is sometimes hard to access. For example, do you remember the name of the African American agricultural chemist who pioneered crop rotation methods and invented peanut butter? If his name doesn't come to mind, look at this list:

Marconi   Carver   Fulton   Luther

Now do you know the answer? (If not, it appears before "Check Your Learning," on page 193.) Just as books are sometimes misplaced in a library, you sometimes cannot find a fact in long-term memory. Given a list of names, though, you can go directly to the location in long-term memory associated with each name and determine which is the famed chemist.

Coordinating all these activities is the *central executive,* **which is like the computer's operating system** (e.g., Windows 7 or Linux). The central executive, for example, moves information from working memory to long-term memory, selects strategies that are needed to accomplish particular goals, and executes needed responses.

When children are thinking—be it reading, finding their way to a friend's house, or deciding what to eat for dessert—the system in Figure 6-3 is involved, usually in conjunction with specialized strategies that are designed for particular tasks. Reading, for example, calls upon strategies for identifying sounds associated with specific letters; way-finding calls upon strategies for recognizing familiar landmarks as a way to verify that one is "on course." Thus, in the information-processing view, thinking involves the general system shown in Figure 6-3 implementing specialized strategies, just as a computer is a general-purpose system that runs specialized software (e.g., word-processing software, graphing software) to accomplish different tasks.

> Information-processing theorists propose several mechanisms of change, including use of better strategies, increased capacity of working memory, and more effective executive functioning.

HOW INFORMATION PROCESSING CHANGES WITH DEVELOPMENT. A fundamental question for child-development researchers is "Why do cognitive processes become steadily more powerful during childhood and adolescence?" That is, what is responsible for the steady age-related march to ever-more sophisticated thinking? Information-processing psychologists describe several mechanisms that drive cognitive development (Halford & Andrews, 2011; Siegler & Alibali, 2005). Let's look at some of them.

BETTER STRATEGIES. Older children usually use better strategies to solve problems (Bjorklund, 2005). That is, as children develop, they use strategies that are faster, more accurate, and easier. For example, trying to find a parent in a crowded auditorium, a younger child might search each row, looking carefully at every person; an older child might remember that the parent is wearing a purple sweater and only look at people in purple. Both children will probably find the parent, but the older child's approach is more efficient. Thus, as children get older and more knowledgeable, their mental software becomes more sophisticated and more powerful, just as the current version of PowerPoint is vastly more capable than PowerPoint 1.0 (which ran only in black and white when it was released in 1987!).

How do children learn more effective strategies? Of course, parents and teachers often help youngsters learn new strategies. By structuring children's actions and providing hints, adults demonstrate new strategies and how best to use them. However, youngsters also learn new strategies by watching and working with more-skilled children (Tudge, Winterhoff, & Hogan, 1996). For example, children and adolescents watch others play video games in order to learn good game strategies. Children also discover new strategies on their own (Siegler, 2000). For example, when my daughter was 5, I watched her match words with their antonyms in a language workbook. The pages always had an equal number of words and antonyms, so she quickly learned to connect the last word with the one remaining antonym, without thinking about the meaning of either.

INCREASED CAPACITY OF WORKING MEMORY. Modern personal computers can run more complex software than ever before, in part because they have much more RAM than their counterparts from the 1980s and 1990s. If you use this technological change as a metaphor for children's development, the implication is clear. Compared to younger children, it's as if older children have more working memory "chips" to allocate to mental software and to information storage (Case, 1992; Kail, 2004). Consequently, older children usually outperform younger children on tasks where working memory is important for performance, such as reading or solving complicated problems.

MORE EFFECTIVE INHIBITORY PROCESSES AND EXECUTIVE FUNCTIONING. Yesterday I was listening to the radio and heard that classic oldie "The Lion Sleeps Tonight." Unfortunately, I spent the rest of the afternoon hearing "aweem away, aweem away" over and over in my mind. Undoubtedly, you, too, have had this experience—a thought gets into your head and you can't get rid of it.

Fortunately, most of the time, irrelevant and unwanted ideas do not intrude on our thinking. Why not? *Inhibitory processes* **prevent task-irrelevant information from entering working memory.** These processes, which were described in Module 5.2, improve steadily during childhood (Cragg & Nation, 2008). Consequently, thinking in older children and adolescents is more sophisticated because better inhibition means fewer disruptions from irrelevant stimulation and, therefore, more efficient working memory. When an older child is trying to write an essay for social studies, the sound of popcorn popping or thoughts of an upcoming swim meet are less likely to intrude on working memory and disrupt his planning (Kail, 2002).

Inhibitory processes, along with planning and cognitive flexibility, define *executive functioning* (i.e., the actions of the central executive shown in Figure 6-3). In many ways, executive functioning is synonymous with skilled problem solving, which helps to explain the presence of each of the elements in the definition. That is, good problem solving usually involves a plan and often requires flexibility (the ability to respond differently when the old response no longer works) and the ability to inhibit irrelevant responses (Best, Miller, & Jones, 2009). Executive functioning has been linked to several brain regions, including, for example, the frontal cortex, a region known to develop throughout infancy and childhood (Crone, 2009). Thus, with age children are better able to inhibit irrelevant responses, to formulate effective plans, and to adjust those plans as needed.

INCREASED AUTOMATIC PROCESSING. Think back to when you were learning a new skill, such as how to type. At first, you had to think about every single step in the process. If you were asked to type "child," you probably started, like the child in the photo, by trying to remember the location of "c" on the keyboard and then deciding which finger to use to reach that key. You had to repeat this process for each of the remaining four letters. But, as your skill grew, each step became easier until you could type "child" without even thinking about it; your fingers seem to move automatically to the right keys, in the right sequence. **Cognitive activities that require virtually no effort are known as** *automatic processes.*

To understand how automatic processes affect developmental change, we need to return to working memory. In the early phases of learning a skill, each individual step (such as finding a "c" on the keyboard) must be stored in working memory. Because there are so many steps, an unmastered skill can easily occupy much of the capacity of working memory. In contrast, when a skill has been mastered, individual steps are no longer stored in working memory, which means that more capacity is available for other activities.

Compared to adolescents and adults, children have limited experience in most tasks, so they perform few processes automatically. Instead, their processing requires substantial working memory capacity. As children gain experience, however, some

As children and adolescents acquire greater skill at new tasks such as typing, some aspects of the task are performed automatically, which means they require no effort.

QUESTION 6.2
Fifteen-year-old Quinn has just completed driver's ed, and he loves to get behind the wheel. For the most part, his parents are okay with his performance, but they absolutely refuse to let him listen to the radio while he's driving. Quinn thinks this is a stupid rule. Do you? *(Answer is on page 193.)*

processes become automatic, freeing working memory capacity for other processes (Rubinstein et al., 2002). Thus, when faced with complex tasks involving many processes, older children are more likely to succeed because they can perform some of the processes automatically. In contrast, younger children must think about all or most of the processes, taxing or even exceeding the capacity of their working memory.

INCREASED SPEED OF PROCESSING. As children develop, they complete most mental processes at an ever-faster rate (Cerella & Hale, 1994). Improved speed is obvious when we measure how fast children of different ages respond on tasks. Across a wide range of cognitive tasks, such as deciding which of two numbers is greater, naming a pictured object, and searching memory, 4- and 5-year-olds are generally one-third as fast as adults, whereas 8- and 9-year-olds are one-half as fast as adults (Kail, 2008).

Age differences in processing speed are critical when a specified number of actions must be completed in a fixed period of time. For example, perhaps you've had the unfortunate experience of trying to understand a professor who lectures at warp speed. The instructor's speech was so rapid that your cognitive processes couldn't keep up, which meant that you didn't get much out of the lecture. The problem is even more serious for children, who process information much more slowly than adults.

With the five types of change interacting in this fashion (and functioning independently), information processing provides a set of powerful mechanisms to drive cognitive development during childhood and adolescence. The combined result of these mechanisms is a steady age-related increase in cognitive skill. In contrast to Piaget's theory, there are no abrupt or qualitative changes that create distinct cognitive stages.

SUMMARY TABLE

TYPES OF DEVELOPMENTAL CHANGE IN INFORMATION PROCESSING

Type of Developmental Change	Defined	Example
Better strategies	Older children use faster, more accurate, and easier strategies.	Younger children may "sound out" a word's spelling, but older children simply retrieve it from memory.
Increased capacity of working memory	Older children have a larger mental workspace for cognitive processes.	An older child could simultaneously watch TV and converse with a friend; a young child could do one but not both.
Greater inhibitory control and executive functioning	Older children are less prone to interference from irrelevant stimulation and are more flexible in their thinking.	Asked by a teacher to format assignments in a new way (e.g., place a name in a different location, provide the day but not the date), older children are more successful in adapting to the new format.
Increased automatic processing	Older children execute more processes automatically (without using working memory).	Asked to get ready for bed, an older child goes through all the tasks (e.g., brush teeth, put on pajamas) while thinking about other things, but a younger child focuses on each task as well as what to do next.
Increased speed of processing	Older children can execute mental processes more rapidly than younger children.	Shown a picture of a dog, older children can retrieve the name "dog" from memory more rapidly.

Finally, what would information-processing researchers say about Victoria, from the module-opening vignette? They would probably want to explain why she finds some puzzles harder than others. Using the list of developmental mechanisms that we've examined in the past few pages, they would note that complex puzzles may require more sophisticated strategies that are too demanding for her limited working-memory capacity. However, as she does more and more puzzles with her dad, some parts of these complex strategies may become automated, making it easier for Victoria to use the strategy.

Core-Knowledge Theories

Imagine a 12-year-old (a) trying to download apps for her new iPad, (b) wondering why her dad is grouchy today, and (c) taking her pet dog for a walk. According to Piaget and most information-processing theories, in each case the same basic mechanisms of thinking are at work, even though the contents of the child's thinking range from objects to people to pets. In this view, different types of knowledge are like different kinds of cars—they come in countless numbers of makes, models, and colors, but down deep they are alike in consisting of an engine, four wheels, doors, windows, and so on.

> According to core-knowledge theories, infants are endowed with specialized knowledge in domains that were historically significant for survival.

In contrast to this view, *core-knowledge theories* **propose distinctive domains of knowledge, some of which are acquired very early in life** (Spelke & Kinzler, 2007; Wellman & Gelman, 1998). In this view, knowledge is more like the broader class of vehicles: Much knowledge is general, represented by the large number of cars. But there are also distinct, specialized forms of knowledge, represented by buses, trucks, and motorcycles. Returning to our hypothetical 12-year-old, core-knowledge theorists would claim that her thinking about objects, people, and pets may reflect fundamentally different ways of thinking.

Core-knowledge theories were created, in part, to account for the fact that most children acquire some kinds of knowledge relatively easily and early in life. For example, think about learning language (a native language, not a second language) versus learning calculus. Most children learn to talk—in fact, the *inability* to talk is a sign of atypical development—and they do so with little apparent effort. (When was the last time you heard a 3-year-old complaining that learning to talk was just *too* hard?) Calculus, in comparison, is mastered by relatively few, usually only after hours of hard work solving problem after problem.

According to core-knowledge theorists, some forms of knowledge are so important for human survival that specialized systems have evolved to simplify learning of those forms of knowledge. In the case of language, for example, spoken communication has been so essential throughout human history that mental structures evolved to simplify language learning. Other evolutionarily important domains of knowledge include knowledge of objects and simple understanding of people.

The nature of these mental structures, or *modules*, is very much a matter of debate. Some core-knowledge theorists believe they're like the math or graphics coprocessor on a computer: They're prewired to analyze one kind of data very efficiently (numbers and images, respectively, for the computer) but nothing else. The language module, for example, would be very sensitive to speech sounds and would be prewired to derive grammatical rules from sequences of words. Another view of these specialized mental structures borrows from Piaget's metaphor of the child as a scientist who creates informal theories of the world. However, core-knowledge theorists believe that children's theories are focused on core domains, rather than being all-encompassing as Piaget proposed. Also, in creating their theories, children don't start from scratch; instead, a few innate principles provide the starting point. For example, infants' early theories of objects seem to be rooted in a few key principles, such as the principle of cohesion, the idea that objects move as connected wholes (Spelke, 1994). Both of these ideas of mental structures may be right: that is, some forms of knowledge may be better described as modular, but others may be more consistent with the child-as-scientist view.

What are the domains of knowledge that have these specialized mental structures? Language was the first core domain identified by scientists; there is so much to learn about children's mastery of language that I've devoted an entire chapter to it (Chapter 9). In addition, many child-development researchers agree that young children rapidly acquire knowledge of objects, people, and living things. That is, they create informal or naïve theories of physics, psychology, and biology. Like language, acquiring knowledge in each of these domains has been central to human existence: Naïve physics allows children to predict where and how objects will move in the environment; naïve psychology makes for more successful interactions with others; and naïve biology is important in avoiding predators and maintaining health.

Finally, if core-knowledge theorists were asked to comment on Victoria (from the module-opening vignette), they would emphasize the contrast between her sophisticated language skill and her relatively undeveloped puzzle-solving skill. Language represents an evolutionarily important domain, so Victoria's precocity here is not surprising; doing jigsaw puzzles is not a specialized domain with evolutionary significance, which explains her relative lack of skill in that task.

We'll see how knowledge in several fundamental domains changes with development in Module 6.3. For now, the Summary Table reviews the defining features of the three theories that we've explored in Module 6.2.

SUMMARY TABLE

CHARACTERISTICS OF MODERN THEORIES OF COGNITIVE DEVELOPMENT

Approach	Characteristics
Vygotsky's sociocultural theory	Views cognitive development as a sociocultural enterprise; experts use scaffolding to help a novice acquire knowledge; children use private speech to regulate their own thinking.
Information processing	Based on the computer metaphor, views cognitive change in terms of better strategies, increased capacity of working memory, more effective inhibitory and executive processing, more automatic processing, and faster processing speed.
Core knowledge	Views cognitive development as an innate capability to easily acquire knowledge in such specialized domains of evolutionary importance as language, knowledge of objects, and understanding of people.

As you think about the three theoretical perspectives listed in the Summary Table, keep in mind that each goes beyond Piaget's theory in a unique direction. The sociocultural approach expands the focus of cognitive development research from a solitary child to one who is surrounded by people and the culture they represent; the information-processing perspective expands the focus of developmental mechanisms from accommodation and assimilation to working memory, processing speed, and other mechanisms derived from mental hardware and mental software; core-knowledge theories expand the focus to recognize distinct domains of evolutionarily significant knowledge. Thus, these three perspectives provide complementary, not competing, accounts of cognitive development.

> *Response to question on page 187:* The agricultural chemist who pioneered crop rotation while on the faculty of Tuskegee Institute of Technology is George Washington Carver.

 ## Check Your Learning

RECALL What three concepts are fundamental to Vygotsky's sociocultural theory?

What specialized domains of knowledge have been identified by core-knowledge theorists?

INTERPRET Do the developmental mechanisms in the information-processing perspective emphasize nature, nurture, or both? How?

APPLY How might an information-processing theorist explain sociocultural influences on cognitive development (e.g., scaffolding)?

 ANSWER 6.2
Though Quinn may not like the rule, it's probably a good one. Beginning drivers like Quinn are told to keep the music turned off because listening would consume working-memory capacity that is needed for driving. However, with more experience behind the wheel, many driving skills will become automatic, freeing capacity that can be used to listen to the radio. Patience, Quinn, your time will come!

 # 6.3 Understanding in Core Domains

OUTLINE	LEARNING OBJECTIVES
Understanding Objects and Their Properties	• What do infants understand about the nature of objects?
Understanding Living Things	• When and how do young children distinguish between living and nonliving things?
Understanding People	• How do young children acquire a theory of mind?

Amy, a reporter for a magazine that reviews products, was assigned to do a story on different kinds of "sippy cups"—plastic cups with a lid and spout that are spill-proof and so are perfect for babies who are learning to use a cup. Amy brought home the sippy cups—12 different models in all—and used each one for a day with her 14-month-old son. She discovered that some definitely worked better than others, but what amazed her was that after the first day her son always knew what to do with the cup. Despite differences in color, size, and the shape of the spout, he apparently recognized each one as a sippy cup because he immediately lifted each new style to his mouth and started drinking. Amy wondered how he could do this.

The world is filled with endless varieties of "stuff," including sippy cups, cats, and basketball players. Recognizing different instances of the same kind of thing—that is, being able to categorize—is an essential skill for young children. By knowing that an object belongs to a category, we learn some of its properties, including what it can do, and where we're likely to find it. Amy's son, for example, quickly learned the essentials of a sippy cup; later he recognized each different cup as being a member of the general category of sippy cups and knew exactly what to do with them. If he couldn't categorize, every experience would be novel—upon seeing yet another slightly different sippy cup, he'd need to figure out what to do with it as if it were a uniquely new object.

How do infants form categories? Important clues come from perceptual features and their organization. A sippy cup, for example, consists of a cylinder with a spout at one end. After infants have learned these features and how they're related, they can recognize sippy cups regardless of their color or size (Quinn, 2004, 2011). Similarly, they can learn the features that distinguish, for example, dogs from cats, or flowers from chairs. One popular view is that infants' first categories denote groups of objects with many similar perceptual features—the "dog" category includes four-legged animals with a distinctive snout, the "tree" category includes large bark-covered objects with limbs (Horst, Oakes, & Madole, 2005).

By 18 months, children combine many of these categories to form more general categories: Children learn that trees and flowers are part of the more general category of plants and they learn that dogs and birds are part of the more general category of animals (Mareschal & Tan, 2007). At the same time, children learn that their first categories can also be subdivided; for example, they recognize that flowers include the subcategories of rose, tulip, and daisy.

Parents and other adults help children create general categories and subcategories, often by identifying features common to existing categories: "Trees and flowers are both plants—they need water and sunlight to grow." By pointing out differences between category members, parents help children to form subcategories: "Dogs with curly hair are poodles" (Gelman et al., 1998; Nelson & O'Neil, 2005).

In the remainder of this module, we'll see how infants and older children use these categorization skills to carve the world into domains and create theories within those domains. We'll consider infants' knowledge of objects, living things, and people.

Understanding Objects and Their Properties

As adults, we know much about objects and their properties. For example, we know that if we place a coffee cup on a table, it will remain there unless moved by another person; it will not move by itself or simply disappear. And we don't release a coffee cup in midair because we know that an unsupported object will fall. Child-development researchers have long been interested in young children's understanding of objects, in part because Piaget claimed that understanding of objects develops slowly, taking many months to become complete. However, by devising some clever procedures, other investigators have shown that babies understand objects much earlier than Piaget claimed. Renée Baillargeon (1987, 1994), for example, assessed object permanence using a procedure in which infants first saw a silver screen that appeared to be rotating back and forth. When they were familiar with this display, one of two new displays was shown. In the realistic event, a red box appeared in a position behind the screen, making it impossible for the screen to rotate as far back as it had previously. Instead, the screen rotated until it made contact with the box, then rotated forward. In the unrealistic event, shown in Figure 6-4, the red box appeared but the screen continued to rotate as before. The screen rotated back until it was flat, then rotated forward, again revealing the red box. The illusion was possible because the box was mounted on a movable platform that allowed it to drop out of the way of the moving screen. However, from the infant's perspective, the box seemed to vanish behind the screen, only to reappear.

Contrary to Piaget's claims, infants know much about the properties of objects.

1. The silver screen is lying flat on the table and the red box is fully visible.

2. The silver screen has begun to rotate, but the red box is largely visible.

3. The silver screen is now vertical, blocking the red box.

4. The silver screen continues to rotate, blocking the red box, which has started to drop through the trap door.

5. The silver screen is completely flat, apparently having "rotated through" the red box, which is actually now under the table.

6. The silver screen is rotating back toward the infant but still blocks the red box.

7. The silver screen is again flat and the box fully visible to the infant.

FIGURE 6-4

The disappearance and reappearance of the box violates the idea that objects exist permanently. Consequently, an infant who understands the permanence of objects should find the unrealistic event a truly novel stimulus and look at it longer than the realistic event. Baillargeon found that 4½-month-olds consistently looked longer at the unrealistic event than the realistic event. Infants apparently thought that the unrealistic event was novel, just as we are surprised when an object vanishes from a magician's scarf. Evidently, then, infants have some understanding of object permanence early in the first year of life.

Of course, understanding that objects exist independently is just a start; objects have numerous other important properties and infants know many of them (Baillargeon et al. (2011). By about 6 months, infants are surprised when an object that's released in mid-air doesn't fall, when an object remains stationary after being hit, or when an object passes through another solid object (Luo, Kaufman, & Baillargeon, 2009). At this age, infants are surprised when a tall object is completely hidden when placed behind a shorter object, apparently because it violates their expectations about concealment (Walden et al., 2007; Wang & Baillargeon, 2005). Finally, as we'll see in the "Focus on Research" feature, infants distinguish properties of liquids and solids.

Focus on Research

Distinguishing Liquids from Solids

Who were the investigators, and what was the aim of the study? A property of solid objects is that they have a shape that is maintained as the object moves; in contrast, liquids don't have a constant shape but instead change their "shape" depending upon the kind of vessel that contains them. Susan Hespos, Alissa Ferry, and Lance Rips (2009) wanted to determine whether 5-month-olds understand these unique properties of solids and liquids.

How did the investigators measure the topic of interest? Infants were assigned to one of two conditions, shown in Figure 6-5: In a liquid condition, they saw a clear plastic drinking cup filled with a blue liquid. For several familiarization trials, the experimenter rotated the cup back and forth; as she did, of course, movement was apparent as the surface of the liquid remained horizontal. In the solid condition, the clear plastic drinking cup was filled with a blue resin that looked just like the blue liquid. However, when the experimenter rotated the cup back and forth, the resin did not move and the top of the resin remained perpendicular to the sides of the glass. On test trials, infants in both conditions saw two events, shown at the bottom of Figure 6-5. In one, a drinking cup containing blue liquid was lifted and tilted so that the liquid poured into the second cup; in the other event, a drinking cup containing the blue resin was lifted and tilted so that the resin slid into the second cup. Research assistants recorded how long infants looked at each event. If infants distinguish liquids and solids, those familiarized with the liquid should be surprised (and look longer) at the event showing the resin slide from one cup to the other (because they believe that the blue entity is a liquid). By the same logic, infants familiarized with the solid should be surprised at the event showing the liquid pour from one cup to the other (because they believe that the entity is a solid).

FIGURE 6-5

Who were the children in the study? Hespos and her colleagues tested 32 5-month-olds: 16 in the liquid condition and 16 in the solid condition.

What was the design of the study? The study was experimental. The independent variables were the type of entity shown on the familiarization trials (solid vs. liquid) and the kind of event shown on the test trials (pouring vs. sliding). The dependent variable was the time spent looking at each event. The study was not developmental because only 5-month-olds were tested.

Were there ethical concerns with the study? No. Most babies apparently enjoy watching these events. Occasionally babies would get fussy during the course of the experiment—perhaps because they were bored or tired—and when this happened the experiment was stopped.

What were the results? Figure 6-6 shows the amount of time that infants spent looking at sliding and pouring, separately for the infants who were familiarized with liquids and those familiarized with solids. In each case, infants looked longer at the unexpected events: When familiarization trials led infants to believe that the cup contained a solid, they were surprised when the "solid" poured from one cup into the other. When familiarization trials led infants to believe that the cup contained a liquid, they were surprised when the "liquid" slid from one cup into the other.

What did the investigators conclude? By 5 months, infants know some of the differences between liquids and solids. They understand that solids keep their shape when moved but that liquids do not. In other words, "[i]nfants are capable of noticing the characteristic difference between the movement of liquids and solids, and they can use this difference to predict later properties of these entities" (p. 609).

What converging evidence would strengthen these conclusions? Rigid versus changing shape is just one property that distinguishes solids and liquids. One way to strengthen conclusions about infants' understanding of objects would be to test their expectations about other properties that distinguish solids and liquids. For example, objects can pass through a liquid but not through a solid; solids can be carried in containers that have holes (e.g., a sieve or colander) but liquids cannot. Showing that infants recognize these differences would provide additional evidence that they understand the unique properties of solids and liquids.

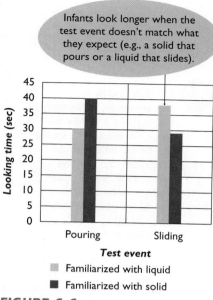

FIGURE 6-6

These amazing demonstrations attest to the fact that the infant is indeed an accomplished naïve physicist (Baillargeon, 2004). Of course, the infant's theories are far from complete; physical properties can be understood at many different levels (Hood, Carey, & Prasada, 2000). Using gravity as an example, infants can expect that unsupported objects will fall, elementary-school children know that such objects fall due to gravity, and physics students know that the force of gravity equals the mass of an object times the acceleration caused by gravity. Obviously, infants do not understand objects at the level of physics students. However, the important point is that infants rapidly create a reasonably accurate theory of some basic properties of objects, a theory that helps them to expect that objects such as toys will act in predictable ways.

Understanding Living Things

Fundamental to adults' naïve theories is the distinction between living and nonliving things. Adults know that living things, for example, are made of cells, inherit properties from parents, and move spontaneously. Knowledge of living things begins in infancy, when babies first distinguish animate objects (e.g., people, insects, other animals) from inanimate objects (e.g., rocks, plants, furniture, tools). Motion is critical in early understanding of the difference between animate and inanimate objects: That is, infants and toddlers use motion to identify animate objects; by 12 to 15 months children have determined that animate objects are self-propelled, can move in irregular paths, and act to achieve goals (Biro & Leslie, 2007; Opfer & Gelman, 2011; Rakison & Hahn, 2004).

By the preschool years, children's naïve theories of biology have come to include many of the specific properties associated with living things (Wellman & Gelman, 1998). Many 4-year-olds' theories of biology include the following elements:

- *Movement:* Children understand that animals can move themselves but inanimate objects can only be moved by other objects or by people. Shown the events in Figure 6-7—an animal and a toy car hopping across a table in exactly the same manner—preschoolers claim that only the animal can really move itself (Gelman & Gottfried, 1996).

- *Growth:* Children understand that, from their first appearance, animals get bigger and physically more complex but that inanimate objects do not change in this way. They believe, for example, that sea otters and termites become larger as time goes by but that teakettles and teddy bears do not (Rosengren et al., 1991).

- *Internal parts:* Children know that the insides of animate objects contain different materials than the insides of inanimate objects. Preschool children judge that blood and bones are more likely to be inside an animate object but that cotton and metal are more likely to be inside an inanimate object (Simons & Keil, 1995).

 QUESTION 6.3
One afternoon, 15-month-old Brandon and 6-month-old Justin saw a dragonfly for the first time as it flew around in the backyard, hunting mosquitoes. Would either Brandon or Justin be likely to conclude that a dragonfly is a living thing?
(Answer is on page 204.)

FIGURE 6-7

- *Inheritance:* Children realize that only living things have offspring that resemble their parents. Asked to explain why a dog is pink, preschoolers believe that some biological characteristic of the parents probably made the dog pink; asked to explain why a phone is pink, preschoolers rely on mechanical causes (e.g., a worker used a machine), not biological ones (Springer & Keil, 1991; Weissman & Kalish, 1999). Both U.S. and Brazilian children believe that a baby pig that is adopted by a cow would grow up to look and behave like a pig (Sousa, Altran, & Medin, 2002).

- *Illness:* Preschoolers believe that permanent illnesses such as color blindness or food allergies are more likely to be inherited from parents, but that temporary illnesses such as a sore throat or a runny nose are more likely to be transmitted through contact with other people (Raman & Gelman, 2005). They also understand that people can become ill when they eat contaminated food (Legare, Wellman, & Gelman, 2009).

- *Healing:* Children understand that, when injured, animate things heal by regrowth whereas inanimate things must be fixed by humans. Preschoolers know that hair will grow back when cut from a child's head but must be repaired by a person when cut from a doll's head (Backscheider, Shatz, & Gelman, 1993).

> Preschoolers know that living things move, grow, and heal when injured.

By 4 years, children's understanding of living things is so sophisticated that children aren't fooled by lifelike robots: 4-year-olds know that robots are machines that (a) do not eat or grow and (b) are made by people and can break (Jipson & Gelman, 2007).

A fundamental part of young children's theory of living things is a commitment to *teleological explanations*—**children believe that living things and parts of living things exist for a purpose.** A child like the one in the photo may say that fish have smooth skin so that they won't cut other fish that swim alongside them (Kelemen, 2003). Similarly, a child may explain that lions exist so that people can see them in a zoo. One view is that teleological explanations are based on children's knowledge that objects such as tools and machines are usually made with a purpose in mind. Children may follow a similar logic in thinking that living things (and their parts) were designed with a specific purpose in mind (Kelemen & DiYanni, 2005). This teleological thinking has echoes of the animistic thinking described on page 176: children attribute their own intentions and goals to other living objects.

Young children's theories of living things are also rooted in *essentialism:* **children believe that all living things have an essence that can't be seen but gives a living thing its identity.** All birds share an underlying "bird-ness" that distinguishes them from dogs, which, of course, share an underlying "dog-ness." And bird-ness is what allows birds to fly and sing (Gelman, 2003). Young children's essentialism explains why 4-year-olds believe that a baby kangaroo adopted by goats will still hop and have a pouch and why they believe that a watermelon seed planted in a cornfield will produce watermelons (Gelman & Wellman, 1991). The baby kangaroo and the watermelon seed have kangaroo-ness and

Young children's thinking about living things is often teleological: Children believe that objects and parts of objects were created with a purpose in mind. For example, a fish has smooth skin so that it won't cut other fish swimming next to it.

watermelon-ness that cause properties of kangaroos and watermelons to emerge in maturity.

Most children in Western cultures do not have well-defined ideas about what essences are. They believe that essences are inside an animal because they think that removing an animal's inside parts changes the animal's identity: for example, a dog that has blood and bones removed is no longer a dog (Gelman & Wellman, 1991). But their ideas about essences are limited to a vague notion of "inside parts" located near the center of the body (Newman & Keil, 2008). However, preschool children living in a Native American community in Wisconsin—the Menominee—have more refined ideas. Blood relations matter a great deal in this community because, for example, regulations regarding school funding and hunting are based in part on the number of "full-blooded" Menominee living in the community. Preschool Menominee children believe that a baby cow raised by pigs would grow up to look and act like a cow, which is the usual essentialist response. But, when told that a baby cow received a complete blood transfusion from its adoptive pig parent, now preschool children believed that the cow would grow up to be a pig. For Menominee preschoolers, blood is the essence of cow-ness or pig-ness (Waxman, Medin, & Ross, 2007).

Where do children get this knowledge of living things? Some of it comes just by watching animals, which children love to do. But parents also contribute: When reading books about animals to preschoolers, they frequently mention the properties that distinguish animals, including self-initiated motion (e.g., "the seal is jumping in the water") and psychological properties (e.g., "the bear is really mad!"). Such talk helps to highlight important characteristics of animals for youngsters (Gelman et al., 1998).

Of course, although preschoolers' naïve theories of biology are complex, their theories aren't complete. Preschoolers don't know, for instance, that genes are the biological basis for inheritance (Springer & Keil, 1991). And, although preschoolers know that plants grow and heal, they nevertheless don't consider plants to be living things. It's not until 7 or 8 years that children routinely decide that plants are alive. Preschoolers' reluctance to call plants living things may stem from their belief in goal-directed motion as a key property of living things: This is not easy to see in plants, but when 5-year-olds are told that plants move in goal-directed ways—for example, tree roots turn toward a source of water or a Venus flytrap closes its leaves to trap an insect—they decide that plants are alive after all (Opfer & Siegler, 2004).

Despite these limits, children's naïve theories of biology, when joined with their naïve theory of physics, provide powerful tools for making sense of their world and for understanding new experiences.

Understanding People

The last of the three fundamental theories concerns *naïve psychology,* **which refers to our informal beliefs about other people and their behavior.** Think back to the last time you wanted to figure out why someone—a friend, lover, coworker, sibling, or parent—acted as he or she did. Why did your friend go to a movie with someone else instead of going to a concert with you? Why did your brother say nothing about your brand-new coat? In common situations like this, adults are often naïve psychologists: we try to explain why people act as they do and usually our explanations emphasize that desires or goals cause people's behavior. Your friend went to the movie because she was mad at you for not loaning her your car; your brother didn't comment on your coat because he was preoccupied with something else. Just as naïve physics allows us to predict how objects act and naïve biology allows us to understand living things, naïve psychology allows us to predict how people act.

Amazingly, even infants understand some important psychological phenomena. For example, they understand that people's behavior is often intentional—designed to achieve a goal (Woodward, 2009). Imagine a father who says, "Where are the crackers?" in front of his 1-year-old daughter, then begins opening kitchen cabinets, moving some objects to look behind them. Finding the box of crackers, he says, "There they are!" An infant who understands intentionality would realize how her father's actions—searching, moving objects—were related to the goal of finding the crackers.

Many clever experiments have revealed that 1-year-olds do indeed have this understanding of intentionality. For example, in one study infants observed an adult reaching over a barrier for a ball, but failing because the ball was just out of reach. Then the barrier was removed and infants saw an adult either using the same "over the barrier" reaching motion or reaching directly for the ball; in both cases, the adult grasped the ball. By 10 months, infants were surprised to see the adult relying on the "over the barrier" reach when it was no longer needed. In other words, with the barrier removed, infants expected to see the adult reach directly because that was the best way to achieve the goal of getting the ball; they were surprised when the actor relied on the familiar but no longer necessary method of reaching (Brandone & Wellman, 2009).

Many studies yield results like this one, in which infants are able to identify the goal from the adult's actions (e.g., Sommerville & Woodward, 2005; Southgate & Csibra, 2009). What's more, the regions of the brain that control goal-related motions (e.g., grasping a cup) often become active in the infant's brain *before* the adult achieves a goal, as if the infant knows what goal the adult has in mind (e.g., Southgate et al., 2010).

From this early understanding of intentionality, young children's naïve psychology expands rapidly. **Between ages 2 and 5, children develop a** *theory of mind,* **a naïve understanding of the relations between mind and behavior.** One of the leading researchers on theory of mind, Henry Wellman (1992, 1993, 2002, 2011), believes that children's theory of mind moves through three phases during the preschool years. In the earliest phase, common in 2-year-olds, children are aware of desires, and they often speak of their wants and likes, as in "Lemme see" or "I wanna sit." Also, they often link their desires to their behavior, as in "I happy there's more cookies" (Wellman, 1992). Thus, by age 2, children understand that they and other people have desires and that desires can cause behavior. ⊙⎯Watch the **Video** on **mydevelopmentlab.com**

By about age 3, an important change takes place. Now children clearly distinguish the mental world from the physical world. For example, if told about one girl who has a cookie and another girl who is thinking about a cookie, 3-year-olds know that only the first girl's cookie can be seen, touched, and eaten (Harris et al., 1991). And, most 3-year-olds use "mental verbs" like *think, believe, remember,* and *forget,* which suggests that they have a beginning understanding of different mental states (Bartsch & Wellman, 1995). Although 3-year-olds talk about thoughts and beliefs, they nevertheless emphasize desires when trying to explain why people act as they do.

Not until age 4 do mental states really take center stage in children's understanding of their own and other people's actions. That is, by 4 years, children understand that their own and other people's behavior is based on their beliefs about events and situations, even when those beliefs are wrong.

This developmental transformation is particularly evident when children are tested on false-belief tasks like the one shown in Figure 6-8 on page 202. In all

> Preschool children acquire a theory of mind—a naïve understanding of the links between thoughts, beliefs, and behaviors.

⊙⎯**Watch** the **Video** *Theory of Mind* on **mydevelopmentlab.com.** This video shows a schoolage child who understands that people sometimes act on false beliefs and a preschool child who doesn't understand this. As you watch the video, think about similarities between preschool children's developing theory of mind and their egocentrism.

This is Sally.
Sally has
a basket.

This is Anne.
Anne has
a box.

Sally has
a marble.

She puts the marble
into her basket.

Sally goes
out for
a walk.

Anne takes the marble
out of the basket and
puts it into the box.

Now Sally comes back.
She wants to play with
her marble. Where will
she look for her marble?

FIGURE 6-8

false-belief tasks, a situation is set up so that the child being tested has accurate information, but someone else does not. For example, in the story in the figure, the child being tested knows that the marble is really in the box, but Sally, the girl in the story, believes that the marble is still in the basket. Remarkably, although 4-year-olds correctly say that Sally will look for the marble in the basket (acting on her false belief), most 3-year-olds say she will look in the box. The 4-year-olds understand that Sally's behavior is based on her beliefs, despite the fact that her beliefs are incorrect (Frye, 1993).

This basic developmental progression is remarkably robust. Wellman, Cross, and Watson (2001) conducted a meta-analysis of approximately 175 studies in which more than 4,000 young children were tested on false-belief tasks. Before the age of 3½ years, children typically make the false-belief error: Attributing their own knowledge of the marble's location to Sally, they say she will search in the correct location. Yet, only 6 short months later, children now understand that Sally's false belief will cause her to look for the marble in the basket. This general developmental pattern is evident in many different cultures around the world (Callaghan et al., 2005; Liu et al., 2008).

Thus, at about 4 years of age there is a fundamental change in children's understanding of the centrality of beliefs in a person's thinking about the world. Children now "realize that people not only have thoughts and beliefs, but also that thoughts and beliefs are crucial to explaining why people do things; that is, actors' pursuits of their desires are inevitably shaped by their beliefs about the world" (Bartsch & Wellman, 1995, p. 144).

The early stages of children's theory of mind seem clear. How this happens is very much a matter of debate, however. One of the first explanations for the development of a theory of mind suggested that it is based on an innate, specialized module coming online in the preschool years that automatically recognizes behaviors associated with different mental states such as wanting, pretending, and believing. This view was prompted, in part, by the finding that children with autism, a disorder in which individuals are uninterested in other people and have very limited social skills, lag far behind typically developing children in understanding false belief, as if an "understanding other people" module is not working properly (Peterson, Wellman, & Liu, 2005). As we'll see in the "Improving Children's Lives" feature, although autistic children definitely find false-belief tasks to be challenging, the proper interpretation of that result is very much debated.

Improving Children's Lives

Theory of Mind in Autism

Autism is the most serious of a family of disorders known as Autism Spectrum Disorders (ASD). Individuals with ASD acquire language later than usual and their speech often echoes what others say to them. They sometimes become intensely interested in objects (e.g., making the same actions with a toy over and over), sometimes to the exclusion of everything else. They often seem uninterested in other people, and when they do interact, those exchanges are often awkward, as if the individuals with ASD aren't following the rules that govern social interactions. Symptoms usually emerge early in life, typically by 18 to 24 months of age. Roughly one out of every 200–300 U.S. children is diagnosed with ASD; about 80% of them are boys (Mash & Wolfe, 2010). ASD is heritable and many studies point to atypical brain functioning, perhaps due to abnormal levels of neurotransmitters (NINDS, 2009).

As I mentioned, children with ASD grasp false belief very slowly, and this performance leads some researchers to conclude that the absence of a theory of mind—sometimes called "mindblindness" (Baron-Cohen, 1995)—is the defining characteristic of ASD (Tager-Flusberg, 2007). Other scientists aren't convinced. Although no one doubts that autistic children find false-belief tasks puzzling, some scientists say that mindblindness is a by-product of other deficits and not the cause of the symptoms associated with ASD. One idea is that ASD reflects problems in executive function (described on page 189): According to this view, autistic children's social interactions are impaired because they are relatively unable to plan, to inhibit irrelevant actions, and to shift smoothly between actions (Pellicano, 2010). Another idea emphasizes a focused processing style that is common in ASD. For example, children with ASD find hidden objects faster than typically developing children do (Joseph et al., 2009), but this emphasis on perceptual details usually comes at the expense of maintaining a coherent overall picture. Consequently, in social interactions, children with ASD may focus on one facet of another person's behavior (e.g., her gestures) but ignore other verbal and nonverbal cues (e.g., speech, facial expressions, body language) that collectively promote fluid interactions. Research to evaluate these claims is still ongoing; it's likely that the answers will indicate that multiple factors contribute to ASD.

> Children with autism acquire language later than usual, are sometimes very interested in objects, and don't interact easily with others.

ASD can't be cured. However, therapy can be used to improve language and social skills in children with autism. In addition, medications can be used to treat some of the symptoms, such as reducing repetitive behavior (NINDS, 2009). When ASD is diagnosed early and autistic children grow up in supportive, responsive environments and receive appropriate treatments, they can lead satisfying and productive lives.

The theory-of-mind module that some suspect is missing in autistic children is thought to emerge during the preschool years in typical development. But, just as the role for this module has been challenged in autism, not everyone is convinced that it drives theory of mind in typical development. Some evidence points to a role for executive function in the onset of theory of mind: Children's scores on tasks designed to measure executive function predict their scores on false-belief tasks (e.g., Hughes & Ensor, 2007). Other evidence emphasizes the contribution of language, which develops rapidly during the same years that theory of mind emerges (as we'll see in Chapter 9). Some scientists believe that children's language skills contribute to growth of theory of mind, perhaps reflecting the benefit of an expanding vocabulary that includes verbs describing mental states, such as *think, know, believe* (Pascual et al., 2008). Or the benefits may reflect children's mastery of grammatical forms that can be used to describe a setting where a person knows that another person has a false belief (Low, 2010).

A very different view is that a child's theory of mind emerges from interactions with other people, interactions that provide children with insights into different mental states (Dunn & Brophy, 2005; Peterson & Slaughter, 2003). Through conversations with parents and older siblings that focus on other people's mental states, children learn facts of mental life, and this helps children to see that others often have different perspectives than they do. In other words, when children frequently participate in conversations that focus on other people's moods, their feelings, and their intentions, they learn that people's behavior is based on their beliefs, regardless of the accuracy of those beliefs. Consistent with this view, Taumoepeau and Ruffman (2008) found that when mothers frequently mentioned others' thoughts and knowledge during conversations with their 15-month-olds, as 33-month-olds the children were more advanced in their own description of others' mental states.

Probably through some combination of these forces, preschool children attain a theory of mind. After these years, their naïve psychology moves beyond theory of mind and embraces an ever-expanding range of psychological phenomena. For example, at about age 7, children understand that the same event can trigger different thoughts in different people: They understand that seeing a fish may make one child happy because it reminds her of her pet goldfish, but the same fish may make another child sad because her goldfish died recently (Eisbach, 2004). At about age 10, children know that such psychological states as being nervous or frustrated can produce physical states such as vomiting or having a headache (Notaro, Gelman, & Zimmerman, 2001). Furthermore, as children develop they come to understand the links among emotions, thoughts, and behavior. For example, although 8-year-olds understand that mental states—thoughts and feelings—can cause a person's mood, most 5-year-olds attribute such mood changes to external, observable causes (Flavell, Flavell, & Green, 2001). We'll look at these links more carefully in Module 10.1. Finally, as children develop, their descriptions of other people become more abstract and more psychological, a phenomenon that we'll consider in more detail in Module 11.3.

For now, the important point is that children's naïve psychology flourishes in the preschool years. Armed with this theory, children see that other people's behavior is not unpredictable, but follows regular patterns. When joined with their theories of naïve biology and naïve physics, very young children have extensive knowledge of the physical and social world, knowledge that they can use to function successfully in those worlds.

 ANSWER 6.3
By 12 to 15 months, toddlers know that living things are self-propelled, move along irregular paths, and act to achieve goals. They saw evidence of these last two (movement along an irregular path to achieve a goal), so it's likely that Brandon—but not Justin—was old enough to decide that the dragonfly was alive.

✔ Check Your Learning

RECALL Summarize the evidence indicating that Piaget underestimated infants' understanding of object permanence.

What properties of living things are featured in young children's theories of biology?

INTERPRET A typical 1-year-old's understanding of objects exceeds her understanding of people. Why might this be the case?

APPLY A meta-analysis of children's performance on false-belief tasks (Wellman et al., 2001) showed that the pattern of age-related change in growth of theory of mind was much the same worldwide. What do you think would happen if you conducted a similar meta-analysis on studies of infants' understanding of objects? Would the pattern of age-related change in understanding objects be much the same around the world?

UNIFYING THEMES Active Children

This chapter emphasizes that *children influence their own development.* This idea is the cornerstone of Piaget's theory and of the core-knowledge account of development. Beginning in infancy and continuing through childhood and adolescence, children are constantly trying to make sense out of what goes on around them. Experiences provide intellectual food for children to digest. Parents, teachers, and peers are important in cognitive development, not so much for what they teach directly as for the guidance and challenges they provide. Thus, throughout the developmental journey, the child is a busy navigator, trying to understand the routes available and trying to decide among them.

See for Yourself

The best way to see some of the developmental changes that Piaget described is to test some children with the same tasks that Piaget used. The conservation task shown on page 176 is good because it's simple to set up and children usually enjoy it. Get yourself some glasses and colored liquids, then ask a 3- or 4-year-old and a 7- or 8-year-old to confirm that the two quantities are the same. Then pour one liquid as shown on page 176 and ask children if the quantities are still the same. Ask them to explain their answers. The differences between 3- and 7-year-olds' answers are truly remarkable. See for yourself!

Summary

6.1 Setting the Stage: Piaget's Theory

Basic Principles of Piaget's Theory

In Piaget's view, children construct theories that reflect their understanding of the world. Children's theories are constantly changing, based on their experiences. In assimilation, experiences are readily incorporated into existing theories. In accommodation, experiences cause theories to be modified to encompass new information.

When accommodation becomes much more frequent than assimilation, it is a sign that children's theories are inadequate, so children reorganize them. This reorganization produces four different stages of mental development from infancy through adulthood. All individuals go through all four phases, but not necessarily at the same rate.

Stages of Cognitive Development

The first 2 years of life constitute Piaget's sensorimotor stage. Over these 2 years, infants adapt to and explore their environment, understand objects, and begin to use symbols.

From ages 2 to 7 years, children are in Piaget's preoperational stage. Although now capable of using symbols, their thinking is limited by egocentrism, the inability to see the world from another's point of view. Preoperational children also are centered in their thinking, focusing narrowly on particular parts of a problem.

Between ages 7 and 11, children begin to use and can reverse mental operations to solve perspective-taking and conservation problems. The main limit to thinking at this stage is that it is focused on the concrete and real.

With the onset of formal operational thinking, adolescents can think hypothetically and reason abstractly. In deductive reasoning, they understand that conclusions are based on logic, not experience.

Piaget's Contributions to Child Development

Among Piaget's enduring contributions are emphasizing the importance of cognitive processes in development, viewing children as active participants in their own development, and discovering many counterintuitive developmental phenomena. The theory's weaknesses include poorly defined mechanisms of change and an inability to account for variability in children's performance.

6.2 Modern Theories of Cognitive Development

The Sociocultural Perspective: Vygotsky's Theory

Vygotsky believed that cognition develops first in a social setting and only gradually comes under the child's independent control. The difference between what children can do with assistance and what they can do alone defines the zone of proximal development.

Control of cognitive skills is most readily transferred from others to the child through scaffolding, a teaching style that allows children to take on more and more of a task as they master its different components.

Information Processing

According to the information-processing approach, cognition involves a general-purpose information-processing system that includes a central executive along with sensory, working, and long-term memories. Any specific cognitive activity involves this system plus specialized "software" that is specific to the task at hand.

Information-processing psychologists believe that cognitive development reflects more effective strategies, increased capacity of working memory, more effective inhibitory processes, increased automatic processing, and increased speed of processing.

Core-Knowledge Theories

According to core-knowledge theories, there are distinctive domains of knowledge (e.g., language, understanding of objects), some of which are acquired by infants, toddlers, and preschoolers. These domains have typically evolved because they were essential for human survival. Some theorists believe these domains of knowledge are rooted in prewired systems; others use Piaget's metaphor of child-as-scientist and describe them as specialized theories.

6.3 Understanding in Core Domains

Understanding Objects and Their Properties

Infants understand that objects exist independently. They also know that objects move along continuous paths and do not move through other objects.

Understanding Living Things

Infants and toddlers use motion to distinguish animate from inanimate objects. By the preschool years, children know that living things move themselves, grow bigger and physically more complex, have different internal parts than objects, resemble their parents, inherit some diseases from parents but contract other diseases from contact with people, and heal when injured. Preschoolers' thinking about living things is often marked by teleological explanations and essentialism.

Understanding People

By age 1, infants recognize that people perform many acts intentionally, with a goal in mind. At about age 2, children understand that people have desires and that desires can cause behavior. Beginning at 3 years of age, children distinguish the mental world from the physical world, although they still emphasize desires when explaining behavior. By 4 years of age, children understand that people's behavior is based on beliefs about events and situations, even when those beliefs are wrong. Contributing to children's acquisition of a theory of mind are a specialized cognitive module, basic psychological processes such as language, and social interactions that allow children to experience different mental states.

Test Yourself

✓—⎡Study and Review on mydevelopmentlab.com

1. Piaget's theory is built around the metaphor of children as _____.

2. In Piaget's theory, _____ is illustrated by a breast-fed baby who changes the way that she sucks to get milk from a bottle.

3. The accomplishments of the sensorimotor stage include adapting to and exploring the environment, understanding objects, and _____.

4. A defining feature of children in the _____ stage of development is that they are often egocentric—they are unable to take the perspective of other people.

5. During the _____ stage, thinking is rule-oriented and logical but limited to the tangible and real.

6. Piaget underestimated the ability of _____ but overestimated the ability of adolescents.

7. The _____ refers to the difference between what children can accomplish alone and what they can do with assistance.

8. According to Vygotsky, young children often rely on _____ to help them regulate their own behavior.

9. In information-processing theories, the _____ is like a computer's operating system in coordinating the flow of information through the system.

10. According to the information-processing account, cognitive development reflects several age-related changes, including better strategies, increased capacity of working memory, more effective inhibitory processes, more automatic processing, and _____.

11. _____ propose that specialized processing systems evolved to simplify learning of certain kinds of knowledge, such as language.

12. Research on infants' understanding of objects suggests that babies have _____ understanding than Piaget suggested.

13. Infants and toddlers rely upon _____ to identify animate objects.

14. Preschoolers' beliefs about living things are rooted in teleology (living things exist for a reason) and _____.

15. By age 4, children have a reasonably sophisticated _____, understanding, for example, that people will act on their beliefs even when those beliefs are false.

Answers: (1) scientists; (2) accommodation; (3) using symbols; (4) preoperational; (5) concrete operational; (6) infants; (7) zone of proximal development; (8) private speech; (9) central executive; (10) faster speed of processing; (11) Core-knowledge theories; (12) greater; (13) self-propelled motion; (14) essentialism—the idea that living things have a hidden "essence" that defines them; (15) theory of mind

Key Terms

accommodation   172
animism   176
assimilation   172
automatic processes   189
central executive   188
centration   176
concrete operational stage   177
constructivism   179
core-knowledge theories   191
deductive reasoning   178
egocentrism   175
equilibration   173

essentialism   199
executive functioning   189
formal operational stage   177
guided participation   183
information-processing theory   186
inhibitory processes   189
inner speech   185
intersubjectivity   183
long-term memory   186
mental operations   177
naïve psychology   200
object permanence   174

preoperational stage   175
private speech   185
scaffolding   184
sensorimotor stage   173
sensory memory   186
sociocultural perspective   182
teleological explanations   199
theory of mind   201
working memory   186
zone of proximal development   183

7 Cognitive Processes and Academic Skills

 7.1
Memory

 7.2
Problem Solving

 7.3
Academic Skills

A few weeks ago I spent a morning in a first-grade classroom watching 6- and 7-year-olds learn to read, to spell simple words, and to do simple addition problems. I then spent the afternoon in a fifth-grade classroom. Like the younger students, these 10- and 11-year-olds devoted much of their time to the traditional three Rs, but with much more complicated material. They were reading books with hundreds of pages, writing two-page essays, and solving story problems that involved multiplication and division.

This remarkable transformation over the course of just a few years became possible, in part, because of profound changes in children's thinking. We'll examine these changes in **Module 7.1**, where we'll see how memory expands as children grow, and also in **Module 7.2**, where we'll consider children's and adolescents' problem-solving skills. Finally, in **Module 7.3** we'll take a closer look at academic skills, tracing children's evolving mastery of reading, writing, and mathematics.

7.1 Memory

OUTLINE

Origins of Memory

Strategies for Remembering

Knowledge and Memory

Learning Objectives

- **How well do infants remember?**
- **How do strategies help children to remember?**
- **How does children's knowledge influence what they remember?**

One afternoon 4-year-old Cheryl came home sobbing and reported that Mr. Johnson, a neighbor and long-time family friend, had taken down her pants and touched her "private parts." Her mother was shocked. Mr. Johnson had always seemed an honest, decent man, which made her wonder if Cheryl's imagination had simply run wild. Yet, at times, he did seem a bit peculiar, so her daughter's claim had a ring of truth.

Regrettably, episodes like this are all too common in America today. When child abuse is suspected and the child is the sole eyewitness, the child often testifies during prosecution of the alleged abuser. But can preschool children like Cheryl be trusted to recall events accurately on the witness stand? To answer this question, we need to understand more about how memory develops. We'll start by examining the origins of memory in infancy, then see what factors contribute to its development in childhood and adolescence.

Origins of Memory

The roots of memory are laid down in the first few months after birth (Bauer, Larkina, & Deocampo, 2011). Young babies remember events for days or even weeks at a time. Among the studies that opened our eyes to the infant's ability to remember were those conducted by Carolyn Rovee-Collier (1997, 1999). The method used in her studies is shown in the photo. A ribbon from a mobile is attached to a 2- or 3-month-old's leg; in each case, within a few minutes, the babies learn to kick to make the mobile move. When Rovee-Collier brought the mobile to the infants' homes several days or a few weeks later, babies would still kick to make the mobile move.

Infants rapidly learn that kicking moves the mobile; days later, babies will kick immediately, showing that they remember the connection between their action and the mobile's movement.

If Rovee-Collier waited several weeks to return, most babies forgot that kicking moved the mobile. When that happened, she gave them a reminder—she moved the mobile herself without attaching the ribbon to the infant's foot. Then she would return the next day, hook up the apparatus, and the babies would kick to move the mobile.

Rovee-Collier's experiments show that three important features of memory exist as early as 2 and 3 months of age: (1) an event from the past is remembered; (2) over time, the event can no longer be recalled; and (3) a cue can serve to dredge up a forgotten memory.

From these humble origins, memory improves rapidly in older infants and toddlers. Youngsters can recall more of what they experience and remember it longer (Bauer & Lukowski, 2010; Pelphrey et al., 2004). When shown novel actions with toys and later asked to imitate what they saw, toddlers can remember more than infants and can remember the actions for longer periods (Bauer, 2007b). For example, if shown how to make a rattle by first placing a wooden block inside a container, then putting a lid on the container, toddlers are more likely than infants to remember the necessary sequence of steps. Similarly, when infants and toddlers learn to push a lever to move a toy train, older children remember the lever–train link longer (Rovee-Collier, 1999). Combining the results for this task with those of the mobile task used with infants reveals steady growth in memory over the first 18 months. Figure 7-1 shows remarkable change in the length of time that children can remember the connection between actions (kicking, pushing) and consequences (movements of mobile or train): from a week or less in young babies to more than 3 months for 1½-year-olds.

BRAIN DEVELOPMENT AND MEMORY.   These improvements in memory can be traced, in part, to growth in the brain regions that support memory (Bauer, 2007a; Richmond & Nelson, 2007). The brain structures primarily responsible for the initial storage of information, including the hippocampus and amygdala, seem to develop very early—by age 6 months. However, structures responsible for retrieving these stored memories—the frontal cortex, for example—develop much later, into the second year. In addition, part of the hippocampus is not mature until about 20 to 24 months. Thus, development of memory during the first 2 years reflects growth in these two different brain regions. In other words, as the hippocampus and prefrontal cortex mature over the first 24 months, children's memory skills gradually improve.

Once youngsters begin to talk, we can study their memory skills using most of the same methods we use with older children and adults. Research using these methods has linked age-related improvement in memory to two factors (Pressley & Hilden, 2006). First, as children grow, they use more effective strategies for remembering. Second, children's growing factual knowledge of the world allows them to organize information more completely and, therefore, to remember better. We'll look at each of these factors in the next few pages.

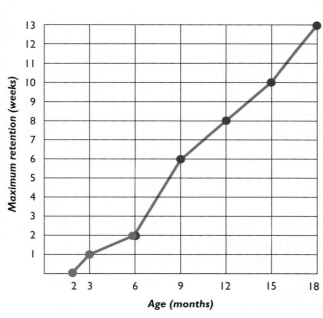

FIGURE 7-1

Strategies for Remembering

When you've studied for exams, you have may outlined chapters in a text or high-lighted important passages; when you've had several errands to complete, you have created a list; and when you've misplaced your iPad, you may have thought back to where you know you had it last. **Each of these actions is a** *memory strategy,* **an action to promote remembering.** Children begin to use memory strategies early. Preschool children look at or touch objects that they've been told to remember (DeLoache, 1984). Looking and touching aren't very effective strategies, but they tell us that preschoolers understand that they should be doing *something* to try to remember; remembering doesn't happen automatically! During the elementary-school years, children begin to use more powerful strategies (Schwenck, Bjorklund, & Schneider, 2009). **For example, 7- and 8-year-olds use** *rehearsal,* **a strategy of repetitively naming information that is to be remembered.** A child wanting to call a new friend will rehearse the phone number from the time she hears it until she places the call.

As children develop, they begin to use different strategies to improve memory.

As children get older, they learn other memory strategies. **One is** *organization:* **structuring material to be remembered so that related information is placed together.** For example, a seventh-grader trying to remember major battles of the American Civil War could organize them geographically (e.g., Shiloh and Fort Donelson in Tennessee, Antietam and Monocacy in Maryland) or chronologically (e.g., Fort Sumter and First Manassas in 1861, Gettysburg and Vicksburg in 1863). **Another strategy is** *elaboration,* **embellishing information to be remembered to make it more memorable.** To see elaboration in action, imagine a child who can never remember if the second syllable of *rehearsal* is spelled *her* (as it sounds) or *hear.* The child could remember the correct spelling by reminding herself that *rehearsal* is like *re-hear-ing.* Thus, imagining herself "re-hearing" a sound would make it easier to remember the spelling of *rehearsal.* Finally, as children grow they're also more likely to use external aids to memory: They are more likely to make notes and to write down information on calendars so that, like the girl in the photo, they won't forget future events (Eskritt & Lee, 2002; Eskritt & McLeod, 2008).

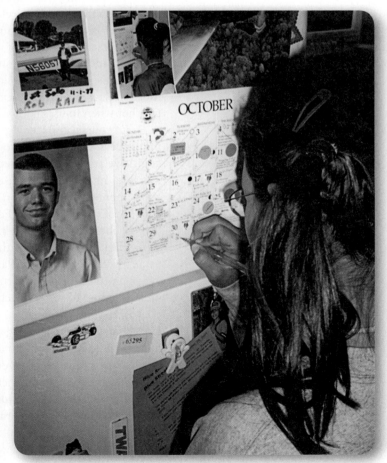

School-age children often use external aids to help them remember, such as writing down events on a calendar.

METACOGNITION. Just as there's not much value to a filled toolbox if you don't know how to use the tools, memory strategies aren't much good unless children know when to use them. For example, rehearsal is a great strategy for remembering phone numbers, but a lousy one for remembering amendments to the U.S. Constitution or the plot of *Hamlet.* During the elementary-school years and adolescence, children gradually learn to identify different kinds of memory problems and the memory strategies most appropriate to each. For example, when reading a textbook or watching a television newscast, outlining or writing a summary are good strategies because they identify the main points and organize them. Children gradually become more skilled at selecting appropriate strategies, but even high-school students do not always use effective learning strategies when they should (Pressley & Hilden, 2006).

After children choose a memory strategy, they need to monitor its effectiveness. That is, they need to decide if the strategy is working. For example, by self-testing—asking themselves questions about the material—children can determine if the strategy is helping them learn. If it's not, they need to begin anew, reanalyzing the memory task to select a better approach. If the strategy is working, they should determine the portion of the material they have not yet mastered and concentrate their efforts there. Monitoring improves gradually with age. For example, elementary-school children can accurately identify which material they have not yet learned, but they do not consistently focus their study efforts on this material (Bjorklund, 2005).

> Metamemory includes the ability to diagnose problems accurately and to monitor the effectiveness of a memory strategy.

Diagnosing memory problems accurately and monitoring the effectiveness of memory strategies are two important elements of *metamemory,* **which refers to a child's informal understanding of memory.** As children develop, they learn more about how memory operates and devise intuitive theories of memory that represent an outgrowth of the theory of mind described in Module 6.3 (Lockl & Schneider, 2007). For example, children learn that memory is fallible (i.e., they sometimes forget!) and that some types of memory tasks are easier than others (e.g., remembering the main idea of the Gettysburg Address is simpler than remembering it word for word). This growing knowledge of memory helps children to use memory strategies more effectively, just as an experienced carpenter's accumulated knowledge of wood tells her when to use nails, screws, or glue to join two boards.

Of course, children's growing understanding of memory is paralleled by growing understanding of all cognitive processes. **Such knowledge and awareness of cognitive processes is called** *metacognitive knowledge.* Metacognitive knowledge increases rapidly during the elementary-school years: Children come to know much about perception, attention, intentions, knowledge, and thinking (Flavell, 1999, 2000; McCormick, 2003). For example, school-age children know that sometimes they deliberately direct their attention—as when searching for a parent's face in a crowd. But they also know that sometimes events capture attention—as with an unexpected clap of thunder (Parault & Schwanenflugel, 2000).

One of the most important features of children's metacognitive knowledge is their understanding of the connections among goals, strategies, monitoring, and outcomes. That is, as shown in Figure 7-2, children come to realize that on a broad spectrum of tasks—ranging from learning words in a spelling list to learning how to spike a volleyball to learning to get along with an overly talkative classmate seated nearby—they need to regulate their learning by understanding the goal and selecting a means to achieve that goal. Then they determine whether the chosen method is working. **Effective** *cognitive self-regulation*—**that is, skill at identifying goals, selecting effective strategies, and monitoring accurately—is a characteristic of successful students** (Usher & Pajares, 2009; Zimmerman, 2001). A student may decide that writing each spelling word twice before the test is a good way to get all the words right. When the student gets only 70% correct on the first test, he switches to a new strategy (e.g., writing each word four times, plus writing its definition), showing the adaptive nature of cognitive processes in self-regulated learners.

Some students do not master these learning strategies spontaneously, but they may acquire them when teachers emphasize them in class (Coffman et al., 2008).

FIGURE 7-2

In addition, several programs have been created to teach students strategies for reading more effectively (Pressley, 2002). Teachers explain and demonstrate several basic strategies that promote greater reading comprehension, including: first selecting a goal for reading, making a mental picture of what's going on in the text, periodically predicting what will happen next, and summarizing aloud what's happened so far. Children practice these strategies separately and as part of a reading "tool kit." Empowered with reading strategies like these, students' understanding of text is deeper and they typically obtain greater scores on standardized tests of reading comprehension (Pressley & Hilden, 2006).

Strategies, metamemory, and metacognition are essential for effective learning and remembering, but as you'll see in the next few pages, knowledge is also an aid to memory (Schneider, 2011).

Knowledge and Memory

To see how knowledge influences memory, let's look at a study in which 10-year-olds and adults tried to remember sequences of numbers (Chi, 1978). As shown in Figure 7-3, adults remembered more numbers than children. Next participants tried to remember the positions of objects in a matrix. This time, 10-year-olds' recall was much better than that of adults.

What was responsible for this surprising outcome? Actually, the objects were chess pieces on a chessboard; the children were skilled chess players, but the adults were novices. The positions of the pieces were taken from actual games, so the configurations were familiar to the child chess players. For the adults, who lacked knowledge of chess, the patterns seemed arbitrary. The children, in contrast, had prior knowledge that helped them organize and give meaning to the patterns, and thus could recognize and then recall the whole configuration instead of many isolated pieces. It was as if the adults were seeing this meaningless pattern:

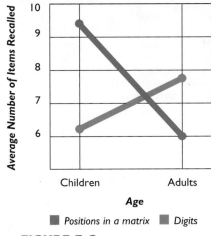

FIGURE 7-3

> nnccbasbccbn

but children were seeing this:

> nbc cbs abc cnn

Usually, of course, the knowledge that allows a child to organize information and give it meaning increases gradually with age (Schneider & Bjorklund, 1998). Researchers often depict knowledge as a network like the one in Figure 7-4, which shows part of a 13-year-old's knowledge of animals. The entries in the network are linked by different types of associations. Some of the links denote membership in categories (a Dalmatian is a dog), and others denote properties (an elephant has a trunk). **Still others denote a** *script,* **a memory structure used to describe the sequence in which events occur.** The list of events in walking the dog is a script.

A network diagram like this for a younger child would have fewer entries and fewer and weaker connecting links. Consequently, the youngster cannot organize information as extensively, which makes remembering more difficult than for an older child.

FIGURE 7-4

Highly familiar activities, such as baking cookies, are often stored in memory as scripts, which denote the events in the activity and the sequence in which they occur.

Nevertheless, the knowledge that young children have is organized; and this turns out to be a powerful asset. In the case of events that fit scripts, for example, they needn't try to remember each individual activity; instead, they simply remember the script. When the preschoolers in the photo want to tell their dad about baking cookies, they can simply retrieve the "baking cookies" script and use it to organize their recall. Knowledge can also distort memory. If a specific experience does not match a child's knowledge (e.g., it differs from a script), the experience is sometimes forgotten or distorted so that it conforms to the existing knowledge (Farrar & Boyer-Pennington, 1999; Levy & Boston, 1994). For example, told a story about a female helicopter pilot, many youngsters will remember the pilot as a man because their knowledge network specifies that pilots are men.

Because older children often have more knowledge than younger children, they are sometimes more prone to memory distortions than younger children (Brainerd, Reyna, & Ceci, 2008). In the "Spotlight on Theories" feature, we'll see one theory that accounts for this surprising finding.

Spotlight on Theories

Fuzzy Trace Theory

BACKGROUND　Children's knowledge of the world usually helps them remember, but sometimes it leads to inaccurate or distorted memory. Such memory errors, although common for children and adolescents, are still poorly understood.

THE THEORY　According to *fuzzy trace theory,* developed by Charles J. Brainerd and Valerie Reyna (2004, 2005), most experiences can be stored in memory exactly (verbatim) or in terms of their basic meaning (gist). A 10-year-old who reads an invitation to a birthday party may store the information in memory as "the party starts at 7:30 PM" (verbatim) or as "the party is after dinner" (gist). A 14-year-old who gets a grade on a science test may store it as "I got 75% correct" (verbatim) or "I got an average grade" (gist).

Throughout development, children store information in memory in both verbatim and gist formats, but young children are biased toward verbatim memory traces; during childhood and adolescence, a bias toward gist traces emerges. That is, older children and adolescents typically represent experiences and information in terms of gist, instead of verbatim. (The theory gets its name from its emphasis on gist memory traces that are vague or fuzzy.)

Hypothesis: Some memory errors depend on gist processing. If older children and adolescents are biased to gist processing, they should be more prone to those errors than are younger children. For example, a common error occurs when people are asked to remember related words such as *rest, awake, bed, snooze, blanket, snore,* and *dream*. Typically, about three-fourths of adults will claim to have seen *sleep* even though it was not presented. Because older children and adolescents extract the gist of the meanings of these words ("they're about sleep"), they should be more susceptible to the illusion than younger children, who more often store the words verbatim.

Test: Brainerd and Reyna (2007) presented words to 6-, 10-, and 14-year-olds. As in the previous example, many words in the list were highly associated with a critical word that was not presented. Later, another list of words was presented, including some that were part of the first list and some that were not. Participants were asked to recognize the words that were part of the first list. Not surprisingly, word recognition increased substantially with age: 14-year-olds recognized 94% of the words, compared to 81% for 10-year-olds and 73% for 6-year-olds. More interesting is how frequently children and adolescents "recognized" the critical word that had not actually been presented: 14-year-olds did so 76% of the time, compared to 67% for 10-year-olds and 42% for 6-year-olds.

> According to fuzzy trace theory, younger children more often remember verbatim but older children and adolescents typically remember the gist.

Conclusion: False memories—in this case "recognizing" a word that was never presented—were less common in young children than in older children and adolescents. This result is consistent with fuzzy trace theory, in which these memory errors are a consequence of the greater tendency for older children and adults to remember the gist of what they've experienced. Fuzzy trace theory is also supported by the finding that when children are encouraged to abstract the gist of the words in the list—to look for similar meanings—they respond like adults in "recognizing" the critical word (Odegard et al., 2008).

Application: Siblings sometimes argue about past events—who did (or said) something in the past. For example:

OLDER CHILD: "I took the trash out last night just like I always do."

YOUNGER CHILD: "Nuh-uh. You were too busy. So I did it."

Listening to these arguments, it's tempting for parents to side with the older child, assuming that older children usually remember past events more accurately. That's not a bad assumption, but the paradox is that the same processes that enhance older children's remembering also make them more prone to certain kinds of memory errors. Consequently, parents need to be cautious and be certain that the situation is not one in which an older child's memory is likely to be inaccurate, an illusion caused by the older child's greater reliance on gist processing. In the example here, the older child's memory of what happened may actually be based on his well-established script of what he *usually* does in the evening.

Thus, although children's growing knowledge usually helps them to remember, sometimes it can interfere with accurate memory. In the next section, we'll look at another link between knowledge and memory: children's memory of their own lives.

AUTOBIOGRAPHICAL MEMORY.   Start by answering these questions:

Who was your teacher in fourth grade?

Where (and with whom) was your first kiss?

Was your high-school graduation indoors or outdoors?

In answering these questions, you searched memory, just as you would search memory to answer questions such as "What is the capital of Canada?" and "Who invented the sewing machine?" However, answers to questions about Canada and sewing machines are based on general knowledge that you have not experienced personally; in contrast, answers to questions about your fourth-grade teacher, your first kiss, and your high-school graduation are based on knowledge unique to your own life. *Autobiographical memory* **refers to people's memory of the significant events and experiences of their own lives.** Autobiographical memory is important because it helps people construct a personal life history. In addition, autobiographical memory allows people to relate their experiences to others, creating socially shared memories (Bauer, 2006).

Autobiographical memory originates in the preschool years. According to one influential theory (Nelson & Fivush, 2004), autobiographic memory emerges gradually, as children acquire the component skills. Infants and toddlers have the basic memory skills that allow them to remember past events. Layered on top of these memory skills during the preschool years are language skills and a child's sense of self. Language allows children to become conversational partners. After infants begin to talk, parents often converse with them about past and future events—particularly about personal experiences in the child's past and future. Parents may talk about what the child did today at day care or remind the child about what she will be doing this weekend. In conversations like these, parents teach their children the important features of events and how events are organized (Fivush, Reese, & Haden, 2006). Children's autobiographical memories are richer when parents talk about past events in detail and, specifically, when they encourage children to expand their description of past events by, for example, using open-ended questions (e.g., "Where did Mommy go last night?"). When parents use this conversational style with their preschool children, as young adolescents they have earlier memories of childhood (Jack et al., 2009).

> Infantile amnesia, in which people can't recall events from early in life, may be due to limits in toddlers' language and their sense of self.

The richness of parent–child conversations also helps to explain a cultural difference in autobiographical memory. Compared to adults living in China, Japan, and Korea, Europeans and North Americans typically remember more events from their early years and remember those events in more detail (Peterson, Wang, & Hou, 2009; Wang, 2006). This difference in early memories can be traced to cultural differences in parent–child conversational styles: The elaborative style is less common among Asian parents, which means that Asian youngsters have fewer opportunities for the conversations about past events that foster autobiographical memory (Kulkofsky, Wang, & Koh, 2009; Wang, 2007).

An emergent sense of self also contributes to autobiographical memory. I describe sense of self in detail in Module 11.1, but the key idea is that 1- and 2-year-olds rapidly acquire a sense that they exist independently, in space and time. An emerging sense of self thus provides coherence and continuity to children's experience. Children realize that the self who went to the park a few days ago is the same self who is now at a birthday party and is the same self who will read a book with Dad before bedtime. The self provides a personal timeline that anchors a child's recall of the past (and anticipation of the future). Thus, a sense of self, language skills that allow children to converse with parents about past and future, and basic memory skills all contribute to the emergence of autobiographical memory in preschool children.

Older children, adolescents, and adults remember few events from their lives that took place before autobiographical memory is in place. *Infantile amnesia* **refers to the inability to remember events from one's early life.** Adults and school-age children recall nothing from infancy, but they remember an ever-increasing number of events from about age 3 or 4 years (Bauer, 2007b; Bauer et al., 2007). For example, when the 2-year-old in the photo is older, he won't remember his brother's birth (Peterson & Rideout, 1998; Quas et al., 1999).* But there's a good chance that the older boy will remember his brother's second—and certainly his third—birthday.

Many of the same factors that forge an autobiographical memory contribute to infantile amnesia. For example, once children learn to talk (at about 2 years of age), they tend to rely on language to represent their past (Nelson, 1993). Consequently, their earlier, prelingual experiences may be difficult to retrieve from memory, just as after you reorganize your bedroom you may have trouble finding things (Simcock & Hayne, 2002). Some theorists also argue that because infants and toddlers have no sense of self, they lack the autobiographical timeline that's used to organize experiences later in life (Howe & Courage, 1997).

Thus, personal experiences from our earliest years usually can't be recalled, because of inadequate language or inadequate sense of self (Harley & Reese, 1999). Beginning in the preschool years, however, autobiographical memory provides a cohesive framework for remembering significant life events. Unfortunately, some children's autobiographical memories include memories of abuse. Can these memories be trusted? We'll see in the next section.

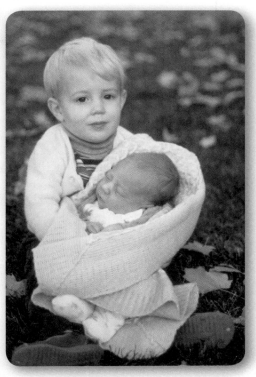

Infantile amnesia is the inability to remember events from early in one's life, such as the birth of a younger sibling.

EYEWITNESS TESTIMONY. Remember Cheryl, the 4-year-old in the module-opening vignette who claimed that a neighbor had touched her "private parts"? If Cheryl's comments lead to a police investigation, Cheryl's testimony will be critical. But can her recall of events be trusted? This question is difficult to answer. In legal proceedings, children are often interviewed repeatedly—sometimes as many as 10 to 15 times—with interviewers sometimes asking leading questions or making suggestive remarks. Over the course of repeated questioning, the child may confuse what actually happened with what others suggest may have happened. For example, in one famous case in which a preschool teacher named Kelly was accused of sexually abusing children in her class, the children were asked the following leading questions (among many, many others):

> Do you think that Kelly was not good when she was hurting you all?
> When did Kelly say these words? Piss, shit, sugar?
> When Kelly kissed you, did she ever put her tongue in your mouth? (Bruck & Ceci, 1995)

Each of the questions is misleading by implying that something happened when actually it might not have. When, as in the situation in the photo on page 218, the questioner is an adult in a position of authority, children often believe that what is suggested by the adult actually happened (Candel et al., 2009; Ceci & Bruck, 1998).

 QUESTION 7.1

When Courtney was 12 months old, she fell on the sidewalk and went to the emergency room for stitches in her chin. Now she's a mother and enjoys telling her children how brave she was at the hospital. What aspect of this story doesn't ring true? *(Answer is on page 219.)*

---

*Perhaps you're not convinced because you vividly recall significant events that occurred when you were 2, such as the birth of a sibling, a move to a different home, or the death of a close friend or relative. In reality, you are probably not remembering the actual event. Instead, I can almost guarantee that you're remembering others' retelling of these events and your role in them, not the events themselves. Events like these are often socially shared memories, and that's the basis for your memory.

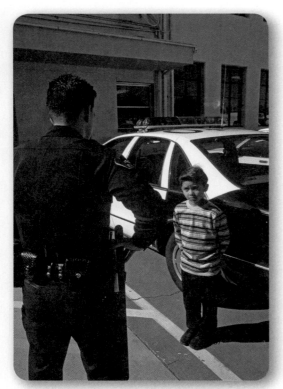

When trying to remember past events, young children sometimes "remember" what others suggest might have happened in the past, particularly when the suggestion comes from a person in authority.

Children's memories can also be tainted simply by overhearing others—adults or peers—describe events. When, for example, some children in a class experience an event (e.g., a special class visitor, such as a magician), they often talk about the event with classmates who weren't there; later, these absent classmates readily describe what happened and often insist that they were actually there (Principe & Ceci, 2002; Principe et al., 2006).

Preschool children are particularly suggestible. Why? One idea is that they are less able than older children and adults to know the source of information that they remember (Poole & Lindsay, 1995). For example, a father recalling his daughter's piano recitals will know the source of many of his memories: Some are from personal experience (he attended the recital), some he saw on videotape, and some are based on his daughter's descriptions. Preschool children are not particularly skilled at such source monitoring. When recalling past events, preschoolers become confused about who did or said what and, when confused in this manner, they frequently assume that they must have experienced something personally. Consequently, when preschool children are asked leading questions (e.g., "When the man touched you, did it hurt?'), this information is also stored in memory, but without the source. Because preschool children are not skilled at monitoring sources, they have trouble distinguishing what they actually experienced from what interviewers imply that they experienced (Ghetti, 2008).

Perhaps you're skeptical of findings like these. Surely it must be possible to tell when a young child is describing events that never happened. In fact, although law enforcement officials and child-protection workers believe they can usually tell whether children are telling the truth, research shows that they often cannot (Gordon, Baker-Ward, & Ornstein, 2001).

Findings like these emphasize the need to find effective ways of interviewing children that increase the chances of obtaining accurate descriptions of past events. The "Child Development and Family Policy" feature tells how this has been done.

Child Development and Family Policy

Interviewing Children Effectively

Toward the end of the 20th century, the number of child-abuse cases had skyrocketed, followed soon by reports that some adults had been wrongly convicted based on children's false memories. Consequently, many state and federal agencies created task forces to determine the best way to respond to the challenges of evaluating allegations of child abuse. In Michigan, for example, the Governor's Task Force on Children's Justice, created in 1992, quickly identified the need for a standard protocol for interviewing children in child-abuse cases: a protocol that would avoid contaminating children's testimony by using, for example, misleading questions like those listed on page 217. Debra Poole, a psychologist at Central Michigan University and a leading expert on children's eyewitness testimony, was hired to develop the protocol. Poole was an obvious choice because she had recently written a book with Michael E. Lamb, *Investigative Interviews of Children: A Guide for Helping Professionals,* which was published by the American Psychological Association in 1998. Working with agencies in nine Michigan counties, Poole devised a preliminary interview protocol that was tested in those counties. The revised protocol was then published by the Governor's Task Force (1998) and the procedures were implemented statewide. These procedures, derived largely from the research described here, are designed to meet the needs of all parties involved: The procedures "will reduce trauma to children, make the information gained more credible in the court process, and protect the rights of the accused" (Governor's Task Force, 1998, p. v).

Revised versions of the Michigan protocol were released in 2004 and 2011. Similar protocols have been created in other U.S. states, and the National Institutes of Child Health and Human Development have also developed a structured-interview protocol. Most of these protocols make similar recommendations regarding "best practices" for interviewing children. Specifically, interviewers should:

- Interview children as soon as possible after the event in question.
- Encourage children to tell the truth, to feel free to say "I don't know" to questions, and to correct interviewers when they say something that's incorrect.
- Start by asking children to describe the event in their own words ("Tell me what happened after school . . .") and follow up with open-ended questions ("Can you tell me more about what happened while you were walking home?") and minimize the use of specific questions (because they may suggest to children events that did not happen).
- Allow children to understand and feel comfortable in the interview format by beginning with a neutral event (e.g., a birthday party or holiday celebration) before moving to the event of interest.
- Ask questions that consider alternate explanations of the event (i.e., explanations that don't involve abuse).

Following guidelines like these foster the conditions under which children are likely to recall past events more accurately and thereby be better witnesses (Lamb et al., 2007). And the new procedures document that research findings can be a stable foundation for public policy.

> When interviewed appropriately, preschool children can remember past events accurately and won't recall events that didn't happen.

 ANSWER 7.1
Due to infantile amnesia, it's not very likely that Courtney is remembering her actual experience at the emergency room. Instead, her recall of these events is based on what she remembers others saying about what happened that day. She's heard these stories so many times, she can easily imagine seeing herself in the emergency room as a 12-month-old.

 Check Your Learning

RECALL Describe how children use strategies to help them remember.

Summarize the processes that give rise to autobiographical memory in toddlers.

INTERPRET Distinguish the situations in which gist processing of experience is advantageous (i.e., it leads to better memory) from those in which it is not.

APPLY Describe how research on children's eyewitness testimony illustrates connections among emotional, cognitive, and social development.

7.2 Problem Solving

OUTLINE	LEARNING OBJECTIVES
Developmental Trends in Solving Problems	• Do older children and adolescents typically solve problems better than younger children?
Features of Children's and Adolescents' Problem Solving	• What factors contribute to children's and adolescents' success in solving problems?
Scientific Problem Solving	• Can children and adolescents reason scientifically?

Brad, age 12, wanted to go to a hobby shop on New Year's Day. His mother, Terri, doubted that the store would be open on a holiday, so she asked Brad to call first. Moments later Brad returned and said, "Let's go!" When they arrived at the hobby shop, it was closed. Annoyed, Terri snapped, "I thought you called!" Brad answered, "I did. They didn't answer, so I figured they were too busy to come to the phone." Later that day, Brad's 3-year-old sister grabbed an opened can of soda from the kitchen counter, looked at Terri, and said, "This isn't yours 'cause there's no lipstick." Terri thought her daughter's inference was sophisticated, particularly when compared to her son's illogical reasoning earlier in the day.

According to Piaget's theory, reasoning and problem solving become progressively more sophisticated as children develop. Piaget believed that young children's reasoning (reflected in the name "preoperational thought") was particularly limited and that adolescents' reasoning (reflected in the name "formal operational thought") was quite powerful. But research has since shown that this account was wrong in two ways. First, it underestimated young children, who, like Brad's sister, often astonish us with the inferences they draw. Second, it overestimated adolescents who, like Brad, frequently frustrate us with their flawed logic.

In this module, we'll trace the growth of problem-solving skills in childhood and adolescence. We'll see that young children do indeed solve problems with far greater skill than predicted by Piaget but that, throughout development, many factors limit the success with which children, adolescents, and adults solve problems.

Developmental Trends in Solving Problems

Solving problems is as much a part of children's daily lives as eating and sleeping. Think about some common examples:

- After dinner, a child tries to figure out how to finish homework and watch his favorite TV program.
- A child wants to get her bike out of the garage, where it's trapped behind the car and the lawn mower.
- At school, a first-grader tries to decide the surest way to be at the head of the line for lunch.
- A teenager wants to come up with a way to avoid raking the leaves.

In each case, there's a well-defined goal (e.g., riding the bike, being at the head of the line) and the child is deciding how to achieve it.

As a general rule, as children get older they solve problems like these more often and solve them more effectively. Of course, this doesn't mean that younger children are always inept at solving problems. In fact, research has produced many instances in which young children solve problems successfully. For example, when asked what they could do if they went to the grocery store but didn't have enough money or if they went to the beach but forgot to bring lunch, most 4- and 5-year-olds suggest plausible, effective solutions. For example, they suggest borrowing money from someone they know and buying lunch at the concession stand (Hudson, Shapiro, & Sosa, 1995). What's more, even infants can solve simple problems (Barrett, Davis, & Needham, 2007). If an attractive toy is placed out of reach, like the baby in the photo infants will use other means to bring the toy to them, such as pulling on a string, or, if the toy is on a cloth, pulling the cloth. Both are simple but wonderfully effective methods of achieving the goal of playing with an interesting toy (Willatts, 1999).

Even infants can solve some problems effectively, for example, by pulling on the string to bring the toy within reach.

Also, as Brad's behavior in the vignette reveals, adolescents are not always skilled problem solvers. It's not hard to find instances in which their problem solving is inefficient, haphazard, or just plain wrong. Think about the following problem:

> Imagine that you want to enter one of two raffles. The first one advertises, "50 tickets, 5 winners, so you have a 10% chance of winning!" The second advertises, "500 tickets, 40 winners, so you have an 8% chance of winning!" Which raffle would you enter?

Many adolescents choose to enter the second raffle—even though they've just read that the odds of winning are less (8% versus 10%)—apparently because they see that there are 40 winning tickets, not just 5 (Kokis et al., 2002). In the process, of course, they ignore the fact that the second raffle has 460 losing tickets compared to only 45 in the first raffle!

Thus, research confirms what we saw in the vignette with Brad and his sister: Although children tend to become more effective problem solvers as they get older, even young children sometimes show remarkable problem-solving skill and adolescents can be error prone. In the next section, we'll look at some of the elements that govern children's success in solving problems.

Features of Children's and Adolescents' Problem Solving

Because problem solving is such an important skill, child-development scientists have been eager to reveal the circumstances that promote children's problem solving. The results of this work are described in the next few pages, organized around important themes that characterize children's problem solving.

YOUNG CHILDREN SOMETIMES FAIL TO SOLVE PROBLEMS BECAUSE THEY DON'T ENCODE ALL THE IMPORTANT INFORMATION IN A PROBLEM. When solving a problem, people construct a mental representation that includes the important features of a problem. *Encoding processes* **transform the information in a problem into a mental representation.** When the problem is to get the bike that's trapped in the back of the garage, for example, encoding creates a representation that includes the goal (get the bike) as well as other critical elements of the problem (e.g., the location of the obstacles).

Quite often children's representations of problems are incorrect or incomplete. They fail to encode problem features (or encode them incorrectly), making it unlikely that they will solve problems. On conservation of liquid problems like the one shown on page 176, young children's representations often include the heights of the containers but not their diameters. A more subtle form of flawed encoding emerges in transitive inference problems, in which children might be told, "Jon is older than Dave. Dave is older than Rob. Who's older, Jon or Rob?" Young children often encode these statements in absolute terms, not relative ones, like this:

Jon = OLD; Dave = NOT OLD
Dave = OLD; Rob = NOT OLD

> Young children sometimes fail to solve problems because they don't encode the needed information, they don't plan ahead, and they lack necessary knowledge.

Encoding in this way leaves children with the conflicting information that Dave is both OLD and NOT OLD, and no way to determine the relative ages of Jon and Rob (Halford, 1993).

When young children's representations lack these key features, it's not surprising that they fail to solve problems. As children grow, their encodings are more likely to be complete, perhaps due to increases in the capacity of working memory and because of greater knowledge of the world (as we'll see in the next section).

YOUNG CHILDREN SOMETIMES FAIL TO SOLVE PROBLEMS BECAUSE THEY DON'T PLAN AHEAD.   Solving problems, particularly complex ones, often requires planning ahead. For example, the goal "get ready for school" requires planning because it involves coordinating a number of goals—get dressed, eat breakfast, brush teeth, find backpack—which must be completed under time pressure. Faced with problems like this one, young children rarely come up with effective plans. Why? Several factors contribute (Ellis & Siegler, 1997):

- Young children often believe—unrealistically—that they can solve a problem by boldly forging ahead without an explicit plan. Like many people who hate to read directions that come with new toys, games, or software, young children often find it difficult to inhibit the urge to "let's get moving" in favor of "let's figure this out."
- Planning is hard work, and if young children find that their plans often fail, they may see little point in investing the effort.
- Young children may expect parents and other adults to solve complex problems for them.

These factors don't mean that young children never plan or can't plan. For example, when 4-year-olds are asked to solve mazes and are urged to avoid "dead ends" in the maze, they typically pause before drawing and look ahead to find a solution. Often they trace it with their finger first, then draw it (Gardner & Rogoff, 1990). Thus, young children can plan, if they're asked to and the problem is not too complex. But many problems make it difficult or even pointless for young children to plan.

SUCCESSFUL PROBLEM SOLVING TYPICALLY DEPENDS UPON KNOWLEDGE SPECIFIC TO THE PROBLEM AS WELL AS GENERAL PROCESSES.   Solving a problem often requires that children know some critical facts. For example, during the elementary-school years, children become much more adept at solving arithmetic word problems such as this one: "Joe has two candy bars, then Jessica gives him four more. How many candy bars does Joe have in all?" This improvement comes about as children master their basic arithmetic facts and as they learn how to map different types of word problems onto arithmetic problems (Kail & Hall, 1999).

More often than not, of course, older children have more of the knowledge relevant to solving a problem and so they will be more successful. Still, effective problem solving depends on more than problem-specific knowledge. Children often use generic strategies—ones not specific to particular tasks or problems—to find a solution. **An example is** *means-ends analysis,* **in which a person determines the difference between the current and desired situations, then does something to reduce the difference**. If no single action leads directly to the goal, then a person establishes a subgoal, one that moves her closer to the goal. To illustrate, think of a 9-year-old who has pangs of hunger while reading in her bedroom. Her goal is getting something to eat. There's no food in her bedroom, so "go to the kitchen" becomes a subgoal and, once there, she can achieve her goal. Likewise, the baby on page 221 used means-ends analysis in pulling the string toward himself to achieve the main goal of grabbing the toy.

Even preschool children use means-ends analyses to solve problems. This is evident in their efforts to solve the dog-cat-mouse problem shown in Figure 7-5. Three animals and their favorite foods are placed on corners and the child is asked to move the animals along the paths, one at a time, until each animal is paired with its favorite food. In the problem in the figure, moving the cat to the opposite corner would achieve part of that goal, and that's what most children do. In contrast, they rarely move an animal away from its favorite food (even though that's often required temporarily) because that is a "bad move" according to means-end analyses (Klahr, 1985). Even though young children often use means-end analyses, such analyses are usually successful only for relatively simple problems in which the difference between the current and desired situations can be achieved in a few moves. Younger children struggle with more complex problems that require generating many subgoals and keeping track of them while en route to the overall goal (DeLoache, Miller, & Pierroutsakos, 1998).

 QUESTION 7.2
Ten-year-old Kayla wakes to see the season's first snowfall. She can hardly wait to get outside, but then remembers that her sled is hanging on a hook in the garage, beyond her reach. Use means-ends analysis to show how she could achieve her goal of sledding.
(Answer is on page 228.)

CHILDREN AND ADOLESCENTS USE A VARIETY OF STRATEGIES TO SOLVE PROBLEMS. In Piaget's view, children and adolescents solve problems in fundamentally different ways: 8-year-olds, for example, consistently do so using concrete operational logic, but 13-year-olds do so using formal operational logic. The modern view, introduced in Module 6.2, differs: Children and adolescents call upon several different strategies to solve problems. For example, while playing board games in which a roll of the dice determines how many spaces to move, young children use many strategies to determine the number of moves from the dice (Bjorklund & Rosenblum, 2002). If the dice show 5 and 2, sometimes a child counts aloud "1, 2, 3, 4, 5, 6, 7" and then moves seven spaces; sometimes the child simply counts "5 . . . 6, 7" and moves; and other times the child glances briefly at the dice, then moves, as if she recalled the sum from memory.

Much the same thing happens, of course, when older children or adolescents learn a new game or a new skill. Initially, they try many different ways to solve a problem. Given enough experience in solving a particular type of problem, they learn the easiest, most effective strategy and use it as often as possible (Siegler, 2000).

This general approach is captured in Siegler's (1996, 2007) overlapping waves model. According to Siegler (1996), children

Bone

Fish

Cheese

FIGURE 7-5

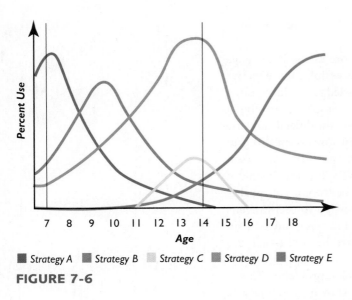

Percent Use

7 8 9 10 11 12 13 14 15 16 17 18
Age

■ *Strategy A* ■ *Strategy B* ■ *Strategy C* ■ *Strategy D* ■ *Strategy E*

FIGURE 7-6

use multiple strategies to solve problems and, over time, they tend to use strategies that are faster, more accurate, and take less effort. The model is illustrated in Figure 7-6, which shows how often different hypothetical strategies are used, based on a person's age. Strategy A, for example, is very common among young children but becomes less common with age; Strategy E shows the opposite profile, becoming more common with age. The vertical lines make it easy to see how often various strategies are used at different ages. Among 7-year-olds, Strategy A is most common, followed by B and D; in contrast, among 14-year-olds, Strategy D is most common, followed by C and E. Thus, children and adolescents are alike in choosing from a well-stocked tool kit to solve problems; they differ in that adolescents typically have a more sophisticated set of tools.

Some theorists go further and imagine that the problem-solving toolbox includes two general kinds of tools (Klaczynski, 2004; Stanovich, Toplak, & West, 2008). Sometimes children and adolescents solve problems using *heuristics*—**rules of thumb that do not guarantee a solution but are useful in solving a range of problems**. Heuristics tend to be fast and require little effort. But sometimes children solve problems analytically; depending on the nature of the problem, they may compute an answer mathematically or use logical rules.

To see the difference between heuristic and analytic solutions, think about the following problem:

> Erica wants to go to a baseball game to try to catch a fly ball. She calls the main office and learns that almost all fly balls have been caught in section 43. Just before she chooses her seats, she learns that her friend Jimmy caught 2 fly balls last week while sitting in section 10. Which section is most likely to give Erica the best chance to catch a fly ball? (Kokis et al., 2002, p. 34)

The heuristic solution relies on personal experience: When in doubt, imitate other people who have been successful. In this case, that means sitting where the friend sat.

Children and adolescents both rely on heuristic and analytic solutions, but adolescents are more likely to use analytic solutions.

The analytic solution, in contrast, involves relying upon the statistical information that, historically, the odds of catching a fly ball are greatest in section 43. Adolescents are more likely than children to solve problems like this one analytically, but some children solve them analytically and some adolescents rely on the heuristic approach (Kokis et al., 2002). In fact, this is a general pattern: heuristic and analytic solutions are both used throughout childhood and adolescence, but use of analytic solutions becomes more frequent as children develop.

COLLABORATION OFTEN ENHANCES CHILDREN'S PROBLEM SOLVING. In research, children typically solve problems by themselves, but in everyday life they often collaborate with parents, siblings, and peers. This collaboration is usually beneficial when the partner is a parent, older child, or more knowledgeable peer. As we saw in Module 6.2, parents and older children often scaffold children's efforts to solve problems, providing structure and direction that allow younger children to accomplish more than they could alone. In laboratory studies, for example, parents often tailor help to the child's needs, watching quietly when children are making headway but giving words of encouragement and hints when their children are stumped (Rogoff, 1998).

Collaboration with peers is sometimes but not always productive, and the settings that are conducive to effective peer collaboration remain something of a mystery (Siegler & Alibali, 2004). On the one hand, collaboration involving young children like the ones shown in the photo often fails, simply because preschool children lack many of the social and linguistic skills needed to work as part of a team. Peer collaboration is also often unproductive when problems are so difficult that neither child has a clue about how to proceed. On the other hand, peer collaboration works when both children are invested in solving the problem and when they share responsibility for doing so.

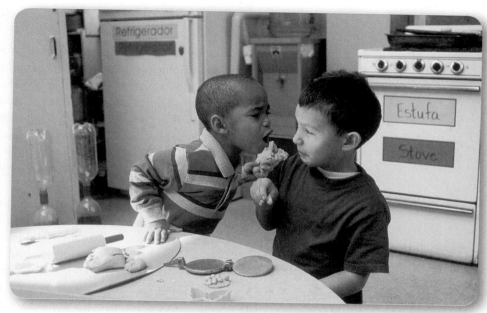

Collaborative problem solving is often ineffective with young children because they lack the cognitive and social skills needed to work together.

Despite its virtues, collaboration doesn't come easily to children attending traditional Western schools, where the common teacher–student "dialog" consists of a teacher asking a question with a well-defined answer, a student responding, and the teacher evaluating that response. In other words, children attending traditional Western schools are exposed to instruction that emphasizes an individual student's participation and achievement. In contrast, in some schools in the rest of the world— for example, in Mexico and Japan—students are taught to support their classmates, to learn from and build on their ideas and suggestions, and to view classmates as resources. In this setting, collaboration comes naturally to children (Chavajay, 2008; Silva, Correa-Chávez, & Rogoff, 2010).

Scientific Problem Solving

In Chapter 6, we saw that many child-development researchers rely on the child-as-scientist metaphor, in which experiences provide the "data" from which children construct theories that capture their understanding of the material and social world. These theories are usually described as informal because they lack the rigor of real scientific theories and because children and adolescents rarely conduct true experiments designed to test their theories. However, when it comes to the skills associated with real scientific reasoning, children and even adolescents typically have some conspicuous faults:

- *Children and adolescents often devise experiments in which variables are confounded—they are combined instead of evaluated independently—so that the results are ambiguous.* For example, if asked to determine how the size of a car's engine, wheels, and tail fins affect its speed, children often manipulate more than one variable at a time. They compare a car with a large engine, large wheels, and large tail fins against a car with a small engine, small wheels, and small tail fins. Not until adulthood do individuals commonly devise experiments in which only one variable is manipulated (e.g., size of the wheels) and the rest are held constant, which allows clear conclusions regarding cause and effect (Schauble, 1996).

- *Children and adolescents often have difficulty integrating theory and data.* For example, if the results of an experiment don't support adolescents' own beliefs, they tend to discount the value of the study (Klaczynski, 2004). To illustrate, if Baptist adolescents read about a flawed experiment, they tend to overlook the flaws if the results show that Baptists make better parents but not when the results show that Baptists make worse parents. (The same is true of adolescents of other faiths.) In these cases, adolescents use less rigorous standards to evaluate experiments when the evidence supports what they believe (Jacobs & Klaczynski, 2002; Klaczynski, 2000).

- *Children and adolescents often reach conclusions prematurely, basing them on too little evidence.* Instead of conducting all of the experiments necessary to isolate the impact of variables, children and adolescents typically conduct a subset of the experiments, and then reach conclusions prematurely (Zimmerman, 2007). In the previous example about determining a car's speed, children rarely do enough experimentation to provide conclusive evidence about each variable. They might perform experiments showing that a car runs fast with a large engine and slower with large tail fins, but also assume that wheel size has no effect without actually doing the critical experiments (Kuhn et al., 1995). The "Focus on Research" feature shows one specific way in which children jump to conclusions without considering evidence carefully.

> Despite the popularity of the "child-as-scientist" metaphor, children and adolescents have limited skill in designing and evaluating real experiments.

Focus on Research

Developmental Change in Sensitivity to Sample Size

Who were the investigators, and what was the aim of the study? Scientists and laypeople alike know that conclusions from research are more convincing when they are based on larger samples rather than smaller ones. For example, an election poll based on 1,000 voters is trusted more than one based on 50 voters. Amy M. Masnick and Bradley J. Morris (2008) wanted to know whether children understood the impact that sample size has on the confidence in the conclusions that can be drawn from scientific research.

How did the investigators measure the topic of interest? Masnick and Morris told participants in their study that coaches tested two players to decide who should be on a sports team. The players were described as taking turns kicking, hitting, or throwing a ball, taking 1 to 6 turns. For example, participants might be told that Alan kicked a ball 56, 47, 52, and 60 feet on his four tries but Bill kicked it 59, 52, 60, and 65 feet—on every turn, Bill kicked it farther. There were 14 problems like these. Each consisted of different pairs of players and the number of turns—in other words, the sample size—varied from one to six. After participants had studied the results of testing, they were asked to select the better player and to indicate their confidence in that decision on a 7-point scale where 7 meant totally confident that one player was better.

Who were the children in the study? The children included 39 9-year-olds and 44 12-year-olds. In addition, 50 college students participated.

What was the design of the study? This study was experimental. There were two independent variables: (a) the age of the child, and (b) the size of the sample (i.e., the number of turns), which was 1, 2, 4, or 6 pairs. The dependent variable was the participant's rated confidence that one player was better. The study was cross-sectional because it included three age groups and each participant was tested once.

Were there ethical concerns with the study? The hypothetical problems were straightforward and posed no special risks to children.

What were the results? Nearly everyone identified the better player in each pair (i.e., the one who consistently kicked, hit, or threw the ball farther). But there were striking age differences in the impact of sample size on confidence, as shown in Figure 7-7. The 9-year-olds' judgments were unaffected by the size of the sample. These children were just as confident with a sample of one pair as with six pairs. Notice, too, that they were very confident: Their average scores were consistently nearly 7, which was the maximum value on the confidence scale. In contrast, adults' confidence increased steadily as the sample size increased: They were relatively unconfident with the smaller samples (1, 2 pairs) and relatively more confident with the larger samples (4, 6 pairs). The 12-year-olds' responses were in between, showing a small influence of sample size on confidence.

What did the investigators conclude? The college students in this study were very sensitive to the impact of sample size, but 9-year-olds ignored it. According to Masnick and Morris, at this age children may "find multiple data points to be more confusing than informative" (p. 1039). Masnick and Morris also suggest that this age-related increase in sensitivity to sample size may come about due to increases in processing capacity and strategy-use (i.e., the sorts of factors described on pages 188–190).

What converging evidence would strengthen these conclusions? Of course, sample size is just one feature that affects level of confidence in the results of a scientific study. The consistency of the data (i.e., variability) can also influence confidence, as can the manner in which the impact of these variables is measured. Thus, it would be valuable to examine age-related changes in sensitivity to the impact of variability on children's ratings of confidence and to use different task formats to ensure that the results are not specific to comparing pairs of athletes.

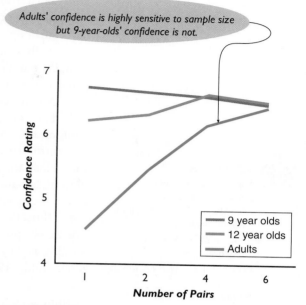

FIGURE 7-7

These findings suggest that children and adolescents have limited scientific skills. Other findings, however, indicate that young children have some rudimentary scientific skill. For example, children can sometimes identify the kind of evidence that would support a hypothesis. If trying to determine whether an animal has a good sense of smell, 6- to 8-year-olds know that it's better to conduct an experiment that uses a weak-smelling food than a strong-smelling food. If trying to decide whether a mouse that's loose in a house is large or small, they know that it's better to place a piece of food in a box that has a small opening instead of one with a large opening (Sodian, Zaitchik, & Carey, 1991). In these studies, young children are not designing complete experiments on their own; instead, they are simply evaluating part of an experiment that someone else has planned, which may explain their improved skill (DeLoache et al., 1998).

And it's clear that even young children can be trained to think more scientifically. For example, elementary-school children can be trained in the need to avoid confounded experiments by manipulating one variable at a time. Such training is straightforward—by showing both confounded and unconfounded experiments, then illustrating the difficulty in drawing clear conclusions from confounded experiments—and results in long-lasting improvements in children's understanding of well-designed experiments (Lorch et al., 2010).

Thus, the general developmental trend for scientific reasoning resembles the one we saw previously for general problem solving: Overall, children's skill improves steadily as they grow, but young children are sometimes amazingly skilled whereas older children and adolescents are sometimes surprisingly inept (Kuhn, 2011). In the next module, we'll see whether children's academic skills (reading, writing, arithmetic) develop in a similar manner.

 ANSWER 7.2
Top goal: Go sledding
Subgoal 1: Get sled
Fact: Sled is on hook in garage, out of reach
Subgoal 2: Get parent to reach sled
Fact: Mom left for work, Dad is asleep
Subgoal 3: Wake Dad

 Check Your Learning

RECALL Describe findings that counter the general trend in which children are more successful at solving problems as they get older.

Summarize the reasons why young children often fail to solve problems.

INTERPRET Compare the widely held metaphor of "children as scientists" with the outcomes from research on actual scientific reasoning by children and adolescents.

APPLY Based on what you know about children's success at solving problems collaboratively, would you recommend that children and adolescents work together on homework?

 Academic Skills

OUTLINE	LEARNING OBJECTIVES
Reading	● **What are the components of skilled reading?**
Writing	● **As children develop, how does their writing improve?**
Knowing and Using Numbers	● **When do children understand and use quantitative skills?**

When Jasmine, a bubbly 3-year-old, is asked how old she'll be on her next birthday, she proudly says, "Four!" while holding up five fingers. Asked to count four objects, whether they're candies, toys, or socks, Jasmine almost always says, "1, 2, 6, 7 . . . SEVEN!" Jasmine's older brothers find all this very funny, but her mother thinks that, notwithstanding the obvious mistakes, Jasmine's behavior shows that she knows a lot about numbers and counting. But what, exactly, does Jasmine understand? That question has her mother stumped!

Children and adolescents use their cognitive skills to accomplish many tasks in a variety of settings. Among the most important of these, however, are the school-related tasks of learning to read, write, and do math. Child-development researchers have studied these domains extensively, as you'll see in this module, which examines the traditional three Rs. We'll start with reading, then examine writing, and end with numbers, where you'll learn why Jasmine counts as she does.

Reading

Try reading the following sentence:

Андрей достал билеты на концерт.

Unless you know Russian, you probably didn't make much headway, did you? Now try this one:

Snore secretary green plastic sleep trucks.

These are English words and you probably read them quite easily, but did you get anything more out of this sentence than the one in Russian? These examples show two important processes involved in skilled reading. *Word decoding* **is the process of identifying a unique pattern of letters.** Without knowing Russian, your word recognition was not successful in the first sentence. You did not know that *билеты* means "tickets" or that концерт means "concert." What's more, because you could not recognize individual words, you had no idea of the meaning of this sentence. *Comprehension* **is the process of extracting meaning from a sequence of words.** In the second sentence, your word recognition was perfect, but comprehension was still impossible because the words were presented in a random sequence. These examples remind us just how difficult learning to read can be.

In the next few pages, we'll look at how children read. We'll start with the skills that children must have if they are to learn to read, then move to word recognition and comprehension.

FOUNDATIONS OF READING SKILL. Reading involves extracting meaning from print, and children have much to learn to do this successfully. Children need to know that reading is done with words made of letters, not with pictures or scribbles; that words on a page are separated by spaces; and that in English words are read from left to right. And, of course, they need to know the names of individual letters. These skills improve gradually over the preschool years; for example, U.S. and Canadian 4-year-olds know the names for about half of the letters (Levy et al., 2006; Treiman & Kessler, 2003).

Children learn more about letters and word forms when they're frequently involved in literacy-related activities such as reading with an adult, playing with magnetic letters, or trying to print simple words. Not surprisingly, children who know more about letters and word forms learn to read more easily than their peers who know less (Levy et al., 2006; Treiman & Kessler, 2003).

Important prereading skills include knowing the letters of the alphabet and the sounds they make.

A second essential skill is sensitivity to language sounds. **The ability to distinguish the sounds in spoken words is known as** *phonological awareness.* English words consist of syllables and a syllable is made up of a vowel that's usually but not always accompanied by consonants. For example, *dust* is a one-syllable word that includes the initial consonant *d*, the vowel *u*, and the final consonant cluster *st*. Phonological awareness is shown when children can decompose words in this manner by, for example, correctly answering "What's the first sound in *dust*?" or "*Dust* without the *d* sounds like what?"

Phonological awareness is strongly related to success in learning to read: Children who can readily identify different sounds in spoken words learn to read more readily than children who do not (Muter et al., 2004). In fact, as we'll see in Module 8.3, an insensitivity to language sounds is one of the core features of reading disability.

Learning to read in English is particularly challenging because English is often inconsistent in the way that letters are pronounced (e.g., compare the sound of "a" in *bat, far, rake,* and *was*) and the way that sounds are spelled (e.g., the long "e" sound is the same in each of these spellings: team, feet, piece, lady, receive, magazine).[**] In contrast, many other languages—Greek, Finnish, German, Italian, Spanish, Dutch—are far more consistent, which simplifies the mapping of sounds to letters. In Italian, for example, most letters are pronounced in the same way; reading a word like *domani* (tomorrow) is simple because beginning readers just move from left to right, converting each letter to sound using simple rules: *d, m,* and *n* are pronounced as in English, *o* as in *cold, a* as in *car,* and *i* as in *see* (Barca, Ellis, & Burani, 2007). In fact, even though children learn to read more rapidly in languages where letter-sound rules are more consistent, phonological awareness remains the single best predictor of reading success in many languages (Lervåg, Bråten, & Hulme, 2009; Ziegler et al., 2010).

If cracking the letter-sound code is so essential for learning to read in so many languages, how can we help children master language sounds? The "Improving Children's Lives" feature describes one easy way.

Improving Children's Lives

Rhyme Is Sublime Because Sounds Abounds

The Cat in the Hat and *Green Eggs and Ham* are two books in the famous Dr. Seuss series. You probably know these stories for their zany plots and extensive use of rhyme. When parents frequently read rhymes—not just Dr. Seuss, but also Mother Goose and other nursery rhymes—their children become more aware of word sounds. Passages like the following draw children's attention to the different sounds that make up words:

> I do not like them in a house. I do not like them with a mouse. I do not like them here or there. I do not like them anywhere. I do not like green eggs and ham. I do not like them, Sam-I-Am (Geisel, 1960, p. 20)

The more parents read rhymes to their children, the greater their children's phonological awareness, which makes learning to read much easier (Bradley & Bryant, 1983; Ehri et al., 2001).

So, the message is clear: Read to children—the more, the better. As the photo shows, children love it when adults read to them, and learning more about word sounds is icing on the cake!

Picture-book reading is mutually enjoyable for parent and child and often fosters a child's prereading skills.

[**]The famous British playwright George Bernard Shaw ridiculed English spelling by writing *fish* as *ghoti,* with *gh* as in *laugh, o* as in *women,* and *ti* as in *motion*!

Storybook reading like that described in the feature is an informal way that parents can foster prereading skills. Sometimes, however, parents go beyond simply reading and take on the role of teacher. They may talk about the names of letters and the sounds they make: "This is a *u*. Sometimes it goes *oo-oo-oo* and sometimes it goes *uh*." Both activities—reading for fun and teaching letter names and sounds while reading—promote phonological awareness and early reading skill, in part because they draw children's attention to the printed words on a page (Justice, Pullen, & Pence, 2008; Raikes et al., 2006). The benefits are not limited to the first steps in learning to read; rather, they persist into the middle elementary-school years and are just as useful for children learning to read other languages, such as Chinese (Chow et al., 2008; Sénéchal & LeFevre, 2002).

RECOGNIZING WORDS.   At the very beginning of reading, children sometimes learn to read a few words "by sight," but they have no understanding of the links between printed letters and the word's sound. However, the first step in true reading is learning to decode printed words by sounding out the letters in them: Beginning readers like the boy in the photo often say the sounds associated with each letter and then blend the sounds to produce a recognizable word. After a word has been sounded out a few times, it becomes a known word that can be read by retrieving it directly from long-term memory: As the individual letters in a word are identified, long-term memory is searched to see if there is a matching sequence of letters. After the child knows that the letters are, in sequence, *c-a-t*, he searches long-term memory for a match and recognizes the word as *cat* (Rayner et al., 2001).

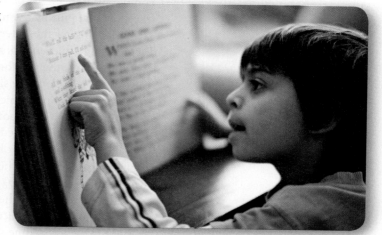

Beginning readers rely heavily on "sounding out" to recognize words, but even beginning readers retrieve some words from memory.

Thus, from their very first efforts to read, most children use retrieval for some words. From that point on, the general strategy is to try retrieval first and then, if that fails, to sound out the word or ask a more skilled reader for help (Siegler, 1986). For example, when my daughter Laura was just beginning to read, she knew *the, Laura,* and several one-syllable words that ended in *at,* such as *bat, cat,* and *fat.* Shown a sentence like

Laura saw the fat cat run.

she would say, "Laura s-s-s . . . ah-h . . . wuh . . . saw the fat cat er-r-r . . . uh-h-h . . . n-n-n . . . run." Familiar words were retrieved rapidly, but the unfamiliar ones were slowly sounded out.

With more experience, children sound out fewer words and retrieve more (Siegler, 1986). That is, by sounding out novel words, children store information about words in long-term memory that is required for direct retrieval (Cunningham et al., 2002; Share, 2008).

> Beginning readers sound out novel words but retrieve familiar words.

So far, word recognition may seem like a one-way street, where readers first recognize letters and then recognize words. In reality, we know that information flows both ways: Readers constantly use context to help them recognize letters and words (Rayner et al., 2001). For example, read these two sentences:

The last word in this sentence is cat.
The little girl's pet dog chased the cat.

Most readers recognize *cat* more rapidly in the second sentence. The reason is that the first seven words put severe limits on the last word: It must be something "chase-able," and because the "chaser" is a dog, *cat* is a very likely candidate. In contrast, the first seven words in the first sentence put no limits on the last word; virtually any word could end the sentence. Readers use sentence context like this to help them recognize words, particularly difficult ones (Archer & Bryant, 2001; Kim & Goetz, 1994).

EDUCATIONAL IMPLICATIONS FOR TEACHING READING. Teaching young children to read is probably the most important instructional goal for most American elementary schools. Historically, teachers have used one of three methods to teach reading (Rayner et al., 2001, 2002). The oldest is teaching phonics: for hundreds of years, American children have learned to read by first focusing on letter names, then their typical sounds, and then moving on to syllables and words. Young children might be taught that *b* sounds like "buh" and that *e* sounds like "eeee," so that putting them together makes "buh-eee . . . be."

Learning all the letters and their associated sounds can be tedious, perhaps discouraging children from their efforts to learn to read. Consequently, teachers have looked to other methods. In the whole-word method, children are taught to recognize whole words by sight. This usually begins with a small number (50 to 100) of very familiar words, which are repeated over and over to help children learn their appearance (e.g., "Run, Spot, run!"). In the whole-language method, which has been quite popular in the United States for 20 years, learning to read is thought to occur naturally as a by-product of immersing the child in language-related activities, such as following print as a teacher reads aloud or writing their own stories, inventing their own spellings as necessary (e.g., "Hr nak wz sor."). Teaching phonics is discouraged.

Although each of these three methods has some strengths, research clearly shows that phonics instruction is *essential* (Rayner et al., 2001, 2002). Children are far more likely to become successful readers when they're taught letter–sound correspondences, and this is particularly true for children at risk for reading failure. That is, the mapping of sounds onto letters, which is the basis of all alphabet-based languages such as English and German, is not something that most children master naturally and incidentally; most children need to be taught letter–sound relations explicitly.

Of course, mindless drilling of letter–sound combinations can be deathly boring. But flash cards and drills aren't the only way to master this knowledge; children can acquire it in the context of language games and activities that they enjoy. And, teaching children to read some words visually is a good practice, as is embedding reading instruction in other activities that encourage language literacy. However, these practices should be designed to complement phonics instruction, not replace it (Rayner et al., 2001, 2002).

COMPREHENSION. As children become more skilled at decoding words, reading begins to have a lot in common with understanding speech. That is, the means by which people understand a sequence of words is much the same whether the source of those words is printed text or speech or, for that matter, Braille or sign language (Oakhill & Cain, 2004). **In all these cases, children derive meaning by combining words to form** *propositions* **or ideas and then combining propositions.** For example, as you read

The tall boy rode his bike.

you spontaneously derive a number of propositions, including "There is a boy," "The boy is tall," and "The boy was riding." If this sentence were part of a larger body of text, you would derive propositions for each sentence, then link the propositions together to derive meaning for the passage as a whole (Perfetti & Curtis, 1986).

As children gain more reading experience, they better comprehend what they read. Several factors contribute to this improved comprehension (Siegler & Alibali, 2004):

- *Children become more skilled at recognizing words, allowing more working memory capacity to be devoted to comprehension* (Zinar, 2000): When children struggle to recognize individual words, they often cannot link them to derive the meaning of a passage. In contrast, when children recognize words effortlessly, they can focus their efforts on deriving meaning from the whole sentence.

- *Working memory capacity increases, which means that older and better readers can store more of a sentence in memory as they try to identify the propositions it contains* (De Beni & Palladino, 2000; Nation et al., 1999): This extra capacity is handy when readers move from sentences like "Kevin hit the ball" to "In the bottom of the ninth, with the bases loaded and the Cardinals down 7 to 4, Kevin put a line drive into the left-field bleachers, his fourth home run of the series."

- *Children acquire more general knowledge of their physical, social, and psychological worlds, which allows them to understand more of what they read* (Ferreol-Barbey, Piolat, & Roussey, 2000; Graesser, Singer, & Trabasso, 1994): For example, even if a 6-year-old could recognize all of the words in the longer sentence about Kevin's home run, the child would not fully comprehend the meaning of the passage because he or she lacks the necessary knowledge of baseball.

> Older children comprehend more because they recognize words easier, have more working memory, know more of the world, monitor their reading, and use appropriate reading strategies.

- *With experience, children better monitor their comprehension:* When skilled readers don't grasp the meaning of a passage because it is difficult or confusing, they read it again (Baker & Brown, 1984). Try this sentence (adapted from Carpenter & Daneman, 1981): "The Midwest State Fishing Contest would draw fishermen from all around the region, including some of the best bass guitarists in Michigan." When you first encountered "bass guitarists," you probably interpreted *bass* as a fish. This didn't make much sense, so you reread the phrase to determine that *bass* refers to a type of guitar. Older readers are better able to realize that their understanding is not complete and take corrective action.

- *With experience, children use more appropriate reading strategies:* The goal of reading and the nature of the text dictate how you read. When reading a popular or romance novel, for example, do you often skip sentences (or perhaps paragraphs or entire pages) to get to the "good parts"? This approach makes sense for casual reading, but not for reading textbooks, recipes, or how-to manuals. Reading a textbook requires attention to both the overall organization and the relationship of details to that organization. Older, more experienced readers are better able to select a reading strategy that suits the material being read; in contrast, younger, less-skilled readers less often adjust their reading strategies to fit the material (Brown et al., 1996; Cain, 1999).

Greater word recognition skill, greater working memory capacity, greater world knowledge, greater monitoring skill, and use of more appropriate reading strategies are all part of the information-processing explanation of how older and more experienced readers get more meaning from what they read. One way to summarize what we've learned about reading comprehension is with the Simple View of Reading model proposed by Gough and Tunmer (1986). In their model, reading comprehension is viewed as the product of two general processes: word decoding and language comprehension. Children can't comprehend what they read when either a word can't be decoded or it's decoded but not recognized as a familiar word. Thus, the best way to ensure that children understand what they read is to help them master fast, accurate decoding and language comprehension (e.g., increasing their vocabulary, their mastery of grammar). Reading instruction is most likely to succeed when it is tailored to a child's weaknesses, emphasizing letter-sound skills for children whose decoding skills are limited but vocabulary and grammar for children who need stronger language-comprehension skills (Connor et al., 2007).

Writing

Though few of us end up being a Maya Angelou, a Sandra Cisneros, or a John Grisham, most adults do write, both at home and at work. Learning to write begins early but takes years. Before children enter school, they know some of the essentials of writing. For example, 4- and 5-year-olds often know that writing involves placing letters on a page to communicate an idea (McGee & Richgels, 2004). But skilled writing develops very gradually, because it's a complex activity that requires coordinating cognitive and language skills to produce coherent text.

Developmental improvements in children's writing can be traced to a number of factors (Adams, Treiman, & Pressley, 1998; Siegler & Alibali, 2004).

GREATER KNOWLEDGE OF AND ACCESS TO KNOWLEDGE ABOUT TOPICS. Writing is about telling "something" to others. With age, children have more to tell as they gain more knowledge about the world and incorporate this knowledge into their writing (Benton et al., 1995). For example, asked to write about a mayoral election, children are apt to describe it as much like a popularity contest; in contrast, adolescents more often describe it in terms of political issues that are both subtle and complex. Of course, students are sometimes asked to write about topics quite unfamiliar to them. In this case, older children's and adolescents' writing is usually better because they are more adept at finding useful reference material and incorporating it into their writing.

GREATER UNDERSTANDING OF HOW TO ORGANIZE WRITING. One difficult aspect of writing is organization: arranging all the necessary information in a manner that readers find clear and interesting. In fact, children and young adolescents organize their writing differently than older adolescents and adults (Bereiter & Scardamalia, 1987). **Young writers often use a** *knowledge-telling strategy,* **writing down information on the topic as they retrieve it from memory.** For example, asked to write about the day's events at school, a second-grader wrote:

> It is a rainy day. We hope the sun will shine. We got new spelling books. We had our pictures taken. We sang "Happy Birthday" to Barbara (Waters, 1980, p. 155).

The story has no obvious structure. The first two sentences are about the weather, but the last three deal with completely independent topics. Apparently, the writer simply described each event as it came to mind.

During adolescence, writers begin to use a *knowledge-transforming strategy,* **deciding what information to include and how best to organize it for the point they wish to convey to their readers.** This approach involves considering the purpose of writing (e.g., to inform, to persuade, to entertain) and the information needed to achieve this purpose. It also involves considering the needs, interests, and knowledge of the anticipated audience.

Asked to describe the day's events, most older adolescents can select from among genres in creating a piece of writing, depending on their purpose for writing and the intended audience. An essay written to entertain peers about humorous events at school, for example, would differ from a persuasive one written to convince parents about problems with the required course load (Midgette, Haria, & MacArthur, 2008). And both of these essays would differ from one written to inform an exchange student about a typical day in a U.S. high school. In other words, although children's knowledge-telling strategy gets words on paper, the more mature knowledge-transforming strategy produces a more cohesive text for the reader.

> Older children write better because they know how to organize their writing, have mastered the mechanical aspects of writing, and revise more effectively.

GREATER EASE IN DEALING WITH THE MECHANICAL REQUIREMENTS OF WRITING. Soon after I earned my pilot's license, I took my son Matt for a flight. A few days later, he wrote the following story for his second-grade weekly writing assignment:

> This weekend I got to ride in a one propellered plane. But this time my dad was alone. He has his license now. It was a long ride. But I fell asleep after five minutes. But when we landed I woke up. My dad said, "You missed a good ride." My dad said, "You even missed the jets!" But I had fun.

Matt spent more than an hour writing this story, and the original (hanging in my office) is filled with erasures where he corrected misspelled words, ill-formed letters, and incorrect punctuation. Had Matt simply described our flight aloud (instead of writing it), his task would have been much easier. In oral language, he could ignore capitalization, punctuation, spelling, and printing of individual letters. These many mechanical aspects of writing can be a burden for all writers, but particularly for young writers.

In fact, research shows that when youngsters such as the one in the photo are absorbed by the task of printing letters correctly, the quality of their writing usually suffers; as children master printed and cursive letters, they can pay more attention to other aspects of writing (Graham, Harris, & Fink, 2000; Olinghouse, 2008). Similarly, correct spelling and good sentence structure are particularly hard for younger writers; as they learn to spell and to generate clear sentences, they write more easily and more effectively (Graham et al., 1997; McCutchen et al., 1994).

Young children often find writing difficult because of the problems they experience in printing letters properly, spelling words accurately, and using correct punctuation.

GREATER SKILL IN REVISING. Few authors get it down right the first time. Instead, they revise and revise, then revise some more. In the words of one expert, "Experienced writers get something down on paper as fast as they can, just so they can revise it into something clearer" (Williams, 1997, p. 11).

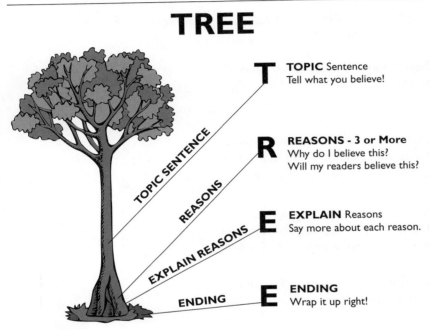

POW

P   Pick my Idea

O   Organize my Notes

W   Write and Say More

TREE

T   **TOPIC** Sentence
Tell what you believe!

R   **REASONS - 3 or More**
Why do I believe this?
Will my readers believe this?

E   **EXPLAIN** Reasons
Say more about each reason.

E   **ENDING**
Wrap it up right!

TOPIC SENTENCE

REASONS

EXPLAIN REASONS

ENDING

FIGURE 7-8

Unfortunately, young writers often don't revise at all—the first draft is usually the final draft. To make matters worse, when young writers revise, the changes do not necessarily improve their writing (Fitzgerald, 1987). Effective revision requires being able to detect problems and knowing how to correct them (Baker & Brown, 1984; Beal, 1996). As children develop, they're better able to find problems with their writing and to know how to correct them. Children and adolescents are more likely to find flaws in others' writing than in their own (Cameron et al., 1997). They are also more likely to revise successfully when the topic is familiar to them and when more time passes between initial writing and revising (Chanquoy, 2001; McCutchen, Francis, & Kerr, 1997).

If you look over these past few paragraphs, it's quite clear why good writing is so gradual in developing. Many different skills are involved and each is complicated in its own right. Word-processing software makes writing easier by handling some of these skills (e.g., checking spelling, simplifying revision), and research indicates that writing improves when people use word processors (Clements, 1995; Rogers & Graham, 2008).

Fortunately, students *can* be taught to write better. When instruction focuses on the building blocks of effective writing—strategies for planning, drafting, and revising text—students' writing improves substantially (Graham & Perin, 2007; Tracy, Reid, & Graham, 2009). For example, one successful program for teaching writing—the Self-Regulated Strategy Development in Writing program—tells students that POW + TREE is a trick that good writers use. As you can see in Figure 7-8, POW provides young writers with a general plan for writing, and TREE tells them how to organize their writing in a nicely structured paragraph (Harris et al., 2008).

Of course, mastering the full set of writing skills is a huge challenge, one that spans all of childhood, adolescence, and adulthood. Much the same can be said for mastering quantitative skills, as we'll see in the next section.

Knowing and Using Numbers

Basic number skills originate in infancy, long before babies learn names of numbers. Many babies experience daily variation in quantity. They play with two blocks and see that another baby has three; they watch as a father sorts laundry and finds two black socks but only one blue sock, and they eat one hot dog for lunch while an older brother eats three.

From these experiences, babies apparently come to appreciate that quantity or amount is one of the ways in which objects in the world can differ. This conclusion is based on research in which babies are tested with sequences of pictures like those shown in Figure 7-9. The actual objects in the pictures differ, as do their size, color, and position. Notice, however, that the first three pictures each show two things: two flowers, two cats, two butterflies.

FIGURE 7-9

When the first of these pictures is shown, infants look at it for several seconds. But, as more pictures of two things are presented, infants habituate (become familiar with them; see Module 5.1): They glance at the picture briefly, then look away. But if a picture of a single object or, like the last drawing in the figure, a picture of three objects is then shown, infants again look for several seconds, their interest apparently renewed. Because the only systematic change is the number of objects depicted in the picture, we know that babies can distinguish stimuli on the basis of number. Typically, 5-month-olds can distinguish two objects from three and, less often, three objects from four (Cordes & Brannon, 2009; Wynn, 1996).

How do infants distinguish differences in quantity? Older children might count, but, of course, infants have not yet learned names of numbers. Instead, the process is probably more perceptual in nature. As we saw in Module 5.1, the infant's perceptual system is sensitive to characteristics such as shape and color (Bornstein, 1981). Quantity may well be another characteristic of stimuli to which infants are sensitive. That is, just as colors (reds, blues) and shapes (triangles, squares) are basic perceptual properties, small quantities ("twoness" and "threeness") may be perceptually obvious (Strauss & Curtis, 1984).

> Infants can distinguish different quantities and do simple arithmetic, as long as the quantities are small.

What's more, young babies can do simple addition and subtraction—as long as it's *very* simple. In experiments using the method shown in Figure 7-10 on page 238, infants view a stage with one mouse. A screen hides the mouse and then a hand appears with a second mouse, which is placed behind the screen. When the screen is removed and reveals one mouse, 5-month-olds look longer than when two mice appear. Apparently, 5-month-olds expect that one mouse plus another mouse should equal two mice and they look longer when this expectancy is violated (Wynn, 1992). And when the stage first has two mice, one of which is removed, infants are surprised when the screen is removed and two mice are still on the stage. These experiments only work with very small numbers, indicating that the means by which infants add and subtract are very simple and probably unlike the processes that older children use (Mix, Huttenlocher, & Levine, 2002).

Finally, scientists have shown that infants can compare quantities. One way to relate two quantities is their ratio, and, amazingly, 6-month-olds are sensitive to ratio (McCrink & Wynn, 2007). Shown stimuli that features two blue circles for

Sequence of events 1+1=1 or 2

1. Object placed in case

2. Screen comes up

3. Second object added

4. Hand leaves empty

Then either: possible outcome

5. Screen drops . . .   revealing 2 objects

or: impossible outcome

5. Screen drops . . .   revealing 1 object

FIGURE 7-10

every yellow circle (e.g., 8 blue, 4 yellow; 30 blue, 15 yellow), infants look longer when they're next shown stimuli that have a ratio of four blue circles to every yellow circle (e.g., 36 blue, 9 yellow). Infants are also aware of the larger of two quantities. If 10-month-olds watch an adult place two crackers in one container but three crackers in a second container, the infants usually reach for the container with more crackers (Feigenson, Carey, & Hauser, 2002).

LEARNING TO COUNT. Names of numbers are not among most babies' first words, but by 2 years, youngsters know some number words and have begun to count. Usually, their counting is full of mistakes. In Jasmine's counting sequence that was described in the vignette—"1, 2, 6, 7"—she skips 3, 4, and 5. But research has shown that if we ignore her mistakes momentarily, the counting sequence reveals that she does understand a great deal. Gelman and Meck (1986) simply placed several objects in front of a child and asked, "How many?" By analyzing children's answers to many of these questions, they discovered that by age 3 most children have mastered three basic principles of counting, at least when it comes to counting up to five objects.

- *One-to-one principle:* **There must be one and only one number name for each object that is counted.** A child who counts three objects as "1, 2, a" understands this principle because the number of number words matches the number of objects to be counted.

- *Stable-order principle:* **Number names must be counted in the same order.** A child who counts in the same sequence—for example, consistently counting four objects as "1, 2, 4, 5"—shows understanding of this principle.

- *Cardinality principle:* **The last number name differs from the previous ones in a counting sequence by denoting the number of objects.** Typically, 3-year-olds reveal their understanding of this principle by repeating the last number name, often with emphasis: "1, 2, 4, 8 . . . EIGHT!"

During the preschool years, children master these basic principles and apply them to ever-larger sets of objects. By age 5, most youngsters apply these counting principles to as many as nine objects. (To see whether you understand the counting principles, go back to Jasmine's counting in the vignette and decide which principles she has mastered; my answer is given before "Check Your Learning" on page 243.)

Of course, children's understanding of these principles does not mean that they always count accurately. To the contrary, children can apply all these principles consistently while counting incorrectly. They must master the conventional sequence of the number names and the counting principles to learn to count accurately. Learning the number names beyond 9 is easier because the counting words can be generated based on rules for combining decade number names (20, 30, 40) with unit names (1, 2, 3, 4). Later, similar rules are used for hundreds, thousands, and so on. By age 4, most youngsters know the numbers to 20, and some can count to 99 (Siegler & Robinson, 1982).

> Preschoolers know many counting principles even though they often count inaccurately.

Learning to count beyond 10 is more complicated in English than in other languages. For example, *eleven* and *twelve* are completely irregular names, following no rules. Also, the remaining "teen" number names differ from the 20s, 30s, and the rest in that the decade number name comes after the unit (thir-*teen*, four-*teen*) rather than before (*twenty*-three, *thirty*-four). Also, some decade names only loosely correspond to the unit names on which they are based: *twenty, thirty,* and *fifty* resemble *two, three,* and *five* but are not the same.

In contrast, the Chinese and Korean number systems are almost perfectly regular. *Eleven* and *twelve* are expressed as *ten-one* and *ten-two*. There are no special names for the decades: *Two-ten* and *two-ten-one* are names for 20 and 21. These simplified number names help explain why youngsters growing up in Asian countries count more accurately than U.S. preschool children of the same age (Miller et al., 1995). What's more, the direct correspondence between the number names and the base-10 system makes it easier for Asian youngsters to learn some mathematical concepts. For example, if a child has 10 blocks, then gets 6 more, an American 5-year-old will carefully count the additional blocks to determine that he now has 16. In contrast, a Chinese 5-year-old will not count but quickly say "16" because she understands that in the base-10 system, 10 + 6 = 16 (Ho & Fuson, 1998).

By the time children are ready to begin school, their grasp of arithmetic concepts has progressed considerably. For example, they implicitly understand that addition is commutative (e.g., 4 + 2 = 2 + 4). Shown one bear who receives four candies, then three more, as well as a second bear who receives three candies then four more, 5-year-olds believe that the two bears have the same number of candies (Canobi, Reeve, & Pattison, 2002). But some of their understanding is distorted, such as their grasp of the number line. If 5-year-olds are shown a line with 0 and 100 at the ends, then asked to place marks corresponding to 2, 8, 16, 46, and 81 on the line, they'll usually produce something like Figure 7-11 (Booth & Siegler, 2006; Siegler & Mu, 2008). Preschool children's representation of numbers is skewed, with much larger gaps between the digits 1 through 10 and much smaller gaps between the digits 10 through 100.

FIGURE 7-11

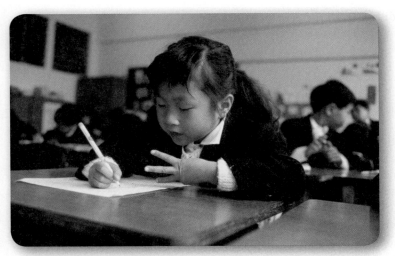

Young children use many strategies to solve simple arithmetic problems, including counting on their fingers.

ADDING AND SUBTRACTING. By 4 or 5 years of age, most children have encountered arithmetic problems that involve simple addition or subtraction. A 4-year-old might put one green bean on her plate, then watch in dismay as her dad gives her three more. Now she wonders, "Now how many do I have to eat?" Like the child in the photo, many youngsters solve this sort of problem by counting. They first count out four fingers on one hand, then count out two more on the other. Finally, they count all six fingers on both hands. To subtract, they do the same procedure in reverse (Siegler & Jenkins, 1989; Siegler & Shrager, 1984).

Youngsters soon abandon this approach for a slightly more efficient method. Instead of counting the fingers on the first hand, they simultaneously extend the number of fingers on the first hand corresponding to the larger of the two numbers to be added. Next, they count out the smaller number with fingers on the second hand. Finally, they count all of the fingers to determine the sum (Groen & Resnick, 1977).

After children begin to receive formal arithmetic instruction in first grade, addition problems are solved less frequently by counting aloud or by counting fingers (Jordan et al., 2008). Instead, children add and subtract by counting mentally. That is, children act as if they are counting silently, beginning with the larger number, and adding on. By age 8 or 9, children have learned the addition tables so well that sums of the single-digit integers (from 0 to 9) are facts that are simply retrieved from memory (Ashcraft, 1982).

These counting strategies do *not* occur in a rigid developmental sequence. Instead, as I mentioned in describing the overlapping waves model (on page 223), individual children use many different strategies for addition, depending on the problem. Children usually begin by trying to retrieve an answer from memory. If they are not reasonably confident that the retrieved answer is correct, then they resort to counting aloud or on fingers (Siegler, 1996). Retrieval is most likely for problems with small addends (e.g., 1 + 2, 2 + 4) because these problems are presented frequently in textbooks and by teachers. Consequently, the sum is highly associated with the problem, which makes the child confident that the retrieved answer is correct. In contrast, problems with larger addends, such as 9 + 8, are presented less often. The result is a weaker link between the addends and the sum and, consequently, a greater chance that children need to determine an answer by resorting to a backup strategy such as counting.

Of course, arithmetic skills continue to improve as children move through elementary school. They become more proficient in addition and subtraction, learn multiplication and division, and in high school and college move on to the more sophisticated mathematical concepts involved in algebra, geometry, trigonometry, and calculus (De Brauwer & Fias, 2009). But just as basic word decoding skills set the stage for more complicated comprehension skills, basic understanding of numbers that is acquired in the preschool years provides the foundation for more complex arithmetic and mathematical operations (Jordan et al., 2009). And, just as parents can promote their children's reading skills by reading with them, playing number games (e.g., board games in which children must count the number of spaces to move a

 QUESTION 7.3

Barb enjoys asking her 6-year-old, Erin, to solve simple arithmetic problems, such as 4 + 2 and 3 + 1. Erin likes solving these problems, but Barb finds it puzzling that Erin may solve a problem by counting on her fingers one day and simply saying the answer aloud on the next day. Is Erin's behavior unusual? *(Answer is on page 243.)*

game piece) can foster children's early number skills (Ramani & Siegler, 2008).

COMPARING U.S. STUDENTS WITH STUDENTS IN OTHER COUNTRIES. Let's return to the issue of cultural differences in mathematical competence. When compared to students worldwide in terms of math skills, U.S. students don't fare well. For example, Figure 7-12 shows the math results from a major international comparison (Gonzales et al., 2008). U.S. eighth-graders have substantially lower scores than eighth-graders in several nations. Phrased another way, the very best U.S. students only perform at the level of average students in many Asian countries. What's more, the cultural differences in math achievement hold for both math operations and math problem solving (Stevenson & Lee, 1990).

Why do American students rate so poorly? The "Cultural Influences" feature gives some answers.

FIGURE 7-12

Cultural Influences

Fifth Grade in Taiwan

Shin-ying is an 11-year-old attending school in Taipei, the largest city in Taiwan. Like most fifth-graders, Shin-ying is in school from 8:00 AM until 4:00 PM daily. Most evenings, she spends 2 to 3 hours doing homework. This academic routine is grueling by U.S. standards, where fifth-graders typically spend 6 to 7 hours in school each day and less than an hour doing homework. I asked Shin-ying what she thought of school and schoolwork. Her answers surprised me.

RK: Why do you go to school?

SHIN-YING: I like what we study.

RK: Any other reasons?

SHIN-YING: The things that I learn in school are useful.

RK: What about homework? Why do you do it?

SHIN-YING: My teacher and my parents think it's important. And I like doing it.

RK: Do you think that you would do nearly as well in school if you didn't work so hard?

SHIN-YING: Oh no. The best students are always the ones who work the hardest.

Schoolwork is the focal point of Shin-ying's life. Although many American school-children are unhappy when schoolwork intrudes on time for play and television, Shin-ying is enthusiastic about school and school-related activities.

Students in Asia spend more time on school tasks and their parents set high standards for academic achievement.

Shin-ying is not unusual among Chinese elementary-school students. Many of her comments illustrate findings that emerge from detailed analyses of classrooms, teachers, students, and parents in studies comparing students in Japan, Taiwan, and the United States (Perry, 2000; Stevenson & Lee, 1990; Stigler, Gallimore, & Hiebert, 2000):

- ***Time in school and how it is used.*** By fifth grade, students in Japan and Taiwan spend 50% more time than American students in school, more of this time is devoted to academic activities than in the United States, and instruction in Asian schools is often better organized and more challenging.

- ***Time spent on homework and attitudes toward it.*** Students in Taiwan and Japan spend more time on homework and value homework more than American students do.

- ***Parents' attitudes.*** American parents are more often satisfied with their children's performance in school; in contrast, Japanese and Taiwanese parents set much higher standards for their children.

Many Asian schoolchildren have a quiet area at home where they can study undisturbed.

- ***Parents' beliefs about effort and ability.*** Japanese and Taiwanese parents believe more strongly than American parents that effort, not native ability, is the key factor in school success.

Thus, students in Japan and Taiwan excel because they spend more time both in and out of school on academic tasks. Furthermore, their parents (and teachers) set loftier scholastic goals and believe that students can attain these goals with hard work. Japanese classrooms even post a motto describing ideal students: *gambaru kodomo*—those who strive the hardest.

Parents underscore the importance of schoolwork in many ways to their children. For example, even though homes and apartments in Japan and China are very small by U.S. standards, Asian youngsters, like the child in the photo, typically have a desk in a quiet area where they can study undisturbed (Stevenson & Lee, 1990). For Japanese and Taiwanese teachers and parents, academic excellence is paramount, and it shows in their children's success.

EDUCATIONAL IMPLICATIONS OF CROSS-CULTURAL FINDINGS ON ACADEMIC ACHIEVEMENT. What can Americans learn from Japanese and Taiwanese educational systems? From their experiences with Asian students, teachers, and schools, Stevenson and Stigler (1992) suggest several ways American schools could be improved:

- Give teachers more free time to prepare lessons and correct students' work.

- Improve teachers' training by allowing them to work closely with older, more experienced teachers.

- Organize instruction around sound principles of learning, such as providing multiple examples of concepts and giving students adequate opportunities to practice newly acquired skills.

- Set higher standards for children, who need to spend more time and effort in school-related activities in order to achieve those standards.

Changing teaching practices and attitudes toward achievement would begin to reduce the gap between American students and students in other industrialized countries, particularly Asian countries. Ignoring the problem will mean an increasingly undereducated workforce and citizenry in a more complex world—an alarming prospect.

Response to question about Jasmine's counting on page 239: Because Jasmine uses four number names to count four objects ("1, 2, 6, 7 . . . SEVEN!"), she understands the one-to-one principle. The four number names are always used in the same order, so she grasps the stable-order principle. Finally, she repeats the last number name with emphasis, so she understands the cardinality principle.

 ANSWER 7.3

No. In many domains, including simple arithmetic, children use multiple strategies. They will solve a problem one way (e.g., counting on their fingers) and when asked the problem again, solve it a different way (e.g., retrieving the answer from memory).

 Check Your Learning

RECALL What are some of the prerequisite skills that children must master to learn to read?

Summarize the differences between education in China and education in the United States.

INTERPRET Compare the mathematical skills that are mastered before children enter school with those that they master after beginning school.

APPLY Review the research on page 233 regarding factors associated with skilled reading comprehension. Which of these factors—if any—might also contribute to skilled writing?

UNIFYING THEMES Active Children

This chapter highlights the theme that *children influence their own development:* Japanese and Chinese elementary-school children typically enjoy studying (an attitude fostered by their parents), and this makes them quite willing to do homework for 2 or 3 hours nightly. This, in turn, contributes to their high levels of scholastic achievement.

American schoolchildren usually detest homework and do as little of it as possible, which contributes to their relatively lower level of scholastic achievement. Thus, children's attitudes help to determine how they behave, which determines how much they will achieve over the course of childhood and adolescence.

See for Yourself

Create several small sets of objects that vary in number. You might have two pennies, three candies, four buttons, five pencils, six erasers, seven paper clips, and so on. Place each set of objects on a paper plate. Then find some preschool children; 4- and 5-year-olds would be ideal. Put a plate in front of each child and ask, "How many?" Then watch to see what the child does. If possible, tape-record the children's counting

so that you can analyze it later. If this is impossible, try to write down exactly what each child says as he or she counts. Later, go back through your notes and determine whether the children follow the counting principles described on pages 238–239. You should see that children, particularly younger ones, more often follow the principles while counting small sets of objects than larger sets. See for yourself!

Summary

7.1 Memory

Origins of Memory

Rovee-Collier's studies of kicking show that infants can remember, forget, and be reminded of events that occurred in the past.

Strategies for Remembering

Beginning in the preschool years, children use strategies to help them remember. With age, children use more powerful strategies, such as rehearsal and outlining. Using memory strategies successfully depends, first, on analyzing the goal of a memory task and, second, on monitoring the effectiveness of the chosen strategy. Analyzing goals and monitoring are two important elements of metamemory, which is a child's informal understanding of how memory operates.

Knowledge and Memory

A child's knowledge of the world can be used to organize information that is to be remembered. When several events occur in a specific order, they are remembered as a single script. Knowledge improves memory for children and adolescents, although older individuals often reap more benefit because they have more knowledge. Knowledge can also distort memory by causing children and adolescents to forget information that does not conform to their knowledge or to remember events that are part of their knowledge but that did not actually take place.

Autobiographical memory refers to a person's memory about his or her own life. Autobiographical memory emerges in the early preschool years, often prompted by parents' asking children about past events. Infantile amnesia—children's and adults' inability to remember events from early in life—may reflect the absence of language or a sense of self.

Young children's memory in court cases is often inaccurate because children are questioned repeatedly, which makes it hard for them to distinguish what actually occurred from what adults suggest may have occurred. Children's testimony would be more reliable if children are interviewed promptly, they're encouraged to tell the truth, they're first asked to explain what happened in their own words, and interviewers ask questions that test alternate accounts of what happened.

7.2 Problem Solving

Developmental Trends in Solving Problems

As a general rule, as children develop they solve problems more often and solve them more effectively. However, exceptions to the rule are not uncommon: Young children sometimes solve problems successfully while adolescents sometimes fail.

Features of Children's and Adolescents' Problem Solving

Young children sometimes fail to solve problems because they don't plan ahead and because they don't encode all of the necessary information in a problem. Successful problem solving typically depends on knowledge specific to the problem, along with general processes; involves the use of a variety of strategies; and is enhanced by collaborating with an adult or older child.

Scientific Problem Solving

Although the "child-as-scientist" metaphor is popular, in fact, children and adolescents lack many of the skills associated with real scientific reasoning: They tend to design confounded experiments; they reach conclusions prematurely, based on inadequate evidence; and they have difficulty integrating theory and data.

7.3 Academic Skills

Reading

Reading encompasses a number of component skills. Prereading skills include knowing letters and the sounds associated with them. Word recognition is the process of identifying a word. Beginning readers more often accomplish this by sounding out words; advanced readers more often retrieve a word from long-term memory. Comprehension (the act of extracting meaning from text) improves with age because of several factors: working memory capacity increases, readers gain more world knowledge, and readers are better able to monitor what they read and to match their reading strategies to the goals of the reading task.

Writing

As children develop, their writing improves, reflecting several factors: They know more about the world and so they have more to say; they use more effective ways of organizing their writing; they master the mechanics (e.g., handwriting, spelling) of writing; and they become more skilled at revising their writing.

Knowing and Using Numbers

Infants can distinguish quantities, probably by means of basic perceptual processes. Children begin to count by about age 2, and by 3 years most children have mastered the one-to-one, stable-order, and cardinality principles, at least when counting small sets of objects. Counting is how children first add, but it is replaced by more effective strategies such as retrieving sums directly from memory.

In mathematics, American students lag behind students in most other industrialized nations, chiefly because of cultural differences in the time spent on schoolwork and homework and in parents' attitudes toward school, effort, and ability.

Test Yourself

✔●—Study and Review on mydevelopmentlab.com

1. Important features of memory are evident in young infants: They can remember past events, but with the passage of time some events are no longer recalled, although _____.

2. A strategy that preschool children often use to help them remember is to _____.

3. Diagnosing memory problems and monitoring the effectiveness of memory strategies are two important elements of _____.

4. According to fuzzy trace theory, older children and adolescents are more prone to memory errors because they tend to remember _____.

5. Autobiographical memory develops early as children acquire basic memory skills, language, and _____.

6. Young children often fail to solve problems because they don't encode all the information that's necessary and because _____.

7. Children and adolescents both rely on heuristic and analytic solutions, but _____ solutions are more common among adolescents.

8. Young children often have trouble solving problems collaboratively because neither child knows how to proceed and because _____.

9. When children try to reason scientifically, they often devise confounded experiments, frequently reach conclusions prematurely, and have difficulty _____.

10. In many languages, _____ is the best predictor of a child's success in learning to read.

11. _____ instruction is an essential part of programs designed to teach children to read.

12. When young children write, they often rely upon a _____ strategy.

13. Infants can distinguish different quantities because _____.

14. By three years, children have mastered the _____, stable-order, and cardinality principles of counting (for small sets of objects).

15. Two reasons why students in Asian countries often excel in math achievement are that their parents set higher standards and their parents believe that _____.

Answers: (1) a cue can help to retrieve a forgotten memory; (2) look at or touch objects that they've been asked to remember; (3) metamemory; (4) gist (not verbatim); (5) a sense of self; (6) they don't plan ahead; (7) analytic; (8) young children typically lack the social and linguistic skills to make collaboration effective; (9) integrating theory and data; (10) phonological awareness; (11) Phonics; (12) knowledge-telling; (13) the perceptual system is sensitive to quantity; (14) one-to-one; (15) hard work, not ability, is the key to achievement.

Key Terms

autobiographical memory   216
cardinality principle   239
cognitive self-regulation   212
comprehension   229
confounded   225
elaboration   211
encoding processes   221
fuzzy trace theory   214
heuristics   224

infantile amnesia   216
knowledge-telling strategy   234
knowledge-transforming strategy   235
means-ends analysis   223
memory strategy   211
metacognitive knowledge   212
metamemory   212

one-to-one principle   238
organization   211
phonological awareness   229
propositions   232
rehearsal   211
script   213
stable-order principle   238
word decoding   229

8

Intelligence and Individual Differences in Cognition

What Is Intelligence?

Measuring Intelligence

Special Children, Special Needs

Have you ever stopped to think how many standardized tests you've taken in your student career? You probably took either the SAT or the ACT to enter college. Before that, you took countless achievement and aptitude tests during elementary school and high school. Psychological testing began in schools early in the 20th century and continues to be an integral part of American education in the 21st century.

Of all standardized tests, none attracts more attention and generates more controversy than tests designed to measure intelligence. Intelligence tests have been hailed by some as one of psychology's greatest contributions to society and cursed by others. Intelligence tests and what they measure are the focus of Chapter 8. We'll start, in **Module 8.1**, by looking at different definitions of intelligence. In **Module 8.2**, we'll see how intelligence tests work and examine some factors that influence test scores. Finally, in **Module 8.3**, we'll look at special children—youngsters whose intelligence sets them apart from their peers.

8.1 What Is Intelligence?

OUTLINE

Psychometric Theories

Gardner's Theory of Multiple Intelligences

Sternberg's Theory of Successful Intelligence

LEARNING OBJECTIVES

- What is the psychometric view of the nature of intelligence?
- How does Gardner's theory of multiple intelligences differ from the psychometric approach?
- What are the components of Sternberg's theory of successful intelligence?

Diana is an eager fourth-grade teacher who loves history. Consequently, every year she's frustrated when she teaches a unit on the American Civil War. Although she's passionate about the subject, her enthusiasm is not contagious. Instead, her students' eyes glaze over and she can see young minds drifting off—and, of course, they never seem to grasp the historical significance of this war. Diana wishes there was a different way to teach this unit, one that would engage her students more effectively.

Before you read further, how would you define *intelligence*? If you're typical of most Americans, your definition probably includes the ability to reason logically, connect ideas, and solve real problems. You might mention *verbal ability*, meaning the ability to speak clearly and articulately. You might also mention *social competence*, referring, for example, to an interest in the world at large and an ability to admit when you make a mistake (Sternberg & Kaufman, 1998).

As you'll see in this module, many of these ideas about intelligence are included in psychological theories of intelligence. We'll begin by considering the oldest theories of intelligence, those associated with the psychometric tradition. Then we'll look at two newer approaches and, along the way, get some insights into ways that Diana could make the Civil War come alive for her class.

Psychometric Theories

Psychometricians **are psychologists who specialize in measuring psychological characteristics such as intelligence and personality.** When psychometricians want to research a particular question, they usually begin by administering a large number of tests to many individuals. They then look for patterns in performance across the different tests. The basic logic underlying this technique is similar to the logic a jungle hunter uses to decide whether some dark blobs in a river are three separate rotting logs or a single alligator (Cattell, 1965). If the blobs move together, the hunter decides that they are part of the same structure, an alligator. If they do not move together, they are three different structures—three logs. Similarly, if changes in performance on one psychological test are accompanied by changes in performance on a second test—that is, if the scores move together—then the tests appear to measure the same attribute or factor.

Patterns of test scores provide evidence for general intelligence as well as for specific abilities.

Suppose, for example, that you believe intelligence is very broad and general. In other words, you believe that some people are smart regardless of the situation, task, or problem, whereas others are not so smart. According to this view, children's performance should be very consistent across tasks. Smart children should always receive high scores and less smart youngsters should always get lower scores. In fact, more than 100 years ago, Charles Spearman (1904) reported findings supporting the idea that a general factor for intelligence, or *g*, is responsible for performance on all mental tests.

Other researchers, however, have found that intelligence consists of distinct abilities. For example, Thurstone and Thurstone (1941) analyzed performance on a wide range of tasks and identified seven distinct patterns, each reflecting a unique ability: perceptual speed, word comprehension, word fluency, space, number, memory, and induction. Thurstone and Thurstone also acknowledged a general factor that operated in all tasks, but they emphasized that the specific factors were more useful in assessing and understanding intellectual ability.

These conflicting findings have led many psychometric theorists to propose hierarchical theories of intelligence that include both general and specific components. John Carroll (1993, 1996), for example, proposed a hierarchical theory with three levels, shown in Figure 8-1. At the top of the hierarchy is *g*, general intelligence. In the middle level are eight broad categories of intellectual skill. **For example,** *fluid intelligence* **refers to the ability to perceive relations among stimuli.** Each of the abilities in the second level is further divided into the skills listed in the bottom and most specific level. *Crystallized intelligence,* **for example, comprises a person's culturally influenced accumulated knowledge and**

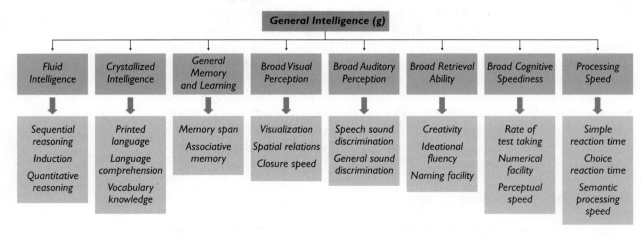

Source: Carroll, 1993.

FIGURE 8-1

skills, including understanding printed language, comprehending language, and knowing vocabulary.

Carroll's hierarchical theory is, in essence, a compromise between the two views of intelligence—general versus distinct abilities. But some critics still find it unsatisfactory because it ignores the research and theory on cognitive development described in Chapters 6 and 7. They believe we need to look beyond the psychometric approach to understand intelligence. In the remainder of this module, then, we'll look at two newer theories that have done just this.

Gardner's Theory of Multiple Intelligences

Only recently have child-development researchers viewed intelligence from the perspective of modern theories of cognition and cognitive development. These new theories present a much broader perspective on intelligence and how it develops. Among the most ambitious is Howard Gardner's (1983, 1999, 2002, 2006) theory of multiple intelligences. Rather than using test scores as the basis for his theory, Gardner drew on research in child development, studies of brain-damaged persons, and studies of exceptionally talented people. Using these resources, Gardner identified seven distinct intelligences when he first proposed the theory in 1983. In subsequent work, Gardner (1999, 2002) has identified two additional intelligences; the complete list is shown in Table 8-1.

The first three intelligences in this list—linguistic intelligence, logical-mathematical intelligence, and spatial intelligence—are included in psychometric theories of intelligence. The last six intelligences are not: Musical, bodily-kinesthetic, interpersonal, intrapersonal, naturalistic, and existential intelligences are unique to Gardner's theory. According to Gardner, Carlos Santana's wizardry on the guitar, the Williams sisters' remarkable shots on the tennis court, and Oprah Winfrey's

TABLE 8-1

NINE INTELLIGENCES IN GARDNER'S THEORY OF MULTIPLE INTELLIGENCES

Type of Intelligence	Definition
Linguistic	Knowing the meanings of words, having the ability to use words to understand new ideas, and using language to convey ideas to others
Logical-mathematical	Understanding relations that exist among objects, actions, and ideas, as well as the logical or mathematical operations that can be performed on them
Spatial	Perceiving objects accurately and imagining in the "mind's eye" the appearance of an object before and after it has been transformed
Musical	Comprehending and producing sounds varying in pitch, rhythm, and emotional tone
Bodily-kinesthetic	Using one's body in highly differentiated ways, as dancers, craftspeople, and athletes do
Interpersonal	Identifying different feelings, moods, motivations, and intentions in others
Intrapersonal	Understanding one's emotions and knowing one's strengths and weaknesses
Naturalistic	Understanding the natural world, distinguishing natural objects from artifacts, grouping and labeling natural phenomena
Existential	Considering "ultimate" issues, such as the purpose of life and the nature of death

Source: Gardner, 1983, 1999, 2002.

grace and charm in dealing with people are all features of intelligence that are totally ignored in traditional theories.

How did Gardner arrive at these nine distinct intelligences? First, each has a unique developmental history. Linguistic intelligence, for example, develops much earlier than the other eight. Second, each intelligence is regulated by distinct regions of the brain, as shown by studies of brain-damaged persons. Spatial intelligence, for example, is regulated by particular regions in the brain's right hemisphere. Third, each has special cases of talented individuals. The field of music, for example, is well known for individuals with incredible talent that's apparent at an early age. Claudio Arrau, one of the 20th century's greatest pianists, could read musical notes before he could read words; Yo-Yo Ma, the famed cellist, performed in concert at seven years of age for President John F. Kennedy.

> From research in child development, studies of people with brain damage, and studies of talented people, Gardner proposed nine distinct intelligences.

Prompted by Gardner's theory, researchers have begun to look at other nontraditional aspects of intelligence. **Probably the best known is** *emotional intelligence,* **which is the ability to use one's own and others' emotions effectively for solving problems and living happily.** Emotional intelligence made headlines in 1995 because of a best-selling book, *Emotional Intelligence,* in which the author, Daniel Goleman, argued that "emotions [are] at the center of aptitudes for living" (1995, p. xiii). One major model of emotional intelligence (Salovey & Grewal, 2005; Mayer, Salovey, & Caruso, 2008) includes several distinct facets, including perceiving emotions accurately (e.g., recognizing a happy face), understanding emotions (e.g., distinguishing happiness from ecstasy), and regulating emotions (e.g., hiding one's disappointment). People who are emotionally intelligent tend to have more satisfying interpersonal relationships, have greater self-esteem, and be more effective in the workplace (Joseph & Newman, 2010; Mayer, Roberts, & Barsade, 2008).

Most of the research on emotional intelligence has been done with adults, in large part because Goleman (1998; Goleman, Boyatzis, & McKee, 2002) has argued that emotional intelligence can be the key to a successful career. Child-development researchers have studied emotion, but usually from a developmental angle—they've wanted to know how emotions change with age. We'll look at their research in Module 10.1.

IMPLICATIONS FOR EDUCATION. The theory of multiple intelligence has important implications for education. Gardner (1993, 1995) believes that schools should foster all intelligences, rather than just the traditional linguistic and logical-mathematical intelligences. Teachers should capitalize on the strongest intelligences of individual children. That is, teachers need to know a child's profile of intelligence—the child's strengths and weaknesses—and gear instruction to the strengths (Chen & Gardner, 2005). For example, Diana, the fourth-grade teacher in the opening vignette, could help some of her students understand the Civil War by studying music of that period (musical intelligence). Other students might benefit by emphasis on maps that show the movement of armies in battle (spatial intelligence). Still others might profit from focusing on the experiences of African Americans living in the North and the South (interpersonal intelligence).

These guidelines do not mean that teachers should gear instruction solely to a child's strongest intelligence, pigeonholing youngsters as numerical learners or spatial learners. Instead, whether the topic is the signing of the Declaration of Independence or Shakespeare's *Hamlet,* instruction should try to engage as many different intelligences as possible (Gardner, 1999, 2002). The typical result is a much richer understanding of the topic by all students.

Some American schools have enthusiastically embraced Gardner's ideas (Gardner, 1993). Are these schools better than those that have not? Educators in schools using the theory think so; they cite evidence that their students benefit in many ways (Kornhaber, Fierros, & Veenema, 2004), although some critics are not yet convinced (Waterhouse, 2006). Nevertheless, there is no doubt that Gardner's work has helped liberate researchers from narrow, psychometric-based views of intelligence.

A comparably broad but different view of intelligence comes from another new theory that we'll look at in the next section.

Sternberg's Theory of Successful Intelligence

Robert Sternberg has studied intelligence for more than 35 years. He began by asking how adults solve problems on intelligence tests. Over the years, this work led to a comprehensive theory of intelligence, one that is the focus of the "Spotlight on Theories" feature.

Spotlight on Theories

The Theory of Successful Intelligence

BACKGROUND Traditional theories of intelligence have been rooted in test scores. Today, however, many scientists believe that these classic theories are too narrow; they argue that we need to look to modern theories of thinking and development for broader, more comprehensive views of intelligence.

THE THEORY Robert Sternberg (1999) defines *successful intelligence* as using one's abilities skillfully to achieve one's personal goals. Goals can be short term: getting an A on a test, making a snack in the microwave, or winning the 100-meter hurdles. Or they can be longer term: having a successful career and a happy family life. Achieving these goals by using one's skills defines successful intelligence. ⊙—Watch the **Video** on **mydevelopmentlab.com**

In achieving personal goals, people use three different kinds of abilities. *Analytic ability* **involves analyzing problems and generating different solutions.** Suppose a teenager wants to download songs to her iPod but something isn't working. Analytic intelligence is shown when she considers different causes of the problem—maybe the iPod is broken or maybe the software to download songs wasn't installed correctly. Analytic intelligence also involves thinking of different solutions: She could surf the Internet for clues about what's wrong or ask a sibling for help.

Creative ability **involves dealing adaptively with novel situations and problems.** Returning to our teenager, suppose that she discovers her iPod is broken just as she's ready to leave on a day-long car trip. Lacking the time (and money) to buy a new player, she might show creative intelligence in dealing successfully with a novel goal: finding something enjoyable to do to pass the time on a long drive.

Finally, *practical ability* **involves knowing what solution or plan will actually work.** That is, although problems can often be solved in different ways in principle, in reality only one solution is practical. Our teenager may realize that surfing the Net for

⊙—Watch the **Video** *Robert Sternberg's Views on Intelligence* on **mydevelopmentlab .com** to learn more about some of the events from Sternberg's childhood that led him to become fascinated with intelligence.

a way to fix the player is the only real choice, because her parents wouldn't approve of many of the songs and she doesn't want a sibling to know that she's downloading them anyway.

Hypothesis: If successful intelligence consists of three distinct abilities—analytic, creative, and practical—then this leads to an important hypothesis: Scores from tests that measure different abilities should be unrelated. Creative ability scores should be unrelated to practical ability scores; and both should be unrelated to analytic ability scores.

Test: Sternberg and his colleagues (2006) had high-school and college students complete 45 test items, 15 for each ability. For example, on one item measuring analytic creative ability, students read a novel word in a paragraph, then had to use the context to determine the meaning of that word. On an item assessing creative ability, students were given a false statement (e.g., "Money grows on trees") and then asked to solve reasoning problems as if the statement were true. Finally, an item testing practical ability described common problems facing teenagers (e.g., a friend seems to have a substance-abuse problem) and students selected the best solution.

> According to Robert Sternberg, intelligence involves using analytic, creative, and practical abilities to achieve personal goals.

The critical finding concerns correlations between test scores. If analytic, creative, and practical abilities are completely distinct, then test scores should be unrelated: The correlations between analytic test scores and creative test scores, for example, should be 0. At the other extreme, if analytic, creative, and practical abilities are really all the same "thing"—such as general intelligence, g—then the correlation between test scores should be 1. In reality, the pattern was midway between these two alternatives: Scores were related—correlations were about .6—but not perfectly, as they would be if all tests were simply measuring general intelligence.

Conclusion: The results are not perfectly consistent with the hypothesis, but do provide some support for it: Intelligence includes analytic, creative, and practical abilities, but these may not be completely independent as Sternberg initially proposed.

Application: If people differ in their analytic, creative, and practical abilities, then they may learn best when instruction is geared to their strength. A child with strong analytic ability, for example, may find algebra simpler when the course emphasizes analyses and evaluation; a child with strong practical ability may be at his best when the material is organized around practical applications. Thus, the theory of successful intelligence shows how instruction can be matched to students' strongest abilities, enhancing students' prospects for mastering the material (Grigorenko, Jarvin, & Sternberg, 2002).

Q&A QUESTION 8.1

Kathryn is convinced that her daughter is really smart because she has a huge vocabulary for her age. Would a psychometrician, Howard Gardner, and Robert Sternberg agree with Kathryn's opinion? *(Answer is on page 254.)*

Sternberg emphasizes that successful intelligence is revealed in people's pursuit of goals. Of course, these goals vary from one person to the next and, just as importantly, often vary even more in different cultural, ethnic, or racial groups. This makes it tricky—at best—to compare intelligence and intelligence-test scores for individuals from different groups, as we'll see in the "Cultural Influences" feature.

Cultural Influences

How Culture Defines What Is Intelligent

In Brazil, many elementary-school-age boys like the two in the top photo sell candy and fruit to bus passengers and pedestrians. These children often cannot identify the numbers on paper money, yet they know how to purchase their goods from wholesale stores, make change for customers, and keep track of their sales (Saxe, 1988).

Adolescents who live on Pacific Ocean islands near New Guinea learn to sail boats, like the one in the bottom photo, hundreds of miles across open seas to get from one small island to the next. They have no formal training in mathematics, yet they can use a complex navigational system based on the positions of stars and estimates of the boat's speed (Hutchins, 1983).

If either the Brazilian vendors or the island navigators were given the tests that measure intelligence in U.S. students, they would fare poorly. And they probably couldn't download music to an iPod. Does this mean they are less intelligent than U.S. children? Of course not. The specific skills and goals that are important to American conceptions of successful intelligence and that are assessed on many intelligence tests are less valued in these other cultures and so are not cultivated in the young. By the same token, most bright U.S. children would be lost trying to navigate a boat in the open sea. Each culture defines what it means to be intelligent, and the specialized computing skills of vendors and navigators are just as intelligent in their cultural settings as verbal skills are in American culture (Sternberg & Kaufman, 1998).

In Brazil, many school-aged boys sell candy and fruit on the streets, yet they often cannot identify the numbers on money.

As with Gardner's theory, researchers are still evaluating Sternberg's theory. As you can see in the table that summarizes the different approaches, theorists are still debating the question of what intelligence *is*. But, however it is defined, the fact remains that individuals differ substantially in intellectual ability, and numerous tests have been devised to measure these differences. The construction, properties, and limits of these tests are the focus of the next module.

Adolescents living on islands in the Pacific Ocean near New Guinea navigate small boats across hundreds of miles of open water, yet they have no formal training in mathematics.

SUMMARY TABLE

FEATURES OF MAJOR APPROACHES TO INTELLIGENCE

Approach	Distinguishing Features
Psychometric	Intelligence is a hierarchy of general and specific skills.
Gardner's theory of multiple intelligences	Nine distinct intelligences exist: linguistic, logical-mathematical, spatial, musical, bodily-kinesthetic, interpersonal, intrapersonal, naturalistic, and existential.
Sternberg's theory of successful intelligence	Successful intelligence is defined as the use of analytic, creative, and practical abilities to pursue personal goals.

ANSWER 8.1

Each of them would agree that verbal ability is one part of intelligence. A psychometrician and Howard Gardner would both tell her that intelligence includes other skills (although they wouldn't mention the same ones); Sternberg would emphasize that it's the application of verbal skill in the context of analytic, creative, and practical abilities that really matters.

 Check Your Learning

RECALL Describe the psychometric perspective on intelligence.

Summarize the main features of Sternberg's theory of successful intelligence.

INTERPRET Compare and contrast the major approaches to intelligence in terms of the extent to which they make connections among different aspects of development. That is, to what extent does each perspective emphasize cognitive processes versus integrating physical, cognitive, social, and emotional processes?

APPLY On page 250, I mentioned activities that would allow Diana, the fourth-grade teacher, to take advantage of musical, spatial, and interpersonal intelligences to help engage more of her students in a unit on the American Civil War. Think of activities that would allow her to engage Gardner's remaining intelligences in her teaching.

 8.2   Measuring Intelligence

OUTLINE	LEARNING OBJECTIVES
Binet and the Development of Intelligence Testing	• Why were intelligence tests devised initially? What are modern tests like?
What Do IQ Scores Predict?	• How stable are IQ scores? What do they predict?
	• What is dynamic testing? How does it differ from traditional testing?
Hereditary and Environmental Factors	• What are the roles of heredity and environment in determining intelligence?
Impact of Ethnicity and Socioeconomic Status	• How do ethnicity and socioeconomic status influence intelligence test scores?

Charlene, an African American third-grader, received a score of 75 on an intelligence test administered by a school psychologist. Based on the test score, the psychologist believes that Charlene is mildly mentally retarded and should receive special education. Charlene's parents are indignant; they believe that the tests are biased against African Americans and that the score is meaningless.

Between 1890 and 1915, enrollment in U.S. schools nearly doubled nationally as great numbers of immigrants arrived and as reforms restricted child labor and emphasized education. Increased enrollment meant that teachers now had larger numbers of students who did not learn as readily as the "select few" who had populated their classes previously. How to deal with these less-capable children was one of the pressing issues of the day (Giordano, 2005). In this module, you'll see how intelligence tests were devised initially to address a changed school population. Then we'll look at a simple question: "How well do modern tests work?" Finally, we'll examine how race, ethnicity, social class, environment, and heredity influence intelligence, and we'll learn how to interpret Charlene's test score.

Binet and the Development of Intelligence Testing

The problems facing educators at the beginning of the 20th century were not unique to the United States. In 1904, the minister of public instruction in France asked two noted psychologists, Alfred Binet and Theophile Simon, to formulate a way to identify children who were likely to succeed in school. Binet and Simon's approach was to select simple tasks that French children of different ages ought to be able to do, such as naming colors, counting backwards, and remembering numbers in order. Based on preliminary testing, Binet and Simon determined problems that normal 3-year-olds could solve, that normal 4-year-olds could solve, and so on. **Children's** *mental age or MA* **referred to the difficulty of the problems that they could solve correctly.** A child who solved problems that the average 7-year-old could pass would have an MA of 7.

Binet and Simon used mental age to distinguish "bright" from "dull" children. A bright child would have the MA of an older child; for example, a 6-year-old with an MA of 9 was considered bright. A dull child would have the MA of a younger child, for example, a 6-year-old with an MA of 4. Binet and Simon confirmed that bright children did better in school than dull children. Voilá—the first standardized test of intelligence!

THE STANFORD-BINET. Lewis Terman, of Stanford University, revised Binet and Simon's test and published a version known as the *Stanford-Binet* in 1916. **Terman described performance as an** *intelligence quotient, or IQ,* **which was simply the ratio of mental age to chronological age, multiplied by 100:**

$$IQ = MA/CA \times 100$$

At any age, children who are perfectly average will have an IQ of 100 because their mental age equals their chronological age. Figure 8-2 on page 256 shows the typical distribution of test scores in the population. Roughly two-thirds of children taking a test will have IQ scores between 85 and 115 and 95% will have scores between 70 and 130.

Binet and Simon created the first intelligence test by using simple tasks to distinguish children who would do well in school from those who wouldn't.

The IQ score can also be used to compare intelligence in children of different ages. A 4-year-old with an MA of 5 has an IQ of 125 ($5/4 \times 100$), the same as an 8-year-old with an MA of 10 ($10/8 \times 100$).

IQ scores are no longer computed in this manner. Instead, children's IQ scores are determined by comparing their test performance to that of others their age. When children perform at the average for their age, their IQ is 100. Children who perform above the average have IQs greater than 100; children who perform below the average have IQs less than 100. Nevertheless, the concept of IQ as the ratio of MA to CA helped popularize the Stanford-Binet test.

By the 1920s, the Stanford-Binet had been joined by many other intelligence tests. Educators enthusiastically embraced the tests as an efficient and objective

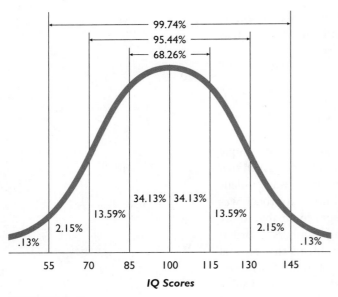

FIGURE 8-2

way to assess a student's chances of succeeding in school (Chapman, 1988). Nearly 100 years later, the Stanford-Binet remains a popular test; the latest version was revised in 2003. Like the earlier versions, the modern Stanford-Binet consists of various cognitive and motor tasks, ranging from the extremely easy to the extremely difficult. The test may be administered to individuals ranging in age from approximately 2 years to adulthood, but the test items used depend on the child's age. For example, preschool children may be asked to name pictures of familiar objects, string beads, answer questions about everyday life, or fold paper into shapes. Older individuals may be asked to define vocabulary words, solve an abstract problem, or decipher an unfamiliar code. Based on a person's performance, a total IQ score is calculated, along with scores measuring five specific cognitive factors: fluid reasoning, knowledge, quantitative reasoning, visual-spatial processing, and working memory.

Another test used frequently with 6- to 16-year-olds is the Wechsler Intelligence Scale for Children-IV, or WISC-IV for short. The WISC-IV includes subtests for verbal and performance skills, some of which are shown in Figure 8-3. Based on their performance, children receive an overall IQ score as well as scores for verbal comprehension, perceptual reasoning, working memory, and processing speed.

The Stanford-Binet and the WISC-IV are alike in that they are administered to one person at a time. Other tests can be administered to groups of individuals, with the advantage of providing information about many individuals quickly and inexpensively, typically without the need of trained psychologists. But individual testing like that shown in the photo optimizes the motivation and attention of the child and provides an opportunity for a sensitive examiner to assess factors that may influence test performance. The examiner may notice that the child is relaxed and that test performance is therefore a reasonable sample of the individual's talents. Or the examiner may observe that the child is so anxious that she cannot do her best. Such determinations are not possible with group tests. Consequently, most psychologists prefer individualized tests of intelligence over group tests.

INFANT TESTS. The Stanford-Binet and the WISC-IV cannot be used to test intelligence in infants. For this purpose, many psychologists use the Bayley Scales of Infant Development (Bayley, 1970, 1993, 2006). Designed for use with 1- to 42-month-olds, the Bayley Scales consist of five scales: cognitive, language, motor, social-emotional, and adaptive behavior. To illustrate, the motor scale assesses an infant's control of its body, its coordination, and its ability to manipulate objects. For example, 6-month-olds should turn the head toward an object that the examiner drops on the floor, 12-month-olds should imitate the examiner's actions, and 16-month-olds should build a tower from three blocks.

An advantage of an individual intelligence test is that the examiner can be sure that the child is attentive and not anxious during testing.

STABILITY OF IQ SCORES. If intelligence is a stable property of a child, then scores obtained at younger ages should predict IQ scores at older ages. In other

Items Like Those Appearing on Different Subtests of the WISC-IV

Verbal Scale	*Information: The child is asked questions that tap his or her factual knowledge of the world.* 1. How many wings does a bird have? 2. What is steam made of?
	Comprehension: The child is asked questions that measure his or her judgment and common sense. 1. What should you do if you see someone forgot his book when he leaves a restaurant? 2. What is the advantage of keeping money in a bank?
	Similarities: The child is asked to describe how words are related. 1. In what way are a lion and a tiger alike? 2. In what way are a saw and a hammer alike?
Performance Scale	*Picture arrangement: Pictures are shown and the child is asked to place them in order to tell a story.*
	Picture completion: The child is asked to identify the part that is missing from the picture.

FIGURE 8-3

words, smart babies should become smart elementary-school students, who should become smart adults. In fact, scores from infant intelligence tests are *not* related to IQ scores obtained later in childhood, adolescence, or adulthood (McCall, 1993). Not until 18 or 24 months of age do infant IQ scores predict later IQ scores (Kopp & McCall, 1982). Why? Infant tests measure different abilities than tests administered to children and adolescents: Infant tests place more emphasis on sensorimotor skills and less on tasks involving cognitive processes such as language, thinking, and problem solving.

According to this reasoning, a measure of infant cognitive processing might yield more accurate predictions of later IQ. In fact, *habituation*, a measure of information processing described in Module 6.1, does predict later IQ more effectively than do scores from the Bayley. The average correlation between habituation and IQ in childhood is approximately .5 (Bornstein, 1997), and one study found that infants' information-processing efficiency was correlated .34 with their intelligence as young adults (Fagan, Holland, & Wheeler, 2007). That is, infants who habituate to visual stimuli more rapidly tend to have higher IQs as children and adults. Apparently, infants who rapidly make sense of their world—in this case, thinking "I've seen this picture before, so let's see something new!"—are smarter during the elementary-school years.

If scores on the Bayley Scales do not predict later IQs, why are these tests used at all? The answer is that they are important diagnostic tools: Researchers and health care professionals use scores from the Bayley Scales to determine whether development is progressing normally. That is, low scores on these tests are often a signal that a child may be at risk for problems later.

Although infant test scores don't reliably predict IQ later in life, scores obtained in childhood do. For example, the correlation between IQ scores at 6 years of age and adult IQ scores is about .7 (Brody, 1992; Kaufman & Lichtenberger, 2002). This is a relatively large correlation and shows that IQ scores are reasonably stable during childhood and adolescence. Nevertheless, during these years many children's IQ scores will fluctuate between 10 and 20 points (McCall, 1993; Weinert & Haney, 2003).

What Do IQ Scores Predict?

IQ scores are remarkably powerful predictors of developmental outcomes. In fact, one expert argued that "IQ is the most important predictor of an individual's ultimate position within American society" (Brody, 1992). Of course, because IQ tests were devised to predict school success, it's not surprising that they do this quite well. IQ scores predict school grades, scores on achievement tests, and number of years of education; the correlations are usually between .5 and .7 (Brody, 1992; Geary, 2005).

These correlations are far from perfect, which reminds us that some youngsters with high test scores do not excel in school and others with low test scores manage to get good grades. In fact, some researchers find that self-discipline predicts grades in school even better than IQ scores do (Duckworth & Seligman, 2005). In general, however, tests do a reasonable job of predicting school success.

Not only do intelligence scores predict success in school, they also predict occupational success (Deary, Batty, & Gale, 2008; Strenze, 2007). Individuals with higher IQ scores are more likely to hold high-paying, high-prestige positions within medicine, law, and engineering (Schmidt & Hunter, 2004); among scientists with equal education, those with higher IQ scores hold more patents and have more articles published in scientific journals (Park, Lubinski, & Benbow, 2008). Some of the linkage between IQ and occupational success occurs because these professions require more education, and we've already seen that IQ scores predict educational success. However, even within a profession—where all individuals have the same amount of education—IQ scores predict job performance and earnings, particularly for more complex jobs (Henderson, 2010; Schmidt & Hunter, 2004). If, for example, two teenagers have summer jobs running tests in a biology lab, the smarter of the two will probably learn the procedures more rapidly and, once learned, conduct them more accurately and efficiently.

IMPROVING PREDICTIONS WITH DYNAMIC TESTING. Traditional tests of intelligence, such as the Stanford-Binet and the WISC-IV, measure knowledge and skills that a child has accumulated up to the time of testing. These tests do not directly measure a child's potential for future learning; instead, the usual assumption is that children who have learned more in the past will probably learn more

QUESTION 8.2

Amanda's 12-month-old son completed an intelligence test and received a slightly below-average score. Amanda is distraught because she's afraid her son's score means that he'll struggle in school. What advice would you give Amanda?

(Answer is on page 264.)

Scores on IQ tests predict grades in school and occupational success.

in the future. Critics argue that tests would be more valid if they directly assessed a child's potential for future learning.

Dynamic testing **measures a child's learning potential by having the child learn something new in the presence of the examiner and with the examiner's help.** Thus, dynamic testing is interactive and measures new achievement rather than past achievement. It is based on Vygotsky's ideas of the zone of proximal development and scaffolding (see pages 183–185). Learning potential can be estimated by the amount of material the child learns during interaction with the examiner and from the amount of help the child needs to learn the new material (Grigorenko & Sternberg, 1998; Sternberg & Grigorenko, 2002).

To understand the difference between traditional, static methods of intelligence testing and new, dynamic approaches, imagine a group of children attending a week-long basketball camp. On the first day, all children are tested on a range of basketball skills and receive a score that indicates their overall level of basketball skill. If this score were shown to predict later success in basketball, such as number of points scored in a season, this would be a valid static measure of basketball skill. To make this a dynamic measure of basketball skill, children would spend all week at camp being instructed in new skills. At the end of the week, the test of basketball skills would be re-administered. The amount of the child's improvement over the week would measure learning potential, with greater improvement indicating greater learning potential.

Dynamic testing is a recent innovation that is still being evaluated. Preliminary research does indicate, however, that static and dynamic testing both provide useful and independent information. If the aim is to predict future levels of a child's skill, it is valuable to know a child's current level of skill (static testing) as well as the child's potential to acquire greater skill (dynamic testing). By combining both forms of testing, we achieve a more comprehensive view of a child's talents than by relying on either method alone (Day et al., 1997; Grigorenko et al., 2006).

Hereditary and Environmental Factors

In a typical U.S. elementary school, several first-graders will have IQ scores greater than 120 and a similar number will have IQ scores in the low 80s. What accounts for the 40-point difference in these youngsters' scores? Heredity plays an important role (Bouchard, 2009), as does experience (Bronfenbrenner & Morris, 2006).

Some of the evidence for hereditary factors is shown in Figure 8-4. If genes influence intelligence, then siblings' test scores should become more alike as siblings become more similar genetically (Plomin & Petrill, 1997). In other words, because

FIGURE 8-4

Children who achieve high scores on intelligence tests often come from homes that are well organized and include many age-appropriate books and toys to stimulate a child's intellectual growth.

Two findings show the impact of heredity on intelligence: Identical twins' IQ scores are more alike than fraternal twins' scores and adopted children's IQ scores are more like their biological parents' scores than their adoptive parents' scores.

identical twins are identical genetically, they typically have virtually identical test scores, which would be a correlation of 1. Fraternal twins have about 50% of their genes in common, just like nontwin siblings of the same biological parents. Consequently, we could predict that their test scores should be (a) less similar than scores for identical twins, (b) similar to scores of other siblings who have the same biological parents, and (c) more similar than scores of children and their adopted siblings. You can see in the graph of Figure 8-4 that each of these predictions is supported.

Studies of adopted children also suggest the impact of heredity on IQ: If heredity helps determine IQ, then children's IQs should be more like those of their biological parents than of their adoptive parents. In fact, throughout childhood and adolescence, the correlation between children's IQ and their biological parents' IQ is greater than the correlation between children's IQ and their adoptive parents' IQ. What's more, as adopted children get older, their test scores increasingly resemble those of their biological parents (Plomin & Petrill, 1997). These results are evidence for the greater impact of heredity on IQ as a child grows.

Do these results mean that heredity is the sole determinant of intelligence? No. Three areas of research show the importance of environment on intelligence. The first is research on characteristics of families and homes. If intelligence were solely due to heredity, environment should have little or no impact on children's intelligence. But we know that many characteristics of parents' behavior and home environments are related to children's intelligence. For example, children with high test scores tend to come from homes that are well organized and, like the one in the photo, have plenty of appropriate play materials (Bradley et al., 2001; Tamis-LeMonda et al., 2004).

The impact of the environment on intelligence is also implicated by a dramatic rise in IQ test scores during the 20th century (Flynn & Weiss, 2007). For example, scores on the WISC increased by nearly 10 points over a 25-year period (Flynn, 1999). The change might reflect smaller, better-educated families with more leisure time (Daley et al., 2003; Dickens & Flynn, 2001). Or it might be due to movies, television, and, more recently, the computer and the Internet providing children with an incredible wealth of virtual experience (Greenfield, 1998). Yet another possibility is suggested by the fact that improvements in IQ scores are particularly striking at the lower end of the distribution: Fewer children are receiving very low IQ scores, which may show the benefits of improved health care, nutrition, and education for children who had limited access to these resources in previous generations (Geary, 2005). Although the exact cause of increased IQ scores remains a mystery, the increase per se shows the impact of changing environmental conditions on intelligence.[*]

The importance of a stimulating environment for intelligence is also demonstrated by intervention programs that prepare economically disadvantaged children for school. Without preschool, children from low-income families often enter

---

[*]Another possibility suggests that improved IQ scores is due to heredity, not the environment. According to one intriguing theory (Mingroni, 2007), IQ scores have risen because mating has become more random over the decades, which has caused more mixing of individuals with high- and low-IQ genotypes. Assuming that genes leading to higher IQ are dominant, this would yield a gradual increase in IQ scores.

kindergarten or first grade lacking key readiness skills for academic success, which means they rapidly fall behind their peers who have these skills. Consequently, providing preschool experiences for children from poor families has long been a part of U.S. federal policy to eliminate poverty. The "Child Development and Family Policy" feature traces the beginnings of these programs.

Child Development and Family Policy

Providing Children with a Head Start for School

For more than 40 years, Head Start has been helping to foster the development of preschool children from low-income families. This program's origins can be traced to two forces. First, in the early 1960s, child-development researchers argued that environmental influences on children's development were much stronger than had been estimated previously. The year 1961 marked the appearance of *Intelligence and Experience* by psychologist Joseph McVicker Hunt. Hunt reviewed the scientific evidence concerning the impact of experience on intelligence and concluded that children's intellectual development could reach unprecedented heights once child-development scientists identified optimal environmental influences. In addition, a novel program in Tennessee directed by Susan Gray (Gray & Klaus, 1965) gave credibility to the argument by showing that a summer program coupled with weekly home visits throughout the school year could raise intelligence and language skills in preschool children living in poverty. Gray's findings suggested that Hunt's claims were not simply pipe dreams.

The second force was a political twist of fate. When President Lyndon Johnson launched the War on Poverty in 1964, the Office of Economic Opportunity (OEO) was the command center. Sargent Shriver, the OEO's first director, found himself with a huge budget surplus. Most of the War on Poverty programs targeted adults; and because many of these programs were politically unpopular, Shriver was reluctant to spend more money on them. Shriver realized that no programs were aimed specifically at children and that such programs would be much less controversial politically. (After all, critics may contend that poor adults "deserve their fate" because they're lazy or irresponsible, but such arguments are not very convincing when applied to young children.) What's more, he was personally familiar with the potential impact of programs targeted at young children through his experience as the president of the Chicago School Board and his wife's work on the President's Panel on Mental Retardation (Zigler & Muenchow, 1992).

Shriver envisioned a program that would better prepare poor children for first grade. In December 1964, he convened a 14-member planning committee that included professionals from medicine, social work, education, and psychology. Over a six-week period, the planning committee devised a comprehensive program that would, by involving professionals and parents, meet the health and educational needs of young children. In May 1965, President Johnson announced the opening of Head Start; by that summer, half a million American youngsters were enrolled. The program now enrolls nearly a million American children living in poverty and has, since its inception in 1965, met the needs of more than 25 million children (Administration for Children and Families, 2010).

High-quality Head Start programs are effective: Graduates of such programs are less likely to repeat a grade in school and are more likely to graduate from high school.

The role of the environment on intelligence is documented by the impact on IQ of well-organized home environments, historical change, and intervention programs.

How effectively do intervention programs like these meet the needs of preschool youngsters? Head Start takes different forms in different communities, which makes it difficult to make blanket statements about the overall effectiveness of the program. However, high-quality Head Start programs *are* effective overall. When children such as those in the photo attend good Head Start programs, they are healthier and do better in school (Ludwig & Phillips, 2007; Zigler & Styfco, 1994). For example, Head Start graduates are less likely to repeat a grade level or to be placed in special education classes, and they are more likely to graduate from high school.

One of the most successful interventions is the Carolina Abecedarian Project (Campbell et al., 2001; Ramey & Campbell, 1991; Ramey & Ramey, 2006). This project included 111 children; most were born to African American mothers who had less than a high-school education, an average IQ score of 85, and typically no income. About half the children were assigned to a control group in which they received no special attention. The others attended a special day-care facility daily from age 4 months until 5 years. The curriculum emphasized mental, linguistic, and social development for infants, and prereading skills for preschoolers.

During elementary school and high school, children in the intervention program consistently had higher scores on a battery of cognitive tests (Campbell et al., 2001). What's more, as adults (the infants enrolled in the first year of the project are now nearly 40 years old), those who experienced the intervention were roughly four times more likely to have attended college and nearly three times more likely to have skilled rather than unskilled employment (Pungello et al., 2010).

Thus, intervention works. Of course, massive intervention over many years is expensive. But so are the economic consequences of poverty, unemployment, and their by-products. In fact, economic analyses show that, in the long term, these programs more than pay for themselves in the form of increased earnings (and tax revenues) for participating children and lowered costs associated with the criminal justice system (Reynolds et al., 2011). Programs like the Abecedarian Project show that the repetitive cycle of school failure and education can be broken. In the process, they show that intelligence is fostered by a stimulating and responsive environment.

Impact of Ethnicity and Socioeconomic Status

Ethnic groups differ in their average scores on many intelligence tests: Asian Americans tend to have the highest scores, followed by European Americans, Hispanic Americans, and African Americans (Hunt & Carlson, 2007). To a certain extent, these differences in test scores reflect group differences in socioeconomic status. Children from economically advantaged homes tend to have higher test scores than children from economically disadvantaged homes; and European American and Asian American families are more likely to be economically advantaged, whereas Hispanic American and African American families are more likely to be economically disadvantaged. Nevertheless, when children of comparable socioeconomic status are compared, group differences in IQ test scores are reduced but not eliminated (Magnuson & Duncan, 2006). Let's look at four explanations for this difference.

A ROLE FOR GENETICS?   On page page 259, you learned that heredity helps determine a child's intelligence: Smart parents tend to beget smart children. Does this also mean that group differences in IQ scores reflect genetic differences? No. Most researchers agree that there is no evidence that some ethnic groups have more "smart genes" than others. Instead, they believe that the environment is largely responsible for these differences (Bronfenbrenner & Morris, 2006; Neisser et al., 1996).

A popular analogy (Lewontin, 1976) demonstrates the thinking here. Imagine two kinds of corn: Each kind produces both short and tall plants; and height is known to be due to heredity. If one kind of corn grows in a good soil—with plenty of water and nutrients—the mature plants will reach their genetically determined heights; some short, some tall. If the other kind of corn grows in poor soil, few of the plants will reach their full height and overall the plants of this kind will be much shorter. Even though height is quite heritable for each type of corn, the difference in height between the two groups is due solely to the quality of the environment. Similarly, though IQ scores may be quite heritable for different groups, limited exposure to stimulating environments may mean that one group ends up with lower IQ scores overall, just like the group of plants growing up in poor soil.

EXPERIENCE WITH TEST CONTENTS.   Some critics contend that differences in test scores reflect bias in the tests themselves. They argue that test items reflect the cultural heritage of the test creators, most of whom are economically advantaged European Americans, and so tests are biased against economically disadvantaged children from other groups (Champion, 2003). They point to test items like this one:

A conductor is to an orchestra as a teacher is to what?
book   school   class   eraser

Children whose background includes exposure to orchestras are more likely to answer this question correctly than children who lack this exposure.

The **problem of bias led to the development of** *culture-fair intelligence tests,* **which include test items based on experiences common to many cultures.** An example is Raven's Progressive Matrices, which consist solely of items like the one shown in Figure 8-5. Examinees are asked to select the piece that would complete the design correctly (6, in this case). Although items like this are thought to reduce the impact of specific experience, ethnic group differences still remain in performance on

FIGURE 8-5

so-called culture-fair intelligence tests (Anastasi, 1988; Herrnstein & Murray, 1994). Apparently, familiarity with test-related items per se is not the key factor responsible for group differences in performance.

STEREOTYPE THREAT. When people know they belong to a group that is said to lack skill in a domain, this makes them anxious when performing in that domain for fear of confirming the stereotype, and they often do poorly as a result. **This self-fulfilling prophecy, in which knowledge of stereotypes leads to anxiety and reduced performance consistent with the original stereotype, is called** *stereotype threat.* Applied to intelligence, the argument is that African American children experience stereotype threat when they take intelligence tests, and this contributes to their lower scores (Steele, 1997; Steele & Aronson, 1995). For example, imagine two 10-year-olds taking an intelligence test for admission to a special program for gifted children. The European American child worries that if he fails the test, he won't be admitted to the program. The African American child has this same fear, but also worries that if he does poorly, it will confirm the stereotype that African American children don't get good scores on IQ tests (Suzuki & Aronson, 2005). Consistent with this idea, when African American students experience self-affirmation—they remind themselves of values that are important to them and why—threat is reduced and their performance improves (Cohen et al., 2006).

> European Americans and Asian Americans often get higher scores on IQ tests, in part because they are more familiar and more comfortable with the testing situation.

TEST-TAKING SKILLS. The impact of experience and cultural values can extend beyond particular items to a child's familiarity with the entire testing situation. Tests underestimate a child's intelligence if, for example, the child's culture encourages children to solve problems in collaboration with others and discourages them from excelling as individuals. What's more, because they are wary of questions posed by unfamiliar adults, many economically disadvantaged children often answer test questions by saying, "I don't know." Obviously, this strategy guarantees an artificially low test score. When these children are given extra time to feel at ease with the examiner, they respond less often with "I don't know" and their test scores improve considerably (Zigler & Finn-Stevenson, 1992).

CONCLUSION: INTERPRETING TEST SCORES. If all tests reflect cultural influences, at least to some degree, how should we interpret test scores? Remember that tests assess successful adaptation to a particular cultural context: They predict success in a school environment, which usually espouses middle-class values. Regardless of ethnic group—African American, Hispanic American, or European American—a child with a high test score is more likely to have the intellectual skills needed for academic work based on middle-class values (Hunt & Carlson, 2007). A child with a low test score, like Charlene in the module-opening vignette, apparently lacks those skills. Does a low score mean that Charlene is destined to fail in school? No. It simply means that, based on her current skills, she's unlikely to do well. Improving Charlene's skills will improve her school performance.

Q&A ANSWER 8.2
Tell her to relax. Scores on intelligence tests for infants are not related to scores taken on tests in childhood or adolescence, so the lower-than-average score has virtually no predictive value.

I want to end this module by emphasizing a crucial point: By focusing on groups of people, it's easy to overlook the fact that the average difference in IQ scores between various ethnic groups is relatively small compared to the entire range of scores for these groups (Sternberg, Grigorenko, & Kidd, 2005). You can easily find youngsters with high IQ scores from all ethnic groups, just as you can find youngsters with low IQ scores from all groups. In the next module we'll look at children at these extremes of ability.

Check Your Learning

RECALL What are modern intelligence tests like? How well do they work?

Describe the reasons why ethnic groups differ in their average scores on intelligence tests.

INTERPRET Explain the evidence that shows the roles of heredity and environment on intelligence.

APPLY Suppose that a local government official proposes to end all funding for pre-school programs for disadvantaged children. Write a letter to this official in which you describe the value of these programs.

 ## 8.3 Special Children, Special Needs

OUTLINE

Gifted and Creative Children

Children with Disability

LEARNING OBJECTIVES

- **What are the characteristics of gifted and creative children?**
- **What are the different forms of disability?**

Sanjit, a second-grader, has taken two separate intelligence tests, and both times he had above-average scores. Nevertheless, Sanjit absolutely cannot read. Letters and words are as mysterious to him as Metallica's music would be to Mozart. His parents took him to an ophthalmologist, who determined that Sanjit's vision was 20-20; nothing is wrong with his eyes. What is wrong?

Throughout history, societies have recognized children with disabilities as well as those with extraordinary talents. Today, we know much about the extremes of human talents. We'll begin this module with a look at gifted and creative children. Then we'll look at children with disabilities and discover why Sanjit can't read.

Gifted and Creative Children

In many respects the boy in the photo, Bernie, is an ordinary middle-class 12-year-old: He is the goalie on his soccer team, takes piano lessons on Saturday mornings, sings in his church youth choir, and likes to go roller blading. However, when it comes to intelligence and academic prowess, Bernie leaves the ranks of the ordinary. He received a score of 175 on an intelligence test and is taking a college calculus course. **Bernie is** *gifted,* **which traditionally has referred to individuals with scores of 130 or greater on intelligence tests** (Horowitz & O'Brien, 1986).

Because giftedness was traditionally defined in terms of IQ scores, exceptional ability is often associated primarily with academic skill. But modern definitions

Traditional definitions of giftedness emphasized test scores; modern definitions emphasize exceptional talent in a variety of areas, beginning with academic areas but also including the arts and sports.

of giftedness are broader and include exceptional talent in an assortment of areas, including art, music, creative writing, and dance (Robinson & Clinkenbeard, 1998; Winner, 2000).

Whether the field is music or math, though, exceptional talent seems to have several prerequisites (Rathunde & Csikszentmihalyi, 1993):

- The child loves the subject and has an almost overwhelming desire to master it.
- Instruction to develop the child's special talent usually begins at an early age with inspiring and talented teachers.
- Parents are committed to promoting their child's talent.

The message here is that exceptional talent must be nurtured. Without encouragement and support from parents and stimulating and challenging mentors, a youngster's talents will wither. Talented children need a curriculum that is challenging and complex; they need teachers who know how to foster talent; and they need likeminded peers who stimulate their interests (Feldhusen, 1996). With this support, gifted children's achievement can be remarkable. In a 20-year-longitudinal study, gifted teens were, as adults, extraordinarily successful in school and in their careers (Lubinski et al., 2006).

The stereotype is that gifted children are often emotionally troubled and unable to get along with their peers. In reality, gifted children and adults tend to be more mature than their peers and have fewer emotional problems (Luthar, Zigler, & Goldstein, 1992; Simonton & Song, 2009), and as adults, they report being highly satisfied with their careers, relationships with others, and life in general (Lubinski et al., 2006).

CREATIVITY. Mozart and Salieri were rival composers in Europe during the 18th century. Both were talented, ambitious musicians. Yet, more than 200 years later, Mozart is revered and Salieri is all but forgotten. Why? Then and now, Mozart was considered creative but Salieri was not. What is creativity, and how does it differ from intelligence?

Intelligence is associated with *convergent thinking*, using information that is provided to determine a standard, correct answer. In contrast, creativity is associated with *divergent thinking*, where the aim is not a single correct answer (often there isn't one) but novel and unusual lines of thought (Callahan, 2000).

Divergent thinking is often measured by asking children to produce many ideas in response to some specific stimulus (Kogan, 1983). For example, children might be asked to name different uses for a common object, such as a coat hanger. Or they might be shown a page filled with circles and asked to draw as many different pictures as they can, as shown in Figure 8-6. Both the number of responses and the originality of the responses are used to measure creativity.

Creativity, like giftedness, must be cultivated. The "Improving Children's Lives" feature gives some guidelines for fostering children's creativity.

FIGURE 8-6

Improving Children's Lives

Fostering Creativity

Here are some guidelines for helping children to be more creative.

1. **Encourage children to take risks.** Not all novel ideas bear fruit; some won't work and some are silly. But only by repeatedly thinking in novel and unusual ways are children likely to produce something truly original.

2. **Encourage children to think of alternatives to conventional wisdom.** Have them think what would happen if accepted practices were changed. For example, "What would life be like without cars?" or "Why not eat breakfast in the evening and dinner in the morning?"

3. **Praise children for working hard.** As the saying goes, creativity is one part inspiration and nine parts perspiration. The raw creative insight must be developed and polished to achieve the luster of a finished product.

4. **Help children get over the "I'm not creative" hurdle.** Too often they believe that only others are creative. Assure children that following these guidelines will make anyone more creative.

Gifted and creative children represent one extreme of human ability. At the other extreme are youngsters with disability, the topic of the next section.

Children with Disability

"Little David," so named because his father was also named David, was the oldest of four children. He learned to sit only days before his first birthday, he began to walk at 2, and he said his first words as a 3-year-old. By age 5, David was far behind his agemates developmentally. David had Down syndrome, a disorder (described in Module 2.2) that is caused by an extra 21st chromosome.

CHILDREN WITH INTELLECTUAL DISABILITY. Down syndrome is an example of a condition that leads to *intellectual disability*, **which refers to substantial limitations in intellectual ability as well as problems in adapting to an environment, with both emerging before 18 years of age.** Limited intellectual skill is often defined as a score of 70 or less on an intelligence test such as the Stanford-Binet. Adaptive behavior includes conceptual skills important for successful adaptation (e.g., literacy, understanding money and time), social skills (e.g., interpersonal skill), and practical skills (e.g., personal grooming, occupational skills). It is usually evaluated from interviews with a parent or other caregiver. Only individuals who are under the age of 18, have problems adapting in these areas, and IQ scores of 70 or less are considered to have an intellectual disability (AAIDD Ad Hoc Committee on Terminology and Classification, 2010).[1]

> Intellectual disability is defined by below-average scores on intelligence tests and problems adapting to the environment.

[1]What we now call intellectual disability was long known as mental retardation, and much federal and state law in the United States still uses the latter term. However, *intellectual disability* is the preferred term because it better reflects the condition not as a deficit in the person but as a poor "fit between the person's capacities and the context in which the person is to function" (AAIDD Ad Hoc Committee on Terminology and Classification, 2010, p. 13).

Modern explanations pinpoint four factors that place individuals at risk for intellectual disability:

- Biomedical factors, including chromosomal disorders, malnutrition, and traumatic brain injury
- Social factors, such as poverty and impaired parent–child interactions
- Behavioral factors, such as child neglect or domestic violence
- Educational factors, including impaired parenting and inadequate special education services

No individual factor in this list *necessarily* leads to intellectual disability. Instead, the risk for intellectual disability grows as more of these are present (AAIDD Ad Hoc Committee on Terminology and Classification, 2010). For example, the risk is great for a child with Down syndrome whose parents live in poverty and cannot take advantage of special education services.

As you can imagine, the many factors that can lead to intellectual disability mean that the term encompasses an enormous variety of individuals. One way to describe this variation is in terms of the kind and amount of support that they need. At one extreme, some people have so few skills that they must be supervised constantly. Consequently, they usually live in institutions for persons with intellectual disability, where they can sometimes be taught self-help skills such as dressing, feeding, and toileting (Reid, Wilson, & Faw, 1991). At the other extreme are individuals who go to school and master many academic skills, but not as quickly as a typical child does. They often work and many marry. With comprehensive training programs that focus on vocational and social skills, they're often productive citizens and satisfied human beings (Ellis & Rusch, 1991).

CHILDREN WITH LEARNING DISABILITY.   A key element of the definition of intellectual disability is substantially below-average intelligence. In contrast, by definition children with learning disability have normal intelligence. That is, **children with** *learning disability:* **(a) have difficulty mastering an academic subject, (b) have normal intelligence, and (c) are not suffering from other conditions that could explain poor performance, such as sensory impairment or inadequate instruction.**

In the United States, about 5% of school-age children are classified as learning disabled, which translates into nearly 3 million youngsters. The number of distinct disabilities and the degree of overlap among them are still debated (Torgesen, 2004). However, most scientists agree that three are particularly common (Hulme & Snowling, 2009): difficulties in reading individual words, sometimes known as *developmental dyslexia*; difficulties in understanding words that have been read successfully, which is called *impaired reading comprehension*; and, finally, difficulties in mathematics, which is termed *mathematical learning disability* or *developmental dyscalculia*.

Children with developmental dyslexia struggle to read because they have problems understanding and using language sounds.

Understanding learning disabilities is complicated because each type has its own causes (Landerl et al., 2009) and thus requires its own treatment. For example, developmental dyslexia is the most common type of learning disability. (It's so common that sometimes it's just referred to as *reading disability*.) Many children with this disorder have problems in phonological awareness (described in Module 7.3), which refers to distinguishing sounds in written and oral language. For children with developmental dyslexia—like Sanjit (in the opening vignette) or the boy in the photograph—distinguishing *bis* from *bep* or *bis* from *dis* is very difficult; apparently the words all sound very similar (Ziegler et al., 2010). The "Focus on Research" feature illustrates research that has examined this problem in detail.

Youngsters with reading disability often struggle to distinguish different letter sounds.

Focus on Research

Phonological Representations in Children with Developmental Dyslexia

Who were the investigators, and what was the aim of the study? Most reading experts agree that, compared to children who read normally, disabled readers have difficulty with phonological processing, that is, in translating print into sound. Where experts disagree is in the nature of this problem. One idea is that phonological representations—information in long-term memory about the sounds of words—may be less detailed or less precise in children who have reading disability. For example, think about pairs of similar-sounding words such as *bit* and *bet* or *but* and *bet*. In each pair, only the vowels distinguish the two words and the vowels themselves sound similar. If phonological representations in children with reading disability have less precise information about vowel sounds, this could cause children to read more slowly and less accurately.

According to this hypothesis, reading disability should be apparent when children use language sounds in nonreading tasks. Jennifer Bruno and her colleagues—Frank Manis, Patricia Keating, Anne Sperling, Jonathan Nakamoto, and Mark Seidenberg (2007)—tested this hypothesis by determining how well children with reading disability recognized familiar words that were presented auditorily.

How did the investigators measure the topic of interest? The task was simple: Familiar one-syllable words (e.g., *bone, boat*) were presented on audiotape and children were asked to say what they were. What made the task difficult for children is that only a portion of the word was presented at a time, beginning with just the initial consonant and a small portion of the vowel. If children could not recognize the word on this initial presentation (most couldn't), the word was repeated with a bit more of the vowel presented. This process was repeated, adding more of the vowel and, later, the final consonant, until the child recognized the word. (All of this was possible because the experimenters recorded an adult saying each of the words, then used specially designed software that allowed them to edit each word so that a precise amount of vowel was presented.)

Who were the children in the study? Bruno and her colleagues tested 23 8- to 14-year-olds with reading disability, along with 23 8- to 14-year-olds with normal reading skills.

What was the design of the study? The study was both experimental and correlational. In the experimental part of the study, the independent variable was the type of consonant sound that ended the word. Some words ended in stop consonants (*dot, seat*), some ended in lateral consonants (*coal, feel*), and some in nasal consonants (*cone, pan*).** The dependent variable was the proportion of the word that had to be presented until children recognized it. The study was also correlational because the investigators were interested in the relation between reading skill (reading disability versus normal reading skill) and ease of word recognition. The investigators did not look at age differences, so the study was neither longitudinal nor cross-sectional.

Were there ethical concerns with the study? No. The tasks are frequently used in research, with no known risks.

What were the results? Figure 8-7 shows what proportion of a word had to be presented until children recognized it. Words ending in stop consonants were easiest for both groups of readers—they recognized these words based on hearing just less than half of the word. Words ending in lateral and nasal consonants were harder—children needed to hear more of the word to recognize it—and this was particularly true for children with reading disability.

What did the investigators conclude? For words that end with lateral and nasal consonants, children with reading disability need to hear more of a word to recognize it. Bruno et al. argued that this reflects subtle differences in the phonological representations of these simple words in long-term memory of disabled readers. That is, because phonological representations are less precise for these children, they must hear more of a word to be able to recognize it for sure. Of course, the differences in Figure 8-7 are small, but these small differences add up quickly when children must repeatedly access the sounds of words during reading.

What converging evidence would strengthen these conclusions? This study focused on stop, lateral, and nasal consonants; it would be useful to extend this work to a broader range of vowel and consonant sounds. This would allow researchers to generate a more complete profile of the phonological representations of children with developmental dyslexia.

Children with a reading disability need to hear more of a word to recognize it.

■ Reading disabled   ■ Reading normally

FIGURE 8-7

Percent of word presented

Stop

Lateral

Nasal

**All consonants are produced by disrupting air from the lungs as it flows through the vocal tract. In stop consonants, the flow of air is stopped briefly; in lateral consonants, the flow of air is diverted to the side of the tongue; in nasal consonants, air flows through the nose.

Children with developmental dyslexia typically benefit from two kinds of instruction: training in phonological awareness—experiences that help them to identify subtle but important differences in language sounds—along with explicit instruction on the connections between letters and their sounds. With intensive instruction of this sort, youngsters with developmental dyslexia can read much more effectively (Hulme & Snowling, 2009).

Children with impaired reading comprehension have no trouble reading individual words, but they understand far less of what they read. Asked to read sentences such as *The man rode the bus to go to work* or *The dog chased the cat through the woods*, they do so easily but find it difficult to answer questions about what they've read (e.g., *What did the man ride? Where did the man go?*). These problems seem to reflect a limited spoken vocabulary (they simply know fewer words), as well as problems with linking words in a sentence together to create coherent meaning (Hulme & Snowling, 2009). Told to select the picture showing children sitting on a table, they may point to a picture of children sitting on a rug or to a picture of children playing a game on a table, but not sitting on it (Nation et al., 2004). In other words, for these youngsters, impaired reading comprehension seems to be a by-product of impaired oral (spoken) language. Consistent with this view, these children understand much more of what they read following extensive instruction in vocabulary and other language skills that are not specific to reading (Clark et al., 2010).

A third common form of learning disability is mathematical disability. Roughly 5–10% of young children struggle with arithmetic instruction from the very beginning. These youngsters progress slowly in their efforts to learn to count, to add, and to subtract; many are also diagnosed with reading disability. As they move into second and third grade (and beyond), these children often use inefficient methods for computing solutions, such as continuing (as third-graders) to use their fingers to solve problems such as 9 + 7 (Geary, 2010; Jordan, 2007).

We know far less about mathematical learning disability, largely because mathematics engages a broader set of skills than reading (which really involves just two broad classes: decoding and comprehension). Some scientists propose that the heart of the problem is a poorly developed number sense, which includes such skills as understanding and comparing quantities (e.g., 9 > 6) and representing quantity on a number line (Berch, 2005; Jordan, 2007). Another possibility is that youngsters with mathematical disability are impaired in counting and retrieving arithmetic facts from memory (Hulme & Snowling, 2009). Still others suggest that mathematical disability reflects problems in the basic cognitive processes that are used in doing arithmetic, such as working memory and processing speed (Geary et al., 2007).

Because mathematical disability is so poorly understood, effective interventions are not yet available. When the core problems that define mathematical disability have been defined, researchers and educators should be able to craft instruction specifically tailored to improve these children's math skills. When that happens, children with mathematical disability, like children with developmental dyslexia and impaired reading comprehension, will be able to develop their full intellectual potential.

 QUESTION 8.3
Ryan's 8-year-old daughter has been diagnosed with a reading disability. Ryan is concerned that this is just a politically correct way of saying that his daughter is stupid. Is he right? *(Answer is on page 271.)*

Mathematical learning disability is not well understood, mainly because mathematics involves such a broad set of skills.

 ANSWER 8.3
No. Part of the definition of learning disability is normal intelligence; children with learning disability have a specific, well-defined disability in conjunction with normal intelligence.

Check Your Learning

RECALL Summarize the different factors that put children at risk for intellectual disability.

How is learning disability defined? What are the different types of learning disability?

INTERPRET Compare and contrast traditional and modern definitions of giftedness.

APPLY How might Jean Piaget, Howard Gardner, and Robert Sternberg define intellectual disability?

UNIFYING THEMES   Nature and Nurture

In this chapter, I want to underscore the theme that *development is always jointly influenced by heredity and environment*. In no other area of child development is this theme as important, because the implications for social policy are so profound. If intelligence were completely determined by heredity, for example, intervention programs would be a waste of time and tax dollars, because no amount of experience would change nature's prescription for intelligence. But we've seen several times in this chapter that neither heredity nor environment is all-powerful when it comes to intelligence. Studies of twins, for example, remind us that heredity clearly has substantial impact on IQ scores.

Identical twins' IQs are consistently more alike than are fraternal twins' IQs, a result that documents heredity's influence on intelligence. Yet, at the same time, intervention studies such as Head Start and the Carolina Abecedarian Project show that intelligence is malleable. Children's intelligence can be enhanced by intensely stimulating environments.

Thus, heredity imposes some limits on how a child's intelligence will develop, but the limits are fairly modest. We can nurture all children's intelligence considerably if we are willing to invest the time and effort.

See for Yourself

We've seen that the definition of intelligence differs across cultural settings. See how parents define intelligence by asking them to rate the importance of four common aspects of intelligence:

- Problem-solving skill (thinking before acting, seeing different sides to a problem)
- Verbal skill (speaking clearly, having a large vocabulary)
- Creative skill (asking many questions, trying new things)
- Social skill (playing and working well with other people, respecting and caring for others)

Ask parents to rate the importance of each element on a 6-point scale, where 1 means extremely unimportant to intelligence and 6 means extremely important. Try to ask parents from different ethnic groups; then compare your results with other students' results to see if parents' views of intelligence are similar or different and if cultural background affects parents' definitions. See for yourself!

Summary

8.1 What Is Intelligence?

Psychometric Theories

Psychometric approaches to intelligence include theories that describe intelligence as a general factor as well as theories that include specific factors. Hierarchical theories include general intelligence as well as various specific skills, such as verbal and spatial ability.

Gardner's Theory of Multiple Intelligences

Gardner's theory of multiple intelligences proposes nine distinct intelligences. Three are found in psychometric theories (linguistic, logical-mathematical, and spatial intelligence), but six are new (musical, bodily-kinesthetic, interpersonal, intrapersonal, naturalistic, and existential intelligence). Gardner's theory has stimulated research on nontraditional forms of intelligence, such as emotional intelligence. The theory also has implications for education, suggesting, for example, that schools should adjust teaching to each child's unique intellectual strengths.

Sternberg's Theory of Successful Intelligence

According to Robert Sternberg, intelligence is defined as using abilities to achieve short- and long-term goals and depends upon three abilities: analytic ability to analyze problems and generate solutions, creative ability to deal adaptively with novel situations, and practical ability to know what solutions will work.

8.2 Measuring Intelligence

Binet and the Development of Intelligence Testing

Binet created the first intelligence test to identify students who would have difficulty in school. Using this work, Terman created the Stanford-Binet, which introduced the concept of the intelligence quotient (IQ). Another widely used test, the WISC-IV, yields IQ scores based on verbal and performance subtests. Infant tests, such as the Bayley Scales, typically assess mental and motor development.

Scores on infant intelligence tests do not predict adult IQ scores, but infant habituation predicts childhood IQs, and preschool IQ scores predict adult IQs.

What Do IQ Scores Predict?

Intelligence tests are reasonably valid measures of achievement in school. They also predict people's performance in the workplace.

Dynamic tests measure children's potential for future learning and complement traditional tests, which emphasize knowledge acquired prior to testing.

Hereditary and Environmental Factors

Evidence for the impact of heredity on IQ comes from the findings that (a) siblings' IQ scores are more alike when siblings are more similar genetically, and (b) adopted children's IQ scores are more like their biological parents' test scores than their adoptive parents' scores. Evidence for the impact of the environment comes from the impact of home environments, historical change, and intervention programs on IQ scores.

Impact of Ethnicity and Socioeconomic Status

Ethnic groups differ in their average scores on IQ tests. This difference is not due to genetics or to familiarity with specific test items, but rather to children's familiarity and comfort with the testing situation. Nevertheless, IQ scores remain valid predictors of school success because middle-class experience is often a prerequisite for school success.

8.3 Special Children, Special Needs

Gifted and Creative Children

Traditionally, gifted children have been those with high scores on IQ tests. Modern definitions of giftedness are broader and include exceptional talent in, for example, the arts. Gifted children are usually socially mature and emotionally stable.

Creativity is associated with divergent thinking, that is, thinking in novel and unusual directions. Tests of divergent thinking can predict which children are most likely to be creative when they are older. Creativity can be fostered by experiences that encourage children to think flexibly and explore alternatives.

Children with Disability

Individuals with intellectual disability have IQ scores of 70 or lower and problems in adaptive behavior. Biomedical, social, behavioral, and educational factors place individuals at risk for intellectual disability.

Children with a learning disability have normal intelligence but have difficulty mastering specific academic subjects. Common variants include developmental dyslexia (difficulty decoding individual words), impaired reading comprehension (problems understanding what one has read), and mathematical learning disability. The most common is reading disability, which often can be traced to inadequate understanding and use of language sounds. When such language-related skills are taught, children's reading improves.

Test Yourself

✓●─Study and Review on mydevelopmentlab.com

1. The psychometric approach to intelligence relies upon _____.

2. _____ theories of intelligence measure both *g* (general intelligence) and specific components, such as fluid intelligence.

3. In formulating his theory of multiple intelligences, Gardner drew upon _____, studies of brain-damaged persons, and studies of persons with exceptional talent.

4. Linguistic, logical-mathematical, and _____ intelligences are included in psychometric theories as well as in Gardner's theory of multiple intelligence.

5. Sternberg's theory of successful intelligence includes _____, creative, and practical abilities.

6. Two commonly used intelligence tests are the _____ and the WISC-IV.

7. Infant IQ tests do not predict childhood IQ accurately, but are still valuable because _____.

8. IQ scores predict success in school as well as predicting _____.

9. Evidence for the impact of heredity on IQ comes from studies of twins (in which identical twins had more similar scores than fraternal twins) and from _____.

10. The role of the environment on intelligence is revealed by research linking home environments to intelligence, _____, and the impact of intervention programs.

11. Ethnic group differences have been linked to _____, stereotype threat, and test-taking skills.

12. Intelligence is associated with convergent thinking, whereas creativity is associated with _____ thinking.

13. Intellectual disability is defined by limited intellectual ability and _____, both of which emerge before age 18.

14. Children with _____ have normal intelligence and sensory functioning, yet have difficulty mastering an academic subject.

15. Common learning disabilities include developmental dyslexia, _____, and mathematical learning disability (developmental dyscalculia).

Answers: (1) performance on intelligence tests; (2) Hierarchical; (3) child-development research; (4) spatial; (5) analytic; (6) Stanford-Binet; (7) they can be used to determine whether development is progressing normally; (8) occupational success; (9) adopted children (adoptees' scores resembled the scores of their biological parents, not their adoptive parents); (10) increases in IQ scores during the latter part of the 20th century; (11) experience with test contents; (12) divergent; (13) problems adapting to the environment; (14) learning disability; (15) impaired reading comprehension.

Key Terms

analytic ability   251
convergent thinking   266
creative ability   251
crystallized intelligence   248
culture-fair intelligence tests   263
divergent thinking   266

dynamic testing   259
emotional intelligence   250
fluid intelligence   248
gifted   265
intellectual disability   267
intelligence quotient (IQ)   255

learning disability   268
mental age (MA)   255
practical ability   251
psychometricians   247
stereotype threat   264

9

Language and Communication

9.1

The Road to Speech

9.2

Learning the Meanings of Words

9.3

Speaking in Sentences

9.4

Using Language to Communicate

Toni Morrison, a contemporary African American writer who won the Nobel Prize in literature in 1993, said, "We die. That may be the meaning of life. But we do language. That may be the measure of our lives." Language is indeed a remarkable human tool. Language allows us to express thoughts and feelings to others and to preserve our ideas and learn from the past.

What's truly amazing, given the complexities of language, is that most children master it rapidly and easily. In this chapter we'll study that mastery, focusing on four different facets of language. We begin, in **Module 9.1**, by looking at the first steps in acquiring language: learning about speech sounds. **Module 9.2** concerns how children learn to speak and how they learn new words thereafter. In **Module 9.3**, we'll examine children's early sentences and the rules that children follow in creating them. Finally, in **Module 9.4**, we'll learn how children use language to communicate with others.

9.1 The Road to Speech

OUTLINE

Elements of Language

Perceiving Speech

First Steps to Speech

LEARNING OBJECTIVES

- **What are the basic sounds of speech, and how well can infants distinguish them?**
- **How does infant-directed speech help children learn about language?**
- **What is babbling, and how does it become more complex in older infants?**

As a 7-month-old, Chelsea began to make her first word-like sounds, saying "dah" and "nuh." Several weeks later, she began to repeat these syllables, saying "dah-dah" and "nuh-nuh." By 11 months her speech resembled sentences with stressed words: "dah-NUH-bah-BAH!" Chelsea's parents were astonished that her sentences could sound so much like real speech yet still be absolutely meaningless!

From birth, infants make sounds—they laugh, cry, and, like Chelsea, produce sounds that resemble speech. Yet, for most of their first year, infants do not talk. This contrast raises two important questions about infants as nonspeaking creatures. First, can babies who are unable to speak understand any of the speech that is directed to them? Second, how do infants like Chelsea progress from crying to more effective methods of oral communication, such as speech? We'll answer both questions in this module, but let's begin by considering exactly what we mean by *language*.

Elements of Language

When you think of language, what comes to mind? English, perhaps? Or maybe German, Spanish, Korean, or Zulu? What about American Sign Language? **Defined broadly, *language* is a system that relates sounds (or gestures) to meaning.** Languages are expressed in many forms—through speech, writing, and gestures. Furthermore, languages consist of different subsystems. Spoken languages usually involve four distinct but interrelated elements:

- *Phonology* **refers to the sounds of a language.** About 200 different sounds are used in all known spoken languages; all the different words in English are constructed from only about 45 of them.

The elements of language include phonology, semantics, syntax, and pragmatics.

- *Semantics* **denotes the study of words and their meaning.** *Webster's Third New International Dictionary* includes roughly half a million words; a typical college-educated English speaker has a vocabulary of about 150,000 words.

- *Syntax* **refers to rules that specify how words are combined to form sentences.** For example, one simple rule specifies that a noun followed by a verb (e.g., *dog barks, ball rolls*) is a sentence.

- *Pragmatics* **refers to the communicative functions of language and the rules that lead to effective communication.** For example, rules for effective communication specify that speakers should be clear and their comments relevant to the topic of conversation.

Learning language involves mastering each of these elements. Children must learn to hear the differences in speech sounds and how to produce them; they must learn the meaning of words and rules for combining words in sentences; and they must learn appropriate and effective ways to talk with others. In the remainder of this module (and the other three in this chapter), we'll see how children come to understand language and speak it themselves.

Perceiving Speech

We learned in Module 5.1 that even newborn infants hear remarkably well. Newborns also prefer to listen to speech over comparably complex nonspeech sounds (Vouloumanos et al., 2010). But can babies distinguish speech sounds? To answer this question, we first need to know more about the elements of speech. **The basic building blocks of language are** *phonemes,* **unique sounds that can be joined to create words.** Phonemes include consonant sounds, such as the sound of *t* in *toe* and *tap,* along with vowel sounds, such as the sound of *e* in *get* and *bed.* Infants can distinguish most of these sounds, many of them by as early as 1 month after birth (Aslin, Jusczyk, & Pisoni, 1998).

How do we know that infants can distinguish different vowels and consonants? Researchers have devised a number of clever techniques to determine if babies respond differently to distinct sounds. One approach is illustrated in Figure 9-1. A rubber nipple is connected to a computer so that sucking causes the computer to play a sound out of a loudspeaker. In just a few minutes, 1-month-olds learn the relation between their sucking and the sound: They suck rapidly to hear nothing more than repeated presentation of the sound of *p* as in *pin, pet,* and *pat* (pronounced "puh").

After a few more minutes, infants seemingly tire of this repetitive sound and suck less often, which represents the habituation phenomenon described in Module 5.1. But, if the computer presents a new sound, such as the sound of *b* in *bed, bat,* or *bird* (pronounced "buh"), babies begin sucking rapidly again. Evidently, they recognize that the sound of *b* is different from *p* because they suck more often to hear the new sound (Jusczyk, 1995).

Of course, the same sound is not pronounced exactly the same way by all people. For example, two native speakers of English may say *baby* differently and a nonnative speaker's pronunciation could differ even more. Only older infants consistently recognize the same words across variations in pronunciation (Schmale & Seidl, 2009).

THE IMPACT OF LANGUAGE EXPOSURE. Not all languages use the same set of phonemes; a distinction that is important in one language may be ignored in another. For example, unlike English, French and Polish differentiate between nasal

"puh"

FIGURE 9-1

and nonnasal vowels. To hear the difference, say the word *rod*. Now repeat it, but holding your nose. The subtle difference between the two sounds illustrates a nonnasal vowel (the first version of *rod*) and a nasal one (the second).

Because an infant might be exposed to any of the world's languages, it would be adaptive for young infants to be able to perceive a wide range of phonemes. In fact, research shows that infants can distinguish phonemes that are not used in their native language. For example, Japanese does not distinguish the consonant sound of *r* in *rip* from the sound of *l* in *lip*, and Japanese adults trying to learn English have great difficulty distinguishing these sounds. At about 6 to 8 months, Japanese and American infants can distinguish these sounds equally well. However, by 10 to 12 months, perception of *r* and *l* improves for American infants—presumably because they hear these sounds frequently—but declines for Japanese babies (Kuhl et al., 2006).

Newborns apparently are biologically capable of hearing the entire range of phonemes in all languages worldwide. But as babies grow and are more exposed to a particular language, they only notice the linguistic distinctions that are meaningful in their own language (Maye, Weiss, & Aslin, 2008). Thus, specializing in one language apparently comes at the cost of making it more difficult to hear sounds in other languages (Best, 1995). And this pattern of greater specialization in speech perception is very reminiscent of the profile for face perception (pages 151–153). With greater exposure to human faces, babies develop a more refined notion of a human face, just as they develop a more refined notion of the sounds that are important in their native language.

IDENTIFYING WORDS.   Of course, hearing individual phonemes is only the first step in perceiving speech. One of the biggest challenges for infants is identifying recurring patterns of sounds—words, that is. Imagine, for example, an infant overhearing this conversation between a parent and an older sibling:

SIBLING: Jerry got a new *bike*.

PARENT: Was his old *bike* broken?

SIBLING: No. He'd saved his allowance to buy a new mountain *bike*.

An infant listening to this conversation hears *bike* three times. Can the infant learn from this experience? Yes. When 7- to 8-month-olds hear a word repeatedly in different sentences, they later pay more attention to this word than to words they haven't heard previously. Evidently, 7- and 8-month-olds can listen to sentences and recognize the sound patterns that they hear repeatedly (Houston & Juscyzk, 2003; Saffran, Aslin, & Newport, 1996). Also, by 6 months of age, infants pay more attention to content words (e.g., nouns, verbs) than to function words (e.g., articles, prepositions), and they look at the correct parent when they hear "mommy" or "daddy" (Shi & Werker, 2001; Tincoff & Jusczyk, 1999).

In normal conversation, there are no silent gaps between words, so how do infants pick out words? Stress is one important clue. English contains many one-syllable words that are stressed and many two-syllable words that have a stressed syllable followed by an unstressed syllable (e.g., dough´ -nut, tooth´ -paste, bas´ -ket). Infants pay more attention to stressed syllables than unstressed syllables, which is a good strategy for identifying the beginnings of words (Bortfeld & Morgan, 2010; Thiessen & Saffran, 2003). And infants learn words more readily when the words appear at the beginning and ends of sentences, probably because the brief pause between sentences makes it easier to identify first and last words (Seidl & Johnson, 2006).

Another useful method is statistical. Infants notice syllables that go together frequently (Jusczyk, 2002). For example, in many studies, 8-month-olds heard the following sounds, which consisted of 4 three-syllable artificial words, said over and over in a random order.

pa bi ku go la tu da ro pi ti bu do da ro pi go la tu pa bi ku da ro pi

I've underlined the words and inserted gaps between them so that you can see them more easily, but in the actual studies there were no breaks at all, just a steady flow of syllables for 3 minutes. Later, infants listened to these words less than to new words that were novel combinations of the same syllables. They had detected *pa bi ku, go la tu, da ro pi,* and *ti bu do* as familiar patterns and listened to them less than to words like *tu da ro,* a new word made up from syllables they'd already heard (Aslin, Saffran, & Newport, 1998; Pelucci, Hay, & Saffran, 2009).

> Infants use the co-occurence of sounds and familiar function words to break up the speech stream and identify words.

Yet another way in which infants identify words is through their emerging knowledge of how sounds are used in their native language. For example, think about these two pairs of sounds: *s* followed by *t* and *s* followed by *d*. Both pairs are quite common at the end of one word and the beginning of the next: bu*s t*akes, ki*ss t*ook; thi*s d*og, pa*ss d*irectly. However, *s* and *t* occur frequently within a word (*st*op, li*st*, pe*st*, *st*ink) but *s* and *d* do not. Consequently, when *d* follows an *s*, it probably starts a new word. In fact, 9-month-olds follow rules like this one because when they hear novel words embedded in continuous speech, they're more likely to identify the novel word when the final sound in the preceding word occurs infrequently with the first sound of the novel word (Mattys & Jusczyk, 2001).

Another strategy that infants use is to rely on familiar function words, such as the articles *a* and *the,* to break up the speech stream. These words are very common in adults' speech; by six months most infants recognize them and use them to determine the onset of a new word (Shi & Lepage, 2008). For example, for infants familiar with *a,* the sequence like *aballabataglove* becomes *a ball a bat a glove.* The new words are isolated by the familiar ones.

Thus, infants use many powerful tools to identify words in speech. Of course, they don't yet understand the meanings of these words; at this point, they simply recognize a word as a distinct configuration of sounds. Nevertheless, these early perceptual skills are important because infants who are more skilled at detecting speech sounds know more words as toddlers (Conboy, Sommerville, & Kuhl, 2008), and overall their language is more advanced at 4 to 6 years of age (Newman et al., 2006).

Parents (and other adults) often help infants to master language sounds by talking in a distinctive style. **In** *infant-directed speech,* **adults speak slowly and with exaggerated changes in pitch and loudness.** If you could hear the mother in the photo talking to her baby, you would notice that she alternates between speaking softly and loudly and between high and low pitches and that her speech seems very expressive emotionally (Liu, Tsao, & Kuhl, 2007; Trainor, Austin, & Desjardins, 2000). (Infant-directed speech is also known as *motherese,* because this form of speaking was first noted in mothers, although it's now known that most caregivers talk this way to infants.) ●─ Watch the Video on **mydevelopmentlab.com**

When parents talk to babies, they often use *infant-directed speech,* which is slower and more varied in pitch and volume than adult-directed speech.

Infant-directed speech attracts infants' attention, perhaps because its slower pace and accentuated changes provide infants with increasingly more salient language clues (Cristia, 2010). For example, infants can segment words more effectively when they hear them in infant-direct speech (Thiessen, Hill, & Saffran, 2005). In addition, infant-directed speech includes especially good examples of vowels (Kuhl et al., 1997), which may help infants learn to distinguish these sounds. And when talking to infants, speaking clearly is a good idea. In one study (Liu, Kuhl, & Tsao, 2003), infants who could best distinguish speech sounds had the mothers who spoke the most clearly. **Watch** the **Video** on **mydevelopmentlab.com**

Infant-directed speech, then, helps infants perceive the sounds that are fundamental to their language. Unfortunately, some babies cannot hear speech sounds because they are deaf. How can these infants best learn language? The "Child Development and Family Policy" feature addresses this question.

Child Development and Family Policy

Are Cochlear Implants Effective for Young Children?

About 1 child out of 1,000 is born deaf or has profound hearing loss before mastering language. Of these youngsters, about 10% are born to deaf parents. In these cases, the child's deafness is usually detected early and parents communicate with their children using sign language. Deaf infants and toddlers seem to master sign language in much the same way and at about the same pace that hearing children master spoken language. For example, deaf 10-month-olds often babble in signs: They produce sequences of signs that are meaningless but resemble the tempo and duration of real signs.

The remaining 90% of deaf infants and toddlers have parents with normal hearing. For these children, communicating with signs is not really an option because their parents don't know sign language. Consequently, the usual recommendation for deaf children of hearing parents is to master spoken language, sometimes through methods that emphasize lipreading and speech therapy and sometimes with these methods along with signs and gestures. Unfortunately, with any of these methods, deaf children and parents rarely master spoken language. Their ability to produce and comprehend spoken language falls years behind their peers with normal language (Hoff, 2009).

Since the mid-1990s, however, deaf children have had a new option. As I described on page 142, the *cochlear implant* is a device that picks up speech sounds and converts them to electrical impulses that stimulate nerve cells in the ear. Cochlear implants are a tremendous benefit for people who lose their hearing after they master language. Adults with cochlear implants can converse readily with hearing speakers and some can converse on the phone (which is difficult otherwise because they can't lipread and because telephone lines sometimes distort speech sounds).

Cochlear implants also promote language acquisition in deaf children. When children deaf from birth receive cochlear implants, their spoken language skills end up substantially better than those of children who do not have cochlear implants. In fact, after receiving cochlear implants, many deaf children acquire language at

Watch the **Video** *Language Development* on **mydevelopmentlab .com** to learn more about infant-directed speech. The only example of actual infant-directed speech occurs early in the video, so pay attention or you'll miss it. The rest of the video describes how children benefit from hearing infant-directed speech.

Q&A **QUESTION 9.1**
Kristin spends hours talking to her infant son. Her husband enjoys spending time with his wife and son, but wishes that Kristin would stop using "baby talk" with their son and just talk in her regular voice. The sing-song pattern drives him crazy and he can't believe that it's of any good for their son. Is he right?
(Answer is on page 283.)

roughly the same rate as children with normal hearing (Svisky et al., 2000; Wie et al., 2007).

But this good news comes with several cautions. First, because some children do not receive their cochlear implants until 4 or 5 years of age, their language skills are still substantially behind that of hearing children. Second, a cochlear implant does not replace other forms of therapy for deaf children; a cochlear implant is used along with these other forms to make them more effective. Third, the benefits of a cochlear implant are not the same for all children: Improvements in language are astonishing for some children but modest for others.

Thus, a cochlear implant is an effective tool that can enhance children's language; it should be made available to deaf children, and the younger the better (Svirsky, Chin, & Jester, 2007). At the same time, research is needed to determine, first, the value of cochlear implants for younger infants; second, the sorts of language therapy that are most effective following a cochlear implant; and third, why cochlear implants benefit some children but not others.

First Steps to Speech

As any new parent can testify, newborns and young babies make many sounds: they cry, burp, and sneeze. However, language-based sounds don't appear immediately. **At 2 months, infants begin to produce vowel-like sounds, such as "ooooooo" or "ahhhhhh," a phenomenon known as** *cooing.* Sometimes infants become quite excited as they coo, perhaps reflecting the joy of simply playing with sounds.

Babbling appears at 5 or 6 months of age with a single consonant and vowel, then combines different speech sounds, and, later, adds intonation.

After cooing comes *babbling,* **speech-like sound that has no meaning.** A typical 6-month-old might say "dah" or "bah," utterances that sound like a single syllable consisting of a consonant and a vowel. Over the next few months, babbling becomes more elaborate as babies apparently experiment with more complex speech sounds. Older infants sometimes repeat a sound, as in "bahbahbah," and begin to combine different sounds, "dahmahbah" (Hoff, 2009).

Babbling is not just mindless playing with sounds; instead, it's a precursor to real speech. We know this, in part, from video records of people's mouths while speaking. When adults speak, the mouth is open somewhat wider on the right side than on the left side, reflecting the left hemisphere's control of language and muscle movements on the body's right side (Graves & Landis, 1990). Infants do the same when they babble, but not when making other nonbabbling sounds, which suggests that babbling is fundamentally linguistic (Holowka & Petitto, 2002).

Other evidence for the linguistic nature of babbling comes from studies of developmental change in babbling: At roughly 8 to 11 months, infants' babbling sounds more like real speech because infants, like Chelsea (in the vignette), stress some syllables and vary the pitch of their speech (Snow, 2006). In English declarative sentences, for example, pitch first rises, then falls toward the end of the sentence. In questions, however, the pitch is level, then rises toward the end of the question. **This pattern of rising or falling pitch is known as** *intonation.* Older babies' babbling reflects these patterns: Babies who are brought up by English-speaking parents have both the declarative and question patterns of intonation in their babbling. Babies exposed to a language with different patterns of intonation, such as Japanese or French, reflect their language's intonation in their babbling (Levitt & Utman, 1992).

The appearance of intonation in babbling indicates a strong link between perception and production of speech: Infants' babbling is influenced by the characteristics of the speech that they hear (Goldstein & Schwade, 2008). Beginning in the middle of the first year, infants try to reproduce the sounds of language that others use in trying to communicate with them (or, in the case of deaf infants with deaf parents, the signs that others use). Hearing *dog*, an infant may first say "dod," then "gog" before finally saying "dog" correctly. In the same way that beginning typists gradually link movements of their fingers with particular keys, through babbling infants learn to use the lips, tongue, and teeth to produce specific sounds, gradually making sounds that approximate real words (Poulson et al., 1991). Fortunately, learning to produce language sounds is easier for most babies than the cartoon suggests!

 ANSWER 9.1

No, he's wrong. Infant-directed speech helps babies to learn language, in part because changes in pitch attract an infant's attention and because the slower pace and accentuated changes help infants to detect differences in speech sounds. But I'll agree with Kristin's husband that infant-directed speech can become grating after a while!

The ability to produce sound, coupled with the 1-year-old's advanced ability to perceive speech sounds, sets the stage for the infant's first true words. In Module 9.2, we'll see how this happens.

 ## Check Your Learning

RECALL How do infants distinguish words in the speech they hear?

What evidence indicates that babbling is a precursor to speech?

INTERPRET Compare the developmental milestones during infancy for perceiving speech and those for producing speech.

APPLY Suppose that a 3-month-old baby born in Romania was adopted by a Swedish couple. How would the change in language environment affect the baby's language learning?

9.2 Learning the Meanings of Words

OUTLINE

Understanding Words
as Symbols

Fast Mapping Meanings
to Words

Individual Differences
in Word Learning

Encouraging Word Learning

Beyond Words: Other Symbols

LEARNING OBJECTIVES

• **How do children make the transition from babbling to talking?**

• **What rules do children follow to learn new words?**

• **What different styles of language learning do young children use?**

• **What conditions foster children's learning of new words?**

• **How does children's understanding of symbols progress beyond language?**

Sebastien is 20 months old and loves to talk. What amazes his parents is how quickly he adds words to his vocabulary. For example, the day his parents brought home a computer, Sebastien watched as they set it up. The next day, he spontaneously pointed to the computer and said, "puter." This happens all the time—Sebastien hears a word once or twice, then uses it correctly himself. Sebastien's parents wonder how he does this, particularly because learning vocabulary in a foreign language is so difficult for them!

At about their first birthday, most youngsters say their first words. In many languages, those words are similar (Nelson, 1973; Tardif et al., 2008) and include terms for mother and father, and greetings (*Hi*, *bye-bye*), as well as foods and toys (*juice*, *ball*). By age 2, most youngsters have a vocabulary of a few hundred words, and by age 6, a typical child's vocabulary includes more than 10,000 words (Bloom, 1998).

Like Sebastien, most children learn new words with extraordinary ease and speed. How do they do it? We'll answer that question in this module.

Understanding Words as Symbols

When my daughter, Laura, was 9 months old, she sometimes babbled "bay-bay." A few months later, she still said "bay-bay," but with an important difference. As a 9-month-old, "bay-bay" was simply an interesting set of sounds that had no special meaning to her. As a 13-month-old, "bay-bay" was her way of saying "baby." What had happened between 9 and 13 months? Laura had begun to understand that speech is more than just entertaining sound. She realized that sounds form words that refer to objects, actions, and properties. Put another way, Laura recognized that words are symbols, entities that stand for other entities. She already had formed concepts such as "round, bouncy things" and "furry things that bark" and "little humans that adults carry" based on her own experiences. With the insight that speech sounds can denote these concepts, she began to match sound patterns (words) and concepts (Reich, 1986).

If this argument is correct, we should find that children use symbols in other areas, not just in language. They do. Gestures are symbols, and like the baby in the photo, infants begin to gesture shortly before their first birthday (Goodwyn & Acredolo, 1993). Young children may smack their lips to indicate hunger or wave "bye-bye" when leaving. In these cases, gestures and words convey a message equally well.

What's more, gestures sometimes pave the way for language. Before knowing an object's name, infants often point to it or pick it up for a listener, as if saying, "I want this!" or "What's this?" In one study, 50% of all objects were first referred to by gesture and, about 3 months later, by word (Iverson & Goldin-Meadow, 2005). Given this connection between early gestures and first spoken words, it's not surprising that toddlers who are more advanced in their use of gesture tend to have, as preschoolers, more complex spoken language (Rowe & Goldin-Meadow, 2009).

Fast Mapping Meanings to Words

Once children have the insight that a word can symbolize an object or action, their vocabularies grow slowly at first. A typical 15-month-old, for example, may learn two to three new words each week. **However, at about 18 months, many children experience a** *naming explosion* **during which they learn new words—particularly names of objects—much more rapidly than before.** Children now learn 10 or more new words each week (Fenson et al., 1994; McMurray, 2007).

This rapid rate of word learning is astonishing when we realize that most words have many plausible but incorrect referents. To illustrate, imagine what's going through the mind of the child in the bottom photo. The mother has just pointed to the flowers, saying, "Flowers. These are flowers. See the flowers." To the mother (and you), this all seems crystal clear and incredibly straightforward. But what might a child learn from this episode? Perhaps the correct referent for "flowers." But a youngster could, just as reasonably, conclude that "flowers" refers to the petals, to the color of the flowers, or to the mother's actions in pointing to the flowers.

Surprisingly, though, most youngsters learn the proper meanings of simple words in just a few presentations. **Children's ability to connect new words to their meanings so rapidly that they cannot be considering all possible meanings for the new word is termed** *fast mapping.* How can young children learn new words so rapidly? Researchers believe that many distinct factors contribute to young children's rapid word learning (Hollich, Hirsh-Pasek, & Golinkoff, 2000).

JOINT ATTENTION. Parents encourage word learning by carefully watching what interests their children. When toddlers touch or look at an object, parents often label it for them. When a youngster points to a banana, a parent may say, "Banana, that's a banana." Most parents also do their best to simplify the task for children by using one label consistently for an object (Callanan & Sabbagh, 2004).

Of course, to take advantage of this help, infants must be able to tell when parents are labeling instead of just conversing. In fact, when adults label an unfamiliar

Babies begin to gesture at about the same time that they say their first words; both accomplishments show that infants are mastering symbols.

When a parent points to an object and says a word, babies conceivably could link the name to the object, to a property of the object (e.g., color), or to the act of pointing. In fact, babies consistently interpret the word as the object's name, an assumption that allows them to learn words rapidly.

object, young children are much more likely to assume that the label is the object's name when adults show signs that they are referring to the object, either by looking or pointing at it while labeling (Liebal et al., 2009; Nurmsoo & Bloom, 2008). Young children also consider an adult's credibility as a source: If an adult seems uncertain or has given incorrect names for words in the past, preschoolers are less likely to pick up words from them (Birch, Akmal, & Frampton, 2010; Koenig & Woodward, 2010). Thus, beginning in the toddler years, parents and children work together to create conditions that foster word learning: Parents label objects and youngsters rely on adults' behavior to interpret the words they hear. Finally, although joint attention helps children to learn words, it is not required: Children learn new words when those words are used in ongoing conversation and when they overhear others use novel words (Akhtar, Jipson, & Callanan, 2001).

CONSTRAINTS ON WORD NAMES.   Joint attention simplifies word learning for children, but the problem still remains: How does a toddler know that *banana* refers to the object that she's touching, as opposed to her activity (touching) or to the object's color? Many researchers believe that young children follow several simple rules that limit their conclusions about what labels mean.

A study by Au and Glusman (1990) shows how researchers have identified some of the rules that young children use. These investigators presented preschoolers with a stuffed animal with pink horns that otherwise resembled a monkey and called it a *mido*. *Mido* was then repeated several times, always referring to the monkey-like stuffed animal with pink horns. Later, these youngsters were asked to find a *theri* in a set of stuffed animals that included several *mido*. Never having heard of a *theri*, what did the children do? They never picked a *mido*; instead, they selected other stuffed animals. Knowing that *mido* referred to monkey-like animals with pink horns, evidently they decided that *theri* had to refer to one of the other stuffed animals.

> Young children use several simple rules to learn word names, such as the rule that a name applies to an entire object.

Apparently children were following this simple but effective rule for learning new words:

- If an unfamiliar word is heard in the presence of objects that already have names and objects that don't, the word refers to one of the objects that doesn't have a name.

Researchers have discovered several other simple rules that help children match words with the correct referent (Hoff, 2009; Woodward & Markman, 1998):

- A name refers to a whole object, not its parts or its relation to other objects, and refers not just to this particular object but to all objects of the same type (Hollich, Gollinkoff, & Hirsh-Pasek, 2007). For example, when a grandparent points to a stuffed animal on a shelf and says "dinosaur," children conclude that *dinosaur* refers to the entire dinosaur, not just its ears or nose, not to the fact that the dinosaur is on a shelf, and not to this specific dinosaur but to all dinosaur-like objects.
- If an object already has a name and another name is presented, the new name denotes a subcategory of the original name. If a child who knows the meaning of *dinosaur* sees a brother point to another dinosaur and say "T-rex," the child will conclude that *T-rex* is a special type of dinosaur.
- Given many similar category members, a word applied consistently to only one of them is a proper noun. If a child who knows *dinosaur* sees that one of a group of dinosaurs is always called "Dino," the child will conclude that *Dino* is the name of that particular dinosaur.

Rules like these make it possible for children such as Sebastien, the child in the vignette, to learn words rapidly because they reduce the number of possible referents. The child in the photo on page 285 follows these rules to decide that *flower* refers to the entire object, not its parts or the action of pointing to it.

SENTENCE CUES.   Children hear many unfamiliar words embedded in sentences containing words they already know. The other words and the overall sentence structure can be helpful clues to a word's meaning (Yuan & Fisher, 2009). For example, when a parent describes an event using familiar words but an unfamiliar verb, children often infer that the verb refers to the action performed by the subject of the sentence (Fisher, 1996; Woodward & Markman, 1998). When the youngsters in the photo hear, "The man is juggling," they will infer that *juggling* refers to the man's actions with the bats, because they already know *man* and because *-ing* refers to ongoing actions.

Preschool children know that *-ing* is added to a verb to indicate an ongoing action; consequently, when they hear an unfamiliar verb (e.g., "juggle") with *-ing* they infer that the unfamiliar verb must refer to the current action.

As another example of how sentence context aids word learning, look at the blocks in Figure 9-2 and point to "the boz block." I imagine you pointed to the middle block. Why? In English, adjectives usually precede the nouns they modify, so you inferred that *boz* is an adjective describing *block*. Since *the* before *boz* implies that only one block is *boz*, you picked the middle one, having decided that *boz* means "winged." Toddlers, too, use sentence cues like these to judge word meanings. Hearing "This is a Zav," 2-year-olds will interpret *Zav* as a category name, but hearing "This is Zav" (without the *a*), they interpret *Zav* as a proper name (Hall, Lee, & Belanger, 2001).

COGNITIVE FACTORS.   The naming explosion coincides with a time of rapid cognitive growth, and children's increased cognitive skill helps them to learn new words. As children's thinking becomes more sophisticated and, in particular, as they start to have goals and intentions, language becomes a means to express those goals and to achieve them. Thus, intention provides children with an important motive to learn language: to help achieve their goals (Bloom & Tinker, 2001).

FIGURE 9-2

In addition, young children's improving attentional and perceptual skills also promote word learning. In the "Spotlight on Theories" feature, we'll see how children's attention to shape (e.g., balls are round, pencils are slender rods) helps them learn new words.

Spotlight on Theories

A Shape-Bias Theory of Word Learning

BACKGROUND   Many developmental scientists believe that young children could master a complex task like word learning only by using built-in, language-specific mechanisms (e.g., fast-mapping rules such as "unfamiliar words refer to objects that don't have names"). However, not all scientists agree that specialized processes are required. Instead, they argue that word learning can be accomplished by applying basic processes of attention and learning.

THE THEORY   Linda B. Smith (2000, 2009) argues that shape plays a central role in learning words. Infants and young children spontaneously pay attention to an object's shape and they use this bias to learn new words. In Smith's theory, children first associate names with a single object: "ball" is associated with a specific tennis ball and "cup" is associated with a favorite sippy cup. As children encounter new balls and new cups, however, they hear the same words applied to similarly shaped objects and reach the conclusion that balls are round and cups are cylinders with handles. With further experience, children derive an even more general rule: Objects that have the same shape have the same name. From this, children realize that paying attention to shape is an easy way to learn names.

Hypothesis: If bias to attend to shape helps children learn names of words, then the age at which children first show the shape bias should coincide with a jump in the number of names that children learn. In other words, as soon as children realize that similarly shaped objects have the same name, they should start learning names much more rapidly.

Young children use an object's shape to help them learn its name.

Test: Gershkoff-Stowe and Smith (2004) conducted a longitudinal study in which parents kept detailed records of their toddlers' word learning for several months. In addition, toddlers were tested every three weeks. They were shown a multicolored U-shaped wooden object and told it was a "dax." Then they were shown several objects, some of which were also U-shaped but differed in color and material (e.g., a blue U-shaped sponge). Other objects were the same color (i.e., multicolored) or the same material (i.e., wood) but not U-shaped. Children were asked to give all the "dax" to the experimenter.

The crucial findings concern the age at which shape bias emerges and the age at which the naming explosion begins. Gershkoff-Stowe and Smith defined the onset of shape bias as the first session in which toddlers gave both U-shaped objects—but no others—to the experimenter. The onset of the naming explosion was defined as the first week in which toddlers learned 10 or more new words. These two ages were highly correlated—$r = .85$—indicating a tight link between onset of shape bias and the naming explosion.

Conclusion: As predicted, once toddlers showed a shape bias—that is, they realized that a name applies to objects that have the same shape but not to objects of the same color or made of the same material—they used this knowledge to learn new words faster. This result supports Smith's theory and the general idea that word learning may not require specialized mechanisms.

Application: If shape bias helps children learn words, can we teach this bias and foster word learning? Yes. Smith and colleagues (2002) had toddlers and an experimenter play with four pairs of novel objects; each pair of objects had the same name and the same shape but differed in color and material. A "dax" was still a U-shaped object; a "zup" referred to an elliptical-shaped object with a slot in one end. During play, the experimenter named each object 10 times. When children played with objects in this way, they learned the names of real words rapidly. From playing with "dax" and "zup," toddlers apparently learned that paying attention to shape is a good way to learn object names. Likewise, by systematically showing toddlers that the same name applies to many similarly shaped objects (e.g., book, crayon, comb, spoon), parents can teach youngsters the value of paying attention to shape to learn word names.

DEVELOPMENTAL CHANGE IN WORD LEARNING. Some of the word-learning tools described in the past few pages are particularly important at different ages (Hirsh-Pasek & Golinkoff, 2008). Before 18 months, infants learn words relatively slowly—often just one new word each day. At this age, children rely heavily on simple attentional processes (e.g., the shape bias) to learn new words. But by 24 months, most children are learning many new words daily. This faster learning reflects children's greater use of language cues (e.g., constraints on names) and a speaker's social cues. At any age, infants and toddlers rely on a mixture of word-learning tools, but with age they gradually move away from attentional cues and toward language and social cues.

NAMING ERRORS. Of course, these many ways of learning new words are not perfect; initial mappings of words onto meanings are often only partially correct (Hoff & Naigles, 2002). **A common mistake is** *underextension,* **defining a word too narrowly.** Using *car* to refer only to the family car and *ball* to a favorite toy ball are examples of underextension. **Between 1 and 3 years, children sometimes make the opposite error,** *overextension,* **defining a word too broadly.** Children may use *car* to also refer to buses and trucks or use *doggie* to refer to all four-legged animals.

The overextension error occurs more frequently when children are producing words than when they are comprehending words. Two-year-old Jason may say "doggie" to refer to a goat but nevertheless correctly point to a picture of a goat when asked. Because overextension is more common in word production, it may actually reflect another fast-mapping rule that children follow: "If you can't remember the name for an object, say the name of a related object" (Naigles & Gelman, 1995).

Both underextension and overextension disappear gradually as youngsters refine meanings for words with more exposure to language.

Individual Differences in Word Learning

The naming explosion typically occurs at about 18 months, but like many developmental milestones, the timing of this event varies widely for individual children. Some youngsters have a naming explosion as early as 14 months but for others it may be as late as 22 months (Goldfield & Reznick, 1990). Another way to make this point is to look at variation in the size of children's vocabulary at a specific age. At 18 months, for example, an average child's vocabulary would have about 75 words, but a child in the 90th percentile would know nearly 250 words and a child in the 10th percentile fewer than 25 words (Fenson et al., 1994).

The range in vocabulary size for normal 18-month-olds is huge—from 25 to 250 words! What can account for this difference? Heredity contributes: Twin studies find that vocabulary size is more similar in identical twins than in fraternal twins (Dionne et al., 2003). But the difference is fairly small, indicating a relatively minor role for genetics.

More important are two other factors. **One is** *phonological memory,* **the ability to remember speech sounds briefly.** This is often measured by saying a nonsense word to children—"ballop" or "glistering"—and asking them to repeat it immediately. Children's skill in recalling such words is strongly related to the size of their vocabulary (Gathercole et al., 1992; Leclercq & Majerus, 2010). Children who have difficulty remembering speech sounds accurately find word learning particularly challenging, which is not surprising since word learning involves associating meaning with an unfamiliar sequence of speech sounds.

QUESTION 9.2
Gavin and Mitch are both
16-month-olds. Gavin's
vocabulary includes about
14 words but Mitch's has
about 150 words, more than
10 times as many as Gavin.
What factors contribute
to this difference?
(Answer is on page 296.)

However, the single most important factor in growth of vocabulary is the child's language environment. Children have larger vocabularies when they are exposed to a lot of high-quality language. The more words children hear, the better (Hurtado, Marchman, & Fernald, 2008). Specifically, children learn more words when their parents' speech is rich in different words and is grammatically sophisticated (Hoff, 2003; Huttenlocher et al., 2010), and when parents respond promptly and appropriately to their children's talk (Tamis-Lemonda & Bornstein, 2002).

WORD LEARNING STYLES.   Size of vocabulary is not the only way in which young children differ in their word learning. As youngsters expand their vocabulary, they often adopt a distinctive style of learning language (Bates, Bretherton, & Snyder, 1988; Nelson, 1973). **Some children have a** *referential style:* **their vocabularies consist mainly of words that name objects, persons, or actions.** For example, Caitlin, a referential child, had 42 name words in her 50-word vocabulary but only 2 words for social interaction or questions. **Other children have an** *expressive style:* **their vocabularies include some names but also many social phrases that are used like a single word, such as "go away," "what'd you want?" and "I want it."** A typical expressive child, Candace, had a more balanced vocabulary, with 22 name words and 13 for social interactions and questions.

Referential and expressive styles represent end points on a continuum; most children are somewhere in between. For children with referential emphasis, language is primarily an intellectual tool—a means of learning and talking about objects (Masur, 1995). In contrast, for children with expressive emphasis, language is more of a social tool—a way of enhancing interactions with others. Of course, both of these functions—intellectual and social—are important functions of language, which explains why most children blend the referential and expressive styles of learning language.

> Language is primarily an intellectual tool for referential children and primarily a social tool for expressive children.

Encouraging Word Learning

How can parents and other adults help children learn words? If children are to expand their vocabularies, they need to hear others speak. Not surprisingly, then, children learn words more rapidly if their parents speak to them frequently (Huttenlocher et al., 1991; Roberts, Burchinal, & Durham, 1999). Of course, sheer quantity of parental speech is not all that matters. Parents can foster word learning by naming objects that are the focus of a child's attention (Dunham, Dunham, & Curwin, 1993). Parents can name different products on store shelves as they point to them. During a walk, parents can label the objects—birds, plants, vehicles—that the child sees.

Parents can also help children learn words by reading books with them. Reading together is fun for parents and children alike, and it provides opportunities for children to learn new words. However, the way that parents read makes a difference. When parents carefully describe pictures as they read, preschoolers' vocabularies increase (Reese & Cox, 1999). Asking children questions also helps (Sénéchal, Thomas, & Monker, 1995). When an adult reads a sentence (e.g., "Arthur is *angling*"), then asks a question (e.g., "What is Arthur doing?"), a child must match the new word (*angling*) with the pictured activity (fishing) and say the word aloud. When parents read without questioning, children can ignore words they don't understand. Questioning forces children to identify meanings of new words and practice saying them.

For school-age children, parents remain an important influence on vocabulary development: Children learn words when exposed to a parent's advanced vocabulary, particularly in the context of instructive and helpful interactions (Weizman & Snow, 2001). Reading is another great way to learn new words. Written material—books, magazines, newspapers, textbooks—almost always contains more unfamiliar words than conversational language, so reading is rich in opportunities to expand vocabulary (Hayes, 1988). Not surprisingly, children who read frequently tend to have larger vocabularies than children who read less often (Allen, Cipielewski, & Stanovich, 1992).

IMPACT OF VIDEO.   Television has been a regular part of American children's lives since the 1950s, but video has assumed an even larger role with the ready availability of inexpensive DVD players and child-oriented DVDs. A typical preschool child in the United States spends more than two hours watching video, and infants like the one in the photo spend more than an hour watching (Linebarger & Vaala, 2010). We'll learn more about the impact of video in general in Module 15.2; for now, the issue is the influence of video in helping children to learn new words.

Although U.S. babies typically spend more than an hour every day watching video, they learn little language from such exposure.

For preschool children, viewing video can help word learning, under some circumstances. For example, preschool children who regularly watch *Sesame Street* usually have larger vocabularies than preschoolers who watch *Sesame Street* only occasionally (Wright et al., 2001). Other programs that promote word learning are those that tell a story (e.g., *Thomas the Tank Engine*), as well as programs like *Blue's Clues* and *Dora the Explorer*, which directly ask questions of the viewer. The benefits of these programs are greatest when preschoolers watch them with adults, in part because the video contents become the focus of joint attention, as described on page 285. In contrast, most cartoons have no benefit for language learning (Linebarger & Vaala, 2010).

What about videos claiming that they promote word learning in infants? Most of the evidence suggests that before 18 months of age, infant-oriented videos (e.g., Baby Einstein, Brainy Baby) are not effective in promoting infants' word learning (Linebarger & Vaala, 2010). The "Focus on Research" feature describes a study (first mentioned on page 27 as a good example of a field experiment) that reports this sort of negative evidence.

Focus on Research

Do Infants Learn Words from Watching Infant-Oriented Media?

Who were the investigators, and what was the aim of the study? Although marketing and some testimonials suggest that infants expand their vocabulary from watching infant-oriented video, there's very little experimental work on the issue. Because correlational studies (e.g., Zimmerman, 2007) suggested a negative relation between exposure to infant videos and the size of infants' vocabularies (i.e., more exposure was associated with smaller vocabularies), Judy DeLoache and her colleagues (2010) conducted an experiment to determine the impact of exposure to infant-oriented videos on word learning.

How did the investigators measure the topic of interest? DeLoache et al. created four different conditions. In two of them, parents were given a commercially available DVD that was designed to teach new words to young children. The video included 25 common objects, and each was labeled 3 times (e.g., This is a *clock*). In both conditions, infants watched the video at home five times a week for four weeks. However, in one condition they watched it together with a parent; in another condition, they watched it alone (although the parent was usually in the same room). In a third condition, parents were given a list of the 25 words presented in the video and encouraged to teach the words to their infant "in whatever way seems natural to you" (p. 1571) over the same four-week period. Finally, in a control condition, infants were not exposed to the 25 words in any way; instead, they were simply tested at the beginning and the end of the four-week period to determine which words they understood. Infants in the other three conditions were also tested in this manner: Infants were shown a replica of one of the objects shown in the video (e.g., a clock) along with a replica of an object not shown in the video (e.g., a fan) and the experimenter asked infants to show the target object (e.g., "Can you show me the clock?).

Who were the children in the study? DeLoache et al. tested 72 12- to 18-month-olds.

What was the design of the study? This study was experimental: The independent variable was the nature of infants' exposure to the 25 words in the video (video with parental interaction, video only, parental teaching, no systematic exposure). The dependent variable was the percentage of times that the infants selected the correct replica. The study was not developmental (12- to 18-month-olds were tested just once), so it was neither cross-sectional nor longitudinal. However, as I mentioned previously, the study nicely illustrates a field experiment (i.e., an experiment conducted in infants' homes).

Were there ethical concerns with the study? No. The task posed no danger to the infants.

What were the results? During the initial testing, most infants knew 6 to 7 words; these words were not presented during the final testing. During final testing, infants learned the most words when parents taught them directly. These infants learned about half of the words. In contrast, the infants in the remaining conditions (two video conditions and the control condition) only learned about one-third of the words. In other words, regularly daily exposure to the 25 words through the video produced no greater word learning than the incidental, casual exposure that took place in the control condition.

What did the investigators conclude? The findings indicate that the video was ineffective in promoting word learning. In the words of DeLoache et al., "the degree to which babies actually learn from baby videos is negligible" (p. 1573).

What converging evidence would strengthen these conclusions? DeLoache and colleagues tested only a single video; extending the work to other DVDs would be useful. In addition, most of the infants came from middle-class homes; it would be important to determine whether these videos have any effectiveness in promoting language for infants from families with lower socioeconomic status.

Why do baby videos seem to have no benefit for infants' word learning, particularly when videos for preschool children are effective? According to Linebarger and Vaala, one reason is that these videos are "poorly designed, insufficient to support language processing, and developmentally inappropriate" (2010, p. 184). Another reason stems from a phenomenon that we'll consider in detail at the end of this module: 12- to 18-month olds have limited understanding of relationships between real objects and their depictions in photographs and video. In other words, they have difficulty relating what they see in the video to those objects and actions as experienced in their own lives.

Research on video and on parents' influence points to a simple but powerful conclusion: Children are most likely to learn new words when they participate in activities that force them to understand the meanings of new words and use those new words. Is learning new words (and other aspects of language) more difficult for children learning two languages? The "Cultural Influences" feature has the answer.

> **Baby videos seem to have no benefit for infants' word learning.**

Cultural Influences

Growing Up Bilingual

More than 10 million American children and adolescents come from homes where English is not the primary language. In many states, 25% or more of the children are bilingual, and the percentages are even higher in some urban areas (Shin & Kominski, 2010). These youngsters usually speak English and another language, such as Spanish or, like the children in the photo, Chinese.

Is learning two languages easier or harder than learning just one language? For much of the 20th century, the general view was that bilingualism harmed children's development. One child psychology text published roughly 60 years ago surveyed the research and concluded, "There can be no doubt that the child reared in a bilingual environment is handicapped in his language growth" (Thompson, 1952, p. 367). Today, we know this conclusion is wrong because it was based on studies of poor, immigrant children's scores on intelligence tests. In retrospect, immigrant children's test scores had more to do with their poverty and unfamiliarity with a new culture than with their bilingualism.

In fact, modern studies lead to a different picture. When infants learn two languages simultaneously, they often progress somewhat slowly at first. They mix words from the two languages, and are less skilled at using language-specific sounds to guide word learning (Fennell, Byers-Heinlein, & Werker, 2007). Soon, however, they separate the languages, and bilingual children reach most language milestones at about the same age as monolingual children (Pettito et al., 2001). When each language is considered separately, bilingual children often have somewhat smaller vocabularies than monolingual children (Umbel et al., 1992). However, since bilingual youngsters often know words in one language but not the other, their total vocabulary (i.e., words known in both languages plus words known in either language but not both) is greater than that of monolingual children.

Bilingual children learn language at about the same rate as monolingual children and often have more sophisticated understanding of the underlying symbolic nature of language.

What's more, bilingual children surpass monolingual children in other language skills. Bilingual preschoolers are more likely to understand that the printed form of a word is unrelated to the meaning of the word (Bialystok, 1997; Bialystok, Shenfield, & Codd, 2000). For example, bilingual preschoolers are less likely to believe that words denoting large objects (e.g., *bus*) are longer than words denoting small objects (e.g., *bug*). Bilingual children also better understand that words are simply arbitrary symbols. Bilingual youngsters, for instance, are more likely than monolingual children to understand that, as long as all English speakers agreed, *dog* could refer to cats and *cat* could refer to dogs (Bialystok, 1988; Campbell & Sais, 1995).

Finally, bilingual children are more skilled at switching back and forth between tasks and often are better able to inhibit inappropriate responses (Bialystok, 2010; Carlson & Meltzoff, 2008). If asked to sort cards first by color, then by shape, children often sort by the first rule: Instead of sorting by shape, they revert to sorting by color (the first rule). Bilingual children are less prone to this sort of mistake, perhaps because they must routinely inhibit relevant words while speaking, listening, or reading. For example, when shown a photo of a dog and asked, "What's this?," preschoolers bilingual in French and English must respond "dog" while suppressing "chien." Apparently, this experience makes bilingual children generally better at inhibiting competing responses.

> Compared to monolingual children, bilingual children better understand the symbolic nature of words.

Of course, many children in America can't speak English at the time when they should begin school. How to teach these children has prompted much national debate. One view is that all Americans should speak English and so all teaching should be in English. Another view is that children learn more effectively in their native tongue and so all teaching should be done in that language.

Much of the debate over the proper language of instruction is political, reflecting people's desire for a society with a universal cultural heritage and language rather than a society with pluralistic heritages and languages. Ignoring the political aspects, research shows that the best method uses both the child's native language *and* English (Padilla et al., 1991; Wong-Fillmore et al., 1985). Initially, children receive basic English-language teaching while they are taught other subjects in their native language. Gradually, more instruction is done in English, in step with children's growing proficiency in the second language. When instruction is in children's native language and English, they are most likely to master academic content and literacy skills in both languages (Farver, Lonigan, & Eppe, 2009).

Beyond Words: Other Symbols

To end this module, let's return to the topic that began the module—symbols. Words are indeed powerful and immensely useful symbols. However, as children grow they learn other symbol systems. Pictures, for example, are symbols that represent something else. The link between a picture and what it represents is often very clear. Wallet photos, for example, are easily recognized as representations of familiar people (at least to the wallet's owner!). But the seemingly transparent connection between photographs and the object photographed actually poses a problem for young children—photos are not the actual object but simply a representation of it. Young children must learn that shaking a picture of a rattle will not make a noise and inverting a picture of a glass of juice will not cause it to spill. In fact, if shown realistic photos of familiar toys, 9-month-olds often try to grasp the toy in the photo, much as they would grasp the real object. By 18 months, toddlers rarely do this, indicating that toddlers understand that photos are representations of objects, not the objects themselves (Troseth, Pierroutsakos, & DeLoache, 2004).

A scale model is another kind of symbolic representation. A scale model of the solar system helps students to understand the relative distances of planets from the sun; a scale model of a college campus shows the location of campus landmarks to new students; and a scale model of an airplane allows aeronautical engineers to measure how air flows over a wing. Scale models are useful because they are realistic-looking—simply smaller versions of the real thing. Nevertheless, young children do not understand the relation between scale models and the objects the models represent: The ability to use scale models develops early in the preschool years. To illustrate, if young children watch an adult hide a toy in a full-size room, then try to find the toy in a scale model of the room that contains all the principal features of the full-scale room (e.g., carpet, window, furniture), 3-year-olds find the hidden toy readily but 2½-year-olds do not (DeLoache, 1995).

Why is this task so easy for 3-year-olds and so difficult for 2½-year-olds? Do the younger children simply forget the location of the toy by the time they look at the scale model of the room? No. If returned to the full-size room, they easily find the hidden toy. Judy DeLoache and her colleagues believe that 2½-year-olds "attention to a scale model as an interesting and attractive object makes it difficult for them to simultaneously think about its relation to something else" (DeLoache, Miller, & Rosengren, 1997, p. 308). In other words, young children are drawn to the model as a real object and therefore find it hard to think about the model as a symbol of the full-size room.

If this argument is correct, 2½-year-olds should be more successful using the model if they don't have to think of it as a symbol for the full-size room. DeLoache and her colleagues tested this hypothesis in what is my favorite study of all time, for reasons that should soon be obvious. To test this argument, they created a condition designed to eliminate the need for children to think of the model as both an object and a symbol. Children saw the oscilloscope shown in the photograph, which was described as a shrinking machine. They saw a toy doll—"Terry the Troll"—placed in front of the oscilloscope; then the experimenter and child left the room briefly while a tape recorder played sounds that were described as sounds "the machine makes when it's shrinking something." When experimenter and child returned, Terry had shrunk from 8 inches to 2 inches. Next, Terry was hidden in the full-size room, the experimenter aimed the "shrinking machine" at the full-size room, then experimenter and child left the room. While the tape recorder played shrinking sounds, research assistants quickly removed everything from the full-size room and substituted the model. Then the experimenter and child returned and the child was asked to find Terry.

Children rarely found the toy when tested with the usual instructions, but they usually did in the "shrinking machine" condition. Apparently, 2½-year-olds find it very difficult to think of the model as an object and as a symbol, and, consequently, cannot find the hidden toy, even though the model is an exact replica of the full-size room. In contrast, when children can think of the model as the room, but much smaller, they readily find the toy.

A map is more demanding for children because it is only a two-dimensional (flat) representation of objects in the world. Nevertheless, by 4 years of age

In a study that examined children's understanding of scale models as symbols, Judy DeLoache and her colleagues convinced 2½-year-olds that this oscilloscope could shrink the doll and other objects.

ANSWER 9.2
The two main factors are phonological memory and the boys' language environments. It's likely that Mitch has a better phonological memory—he can remember speech sounds more accurately and longer—and he gets exposed to more speech and more sophisticated speech.

children can use simple maps to find objects (Shusterman, Lee, & Spelke, 2008). What's more, this skill emerges when children have no exposure to maps: In a study conducted in isolated villages in South America where there were no maps, rulers, or schools, children used simple maps as capably as U.S. children did (Dehaene et al., 2006).

Of course, after children have mastered scale models and maps, a host of other symbolic forms awaits them, including graphs and musical notation. But children take their first steps toward lifelong access to symbols as infants, when they master words and gestures.

 ## Check Your Learning

RECALL What factors help children learn new words so rapidly?

Summarize some of the ways in which children's vocabularies differ quantitatively and qualitatively.

INTERPRET Explain why a child's first words are best viewed as a breakthrough in children's understanding of symbols.

APPLY Suppose you've been asked to write a brochure for first-time parents about ways they can foster word learning in their toddlers. What would you say?

 ## 9.3 Speaking in Sentences

OUTLINE
From Two-Word Speech to Complex Sentences
How Do Children Acquire Grammar?

LEARNING OBJECTIVES
- How do children progress from speaking single words to creating complicated sentences?
- How do children acquire the grammar of their native language?

Jaime's daughter, Luisa, is a curious 2½-year-old who bombards her father with questions. Jaime enjoys Luisa's questioning, but he is bothered by the way she phrases her questions. Luisa will say, "What you are doing?" and "Why not she sleep?" Obviously, Jaime doesn't talk this way, so he wonders where Luisa learned to ask questions like this. Is it normal, or is it a symptom of some type of language disorder?

Not long after children begin to talk, they start combining words to form simple sentences. These simple sentences are the first step in a new area of language learning, mastering *syntax*—a language's rules for combining words to create sentences. We'll begin this module by tracing the stages in children's acquisition of syntax and, along the way, see that Luisa's way of asking questions is quite normal for youngsters learning English. Then we'll examine different factors that influence children's mastery of syntax.

From Two-Word Speech to Complex Sentences

At about 1½ years, children begin to combine individual words to create two-word sentences, like *more juice, gimme cookie, truck go, my truck, Mommy go, Daddy bike.* **Researchers call this kind of talk** *telegraphic speech* **because, like telegrams of days gone by, it consists of only words directly relevant to meaning.** Before text messages and e-mail, people sent urgent messages by telegraph, and the cost was based on the number of words. Consequently, telegrams were brief and to the point, containing only the important nouns, verbs, adjectives, and adverbs, much like children's two-word speech.

Children use a small set of rules to create two-word sentences that describe people, actions, and properties.

In their two-word speech, children follow rules to express different meanings. For example, the sentences *truck go* and *Daddy eat* are both about agents—people or objects that do something and the actions they perform. Here the rule is "agent + action." In contrast, *my truck* is about a possessor and a possession; the rule for creating these sentences is "possessor + possession."

When children are in the two-word stage, they use several basic rules to express meaning (Brown, 1973). These are listed in Table 9-1. Of course, not all children use all eight rules listed in the table, but most do. And this is true of children around the world (Tager-Flusberg, 1993). Regardless of the language they learn, children's two-word sentences follow a common set of rules that are very useful in describing ideas concerning people and objects, their actions, and their properties.

TABLE 9-1

RULES USED TO EXPRESS MEANING DURING THE TWO-WORD STAGE

Rule	Example
agent + action	Daddy eat
possessor + possession	my truck
action + object	gimme cookie
agent + object	boy car (meaning the boy is pushing the car)
action + location	put chair (meaning put the object on the chair)
entity + location	truck chair (meaning the truck is on the chair)
attribute + entity	big car
demonstrative + entity	that cup

Source: Based on Brown, 1973.

BEYOND TELEGRAPHIC SPEECH.   Beginning at about the second birthday, children move to three-word and even longer sentences. For example, at 1½ years, my daughter Laura would say, "gimme juice" or "bye-bye, Mom." As a 2½-year-old, she had progressed to "When I finish my ice cream, I'll take a shower, okay?" and "Don't turn the light out—I can't see better!" **Children's longer sentences are filled with** *grammatical morphemes,* **words or endings of words (such as** *-ing, -ed,* **or** *-s)* **that make a sentence grammatical.** To illustrate, a 1½-year-old might say, "kick ball," but a 3-year-old would be more likely to say, "I am kicking the ball." Compared to the 1½-year-old's telegraphic speech, the 3-year-old has added several elements,

This is a wug.

*Now there is another one.
There are two of them.
There are two _____ .*

FIGURE 9-3

 QUESTION 9.3

Describing her vacation,
3-year-old Kelly said, "I sleeped
in a tent!" What feature of
grammatical development
does her comment illustrate?
(Answer is on page 303.)

including a pronoun, *I*, to serve as the subject of the sentence; the auxiliary verb *am*; *-ing* to the verb *kick*; and an article, *the*, before *ball*. Each of these grammatical morphemes makes the older child's sentence slightly more meaningful and much more grammatical.

How do children learn all of these subtle nuances of grammar? Conceivably, a child might learn that *kicking* describes kicking that is ongoing and that *kicked* describes kicking that occurred in the past. Later, the child might learn that *raining* describes current weather and *rained* describes past weather. But learning different tenses for individual verbs—one by one—would be remarkably slow. More effective would be to learn the general rules that "verb + *-ing*" denotes an ongoing activity and "verb + *-ed*" denotes a past activity. In fact, this is what children do: They learn general rules about grammatical morphemes. For example, suppose you show preschoolers pictures of nonsense objects like the one in Figure 9-3 and label it: "This is a wug." Then you show pictures of two of the objects while saying, "Now there is another one. There are two of them. There are two . . ." Preschoolers usually say, "Wugs" (Berko, 1958). Because *wug* is a novel word, children can answer correctly only by applying the rule of adding *-s* to indicate plural.

Sometimes, of course, applying the general rule can lead to very creative communication. As a 3-year-old, my daughter would say, "unvelcro it," meaning detach the Velcro. She had never heard *unvelcro*, but she created this word from the rule that "*un-* + verb" means to reverse or stop the action of a verb. Creating such novel words is, in fact, evidence that children learn grammar by applying rules, not by learning individual words.

Additional evidence that children master grammar by learning rules comes from preschoolers' *overregularization,* **applying rules to words that are exceptions to the rule.** Youngsters learning English may incorrectly add an *-s* instead of using an irregular plural—*two mans* instead of *two men* or *two foots* instead of *two feet*. With the past tense, children may add *-ed* instead of using an irregular past tense—*I goed* instead of *I went* or *she runned* instead of *she ran* (Maratsos, 2000; Marcus et al., 1992). Children apparently know the general rule but not all the words that are exceptions.

The rules governing grammatical morphemes range from fairly simple to very complex. The rule for plurals—add *-s* —is simple to apply, and, as you might expect, it's one of the first grammatical morphemes that children master. Adding *-ing* to denote ongoing action is also simple, and it too is mastered early. More complex forms, such as the various forms of the verb *to be*, are mastered later; but, remarkably, by the end of the preschool years, children typically have mastered most of the rules that govern grammatical morphemes.

At the same time that preschoolers are mastering grammatical morphemes, they extend their speech beyond the subject-verb-object construction that is basic in English. You can see these changes in the way children ask questions. Children's questions during two-word speech are marked by intonation alone. Soon after a child can declare, "My ball," he can also ask, "My ball?" Children quickly discover *wh* words (*who, what, when, where, why*), but they don't use them correctly. Like Luisa, the 2½-year-old in the module-opening vignette, many youngsters merely attach the *wh* word to the beginning of a sentence without changing the rest of the sentence: *What he eating? What we see?* But by 3 or 3½ years, youngsters insert the required auxiliary verb before the subject, creating *What is he eating?* or *What will we see?* (Rowland et al., 2005; deVilliers & deVilliers, 1985).

Between ages 3 and 6, children also learn to use negation ("That isn't a butterfly") and embedded sentences ("Jennifer thinks that Bill took the book"). They begin to comprehend passive voice ("The ball was kicked by the girl") as opposed to the active voice ("The girl kicked the ball"), although full understanding of this form continues to develop into the elementary-school years (Hoff, 2009). In short, by the time most children enter kindergarten, they use most of the grammatical forms of their native language with great skill.

As children move beyond two-word speech, they begin to master questions, negation, and other more complex sentences.

How Do Children Acquire Grammar?

Ponder young children's grammatical accomplishments for a moment, particularly in light of their other cognitive skills. Most youngsters can neither read nor do arithmetic, and some don't know the letters of the alphabet, but virtually all have mastered the fundamentals of grammar of their native tongue. How do they do it? Theorists have proposed several different answers to this question.

THE BEHAVIORIST ANSWER. The simplest explanation for learning grammar is that children imitate the grammatical forms they hear. In fact, B. F. Skinner (1957) and other learning theorists once claimed that all aspects of language—sounds, words, grammar, and communication—are learned through imitation and reinforcement (Moerk, 2000; Whitehurst & Vasta, 1975).

Critics were quick to point to some flaws in this explanation, however. One problem is that most of children's sentences are novel, which is difficult to explain in terms of simple imitation of adults' speech. For example, when young children create questions by inserting a *wh* word at the beginning of a sentence ("What she doing?"), who are they imitating?

Also troublesome for the learning view is that even when children imitate adult sentences, they do not imitate adult grammar. In simply trying to repeat "I am drawing a picture," young children will say "I draw picture." Furthermore, linguists, particularly Noam Chomsky (1957, 1995), argued that grammatical rules are far too complex for toddlers and preschoolers to infer them solely on the basis of the speech that they hear.

THE LINGUISTIC ANSWER. Beginning with Chomsky (1957), linguists proposed that children are born with mechanisms that simplify the task of learning grammar (Slobin, 1985). According to this view, children are born with neural circuits in the brain that allow them to infer the grammar of the language that they hear. That is, grammar itself is not built into the child's nervous system, but processes that guide the learning of grammar are. **For example, according to** *semantic bootstrapping theory,* **children are born knowing that nouns usually refer to people or objects and that verbs are actions; they use this knowledge to infer grammatical rules.*** Hearing sentences such as "Billy drinks," "Susan sleeps," and "Jen reads," children infer that noun + verb makes a grammatical sentence in English. Consistent with this idea, by 2 years of age, English-speaking children know that a typical transitive sentence (e.g., "the bunny ate the carrot") includes an agent (the subject), an action (the transitive verb), and a patient (the object of the action). Told that "the pig is dorping the cow," 2-year-olds match this with a video of a pig performing an action on a cow (Gertner, Fisher, & Eisengart, 2006).

*The name for this theory comes from the phrase "pull yourself up by your bootstraps," which means improving your situation by your own efforts. The phrase is from an 18th-century fantasy tale about a baron who falls into a deep hole and escapes by pulling up on his bootstraps.

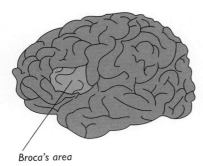

Broca's area

FIGURE 9-4

The proposal that inborn mechanisms help children learn grammar might not be as intuitively appealing as imitation, but many findings indirectly support this view:

1. **Specific regions of the brain are known to be involved in language processing.** If children are born with a "grammar-learning processor," it should be possible to locate a specific region or regions of the brain that are involved in learning grammar. In fact, you may remember from Module 4.3 that for most people the left hemisphere of the brain plays a critical role in understanding language. Some functions of language have been located even more precisely. For example, the area in blue in Figure 9-4 is Broca's area—a region in the left frontal cortex that is necessary for combining words into meaningful sentences. By 2 years of age, specific regions of the left hemisphere are activated when sentences break simple grammatical rules, such as a noun appearing when a verb would be expected (Bernal et al., 2010). The fact that specific areas in the brain have well-defined functions for language makes it plausible that children have specialized neural circuits that help them learn grammar.

2. **Only humans learn grammar readily.** If grammar is learned solely through imitation and reinforcement, then it should be possible to teach rudimentary grammar to nonhumans. If, instead, learning grammar depends on specialized neural mechanisms that are unique to humans, then efforts to teach grammar to nonhumans should fail. This prediction has been tested many times by trying to teach grammar to chimpanzees, the species closest to humans on the evolutionary ladder. For example, chimps like the one in the photo have been taught to communicate using gestures taken from sign language. Other chimps have been taught using plastic chips to stand for words. The result? Chimps master a handful of grammatical rules governing two-word speech, but only with massive effort that is completely unlike the preschool child's learning of grammar (Savage-Rumbaugh, 2001; Seyfarth & Cheney, 1996). And the resulting language is unlike children's grammar in many ways (Kako, 1999). For example, one chimp, Nim, gradually used longer sentences, but they were longer only because he repeated himself (e.g., "eat Nim eat Nim"), not because he expressed more complicated ideas. Because numerous efforts to teach grammar to chimps have failed, this suggests that children rely on some type of mechanism specific to humans to master grammar.

3. **There is a critical period for learning language.** The period from birth to about 12 years is a critical period for acquiring language generally and mastering grammar particularly. If children do not acquire language in this period, they will never truly master language later. Evidence of a critical period for language comes from studies of isolated children. In one tragic instance, a baby girl named Genie was restrained by a harness during the day and a straitjacket-like device at night. No one was permitted to talk to Genie, and she was beaten when she made

Chimpanzees can be taught very simple grammatical rules, but only after massive training that is unlike what toddlers and preschoolers experience.

any noise. When Genie was discovered, at age 13, she did not speak at all. After several years of language training, her mastery of grammar remained limited, resembling the telegraphic speech of a 2-year-old (Curtiss, 1989; Rymer, 1993).

Further evidence for a critical period for language comes from studies of individuals learning second languages. Individuals master the grammar of a foreign language at the level of a native speaker only if they are exposed to the language prior to adolescence (Newport, 1991). Why can one period of time be so much more influential for language than others? Why can't missed language experiences be made up after age 12? A critical period for language answers these questions. That is, just as females ovulate for only a limited portion of the life span, the neural mechanisms involved in learning grammar may function only during infancy and childhood.

Children master grammar only when they are exposed to a language before adolescence.

4. **The development of grammar is tied to the development of vocabulary.** The mastery of grammar is closely related to vocabulary growth, in a way that suggests both are part of a common, emerging language system (Dixon & Marchman, 2007). One idea, for example, is that as children learn words, they learn not only a word's meaning, but also about the kinds of sentences in which a word appears and its position in those sentences. They learn the meaning of "teacher" and that "teacher" can appear as the actor and object in transitive sentences. Grammar then emerges naturally as children learn more and more words.

Two fascinating findings document this tight link between growth of vocabulary and emergence of grammar. First, in bilingual children, growth of vocabulary and grammar are related within each language, but not across languages (Conboy & Thal, 2006). In other words, children's English vocabulary predicts the complexity of their English sentences (but not their Spanish sentences) while their Spanish vocabulary predicts the complexity of their Spanish sentences (but not their English sentences). In each language, children need a "critical mass" of words before grammar can emerge.

Second, children who are adopted by adults who speak another language (typically, through an international adoption) represent a valuable natural experiment. Most children are adopted as infants, toddlers, or preschoolers, which means they differ considerably in the cognitive skills they can use to learn grammar. Nevertheless, the size of children's vocabulary, not their age, predicts the complexity of their grammar (Snedeker, Geren, & Shafto, 2007). That is, if a 3-year-old and a 7-year-old each know 400 words, their grammar will be comparable, despite the age difference. This tight coupling of vocabulary and grammar in adopted and bilingual children goes well with the idea that development of vocabulary and grammar is regulated by a common, language-specific system.

Although these findings are consistent with the idea that children have innate grammar-learning mechanisms, they do *not* prove the existence of such mechanisms. Consequently, scientists have continued to look for other explanations.

THE COGNITIVE ANSWER.   Not all researchers believe that children must have specialized mechanisms to learn grammar. Some theorists (e.g., Braine, 1992) believe that children learn grammar through powerful cognitive skills that help them rapidly detect regularities in their environments, including patterns in the speech they hear. According to this approach, it's as if children establish a huge Excel spreadsheet that has the speech they've heard in one column and the context in which they heard it in a second column; periodically infants scan the columns looking for recurring patterns (Maratsos, 1998). For example, children might be confused the first time they hear -*s* added to the end of a familiar noun. However, as the database expands to include many instances of familiar nouns with an added -*s*, children discover that -*s* is always added to a noun when there are multiple instances of the object. Thus, they create the rule: noun + -*s* = plural. With this view, children learn language by searching for regularities across many examples that are stored in memory, not through an inborn grammar-learning device (Bannard & Matthews, 2008). Scientists who subscribe to this view argue that infants' impressive ability to extract regularities in the speech sounds that they hear (described on page 280) would work just as effectively to extract regularities in sentence structure (Gerken, 2006).

THE SOCIAL-INTERACTION ANSWER.   This approach is eclectic, drawing on each of the views we've considered so far. From the behaviorist approach, it takes an emphasis on the environment; from the linguistic approach, that language learning is distinct; and, from the cognitive view, that children have powerful cognitive skills they can use to master language. The unique contribution of this perspective is emphasizing that children master language generally and grammar specifically in the context of social interactions (Bloom & Tinker, 2001). That is, much language learning takes place in the context of interactions between children and adults, with both parties eager for better communication. Children have an ever-expanding repertoire of ideas and intentions that they wish to convey to others, and caring adults want to understand their children, so both parties work to improve language skills as a means toward better communication. Thus, improved communication provides an incentive for children to master language and for adults to help them.

You can see the nature of these interactions in the following example, in which a child wants a cookie (after Hulit & Howard, 2002, pp. 37–38). Like the child in the photo, a 9-month-old who wants a brownie might point to it while looking at the mother. In turn, the mother gives the cookie, saying, "Here's the cookie." By age 2, a child might say, "Gimme cookie, please?" with the mother responding, "Yes, I'll give you the cookie." At 9 months and 2 years, the child's desire to have the cookie motivates communication (pointing at 9 months, spoken language at 2 years) and gives the mother opportunities to demonstrate more advanced forms of language.

None of these accounts, summarized in the accompanying table, provides a comprehensive account of how grammar is mastered. But many scientists believe the final explanation will include contributions from the linguistic, cognitive, and social-interaction accounts. That is, children's learning of grammar will be explained in terms of some mechanisms specific to learning

According to the social-interaction account of language learning, children are eager to master grammar because it allows them to communicate their wishes and needs more effectively.

SUMMARY TABLE		
DIFFERENT APPROACHES TO EXPLAINING CHILDREN'S ACQUISITION OF GRAMMAR		
Approach	**Children Are Thought to Master Grammar . . .**	
Behaviorist	by imitating speech they hear.	
Linguistic	with inborn mechanisms that allow children to infer the grammatical rules of their native language.	
Cognitive	using powerful cognitive mechanisms that allow children to find recurring patterns in the speech they hear.	
Social Interaction	in the context of social interactions with adults in which both parties want improved communication.	

grammar, children actively seeking to identify regularities in their environment, and linguistically rich interactions between children and adults (MacWhinney, 1998).

Of course, many parents don't care much about theories of language, but they do want to know how they can help their children master grammar and other aspects of language. The "Improving Children's Lives" feature provides some guidelines.

Children learn grammar by relying on language-specific mechanisms, by noting regularities in speech, and by participating in linguistically rich interactions.

Improving Children's Lives

Promoting Language Development

Adults eager to promote children's language development can follow a few guidelines:

1. Talk with children frequently and treat them as partners in conversation. That is, try talking with children interactively, not directively.

2. Use a child's speech to show new language forms. Expand a child's remark to introduce new vocabulary or new grammatical forms. Rephrase a child's ungrammatical remark to show the correct grammar.

3. Encourage children to go beyond minimal use of language. Have them answer questions in phrases and sentences, not single words. Have them replace vague words such as *stuff* or *somebody* with more descriptive ones.

4. Listen. This guideline has two parts. First, because children often talk slowly, it's tempting for adults to complete their sentences for them. Don't. Let children express themselves. Second, pay attention to what children are saying and respond appropriately. Let children learn that language works.

5. Make language fun. Use books, rhymes, songs, jokes, and foreign words to increase a child's interest in learning language.

Of course, as children's language improves during the preschool years, others can understand it more readily, which means that children become better at communicating. The emergence and growth of communication skills is the topic of the next module.

 ANSWER 9.3
Saying "sleeped" instead of "slept" shows that Kelly knows the rule about adding –*ed* to a verb to make it past tense. It also shows that children overgeneralize rules—they use rules with verbs to which the rules don't apply.

 ## Check Your Learning

RECALL Describe the major milestones that mark children's progress from two-word speech to complex sentences.

What are the main accounts of how children master grammar?

INTERPRET How do the various explanations of grammatical development differ in their view of the child's role in mastering grammar?

APPLY How might the cognitive processes described in Chapter 7 help children learn grammar?

9.4 Using Language to Communicate

LEARNING OBJECTIVES

• When and how do children learn to take turns in conversation?

• What are the skills required to be an effective speaker?

• What is involved in becoming a good listener?

Marla and Kitty, both 9-year-olds, usually are good friends, but right now they're boiling mad at each other. Marla was going to the store with her dad to buy some new markers. Kitty found out and gave Marla money to buy some markers for her, too. Marla returned with the markers, but they weren't the kind that Kitty liked, so she was angry. Marla was angry because she didn't think Kitty should be mad; after all, it was Kitty's fault for not telling her what kind to buy. Meanwhile, Marla's dad hopes they come to some understanding soon and cut out all the shouting.

Imagining these girls arguing is an excellent way to learn what is needed for effective communication. Both talk at the same time, their remarks are rambling and incoherent, and neither bothers to listen to the other. For effective oral communication these girls need to follow a few simple guidelines:

• People should take turns, alternating as speaker and listener.

• A speaker's remarks should relate to the topic and be understandable to the listener.

• A listener should pay attention and let the speaker know if his or her remarks don't make sense.

Complete mastery of these guidelines is a lifelong pursuit; after all, even adults often miscommunicate with one another because they don't observe one or more of these rules. However, in this module, we'll trace the development of effective communication skills and, along the way, discover why young children like Marla and Kitty sometimes fail to communicate.

Taking Turns

Many parents begin to encourage turn-taking long before infants say their first words. Parents such as the mother in the photo often structure a "conversation" around a baby's early sounds, even when those sounds lack any obvious communicative intent (Field & Widmayer, 1982):

PARENT:	Can you see the bird?
INFANT (COOING):	ooooh
PARENT:	It *is* a pretty bird.
INFANT:	ooooh
PARENT:	You're right, it's a cardinal.

Soon after 1-year-olds begin to speak, parents encourage their youngsters to participate in conversational turn-taking. To help children along, parents often carry both sides of a conversation to demonstrate how the roles of speaker and listener alternate (Shatz, 1983):

PARENT (TO INFANT): What's Amy eating?

PARENT (ILLUSTRATING REPLY): She's eating a cookie.

Parents and other caregivers often work hard to allow infants and toddlers to "fit in" to a conversation. That is, caregivers scaffold youngsters' attempts to converse, making it more likely that children will succeed. However, such early conversations between caregivers and infants are not universal. In some non-Western cultures, preverbal infants are not considered appropriate conversational partners, so adults don't talk to them. Only after infants are older do others begin to converse with them (Hoff, 2009).

By age 2, spontaneous turn-taking is common in conversations between youngsters and adults (Barton & Tomasello, 1991). By age 3, children have progressed to the point that if a listener fails to reply promptly, the child will repeat his or her remark in order to elicit a response (Garvey & Beringer, 1981). A 3-year-old might say, "Hi, Paul" to an older sibling who's busy reading. If Paul doesn't answer in a few seconds, the 3-year-old might say, "Hi, Paul" again. When Paul remains unresponsive, the 3-year-old is likely to shout, "PAUL!"—showing that by this age children understand the rule that a comment deserves a response. Preschool children seem to interpret the lack of a response as, "I guess you didn't hear me, so I'll say it again, louder!"

When parents speak with young babies, they often alternate roles of speaker and listener, showing conversational turn-taking.

Speaking Effectively

When do children first try to initiate communication with others? In fact, what appear to be the first deliberate attempts to communicate typically emerge at about 10 months (Golinkoff, 1993). Infants at this age may touch or point to an object while simultaneously looking at another person. They continue this behavior until the person acknowledges them. It's as if the child is saying, "This is a neat toy! I want you to see it, too."

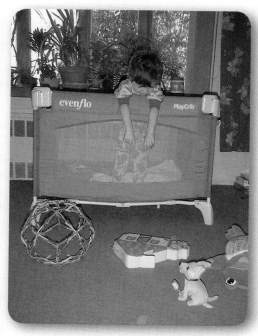

Beginning at 10 months, an infant may point, touch, or make noises to get an adult to do something. An infant in a playpen like the one in the photo who wants a toy that is out of reach may make noises while pointing to the toy. The noises capture an adult's attention, and the pointing indicates what the baby wants (Tomasello, Carpenter, & Liszkowski, 2007). The communication may be a bit primitive by adult standards, but it works for babies! And mothers typically translate their baby's pointing into words, so that gesturing paves the way for learning words (Goldin-Meadow, Mylander, & Franklin, 2007).

After their first birthday, children begin to use speech to communicate and often initiate conversations with adults (Bloom et al., 1996). Toddlers' first conversations are about themselves, but their conversational scope expands rapidly to include objects in the environment (e.g., toys, food). Later, conversations begin to include more abstract notions, such as hypothetical objects and past or future events (Foster, 1986).

Even before children can speak, they make gestures to communicate with others.

Of course, young children are not always skilled conversational partners. At times their communications are confusing, leaving a listener to wonder, "What was that all about?" Saying something clearly is often difficult because clarity can be judged only by considering the listener's age, experience, and knowledge of the topic, along with the context of the conversation. For example, think about the simple request, "Please hand me the Phillips-head screwdriver." This message may be clear to older listeners familiar with different types of screwdrivers, but it won't mean much to younger listeners who think all screwdrivers are alike. And, if the toolbox is filled with Phillips-head screwdrivers of assorted sizes, the message won't be clear even to a knowledgeable listener.

Constructing clear messages is a fine art, but, amazingly, by the preschool years, youngsters begin to adjust their messages to match the listener and the context. In a classic study, Marilyn Shatz and Rochel Gelman (1973) asked 4-year-olds to explain how a toy worked, once to a 2-year-old and once to an adult. Shatz and Gelman found that 4-year-olds talked more overall to adults than to 2-year-olds and used longer sentences with adult listeners than with 2-year-old listeners. Also, children used simpler grammar and more attention-getting words, such as *see*, *look*, *watch*, and *hey*, when speaking with 2-year-olds. Here, for example, is how one 4-year-old child explained the toy to her two different listeners (the toy was a garage with drivers and trucks that carry marbles to a dumping station):

QUESTION 9.4

Shauna's older brother asked, "Where's your locker this year?" Shauna replied, "Next to Mrs. Rathert's room." When Shauna's grandmother, who lived in another city, asked the same question, Shauna's reply was much longer: "After you go in the front door, you turn left and go down a long hall until you get to some stairs. Then. . . ." What feature of effective communication is shown in Shauna's two answers to the same question? *(Answer is on page 308.)*

ADULT LISTENER: You're supposed to put one of these persons in, see? Then one goes with the other little girl. And then the little boy. He's the little boy and he drives. And then they back up. . . . And then the little girl falls out and then it goes backwards.

2-YEAR-OLD LISTENER: Watch, Perry. Watch this. He's back in here. Now he drives up. Look, Perry. Look here, Perry. Those are marbles, Perry. Put the men in here. Now I'll do it (Shatz & Gelman, 1973, p. 13).

Shatz and Gelman's findings show that preschoolers are already sensitive to characteristics of the listener in formulating a clear message. Subsequent findings also show that children consider the listener and setting in devising clear messages:

- Preschool children give more elaborate messages to listeners who lack critical information than to listeners who have the information (Nadig & Sedivy, 2002; O'Neill, 1996). For example, a child describing where to find a toy will give more detailed directions to a listener whose eyes were covered when the toy was hidden. Also, if a word's meaning might be ambiguous in the context of the conversation (e.g., *bat* as an animal versus a piece of sporting equipment), young children sometimes gesture to indicate the meaning (Kidd & Holler, 2009).

- School-age children speak differently to adults and peers. They are more likely to speak politely with adults and be more demanding with peers (Anderson, 2000; Warren-Leubecker & Bohannon, 1989). A child might ask a parent, "May I have one of your cookies?" but say to a peer, "Gimme one of your cookies."

- Some African Americans speak *African American English,* **a variant of standard English that has slightly different grammatical rules.** For example, "He be tired" in African American English is synonymous with "He usually is tired" in standard English. Many African American children learn both African American English and standard English, and they switch back and forth, using standard English more often in school and when talking with European Americans but using African American English more often at home and when talking with African American peers (Warren & McCloskey, 1993).

> Young children adjust their messages based on a listener's age and knowledge.

All these findings show that school-age children (and sometimes preschoolers) are well on their way to understanding the factors that must be considered in creating clear messages. From a surprisingly young age, children express themselves to others and adjust their conversations to fit listeners. Are young children equally adept at listening? We'll find out in the next section.

Listening Well

To listen well, a person must continuously decide whether a speaker's remarks make sense. If they do, then a listener needs to reply appropriately, typically by extending the conversation with another remark that's on the topic. Otherwise, the listener needs to provide feedback that the speaker was confusing (e.g., "I don't get what you mean").

Few toddlers master these fundamental conversation skills. Their replies are more likely to be unrelated to the topic than related to it (Bloom, Rocissano, & Hood, 1976). Asked "Where's the sock?," a 1½-year-old may say something like "I'm hungry!" By 3 years, children are more adept at continuing conversations by making remarks that relate to the topic being discussed.

When a message is vague or confusing, young children rarely provide feedback because they don't realize that the message is ambiguous. Told to find "the red toy," they may promptly select the red ball from a pile that includes a red toy car, a red block, and a red toy hammer. Instead of asking the speaker which *specific* red toy, young listeners often assume that they know which toy the speaker had in mind (Beal & Belgrad, 1990). Only when messages almost defy comprehension—when they are too quiet to be heard or when they impart obviously ambiguous or even conflicting information—do youngsters detect a problem.

Because young children's remarks often contain ambiguities and because, as listeners, they often do not detect ambiguities, young children often miscommunicate, just like Marla and Kitty in the opening vignette. Kitty probably didn't communicate exactly what kind of markers she wanted, and Marla didn't realize that the directions were unclear. Throughout the elementary-school years, youngsters gradually master the many skills involved in determining whether a message is consistent and clear (Ackerman, 1993).

Sometimes messages are confusing because they conflict with what a listener thinks is true. For example, suppose a child is told that the family cat, which always stays indoors, has run away. Even preschoolers are more likely to believe such a message when told by a parent than by a classmate, because they know the parent is better informed about this particular topic (Robinson, Champion, & Mitchell, 1999). By the age of 7 or 8 years, children can be skeptical listeners—taking what a speaker says with a grain of salt—when, for example, a speaker has a vested interest in a topic. When a child announces to an entire class that her birthday party is going to be the "best one all year," school-age children believe her less than if they heard the information from an independent, third party (Mills & Keil, 2005).

Sometimes listeners must go beyond the words to understand the real meaning of a message. Metaphor is one example. When parents tell their teenagers, "Your bedroom is a junk yard," the remark is not to be taken literally but highlights the fact that the bedroom is a mess and filled with things that could be thrown away. Understanding of nonliteral meanings of messages develops slowly (e.g., Dews et al., 1996). In the case of metaphor, young children easily understand simple metaphors in which the nonliteral meaning is based on references to concrete objects and their properties. For example, a parent might say to a 5-year-old, "You're a fish," referring to how well the child swims and enjoys the water, and the child will likely understand.

More complex metaphors require that children make connections based on abstract relations. For example, in Shakespeare's *Romeo and Juliet*, Romeo proclaims that "Juliet is the Sun." You might interpret this line to mean that Juliet is the center of Romeo's universe or that without Juliet, Romeo will die. The first interpretation depends on your knowledge of astronomy; the second, on your knowledge of biology. Younger children lack this sort of knowledge to comprehend metaphors, so they try to interpret them literally. Only when children gain the necessary content knowledge do they understand metaphors based on abstract relations (Franquart-Declercq & Gineste, 2001).

Sarcasm is another form of communication that is not to be interpreted literally. When a soccer player misses the ball entirely and a teammate says, "Nice kick," the literal meaning of the remark is the opposite of the intended meaning. Like understanding of metaphor, understanding of sarcasm develops gradually (Creusere, 1999). When people emphasize their sarcasm by speaking in mocking or overly enthusiastic tones, school-age children can detect their meaning. However, if sarcasm must be detected solely from the context—by realizing that the comment is the opposite of what would be expected—only adolescents and adults are likely to understand the real meaning of the remark (Capelli, Nakagawa, & Madden, 1990).

This discussion of listening skills completes our catalog of the important accomplishments in communication that take place during childhood. By the time most children enter kindergarten, they have mastered many of the fundamental rules of communication, and as they grow older, they acquire even greater proficiency.

 ANSWER 9.4
Shauna has changed her description to reflect her listener's knowledge. Her description is more elaborate for her grandmother (who's unfamiliar with her school) than for her brother (who knows it well).

✓ Check Your Learning

RECALL What findings illustrate that preschool children are sometimes effective speakers?

Summarize children's understanding of messages that are not meant to be taken literally.

INTERPRET What are the strengths and weaknesses of infants as communicators?

APPLY In Chapter 6, we saw that Piaget characterized preschool children as egocentric. Are the findings described in this module consistent with Piaget's view?

UNIFYING THEMES Connections

This chapter is an appropriate occasion to stress the theme that *development in different domains is connected:* Language has important connections to biological, cognitive, and social development. A link to biological development would be children's mastery of grammar: In ways that we don't yet fully understand, children seem to be endowed with a

mechanism that smoothes the path to mastering grammar. A link to cognitive development would be children's first words: Speaking words reflects the cognitive insight that speech sounds are symbols. A link to social development would be the communication skills that enable children to interact with peers and adults.

See for Yourself

Berko's (1958) "wugs" task is fun to try with preschool children. Photocopy the drawing on page 298 and show it to a preschooler, repeating the instructions that appear on that page. You should find that the child quite predictably says,

"two wugs." Create some pictures of your own to examine other grammatical morphemes, such as adding *-ing* to denote ongoing activity or adding *-ed* to indicate past tense. See for yourself!

Summary

9.1 The Road to Speech

Elements of Language

Language includes four distinct elements: phonology (sounds), semantics (word meaning), syntax (rules for language structure), and pragmatics (rules for communication).

Perceiving Speech

Phonemes are the basic units of sound that make up words. Infants can hear phonemes soon after birth. They can even hear phonemes that are not used in their native language, but this ability is lost by the first birthday. Before they speak, infants can recognize words, apparently by noticing stress and syllables that go together. Infants prefer infant-directed speech—adults' speech to infants that is slower and has greater variation in pitch—because it provides them with additional language clues.

First Steps to Speech

Newborns are limited to crying, but at about 3 months, babies coo. Babbling soon follows, consisting of a single syllable; over several months, infants' babbling includes longer syllables and intonation.

9.2 Learning the Meanings of Words

Understanding Words as Symbols

Children's first words represent a cognitive accomplishment that is not specific to language. Instead, the onset of speech is due to a child's ability to interpret and use symbols. Consistent with this view, there are parallel developments in the use of gestures.

Fast Mapping Meanings to Words

Most children learn the meanings of words too rapidly for them to consider all plausible meanings systematically. Instead, children use a number of fast-mapping rules to determine probable meanings of new words. Joint attention, constraints, sentence cues, and cognitive skills all help children learn words. The rules do not always lead to the correct meaning. An underextension denotes a child's meaning that is narrower than an adult's meaning; an overextension denotes a child's meaning that is broader.

Individual Differences in Word Learning

Individual children differ in vocabulary size; these differences are attributable to phonological memory and the quality of the child's language environment. Some youngsters use a referential word-learning style that emphasizes words as names and that views language as an intellectual tool. Other children use an expressive style that emphasizes phrases and views language as a social tool.

Encouraging Word Learning

Children's word learning is fostered by experience, including being read to, watching television, and, for school-age children, reading to themselves. The key ingredient is making children think about the meanings of new words.

Beyond Words: Other Symbols

As children learn language, they also learn about other symbol systems. By 18 months, toddlers understand that photos are representations of other objects; by 3 years, children understand that a scale model is a representation of an identical but larger object. Preschoolers can use simple maps.

9.3 Speaking in Sentences

From Two-Word Speech to Complex Sentences

Not long after their first birthday, children produce two-word sentences that are based on simple rules for expressing ideas or needs. These sentences are sometimes called *telegraphic* because they use the fewest possible words to convey meaning. Moving from two-word to more complex sentences involves adding grammatical morphemes. Children first master grammatical morphemes that express simple relations, then those that denote complex relations.

As children acquire grammatical morphemes, they also extend their speech to other sentence forms, such as questions, and later to more complex constructions, such as passive sentences.

How Do Children Acquire Grammar?

Behaviorists proposed that children acquire grammar through imitation, but that explanation is incorrect. Today's explanations come from three perspectives: The linguistic emphasizes inborn mechanisms that allow children to infer the grammatical rules of their native language, the cognitive perspective emphasizes cognitive processes that allow children to find recurring patterns in the speech they hear, and the social-interaction perspective emphasizes social interactions with adults in which both parties want improved communication.

9.4 Using Language to Communicate

Taking Turns

Parents encourage turn-taking even before infants talk and later demonstrate both the speaker and listener roles for their children. By age 3, children spontaneously take turns and prompt one another to speak.

Speaking Effectively

Before they can speak, infants use gestures and noises to communicate. During the preschool years, children gradually become more skilled at constructing clear messages, in part by adjusting their speech to fit their listeners' needs. They also begin to monitor their listeners' comprehension, repeating messages if necessary.

Listening Well

Toddlers are not good conversationalists because their remarks don't relate to the topic. Preschoolers are unlikely to identify ambiguities in another's speech. Also, they sometimes have difficulty understanding messages that are not to be taken literally, such as metaphor and sarcasm.

Test Yourself

✓●─Study and **Review** on mydevelopmentlab.com

1. Newborns can hear a wide range of language sounds, but by the first birthday infants readily distinguish only those sounds _____.

2. To pick out individual words from a steady stream of speech, infants use _____, knowledge of what phonemes sound good together and where they appear in words, and familiar function words.

3. In _____, adults speak slowly and with exaggerated changes in pitch and loudness.

4. During the first year, babbling becomes progressively more language-like, and at about 8 to 11 months sounds like real speech because _____.

5. A child's first word probably reflects the child's mastery of symbols because _____.

6. At about 18 months children experience a _____: they start to learn new words much more rapidly than before.

7. Children's rapid learning of words reflects joint attention, rules that constrain word meanings, _____, and cognitive growth.

8. _____ and the child's language environment contribute to individual differences in the size of children's vocabulary.

9. There are many ways that parents can help infants to learn new words (e.g., reading books to them), but _____ is not one of them.

10. The benefits of bilingualism include greater understanding of the symbolic nature of language and _____.

11. In the telegraphic speech that's common among 1½-year-olds, children _____.

12. Overregularizations in children's speech (e.g., "I goed to the store") show that children master grammar by _____.

13. The development of grammar includes contributions from language-specific processes, cognitive skills, and _____.

14. An example of preschoolers' communicative skill is that when talking with younger children, 4-year-olds _____.

15. Preschoolers aren't very skilled listeners; when a message is confusing, they _____.

Answers: (1) that are meaningful in their own language; (2) stress cues; (3) infant-directed speech; (4) it mimics the intonation patterns of the infant's native language; (5) children begin to use other symbols, such as gestures, at about the same time that they start to speak; (6) naming explosion; (7) cues to a word's meaning that are provided by sentences; (8) Phonological memory; (9) showing them infant-oriented language videos; (10) greater skill at task-switching and inhibiting inappropriate responses; (11) include only words that are directly relevant to meaning; (12) learning rules; (13) social interaction; (14) use simpler grammar and more attention-getting words; (15) often fail to provide feedback to the speaker; instead, they assume that they knew what the speaker meant.

Key Terms

African American English   306
babbling   282
cooing   282
expressive style   290
fast mapping   285
grammatical morphemes   297
infant-directed speech   280
intonation   282

language   277
naming explosion   285
overextension   289
overregularization   298
phonemes   278
phonological memory   289
phonology   277
pragmatics   278

referential style   290
semantic bootstrapping theory   299
semantics   278
syntax   278
telegraphic speech   297
underextension   289

10

Emotional Development

10.1

Emerging Emotions

10.2

Temperament

10.3

Attachment

If you're a fan of *Star Trek*, you know that Mr. Spock feels little emotion because he's half Vulcan and people from the planet Vulcan don't have emotions. Few of us would like to live an emotionless life like Mr. Spock, because feelings enrich our lives. As partial testimony to their importance, the English language has more than 500 words that refer to emotions (Averill, 1980). Joy, happiness, satisfaction, and yes, anger, guilt, and humiliation are just a few of the feelings that give life meaning.

In this chapter, we'll see how emotions emerge and how they affect development. In **Module 10.1**, we'll discuss when children first express different emotions and recognize emotions in others. Next, in **Module 10.2**, we'll see that children have different behavioral styles and that these styles are rooted, in part, in emotions. Finally, in **Module 10.3**, we'll examine the infant's first emotional relationship, the one that develops with the primary caregiver.

 10.1 **Emerging Emotions**

OUTLINE

The Function of Emotions

Experiencing and Expressing Emotions

Recognizing and Using Others' Emotions

Regulating Emotions

LEARNING OBJECTIVES

- Why do people "feel"? Why do they have emotions?
- At what ages do children begin to experience and express different emotions?
- When do children begin to understand other people's emotions? How do they use this information to guide their own behavior?
- When do children show evidence of regulating emotion, and why is this an important skill?

Nicole was ecstatic that she was finally going to see her 7-month-old nephew, Claude. She rushed into the house and, seeing Claude playing on the floor with blocks, swept him up in a big hug. After a brief, puzzled look, Claude burst into angry tears and began thrashing around, as if saying to Nicole, "Who are you? What do you want? Put me down! Now!" Nicole quickly handed Claude to his mother, who was surprised by her baby's outburst and even more surprised that he continued to sob while she rocked him.

This vignette illustrates three common emotions. Nicole's initial joy, Claude's anger, and his mother's surprise are familiar to all of us. In this module, we begin by discussing *why* people have feelings at all. Then we look at when children first express emotions, how children come to understand emotions in others, and, finally, how children regulate their emotions. As we do, we'll learn why Claude reacted to Nicole as he did and how Nicole could have prevented Claude's outburst.

The Function of Emotions

Why do people feel emotions? Wouldn't life be simpler if people were emotionless like computers or residents of Mr. Spock's Vulcan? Probably not. Think, for example, about activities that most adults find pleasurable: a good meal, sex, holding one's children, and accomplishing a difficult but important task. These activities were and remain essential to the continuity of humans as a species, so it's not surprising that they elicit emotions (Gaulin & McBurney, 2001).

Modern theories emphasize the functional value of emotion. That is, according to the functional approach, emotions are useful because they help people adapt to their environment (Izard & Ackerman, 2000; Saarni et al., 2006). Take fear as an example. Most of us would rather not be afraid, but there are instances in which feeling fearful is very adaptive. Imagine you are walking alone, late at night, in a poorly lighted section of campus. You become frightened and, as a consequence, are particularly attentive to sounds that might signal the presence of threat, and you probably walk quickly to a safer location. Thus, fear is adaptive because it organizes your behavior around an important goal: avoiding danger (Cosmides & Tooby, 2000).

Similarly, other emotions are adaptive. Happiness, for example, is adaptive in contributing to stronger interpersonal relationships: When people are happy with another person, they smile, and this often causes the other person to feel happy too, strengthening their relationship (Izard & Ackerman, 2000). Disgust is adaptive in keeping people away from substances that might make them ill: As we discover that the milk in a glass is sour, we experience disgust and push the glass away (Oaten, Stevenson, & Case, 2009). Thus, in the functional approach, most emotions developed over the course of human history to meet unique life challenges and help humans to survive.

Experiencing and Expressing Emotions

DEVELOPMENT OF BASIC EMOTIONS. The three emotions from the vignette—happiness, anger, and surprise—are considered "basic emotions," as are interest, disgust, sadness, and fear (Draghi-Lorenz, Reddy, & Costall, 2001). *Basic emotions* **are experienced by people worldwide, and each consists of three elements: a subjective feeling, a physiological change, and an overt behavior** (Izard, 2007). For example, suppose you wake to the sound of a thunderstorm and then discover that your roommate has left for class with your umbrella. Subjectively, you might feel ready to explode with anger; physiologically, your heart would beat faster; and behaviorally, you would probably be scowling.

Using facial expressions and other overt behaviors, scientists have traced the growth of basic emotions in infants. According to one influential theory (Lewis, 2000), newborns experience only two general emotions: pleasure and distress. Rapidly, though, more discrete emotions emerge, and by 8 or 9 months of age, infants are thought to experience all basic emotions. The onset of happiness, for example, is evident in a baby's smiles. In the first month, infants may smile while asleep or when touched softly. The meaning of these smiles isn't clear; they may just represent a reflexive response to bodily states. However, an important change occurs at about 2–3 months of age. *Social smiles* **first appear: Infants smile when they see another person.** As with the baby in the photo, the social smile seems to reflect the infant's pleasure in simple interactions with others. When smiling, they sometimes coo (the early form of vocalization described in Module 9.1) and they may move their arms and legs to express excitement.

Social smiles emerge at 2–3 months of age and seem to express an infant's happiness at interacting with others.

Anger is one of the first negative emotions to emerge from generalized distress, and typically does so between 4 and 6 months. Infants will become angry, for example, if a favorite food or toy is taken away (Sullivan & Lewis, 2003). Reflecting their growing understanding of goal-directed behavior (see Module 6.1), older infants become increasingly angry when their attempts to achieve a goal are frustrated (Braungart-Rieker, Hill-Soderlund, & Karrass, 2010). For example, if a parent restrains an infant who is trying to pick up a toy, the guaranteed result is a very angry baby.

Like anger, fear emerges later in the first year. **At about 6 months, infants become wary in the presence of an unfamiliar adult, a reaction known as** *stranger wariness.* When a stranger approaches, a 6-month-old typically looks away and begins to fuss (Mangelsdorf, Shapiro, & Marzolf, 1995). The baby in the photo is showing the signs of stranger wariness. The grandmother has picked him up without giving him a chance to warm up to her, and the outcome is as predictable as it was with Claude, the baby in the vignette who was frightened by his aunt: He cries, looks frightened, and reaches with arms outstretched in the direction of someone familiar.

How wary an infant feels around strangers depends on a number of factors (Thompson & Limber, 1991). First, infants tend to be less fearful of strangers when the environment is familiar and more fearful when it is not. Many parents know this firsthand from traveling with their infants: Enter a friend's house for the first time and the baby clings tightly to its mother. Second, the amount of anxiety depends on the stranger's behavior. Instead of rushing to greet or pick up the baby, as Nicole did in the vignette, a stranger should talk with other adults and, in a while, perhaps offer the baby a toy (Mangelsdorf, 1992). Handled this way, many infants will soon become curious about the stranger instead of afraid.

Wariness of strangers is adaptive because it emerges at the same time that children begin to master creeping and crawling (described in Module 5.3). Like Curious George, the monkey in a famous series of children's books, babies are inquisitive and want to use their new locomotor skills to explore their worlds. Being wary of strangers provides a natural restraint against the tendency to wander away from familiar caregivers. However, as youngsters learn to interpret facial expressions and recognize when a person is friendly, their wariness of strangers declines.

By 6 months, infants are wary of strangers and often become upset when they encounter people they don't know, particularly when strangers rush to greet or hold them.

Of the negative emotions, we know the least about disgust. Preschool children may respond with disgust at the odor of feces or at being asked to touch a maggot or being asked to eat a piece of candy that's resting on the bottom of a brand-new potty seat. Parents likely play an important role in helping children to identify disgusting stimuli: Mothers respond quite vigorously to disgust-eliciting stimuli when in the presence of their children. They might say "That's revolting!" while moving away from the stimulus (Stevenson et al., 2010). This early sensitivity to disgust is useful because many of the cues that elicit disgust are also signals of potential illness: disgusting stimuli such as feces, vomit, and maggots can all transmit disease.

> Basic emotions include a subjective feeling, a physiological response, and an overt behavior.

EMERGENCE OF COMPLEX EMOTIONS. In addition to basic emotions such as happiness and anger, people feel complex emotions such as pride, shame, guilt, and embarrassment. **Sometimes known as the** *self-conscious emotions,* **they involve feelings of success when one's standards or expectations are met and feelings of failure when they aren't.** These emotions don't surface until 18 to 24 months of age, because they depend on the child having some understanding of the self, which typically occurs between 15 and 18 months. Children feel guilty, for example, when they've done something they know they shouldn't have done (Kochanska et al., 2002). A child who breaks a toy is thinking, "You told me to be careful. But I wasn't!" A child may show embarrassment at being asked

By 18 to 24 months, children start to experience complex emotions, including pride in accomplishing a difficult task.

QUESTION 10.1

Courtney often expresses her joy, anger, and fear, but has yet to show pride, guilt, or embarrassment. Based on this profile, how old do you think Courtney is?

(Answer is on page 321.)

to "perform" for grandparents by burying his face in his hands. However, children feel pride when they accomplish a challenging task for the first time. The toddler in the photo is probably thinking something like, "I've never done this before, but this time I did it—all by myself!" Thus, children's growing understanding of themselves (which I discuss in detail in Module 11.1) allows them to experience complex emotions such as pride and guilt (Lewis, 2000).

The features of basic and self-conscious emotions are summarized in the accompanying table.

SUMMARY TABLE			
INFANTS' EXPRESSION OF EMOTIONS			
Type	**Defined**	**Emerge**	**Examples**
Basic	Experienced by people worldwide; include a subjective feeling, a physiological response, and an overt behavior	Birth to 9 months	Happiness, anger, fear
Self-conscious	Responses to meeting or failing to meet expectations or standards	18 to 24 months	Pride, guilt, embarrassment

LATER DEVELOPMENTS.   As children grow, their catalog of emotions continues to expand. For example, think about regret and relief, emotions that adults experience when they compare their actions with alternatives. Imagine, for example, that you're cramming for a test and decide that you have time to review your lecture notes but not reread the text. If the test questions turned out to be based largely on the lectures, you'll feel a sense of relief because your decision led to a positive outcome compared to "what might have been." If, instead, test questions cover only the text, you'll feel regret because your decision led to a terrible outcome; "If only I had reread the text!" In fact, by 7 years of age children experience feelings of regret, but they're less likely to experience feelings of relief (Guttentag & Ferrell, 2004).

In addition to adding emotions to their repertoire, older children experience basic and complex emotions in response to different situations or events. In the case of complex emotions, cognitive growth means that elementary-school children experience shame and guilt in situations where they would not have when they were younger (Reimer, 1996). For example, unlike preschool children, many school-age children would be ashamed if they neglected to defend a classmate who had been wrongly accused of a theft.

Fear is another emotion that can be elicited in different ways, depending on a child's age. Many preschool children are afraid of the dark and of imaginary creatures. These fears typically diminish during the elementary-school years as children grow cognitively and better understand the difference between appearance and reality. Replacing these fears are concerns about school, health, and personal harm (Silverman, La Greca, & Wasserstein, 1995). Such worries are common and not cause for concern in most children. In some youngsters, however, they become so extreme that they overwhelm the child (Chorpita & Barlow, 1998). For example, a 7-year-old's worries about school would not be unusual unless her concern grew to the point that she refused to go to school. In the "Improving Children's Lives" feature, we'll look at this form of excessive fear and how it can be treated.

Improving Children's Lives

"But I Don't Want to Go to School!"

Many youngsters plead, argue, and fight with their parents daily over going to school. For example, every school day, 9-year-old Keegan would cling to his mother and start to sob as soon as he finished his breakfast. When it was time to leave the house to catch the bus, he would drop to the floor and start kicking.

Understanding the reasons for such school refusal behavior is essential because, not surprisingly, refusing to go to school puts children on a path that leads to academic failure and leaves them with few options in the workplace. School refusal behavior sometimes reflects a child's desire to avoid school-related situations that are frightening (e.g., taking a test, speaking in front of a class, meeting new people). School refusal is sometimes an effort to get attention from parents, and sometimes reflects a child's desire to pursue enjoyable activities, such as playing video games, instead of aversive ones, such as doing schoolwork (Kearney, 2007).

Fortunately, school refusal behavior can be treated effectively, typically with a combination of behavioral and cognitive strategies (Pina et al., 2009). The former include gradual exposure to fear-provoking school situations, techniques for relaxing when confronting these situations, and reinforcement for attending school. The latter include providing children with strategies for coping with their anxiety and helping them reinterpret school situations (e.g., realize that teachers are *not* picking on them). Using these techniques, school refusal becomes much less common. In one meta-analysis (Pina et al., 2009), school attendance increased from 30% before treatment to 75% after. What's more, children's school-related fears were much reduced.

CULTURAL DIFFERENCES IN EMOTIONAL EXPRESSION. Children worldwide express many of the same basic and complex emotions. However, cultures differ in the extent to which emotional expression is encouraged (Hess & Kirouac, 2000). In many Asian countries, for example, outward displays of emotion are discouraged in favor of emotional restraint. Consistent with these differences, in one study (Camras et al., 1998), European American 11-month-olds cried and smiled more often than Chinese 11-month-olds. In another study (Camras et al., 2006), U.S. preschoolers were more likely than Chinese preschoolers to smile at funny pictures and to express disgust after smelling a cotton swab dipped in vinegar.

Cultures also differ in the events that trigger emotions, particularly complex emotions. Situations that evoke pride in one culture may evoke embarrassment or shame in another. For example, American elementary-school children often show pride at personal achievement, such as getting the highest grade on a test or, as shown in the photo on page 318, winning a spelling bee. In contrast, Asian elementary-school children are embarrassed by a public display of individual achievement but show great pride when their entire class is honored for an achievement (Lewis et al., 2010; Stevenson & Stigler, 1992).

Cultures differ in the extent to which they encourage children to express emotions and in the circumstances that lead to emotions.

Expression of anger also varies around the world. Imagine that one child has just completed a detailed drawing when a classmate spills a drink, ruining the drawing. Most American children would respond with anger. In contrast, children growing up in east Asian countries that practice Buddhism (e.g., Mongolia, Thailand, Nepal) rarely

Children living in the United States, Canada, and Europe often express great pride at personal achievement.

respond with anger because this goes against the Buddhist tenet to extend loving kindness to all people, even those whose actions hurt others. Instead, they would probably remain quiet and experience shame that they had left the drawing in a vulnerable position (Cole, Tamang, & Shrestha, 2006).

Thus, culture can influence when and how much children express emotion. Of course, expressing emotion is only part of the developmental story. Children must also learn to recognize others' emotions, which is our next topic.

Recognizing and Using Others' Emotions

Imagine that you are broke and plan to borrow $20 from your roommate when she returns from class. Shortly, she storms into your apartment, slams the door, and throws her backpack on the floor. You change your plans immediately, realizing that now is hardly a good time to ask for a loan. This example reminds us that, just as it is adaptive to be able to express emotions, it is adaptive to be able to recognize others' emotions and sometimes change our behavior as a consequence.

When can infants first identify emotions in others? Perhaps as early as 4 months, and definitely by 6 months, infants begin to distinguish facial expressions associated with different emotions. They can, for example, distinguish a happy, smiling face from a sad, frowning face (Bornstein & Arterberry, 2003; Montague & Walker-Andrews, 2001) and fearful, happy, and neutral faces elicit different patterns of electrical activity in the infant's brain (Leppanen et al., 2007), which also indicates their ability to differentiate facial expressions of emotion. What's more, like adults, infants are biased toward negative emotions (Vaish, Woodward, & Grossmann, 2008). They attend more rapidly to faces depicting negative emotions (e.g., anger) and pay attention to them longer than emotionless or happy faces (LoBue & DeLoache, 2010; Peltola et al., 2008).

Of course, infants might be able to distinguish an angry face from a happy one but not know the emotional significance of the two faces. How can we tell whether infants understand the emotions expressed in a face? The best evidence is that infants often match their own emotions to other people's emotions. When happy mothers smile and talk in a pleasant voice, infants express happiness themselves. If mothers are angry or sad, infants become distressed, too (Haviland & Lelwica, 1987; Montague & Walker-Andrews, 2001).

Also like adults, infants use others' emotions to direct their behavior. **Infants in an unfamiliar or ambiguous environment often look at their mother or father, as if searching for cues to help them interpret the situation, a phenomenon known as** *social referencing.* If a parent looks afraid when shown a novel object, 12-month-olds are less likely to play with the new toy than if a parent looks happy (Repacholi, 1998). Furthermore, an infant can use parents' facial expressions or their vocal expressions alone to decide whether they want to explore an unfamiliar object (Mumme, Fernald, & Herrera, 1996). Infants' use of their parents' cues is precise. If two unfamiliar toys are shown to a parent, who expresses disgust at one toy but not the other, 12-month-olds will avoid the toy that elicited the disgust but not the other toy (Moses et al., 2001). By 14 months of age, infants remember this information: They avoid a toy that elicited disgust an hour earlier (Hertenstein & Campos, 2004). By 18 months, they're even more sophisticated: When one adult demonstrates an unfamiliar toy and a second adult comments, in an angry tone, "That's really annoying! That's so irritating!" 18-month-olds play less with the toy, compared to when the second adult makes neutral remarks in a mild manner. These youngsters apparently decided that it wasn't such a good idea to play with the toy if it might upset the second adult again (Repacholi & Meltzoff, 2007; Repacholi, Meltzoff, & Olsen, 2008). Thus, social referencing shows that infants are remarkably skilled in using their parents' emotions to help them direct their own behavior.

Although infants and toddlers are remarkably adept at recognizing others' emotions, their skills are far from mature. Adults are much more skilled than infants—and school-aged children, for that matter—in recognizing the subtle signals of an emotion (Thomas et al., 2007), and adults are better able to tell when others are "faking" emotions; they can distinguish the face of a person who's really happy from the face of a person who's faking happiness (Del Giudice & Colle, 2007). Thus, facial expressions of emotion are recognized with steadily greater skill throughout childhood and into adolescence.

> By the first birthday, infants can recognize others' emotions and use these emotions to direct their own behavior.

UNDERSTANDING EMOTIONS.   As their cognitive skills grow, children begin to understand why people feel as they do. By kindergarten, for example, children know that undesirable or unpleasant events often make a person feel angry or sad (Levine, 1995). Children even know that they more often feel sad when they think about the undesirable event itself (e.g., a broken toy or a friend who moves away) but feel angry when they think about the person who caused the undesirable event (e.g., the person who broke the toy or the friend's parents who wanted to live in another city). Kindergarten children also understand that a child who is feeling sad or angry may do less well on school tasks like spelling or math (Amsterlaw, Lagattuta, & Meltzoff, 2009) and that people worry when faced with the possibility that an unpleasant event may recur (Lagattuta, 2007).

During the elementary-school years, children begin to comprehend that people sometimes experience "mixed feelings." They understand that some situations may lead people, for example, to feel happy and sad at the same time (Larsen, To, & Fireman, 2007). The increased ability to see multiple, differing emotions coincides with the freedom from centered thinking that characterizes the concrete operational stage (Module 6.1).

As children develop, they also begin to learn *display rules,* **culturally specific standards for appropriate expressions of emotion in a particular setting or with a particular person or persons.** Adults know, for example, that expressing sadness is appropriate at funerals but expressing joy is not. Similarly, expressing sadness is appropriate with relatives and close friends but less so with strangers. Preschool children's understanding of display rules is shown by the fact that they control their anger more when provoked by peers they like than when provoked by peers they don't like (Fabes et al., 1996). Also, school-age children and adolescents are more willing to express anger than sadness and, like the child in the photo on page 320, more willing to express both anger and sadness to parents than to peers (Zeman & Garber, 1996; Zeman & Shipman, 1997).

What experiences contribute to children's understanding of emotions? Parents and children frequently talk about past emotions and why people felt as they did; this is particularly true for negative emotions such as fear and anger

As children develop, they learn their culture's rules for expressing emotions. For example, many children living in North America might cry in private or with parents, but would avoid crying in public, particularly when with their peers.

(Lagattuta & Wellman, 2002). Not surprisingly, children learn about emotions by hearing parents talk about feelings, explaining how they differ and the situations that elicit them (Brown & Dunn, 1996; Cervantes & Callanan, 1998). Also, a positive, rewarding relationship with parents and siblings is related to children's understanding of emotions (Brown & Dunn, 1996; Thompson, Laible, & Ontai, 2003). The nature of this connection is still a mystery. One possibility is that within positive parent–child and sibling relationships, people express a fuller range of emotions (and do so more often) and are more willing to talk about why they feel as they do, providing children with more opportunities to learn about emotions.

Children's growing understanding of emotions in others contributes in turn to a growing ability to help others. They are more likely to recognize the emotions that signal a person's need. Better understanding of emotions in others also contributes to children's growing ability to play easily with peers because they can see the impact of their behavior on others. We'll cover empathy and social interaction in detail later in the book; for now, the important point is that recognizing emotions in others is an important prerequisite for successful, satisfying interactions. Another element of successful interactions is regulation of emotions, our next topic.

Regulating Emotions

Think back to a time when you were *really* angry at a good friend. Did you shout at the friend? Did you try to discuss matters calmly? Or did you simply ignore the situation altogether? Shouting is a direct expression of anger, but calm conversation and overlooking a situation are deliberate attempts to regulate emotion. People often regulate emotions; for example, we routinely try to suppress fear (because we know there's no real need to be afraid of the dark), anger (because we don't want to let a friend know just how upset we are), and joy (because we don't want to seem like we're gloating over our good fortune).

As these examples illustrate, regulating emotions skillfully depends on cognitive processes like those described in Chapters 6 through 9 (Zelazo & Cunningham, 2007). Attention is an important part of emotion regulation: We can control emotions such as fear by diverting attention to other less emotional stimuli, thoughts, or feelings (Rothbart & Sheese, 2007). We can also use strategies to reappraise the meaning of an event (or of feelings or thoughts), so that it provokes less emotion (John & Gross, 2007). For example, a soccer player nervous about taking a penalty kick can reinterpret her state of physiological arousal as being "pumped up" instead of being "scared to death."

Because cognitive processes are essential for emotional regulation, the research described in Chapters 6 through 9 would lead us to expect that successful regulation develops gradually through childhood and adolescence and that at any age some children will be more skilled than others at regulating emotions (Thompson, Lewis, & Calkins, 2008). In fact, child-development researchers have documented both patterns. Emotion regulation clearly begins in infancy. By 4 to 6 months, infants use simple strategies to regulate their emotions (Buss & Goldsmith, 1998; Rothbart & Rueda, 2005). When something frightens or confuses an infant—for example, a stranger or a mother who suddenly stops responding—he or she often looks away (just as older children and even adults often turn away or close their eyes to block out disturbing stimuli). Frightened infants also move closer to a parent, another effective way of helping to control their fear (Parritz, 1996). By 24 months, a distressed toddler's face typically expresses sadness instead of fear or anger; apparently by this age toddlers have learned that a sad facial expression is the best way to get a mother's attention and support (Buss & Kiel, 2004). Of course, because infants and toddlers have limited ability to regulate their emotions, parents and other caregivers often help: As we saw in Module 3.4, holding, rocking, and talking softly are effective in soothing an infant who's upset (Jahromi, Putnam, & Stifter, 2004).

Even infants can regulate their emotions and school-age children have mastered several techniques for regulating emotions.

Older children and adolescents encounter a wider range of emotional situations, so it's fortunate that they develop a number of related new ways to regulate emotion (Eisenberg & Morris, 2002):

- Children begin to regulate their own emotions and rely less on others to do this for them. A fearful child no longer runs to a parent, but instead devises her own methods for dealing with fear. For example, she might reassure herself by saying, "I know the thunderstorm won't last long and I'm safe inside the house."

- Children more often rely on mental strategies to regulate emotions. For example, a child might reduce his disappointment at not receiving a much-anticipated and hoped-for gift by telling himself that he didn't really want the gift in the first place.

- Children more accurately match the strategies for regulating emotion with the particular setting. For example, when faced with emotional situations that are unavoidable, such as going to the dentist to have a cavity filled, children adjust to the situation (for instance, by thinking of the positive consequences of treating the tooth) instead of trying to avoid the situation.

Collectively, these age-related trends give older children and adolescents plenty of tools for regulating emotions. Nevertheless, not all children regulate their emotions well, and those who don't tend to have problems interacting with peers and have adjustment problems (Eisenberg et al., 2005; Feng et al., 2009). When children can't control their anger, worry, or sadness, they often have difficulty resolving the conflicts that inevitably surface in peer relationships (Fabes et al., 1999). For example, when children argue over which game to play or which movie to watch, their unregulated anger can interfere with finding a mutually satisfying solution. Thus, ineffective regulation of emotions leads to more frequent conflicts with peers, and, consequently, less satisfying peer relationships and less adaptive adjustment to school (Eisenberg et al., 2001; Olson et al., 2005).

In this module, we've seen how children express, recognize, and regulate emotions; in the next module, we'll discover that emotion is an important feature of children's temperament.

 ANSWER 10.1
Because Courtney expresses joy, anger, and fear, she's at least 6 months old. Because she hasn't expressed any of the complex emotions (pride, guilt, embarrassment), she's not yet 18 months old. Thus, she's probably between 6 and15 months old.

Check Your Learning

RECALL Describe biological and cultural contributions to children's expression of emotion.

How do infants and children regulate their emotions? What are the consequences when children can't regulate their emotions well?

INTERPRET Distinguish basic emotions from self-conscious emotions.

APPLY Cite similarities between developmental change in infants' expression and regulation of emotion and developmental change in infants' comprehension and expression of speech (described in Module 9.1).

 Temperament

OUTLINE

What Is Temperament?

Hereditary and Environmental Contributions to Temperament

Stability of Temperament

Temperament and Other Aspects of Development

LEARNING OBJECTIVES

- What are the different features of temperament?
- How do heredity and environment influence temperament?

- How stable is a child's temperament across childhood?
- What are the consequences of different temperaments?

Soon after Yoshimi arrived in the United States from Japan to begin graduate studies, she enrolled her 5-month-old son in day care. She was struck by the fact that, compared to her son, the European American babies in the day-care center were "wimps" (slang she had learned from American television). The other babies cried often and with minimal provocation. Yoshimi wondered whether her son was unusually "tough" or whether he was just a typical Japanese baby.

When you've observed young babies—perhaps as part of "See for Yourself" in Chapter 3—were some babies like Yoshimi's, quiet most of the time, while others cried often and impatiently? Maybe you saw some infants who responded warmly to strangers and others who seemed very shy. **Such behavioral styles, which are fairly stable across situations and are biologically based, make up an infant's** *temperament.* For example, all babies become upset occasionally and cry. However, some, like Yoshimi's son, recover quickly, but others are very hard to console. These differences in emotion and style of behavior are evident in the first few weeks after birth and are important throughout life.

We'll begin this module by looking at different ways that scientists define temperament.

What Is Temperament?

Alexander Thomas and Stella Chess (Thomas, Chess, & Birch, 1968; Thomas & Chess, 1977) pioneered the study of temperament with the New York Longitudinal Study, in which they traced the lives of 141 individuals from infancy through adulthood. Thomas and Chess interviewed parents about their babies and had individuals unfamiliar with the children observe them at home. From these interviews and observations, Thomas and Chess suggested that infants' behavior varies along nine temperamental dimensions. One dimension was *activity*, which referred to an infant's typical level of motor activity. A second was *persistence*, which referred to the amount of time that an infant devoted to an activity, particularly when obstacles were present.

Using these and other dimensions, Thomas and Chess identified three patterns of temperament. Most common were "easy" babies, who were usually happy and cheerful, tended to adjust well to new situations, and had regular routines for eating, sleeping, and toileting. A second, less common group included "difficult" babies, who tended to be unhappy, were irregular in their eating and sleeping, and often responded intensely to unfamiliar situations. Another less common group was made up of "slow-to-warm-up" babies. Like difficult babies, slow-to-warm-up babies were often unhappy; but unlike difficult babies, slow-to-warm-up babies were not upset by unfamiliar situations. ● ▶ |Watch the **Video** on **mydevelopmentlab.com**

The New York Longitudinal Study launched research on infant temperament, but today's researchers no longer emphasize creating different categories of infants, such as "easy" or "slow to warm up." Instead, researchers want to determine the different dimensions that underlie temperament. One modern approach to temperament is described in the "Spotlight on Theories" feature.

 QUESTION 10.2
Ten-month-old Nina is usually cheerful, enjoys going on outings with her dad, and sleeps soundly every night. How would Thomas and Chess describe Nina's temperament? *(Answer is on page 330.)*
. . . .

● ▶|Watch the **Video** *Temperament* on **mydevelopmentlab.com** to learn more about temperamental differences in three preschool children.

 ## Spotlight on Theories

A Theory of the Structure of Temperament in Infancy

BACKGROUND   Most scientists agree that *temperament* refers to biologically based differences in infants' and children's emotional reactivity and emotional self-regulation. However, scientists disagree on the number and nature of the dimensions that make up temperament.

THE THEORY   Mary K. Rothbart (2007) has devised a theory of temperament that includes three different dimensions:

- *Surgency/extraversion* **refers to the extent to which a child is generally happy, active, vocal, and regularly seeks interesting stimulation.**
- *Negative affect* **refers to the extent to which a child is angry, fearful, frustrated, shy, and not easily soothed.**
- *Effortful control* **refers to the extent to which a child can focus attention, is not readily distracted, and can inhibit responses.**

Rothbart claims that these dimensions of temperament are evident in infancy, continue into childhood, and are related to dimensions of personality that are found in adolescence and adulthood. However, the dimensions are not independent: Specifically, infants who are high on effortful control tend to be high on surgency/extraversion and low on negative affect. In other words, babies who can control their attention and inhibit responses tend to be happy and active but not angry or fearful.

Hypothesis: If temperament is biologically based and includes the three dimensions of Rothbart's theory, then those dimensions of temperament should be observed in children around the world. That is, cross-cultural studies of temperament should consistently reveal the dimensions of surgency/extraversion, negative affect, and effortful control.

Test: Gartstein, Knyazev, and Slobodskaya (2005) conducted a cross-cultural study in which they examined the structure of temperament in infants growing up in the United States and in Russia. The sample in the United States included approximately 600 parents of 3- to 12-month-olds; the sample in Russia included about 200 parents of 3- to 12-month-olds. Both samples included roughly the same number male and female babies, and most were Caucasian. Parents in both countries completed the revised version of the Infant Behavior Questionnaire (IBQ-R), which consists of 184 items assessing different dimensions of Rothbart's theory of temperament. For example, the items "When given a new toy, how often did the baby get very excited about getting it?" and "When put into the bath water, how often did the baby splash or kick?" both measure the surgency/extraversion dimension; "When frustrated with something, how often did the baby calm down within 5 minutes?" measures the negative-affect dimension. For each item, parents rated how often the behavior had been observed in the past 7 days, using a scale that ranged from "never" to "always."

> In Mary Rothbart's theory, temperament includes surgency/extraversion, negative affect, and effortful control.

Gartstein et al. used factor analysis (described on page 248 in Module 8.1) to examine relations between parents' responses to different questionnaire items. This method looks for patterns in parents' responses. To illustrate, the surgency/extraversion dimension would be supported if parents who judged that their infants were always excited about a new toy also said that their babies always splashed or kicked during a bath (because both items are thought to measure surgency/extraversion). In fact, factor analyses revealed that three temperamental dimensions—surgency/extraversion, negative affect, and effortful control—were evident in the pattern of parents' responses to the 184 items on the IBQ-R. That is, the basic dimensions of temperament are evident in U.S. infants and Russian infants, at least based on parents' ratings.

Conclusion: As predicted, the structure of temperament was the same in two cultures. This supports Rothbart's claim that the dimensions of her theory of temperament are biologically rooted and, consequently, should be evident regardless of the specific environment or culture in which a child develops.

Application: An important theme of temperament research is that children's development proceeds best when there is a good fit between their temperament and the environment in which they grow up. That is, because temperament is rooted in biological factors, parents should accept their baby's unique temperamental characteristics and adjust their parenting accordingly. For example, babies who are quiet and shy clearly benefit when parents actively stimulate them (e.g., by describing and explaining). But these same activities are actually counterproductive with active, outgoing babies who would rather explore the world on their own (Miceli et al., 1998). Thus, Rothbart's theory, and other research on temperament, reminds us that parent–child interactions represent a two-way street in which interactions are most successful when both parties—child and parent—adjust to the needs of the other.

Hereditary and Environmental Contributions to Temperament

Most theories agree that temperament reflects both heredity and experience (Caspi, Roberts, & Shiner, 2005). The influence of heredity is shown in twin studies: Identical twins are more alike in most aspects of temperament than fraternal twins (Goldsmith, Pollak, & Davidson, 2008). In other words, like the youngsters in the photo, if one identical twin is temperamentally active, the other usually is, too. However, the impact of heredity also depends on the temperamental dimension and the child's age. For example, negative affect is more influenced by heredity than the other dimensions; and temperament in childhood is more influenced by heredity than is temperament in infancy (Wachs & Bates, 2001).

The environment also contributes to children's temperament. Positive emotionality—laughing often, being generally happy, and often expressing pleasure— seems to reflect environmental influences (Goldsmith, Buss, & Lemery, 1997). Infants are less emotional when parents are responsive (Hane & Fox, 2006; Leerkes, Blankson, & O'Brien, 2009). Conversely, infants become increasingly fearful when their mothers are depressed (Gartstein et al., 2010).

Heredity and experience may also explain why Yoshimi, the Japanese mother in the vignette, has such a hardy son. The "Cultural Influences" feature tells the story.

The hereditary contribution to temperament is shown by the fact that twins are typically similar in their level of activity.

Cultural Influences

Why Is Yoshimi's Son So Tough?

If you've ever watched an infant getting an injection, you know the inevitable response. After the syringe is removed, the infant's eyes open wide and then the baby begins to cry, as if saying, "Wow, that hurt!" Infants differ in how intensely they cry and in how readily they are soothed, reflecting differences in the emotionality dimension of temperament, but virtually all European American babies cry. It's easy to suppose that crying is a universal response to the pain from the inoculation, but it's not.

In such stressful situations, Japanese and Chinese infants are less likely to become upset (Kagan et al., 1994). Lewis, Ramsay, and Kawakami (1993) found that most European American 4-month-olds cried loudly within 5 seconds of an injection, but only half the Japanese babies in their study cried. What's more, when Japanese and Chinese babies did become upset, they were soothed more readily than European American babies. Lewis and his colleagues found that about three-fourths of the Japanese babies were no longer crying 90 seconds after the injection, compared to fewer than half of the European American babies. The conclusion seems clear: Yoshimi's son appears to be a typical Japanese baby in crying less often and less intensely than the European American babies at his day-care center.

Why are Asian infants less emotional than their European American counterparts? Heredity may be involved. Perhaps the genes that contribute to emotionality are less common among Asians than among European Americans. But we can't overlook experience. Compared to European American mothers, Japanese mothers spend more time in close physical contact with their babies, constantly and gently soothing them; this may reduce the tendency to respond emotionally.

Of course, in trying to determine the contributions of heredity and environment to temperament, the most likely explanation is that both contribute (Henderson & Wachs, 2007). In fact, one view is that temperament may make some children particularly susceptible to environmental influences— either beneficial or harmful (Belsky, Bakermans-Kranenburg, & van IJzendoorn, 2007). For example, in one study (Kochanska, Aksan, & Joy, 2007), emotionally fearful children were more likely to cheat in a game when their parents' discipline emphasized asserting power (e.g., "Do this now and don't argue!"). Yet these children were the least likely to cheat when parents were nurturing and supportive. In other words, temperamentally fearful preschoolers can become dishonest or scrupulously honest, depending on their parents' disciplinary style.

Other exciting evidence comes from work on the DRD4 gene on chromosome 11. This gene is linked to brain systems that regulate attention, motivation, and reward, and one allele for this gene is associated with novelty-seeking in adults (Schinka, Letsch, & Crawford, 2002). In one study (Bakermans-Kranenburg et al., 2008), preschool children with this allele were more likely (than children without the allele) to be overactive, aggressive, and oppositional with others. However, when mothers participated in an intervention program designed to improve discipline by making parents more sensitive to their children's needs, preschoolers with this allele were *less* likely to be overactive, aggressive, and oppositional. Thus, children with this particular variant of the DRD4 gene are particularly susceptible to quality of parenting, be it sensitive or insensitive.

DRD4 is *not* a temperament gene, but it is linked to behaviors that make up temperament (e.g., novelty-seeking, fearlessness). Consequently, these findings, along with work on fearful preschoolers (Kochanska et al., 2007), show that temperamental features may make some children particularly sensitive to environmental influences. It's as if some children are sailboats with small rudders so that wind—representing environmental influence—can easily change their developmental course; other children have temperamentally larger rudders and are less affected by these environmental winds.

Stability of Temperament

Do calm, easygoing babies grow up to be calm, easygoing children, adolescents, and adults? Are difficult, irritable infants destined to grow up to be cranky, whiny children? In fact, temperament is moderately stable throughout infancy, childhood, and adolescence (Janson & Mathiesen, 2008; Wachs & Bates, 2001). For example, newborns who cry under moderate stress tend, as 5-month-olds, to cry when they are placed in stressful situations like the one in the photo, in which the mother is not allowing her baby to move its body (Stifter & Fox, 1990). In addition, when inhibited toddlers are adults, they respond more strongly to unfamiliar stimuli. Schwartz et al. (2003) had adults who were either inhibited or uninhibited as toddlers view novel and familiar faces. Records of brain activity showed that when adults who had been inhibited as toddlers viewed novel faces, they had significantly more activity in the amygdala, a brain region that regulates perception of fearful stimuli. Thus, the same individuals who avoided strangers as 2-year-olds had, as adults, the strongest response to novel faces.

The finding of modest stability in temperament means that Sam, an inhibited 1-year-old, is more likely to be shy as a 12-year-old than Dave, an outgoing 1-year-old. However, it's not a "sure thing" that Sam will still be shy as a 12-year-old.

Instead, think of temperament as a predisposition. Some infants are naturally predisposed to be sociable, emotional, or active; others *can* act in these ways, too, but only if the behaviors are nurtured by parents and others.

In many respects, temperament resembles personality, so it's not surprising that many child-development researchers have speculated about potential connections between the two. In fact, personality in adulthood includes many of the same dimensions observed for temperament in infancy and childhood (Caspi et al., 2005; Rothbart, 2007). For example, extroversion is a dimension of personality that refers to a person's warmth, gregariousness, and activity level. Extroverted individuals tend to be affectionate, prefer the company of others, and like being active; introverted people tend to be more reserved, enjoy solitude, and prefer a more sedate pace (Costa & McCrae, 2001).

Extroversion looks like a blend of the temperamental dimensions of positive affect and activity level, and longitudinal studies find that inhibited children are more likely as adults to be introverted than extroverted (Caspi et al., 2005). However, research of this sort also reveals many instances in which temperament is poorly related to personality in adulthood (Wachs & Bates, 2001). This may seem surprising, but remember that temperament changes as children develop, depending on their experiences. An inhibited child who finds herself in a school group with children who have similar interests may "open up" and become much more outgoing over time; her early inhibited temperament is not related to her later outgoing personality. Thus, we should not expect children's temperament to be consistently related to their personality as adults.

In the next section, we'll see some of the connections between temperament and other aspects of development.

Temperament is moderately stable throughout infancy. For example, babies who as newborns cry when they experience stress tend, as 5-month-olds, to cry when they experience stress from being restrained.

Temperament and Other Aspects of Development

In their New York Longitudinal Study, Thomas and Chess discovered that about two-thirds of the preschoolers with difficult temperaments had developed behavioral problems by the time they entered school. In contrast, fewer than one-fifth of the children with easy temperaments had behavioral problems (Thomas et al., 1968). Later studies have documented this link between a difficult temperament—youngsters who anger easily and have relatively little control—and later behavior problems, both in the United States and China (Zhou, Lengua, & Wang, 2009). However, difficult temperament does not necessarily lead to adjustment problems: Children with difficult temperaments can fare well when parents are warm, supportive, and respect their children's autonomy (Stright, Gallagher, & Kelley, 2008).

Other scientists have followed the lead of the New York Longitudinal Study in looking for links between temperament and outcomes of development, and they've found that temperament is an important influence on development. Consider these examples:

- Persistent children are likely to succeed in school, whereas active and distractible children are less likely to succeed (Martin, Olejnik, & Gaddis, 1994).
- Shy, inhibited children often have difficulty interacting with their peers and often do not cope effectively with problems (Eisenberg et al., 1998).

Temperament is linked to school success, good peer relations, compliance with requests, and to depression.

- Anxious, fearful children are more likely to comply with a parent's rules and requests, even when the parent is not present (Kochanska et al., 2007).
- Children who are frequently angry or fearful are more prone to depression (Lengua, 2006).
- Children who are capable of greater effortful control, as 3- and 4-year-olds, have higher scores on measures of working memory (Wolfe & Bell, 2007) and, as school-age children, are less likely to be diagnosed with ADHD (Martel & Nigg, 2006).

The "Focus on Research" feature shows that temperament is also related to children's tendency to help people in distress.

Focus on Research

Temperament Influences Helping Others

Who were the investigators, and what was the aim of the study? When people are in obvious distress, some children readily step forward to help, but others seem reluctant to help. Why are some children so helpful whereas others aren't? Shari Young, Nathan Fox, and Carolyn Zahn-Waxler (1999) argued that temperament may be part of the answer. Specifically, inhibited, shy youngsters may find it difficult to overcome their reticence to help another, particularly when they do not know the person and when the other person does not specifically request help. Young and her colleagues examined this hypothesis by studying inhibition and helping in 2-year-olds.

How did the investigators measure the topic of interest? The researchers videotaped children as they interacted with their mother and a stranger during free play. At some point during the session, the experimenter feigned injury (e.g., she pretended that she had caught her fingers in the clipboard). Later in the session, the mother also feigned injury (e.g., she pretended to bump into a chair). While feigning injury, the experimenter and the mother did not solicit the child's help in any way, either directly (e.g., by saying, "Help me, help me") or indirectly (e.g., by calling the child's name). Later, observers scored children's behaviors on several dimensions, including:

- *Inhibition:* The extent to which children avoided the experimenter, even when he began playing with a novel, attractive toy.
- *Concerned expression:* The extent to which children displayed obvious concern for the injured experimenter or mother, as shown by, for example, expressions of sadness.
- *Helpful behavior:* The extent to which children acted in ways apparently aimed at reducing distress, such as sharing a toy or stroking the injured body part.

Who were the children in the study? The study involved 50 2-year-olds. Children were tested within 2 weeks of their second birthday.

What was the design of the study? This study was correlational because Young and her colleagues were interested in the relation that existed naturally between inhibition and helping. The study was actually longitudinal (children were also tested at

4 months), but I'm only describing the results from the second testing session, which took place at age 2 years.

Were there ethical concerns with the study? No. The children enjoyed most of the free-play session. The experimenters and mothers "recovered" quickly from their feigned injuries—in approximately 1 minute—and no children were visibly upset by the apparent injuries.

What were the results? The graph in Figure 10-1 shows some correlations between inhibition and (a) expressing concern, and (b) helping behavior, separately for helping the mother and helping the experimenter. Let's begin with the correlations for mothers. Neither correlation is significant, which indicates that when interacting with their moms, shy and outgoing children were equally likely to express concern and to provide help. The results differ for helping the experimenter. The correlation between inhibition and expressing concern is again small, indicating that shy and outgoing youngsters were equally likely to express concern when the experimenter feigned injury. However, the correlation between inhibition and helping is negative: shy, inhibited 2-year-olds were less likely than outgoing 2-year-olds to help an experimenter who appeared to be hurt.

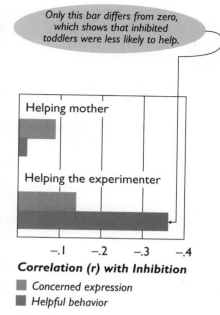

FIGURE 10-1

What did the investigators conclude? A young child's temperament helps determine whether that child will help. When mothers and experimenters feigned injury, both shy and outgoing children noticed and were disturbed by their distress. Outgoing children typically translated this concern into action, helping both mothers and experimenters. In contrast, shy youngsters helped mothers but could not overcome their reticence to help an unfamiliar adult who did not specifically ask for help. Even though shy children see that a person is suffering, their apprehensiveness in unfamiliar social settings often prevents them from helping.

What converging evidence would strengthen these conclusions? One way to test the generality of these results would be to repeat the experiment, replacing the mother and adult experimenter with an older sibling and an unfamiliar child who is the same age as the older sibling. The prediction is that shy and outgoing children would help the familiar older sibling, but only outgoing children would help the unfamiliar older child.

Although these findings underscore that temperament is an important force in children's development, temperament rarely is the sole determining factor. Instead, the influence of temperament often depends on the environment in which children develop. To illustrate, let's consider the link between temperament and behavior problems. Infants and toddlers who temperamentally resist control—those who are difficult to manage, who are often unresponsive, and who are sometimes impulsive—tend to be prone to behavior problems, particularly aggression, when they are older. However, more careful analysis shows that resistant temperament leads to behavior problems primarily when mothers do not exert much control over their children. Among mothers who do exert control—those who prohibit, warn, and scold their children when necessary—resistant temperament is not linked to behavior problems (Bates et al., 1998).

Similarly, young adolescents are more likely to drink, smoke, and use drugs when they experience many life stressors (e.g., when someone in the family has a serious accident or illness, when a parent loses a job, or when parents and the child are frequently in conflict) and their parents themselves smoke and drink. But this is less true for young adolescents with temperaments marked by positive affect (Wills et al., 2001). That is, young adolescents who are temperamentally cheerful apparently are less affected by life stressors and consequently are less likely to drink, smoke, or use drugs.

This research reminds us that emotion is a fundamental element of temperament. In the next module, we'll look at emotion from yet another perspective, that of the emotional relationship formed between an infant and its primary caregiver.

Q&A ANSWER 10.2
Thomas and Chess would say that she's a prototypic "easy" baby: she's happy, she adjusts well to new situations (shown by how much she enjoys going to new places with her dad), and she has a regular routine for sleeping.

 ## Check Your Learning

RECALL How is temperament influenced by heredity and environment?

Summarize the influence of temperament on other aspects of development.

INTERPRET Compare and contrast the Thomas and Chess approach to temperament with Rothbart's theory of temperament.

APPLY Based on what you know about the stability of temperament, what would you say to a parent who's worried that her 15-month-old seems shy and inhibited?

 ## 10.3 Attachment

OUTLINE
The Growth of Attachment

The Quality of Attachment

LEARNING OBJECTIVES
• How does an attachment relationship develop between an infant and the primary caregiver?
• What different types of attachment relationships are there? What are the consequences of different types of relationships?

Ever since Samantha was a newborn, Karen and Dick looked forward to going to their favorite restaurant on Friday night. Karen enjoyed the break from child-care responsibilities and Dick liked being able to talk to Karen without interruptions. But recently they've had a problem. When they leave her with a sitter, 8-month-old "Sam" gets a frightened look on her face and usually begins to cry hysterically. Karen and Dick wonder if Sam's behavior is normal and if their Friday-night dinners are coming to an end.

The social-emotional relationship that develops between an infant and a parent (usually, but not necessarily, the mother) is special. This is a baby's first social-emotional relationship, so scientists and parents alike believe that it should be satisfying and trouble-free to set the stage for later relationships. In this module, we'll look at the steps involved in creating the baby's first emotional relationship. Along the way, we'll see why 8-month-old Sam has begun to cry when Karen and Dick leave her with a sitter.

The Growth of Attachment

Today's parents are encouraged to shower their babies with hugs and kisses; the more affection young children receive, the better! This advice may seem obvious, but actually it's a relatively recent recommendation, dating from the middle of the 20th century. It emerged, in part, from observations of European children whose parents were killed during World War II. Despite being well fed and receiving necessary health care, the children's development was far from normal: their mental development was slow and they often seemed withdrawn and listless (Bowlby, 1953; Spitz, 1965). Some scientists claimed that these problems came about because the children lived in institutions (e.g., orphanages and refugee camps) where they could not form a close social-emotional bond with adults.

Soon after, studies of monkeys that were reared in isolation confirmed this idea. Although the monkeys received excellent physical care, they stayed huddled in a corner of their cages, clutching themselves, and rocking constantly; when placed with other monkeys, they avoided the others as much as they could (Harlow & Harlow, 1965). Clearly, in the absence of regular social interactions with caring adults, normal development is thrown way off course.

In explaining the essential ingredients of these early social relationships, most modern accounts take an evolutionary perspective. **According to** *evolutionary psychology,* **many human behaviors represent successful adaptation to the environment.** That is, over human history, some behaviors have made it more likely that people will reproduce and pass on their genes to following generations. For example, we take it for granted that most people enjoy being with other people. But evolutionary psychologists argue that our "social nature" is a product of evolution: For early humans, being in a group offered protection from predators and made it easier to locate food. Thus, early humans who were social were more likely than their asocial peers to live long enough to reproduce, passing on their social orientation to their offspring (Gaulin & McBurney, 2001). Over many, many generations, "being social" had such a survival advantage that nearly all people are socially oriented (though in varying amounts, as we know from research on temperament in Module 10.2).

Applied to child development, evolutionary psychology highlights the adaptive value of children's behavior at different points in development (Bjorklund & Pellegrini, 2000). For example, think about the time and energy that parents invest in child rearing. Without such effort, infants and young children would die before they were sexually mature, which means that a parent's genes could not be passed along to grandchildren (Geary, 2002). Here, too, although parenting just seems "natural," it really represents an adaptation to the problem of guaranteeing that one's helpless offspring can survive until they're sexually mature.

An evolutionary perspective of early human relationships comes from John Bowlby (1969, 1991). **According to Bowlby, children who form an** *attachment*—**that is, an enduring social-emotional relationship to an adult—are more likely to survive.** This person is usually the mother but need not be; the key is a strong emotional relationship with a responsive, caring person. Attachments can form with fathers, grandparents, or someone else. Bowlby described four phases in the growth of attachment:

- *Preattachment* (birth to 6–8 weeks). During prenatal development and soon after birth, infants rapidly learn to recognize their mothers by smell and sound, which sets the stage for forging an attachment relationship (Hofer, 2006). What's more, evolution has endowed infants with many behaviors that elicit caregiving from an adult. When babies cry, smile, or gaze intently at a parent's face, parents usually smile back or hold the baby. The infant's behaviors and the responses they evoke in adults create an interactive system that is the first step in the formation of attachment relationships.

- *Attachment in the making* (6–8 weeks to 6–8 months). During these months, babies begin to behave differently in the presence of familiar caregivers and unfamiliar adults. Babies now smile and laugh more often with the primary caregiver; when babies are upset, they're more easily consoled by the primary caregiver. Babies are gradually identifying the primary caregiver as the person they can depend on when they're anxious or distressed.

- *True attachment* (6–8 months to 18 months). By approximately 7 or 8 months, most infants have singled out the attachment figure—usually the mother—as a special individual. The attachment figure is now the infant's stable social-emotional base. For example, a 7-month-old like the one in the photo will explore a novel environment but periodically look toward his mother, as if seeking reassurance that all is well. The behavior suggests that the infant trusts his mother and indicates that the attachment relationship has been established. In addition, this behavior reflects important cognitive growth: It means that the infant has a mental representation of the mother, an understanding that she will be there to meet the infant's needs (Lewis, 1997). This is why infants like 8-month-old Sam from the vignette are distressed when they're separated from the attachment figure: because they've lost their secure base.

> According to Bowlby, mother-infant attachment progresses through four stages.

- *Reciprocal relationships* (18 months on). Infants' growing cognitive and language skills and their accumulated experience with their primary caregiver make infants better able to act as true partners in the attachment relationship. They often take the initiative in interactions and negotiate with parents ("Please read me another story!"). They begin to understand parents' feelings and goals and sometimes use this knowledge to guide their own behavior (e.g., social referencing, described on page 318). And they cope with separation more effectively because they can anticipate that parents will return.

When an infant has formed an attachment with a caregiver, that person becomes a secure, stable emotional base for the infant.

THE ROLE OF FATHERS. Attachment typically first develops between infants and their mothers because mothers are usually the primary caregivers of American infants. Babies soon become attached to fathers, too, even though fathers spend less time in caregiving tasks (e.g., feeding or bathing a child) than mothers do (Pleck & Masciadrelli, 2004). Instead, fathers spend more time playing with their babies than taking care of them— and even their style of play differs. Physical play like that shown in the photo is the norm for fathers, whereas mothers spend more time reading and talking to babies, showing them toys, and playing games like patty-cake (Paquette, 2004). Given the opportunity to play with mothers or fathers, infants more often choose their fathers. However, when infants are distressed, mothers are preferred (Field, 1990). Thus, although most infants become attached to both parents, mothers and fathers typically have distinctive roles in their children's early social development.

The Quality of Attachment

Attachment between infant and mother usually occurs by 8 or 9 months of age, but the attachment can take on different forms. Mary Ainsworth (1978, 1993) pioneered the study of attachment relationships using a procedure that has come to be known as the Strange Situation. You can see in Figure 10-2 that the Strange Situation involves a series of episodes, each about 3 minutes long. The mother and infant enter an unfamiliar room filled with interesting toys. The mother leaves briefly, then mother and baby are reunited. Meanwhile, the experimenter observes the baby, recording its response to both events.

Based on how the infant reacts to separation from the mother and then reunion, researchers identify four different types of attachment relationships (Ainsworth, 1993; Thompson, 2006). One is a secure attachment and three are insecure attachments (avoidant, resistant, disorganized):

- *Secure attachment:* **The baby may or may not cry when the mother leaves, but when she returns, the baby wants to be with her and if the baby is crying, it stops.** Babies in this group seem to be saying, "I missed you terribly, but now

Fathers spend much of their time with babies playing with them (instead of taking care of them) and tend to play with them more vigorously and physically than mothers do.

Steps in the Strange Situation

1. Observer shows the experimental room to mother and infant, then leaves the room.

2. Infant is allowed to explore the playroom for 3 minutes; mother watches but does not participate.

3. A stranger enters the room and remains silent for 1 minute, then talks to the baby for a minute, and then approaches the baby. Mother leaves unobtrusively.

4. The stranger does not play with the baby but attempts to comfort it if necessary.

5. After 3 minutes, the mother returns, greets, and consoles the baby.

6. When the baby has returned to play, the mother leaves again, this time saying "bye-bye" as she leaves.

7. Stranger attempts to calm and play with the baby.

8. After 3 minutes, the mother returns and the stranger leaves.

FIGURE 10-2

that you're back, I'm okay." Approximately 60 to 65% of American babies have secure attachment relationships.

- *Avoidant attachment:* **The baby is not visibly upset when the mother leaves and, when she returns, may ignore her by looking or turning away.** Infants with an avoidant attachment look as if they're saying, "You left me again. I always have to take care of myself!" About 20% of American infants have avoidant attachment relationships, which is one of the three forms of insecure attachment.

- *Resistant attachment:* **The baby is upset when the mother leaves and remains upset or even angry when she returns, and is difficult to console.** Like the baby in the photo, these babies seem to be telling the mother, "Why do you do this? I need you desperately and yet you just leave me without warning. I get so angry when you're like this." About 10 to 15% of American babies have this resistant attachment relationship, which is another form of insecure attachment.

- *Disorganized (disoriented) attachment:* **The baby seems confused when the mother leaves and, when she returns, seems not to really understand what's happening.** The baby often has a dazed look on its face, as if wondering, "What's going on here? I want you to be here, but you left and now you're back. I don't know whether to laugh or cry!" About 5 to 10% of American babies have this disorganized attachment relationship, the last of the three kinds of insecure attachment.

The Strange Situation is an important tool for studying attachment, but some scientists have criticized its emphasis on separation and reunion as the primary means for assessing quality of attachment. They suggest that what is considered an appropriate response to separation may not be the same in all cultures (Rothbaum et al., 2000). Consequently, investigators now use other methods to complement the Strange Situation. One of them, the Attachment Q-Set, can be used with young children as well as infants and toddlers. In this method, trained observers watch mothers and children interact at home; then the observer rates the interaction on many attachment-related behaviors (e.g., "Child greets mother with a big smile when she enters the room"). The ratings are totaled to provide a measure of the security of the child's attachment. Scores obtained with the Q-Set converge with assessments derived from the Strange Situation (van IJzendoorn et al., 2004).

An infant with a resistant attachment is upset or angry with the mother when reunited following a separation from her.

STABILITY OF ATTACHMENT. The quality of attachment during infancy predicts parent–child relations during childhood, adolescence, and young adulthood. Infants with secure attachment relationships tend to report, as adolescents and young adults, that they depend on their parents for care and support. In contrast, infants with insecure attachment relationships often report, as adolescents and young adults, being angry with their parents or deny being close to them. However, consistency is far from perfect. Stressful life events—death of a parent, divorce, life-threatening illness, poverty—help to determine stability and change in attachment. Stressful life events are associated with insecure attachments during adolescence and young adulthood. Consequently, when infants with insecure attachments experience stressful life events, their attachment tends to remain insecure; when infants with secure attachment experience these same events, their attachment often becomes insecure, perhaps because stress makes parents less available and less responsive to their children (Moss et al., 2005; Waters et al., 2000).

PATTERNS OF ATTACHMENT WORLDWIDE. Worldwide, secure attachment is the most common form: In most countries, roughly 55 to 70% of infants are classified as being securely attached (van IJzendoorn, Schuengel, & Bakermans-Kranenburg, 1999). However, the percentage of infants falling in the different categories of insecure attachment differs substantially across cultures. For example, in Japan, resistant attachment (where the infant wants to be picked up at reunion but squirms as if to avoid the mother's hugs) is much more common than avoidant attachment (where the infant does not wish to be picked up at all following reunion). The reverse pattern has been found in Germany (Sagi et al., 1995).

These differences may reflect cultural variations in parents' expectations about infant behavior. German parents, for example, are more likely to encourage independence, which may explain why avoidant attachment is more common in German infants. In contrast, Japanese parents see the mother–child relationship as particularly interdependent and Japanese mothers spend much time holding their infants closely (Rothbaum et al., 2000). This may explain why Japanese infants rarely avoid their mothers during reunion after separation.

These cultural variations in frequency of different types of insecure attachment should not overshadow the substantial cultural consistency in the prevalence of secure attachment. Evolutionary psychologists would argue that this prevalence must mean that secure attachment is adaptive relative to the other forms. In the next section, we'll see that this is true.

CONSEQUENCES OF QUALITY OF ATTACHMENT. Erikson, Bowlby, and other theorists (Waters & Cummings, 2000) believe that attachment, as the first social relationship, provides the basis for all of an infant's later social relationships. In this view, infants who experience the trust and compassion of a secure attachment should develop into preschool children who interact confidently and successfully with their peers. In contrast, infants who do not experience a successful, satisfying first relationship should be more prone to problems in their social interactions as preschoolers.

> Infants with secure attachment tend to interact successfully with peers.

In fact, children with secure attachment relationships have higher-quality friendships and fewer conflicts in their friendships than children with insecure attachment relationships (McElwain et al., 2008). What's more, secure attachment in infancy is associated with more stable and higher-quality romantic relationships in adolescence (Collins, Welsh, & Furman, 2009). Finally, research consistently points to links between disorganized attachment and behavior problems involving anxiety, anger, and aggressive behavior (Fearon et al., 2010; Moss et al., 2006).

The conclusion seems inescapable: As they grow, infants who have secure attachment relationships tend to have satisfying social interactions, but infants with disorganized attachment do not. Why? One explanation focuses on the lasting impact of this first social relationship. Secure attachment evidently leads infants to trust and confide in other humans, which leads to more skilled social interactions later in childhood. Another view does not discount the impact of this early relationship, but adds another wrinkle: Theorists who emphasize continuity of caregiving argue that parents who establish secure attachments with infants tend to be warm and supportive throughout their child's development (Lamb et al., 1985; Thompson, 2006). Thus, it is continuous exposure to high-quality parenting that promotes secure attachment in infancy and positive social relationships in childhood and adolescence. These accounts are *not* mutually exclusive: A successful first relationship and continued warm parenting likely work together to foster children's development.

FACTORS DETERMINING QUALITY OF ATTACHMENT. Because secure attachment is so important to a child's later development, researchers have tried to identify the factors involved. Undoubtedly the most important is the interaction between parents and their babies. A secure attachment is most likely when parents respond to infants predictably and appropriately (De Wolff & van IJzendoorn, 1997; Tomlinson, Cooper, & Murray, 2005). For example, the mother in the photo has promptly responded to her baby's crying and is trying to reassure the baby. The mother's behavior evidently conveys that social interactions are predictable and satisfying, and apparently this behavior instills in infants the trust and confidence that are the hallmark of secure attachment.

A key ingredient in creating a secure mother–infant attachment is for the mother to respond appropriately and predictably to her infant's needs.

Why does predictable and responsive parenting promote secure attachment relationships? To answer this question, think about your own friendships and romantic relationships. These relationships are usually most satisfying when we believe we can trust the other people and depend on them in times of need. The same formula seems to hold for infants. **Infants develop an** *internal working model,* **a set of expectations about parents' availability and responsiveness, both generally and in times of stress.** When parents are dependable and caring, babies come to trust them, knowing they can be relied upon for comfort. That is, babies develop an internal working model in which they believe their parents are concerned about their needs and will try to meet those needs (Huth-Bocks et al., 2004; Thompson, 2000).

In a particularly clever demonstration of infants' working models of attachment (Johnson, Dweck, & Chen, 2007), 13-month-olds were shown animated videos depicting a large ellipse (mother) paired with a small ellipse (child). The video began with the mother and child ellipses together, then the mother moved away from the child, who began to cry. On some trials, the mother ellipse returned to the child ellipse; on other trials, she continued to move away. Securely attached 13-month-olds looked longer at the trials depicting an unresponsive mother but insecurely attached infants looked longer at the trials when the mother returned. Evidently, each group has a working model of how parents respond—securely attached infants expect parents to respond but insecurely attached infants do not—and they look longer at the trials that violate their expectations of maternal behavior.

Many research findings attest to the importance of a caregiver's sensitivity for developing secure attachment:

- In a study conducted in Israel, infants were less likely to develop secure attachment when they slept in dormitories with other children, where they received inconsistent (if any) attention when they became upset overnight (Sagi et al., 1995).

- In a study conducted in the Netherlands, infants were more likely to form a secure attachment when their mother had 3 months of training that emphasized monitoring an infant's signals and responding appropriately and promptly (van den Boom, 1994, 1995).

- Infants living in orphanages in Romania were more likely to be attached to their institutional caregivers when the caregivers were emotionally involved and responsive to them (Zeanah et al., 2005).

Thus, secure attachment is most likely when parents are sensitive and responsive. Of course, not all caregivers react to babies in a reliable and reassuring manner. Some respond intermittently or only after the infant has cried long and hard. And when these caregivers finally respond, they are sometimes annoyed by the infant's demands and may misinterpret the infant's intent. Over time, these babies tend to see social relationships as inconsistent and often frustrating, conditions that do little to foster trust and confidence.

When parents respond appropriately and predictably, secure attachments usually result.

Why are some parents more responsive (and thus more likely to foster secure attachment) than others? According to modern attachment theory (e.g., Cassidy, 1994), parents have internal working models of the attachment relationship with their own parents, and these working models guide interactions with their own infants. When questioned about attachment relationships with the Adult Attachment Interview (George, Kaplan, & Main, 1985), adults can be classified into one of three groups, one corresponding to the secure attachment of childhood and the other two corresponding to insecure attachments:

- *Secure adults* **describe childhood experiences objectively and value the impact of the parent–child relationship on their development.**
- *Dismissive adults* **sometimes deny the value of childhood experiences and sometimes are unable to recall those experiences precisely, yet they often idealize their parents.**
- *Preoccupied adults* **describe childhood experiences emotionally and often express anger or confusion regarding relationships with their parents.**

According to attachment theory, only parents with secure attachment representations are likely to provide the sensitive caregiving that promotes secure attachment relationships. In fact, many studies show that parents' secure attachment representations are associated with sensitive caregiving, and, in turn, with secure attachment in their infants (Pederson et al., 1998; Tarabulsy et al., 2005; van IJzendoorn, 1995). Furthermore, as I mentioned earlier, infants with secure attachment relations often become young adults with secure attachment representations, completing the circle.

The sensitive and responsive caregiving that is essential for secure attachments is often taxing, particularly for babies with difficult temperaments. That is, babies who fuss often and are difficult to console are more prone to insecure attachment (van IJzendoorn et al., 2004). Insecure attachment may also be more likely when a difficult, emotional infant has a mother whose personality is rigid and traditional than when the mother is accepting and flexible (Mangelsdorf et al., 1990). Rigid mothers do not adjust well to the often erratic demands of their difficult babies; instead, they want the baby to adjust to them. This means that rigid mothers less often provide the responsive, sensitive care that leads to secure attachment.

Fortunately, even brief training for mothers of newborns can help them respond to their babies more effectively (Bakermans-Kranenburg, van IJzendoorn, & Juffer, 2003). Mothers can be taught how to interact more sensitively, affectionately, and responsively, paving the way for secure attachment and the lifelong benefits associated with a positive internal working model of interpersonal relationships.

WORK, ATTACHMENT, AND CHILD CARE.   Since the 1970s, more women in the workforce and more single-parent households have made child care a fact of life for many American families. I describe child care in detail in Module 15.3, but here I want to focus on one specific aspect: What happens to mother–infant attachment when other people care for the infant much of the time? Parents and policymakers alike have been concerned about the impact of such care. Is there, for example, a maximum amount of time per week that infants should spend in care outside the home? Is there a minimum age below which infants should not be placed in care outside the home? The "Child Development and Family Policy" feature describes work that has attempted to answer these and other questions about the impact of early child care on children's development.

Child Development and Family Policy

Determining Guidelines for Child Care for Infants and Toddlers

Because so many American families need child care for their infants and toddlers, a comprehensive study of early child care was required to provide parents and policymakers with appropriate guidelines. The task fell to the U.S. National Institute of Child Health and Human Development, which began the Early Child Care study in 1991. Researchers recruited 1,364 mothers and their newborns from 12 U.S. cities. Both mothers and children have been tested repeatedly (and the testing continues, because the study is ongoing).

From the outset, one of the concerns was the impact of early child care on mother–infant attachment—but the results so far show no overall effects of child-care experience on mother–infant attachment, for either 15- or 36-month-olds (NICHD Early Child Care Research Network, 1997, 2001). In other words, a secure mother–infant attachment was just as likely, regardless of the quality of child care, the amount of time the child spent in care, the age when the child began care, how frequently the parents changed child-care arrangements, and the type of child care (e.g., at a child-care center or in the home with a nonrelative).

However, when the effects of child care were considered along with characteristics of mothers, an important pattern was detected: At 15 and 36 months, insecure attachments were more common when less-sensitive mothering was combined with low-quality or large amounts of child care (NICHD Early Child Care Research Network, 1997, 2001). As the investigators put it, "poor quality, unstable, or more than minimal amounts of child care apparently added to the risks already inherent in poor mothering, so that the combined effects were worse than those of low maternal sensitivity and responsiveness alone" (1997, p. 877). These conclusions are particularly convincing because the same pattern of results was found in Israel in a large-scale study of child care and attachment that was modeled after the NICHD Early Child Care study (Sagi et al., 2002). What's more, although children in child care often become attached to their nonparental caregivers, this is not at the expense of secure attachment to parents (Ahnert, Pinquart, & Lamb, 2006).

These results provide clear guidelines for parents. The essential ingredient for secure attachment is high-quality parenting. With such parenting, a secure attachment is likely regardless of a child's experience in child care. Of course, parents should still look for high-quality child care; we'll explore this topic in detail in Module 15.3.

QUESTION 10.3

Chantal is the mother of a 3-month-old. She's eager to return to her job as a civil engineer, but she worries that she may harm her baby by going back to work so soon. What could you say to reassure her?

(Answer is on page 339.)

Check Your Learning

RECALL   Describe the evolutionary perspective on mother–infant attachment.

What are the different forms of mother–infant attachment? What are the consequences of these different forms?

INTERPRET   Compare the infant's contributions to the formation of mother–infant attachment with the mother's contributions.

APPLY   Based on what you know about the normal developmental timetable for the formation of mother–infant attachment, what would seem to be the optimal age range for children to be adopted?

 ANSWER 10.3
Tell her that the findings of the NICHD Early Child Care Study make it clear that as long as Chantal provides high-quality parenting—that is, as long as she responds appropriately and predictably to her baby's needs—she and her baby should have a secure attachment even if the baby is in day care full time.

UNIFYING THEMES   Active Children

Temperament is one of the best examples in this book of the theme that *children influence their own development*. Temperament helps determine how parents, peers, and other adults respond to children. Parents and peers, for example, usually respond positively to temperamentally easy children. Parents find it more straightforward to establish a secure attachment with an easy child than with a difficult child. Peers get along better with easy children than with shy, inhibited children. Children's temperament does not alone dictate the direction of their development, but it makes some directions much easier to follow than others.

See for Yourself

Arrange to visit a local day-care center where you can unobtrusively observe preschoolers for several days. As you watch the children, see if you can detect the temperamental differences that are described in Module 10.2. Can you identify an emotional child, an active child, and a social child? Also, notice how adults respond to the children. Notice if the same behaviors lead to different responses from adults, depending on the child's temperament. See for yourself!

Summary

10.1 Emerging Emotions

The Function of Emotions
Modern theories emphasize the functional value of emotion. Emotions such as fear, happiness, and disgust are valuable because they help people adapt: keeping them away from danger and strengthening social relationships.

Experiencing and Expressing Emotions
Basic emotions, which include joy, anger, and fear, emerge in the first year. Fear first appears in infancy as stranger wariness. Self-conscious emotions have an evaluative component and include guilt, embarrassment, and pride. They appear between 18 and 24 months and require more sophisticated cognitive skills than basic emotions such as happiness and fear. Cultures differ in the rules for expressing emotions and the situations that elicit particular emotions.

Recognizing and Using Others' Emotions
By 6 months, infants have begun to recognize the emotions associated with different facial expressions. They use this information to help them evaluate unfamiliar situations. Beyond infancy, children understand the causes and

consequences of different emotions, that people can feel multiple emotions simultaneously, and the rules for displaying emotions appropriately.

Regulating Emotions

Infants use simple strategies to regulate emotions such as fear. As children grow, they become better skilled at regulating their emotions. Children who do not regulate emotions well tend to have problems interacting with others.

10.2 Temperament

What Is Temperament?

Temperament refers to biologically based, stable patterns of behavior that are evident soon after birth. The New York Longitudinal Study suggested three main categories of temperament, but most modern theories focus on dimensions of temperament. According to Rothbart's theory, temperament includes three main dimensions: surgency/extraversion, negative affect, and effortful control.

Hereditary and Environmental Contributions to Temperament

The major theories agree that both heredity and environment contribute to temperament. For many dimensions of temperament, identical twins are more alike than fraternal twins. Positive emotionality reflects environmental influences.

Stability of Temperament

Temperament is moderately stable in infancy, childhood, and adolescence. Temperament in childhood is somewhat related to personality in adulthood. The relations are not very strong because temperament itself changes as children develop.

Temperament and Other Aspects of Development

Many investigators have shown that temperament is related to other aspects of development. Difficult babies are more likely to have behavioral problems by the time they are old enough to attend school. Persistent children are more successful in school, shy children sometimes have problems with peers, anxious children are more compliant with parents, and angry or fearful children are prone to depression. However, the impact of temperament always depends on the environment in which children develop.

10.3 Attachment

The Growth of Attachment

Attachment is an enduring social-emotional relationship between infant and parent. Bowlby's theory of attachment is rooted in evolutionary psychology and describes four stages in the development of attachment: preattachment, attachment in the making, true attachment, and reciprocal relationships.

The Quality of Attachment

Research with the Strange Situation, in which infant and mother are separated briefly, reveals four primary forms of attachment. Most common is a secure attachment, in which infants have complete trust in the mother. Less common are three types of insecure attachment relationships that lack this trust. In avoidant relationships, infants deal with the lack of trust by ignoring the mother; in resistant relationships, infants often seem angry with her; in disorganized (disoriented) relationships, infants seem not to understand the mother's absence.

Children who have had secure attachment relationships during infancy often interact with their peers more readily and more skillfully. Secure attachment is most likely to occur when mothers respond sensitively and consistently to their infants' needs. Adults who value their relationship with their own parents are most likely to use the sensitive caregiving that promotes secure attachments with their own infants.

Test Yourself

✓─ **Study** and **Review** on mydevelopmentlab.com

1. Modern approaches to emotion emphasize the _____ of emotions in helping people to adapt to their environment.

2. _____ are experienced by people worldwide and consist of a subjective feeling, a physiological change, and an overt behavior.

3. Complex emotions (sometimes called *self-conscious emotions*) develop between 18 and 24 months of age because they depend on the child having _____.

4. In _____, infants look to a parent to help them interpret an unfamiliar or ambiguous environment.

5. Compared to younger children's emotion regulation, older children and adolescents rely on themselves, not parents, to regulate emotions; more often rely on mental strategies to regulate emotions; and _____.

6. In the New York Longitudinal Study, most babies were happy and cheerful; they were called _____ babies.

7. Rothbart's theory of temperament includes three dimensions: surgency/extraversion, negative affect, and _____.

8. _____ is the dimension of temperament that's most influenced by heredity.

9. Inhibited children are more likely as adults to have an _____ personality.

10. When young children with difficult temperaments grow up, they are prone to _____.

11. Modern theories view attachment from an evolutionary perspective and emphasize the _____.

12. Young infants are interested in people and can identify their mothers, but not until _____ months of age do infants identify a single attachment figure who provides a stable social-emotional base.

13. In the Strange Situation, infants with _____ attachment are not upset when the mother leaves and ignore her when she returns.

14. Around the world, _____ attachment is the most common form.

15. The most important factor in determining a secure attachment is _____.

Answers: (1) functional value; (2) Basic emotions; (3) some understanding of himself or herself; (4) social referencing; (5) match regulation strategies more accurately to the setting; (6) easy; (7) effortful control; (8) Negative affect; (9) introverted; (10) behavioral problems; (11) survival value of a strong social-emotional relationship between parent and child; (12) 6 to 8; (13) avoidant; (14) secure; (15) parents responding predictably and appropriately to their baby.

Key Terms

attachment 331
avoidant attachment 334
basic emotions 314
dismissive adults 337
disorganized (disoriented)
  attachment 334
display rules 319

effortful control 323
evolutionary psychology 331
internal working model 336
negative affect 323
preoccupied adults 337
resistant attachment 334
secure adults 337

secure attachment 333
self-conscious emotions 315
social referencing 318
social smiles 314
stranger wariness 315
surgency/extraversion 323
temperament 322

11

Understanding Self and Others

11.1

**Who Am I?
Self-Concept**

11.2

Self-Esteem

11.3

Understanding Others

A century ago, G. Stanley Hall, an influential American developmental psychologist, wrote that adolescence was "strewn with wreckage of mind, body and morals" (1904, p. xiv). Judging by today's movies and media, Hall's portrayal persists: When teens aren't presented as runaways, drug addicts, and shoplifters, they're moody and withdrawn or manic. But how accurate is this picture? What does current research show about adolescence and the process of developing independence and identity?

In **Module 11.1**, we'll look at the mechanisms that give rise to a person's identity, and we'll see if adolescent "storm and stress" is a necessary step in achieving an identity. Of course, people are often happier with some aspects of themselves than with others. These evaluative aspects of identity are the focus of **Module 11.2**. Finally, in **Module 11.3**, we'll look at how we develop an understanding of others, because as we learn more about ourselves, we learn more about other people, too.

11.1 Who Am I? Self-Concept

OUTLINE	LEARNING OBJECTIVES
Origins of Self-Recognition	• When do infants first acquire a sense of self?
The Evolving Self-Concept	• How does self-concept become more elaborate as children grow?
The Search for Identity	• How do adolescents achieve an identity?

Dea was born in Seoul of Korean parents but was adopted by a Dutch couple in Michigan when she was 3 months old. Growing up, she considered herself a red-blooded American. In high school, however, Dea realized that others saw her as an Asian American, an identity to which she had never given much thought. She began to wonder: Who am I, really? American? Dutch American? Asian American?

Like Dea, do you sometimes wonder who you are? **Answers to "Who am I?" reflect a person's** *self-concept,* **which refers to the attitudes, behaviors, and values that a person believes make him or her a unique individual.** One answer to "Who am I?"—from a teenage girl—shows just how complex a person's self-concept can be:

> I'm sensitive, friendly, outgoing, popular, and tolerant, though I can also be shy, self-conscious, and even obnoxious! I'd like to be friendly and tolerant all of the time. That's the kind of person I want to be, and I'm disappointed when I'm not. I'm responsible, even studious now and then, but on the other hand, I'm a goof-off, too, because if you're too studious, you won't be popular (Harter, 1990, p. 352).

As an adult, your answer is probably even more complex, because, after all, most people are complex creatures. But how did you acquire this complex self-concept? We'll answer that question in this module, beginning with the origins of an infant's sense of self. Later, we'll see how identity becomes elaborated after infancy and see how individuals like Dea develop an ethnic identity.

Origins of Self-Recognition

What is the starting point for self-concept? Following the lead of the 19th-century philosopher and psychologist William James, modern researchers believe that the foundation of self-concept is the child's awareness that he or she exists. At some point early in life, children must realize that they exist independently of other people and objects in the environment and that their existence continues over time.

Although even very young babies enjoy looking at that "thing" in the mirror, not until about 15 months of age do babies realize that *they* are the thing in the mirror; this is one of the first signs of an emerging sense of self.

Measuring the onset of this awareness is not easy. Obviously, we can't simply ask a 3-year-old, "So, tell me, when did you first realize that you existed and weren't simply part of the furniture?" A less direct approach is needed, and the photo shows one route that many investigators have taken. Like many babies his age, the 9-month-old in the photo is looking at the face he sees in the mirror. Babies at this age sometimes touch the face in the mirror or wave at it, but none of their behaviors indicates that they recognize themselves in the mirror. Instead, babies act as if the face in the mirror is simply a very interesting stimulus.

How would we know that infants recognize themselves in a mirror? One clever approach is to have the mother place a red mark on her infant's nose; she does this surreptitiously, while wiping the baby's face. Then the infant is returned to the mirror. Many 1-year-olds touch the red mark on the mirror, showing that they notice the mark on the face in the mirror. At about 15 months, however, an important change occurs: Many babies see the red mark in the mirror, then reach up and touch *their own* noses. By age 2, most children do this (Bullock & Lütkenhaus, 1990; Lewis, 1997). When these older toddlers notice the red mark in the mirror, they understand that the funny-looking nose in the mirror is their own. And this pattern of age-related change is found among infants living in desert communities that have no mirrors (or other reflective surfaces), which shows that toddlers' behavior is not due to their growing understanding of mirrors (Priel & deSchonen, 1986).

We don't need to rely solely on the mirror task to know that self-awareness emerges between 18 and 24 months. During this same period, toddlers look more at photographs of themselves than at photos of other children. They also refer to themselves by name or with a personal pronoun, such as *I* or *me*, and sometimes they know their age and their gender. These changes, which often occur together, suggest that self-awareness is well established in most children by age 2 (Lewis & Ramsay, 2004; Moore, 2007). ◉─⌐Watch the **Video** on **mydevelopmentlab.com**

◉─⌐Watch the **Video** *Self-Awareness Task* on **mydevelopmentlab.com** to learn more about children doing the mirror task. Notice how the 12-month-old is oblivious to the mark on her nose; she pays no attention to it. In contrast, as soon as the 15-month-old sees the mark, he touches it with his finger.

The self-awareness that's evident in toddlers clearly has its roots in infancy (Rochat, 2001). Some of the roots are social. From regular, predictable interactions with caregivers, infants learn that those interactions involve different roles—one for the infant and one for the caregiver. Such differentiation of roles into the "my" and "other" roles is an important early step toward self-awareness. Other roots of self-awareness involve infants' understanding of their own bodies. As adults, we know that when we raise a hand to scratch our nose, the hand we see "doing the scratching" is our hand; it's part of our physical self. From experience watching their bodies move, infants learn this aspect of self-awareness—"that's not any old hand, that's *my* hand"—by 3 to 5 months of age. Play with objects also contributes to self-recognition

By 2 years of age, most children recognize themselves and refer to themselves by name or with I and me.

(Keller et al., 2004), perhaps because it provides many opportunities for infants to explore how their arm and hand movements relate to the physical world.

Soon after children are self-aware, autobiographical memory (described in Module 7.1) begins to emerge (Harley & Reese, 1999). That is, children begin to recognize continuity in the self over time; the "I" in the present is linked to the "I" in the past (Nelson, 2001). Awareness of a self that is extended in time is fostered by conversations with parents about the past and the future. Through such conversations, a 3-year-old celebrating a birthday understands that she's an older version of the same person who had a birthday a year previously.

Children's growing awareness of a self extended in time is also revealed by their understanding of ownership (Fasig, 2000). When a toddler sees his favorite toy and says "mine," this implies awareness of continuity of the self over time: "In the past, I played with that." Notably, when toddlers, like the girl in the photo, say "Mine!" they are often not being aggressive or selfish; instead, "mine" is a way of indicating ownership and, in the process, defining themselves. Thus, the girl in the photo is not trying to deny the doll to the other girl; she is simply saying that playing with dolls is part of who she is (Levine, 1983).

Young children often use their toys as a way to tell others who they are; "Mine!" means "That's part of me!" not "That belongs to me—hands off!"

Once self-awareness is established, children begin to acquire a self-concept. That is, once children fully understand that they exist and that they have a unique mental life, they begin to wonder who they are. They want to define themselves. In the next section, we'll see how this self-concept becomes more complex as children develop.

The Evolving Self-Concept

Before you go any further, return to the teenager's quotation on page 343. In describing herself, this girl relies heavily on psychological traits. The first sentence alone includes eight adjectives referring to these traits: *sensitive, friendly, outgoing, popular, tolerant, shy, self-conscious,* and *obnoxious.* How do children develop such a complex view of themselves? For toddlers and preschoolers, self-concept is much simpler. If asked to describe themselves, preschoolers are likely to mention physical characteristics ("I have blue eyes"), their preferences ("I like cookies"), their possessions ("I have trucks"), and their competencies ("I can count to 50").

These features all share a focus on attributes of children that are observable and concrete (Harter, 2006). They also emphasize personal characteristics that are (relatively) unchanging across time and setting. All preschool children mention such characteristics, but they dominate European American preschoolers' descriptions of themselves. In contrast, in many Asian cultures, the self is defined, to a much greater extent, by children's social relationships. For example, in describing themselves, Chinese preschoolers are more likely than European American preschoolers to say, "I love my mommy" or "I play with Qi at school," showing that the self is embedded in relationships with others (Wang, 2006).

At about 5 to 7 years of age, children's self-descriptions begin to change (Harter, 2005). Children are more likely to mention emotions ("Sometimes I get angry"). They are also more likely to mention the social groups to which they belong ("I'm on the lacrosse team"). Finally, in contrast to preschool children, who simply mention their competencies, elementary-school children describe their level of skill in relation to their peers ("I'm the best speller in my whole class").

Self-concepts change again as children enter adolescence (Harter, 2006). They now include attitudes ("I love algebra") and personality traits ("I'm usually a very happy person"). Adolescents also begin to make religious and political beliefs part of their self-concept ("I'm a Catholic" or "I'm a conservative Republican"). Another change is that adolescents' self-concepts often vary with the setting. A teenager might say, "I'm really shy around people I don't know, but I let loose when I'm with my friends and family."

> A preschooler's self-concept is linked to the concrete and real but an adolescent's self-concept is more abstract and psychological.

Yet another change is that adolescents' self-concepts are often future oriented: Adolescents often describe themselves in terms of what they will be when they reach adulthood (Harter, 2005; Steinberg et al., 2009). These descriptions may include occupational goals ("I'm going to be an English teacher"), educational plans ("I plan to go to a community college to learn about computers"), or social roles ("I want to get married as soon as I finish high school").

The gradual elaboration of self-concept from the preschool years to adolescence is described in the Summary Table. Two general changes are evident: First, self-concept becomes richer as children grow; adolescents simply know much more about themselves than preschoolers. Second, the type of knowledge that children have of themselves changes. Preschoolers' understanding is linked to the concrete, the real, and the here-and-now. Adolescents' understanding, in contrast, is more abstract and more psychological, and sees the self as evolving over time. The change in children's knowledge of themselves should not surprise you, because it's exactly the type of change that Piaget described. Concrete operational children's focus on the real and tangible extends to their thoughts about themselves, just as formal operational adolescents' focus on the abstract and hypothetical applies to their thoughts about themselves.

Adolescence is also a time of increasing self-reflection. Adolescents look for an identity that integrates the many different and sometimes conflicting elements of the self (Marcia, 1991). We'll look at this search for identity in detail in the next section.

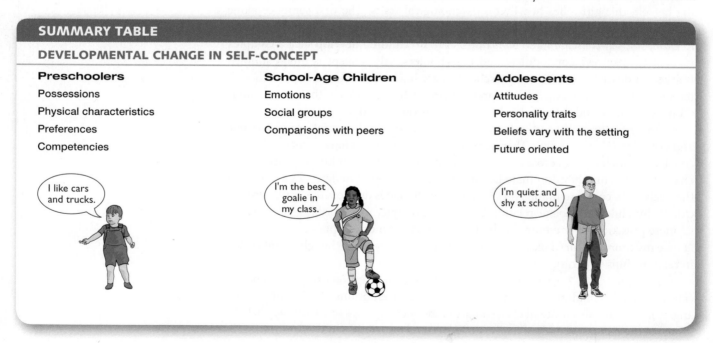

SUMMARY TABLE

DEVELOPMENTAL CHANGE IN SELF-CONCEPT

Preschoolers	School-Age Children	Adolescents
Possessions	Emotions	Attitudes
Physical characteristics	Social groups	Personality traits
Preferences	Comparisons with peers	Beliefs vary with the setting
Competencies		Future oriented

I like cars and trucks.

I'm the best goalie in my class.

I'm quiet and shy at school.

The Search for Identity

Erik Erikson (1968) believed that adolescents struggle to achieve an identity that will allow them to participate in the adult world. How exactly do they accomplish this? To learn more about possible identities, adolescents use the hypothetical reasoning skills of the formal operational stage to experiment with different selves. Adolescents' advanced cognitive skills allow them to imagine themselves in different roles.

Much of the testing and experimentation is career oriented. Some adolescents, like the ones shown in the photo, may envision themselves as rock stars; others may imagine being a professional athlete, a Peace Corps worker, or a best-selling novelist. Other testing is romantically oriented. Teens may fall in love and imagine living with the loved one. Still other exploration involves religious and political beliefs (Harre, 2007; King, Elder, & Whitbeck, 1997). Teens give different identities a trial run, just as you might test-drive different cars before selecting one. By fantasizing about their future, adolescents begin to discover who they will be.

As part of their search for an identity, adolescents often try on different roles, such as trying to imagine what life might be like as a rock star.

The self-absorption that marks the teenage search for identity is referred to as *adolescent egocentrism* (Elkind, 1978; Schwartz, Maynard, & Uzelac, 2008). Unlike preschoolers, adolescents know that others have different perspectives on the world. At the same time, many adolescents believe, wrongly, that they are the focus of others' thinking and attention. A teen like the one in the photo who spills food on herself may imagine that all her friends are thinking only about the stain on her blouse and how sloppy she is. **Many adolescents feel that they are, in effect, actors whose performance is being watched constantly by their peers, a phenomenon known as the** *imaginary audience.* 👁 Watch the **Video** on **mydevelopmentlab.com**

Adolescent self-absorption is also demonstrated by the *personal fable,* **teenagers' tendency to believe that their experiences and feelings are unique, that no one has ever felt or thought as they do.** Whether feeling the excitement of first love, the despair of a broken relationship, or the confusion of planning for the future, adolescents often believe that they are the first to experience these feelings and that no one else could possibly understand the power of their emotions (Elkind & Bowen, 1979). **Adolescents' belief in their uniqueness also contributes to an** *illusion of invulnerability*—**the belief that misfortune only happens to others.** They think they can have sex without becoming pregnant or drive recklessly without being in an auto accident. Those misfortunes, according to them, only happen to others.

Adolescents often believe that others are constantly watching them, a phenomenon known as *imaginary audience*; consequently, they're often upset or embarrassed when they make obvious mistakes or blunders, such as spilling food or drink.

Adolescent egocentrism, imaginary audiences, personal fables, and the illusion of invulnerability become less common as adolescents make progress toward achieving an identity. What exactly is involved in achieving an identity? Most adolescents

👁-Watch the **Video** *Imaginary Audience* on **mydevelopmentlab.com**, to view a teenager describing a "bad hair day" in which she imagined that everyone was looking at her weird hair. Perhaps this reminds you of similar experiences during your high-school years?

progress through different phases or *statuses*, though not necessarily in this order (Marcia, 1980, 1991):

- *Diffusion:* **Individuals in this status are confused or overwhelmed by the task of achieving an identity and are doing little to achieve one.**
- *Foreclosure:* **Individuals in this status have an identity determined largely by adults, rather than from personal exploration of alternatives.**
- *Moratorium:* **Individuals in this status are still examining different alternatives and have yet to find a satisfactory identity.**
- *Achievement:* **Individuals in this status have explored alternatives and have deliberately chosen a specific identity.**

Unlike Piaget's stages, these four phases do not necessarily occur in sequence. Most young adolescents are in a state of diffusion or foreclosure. The common element in these phases is that teens are not exploring alternative identities. They are avoiding the crisis altogether or have resolved it by taking on an identity suggested by parents or other adults. However, as individuals move beyond adolescence and into young adulthood and have more opportunity to explore alternative identities, diffusion and foreclosure become less common, and achievement and moratorium become more common (Meeus et al., 2010).

Typically, young people do not reach the achievement status for all aspects of identity at the same time (Goossens, 2001; Kroger & Greene, 1996). Some adolescents may reach the achievement status for occupation before achieving it for religion and politics. Others reach the achievement status for religion before other domains. Evidently, few youth achieve a complete sense of identity all at once; instead, the crisis of identity is resolved first in some areas and then in others.

Q&A QUESTION 11.1
Jenny thinks she might like to be an engineer, but she also enjoys dance. To help decide what path would be best for her, Jenny has taken a battery of interest inventories and her guidance counselor has suggested colleges where she could pursue both engineering and dance. Which of the four statuses best describes Jenny, at least as far as a possible occupation is concerned?
(Answer is on page 353.)

What circumstances help adolescents to achieve identity? Parents are influential (Marcia, 1980). When parents encourage discussion and recognize their children's autonomy, their children are more likely to reach the achievement status. Apparently, these youth feel encouraged to undertake the personal experimentation that leads to identity. In contrast, when parents set rules with little justification and enforce them without explanation, children are more likely to remain in the foreclosure status. These teens are discouraged from experimenting personally; instead, their parents simply tell them what identity to adopt. Overall, adolescents are most likely to establish a well-defined identity in a family atmosphere where parents encourage children to explore alternatives on their own but do not pressure them or provide explicit direction (Luyckx et al., 2007; Smits et al., 2010).

Beyond parents, peers are also influential. When adolescents have close friends whom they trust, they feel more secure exploring alternatives (Meeus, Oosterwegel, & Vollebergh, 2002). The broader social context also contributes (Bosma & Kunnen, 2001). Exploration takes time and access to resources; neither may be readily available to adolescents living in poverty (e.g., they can't explore because they drop out of school to support themselves and their family). Finally, through their personality, adolescents themselves may affect the ease with which they achieve an identity. Individuals who are more open to experience and are more agreeable (friendly, generous, helpful) are more likely to achieve an identity (Crocetti et al., 2008).

ETHNIC IDENTITY. For many adolescents growing up in North America today, achieving an identity is even more challenging because they are members of ethnic minority groups. The "Cultural Influences" feature describes one example.

Cultural Influences

Dea's Ethnic Identity

Dea, the adolescent in the opening vignette, belongs to the one-third of adolescents and young adults living in the United States who are members of ethnic minority groups. They include African Americans, Asian Americans, Hispanic Americans, and Native Americans. **These individuals typically develop an** *ethnic identity:* **They feel they are a part of their ethnic group and learn the special customs and traditions of their group's culture and heritage** (Phinney, 2005).

An ethnic identity seems to be achieved in three phases. Initially, adolescents have not examined their ethnic roots. A teenage African American girl in this phase remarked, "Why do I need to learn about who was the first Black woman to do this or that? I'm just not too interested" (Phinney, 1989, p. 44). For this girl, ethnic identity is not yet an important personal issue.

In the second phase, adolescents begin to explore the personal impact of their ethnic heritage. The curiosity and questioning that are characteristic of this stage are captured in the comments of a teenage Mexican American girl who said, "I want to know what we do and how our culture is different from others. Going to festivals and cultural events helps me to learn more about my own culture and about myself" (Phinney, 1989, p. 44). Part of this phase involves learning cultural traditions; for example, like the girl in the photo, many adolescents learn to prepare ethnic foods.

Part of the search for an ethnic identity involves learning cultural traditions, such as learning how to prepare foods associated with one's ethnic group.

In the third phase, individuals achieve a distinct ethnic self-concept. One Asian American adolescent explained his ethnic identification like this: "I have been born Filipino and am born to be Filipino. I'm here in America, and people of many different cultures are here, too. So I don't consider myself only Filipino, but also American" (Phinney, 1989, p. 44).

To see if you understand the differences between these stages of ethnic identity, reread the vignette on page 343 about Dea and decide which stage applies to her. The answer appears on page 353, just before "Check Your Learning."

Older adolescents are more likely than younger ones to have achieved an ethnic identity because they are more likely to have had opportunities to explore their cultural heritage (French et al., 2006). As adolescents explore their ethnic identity, they often change the way they refer to themselves. For example, a U.S. teen whose parents were born in Vietnam might refer to herself at different times as Vietnamese, Vietnamese American, or Asian American, in no particular order (Fuligni et al., 2008).

As is true for identity formation in general, parents matter. Adolescents are most likely to achieve an ethnic self-concept when their parents encourage them to learn about their cultural heritage and prepare them for possible discrimination.

For example, African American adolescents have a more advanced ethnic identity when their mothers tell them about Black history and racism (McHale et al., 2006). Similarly, Latino teens have a more advanced ethnic identity when their parents emphasize the importance of knowing their cultural heritage and routinely highlight that heritage by, for example, displaying cultural artifacts in the home (Umaña-Taylor & Guimond, 2010).

Do adolescents benefit from a strong ethnic identity? Yes. Adolescents who have achieved an ethnic identity tend to have higher self-esteem and find their interactions with family and friends more satisfying (Mandara et al., 2009; Roberts, Burchinal, & Durham, 1999). They're also happier and worry less (Kiang et al., 2006). In addition, adolescents with a strong ethnic identity do better in school, and are more likely to go to college, than adolescents whose ethnic identities are weaker (Altschul, Oyserman, & Bybee, 2006; Chavous et al., 2003).

> Adolescents with an ethnic identity have higher self-esteem, find interactions with others more satisfying, and do better in school.

Some individuals achieve a well-defined ethnic self-concept and, at the same time, identify strongly with the mainstream culture. In the United States, for example, many Chinese Americans embrace both Chinese and American culture; in England, many Indians identify with both Indian and British cultures. For other individuals, the cost of strong ethnic identification is a weakened tie to mainstream culture. Some investigators report that, for Hispanic Americans, strong identification with American culture is associated with a weaker ethnic self-concept (Phinney, 1990).

We shouldn't be too surprised that identifying with mainstream culture weakens ethnic identity in some groups but not others. Racial and ethnic groups living in the United States are diverse. African American, Asian American, Hispanic American, and Native American cultures and heritages differ; thus, we should expect that the nature and consequences of a strong ethnic self-concept will differ across these and other ethnic groups (Phinney, 2005).

Even within any particular group, the nature and consequences of ethnic identity may change over successive generations (Cuellar et al., 1997). As successive generations become more assimilated into mainstream culture, they may identify less strongly with ethnic culture (Marks, Patton, & García Coll, 2011). When parents maintain strong feelings of ethnic identity that their children don't share, problems sometimes develop, as immigrant parents cling to the "old ways" but their children embrace the new culture. For example, in one study of Chinese immigrants to Canada (Costigan & Dokis, 2006), children were less interested in school and had more conflicts with parents when they strongly identified with Canada but their parents did not. In another study (Schofield et al., 2008), Mexican American children had more conflicts with parents and more behavioral problems when they identified themselves as Anglo but their parents identified themselves as Mexican. ●─Watch the **Video** on **mydevelopmentlab.com**

Finally, let's think about adolescents for whom an ethnic identity is a particular challenge: those whose parents come from different racial or ethnic groups. As recently as 1970, only 1% of U.S. children were multiracial; now 5% are multiracial (Jones & Smith, 2001). When children have one European American parent and the other is African American, Asian American, or Hispanic, children tend to adopt the ethnic minority identity. A child with an Asian mother and a European American father will probably consider herself Asian (Herman, 2004).

Identity in biracial adolescents can be quite fluid. Some biracial adolescents first identify themselves as monoracial, then embrace a biracial identity; others shift in the opposite direction, converging on a single racial identity; still others shift from one racial identity to another (Doyle & Kao, 2007). Collectively, youth with shifting

●─**Watch** the **Video** *Adolescence: Identity and Role Development and Ethnicity* on **mydevelopmentlab.com**, which shows an Asian American teenager who's caught between her parents' traditional ways and her desire to be "more American."

racial identities tend to have lower self-esteem than those with a consistent biracial identity (Hitlin, Brown, & Elder, 2006).

STORM AND STRESS. According to novelists and film-makers, the search for identity that I've described in the past few pages is inherently a struggle, a time of storm and stress for adolescents. Although this view may make for best-selling novels and hit movies, in reality teen rebelliousness is vastly overstated. Adolescents generally enjoy happy and satisfying relationships with their parents (Steinberg, 2001). Most teens love their parents and feel loved by them. And they embrace many of their parents' values and look to parents for advice.

Cross-cultural research provides further evidence that for most teens, adolescence is not a time of turmoil and conflict. Offer and his colleagues (1988) interviewed adolescents from 10 different countries and found that most adolescents were moving confidently and happily toward adulthood. As the graphs in Figure 11-1 show, most adolescents around the world reported that they were usually happy, and few avoided their homes.

The Offer et al. (1988) work is nearly a quarter-century old, but newer studies paint much the same picture. In one study of Arab adolescents living in Israel (Azaiza, 2005), 82% of adolescents said they felt wanted by their family and 89% reported that they appreciated their family. In another study (Güngör & Bornstein, 2010), adolescents in Turkey and Belgium rated their mothers as being very supportive, endorsing items such as "My mother supports me in dealing with problems" and "My mother talks to me in a comforting way." These findings are consistent with the older studies and undercut the myth of adolescence as necessarily being a time when adolescent storms rain on parent–child relationships.

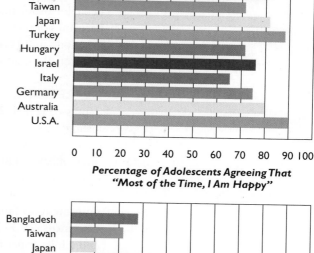

Percentage of Adolescents Agreeing That "Most of the Time, I Am Happy"

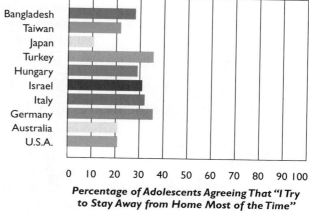

Percentage of Adolescents Agreeing That "I Try to Stay Away from Home Most of the Time"

Source: Offer et al., 1988.

FIGURE 11-1

Of course, parent–child relations *do* change during adolescence. As teens become more independent, their relationships with their parents become more egalitarian. Parents must adjust to their children's growing sense of autonomy by treating them more like equals (Laursen & Collins, 1994). This growing independence means that teens spend less time with their parents, are less affectionate toward them, and argue more often with them about matters of style, taste, and freedom (Shanahan et al., 2007). Although adolescents do have more disagreements with parents, these disputes are usually relatively mild—bickering, not all-out shouting matches—and usually concern personal choices (e.g., hairstyle, clothing). These changes are natural by-products of an evolving parent–child relationship in which the "child" is nearly a fully independent young adult (Steinberg & Silk, 2002).

Before you think that this portrait of parent–child relationships in adolescence is too good to be true, I want to add two cautionary notes. First, conflicts between parents and their adolescent children are often very distressing for *parents*, who may read far more into these conflicts than their teenagers do (Steinberg, 2001). Parents sometimes fear that arguments over attire or household chores may reflect much more fundamental disagreements about values: A mother may interpret her son's refusal to clean his room as a rejection of values concerning the need for order and cleanliness, when the son simply doesn't want to waste time cleaning a room that he knows will become a mess again in a matter of days. Second, for a minority of families—roughly 25%—parent–child conflicts in adolescence are more serious and are associated with behavior problems in adolescents (van Doorn, Branje, & Meeus, 2008). These more harmful conflicts are more common among adolescents who don't regulate their emotions well (Eisenberg et al., 2008), and they often predate adolescence; even as children, these adolescents were prone to conflict with their parents (Steinberg, 2001).

DEPRESSION.　The challenges of adolescence can lead some youth to become depressed (Fried, 2005). As we saw in Chapter 3, depressed individuals have pervasive feelings of sadness, are irritable, have low self-esteem, sleep poorly, and are unable to concentrate. About 5% to 15% of adolescents are depressed; adolescent girls are more often affected than boys, probably because social challenges in adolescence are often greater for girls than boys (Dekker et al., 2007; Hammen & Rudolph, 2003).

Depression is often triggered when adolescents experience a serious loss, disappointment, or failure, such as the death of a loved one or when a much-anticipated date turns out to be a fiasco (Schneiders et al., 2006). Of course, many adolescents and adults experience negative events like these, but most don't become depressed. Why? One contributing factor is temperament: Children who are less able to regulate their emotions are, as adolescents, more prone to depression (Karevold et al., 2009). Another factor is a belief system in which adolescents see themselves in an extremely negative light. Depression-prone adolescents are, for example, more likely to blame themselves for failure (Gregory et al., 2007). Thus, after the disappointing date, a depression-prone teen is likely to think, "I acted like a fool" instead of placing blame elsewhere by thinking, "Gee. He was a real jerk!"

> Depression is often triggered when adolescents blame themselves for a negative event.

Parents and families can also put an adolescent at risk for depression. Not surprisingly, adolescents more often become depressed when their parents are emotionally distant and uninvolved, and when family life is stressful due to economic disadvantage or marital conflict (Karevold et al., 2009; Yap, Allen, & Ladouceur, 2008). Because African American and Hispanic adolescents more often live in poverty, they're more often depressed (Brown, Meadows, & Elder, 2007). Finally, when parents rely on punitive discipline—hitting and shouting—adolescents often resort to the negative attributions (e.g., blaming themselves) that can lead to depression (Lau et al., 2007).

Heredity also plays a role, putting some adolescents at greater risk for depression (Haeffel et al., 2008). Neurotransmitters may be the underlying mechanism: Some adolescents may feel depressed because lower levels of neurotransmitters make it difficult for them to experience happiness, joy, and other pleasurable emotions (Kaufman & Charney, 2003).

To treat depression, some adolescents take antidepressant drugs designed to correct the imbalance in neurotransmitters. However, drug treatment has no lasting effects—it only works while a person is taking the drugs—and it has been linked to increased risk of suicide (Vitiello & Swedo, 2004). Consequently, psychotherapy is a better choice for treating depressed adolescents. One common approach emphasizes cognitive and social skills; that is, adolescents learn how to have rewarding social interactions and to interpret them appropriately. These treatments *are* effective (Weisz, McCarty, & Valeri, 2006)—and depressed adolescents do need help. Left untreated, depression can interfere with performance in school and social relationships, and may also lead to recurring depression in adulthood (Nevid, Rathus, & Greene, 2003; Rudolph, Ladd, & Dinella, 2007). Also effective are prevention programs, which can substantially reduce the number of depressive episodes in high-risk youth (Stice et al., 2009).

Response to question on page 349 about Dea's ethnic identity: Dea, the Dutch Asian American high-school student, doesn't know how to integrate the Korean heritage of her biological parents with the Dutch American culture in which she was reared. This would put her in the second phase of acquiring an ethnic identity. On the one hand, she is examining her ethnic roots, which means she's progressed beyond the initial stage. On the other hand, she has not yet integrated her Asian and European roots, and so has not reached the third and final phase.

 ANSWER 11.1
Jenny appears to be in the moratorium status because she is actively exploring different alternatives.

 Check Your Learning

RECALL What evidence indicates that sense of self emerges during the second year of life? What contributes to the emergence of a sense of self?

Describe research that undermines the view of adolescence as a period of "storm and stress."

INTERPRET Compare and contrast the three stages in the achievement of an ethnic identity with Piaget's description of the concrete and formal operational stages of cognitive development.

APPLY The Tran family has just immigrated to the United States from Vietnam. The mother and father want their two children to grow up appreciating their Vietnamese heritage, but worry that a strong ethnic identity may not be good for their kids. What advice would you give Mr. and Mrs. Tran about the impact of ethnic identity on children's development?

 11.2 **Self-Esteem**

OUTLINE	LEARNING OBJECTIVES
Developmental Change in Self-Esteem	• How does self-esteem change as children develop?
Variations in Self-Esteem Associated with Ethnicity and Culture	• How does self-esteem vary depending on ethnicity and culture?
Sources of Self-Esteem	• What factors influence the development of self-esteem?
Low Self-Esteem: Cause or Consequence?	• Is children's development affected by low self-esteem?

Darnel, age 10, loves school, and for good reason: Every year, he is always one of the best students in his class. Darnel's mother, Karen, wants to enroll him in a program for gifted children, where she believes the pace will be more appropriate for her talented son. Darnel's dad, Jon, doesn't think this is such a great idea. He's afraid that if Darnel doesn't do well against all those other bright kids, his son will begin to doubt his academic ability.

Jon is concerned about Darnel's *self-esteem,* **which refers to a person's judgment and feelings about his or her own worth.** Children with high self-esteem judge themselves favorably and feel positive about themselves. In contrast, children with low self-esteem judge themselves negatively, are unhappy with themselves, and often would rather be someone else. In this module, we'll see how self-esteem changes as children develop and what forces shape it.

Developmental Change in Self-Esteem

Think about your own self-esteem. Do you think you have high self-esteem or low self-esteem? To help you answer this question, read each of these sentences and decide how well each applies to you:

> I'm very good at schoolwork.
>
> I find it very easy to make friends.
>
> I do very well at all kinds of different sports.
>
> I'm happy with the way I look.

If you agreed strongly with each of these statements, you definitely have high self-esteem.

When children and adolescents read these sentences, their responses reveal two important developmental changes in self-esteem: change in the structure of self-esteem and change in overall levels of self-esteem.

STRUCTURE OF SELF-ESTEEM.   By 4 or 5 years of age, which is the earliest we can measure self-esteem, children have a differentiated view of themselves. They can distinguish overall self-esteem as well as self-esteem in specific domains (Marsh, Ellis, & Craven, 2002). This structure should seem familiar because it's like intelligence: In Module 8.1, we saw that hierarchical theories of intelligence begin with a general intelligence that is divided into more specific abilities, such as verbal ability and spatial ability. In the case of self-esteem, overall self-esteem is at the top of the hierarchy, with self-esteem in more specialized areas underneath (Harter, 2006). In the elementary-school years, four specialized areas stand out:

In the elementary-school years, self-esteem reflects scholastic competence, athletic competence, social competence, and physical appearance.

- *Scholastic competence:* How competent or smart the child feels in doing schoolwork
- *Athletic competence:* How competent the child feels at sports and games requiring physical skill or athletic ability
- *Social competence:* How competent the child feels in relationships with parents and peers
- *Physical appearance:* How good-looking the child feels and how much the child likes his or her physical characteristics, such as height, weight, face, and hair

During the elementary-school years, children's academic self-concepts become even more specialized (Marsh & Craven, 2006; Marsh & Yeung, 1997). As children accumulate successes and failures in school, they form beliefs about their ability in different content areas (e.g., English, math, science), and these beliefs contribute to their overall academic self-concept. A child who believes that she is skilled at English and math but not so skilled in science will probably have a positive academic self-concept overall. But a child who believes he is untalented in most academic areas will have a negative academic self-concept.

During adolescence, other domains of self-esteem are added, including job competence, close friendships, and romantic appeal. What's more, the social component of self-esteem becomes particularly well differentiated. Adolescents distinguish self-worth in many different social relationships. A teenager may, for example, feel very positive about her relationships with her parents but believe that she's a loser in romantic relationships. Another teen may feel loved and valued by his parents but think that coworkers at his part-time job can't stand him (Harter, Waters, & Whitesell, 1998).

Children's overall self-worth is *not* simply the average of their self-worth in specialized areas. Instead, self-esteem in some domains contributes more than others. For many children and adolescents, self-esteem concerning appearance has the biggest influence on overall self-esteem (Shapka & Keating, 2005). Thus, Allison, whose self-worth in the academic, athletic, and social domains is just average, has high self-esteem overall because she believes that she's very good looking. In contrast, although Colleen has high self-esteem in academics and athletics, her overall self-esteem is only average because she considers herself relatively unattractive.

Thus, between the late preschool years and adolescence, self-esteem becomes more complex, as older children and adolescents identify distinct domains of self-worth. This growing complexity is not surprising—it reflects the older child's and adolescent's greater cognitive skill and the more extensive social world of older children and adolescents.

CHANGES IN LEVEL OF SELF-ESTEEM. At what age is self-esteem greatest? The answer may surprise you: it's during the preschool years. Most preschool children have very positive views of themselves across many different domains (Marsh, Ellis, & Craven, 2002). This outcome isn't surprising if you think back to Piaget's description of the preoperational period (Module 6.1). Preschool children are egocentric; they have difficulty taking another person's viewpoint. Unable to see themselves as others do, preschoolers blissfully believe that they are extremely competent in all domains.

As children progress through the elementary-school years, self-esteem usually drops somewhat. Why? In reality, of course, all children are *not* above average. During the elementary-school years, children begin to compare themselves with peers (Ruble et al., 1980). When they do, they discover that they are not necessarily the best readers or the fastest runners. They may realize, instead, that they are only average readers. Or, like the girl in the background of the photo, they come to understand that they are among the slowest runners in the class. This realization means that children's self-esteem usually drops somewhat at the beginning of elementary school.

By the end of the elementary-school years, children's self-esteem has usually stabilized (Harter, Whitesell, & Kowalski, 1992) as children learn their place in the "pecking order" of different domains and adjust their self-esteem accordingly. However, self-esteem sometimes drops when children move from elementary school to middle school or junior high (Twenge & Campbell, 2001). Apparently, when students from different elementary schools enter the same middle school or junior high, they know where they stand compared to their old elementary-school classmates but not compared to students from other elementary schools. Thus, peer comparisons begin anew, and self-esteem often suffers temporarily. But, as a new school becomes familiar and students gradually adjust to the new pecking order, self-esteem again increases.

Children's self-esteem is often influenced by comparisons with peers; a child who discovers that she's not a very fast runner may lose athletic self-esteem.

 QUESTION 11.2
During the summer, Karina moved with her family to a new city, where she will begin middle school. What will probably happen to Karina's self-esteem as she enters her new school?
(Answer is on page 359.)

Variations in Self-Esteem Associated with Ethnicity and Culture

The developmental changes in structure and average levels of self-esteem that I've just described are not universals. Instead, ethnicity and culture each influence important variations on these developmental trends. For example, growth of self-worth among U.S. children and adolescents varies depending on their ethnicity. Compared to European American children, African Americans and Hispanic Americans have lower self-esteem during most of the elementary-school years. However, in adolescence the gap narrows for Hispanic Americans and actually reverses for African American adolescents, who have greater self-esteem than their European American peers (Gray-Little & Hafdahl, 2000; Herman, 2004; Twenge & Crocker, 2002). Scientists don't fully understand why these changes take place, but one hypothesis involves ethnic identity. The idea is that beginning in early adolescence, many African American and Hispanic American teens take pride in belonging to a distinct social and cultural group, and this raises their sense of self-worth (Gray-Little & Hafdahl, 2000; Umaña-Taylor, Diversi, & Fine, 2002).

Cross-cultural studies reveal one consistent difference in self-esteem: Children from Asian countries (e.g., China, Japan, Korea) tend to have lower self-esteem than children from North America and Europe, and the difference increases in adolescence (Harter, 2006). Part of this difference is that Asian cultures emphasize modesty to a greater extent than Western cultures; as Asian youngsters internalize this cultural standard, they are reluctant to proclaim extremely positive feelings of self-worth (Cai et al., 2007).

Youth from Asian countries typically have lower self-esteem than youth from North America and Europe, particularly in adolescence.

But that's not the whole story. Asian adolescents are also more willing to admit their weaknesses (Hamamura, Heine, & Paulhus, 2008). Consequently, although Western adolescents often emphasize areas of strength but ignore weaknesses when estimating overall self-esteem (e.g., the example with Allison), Asian adolescents' global self-esteem is lower because it reflects strengths *and* weaknesses. Finally, the social-comparison process that fuels self-worth in Western countries is far less common in Asian cultures. Children in Western cultures compare themselves with others in their group and feel good about themselves when they come out on top. In contrast, Asian children and adolescents see themselves as integral parts of their social groups and eschew social comparisons because they can undermine group harmony (Falbo et al., 1997).

Sadly, at any age, in any domain, and in any group, it's easy to find children who do not view themselves very positively. Some children are ambivalent about their self-worth; others actually feel negative about themselves. In one study (Cole, 1991), roughly 25% of 9- and 10-year-olds had negative self-esteem in at least three domains. Why do these children have so little self-worth compared to their peers? We'll answer this question in the next section.

Sources of Self-Esteem

Why do some children feel so positive about themselves while others feel so negative? Research indicates two important sources of children's self-esteem. One is based on children's actual competence in domains that are important to them: Children's self-worth is greater when they are skilled in areas that matter to them. In other words, children's interests, abilities, and self-concept are coupled.

Children tend to like domains in which they do well, and their self-concepts reflect this (Denissen, Zarrett, & Eccles, 2007). Mark, who likes math and gets good grades in math, has a positive math self-concept: "I'm good at math and do well when I have to learn something new in math. And I'd probably like a job that involved math."

This explanation of self-esteem has implications for academically talented youngsters, like Darnel in the opening vignette, who might be placed in classes for gifted children. We examine these implications in the "Improving Children's Lives" feature.

Improving Children's Lives

Self-Esteem in Gifted Classes

In a traditional classroom of students with a wide range of ability, talented youngsters see that they're doing very well in class, and their academic self-esteem flourishes. But in classes for gifted students, many talented youngsters do only "average" work and some are "below average." Consequently, they sometimes lose sight of the bigger picture, believing themselves to be incompetent in a domain that's important to them, causing their academic self-esteem to drop (Marsh et al., 1995). Thus, accelerated academic progress may come at a price: Children's academic self-esteem may decline somewhat, even though their actual skills are improving.

What should parents like Karen and Jon (from the module-opening vignette) do when deciding whether to enroll their child in classes for gifted children? First, they should look honestly at their child and decide whether he or she values learning per se versus getting good grades. Students who insist on getting straight As will be more affected by the lower grades in a gifted class than students who are excited about mastering challenging academic material. Second, parents should find out whether common assignments and comparative evaluations are made, as in typical classrooms, or whether the gifted class emphasizes individualized work. The latter is more conducive to self-esteem because students can evaluate their performance based on the progress they've made, not by comparing their grades with other students' grades. Carefully considering these factors can help parents decide if a gifted program is likely to lower their child's self-esteem—a very unwelcome side effect.

Children's and adolescents' self-worth is also affected by how others view them, particularly other people who are important to them. Parents matter, of course—even to adolescents. Children are more likely to view themselves positively when their parents are affectionate toward them and involved with them (Lord, Eccles, & McCarthy, 1994; Ojanen & Perry, 2007). Around the world, children have higher self-esteem when families live in harmony and parents nurture their children (Scott, Scott, & McCabe, 1991). A father who routinely hugs his daughter and gladly takes her to piano lessons is saying to her, "You are important to me." When children hear this regularly from parents, they evidently internalize the message and come to see themselves positively.

Parents' discipline also is related to self-esteem. Children with high self-esteem generally have parents who have reasonable expectations for their children and are also willing to discuss rules and discipline with their children (Laible & Carlo, 2004). Parents who fail to set rules are, in effect, telling their children that they don't care; they don't value them enough to go to the trouble of creating rules and enforcing them. In much the same way, parents who refuse to discuss discipline with their children are saying, "Your opinions don't matter to me." Not surprisingly, when children internalize these messages, the result is lower overall self-worth.

Peers' views are important, too. Children's and particularly adolescents' self-worth is greater when they believe that their peers think highly of them (Harter, 2005). Lauren's self-worth increases, for example, when she hears that Pedro, Matt, and Michael think she's the hottest girl in the eighth grade. Conversely, self-esteem drops when peers provide negative feedback, especially when those peers are popular themselves (Thomas et al., 2010).

Thus, children's and adolescents' self-worth depends on their being competent at something they value and in being valued by people who are important to them. By encouraging children to find their special talents and by being genuinely interested in their progress, parents and teachers can enhance the self-esteem of all students.

Low Self-Esteem: Cause or Consequence?

Having low self-esteem is associated with many developmental problems (Baumeister et al., 2003). Children with low self-esteem are:

- More likely to have problems with peers (Parker et al., 2005; Rubin, Copland, & Bowker, 2009)
- More prone to psychological disorders such as depression (Boden, Fergusson, & Horwood, 2008; McDonald et al., 2005)
- More likely to be involved in bullying, aggressive behavior, and criminal activity (Donnellan et al., 2005; Trzesniewski et al., 2006)
- More likely to do poorly in school (Marsh & Yeung, 1997)

These outcomes provide an excellent opportunity to remember the difficulty in identifying causal forces from correlational studies. Does low self-esteem cause children to have few friends, because peers want to avoid them? Or do poor peer relations cause children to have low self-esteem? Either claim is plausible, and what often happens is that low self-esteem contributes to the outcome but is itself also caused by the outcome. For example, the claim that "low self-esteem leads to poor peer relations" is supported by findings that over the course of a school year, children with low social self-esteem often withdraw from peer interactions, and by year's end are more likely to be left out of social activities and to have few or no friends. But the claim that "poor peer relations reduce social self-worth" is also supported, this time by findings that children who have few friends at the beginning of a school year (but adequate social self-worth) tend to withdraw socially, and by year's end, their self-worth has dropped (Caldwell et al., 2004). Thus, poor peer relations reduce self-esteem in the peer context and disrupt future peer interactions,

> Children with low self-esteem typically have poor peer relations, are at risk for psychological disorders, are involved in antisocial activities, and do poorly in school.

causing social self-worth to drop even more, making children even less likely to have good peer relations—the cycle goes on and on.

A similar vicious circle applies to the link between low academic self-esteem and poor performance in school: Over time, children who are unskilled academically do not keep up in school, which causes a drop in their academic self-esteem, making them less confident and probably less successful in future school learning, causing their academic self-esteem to continue to fall (Marsh et al., 2005). Thus, low self-esteem is a cause of future harmful outcomes *and* a consequence of past harmful outcomes. Of course, the same kind of cycle can increase children's self-worth: success in academics, athletics, or social relationships can breed positive self-worth, which breeds more success.

Understanding this complex cause-effect-cause pattern is important in deciding how to help children with low self-esteem. Some children benefit directly from therapy that increases their low self-esteem. Others, however, who need to change their own behavior, also benefit from learning how to improve their social skills (a topic that I discuss again in Modules 12.4 and 15.1). And, we need to remember that all children have some talents that can be nurtured. Taking the time to recognize each child creates the feeling of "being special" that promotes self-esteem.

But I want to end this module on a cautionary note: There is widespread agreement that low self-esteem is not desirable and that parents and teachers should promote a child's sense of self-worth. However, for children and adolescents who are antisocial and aggressive, high self-esteem actually has a cost. These children and adolescents sometimes use their lofty sense of self-worth to justify their aggressive behavior. In other words, their sense of self-worth leads them to believe that they deserve the rewards that can be achieved with aggression and that they are entitled to push around their "lesser" peers (Menon et al., 2007). Thus, high self-worth actually puts antisocial, aggressive youth at risk for poor relationships with their peers, which can be quite harmful in the long run (as we'll see in Modules 12.4 and 15.1).

Thus far in this chapter, we've focused on children's growing understanding of themselves. In the next module, we'll look at parallel changes that occur in children's understanding of other people.

 ANSWER 11.2
Karina's self-esteem is likely to drop, at least temporarily, because she won't know "where she stands" in comparison to her new classmates (e.g., whether she still is one of the smartest kids, one of the best basketball players, etc.). After she's discovered where she fits in, her self-esteem will increase.

 ## Check Your Learning

RECALL What are the salient features of self-esteem during the elementary-school years?

Summarize the ways in which self-esteem changes during childhood and adolescence.

INTERPRET Explain the forces that lead some children to have high self-esteem but others to have low self-esteem.

APPLY Suppose you attended a presentation for parents of middle-school students in which a counselor emphasized the importance of children having high self-esteem. The counselor asserts that when children have low self-esteem, they do poorly in school and don't get along well with their peers. Would you agree or disagree with the counselor's claims? Why?

11.3   Understanding Others

OUTLINE

Describing Others

Understanding What Others
Think

Prejudice

LEARNING OBJECTIVES

● **As children develop, how do they describe others differently?**

● **How does understanding of others' thinking change as children develop?**

● **When do children develop prejudice toward others?**

When 12-year-old Ian agreed to baby-sit for his 5-year-old brother, Kyle, his mother reminded him to keep Kyle out of the basement because Kyle's birthday presents were there, unwrapped. But as soon as their mother left, Kyle wanted to go to the basement to ride his tricycle. When Ian told him no, Kyle burst into angry tears and shouted, "I'm gonna tell Mom you were mean to me!" Ian wished he could explain to Kyle, but he knew that would just cause more trouble!

We know from Modules 11.1 and 11.2 that Ian, as a young adolescent, has a growing understanding of himself. This vignette suggests that his understanding of other people is also growing. He understands why Kyle is angry, and he also knows that if he gives in to Kyle, his mother will be angry when she returns. Children's growing understanding of others is the focus of this module. We'll begin by looking at how children describe others, then examine their understanding of how others think. We'll also see how children's recognition of different social groups can lead to prejudices.

Describing Others

As children develop, their self-descriptions become richer, more abstract, and more psychological. These same changes occur in children's descriptions of others. Classic research conducted by Livesley and Bromley (1973) showed that children begin by describing other people in terms of concrete features, such as behavior and appearance, and progress to describing them in terms of abstract traits. For instance, when asked to describe a girl that she liked a lot, 5-year-old Tamsen said,

> Vanessa is short. She has black hair and brown eyes. She uses a wheelchair because she can't walk. She's in my class. She has dolls just like mine. She likes to sing and read.

Tamsen's description of Vanessa is probably not too different from the way she would have described herself: The emphasis is on concrete characteristics, such as Vanessa's appearance, possessions, and preferences. Contrast this with the following description, which Tamsen gave as a 10-year-old:

> Kate lives in my apartment building. She is a very good reader and is also good at math and science. She's nice to everyone in our class. And she's very funny. Sometimes her jokes make me laugh so-o-o hard! She takes piano lessons and likes to play soccer.

Tamsen's account still includes concrete features, such as where Kate lives and what she likes to do. However, psychological traits are also evident: Tamsen describes

Kate as nice and funny. By age 10, children move beyond the purely concrete and observable in describing others. During adolescence, descriptions become even more complex, as you can see in the following, from Tamsen as a 16-year-old:

> Jeannie is very understanding. Whenever someone is upset, she's there to give a helping hand. Yet, in private, Jeannie can be so sarcastic. She can say some really nasty things about people. But I know she'd never say that stuff if she thought people would hear it because she wouldn't want to hurt their feelings.

This description is more abstract: Tamsen now focuses on psychological traits such as understanding and concern for others' feelings. It's also more integrated: Tamsen tries to explain how Jeannie can be both understanding and sarcastic. Although she began, as a 7-year-old, by emphasizing concrete characteristics, as a 16-year-old she tries to integrate traits to form a cohesive picture.

More recent work also supports the trend to more abstract and richer psychological descriptions of others, but indicates that young children's understanding of other people is more sophisticated than is suggested by their verbal descriptions of people they know (Heyman, 2009). Indeed, modern work indicates that 4- and 5-year-olds have begun to think about other people in terms of psychological traits such as being smart, friendly, helpful, and shy. They can use behavioral examples to infer an underlying trait: Told about a child who won't share cookies or won't allow another child to play with a toy, 4- and 5-year-olds accurately describe the child as selfish. In addition, given information about a trait, they correctly predict future behavior: Told about a child who is shy, they believe that the child will not volunteer to help a puppeteer and will be quiet at a meal with many relatives (Liu, Gelman, & Wellman, 2007).

> *Children's descriptions of others first focus on concrete features, then on psychological traits, then on integrating different characteristics.*

One idiosyncrasy of young children's descriptions of others is they see others "through rose-colored glasses"—that is, until about 10 years of age, children have a bias to look for positive traits, not negative traits, in others. Young children are willing to believe that someone is smart (or friendly or helpful) based on relatively little evidence (and based on inconsistent evidence), but require much more evidence (and more consistent evidence) to decided that someone is mean or stupid. This bias may simply be an extension of children's positive evaluations of themselves—recall from page 355 that self-esteem is greatest in preschoolers and declines gradually during the elementary-school years (Boseovski, 2010).

Understanding What Others Think

One trademark of the preschool child's thinking is difficulty in seeing the world from another's point of view. Piaget's term for this was *egocentrism*, and it was a defining characteristic of his preoperational stage of development (see Module 6.1). In much the same way, preschool children's communication is often ineffective because they don't consider the listener's perspective when they talk (see Module 9.4). As children move beyond the preschool years, though, they realize that others see the world differently, both literally and figuratively. For example, in the module-opening vignette, 12-year-old Ian knows why his little brother, Kyle, is angry: Kyle thinks that Ian is being bossy and mean. Ian understands that Kyle doesn't know there is a good reason why he can't go to the basement.

Sophisticated understanding of how others think is achieved gradually throughout childhood and adolescence. Robert Selman (1980, 1981) has proposed a theory of how understanding others' thinking—or *perspective taking*—occurs. Selman's theory is based on two of Piaget's key assumptions: namely, that understanding of others occurs in stages and that movement from one stage to the next is based on cognitive development. Table 11-1 shows Selman's five stages of perspective taking.

TABLE 11-1

SELMAN'S STAGES OF PERSPECTIVE TAKING

Stage	Approximate Ages	Description
Undifferentiated	3–6 years	Children know that self and others can have different thoughts and feelings, but often confuse the two.
Social-informational	4–9 years	Children know that perspectives differ because people have access to different information.
Self-reflective	7–12 years	Children can step into another's shoes and view themselves as others do; they know that others can do the same.
Third-person	10–15 years	Children and adolescents can step outside the immediate situation to see how they and another person are viewed by a third person.
Societal	14 years to adult	Adolescents realize that a third person's perspective is influenced by broader personal, social, and cultural contexts.

To see the progression from stage to stage, imagine two boys arguing about what to do after school. One wants to go to a playground and the other wants to watch TV. If the boys were 5-year-olds (undifferentiated stage), neither would really understand why the other wants to do something different. Their reasoning is stone simple: "If I want to go to the playground, you should too!"

During the early elementary-school years (social-informational stage), each child understands that the other wants to do something different, and they explain their differing views in terms of the other person lacking essential information. Their thinking is along the lines, "I know that you want to watch TV, but if you knew what I knew, you'd want to go to the playground." By the late elementary-school years (self-reflective stage), the boys would understand that each wants to do something different and they could "step into the other's shoes" to understand why: "I know you want to go to the playground because you haven't been there all week."

In early adolescence (third-person stage), the boys could step even farther apart and imagine how another person (e.g., a parent or teacher) could view the disagreement. Finally, in late adolescence (societal stage), the boys (now young men, really) can remove themselves even further and appreciate, for example, that many people would think it's silly to watch TV on a beautiful sunny day.

> In Selman's theory, young children confuse their own and others' views, but adolescents can see their own and another's views from a third person's perspective.

As predicted by Selman's theory, as children get older, their reasoning moves through each stage, in sequence. In addition, regardless of age, children at more advanced cognitive levels tend to be at more advanced stages in perspective taking (Gurucharri & Selman, 1982; Krebs & Gillmore, 1982). However, many scientists are not convinced that more sophisticated perspective taking occurs in such a stage-like fashion; they believe that it improves steadily throughout childhood and adolescence (just as cognitive development is now seen to be more continuous than Piaget's theory predicted).

Some investigators have linked improved perspective taking to the developing theory of mind, described in Module 7.3 (Chandler & Carpendale, 1998). The traditional false-belief task, for example, reveals children's understanding that another person's actions are often based on their beliefs, even when those beliefs are wrong. As an illustration, suppose children hear the following story:

> Lindsay and Angela are in the park and see some kids playing softball. Lindsay wants to play, so she runs home for her glove. Angela waits at the park for her, but while Lindsay's away, the kids decide it's too hot for softball and leave to get some ice cream.

Children understand false belief if they say that Lindsay will return to the ball field (acting on her false belief that the kids are still playing ball). But we can add a new wrinkle to the story.

> As the kids are leaving the park, one of them thinks that Lindsay might like to join them for ice cream, so she calls Lindsay and tells her the plan.

Now children are asked: "Where does Angela think Lindsay thinks the kids are?" Children understand second-order belief if they say that Angela thinks that Lindsay will go to the ball field. **This sort of "he thinks that she thinks . . . " reasoning is known as** *recursive thinking.* It emerges at about 5 or 6 years of age and improves steadily during the elementary-school years, due to the combined effects of increased language skill and greater executive functioning (Miller, 2009).

One of the benefits of a developing appreciation of others' thoughts and viewpoints is that it allows children to get along better with their peers. That is, children who can readily take another's perspective are typically well liked by their peers (FitzGerald & White, 2003; LeMare & Rubin, 1987). Of course, mere understanding does not guarantee good social behavior; sometimes children who understand what another child is thinking take advantage of that child. In general, though, greater understanding of others seems to promote positive interactions, a topic that we'll discuss further in Chapter 12 on moral understanding and behavior.

 QUESTION 11.3

Gracie can hardly wait for her cousin Andrew to arrive for a week-long visit. Gracie knows that Andrew will want to go swimming right away because Gracie loves to swim. Based on this example, what stage of perspective taking is Gracie in? About how old is she?
(Answer is on page 369.)

Prejudice

As children learn more about others, they discover that people belong to different social groups, based on variables such as sex, ethnicity, and social class. By the preschool years, most children can distinguish males from females and can identify people from different racial groups (Nesdale, 2001). After children learn their membership in a specific group, they typically have an enhanced view of their own group. That is, preschool and kindergarten children attribute many positive traits, such as being friendly and smart, and few negative traits, such as being mean, to their own group (Bigler, Jones, & Lobliner, 1997; Patterson & Bigler, 2006).

Negative views of other groups form more slowly. In young children, negative views typically don't involve overt hostility; it's simply that other groups "come up short" when compared to one's own group (Aboud, 2003). However, when children believe that children from other groups dislike them or think they're better, then children's views of other groups become more negative (Nesdale et al., 2005).

As children move into the elementary-school years, their knowledge of racial stereotypes and prejudices increases steadily; by 10 or 11 years of age, most children are aware of broadly held racial stereotypes (Pauker, Ambady, & Apfelbaum, 2010). During these years, prejudice declines some, in part because children learn norms that discourage openly favoring their own group over others (Apfelbaum et al., 2008). But, as we'll see in the "Focus on Research" feature, this decline in overt bias does not mean that implicit bias declines.

Focus on Research

Developmental Profiles for Implicit and Explicit Racial Bias

Who were the investigators, and what was the aim of the study? Children's explicit bias for their own race usually declines during elementary school and continues to decline in adolescence and adulthood. Much less is known about the implicit or unconscious attitudes that children and adolescents harbor toward various groups. Andrew Scott Baron and Mahzarin R. Banaji (2006) wanted to learn whether the developmental decline in overt bias against other groups was accompanied by a similar decline in implicit bias.

How did the investigators measure the topic of interest? To measure explicit bias, participants were shown pairs of faces—one African American and one European American—and were asked which one they preferred. To measure implicit bias, Baron and Banaji used a version of the Implicit Association Test. On each trial, participants are presented one of four stimuli: an African American face, a European American face, a "good" word (love, nice), or a "bad" word (hate, mad). For some trials, participants are told to push one button when they see an African American face or a good word but a second button when they see a European American face or a bad word. For other trials, the rules are reversed: Now they push one button for an African American face or a bad word and a second button for a European American face or a good word. Participants are asked to answer as quickly as possible; if they have no implicit bias, then the pairing of race with good and bad words shouldn't affect how quickly they reply. But if participants have subtle, unconscious bias, it may take a fraction of a second longer to classify an African American face when the response involves pushing the same button as for "good" words. Consequently, the measure of implicit bias is the difference in response times on the two kinds of trials.

Who were the children in the study? They tested 27 6-year-olds, 30 10-year-olds, and 22 19-year-olds. All were European American and of middle-class status.

What was the design of the study? This study was part experimental, part correlational. The experimental part was in the Implicit Association Test, where response times were compared for two kinds of pairing: (1) African American/good words versus European American/bad words, and (2) African American/bad words versus European American/good words. The correlational part involved relations between the age of the participants and their biases (implicit and explicit). The study was cross-sectional because individuals at three ages (6, 10, and 19 years) were each tested once.

Were there ethical concerns with the study? No. The measures had been used extensively and posed no apparent risks to participants.

Explicit racial bias declines during the elementary-school years, but implicit racial bias does not.

What were the results? The top graph in Figure 11-2 shows explicit prejudice, which was measured as the percentage of times that a participant preferred European American faces. At 6 years of age, children are strongly biased, selecting European American faces four times more often than they pick African American faces. By adulthood, bias had disappeared. The bottom graph in Figure 11-2 shows implicit prejudice. At all ages, participants respond faster when African American faces are paired with bad words but European American faces are paired with good words, and there's no hint of a decline. (Although the values increase slightly in the graph, those differences were not statistically significant.)

What did the investigators conclude? Explicit and implicit measures of bias show very different profiles. As Baron and Banaji put it, "implicit race attitudes are acquired early and remain relatively stable across development, even though explicit attitudes become more egalitarian" (2006, p. 57).

What converging evidence would strengthen these conclusions? One limitation of the study concerns the sample. The results may be specific to children and adolescents who are middle-class European Americans. Testing samples from other populations—particularly from ethnic and racial minorities—would provide a much broader perspective on the development of implicit biases. Another limit is that the study only measured bias toward African Americans; assessing bias toward other groups (e.g., other racial groups as well as other common targets of discrimination, such as the elderly) would tell more about the extent of implicit biases during childhood and adolescence.

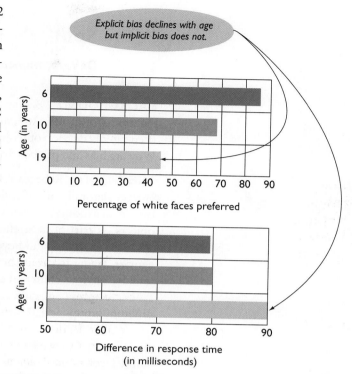

FIGURE 11-2

During early adolescence, prejudice sometimes increases again. This resurgence apparently reflects two different processes (Black-Gutman & Hickson, 1996; Teichman, 2001). One is experiential: Exposed to prejudices of those around them, children and adolescents internalize some of these views (Castelli, Zogmaister, & Tomelleri, 2009). A second process concerns adolescents' identity. In the search for identity (described on pages 347–350), adolescents' preferences for their own groups often intensify (Rutland, Killen, & Abrams, 2010). Thus, greater prejudice in older children and adolescents reflects both a more positive view of their own group and a more negative view of other groups. For example, Bob, a 14-year-old European American growing up in Arizona, becomes more prejudiced because he views his own European American heritage more positively and acquires prejudicial attitudes toward Native Americans from his parents and peers.

Identifying *how* children form actual prejudices is challenging because ethical concerns limit us to correlational studies. In the "Spotlight on Theories" feature, we'll look at one approach in which bias and prejudice is a natural by-product of children's efforts to understand their social worlds.

Spotlight on Theories

Developmental Intergroup Theory

BACKGROUND   Bias and prejudice emerge early in development and are found in children worldwide. And, although I've emphasized racial bias in this module, children rapidly develop other biases as well, such as gender bias (the topic of Chapter 13). Why are bias and prejudice so prevalent, and why do they develop so early?

THE THEORY   Rebecca Bigler and Lynn Liben (2007) believe that bias and prejudice emerge naturally out of children's efforts to understand their social world. You'll recall, from Module 6.3, that young children actively categorize animate and inanimate objects, as part of their effort to understand the world around them. As children's social horizons expand beyond their parents to include peers, they continue to categorize, trying to decide how different groups of people "go together." That is, they look for obvious clues that could be used to distinguish people. They use perceptually salient features (e.g., race, gender, age) as well as verbal labels that adults may apply to different groups (e.g., "Girls go to lunch first, then the boys").

After children have identified the salient features that define peers in their environment, they begin to classify people whom they encounter along these dimensions. Jacob is now seen as a White boy; Kalika is now seen as a Black girl. Finally, children seek to learn more about each of the groups that they have defined. As they do this, their thinking is guided by essentialism, the belief that individuals who belong to the same group share internal, unseen similarities (i.e., essences). In addition, they are biased toward their own group and generate more favorable characterizations of its members.

> Bias and prejudice develop, in part, out of children's efforts to understand the social world, which leads them to group people based on salient features.

Hypothesis: The first step in forming bias is detecting features in a setting that distinguish groups of people. Consequently, making a person-related feature more salient in an environment should make it more likely that this feature will contribute to bias. In other words, if teachers insisted that all left-handed children wear gloves on the left hand and right-handed children wear gloves on the right hand, this would make handedness a salient feature of people in the environment and should lead children to favor same-handed peers.

Test: Patterson and Bigler (2006) tested 3- to 5-year-olds attending day care. They were assigned to a "red group" or a "blue group" and wore red or blue T-shirts every day. In classrooms in the experimental group, teachers used the color names to refer to children (e.g., "Good morning, Blues!") and to organize the classroom (e.g., they created lines of Reds and Blues to leave the classroom). In classrooms in the control group, the children wore colored T-shirts but teachers never referred to them or used color names in any way.

After 3 weeks, children's perceptions and preferences were measured. As predicted, when teachers made color an important feature of the social world, children developed bias toward their own group. For example, children in these classrooms (a) believed that a new student would want to join their group, (b) said that they were happier than students in the other group, and (c) expressed greater liking for children in their own group and played with those children more often. In the control classrooms—where teachers did not mention color—children developed none of these biases.

Conclusion: As predicted, children developed bias in favor of their own color group when teachers made color salient in the day-care environment. This finding supports the general view that bias and prejudice are a natural by-product of children's efforts to determine the features in an environment that distinguish different groups.

Application: Because children are eager to know more about their social worlds and they categorize so skillfully, they easily notice features that signal group differences. This means that parents in particular and society in general face a huge challenge in reducing or eliminating bias. Parents can encourage their children to interact in multiracial groups of boys and girls, so that neither race nor gender is as salient for children. Institutions can have comparable policies. For example, teachers can be very careful to avoid use of gender labels in their classrooms (just as they avoid racial labels).

Unfortunately, the best efforts along these lines may reduce bias, but are unlikely to eliminate it. Hence, it is important to know about ways to deal with bias after it's formed. We'll look at this next.

What can parents, teachers, and other adults do to rid children of prejudice? One way is to encourage contacts between children from different groups. However, contact alone usually accomplishes little. Instead, intergroup contact reduces prejudice:

- When the participating groups of children are equal in status
- When the contact between groups involves pursuing common goals (instead of competing) and encourages children to think of groups as part of a larger, common group, and
- When parents and teachers support the goal of reducing prejudice (Cameron et al., 2006; Killen & McGlothlin, 2005)

To illustrate, adults might have children from different groups work together on a class project, as shown in the photo. In sports, the common task might be mastering a new skill. By working together, Gary starts to realize that Vic acts, thinks, and feels as he does simply because he's Vic, not because he's an Italian American.

Another useful approach is to ask children to play different roles (Davidson & Davidson, 1994; Tynes, 2007). They can be asked to imagine that, because of their race, ethnic background, or sex, they have been insulted verbally or not allowed to participate in special activities. A child might be asked to imagine that she can't go to a private swimming club because she's African American or that she wasn't invited to a party because she's Hispanic. Afterward, children reflect on how they felt when prejudice and discrimination were directed at them. They're also asked to think about what would be fair—what should be done in situations like these?

One way to reduce children's prejudice is to have children from different groups work together toward a common goal, such as completing a school assignment.

A final strategy involves education. In one study (Hughes, Bigler, & Levy, 2007), European American elementary-school children learned about the racism that famous African Americans experienced. For example, they learned that Jackie Robinson played for a team in the old Negro Leagues because the White people in charge of Major League Baseball wouldn't allow any African Americans to play. There was also a control group in which the biographies omitted the experiences of racism. When children learned about racism directed at African Americans, they had much more positive attitudes toward African Americans.

From such experiences, children and adolescents discover for themselves that a person's membership in a social group tells us very little about that person. They learn, instead, that all children are different, each a unique mix of experiences, skills, and values.

Increasing interaction between children of different racial groups was one of the consequences of the U.S. Supreme Court's decision in *Brown v. Board of Education*, a case that shows how child-development research influenced social policy.

Child Development and Family Policy

Ending Segregated Schools

In 1950, African American and White children in much of the United States attended separate schools. Segregated schooling had been the law of the land for more than 100 years, bolstered by several famous Supreme Court decisions. In the fall of 1950, the chapter of the National Association for the Advancement of Colored People (NAACP) in Topeka, Kansas, decided to test the constitutionality of the law. Thirteen African American parents, including Oliver Brown, attempted to enroll their children in White-only schools; when they were turned away, the NAACP sued the Topeka Board of Education.

A key element in the NAACP's case was that separate schools were inherently harmful to African American children because such schools apparently legitimized their second-class status. To support this claim, the NAACP legal team relied on testimony from Dr. Kenneth B. Clark. In previous work, Clark (1945; Clark & Clark, 1940) had shown that African American children typically thought that White dolls were "nice" but that brown dolls were "bad." He found the same results in African American children attending segregated Topeka schools, leading him to testify that:

> these children . . . like other human beings who are subjected to an obviously inferior status in the society in which they live, have been definitely harmed in the development of their personalities. . . .

In May 1954, the Supreme Court rendered the landmark decision that segregated schools were unconstitutional. The impact of Clark's research and testimony was evident in the decision in *Brown v. Board of Education*, delivered by Chief Justice Earl Warren:

> Segregation of white and colored children in public schools has a detrimental effect upon the colored children. The impact is greater when it has the sanction of the law, for the policy of separating the races is usually interpreted as denoting the inferiority of the negro group. A sense of inferiority affects the motivation of

Dr. Kenneth B. Clark's research on prejudice was influential in the Supreme Court's ruling that segregated schools are unconstitutional.

a child to learn. Segregation with the sanction of law, therefore, has a tendency to [retard] the educational and mental development of negro children and to deprive them of . . . benefits they would receive in a racial[ly] integrated school system.

After the *Brown* decision, Clark continued his work on civil rights and worked on behalf of African American youth. For his lifelong effort to inform public policy on African American children and their families, in 1987 he received the Gold Medal for Life Achievement in Psychology in the Public Interest from the American Psychological Foundation; he died in 2005.

Clark's work is a compelling demonstration of the manner in which child-development research can have far-reaching implications for policy—in this case, helping to eliminate racially segregated schools in America. The integrated schools that resulted have helped to reduce prejudice by providing children with opportunities to learn about peers from other ethnic and racial groups.

 ## Check Your Learning

RECALL Describe the different stages in Selman's theory of perspective taking.

Summarize developmental change in prejudice.

INTERPRET Compare developmental change in children's descriptions of others with developmental change in children's self-concept (described in Module 11.1).

APPLY Based on what you've learned in this module, what can parents and teachers do to discourage prejudice in children?

 ANSWER 11.3
Gracie is confusing what she wants to do ("I love to swim and can't wait to go!") with what Andrew wants to do (which she doesn't know). This would put her in Selman's un-differentiated stage because she is confusing her thoughts with his. And this means she's probably between 3 and 6 years old.

UNIFYING THEMES   Nature and Nurture

This chapter is a good occasion to feature the theme that *development is always jointly influenced by heredity and environment.* The emergence of self-awareness between 15 and 24 months is primarily due to biological forces. Regardless of circumstances, children become self-aware between the ages of 1 and 2. However, elaborating self-awareness into a specific self-concept depends largely on a child's experiences at home and in school. The specific direction that children take in establishing an identity is strongly influenced by those around them, particularly their parents and teachers.

See for Yourself

The mirror recognition task, described on page 344, is great fun to do, and you'll be astonished by the rapid change in children's responses between 1 and 2 years. For this task, you simply need a mirror, some tissue, blush, and a few cooperative parents of 12- to 18-month-olds. Have the parents play with their toddler near the mirror and, in the process, wipe the toddler's nose with a tissue that has blush on it. Then see how the toddler responds to the now-red nose.

Some 12-month-olds will do nothing; others will touch the red nose in the mirror. When the 15- or 18-month-olds see themselves, though, they should stop, get a curious expression on their faces, and then reach up to touch their own noses. See for yourself!

Summary

11.1 Who Am I? Self-Concept

Origins of Self-Recognition

At about 15 months, infants begin to recognize themselves in the mirror, one of the first signs of self-recognition. They also begin to prefer to look at pictures of themselves, to refer to themselves by name and with personal pronouns, and sometimes to know their age and gender. Evidently, by 2 years, most children have the rudiments of self-awareness.

The Evolving Self-Concept

Preschoolers often define themselves in terms of observable characteristics, such as possessions, physical characteristics, preferences, and competencies. During the elementary-school years, self-concept begins to include emotions, a child's membership in social groups, and comparisons with peers. During adolescence, self-concept includes attitudes, personality traits, beliefs, and future plans. In general, adolescents' self-concepts are more abstract, more psychological, and more future oriented than self-concepts in younger children.

The Search for Identity

The search for identity typically involves four statuses. Diffusion and foreclosure are more common in early adolescence; moratorium and achievement are more common in late adolescence and young adulthood. Adolescents are most likely to achieve an identity when parents encourage discussion and recognize their autonomy; they are least likely to achieve an identity when parents set rules and enforce them without explanation.

Adolescents from ethnic groups often progress through three phases in acquiring an ethnic identity: initial disinterest, exploration, and identity achievement. Achieving an ethnic identity usually results in higher self-esteem but is not consistently related to the strength of one's identification with mainstream culture.

Contrary to myth, adolescence is not usually a period of storm and stress. Most adolescents love their parents, feel loved by them, rely on them for advice, and adopt their values. The parent–child relationship becomes more egalitarian during the adolescent years, reflecting adolescents' growing independence. A small number of adolescents become depressed, often because their explanations of their own behavior are flawed.

11.2 Self-Esteem

Developmental Change in Self-Esteem

Global self-esteem is very high during the preschool years but declines in the elementary-school years as children start to compare themselves to peers. Self-esteem also declines, temporarily, when children make school transitions. Self-esteem becomes more differentiated in older children and adolescents as they evaluate themselves on more aspects of self-esteem, including different types of academic skills.

Variations in Self-Esteem Associated with Ethnicity and Culture

Ethnicity and culture each influence important variations on the developmental changes in structure and average levels of self-esteem. African American and Hispanic American children have lower self-esteem in childhood but self-esteem increases in adolescence. Children from Asian countries tend to have lower self-esteem than children from North America and Europe, reflecting internalization of a cultural standard of modesty, ready admission of weaknesses, and less frequent comparison with peers.

Sources of Self-Esteem

Children's self-esteem is greater when parents are affectionate and involved with them and when parents set rules and discuss disciplinary action. Self-esteem also depends on peer comparisons. Self-esteem is usually greater when children know that others view them positively.

Low Self-Esteem: Cause or Consequence?

When children have low self-esteem, they are more likely to have poor peer relations, suffer psychological disorders such as depression, be involved in antisocial activities, and do poorly in school. Therapy and improved social skills can enhance children's self-esteem.

11.3 Understanding Others

Describing Others

Children's descriptions of others change in much the same way that their descriptions of themselves change. During the early elementary-school years, descriptions emphasize concrete characteristics. In the late elementary-school years, they emphasize personality traits. In adolescence, they emphasize an integrated picture of a person. Children use their descriptions to predict others' behaviors.

Understanding What Others Think

According to Selman's perspective-taking theory, children's understanding of how others think progresses through five stages. In the first, the undifferentiated stage, children often confuse their own and another's view. In the last, the societal stage, adolescents take a third person's perspective and understand that this perspective is influenced by context.

Prejudice

Prejudice emerges in the preschool years, soon after children recognize different social groups. Prejudice declines during childhood but often increases in older children and adolescents. The best way to reduce prejudice is with additional exposure to individuals from other social groups, through role play that allows children to experience prejudice and discrimination, and by educating children about racism.

Test Yourself

✓•⌐Study and Review on mydevelopmentlab.com

1. Because toddlers _____, use personal pronouns, and point to themselves in photos, scientists conclude that they have (at least) rudimentary self-awareness.

2. _____ define themselves in terms of their physical characteristics, possessions, and preferences.

3. An emphasis on the future is unique to self-concept during _____.

4. In the _____ status, individuals have not explored alternatives but have an identity determined largely by adults.

5. Adolescents are more likely to achieve an ethnic identity when _____.

6. Adolescence is not a period of storm and stress for most families, but it can be for adolescents who _____.

7. During the elementary-school years, domains of self-esteem include scholastic competence, _____, social competence, and physical appearance.

8. Self-esteem is greatest during _____.

9. During childhood, Hispanic Americans and African Americans often have lower self-esteem than European Americans; but during adolescence _____.

10. Children with high self-esteem often have parents whose disciplinary practices are characterized by _____.

11. Research designed to determine whether low self-esteem is a cause or consequence of developmental problems suggests that _____.

12. Young children's descriptions of others are unusual in that they _____.

13. Children who are more skilled in taking the perspective of others typically _____.

14. Prejudice typically increases in adolescence because teens internalize some prejudiced views of those around them and _____.

15. Contact between diverse groups of children can reduce prejudice when the groups have equal status, the contact involves pursuit of mutual goals, and _____.

Answers: (1) recognize themselves in a mirror; (2) Preschool children; (3) adolescence; (4) foreclosure; (5) their parents encourage them to learn about their heritage and prepare them for discrimination; (6) don't regulate their emotions well; (7) athletic competence; (8) the preschool years; (9) the gap narrows for Hispanic Americans and reverses for African Americans; (10) rules and reasonable expectations, paired with a willingness to discuss discipline; (11) both are true, in that low self-esteem can lead to developmental problems, which further lower self-esteem, creating a vicious circle; (12) consistently look for good things in others, not bad things; (13) get along better with peers; (14) their search for identity leads them to have a more positive view of their own group; (15) parents support the goal of reducing prejudice.

Key Terms

achievement   348
adolescent egocentrism   347
diffusion   348
ethnic identity   349

foreclosure   348
illusion of invulnerability   347
imaginary audience   347
moratorium   348

personal fable   347
recursive thinking   363
self-concept   343
self-esteem   354

12

Moral Understanding and Behavior

12.1

Self-Control

12.2

Reasoning About Moral Issues

12.3

Helping Others

12.4

Aggression

Consider the following hypothetical situation. You enter a nursery filled with 2-day-olds. The babies look like babies in any nursery—some are asleep, some are crying, others are simply lying quietly. However, the nurse tells you that the newborns include Mother Teresa, Adolf Hitler, Mohandas Gandhi, and Martin Luther King, Jr. Although seemingly identical now, three of the newborns will rank among the 20th century's greatest figures and one will be guilty of unspeakable horrors. Why? What determines whether children act morally or immorally? Whether they care about others or take from others? Whether they become samaritans or follow a path of evil? The four modules in this chapter provide some answers to these questions. In **Module** **12.1**, we'll see how children learn to control their behavior. In **Module 12.2**, we'll look at how children and adolescents reason about moral issues, and in **Module 12.3**, we'll look at factors that encourage children to be kind to others. Finally, in **Module 12.4**, we'll see why children act aggressively toward others.

12.1 Self-Control

OUTLINE

Beginnings of Self-Control

Influences on Self-Control

Improving Children's Self-Control

LEARNING OBJECTIVES

- **When does self-control begin, and how does it change as children develop?**
- **What factors influence children's ability to maintain self-control?**
- **What strategies can children use to improve their self-control?**

Shirley returned from a long day at work tired but eager to celebrate her son Ryan's fourth birthday. Her excitement quickly turned to dismay when she discovered that Ryan had taken a huge bite of icing from the birthday cake while the babysitter fixed lunch. Before she had left for work that morning, Shirley had explicitly told Ryan not to touch the cake. Why couldn't Ryan wait? Why did he give in to temptation? What could she do to help Ryan control himself better in the future?

In this vignette, Shirley wishes that Ryan had greater *self-control,* **the ability to control one's behavior and to inhibit impulsive responding to temptations.** A child who obeys a parent's request that she not touch a nicely wrapped present is showing self-control, as is an adolescent who studies for an exam instead of going to the mall with his friends, knowing that tomorrow he can enjoy the mall and a good grade on his exam.

Self-control is one of the first steps toward moral behavior, because children must learn that they cannot constantly do whatever tempts them at the moment. Instead, society has rules for behavior in certain situations, and children must learn to restrain themselves.

In this module, we'll first see how self-control emerges during the preschool years. Then we'll learn some of the factors that determine how well children control themselves. Finally, we'll look at strategies that children use to improve their self-control.

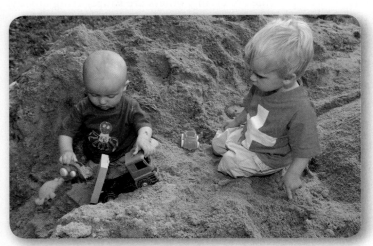

By 2 years of age, many children have enough self-control that they can resist the temptation to take an interesting toy away from another child.

 QUESTION 12.1

Two-year-old Amanda spilled a cup filled with juice, just after she'd been asked to leave it on the counter. Amanda's dad thinks she should be disciplined for disobeying a direct instruction; her mom thinks Amanda is too young to control herself. How would you advise Amanda's parents? *(Answer is on page 378.)*

Beginnings of Self-Control

In the cartoon at the bottom of the page, Calvin shows little self-control. Is he typical for his age? Thankfully, no. Self-control emerges in infancy and gradually improves during the preschool years (Kopp, 1997; Li-Grining, 2007). A rough chronology looks like this:

- At approximately the first birthday, infants become aware that people impose demands on them and they must react accordingly. Infants learn that they are not entirely free to behave as they wish; instead, others set limits on what they can do. These limits reflect both concern for their safety ("Don't touch! It's hot") as well as early socialization efforts ("Don't grab Ravisha's toy").

- At about 2 years, toddlers have internalized some of the controls imposed by others and are capable of some self-control in parents' absence. For example, although the boy on the left in the photo certainly looks as if he wants to play with the toy that the other toddler has, so far he has inhibited his desire to grab the toy, perhaps because he remembers that his parents have told him not to take things from others.

- At about 3 years, children become capable of self-regulation; they can devise ways to control their own behavior. To return to the example of a playmate's interesting toy, children might tell themselves that they really don't want to play with it, or they might turn to another activity that removes the temptation to grab the toy.

Of course, although preschoolers are able to regulate impulsive behavior somewhat, effective control is achieved only gradually throughout the elementary-school years (Vazsonyi & Huang, 2010). One way to chart this long developmental trek is with studies of delay of gratification, in which children are offered the choice of a relatively small reward immediately or a much larger reward if they wait. In one study (Lemmon & Moore, 2007), 3-year-olds preferred to earn one sticker immediately

Calvin and Hobbes
by Bill Watterson

MOM AND DAD SAY I SHOULD MAKE MY LIFE AN EXAMPLE OF THE PRINCIPLES I BELIEVE IN.

BUT EVERY TIME I DO, THEY TELL ME TO STOP IT.

I'M NOT SURE THAT TOTAL SELF-INDULGENCE IS REALLY A PRINCIPLE.

6-28 © 1993 Watterson/Distributed by Universal Press Syndicate instead of receiving five stickers later, at the end of the game. Basically, these youngsters were not willing to delay gratification at all! In contrast, 4-year-olds were willing to wait for four or five stickers but not for two or three stickers. In another study (Rotenberg & Mayer, 1990), children and adolescents were offered the choice of a small piece of candy immediately or an entire bag of chips if they waited 1 day. About one-third of the 6- to 8-year-olds opted to wait for the chips. In contrast, half of the 9- to 11-year-olds and nearly all of the 12- to 15-year-olds waited a day for the chips. Thus, although self-control may be evident in toddlers, mastery occurs gradually throughout childhood.

> Preschool children who have better self control often become adolescents who are more attentive and have higher SAT scores and become adults who have higher self-esteem.

Perhaps you wonder about the validity of these tasks. That is, are these tasks measuring important aspects of self-control in children's natural environments? Mothers' reports of their youngsters' self-control represent one source of evidence for the validity of these tasks. Children who are less likely to touch prohibited toys are, according to their mothers' reports, more likely to spontaneously confess to misdeeds at home and more likely to do as asked at home, without parental supervision (Kochanska et al., 1994).

Even more remarkable are the results from longitudinal studies on the long-term consistency of self-control. These studies find that preschoolers' self-control predicts outcomes in adolescence and young adulthood. For example, preschoolers who show the greatest self-control are, as adolescents, more attentive, have higher SAT scores, and are less likely to experiment with drugs and alcohol (Shoda, Mischel, & Peake, 1990). What's more, as young adults, they are better educated, have higher self-esteem, and have better cognitive control (Ayduk et al., 2000; Eigsti et al., 2006).

Obviously, individuals differ in their ability to resist temptation, and this characteristic is remarkably stable over time. But why are some children and adults better able than others to exert self-control? As you'll see in the next section of this module, parents and children's temperament both contribute to children's self-control.

Influences on Self-Control

Parents like Shirley are disappointed and upset when their children lack self-control. What can parents do? Research consistently links greater self-control with a disciplinary style in which parents are warm and loving but establish well-defined limits on what behavior is acceptable (Feldman & Klein, 2003; Vazsonyi & Huang, 2010). Self-control is enhanced when parents discuss disciplinary issues with their children instead of simply asserting their power as parents (e.g., "You'll do it because I say so"). When Shirley disciplines Ryan, she should remind him of the clear behavioral standard (not touching the cake), explain her disappointment ("Now nobody else will see how pretty your cake was!"), and suggest ways that he could resist similar temptations in the future.

Research also shows that children's self-control is usually *lower* when parents are very strict with them (Donovan, Leavitt, & Walsh, 2000; Feldman & Wentzel, 1990). By constantly directing them to do one thing but not another, parents do not give their children either the opportunity or the incentive to internalize control (Kochanska, Coy, & Murray, 2001).

But parents aren't the only important influence on children's self-control; remember, from Module 10.2, that temperament also matters. One dimension of temperament is effortful control, which describes a child's ability to focus attention, to ignore distraction, and to inhibit inappropriate responses. Thus, some children are simply temperamentally better suited to maintain self-control and regulate their behavior (Stifter et al., 2009).

Temperament also influences how children respond to parents' efforts to teach self-control. Youngsters who are temperamentally fearful and anxious usually comply with parental requests because they are typically anxious about not following instructions, getting caught, or having to confess to a misdeed. In contrast, children who are not naturally fearful at the thought of misdeeds are more likely to comply when parents appeal to the child to cooperate, based on the strong attachment relationship between parent and child. In other words, temperamentally fearless children comply with parental requests out of positive feelings for a loved one, not out of distress caused by fear of misdeeds (Kochanska & Aksan, 2006).

Of course, regardless of their temperament, children are not perfectly consistent in their self-control. Children who are able to resist temptation on one occasion may give in the next time. Why do children show self-control on some tasks but not on others? As we'll see in the next section, the answer lies in children's plans for resisting temptation.

Improving Children's Self-Control

Imagine it's one of the first nice days of spring. You have two major exams that you should study for, but it's so-o-o-o tempting to spend the entire day with your friends, sitting in the sun. What do you do to resist this temptation and stick to studying? You might remind yourself that these exams are very important. You might also move to a windowless room to keep your mind off the tempting weather. Stated more generally, effective ways to resist temptation include (a) reminding yourself of the importance of long-term goals over short-term temptations and (b) reducing the attraction of the tempting event or circumstance.

During the preschool years, some youngsters begin to use both of these methods spontaneously. In an experiment by Mischel and Ebbesen (1970), 3- to 5-year-olds were asked to sit alone in a room for 15 minutes. If they waited the entire time, they would receive a desirable reward. Children could call the experimenter back to the room at any time by a prearranged signal; in this case, they would receive a much less desirable reward.

Some children, of course, were better able than others to wait the full 15 minutes. How did they do it? Some children talked to themselves: "I've gotta wait to get the best prize!" As Vygotsky described (Module 6.2), these youngsters were using private speech to control their own behavior. Others, like the child in the photograph, sang. Still others invented games. All were effective techniques for enduring 15 boring minutes to receive a desired prize.

Later studies show that children are far better able to delay gratification when they have a concrete way of handling tempting situations (Mischel & Ayduk, 2004). Effective plans include (a) reminders to avoid looking at the tempting object; (b) reminders of rules against touching a tempting object; and (c) activities designed to divert attention from the tempting object, such as playing with other objects. The Focus on Research feature shows the benefits of plans like these.

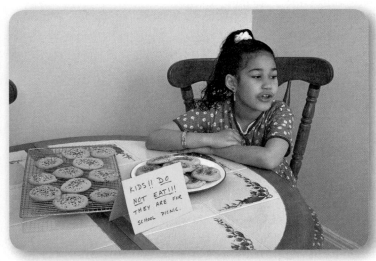

One way to resist the temptation of desirable objects is to think about something else or do something else, such as singing.

Focus on Research

Engaging Preschool Children to Help Them Delay Gratification

Who were the investigators, and what was the aim of the study? Philip Peake and his colleagues Michelle Hebl and Walter Mischel (2002) wanted to determine the conditions that would help children delay gratification. That is, they hoped to learn ways to help children resist the temptation to take a lesser reward immediately and instead wait for a better reward later.

How did the investigators measure the topic of interest? Peake and his colleagues tested children on a classic task. Children were shown two rewards and asked which they preferred. Children in a control condition were told that the experimenter had to leave the room for a while but that if they waited patiently until the experimenter returned, they would get their chosen reward. They were also told that at any time they could ring a bell for the experimenter to return, but if they did so they would receive the less-preferred reward. Children in another condition were given these same instructions but were also shown a large bucket of colored marbles and told that they could pass the time by sorting the marbles into color-coded cups. In a third condition, a jar with a tube was decorated to look like a baby bird; children were told that they could pass the time by putting marbles down the tube to "feed the bird." (Prior work had shown that children considered this much more fun than sorting marbles.) The experimenter recorded the length of time that children waited and recorded where they looked while waiting. For all children, both rewards remained on display, thus serving as tempting objects while they waited.

Who were the children in the study? Peake and his colleagues tested 30 3- to 5-year-olds.

What was the design of the study? This study was experimental. The independent variable was the conditions under which children waited: alone with nothing to do, with marbles to sort, or feeding the bird. The study had two dependent variables: the length of time that children waited and the amount of time they spent looking at the rewards. The study was neither longitudinal nor cross-sectional because all children were approximately the same age and each was only tested once.

Were there ethical concerns with the study? No. The tasks involved minimal risk and weren't much different from experiences that children would encounter in daily life.

What were the results? Let's begin by looking at how long children waited. The top panel of Figure 12-1 shows that children waited longest when they performed an engaging task (feeding the bird). They waited next longest when performing the boring task (sorting marbles), and waited the least when they had nothing to do. The bottom panel of Figure 12-1 helps to explain why: With nothing to do, children spent nearly half the time just looking at the rewards. It's no wonder that they gave into temptation early. In contrast, when children were engaged in tasks, they rarely looked at the rewards.

What did the investigators conclude? Left to their own devices—"just wait here"—preschool children weren't very successful in controlling their behavior in the face of temptation. But when their attention was engaged elsewhere—particularly with the interesting task—they were much more successful in delaying gratification. Thus, a critical part of resisting temptation is "the ability to control the direction of attention, to strategically self-distract, and to move the focus of attention flexibly across a situation" (p. 325).

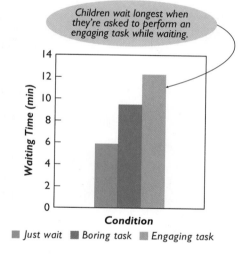

Children wait longest when they're asked to perform an engaging task while waiting.

■ *Just wait* ■ *Boring task* ■ *Engaging task*

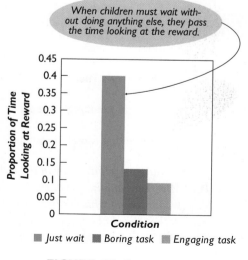

When children must wait without doing anything else, they pass the time looking at the reward.

■ *Just wait* ■ *Boring task* ■ *Engaging task*

FIGURE 12-1

What converging evidence would strengthen these conclusions? Peake and his colleagues measured children's self-control with a specially designed task. Consequently, a useful next step would be to complement the results from those tasks with observations of self-control as it occurs naturally in children's homes. Also, because 3- to 5-year-olds have hardly mastered self-control, another logical extension would be to test older children.

 ANSWER 12.1
All other things being equal, I'd side with Amanda's dad. A typical 2-year-old should be able to control himself or herself when the standard is clear and reasonable, which it seems to be in this case.

Overall, then, how children think about tempting objects or outcomes makes all the difference. Even preschoolers can achieve self-control by making plans that include appropriate self-instruction. For example, in the vignette, Shirley could have helped Ryan make a plan to resist temptation. She might have told him, "When you feel like you want to eat some cake, tell yourself, 'No cake until Mom gets home' and go play in your bedroom."

As children learn to regulate their own behavior, they also begin to learn about moral rules—cultural rights and wrongs—which are described in the next module.

 ## Check Your Learning

RECALL Describe the three phases in the emergence of self-control during infancy and the preschool years.

How does temperament influence a child's self-control?

INTERPRET What does longitudinal research on preschool children's ability to delay gratification tell us about the continuity of development?

APPLY Shirley described the birthday cake episode to her own mother, who replied, "It's simple, my dear. You're the parent. He's the kid. You're the boss. Tell him what to do." What would you say to Shirley's mom?

 12.2 ## Reasoning About Moral Issues

OUTLINE	LEARNING OBJECTIVES
Piaget's Views	• How does reasoning about moral issues change during childhood and adolescence?
Kohlberg's Theory	• How do concern for justice and caring for other people contribute to moral reasoning?
Beyond Kohlberg's Theory	• What factors help promote more sophisticated reasoning about moral issues?
Promoting Moral Reasoning	• How can youth be encouraged to reason at more advanced levels?

Howard, the least popular boy in the eighth grade, had been wrongly accused of stealing a sixth-grader's iPod. Min-shen, another sixth-grader, knew that Howard was innocent but said nothing to the school principal for fear of what his friends would say about siding with Howard. A few days later, when Min-shen's father heard about the incident, he was upset that his son apparently had so little "moral fiber." Why hadn't Min-shen acted in the face of an injustice?

On one of the days when I was writing this module, my local paper had two articles about youth from the area. One article was about a 14-year-girl who was badly burned while saving her younger brothers from a fire in their apartment. Her mother said she wasn't surprised by her daughter's actions, because the daughter had always been an extraordinarily caring person. The other article was about two 17-year-old boys who had beaten an elderly man to death. They had only planned to steal his wallet, but when he insulted them and tried to punch them, they became enraged.

In Piaget's view, 5- to 7-year-olds believe that rules are absolute; by age 8, children understand that rules are created by people to help them get along.

Reading articles like these, you can't help but question why some people act in ways that earn our deepest respect and admiration, whereas others earn our utter contempt as well as our pity. At a more mundane level, we wonder why Min-shen didn't tell the truth about the theft to the school principal. In this module, we'll begin our exploration of moral understanding and behavior by looking at children's thinking about moral issues: How do children judge what is "good" and what is "bad"? Let's start by looking at Jean Piaget's ideas about the development of moral reasoning.

Piaget's Views

I remember playing Chutes and Ladders® with my son Matt when he was about 6. This is a board game in which you can advance rapidly when you land on a space that has a ladder but must go backward if you land on a chute. To speed up the game, I suggested to Matt that we be allowed to advance if we landed on a chute as well as a ladder. I reminded him that he liked to climb up slides at playgrounds, so my suggestion had some logic to it. Matt would have none of this. He told me, "It's a rule that you have to go backward when you land on a chute. You can't go forward. The people who made Chutes and Ladders® say so. Just read the instructions, Daddy." I tried again to persuade him (because, in my humble opinion, Chutes and Ladders® gives new meaning to "bored" games), but he was adamant.

Matt's inflexibility, which is typical of 6-year-olds, can be explained by Piaget's stage theory of moral development, which includes three stages. In the first stage, which lasts from age 2 years to about 4, children have no well-defined ideas about morality. **But, beginning at about 5 years and continuing through age 7, children are in a stage of** *moral realism;* **they believe that rules are created by wise adults and therefore must be followed and cannot be changed. Another characteristic of the stage of moral realism is that children believe in** *immanent justice,* **the idea that breaking a rule always leads to punishment.** Suppose I had forced Matt to use my new rules for Chutes and Ladders® and that, the next day, he had tripped on his way to school, scraping his knee. Believing in immanent justice, he would have seen the scraped knee as the inevitable consequence of breaking the rule the previous day.

At about age 8, children progress to the stage of *moral relativism,* **the understanding that rules are created by people to help them get along.** Children progress to this more advanced level of moral reasoning in part because advances in cognitive development allow them to understand the reasons for rules. Furthermore, from interactions with their peers, children come to understand the need for rules and how they are created. For example, as the boys in the photo on page 380 decide where to ride their skateboards, they might follow a rule that everybody can suggest some place and then they'll vote. The boys understand that this rule isn't absolute; they follow it because it's reasonably fair and, by using this rule, they spend more time skating and less time arguing.

By 8 years of age, children understand that people create rules to get along; for example, these boys may follow the rule that they'll vote to decide where to ride their skateboards.

Children in the stage of moral relativism also understand that because people agree to set rules in the first place, they can also change them if they see the need. If the skateboarding boys decided another rule would be fairer and would help them get along better, they could adopt the new rule.

Some of Piaget's ideas about moral reasoning have stood the test of time better than others. For example, later research has showed that children's early moral reasoning does not consider adult authority final and absolute. Instead, preschool children believe adults' authority is limited. Preschoolers believe that pushing a child or damaging another child's possession is wrong even when an adult says that it's okay (Tisak, 1993). A lasting contribution of Piaget's work, however, is the idea that moral reasoning progresses through a sequence of stages, driven by cognitive development and interactions with peers. One important theory that builds on Piaget's stage approach comes from Lawrence Kohlberg; it's the focus of the next section.

Kohlberg's Theory

To begin, I'd like to tell you a story about Heidi, a star player on a soccer team that I coached several years ago. Heidi was terribly upset because our team was undefeated and scheduled to play in a weekend tournament to determine the league champion. But on Sunday of this same weekend, a Habitat-for-Humanity house was to be dedicated to her grandfather, who had died a few months previously. If Heidi skipped the tournament game, her friends on the team would be upset; if she skipped the dedication, her family would be disappointed. Heidi couldn't do both and didn't know what to do.

Kohlberg created stories like this one to study how people reason about moral dilemmas. He made it very difficult to reach a decision in his stories because every alternative involved some undesirable consequences. In fact, there is no "correct" answer—that's why the stories are referred to as moral "dilemmas." For Heidi, pleasing her teammates means disappointing her family; pleasing her family means letting down her teammates. Kohlberg was more interested in the reasoning used to justify a decision—Why should Heidi go to the tournament? Why should she go to the dedication?—not in the decision itself.*

Kohlberg's best-known moral dilemma is about Heinz, whose wife is dying:

> In Europe, a woman was near death from cancer. One drug might save her, a form of radium that a druggist in the same town had recently discovered. The druggist was charging $2,000, ten times what the drug cost him to make. The sick woman's husband, Heinz, went to everyone he knew to borrow the money, but he could only get together about half of what it cost. He told the druggist that his wife was dying and asked him to sell it cheaper or let him pay later. But the druggist said, "No." The husband got desperate and broke into the man's store to steal the drug for his wife (Kohlberg, 1969, p. 379).

Although more hangs in the balance for Heinz than for Heidi, both are moral dilemmas in that the alternative courses of action have desirable and undesirable features.

Kohlberg analyzed children's, adolescents', and adults' responses to a large number of dilemmas and identified three levels of moral reasoning, each

*As it turned out, Heidi didn't have to resolve the dilemma. We lost our tournament game on Saturday, so she went to the dedication on Sunday.

divided into two stages. Across the six stages, the basis for moral reasoning shifts. In the earliest stages, moral reasoning is based on external forces, such as the promise of reward or the threat of punishment. At the most advanced levels, moral reasoning is based on a personal, internal moral code and is unaffected by others' views or society's expectations. You can clearly see this gradual shift in the three levels: ◉─|Watch the **Video** on **mydevelopmentlab.com**

◉─|Watch the **Video** *Moral Development: Preconventional* on **mydevelopmentlab .com** to learn more about Kohlberg's theory. As you watch these video segments, look for the ways in which the child's reasoning about the dilemma differs from the adolescent's reasoning.

- *Preconventional level:* **For most children, many adolescents, and some adults, moral reasoning is controlled almost solely by obedience to authority and by rewards and punishments.**

Stage 1: Obedience orientation. People believe that adults know what is right and wrong. Consequently, a person should do what adults say is right to avoid being punished. A person at this stage might argue that Heinz should not steal the drug because it is against the law (which was set by adults).

Stage 2: Instrumental orientation. People look out for their own needs. They often are nice to others because they expect the favor to be returned in the future. A person at this stage might say it was all right for Heinz to steal the drug because his wife might do something nice for him in return (that is, she might reward him).

> In Kohlberg's theory, moral reasoning is first based on reward and punishment but ultimately is based on a personal moral code.

- *Conventional level:* **For most adolescents and most adults, moral decision making is based on social norms—what is expected by others.**

Stage 3: Interpersonal norms. Adolescents and adults believe that they should act according to others' expectations. The aim is to win the approval of others by behaving like "good boys" and "good girls." An adolescent or adult at this stage might argue that Heinz should not steal the drug because then others would see him as an honest citizen who obeys the law.

Stage 4: Social system morality. Adolescents and adults believe that social roles, expectations, and laws exist to maintain order within society and to promote the good of all people. An adolescent or adult in this stage might reason that Heinz should steal the drug because a husband is obligated to do all that he possibly can to save his wife's life. Or a person in this stage might reason that Heinz should not steal the drug because stealing is against the law and society must prohibit theft.

- *Postconventional level:* **For some adults, typically those older than 25, moral decisions are based on personal, moral principles.**

Stage 5: Social contract orientation. Adults agree that members of cultural groups adhere to a "social contract" because a common set of expectations and laws benefits all group members. However, if these expectations and laws no longer promote the welfare of individuals, they become invalid. Consequently, an adult in this stage might reason that Heinz should steal the drug because social rules about property rights are no longer benefiting individuals' welfare.

Stage 6: Universal ethical principles. Abstract principles such as justice, compassion, and equality form the basis of a personal moral code that may sometimes conflict with society's expectations and laws. An adult at this stage might argue that Heinz should steal the drug because life is paramount and preserving life takes precedence over all other rights.

The Summary Table puts all the stages together, providing a quick review of Kohlberg's theory.

SUMMARY TABLE
STAGES IN KOHLBERG'S THEORY OF MORAL DEVELOPMENT
Preconventional Level: Punishment and Reward
Stage 1: Obedience to authority
Stage 2: Nice behavior in exchange for future favors
Conventional Level: Social Norms
Stage 3: Live up to others' expectations
Stage 4: Follow rules to maintain social order
Postconventional Level: Moral Codes
Stage 5: Adhere to a social contract when it is valid
Stage 6: Personal morality based on abstract principles

 QUESTION 12.2

When Paige was told the Heinz dilemma, she replied, "He should steal the drug. Everyone would understand why he did it. And if he just let his wife die, his family and friends would think he's a terrible husband. They would never speak to him again." Which of Kohlberg's stages best describes Paige's thinking? About how old is she? *(Answer is on page 386.)*

SUPPORT FOR KOHLBERG'S THEORY. Kohlberg proposed that individuals move through the six stages in the order listed and in only that order. Consequently, older and more advanced thinkers should be more advanced in their moral development, and indeed they usually are (Stewart & Pascual-Leone, 1992). In addition, longitudinal studies show that individuals progress through each stage in sequence, and virtually no individuals skip stages (Colby et al., 1983).

Further support for Kohlberg's theory comes from research on the link between moral reasoning and moral behavior. Less advanced moral reasoning reflects the influence of external forces (e.g., rewards), but more advanced reasoning is based on a personal moral code. Therefore, individuals at the preconventional and conventional levels would act morally when external forces so demand, but otherwise they might not. In contrast, individuals at the postconventional level, where reasoning is based on personal principles, should be compelled to moral action even when external forces may not favor it.

Consistent with this claim, adolescents who would defend their principles in difficult situations tend to be more advanced in Kohlberg's stages (Gibbs et al., 1986). For example, students like those in the photograph who protest social conditions tend to have higher moral reasoning scores. This explains why Min-shen, the boy in the vignette, said nothing. Speaking out on behalf of the unpopular student is unlikely to lead to reward and violates social norms against "squealing" on friends. Consequently, a sixth-grader—who is probably in the preconventional or conventional level of moral reasoning—would probably let the unpopular student be punished unfairly.

On some other features, Kohlberg's theory does not fare as well. One is that moral reasoning is not as consistent as would be expected from the theory. Teenagers reasoning at the conventional level should always base their moral decisions on others' expectations—but, in reality, such consistency is not the norm. Moral reasoning may be advanced for some problems but much less sophisticated for others (Krebs & Denton, 2005).

Students who show moral courage by participating in protest movements typically have more advanced moral reasoning.

Another concern is Kohlberg's claim that his sequence of stages is universal: All people in all cultures should progress through the six-stage sequence. Indeed, children and adolescents in cultures worldwide reason about moral dilemmas at stages 2 or 3, just like North American children and adolescents (Gibbs et al., 2007). But, beyond the earliest stages, moral reasoning in other cultures is often not described well by Kohlberg's theory. Many critics note that Kohlberg's emphasis on individual rights and justice reflects traditional American culture and Judeo-Christian theology. Not all cultures and religions share this emphasis; consequently, moral reasoning might be based on different values in other cultures (Turiel, 2006).

The Hindu religion, for example, emphasizes duty and responsibility to others, not individual rights and justice (Simpson, 1974). Consistent with this emphasis, when Hindu children and adults living in India respond to moral dilemmas, they put a priority on solutions that provide care for others, even when individual rights or justice may suffer (Miller & Bersoff, 1992). For example, Hindu children and adults sometimes condone theft if it's the best way to meet one's responsibilities to care for others. Thus, the bases of moral reasoning are not universal as Kohlberg claimed; instead, they reflect cultural values.

Beyond Kohlberg's Theory

Kohlberg's theory obviously is not the final word on moral development. Much about his theory seems valid, but investigators have addressed its shortcomings. In the next few pages I describe some work that helps complete our picture of the development of moral thinking.

> Gilligan's theory emphasizes that moral judgments are based on a concern with caring for others.

GILLIGAN'S ETHIC OF CARING.   Carol Gilligan (1982; Gilligan & Attanucci, 1988) argued that Kohlberg's emphasis on justice applies more to males than to females, whose reasoning about moral issues is often rooted in concern for others. According to Gilligan, this "ethic of care" leads females like the girls in the photo to put a priority on fulfilling obligations to other people, and those obligations guide their moral decision making.

What does research tell us about the importance of justice and care in moral reasoning? Do females and males differ in the bases of their moral reasoning? In a comprehensive meta-analysis (Jaffee & Hyde, 2000), males tended to get slightly greater scores on problems that emphasized justice, whereas females tended to get slightly greater scores on problems that emphasized caring. But the differences were small and do not indicate that moral reasoning by females is predominated by a concern with care or that moral reasoning by males is predominated by a concern with justice. Instead, girls and boys as well as men and women reason about moral issues similarly. Most people think about moral issues in terms of *both* justice and caring, depending on the nature of the moral dilemma and the context (Turiel, 2006).

DEVELOPMENT OF DOMAINS OF SOCIAL JUDGMENT. Another approach notes that moral judgments (whether based on justice or care) represent just one of several important domains in which children and adults make social judgments (Smetana, 2006; Turiel, 1998). To illustrate the domains, think about the following preschool children:

In Gilligan's theory, the most advanced level of moral reasoning is based on the understanding that caring is the cornerstone of all human relationships, ranging from parent–child relationships to the one that exists between a homeless person and a volunteer at a shelter.

- Brian often kicks or pushes his younger brother when their mom isn't looking.
- Kathryn never puts her toys away when she's done playing with them.
- Brad likes to wear his underpants inside out.

Although each child's behavior is in some sense "wrong," only the first child's behavior—kicking and pushing—represents a moral transgression, because Brian's actions can harm another person. **In contrast,** *social conventions* **are arbitrary standards of behavior agreed to by a cultural group to facilitate interactions within the group.** Thus social convention says that we can eat French fries but not green beans with our fingers and that, in the case of Kathryn, children should clean up after themselves. **Finally, the** *personal domain* **pertains to choices concerning one's body (e.g., what to eat and wear) and choices of friends or activities.** Decisions here are not right or wrong, but instead are seen as personal preferences left up to the individual (Smetana, 2002). Thus, Brad's decision to wear his underpants inside out is unusual but not wrong.

During the preschool years, children begin to differentiate these domains (Lagattuta, Nucci, & Bosacki, 2010; Turiel, 1998; Yau, Smetana, & Metzger, 2009). For example, they believe that breaking a moral rule is more serious and should be punished more severely than breaking a social convention. And preschool children

> Preschool children distinguish moral decisions and social conventions from the personal domain.

believe that moral rules apply regardless of the situation (e.g., it's *never* okay to hit other children) and can't be overruled by adults. In contrast, preschoolers claim that social conventions are established by adults, which means they can be changed (e.g., it's okay for a school to say that students should address teachers by their first names). Finally, even preschoolers believe that the personal domain is just that: one where the individual should choose and not have the choices dictated by others.

Of course, although preschoolers can distinguish the different domains, reasoning within the domains changes as children develop. For example, preschool children claim that lying is always wrong, but older children have a more nuanced view and claim that "polite lying" is justified if it helps the welfare of others or would prevent an injustice (Perkins & Turiel, 2007). An Asian American teenager who knows that her parents would disapprove of her African American friends will lie to her parents about her companions and justify it on the ground that her parents' views are unethical. As another example, children and particularly adolescents expand the scope of decisions that fall under the personal domain and object when adults (parents, especially) intervene (Lins-Dyer & Nucci, 2007).

When domains of social justice are examined across cultures, both similarities and differences emerge, as we'll see in the "Cultural Influences" feature.

 ## Cultural Influences

Similarity in Structure of Domains of Social Judgment but Differences in Content

Children and adolescents in many different Western and non-Western countries distinguish the three different domains and reason similarly within each domain. For instance, young children in many countries worldwide share the view that decisions in the personal domain should be left to the individual and that adults should not interfere. Similarly, moral sanctions against hurting other people are upheld by children around the world (Wainryb, 2006).

But cultures sometimes differ in how they categorize actions. A good example is helping others when their need is only moderate (e.g., not life-threatening or an emergency, such as helping a friend with homework). For most American children and adolescents, this does not have the force of a moral imperative. In the words of a 15-year-old boy who was asked about helping an acquaintance with homework, "You should help if you can but there are reasons why you might not be able to, like studying for a big test or because you already had plans." In contrast, as we've already seen (page 383), helping others, regardless of their state of need, is an absolute for Hindu children and adolescents (Killen & Turiel, 1998).

Prosocial lying is another example of a cultural difference. Although most cultures have moral rules about being truthful, many cultures have social conventions that approve polite lies told to protect someone else from harm (Xu et al., 2010). Nevertheless, the circumstances that justify polite lying vary with culture. Chinese school children believe that polite lying is acceptable when it helps the group and, in the process, hurts an individual. The reverse is true for North American children. If a classmate who sings poorly wants to join the choir, Chinese children believe that lying to the child ("Sorry, but there are no spaces left in the choir") is acceptable because it protects the quality of the choir; North American children believe that lying to the choir ("My friend sings really well") is acceptable because it makes the friend happy (Fu et al., 2007). These cultural standards for polite lying reflect more general differences between Asian and Western cultures in their emphasis on the group and the individual (e.g., recall, from Module 10.1, that Asian children take pride in group achievement but North American children take pride in individual achievement).

Thus, the domains of morality, social convention, and personal autonomy are seen in development worldwide. However, the actions that make up the different domains vary, reflecting culturally specific values (Smetana, 2006).

How do children come to understand these different domains? For children in North America, this understanding is rooted in their experiences and parents' responses to different kinds of transgressions (Turiel, 1998). When a child breaks a moral rule, adults talk about the impact of the act on the victim and how that person could be hurt. In contrast, when a child violates a social convention, adults more often talk about the need to follow rules and to obey parents, teachers, and other people in authority. Finally, conversations about the personal domain are different: Here adults typically do not specify a "right" or "wrong" choice, but instead encourage children to make their own choices (Nucci & Weber, 1995).

Thus, from the viewpoint of domains of social judgment, moral reasoning is part of a much larger developmental accomplishment: Children understand that there are different domains of social decision making, each with unique rules of authority and sanctions for misbehavior. By the preschool years, children have made remarkable progress in understanding the distinction between the moral, social-conventional, and personal domains (Turiel & Neff, 2000).

THE ROLE OF EMOTIONS. So far we've considered moral development primarily in cognitive terms: as a rational decision-making process in which children deliberately evaluate the virtues of different actions. Yet moral decision making is often quite emotional (e.g., in the module-opening vignette, Min-shen actually became quite upset as he debated whether to tell authorities who had stolen the iPod) and activates emotional centers in the brain (Greene, 2007). Consequently, scientists have begun to study the interplay of cognition and emotion in shaping the development of moral judgments (Nucci & Gingo, 2011).

One idea is that emotional responses to events provide the raw data that allow children to create different categories of morally relevant concepts (Arsenio, Gold, & Adams, 2006). For example, even preschool children know that a boy would feel sad if someone stole his dessert or took his turn on a swing. And they know that a girl would feel happy if she helped a peer who dropped a stack or papers or shares her lunch with a friend who forgot hers. Repeated experience with these kinds of events leads children to form scripts (see page 213) about the emotional consequences of different actions, and children then create categories of events that lead to similar emotional outcomes. For example, one script in which a child becomes sad after a theft or another script in which a child becomes sad following unprovoked aggression may lead children to create a concept of unfair victimization.

Thus, children's emotional response to social-moral events is an important step in creating different categories of moral concepts. In Modules 12.3 and 12.4, we'll see that the nature of children's emotional responses to social interactions predicts whether they act prosocially or act aggressively.

Promoting Moral Reasoning

Whether it is based on justice or care, most cultures and most parents want to encourage adolescents to think carefully about moral issues. What can be done to help adolescents develop more mature forms of moral reasoning? Sometimes simply being exposed to more advanced moral reasoning is sufficient to promote developmental change (Walker, 1980). Adolescents may notice, for example, that older friends do not wait to be rewarded before they help others. Or a teenager may notice that respected peers take courageous positions regardless of the social consequences. Such experiences apparently cause adolescents to reevaluate their reasoning on moral issues and propel them toward more sophisticated thinking.

> Adolescents' moral reasoning often becomes more advanced when they are exposed to more advanced reasoning and when they participate in discussions with others who reason at more advanced levels.

Discussion can be particularly effective in revealing shortcomings in moral reasoning (Berkowitz et al., 2006). When people reason about moral issues with others whose reasoning is at a higher level, the usual result is that individuals reasoning at lower levels improve. This is particularly true when the conversational partner with the more sophisticated reasoning makes an effort to understand the other's view, by requesting clarification or paraphrasing what the other child is saying (Walker, Hennig, & Krettenauer, 2000).

Adolescents' moral reasoning (and moral behavior) is also influenced by their involvement in religion. Adolescents who are more involved in religion have greater concern for others and place more emphasis on helping them (Youniss, McLellan, & Yates, 1999). An obvious explanation for this link is that religion provides moral beliefs and guidelines for adolescents. But participation in religion can promote moral reasoning in a second, less direct way. Involvement in a religious community—typically through youth groups associated with a church, synagogue, or mosque—connects teens to an extended network of caring peers and adults. From interacting with individuals in this network, earning their trust, and sharing their values, adolescents gain a sense of responsibility to and concern for others (King & Furrow, 2004).

In this module, we've seen how moral reasoning changes as children develop. To see how these changes lead to changes in moral action, we'll look at children's prosocial behavior in the next module.

 ANSWER 12.2

Paige's thinking conforms to Kohlberg's stage 3, in which morality is based on living up to others' expectations. That is, Paige believes that Heinz should steal the drug because he needs to act as others expect a husband should act. Stage 3 reasoning is common in older adolescents and young adults, so Paige is probably at least 15 years old.

Check Your Learning

RECALL Summarize research that supports and refutes Kohlberg's theory of moral reasoning.

What are the different domains of social judgment? What do young children understand about each of them?

Describe ways to foster children's moral reasoning.

INTERPRET How do Piaget's stages of moral realism and moral relativism fit with Kohlberg's six stages?

APPLY Imagine that you were the father of Min-shen, the boy in the vignette who did not stand up for the boy who was wrongly accused of stealing the iPod. Based on the research described in this module, what might you do to try to advance Min-shen's level of moral reasoning?

 12.3 **Helping Others**

OUTLINE	LEARNING OBJECTIVES
Development of Prosocial Behavior	• At what age do children begin to act prosocially? How does prosocial behavior change with age?
Skills Underlying Prosocial Behavior	• What skills do children need to behave prosocially?
Situational Influences	• What situations influence children's prosocial behavior?
The Contribution of Heredity	• How does heredity contribute to children's prosocial behavior?
Socializing Prosocial Behavior	• How can parents encourage their children to act prosocially?

Six-year-old Juan got his finger trapped in the DVD player when he tried to remove a disc. While he cried and cried, his 3-year-old brother, Antonio, and his 2-year-old sister, Carla, watched but did not help. Later, when their mother had soothed Juan and saw that his finger was not injured, she worried about her younger children's reactions. In the face of their brother's obvious distress, why had Antonio and Carla done nothing?

Most parents, most teachers, and most religions try to teach children to act in cooperative, helping, giving ways—at least most of the time and in most situations. **Actions that benefit others are known as** *prosocial behavior.* Of course, cooperation often "works" because individuals gain more than they would by not cooperating. *Altruism* **is prosocial behavior that helps another with no direct benefit to the individual.** Altruism is driven by feelings of responsibility for other people. Two youngsters pooling their funds to buy a candy bar to share demonstrates cooperative behavior. One youngster giving half her lunch to a friend who forgot his own lunch demonstrates altruism.

Many scientists believe that humans are biologically predisposed to be helpful, to share, to cooperate, and to be concerned for others (Hastings, Zahn-Waxler, & McShane, 2006). Why has prosocial behavior evolved over time? The best explanation has nothing to do with lofty moral principles; instead, it's much more pragmatic: People who frequently help others are more likely to receive help themselves, and this increases the chance that they'll pass along their genes to future generations.

But, as the story of Juan and his siblings shows, children (and adults, for that matter) are not always helpful or cooperative. In this module, you'll learn how prosocial behavior changes with age and discover some factors that promote prosocial behavior.

Development of Prosocial Behavior

Even toddlers recognize when others are upset, and try to comfort them.

Simple acts of altruism can be seen by 18 months of age. When toddlers and preschoolers see other people who are obviously hurt or upset, they appear concerned, like the child in the photo. They try to comfort the person by hugging him or patting him (Zahn-Waxler et al., 1992). Apparently, at this early age, children recognize signs of distress. And if an adult is in obvious need of help—a teacher accidentally drops markers on a floor—most 18-month-olds spontaneously help get the markers (Warneken & Tomasello, 2006).

During the toddler and preschool years, children gradually begin to understand others' needs and learn more appropriate altruistic responses (van der Mark, van IJzendoorn, & Bakermans-Kranenburg, 2002). When 3-year-old Alexis sees that her infant brother is crying because he's dropped his favorite bear, she retrieves it for him; when 4-year-old Darren sees his mom crying while watching a TV show, he may turn off the TV. These early attempts at altruistic behavior are limited because young children's knowledge of what they can do to help is modest. As youngsters acquire more strategies to help others, their preferred strategies become more adult-like (Eisenberg, Fabes, & Spinrad, 2006).

Thus, as a general rule, intentions to act prosocially increase with age, as do children's strategies for helping. Of course, not all children respond to the needs of others, either in toddlerhood or at later ages. Some children attach greater priority to looking out for their own interests. What makes some children more likely than others to help? We'll answer this question in the next section.

Skills Underlying Prosocial Behavior

Think back to an occasion when you helped someone. How did you know that the person needed help? Why did you decide to help? Although you didn't realize it at the time, your decision to help was probably based on several skills:

- *Perspective taking.* In Module 6.1, you learned about Piaget's concept of egocentrism, the preoperational youngster's inability to see things from another's point of view. Egocentrism limits children's ability to share or help because they simply do not realize the need for prosocial behavior. They have only one perspective—their own. For example, young children might not help someone carrying many packages because they cannot envision that carrying lots of bulky things is a burden. Older children, however, can take the perspective of others, so they recognize the burden and are more inclined to help. In general, the better children understand the thoughts and feelings of other people, the more willing they are to share and help others (Strayer & Roberts, 2004; Vaish, Carpenter, & Tomasello, 2009).

- *Empathy.* **The ability to experience another person's emotions is** *empathy.* Children who deeply feel another person's fear, disappointment, sorrow, or loneliness are more inclined to help that person than are children who do not feel these emotions (Eisenberg et al., 2006; Malti et al., 2009). In other words, youngsters like the one in the photo, who is obviously distressed by what she is seeing, are most likely to help others.

- *Moral reasoning.* In Module 12.2, you learned that reward and punishment influence young children's moral reasoning, whereas a concern for moral principles characterizes adolescents' and adults' moral decision making. Therefore, as you would expect, prosocial behavior in young children is usually determined by the chance of reward or punishment. It also follows that, as children mature and begin to make moral decisions on the basis of fairness and justice, they become more prosocial. Consistent with this idea, Eisenberg, Zhou, and Koller (2001) found that Brazilian 13- to 16-year-olds were more likely to act prosocially when their moral reasoning was more advanced (e.g., based on internalized moral standards).

Children who are empathic—they understand how others feel—are more likely to help others in need.

In sum, children and adolescents who help others tend to be better able to take another's view, to feel another's emotions, and to act on the basis of principles, rather than rewards, punishments, or social norms. For example, a 15-year-old who spontaneously loans his favorite video game to a friend does so because he sees that the friend would like to play the game, he feels the friend's disappointment at not owning the game, and he believes that friends should share with each other.

Of course, perspective taking, empathy, and moral reasoning skills do not guarantee that children always act altruistically. Even though children have the skills needed to act altruistically, they may not because of the particular situation, as we'll see in the next section.

Situational Influences

Kind children occasionally disappoint us by being cruel, and children who are usually stingy sometimes surprise us with their generosity. Why? The setting helps determine whether children act altruistically or not.

- *Feelings of responsibility.* Children act altruistically when they feel responsible to the person in need. They are more likely to help siblings and friends than strangers, simply because they feel a direct responsibility to people whom they know well (Costin & Jones, 1992). And they're more likely to help when prompted with photos showing two people who look to be friends (Over & Carpenter, 2009). In other words, a simple reminder of the importance of friendship (or affiliation with others) can be enough to elicit helping (Over & Carpenter, 2009).

  Children are most likely to help when they feel responsible, have the needed skills, are happy, and believe that they will lose little.

- *Feelings of competence.* Children act altruistically when they feel that they have the skills necessary to help the person in need. Suppose, for example, that a preschooler is growing more and more upset because she can't figure out how to work a computer game. A classmate who knows little about computer games is not likely to help, because he doesn't know what to do to help. By helping, he could end up looking foolish (Peterson, 1983).

- *Mood.* Children act altruistically when they are happy or feeling successful but not when they are sad or feeling as if they have failed (Wentzel, Filisetti, & Looney, 2007). In other words, a preschooler who has just spent an exciting morning as the "leader" in nursery school is more inclined to share treats with siblings than is a preschooler who was punished by the teacher (Eisenberg, 2000).

- *Cost of altruism.* Children act altruistically when it entails few or modest sacrifices. A preschooler who has received a snack that she doesn't particularly like is more inclined to share it than is a child who has received her very favorite snack (Eisenberg & Shell, 1986).

When, then, are children most likely to help? When they feel responsible to the person in need, have the skills that are needed, are happy, and do not think they have to give up a lot by helping. When are children least likely to help? When they feel neither responsible for nor capable of helping, are in a bad mood, and believe that helping will entail a large personal sacrifice.

Using these guidelines, how do you explain why Antonio and Carla, the children in the vignette, watched idly as their older brother cried? Hint: The last two factors—mood and cost—are not likely to be involved. However, the first two factors may explain Antonio and Carla's failure to help their older brother. My explanation appears on page 392, just before "Check Your Learning."

So far, we've seen that altruistic behavior is determined by children's skills (such as perspective taking) and by characteristics of situations (such as whether children feel competent to help in a particular situation). Whether children are altruistic is also determined by genetics and by socialization, the topic of the remaining two sections in this module.

The Contribution of Heredity

As I mentioned on page 388, many scientists believe that prosocial behavior represents an evolutionary adaptation: People who help others are more likely to be helped themselves and thus are more likely to survive and have offspring. According to this argument, we should expect to find evidence for heritability of prosocial behavior, and in fact that's the case: Twin studies consistently find that identical twins are more alike in their prosocial behavior than are fraternal twins (Gregory et al., 2009).

Heredity may influence prosocial behavior through temperament: children are less likely to help when they don't regulate their emotions well and when they're shy.

Genes probably affect prosocial behavior indirectly, by their influence on temperament. For example, children who are temperamentally less able to regulate their emotions (in part due to heredity) may help less often because they're so upset by another's distress that taking action is impossible (Eisenberg et al., 2007). Another temperamental influence may be via inhibition (shyness). Children who are temperamentally shy are often reluctant to help others, particularly people they don't know well (Young, Fox, & Zahn-Waxler, 1999). Even though these children realize that others need help and are upset by another person's apparent distress, shy children's reticence means that these feelings don't translate into action. Thus, in both cases, children are aware that others need help. But in the first instance, they're too upset themselves to figure out how to help, and in the second instance they know how to help but are too inhibited to follow through.

Socializing Prosocial Behavior

Dr. Martin Luther King, Jr. said that his pursuit of civil rights for African Americans was particularly influenced by three people: Henry David Thoreau (a 19th-century American philosopher), Mohandas Gandhi (the leader of the Indian movement for independence from England), and his father, Dr. Martin Luther King, Sr. As is true of many humanitarians, Dr. King's prosocial behavior started in childhood, at home. But how do parents foster altruism in their children? Several factors contribute:

- *Modeling.* When children see adults helping and caring for others, they often imitate such prosocial behavior (Eisenberg et al., 2006). Of course, parents are the models to whom children are most continuously exposed, so they exert a powerful influence. Parents who report frequent feelings of warmth and concern for others tend to have children who experience stronger feelings of empathy. When a mother is helpful and responsive, her children often imitate her by being cooperative, helpful, sharing, and less critical of others. In a particularly powerful demonstration of the impact of parental modeling, people who had risked their lives during World War II to protect Jews from the Nazis often reported their parents' emphasis on caring for all people (Oliner & Oliner, 1988).

- *Disciplinary practices.* Children behave prosocially more often when their parents are warm and supportive, set guidelines, and provide feedback; in contrast, prosocial behavior is less common when parenting is harsh, threatening, and includes frequent physical punishment (Asbury et al., 2003; Eisenberg & Fabes, 1998; Moreno, Klute, & Robinson, 2008). Particularly important is parents' use of reasoning as a disciplinary tactic, with the goal of helping children see how their actions affect others. For example, after 4-year-old Annie grabbed some crayons from a playmate, her father told Annie, "You shouldn't just grab things away from people. It makes them angry and unhappy. Ask first, and if they say 'no,' then you mustn't take them."

- *Opportunities to behave prosocially.* You need to practice to improve motor skills, and the same is true of prosocial behaviors: Children and adolescents are more likely to act prosocially when they're routinely given the opportunity to help and cooperate with others. At home, children can help with household tasks, such as cleaning and setting the table. Adolescents can be encouraged to participate in community service, such as working at a food pantry or, like the teenager in the photo, helping older adults. Experiences like these help to sensitize children and adolescents to the needs of others and allow them to enjoy the satisfaction of helping (Grusec, Goodnow, & Cohen, 1996; McLellan & Youniss, 2003).

Thus, many factors, summarized in the following table, contribute to children's prosocial behavior. Combining all these ingredients, we can describe the development of children's altruistic behavior this way: As children get older, their perspective-taking and empathic skills develop, which enables them to see and feel another's needs. Nonetheless, children are never invariably altruistic (or, fortunately, invariably nonaltruistic), because properties of situations dictate altruistic behavior, too.

 QUESTION 12.3
Paula worries that her son Elliot is too selfish and wishes that he was more caring and compassionate. As a parent, what could Paula do to encourage Elliot to be more concerned about others' welfare? (*Answer is on page 392.*)

After children and adolescents have had the opportunity to help others, they often continue to be helpful because they better understand the needs of others.

SUMMARY TABLE

FACTORS CONTRIBUTING TO CHILDREN'S PROSOCIAL BEHAVIOR

General Category	Types of Influence	Children Are More Likely to Help When . . .
Skills	Perspective taking	they can take another person's point of view.
	Empathy	they feel another person's emotions.
	Moral reasoning	they base moral decisions on fairness.
Situational influences	Feelings of responsibility	they feel responsible to the person in need.
	Feelings of competence	they feel competent to help.
	Mood	they're in a good mood.
	Cost of altruism	the cost of prosocial behavior is small.
Heredity	Temperament	they're not shy and can control their emotions.
Parents' influence	Modeling	parents behave prosocially themselves.
	Discipline	parents reason with them.
	Opportunities	they practice at home and elsewhere.

 ANSWER 12.3

First, Paula can be sure to model the same behavior that she'd like to encourage in her son—she needs to be compassionate herself. Second, when disciplining Elliot, Paula should try to reason with him, emphasizing how his behavior causes others to feel. Third, Paula can ask Elliot to help around the house and suggest that he do some volunteer activity in the community.

As parents and other adults try to encourage children's prosocial behavior, one of the biggest obstacles is aggressive behavior, which is common throughout childhood and adolescence. In the next module, we'll look at some of the forces that contribute to children's aggression.

Answer to question on page 390 about why Antonio and Carla didn't help: Here are two explanations: First, neither Antonio nor Carla may have felt sufficiently responsible to help because (a) with two children who could help, each child's feeling of individual responsibility is reduced, and (b) younger children are less likely to feel responsible for an older brother. Second, I imagine that both children have been told not to use the DVD player by themselves. Consequently, they don't feel competent to help: they don't know what to do to help Juan remove his finger.

 ## Check Your Learning

RECALL Describe developmental change in prosocial behavior.

What are the situations in which children are most likely to help others?

INTERPRET Why must a full account of children's prosocial behavior include an emphasis on skills (e.g., empathy) as well as situations (e.g., whether a child feels responsible)?

APPLY Helping with household chores and voluntary community service often increase children's prosocial behavior. Of the skills underlying prosocial behavior (pages 388–389), which do you think are most affected by children's experiences helping at home and elsewhere?

12.4 Aggression

OUTLINE

Change and Stability

Roots of Aggressive
Behavior

Victims of Aggression

LEARNING OBJECTIVES

- When does aggressive behavior first emerge? How stable is aggression across childhood, adolescence, and adulthood?
- How do families, television, and the child's own thoughts contribute to aggression?
- Why are some children victims of aggression?

Every day, 7-year-old Reza follows the same routine when he gets home from school: He watches one action-adventure cartoon on TV after another until it's time for dinner. Reza's mother is disturbed by her son's constant TV viewing, particularly because of the amount of violence in the shows that he likes. Her husband tells her to stop worrying: "Let him watch what he wants to. It won't hurt him and, besides, it keeps him out of your hair."

If you think back to your years in elementary school, you can probably remember a class "bully"—a child who was always teasing classmates and picking fights. **Such acts typify** *aggression,* **behavior meant to harm others.** Aggressiveness is not the same as assertiveness, even though laypeople often use these words interchangeably. You've probably heard praise for an "aggressive businessperson" or a ballplayer who was "aggressive at running the bases." Psychologists and other behavioral scientists, however, would call these behaviors *assertive.* Assertive behaviors are goal-directed actions to further the legitimate interests of individuals or the groups they represent, while respecting the rights of other persons. In contrast, aggressive behavior, which may be physical or verbal, is intended to harm, damage, or injure and is carried out without regard for the rights of others.

In this module, we will examine aggressive behavior in children and see how it changes with age. Then we'll examine some causes of children's aggression and, in the process, learn more about the impact of Reza's TV watching on his behavior.

Change and Stability

By the time youngsters are old enough to play with one another, they show aggression. When 1- and 2-year-olds play, conflicts frequently arise over contested playthings, and youngsters often use aggression to resolve their conflicts (Dodge, Coie, & Lynam, 2006). **In** *instrumental aggression,* **a child uses aggression to achieve an explicit goal.** Instrumental aggression would include shoving a child to get to the head of a lunch line or, as shown in the photo on page 394, grabbing a toy away from another child. By the start of the elementary-school years, another form of aggression emerges (Coie et al., 1991). *Hostile aggression* **is unprovoked; apparently, its sole goal is to intimidate, harass, or humiliate another child.** Hostile aggression is illustrated by a child who spontaneously says, "You're stupid!" and then kicks the other child. **Yet another common type of aggression is** *reactive aggression,* **in which one child's behavior leads to another child's aggression.**

Watch the **Video** *Reactive Aggression* on **mydevelopmentlab.com** to view a nice example of a preschool child displaying aggression toward a peer who has taken a toy from him.

In instrumental aggression, children use force to achieve a goal, such as taking a toy from another child.

Reactive aggression would include a child who loses a game and then punches the child who won, or a child not chosen for the starring role in a play kicking the child who was selected. ◉─⎸Watch the Video on mydevelopmentlab.com

Instrumental, hostile, and reactive aggression are most likely to be expressed physically by younger children. As children get older, they more often use language to express their aggression (Dodge, Coie, & Tremblay, 2006). **A particularly common form of verbal aggression is** *relational aggression,* **in which children try to hurt others by undermining their social relationships.** In relational aggression, which is more typical of girls than boys, children try to hurt others by telling friends to avoid a particular classmate, by spreading malicious gossip, or by making remarks meant to hurt others (Côté et al., 2007; Crick et al., 2004). Two true stories from my child-development students portray relational aggression. After a heated argument in second grade, one student's former friend wrote "Erin is a big jerk" in block letters on the sidewalk where everyone walking to school would see the message. Another student, Beth, told me that after she'd beaten a classmate in the fifth-grade spelling bee, the classmate's friends formed the "I Hate Beth" club.

STABILITY OF AGGRESSION OVER TIME. Forms of aggression change with development, but individual children's tendencies to behave aggressively are stable over time, particularly among those children who are highly aggressive at a young age. Each of the following longitudinal studies shows that many aggressive young children grow up to be adolescents and adults who are aggressive, sometimes violent, and often commit crimes:

- In a study of about 500 boys growing up in Pittsburgh (Raine et al., 2005), among the 7-year-olds judged by their teachers to be highly aggressive, more than half had committed serious acts of delinquency (e.g., stealing a car, attacking others with the aim to hurt or kill) by age 17.

- In a study of more than 900 Canadian girls (Côté et al., 2001), 6-year-olds who had been rated by their teachers as frequently disrupting class (e.g., they were disobedient or they bullied classmates) were four to five times more likely to be diagnosed, as teenagers, with conduct disorder, a disorder in which individuals are chronically aggressive, destroy property, and lie or steal.

- In a study involving more than 200 German preschool children (Asendorpf, Denissen, & van Aken, 2008), those children who were judged by teachers to be most aggressive were, as young adults, 12 times more likely than the least aggressive children to have been charged for criminal activity.

Violent behavior in adulthood is not the only long-term outcome of childhood aggression; poor adjustment to high school (e.g., dropping out, failing a grade) and unemployment are others (Asendorpf et al., 2008; Ladd, 2003). In one study, aggressive 8-year-olds tended to do poorly in high school, leaving them few options for work as young adults and putting them at risk for problem drinking. By their early 30s, many highly aggressive 8-year-olds had been unemployed for more than 2 years (Kokko & Pulkkinen, 2000).

Findings from these and similar studies show that aggression is *not* simply a case of playful pushing and shoving that children always outgrow. To the contrary, a small minority of children who are highly aggressive develop into young adults who create havoc in society. What causes children to behave aggressively? Let's look at some of the roots of aggressive behavior.

Highly aggressive children often grow up to be adults who are aggressive, violent, and commit crimes.

Roots of Aggressive Behavior

Psychologists once believed that aggression was caused by frustration. The idea was that when children or adults were blocked from achieving a goal, they became frustrated and acted aggressively, often against the interfering person or object. Today, however, scientists look to many other causes, including biological factors, the family, the child's community and culture, and the child's own thoughts.

BIOLOGICAL CONTRIBUTIONS. *Born to Be Bad* is the title of at least two movies, two CDs (one by George Thorogood and one by Joan Jett), and three books. Implicit in this popular title is the idea that, from birth, some individuals follow a developmental track that leads to destructive, violent, or criminal behavior. In other words, the claim is that biology sets the stage for people to be aggressive long before experience can affect development.

Is there any truth to this idea? In fact, biology and heredity *do* contribute to aggressive and violent behavior, but not in the manner suggested by the epithet "born to be bad" (van Goozen, Fairchild, & Harold, 2008). Twin studies make it clear that heredity contributes: Identical twins are usually more alike in their levels of physical aggression than are fraternal twins (Brendgen et al., 2006). But these studies do not tell us that aggression per se is inherited; instead, they indicate that some children inherit factors that place them at risk for aggressive or violent behavior. Temperament seems to be one such factor: Youngsters who are temperamentally difficult, overly emotional, or inattentive are, for example, more likely to be aggressive (Joussemet et al., 2008; Xu, Farver, & Zhang, 2009). Hormones represent another factor: Boys with higher levels of the hormone testosterone are often more irritable and have greater body mass (Olweus et al., 1988; Tremblay et al., 1998). A third factor is a deficit in the neurotransmitters that inhibit aggressive behavior (van Goozen et al., 2007).

None of these factors—temperament, testosterone, or neurotransmitters—*causes* a child to be aggressive, but they do make aggressive behavior more likely. For instance, children who are emotional and easily irritated may be disliked by their peers and be in frequent conflict with them, opening the door for aggressive responses. Thus, biological factors place children at risk for aggression. To understand which children actually become aggressive, we need to look at interactions between inherited factors and children's experiences (Moffitt, 2005).

IMPACT OF THE FAMILY. Although few parents deliberately teach their children to harm others, early family experiences are a prime training ground for learning patterns of aggression. Parents' approach to discipline is crucial. When parents use physical punishment or threats to discipline their children, the hidden message to children is that physical force "works" as a means of controlling others. A parent like the one in the photo is saying, in effect, "The best way to get people to do what you want is to hurt them" (Bradley & Corwyn, 2007). In one study (Dodge, Bates, & Pettit, 1990), children who had been punished so harshly that they were injured were rated twice as aggressive as children who had not experienced such harsh punishment. But strong or aggressive parental responses are not essential in making a child aggressive. When parents are coercive, unresponsive, depressed, and emotionally uninvested, their children are more likely to be aggressive (Blatt-Eisengart et al., 2009; Rubin, Bukowski, & Parker, 2006).

When parents often use physical punishment, their children are more likely to become aggressive.

In many families with aggressive children, a vicious circle seems to develop. Compared to families with nonaggressive children, both aggressive children and their parents are more likely to respond to neutral behavior with aggression. What's more, after an aggressive exchange has begun, both parents and children are likely to escalate the exchange, rather than break it off. And once a child has been labeled aggressive by parents and others, that child is more likely to be accused of aggression and to be singled out for punishment, even when the child has been behaving entirely appropriately on the occasion in question (Patterson, 2002). The "aggressive child" will be accused of all things that go wrong—from missing cookies to broken appliances—and other children's misbehaviors will be ignored.

Another aspect of parental behavior that's been linked to aggression is *monitoring,* **which refers to parents' knowledge of where their children are, what they're doing, and who they're with.** When parents don't monitor their children's behavior, the children are more frequently aggressive (Patterson, 2008; Vieno et al., 2009). Of course, monitoring requires children's cooperation to a certain extent, and children who are chronically aggressive often do not cooperate (e.g., teenagers not answering their cell phones when they see that a parent is calling), in part because they see monitoring as intrusive (Laird et al., 2003).

Parents contribute to aggressive behavior by using physical punishment and by failing to monitor their children's behavior.

So far we've seen that children's aggression is linked to parents' use of physical punishment and to their lack of monitoring. To this list we need to add another critical aspect of family life: the presence of conflict. When parents constantly argue and fight, their children are much more likely to be aggressive (Cummings et al., 2006; Feldman, Masalha, & Derdikman-Eiron, 2010). Of course, children have ringside seats for many of these confrontations, and thus they can see firsthand how parents use verbal and physical aggression against each other. Sadly, children often come to believe that these patterns of interacting represent "natural" ways of solving problems within a family (Graham-Bermann & Brescoll, 2000).

INFLUENCE OF COMMUNITY AND CULTURE. Parents are hardly alone in giving important lessons about aggression. Other influential voices within children's lives deliver powerful messages about aggressive behavior:

- *Television and media games.* Most TV programs targeted at children contain acts of physical aggression (Wilson et al., 2002). The average American youngster will see several *thousand* murders on TV before reaching adolescence (Waters, 1993). (If you find these numbers hard to believe, try the activities described in "See for Yourself" at the end of this chapter.) What does research tell us about this steady diet of televised mayhem and violence? Will Reza, the avid cartoon watcher in the vignette at the beginning of the module, become more aggressive? Or, as his father believes, is his TV watching simply fun? In fact, longitudinal studies have consistently found that children exposed to much media violence often grow up to be aggressive and violent adults. This is true even when confounding variables such as parents' education and family income are controlled (Fuld et al., 2009). What's more, playing violent video games seems to lead to aggressive and violent behavior in much the same way that watching violent TV does (Anderson et al., 2003), particularly when children play habitually and identify with aggressive game characters (Konijn, Nije Bijvank, & Bushman, 2007). In short, Reza's father is clearly wrong: Frequent exposure to media violence makes children more aggressive.

- *Peers.* Aggressive children often befriend other aggressive children. The outcome is hardly surprising: Aggressive friends support and encourage each other's aggressive behavior (Brendgen et al., 2008; Monahan, Steinberg, & Cauffman, 2009). Just as friends drawn together by a mutual interest in music enjoy listening to CDs together, friends whose bond is their aggressive behavior enjoy teaming up to attack their peers; they often "share" targets of aggression (Card & Hodges, 2006). Aggressive adolescents often join gangs, which has a catalytic effect on aggressive and violent behavior. That is, even though adolescents who join gangs are already aggressive, their membership in a gang leads to more frequent and more violent antisocial behavior (Thornberry et al., 2003). 👁—[**Watch** the **Video** on **mydevelopmentlab.com**

👁—[**Watch** the **Video** *Relational Aggression* on **mydevelopmentlab.com** which provides a vivid illustration of teenage girls being particularly nasty in their remarks about a peer they dislike. If you want to see more of the same, watch all 97 minutes of Mean Girls starring Lindsay Lohan (not available in the Multimedia Library of MyDevelopmentLab—sorry!).

- *Failure in school.* Aggressive children are often uninterested in school and their grades reflect this disinterest. One interpretation of this finding is that aggressive children's behavior interferes with their learning. Instead of spending time on school tasks such as learning to add, aggressive youngsters are busy creating mayhem or being disciplined; in the process, they create conflicted relationships with their teachers—another impediment to school success (Stipek & Miles, 2008). Another interpretation is that children who have difficultly learning in school become frustrated and unhappy; they express their frustration by aggressing against their peers.

  Both views may be right (Masten et al., 2005; Miles & Stipek, 2006). School failure may breed aggressive behavior and aggressive behavior, in turn, leads to school failure. In other words, this may be a vicious circle in which the starting point can be either aggressive behavior or school failure. Once started, the other soon follows and the cycle grows. A 5-year-old boy who kicks and pushes classmates struggles to learn to read. His failure breeds even greater anger and aggression toward his classmates, which causes him to fall further behind academically. Over time, he becomes more aggressive and more of a failure in school (Masten et al., 2005).

- *Poverty.* Aggressive and antisocial behavior is more common among children living in poverty than among children who are economically advantaged (Williams, Conger, & Blozis, 2007). Some of the impact of poverty can be explained by factors that we've already considered. For example, living in poverty is extremely stressful for parents and often leads to the very parental behaviors that promote aggression—harsh discipline and lax monitoring (Tolan, Gorman-Smith, & Henry, 2003). But poverty also contributes to violent behavior in another manner, by helping to create a culture of violence.

- *Culture of violence.* Violent crime is far more common in poverty-stricken neighborhoods, and exposure to such violence fosters aggressive behavior in adolescents. For example, in a group of Chicago adolescents, those living in poverty were more likely to be exposed to firearms violence (e.g., seeing someone shot) and, as they got older, were more likely to be aggressive and violent themselves (Bingenheimer, Brennan, & Earls, 2005). Similarly, individuals living in the South and West regions of the United States often endorse a "culture of honor" that endorses aggressive and violent behavior to defend one's honor, family, and property (Hayes & Lee, 2005). In such states, adolescents are more likely to report carrying firearms to school, and school shootings like those at Columbine High School are more common, even after controlling for numerous relevant variables (Brown, Osterman, & Barnes, 2009). In other words, just as frequent exposure within a family to physical punishment and marital conflict leads children to believe that aggression is a natural way to solve problems, exposure at the community level to violence and pro-aggression attitudes leads adolescents to condone aggressive and violent behavior.

COGNITIVE PROCESSES. The perceptual and cognitive skills described in Chapters 6 through 8 also play a role in aggression. Aggressive boys often respond aggressively because they are not skilled at interpreting other people's intentions and, without a clear interpretation in mind, they respond aggressively by default (Dodge, Bates, & Pettit, 1990). Far too often, they think, "I don't know what you're up to, and, when in doubt, attack." In the "Spotlight on Theories" feature, we'll learn more about a theory of cognitive processing that's helping to reveal how aggressive children think about other people.

Spotlight on Theories

Social-Information-Processing Theory and Children's Aggressive Behavior

BACKGROUND Genetics, parents, TV, peers, and poverty all contribute to make some children prone to aggression. What these influences have in common is that they lead some children to see the world as a hostile place in which they must be wary of other people. Nonetheless, precisely characterizing the aggressive child's hostile view has been a challenge.

THE THEORY To explain how children perceive, interpret, and respond to people, Nicki R. Crick and Kenneth Dodge (1994; Dodge & Crick, 1990; Fontaine & Dodge, 2006) formulated an information-processing model of children's thinking, which is shown in Figure 12-2. According to the model, responding to a social stimulus involves several steps. First, children selectively attend to certain features of the social stimulus but do not attend to others. Second, children try to interpret the features that they have processed; that is, they try to give meaning to the social stimulus. Third, children evaluate their goals for the situation. Fourth, children retrieve from memory a behavioral response that is associated with the interpretation and goals of the situation. Fifth, children evaluate this response to determine if it is appropriate. Finally, the child proceeds with the behavior.

Applied to aggressive children, the theory says that aggressive children's processing is biased and restricted in many of the steps in the diagram, and that this flawed information processing is part of what leads these children to be more aggressive: They systematically misperceive people's actions (Crick & Werner, 1998; Egan, Monson, & Perry, 1998).

Hypothesis: According to social-information-processing theory, aggressive children's processing of social information (e.g., people) is biased in each of the stages depicted in Figure 12-2. In the fourth and fifth stages of processing—accessing response options and evaluating them—this bias leads to the hypothesis that aggressive children should respond hostilely when this interpretation is not warranted. For example, when an aggressive child picks up a book from a desk and another child says, "That's my book" in a nonprovocative manner, aggressive children are expected to be more likely to respond in a hostile way ("I was just looking at it. I didn't know it was yours. No need to jump all over me.") than in a neutral way ("Okay, I was wondering whose it was.").

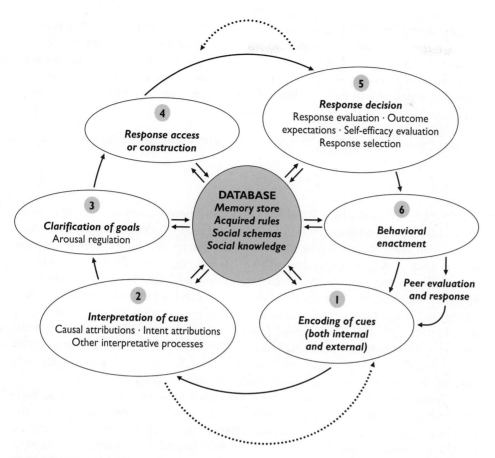

FIGURE 12-2

Test: Fontaine et al. (2009) evaluated this hypothesis by asking adolescents to watch videos in which one person's action (e.g., picking up a book) leads to another person's neutral response ("That's my book."). Then the videos showed hostile and nonhostile responses; adolescents in the study were asked how easily they would act in these ways and how they would feel in doing so. Aggressive adolescents more often endorsed the hostile response but less aggressive adolescents tended to endorse the nonhostile response.

Conclusion: When confronted with situations in which a person's actions aren't clear, aggressive children and adolescents often respond in a hostile manner by default. In other words, aggressive children view the world through suspicious eyes—as if the others are always "out to get them," and consequently they respond to many neutral interactions with unwarranted hostility and anger.

Aggressive children often interpret neutral behavior in hostile terms.

Application: If aggressive children are unskilled at interpreting and responding to others' actions, would training in these skills improve their social behavior? The answer seems to be yes (Dodge & Crick, 1990). One approach is to teach aggressive children that aggression is painful and does not solve problems; that intentions can be understood by attending to relevant cues; and that there are more effective, prosocial ways to solve interpersonal disputes. In a study by Guerra and Slaby (1990), adolescents incarcerated for committing violent acts received training designed to increase their understanding of social situations. For example, they were taught to pay attention to nonhostile cues in a social situation, to think of alternative ways of responding to social problems, and to evaluate responses in terms of their consequences. Supervisors at the correctional facility judged that the adolescents were better adjusted following training than before. They were less aggressive, less impulsive, and more flexible in their solutions.

MULTIPLE, CASCADING RISKS. Obviously, many factors contribute to make some children and adolescents more prone to aggressive, sometimes violent behavior. As you can imagine, when risk factors mount up in children's lives, they are at ever-greater risk for aggressive behavior (Greenberg et al., 1999). What's more, many of the factors operate in a cascading fashion, such that later risk factors build on prior factors: Poverty or maternal depression can lead to harsh, ineffective parenting. In turn, this leads children to be unprepared for school (both academically and socially), which leads to school failure and conduct problems. These difficulties cause some parents to become less active and less invested in parenting, which means that they monitor their children less often, allowing them to associate with deviant, aggressive peers (Dodge, Greenberg, & Malone, 2008).

Thus, the developmental journey that leads to a violent, aggressive, antisocial adolescent starts in early childhood but gains momentum along the way. Consequently, efforts to prevent children from taking this path must begin early, be maintained over childhood, and target both children and their parents. An example of a successful intervention program is Fast Track (Conduct Problems Prevention Research Group, 2011), which is designed to teach academic and social skills to elementary-school children plus life and vocational skills to adolescents. In addition, parents are taught skills for effective child rearing and, later, how to stay involved with their children and to monitor their behavior. At 12th grade—two years after the program had ended—aggressive and destructive behavior among children who were at highest risk in kindergarten was cut in half compared to similar high-risk children assigned to a control condition.

Of course, this sort of successful program comes with a very high price tag. But its cost is a fraction of that associated with the by-products of aggressive behavior: One analysis suggests that each violent and aggressive American adolescent costs $2–$5 million in payments to victims, court costs, and costs of incarceration (Cohen & Piquero, 2009). Thus, programs like Fast Track not only improve children's lives (and the lives of people around them) but are also cost-effective.

Victims of Aggression

Every aggressive act is directed at someone. Most children are the targets of an occasional aggressive act—a shove or kick to gain a desired toy, or a stinging insult by someone trying to save face. However, a small percentage of children are chronic targets of bullying. In both Europe and the United States, about 15% of elementary-school children and adolescents are chronic victims of aggression (Nansel et al., 2001). In recent years, some youth have become victims of electronic bullying, in which they are harassed via cell phones or the Internet (Raskauskas & Stoltz, 2007). In her novel *Bastard Out of Carolina*, Dorothy Allison provides a frightening glimpse of this victimization when a girl, Shannon, boards a school bus:

> As she made her way up the aisle, I watched each boy slide to the end of his seat to block her sitting with him and every girl flinch away as if whatever Shannon had might be catching. In the seat ahead of us Danny Yarboro leaned far over into the aisle and began making retching noises. "Cootie train! Cootie train" somebody yelled as the bus lurched into motion and Shannon still hadn't found a seat (1993, pp. 153–154).

> Some children who are chronic victims of aggression overreact when provoked, others withdraw and submit to aggression.

In this episode, Shannon is the victim of verbal bullying. But victimization by physical force also occurs frequently: Think of a child who is beat up daily on the playground. Other children are chronic targets of relational aggression: Think of children who are constantly the subject of rumors spread by their classmates (Crick, Casas, & Nelson, 2002).

As you can imagine, being tormented daily by their peers is hard on children. Research consistently shows that children who are chronic victims of aggression are often lonely, anxious, and depressed; they dislike school and their peers; and they have low self-esteem (Ladd & Ladd, 1998; Rudolph, Troop-Gordon, & Flynn, 2009). Ironically, the impact of bullying is reduced when children see others being bullied, apparently because they feel that they're not being singled out for harassment (Nishina & Juvonen, 2005). Also, though most children are happier when no longer victimized, the harmful effects linger for some children: They are still lonely and sad despite not having been victims for one or two years (Kochenderfer-Ladd & Wardrop, 2001).

Why do some children suffer the sad fate of being victims? Some victims are actually aggressive themselves (Schwartz et al., 1997; Veenstra et al., 2005). These youngsters often overreact, are restless, and are easily irritated. Their aggressive peers soon learn that these children are easily baited. A group of children will, for example, insult or ridicule such a child, knowing that he or she will probably start a fight even though he or she is outnumbered. Other victims tend to be withdrawn, submissive, and have low self-esteem. They are unwilling or unable to defend themselves from their peers' aggression, and so they are usually referred to as *passive victims* (Guerra, Williams, & Sadek, 2011; Ladd & Ladd, 1998; Salmivalli & Isaacs, 2005). When attacked, like the child in the photo, they show obvious signs of distress and usually give in to their attackers, thereby rewarding the aggressive behavior. Thus, both aggressive and withdrawn–submissive children end up as victims—and this pattern holds for children in China as well as for children in North America (Schwartz, Chang, & Farver, 2001).

When children give in to aggressive children, they often become chronic victims.

How do children end up as victims? Family history and parenting help decide. To understand these forces, we need to distinguish victims who overreact from those who respond passively, and within the latter group, distinguish boys from girls. Victims who overreact often come from hostile, punitive, or even abusive family environments (Schwartz et al., 1997). Among passive victims, boys tend to have mothers who are overprotective or emotionally overinvolved with them; in

 QUESTION 12.4
Brandon is constantly picked on by other kids at his school: The girls tease him and the boys often start fights with him. What could he and his parents do to improve his peer relations?
(Answer appears on page 402.)

contrast, girls who are passive victims tend to have mothers who are controlling and unresponsive (Ladd & Ladd, 1998).

Some victims try to cope with the problem themselves, but this is complicated because different strategies seem to work best for boys and girls (Kochendefer-Ladd & Skinner, 2002). One strategy for victimized children is to turn to peers for support, by telling them how it feels to be victimized or by asking them for help directly. This strategy works for girls but backfires for boys: Boys' classmates like them even less as a result, perhaps because boys are expected to cope with problems alone and peers shun boys who seek help. A strategy that has both costs and benefits for boys is ignoring the victimization—pretending that it's not happening or saying that it doesn't matter. When victimized boys do this, they tend to be more anxious (the cost), but their peers like them more (the benefit).

Rather than letting children cope alone with victimization (using strategies that may or may not work), a better approach is to teach victimized children ways of dealing with bullying that are more effective than either overreacting or withdrawing passively (e.g., don't lash out when you're insulted; don't show that you're afraid when you're threatened). In addition, increasing self-esteem can help. When attacked, children with low self-esteem may think, "I'm a loser and have to put up with this because I have no choice." Increasing children's self-esteem makes them less tolerant of personal attacks (Egan et al., 1998). Another useful way to help victims is to foster their friendships with peers. When children have friends, they're not as likely to be victimized (Veenstra et al., 2010). Finally, the best solution is to prevent bullying and victimization altogether; an effective way to do this is to create a school climate in which bullying is not condoned and victims are supported by their peers (Kärnä et al., 2011).

Throughout this module, we've seen the harm caused by aggression: Both victims who are hurt and children who are chronically aggressive often lead problem-filled lives. Yet, the research described in this module has also identified many of the roots of aggressive behavior and suggested how children can learn other, more constructive ways to interact with peers.

 ANSWER 12.4
In the short term, Brandon should try to look and act as if the teasing and fighting don't bother him; in the longer term, one of the best things he can do is to make more friends in his class.

✓ Check Your Learning

RECALL Describe the different forms of aggression and the ages when they typically appear.

Summarize the primary phases of decision making in Crick's and Dodge's information-processing model and the biases that are found in aggressive children's decision making.

INTERPRET Compare the impact of nature and nurture on children's aggressive behavior.

APPLY Suppose that a group of elementary-school teachers wanted to know how to reduce the amount of aggressive behavior in their classrooms. What advice would you give them?

UNIFYING THEMES   Continuity

This chapter has some nice illustrations of the theme that *early development is related to later development, but not perfectly.* For example, we learned on page 375 that preschoolers who were best able to delay gratification were, as adolescents, less likely to yield to temptation and to be distractible. Yet the relation was not perfect: Many preschoolers who quickly gave into temptation became adolescents who were not distractible. The same conclusion is evident in the results of longitudinal studies of aggressive children (page 394). Many of these children commit serious crimes as adults, but not all do. Behaving aggressively in childhood definitely increases the odds of adult criminal activity, but it does not guarantee it.

See for Yourself

This assignment may seem like a dream come true—you are being required to watch TV! Pick an evening when you can watch network television programming from 8:00 until 10:00 PM (prime time). Your job is to count each instance of (a) physical force by one person against another and (b) threats of harm to compel another to act against his or her will. Select one network randomly and watch the program for 10 minutes. Then turn to another network and watch that program for 10 minutes. Continue changing the channels every 10 minutes until the 2 hours are over. Of course, it won't be easy to follow the plots of all these programs, but you will end up with a wider sample of programming this way. Repeat this procedure on a Saturday morning when you can watch 2 hours of children's cartoons (not *South Park!*).

Now simply divide the total number of aggressive acts by 4 to estimate the amount of aggression per hour. Then multiply this figure by 11,688 to estimate the number of aggressive acts seen by an average adolescent by age 19. (Why 11,688? Two hours of daily TV viewing—a very conservative number—multiplied by 365 days and 16 years.) Then ponder the possible results of that very large number. If your parents told you, nearly 12,000 times, that stealing was okay, would you be more likely to steal? Probably. Then what are the consequences of massive exposure to the televised message, "Solve conflicts with aggression"? See for yourself!

Summary

12.1 Self-Control

Beginnings of Self-Control

At 1 year, infants are first aware that others impose demands on them; by 3 years, youngsters can devise plans to regulate their behavior. During the school-age years, children become better able to control their behavior.

Children differ in their self-control, but individuals are fairly consistent over time: Preschoolers who have good self-control tend to become adolescents and adults with good self-control.

Influences on Self-Control

Children who have the best self-control tend to have parents who are loving, set limits, and discuss discipline with them. When parents are overly strict, their children have less self-control, not more.

Temperament helps determine how parents influence their children's self-control. With temperamentally fearful children, gentle reminders are effective; with fearless children, parents should appeal to the attachment relationship.

Improving Children's Self-Control

Children are better able to regulate their own behavior when they have plans to help them remember the importance of the goal and something to distract them from tempting objects.

12.2 Reasoning About Moral Issues

Piaget's Views

Piaget theorized that 5- to 7-year-olds are in a stage of moral realism. They believe that rules are created by wise adults; therefore, rules must be followed and cannot be changed. At about 8 years, children enter a stage of moral relativism, believing that rules are created by people to help them get along.

Kohlberg's Theory

Kohlberg proposed that moral reasoning includes preconventional, conventional, and postconventional levels. Moral reasoning is first based on rewards and punishments, and, later, on personal moral codes. As predicted by Kohlberg's theory, people progress through the stages in sequence and do not regress, and morally advanced reasoning is associated with more frequent moral behavior. However, few people attain the most advanced levels, and cultures differ in the bases for moral reasoning.

Beyond Kohlberg's Theory

Gilligan proposed that females' moral reasoning is based on caring and responsibility for others, not justice. Research does not support consistent sex differences, but has found that males and females both consider caring as well as justice in their moral judgments, depending on the situation.

During the preschool years, children differentiate moral rules, social conventions, and personal choices. They believe, for example, that social conventions can be changed but moral rules cannot. And, they understand that breaking a moral rule produces a harsher punishment than breaking a social convention.

Promoting Moral Reasoning

Many factors can promote more sophisticated moral reasoning, including observing others reason at more advanced levels, and discussing moral issues with peers, teachers, and parents.

12.3 Helping Others

Development of Prosocial Behavior

Even toddlers know when others are upset, and they try to offer comfort. As children grow older, they more often see the need to act prosocially and are more likely to have the skills to do so.

Skills Underlying Prosocial Behavior

Children are more likely to behave prosocially when they are able to take others' perspectives, are empathic, and have more advanced moral reasoning.

Situational Influences

Children's prosocial behavior is often influenced by situational characteristics. Children more often behave prosocially when they feel that they should and can help, when they are in a good mood, and when they believe that they have little to lose by helping.

The Contribution of Heredity

Genes influence prosocial behavior through temperament: Some children are unlikely to help because they're too shy or they become too upset themselves (because they can't control their emotions).

Socializing Prosocial Behavior

Parenting approaches that promote prosocial behavior include modeling prosocial behavior, using reasoning in discipline, and giving children frequent opportunities inside and outside the home to use their prosocial skills.

12.4 Aggression

Change and Stability

Typical forms of aggression in young children include instrumental, hostile, and reactive aggression. As children grow older, physical aggression decreases and relational aggression becomes more common. Overall levels of aggression are fairly stable, which means that very aggressive young children often become involved in violent and criminal activities as adolescents and adults.

Roots of Aggressive Behavior

Children's aggressive behavior has many sources: genetics, harsh parenting, viewing violence on TV and in other media, aggressive peers, school failure, living in poverty, and biased interpretation of people's behavior.

Victims of Aggression

Children who are chronic targets of aggression are often lonely and anxious. Some victims of aggression tend to overreact when provoked; others tend to withdraw and submit. Victimization can be overcome by increasing children's social skills, their self-esteem, and their number of friends.

Test Yourself

✓•—[Study and **Review** on **mydevelopmentlab.com**

1. The first step in the development of self-control occurs when infants _____.

2. Children's self-control is affected by parents' discipline and by a child's _____.

3. Self-control can be improved by reminding children of the need to avoid temptation and by _____.

4. According to Piaget, until about 8 years of age children are in a stage of moral realism in which they believe that _____.

5. At the _____ level in Kohlberg's theory, people believe that moral decision making is based on social norms (i.e., how others expect them to behave).

6. Gilligan argued that Kohlberg's theory places too much emphasis on justice in moral decision making and ignores the role of _____.

7. Domains of social judgment include moral transgressions, _____, and the personal domain.

8. Emotions may influence children's moral development by _____.

9. Skills necessary for prosocial behavior include perspective taking, _____, and moral reasoning.

10. Aspects of a situation that influence helping include _____, feelings of competence, a child's mood, and the cost of altruism.

11. Parents foster altruistic behavior by modeling it for children to see, by _____, and by providing children with the opportunity to behavior prosocially.

12. In _____ aggression, children use aggression to achieve their goals.

13. Children are more likely to behave aggressively when their parents use physical punishment frequently, _____, and are in frequent conflict with each other.

14. Cultural influences on aggression include the media, peers, experiences in school, _____, and a culture of violence.

15. According to the social-information-processing framework, aggressive children are biased _____.

Answers: (1) become aware that others impose demands on them and they must react accordingly; (2) temperament; (3) activities that divert attention from temptation; (4) rules are created by wise adults and must be followed and cannot be changed; (5) conventional; (6) caring for others; (7) social conventions; (8) helping children create different categories of morally relevant concepts; (9) empathy; (10) a child's feelings of responsibility; (11) their disciplinary practices; (12) instrumental; (13) don't monitor their children's behavior; (14) poverty; (15) to interpret actions in terms of aggressive intent and to respond aggressively by default.

Key Terms

13 Gender and Development

13.1
Gender Stereotypes

13.2
Differences Related to Gender

13.3
Gender Identity

13.4
Gender Roles in Transition

You barely have the phone to your ear before your brother-in-law shouts, "Camille had the baby!"

"A boy or a girl?" you ask. Why are people so interested in a baby's sex? The answer is that being a boy or a girl is not simply a biological distinction. **Instead, these terms are associated with distinct** *social roles* **that are cultural guidelines for people's behavior. Starting in infancy, children learn about** *gender roles*—**behaviors considered appropriate for males and females.** As youngsters learn these roles, they begin to identify with one of these groups. **Children forge a** *gender identity*, **the perception of the self as either male or female.**

In this chapter, we will see how children acquire a gender role and a gender identity. We'll begin, in **Module 13.1,** by considering cultural stereotypes of males and females. In **Module 13.2,** we will examine actual psychological differences between boys and girls. In **Module 13.3,** we'll focus on how children come to identify with one sex. Finally, in **Module 13.4,** we'll discuss recent changes in gender roles. Throughout this chapter, I'll use *sex* to refer to aspects of males and females that are clearly biological (such as differences in anatomy) and the term *gender* to refer to all other characteristics that relate to maleness and femaleness.

13.1 Gender Stereotypes

OUTLINE

How Do We View Men and Women?

Learning Gender Stereotypes

LEARNING OBJECTIVES

- What are gender stereotypes, and how do they differ for males and females?
- How do gender stereotypes influence behavior?
- When do children learn their culture's stereotypes for males and females?

When Nancy was 7 months pregnant, her 11-year-old son, Clark, announced that he really wanted a brother, not a sister. Clark explained, "A sister would drive me crazy. Girls never make up their minds about stuff, and they get all worked up over nothin'." "Where did Clark get these ideas?" Nancy wondered. "Is this typical for 11-year-olds?"

All cultures have *gender stereotypes*: **beliefs about how males and females differ in personality traits, interests, and behaviors.** Of course, because stereotypes are beliefs, they may or may not be true. In this module, we'll look at the features associated with gender stereotypes and discover when children like Clark learn about gender stereotypes.

How Do We View Men and Women?

"Terry is active, independent, competitive, and aggressive." As you were reading this sentence, did you assume that Terry was a male? Why? *Terry* is a common name for both males and females, but the adjectives used here to describe Terry are more commonly associated with men than with women. In fact, most adults associate different traits with men and women, and these views have changed very little since the 1960s (Ruble, Martin, & Berenbaum, 2006). Men are said to be independent, competitive, aggressive, outgoing, ambitious, self-confident, and dominant. **These male-associated traits are called** *instrumental* **because they describe individuals who act on the world and influence it.** In contrast, women are said to be emotional, kind, creative, considerate, gentle, excitable, and aware of others' feelings. **Female-associated traits are called** *expressive***, because they describe emotional functioning and individuals who value interpersonal relationships.**

Are these views shared by adults worldwide? The graphs in Figure 13-1 provide the answer for four traits from seven countries (Williams & Best, 1990). You can see that each trait shows cultural variation. For example, virtually all American participants consider men aggressive, but only a slight majority of Nigerian participants do. Thus, American views of men and women are not shared worldwide. In fact, what's notable about the research results is that Americans' gender stereotypes are more extreme than those of any other country listed. Keep this in mind as you think about what men and women can and cannot do and what they should and should not do. Your ideas about gender are shaped by your culture's beliefs, which are not held universally.

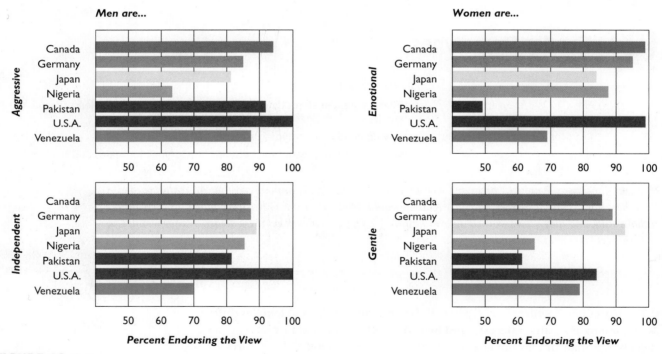

FIGURE 13-1

Understanding our tendency to stereotype gender behavior is important because stereotypes are very limiting (Smith & Mackie, 2000). If we have stereotyped views, we expect males to act in particular ways and females to act in other ways, and we respond to males and females solely on the basis of gender, not as individuals. For example, do you assume the youngster in the photo is a girl based on her taste in toys? Assuming the child is a girl would, in turn, probably lead you to think she plays more quietly and is more easily frightened than if you assume the child is a boy (Karraker, Vogel, & Lake, 1995). Making stereotyped assumptions about gender leads to a whole host of inferences about behavior and personality that may not be true.

When do children begin to learn their culture's stereotypes for males and females? We'll answer this question in the next section.

Learning Gender Stereotypes

Children don't live in a gender-neutral world for long. Although 12-month-old boys and girls look equally at gender-stereotyped toys, 18-month-olds do not: Girls look longer at pictures of dolls than pictures of trucks, but boys look longer at pictures of trucks (Serbin et al., 2001). By 4 years, children's knowledge of gender-stereotyped activities is extensive: They believe that girls play hopscotch but that boys play football; girls help bake cookies but boys take out the trash; and women feed babies but men chop wood (Gelman, Taylor, & Nguyen, 2004). And they've begun to learn about behaviors and traits that are stereotypically masculine or feminine. Preschoolers believe that boys are more often aggressive physically but girls tend to be aggressive verbally (Giles & Heyman, 2005).

During the elementary-school years, children expand their knowledge of gender-stereotyped traits and behaviors and they begin to include personality traits (Heyman & Legare, 2004). By the time they enter middle school, their ideas of gender stereotypes are virtually as well formed as those of adults.

During the elementary-school years, children also learn that occupations associated with males tend to earn more money and have greater power than those associated with females (Weisgram, Bigler, & Liben, 2010). Children apparently learn a simple rule—something like "Jobs for men are more prestigious than jobs for women"—because children learning unfamiliar jobs (e.g., a chandler makes candles) rate these occupations as more prestigious if they're illustrated with men than with women (Liben, Bigler, & Krogh, 2001).

As children develop, they also begin to understand that gender stereotypes do not always apply; older children are more willing than younger children to ignore stereotypes when judging other children. For example, told about a boy who likes to play with girls and pretend to iron, preschoolers think he would still want to play with masculine toys. By the middle elementary-school years, however, children realize that this boy's interests are not stereotypic and he would rather play with stereotypically feminine toys (Blakemore, 2003).

Thus, although older children are more familiar with gender stereotypes, they see these stereotypes as general guidelines for behavior that are not necessarily binding for all boys and girls (Banse et al., 2010). This developmental trend toward greater flexibility is evident in the study described in the "Focus on Research" feature.

Gender stereotypes lead us to assume that this child is a girl simply because the child is playing with a doll.

 QUESTION 13.1
Abigail believes that girls are gentler than boys, and that boys are stronger than girls, but that boys and girls are equally talkative and confident. With these stereotypic beliefs, how old is Abigail likely to be?
(Answer is on page 411.)

Focus on Research

Reasoning About Gender-Related Properties

Who were the investigators, and what was the aim of the study? Do children believe that physical and behavioral properties of boys and girls are inherent and stable? Do they believe, for example, that boys *necessarily* like to build things and will grow up to have a beard? Do they believe that girls *necessarily* like to play with dolls and will grow up to have breasts? Marianne Taylor, Marjorie Rhodes, and Susan Gelman (2009) conducted a study to answer these questions.

How did the investigators measure the topic of interest? Taylor and colleagues told participants about a baby girl who, right after birth, went to live on an island inhabited only by men, including her uncle. She had no contact with females. Participants were then shown a photo of the baby as a "big kid" and were asked several questions about her physical properties (e.g., "Will she grow up to be a mommy or a daddy?" Will she grow up to have breasts or a beard?") and some about her behavioral properties (e.g., "Will she like to play with a tea set or with trucks?" "Will she want to be a nurse or a firefighter?"). They were also told about a baby boy who lives on an island with his aunt and other women and then were asked the same questions.

Who were the participants in the study? The study included 68 5-year-olds, 64 10-year-olds, and 32 college students. At each age, half of the children were girls.

What was the design of the study? This study was experimental because Taylor and colleagues were interested in the impact of the domain—physical versus behavioral—on participants' judgments. The study was cross-sectional because it included 5-year-olds, 10-year-olds, and college students, each tested once.

Were there ethical concerns with the study? No; the children enjoyed hearing stories about babies growing up on the island.

What were the results? The investigators recorded the percentage of responses that were consistent with the baby's biological sex (e.g., predicting that the baby girl would like a tea set and want to be a nurse, and that she'll grow up to be a mom and have breasts). The results are shown in Figure 13-2, separately for physical and behavioral properties.

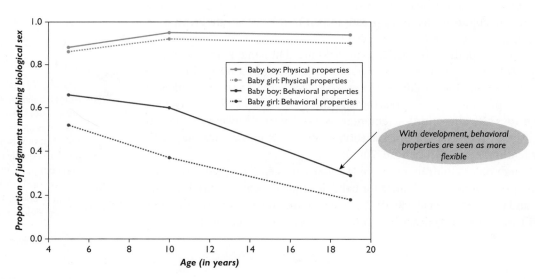

FIGURE 13-2

Let's start with the physical properties. There's little developmental change in these judgments: at all ages, participants expected the baby to acquire physical properties associated with its biological sex. However, the pattern is quite different for behavioral properties, where there is a steady downward developmental trend. Five-year-olds tend to believe that boys and girls will engage in gender-stereotypic behaviors, though they see these as slightly more flexible than physical properties. In contrast, adults believe that a boy brought up by women will behave in a feminine-stereotypic manner and that a girl brought up by men will behave in a masculine-stereotypic manner. A final result to note is that participants at all ages claimed greater flexibility in behavioral properties for girls than for boys; they thought that girls were more likely to be influenced in a masculine direction than boys were to be influenced in a feminine direction.

What did the investigators conclude? Taylor and colleagues concluded that "young children treat the concepts of 'boy' and 'girl' as equivalent to species, in the extent to which features are inborn, inflexible, and intrinsically linked to category membership. . . . [By] adulthood, participants viewed both male and female behavior as more open to the environment and flexible . . ." (2009, p. 475).

What converging evidence would strengthen these conclusions? The children in this sample came from university towns in the U.S. Midwest, and most were European American. It would be important to see whether children from different backgrounds responded in a similar fashion. In addition, it would be valuable to extend the list of properties to, for example, psychological properties (e.g., personality) to determine whether they're considered more like physical properties or more like behavioral properties in terms of flexibility.

Increased age is not the only factor leading to more flexible views of stereotypes. Girls tend to be more flexible about stereotypes (Ruble & Martin, 1998), perhaps because they see that male-stereotypic traits are more attractive and have more status than female-stereotypic traits. Social class also contributes. Adolescents and young adults (but not children) from middle-class homes tend to have more flexible ideas about gender than individuals from lower-class homes (e.g., Serbin, Powlishta, & Gulko, 1993). This difference may be due to education: Better-educated, middle-class parents may impart less rigid views of gender to their children.

Ethnicity is another factor associated with flexible views of gender. Some studies find that African American youngsters have more flexible ideas about gender than their European American peers (e.g., Bardwell, Cochran, & Walker, 1986). Compared to European American mothers, African American mothers are more frequently employed outside the home, and this may contribute to their children's more open attitudes.

At this point, perhaps you're wondering whether there's any truth to gender stereotypes. For example, are boys really more dominant than girls? Are girls really more excitable than boys? For answers to these questions, let's go to Module 13.2.

> By the end of elementary school, children know adults' stereotypes of males and females but understand that these stereotypes are not binding on individuals.

 ANSWER 13.1

She's probably about 5 years old. (A more conservative estimate would be to say that she's in the early elementary-school years.) The logic behind this estimate is that she has learned some of the typical stereotypes of boys and girls (e.g., that girls are gentler than boys) but has yet to learn others (e.g., that boys are more confident than girls).

Check Your Learning

RECALL How do older children's gender stereotypes differ from those of younger children?

What groups of children tend to have more flexible views of gender stereotypes?

INTERPRET Compare and contrast instrumental traits with expressive traits.

APPLY How might Piaget have explained older children's more flexible views of gender stereotypes?

13.2 Differences Related to Gender

OUTLINE

Differences in Physical Development and Behavior

Differences in Intellectual Abilities and Achievement

Differences in Personality and Social Behavior

Frank Talk About Gender Differences

LEARNING OBJECTIVES

• How do boys and girls differ in physical development, intellectual abilities, and social behavior?

• What factors are responsible for these gender differences?

• What are the implications of these gender differences for boys' and girls' development?

The high-school student council was discussing a proposal to hold the prom in an expensive hotel in a nearby big city. Maggie thought this was a truly terrible idea, but most of the group seemed to like the plan, so she decided not to say anything. Just as she decided to keep quiet, her friend Charles announced that he was going to vote against the proposal and, as he described his reasons, Maggie realized that they were exactly the ones that she'd thought of but hadn't voiced.

Maggie and Charles both thought the proposal was flawed, but only Charles expressed those concerns. Why? We'll answer that question in this module as we explore gender-related differences in different domains of development. This territory was first charted in *The Psychology of Sex Differences*, a book by Eleanor Maccoby and Carol Jacklin published in 1974, that summarized results from approximately 1,500 research studies. Maccoby and Jacklin concluded that gender differences had been established in only four areas: Girls have greater verbal ability, whereas boys have greater mathematical and visual–spatial ability, and boys are more aggressive than girls. Just as importantly, Maccoby and Jacklin did *not* find evidence to support popular ideas that girls are more social and suggestible than boys, have lower self-esteem, are less analytic in thinking, and lack achievement motivation.

> Maccoby and Jacklin concluded that girls have greater verbal ability but that boys have greater mathematical and spatial ability and are more aggressive.

Some critics challenged Maccoby and Jacklin on the grounds that they had included some weak studies and defined behaviors in ways that other researchers might not (Block, 1978). The debate stimulated more research; some of this research applied new statistical techniques that allowed for finer analysis, such as meta-analysis. Many developmentalists now believe that gender differences are more extensive than Maccoby and Jacklin suggested, but their book remains a classic because its comprehensiveness provided an excellent starting point for further research.

In the remainder of this module, we'll see what we've discovered about gender differences since Maccoby's and Jacklin's classic analysis. We'll focus on differences in physical development, cognitive processes, and social behavior.

Differences in Physical Development and Behavior

Of course, differences in the reproductive system are what differentiate boys from girls, along with differences in secondary sex characteristics such as lower voice and facial hair in boys and breast development and wider hips in girls. Boys are usually

FIGURE 13-3

larger and stronger than girls, which means that they often physically outperform girls. You can see the difference at high-school track meets: Boys usually run faster, jump higher, and throw objects farther and more accurately. And, as Figure 13-3 shows, long before high school, boys throw and jump farther than girls. Outside of sports, on tasks that involve fine-motor coordination, such as tracing and drawing, girls do better than boys (Thomas & French, 1985).

Some of the gender differences in gross-motor skills that require strength reflect the fact that as children approach and enter puberty, girls' bodies have proportionately more fat and less muscle than boys' bodies. This difference explains why, for example, boys can hang from a bar using their arms and hands much longer than girls can. However, for other gross-motor skills, such as running, throwing, and catching, body composition is much less important (Smoll & Schutz, 1990). In these cases, children's experience is crucial. Many girls and their parents believe that sports and physical fitness are less valuable for girls than for boys. Consequently, girls spend less time in these sports- and fitness-related activities than boys, depriving them of opportunities to practice, which is essential for developing motor skills (Eccles & Harold, 1991). During recess, for example, elementary-school girls are more often found swinging, jumping rope, or perhaps talking quietly in a group; in contrast, boys are often playing football or shooting baskets. Consistent with this argument, gender differences in throwing are much smaller among Australian Aborigines, a group that traditionally expected girls to be able to throw during hunting (Thomas et al., 2010).

As infants, boys are more active than girls, and this difference increases during childhood (Else-Quest et al., 2006; Saudino, 2009). For example, in a classroom, boys are more likely than girls to have a hard time sitting still. On playgrounds like those in the photos on page 414, boys more often play vigorously and girls quietly. And, recall

Boys are physically more active than girls, a difference that's evident when you watch children on a playground.

from Module 5.2 that boys are three times more likely than girls to be diagnosed with attention deficit hyperactivity disorder.

Girls tend to be healthier than boys. Female embryos are more likely than male embryos to survive prenatal development. This trend continues after birth. Infant boys are more prone to birth complications, and throughout life boys are more prone to many diseases and dysfunctions (Jacklin, 1989). Finally, adolescent boys and young men are more likely to engage in unhealthy, risk-taking behaviors, including drinking, reckless driving, and sexual activity (Byrnes, Miller, & Schafer, 1999; Granie, 2009).

To summarize, boys tend to be bigger, stronger, and more active; girls tend to have better fine-motor coordination and to be healthier. In the next section, which concerns intellectual skills, you'll again see that gender differences vary from one skill to the next.

Differences in Intellectual Abilities and Achievement

Of the four gender-based differences discovered by Maccoby and Jacklin (1974), three concern intellectual skills: Girls tend to have greater verbal skill but boys tend to have greater mathematical and visual–spatial skill. Since Maccoby's and Jacklin's work was published, we've learned much about the nature of gender differences in these areas.

VERBAL ABILITY. Girls have larger vocabularies than boys and are more talkative (Feldman et al., 2000; Leaper & Smith, 2004). During elementary school and high school, girls read, write, and spell better than boys, and this difference is found in virtually all industrialized countries (Halpern et al., 2007). Finally, more boys are diagnosed with language-related problems such as reading disability or specific language impairment (Wicks-Nelson & Israel, 2006).

Differences in verbal ability and spatial ability likely reflect the impact of biological forces and children's experiences.

Why are girls more talented verbally than boys? Part of the explanation may lie in biological forces. The left hemisphere of the brain, which is central to language (see Module 4.3), may mature more rapidly in girls than in boys (Diamond et al., 1983). However, experience also contributes. During the toddler years, mothers talk more to daughters than to sons (Fivush et al., 2000). And by the elementary-school years, reading is often stereotyped as an activity for girls (Huston, 1983), which may make girls more willing than boys to invest time and effort in mastering verbal skills such as reading.

SPATIAL ABILITY.   In Module 8.1, you saw that spatial ability is a component of most models of intelligence. **One aspect of spatial ability is** *mental rotation*, **the ability to imagine how an object will look after it has been moved in space.** The items in Figure 13-4 test mental rotation: The task is to determine which of the figures labeled A through E are rotated versions of the figure in the box on the left. During childhood and adolescence, boys tend to have better mental-rotation skill than girls (Govier & Salisbury, 2000; Voyer, Voyer, & Bryden, 1995). (The correct answers are C and D.)

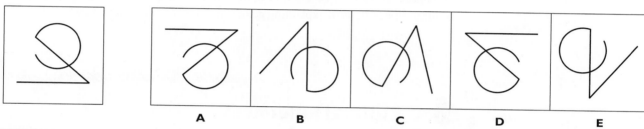

FIGURE 13-4

There's even evidence that the sexes differ in mental-rotation ability in infancy. In one study (Quinn & Liben, 2008), 4-month-olds were shown a stimulus in various orientations (e.g., upright, rotated 90 degrees, rotated 180 degrees). Later, when the stimulus was shown at a novel orientation (e.g., rotated 45 degrees), infant boys recognized it but infant girls did not. Similarly, in another study (Moore & Johnson, 2008), 5-month-olds watched a video showing an unfamiliar object rotating through a 240-degree arc. Later, when the object was shown rotating through the other 120 degrees, infant boys recognized it but infant girls did not. Together these findings suggest an early start to the sex differences in mental rotation.

Some explanations for gender differences in mental rotation and other spatial abilities emphasize biology. Some scientists argue that spatial skill was essential for successful hunting—in navigating and in calculating trajectories for weapons—and may represent an evolutionary adaptation for males (Halpern et al., 2007). A related idea is that the right hemisphere of the brain may be more specialized for spatial processing in males than in females, perhaps because boys mature more slowly than girls (Rilea, Roskos-Ewoldsen, & Boles, 2004; Waber, 1977).

But experience certainly contributes too. Boys are more likely than girls to participate in activities that foster spatial skill, such as estimating the trajectory of an object moving through space (e.g., a baseball), using two-dimensional plans to assemble an object such as a scale model (Baenninger & Newcombe, 1995), or, like the boy in the photo on page 416 playing video games that involve visual–perceptual skills (Okagaki & Frensch, 1994; Terlecki & Newcombe, 2005). Among children from lower-socioeconomic-status homes, boys and girls have comparable spatial skills (Levine et al., 2005), which suggests that some experience associated with middle-class living is critical for the sex differences to emerge.

Playing video games can enhance a child's spatial skill; because boys play video games more often than girls, this may contribute to a gender difference in spatial skill.

Of course, these explanations are not necessarily mutually exclusive. Biological and experiential forces may both contribute to gender differences in spatial ability, just as both contribute to gender differences in verbal ability. Thus, parents and others can foster verbal and spatial abilities in both boys and girls because each is influenced considerably by experience (Newcombe, 2002).

MATHEMATICS. On standardized tests of math achievement, during the elementary-school years, girls usually get greater scores than boys. For tests administered during high school and college, boys used to get higher scores, but that difference has diminished substantially over the past 25 years; now boys have a negligible advantage (Lindberg et al., 2010). This change apparently reflects efforts to encourage girls to pursue mathematics generally and to take more math courses specifically. For example, American boys and girls are now equally likely to take calculus courses in high school (National Science Foundation, 2008). And, as we'll see in the "Cultural Influences" feature, cross-cultural comparisons also point to an important role for cultural expectations in explaining gender differences in mathematics.

Cultural Influences

A Cross-Cultural Look at Gender Differences in Math

Several math achievement tests are administered internationally, and the results provide useful insights into the forces that drive gender differences in math. For example, the Programme for International Student Assessment (PISA) is administered in more than 60 countries, with thousands of high-school students in each country taking tests measuring math, reading, and science abilities (Organisation for Economic Co-operation and Development, 2010). In many countries, there are small differences favoring boys (e.g., France, Germany). However, in some countries (e.g., Republic of Korea, the Slovak Republic), boys have substantially greater scores. And in Iceland, girls have the advantage (Else-Quest, Hyde, & Linn, 2010).

Why should the pattern vary so much? One view is that it reflects cultural differences in math-related career opportunities for men and women. When girls (and their parents and their teachers) see math as a means to achieve success, they will be interested in math and take math courses. In contrast, if girls see math-related careers as "for boys only," they will have little reason to invest time and energy in mastering math. This line of thinking leads to a straightforward prediction: In countries where women have much the same access to education, occupations, and political power as men, gender differences in math should be negligible. In contrast, where women are limited to traditionally feminine-stereotypic occupations that do not require math skills, gender differences in math should remain. Exactly this pattern is found in international comparisons of PISA math data (Else-Quest et al., 2010). For example, educational and professional opportunities are substantial in Iceland (where girls excel in math) but not in the Republic of Korea (where test results favor boys). In other words, these cross-cultural comparisons seem to suggest that "girls will perform at the same level as their male classmates when they are encouraged to succeed, are given the necessary educational tools, and have visible female role models excelling in mathematics" (Else-Quest et al., 2010, p. 125).

Differences in Personality and Social Behavior

Are there differences in personality and social behavior between boys and girls? In the 1970s, Maccoby and Jacklin (1974) found convincing evidence of only one gender difference in this realm: Boys were more aggressive than girls. In this section, we'll see what researchers have discovered in the ensuing 35 years.

AGGRESSIVE BEHAVIOR.   No one doubts Maccoby's and Jacklin's conclusion that boys are more aggressive physically than girls. As mentioned in Module 12.4 and as you can see in the photo, the gender difference in physical aggression is readily observed. No matter how you slice it, boys are more aggressive than girls, and this is true as early as 17 months of age (Baillargeon et al., 2007; Card et al., 2008). Of course, some qualifications apply. Boys are not always aggressive. They are, for example, more likely to be physically aggressive toward other boys than toward girls (Maccoby & Jacklin, 1980): Boys may try to beat up other boys, but, as a general rule, they don't try to beat up girls. And, when they're provoked, girls can be physically aggressive, too (Bettencourt & Miller, 1996).

Because boys and men are more aggressive in virtually all cultures, and because males in nonhuman species are also more aggressive, scientists are convinced that biology contributes heavily to this gender difference. **Aggressive behavior has been linked to** *androgens*, **hormones secreted by the testes.** Androgens do not lead directly to aggression. Instead, androgens make it more likely that boys will be aggressive by making them more excitable or easily angered and by making boys stronger (e.g., Marcus et al., 1985).

Just because hormones are involved, though, we can't ignore experience. The media are filled with aggressive male models—from Vin Diesel to Jedi knights—who are rewarded for their behavior. What's more, parents are more likely to use physical punishment with sons than with daughters and are more tolerant of aggressive behavior in sons than in daughters (Block, 1978; Condry & Ross, 1985). As we saw in Module 12.4, these are just the sort of experiences that precipitate a vicious cycle of increasing aggression; and this cycle is much more common for boys than for girls. Although biology may make boys more prone to aggression, experience encourages boys rather than girls to express their aggression physically.

Boys' aggression may be more obvious because of its physical nature, but girls can be aggressive, too (Ostrov & Godleski, 2010). In Module 12.4, we saw that girls often rely upon relational aggression, in which they try to hurt others by damaging their relationships with peers (Crick & Grotpeter, 1995). They may call other children names, make fun of them, spread rumors about them, or—just as bad—pointedly ignore them. Thus, when boys want to harm peers, they try to hurt them physically, but girls try to damage their relationships with peers.

 QUESTION 13.2
Brianna is the mother of fraternal twins, a boy and a girl, who are just starting elementary school. She's determined that both of her children will excel in reading and math. Are Brianna's goals realistic?
(Answer is on page 420.)

Physical aggression is far more common among boys than among girls.

Worldwide, boys are more physically aggressive than girls, who favor relational aggression.

EMOTIONAL SENSITIVITY.   According to the stereotypes listed on page 408, girls are better able to express their emotions and interpret others' emotions. In fact, this is a gender difference supported by research (Hall & Halberstadt, 1981; Weinberg et al., 1999). For example, throughout infancy, childhood, and adolescence, girls identify facial expressions (e.g., happy face versus a sad face) more accurately than boys do (McClure, 2000). And in their interactions with peers, girls are more empathic—they're better able to understand and "feel" how other children and adolescents are feeling (Rose & Rudolph, 2006).

Most developmentalists believe that the gender difference in emotional sensitivity reflects both nature and nurture. On the nature side, regions of the brain's temporal lobe that play a leading role in processing emotional expression develop more rapidly in girls than in boys (McClure, 2000). On the nurture side, parents behave in more "feeling-oriented" manners with daughters than with sons. They are more likely to talk about emotions with daughters than with sons and to emphasize the importance of considering others' feelings (Kuebli, Butler, & Fivush, 1995; Zahn-Waxler, Cole, & Barrett, 1991).

SOCIAL INFLUENCE.   Another gender stereotype is that females are more easily influenced by others—that is, that they are more persuadable. In fact, young girls are more likely than young boys to comply with an adult's request, and they are more likely to seek an adult's help (Jacklin & Maccoby, 1978). Girls and women are also influenced more than boys and men by persuasive messages and others' behavior, especially when they are under group pressure (Becker, 1986; Eagly, Karau, & Makhijani, 1995). However, these gender differences may stem from the fact that females value group harmony more than boys and thus seem to give in to others (Miller, Danaher, & Forbes, 1986; Strough & Berg, 2000). For instance, at a meeting like the one described in the module-opening vignette, girls are just as likely as boys to recognize the flaws in a bad idea, but, like Maggie, girls are more willing to go along simply because they don't want the group to start arguing.

DEPRESSION.   *Depression*, a disorder in which individuals are chronically sad and irritable and have low self-esteem, is rare in childhood but becomes much more common in adolescence, particularly among teenage girls (Avenevoli & Steinberg, 2001). According to current theories (Hankin & Abramson, 2001), depression is often triggered when adolescents experience a negative life event (e.g., flunk a major exam) and interpret this event negatively (e.g., "I'm so stupid; my friends won't want to be with me if they know I'm this dumb").

Applied to the sex difference in depression during adolescence, theorists emphasize that girls experience more frequent stressors, such as dissatisfaction with their appearance after pubertal change or conflict with close friends (Hankin, Mermelstein, & Roesch, 2007). Also, girls like the one in the photo are more apt to interpret these negative life events in harmful terms, emphasizing social-emotional consequences to a far greater extent than boys do. For example, I knew a 15-year-old boy who, after 9 years of playing soccer, was the only player cut from the high-school team. Although upset briefly, within days he had decided to go out for cross-country and ended up having a successful and rewarding running career. In the same circumstances, a girl might well have spent more time focusing on the harmful consequences— "I won't be able to hang with my soccer friends," "I stink at sports"—the kind of thinking that would put her at risk for a bout of depression. Much more than boys, girls are prone to ruminate about their problems: thinking about them over and over, and talking about them with friends (Cox, Mezulis, & Hyde, 2010).

Depression is more common among adolescent girls than adolescent boys.

At this point, perhaps you're wondering about the role of hormones in depression. After all, adolescence is often portrayed as a time when hormones run wild and cause huge mood swings. In fact, researchers have found few consistent connections between depression (and other mood disorders) and levels of hormones (Buchanan, Eccles, & Becker, 1992). That is, although levels of female hormones such as progesterone and estrogen definitely rise with the onset of puberty, these changes play no more than a small role in the onset of depression in teenage girls.

Frank Talk About Gender Differences

The gender differences we've discussed in this module are listed in the Summary Table on page 420. What should we make of these differences? What do they tell us about the experience of growing up male versus growing up female?

During adolescence, girls are more likely than boys to suffer from depression.

First, remember that the gender differences described in this module represent differences in the *average scores* for boys and girls—differences that are relatively small. For example, Figure 13-5 shows the distribution of scores on a hypothetical reading test. As we would expect, overall girls do better than boys. However, the distributions of girls' and boys' scores overlap substantially. The area shaded in yellow shows the large percentage of boys who have higher reading scores than the average girl, and the area shaded in red shows the large percentage of girls who have lower reading scores than the average boy. The diagram makes it obvious that a difference in average scores does *not* mean that girls read well and boys read poorly. Consequently, a boy who wants to become a writer should not be deterred because of small differences in average scores for boys and girls. Of course, we could draw similar diagrams in the other domains in which boys and girls differ, with the same conclusion. The vast majority of gender differences are small, which means that boys' and girls' scores overlap considerably (Hyde, 2007).

Second, think about the large number of abilities, behaviors, and traits that have not been considered in this module. Boys and girls do not differ in many, many

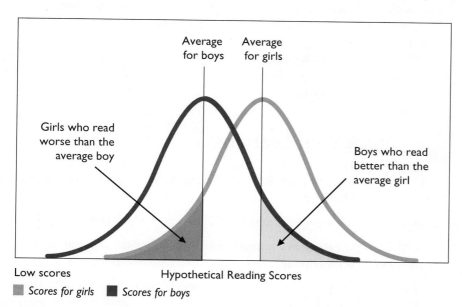

FIGURE 13-5

SUMMARY TABLE

SEX DIFFERENCES IN PHYSICAL AND BEHAVIORAL DEVELOPMENT

General	Specific Domain	Nature of Difference
Physical Development		
	Motor skills	Boys excel at tasks that require strength, but girls do better on tasks that require fine-motor coordination.
	Activity	Beginning in infancy, boys are more active than girls.
	Health	From conception through adulthood, girls are healthier.
Intellectual Abilities		
	Verbal ability	Girls have larger vocabularies; they also read, write, and spell better.
	Spatial ability	Boys are better on mental-rotation tasks and in determining relations between objects in space.
	Mathematics	Boys get higher scores on standardized tests, but primarily in countries where girls have limited educational and career opportunities.
Personality and Social Behavior		
	Aggression	Boys are more aggressive physically; girls rely more on relational aggression.
	Emotional sensitivity	Girls are better able to identify and express emotions.
	Social influence	Because girls value group harmony more than boys do, girls are more susceptible to others' influence.
	Depression	Beginning in adolescence, girls are more prone to depression than boys.

---

aspects of cognition, personality, and social behavior, a point that is easily lost when focusing on gender differences. In reality, a list of ways in which boys and girls are similar is much longer than a list of differences (Hyde, 2007). In cognitive processing, memory, and understanding of people—to name just a few areas—boys and girls are much more alike than different. If development is a journey, both boys and girls have many choices as they travel; few, if any, routes have signs that say "for girls only" or "for boys only."

In this module, we've focused on the behaviors and skills on which boys and girls differ; in the next, we'll see how children acquire a gender identity, a sense of "being a boy" or "being a girl."

 ANSWER 13.2
Yes, her son and daughter may both excel in math. But if the typical pattern of gender differences holds, her daughter may be the better reader.

 ## Check Your Learning

RECALL What were the primary gender differences that Maccoby and Jacklin described in their 1974 book?

Summarize features of personality and social behavior in which boys and girls differ.

INTERPRET How do nature and nurture contribute to gender differences in intellectual abilities and achievement?

APPLY Based on what you know about differences between boys and girls in intellectual abilities and social behavior, how might this module differ in the 40th edition of this book, published in 2106?

13.3 Gender Identity

OUTLINE

The Socializing Influences of People and the Media

Cognitive Theories of Gender Identity

Biological Influences

LEARNING OBJECTIVES

• How do parents, peers, and the media influence children's learning of gender roles?

• How do cognitive theories explain children's learning of gender roles?

• How does biology influence children's learning of gender roles?

Taryn, who has just turned 4, knows that she's a girl but is convinced that she'll grow up to be a man. Taryn plays almost exclusively with boys and her favorite toys are trucks and cars. Taryn tells her parents that when she's bigger, she'll grow a beard and be a daddy. Taryn's father is confident that his daughter's ideas are a natural part of a preschooler's limited understanding of gender, but her mother wonders if they've neglected some important aspect of Taryn's upbringing.

A ccording to the old saying, "Boys will be boys and girls will be girls"—but how, in fact, do boys become boys and girls become girls when it comes to gender roles? That is, how do children acquire and internalize their culture's roles for males and females? And how do children develop a sense of identity as a male or female? We'll answer these questions in this module and, as we do, learn whether Taryn's wish to grow up to be a man is typical for youngsters her age.

The Socializing Influences of People and the Media

Folklore holds that parents and other adults—teachers and television characters, for example—directly shape children's behavior regarding the roles associated with their sex. Boys are rewarded for boyish behavior and punished for girlish behavior.

The folklore even has a theoretical basis: According to social cognitive theorists such as Albert Bandura (1977, 1986; Bandura & Bussey, 2004) and Walter Mischel (1970), children learn gender roles in much the same way they learn other social behaviors—by watching the world around them and learning the outcomes of actions. Thus, children learn what their culture considers appropriate behavior for males and females simply by watching how adults and peers act. How well does research support social cognitive theory? Let's look first at research done with parents.

> Parents treat sons and daughters similarly, except for behavior explicitly related to gender roles.

PARENTS.   An extensive meta-analysis of 172 studies involving 27,836 children (Lytton & Romney, 1991) found that parents often treat sons and daughters similarly: Parents interact equally with sons and daughters, are equally warm to both, and encourage both sons and daughters to achieve and be independent. However, in behavior related to gender roles, parents respond differently to sons and daughters (Lytton & Romney, 1991). Activities such as playing with dolls, dressing up, or helping an adult are encouraged more often in daughters than in sons; rough-and-tumble play and playing with blocks are encouraged more in sons than in daughters.

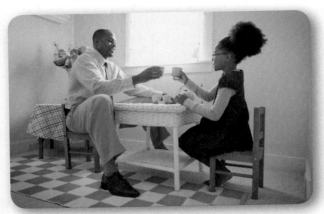

Fathers are more likely than mothers to treat their children in a stereotyped manner.

Parents tolerate mild aggression more in sons than in daughters (Martin & Ross, 2005), and, following the birth of a child (especially a firstborn), parents become more traditional in their attitudes regarding gender (Katz-Wise, Priess, & Hyde, 2010).

Fathers are more likely than mothers to treat sons and daughters differently. More than mothers, fathers such as the one in the photo often encourage gender-related play. Fathers also push their sons to achieve more but accept dependence in their daughters (Snow, Jacklin, & Maccoby, 1983). A father, for example, may urge his frightened young son to jump off the diving board ("Be a man!") but not be so insistent with his daughter ("That's okay, honey"). Apparently, mothers are more likely to respond based on their knowledge of the individual child's needs, but fathers respond based on gender stereotypes. A mother responds to her son knowing that he's smart but unsure of himself; a father may respond because of what he thinks boys should be like.

Of course, adults differ in their views on the relative rights and roles of males and females. Some have very traditional views, believing, for example, that men should be hired preferentially for some jobs and that it's more important for sons than daughters to attend college; others have more gender-neutral views, believing, for example, that women should have the same business and professional opportunities as men and that daughters should have the same educational opportunities as sons. It would be surprising if parents did not convey these attitudes to their children, and indeed they do (Crouter et al., 2007). A meta-analysis of 48 studies, including more than 10,000 pairs of parents and children, showed that children's gender-related interests, attitudes, and self-concepts are more traditional when their parents have traditional views and more gender-neutral when their parents have nontraditional views (Tenenbaum & Leaper, 2002).

TEACHERS.   After parents, teachers may be the most influential adults in children's lives. Many teachers help to differentiate gender roles by making gender salient in the classroom. In elementary schools, students may be told to form separate lines for boys and girls; teachers may praise the girls as a group for being quiet during a video while criticizing the boys for laughing (Thorne, 1993). In addition, teachers spend more time interacting with boys than with girls. Teachers call on boys more frequently, praise them more for their schoolwork, and spend more time scolding them for disruptive classroom behavior (Good & Brophy, 1996). By using sex as a basis for differentiating children and by giving boys more attention, teachers foster gender-role learning (Ruble, Martin, & Berenbaum, 2006).

PEERS.   By the age of 3, most children's play shows the impact of gender stereotypes—boys prefer blocks and trucks, whereas girls prefer tea sets and dolls—and youngsters are critical of peers who engage in gender-inappropriate play (Aspenlieder, 2009). This is particularly true of boys who like feminine toys or who choose feminine activities. Boys who play with dolls and girls (like the one in the photo) who play with trucks will both be ignored, teased, or ridiculed by their peers, but a boy will receive harsher treatment than a girl (Levy, Taylor, & Gelman, 1995). Once children learn rules about gender-typical play, they often harshly punish peers who violate those rules.

Peers influence gender roles in another way, too. Between 2 and 3 years of age, children begin to prefer playing with same-sex peers (Martin & Fabes, 2001). Little boys play together with cars, and little girls play together with dolls. This preference increases during childhood, reaching a peak in preadolescence. By age 10 or 11, the vast majority of peer activity is with same-sex children, and most of this involves sex-typed play: Boys are playing sports or playing with cars or action figures; girls are doing artwork or playing with pets or dolls (McHale et al., 2004). Then the tide begins to turn, but even in adulthood time spent at work and at leisure is quite commonly segregated by gender (Hartup, 1983). This tendency for boys to play with boys and girls with girls has several distinctive features (Maccoby, 1990, 1998):

Preschool children often tease their peers who engage in cross-gender play.

- Given the opportunity, children spontaneously select same-sex playmates. Adult pressure ("James, why don't you play with John, not Amy?") is not necessary.

- Children resist parents' efforts to get them to play with members of the opposite sex. Girls are often unhappy when parents encourage them to play with boys, and boys complain when parents urge them to play with girls.

- Children's reluctance to play with members of the opposite sex is not restricted to gender-typed games, such as playing house or playing with cars. Boys and girls prefer same-sex playmates even in gender-neutral activities such as playing tag or doing puzzles.

Why do boys and girls seem so attracted to same-sex play partners? One reason is that their styles of play are very different. Boys specifically prefer rough-and-tumble play and generally are more competitive and dominating in their interactions. In contrast, when girls play, they are much more cooperative, prosocial, and conversation-oriented (Rose & Rudolph, 2006). Generally, boys don't enjoy the way that girls play and girls are averse to boys' style of play (Maccoby, 1990, 1998).

> Boys and girls don't play together because girls don't like boys' style of play and because girls' enabling style of interacting is ineffective with boys.

Second, when girls and boys play together, girls do not readily influence boys. **Girls' interactions with one another are typically** *enabling*—**their actions and remarks tend to support others and sustain the interaction.** When drawing together, one girl might say to another, "Cool picture" or "What do you want to do now?" **In contrast, boys' interactions are often** *constricting*—**one partner tries to emerge as the victor by threatening or contradicting the other, by exaggerating, and so on.** In the same drawing task, one boy might say to another, "My picture's better" or "Drawing is stupid—let's watch TV." When these styles are brought together, girls find that their enabling style is ineffective with boys. The same subtle overtures that work with other girls have no impact on boys. Boys ignore girls' polite suggestions about what to do and ignore girls' efforts to resolve conflicts with discussion (Rose & Rudolph, 2006).

Some theorists believe that these contrasting styles may have an evolutionary basis (Geary et al., 2003). Boys' concerns about dominating others may stem from a concern with establishing one's rank among a group of males, because those males at the upper ranks have better access to mates and better access to resources needed for offspring. Girls' concerns about affiliation may be a by-product of the fact that women traditionally left their own communities (and relatives) to live in a husband's community. Having no relatives nearby enhanced the value of a close friend, which placed a premium on the affiliative behaviors that lead to and maintain friendships.

Regardless of the exact cause, early segregation of playmates by style of play means that boys learn primarily from boys and girls from girls. Over time, such social segregation by sex reinforces gender differences in play. Martin and Fabes (2001), for example, conducted a longitudinal study of same-sex play in preschool and kindergarten children. When young boys spent most of their time playing with other boys at the beginning of the school year, by the end of the year their play was more active and more aggressive. In contrast, when young girls spent most of their time playing with other girls at the beginning of the school year, by the end of the year their play was less active and less aggressive. Boys and girls who spent more time playing with other-sex children didn't show these changes. Thus, young boys and girls teach each other gender-appropriate play. As they do, this helps solidify a youngster's emerging sense of membership in a particular gender group and sharpens the contrast between genders.

QUESTION 13.3

Rick has encouraged his 4-year-old son to play with the 5-year-old girl who lives next door, but his son will have none of it—he refuses every time. Rick thinks that his son is being unreasonable and stubborn. Do you agree?

(Answer is on page 427.)

TELEVISION.   Another source of influence on gender-role learning is television, which often portrays males and females in stereotyped ways. Women on television tend to be cast in romantic, marital, or family roles; they are depicted as emotional, passive, and weak. Men are more often cast in leadership or professional roles and are depicted as rational, active, and strong. As you can imagine, children who watch a lot of TV end up with more stereotyped views of males and females. In other words, TV viewing causes children to adopt many of the distorted portraits of males and females that dominate television programming (Signorielli & Lears, 1992).

TV often portrays males and females in stereotyped ways and children who watch TV frequently learn these stereotypes.

Let's now return to our original question: How well does research support the social learning explanation of gender roles? Studies of parents, teachers, and peers show that children learn much about gender roles simply by observing males and females, but simple observation of real-life models or television characters cannot be the entire explanation. After all, young boys traditionally have far more opportunities to observe their mother's behavior than their father's, but are more likely to imitate their father (for example, by using hammer and saw) than their mother (for example, by cooking). Thus, an important element in learning about gender is identifying with one gender and then actively seeking out activities that are typical for that gender. This aspect of gender-role learning is the focus of cognitive theories, which we'll examine in the next section.

Cognitive Theories of Gender Identity

According to Lawrence Kohlberg (1966; Kohlberg & Ullian, 1974), full understanding of gender develops gradually and involves three elements.

- *Gender labeling*: **By age 2 or 3, children understand that they are either boys or girls and label themselves accordingly.**

- *Gender stability*: **During the preschool years, children begin to understand that gender is stable—boys become men and girls become women.** That is, they realize that gender is stable over time, but they do not yet believe that it is consistent across situation or context. Children in this stage believe that a girl who wears her hair like a boy will become a boy and that a boy who plays with dolls will become a girl (Fagot, 1985).

- *Gender consistency*: **Between the ages of 4 and 7, most children come to understand that maleness and femaleness do not change over situations or according to personal wishes.** They understand that a child's sex is unaffected by the clothing that a child wears or the toys that a child likes.

Taryn, the 4-year-old in the opening vignette, is in the first stage: she knows that she's a girl. However, she has yet to develop a sense of gender stability or gender consistency. **When children understand labels, stability, and consistency, they have mastered** *gender constancy*.   👁—|Watch the Video on mydevelopmentlab.com

According to Kohlberg's theory, children begin learning about gender roles after they master gender constancy; that is, after they know that gender is fixed across time and situation. Research generally supports this prediction (Martin, Ruble, & Szkrybalo, 2002). However, some work suggests that children begin learning about gender-typical behavior as soon as they master gender stability (invariance across time); as they understand gender consistency (invariance across situation), their understanding of gender roles becomes more flexible. They agree that it's okay for boys to play with dolls or for girls to play with trucks (Ruble et al., 2007).

Kohlberg's theory specifies *when* children begin learning about gender-appropriate behavior and activities, but not *how* such learning takes place. A theory that addresses the "how" of gender learning is the focus of the "Spotlight on Theories" feature.

👁—|Watch the Video *Gender Constancy* on **mydevelopmentlab.com** to learn more about the development of gender identity. As you watch, notice how quickly and easily the younger girl decides that the boy becomes a girl when he has a purse; in contrast, the older girl fully understands that the boy is just a boy with a purse, not a girl.

Spotlight On Theories

Gender-Schema Theory

BACKGROUND   Preschool children learn gender roles rapidly. The environment, of course, provides many clues about typical roles for males and females. But how do children use these clues to learn about the behaviors and characteristics typically associated with their sex?

THE THEORY   A theory proposed by Carol Martin (Martin & Ruble, 2004; Martin et al., 1999), illustrated in Figure 13-6, addresses how children learn about gender. In *gender-schema theory*, **children first decide if an object, activity, or behavior is female or male, then use this information to decide whether or not they should learn more about the object, activity, or behavior.** That is, once children know

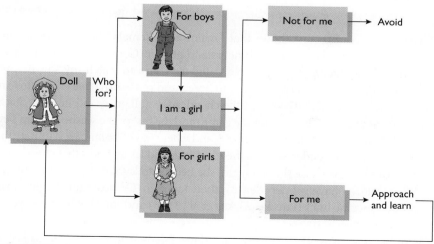

FIGURE 13-6

their gender, they pay attention primarily to experiences and events that are gender appropriate (Martin & Halverson, 1987). According to gender-schema theory, a preschool boy who is watching a group of girls playing in sand will decide that playing in sand is for girls and that, because he is a boy, playing in sand is not for him. Seeing a group of older boys playing football, he will decide that football is for boys, and because he is a boy, football is acceptable and he should learn more about it.

Hypothesis: According to gender-schema theory, children first establish gender identity, then begin actively learning about gender roles. Consequently, children who have established a gender identity should know much about gender roles, but children who have not established a gender identity should know little about gender roles.

Test: Zosuls et al. (2009) recorded children's language development from 10 to 21 months, looking for occasions when children referred to themselves as a boy or as a girl. In addition, at 17 and 21 months, children were observed as they played with several gender-stereotypic toys (truck, doll) and gender-neutral toys (telephone, miniature people). The investigators found that children who referred to themselves by gender played more often with gender-stereotypic toys. In other words, Beth, who has referred to herself as a girl, plays with dolls but not with trucks. In contrast, James, who has never referred to himself as a boy, plays with dolls and trucks equally.

Conclusion: As predicted, children's understanding that they are a boy (or girl)— is the catalyst for learning about gender roles. As Martin and Ruble put it, "Children are gender detectives who search for cues about gender—who should or should not engage in a particular activity, who can play with whom, and why girls and boys are different" (2004, p. 67).

Application: After children understand gender, it's as if they see the world through special glasses that allow only gender-typical activities to be in focus (Liben & Bigler, 2002). For parents who don't want their children limited to traditional views of gender and traditional gender roles, it may be tempting to encourage children to remove the gender-tinted glasses in favor of more neutral glasses. But, once a child has acquired gender identity, that's probably easier said than done. A better strategy may be to expose children to many counterstereotypical examples: By showing girls women who fly planes, work in construction, and manage companies, and by showing boys men who are nurses, preschool teachers, or dental hygienists, children can learn a much broader definition of what it means to be male or female.

Gender-schema theory shows that "male" and "female" become much more salient in children's worlds after they understand gender. Consistent with this theory, I remember vividly taking my 4-year-old daughter Laura to watch my son Ben play football. I wondered if she would become so bored and restless that we'd have to leave. Wrong. Laura immediately discovered the cheerleaders (all girls) and insisted that we sit right in front of them. Throughout the game (and the rest of the season), Laura's eyes were riveted to the cheerleaders' every move, and when we got home, she'd imitate their routines. According to gender-schema theory, 4-year-old Laura knew that cheerleading was for girls and that because she was a girl, she needed to learn everything about it.*

After children have gender identity, their tastes in TV programs begin to shift along gender-specific lines (Luecke-Aleksa et al., 1995) and they begin to use gender

---

*But, during the elementary school years, she abandoned cheerleading for soccer and basketball.

labels to evaluate toys and activities. Shown an unfamiliar toy and told that children of a specific sex *really* like this toy, children like the toy much more if others of their sex do too (Shutts, Banaji, & Spelke, 2010). This selective viewing of the world explains a great deal about children's learning of gender roles, but, as we'll see in the next section, there is a final important element that must be considered.

Biological Influences

Most child-development researchers agree that biology contributes to gender roles and gender identity. Evolutionary developmental psychology, for example, reminds us that men and women performed vastly different roles for much of human history: Women were more invested in child rearing and men were more invested in providing important resources (e.g., food, protection) for their offspring (Geary, 2002). In adapting to these roles, different traits and behaviors evolved for men and women. For example, men became more aggressive because that was adaptive in helping them to hunt and to ward off predators.

If gender roles are based in part on our evolutionary heritage, then behavioral genetic research should show the impact of heredity on gender-role learning. Indeed, twin studies show a substantial impact on gender-role learning (Iervolino et al., 2005). For identical twins, if one strongly prefers sex-typical toys and activities, the other one usually does, too. Fraternal twins are also similar in their preference for sex-typical toys and activities, but not to the same extent as identical twins.

> According to evolutionary developmental psychology, different traits and behaviors have evolved in males and females.

Twin studies point to a biological basis for gender-role learning, but don't tell us what factors are responsible. Some scientists believe that the sex hormones are key players; consistent with this idea, the amount of testosterone in amniotic fluid predicts a child's preference for masculine sex-typed activities: Auyeung et al. (2009) found that male and female fetuses who were exposed to a greater amount of testosterone at four months after conception had greater interest in masculine sex-typed activities during the elementary-school years. This same conclusion was drawn from studies of children with *congenital adrenal hyperplasia (CAH)*, **a genetic disorder in which, beginning in prenatal development, the adrenal glands secrete large amounts of androgen**. The extra androgen doesn't affect a baby boy's physical development; but in baby girls it can enlarge the clitoris so that it resembles a penis. Girls affected by CAH often undergo surgery during infancy to correct their physical appearance and receive hormone therapy to correct the imbalance of androgen. Nevertheless, during childhood and adolescence, girls with CAH prefer masculine activities (such as playing with cars instead of dolls) and male playmates to a much greater extent than girls not exposed to these amounts of androgen, despite strong encouragement from parents to play with feminine toys (Berenbaum & Snyder, 1995; Pasterski et al., 2005). And these effects are largest for girls who have the greatest exposure to androgen during prenatal development (Berenbaum, Duck, & Bryk, 2000; Servin et al., 2003). Apparently, the androgen not only masculinizes the genitals in baby girls, but also affects the prenatal development of brain regions critical for masculine and feminine gender-role behavior.

Perhaps the most accurate conclusion to draw is that biology, the socializing influence of people and media, and the child's own efforts to understand gender-typical behavior all contribute to gender roles and differences. Recognizing the interactive nature of these influences on gender learning also enables us to better understand how gender roles are changing today, which is the focus of the last module.

 ANSWER 13.3

No. Worldwide, boys rarely pick girls as play partners, and they resist when urged to do so by others. Rick's son is simply acting as most boys his age would (and as most girls would, if the tables were turned).

Check Your Learning

RECALL   Describe the forces of socialization that contribute to a child's development of gender identity.

Describe cognitive theories of gender identity.

INTERPRET   How does children's acquisition of gender identity compare with growth in self-concept, described in Module 11.1?

APPLY   The popular view is that children learn gender roles from adults (and society at large). But children are active participants in gender-role learning. Describe how children influence their own learning of gender roles.

 Gender Roles in Transition

OUTLINE

Emerging Gender Roles

Beyond Traditional Gender Roles

LEARNING OBJECTIVES

- What is androgyny, and how is it related to traditional conceptions of masculinity and femininity?
- Can parents rear gender-neutral children?

Meda and Perry want their 6-year-old daughter, Hope, to pick activities, friends, and ultimately a career based on her interests and abilities, rather than on her gender. They have done their best to encourage gender-neutral values and behavior. Both are therefore astonished that Hope seems to be totally indistinguishable from other 6-year-olds reared by conventional parents. Hope's close friends are all girls. When Hope is with her friends, they play house or play with dolls. What seems to be going wrong with Meda and Perry's plans for a gender-neutral girl?

Gender roles are not etched in stone; they change with the times. In the United States, the range of acceptable roles for girls and boys and women and men has never been greater than today. For example, fathers such as the man in the top photo on page 429 stay home to be the primary caregivers for children, and some women work full time as sole support for the family. What is the impact of these changes on children? In this module, we'll answer this question by looking at new gender roles and at efforts by parents like Meda and Perry to rear gender-neutral children.

Emerging Gender Roles

Traditionally, masculinity and femininity were seen as ends of a continuum: Children possessing many traits associated with males were considered highly masculine, and youngsters possessing many traits associated with females were considered highly feminine. A newer view of gender roles is based on the independent dimensions of instrumentality and expressiveness that were described in Module 13.1. In this view, traditional males are rated high on instrumentality but low on expressiveness, whereas traditional females are low on instrumentality but high on expressiveness.

In other words, this approach recognizes that other combinations of traits are possible. *Androgynous* **persons are rated high on both the instrumental and expressive dimensions.** (The term *androgyny* originated from the Greek words for male, *andro*, and female, *gyn*.) That is, androgynous individuals can be both independent and emotional, self-confident and considerate, ambitious and creative.

Many theorists (e.g., Bem, 1996) argue that the ability to react with both instrumental and expressive behaviors is psychologically healthier than reacting primarily with one or the other. In fact, androgynous children often are better adjusted than children whose gender roles are highly stereotyped (Norlander, Erixon, & Archer, 2000). However, the benefits of androgyny are greater for girls than for boys. Androgynous girls have higher self-esteem than expressive girls and are more likely to express their thoughts and feelings publicly (Harter, Waters, & Whitesell, 1998). For example, a girl like the one in the bottom photo, who is independent and ambitious as well as considerate and creative, is more likely to feel positive about herself than a girl who embodies only the expressive traits traditionally associated with females.

Evidently, a balance of expressiveness and instrumentality may be especially adaptive across life's many tasks. Being independent and confident has benefits at home and work, but so does being kind and considerate. Teaching children to adopt nontraditional views of gender is no simple task, however, as we'll see in the next section.

Gender roles continue to evolve, and the range of acceptable roles for men and women continues to expand.

Beyond Traditional Gender Roles

Many researchers (e.g., Eagly, 1995) believe that gender is overemphasized to children. They argue that adults often unnecessarily group children by gender. Consider, for example, a minister who rewards perfect church attendance with blue pencils for boys and pink pencils for girls. Children's gender is irrelevant to the reason for the reward, yet distinguishing boys and girls makes gender seem important and increases children's gender stereotypes (Bigler, 1995).

Many developmentalists believe that gender should be linked strictly to reproductive function instead of, as it is now, to traits, behaviors, and abilities. Is this possible? Children can certainly learn less stereotyped views of gender, at least in the short run. In one study (Bigler & Liben, 1990), some 6- to 11-year-olds were taught how to decide if a person can perform a particular job or occupation. They were told that the person's sex was not relevant; instead, they should decide if the person would like to do at least some of the activities that are part of the job and if the person has some of the skills necessary for the job. For example, to be a construction worker, a person should like to build things and should know how to drive heavy machinery.

Girls benefit from an androgynous gender role that combines the independence and self-confidence of the instrumental dimension with the emotional and considerate aspects of the expressive dimension.

When tested later on their attitudes toward household activities and occupations, these children had significantly fewer stereotyped responses than children who had not been taught to think of occupations in terms of interests and skills. That is, children who have this type of training are more likely to think it perfectly natural for women to be construction workers or men to be nurses.

 QUESTION 13.4
Ms. Bower has her second-grade class form two lines—one for boys and one for girls—before they walk to the cafeteria for lunch. What do you think of this practice? *(Answer is on page 431.)*

Children can be taught to have fewer gender sterotypes, but changing children's style of play and their playmates is difficult.

Short-term interventions like the one just described show that more balanced attitudes and behaviors are possible (Gash & Morgan, 1993). Nevertheless, accomplishing change over the long term in a natural setting may be more complicated, based on some results of the Family Lifestyles Project (Weisner & Wilson-Mitchell, 1990). This research examined families in which the parents were members of the 1960s and 1970s counterculture and deeply committed to rearing their children without traditional gender stereotypes. In these families, men and women shared the household, financial, and child-care tasks.

The Family Lifestyle Project indicates that parents like Meda and Perry in this module's opening vignette can influence some aspects of gender stereotyping more readily than others. The children studied in the Family Lifestyles Project had few stereotypes about occupations: They agreed that girls could be president of the United States and drive trucks and that boys could be nurses and secretaries. They also had fewer stereotyped attitudes about the use of objects: Boys and girls were equally likely to use an iron, a shovel, hammer and nails, and needle and thread. Nevertheless, children in these families tended to have same-sex friends, and they liked gender-stereotypic activities: The boys enjoyed physical play and the girls enjoyed drawing and reading.

It should not surprise you that some features of gender roles and identities are influenced more readily by experience than others. For 250,000 years, *Homo sapiens* have existed in small groups of families, hunting animals and gathering vegetation. Because women have borne the children and cared for them, it has been adaptive for women to be caring and nurturing. As we saw in Module 10.3, a nurturing caregiver increases the odds of a secure attachment and, ultimately, the survival of the infant. Men's responsibilities included hunting and protecting the family unit from predators, roles for which physical strength and aggressiveness were crucial.

Circumstances of life in the 21st century are, of course, substantially different: Often, both men and women are employed outside the home and both men and women care for children. Nevertheless, the cultural changes of the past few decades cannot erase hundreds of thousands of years of evolutionary history (Geary, 2002). We should not be surprised that boys and girls play differently, that girls tend to be more supportive in their interactions with others, and that boys are usually more aggressive physically.

The "Improving Children's Lives" feature suggests ways children can be helped to go beyond traditional gender roles and learn the best from both roles.

Improving Children's Lives

Encouraging Valuable Traits, Not Gender Traits

Parents and other adults can encourage children to learn the best from both of the traditional gender roles. Being independent, confident, caring, and considerate is valuable for all people, not just for boys or girls. Here are some guidelines to help achieve these aims:

- Because children learn gender roles from those around them, parents should be sure that they themselves are not gender bound. Mothers and fathers can mow lawns, make repairs, and work outside the home. Mothers and fathers can prepare meals, do laundry, and care for the young. This *does* make a difference: I've always done most of the laundry in our house, and my daughter, at age 5, was astonished when I told her that in most homes mothers do the wash.

- Parents should not base decisions about children's toys, activities, and chores on the child's sex. They should decide if a toy, activity, or chore is appropriate for the child as an individual (based on age, abilities, and interests), rather than because the child is a boy or a girl.
- Forces outside the home, such as media and teachers, often work against parents who want their children to go beyond traditional gender roles. It's neither feasible nor wise to shelter children from these influences, but parents can encourage them to think critically about others' gender-based decisions. When band teachers insist that boys play trumpets and trombones while girls play clarinets and flutes, parents should ask children whether this makes sense. When a TV program shows a man coming to aid the stereotypic damsel in distress, parents should ask the child why the woman simply didn't get herself out of her predicament.

 ANSWER 13.4
Forming two lines may be a good idea, but there's no reason why one should be for boys and the other for girls. After all, boys and girls are going to the same place, for the same reason. Segregating boys and girls needlessly, as in this case, simply makes gender seem more important than it really is.

By following these guidelines, adults can help children to develop all of their talents, not just those that fit traditional views associated with males and females.

 ## Check Your Learning

RECALL What characteristics make up androgyny?

What elements of gender stereotyping seem fairly easy to change? What elements seem more resistant to change?

INTERPRET Why might girls benefit more than boys from an androgynous gender role?

APPLY What advice would you give to a mother who wants her daughter to grow to be gender-free in her attitudes, beliefs, and aspirations?

UNIFYING THEMES Connections

Research on gender illustrates the theme that *development in different domains is connected.* Think about how children learn gender roles. According to conventional wisdom, children acquire masculine or feminine traits and behaviors through socialization by parents and other knowledgeable or authoritative persons in the child's culture. This process is important, but we have seen that learning gender roles is not simply a social phenomenon: Cognitive processes are essential. Kohlberg's theory shows that children don't really begin to learn about gender until they understand that they will remain a boy or girl for life. Once they understand gender constancy, gender-schema theory shows how children use this information to decide which experiences are relevant to them. Biology apparently contributes, too, although we still don't really understand how. Biology, cognition, and social forces all shape the unique gender role that individual boys or girls play.

See for Yourself

To see that older children know more about gender stereotypes and understand that stereotypes are not binding, you'll need to create some simple stories that illustrate stereotyped traits. I suggest that you use "independent," "confident," "appreciative," and "gentle." Each story should include two to three sentences that describe a child. Be sure that your stories contain no other clues that would hint that the child in the story is a boy or a girl. For example, this story illustrates "independent":

> I know a child who likes to do things without help from adults. This child likes to do homework without help and enjoys traveling alone to visit cousins who live in another city.

Read your stories to some 11- and 12-year-olds. After you've read each story, ask, "Is this child a boy, a girl, or could it be either?" Record the reply, and then ask, "Would most people think that the child is a boy, or would most think that the child is a girl?"

With the first question, you're measuring children's understanding that gender stereotypes are flexible. You should find that children answer with "either one" about half of the time, indicating that they believe in some, but not total, flexibility in gender stereotypes. With the second question, you're measuring children's awareness of gender stereotypes. You should find that most children always answer the second question stereotypically: that people would identify the independent and confident children as boys and the appreciative and gentle children as girls. See for yourself!

Summary

13.1 Gender Stereotypes

How Do We View Men and Women?
Instrumental traits describe individuals who act on the world, and are usually associated with males. Expressive traits describe individuals who value interpersonal relationships, and are usually associated with females.

Learning Gender Stereotypes
By age 4, children have substantial knowledge of gender-stereotypic activities; during the elementary-school years, they come to know gender-stereotypic traits and behaviors. Older children also understand that traits and occupations associated with males have higher social status and that stereotypes are not necessarily binding.

13.2 Differences Related To Gender

In *The Psychology of Sex Differences*, published in 1974, Eleanor Maccoby and Carol Jacklin concluded that males and females differed in only four areas: verbal ability, spatial ability, math achievement, and aggression. Subsequent investigators have used their work as the starting point for analyzing gender differences.

Differences in Physical Development and Behavior
Boys tend to be bigger, stronger, and more active than girls, who tend to have better fine-motor coordination and to be healthier.

Differences in Intellectual Abilities and Achievement
Girls excel in verbal skills whereas boys excel in spatial ability. Boys once had an advantage in math achievement, but the gap is now negligible as girls have more exposure to women who pursue math-relevant careers. Differences in intellectual abilities reflect both hereditary and environmental factors.

Differences in Personality and Social Behavior
Boys are more aggressive physically than girls, and biology probably contributes heavily to this difference. Girls usually express their aggression by trying to damage other children's relations with peers. Girls are more sensitive to others' feelings and are more influenced by others; both differences are probably due to experience. Adolescent girls are more prone to depression than are adolescent boys.

Frank Talk About Gender Differences
Most gender differences are fairly small, which means that abilities for boys and girls overlap considerably. Also, despite the emphasis on gender differences, boys and girls are quite similar in many aspects of cognition, personality, and social behavior.

13.3 Gender Identity

The Socializing Influences of People and the Media
Parents treat sons and daughters similarly, except in gender-related behavior. Fathers may be particularly important in teaching about gender because they are more likely to treat sons and daughters differently. Teachers foster gender-role learning by making gender salient.

By the preschool years, peers discourage cross-gender play by ridiculing peers who engage in it. Peers also influence gender roles because children play almost exclusively with same-sex peers.

Television depicts men and women in a stereotyped fashion, and children who watch a lot of television are likely to have very stereotyped views of men and women.

Cognitive Theories of Gender Identity
According to Kohlberg's theory, children gradually learn that gender is constant over time and cannot be changed according to personal wishes. After children understand gender constancy, they begin to learn gender-typical behavior. According to gender-schema theory, children learn about gender by paying attention to behaviors of members of their own sex and ignoring behaviors of members of the other sex.

Biological Influences

The idea that biology influences some aspects of gender roles is supported by research on females exposed to male hormones during prenatal development.

13.4 Gender Roles In Transition

Emerging Gender Roles

Androgynous persons embody both instrumental and expressive traits. Androgynous girls have higher self-esteem than traditional girls and are more likely to express themselves publicly; androgynous boys have about the same level of self-esteem as traditional boys.

Beyond Traditional Gender Roles

Training studies show that children can learn less-stereotyped views of gender, but studies of parents trying to rear gender-neutral children suggest that many stereotyped behaviors are resistant to change.

Test Yourself

✓ Study and Review on mydevelopmentlab.com

1. Instrumental traits, which are associated with males, describe people who act on the world; _____ traits, which are associated with females, describe people who value interpersonal relationships.

2. During the _____ years, children's knowledge of gender stereotypes expands to include personality traits.

3. By the middle elementary-school years, children know more gender stereotypes, but they also see stereotypes as _____.

4. Boys tend to be stronger and more active; girls tend to have better fine-motor coordination and _____.

5. In the intellectual domain, boys often have greater spatial ability, but girls tend to have greater _____.

6. Girls do as well as boys in math in cultures where _____.

7. When boys are aggressive, it's usually physical; in contrast, the most common form of aggression with girls is _____.

8. In the domains of personality and social behavior, girls are more sensitive emotionally, are _____, and are more prone to depression.

9. Although boys and girls differ in their average scores in several domains, it's also true that their scores _____.

10. _____ often respond to sons and daughters based on gender stereotypes, not based on knowledge of the individual child's needs.

11. Teachers contribute to gender-role learning by making gender salient in the classroom; peers contribute by _____.

12. Play is usually segregated by sex, in part because girls do not enjoy boys' rough-and-tumble play and because girls _____.

13. According to gender-schema theory, children first decide whether an object, activity, or behavior is _____.

14. Girls exposed to large amounts of male hormones prefer masculine activities and _____.

15. Interventions designed to influence children's gender stereotypes shows that it is fairly easy to change children's views of occupations, but that children usually have same-sex friends and prefer _____.

Answers: (1) expressive; (2) elementary-school; (3) more flexible and not as obligatory; (4) to be healthier; (5) verbal ability; (6) males and females have comparable access to education, occupations, and political power; (7) relational; (8) more easily influenced by others (in part because they value group harmony); (9) overlap considerably; (10) Fathers; (11) being critical of peers who engage in gender-inappropriate play; (12) have an enabling style of play that is often ineffective with boys; (13) appropriate for males or females; (14) male playmates; (15) gender-stereotypic activities.

Key Terms

androgens   417
androgynous   429
congenital adrenal hyperplasia (CAH)   427
constricting   423
enabling   423

expressive   408
gender consistency   424
gender constancy   425
gender identity   407
gender labeling   424
gender roles   407

gender-schema theory   425
gender stability   424
gender stereotypes   407
instrumental   408
mental rotation   415
social roles   407

14

Family Relationships

14.1
Parenting

14.2
The Changing Family

14.3
Brothers and Sisters

14.4
Maltreatment: Parent–Child Relationships Gone Awry

Family. The term is as sacred to most Americans as baseball, apple pie, and Chevrolet. But what comes to mind when you think of family? Television gives us one answer: from *Leave It to Beaver* to *Family Ties* to *the middle,* the American family is portrayed as a mother, a father, and their children. In reality, of course, American families are as diverse as the people in them. Some families consist of a single parent and an only child. Others include two parents, many children, and grandparents or other relatives.

All these family configurations, however, have a common goal: nurturing children and helping them become full-fledged adult members of their culture. To learn how families achieve these goals, we'll begin, in **Module 14.1**, by looking at relationships between parents and children. Next, in **Module 14.2**, we'll see how families are changing in the 21st century. Then, in **Module 14.3**, we'll look at relationships between siblings. Finally, in **Module 14.4**, we'll examine the forces that can cause parents to abuse their children.

14.1 Parenting

OUTLINE	LEARNING OBJECTIVES
The Family as a System	• What is a systems view of family dynamics?
Styles of Parenting	• What are the different styles of parenting?
Parental Behavior	• What parental behaviors affect children's development?
Influences of the Marital System	• How are children influenced by the quality of their parents' marital relationship?
Children's Contributions	• How do children help determine how parents rear them?

Tanya and Sheila, both sixth-graders, wanted to go to a Miley Cyrus concert with two boys from their school. When Tanya asked if she could go, her mom said, "No way!" Tanya responded defiantly, "Why not?" In return, her mother exploded, "Because I say so. That's why. Stop pestering me." Sheila wasn't allowed to go either. When she asked why, her mom said, "I just think you're still too young to be dating. I don't mind your going to the concert. If you want to go just with Tanya, that would be fine. What do you think of that?"

The vignette illustrates what we all know well from personal experience: Parents go about child rearing in many different ways. In this module, you'll learn about different approaches that parents take to raising children. But let's begin by thinking about parents as an important element in the family system.

The Family as a System

Families are rare in the animal kingdom. Only human beings and a handful of other species form family-like units. Why? Compared to the young in other species, children develop slowly. Because children are immature—unable to care for themselves—for many years, the family structure evolved as a way to protect and nurture young children as they develop into full-fledged members of their culture (Bjorklund, Yunger, & Pellegrini, 2002). Of course, modern families serve many other functions as well—they're economic units and they provide emotional support—but child rearing remains the most salient and probably the most important family function.

As we think about original and modern families, it's tempting to believe that parents' actions are all that really matter. That is, through their behavior, parents directly and indirectly determine their children's development. This view of parents as "all powerful" was part of early psychological theories (e.g., Watson, 1925) and is held even today by some first-time parents. But most theorists now view families from a contextual perspective (described in Module 1.2). That is, families form a system of interacting elements, in which parents and children influence one another (Cox & Paley, 2003; Schermerhorn & Cummings, 2008), and families are part of a much larger system that includes extended family, friends, and teachers as well as institutions that influence development (e.g., schools).

This systems view of children and families is exemplified in a theory proposed by Bronfenbrenner (1995; Bronfenbrenner & Morris, 2006), which holds that the developing child is embedded in a series of complex and interactive systems. As Figure 14-1 shows, the environment is divided into five components: the microsystem, the mesosystem, the exosystem, the macrosystem, and the chronosystem. **At any point in life, the** *microsystem* **consists of the people and objects in an individual's immediate environment.** These are the people closest to a child, such as parents or siblings. Some children have more than one microsystem; for example, a young child might have the microsystems of the family and of the day-care setting. As you can imagine, microsystems strongly influence development.

Microsystems themselves are connected to create the *mesosystem.* The mesosystem represents the fact that what happens in one microsystem is likely to influence what happens in others. Perhaps you've found that if you have a stressful day at work or school, you're grouchy at home. This indicates that your mesosystem is alive and well; your microsystems of home and work are interconnected emotionally for you.

The *exosystem* **refers to social settings that a person may not experience firsthand but that still influence development.** For example, a mother's work environment is part of her child's exosystem, because she may pay more attention to her child when her work is going well and less attention when she's under a great deal of work-related stress. Although the influence of the exosystem is at least secondhand, its effects on the developing child can be quite strong. Think about the woman in the photo, who doesn't look as if she's having a good day at work; do you think she'll do her best mothering when she gets home? Probably not, which means that the workplace has affected her child's development.

The broadest environmental context is the *macrosystem,* **the subcultures and cultures in which the microsystem, mesosystem, and exosystem are embedded.**

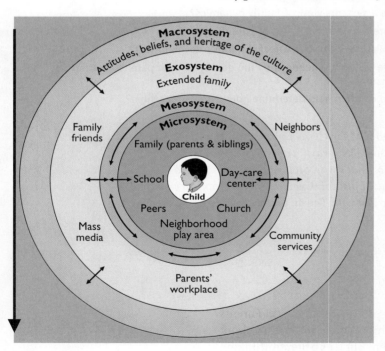

FIGURE 14-1

A mother, her workplace, her child, and the child's school are part of a larger cultural setting, such as Asian Americans living in southern California or Muslim Americans living in large cities on the East Coast. Members of these cultural groups share a common identity, a common heritage, and common values.

Finally, these systems all change over time, a dimension known as the *chronosystem.* This dimension reminds us that microsystem, mesosystem, exosystem, and macrosystem are not static but are constantly in flux. For example, the child's microsystem changes when an older sister leaves home to attend college and the child's exosystem changes when a mother leaves an easy but low-paying job for a more challenging but higher-paying job. And, of course, children themselves are changing over time, which often influences the way in which they are affected by the other elements in the system. For example, a family's move to a distant city may affect a school-age child more than a toddler because the older child must change schools and replace long-term friends (Adams, 2004).

According to a systems approach to parenting, a parent who has a frustrating day at work may be a less effective parent when she gets home.

When viewed as part of an interactive system like the one shown in Figure 14-1, parents still influence their children, both directly—for example, by encouraging them to study hard—and indirectly—for example, by being generous and kind to others. However, the influence is no longer exclusively from parent to children; it is mutual. Children influence their parents, too. By their behaviors, attitudes, and interests, children affect how their parents behave toward them. When children resist discipline, for example, parents may become less willing to reason with them and more inclined to use force.

Even more subtle influences become apparent when families are viewed as systems of interacting elements. For example, fathers' behaviors can affect mother–child relationships. A demanding husband may leave his wife with little time, energy, or interest in helping her daughter with homework. Or, when siblings argue constantly, parents may become preoccupied with avoiding problems rather than encouraging their children's development.

> In the systems view of families, parents and children influence each other and parent-child relations are influenced by other individuals and institutions.

These examples show that narrowly focusing on parents' impact on children misses the complexities of family life. But there is even more to the systems view. The family itself is embedded in other social systems, such as neighborhoods and religious institutions (Parke & Buriel, 1998). These other institutions can affect family dynamics. Sometimes they simplify child rearing, as when neighbors are trusted friends and can help care for each other's children. Other times, however, they complicate child rearing. Grandparents who live nearby can create friction within the family. At times, the impact of the larger systems is indirect, as when work schedules cause a parent to be away from home or when schools must eliminate programs that benefit children.

In the remainder of this module, we'll describe parents' influences on children and then see how children affect their parents' behavior.

Styles of Parenting

Parenting can be described in terms of general dimensions that are like personality traits in that they represent stable aspects of parental behavior—aspects that remain across different situations, creating a characteristic manner or style in which parents interact with their children (Holden & Miller, 1999). When parenting is viewed in this way, two general dimensions of parental behavior emerge. One is the degree of warmth and responsiveness that parents show their children. At one end of the spectrum are parents who are openly warm and affectionate with their children. They are involved with them, respond to their emotional needs, and spend considerable time with them. At the other end of the spectrum are parents who are relatively uninvolved with their children and sometimes even hostile toward them. These parents often seem more focused on their own needs and interests than those of their children. Warm parents enjoy hearing their children describe the day's activities; uninvolved or hostile parents aren't interested, considering it a waste of their time. Warm parents see when their children are upset and try to comfort them; uninvolved or hostile parents pay little attention to their children's emotional states and invest little effort in comforting them when they're upset. As you might expect, children benefit from warm and responsive parenting (Pettit, Bates, & Dodge, 1997; Zhou et al., 2002).

A second general dimension of parental behavior involves control. Some parents are dictatorial: They try to regulate every facet of their children's lives, like a puppeteer controlling a marionette. At the other extreme are parents who exert little or no control over their children: These children do whatever they want without asking parents first or worrying about their parents' response. What's best for children is an intermediate amount of control, when parents set reasonable standards for their children's behavior, expect their children to meet those standards, and monitor their children's behavior (i.e., they also usually know where their children are, what they're doing, and with whom). When parents have reasonable expectations for their children and keep tabs on their activity—for example, a mother knows that her 12-year-old is staying after school for choir practice, then going to the library—their children tend to be better adjusted (Kilgore, Snyder, & Lentz, 2000).

When the dimensions of warmth and control are combined, the result is four prototypic styles of parenting, as shown in Figure 14-2 (Baumrind, 1975, 1991).

Parental Control

	High	Low
High	Authoritative	Permissive
Low	Authoritarian	Uninvolved

(left axis label: **Parental Involvement**)

FIGURE 14-2

- *Authoritarian parenting* **combines high control with little warmth.** These parents lay down the rules and expect them to be followed without discussion. Hard work, respect, and obedience are what authoritarian parents wish to cultivate in their children. There is little give-and-take between parent and child because authoritarian parents do not consider children's needs or wishes. This style is illustrated by Tanya's mother in the opening vignette, who feels no obligation whatsoever to explain her decisions.

- *Authoritative parenting* **combines a fair degree of parental control with warmth and responsivity to children.** Authoritative parents explain rules and encourage discussion. This style is exemplified by Sheila's mother in the opening vignette. She explained why she did not want Sheila going to the concert and encouraged her daughter to discuss the issue with her.

- *Permissive parenting* **offers warmth and caring but little parental control.** These parents generally accept their children's behavior and punish them infrequently. A permissive parent would readily agree to Tanya's or Sheila's request to go to the concert, simply because it is something the child wants to do.

- *Uninvolved parenting* **provides neither warmth nor control.** Uninvolved parents provide for their children's basic physical and emotional needs but little else. These parents try to minimize the amount of time spent with their children and avoid becoming emotionally involved with them. Returning to the vignette, if Tanya had uninvolved parents, she might simply have gone to the concert without asking, knowing that her parents wouldn't care and would rather not be bothered.

Research consistently shows that authoritative parenting is best for most children, most of the time. Children with authoritative parents tend to be responsible, self-reliant, and friendly, and have higher grades (Amato & Fowler, 2002; Simons & Conger, 2007). In contrast, children with authoritarian parents are often unhappy, have low self-esteem, and frequently are overly aggressive (e.g., Silk et al., 2003; Zhou et al., 2008). Finally, children with permissive parents are often impulsive and have little self-control, whereas children with uninvolved parents often do poorly in school and are aggressive (Aunola, Stattin, & Nurmi, 2000; Barber & Olsen, 1997; Driscoll, Russell, & Crockett, 2008). Thus, children typically thrive on a parental style that combines control, warmth, and affection.

> Authoritative parenting fosters achievement in school and self-reliance.

VARIATIONS ASSOCIATED WITH CULTURE AND SOCIOECONOMIC STATUS. The general aim of child rearing—helping children become contributing members of their cultures—is much the same worldwide (Whiting & Child, 1953); and warmth and control are universal aspects of parents' behavior. But views about the "proper" amount of warmth and the "proper" amount of control vary by culture. European Americans want their children to be happy and self-reliant individuals; they believe that these goals are best achieved when parents are warm and exert moderate control (Goodnow, 1992). In many Asian and Latin American countries, however, individualism is less important than cooperation and collaboration (Okagaki & Sternberg, 1993; Wang, Pomerantz, & Chen, 2007). In China, for example, Confucian principles dictate that emotional restraint is the key to family harmony (Chao, 2001), and consistent with their cultural values, mothers and fathers in China are less likely to express affection than are mothers and fathers in the United States (Lin & Fu, 1990). In much the same vein, Latino culture typically places greater emphasis on strong family ties and respecting the roles of all family members, particularly adults; these values lead parents to be more protective of their children and to set more rules for them (Halgunseth, Ispa, & Rudy, 2006). Thus, cultural values help specify culturally appropriate ways for parents to interact with their offspring.

Not only do parental styles vary *across* cultures, they vary *within* cultures, depending on parents' socioeconomic status. Within the United States, parents with lower socioeconomic status tend to be more controlling and more punitive—characteristics associated with the authoritarian parenting style—than are parents with higher socioeconomic status (Hoff-Ginsberg & Tardif, 1995). This difference may reflect educational differences that help to define socioeconomic status. Parents with higher socioeconomic status are, by definition, more educated, and consequently often see development as a more complex process that requires the more nuanced and child-friendly approach that marks authoritative parenting (Skinner, 1985). Another contributing factor derives from another variable that defines socioeconomic status: income (Melby et al., 2008). Due to their limited financial resources, parents with lower socioeconomic status often lead more stressful lives (e.g., they wonder whether they'll have enough money at the end of the month for groceries) and are far more likely to live in neighborhoods where violence, drug abuse, and crime are commonplace. Thus, parents with lower socioeconomic status may be too stressed to invest the energy needed for authoritative parenting, and the authoritarian approach—with its emphasis on the child's immediate compliance—may actually protect children who are growing up in dangerous neighborhoods (Parke & Buriel, 1998).

These different styles are critical for understanding parenting, but there's more to effective child rearing, as we'll see in the next section.

Parents influence children through direct instruction, by acting as models, and by providing feedback.

Parental Behavior

A *style* is a broad characterization of how parents typically behave. If, for example, I describe a parent as using an authoritarian style, you immediately have a sense of that parent's typical ways of interacting with his or her children. Nevertheless, the price for such a general description is that it tells us little about how parents behave in specific situations and how these parental behaviors influence children's development. Put another way, what specific behaviors can parents use to influence their children? Researchers who study parents name three: direct instruction, modeling, and feedback.

DIRECT INSTRUCTION.   Parents often tell their children what to do. But simply playing the role of drill sergeant in ordering children around—"Clean your room!" "Turn off the TV!"—is not very effective. **A better approach is** *direct instruction,* **telling a child what to do, when, and why.** Instead of just shouting "Share your candy with your brother!" a parent should explain when and why it's important to share with a sibling.

In addition, just as coaches help athletes master sports skills, parents can help their youngsters master social and emotional skills. Parents can explain links between emotions and behavior—"Catlin is sad because you broke her crayon" (Gottman, Katz, & Hooven, 1996). They can also teach how to deal with difficult social situations—"When you ask Lindsey if she can sleep over, do it privately so you won't hurt Kaycee's or Hannah's feelings" (Mize & Pettit, 1997). In general, children who get this sort of parental "coaching" tend to be more socially skilled and, not surprisingly, get along better with their peers. (I'll say more about this in Module 15.1.)

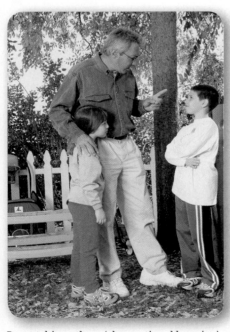

By watching others (observational learning), children can learn behaviors that are expected (and may be rewarded) as well as behaviors that are considered inappropriate (and may lead to punishment).

LEARNING BY OBSERVING.   Children learn a great deal from parents simply by watching them. For example, in Module 12.4 we saw that youngsters often learn how to interact with others by watching how their parents interact. *Observational learning* **can also produce** *counterimitation,* **learning what should not be done.** If an older brother like the one in the photo has been mean to a classmate and the father punishes him, the younger sister may learn to be friendly instead of mean.

Observational learning likely contributes to intergenerational continuity of parenting behavior. Parental behavior is often consistent from one generation to the next. When, for example, parents often use harsh physical punishment to discipline their children, these children will, when they are parents, follow suit (Bailey et al., 2009).

FEEDBACK.   By giving feedback to their children, parents indicate whether a behavior is appropriate and should continue or is inappropriate and should stop. Feedback comes in two general forms. *Reinforcement* **is any action that**

increases the likelihood of the response that it follows. Parents may use praise to reinforce a child's studying or give a reward for completing household chores. *Punishment* **is any action that discourages the reoccurrence of the response that it follows.** Parents may forbid children to watch television when they get poor grades in school or make children go to bed early for neglecting household chores.

Of course, parents have been rewarding and punishing their children for centuries, so what do psychologists know that parents don't know already? **The most surprising discovery is that parents often unwittingly reinforce the very behaviors they want to discourage, a situation called the** *negative reinforcement trap* (Patterson, 1980). This trap occurs in three steps, most often between a mother and her son. In the first step, the mother tells her son to do something he doesn't want to do. She might tell him to clean up his room, to come inside while he's outdoors playing with friends, or to study instead of watching television. In the next step, the son responds with some behavior that most parents find intolerable: He argues, complains, or whines—not just briefly, but for an extended period. In the last step, the mother gives in—saying that the son needn't do as she told him initially—simply to get the son to stop the behavior that is so intolerable.

The feedback to the son is that arguing (or complaining or whining) works; the mother rewards that behavior by withdrawing the request or command that the son did not like. That is, although we usually think a behavior is strengthened when it is followed by the presentation of something that is valued, behavior is also strengthened when it is followed by removing something that is disliked.

As for punishment, research shows that it works best when:

- It is administered directly after the undesired behavior occurs, rather than hours later

- An undesired behavior always leads to punishment, rather than usually or occasionally

- It is accompanied by an explanation of why the child was punished and how punishment can be avoided in the future

- The child has a warm, affectionate relationship with the person administering the punishment.

At the same time, research reveals some serious drawbacks to punishment. One is that the impact of punishment is temporary if children do not learn new behaviors to replace those that were punished. For example, denying TV to brothers who are fighting stops the undesirable behavior, but fighting is likely to recur unless the boys learn new ways of solving their disputes.

A second drawback is that punishment can have undesirable side effects. Children become upset as they are being punished, which means they often miss the feedback that punishment is meant to convey. A child denied TV for misbehaving may become angry over the punishment itself and ignore why he's being punished. What's more, as we saw in Module 12.4, physical punishment often leads children to behave aggressively; this has been found to be true in a range of countries that differ in their general approval of physical punishment (Gershoff et al., 2010). The impact of harsh punishment is not limited to aggression; it's also associated with a range of negative outcomes including mental health problems, impaired parent–child relationships, and delayed cognitive development (Berlin et al., 2009; Gershoff & Bitensky, 2007). Because physical punishment is so harmful to children, many countries around the world (e.g., Costa Rica, the Netherlands, New Zealand, Spain) have banned it

 Q&A QUESTION 14.1

When 10-year-old Dylan's family got a puppy, he agreed to walk it every day after school. But when his mom asks him to do this, he gets angry because he'd rather watch TV. They argue for about 15 minutes, then Dylan's mom gives up and walks the dog herself, while Dylan goes back to watching TV. Analyze this situation. What could Dylan's mom do to prevent these regular arguments?

(Answer is on page 445.)

Time-out, in which children are isolated socially, is a particularly effective form of punishment.

altogether (Global Initiative to End All Corporal Punishment of Children, 2011).

One method retains the best features of punishment but avoids its shortcomings. **In *time-out,* a child who misbehaves must briefly sit alone in a quiet, unstimulating location.** Some parents have children sit alone in a bathroom; others have children sit alone in a room, as shown in the photo. Time-out is punishing because it interrupts the child's ongoing activity and isolates the child from other family members, toys, books, and, generally, all forms of rewarding stimulation.

The period is sufficiently brief—usually just a few minutes—for a parent to use the method consistently. During time-out, both parent and child typically calm down. Then, when time-out is over, a parent can talk with the child and explain why the punished behavior is objectionable and what the child should do instead. "Reasoning" like this—even with preschool children—is effective because it emphasizes why a parent punished initially and how punishment can be avoided in the future.

Thus, parents can influence children by direct instruction, by modeling behavior that they value and not modeling what they don't want their children to learn, by giving feedback, and by adhering to the parenting styles that we examined in the first section of this module. In the next section, we'll explore a final, less direct way in which parents influence their children's development.

Influences of the Marital System

When Derek returned from 7-Eleven with a six-pack of beer and a bag of chips instead of diapers and baby food, Anita exploded in anger. "How could you! I used the last diaper an hour ago!" Huddled in the corner of the kitchen, their son Randy watched yet another episode in the daily soap opera that featured Derek and Anita.

Although Derek and Anita aren't arguing about Randy—in fact, they're so wrapped up in their conflict that they forget he's in the room—it's hard to conceive that a child would emerge unscathed from such constant parental conflict. Indeed, research shows that chronic parental conflict is harmful for children: When parents are constantly in conflict, children and adolescents often become anxious, withdrawn, and aggressive, and they're more prone to chronic diseases (Miller & Chen, 2010; Rhoades, 2008). Parental conflict affects children's development through three distinct mechanisms. First, seeing parents fight jeopardizes a child's feeling that the family is stable and secure, making a child feel anxious, frightened, and sad (Sturge-Apple et al., 2008). Second, chronic conflict between parents often spills over into the parent–child relationship. A wife who finds herself frequently arguing with and confronting her husband may adopt a similarly ineffective style in interacting with her children (Cox, Paley, & Harter, 2001). Third, when parents invest time and energy fighting with each other, they're often too tired or too preoccupied to invest themselves in high-quality parenting (Katz & Woodin, 2002).

Of course, all marriages experience conflict at some point. Does this mean that all children bear at least some scars? Not necessarily. Many parents resolve conflicts in a manner that's constructive instead of destructive. To see this, suppose that one parent believes their child should attend a summer camp, but the other parent believes it's too expensive and not worth it because the child attended the previous summer.

Instead of shouting and name-calling (e.g., "You're always so cheap!"), some parents seek mutually acceptable solutions: The child could attend the camp if she earns money to cover part of the cost or the child could attend a different, less expensive camp. When families like the one in the photo routinely resolve disagreements this way, children actually respond *positively* to conflict, apparently because it shows that their family is cohesive and able to withstand and overcome life's problems (Goeke-Morey et al., 2003).

When parents resolve conflicts constructively, their children respond positively to conflict.

The extent and resolution of conflict is an obvious way in which the parental system affects children, but it's not the only way. Many mothers and fathers form an effective parental team, working together in a coordinated and complementary fashion toward goals that they share for their child's development. For example, Mom and Dad may agree that their daughter is smart and athletically skilled and that she should excel in both domains. Consequently, they're quite happy to help her achieve these goals. Mom gives her basketball tips and Dad edits her school essays.

But not all parents work together well. Sometimes they don't agree on goals: One parent values sports over schoolwork while the other reverses these priorities. Sometimes parents actively compete for their child's attention: Mom may want to take the child shopping but Dad wants to take her to a ball game. Finally, parents sometimes act as gatekeepers, limiting one another's participation in parenting. Mom may feel that infant care is solely her turf and not allow Dad to participate. Or Dad may claim all school-related tasks and discourage Mom from getting involved.

These many examples show that, just as a doubles tennis team won't win many matches when each player ignores his or her partner, parenting is far less effective when parents try to "go it alone" instead of working together, collaborating to achieve goals that they share and using methods that they both accept. Lack of teamwork, competition, and gatekeeping can lead to problems, causing children, for example, to become withdrawn (McHale et al., 2002).

Not all parents work well together, because they disagree about goals, compete for their children's attention, or limit the other parent's participation.

Thus far, we've seen that to understand parents' impact on children's development, we need to consider the nature of the marital relationship as well as parenting style and specific parenting behaviors (e.g., use of feedback). In addition, Figure 14-1 reminds us that forces outside the family can influence parenting and children's development. To illustrate, let's consider work-related influences. One such influence is a parent's job security: Children and adolescents lose self-esteem and find it difficult to concentrate in school when their parents become unemployed, or, for that matter, when they simply worry that their parents may become unemployed (Barling, Zacharatos, & Hepburn, 1999; Kalil & Ziol-Guest, 2005).

Another well-known factor is work-related stress. Not surprisingly, when men and women lead stressful lives at work, they parent less effectively. Sometimes frazzled parents withdraw from family interactions. Over time, this gives the appearance that the parent is detached and disinterested, which makes children anxious and upset. And sometimes work-stressed parents are less accepting and less tolerant, leading to conflicts with their children (Crouter & Bumpus, 2001; Maggi et al., 2008).

Thus, a person's work life can profoundly affect children and adolescents by changing the parenting they experience. In Module 15.3, we'll look at another system-level influence on children: the neighborhood where children live. For now, another way to view family systems in action is by switching perspectives and seeing how children affect parenting behavior.

Children's Contributions

I emphasized earlier that the family is a dynamic, interactive system in which parents and children influence each other. In fact, children begin at birth to influence the way their parents treat them. Let's look at two characteristics of children that influence how parents treat them.

AGE. Parenting changes as children grow. The same parenting that is marvelously effective with infants and toddlers is inappropriate for adolescents. These age-related changes in parenting are evident in the two basic dimensions of parental behavior: warmth and control. Warmth is beneficial throughout development; toddlers and teens alike enjoy knowing that others care about them. But the manifestation of parental affection changes, becoming more reserved as children develop. The enthusiastic hugging and kissing that delights toddlers embarrasses adolescents (Shanahan et al., 2007).

Parental control also changes as children develop (Maccoby, 1984; Vazsonyi, Hibbert, & Snider, 2003). As children enter adolescence, they believe that parents have less authority to make decisions for them, especially in the personal domain (Darling, Cumsille, & Martínez, 2008). In fact, parents gradually relinquish control—though sometimes not as rapidly as adolescents want them to—and increases in decision-making autonomy are associated with greater adolescent well-being (Qin, Pomerantz, & Wang, 2009; Wray-Lake, Crouter, & McHale, 2010).

TEMPERAMENT AND BEHAVIOR. A child's temperament can have a powerful effect on parental behavior (Brody & Ge, 2001). To illustrate the reciprocal influence of parents and children, imagine two preschoolers with different temperaments as they respond to a parent's authoritative style. The first child has an "easy" temperament, complying readily with parental requests and responding well to family discussions about parental expectations. These parent–child relations are a textbook example of successful authoritative parenting. But suppose that, like the child in the photo, the second child has a "difficult" temperament and complies reluctantly and sometimes not at all. Over time, the parent becomes more controlling and less affectionate. The child in turn complies even less in the future, leading the parent to adopt an authoritarian parenting style (Bates et al., 1998; Paulussen-Hoogeboom et al., 2007).

As this example illustrates, parenting behaviors and styles often evolve as a consequence of the child's behavior. With a moderately active young child who is eager to please adults, a parent may discover that a modest amount of control is adequate. But for a very active child who is not as eager to please, a parent may need to be more controlling and directive (Brody & Ge, 2001; Hastings & Rubin, 1999). Influence is reciprocal: Children's behavior helps determine how parents treat them and the resulting parental behavior

An example of the impact of children's behavior on parents is that, when children respond to parents defiantly, their parents often resort to harsher forms of punishment.

influences children's behavior, which in turn causes parents to again change their behavior (Schermerhorn, Chow, & Cummings, 2010).

As time goes by, these reciprocal influences lead many families to adopt routine ways of interacting with each other. Some families end up functioning smoothly: Parents and children cooperate, anticipate each other's needs, and are generally happy. Unfortunately, other families end up troubled: Disagreements are common, parents spend much time trying unsuccessfully to control their defiant children, and everyone is often angry and upset. Still others are characterized by disengagement: Parents withdraw from each other and are not available to their children (Sturge-Apple, Davies, & Cummings, 2010). Over the long term, such troubled families do not fare well, so it's important that these negative reciprocal influences get nipped in the bud (Carrere & Gottman, 1999; Christensen & Heavey, 1999).

 ## Check Your Learning

RECALL Describe ways in which the marital system contributes to children's development.

What are some of the ways in which children influence their own development?

INTERPRET Compare the styles approach to parenting with the approach that focuses on parental behavior per se. What are the strengths of each?

APPLY Imagine a family in which Mom and Dad both work full time outside the home. Mom's employer wants her to take a new position in a distant small town. Mom is tempted because the position represents a promotion with much more responsibility and much higher pay. However, because the town is so small, Dad couldn't get a job comparable to the one he has now, which he loves. Based on what you know about Bronfenbrenner's family systems theory (pages 436–437), how might the move affect the couple's 10-year-old daughter and 4-year-old son?

 ANSWER 14.1
This is a classic negative reinforcement trap: (1) Mom asks her son to do something, (2) he refuses and argues endlessly, and (3) Mom gives in to end the argument, thereby reinforcing the argumentative behavior. Dylan's mom has a couple of alternatives. She could remind Dylan of the original agreement and hold fast to the rule that he can't watch TV until he's walked the dog. But maybe this rule isn't a good one any longer, for reasons that neither Dylan nor his mom could anticipate when they got the puppy. She and Dylan should talk about the agreement and find another way in which he can shoulder part of the responsibility of puppy care.

 ## 14.2 The Changing Family

OUTLINE
Impact of Divorce on Children
Blended Families
The Role of Grandparents
Children of Gay and Lesbian Parents

LEARNING OBJECTIVES
- What are some of the effects of divorce on children?
- How do children adjust to a parent's remarriage?
- How effective as parents are grandparents and gay parents?

Jack has lived with his dad for the four years since his parents' divorce; he visits his mother every other weekend. Although Jack was confused and depressed when his parents divorced, he has come to terms with the new situation. He's excelling in school, where he is well liked by peers and teachers. One of Jack's friends is Troy. Troy's parents are married but bicker constantly since Troy's dad lost his job. His parents are unable to agree on anything; the pettiest event or remark triggers an argument. Troy's grades have fallen, and whereas he was once a leader among the boys in his class, now he prefers to be alone.

The American family has been changing steadily since the middle of the 20th century. First, people are older when they marry; the age of first marriage is up from the early 20s in the 1950s and 1960s to the late 20s today. Second, families are smaller, having decreased from an average of more than three children in 1960 to fewer than two children today (U.S. Census Bureau, 2011). Finally, more children are growing up in single-parent families due to a doubling of the divorce rate since the 1960s and a doubling of the percentage of babies born to unwed mothers (Children's Defense Fund, 2010).

Because of these and other societal changes, today the family takes on many different forms in the United States and in other industrialized nations. In this module, we'll look at several of these forms and see how children develop within them. As we do, we'll look at the impact of divorce on Jack and the impact of marital conflict on Troy.

Impact of Divorce on Children

Like Jack, many American youngsters' parents divorce. According to all theories of child development, divorce is distressing for children because it involves conflict between parents and usually separation from one of them. Do the disruptions, conflict, and stress associated with divorce affect children? Of course they do. Having answered this easy question, however, many more difficult questions remain: Are all aspects of children's lives affected equally by divorce? *How* does divorce influence development? Why is divorce more stressful for some children than others?

WHAT ASPECTS OF CHILDREN'S LIVES ARE AFFECTED BY DIVORCE? Hundreds of studies of divorce have been conducted, involving tens of thousands of preschool- through college-age children. Comprehensive meta-analyses of this research reveal that in school achievement, conduct, adjustment, self-concept, and parent–child relations, children whose parents had divorced fared poorly compared to children from intact families (Amato, 2001; Amato & Keith, 1991; Lansford, 2009). However, the effects of divorce dropped from the 1970s to 1980s, perhaps because as divorce became more frequent in the 1980s, it became more familiar and less frightening. The effects of divorce increased again in the 1990s, perhaps reflecting a widening gap in income between single- and two-parent families (Amato, 2001).

When children of divorced parents become adults, the effects of divorce persist. As adults, children of divorce are more likely to experience conflict in their own marriages, to have negative attitudes toward marriage, and to become divorced themselves. Also, they report less satisfaction with life and are more likely to become depressed (Hetherington & Kelly, 2002; Segrin, Taylor, & Altman, 2005). These findings don't mean that children of divorce are destined to have unhappy, conflict-ridden marriages that inevitably lead to divorce, but children of divorce are at greater risk for such an outcome.

The first year following a divorce is often rocky for parents and children alike. But beginning in the second year, most children begin to adjust to their new circumstances (Hetherington & Kelly, 2002). Children adjust to divorce more readily if their divorced parents cooperate with each other, especially on disciplinary matters (Buchanan & Heiges, 2001). **In** *joint custody,* **both parents retain legal custody**

of the children. Children benefit from joint custody *if* their parents get along well (Bauserman, 2002).

Of course, many parents do not get along well after a divorce, which eliminates joint custody as an option. Traditionally, mothers have been awarded custody; when this happens, children benefit when fathers remain involved in parenting (Fabricius & Luecken, 2007). In recent years fathers have increasingly often been given custody, especially of sons. This practice coincides with findings that children such as Jack, the other boy in the opening vignette, often adjust better when they live with the same-sex parent: Boys often fare better with fathers and girls fare better with mothers (McLanahan, 1999). One reason boys are often better off with their fathers is that boys are likely to become involved in negative reinforcement traps (described in Module 14.1) with their mothers. Another explanation is that both boys and girls may forge stronger emotional relationships with same-sex parents than with other-sex parents (Zimiles & Lee, 1991).

HOW DOES DIVORCE INFLUENCE DEVELOPMENT?   Divorce usually results in several changes in family life that affect children (Amato & Keith, 1991). First, the absence of one parent means that children lose a role model, a source of parental help and emotional support, and a supervisor. For instance, a single parent may have to choose between helping one child complete an important paper or watching another child perform in a school play. Because she can't do both, one child will miss out.

Second, single-parent families often experience economic hardship, which creates stress and often means that activities once taken for granted are no longer available (Lansford, 2009). A single parent may no longer be able to afford books for pleasure reading, music lessons, or other activities that promote child development. Moreover, when a single parent worries about having enough money for food and rent, she has less energy and effort to devote to parenting.

> Divorce affects children through the loss of a role model, economic hardship, and exposure to conflict.

Third, as we saw in Module 14.1, conflict between parents is extremely distressing to children and adolescents (Leon, 2003), particularly for children who are emotionally insecure (Davies & Cummings, 1998). In fact, many of the problems ascribed to divorce are really caused by marital conflict occurring before the divorce (Erel & Burman, 1995; Shaw, Winslow, & Flanagan, 1999). Children like Troy, the boy in the opening vignette whose parents are married but fight constantly, often show many of the same effects associated with divorce (Katz & Woodin, 2002).

WHICH CHILDREN ARE MOST AFFECTED BY DIVORCE? WHY?   Some children are more affected by divorce than others. For example, children who are temperamentally more emotional tend to be more affected by divorce (Lengua et al., 1999). What's more, divorce is more harmful when it occurs during childhood and adolescence than during the preschool or college years (Amato & Keith, 1991), and the consequences differ for children and adolescents. Following divorce, children more often become anxious or develop behavioral problems, but adolescents more often do worse in school (Lansford et al., 2006).

Some children suffer more from divorce because of their tendency to interpret events negatively. We know, from Module 12.4, that two children often have differing interpretations of exactly the same social event. Suppose, for example, that a father forgets to take a child on a promised outing. One child might believe that an emergency prevented the father from taking the child. A second child might believe that the father hadn't really wanted to spend time with the child in the first place and will never make similar plans again. Children who—like the second child—tend to interpret life events negatively are more likely to have behavioral problems following divorce (Mazur et al., 1999).

Finally, children's efforts to cope with divorce-related stress can influence the impact of divorce. When children actively cope with their parents' divorce—either by trying to solve a problem or by trying to make it feel less threatening—they gain confidence in their ability to control future events in their lives. This protects children from behavioral disorders such as anxiety or depression (Sandler et al., 2000).

Just as children can reduce the harm of divorce by being active problem solvers, parents can make divorce easier on their children. The "Improving Children's Lives" feature has some tips on ways parents can make divorce less stressful for their children.

Improving Children's Lives

Helping Children Adjust After Divorce

Divorce causes major changes in children's lives that are very stressful. Here are some ways parents can reduce stress and help children adjust to their new life circumstances. Parents should:

- Explain together to children why they are divorcing and what their children can expect to happen to them
- Reassure children that they will always love them and always be their parents; parents must back up these words with actions by remaining involved in their children's lives, despite the increased difficulty of doing so
- Expect that their children will sometimes be angry or sad about the divorce, and they should encourage children to discuss these feelings with them

Parents should not:

- Compete with each other for their children's love and attention; children adjust to divorce best when they maintain good relationships with both parents
- Take out their anger with each other on their children
- Criticize the ex-spouse in front of the children
- Ask children to mediate disputes; parents should work out problems without putting the children in the middle

Following all these rules all the time is not easy. After all, divorce is stressful and painful for adults, too. Fortunately, there are effective programs available that can help parents and children adjust to life following divorce. The "Focus on Research" feature describes one of them.

Focus on Research

Evaluation of a Program to Help Parents and Children Adjust to Life After Divorce

Who were the investigators, and what was the aim of the study? Throughout this module, we've seen that divorce puts children at risk for reduced school achievement, behavior problems, and other less desirable outcomes. Clorinda Vélez, Sharlene Wolchik, Jenn-Yun Tein, and Irwin Sandler (2011) wanted to determine the benefits for children of an intervention program for mothers that focused primarily on the quality of the mother–child relationship and effective disciplinary methods.

How did the investigators measure the topic of interest? Vélez and her colleagues assigned mothers to one of two conditions: in the intervention condition, mothers participated in five group sessions that discussed ways that a mother can foster quality relationships with her children and three sessions that were devoted to discipline. In the control condition, mothers were simply provided books that described how to adjust to divorce and a reading guide. Before mothers were assigned to conditions and at four points later, mothers and children completed several questionnaires designed to measure parenting quality (defined here as being warm and communicating effectively). In addition, children completed questionnaires designed to measure whether they were coping effectively with divorce-related adjustment (e.g., being proactive in making changes, being optimistic).

Who were the participants in the study? The study included 240 mothers who had been divorced within the previous two years and who had at least one child between 9 and 12 years of age. The mothers had not remarried and had no plans to do so in the near future.

What was the design of the study? This study was experimental because Vélez and her colleagues assigned mothers randomly to either an intervention condition or a control condition. The study was longitudinal because mothers and children were tested five times: prior to the experimental treatment and immediately after the treatment, as well as at three months, sixth months, and six years after.

Were there ethical concerns with the study? No; the questionnaires that parents and children completed were ones commonly used to study parent–child relationships and family interactions.

What were the results? Correlations were computed between experimental conditions, relationship quality, and children's active coping. They revealed that parent–child relationships (as reported by both mothers and children) were of higher quality when mothers participated in the intervention condition and that higher-quality relationships were associated with more active coping on the part of children. In other words, the intervention condition improved mother–child relationships and this improvement, in turn, resulted in children's use of more active coping to deal with their problems.

What did the investigators conclude? Vélez and her colleagues concluded that "by increasing one of children's most important interpersonal resources, mother-child relationship quality, the [intervention program] improved youth's coping efficacy and active coping" (2011, p. 255). In other words, when children have a high-quality relationship with their mother—she is warm to them and communicates well with them—they are empowered to deal with the unique challenges they face as they adjust to life after their mother's divorce.

What converging evidence would strengthen these conclusions? There are two limits to these findings. First, the children were all in middle childhood; would intervention be equally effective with preschool children or with adolescents? Second, mothers and children were mainly middle-class; would intervention work as well with divorced women living in poverty, who face additional stresses and obstacles to effective parenting? Answering these questions would provide more convincing evidence of the effectiveness of intervention programs designed to help children and mothers adjust to life following divorce.

As divorce became more common in the 20th century, so did blended families, in which children live with a stepparent and sometimes with stepsiblings.

Blended Families

Following divorce, most children live in a single-parent household for about five years. However, like the adults in the photo, most men and women eventually remarry (Sweeney, 2010).**The resulting unit, consisting of a biological parent, stepparent, and children, is known as a** *blended family.* (Other terms for this family configuration are *remarried family* and *reconstituted family.*)

Because mothers are more often granted custody of children, the most common form of blended family is a mother, her children, and a stepfather. Most stepfathers do not participate actively in child rearing; they often seem reluctant to become involved (Clarke-Stewart & Bretano, 2005). Nevertheless, children typically benefit from the presence of a stepfather, particularly when he is warm and involved (King, 2006). Preadolescent girls, however, do not adjust readily to their mother's remarriage, apparently because it disrupts the intimate relationship they have established with her (Visher, Visher, & Pasley, 2003).

These adjustments are often more difficult when mothers of adolescents remarry. Adolescents do not adapt to the new family circumstances as easily as children do; they're more likely to challenge a stepfather's authority. And adjustment is more difficult when a stepfather brings his own biological children to the mix. In such families, parents sometimes favor their biological children over their stepchildren, being more involved with and warmer toward their biological children. Such preferential treatment almost always leads to conflict and unhappiness (Dunn & Davies, 2001; Sweeney, 2010). Also, when the mother and stepfather argue, children usually side with their biological parents (Dunn, O'Connor, & Cheng, 2005).

The best strategy for stepfathers is to be interested in their new stepchildren but avoid encroaching on established relationships. Newly remarried mothers must be careful that their enthusiasm for their new spouse does not come at the expense of time and affection for their children. What's more, both parents and children need to have realistic expectations. The blended family can be successful and beneficial for children and adolescents, but it takes effort because of the complicated relationships, conflicting loyalties, and jealousies that usually exist (Sweeney, 2010; White & Gilbreth, 2001).

Daughters in blended families often worry that remarriage will damage the close relationship they have with their biological mother.

Over time, children adjust to the blended family. If the marriage is happy, most children profit from the presence of two caring adults. Nevertheless, when compared to children from intact families, children in blended families do less well in school and experience more symptoms of depression (Halpern-Meekin & Tach, 2008). Unfortunately, second marriages are somewhat more likely than first marriages to end in divorce, particularly when stepchildren are involved (Teachman, 2008). This means that many children relive the trauma of divorce. Fortunately, effective programs are available to help members of blended families adjust to their new roles (Bullard et al., 2010). These emphasize effective co-parenting (described on page 443) and, in particular, ways of dealing with the behavior problems that children often display with stepparents. These programs result in fewer behavior problems and greater marital satisfaction.

The Role of Grandparents

With people living longer, three-generation families—with child, parents, and grandparents—are becoming the norm in many industrialized nations. Many American children see their grandparents at least once a month, more often if they live nearby. Grandmothers, especially maternal grandmothers, are usually more involved with grandchildren than grandfathers, and some scientists believe that this is an evolutionary adaptation (Pollett, Nettle, & Nelissen, 2007). That is, for most of human history, the onset of menopause has coincided, approximately, with the birth of grandchildren. Genetically speaking, middle-aged women may be more valuable in caring for their grandchildren—making sure that they survive to bear further children—than in bearing additional children of their own (Coall & Hartwig, 2010).

What roles do grandparents play in children's lives? One analysis suggests five specific styles of grandparenting (Mueller & Elder, 2003):

- *Influential grandparents* are very close to their grandchildren, are very involved in their lives, and frequently perform parental roles, including discipline.

- *Supportive grandparents* are similar to influential grandparents—close and involved with grandchildren—but do not take on parental roles.

- *Authority-oriented grandparents* provide discipline for their grandchildren but otherwise are not particularly active in their grandchildren's lives.

- *Passive grandparents* are caught up in their grandchildren's development but not with the intensity of influential or supportive grandparents; they do not assume parental roles.

- *Detached grandparents* are uninvolved with their grandchildren.

The first two grandparental roles—influential and supportive—are those in which grandparents are most involved with their grandchildren. Several factors determine whether grandparents assume these involved roles. Some factors are practical: Grandparents are more involved when they live near their grandchildren and when they have few rather than many grandchildren. Other factors relate to grandparents' relationships with their children and their own grandparents: Grandparents are more concerned when their children (i.e., the grandchildren's parents) encourage such involvement and when they knew their own maternal grandparent. Finally, the influential and supportive roles are more often taken by maternal grandparents

Q&A **QUESTION 14.2**

Ollie, a 4-year-old, sees his grandparents several times a week. They take him to preschool on Monday and Wednesday, and try to do something special, such as getting an ice cream cone, each week. And they don't hesitate to remind him to say "please" and "thank you" and to wait his turn. What grandparental role best describes Ollie's grandparents? *(Answer is on page 454.)*

than by paternal grandparents (Mueller & Elder, 2003). Obviously, no single factor determines the extent to which a grandparent takes an active role in a grandchild's development.

Not surprisingly, children and adolescents benefit from close ties with their grandparents. For example, children experience fewer emotional problems and are more prosocial when their grandparents are actively involved in child rearing (Attar-Schwartz et al., 2009; Barnett et al., 2010). Strong grandparent–child relationships are particularly valuable when children and adolescents experience stress, such as that associated with divorce (Henderson et al., 2009): Strong relationships with grandparents are associated with better adjustment by children.

Grandparents are especially active in the lives of immigrant and minority children, often taking on parental roles (Hernandez, 2004; Minkler-Fuller & Thomson, 2005). The "Cultural Influences" feature describes the important role of grandmothers in African American family life.

Cultural Influences

Grandmothers in African American Families

Approximately 1 in 10 African American children lives with a grandmother, compared to only 1 in 25 European-American children (U.S. Census Bureau, 2011). Why is this? A quarter of all African American children grow up in chronic poverty, and living with relatives is one way of sharing—and thereby reducing—the costs associated with housing and child care.

African American grandmothers who live with their daughters and their children frequently become involved in rearing their grandchildren, adopting the role of influential grandparent (Oberlander, Black, & Starr, 2007). When the daughter is a teenage mother, the grandmother may be the child's primary caregiver, an arrangement that benefits both the adolescent mother and the child. Freed from the obligations of child rearing, the adolescent mother is able to improve her situation by, for example, finishing school. The child benefits because grandmothers are often more effective mothers than teenage mothers: Grandmothers are less punitive and, like the grandmother in the photo, are very responsive to their grandchildren (Chase-Lansdale, Brooks-Gunn, & Zamsky, 1994; Smith & Drew, 2002). Another benefit is that when the young mother and young father have positive relationships with grandmothers, they get along better with each other, and parent more effectively (Krishnakumar & Black, 2003).

This family arrangement works well for children. In terms of achievement and adjustment, children living with their mothers and grandmothers resemble children living in two-parent families, and they tend to be better off than children in single-parent families (Wilson, 1989). Even when grandmothers are not living in the house, children benefit when their mothers receive social and emotional support from

African American grandmothers often play an active role in rearing their grandchildren, which benefits the grandchildren.

grandmothers and other relatives: Children are more self-reliant and less likely to become involved in delinquent activities such as drug use and vandalism (Taylor & Roberts, 1995).

Thus, grandmothers and other relatives can ease the burden of child rearing in African American families living in poverty, and, not surprisingly, children benefit from the added warmth, support, and guidance of an extended family.

By acting as surrogate parents, grandparents can affect their grandchildren's lives directly. However, grandparents also affect their grandchildren indirectly, through intergenerational transmission of parental attitudes and practices. For example, if parents are affectionate with their children, when these children become parents themselves, they will tend to be affectionate with their own children. In other words, the grandparents' affectionate behavior results in their grandchildren experiencing affectionate care. Thus, it is important to think about the indirect as well as the direct influences that grandparents have on their grandchildren (Smith & Drew, 2002).

Children of Gay and Lesbian Parents

Many youngsters in the United States have a gay or lesbian parent. In most of these situations, children were born in a heterosexual marriage that ended in divorce when one parent revealed his or her homosexuality. Less frequent, but becoming more common, are children born to single lesbians or to lesbian couples who have children through artificial insemination or adoption.

As parents, gay and lesbian couples are more similar to heterosexual couples than they are different. There is no indication that gay and lesbian parents are less effective parents than heterosexual parents. In fact, some evidence suggests that gay men may be especially responsive to children's needs, perhaps because their self-concepts include emotional sensitivity that is traditionally associated with the female gender role (Patterson, 2004).

Children reared by gay and lesbian parents seem to develop much like children reared by heterosexual couples (Golombok et al., 2003; Patterson, 2006). Preschool boys and girls apparently identify with their own sex and acquire the usual accompaniment of gender-based preferences, interests, activities, and friends. As adolescents, they continue to thrive, and the vast majority are heterosexual (Wainwright, Russell, & Patterson, 2004). In other respects—such as self-concept, social skill, peer relations, moral reasoning, and intelligence—children of lesbian mothers resemble children of heterosexual parents (Patterson, 2006; Wainwright & Patterson, 2008). And, as is the case with heterosexual parents, children benefit from close relationships with warm, caring gay and lesbian parents (Patterson, 2006).

> In most respects—including gender roles, self-concept, and social skill—children of gay and lesbian parents resemble children of heterosexual parents.

Research on children reared by gay and lesbian couples, along with findings concerning African American grandmothers, reminds us that "good parenting" can assume many different forms. These research results also challenge the conventional wisdom that a two-parent family with mother and father both present *necessarily* provides the best circumstances for development. Multiple adults *are* important—that's evident from research on the impact of divorce on children—but *who* the

ANSWER 14.2
Ollie's grandparents are best described as influential because they're very involved in his life and because they take on parental tasks, including discipline.

adults are seems to matter less than what they do. Children benefit from good parenting skills, whether it's a mother and father or grandparents—or two women or two men—doing the parenting.

✓ Check Your Learning

RECALL Describe the different grandparental roles and the factors that influence which roles grandparents take on.

What is known about development in children of gay and lesbian parents?

INTERPRET From a child's perspective, what are the pros and cons of a blended (remarried) family?

APPLY Suppose that a couple argues constantly. They've tried to resolve their differences in counseling, but this was unsuccessful and now they're considering a divorce. They are the parents of two school-age children. What advice would you give them?

14.3 Brothers and Sisters

OUTLINE
Firstborn, Laterborn, and Only Children

Qualities of Sibling Relationships

LEARNING OBJECTIVES
• How do firstborn, laterborn, and only children differ?

• How do sibling relationships change as children grow? What determines how well siblings get along?

Bob and Alice adored their 2-year-old son, Robbie, who was friendly, playful, and always eager to learn new things. In fact, Bob thought Robbie was nearly perfect and saw no reason to tempt fate by having another child. However, Alice had heard stories that only children were conceited, spoiled, and unfriendly. Alice was sure that Robbie would grow up like this unless she and Bob had another child. What to do?

For most of a year, all firstborn children are only children like Robbie. Some children remain "onlies" forever, but most get brothers and sisters, particularly when firstborns are outgoing and smart (Jokela, 2010). Some firstborns are joined by many siblings in rapid succession; others are simply joined by a single brother or sister. As the family acquires these new members, parent–child relationships become more complex (Brody, 2004). Parents can no longer focus on a single child, but must adjust to the needs of multiple children. Just as important, siblings influence each other's development, not just during childhood but throughout life. To understand sibling influence, let's look at differences between firstborns, laterborns, and only children.

Firstborn, Laterborn, and Only Children

Firstborn children are often "guinea pigs" for most parents, who have lots of enthusiasm but little practical experience in rearing children. Parents typically have high expectations for their firstborns and are both more affectionate and more punitive with them. As more children arrive, parents become more adept at their roles, having learned "the tricks of the parent trade" with earlier children. With laterborn children, parents have more realistic expectations and are more relaxed in their discipline (e.g., Baskett, 1985).

The different approaches that parents take with their firstborns and later-borns help explain differences that are commonly observed between these children. Firstborn children generally have higher scores on intelligence tests and are more likely to go to college. They are also more willing to conform to parents' and adults' requests. Laterborn children, perhaps because they are less concerned about pleasing parents and adults but need to get along with older siblings, are more popular with their peers and more innovative (Beck, Burnet, & Vosper, 2006; Bjerkedal et al., 2007).

What about only children? Alice, the mother in the opening vignette, was well acquainted with the conventional wisdom, which says that parents like the ones in the photo dote on "onlies," with the result that the children are selfish and egotistical. Is the folklore correct? From a comprehensive analysis of more than 100 studies, the answer is no. In fact, only children were found more likely to succeed in school than other children and to have higher levels of intelligence, leadership, autonomy, and maturity (Falbo & Polit, 1986).

Contrary to the folklore, only children are not spoiled brats; instead, they tend to do well in school and often are leaders.

This research has important implications for China, where only children are the norm due to government efforts to limit family size. The "Child Development and Family Policy" feature tells the story.

Child Development and Family Policy

Assessing the Consequences of China's One-Child Policy

With more than a billion citizens, the People's Republic of China has the largest population in the world. In the middle of the 20th century, Chinese leaders recognized that a large, rapidly growing population was a serious obstacle to economic growth and improvements in the standard of living. Consequently, the Chinese government implemented several programs to limit family size and since 1979 has had a policy of one child per family. The policy was promoted with billboards, like the one in the photo, advertising the benefits of having only one child. Parents were encouraged to use contraceptives; more importantly, one-child families received many economic benefits, such as cash bonuses, better health and child care, and more desirable housing.

Since 1979, the Chinese government has had a policy of encouraging parents to have only one child.

The policy has been effective in reducing the birth rate in China; and now social scientists are evaluating the impact of the one-child policy on children and their families. For example, traditionally the Chinese have valued well-behaved children who get along well with others. Would the only children in today's China be less cooperative and more self-centered than previous generations of Chinese youngsters? The answer seems to be no. Many studies have compared only and non-only children in China; most comparisons find no differences; when differences are found, the advantage often goes to the only child (Jiao, Ji, & Jing, 1996; Liu, Lin, & Chen, 2010).

As Chinese only children enter adulthood, a new concern will be care of the elderly. Traditionally, children have been responsible for their aging parents. This task becomes more demanding—financially and psychologically—when it cannot be shared with other siblings. Consequently, the Chinese government now encourages older parents and their adult children to sign a Family Support Agreement, which is a voluntary contract specifying the kinds and amounts of support that children will provide for their aging parents (Chou, 2011).

ADOPTED CHILDREN. The U.S. government doesn't keep official statistics on the number of adopted children, but the best estimate is that about 2% to 4% of U.S. children are adopted. The majority of adoptive parents are middle-class European Americans and, until the 1960s, so were adopted children. However, improved birth control and legalized abortion in the late 1960s meant that hardly any European American infants were relinquished for adoption. Consequently, beginning in the 1960s, parents began to adopt children of other races, as shown in the photo, and children from other countries. At the same time, parents began to adopt children with special needs, such as chronic medical problems or exposure to maltreatment (Brodzinsky & Pinderhughes, 2002; Gunnar, Bruce, & Grotevant, 2000).

Beginning in the 1960s, interracial adoption became very common in the United States.

As adoption became more common, the myth of the "adopted child syndrome" blossomed. According to this myth, adopted children are more prone to behavioral problems, substance abuse, and criminal activity, presumably because of the special challenges they face in establishing a unique identity, which we explored in Module 11.1 (Finley, 1999). Is there any truth to the myth? In fact, when compared to children living with biological parents, adopted children are quite similar in terms of temperament, mother–infant attachment, self-esteem, and cognitive development (Brodzinsky & Pinderhughes, 2002; Juffer & van IJzendoorn, 2007).

But some findings *are* consistent with the myth. Adopted children are more prone to problems adjusting to school and to conduct disorders, such as being overly aggressive (Miller et al., 2000; van IJzendoorn & Juffer, 2005). To a certain extent, this finding reflects the fact that adoptive parents are more likely to seek help for their adoptive children because they are more affluent and can afford it, and because they are used to dealing with agencies that provide mental health services (Hellerstedt et al., 2008). Also, the extent of these problems hinges on the age when the child was adopted and the quality of the child's care prior to adoption (Brodzinsky & Pinderhughes, 2002; Lee et al., 2010). Problems are much more common when children are adopted at an older age (and thus probably are separated from an attachment figure) and when their care before adoption was poor (e.g., they were institutionalized or lived in a series of foster homes). For example, the fall of the Ceaușescu regime in Romania in 1989 revealed hundreds of thousands of children living in orphanages under incredibly primitive conditions. Beginning in the 1990s, many of these children were adopted internationally. Some have shown remarkable catch-up growth, but many show multiple impairments, such as delayed cognitive development and disordered attachment (Kreppner et al., 2007).

Perhaps the best way to summarize this research is that although adoption per se is not a fundamental developmental challenge for most children, quality of life before adoption certainly places some adopted children at risk. And it's important to remember that most adopted children fare quite well.

In discussing firstborn, laterborn, only, and adopted children, we have not yet considered relationships that exist between siblings. These can be powerful forces on development, as we'll see in the next section.

> Adopted children are more prone to problems, typically due to poor quality of life before their adoption.

Qualities of Sibling Relationships

From the very beginning, sibling relationships are complicated. On the one hand, most expectant parents are excited by the prospect of another child, and their enthusiasm is contagious: Their children, too, eagerly await the arrival of the newest family member. On the other hand, the birth of a sibling is often distressing for children, who may become withdrawn or revert to more childish behavior because of the changes that occur in their lives, particularly the need to share parental attention and affection (Gottlieb & Mendelson, 1990). However, distress can be avoided if parents remain responsive to their older children's needs (Howe & Ross, 1990). In fact, one of the benefits of a sibling's birth is that fathers become more involved with their older children (Stewart et al., 1987).

Many older siblings enjoy helping their parents take care of newborns. Older children play with the baby, console it, feed it, or change its diapers. In middle-class Western families, such caregiving often occurs in the context of play, with parents nearby. But in some cultures, children—particularly girls like the one in the photo—play an important role in providing care for their younger siblings (Zukow-Goldring, 2002).

As the infant grows, interactions between siblings become more frequent and more complicated. For example, toddlers tend to talk more to parents than to older siblings. But, by the time the younger sibling is 4 years old, the situation is reversed: Now young siblings talk more to older siblings than to their mother (Brown & Dunn, 1992). Older siblings become a source of care and comfort for younger siblings when they are distressed or upset (Kim et al., 2007; Gass, Jenkins, & Dunn, 2007), and older siblings serve as teachers for their younger siblings, teaching them to play games or how to cook simple foods (Maynard, 2002). Finally, when older children do well in school and are popular with peers, younger siblings often follow suit (Brody et al., 2003).

As time goes by, some siblings grow close, becoming best friends in ways that nonsiblings can never be. Other siblings constantly argue, compete, and simply do not get along with each other. The basic pattern of sibling interaction seems to be established early in development and remains fairly stable (Kramer, 2010). In general, siblings who get along as preschoolers continue to get along as young adolescents, but siblings who quarrel as preschoolers often quarrel as young adolescents.

In many developing countries, older siblings are actively involved in caring for their younger siblings.

QUESTION 14.3
Calvin, age 8, and his younger sister, Hope, argue over just about everything and constantly compete for their parents' attention. Teenage sisters Melissa and Caroline love doing everything together and enjoy sharing clothes and secrets about their teen romances. Why might Calvin and Hope get along so poorly but Melissa and Caroline get along so well? *(Answer is on page 459.)*
....

Why are some sibling relationships filled with love and respect, but others are dominated by jealousy and resentment? First, children's sex and temperament matter. Sibling relations are more likely to be warm and harmonious between siblings of the same sex than between siblings of the opposite sex (Dunn & Kendrick, 1981) and when neither sibling is temperamentally emotional (Brody, Stoneman, & McCoy, 1994). Age is also important: Sibling relationships generally improve as the younger child approaches adolescence because siblings begin to perceive one another as equals (Buhrmester & Furman, 1990; Kim et al., 2007).

Parents contribute to the quality of sibling relationships, both directly and indirectly (Brody, 1998). The direct influence stems from parents' treatment. Siblings more often get along when they believe that parents have no "favorites" but treat all siblings fairly (McGuire & Shanahan, 2010). When parents lavishly praise one child's accomplishments while ignoring another's, children notice the difference and their sibling relationship suffers (Updegraff, Thayer, et al., 2005).

This doesn't mean that parents must treat all their children the same. Children understand that parents should treat their kids differently—based on their age or personal needs. Only when differential treatment is not justified do sibling relationships deteriorate (Kowal & Kramer, 1997). In fact, during adolescence, siblings get along better when each has a unique, well-defined relationship with parents (Feinberg et al., 2003).

The indirect influence of parents on sibling relationships stems from the quality of the parents' relationship with each other: A warm, harmonious relationship between parents fosters positive sibling relationships; conflict between parents is associated with conflict between siblings (Erel, Margolin, & John, 1998; Volling & Belsky, 1992). When parents don't get along, they no longer treat their children the same, leading to conflict among siblings (Brody et al., 1994).

Many of the features associated with high-quality sibling relationships, such as the sex of the siblings, are common across different ethnic groups. However, some unique features also emerge. For example, in a study of African American families, sibling relations were more positive when children had a stronger ethnic identity (McHale et al., 2007). And a study of Mexican American families found that siblings feel closer and spend more time together when siblings have a strong commitment to their family—that is, when they felt obligated to their family and viewed it as an important source of support (Updegraff, McHale, et al., 2005).

One practical implication of these findings is that in their pursuit of family harmony (what many parents call "peace and quiet"), parents can influence some of the factors affecting sibling relationships but not others. Parents can help reduce friction between siblings by being equally affectionate, responsive, and caring with all of their children and by caring for one another. And they can encourage the sorts of behaviors that promote positive sibling relationships, including being engaged in mutually enjoyable activities, being supportive of each other, and appreciating their shared experiences (Kramer, 2010).

At the same time, some dissension is natural in families, especially those with young boys and girls: Children's different interests lead to arguments, like the one in the photo. Faced with common simple conflicts—Who decides which TV show to watch? Who gets to eat the last cookie? Who gets to hold the new puppy?—a 3-year-old brother and a 5-year-old sister *will* argue because they lack the social and cognitive skills that allow them to find mutually satisfying compromises.

When siblings do fight—particularly young children—parents should intervene. When parents explain one sibling's behavior to another (e.g., "He covered his eyes 'cause he was scared"), siblings have more positive interactions (Kojima, 2000).

Preschool children often argue because they lack the social skills to settle disagreements in a mutually beneficial manner.

Also, by helping their children to settle differences, parents show children more sophisticated ways to negotiate; later, children often try to use these techniques themselves instead of fighting (Pearlman & Ross, 1997). Parents especially need to intervene when conflicts escalate to the point that siblings are acting aggressively, yelling or swearing, or making denigrating comments. Obviously, parents need to protect their children from each other in the immediate situation. More importantly, though, if left unchecked, over time such conflicts can lead to behavior problems (Garcia et al., 2000).

Fortunately, parents can be shown how to mediate siblings' disputes. Smith and Ross (2007) administered brief training—90 minutes—in which parents were shown how to have children (1) identify points of agreement and disagreement, (2) discuss what they want to achieve (i.e., their goals for the situation), and (3) think of ways to resolve their dispute. After parents know how to mediate, siblings are better able to resolve conflicts successfully, and in doing so, they're more likely to talk calmly (instead of arguing), listen, apologize, and explain their actions. Thus, parents needn't listen to their children argue endlessly; instead, they can show them social skills that will help them solve their conflicts successfully.

Parents can foster good sibling relationships by treating children fairly and by getting along with each other.

 ANSWER 14.3
There are two obvious reasons why Melissa and Caroline get along better than Calvin and Hope. First, they're both girls, and same-sex sibs tend to have better relationships. Second, they're both adolescents, and sibling relationships tend to improve during these years.

 ## Check Your Learning

RECALL Summarize what's known about the psychological development of adopted children.

How do sibling relationships change as children grow?

INTERPRET What research findings suggest continuity in the quality of sibling relationships? What findings suggest discontinuity?

APPLY Suppose your sister has a 2-year-old child. She and her husband are deciding whether to have another child. Describe to her the advantages and disadvantages of having two children versus only one.

 ## 14.4 Maltreatment: Parent–Child Relationships Gone Awry

OUTLINE	LEARNING OBJECTIVES
Consequences of Maltreatment	• What are the consequences of child maltreatment?
Causes of Maltreatment	• What factors cause parents to mistreat their children?
Preventing Maltreatment	• How can maltreatment be prevented?

The first time 7-year-old Max came to school with bruises on his face, he said he'd fallen down the basement steps. When Max showed up with similar bruises a few weeks later, his teacher spoke with the school principal, who contacted local authorities. They discovered that Max's mother hit him with a paddle for even minor misconduct; for serious transgressions, she beat Max and made him sleep alone in an unheated, unlighted basement.

nfortunately, cases like Max's occur far too often in modern America. Maltreatment comes in many forms (Cicchetti & Toth, 2006). The two that often come to mind first are physical abuse involving assault that leads to injuries and sexual abuse involving fondling, intercourse, or other sexual behaviors. Another form of maltreatment is *neglect*, not giving children adequate food, clothing, or medical care. Children can also be gravely harmed by psychological abuse—ridicule, rejection, and humiliation (Wicks-Nelson & Israel, 2006).

The frequency of these various forms of child maltreatment is difficult to estimate because so many cases go unreported. According to the U.S. Department of Health and Human Services (2010), nearly three-quarters of a million children annually suffer maltreatment or neglect. About 75% are neglected, about 15% are abused physically, about 10% are abused sexually, and 5% are maltreated psychologically.

We'll begin this module by looking at the consequences of maltreatment, then look at some causes, and, finally, examine ways to prevent maltreatment. As we do, we'll discover what led Max to suffer as he did.

Consequences of Maltreatment

You probably aren't surprised to learn that the prognosis for youngsters like Max is not very good. Some, of course, suffer permanent physical damage. Even when there is no lasting physical damage, children's social and emotional development is often disrupted. They tend to have poor relationships with peers, often because they are too aggressive (Appleyard, Yang, & Runyan, 2010; Cullerton-Sen et al., 2008). Their cognitive development and academic performance are also disturbed. Abused youngsters typically get lower grades in school, score lower on standardized achievement tests, and are more frequently retained in a grade rather than promoted. Also, school-related behavior problems, such as being disruptive in class, are common, in part because maltreated children are often socially unskilled and don't regulate their emotions well (Burack et al., 2006; Maughan & Cicchetti, 2002). Abuse often leads children and adolescents to become depressed (Appleyard et al., 2010; Harkness, Lumley, & Truss, 2008). Finally, adults who were abused as children are more prone to think about or attempt suicide, and are more likely to abuse spouses and their own children (Malinosky-Rummell & Hansen, 1993). In short, when children are maltreated, the effects are usually widespread and long lasting. ⊙┤Watch the **Video** on **mydevelopmentlab.com**

⊙┤**Watch** the **Video** *Sexual Abuse* on **mydevelopmentlab .com** to learn more about abuse. In this video, a 19-year-old girl describes her experiences of being repeatedly abused sexually by her stepfather and how it continues to affect her.

RESILIENCE. Although the overall picture is bleak, some children are remarkably resilient to the impact of abuse. In other words, in a group of children and adolescents who have been abused, many will show some (or all) of the consequences that I've just described. For a handful, though, the impact of abuse is much reduced. Why are some children protected from the damaging effects of abuse when others are vulnerable?

One factor that protects children is their *ego-resilience,* **which denotes children's ability to respond adaptively and resourcefully to new situations.** For example, Flores, Cicchetti, and Rogosch (2005) found that among a sample of Latino children who had been maltreated, the effects of abuse were smallest for children who were rated by observers as being high in ego-resilience—they were flexible in responding to novel and challenging social situations.

Another preventive factor is a positive mother–child relationship: When children have a positive representation of their mother—they describe her as "kind" and "loving," for example—they suffer relatively few symptoms of maltreatment

(Valentino et al., 2008). However, the buffering value of such a positive view only holds for children who have been neglected. Children who are abused physically suffer the typical maltreatment-related symptoms even when they have a positive representation of their mother.

Causes of Maltreatment

Why would a parent abuse a child? Maybe you think parents would have to be severely disturbed or deranged to harm their own flesh and blood. Not really. The vast majority of abusing parents are not suffering from any specific mental or psychological disorder (Wolfe, 1985). Instead, a host of factors puts some children at risk for abuse and protects others; the number and combination of factors determine if the child is a likely target for abuse (Cicchetti & Toth, 2006). Let's look at three of the most important factors: cultural context and community, the parents, and the children themselves.

CULTURE AND COMMUNITY.   The most general category of contributing factors has to do with cultural values and the social conditions of the community in which parents rear their children. For example, a culture's view of physical punishment may contribute to child maltreatment. Many countries in Europe and Asia have strong cultural prohibitions against physical punishment. It simply isn't done, and would be viewed in much the same way we would view American parents who punished by not feeding their child for a few days. In Sweden and Israel, for example, spanking is against the law and children can report their parents to the police. But, as we saw in Chapter 12, physical punishment is common in the United States. When cultural values condone physical punishment, this opens the door for child maltreatment.

In addition to cultural values, the communities in which children live can put them at risk for maltreatment and abuse. Living in poverty is one important risk factor: Maltreatment is more common in families living in poverty, in part because lack of money increases the stress of daily life (Duncan & Brooks-Gunn, 2000). When parents are worrying about whether they can buy groceries or pay the rent, they are more likely to punish their children physically instead of making the extra effort to reason with them. Similarly, abuse is more common among military families when a soldier is deployed in a combat zone (Gibbs et al., 2007). In this case, maltreatment may be rooted in stress stemming from concern over the absent parent and temporary single parenthood.

A second risk factor is social isolation: Abuse is more likely when families are socially isolated from other relatives or neighbors, because isolation deprives children of adults who could protect them and deprives parents of social support that would help them cope with life stresses (Coulton et al., 2007).

Cultural values and community factors clearly contribute to child abuse, but they are only part of the puzzle. After all, although maltreatment is more common among families living in poverty, it does not occur in a majority of these families and it does occur in middle-class families, too. Consequently, we need to look for additional factors to explain why abuse occurs in some families but not others.

PARENTS.   Faced with the same cultural values and living conditions, why do only a handful of parents abuse or mistreat their children? That is, which

 QUESTION 14.4
Kevin has never physically abused his 10-year-old son, Alex, but he constantly torments him emotionally. For example, when Alex got an *F* on a spelling test, Kevin screamed, "I skipped *Monday Night Football* just to help you but you still flunked. You're such a dummy." When Alex began to cry, Kevin taunted, "Look at Alex, crying like a baby." These interactions occur nearly every day. What are the likely effects of such repeated episodes of emotional abuse?
(Answer is on page 464.)

Children are most likely to be abused when their culture condones physical punishment, their parents lack effective child-rearing skills, and their own behavior is aversive.

characteristics increase the odds that a parent will abuse his or her children? Child-development researchers have identified several important factors (Berlin, Appleyard, & Dodge, 2011; Bugental & Happaney, 2004). First, parents who maltreat their children often were maltreated themselves, which may lead them to believe that abuse is simply a normal part of childhood. This does not mean that abused children inevitably become abusing parents—only about one-third do. But a history of child abuse clearly places adults at risk for mistreating their own children (Cicchetti & Toth, 2006; Serbin & Karp, 2003). Second, parents who mistreat their children often use ineffective parenting techniques (e.g., inconsistent discipline), have such unrealistic expectations that their children can never meet them, and often believe that they are powerless to control their children. For example, when abusive parents do not get along with their children, they often chalk this up to factors out of their control, such as children having a difficult temperament or being tired that day; they're less likely to think that their own behavior contributed to unpleasant interactions. Third, in families where abuse occurs, the couple's interactions are often unpredictable, unsupportive, and unsatisfying for both husbands and wives. In other words, mistreatment of children is simply one symptom of family dysfunction. This marital discord makes life more stressful and makes it more difficult for parents to invest effort in child rearing.

CHILDREN'S CONTRIBUTIONS.   To place the last few pieces in the puzzle, we must look at the abused children themselves. Our discussion in Module 14.1 of reciprocal influence between parents and children should remind you that children may inadvertently, through their behavior, bring on their own abuse (Sidebotham et al., 2003). In fact, infants and preschoolers are abused more often than older children. Why? They are easier targets of abuse and they are less able to regulate aversive behaviors that elicit abuse. You've probably heard stories about a parent who shakes a baby to death because the baby won't stop crying. Because younger children are more likely to cry or whine excessively—behaviors that irritate all parents sooner or later—they are more likely to be the targets of abuse.

For much the same reason, children who are chronically ill or who suffer disabilities like those described in Module 8.3 are more often abused (Govindshenoy & Spencer, 2007; Sherrod et al., 1984). When children are sick, they're more likely to cry and whine, annoying their parents. Also, when children are sick or disabled, they need extra care, which means additional expense. By increasing the level of stress in a family, sick children can inadvertently become the targets of abuse.

Stepchildren form another group at risk for abuse (Daly & Wilson, 1996). Just as Cinderella's stepmother doted on her biological children but abused Cinderella, stepchildren are more prone to be victims of abuse and neglect than are biological children. Adults are less invested emotionally in their stepchildren, and this lack of emotional investment leaves stepchildren more vulnerable.

Obviously, in all of these instances children are *not* at fault and do not deserve the abuse. Nevertheless, normal infant or child behavior can provoke anger and maltreatment from some parents.

Thus, many factors, summarized in the accompanying table, all contribute to child maltreatment. Any single factor will usually not result in abuse; maltreatment is more likely when risk factors start to add up. For example, several factors placed Max, the boy in the module-opening vignette, at risk for abuse: His family had moved to the community recently because his stepfather thought he could find work in the local plant; but the plant wasn't hiring, so his stepfather was unemployed and the family had little money saved. And Max had asthma, which meant there was regular expense for medication and occasional visits to the emergency room when he had a severe attack. All these factors combined to put Max at risk for maltreatment. (How many risk factors? My answer appears just before "Check Your Learning" on page 464.)

SUMMARY TABLE

FACTORS THAT CONTRIBUTE TO CHILD ABUSE

General Category	Specific Factor
Cultural and community contributions	Abuse is more common in cultures that tolerate physical punishment.
	Abuse is more common when families live in poverty because of the stress associated with inadequate income. Abuse is more common when families are socially isolated because parents lack social support.
Parents' contributions	Parents who abuse their children were often maltreated themselves as children. Parents who abuse their children often have poor parenting skills (e.g., unrealistic expectations, inappropriate punishment).
Children's contributions	Young children are more likely to be abused because they cannot regulate their behavior. Ill children are more likely to be abused because their behavior while ill is often aversive. Stepchildren are more likely to be abused because stepparents are less invested in their stepchildren.

Preventing Maltreatment

The complexity of child abuse dashes any hopes for a simple solution (Kelly, 2011). Because maltreatment is more apt to occur when several contributing factors are present, eradicating child maltreatment would entail a massive effort. American attitudes toward "acceptable" levels of punishment and poverty would have to change. American children will be abused as long as physical punishment is considered acceptable and as long as poverty-stricken families live in chronic stress from simply trying to provide food and shelter. Parents also need counseling and training in parenting skills. Abuse will continue as long as parents remain ignorant of effective methods of parenting and discipline.

It would be naïve to expect all of these changes to occur overnight. However, by focusing on some of the more manageable factors, the risk of maltreatment can be reduced. Social supports help. When parents know they can turn to other helpful adults for advice and reassurance, they better manage the stresses of child rearing that might otherwise lead to abuse. Families can also be taught more effective ways of coping with situations that might otherwise trigger abuse (Wicks-Nelson & Israel, 2006). Through role-playing sessions, parents can learn the benefits of authoritative parenting and effective ways of using feedback and modeling (described in Module 14.1) to regulate children's behavior.

Providing social supports and teaching effective parenting are typically done when maltreatment and abuse have already occurred. Of course, preventing

The risk of child abuse can be reduced by providing social supports and by teaching effective parenting skills.

maltreatment in the first place is more desirable and more cost-effective. For prevention, one useful tool is familiar: early childhood intervention programs. That is, maltreatment and abuse can be cut in half when families participate for two or more years in intervention programs that include preschool education along with family support activities aimed at encouraging parents to become more involved in their children's education (Reynolds & Robertson, 2003). When parents participate in these programs, they become more committed to their children's education. This leads their children to be more successful in school, reducing a source of stress and enhancing parents' confidence in their child-rearing skills, reducing the risks of maltreatment in the process.

Another successful approach focuses specifically on parenting skills in families where children are at risk for maltreatment. In one program (Bugental & Schwartz, 2009), mothers of infants at risk for abuse (due to medical problems at birth) participated in an extensive training program in which they learned to identify likely causes of problems associated with recurring problems encountered while caring for their babies (e.g., problems associated with feeding, sleeping, crying). They were then given help in devising methods to deal with those problems and in monitoring the effectiveness of the methods. When mothers participated in the program, they were less likely to use harsh punishment (a known risk factor for child maltreatment) and their children were less likely to suffer injuries at home (a common measure of parental neglect).

There are also effective programs targeting parents of older children who are at risk for maltreatment. One program, Parent-Child Interaction Therapy, focuses on (1) helping parents to build warm and positive relationships with their children, and (2) developing reasonable expectations for their children and using more effective disciplinary practices. When parents of at-risk children participate in this program, they report less stress, their behavior with their children becomes more positive (more praise and fewer commands), and, critically, suspected abuse is less (Thomas & Zimmer-Gimbeck, 2011).

As we end this module, it's important to remember that most parents who have mistreated their children deserve compassion rather than censure. In most cases, parents and children are attached to each other; maltreatment is a consequence of ignorance and burden, not malice.

> *Answer to question on page 463 about the number of risk factors:* Four factors put Max at risk: social isolation (just moved to the community), poverty (unemployed, no savings), he is a stepchild, and he has a chronic illness.

 ANSWER 14.4

If this emotional abuse continues, virtually every aspect of Alex's psychological development is likely to be harmed. That is, Alex will do poorly in school, his social and emotional development will be impaired, he won't get along well with peers, and he'll be at risk for psychological disorders such as depression.

 ## Check Your Learning

RECALL Describe the different factors that lead to child abuse.

How can we prevent child abuse?

INTERPRET How does child abuse demonstrate, in an unfortunate way, that children are sometimes active contributors to their own development?

APPLY Suppose that you read a letter to the editor of your local paper in which the author claims that parents who abuse their children are mentally ill. If you were to write a reply, what would you say?

UNIFYING THEMES Active Children

In this chapter, I want to emphasize the theme that *children influence their own development*. This may seem to be an unusual chapter to emphasize this theme because, after all, we usually think of how parents influence their children. But several times in this chapter we've seen that parenting is determined, in part, by children themselves. We saw that parents change their behavior as their children grow older. Parents also adjust their behavior depending on how their children respond to previous efforts to discipline. And, in discussing causes of child maltreatment, we discovered that younger and sick children often unwittingly place themselves at risk for abuse because of their behavior. Constant whining and crying is trying for all parents and prompts a small few to harm their children.

Of course, parents do influence their children's development in many important ways. Effective parenting recognizes that there is no all-purpose formula that works for all children or, for that matter, for all children in one family. Instead, parents must tailor their child-rearing behavior to each child, recognizing his or her unique needs, strengths, and weaknesses.

See for Yourself

Many students find it hard to believe that parents actually use the different styles described in Module 14.1. To observe how parents differ in their warmth and control, visit a place where parents and children interact together. Shopping malls and fast-food restaurants are two good examples. Observe parents and children, then judge their warmth (responsive to the child's needs versus uninterested) and degree of control (relatively controlling versus uncontrolling). As you observe, decide whether parents are using feedback and modeling effectively. You will most likely observe an astonishing variety of parental behavior, some effective and some not. See for yourself!

Summary

14.1 Parenting

The Family as a System
According to the systems approach, the family is an evolutionary adaptation that consists of interacting elements; parents and children influence each other. The family itself is embedded in a context of interconnected systems that range from the microsystem (people and objects in the child's immediate environment) to the macrosystem (the cultures and subcultures in which all the other systems are embedded).

Styles of Parenting
One dimension of parenting is the degree of parental warmth: Children clearly benefit from warm, caring parents. Another dimension is control. Effective parental control involves setting appropriate standards and enforcing them consistently. Combining warmth and control yields four parental styles: (1) authoritarian parents who are controlling but uninvolved, (2) authoritative parents who are controlling but responsive to their children, (3) indulgent–permissive parents who are loving but exert little control, and (4) indifferent–uninvolved parents who are neither warm nor controlling. Authoritative parenting is usually best for children.

Child rearing is influenced by culture and family configuration. Compared to American parents, Chinese parents are more controlling and less affectionate. Parents living in poverty often rely more heavily on authoritarian parenting.

Parental Behavior
Parents influence development by direct instruction and coaching. In addition, parents serve as models for their children, who sometimes imitate parents' behavior directly and sometimes in ways that are the opposite of what they've seen (counterimitation).

Parents also use feedback to influence children's behavior. Sometimes parents fall into the negative reinforcement trap, inadvertently reinforcing behaviors that they want to discourage. Punishment is effective when it is prompt, consistent, accompanied by an explanation, and delivered by a person with whom the child has a warm relationship. Timeout is one useful form of punishment.

Influences of the Marital System

Chronic conflict is harmful to children, but children can actually benefit when their parents solve problems constructively. Not all parents work well together, because they disagree about child-rearing goals or methods.

Children's Contributions

Parenting is influenced by characteristics of children themselves, such as their age and temperament.

14.2 The Changing Family

Impact of Divorce on Children

Divorce harms children in many ways, ranging from school achievement to adjustment. The impact of divorce stems from less supervision of children, economic hardship, and parental conflict.

Blended Families

The blended family can be successful and beneficial for children and adolescents, but it takes effort because of the complicated relationships, conflicting loyalties, and jealousies that usually exist. When a mother remarries, daughters sometimes have difficulty adjusting because the new stepfather encroaches on an intimate mother–daughter relationship. Best strategies include avoiding preferential treatment of biological children, showing warmth and caring to all family members, and maintaining a harmonious marital relationship.

The Role of Grandparents

Grandparents play many different roles with their grandchildren; the influential and supportive roles are two in which grandparents are particularly active in rearing grandchildren. In African American families, grandmothers often live with their daughters, an arrangement that benefits children. Grandparents also influence their grandchildren indirectly, through the way they reared the child's parents.

Children of Gay and Lesbian Parents

Research on gay and lesbian parents suggests that they are more similar to heterosexual parents than different and that their children develop much like children reared by heterosexual couples.

14.3 Brothers and Sisters

Firstborn, Laterborn, and Only Children

Firstborn children often are more intelligent and more likely to go to college, but laterborn children are more popular and more innovative. Only children are comparable to children with siblings along most dimensions. In many respects, adopted children are similar to children living with their biological parents. Some adopted children have problems, primarily when they were adopted at an older age and when their quality of care before adoption was poor.

Qualities of Sibling Relationships

The birth of a sibling can be stressful for older children, particularly when parents ignore their older child's needs. Siblings get along better when they are of the same sex, believe that parents treat them fairly, enter adolescence, and have parents who get along well.

14.4 Maltreatment: Parent–Child Relationships Gone Awry

Consequences of Maltreatment

Children who are maltreated sometimes suffer permanent physical damage. Their peer relationships are often poor, and they tend to lag in cognitive development and academic performance.

Causes of Maltreatment

A culture's views on violence, poverty, and social isolation can foster child maltreatment. Parents who abuse their children are often unhappy, socially unskilled individuals. Younger, unhealthy children are more likely to be targets of maltreatment, as are stepchildren.

Preventing Maltreatment

Prevention programs often focus on providing families with new ways of coping with problems and providing parents with resources to help them cope with stress.

Test Yourself

✓ Study and Review on mydevelopmentlab.com

1. A systems view of families divides the environment into the microsystem, the mesosystem, the exosystem, the macrosystem, and the _____.

2. The two major dimensions of parental behavior are warmth and _____.

3. _____ parenting combines a fair degree of parental control with warmth.

4. In a _____, parents inadvertently reinforce the behaviors that they hope to discourage.

5. Parental conflict is typically harmful for children, but not when _____.

6. Two features of children that influence how parents treat them are age and _____.

7. Divorce influences children by forcing the loss of a role model and source of parental help, by creating economic hardship, and by _____.

8. Children usually benefit when a mother remarries; the exception is that _____.

9. According to an evolutionary perspective, grandparenting evolved because _____.

10. When children reared by gay and lesbian parents are compared to children reared by heterosexual parents, the usual result is that _____.

11. Adopted children are more likely to experience developmental problems when they are adopted at an older age and when _____.

12. Siblings get along best when they're of the same sex, neither is emotional, when parents treat siblings fairly, and when parents _____.

13. _____ is the most common form of child maltreatment.

14. The impact of maltreatment is less when children can respond adaptively to new situations and when they _____.

15. Factors that contribute to child maltreatment include community values, ineffective parenting, and _____.

Answers: (1) chronosystem; (2) control; (3) Authoritative; (4) negative reinforcement trap; (5) parents solve problems constructively, for example, by looking for mutually acceptable solutions; (6) temperament; (7) the distress produced by parental conflict; (8) sometimes preadolescent girls don't adjust well because the stepfather's presence interferes with a close mother–daughter relationship; (9) it was more valuable for middle-aged women to care for their grandchildren than to produce more children of their own; (10) both groups of children seem to develop similarly and both benefit from close relationships with warm, caring parents; (11) their care before adoption was poor; (12) have a warm, harmonious relationship with little conflict; (13) Neglect; (14) have a positive mother–child relationship; (15) children themselves (e.g., being ill or being a stepchild).

Key Terms

15

Influences Beyond the Family

Peers

15.1

Electronic Media

15.2

Institutional Influences

15.3

If you stand outside a kindergarten classroom on the first day of school, you'll probably see some children crying, fearful of facing a novel environment on their own. What may surprise you is that many parents, too, are struggling to hold back their tears. Why? Parents realize that when children begin school, they are taking an important step toward independence. Other forces now become influential in children's lives, sometimes challenging parents' influence. Among these forces are children's agemates (their peers), the media, and school itself. In this chapter, we'll look at peer influence in **Module 15.1**. Next, in **Module 15.2**, we'll see how electronic media—particularly television and computers—affect children's development. Finally, in **Module 15.3**, we'll examine the influences on children's development of other cultural institutions, including day care, the workplace, neighborhoods, and schools.

15.1 Peers

OUTLINE

Development of Peer Interactions

Friendship

Romantic Relationships

Groups

Popularity and Rejection

LEARNING OBJECTIVES

- When do youngsters first begin to interact with each other, and how do these interactions change during infancy, childhood, and adolescence?
- Why do children become friends, and what are the benefits of friendship?
- When do romantic relationships emerge in adolescence?
- What are the important features of groups in childhood and adolescence? How do groups influence individuals?
- Why are some children more popular than others? What are the causes and consequences of being rejected?

For six months, 17-year-old Gretchen has been dating Jeff, an 18-year-old. They have had sex several times, each time without contraception. Gretchen suggested to Jeff that he buy some condoms, but he didn't want to because someone might see him at the drug store and that would be too embarrassing. She has not pressed the issue because, although she never mentions it to Jeff, Gretchen sometimes thinks that getting pregnant would be cool: Then she and Jeff could move into their own apartment and begin a family.

Many of the major developmental theorists—including Freud, Erikson, Piaget, and Vygotsky—believed that children's development is strongly shaped by their interactions and relationships with peers. Whether occurring with classmates, a small circle of friends, or in a romantic relationship like Gretchen's, children's and adolescents' interactions with peers are important developmental events.

In this module, we'll trace the development of peer interactions. Then we'll look at friendship and romantic relationships; here we'll come to better understand why Gretchen and Jeff are having unprotected sex. Finally, we'll consider children's membership in groups, including their social status within those groups.

Development of Peer Interactions

Peer interactions begin surprisingly early in infancy. Two 6-month-olds together will look, smile, and point at one another. Over the next few months, infants laugh and babble when with other infants (Rubin, Bukowski, & Parker, 2006).

Beginning at about the first birthday and continuing through the preschool years, peer relations rapidly become more complex. **In a classic early study, Parten (1932) identified a developmental sequence that began with** *nonsocial play—* **children playing alone or watching others play but not playing themselves.** Later, children progressed to more elaborate forms of play with each child having a well-defined role. Today, researchers no longer share Parten's view that children move through each stage of play in a rigid sequence, but the different forms of play that she distinguished are useful nonetheless.

The first type of social play to appear—soon after the first birthday—is *parallel play:* **youngsters play alone but maintain a keen interest in what other children are doing.** For example, each boy in the photo has his own toy but is watching the other play, too. During parallel play, exchanges between youngsters begin to occur. When one talks or smiles, the other usually responds (Howes, Unger, & Seidner, 1990).

In parallel play, children play alone but pay close attention to what other nearby children are doing as they play.

Beginning at roughly 15 to 18 months, toddlers no longer just watch one another at play. **In** *associative play,* **youngsters engage in similar activities, talk or smile at one another, and offer each other toys.** Play is now truly interactive (Howes & Matheson, 1992). An example of simple social play would be two 20-month-olds pushing toy cars along the floor, making "car sounds," and periodically trading cars.

Toward the second birthday, *cooperative play* **begins: Now children organize their play around a distinct theme and take on special roles based on the theme.** For example, children may play "hide-and-seek" and alternate roles of hider and finder, or they may have a tea party and alternate being the host and guest. By the time children are 3½ to 4 years old, parallel play is much less common and cooperative play is the norm. Cooperative play typically involves peers of the same sex, a preference that increases until, by age 6, youngsters choose same-sex playmates about two-thirds of the time (LaFreniere, Strayer, & Gauthier, 1984).

MAKE-BELIEVE. During the preschool years, cooperative play often takes the form of make-believe. Preschoolers have telephone conversations with imaginary partners or pretend to drink imaginary juice. In early phases of make-believe, children rely on realistic props to support their play. While pretending to drink, younger preschoolers use a real cup; while pretending to drive a car, they use a toy steering wheel. In later phases of make-believe, children no longer need realistic props; instead, they can imagine that a block is the cup, or, like the girl in the photo, that the pile of sand is pancake batter. Of course, this gradual movement toward more abstract make-believe is possible because of cognitive growth that occurs during the preschool years (Striano, Tomasello, & Rochat, 2001).

Although make-believe is a particularly striking feature of preschoolers' play, it emerges earlier. By 16 to 18 months, toddlers have an inkling of the difference between pretend play and reality. If toddlers see an adult who pretends to fill two glasses with water and then drinks from one of the glasses, they will pretend to drink from the other glass (Bosco, Friedman, & Leslie, 2006).

Of course, the first time that a parent pretends, the activity must be puzzling for toddlers. They probably wonder why Mom is drinking from an empty glass or eating cereal from an empty bowl. But mothers help toddlers make sense out of this behavior: When mothers pretend, they typically look directly at the child and grin, as if to say, "This is just for fun—it's not real!" And toddlers return the smile, as if responding, "I get it! We're playing!" (Nishida & Lillard, 2007). When children are older, they usually tell play partners that they want to pretend ("Let's pretend"), then describe those aspects of reality that are being changed ("I'll be the pilot and this is my plane," referring to the couch). It's as if children mutually agree to enter a parallel universe that's governed by its own set of rules (Rakoczy, 2008; Skolnick Weisberg & Bloom, 2009).

When preschool children engage in make-believe, they often use props to support their play; these props are usually very concrete with younger preschoolers, but can be more abstract with older preschoolers.

As you might suspect, make-believe reflects the values important in a child's culture (Gosso, Morais, & Otta, 2007). For example, adventure and fantasy are favorite themes for European American youngsters, but family roles and everyday activities are favorites of Korean American children. In addition, European American children are more assertive in their make-believe and more likely to disagree with their play partner's ideas about pretending ("*I* want to be the king; *you* be the mom!"), whereas Korean American children are more polite ("Could I *please* be king?"). Thus, cultural values influence both the content and the form of make-believe (Farver & Shin, 1997).

Not only is make-believe play entertaining for children, but it also promotes cognitive development. Children who spend much time in make-believe play tend to be more advanced in language, memory, and reasoning (Bergen & Mauer, 2000). They also tend to have a more sophisticated understanding of other people's thoughts, beliefs, and feelings (Lindsey & Colwell, 2003). ◉ Watch the Video on mydevelopmentlab.com

Yet another benefit of make-believe is that it allows children to explore topics that frighten them. Children who are afraid of the dark may reassure a doll who is also afraid of the dark. By explaining to the doll why she shouldn't be afraid, children come to understand and regulate their own fear of darkness. Or children may pretend that a doll has misbehaved and must be punished, which allows them to experience the parent's anger and the doll's guilt. Make-believe allows children to explore other emotions, too, including joy and affection (Gottman, 1986).

For many preschool children, make-believe play involves imaginary companions. Children can usually describe their imaginary playmates in some detail, mentioning sex and age as well as hair and eye color. Imaginary companions were once thought to be fairly rare, but many preschoolers, particularly firstborn and only children, report imaginary companions (Taylor et al., 2004). What's more, an imaginary companion is associated with many *positive* social characteristics (Gleason & Hohmann, 2006; Roby & Kidd, 2008): Preschoolers with imaginary friends tend to be more sociable and have more real friends than other preschoolers. Among older children who are at risk for developing behavior problems, an imaginary companion promotes better adjustment during adolescence (Taylor, Hulette, & Dishion, 2010).

◉ Watch the Video *Rough-and-Tumble Play* on **mydevelopmentlab.com** to learn more about this unique form of play. As you watch, look at how much fun the boys are having; their facial expressions show that this is very different from aggressive behavior.

Make-believe play promotes cognitive development and lets children explore emotional topics that frighten them.

SOLITARY PLAY. At times throughout the preschool years, many children prefer to play alone. Should parents be worried? Usually, no. Solitary play comes in many forms and most are normal—even healthy. Spending free playtime alone coloring, solving puzzles, or assembling Legos® is not a sign of maladjustment. Many youngsters enjoy solitary activities and, at other times, choose very social play.

Parents influence their children's play by acting as playmate, social director, coach, and mediator.

However, some forms of solitary play *are* signs that children are uneasy about interacting with others (Coplan et al., 2001; Harrist et al., 1997). One type of unhealthy solitary play is wandering aimlessly. Sometimes children go from one preschool activity center to the next, as if trying to decide what to do. But really they just keep wandering, never settling into play with others or into constructive solitary play. Another unhealthy type of solitary play is hovering: A child stands near peers who are playing, watching them play but not participating. Over time, these behaviors do not bode well for youngsters (Coplan & Armer, 2007), so it's best for these youngsters to see a professional who can help them overcome their reticence in social situations.

PARENTAL INFLUENCE.   Parents get involved in their preschool children's play in several ways (Parke & O'Neil, 2000):

- *Playmate.* Many parents enjoy the role of playmate (and many parents deserve an Oscar for their performances). They use the opportunity to scaffold their children's play (see Module 6.2), often raising it to more sophisticated levels (Tamis-LeMonda & Bornstein, 1996). For example, if a toddler is stacking toy plates, a parent might help the child stack the plates (play at the same level) or might pretend to wash each plate (play at a more advanced level). When parents demonstrate more advanced forms of play, their children often play at the more advanced levels later (Lindsey & Mize, 2000).

- *Social director.* It takes two to interact, and young children rely on parents to create opportunities for social interactions. Many parents of young children arrange visits with peers, enroll children in activities (e.g., preschool programs), and take children to settings that attract young children (e.g., parks, swimming pools). All this effort is worth it: Children whose parents provide them with frequent opportunities for peer interaction tend to get along better with their peers (Ladd & Pettit, 2002).

- *Coach.* Successful interactions are based on a host of skills, including how to initiate an interaction, make joint decisions, and resolve conflicts. When parents help their children acquire these skills, children tend to be more competent socially and more accepted by their peers (Parke et al., 2004). But there's a catch: The coaching must be constructive for children to benefit. Parent-coaches sometimes make suggestions that aren't very clear or are actually misguided. Bad coaching is worse than none at all, as it harms children's peer relations (Russell & Finnie, 1990).

- *Mediator.* When young children play, they often disagree, argue, and sometimes fight. As shown in the photo, children play more cooperatively and longer when parents are present to help iron out conflicts (Mize, Pettit, & Brown, 1995). When young children can't agree on what to play, a parent can negotiate a mutually acceptable activity. When both youngsters want to play with the same toy, a parent can arrange for them to share. Here, too, parents scaffold their preschoolers' play, smoothing the interaction by providing some of the social skills that preschoolers lack.

In addition to these direct influences on children's play, parents influence children's play indirectly, via the quality of the parent–child attachment relationship. Recall from Module 10.3 that children's relationships with peers are most successful when, as infants, they had a secure attachment relationship with their mother (Bascoe et al., 2009; Wood, Emmerson, & Cowan, 2004). A child's relationship with his or her parents is the internal working model for all future social relationships. When the parent–child relationship is of high quality and emotionally satisfying, children are encouraged to form relationships with other people. Another possibility is that a secure attachment relationship with the mother makes an infant feel more confident about exploring the environment, which, in turn, provides more opportunities to interact with peers. These two views are not mutually exclusive; both may contribute to the relative ease with which securely attached children interact with their peers (Hartup, 1992).

One way in which parents facilitate their children's play is by taking on the role of mediator; parents help to resolve the disputes that inevitably develop when young children play.

PEER RELATIONS AFTER PRESCHOOL. When children attend elementary school, the context of peer relations changes dramatically (Rubin et al., 2006). Not only does the sheer number of peers increase, but children are also often exposed to a far more diverse set of peers than before. In addition, children find themselves interacting with peers in situations that range from reasonably structured with much adult supervision (e.g., a classroom) to largely unstructured with minimal adult supervision (e.g., a playground during recess).

An obvious change in children's peer relations during the elementary-school years is that, due to more experience with peers as well as cognitive and language development, children get along better than when they were younger. They become more skilled at initiating and maintaining interactions. They also use more sophisticated methods to resolve conflicts, such as negotiation (Laursen, Finkelstein, & Betts, 2001).

What do school-age children do when they're together? In one study (Zarbatany, Hartmann, & Rankin, 1990), investigators asked Canadian students in grades 5 and 6 how they spent their time with peers. The students in the study indicated how often they participated with peers in each of 29 different activities. The results, shown in the graph in Figure 15-1, are not too surprising, eh? The most common activities with peers are simple—just being together and talking. This is true of high-school students as well: They spend more time talking and hanging out with friends than in watching videos, doing homework, or participating in school activities (Nelson & Gastic, 2009).

The graph also highlights another important feature of peer relations during the elementary-school years. Children reported that they played physical games a few times each week, which reflects, in part, the emergence of a special type of play in school-age children. **In** *rough-and-tumble play,* **children**

Rated Frequency of Different Activities
(0 = Never, 7 = More Than Once a Day)

FIGURE 15-1

playfully chase, punch, kick, shove, fight, and wrestle with peers. Notice the word *play* in this definition: Unlike aggression, where the intention is to do harm, rough-and-tumble play is for fun. When children are involved in rough-and-tumble play, they are usually smiling and sometimes laughing (Pellis & Pellis, 2007). When parents or teachers intervene, the youngsters usually explain that there's no problem, they're just playing. Rough-and-tumble play is more common among boys than girls, and girls' rough-and-tumble play tends to emphasize running and chasing over wrestling and fighting.

As children move into adolescence, three features of their peer relationships loom large: Friendships become more intimate, youth have their first romantic relationships, and groups take on greater significance. These changes are so important that we'll consider each one separately. Let's start with friendship.

Friendship

Over time, even young children develop special relationships with certain peers. *Friendship* **is a voluntary relationship between two people involving mutual liking**. By age 4 or 5 years, most children claim to have a "best friend." If you ask them how they can tell a child is their best friend, their response will probably resemble 5-year-old Katelyn's:

INTERVIEWER:	Why is Heidi your best friend?
KATELYN:	Because she plays with me. And she's nice to me.
INTERVIEWER:	Are there any other reasons?
KATELYN:	Yeah, Heidi lets me play with her dolls.

Thus, the key elements of friendship for preschool and younger elementary-school children are that children like each other and enjoy playing together.

As children develop, their friendships become more complex. For older elementary-school children (8 to 11 years), mutual liking and shared activities are joined by features that are more psychological in nature, such as trust and assistance. At this age, children expect that they can depend on their friends—their friends will be nice to them, will keep their promises, and won't say mean things about them to others. And they expect friends to step forward in times of need: A friend should willingly help with homework or willingly share a snack.

Friendship is based on mutual liking and common interests in childhood and adolescence; intimacy becomes part of friendships in adolescence, particularly for girls.

Adolescence adds another layer of complexity to friendships. Mutual liking, common interests, and trust remain. In fact, trust becomes even more important in adolescent friendships. New to adolescence is intimacy: friends now confide in one another, sharing personal thoughts and feelings. Teenagers will reveal their excitement over a new romance or disappointment at not being cast in a school musical. Intimacy is more common in friendships among girls, who are more likely than boys to have one exclusive "best friend" (Markovits, Benenson, & Dolenszky, 2001). Because intimacy is at the core of their friendships, girls are also more likely to be concerned about the faithfulness of their friends and worry about being rejected (Benenson & Christakos, 2003; Poulin & Chan, 2010).

The emergence of intimacy in adolescent friendships means that friends also come to be seen as sources of social and emotional support. Elementary-school children generally rely on close family members—parents, siblings, and grandparents—as primary sources of support when they need help or are upset. But adolescents turn to close friends instead. Because adolescent friends share intimate thoughts and feelings, they can provide support during emotional or stressful periods (del Valle, Bravo, & Lopez, 2010; Levitt, Guacci-Franco, & Levitt, 1993).

Hand in hand with the emphasis on intimacy is loyalty. Having confided in friends, adolescents expect friends to stick with them through good and bad times. If a friend is disloyal, adolescents are afraid that they may be humiliated because their intimate thoughts and feelings will become known to a much broader circle of people (Berndt & Perry, 1990).

QUESTION 15.1
If Heidi is still Katelyn's best friend in high school, how would Katelyn's description of their friendship differ from the description she gave as a 5-year-old?
(Answer is on page 484.)

WHO BECOME FRIENDS?   In childhood and adolescence, most friends are like those in the photo: alike in age, sex, and race (Hamm, 2000; Mehta & Strough, 2009). Because friends are supposed to treat each other as equals, friendships are rare between an older, more experienced child and a younger, less experienced child. Because children typically play with same-sex peers (see Module 13.3), boys and girls become close friends infrequently.

Friendships are more common between children and adolescents from the same race or ethnic group than between those from different groups, reflecting racial segregation in American society. Friendships among children of different groups are more common in schools where classes are smaller (Hallinan & Teixeira, 1987) and when a child's school and neighborhood are ethnically diverse (Quillian & Campbell, 2003). Although such cross-group friendships are uncommon, they are valuable: Children from majority groups typically form more positive attitudes toward a minority group following a friendship with a youth from that group (Feddes, Noack, & Rutland, 2009).

Friends tend to be alike in age, sex, race, and interests.

Of course, friends are usually alike not only in age, sex, and race, but also in attitudes toward school, recreation, drug use, and plans for the future (Hamm, 2000; Newcomb & Bagwell, 1995). Children and adolescents befriend others who are similar to themselves and, as time passes, friends become more similar in their attitudes and values (Popp et al., 2008; Van Zalk et al., 2010). Nevertheless, friends are not photocopies of each other; friends are less similar, for example, than spouses or dizygotic twins (Rushton & Bonds, 2005).

Although children's friendships are overwhelmingly with members of their own sex, a few children have friendships with other-sex children. Children with same- *and* other-sex friendships tend to be very well adjusted, whereas children with only other-sex friendships tend to be unpopular and less competent academically and socially, and to have lower self-esteem. Apparently, children with both same- *and* other-sex friends are so socially skilled and popular that both boys and girls are eager to be their friends. In contrast, children with only other-sex friendships are socially unskilled, unpopular youngsters who are rejected by their same-sex peers and form friendships with other-sex children as a last resort (Bukowski, Sippola, & Hoza, 1999).

Other-sex friendships are more common among teenagers (Arndorfer & Stormshak, 2008). By mid-adolescence, boys make up about 33% of girls' friends, but only 20% of boys' friends are girls. Boys benefit more from these other-sex friendships: Female friends provide more help and support to boys than male friends provide to girls (Poulin & Pedersen, 2007; Sears, Graham, & Campbell, 2009).

QUALITY AND CONSEQUENCES OF FRIENDSHIP.   You probably remember some childhood friendships that were long lasting and satisfying, whereas others rapidly wore thin and soon dissolved. What accounts for these differences in the quality and longevity of friendships? Sometimes friendships are brief because children have the skills to create friendships—they know funny stories, they kid around, they know good gossip—but lack the skills to sustain those friendships—they can't keep secrets, or they're too bossy (Jiao, 1999; Parker & Seal, 1996). Sometimes friendships end because, when conflicts arise, children are more concerned about their own interests and are unwilling to compromise or negotiate (Fonzi et al., 1997; Rose & Asher, 1999). At other times, friendships dissolve when children discover that their needs and interests aren't as similar as they thought initially (Ellis & Zarbatany, 2007; Poulin & Boivin, 2000).

Considering that friendships disintegrate for many reasons, you're probably reminded that truly good friends are to be treasured. In fact, researchers consistently find that children benefit from having good friends. Compared to children who lack friends, children with good friends have higher self-esteem, are less likely to be lonely and depressed, and more often act prosocially—sharing and cooperating with others (Burk & Laursen, 2005; Hartup & Stevens, 1999). Children with good friends cope better with life stresses, such as the transition from elementary school to middle school or junior high (Berndt & Keefe, 1995) or being rejected by peers (McDonald et al., 2010). And they're less likely to be victimized by peers (Schwartz et al., 2000). What's more, the benefits of friendship are long lasting: Children who have friends have greater self-worth as young adults (Bagwell, Newcomb, & Bukowski, 1998). Thus, for many adolescents, friends are important resources. Children learn from their friends and turn to them for support in times of stress.

> When children have good friends, they are more likely to behave prosocially and to be better adjusted.

Although children and adolescents benefit from their friends' support, there can be costs as well. **Sometimes friends spend much of their time together discussing each other's personal problems, which is known as** *co-rumination.* Girls do this more than boys (consistent with the fact that intimacy is more important to girls' friendships). Such co-rumination strengthens girls' friendships but also puts them at risk for greater depression and anxiety. In other words, when Avanti and Mishra spend day after day talking about problems with their parents and their schoolwork, they grow closer but also more troubled (Brendgen et al., 2010; Rose, Carlson, & Waller, 2007).

There are other ways in which friendships can be hazardous (Bagwell, 2004). For example, when aggressive children are friends, they often encourage each other's aggressive behavior (Dishion, Poulin, & Burraston, 2001; Piehler & Dishion, 2007). Similarly, when teens engage in risky behavior (e.g., they drink, smoke, or have sex), they often reinforce the other's risky behavior (Bot et al., 2005; Henry et al., 2007). The "Focus on Research" feature describes a study that shows this impact of friends.

Focus on Research

Influence of Best Friends on Sexual Activity

Who were the investigators, and what was the aim of the study? James Jaccard, Hart Blanton, and Tonya Dodge (2005) set out to determine whether close friends influence adolescents' sexual behavior. That is, they wanted to know whether adolescents were more likely to be sexually active when their closest same-sex friend was sexually active.

How did the investigators measure the topic of interest? Jaccard and his colleagues used data from the *Add Health* database, which includes information obtained from more than 20,000 U.S. adolescents in grades 7–12. They completed questionnaires and were interviewed on a wide range of topics concerning adolescent health and development. Best friends were determined by asking adolescents to name five same-sex friends and then indicate the time spent with each in the past week. Sexual activity was determined by asking teens whether they had ever had sexual intercourse, and, if so, how recently.

Who were the children in the study? The investigators focused on a subsample of nearly 1,700 adolescents—837 boys and 851 girls—who were interviewed twice and who were not married.

What was the design of the study? This study was correlational because Jaccard and colleagues were interested in the relation that existed naturally between two variables: whether an adolescent was sexually active and whether an adolescent's best friend was sexually active. The study was longitudinal because adolescents were interviewed twice, approximately a year apart.

Were there ethical concerns with the study? You bet. This is one of the few child-development studies that's been debated on the floor of the U.S. Congress! The initial version of the project, proposed in the late 1980s, was motivated by the growing AIDS epidemic and focused solely on adolescent sexual risk-taking. After the National Institutes of Health (NIH) decided to fund the project, many conservative groups protested, arguing that the project actually endorsed the adolescent sexual behaviors that it was designed to study. The NIH withdrew the funds but a compromise was reached in 1993: The U.S. Congress passed legislation calling for a much broader longitudinal study, one that would examine adolescent health and well-being, the factors that jeopardize adolescent health, and behaviors that promote health. The result was the National Longitudinal Study of Adolescent Health—*Add Health* for short.

Parents and adolescents both gave consent to participate. In addition, the *Add Health* project went to great lengths to ensure that no individual's name could be linked to his or her responses to any question. For example, for questions on sensitive topics, adolescents listened to questions played on a tape recorder and they entered their answers directly into a laptop computer.

What were the results? When adolescents were interviewed the first time, the correlation between an adolescent being sexually active and an adolescent's best friend being sexually active was .34 for boys and .40 for girls. This shows a tendency for best friends to be alike in their sexual experience. But are adolescents more likely to be sexually active when their best friends are? The investigators answered this question by examining adolescents' sexual activity over the year. They found that when best friends were sexually active over the year, 56% of adolescents were sexually active during the same period; in contrast, when best friends were sexually inactive, only 24% of adolescents were sexually active. Thus, over time, adolescents were more likely to be sexually active when their best friend was, too. This was true for adolescents who were sexually active at the initial interview as well as for those who had been inactive sexually.

What did the investigators conclude? Adolescent friendships are based on similarity and, once friendships are formed, like-minded friends can encourage and support each other's behavior. In this case, they can support each other's sexual activity or inactivity. However, friendships are not all-powerful in this regard. When adolescents' best friends were sexually active over the year, 56%

of the adolescents followed their friends in becoming sexually active but 44% did not. As Jaccard et al. put it, "adolescent peer and social networks exert considerable impact on a wide range of behaviors, such as musical interests, clothing preference, and extracurricular activities. . . . [However] . . . peer influence is just one of a number of factors that contribute to adolescent risk behavior" (2005, p. 144).

What converging evidence would strengthen these conclusions? One useful step would be to continue the longitudinal study to examine the influence of friends over a longer term. Another important addition would be to examine the impact of an extended peer network, not simply an adolescent's best friend.

Finally, it's important to note that many youth are involved in relationships that are just the opposite of friendships. Mutual antipathies are characterized by shared dislike for each other, including some in which the feelings are quite intense (e.g., "I hate your guts!") as well as those in which the feelings are milder (e.g., children simply avoid each other). About one-third of US children and adolescents have mutual antipathic relationships; those who do are more likely to be aggressive and be withdrawn (Card, 2010). These relationships sometimes reflect dissimilarities between children (Nangle et al., 2004). Tom, who enjoys school, likes to read, and plans to go to Harvard, loathes Barry, who thinks that school is stupid, listens to his iPod constantly, and plans to quit high school to become a rock star; Barry feels the same way about Tom. Sometimes antipathies emerge from the wreckage of a broken friendship (Casper & Card, 2010). For example, when Kerri shares Regan's intimate secrets with the rest of their group, Regan retaliates by doing the same with Kerri's secrets; their friendship dissolves and they quickly develop an antipathic relationship.

Romantic Relationships

The social landscape adds a distinctive landmark in adolescence: romantic relationships. These are uncommon during elementary school, but by high school roughly two-thirds of U.S. adolescents have had a romantic relationship within the previous 1½ years and most have been involved in a romance lasting nearly a year (Carver, Joyner, & Udry, 2003).

But cultural factors influence the timing of romantic relationships. Traditional Hispanic American and Asian American parents emphasize family ties and loyalty to parents. Because romantic relationships are a sign of independence and usually result in less time spent with family, it's not surprising that Hispanic American and Asian American adolescents often begin to date at an older age and date less frequently (Collins, Welsh, & Furman, 2009).

Romantic relationships build on friendships. Like friends, romantic partners tend to be similar in popularity and physical attractiveness. And a best friendship serves both as a prototype for and a source of support during ups-and-downs of close relationships (Collins et al., 2009). What's more, romantic relationships change over time in ways that resemble changes in friendship: For younger adolescents, romantic relationships offer companionship (like that provided by a best friend) and an outlet for sexual exploration. For older adolescents like those in the photo, intimacy, trust, and support become important features of romantic relationships (Shulman & Kipnis, 2001).

It's tempting to dismiss teen romances as nothing more than "puppy love," but they are often developmentally significant (Collins et al., 2009). On the one hand, adolescents involved in a romantic relationship are often more self-confident and have higher self-esteem, and high-quality adolescent romances are associated with positive relationships during adulthood. On the other hand, adolescents in romantic relationships report more emotional upheaval and conflict (Joyner & Udry, 2000). In addition, early dating with many different partners is associated with a host of problems in adolescence (e.g., drug use, lower grades) and is associated with less satisfying romantic relationships in adulthood (Collins, 2003).

When older adolescents are romantically involved, they believe that trust and support are an important part of their relationship.

SEXUAL BEHAVIOR. Sexual exploration is an important feature of romantic relationships for younger adolescents. In fact, by the end of high school, roughly two-thirds of American adolescents will have had intercourse at least once (Eaton et al., 2008). No single factor predicts adolescent sexual behavior. Instead, adolescents are more likely to be sexually active when they acquire (from parents and peers) permissive attitudes towards sex, when their parents don't monitor their behavior, when their peers approve and when they believe their peers are also having sex, when they are more physically mature, and when they drink alcohol regularly (Belsky et al., 2010; Hipwell et al., 2010; Zimmer-Gembeck & Helfand, 2008).

Adolescents' sexual behavior is a cause for concern because, among American adolescent girls who have ever had intercourse, approximately 1 in 6 becomes pregnant. The result is that nearly a half million babies are born to American teenagers annually. African American and Hispanic American adolescents are the most likely to become pregnant (Ventura et al., 2008).

Teen pregnancy is common because sexually active teens typically do not use birth control consistently or correctly. Why? Several factors contribute (Gordon, 1996). First, many adolescents are ignorant of basic facts of conception and many believe that they are invulnerable—that only others become pregnant. Second, some teenagers do not know where to obtain contraceptives, and others, like Jeff in the module-opening vignette, are embarrassed to buy them (Ralph & Brindis, 2010). Still others don't know how to use contraceptives. Third, for some adolescent girls, like Gretchen from the vignette, becoming pregnant is appealing (Phipps et al., 2008). They think having a child is a way to break away from parents, gain status as an independent-living adult, and have "someone to love them."

The best way to reduce adolescent sexual behavior and teen pregnancy is with comprehensive sex education programs (Kirby & Laris, 2009). These programs teach the biological aspects of sex and emphasize responsible sexual behavior or abstinence from premarital sex altogether. They also include discussions of the pressures to become involved sexually and ways to respond to this pressure. A key element is that in role-playing sessions, students practice strategies for refusing to have sex. Youth who participate in programs like these are less likely to have intercourse; when they do have intercourse, they are more likely to use contraceptives. In contrast, there is little evidence that programs focusing solely on abstinence are effective in reducing sexual activity or encouraging contraceptive use.

Adolescents often fail to use contraception, which is why so many teens become pregnant.

About 5% of adolescents find themselves attracted to members of their own sex and identify themselves as gay or lesbian.

SEXUAL ORIENTATION. For most adolescents, sexual behavior involves members of the other sex. However, in early and mid-adolescence, roughly 15% of teens experience a period of sexual questioning, during which they sometimes report emotional and sexual attractions to members of their own sex (Carver, Egan, & Perry, 2004). For most adolescents, these experiences are simply a part of the larger process of role experimentation common to adolescence. However, like the teens in the photo, about 5% of teenage boys and girls identify their sexual orientation as gay (Rotherman-Borus & Langabeer, 2001).

The roots of attraction to members of the same sex are poorly understood. Scientists have, however, discredited several theories of sexual orientation. Research (Bell, Weinberg, & Hammersmith, 1981; Golombok & Tasker, 1996; Patterson, 1992) shows that each of the following is *false:*

- Sons become gay when raised by a domineering mother and a weak father.
- Girls become lesbians when their father is their primary role model.
- Children raised by gay or lesbian parents usually adopt their parents' sexual orientation.
- Gay and lesbian adults were, as children, seduced by an older person of their sex.

If all these ideas are false, why are adolescents attracted to members of their own sex? For males, genes and hormones may lead some boys to feel "different" during childhood and early adolescence, and these feelings lead to an interest in gender-atypical activities and, later, attraction to other males. For females, the path to same-sex attraction is less predictable. Attraction to other females usually does not emerge until mid- or late adolescence, and, in some cases, not until middle or old age. What's more, for many lesbian women, same-sex attraction grows out of deep feelings for a particular woman that, over time, extends to other females (Diamond, 2007).

Although the origins of same-sex attraction are not yet well understood, it is clear that gay and lesbian individuals face many challenges. Their family and peer relationships are often disrupted, and they endure verbal and physical attacks. Given these problems, it's not surprising that gay and lesbian youth often experience mental health problems (Toomey et al., 2010). In recent years, social changes have helped gay and lesbian youth respond more effectively to these challenges, including more (and more visible) role models and more centers for gay and lesbian youth. These resources are making it easier for gay and lesbian youth to understand their sexual orientation and to cope with the many other demands of adolescence.

In concluding this section, we need to recognize that sexual behavior and sexuality are enormously complicated and emotionally charged issues, even for adults. Adults who deal with adolescents need to recognize this complexity and help provide teenagers with skills for dealing with the issues involved in their emerging sexuality.

Groups

During adolescence, groups become an important feature of social life. Two types of groups are particularly common during adolescence. **A** *clique* **consists of four to six individuals who are good friends and, consequently, tend to be similar in age, sex, race, and interests**. Members of a clique spend time together and often dress, talk, and act alike. Cliques are often part of a larger group, too. **A** *crowd* **is a larger mixed-sex group of older children or adolescents who have similar values and attitudes and are known by a common label.** Maybe you remember some of the different crowds from your own youth? *Jocks, preppies, burnouts, nerds,* and *brains*—adolescents use these or similar terms to refer to crowds of older children or adolescents (Brown & Klute, 2003). Ethnic minority youth typically belong to such crowds, but some belong to ethnically based crowds instead (Brown et al., 2008).

Some crowds have more status than others. For example, students in many junior and senior high schools claim that the jocks are the most prestigious crowd, whereas the burnouts are among the least prestigious. Self-esteem in older children and adolescents often reflects the status of their crowd. During the school years, youths from high-status crowds tend to have greater self-esteem than those from low-status crowds (Sussman et al., 2007). Some crowds typically dislike others. Crowds that support adult values, such as jocks and preppies, usually dislike crowds that don't support these values (Laursen et al., 2010).

Why do some students become nerds while others join the burnouts? Adolescents' interests and abilities matter, obviously. Brighter students who enjoy school gravitate to the brain or nerd crowds while athletically talented teens become part of the jock crowd (Prinstein & LaGreca, 2004). Adolescents' crowds also reveal parents' influence. When parents practice authoritative parenting—they are warm but controlling—their children become involved with crowds that endorse adult standards of behavior (for example, normals, jocks, brains). But, when parents' style is neglectful or permissive, their children are less likely to identify with adult standards of behavior and, instead, join crowds like druggies that disavow adult standards. This seems to be true of African American, Asian American, European American, and Hispanic American children and their parents (Brown et al., 1993).

GROUP STRUCTURE. Groups—whether in school, at a summer camp, or anyplace else—typically have a well-defined structure. **Most groups have a** *dominance hierarchy* **consisting of a leader to whom all other members of the group defer.** Other members know their position in the hierarchy. They yield to members who are above them in the hierarchy and assert themselves over members who are below them. A dominance hierarchy is useful in reducing conflict and allocating resources within groups, because every member knows his or her place.

What determines where members stand in the hierarchy? With children, especially boys, physical power is often the basis for the dominance hierarchy. The leader is usually the most physically intimidating child (Hawley, 1999). Among girls and older boys, leaders have high self-esteem, good relationships with peers, and skills useful to the group. At a summer camp, for example, the leaders most often are the children with the greatest camping experience. Among Girl Scouts, girls chosen to be patrol leaders tend to be bright and goal oriented and to have new ideas (Edwards, 1994). These characteristics are appropriate because the primary function of patrols is to help plan activities for the entire troop. Similarly, in a study of classroom discussion groups, the children who became leaders had good ideas and were outgoing (Li et al., 2007). Thus, leadership based on key skills is effective because it gives the greatest influence to those with the skills most important to group functioning.

PEER PRESSURE. Groups establish *norms*—standards of behavior that apply to all group members—and groups may pressure members to conform to these

> Students have higher self-esteem when they belong to more prestigious crowds.

norms. Such "peer pressure" is often characterized as an irresistible, harmful force. The stereotype is that teenagers exert enormous pressure on each other to behave antisocially. In reality, peer pressure is neither all-powerful nor always evil. For example, most adolescents resist peer pressure to behave in ways that are clearly antisocial, such as stealing (Cook, Buehler, & Henson, 2009), and such resistance increases from mid- to late adolescence (Steinberg & Monahan, 2007). Peer pressure can be positive, too. Peers often urge one another to work hard in school; to participate in school activities, such as trying out for a play or working on the yearbook; or to become involved in community action projects, such as Habitat for Humanity (Kindermann, 2007; Molloy, Gest, & Rulison, 2011).

Of course, peer influence is common throughout the life span. As we saw in Module 1.1, children and adults often imitate their peers' behavior, particularly when the peer has high status and the behavior is rewarded. But adolescents may be particularly susceptible to peer influence because they are forging an identity (Module 11.1) and matching the behavior of a valued peer group may help to foster that identity. If Jordan sees that popular kids smoke and part of her emerging identity is that she's in the popular group, she may start smoking too (Brechwald & Prinstein, 2011).

Peer pressure is *not* all-powerful. Instead, peer influence is stronger when (1) youth are younger and more socially anxious; (2) peers have high status, (3) peers are friends, and (4) standards for appropriate behavior are not clear-cut, as in the case of tastes in music or clothing, or standards for smoking and drinking (Anderson et al., 2011; Brechwald & Prinstein, 2011). Thus, when 14-year-old Doug's best friend (who's one of the most popular kids in school) gets his hair cut like Justin Beiber, Doug may go along because he's young, the peer is popular and his friend, and there are no fixed standards for hair style. But when an unpopular kid that 18-year-old Kelly barely knows suggests to her that they got to the mall and shoplift some earrings, Kelly will resist because she's older, the peer is unpopular and not a friend, and norms for shoplifting are clear.

Popularity and Rejection

Eileen is definitely the most popular child in her class. Other youngsters always want to play with her and sit near her at lunch or on the school bus. In contrast, Jay is the least popular child in the class. When he tries to join a game of four square, the others quit. Students in the class dislike Jay as much as they like Eileen.

Popular and rejected children like Eileen and Jay can be found in every classroom and neighborhood. In fact, studies of popularity (Hymel et al., 2004) reveal that most children can be placed in one of five categories:

- *Popular children* are liked by many classmates.
- *Rejected children* are disliked by many classmates.
- *Controversial children* are both liked and disliked by classmates.
- *Average children* are liked and disliked by some classmates but without the intensity found for popular, rejected, or controversial children.
- *Neglected children* are ignored by classmates.

Of these categories, we know most about popular and rejected children. Each of these categories actually includes two subtypes. Most popular children are skilled academically and socially. They are good students who are usually friendly, cooperative, and helpful. They are more skillful at communicating and better at integrating themselves into an ongoing conversation or play session—they "fit in" instead of "barging in" (Graziano, Keane, & Calkins, 2007; Rubin et al., 2006; Véronneau et al., 2010). A smaller group of popular children includes physically aggressive boys who pick fights with peers and relationally aggressive girls who, like the "Plastics" in the film *Mean Girls,* thrive on manipulating social relationships. Although these youth are not particularly friendly, their antisocial behavior nevertheless apparently has a certain appeal to peers (Cillessen & Rose, 2005; Xie et al., 2006).

Are these avenues to popularity specific to American children, or do they apply more generally? The "Cultural Influences" feature has the answer.

Cultural Influences

Keys to Popularity

In America, popular children seem to know how to get along with others. These results don't apply just to American children; they hold for children in many cultures around the world, including Canada, European countries, Israel, and China (e.g., Casiglia, Coco, & Zappulla, 1998). Sometimes, however, popular children have other characteristics that are unique to their cultural setting. In Israel, for example, popular children are more likely to be direct and assertive than in other countries (Krispin, Sternberg, & Lamb, 1992). In China, popular children are more likely to be shy than in other countries (Chen et al., 2009). Evidently, good social skills are at the core of popularity in most countries, but other features may also be important, reflecting culturally specific values.

As for rejected children, many are overly aggressive, hyperactive, socially unskilled, and unable to regulate their emotions. These children are usually much more hostile than popular aggressive children, and seem to view aggression as an end—which peers dislike—instead of using aggression as a means toward other ends—which peers may not actually like but grudgingly respect (Prinstein & Cillessen, 2003). Other rejected children are shy, withdrawn, timid, and, not surprisingly, lonely (Asher & Paquette, 2003; Rubin, Coplan, & Bowker, 2009).

CONSEQUENCES OF REJECTION. No one enjoys being rejected. Not surprisingly, peer rejection poses a major obstacle in children's development. Over time, for example, rejected youngsters become less involved in classroom activities; they end up feeling lonely and disliking school (Buhs & Ladd, 2001; Ladd, Herald-Brown, & Reiser, 2008). Repeated peer rejection in childhood can also have serious long-term consequences (Ladd, 2006; Rubin et al., 2009). Rejected youngsters are more likely than youngsters in the other categories to drop out of school, commit juvenile offenses, and suffer from psychopathology.

Most popular children are socially skilled—they're friendly, cooperative, and helpful—but some popular children are aggressive.

CAUSES OF REJECTION. Peer rejection can be traced, at least in part, to parental influence (Ladd, 1998). Children see how their parents respond to different

Many rejected children are too aggressive, and some learn this style of interaction from watching their parents in conflict.

 ANSWER 15.1

As a teenager, Katelyn's description of Heidi would focus more on intimacy. She might say, "I can tell Heidi stuff—special stuff, like secrets—that I wouldn't tell anyone else. And I know she'll keep my secrets." And Katelyn might mention that Heidi is loyal, willing to stand by her when other kids are teasing her.

social situations and often imitate these responses later. Parents who are friendly and cooperative with others demonstrate effective social skills. Parents who are belligerent and combative demonstrate much less effective social skills. In particular, when parents typically respond to interpersonal conflict like the couple in the photo—with intimidation or aggression—their children may imitate them; this hampers their development of social skills and makes them less popular in the long run (Keane, Brown, & Crenshaw, 1990).

Parents' disciplinary practices also affect their children's social skill and popularity. Inconsistent discipline—punishing a child for misbehaving one day and ignoring the same behavior the next—is associated with antisocial and aggressive behavior, paving the way to rejection (Dishion, 1990). Consistent punishment that is tied to parental love and affection is more likely to promote social skill and, in the process, popularity (Dekovic & Janssens, 1992).

In sum, parenting can lead to an aggressive interpersonal style in a child, which in turn leads to peer rejection. The implication, then, is that by teaching youngsters (and their parents) more effective ways of interacting with others, we can make rejection less likely. With improved social skills, rejected children would not need to resort to antisocial behaviors. Rejected children (and other types of unpopular children) can be taught how to initiate interaction, communicate clearly, and be friendly. They can also be discouraged from behaviors that peers dislike, such as whining and fighting. This training is very similar to training for aggressive adolescents, who are typically unpopular (see Module 12.4). Training of this sort does work. Rejected children can learn skills that lead to peer acceptance and thereby avoid the long-term harm associated with being rejected (LaGreca, 1993; Mize & Ladd, 1990).

Throughout this module, we've seen that peers affect children's development in many ways—for example, through different forms of play, through friendships, and through participation in social groups. Beginning in the next module, we'll look at important *nonsocial* influences on children's development, starting with media such as television and computers.

 ## Check Your Learning

RECALL Describe the factors that seem to contribute to an adolescent's or young adult's sexual orientation.

How and when are teenagers most susceptible to peer pressure?

INTERPRET How might developmental change in peer interactions during infancy and the preschool years be explained by Piaget's stages of cognitive development, described in Module 6.1?

APPLY On page 482, you met Jay, who is the least popular child in his class. Jay's mom is worried about her son's lack of popularity and wants to know what she can do to help her son. Jay's dad thinks that Jay's mom is upset over nothing—he argues that, like fame, popularity is fleeting, and that Jay will turn out okay in the end. What advice would you give to Jay's parents?

15.2 Electronic Media

OUTLINE
Television
Computers

LEARNING OBJECTIVES
- How does watching television affect children's attitudes and behavior?
- How does TV viewing influence children's cognitive development?
- How do children use computers at home and in school?

Whenever Bill visits his granddaughter, Harmony, he is struck by the amount of time Harmony spends watching television. Many of the programs she watches are worthwhile. Nevertheless, Bill wonders if such a steady diet of TV watching might somehow be harmful. Images pop on and off the screen so rapidly that Bill wonders how Harmony will ever learn to pay attention, particularly in other settings that aren't as rich in video stimulation.

In generations past, children learned their culture's values from parents, teachers, religious leaders, and print media. These sources of cultural knowledge are still with us, but they coexist with new technologies that do not always incorporate or portray parents' values. Think about some of the technological developments that contemporary children take for granted that were completely foreign to youngsters growing up just a few decades ago. Your list would probably include satellite TV, CD and DVD players, video game players, personal computers, cell phones that take pictures and play music, pagers, and the Internet. More forces than ever before can potentially influence children's development. Two of these technologies—television and computers—are the focus of this module. As we look at their influence, we'll see if Bill's concern for his granddaughter is well founded.

Television

The cartoon exaggerates TV's impact on American children, but only somewhat. If you were a typical U.S. child and adolescent, you spent much more time watching TV than interacting with your parents or friends or in school. The numbers tell an incredible story. School-age children spend about 20 to 25 hours each week watching TV (Roberts, Foehr, & Rideout, 2005). Extrapolated through adolescence, the typical American high-school graduate has watched 15,000 hours of TV—nearly 2 full years of watching TV 24/7! No wonder scientists and laypeople alike think TV plays an important role in socializing American children.

For most youngsters, viewing time increases gradually during the preschool and elementary-school years, reaching a peak just before adolescence. Boys watch more TV than girls. Also, children with lower IQs watch more than those with higher IQs; children from lower-income families watch more TV than children from higher-income families (Huston & Wright, 1998).

It is hard to imagine that all this TV viewing would not affect children's behavior. For this reason, scientists have been studying the impact of TV since the 1950s. Much of the research has addressed the impact of the medium per se; other research

"MRS. HORTON, COULD YOU STOP BY SCHOOL TODAY?"

has examined the impact of the contents of TV programs (Huston & Wright, 1998). In this section, we'll look at the results of both types of research.

THE MEDIUM IS THE MESSAGE—OR IS IT? Some critics argue that the medium itself—independent of the contents of programs—has several harmful effects on viewers, particularly children (Huston & Wright, 1998). Among the criticisms are these:

- Because TV programs consist of many brief segments presented rapidly, children who watch much TV develop short attention spans and have difficulty concentrating in school.
- Because TV provides ready-made, simple-to-interpret images, children who watch a lot of TV become passive, lazy thinkers and become less creative.
- Children who watch TV often spend less time in more productive and valuable activities, such as reading, participating in sports, and playing with friends.

In fact, as stated, none of these criticisms is consistently supported by research. The first criticism—TV watching reduces attention span—is the easiest to dismiss. Research repeatedly shows that increased TV viewing does not lead to reduced attention, greater impulsivity, reduced task persistence, or increased activity levels (Foster & Watkins, 2010). The *contents* of TV programs can influence these dimensions of children's behavior—for example, children who watch impulsive models behave more impulsively themselves—but TV per se does not harm children's ability to pay attention. Bill, the grandfather in the opening vignette, need not worry that his granddaughter's TV viewing will limit her ability to pay attention later in life.

> The contents of TV programs can make children less attentive and more impulsive, but the medium itself does not.

As for the criticism that TV viewing fosters lazy thinking and stifles creativity, the evidence is mixed. Many studies find no link between the amount of TV viewing and creativity. For example, Anderson and colleagues (2001) found that the amount of time spent watching TV during the preschool years was unrelated to creativity during adolescence. Other studies, however, find a negative relation: As children watch more TV, they tend to be less creative on tests of divergent thinking like those described in Module 8.3 (Valkenburg & van der Voort, 1994, 1995). Child-development researchers don't know why the negative effects aren't found more consistently, although one idea is that the effects depend on which programs children watch, rather than simply the amount of TV watched.

Finally, according to the last criticism, TV viewing replaces other socially more desirable activities: The simple-minded view is that every hour of TV viewing replaces an hour of some more valuable activity, such as reading or doing homework. To illustrate the problems with this view, let's look at reading. The correlation between time spent watching TV and reading tends to be negative—heavy TV viewers read less (Ennemoser & Schneider, 2007; Schmidt & Vandewater, 2008). But we need to be cautious in interpreting this correlation (see Figure 1-2 on page 25). The easy interpretation is that watching much TV causes children to read less. However, an alternate interpretation is also plausible: Children who are poor readers (and thus are unlikely to spend much time reading) end up watching a lot of TV. For youngsters who read poorly, an hour spent watching TV replaces some activity, but not necessarily an hour that would have been spent reading (Huston & Wright, 1998).

Research does reveal one way in which the medium itself is harmful. In many homes, the TV is on constantly—from morning until bedtime—even though no one is explicitly watching a specific program. In this case, TV is often a powerful distraction. Young children will make frequent, brief glances at the TV, enough to disrupt the quality of their play. Similarly, during parent–child interaction, parents will steal quick looks at the TV, which reduces the quantity and quality of parent–child interactions (Kirkorian et al., 2009; Schmidt et al., 2008).

When we move past the medium per se and consider the contents of programs, TV does substantially affect children's development (Anderson & Hanson, 2009), as you'll see in the next three sections.

INFLUENCE ON ATTITUDES AND SOCIAL BEHAVIOR. Children are definitely influenced by what they see on TV (Browne & Hamilton-Giachritsis, 2005; Huesmann, 2007). In Module 12.4, for example, we saw how some children become more aggressive after viewing violence on television; and in Module 13.3 we saw how children adopt gender stereotypes from TV. Watching can also help children learn to be more generous and cooperative and have greater self-control. Youngsters who watch TV shows that emphasize prosocial behavior, such as *Mister Rogers' Neighborhood,* are more likely to behave prosocially (Wilson, 2008). However, prosocial behaviors are portrayed on TV far less frequently than aggressive behaviors, so opportunities to learn the former from television are limited; we are far from harnessing the power of television for prosocial uses.

INFLUENCE ON CONSUMER BEHAVIOR. Sugary cereals, hamburgers and French fries, snack foods, toys, jeans, and athletic shoes—a phenomenal number of TV advertisements for these products are directed toward children and adolescents. A typical U.S. youth may see more than 100 commercials a day (Linn, 2004)! Children as young as 3 years can distinguish commercials from programs, though preschoolers believe commercials are simply a different form of entertainment—one designed to inform viewers. Not until age 8 or 9 do children begin to understand the persuasive intent of commercials; a few years later, children realize that commercials are not always truthful (Linn, 2005; Oates, Blades, & Gunter, 2002). They understand that a toy rocket will not really fly or that a doll will not really talk, contrary to how they're shown in commercials.

Even though children and adolescents come to understand the real intent of commercials, commercials are still effective sales tools (Smith & Atkin, 2003). Children grow to know many of the products advertised on TV (Buijzen & Bomhof, 2008) and urge parents to buy products they've seen on television. And among adolescents, exposure to TV programs that contain commercials for alcohol (e.g., beer ads) is associated with more frequent drinking of alcohol (Stacy et al., 2004). This selling power of TV has long concerned advocates for children because so many commercials are for foods that have little nutritional value and can lead to obesity and tooth decay. The U.S. government once regulated the amount and type of advertising on children's TV programs (Huston, Watkins, & Kunkel, 1989), but today the responsibility falls largely to parents.

INFLUENCE ON COGNITION. Big Bird, Bert, Ernie, and other members of the cast of *Sesame Street,* shown in the photo, have been helping to educate preschool children for more than 40 years. Today, mothers and

QUESTION 15.2
Brent is a 6-year-old boy who loves to read. His parents are thinking about limiting his TV viewing because they're afraid it will cut into the time he spends reading. Do research findings suggest that Brent's parents are on the right track? *(Answer is on page 490.)*

For more than four decades, *Sesame Street* has had tremendous success in helping preschool children acquire many of the skills needed for success in school, such as knowing the names of letters and knowing how to count.

fathers who watched *Sesame Street* as preschoolers are watching with their own youngsters. Remarkably, the time preschool children spend watching *Sesame Street* predicts their grades in high school and the amount of time they spend reading as adolescents (Anderson et al., 2001).

Sesame Street has been joined by programs designed to teach young children about language and reading skills (*Arthur, Martha Speaks, Super Why!*) and programs that teach basic science and math concepts (*Curious George, Sid the Science Kid, The Dinosaur Train*). Programs like these (and older programs, such as *Electric Company, 3-2-1 Contact,* and *Square One TV*) show that the power of TV can be harnessed to help children learn important academic skills and useful social skills.

The "Improving Children's Lives" feature includes some guidelines for ensuring that TV's influence on children is positive.

Improving Children's Lives

Get the Kids Off the Couch!

If you know a child who sits glued to the TV screen from after school until bedtime, it's time to take action. Here are some suggestions:

- Children need absolute rules concerning the amount of TV and the types of programs that they can watch. These rules must be enforced consistently.
- Children shouldn't fall into the trap of "I'm bored, so I'll watch TV." Children should be encouraged to know what they want to watch before they turn on the TV.
- Adults should watch TV with children and discuss the programs. For example, parents can express their disapproval of a character's use of aggression and suggest other means of resolving conflicts. Parents can also point to the stereotypes that are depicted. The aim is for children to learn that TV's account of the world is often inaccurate and that TV should be watched critically.
- Parents need to be good TV viewers themselves. The first two tips listed here apply to viewers of all ages. When a child is present, parents shouldn't watch violent programs or others that are inappropriate for the young. And parents should watch TV deliberately and selectively, instead of mindlessly channel surfing.

Computers

Some observers believe that computers are creating a "digital childhood"—an era in which new media are transforming the lives of American children. In this section, we'll look at children's use of computers at home and in school.

COMPUTERS IN THE HOME. More than 80% of American youth live in homes with a computer (Roberts et al., 2005). And they begin to use the computer at a remarkably young age. Many 2½-year-olds play computer games while seated on a parent's lap; by 3½, children play computer games independently, controlling a mouse themselves (Calvert et al., 2005).

Most children and adolescents use home computers primarily to access the Internet. For example, they search the Web for information for school assignments. However, a far more common use of computers, particularly for boys, is to play games online. Research reveals that computer games affect youth in much the same way that TV does—content matters. In other words, just as children and adolescents are influenced by the TV programs they watch, they're influenced by the contents of the computer games they play. On the one hand, many games, including *Tetris* and *Star Fox,* emphasize perceptual–spatial skills, such as estimating the trajectory of a moving object, and responding rapidly. When children play such games frequently, their spatial skills often improve (Subrahmanyam et al., 2001), as does their processing speed (Mackey et al., 2011). On the other hand, many popular games, such *Manhunt* and *Grand Theft Auto,* are violent, with players killing game characters in extraordinarily gruesome ways. Just as exposure to televised violence can make children behave more aggressively, playing violent video games can make children more aggressive (Anderson et al., 2010).

What's more, a minority—roughly 10%—of youth get "hooked" on video games (Gentile, 2009). They show many of the same symptoms associated with pathological gambling: Playing video games comes to dominate their lives, it provides a "high," and it leads to conflict with others. Not surprisingly, extreme video-game playing is associated with less success in school, apparently because youth spend time playing games instead of studying (Weis & Cerankosky, 2010).

The other main use of home computers (and cell phones) is to communicate with peers, often through social networking sites such as Facebook.com. In the early days of the Internet—the 1990s—spending much time online communicating with others had harmful effects: friendships, social connectedness, and well-being suffered. In those days, a small minority of teens had Internet access, so online social connections usually came at the expense of "real" connections. Today, however, most teens are online and they use the Internet (and other communication technologies) to maintain existing "real" social connections. In fact, online communication seems to promote self-disclosure, which produces high-quality friendships and, in turn, adolescents' well-being (Valkenburg & Jochen, 2009). Boys, in particular, benefit from online communication because self-disclosure is much easier for them online than face-to-face (Schouten, Valkenburg, & Peter, 2007).

In many respects, new technologies have changed the *how* of childhood and adolescence but not the *what.* As with previous generations, children and adolescents still play games, connect with peers, and do homework. Technology like a home computer simply provides a different means for accomplishing these tasks. As we'll see in the next section, much the same is true of computers in schools.

COMPUTERS IN THE CLASSROOM. New technologies—whether TV, DVD, or pocket calculator—soon find themselves in the classroom. Personal computers are no exception; virtually all American public schools now use personal computers to aid instruction. Computers serve many functions in the classroom (Roschelle et al., 2000). One is that of instructor: As shown in the photo, children use computers to

Computers are used in schools as tutors, for experiential learning, and to help children accomplish traditional academic goals.

Computerized instruction can be extremely useful because it allows instruction to be individualized and interactive, which allows students to work at their own pace and receive personalized feedback.

learn reading, spelling, arithmetic, science, and social studies. Computers allow instruction to be individualized and interactive. Students proceed at their own pace, receiving feedback and help when necessary (Hurts, 2008; Roschelle et al., 2010). Computers are also a valuable medium for experiential learning. Simulation programs allow students to explore the world in ways that would be impossible or dangerous otherwise. Students can change the law of gravity or see what happens to a city when no taxes are imposed. Finally, computers can help students achieve traditional academic goals (Steelman, 1994). A graphics program can allow artistically untalented students to produce beautiful illustrations. A word-processing program can relieve much of the drudgery associated with revising, thereby encouraging better writing.

Overall, then, computers are like television in that the technology per se doesn't necessarily influence children's development. However, the way the technology is used—for example, watching violent TV programs or using word-processing software to revise a short story—can affect children, positively or negatively depending on the use and content. In the next module, we'll see whether institutions such as neighborhoods and schools also influence children in this manner.

 ANSWER 15.2
Probably not. Children who read well and enjoy reading will find time to read. Research suggests that for these youngsters, TV viewing will not replace time spent reading. Frankly, a better strategy would be to set limits on *what* he watches on TV, not on how much he watches.

 Check Your Learning

RECALL Summarize research that has examined the impact on children of TV as a medium.

What are the primary ways in which computers are used in schools?

INTERPRET Compare and contrast the ways in which TV viewing and Web surfing might affect children's development.

APPLY What if you had the authority to write new regulations for children's TV programs? What shows would you encourage? What shows would you want to limit?

15.3 Institutional Influences

OUTLINE	LEARNING OBJECTIVES
Child Care and After-School Activities	• How are children affected by nonparental child care?
Part-Time Employment	• What is the impact of part-time employment on children's development?
Neighborhoods	• How are children influenced by their neighborhoods?
School	• What are the hallmarks of effective schools and effective teachers?

When 15-year-old Aaron announced that he wanted an after-school job at the local supermarket, his mother was delighted, believing that he would learn much from the experience. Five months later, she had her doubts. Aaron had lost interest in school, and they argued constantly about how he spent his money.

So far in this chapter, we've seen the potent influences of peers and media on children's development. Yet there are other noteworthy influences on children and their development: namely, cultural institutions where children spend much of their lives. In this module, we'll look at four such institutions: day care, the workplace, neighborhoods, and school. As we do, we'll see whether part-time jobs like Aaron's help or harm youth.

Child Care and After-School Activities

Each day, millions of U.S. children age 5 and under are cared for by someone other than their mother, a phenomenon linked to more dual-earner couples and to more single-parent households in the United States in the 21st century. Three forms of child care are most common: (1) children stay at home, where they receive care from a relative such as a father or grandparent, (2) children receive care in the home of a child-care provider, and (3) children attend day-care or nursery-school programs. The patterns are very similar for European American, African American, and Hispanic American youngsters (Singer et al., 1998; U.S. Census Bureau, 2008).

Many parents, particularly mothers, have misgivings about their children spending so much time in the care of others. Should parents worry? Does nonmaternal care harm children? Before turning to research for answers to these questions, let's put them in historical and cross-cultural perspective. Although nonmaternal care of children is often portrayed as unnatural—and therefore potentially harmful—the truth is that for most of history and in most cultures, a majority of children have been cared for by someone other than the mother, at least some of the time (Lamb, 1999). When viewed from the larger perspective of history, there is nothing "natural" or "traditional" about mothers having nearly exclusive responsibility for child care.

Nevertheless, in the United States (and many other industrialized countries) since World War II, the cultural ideal and conviction has been that children are better off when cared for at home by their mothers. Does research support the cultural ideal? In answering this question, most researchers worried about the impact of child care on mother–infant attachment. But, as we saw in Module 10.3, the Early Child-Care study conducted by the National Institute of Child Health and Human Development showed that attachment security was affected by child care only when less sensitive mothers had their infants in low-quality child care.

Of course, the effects of day care need not be limited to attachment; other aspects of children's development might be affected, and these have been investigated in other reports from the Early Child Care study. Here, too, the general finding is that time spent in day care is not a critical factor. There are some exceptions: for example, when children spend many hours each week in day care, they more often have behavior problems. To illustrate, children in the Early Child Care study who had spent the most time in day care as infants and preschoolers were, as elementary-school students, more likely to be aggressive with peers and to have conflicts with adults (Rodkin & Roisman, 2010; Vandell et al., 2010).

However, the more important factor in understanding the impact of child care is the quality of care that children receive: Not surprisingly, better care is linked to better outcomes. High-quality child care means a relatively small number of children per caregiver (e.g., three infants or toddlers per caregiver) along with well-educated and well-trained caregivers (de Schipper, Riksen-Walraven, & Geurts, 2006). In addition, in high-quality child care, caregivers are warm and responsive, and they provide age-appropriate activities that are designed to promote cognitive and social development (Marshall, 2004). When children are enrolled in programs that meet these standards, they often grow cognitively and socioemotionally. For example, when children receive high-quality child care, their cognitive and language development is more advanced (Vandell et al., 2010). What's more, such care seems to be particularly beneficial for children from low-income families: High-quality child care improves their school readiness, which translates into more success after they enter school (Dearing, McCartney, & Taylor, 2009). Thus, working parents can enroll their infants and preschoolers in high-quality day-care programs with no fear of harmful consequences.

Sometimes parents must rely on multiple sources of care, such as a family member for two days and center care for three days. Parents also sometimes switch caregivers. As you might imagine, multiple low-quality caregivers are detrimental to children, as are constantly changing child-care arrangements (Morrissey, 2009). However, multiple child-care providers can be beneficial when they are part of a stable arrangement and when each provider is of high quality (Tran & Weinraub, 2006).

> **Parents can enroll their children in high-quality day care without fearing harmful consequences.**

When children enter elementary school, child care becomes easier for working parents. However, many children still need care after school. Historically, after-school programs have focused on recreation: children played games and sports, did arts and crafts, or participated in musical or dramatic productions. Recently, however, many after-school programs have focused more on academics. Children attending such programs often show modest improvements in school achievement, particularly when they attend higher-quality programs (Vandell, Pierce, & Dadisman, 2005).

In addition, many children and adolescents participate in structured activities after school. The most common activities are sports, school clubs, and community service or religious organizations (Fredricks & Eccles, 2006; Larson, Hansen, & Moneta, 2006). As a general rule, children and adolescents benefit from participating: They often are better adjusted, have higher self-esteem, are less likely to have behavioral problems, and are more likely to continue their education after high school (Beal & Crockett, 2010; Fredricks & Eccles, 2006). The main exception is participation in sports, where the findings are mixed. Some studies (e.g., Fauth, Roth, & Brooks-Gunn, 2007) show that adolescents involved in sports are more likely to drink alcohol and to have lower grades. But not all studies report this outcome; the results may depend, for example, on attitudes toward sports in the school and on the specific sports in which the child is involved (Fredricks & Eccles, 2006; Metzger et al., 2011; Wilson et al., 2010).

Of course, many students participate in many activities, and such diverse participation is beneficial. Students who participate in multiple school activities tend to be better adjusted, more successful in school, less prone to drug use, and more involved in their communities (Busseri et al., 2006; Fredricks & Eccles, 2006). This may surprise you in light of media reports that American youth—particularly affluent youth—are stressed out because they're overscheduled after school. But research suggests that most teenagers are not distressed by a busy after-school schedule; most children participate in activities because they enjoy them, not because they're pressured into them by achievement-oriented parents (Luthar, Shoum, & Brown, 2006).

Many American children care for themselves after school, an arrangement that can be safe, depending on the child's age and maturity, the neighborhood, and the rules established for the child.

Finally, many school-age children and adolescents—about one-third of U.S. middle-school students and one-half of high-school students—care for themselves after school at least once a week (Mahoney & Parente, 2009). **Children who care for themselves are sometimes called** *latchkey children,* **a term that**

originated more than 200 years ago to describe children who raised a door latch to enter their own homes. Some latchkey children, like the child in the photo, stay at home alone (sometimes with parental supervision in absentia via the telephone). Others may stay at friends' homes where adults are sometimes present, or they may be unsupervised in public places such as shopping malls.

The popular perception is that latchkey children are a frightened, endangered lot. In fact, research suggests that self-care can be risky under certain circumstances. Youth who care for themselves can get into trouble—do drugs, become aggressive, and begin to fail in school—when they spend their after-school hours away from home, unsupervised, and when they live in neighborhoods plagued by high crime rates. When these circumstances don't apply, older children and adolescents can care for themselves successfully (Mahoney & Parente, 2009).

Many states provide specific guidelines to help parents decide whether a child is capable of self-care (e.g., Connecticut Department of Children and Families, 2003). Parents are urged to consider their child's age—many experts recommend that children are not capable of self-care until they're 12, but others say that some 8-year-olds can care for themselves briefly (1 to 1½ hours) during the day. More important than age is the child's maturity: Is the child responsible? Does the child make good decisions on his or her own? Parents should also consider the child's attitudes and feelings about being left alone: Is the child anxious about being alone in the house? Finally, it's important for parents to consider their neighborhood: Is it safe? Are there trusted neighbors that the child can turn to if necessary?

If questions like these can be answered yes, then self-care will probably work. But it's important that children be prepared for self-care. They need to know after-school routines (for example, acceptable ways of getting home from school and how to check in with a parent), rules for their own behavior after school (for example, acceptable and unacceptable activities), guidelines on how to handle emergencies, and emergency phone numbers (American Academy of Child and Adolescent Psychiatry, 2000).

Fortunately, employers have begun to realize that convenient, high-quality child care makes for a better employee. Businesses are realizing that the availability of excellent child care helps attract and retain a skilled labor force. And cities help by modifying their zoning codes so that new shopping complexes and office buildings must include child-care facilities, like those in the photo. With effort, organization, and help from the community and businesses, high-quality child care can be available to all families.

Because many employees—particularly mothers who work full-time outside of the home—want high-quality child care available, many companies now provide such care onsite.

Part-Time Employment

The teen in the photo is engaged in an American adolescent ritual: the part-time job. Today, about 25% of first-year high-school students have a part-time job and about 75% of high-school seniors do (Bachman et al., 2011). About two-thirds of these youth work in retail and half of those are employed in the food and beverage industry (U.S. Department of Labor, 2000).

Many American adolescents hold part-time jobs; these can be beneficial, but not when adolescents work more than 20 hours weekly.

Most adults praise teens for working, believing that early exposure to the workplace teaches self-discipline, self-confidence, and important job skills (Snedeker, 1982). For most adolescents, however, the reality is very different. Part-time work can actually be harmful, for several reasons:

1. **School performance suffers.** When students work more than approximately 20 hours per week, they become less engaged in school and are less likely to be successful in college (Bachman et al., 2011; Monahan, Lee, & Steinberg, 2011). Many high-school students apparently do not have the foresight and discipline necessary to consistently meet the combined demands of work and school.

2. **There are mental health and behavioral problems.** Adolescents who work long hours—more than 15 or 20 hours a week—are more likely to experience anxiety and depression, and their self-esteem often suffers. Many adolescents find themselves in jobs that are repetitive and boring but stressful, and such conditions undermine self-esteem and breed anxiety. Extensive part-time work frequently leads to substance abuse and frequent problem behavior, such as theft and cheating in school (Monahan et al., 2011).

   > *When adolescents work many hours in part-time jobs, they do worse in school, often have behavioral problems, and experience misleading affluence.*

   Why employment is associated with all of these problems is not clear. Perhaps employed adolescents turn to drugs to help them cope with the anxiety and depression brought on by work. Arguments with parents may become more common because anxious, depressed adolescents are more prone to argue or because wage-earning adolescents may believe that their freedom should match their income. Whatever the exact mechanism, extensive part-time work is clearly detrimental to the mental health of most adolescents.

3. **Affluence is misleading.** Adults sometimes argue that work is good for teenagers because it teaches them "the value of a dollar." Here, too, the reality is different. The typical teenage pattern is "earn and spend." Working adolescents spend most of their earnings on themselves—to buy clothing, snack food, or cosmetics, and to pay for entertainment. Few working teens set aside much of their income for future goals, such as a college education, or use it to contribute to their family's expenses (Shanahan et al., 1996a, 1996b). Because parents customarily pay for many of the essential expenses associated with truly independent living—rent, utilities, and groceries, for example—working adolescents often have a vastly higher percentage of their income available for discretionary spending than working adults. Thus, for many teens, the part-time work experience provides unrealistic expectations about how income can be allocated, and they often end up spending their income to purchase alcohol and cigarettes (Darling et al., 2006; Zhang, Cartmill, & Ferrence, 2008).

The message that emerges repeatedly from research on part-time employment is hardly encouraging. Like Aaron, the teenage boy in the vignette, many adolescents who work long hours at part-time jobs do not benefit from the experience. To the contrary, they do worse in school, are more likely to have behavioral problems, and learn how to spend money rather than how to manage it. These effects are similar for adolescents from different ethnic groups (Steinberg & Dornbusch, 1991) and are comparable for boys and girls (Bachman & Schulenberg, 1993). Ironically, though, there is a long-term benefit: Young adults who had a stressful part-time job as an adolescent are better able to cope with stressful adult jobs (Mortimer & Staff, 2004). They're apparently better prepared to cope with the corresponding stresses of full-time employment.

Does this mean that teenagers who are still in school should never work part-time? Not necessarily. Part-time employment *can* be a good experience, depending on the circumstances. One key is the number of hours of work. Although the exact number of hours varies, of course, from one student to the next, most students could easily work 5 hours weekly without harm, and many could work 10 hours weekly. Another key is the type of job. When adolescents have jobs that allow them to use existing skills (e.g., computing), acquire new skills, and receive effective mentoring, self-esteem is enhanced, and they learn from their work experience (Staff & Schulenberg, 2010; Vazsonyi & Snider, 2008). Yet another factor is how teens spend their earnings. When they save their money or use it to pay for clothes and school expenses, relations with their parents often improve (Marsh & Kleitman, 2005; Shanahan et al., 1996b).

By these criteria, who is likely to show the harmful effects of part-time work? A teen who spends 30 hours a week bagging groceries and spends most of it on CDs or videos. And who is likely to benefit from part-time work? A teen who likes to tinker with cars, who spends Saturdays working in a repair shop, and who sets aside some of his earnings for college.

Finally, summer jobs typically do not involve conflict between work and school. Consequently, many of the harmful effects associated with part-time employment during the school year do not hold for summer employment. In fact, such employment sometimes enhances adolescents' self-esteem, especially when they save part of their income for future plans (Marsh, 1991).

Neighborhoods

For years, Mr. Rogers greeted preschool children singing, "It's a beautiful day in my neighborhood" and telling young viewers, "I've always wanted a neighbor just like you." Mr. Rogers's neighborhood is indeed safe and nurturing, but not all children are so fortunate; their neighborhoods are neither safe nor nurturing. Do these differences in neighborhoods affect children's lives? Yes; all other things being equal, children benefit from living in a neighborhood where most of the adults are well educated and economically advantaged. These benefits are seen for both school achievement and psychological adjustment. In other words, when children live in economically advantaged neighborhoods, they tend to do better in school and are somewhat less likely to have behavioral and emotional problems (Ackerman & Brown, 2006; Murray et al., 2011).

Researchers agree that neighborhoods per se do not influence children's behavior. Instead, as we would expect from the contextual model of parenting (described in Module 14.1), the impact of neighborhoods is indirect, transmitted through people (parents and peers, primarily) and other social institutions. Several pathways of influence are possible (Leventhal & Brooks-Gunn, 2000). One concerns the availability of institutional resources: Economically advantaged neighborhoods more often have the kinds of resources that enhance children's development: libraries, museums, quality day care, and good schools to foster children's cognitive development; medical services to provide for children's physical and mental health; and opportunities for adolescents to find work. In economically advantaged neighborhoods that tend to have these resources, children are more likely to have experiences that lead to school success, to good health, and to the ability to find part-time jobs as teenagers. In contrast, in economically disadvantaged neighborhoods that frequently lack these resources, children are often prepared inadequately for school, receive little medical

QUESTION 15.3
Nick is a 16-year-old who would love to have a career in the entertainment industry—TV, movies, or maybe in music. For now, he works two nights a week (about 8 hours total) as an usher at a local movie theater. At his parents' request, one-third of his take-home pay goes into a college fund. Will this part-time job be harmful to Nick?
(Answer is on page 501.)

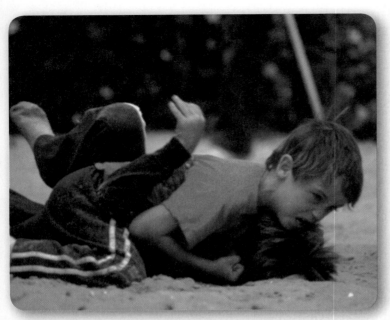

People living in poorer neighborhoods are less likely to know their neighbors and, consequently, are less likely to get involved in their neighbors' lives; for example, when children are fighting, they may be reluctant to stop the fight because they don't know the children.

care, and are unable to find jobs as teenagers, so they turn to delinquent or criminal behavior.

A second way in which neighborhoods affect children and adolescents is based on the fact that, because economically advantaged neighborhoods are more likely to be stable, they are more cohesive and close-knit, which means residents take a greater interest in neighborhood events and activities, including those of children and adolescents (Chung & Steinberg, 2006; Odgers et al., 2009). Suppose, for example, adults see the two boys in the photo slugging it out in the park. In a cohesive neighborhood, adults are more likely to intervene (e.g., break up the fight and scold the children for fighting) because they are committed to its residents; in a less cohesive neighborhood, adults might ignore the children because they don't want the hassle of getting involved. Thus, in cohesive neighborhoods, residents are much more likely to monitor the activities of neighborhood children, making it less likely for children get into trouble.

Yet another link between poverty and children's development reflects the fact that when children live in poverty, their home life is often described as chaotic (Chen, Cohen, & Miller, 2010). Their residence is often crowded and noisy and their lives are often relatively unstructured and unpredictable. For example, children may not have a set time for doing homework, or even a place to do it. Living in such chaos often engenders a sense of helplessness: Children feel as if they have little control over their own lives, and these feelings of helplessness are often associated with mental health problems and school failure (Bradley & Corwyn, 2002; Evans et al., 2005). Finally, children living in poverty often get less sleep and sleep less soundly, which may interfere with school success and contribute to behavior problems (Buckhalt, 2011).

Finally, neighborhoods affect children through their impact on parenting behavior. One account of this link is the focus of the "Spotlight on Theories" feature.

Spotlight on Theories

The Family Economic Stress Model

BACKGROUND The harmful effects of poverty on children have been known for decades; but only recently have researchers attempted to understand the many different ways in which poverty harms children. Among the most difficult to understand is the way in which poverty causes children to receive less effective parenting.

THE THEORY Adults living in chronic poverty often experience much stress, from constantly worrying about whether they will have enough money to buy food and clothing or to pay rent. Rand Conger and Glen Elder (1994) proposed the Family Economic Stress Model (FESM) to explain how such poverty-induced stress could affect children's development. According to the FESM, economic hardship results in a series of consequences:

1. Parents find that their income is not adequate to meet their needs.
2. This economic pressure affects parents' mental health, causing some to become depressed.
3. Once depressed, the quality of the marital relationship declines.
4. This results in less effective parenting (parents are not as warm with their children, praise them less frequently, and, instead, are often angry and impatient with them).
5. Because children receive less effective parenting, behavioral problems are common (e.g., children become anxious or angry).

Thus, in the FESM, poverty harms children's development because parents struggling to make ends meet become depressed and parent less effectively.

Hypothesis: When parents' economic situation changes for the worse—for example, one or both parents lose a job and can't find a comparable new job—this should start the cascade of consequences described in the FESM: Diminished income causes economic stress, which leads to depression, which leads to marital conflict and ineffective parenting, which finally disrupts children's development.

> Poverty creates stress, which leads, in turn, to depression, marital conflict, ineffective parenting, and disrupted child development.

Test: Solantaus, Leinonen, and Punamäki (2004) provided a novel evaluation of this hypothesis by looking at families in Finland in the early 1990s, when that country experienced a deep economic decline that compared to the Great Depression in the United States in the 1930s. They took advantage of the fact that a large cross-section of Finnish families had been studied in the late 1980s, before the onset of the depression. Then, children and their families were studied again in 1994 when the economic recession was at its peak. Solantaus and colleagues obtained measures of all the key constructs in the FESM: family economic hardship, parental mental health, quality of marital interaction, parenting quality, and children's mental health. All were measured with questionnaires, which were completed by parents, children, and the children's teachers. Each of the links in the FESM was supported: (1) families who experienced more economic pressure reported more mental health problems, (2) parents who had more mental problems reported that their marriages were less satisfying, (3) a less-satisfying marriage was associated with lower-quality parenting, and (4) lower-quality parenting was associated with more frequent mental health problems in children.

Conclusion: Solantaus and colleagues found the outcomes predicted by the FESM: Economic hardship triggered a sequence of events that ultimately harmed children's mental health. As they phrased it, "[The family] is a relationship unit, but it is also an economic unit. . . . This means that economic and relationship issues are intertwined, making the relationships vulnerable when the economy collapses" (2004, p. 425).

Application: Based on these findings, we can add "improving children's mental health" to the long list of reasons to eliminate poverty. Until that happens, these findings and the FESM remind us of the difficulties of parenting effectively while living in poverty. Families living in poverty often need immediate help (e.g., services for parents and children who have mental health problems) as they pursue their longer-term goal of leaving poverty.

Chronic poverty is particularly hard for parents because they usually have few social supports to help them cope with stress. When adults living in economically advantaged neighborhoods find life so stressful that they need help, they can turn to neighbors or health care professionals. In contrast, adults living in poverty are less likely to turn either to a neighbor (because they don't know anyone well enough due to instability in the neighborhood) or to a health care professional (because one is not available nearby or they can't afford it). Thus, adults living in chronic poverty experience a "double whammy"—more stress and fewer resources to cope with stress—that contributes to less effective parenting.

Thus, children growing up in economically disadvantaged neighborhoods typically have access to fewer institutional resources, are monitored less often by neighbors, often lead chaotic lives, and experience less effective parenting brought on by chronic stress. At the same time, the research suggests that an effective way to invest in poverty-ridden neighborhoods is by providing additional institutional resources (Huston et al., 2005). When neighborhoods have good child care and good schools, many opportunities for recreation, and effective health care, children benefit directly. They also benefit indirectly because when parents feel less stress, they parent more effectively, and because residents are less likely to move, contributing to neighborhood cohesiveness.

Exposure to disasters such as Hurricane Katrina is very stressful for youth, particularly when they're younger, dealing with other stresses in their lives, and don't regulate their emotions well.

Neighborhoods—be they advantaged or disadvantaged—are usually relatively stable institutions where change occurs gradually, over months or years. But sometimes neighborhoods or entire communities are affected by natural disasters (e.g., floods, earthquakes, or tornados), human-made disasters (e.g., terrorist acts, armed conflicts, industrial accidents), or a combination of the two, as was the case with the 2011 earthquake in northeastern Japan that damaged nuclear reactors. In the United States, roughly one child in seven will experience some sort of disaster during childhood or adolescence (Becker-Blease, Turner, & Finkelhor, 2010). Not surprisingly, exposure to disasters is traumatic for children; mental health problems such as depression are frequent following exposure to disasters and risks typically increase with the degree of exposure (Masten & Osofsky, 2010). As familiar institutions and familiar people are harmed or lost, disasters threaten a child's sense of security, and this loss of security leads to adjustment problems (Cummings et al., 2011).

However, as we've seen several times before, children and adolescents respond differently to adversity. Youth cope better with a disaster-related adversity when they're adolescents, when they're not also trying to deal with other family- or school-related stress, and when they're better able to regulate their emotions (Kithakye et al., 2010; Kronenberg et al., 2010). However, a substantial minority of children still suffer from stress more than a year after exposure to a disaster. These youth can be helped by cognitive-behavioral treatment that helps them modify their disaster-related thinking and teaches them ways to cope with stress-related feelings (LaGreca & Silverman, 2009). Following a disaster, all children are helped when familiar institutions are restored as soon as possible. Foremost among these are schools (Masten & Osofsky, 2010), which are the focus of the next (and last!) section.

School

At age 5 or 6, most American children head off to kindergarten, starting an educational journey that lasts 13 years for most and more than 17 years for some. How do schools influence children's development? Answering this question is difficult because American education is a smorgasbord, reflecting local control by communities throughout the United States. Schools differ on many dimensions, including their emphasis on academic goals and parent involvement. Teachers, too, differ in many ways, such as how they run their classrooms and how they teach. These and other variables affect how much students learn, as you'll see in the next few pages. Let's begin with school-based influences.

SCHOOL-BASED INFLUENCES ON STUDENT ACHIEVEMENT.   Roosevelt High School, in the center of Detroit, has an enrollment of 3,500 students in grades 9 to 12. Opened in 1936, the building shows its age. The rooms are drafty, the desks are decorated with generations of graffiti, and new technology means an overhead projector. Nevertheless, attendance at Roosevelt is good, most students graduate, and many continue their education at community colleges and state universities. Southport High School, in Boston, has about the same enrollment as Roosevelt High and the building is about the same age. Yet truancy is commonplace at Southport, where fewer than half the students graduate and almost none go to college.

> Successful schools emphasize academic excellence, have a safe and nurturing environment, monitor pupils' and teachers' progress, and encourage parents to be involved.

These schools are hypothetical, but accurately portray American education. Some schools are much more successful than others, regardless of whether success is defined in terms of the percentage of students who are literate, graduate, or go to college. Why are some schools successful and not others? Researchers (El Nokali, Bachman, & Votruba-Drzal, 2010; Good & Brophy, 2008; Pianta, 2007) have identified a number of factors linked with successful schools:

- *Staff and students alike understand that academic excellence is the primary goal and standards are set accordingly.* The school day emphasizes instruction, and students are recognized publicly for their academic accomplishments.

- *The school climate is safe and nurturing.* Students know that they can devote their energy to learning (instead of worrying about being harmed in school), and they know the staff truly wants to see them succeed.

- *Parents are involved.* In some cases, this may be through formal arrangements, such as parent–teacher organizations. Or it may be informal. Parents may spend some time each week in school grading papers or, like the dad in the photo, tutoring a child. Such involvement signals both teachers and students that parents are committed to students' success.

- *Progress of students, teachers, and programs is monitored.* The only way to know if schools are succeeding is by measuring performance. Students, teachers, and programs must be

Successful schools encourage parents to become involved; for example, they may encourage parents to tutor students.

evaluated regularly, using objective measures that reflect academic goals. In schools that follow these guidelines, students usually succeed. In schools where the guidelines are ignored, students more often fail.

Of course, on a daily basis, individual teachers have the most potential for impact. Let's see how teachers can influence their students' achievement. ·

TEACHER-BASED INFLUENCES. Take a moment to recall your teachers in elementary school, junior high, and high school. Some you probably remember fondly, because they were enthusiastic and innovative and they made learning fun. You may remember others with bitterness. They seemed to have lost their love of teaching and children, making class a living hell. Your experience tells you that some teachers are better than others, but what exactly makes a good teacher? Personality and enthusiasm are not the key elements. Although you may enjoy warm and eager teachers, research (Good & Brophy, 2008; Pianta, 2007; Walberg, 1995) shows that several other factors are critical when it comes to students' achievement. Students tend to learn the most when teachers:

- *Manage the classroom effectively so they can devote most of their time to instruction.* When teachers spend a lot of time disciplining students, or when students do not move smoothly from one class activity to the next, instructional time is wasted, and students are apt to learn less.

- *Believe they are responsible for their students' learning and that their students will learn when taught well.* When students don't understand a new topic, these teachers repeat the original instruction (in case the student missed something) or create new instruction (in case the student heard everything but just didn't "get it"). These teachers keep plugging away because they feel at fault if students don't learn.

- *Pay careful attention to pacing.* They present material slowly enough that students can understand a new concept, but not so slowly that students get bored.

- *Emphasize mastery of topics.* Teachers should introduce a topic, then give students many opportunities to understand, practice, and apply the topic. Just as you'd find it hard to go directly from driver's ed to driving a race car, students more often achieve when they grasp a new topic thoroughly, then gradually move on to other, more advanced topics.

- *Teach actively.* The best teachers don't just talk or give students an endless stream of worksheets. Instead, they demonstrate topics concretely or have hands-on demonstrations for students. They also have students participate in class activities and encourage students to interact, generating ideas and solving problems together.

- *Value tutoring.* Good teachers work with students individually or in small groups, so they can gear their instruction to each student's level and check each student's understanding. They also encourage peer tutoring, in which more capable students tutor less capable students. Children who are tutored by peers do learn, and so do the tutors, evidently because teaching helps tutors organize their knowledge.

- *Teach children techniques for monitoring and managing their own learning.* Students are more likely to achieve when they are taught how to recognize the aims of school tasks and know effective strategies for achieving those aims (like those described on pages 211–213).

Effective teachers manage classrooms well, believe they are responsible for students' learning, pace their teaching, emphasize mastery, teach actively, value tutoring, and teach students to monitor their learning.

Thus, what makes for effective schools and teachers? No single element is crucial. Instead, many factors contribute to make some schools and teachers remarkably effective. Some of the essential ingredients include parents who are involved, teachers who care deeply about their students' learning and manage classrooms well, and a school that is safe, nurturing, and emphasizes achievement.

Of course, many schools are not very successful. However, as parents, teachers, and concerned citizens, we need to resist the idea that any single magic potion can cure a school's ills. As we have seen throughout this book, the outcome of development—in this case, academic achievement—is determined by many factors, including environmental forces (e.g., parents, teachers) as well as the contributions of children themselves. To foster academic success, we need to consider all these factors, not focus narrowly on only one or two.

Finally, as we consider the features of effective schools and effective teachers, it's important to remember that children's skills when they enter school are powerful predictors of their achievement in school. Longitudinal studies clearly show that kindergarten children who know letters, some words, numbers, and simple quantitative concepts are on the path to success in school; this is true regardless of a child's socioeconomic status or ethnicity (Duncan et al., 2007; Marks & García Coll, 2007). Of course, as we've seen repeatedly, continuity across development is not perfect: Some 5-year-olds who don't know their numbers will get As in calculus as high-school seniors. But they're the exception, not the rule. Consequently, it's crucial for children to begin kindergarten with a solid foundation of pre-reading and pre-arithmetic skills.

On a more general note, understanding why and how children succeed in school (and in other domains of life) is indeed a challenging puzzle. Nevertheless, scientists are making remarkable progress in solving the child-development puzzle; as we end the book, I hope you've enjoyed learning about their discoveries. Thanks for reading.

 ANSWER 15.3
Probably not. He's not working enough for the job to interfere too much with school. Plus, he's interested in working in the entertainment industry, so there's some benefit to learning the business "from the ground up." Finally, he's saving a substantial amount of his pay, which means he's less likely to experience misleading affluence.

 ## Check Your Learning

RECALL What is known about the impact of part-time employment on adolescents?

Summarize the ways in which poverty can influence children's development.

INTERPRET Compare and contrast the ways in which schools (as institutions) affect children's learning with the ways in which teachers affect children's learning.

APPLY Imagine that you've taken a new job, which means that your 10-year-old daughter would need to care for herself at home from after school until about 6:00 PM. What would you do to decide whether she's capable of such self-care? If you decided that she is capable, what would you do to prepare her?

UNIFYING THEMES Continuity

In this last chapter of the book, I want to remind you that *early development is related to later development, but not perfectly*. Children who are rejected by their peers are, over time, more likely to do poorly in school, have lower self-esteem, and have behavioral problems. Of course, not all rejected children suffer this fate. Some do well in school, have high self-esteem, and avoid behavioral problems. Positive outcomes are more likely to occur when children learn effective skills for interacting with others. As we've seen many times in previous chapters, early experiences often point children toward a particular developmental path, but later experiences can cause them to change course.

See for Yourself

The best way to understand the differences between good and bad teaching is to visit some actual school classrooms. Try to visit three or four classes in at least two different schools. (You can usually arrange this by speaking with the school's principal.) Take along the principles of good teaching that are listed on page 500. Start by watching how the teachers and children interact; then decide how much the teacher relies on each of the principles. You'll probably see that most teachers use some but not all of these principles. You'll also see that, in today's classroom, consistently following all the principles is very challenging. See for yourself!

Summary

15.1 Peers

Development of Peer Interactions

Children's first real social interactions, at about 12 to 15 months, take the form of parallel play, in which infants play alone while watching each other. At about 2 years, cooperative play organized around a theme becomes common.

Make-believe play is also common and, in addition to being fun, promotes cognitive development and lets children examine frightening topics. Most solitary play is harmless. Parents foster children's play by acting as skilled playmates, serving as social director for their children, coaching social skills, and mediating disputes.

Beyond preschool, peer relations improve and emphasize talking and being together, as well as rough-and-tumble play.

Friendship

Friendships among preschoolers are based on common interests and getting along well. As children grow, loyalty, trust, and intimacy become more important features in their friendships. Friends are usually similar in age, sex, race, and attitudes. Children with friends are more skilled socially and better adjusted.

Romantic Relationships

For younger adolescents, romantic relationships offer companionship and the possibility of sexual exploration; for older adolescents, they provide trust and support. Pregnancy is common because many adolescents engage in unprotected sex. Comprehensive sex education is effective in reducing teenage sexual activity. Adolescents often wonder about their sexual orientation, but only a small percentage report having homosexual experiences.

Groups

Older children and adolescents often form cliques—small groups of like-minded individuals that become part of a crowd. Members of higher-status crowds often have higher self-esteem.

Most groups have a dominance hierarchy, a well-defined structure with a leader at the top. Physical power often determines the dominance hierarchy, particularly among younger boys. With older children and adolescents, dominance hierarchies are more often based on skills that are important to group functioning.

Peers are particularly influential when standards of behavior are unclear, such as for taste in music or clothing, or concerning drinking.

Popularity and Rejection

Many popular children are socially skilled; they generally share, cooperate, and help others. Other popular children use aggression to achieve social goals. Some children are rejected by their peers because they are too aggressive; others are rejected for being shy. Both groups of rejected children are often unsuccessful in school and have behavioral problems.

15.2 Electronic Media

Television

Many popular criticisms about TV as a medium (e.g., it shortens children's attention span) are not supported by research. However, the content of TV programs can affect children. Youngsters who frequently watch prosocial TV become more skilled socially, and preschoolers who watch programs like *Sesame Street* improve their academic skills and adjust more readily to school.

Computers

At home, children use computers to play video games (and are influenced by the contents of the games they play) and to communicate with friends via the Internet. Computers are used in school as tutors, to provide experiential learning, and as a multipurpose tool to achieve traditional academic goals.

15.3 Institutional Influences

Child Care and After-School Activities

Many U.S. children are cared for by a father or other relative, in a day-care provider's home, or in a day-care center. When children attend high-quality child care, this fosters their cognitive and socioemotional development. After-school programs and structured activities are often beneficial, too. Children can care for themselves after school if they are mature enough, live in a safe neighborhood, and are monitored by a parent.

Part-Time Employment

Adolescents who are employed more than 15 hours per week during the school year typically do poorly in school, often have lowered self-esteem and increased anxiety, and have problems interacting with others. Employed adolescents save relatively little of their income. Instead, they spend most of it on themselves, which can give misleading expectations about how to allocate income.

Part-time employment can be beneficial if adolescents work relatively few hours, if the work allows them to use existing skills or acquire new ones, and if teens save some of their earnings. Summer employment can also be beneficial.

Neighborhoods

Children are more likely to thrive when they grow up in a neighborhood that is economically advantaged and stable. These neighborhoods are better for children because more institutional resources (e.g., schools) are available, because residents are more likely to monitor neighborhood children's behavior, because home life is predictable, and because parents are not living in the chronic stress associated with poverty.

School

Schools influence students' achievement in many ways. Students are most likely to achieve when their school emphasizes academic excellence, has a safe and nurturing environment, monitors pupils' and teachers' progress, and encourages parents to be involved.

Students achieve at higher levels when their teachers manage classrooms effectively, take responsibility for their students' learning, teach mastery of material, pace material well, value tutoring, and show children how to monitor their own learning.

Test Yourself

✓●─Study and Review on mydevelopmentlab.com

1. Make-believe play is fun, promotes children's cognitive development, and helps them _____.

2. Parents are often involved in their children's play, taking on roles as _____, social director, coach, and mediator.

3. Trust is particularly important in friendships between _____.

4. The best way to reduce adolescent sexual behavior and teen pregnancy is with _____.

5. Peer pressure is strongest when youth are younger, peers have high status and are friends, and _____.

6. Some popular children are friendly, cooperative, and helpful; a smaller number tend to be _____.

7. As a general rule, TV as a medium per se has relatively little influence on children, but TV does influence children through _____.

8. Children use computers at home to do schoolwork, play games, and _____.

9. In schools, computers are used as instructors, as _____, and to help students achieve traditional academic goals (e.g., word-processing programs).

10. Youth can care for themselves after school except when they _____ and live in unsafe neighborhoods.

11. When adolescents work many hours in part-time jobs, their school performance suffers and they often experience _____.

12. Part-time work can be a good experience for teens when they work relatively few hours, _____, and they save their money or use it to pay for clothes and school expenses.

13. Disadvantaged neighborhoods affected children indirectly, in that fewer resources such as libraries are available, _____, and home life tends to be more chaotic.

14. Youth cope more effectively with disaster-related adversity when they're _____, not dealing with other stresses, and can regulate their emotions.

15. In effective schools, academic excellence is the main goal, _____, parents are involved, and progress is monitored.

Answers: (1) explore topics that frighten them; (2) playmate; (3) adolescents; (4) comprehensive sex education programs; (5) standards for appropriate behavior are fuzzy (e.g., tastes in music or clothing, standards for smoking and drinking); (6) aggressive (physically aggressive for boys, relationally aggressive for girls); (7) the contents of TV programs (e.g., viewing violent TV programs causes children to behave aggressively); (8) communicate with friends; (9) a medium for experiential learning; (10) spend their after-school time away from home, unsupervised; (11) mental health and behavioral problems; (12) the job allows them to acquire useful new skills; (13) neighborhoods tend to be less cohesive, so that residents take less interest in neighborhood events and people; (14) adolescents; (15) the school climate is safe and nurturing.

Key Terms

associative play   470
clique   480
cooperative play   470
co-rumination   476

crowd   481
dominance hierarchy   481
friendship   474
latchkey children   492

nonsocial play   470
parallel play   470
rough-and-tumble play   473

Glossary

A

accommodation According to Piaget, changing existing knowledge based on new knowledge.

achievement The identity status in Marcia's theory in which adolescents have explored alternative identities and are now secure in their chosen identities.

active–passive child issue The issue of whether children are simply at the mercy of the environment (passive child) or actively influence their own development through their own unique individual characteristics (active child).

adolescent egocentrism The self-absorption that is characteristic of teenagers as they search for identity.

African American English A dialect of standard English spoken by some African Americans; has slightly different grammatical rules than standard English.

age of viability The age at which a fetus can survive because most of its bodily systems function adequately, typically at 7 months after conception.

aggression Behavior meant to harm others.

allele A variation of a specific gene.

altruism Prosocial behavior, such as helping and sharing, in which the individual does not benefit directly from his or her behavior.

amniocentesis A prenatal diagnostic technique that involves withdrawing a sample of amniotic fluid through the abdomen using a syringe.

amniotic fluid Fluid in the amnion that cushions the embryo and maintains a constant temperature.

amniotic sac An inner sac in which the developing child will rest.

amodal information Information that can be presented to different senses, such as duration, rate, and intensity.

analytic ability In Robert Sternberg's theory of intelligence, the ability to analyze problems and generate different solutions.

androgens Hormones secreted by the testes that influence aggressive behavior.

androgynous Having a combination of gender-role traits that includes both instrumental and expressive behaviors.

animism A phenomenon, common in preschool children, in which they attribute life and lifelike properties to inanimate objects.

anorexia nervosa A persistent refusal to eat, accompanied by an irrational fear of being overweight.

Apgar score A measure to evaluate the newborn's condition, based on breathing, heart rate, muscle tone, presence of reflexes, and skin tone.

applied developmental science A scientific discipline that uses child-development research to promote healthy development, particularly for vulnerable children and families.

assimilation According to Piaget, taking in information that is compatible with what one already knows.

associative play A form of play in which toddlers engage in similar activities, talk or smile at one another, and offer each other toys.

attachment The affectionate, reciprocal relationship that is formed at about 6 or 7 months between an infant and his or her primary caregiver, usually the mother.

attention Processes that determine which information will be processed further by an individual.

auditory threshold The quietest sound that a person can hear.

authoritarian parenting A style of parenting that combines high levels of control with low levels of warmth toward children.

authoritative parenting A style of parenting that combines a moderate degree of control with being warm and responsive toward children.

authority-oriented grandparents Grandparents who provide discipline for their grandchildren but otherwise are not particularly active in their grandchildren's lives.

autobiographical memory A person's memory of the significant events and experiences of his or her own life.

automatic processes Cognitive activities that require virtually no effort.

autosomes The first 22 pairs of chromosomes.

avoidant attachment A relationship in which infants turn away from their mothers when they are reunited following a brief separation.

axon A tubelike structure that emerges from the cell body and transmits information to other neurons.

B

babbling Speechlike sounds that consist of vowel–consonant combinations.

baby biographies Detailed, systematic observations of individual children, often by famous scientists, that helped to pave the way for objective research on children.

basal metabolic rate The speed with which the body consumes calories.

basic cry A cry that starts softly and gradually becomes more intense; often heard when babies are hungry or tired.

basic emotions Emotions that are experienced by people worldwide and that consist of a subjective feeling, a physiological change, and an overt behavior; examples include happiness, anger, and fear.

behavioral genetics The branch of genetics that deals with inheritance of behavioral and psychological traits.

blastocyst The fertilized egg 4 days after conception; consists of about 100 cells and resembles a hollow ball.

blended family A family consisting of a biological parent, a stepparent, and children.

body mass index (BMI) An adjusted ratio of weight to height used to define overweight.

breech presentation A birth in which the feet or bottom are delivered first, before the head.

bulimia nervosa An eating disorder in which individuals alternate between bingeing (when they eat uncontrollably) and purging through self-induced vomiting or with laxatives.

C

cardinality principle The counting principle that the last number name denotes the number of objects being counted.

cell body The center of the neuron that keeps the neuron alive.

central executive The component of the information-processing system, analogous to a computer's operating system, that coordinates the activities of the system.

centration Narrowly focused thinking characteristic of Piaget's preoperational stage.

cerebral cortex The wrinkled surface of the brain that regulates many distinctly human functions.

cesarean section (C-section) A surgical procedure in which an incision is made in the mother's abdomen to remove the baby from the uterus.

chorionic villus sampling (CVS) A prenatal diagnostic technique that involves taking a sample of tissue from the chorion.

chromosomes Threadlike structures in the nucleus of the cell that contain genetic material.

chronosystem In Bronfenbrenner's systems view, the idea that the microsystem, mesosystem, exosystem, and macrosystem are not static but change over time.

clique Small groups of friends who are similar in age, sex, race, and interests.

cognitive-developmental perspective An approach to development that focuses on how children think and on how their thinking changes over time.

cognitive self-regulation Skill at identifying goals, selecting effective strategies, and accurate monitoring; a characteristic of successful students.

cohort A group of people born in the same year or same generation.

comprehension The process of extracting meaning from a sequence of words.

concrete operational stage The third of Piaget's stages, from 7 to 11 years, in which children first use mental operations to solve problems and to reason.

cones Specialized neurons in the back of the eye that detect the wavelength of light and, therefore, color.

confounded As applied to the design of experiments, an error in which variables are combined instead of evaluated independently, making the results of the experiment ambiguous.

congenital adrenal hyperplasia (CAH) A genetic disorder in which girls are masculinized because the adrenal glands secrete large amounts of androgen during prenatal development.

constricting An interaction style, common among boys, in which one child tries to emerge as the victor by threatening or contradicting the others, by exaggerating, and so on.

constructivism The view, associated with Piaget, that children are active participants in their own development who systematically construct ever-more-sophisticated understandings of their worlds.

continuity–discontinuity issue An issue concerned with whether a developmental phenomenon follows a smooth progression throughout the life span or a series of abrupt shifts.

conventional level The second level of reasoning in Kohlberg's theory, where moral reasoning is based on society's norms.

convergent thinking Using information to arrive at one standard, correct answer.

cooing Early vowel-like sounds that babies produce.

cooperative play Play that is organized around a theme, with each child taking on a different role; begins at about 2 years of age.

core-knowledge theories The view that infants are born with rudimentary knowledge of the world that is elaborated based on children's experiences.

corpus callosum A thick bundle of neurons that connects the two cerebral hemispheres.

correlation coefficient A statistic that reveals the strength and direction of the relation between two variables.

correlational study A research design in which investigators look at relations between variables as they exist naturally in the world.

co-rumination Conversations with friends that focus on each other's personal problems; thought to contribute to depression in adolescent girls.

counterimitation A type of observational learning in which the child observes and learns what should not be done.

creative ability In Robert Sternberg's theory of intelligence, the ability to deal adaptively with novel situations and problems.

critical period A time in development when a specific type of learning can take place; before or after the critical period, the same learning is difficult or even impossible.

cross-sectional study A research design in which people of different ages are compared at the same point in time.

crowd A large group that includes many cliques with similar attitudes and values.

crowning During labor, the appearance of the top of the baby's head.

crystallized intelligence A person's culturally influenced accumulated knowledge and skills, including understanding printed language, comprehending language, and knowing vocabulary.

culture The knowledge, attitudes, and behavior associated with a group of people.

culture-fair intelligence tests Tests designed to reduce the impact of different experiences by including items based on experiences common to many cultures.

D

deductive reasoning Drawing conclusions from facts; characteristic of formal operational thought.

dendrite The end of the neuron that receives information; looks like a tree with many branches.

deoxyribonucleic acid (DNA) A molecule composed of four nucleotide bases; the biochemical basis of heredity.

dependent variable In an experiment, the behavior that is observed after other variables are manipulated.

detached grandparents Grandparents who are uninvolved with their grandchildren.

differentiation Distinguishing and mastering individual motions.

diffusion The identity status in Marcia's theory in which adolescents do not have an identity and are doing nothing to achieve one.

direct instruction A parental behavior in which adults try to influence their children's behavior by telling them what to do, when, and why.

dismissive adults (attachment representation) A representation of parent–child relations in which adults describe childhood experiences in very general terms and often idealize their parents.

disorganized (disoriented) attachment A relationship in which infants don't seem to understand what's happening when they are separated from and later reunited with their mothers.

display rules Culturally specific standards for appropriate expressions of emotion in a particular setting or with a particular person or persons.

divergent thinking Thinking in novel and unusual directions.

dizygotic (fraternal) twins Twins that are the result of the fertilization of two separate eggs by two sperm.

dominance hierarchy An ordering of individuals within a group in which group members with lower status defer to those with greater status.

dominant The form of an allele whose chemical instructions are followed.

Down syndrome A disorder, caused by an extra chromosome, that causes intellectual disability and a distinctive appearance.

dynamic systems theory A theory that views development as involving many distinct skills that are organized and reorganized over time to meet demands of specific tasks.

dynamic testing An approach to intelligence testing that measures a child's learning potential by having the child learn something new in the presence of the examiner and with the examiner's help.

E

ectoderm The outer layer of the embryo, which becomes the hair, outer layer of skin, and nervous system.

effortful control A dimension of temperament that refers to the extent to which a child can focus attention, is not easily distracted, and can inhibit responses.

ego According to Freud, the rational component of the personality; develops during the first few years of life.

egocentrism Difficulty in seeing the world from another's point of view; typical of children in Piaget's preoperational stage.

ego-resilience The ability to respond adaptively and resourcefully to new situations; a factor that protects children from the impact of maltreatment.

elaboration A memory strategy in which information is embellished to make it more memorable.

electroencephalography A method in which a pattern of brain waves is recorded from electrodes placed on the scalp.

embryo The name given to the developing baby after the zygote is completely embedded in the uterine wall.

emotional intelligence The ability to use one's own and others' emotions effectively for solving problems and living happily.

empathy Experiencing another person's feelings.

enabling An interaction style, common among girls, in which children's actions and remarks tend to support others and to sustain the interaction.

encoding processes The cognitive processes that transform the information in a problem into a mental representation.

endoderm The inner layer of the embryo, which becomes the lungs and the digestive system.

epigenesis The continuous interplay between genes and multiple levels of the environment (from cells to culture).

epiphyses Ends of bone tissue, which are formed first before the center is formed.

equilibration According to Piaget, the process by which children reorganize their schemes and, in the process, move to the next developmental stage.

essentialism The belief, common among young children, that all living things have an underlying essence that cannot be seen but that gives a living thing its identity.

ethnic identity The feeling that one is part of an ethnic group and the understanding of special customs and traditions of the group's culture and heritage.

ethological theory A theory in which development is seen from an evolutionary perspective and behaviors are examined for their survival value.

evolutionary psychology The theoretical view that many human behaviors represent successful adaptation to the environment.

executive functioning A mechanism of growth that includes inhibitory processes, planning, and cognitive flexibility.

exosystem According to Bronfenbrenner, social settings that influence one's development even though one does not experience them firsthand.

experience-dependent growth Changes in the brain due to experiences that are not linked to specific ages and that vary across individuals and across cultures.

experience-expectant growth Changes in the brain from environmental influences that typically occur at specified points in development and for all children.

experiment A systematic way of manipulating factors that a researcher thinks cause a particular behavior.

expressive style A style of language learning that describes children whose vocabularies include many social phrases that are used like one word.

expressive traits Psychological characteristics that describe a person who is focused on emotions and interpersonal relationships.

F

fast mapping The fact that children make connections between new words and referents so quickly that they cannot be considering all possible meanings.

fetal alcohol syndrome disorder (FASD) A disorder affecting babies whose mothers consumed large amounts of alcohol while they were pregnant.

fetal medicine The branch of medicine that deals with treating prenatal problems.

field experiment A type of experiment in which the researcher manipulates independent variables in a natural setting so that the results are more likely to be representative of behavior in real-world settings.

fine-motor skills Motor skills associated with grasping, holding, and manipulating objects.

fluid intelligence The ability to perceive relations among stimuli.

foreclosure The identity status in Marcia's theory in which adolescents have an identity that was chosen based on advice from adults, rather than one that was a result of personal exploration of alternatives.

formal operational stage The fourth of Piaget's stages, from roughly age 11 into adulthood, in which children and adolescents can apply mental operations to abstract entities, allowing them to think hypothetically and reason deductively.

friendship A voluntary relationship between two people involving mutual liking.

frontal cortex A brain region that regulates personality and goal-directed behavior.

functional magnetic resonance imaging (fMRI) A technique for measuring brain activity that uses magnetic fields to track the flow of blood in the brain.

fuzzy trace theory A theory proposed by Brainerd and Reyna in which experiences can be stored in memory verbatim or in terms of their basic meaning (gist).

G

gender consistency The understanding, usually acquired between the ages of 4 and 7 years, that maleness and femaleness do not change over situations or according to personal wishes.

gender constancy A stage in which children have mastered gender labels, gender stability, and gender consistency.

gender identity The perception of oneself as either male or female.

gender labeling Children's understanding, by the age of 2 or 3 years, that they are either boys or girls, and their use of these words to label themselves.

gender role Culturally prescribed behaviors considered appropriate for males and females.

gender-schema theory A theory that children learn gender roles by first deciding if an object, activity, or behavior is female or male, then using this information to decide whether they should learn more about the object, activity, or behavior.

gender stability Children's understanding, during the preschool years, that gender does not change: Boys become men and girls become women.

gender stereotypes Beliefs and images about males and females that are not necessarily true.

gene A group of nucleotide bases that provide a specific set of biochemical instructions.

genetic engineering A branch of fetal medicine in which defective genes are replaced with synthetic normal genes.

genotype A person's hereditary makeup.

germ disc A small cluster of cells near the center of the zygote that develops into the baby.

gifted Traditionally, individuals with intelligence test scores of at least 130.

grammatical morphemes Words or endings of words that make a sentence grammatical.

growth hormone A hormone, secreted by the pituitary gland during sleep, that regulates growth by triggering the release of other hormones that cause muscles and bones to grow.

guided participation According to Vygotsky, structured interactions between a child and another more knowledgeable person; these are thought to promote cognitive growth.

H

habituation Becoming unresponsive to a stimulus that is presented repeatedly.

hemispheres The right and left halves of the cortex.

heritability coefficient A measure of the extent to which heredity contributes to individual differences in a trait for a group of people.

heterozygous When the genes for hereditary characteristics differ from each other.

heuristics Rules of thumb that are handy for solving problems but that do not guarantee a solution.

homozygous When the genes for hereditary characteristics are the same.

hostile aggression Aggression that is unprovoked; its goal seems to be to intimidate, harass, or humiliate others.

Huntington's disease A type of dementia caused by a dominant allele; characterized by degeneration of the nervous system.

hypoxia Lack of oxygen during delivery, typically because the umbilical cord becomes pinched or tangled during delivery.

I

id According to Freud, the element of personality that desires immediate gratification of bodily wants and needs; present at birth.

illusion of invulnerability The belief, common among adolescents, that misfortune only happens to others.

imaginary audience Adolescents' feeling that their behavior is constantly being watched by their peers.

imitation (observational learning) Learning that takes place simply by observing others.

immanent justice A characteristic of the stage of moral realism in which children believe that breaking a rule always leads to punishment.

implantation The process in which the zygote burrows into the uterine wall and establishes connections with the mother's blood vessels.

imprinting Learning that occurs during a critical period soon after birth or hatching, as demonstrated by chicks creating an emotional bond with the first moving object they see.

incomplete dominance The situation in which one allele does not dominate another completely.

independent variable The factor that is manipulated by the researcher in an experiment.

infant-directed speech Speech that adults use with babies that is slow and loud and has exaggerated changes in pitch; thought to foster infants' language learning.

infantile amnesia The inability to remember events from early in one's life.

influential grandparents Grandparents who are very close to their grandchildren, are very involved in their lives, and frequently perform parental roles, including discipline.

information-processing theory A view that human cognition consists of mental hardware and mental software.

informed consent A person's decision to participate in research after having been told enough about the research to make an educated decision; children are not legally capable of giving informed consent.

inhibitory processes Processes that prevent task-irrelevant information from entering working memory.

inner speech Vygotsky's term for thought.

instrumental aggression Aggression used to achieve an explicit goal.

instrumental traits Psychological characteristics that describe a person who acts on and influences the world.

integration Linking individual motions into a coherent, coordinated whole.

intellectual disability A disorder formerly known as mental retardation in which, before 18 years of age, individuals have substantially below-average intelligence and problems adapting to an environment.

intelligence quotient (IQ) A ratio of mental age to chronological age, multiplied by 100.

internal working model An infant's understanding of how responsive and dependable the mother is; thought to influence close relationships throughout the child's life.

interposition A perceptual cue to depth based on the fact that nearby objects partially obscure more distant objects.

intersensory redundancy theory A view, proposed by Bahrick and Lickliter, that the infant's perceptual system is particularly attuned to amodal information that is presented to multiple sensory modes.

intersubjectivity According to Vygotsky, mutual, shared understanding among people who are participating in an activity together.

intonation A pattern of rising and falling pitch in speech or babbling that often indicates whether the utterance is a statement, question, or command.

in vitro fertilization The technique of fertilizing eggs with sperm in a petri dish and then transferring several of the fertilized eggs to the mother's uterus, where they might implant in the lining of the uterine wall.

J

joint custody When both parents retain legal custody of their children following a divorce.

K

kinetic cues Depth cues based on motion, such as visual expansion and motion parallax.

knowledge-telling strategy A strategy for writing, often used by younger writers, in which information is written in sequence as it is retrieved from memory.

knowledge-transforming strategy A strategy for writing, often used by older writers, in which they decide what information to include and how best to organize it for the point they wish to convey to the reader.

L

language Any rule-based system for expressing ideas.

latchkey children Children who care for themselves after school.

learning disability   When a child with normal intelligence has difficulty mastering at least one academic subject.

linear perspective   A cue to depth perception based on the fact that parallel lines come together at a single point in the distance.

locomotion   The ability to move around in the world.

longitudinal study   A research design in which a single cohort is studied over multiple times of measurement.

long-term memory   A permanent storehouse for memories that has unlimited capacity.M

macrosystem   According to Bronfenbrenner, the cultural and subcultural settings in which the microsystems, mesosystems, and exosystems are embedded.

mad cry   A more intense version of a basic cry.

malnutrition   Being small for one's age because of inadequate nutrition.

maturational theory   The view that child development reflects a specific and prearranged scheme or plan within the body.

means-ends analysis   A problem-solving heuristic in which people determine the difference between the current and desired situations, then do something to reduce the difference.

memory strategies   Activities that improve remembering.

menarche   The onset of menstruation.

mental age (MA)   In intelligence testing, a measure of children's performance corresponding to the chronological age of those whose performance equals the child's.

mental operations   Cognitive actions that can be performed on objects or ideas.

mental rotation   One aspect of spatial ability involving the ability to imagine how an object will look after it has been moved in space.

mesoderm   The middle layer of the embryo, which will become the muscles, bones, and circulatory system.

mesosystem   According to Bronfenbrenner, the interrelations between different microsystems.

meta-analysis   A tool that allows researchers to synthesize the results of many studies to estimate relations between variables.

metacognitive knowledge   A person's knowledge and awareness of cognitive processes.

metamemory   A person's informal understanding of memory; includes the ability to diagnose memory problems accurately and to monitor the effectiveness of memory strategies.

microgenetic study   A special type of longitudinal study in which children are tested repeatedly over a span of days or weeks, with the aim of observing change directly as it occurs.

microsystem   According to Bronfenbrenner, the people and objects that are present in one's immediate environment.

monitoring   As applied to parent–child relations, parents' knowledge of where their children are, what they're doing, and with whom.

monozygotic (identical) twins   Twins that result when a single fertilized egg splits to form two new individuals.

moral realism   A stage described by Piaget that begins at about age 5 and continues through age 7, in which children believe that rules are created by wise adults and therefore must be followed and cannot be changed.

moral relativism   A stage described by Piaget that begins at about age 8, in which children understand that rules are created by people to help them get along.

moratorium   The identity status in Marcia's theory in which adolescents are still examining different alternatives and have yet to find a satisfactory identity.

motion parallax   A kinetic depth cue in which nearby moving objects move across a person's visual field faster than distant objects.

motor skills   Coordinated movements of the muscles and limbs.

myelin   A fatty sheath that surrounds neurons in the central nervous system and allows them to transmit information more rapidly.

N

naïve psychology   Our informal beliefs about other people and their behavior.

naming explosion   A period, beginning at about age 18 months, in which children learn new words very rapidly.

naturalistic observation   A method of observation in which children are observed as they behave spontaneously in a real-life situation.

nature–nurture issue   An issue concerning the manner in which genetic and environmental factors influence development.

negative affect   A dimension of temperament that refers to the extent to which a child is angry, fearful, frustrated, shy, and not easily soothed.

negative correlation   A relation between two variables in which larger values on one variable are associated with smaller values on a second variable.

negative reinforcement trap   A situation in which parents often unwittingly reinforce the very behaviors they want to discourage; particularly likely between mothers and sons.

neural plate   A flat group of cells present in prenatal development that becomes the brain and spinal cord.

neuron   A cell that is the basic unit of the brain and nervous system; specializes in receiving and transmitting information.

neurotransmitters   Chemicals released by terminal buttons that carry information to nearby neurons.

niche picking   The process of deliberately seeking environments that are compatible with one's genetic makeup.

non-REM (regular) sleep   Sleep in which heart rate, breathing, and brain activity are steady.

nonshared environmental influences   Forces within a family that make children different from one another.

nonsocial play   An early form of play, identified by Parten (1932), in which children play alone or watch others play but do not play themselves.

O

object permanence   The understanding, acquired in infancy, that objects exist independently of oneself.

observational learning   Learning based on watching others; imitation.

one-to-one principle   The counting principle which states that there must be one and only one number name for each object counted.

operant conditioning   A view of learning, proposed by Skinner, that emphasizes reward and punishment.

organization   A memory strategy in which information to be remembered is structured so that related information is placed together.

orienting response   The response to an unfamiliar or unusual stimulus in which a person startles, fixates the eyes on the stimulus, and shows changes in heart rate and brain-wave patterns.

osteoporosis   A disease, common among women over age 50, in which the bones become thin and brittle, and, as a consequence, sometimes break.

overextension   When children define words more broadly than adults do.

overregularization   Children's application of rules to words that are exceptions to the rule; used as evidence that children master grammar by learning rules.

P

pain cry A cry that begins with a sudden, long burst, followed by a long pause and gasping.

parallel play When children play alone but are aware of and interested in what another child is doing; occurs soon after the first birthday.

passive grandparents Grandparents who are caught up in their grandchildren's development but not with the intensity of influential or supportive grandparents; they do not assume parental roles.

period of the fetus The longest period of prenatal development, extending from the ninth week after conception until birth.

permissive parenting A style of parenting that offers warmth and caring but little parental control over children.

personal domain The domain of decisions concerning one's body (e.g., what to eat and wear) and choices of friends or activities.

personal fable The feeling of many adolescents that their feelings and experiences are unique and have never been experienced by anyone else before.

phenotype The physical, behavioral, and psychological features that are the result of the interaction between one's genes and the environment.

phonemes Unique speech sounds that can be used to create words.

phonological awareness The ability to hear the distinctive sounds associated with specific letters.

phonological memory The ability to remember speech sounds briefly; a key component for learning new words easily.

phonology The sounds of a language.

pictorial cues Depth cues like those used by artists to convey depth in drawings and paintings; examples include linear perspective and interposition.

placenta The structure through which nutrients and wastes are exchanged between the mother and the developing child.

polygenic inheritance When phenotypes are the result of the combined activity of many separate genes.

population A broad group of children that are the usual focus of research in child development.

positive correlation A relation between two variables in which larger values on one variable are associated with larger values on a second variable.

postconventional level The third level of reasoning in Kohlberg's theory, in which

morality is based on a personal moral code.

postpartum depression A condition affecting 10% to 15% of new mothers in which irritability continues for months and is often accompanied by feelings of low self-worth, disturbed sleep, poor appetite, and apathy.

practical ability In Robert Sternberg's theory of intelligence, the ability to know which solutions to problems are likely to work.

pragmatics How people use language to communicate effectively.

preconventional level The first level of reasoning in Kohlberg's theory, where moral reasoning is based on external forces.

premature infant A baby born before the 38th week after conception.

prenatal development The many changes that turn a fertilized egg into a newborn human.

preoccupied adults (attachment representation) A representation of parent–child relations in which adults describe childhood experiences emotionally and often express anger or confusion regarding relationships with their parents.

preoperational stage The second of Piaget's stages, from 2 to 7 years, in which children first use symbols to represent objects and events.

primary sex characteristics Changes in bodily organs directly involved in reproduction (i.e., the ovaries, uterus, and vagina in girls and the scrotum, testes, and penis in boys) that are signs of physical maturity.

private speech Comments that are not intended for others but that help children regulate their own behavior.

propositions Ideas created during reading by combining words.

prosocial behavior Any behavior that benefits another person.

psychodynamic theory A view first formulated by Sigmund Freud in which development is largely determined by how well people resolve conflicts they face at different ages.

psychometricians Psychologists who specialize in the measurement of psychological characteristics such as intelligence and personality.

psychosocial theory A theory proposed by Erik Erikson in which personality development is the result of the interaction of maturation and societal demands.

puberty A collection of physical changes that marks the onset of adolescence, such as the growth spurt and the growth of breasts or testes.

punishment Applying an aversive stimulus (e.g., a spanking) or removing an attractive stimulus (e.g., TV viewing); an action that discourages the reoccurrence of the response that it follows.

Q

quasi-experiment A variation of an experiment in which the impact of an independent variable is examined by groups that are created after the fact, not by random assignment, and are often equated statistically.

R

rapid-eye-movement (REM) sleep (irregular sleep) Irregular sleep in which an infant's eyes dart rapidly beneath the eyelids, while the body is quite active.

reactive aggression Aggression prompted by another child's behavior.

recessive An allele whose instructions are ignored when it is combined with a dominant allele.

recursive thinking A child's ability to think about what others are thinking, particularly when another person's thoughts refer to the child (e.g., "He thinks that I think . . .").

referential style A style of language learning that describes children whose vocabularies are dominated by names of objects, persons, or actions.

reflexes Unlearned responses that are triggered by specific stimulation.

rehearsal A memory strategy that involves repetitively naming information that is to be remembered.

reinforcement A consequence that increases the likelihood that a behavior will be repeated in the future.

relational aggression A form of verbal aggression in which children try to hurt others by undermining their social relationships.

relative size A perceptual cue to depth based on the fact that nearby objects look substantially larger than objects in the distance.

reliability As applied to tests, how consistent test scores are from one testing time to another.

research design An overall conceptual plan for research; the two most common are correlational and experimental designs.

resistant attachment A relationship in which, after a brief separation, infants want to be held but are difficult to console.

response bias The tendency for research participants to respond in ways that are socially more acceptable.

retinal disparity   A perceptual cue to depth based on the fact that, when a person views an object, the retinal images in the left and right eyes differ.

rough-and-tumble play   A form of play common during the elementary-school years in which children playfully chase, punch, kick, shove, fight, and wrestle with peers.

S

sample   A group of children drawn from a population that participates in research.

scaffolding   A teaching style in which adults adjust the amount of assistance that they offer, based on the learner's needs.

script   The means by which people remember common events consisting of sequences of activities.

secondary sex characteristics   Physical signs of maturity in body parts not linked directly to the reproductive organs (e.g., growth of breasts in girls, the appearance of facial hair in boys, the appearance of body hair in both boys and girls).

secular growth trends   Changes in physical development from one generation to the next; for example, the fact that people in industrialized societies are larger and are maturing earlier than in previous generations.

secure adults (attachment representation)   A representation of parent–child relations in which adults describe childhood experiences objectively and mention both positive and negative aspects of their parents.

secure attachment   A relationship in which infants have come to trust and depend on their mothers.

self-concept   Attitudes, behaviors, and values that a person believes make him or her a unique individual.

self-conscious emotions   Emotions, such as pride, guilt, or embarrassment, that involve feelings of success when one's standards or expectations are met and feelings of failure when they aren't; emerge between 18 to 24 months of age.

self-control   The ability to rise above immediate pressures and not give in to impulse.

self-efficacy   The belief that one is capable of performing a certain task.

self-esteem   A person's judgment and feelings about his or her own worth.

self reports   A measurement method in which children respond to questions about specific topics.

semantic bootstrapping theory   A view that children rely on their knowledge of word meanings to discover grammatical rules.

semantics   The study of words and their meaning.

sensorimotor stage   The first of Piaget's four stages of cognitive development, which lasts from birth to approximately 2 years, in which infants progress from responding reflexively to using symbols.

sensory and perceptual processes   The means by which the nervous system receives, selects, modifies, and organizes stimulation from the world.

sensory memory   A type of memory in which information is held in raw, unanalyzed form very briefly (no longer than a few seconds).

sex chromosomes   The 23rd pair of chromosomes; these determine the sex of the child.

sickle-cell trait   A disorder in which individuals show signs of mild anemia only when they are seriously deprived of oxygen; occurs in individuals who have one dominant allele for normal blood cells and one recessive sickle-cell allele.

size constancy   The realization that an object's actual size remains the same despite changes in the size of its retinal image.

small-for-date infants   Newborns who are substantially smaller than would be expected based on the length of time since conception.

social cognitive theory   A theory developed by Albert Bandura in which children use reward, punishment, and imitation to try to understand what goes on in their world.

social conventions   Arbitrary standards of behavior agreed to by a cultural group to help coordinate interactions of individuals within the group.

social influence   As applied to teen pregnancies, the view that when teenage girls give birth, this triggers a set of events that make it harder for them to provide a positive environment for their children's development.

social referencing   A phenomenon in which infants in an unfamiliar or ambiguous environment look at their mother or father, as if searching for cues to help them interpret the situation.

social role   A set of cultural guidelines about how one should behave, especially with other people.

social selection   As applied to teen pregnancies, the view that some teenage girls are more likely than others to become pregnant and these same factors put their children at risk.

social smiles   Smiles that first appear at about 2 months of age, when infants see another human face.

sociocultural perspective   The view, associated with Vygotsky, that children's cognitive development can only be understood by considering the cultural contexts in which children develop.

spermarche   The first spontaneous ejaculation of sperm-laden fluid; typically occurs at age 13.

spina bifida   A disorder in which the embryo's neural tube does not close properly during the first month of pregnancy.

stable-order principle   The counting principle which states that number names must always be counted in the same order.

stereotype threat   The self-fulfilling prophecy in which knowledge of stereotypes leads to anxiety and reduced performance consistent with the original stereotype.

stranger wariness   An infant's apparent concern or anxiety in the presence of an unfamiliar adult; typically observed at about 6 months of age.

stress   A person's physical and psychological responses to threatening or challenging situations.

structured observation   A method in which the researcher creates a setting to elicit the behavior of interest.

sudden infant death syndrome (SIDS)   A disorder in which a healthy baby dies suddenly, for no apparent reason; typically occurs between 2 and 4 months of age.

superego   According to Freud, the moral component of the personality that has incorporated adult standards of right and wrong.

supportive grandparents   Grandparents who are very close to and involved with their grandchildren, but do not take on parental roles.

surgency/extraversion   A dimension of temperament that refers to the extent to which a child is generally happy, active, vocal, and seeks interesting stimulation.

swaddling   A technique for calming a crying baby in which the baby is wrapped tightly in a blanket.

synapse   The gap between one neuron and the next.

synaptic pruning   Gradual loss of unused synapses, beginning in infancy and continuing into early adolescence.

syntax   Rules that specify how words are combined to form sentences.

systematic observation   A method of observation in which investigators watch children and carefully record what they do or say.

T

telegraphic speech A style of speaking, common in 1-year-olds, that includes only words directly relevant to meaning.

teleological explanation As applied to children's naïve theories of living things, the belief that living things and parts of living things exist for a purpose.

temperament A consistent style or pattern of behavior.

teratogen An agent that causes abnormal prenatal development.

terminal buttons Small knobs at the end of an axon that release neurotransmitters.

texture gradient A perceptual cue to depth based on the fact that the texture of objects changes from coarse but distinct for nearby objects to finer and less distinct for distant objects.

theory An organized set of ideas that is designed to explain development.

theory of mind An intuitive understanding of the connections among thoughts, beliefs, intentions, and behavior; develops rapidly in the preschool years.

time-out Punishment that involves removing a child who is misbehaving to a quiet, unstimulating environment.

toddler A young child who has just learned to walk.

U

ultrasound A prenatal diagnostic technique that involves bouncing sound waves off the fetus to generate an image of the fetus.

umbilical cord A structure containing veins and arteries that connects the developing child to the placenta.

underextension When children define words more narrowly than adults do.

uninvolved parenting A style of parenting that provides neither warmth nor control and that minimizes the amount of time parents spend with children.

V

validity As applied to tests, the extent to which the test measures what it is supposed to measure.

variable Any factor subject to change.

vernix A thick, greasy substance that covers the fetus and protects it during prenatal development.

villi Finger-like projections from the umbilical blood vessels that are close to the mother's blood vessels and thus allow nutrients, oxygen, vitamins, and waste products to be exchanged between mother and embryo.

visual acuity The smallest pattern that one can distinguish reliably.

visual cliff A glass-covered platform that appears to have a "shallow" side and "deep" side; used to study infants' depth perception.

visual expansion A kinetic depth cue in which approaching objects fill an ever-greater proportion of the retina.

W

word decoding The ability to identify individual words, either by retrieving them or sounding them out.

word recognition The process of identifying a unique pattern of letters.

working memory A type of memory in which a small number of items can be stored briefly.

Z

zone of proximal development The difference between what children can do with assistance and what they can do alone.

zygote The fertilized egg.

References

AAIDD Ad Hoc Committee on Terminology and Classification. (2010). *Intellectual disability* (11th ed.). Washington, DC: American Association on Intellectual and Developmental Disabilities.

Aboud, F. E. (2003). The formation of in-group favoritism and out-group prejudice in young children: Are they distinct attitudes? *Developmental Psychology, 39,* 48–60.

Ackerman, B. P. (1993). Children's understanding of the speaker's meaning in referential communication. *Journal of Experimental Child Psychology, 55,* 56–86.

Ackerman, B. P., & Brown, E. D. (2006). Income poverty, poverty co-factors, and the adjustment of children in elementary school. In R. V. Kail (Ed.), *Advances in child development and behavior* (Vol. 34, pp. 91–129). Amsterdam: Elsevier Academic Press.

Adams, E. K. (2004). Beyond quality: Parental and residential stability and children's adjustment. *Current Directions in Psychological Science, 13,* 210–213.

Adams, J. (1999). On neurodevelopmental disorders: Perspectives from neurobehavioral teratology. In H. Tager-Flusberg (Ed.), *Neurodevelopmental disorders* (pp. 451–468). Cambridge, MA: MIT Press.

Adams, M. J., Treiman, R., & Pressley, M. (1998). Reading, writing, and literacy. In W. Damon (Ed.), *Handbook of child psychology* (Vol. 4, pp. 275–355). New York, NY: Wiley.

Adams, R. J., & Courage, M. L. (1995). Development of chromatic discrimination in early infancy. *Behavioral Brain Research, 67,* 99–101.

Administration for Children and Families. (2010). *Head Start Facts.* Washington, DC: Author.

Adolph, K. (2002). Learning to keep balance. In R. V. Kail (Ed.), *Advances in child development and behavior* (Vol. 30, pp. 1–40). Orlando, FL: Academic Press.

Adolph, K. E. (1997). Learning in the development of infant locomotion. *Monographs of the Society for Research in Child Development, 62,* Serial No. 251, pp. 1–140.

Adolph, K. E. (2000). Specificity of learning: Why infants fall over a veritable cliff. *Psychological Science, 11,* 290–295.

Adzick, N. S., Thom, E. A., Spong, C Y., Brock, J. W., Burrows, P. K., Johnson, M. P. et al. (2011). A randomized trial of prenatal versus postnatal repair of myelomeningocele. *The New England Journal of Medicine, 364,* 993–1004.

Ahnert, L., Pinquart, M., & Lamb, M. E. (2006). Security of children's relationships with nonparental care providers: A meta-analysis. *Child Development, 77,* 664–679.

Ainsworth, M. S. (1978). The development of infant–mother attachment. In B. M. Caldwell & H. N. Ricciuti (Eds.), *Review of child development research* (Vol. 3, pp. 1–94). Chicago, IL: University of Chicago Press.

Ainsworth, M. S. (1993). Attachment as related to mother–infant interaction. *Advances in Infancy Research, 8,* 1–50.

Akhtar, N., Jipson, J., & Callanan, M. (2001). Learning words through overhearing. *Child Development, 72,* 416–430.

Alberts, A. E. (2005). Neonatal behavioral assessment scale. In C. B. Fisher & R. M. Lerner (Eds.), *Encyclopedia of applied developmental science* (Vol. 1, pp. 111–115). Thousand Oaks, CA: Sage.

Aldridge, V., Dovey, T. M., & Halford, J. C. G. (2009). The role of familiarity in dietary development. *Developmental Review, 29,* 32–44.

Allen, R. J., Cipielewski, J., & Stanovich, K. E. (1992). Multiple indicators of children's reading habits and attitudes: Construct validity and cognitive correlates. *Journal of Educational Psychology, 84,* 489–503.

Allison, D. (1993). *Bastard Out of Carolina.* New York: Plume.

Altschul, I., Oyserman, D., & Bybee, D. (2006). Racial-ethnic identity in mid-adolescence: Content and change as predictors of academic achievement. *Child Development, 77,* 1155–1169.

Amato, P. R. (2001). Children of divorce in the 1990s: An update of the Amato and Keith (1991) meta-analysis. *Journal of Family Psychology, 15,* 355–370.

Amato, P. R., & Fowler, F. (2002). Parenting practices, child adjustment, and family diversity. *Journal of Marriage & the Family, 64,* 703–716.

Amato, P. R., & Keith, B. (1991). Parental divorce and the well-being of children: A meta-analysis. *Psychological Bulletin, 110,* 26–46.

American Academy of Child and Adolescent Psychiatry. (2000). *Home alone.* Retrieved October 7, 2005, from http://www.aacap.org/publications/factsfam/homealon.htm

American Academy of Pediatrics (AAP). (1992, Spring). Bedtime doesn't have to be a struggle. *Healthy Kids,* 4–10.

American Academy of Pediatrics. (2008). *Feeding kids right isn't always easy: Tips for preventing food hassles.* Elk Grove Village, IL: Author.

American Lung Association. (2007). *State of lung disease in diverse communities: 2007.* New York, NY: Author.

American Psychiatric Association. (2004). *Diagnostic and statistical manual of mental disorders* (4th ed.). Washington, DC: Author.

Amso, D., & Johnson, S. P. (2006). Learning by selection: Visual search and object perception in young infants. *Developmental Psychology, 42,* 1236–1245.

Amsterlaw, J., Lagattuta, K. H., & Meltzoff, A. N. (2009). Young children's reasoning about the effects of emotional and physiological states on academic performance. *Child Development, 80,* 115–133.

Anastasi, A. (1988). *Psychological testing* (6th ed.). New York, NY: Macmillan.

Andersen, A. M. N., Wohlfahrt, J., Christens, P., Olsen, J., & Melbye, M. (2000). Maternal age and fetal loss: Population based register linkage study. *British Medical Journal, 320,* 1708–1712.

Anderson, C. A., Berkowitz, L., Donnerstein, E., Huessman, R., Johnson, J. D., Linz, D., Malamuth, N. M., & Wartella, E. (2003). The influence of media violence on youth. *Psychological Science in the Public Interest, 4,* 81–106.

Anderson, C. A., Shibuya, A., Ihori, N., Swing, E. L., Bushman, B. J., Sakamoto, A., et al. (2010). Violent video game effects on aggression, empathy, and prosocial behavior in Eastern and Western countries: A meta-analytic review. *Psychological Bulletin, 136,* 151–173.

Anderson, D. R., & Hanson, K. G. (2009). Children, media, and methodology. *American Behavioral Scientist, 52,* 1204–1219.

Anderson, D. R., Huston, A. C., Schmitt, K. L., Linebarger, D. L., & Wright, J. C. (2001). Early childhood television viewing and adolescent behavior. *Monographs of the Society for Research in Child Development, 66* (Serial No. 264).

Anderson, E. (2000). Exploring register knowledge: The value of "controlled improvisation." In L. Menn & N. B. Ratner (Eds.), *Methods for studying language production* (pp. 225–248). Mahwah, NJ: Erlbaum.

Anderson, K. G., Tomlinson, K., Robinson, J. M., & Brown, S. A. (2011). Friends or foes: Social anxiety, peer affiliation, and drinking in middle school. *Journal of Studies on Alcohol & Drugs, 72,* 61–69.

Anderson, S. W., Damasio, H., Tranel, D., & Damasio, A. R. (2001). Long-term sequelae of prefrontal cortex damage acquired in early childhood. *Developmental Neuropsychology, 18,* 281–296.

Annett, M. (2008). Test of the right shift genetic model for two new samples of family handedness and for the data of McKeever (2000). *Laterality, 13,* 105–123.

Apfelbaum, E. P., Pauker, K., Ambady, N., Sommers, S. R., & Norton, M. I. (2008). Learning (not) to talk about race: When older children underperform in social categorization. *Developmental Psychology, 44,* 1513–1518.

Apgar, V. (1953). A proposal for a new method of evaluation of the newborn infant. *Current Researches in Anesthesia & Analgesia, 32,* 260–267.

Appleyard, K., Yang, C. M., & Runyan, D. K. (2010). Delineating the maladaptive pathways of child maltreatment: A mediated moderation analysis of the roles of self-perception and social support. *Development & Psychopathology, 22,* 337–352.

Archer, N., & Bryant, P. (2001). Investigating the role of context in learning to read: A direct test of Goodman's model. *British Journal of Psychology, 92,* 579–591.

Arndorfer, C. L., & Stormshak, E. A. (2008). Same-sex versus other-sex best friendship in early adolescence: Longitudinal predictors of antisocial behavior throughout adolescence. *Journal of Youth & Adolescence, 37,* 1059–1070.

Arseneault, L., Tremblay, R. E., Boulerice, B., & Saucier, J. F. (2002). Obstetrical complications and violent delinquency: Testing two developmental pathways. *Child Development, 73,* 496–508.

Arsenio, W. F., Gold, J., & Adams, E. (2006). Children's conceptions and displays of moral emotions. In M. Killen & J. G. Smetana (2006), *Handbook of moral development* (pp. 581–609). Mahwah, NJ: Erlbaum.

Asbury, K., Dunn, J. F., Pike, A., & Plomin, R. (2003). Nonshared environmental influences on individual differences in early behavioral development: A monozygotic twin differences study. *Child Development, 74,* 933–943.

Asendorpf, J. B., Denissen, J. J. A., & van Aken, M. A. G. (2008). Inhibited and aggressive preschool children at 23 years of age: Personality and social transitions into adulthood. *Developmental Psychology, 44,* 997–1011.

Ashcraft, M. H. (1982). The development of mental arithmetic: A chronometric approach. *Developmental Review, 2,* 212–236.

Asher, S. R., & Paquette, J. A. (2003). Loneliness and peer relations in childhood. *Current Directions in Psychological Science, 12,* 75–78.

Aslin, R. N. (1987). Visual and auditory discrimination in infancy. In J. D. Osofsky (Ed.), *Handbook of infant development* (2nd ed.). New York, NY: Wiley.

Aslin, R. N., Jusczyk, P. W., & Pisoni, D. B. (1998). Speech and auditory processing during infancy: Constraints on and precursors to language. In W. Damon (Ed.), *Handbook of child psychology* (Vol. 2). New York, NY: Wiley.

Aslin, R. N., Saffran, J. R., & Newport, W. L. (1998). Computation of conditional probability statistics by 8-month-old infants. *Psychological Science, 9,* 321–324.

Aspenlieder, L., Buchanan, C. M., McDougall, P., & Sippola, L. K. (2009). Gender nonconformity and peer victimization in pre- and early adolescence. *European Journal of Developmental Science, 3,* 3–16.

Attar-Schwartz, S., Tan, J. P., Buchanan, A., Fluri, E., & Griggs, J. (2009). Grandparenting and adolescent adjustment in two-parent biological, lone-parent, and step families. *Journal of Family Psychology, 23,* 67–75.

Au, T. K., & Glusman, M. (1990). The principle of mutual exclusivity in word learning: To honor or not to honor? *Child Development, 61,* 1474–1490.

Aunola, K., Stattin, H., & Nurmi, J.-E. (2000). Parenting styles and adolescents' achievement strategies. *Journal of Adolescence, 23,* 205–222.

Auyeung, B., Baron-Cohen, S., Ashwin, E., Knickmeyer, R., Taylor, K., Hackett, G., et al. (2009). Fetal testosterone predicts sexually differentiated childhood behavior in girls and in boys. *Psychological Science, 20,* 144–148.

Avenevoli, S., & Steinberg, L. (2001). The continuity of depression across the adolescent transition. *Advances in Child Development & Behavior, 28,* 139–173.

Averill, J. A. (1980). A constructivist view of emotion. In R. Plutchik & H. Kellerman (Eds.), *Emotion: Theory, research, and experience: Vol. 1 Theories of emotion.* New York, NY: Academic Press.

Ayduk, O., Mendoza-Denton, R., Mischel, W., Downey, G., Peaje, P. K., & Rodriguez, M. (2000). Regulating the interpersonal self: Strategic self-regulation for coping with rejection sensitivity. *Journal of Personality & Social Psychology, 79,* 776–792.

Azaiza, F. (2005). Parent-child relationships as perceived by Arab adolescents living in Israel. *International Journal of Social Welfare, 14,* 297–304.

Bachman, J. G., & Schulenberg, J. (1993). How part-time work intensity relates to drug use, problem behavior, time use, and satisfaction among high school seniors: Are these consequences or merely correlates? *Developmental Psychology, 29,* 229–230.

Bachman, J. G., Staff, J. G., O'Malley, P. M., Schulenberg, J. E., & Freedman-Doan, P. (2011). Twelfth-grade student work intensity linked to later educational attainment and substance use: New longitudinal evidence. *Developmental Psychology, 47,* 344–363.

Backscheider, A. G., Shatz, M., & Gelman, S. A. (1993). Preschoolers' ability to distinguish living kinds as a function of regrowth. *Child Development, 64,* 1242–1257.

Baddeley, A. (1996). Exploring the central executive. *Quarterly Journal of Experimental Psychology: Human Experimental Psychology, 39,* 5–28.

Baenninger, M., & Newcombe, N. (1995). Environmental input to the development of sex-related differences in spatial and mathematical ability. *Learning & Individual Differences, 7,* 363–379.

Bagwell, C. L. (2004). Friendships, peer networks and antisocial behavior. In J. B. Kupersmidt & K. A. Dodge (Eds.), *Children's peer relations* (pp. 37–57). Washington, DC: American Psychological Association.

Bagwell, C. L., Newcomb, A. F., & Bukowski, W. M. (1998). Preadolescent friendship and peer rejection as predictors of adult adjustment. *Child Development, 69,* 140–153.

Bahrick, L. E., & Lickliter, R. (2002). Intersensory redundancy guides early perceptual and cognitive development. In R. V. Kail (Ed.), *Advances in child development and behavior* (Vol. 30, pp. 153–177). Orlando, FL: Academic Press.

Bahrick, L. E., Lickliter, R., & Flom, R. (2004). Intersensory redundancy guides the development of selective attention, perception, and cognition in infancy. *Current Directions in Psychological Science, 13,* 99–102.

Bailey, J. A., Hill, K. G., Oesterle, S., & Hawkins, J. D. (2009). Parenting practices and problem behavior across three generations: Monitoring, harsh discipline, and drug use in the intergenerational transmission of externalizing behavior. *Developmental Psychology, 45,* 1214–1226.

Baillargeon, R. (1987). Object permanence in 3½- and 4½-month-old infants. *Developmental Psychology, 23,* 655–664.

Baillargeon, R. (1994). How do infants learn about the physical world? *Current Directions in Psychological Science, 3,* 133–140.

Baillargeon, R. (2004). Infants' reasoning about hidden objects: Evidence for event-general and event-specific expectations. *Developmental Science, 7,* 391–424.

Baillargeon, R. H., Zoccolillo, M., Keenan, K., Côté, S., Pérusse, D., Wu, H., et al. (2007). Gender differences in physical aggression: A prospective population-based survey of children before and after 2 years of age. *Developmental Psychology, 43,* 13–26.

Baillargeon, R., Lie, J., Gertner, Y., & Wu, D. (2011). How do infants reason about physical events? In U. Goswami (Ed.), *The Wiley-Blackwell handbook of childhood cognitive development* (2nd ed., pp. 11–48). West Sussex, UK: Wiley-Blackwell.

Baker, L., & Brown, A. L. (1984). Metacognitive skills and reading. In P. D. Pearson (Ed.), *Handbook of reading research: Part 2.* New York, NY: Longman.

Bakermans-Kranenburg, M. J., van IJzendoorn, M. H., Pijlman, F. T. A., Mesman, J., & Juffer, F. (2008). Experimental evidence for differential susceptibility: Dopamine D4 receptor polymorphism (DRD4 VNTR) moderates intervention effects on toddlers' externalizing behavior in randomized controlled trial. *Developmental Psychology, 44,* 293–300.

Bakermans-Kranenburg, M., van IJzendoorn, M. H., & Juffer, F. (2003). Less is more: Meta-analyses of sensitivity and attachment interventions in early childhood. *Psychological Bulletin, 129,* 195–215.

Bandura, A. (1977). *Social learning theory.* Englewood Cliffs, NJ: Prentice-Hall.

Bandura, A. (1986). *Social foundations of thought and action: A social-cognitive theory.* Englewood Cliffs, NJ: Prentice-Hall.

Bandura, A. (2000). Social-cognitive theory. In A. E. Kazdin (Ed.), *Encyclopedia of psychology* (Vol. 7, pp. 329–332). Washington, DC: American Psychological Association.

Bandura, A. (2006). Toward a psychology of human agency. *Perspectives on Psychological Science, 1,* 164–180.

Bandura, A., & Bussey, K. (2004). On broadening the cognitive, motivational, and sociostructural scope of theorizing about gender development and functioning: Comment on Martin, Ruble, and Szkrybalo (2002). *Psychological Bulletin, 130,* 691–701.

Bannard, C., & Matthews, D. (2008). Stored word sequences in language learning: The effect of familiarity on children's repetition of four-word combinations. *Psychological Science, 19,* 241–248.

Banse, R., Gawronski, B., Rebetez, C., Gutt, H., & Morton, J. B. (2010). The development of spontaneous gender stereotyping in childhood: Relations to stereotype knowledge and stereotype flexibility. *Developmental Science, 13,* 298–306.

Barber, B. K., & Olsen, J. A. (1997). Socialization in context: Connections, regulation, and autonomy in the family, school, and neighborhood, and with peers. *Journal of Adolescent Research, 12,* 287–315.

Barca, L., Ellis, A. W., & Burani, C. (2007). Context-sensitive rules and word naming in Italian children. *Reading & Writing, 20,* 495–509.

Bardwell, J. R., Cochran, S. W., & Walker, S. (1986). Relationship of parental education, race, and gender to sex role stereotyping in five-year-old kindergartners. *Sex Roles, 15,* 275–281.

Barkley, R. A. (2003). Attention-deficit/hyperactivity disorder. In E. J. Mash & R. A. Barkley (Eds.), *Child psychopathology* (2nd ed., pp. 63–112). New York, NY: Guilford Press.

Barkley, R. A. (2004). Adolescents with attention deficit/hyperactivity disorder: An overview of empirically based treatments. *Journal of Psychiatric Review, 10,* 39–56.

Barling, J., Zacharatos, A., & Hepburn, C. G. (1999). Parents' job insecurity affects children's academic performance through cognitive difficulties. *Journal of Applied Psychology, 84,* 437–444.

Barnett, M. A., Scaramella, L. V., Neppl, T. K., Ontai, L. L., & Conger, R. D. (2010). Grandmother involvement as a protective factor for early childhood social adjustment. *Journal of Family Psychology, 24,* 635–645.

Baron, A. S., & Banaji, M. R. (2006). The development of implicit attitudes: Evidence of race evaluations from ages 6 and 10 and adulthood. *Psychological Science, 17,* 53–58.

Baron-Cohen, S, (1995). *Mindblindness: An essay on autism and theory of mind.* Cambridge MA: MIT Press/Bradford Books.

Barrett, T. M., Davis, E. F., & Needham, A. (2007). Learning about tools in infancy. *Developmental Psychology, 43,* 352–368.

Barton, M. E., & Tomasello, M. (1991). Joint attention and conversation in mother-infant-sibling triads. *Child Development, 62,* 517–529.

Bartsch, K., & Wellman, H. M. (1995). *Children talk about the mind.* New York, NY: Oxford University Press.

Baschat, A. A. (2007). From amniocentesis to selective laser coagulation. *Og.Gyn. News, 42*(17), 17–18.

Bascoe, S. M., Davies, P. T., Sturge-Apple, M. L., & Cummings, E. M. (2009). Children's representations of family relationships, peer information processing, and school adjustment. *Developmental Psychology, 45,* 1740–1751.

Baskett, L. M. (1985). Sibling status effects: Adult expectations. *Developmental Psychology, 21,* 441–445.

Basso, K. H. (1970). *The Cibecue Apache.* New York, NY: Holt, Rinehart, & Winston.

Bates, E., Bretherton, I., & Snyder, L. (1988). *From first words to grammar: Individual differences and dissociable mechanisms.* New York, NY: Cambridge University Press.

Bates, J. E., Pettit, G. S., Dodge, K. A., & Ridge, B. (1998). Interaction of temperamental resistance to control and restrictive parenting in the development of externalizing behavior. *Developmental Psychology, 34,* 982–995.

Bates, J. E., Pettit, G. S., Dodge, K. A., & Ridge, B. (1998). Interaction of temperamental resistance to control and restrictive parenting in the development of externalizing behavior. *Developmental Psychology, 34,* 982–995.

Bauer, P. J. (2006). Event memory. In W. Damon & R. M. Lerner (Eds.), *Handbook of child psychology* (6th ed., Vol. 2). New York, NY: Wiley.

Bauer, P. J. (2007a). Recall in infancy: A neurodevelopmental account. *Current Directions in Psychological Science, 16,* 142–146.

Bauer, P. J. (2007b). *Remembering the times of our lives: Memory in infancy and beyond.* Mahwah, NJ: Erlbaum.

Bauer, P. J., & Lukowski, A. F. (2010). The memory is in the details: Relations between memory for the specific features of events and long-term recall during infancy. *Journal of Experimental Child Psychology, 107,* 1–14.

Bauer, P. J., Burch, M. M., Scholin, S. E., & Guler, O. (2007). Using cue words to investigate the distribution of autobiographical memories in childhood. *Psychological Science, 18,* 910–916.

Bauer, P. J., Larkina, M., & Deocampo, J. (2011). Early memory development. In U. Goswami (Ed.), *The Wiley-Blackwell handbook of cognitive development* (2nd ed., pp.153–179). West Sussex UK: Wiley-Blackwell.

Baumeister, R. F., Campbell, J. D., Krueger, J. I., & Vohs, K. D. (2003). Does high self-esteem cause better performance, interpersonal success, happiness, or healthier lifestyles? *Psychological Science in the Public Interest, 4,* 1–44.

Baumrind, D. (1975). *Early socialization and the discipline controversy.* Morristown, NJ: General Learning Press.

Baumrind, D. (1991). Parenting styles and adolescent development. In R. M. Lerner, A. C. Petersen, & J. Brooks-Gunn (Eds.), *Encyclopedia of adolescence.* New York, NY: Garland.

Bauserman, R. (2002). Child adjustment in joint-custody versus sole-custody arrangements: A meta-analytic review. *Journal of Family Psychology, 16,* 91–102.

Bayley, N. (1970). Development of mental abilities. In P. H. Mussen (Ed.), *Carmichael's manual of child psychology.* New York, NY: Wiley.

Bayley, N. (1993). *Bayley scales of infant development: Birth to two years* (2nd ed.). San Antonio, TX: Psychological Corporation.

Bayley, N. (2006). *Bayley scales of infant and toddler development–Third edition*. San Antonio, TX: Harcourt Assessment, Inc.

Beal, C. R. (1996). The role of comprehension monitoring in children's revision. *Educational Psychology Review, 8*, 219–238.

Beal, C. R., & Belgrad, S. L. (1990). The development of message evaluation skills in young children. *Child Development, 61*, 705–712.

Beal, S. J., & Crockett, L. J. (2010). Adolescents' occupational and educational aspirations and expectations: Links to high school activities and educational attainment. *Developmental Psychology, 46*, 258–265.

Beck, E., Burnet, K. L., & Vosper, J. (2006). Birth-order effects on facets of extraversion. *Personality & Individual Differences, 40*, 953–959.

Becker, B. J. (1986). Influence again: An examination of reviews and studies of gender differences in social influence. In J. S. Hyde & M. C. Linn (Eds.), *The psychology of gender differences. Advances through meta-analysis*. Baltimore, MD: Johns Hopkins University Press.

Becker-Blease, K. A., Turner, H. A., & Finkelhor, D. (2010). Disasters, victimization, and children's mental health. *Child Development, 81*, 1040–1052.

Behnke, M., & Eyler, F. D. (1993). The consequences of prenatal substance use for the developing fetus, newborn, and young child. *International Journal of the Addictions, 28*, 1341–1391.

Bell, A. P., Weinberg, M. S., & Hammersmith, S. K. (1981). *Social preference: Its development in men and women*. New York, NY: Simon & Schuster.

Belsky, J., Bakermans-Kranenburg, M. J., & van IJzendoorn, M. H. (2007). For better and for worse: Differential susceptibility to environmental influences. *Current Directions in Psychological Science, 16*, 300–304.

Belsky, J., Houts, R. M., & Pasco Fearon, R. M. (2010). Infant attachment security and the timing of puberty: Testing an evolutionary hypothesis. *Psychological Science, 21*, 1195–1201.

Belsky, J., Steinberg, L., & Draper, P. (1991). Childhood experience, interpersonal development, and reproductive strategy: An evolutionary theory of socialization. *Child Development, 62*, 647–670.

Belsky, J., Steinberg, L., Houts, R. M., Halpern-Felsher, B., and the NICHD Early Child Care Research Network. (2010). The development of reproductive strategy in females: Early maternal harshness → earlier menarche → increased sexual risk taking. *Developmental Psychology, 46*, 120–128.

Bem, D. J. (1996). Exotic becomes erotic: A developmental theory of sexual orientation. *Psychological Review, 103*, 320–335.

Benenson, J. F., & Christakos, A. (2003). The greater fragility of females' versus males' closest same-sex friendships. *Child Development, 74*, 1123–1129.

Bennett, D. S., Bendersky, M., & Lewis, M. (2008). Children's cognitive ability from 4 to 9 years old as a function of prenatal cocaine exposure, environmental risk, and maternal verbal intelligence. *Developmental Psychology, 44*, 919–928.

Benton, D. (2010). The influence of dietary status on the cognitive performance of children. *Molecular Nutrition & Food Research, 54*, 457–470.

Benton, S. L., Corkill, A. J., Sharp, J M., Downey, R. G., et al. (1995). Knowledge, interest, and narrative writing. *Journal of Educational Psychology, 87*, 66–79.

Berch, D. B. (2005). Making sense of number sense: Implications for children with mathematical disabilities. *Journal of Learning Disabilities, 38*, 333–339.

Bereiter, C., & Scardamalia, M. (1987). *The psychology of written composition*. Hillsdale, NJ: Erlbaum.

Berenbaum, S. A., & Snyder, E. (1995). Early hormonal influences on childhood sex-typed activity and playmate preferences: Implications for the development of sexual orientation. *Developmental Psychology, 31*, 31–42.

Berenbaum, S. A., Duck, S. C., & Bryk, K. (2000). Behavioral effects of prenatal vs. postnatal androgen excess in children with 21-hydroxylase-deficient congenital adrenal hyperplasia. *Journal of Clinical Endocrinology & Metabolism, 85*, 727–733.

Bergen, D., & Mauer, D. (2000). Symbolic play, phonological awareness, and literacy skills at three age levels. In K. A. Roskos & J. F. Christie (Eds.), *Play and literacy in early childhood: Research from multiple perspectives* (pp. 45–62). Mahwah, NJ: Erlbaum.

Berger, S. E., Adolph, K. E., & Lobo, S. A. (2005). Out of the toolbox: Toddlers differentiate wobbly and wooden handrails. *Child Development, 76*, 1294–1307.

Berk, L. E. (2003). Vygotsky, Lev. In L. Nadel (Ed.), *Encyclopedia of cognitive science* (Vol. 6). London: Macmillan.

Berko, J. (1958). The child's learning of English morphology. *Word, 14*, 150–177.

Berkowitz, M. W., Sherblom, S., Bier, M., & Battistich, V. (2006). Educating for positive youth development. In M. Killen & J. G. Smetana (2006), *Handbook of moral development* (pp. 683–702). Mahwah, NJ: Erlbaum.

Berlin, L. J., Appleyard, K., & Dodge, K. A. (2011). Intergenerational continuity in child maltreatment: Mediating mechanisms and implications for prevention. *Child Development, 82*, 162–176.

Berlin, L. J., Ispa, J. M., Fine, M. A., Malone, P. S., Brooks-Gunn, J., Brady-Smith, C., et al. (2009). Correlates and consequences of spanking and verbal punishment for low-income White, African Americans and Mexican American toddlers. *Child Development, 80*, 1403–1420.

Bernal, S., Dehaene-Lambertz, G., Millotte, S., & Christophe, A. (2010). Two-year-olds compute syntactic structure on-line. *Developmental Science, 13*, 69–76.

Berndt, T. J., & Keefe, K. (1995). Friends' influence on adolescents' adjustment to school. *Child Development, 66*, 1312–1329.

Berndt, T. J., & Perry, T. B. (1990). Distinctive features and effects of adolescent friendships. In R. Montemayor, G. R. Adams, & T. P. Gullotta (Eds.), *From childhood to adolescence: A transition period?* London: Sage.

Bertenthal, B. H., & Clifton, R. K. (1998). Perception and action. In W. Damon (Ed.), *Handbook of child psychology* (Vol. 2). New York, NY: Wiley.

Berthier, N. E. (1996). Learning to reach: A mathematical model. *Developmental Psychology, 32*, 811–823.

Best, C. T. (1995). Learning to perceive sound pattern of English. In C. Rovee-Collier (Ed.), *Advances in infancy research*. Norwood, NJ: Ablex.

Best, J. R. (2010). Effects of physical activity on children's executive function: Contributions of experimental research on aerobic exercise. *Developmental Review. 30*, 331–351

Best, J., Miller, P. H., & Jones, L. L. (2009). Executive functions after age 5: Changes and correlates. *Developmental Review, 29*, 180–200.

Bettencourt, B. A., & Miller, N. (1996). Gender differences in aggression as a function of provocation: A meta-analysis. *Psychological Bulletin, 119*, 422–447.

Bhatt, R. S., Bertin, E., Hayden, A., & Reed, A. (2005). Face processing in infancy: Developmental changes in the use of different kinds of relational information. *Child Development, 76*, 169–181.

Bhutta, Z. A., Chopra, M., Axelson, H., Berman, P., Boerma, T., Bryce, J. et al. (2010). Countdown to 2015 decade report (2000–10): Taking stock of maternal, newborn, and child survival. *Lancet, 375*, 2032–2044.

Bialystok, E. (1988). Levels of bilingualism and levels of linguistic awareness. *Developmental Psychology, 24*, 560–567.

Bialystok, E. (1997). Effects of bilingualism and biliteracy on children's emerging concepts of print. *Developmental Psychology, 33*, 429–440.

Bialystok, E. (2010). Global-local and trail-making tasks by monolingual and bilingual children: Beyond inhibition. *Developmental Psychology, 46*, 93–105.

Bialystok, E., Shenfield, T., & Codd, J. (2000). Languages, scripts, and the environment: Factors in developing concepts of print. *Developmental Psychology, 36*, 66–76.

Biederman, J., Monuteaux, M. C., Mick, E., Spencer, T., Wilens, T. E., Silva, J. M., et al. (2006). Young adult outcome of attention deficit hyperactivity disorder: A controlled 10-year follow-up study. *Psychological Medicine, 362*, 167–179.

Biederman, J., Petty, C. R., Evans, M., Small, J., & Faraone, S. V. (2010). How persistent is ADHD? A controlled 10-year follow-up study of boys with ADHD. *Psychiatry Research, 177*, 299–304.

Bigler, R. S. (1995). The role of classification skills in moderating environmental influences on children's gender stereotyping: A study of the functional use of gender in the classroom. *Child Development, 66*, 1072–1087.

Bigler, R. S., & Liben, L. S. (1990). The role of attitudes and interventions in gender-schematic processing. *Child Development, 61*, 1440–1452.

Bigler, R. S., & Liben, L. S. (2007). Developmental intergroup theory: Explaining and reducing children's social stereotyping and prejudice. *Current Directions in Psychological Science, 16*, 162–166.

Bigler, R. S., Jones, L. C., & Lobliner, D. B. (1997). Social categorization and the formation of intergroup attitudes in children. *Child Development, 68*, 530–543.

Bingenheimer, J. B., Brennan, R. T., & Earls, F. J. (2005). Firearm violence exposure and serious violent behavior. *Science, 308*, 1323–1326.

Birch, S. A., Akmal, N., & Frampton, K. (2010). Two-year-olds are vigilant of others' non-verbal cues to credibility. *Developmental Science, 13*, 363–369.

Biro, S., & Leslie, A. M. (2007). Infants' perception of goal-directed actions: Development through cue-based bootstrapping. *Developmental Science, 8*, 36–43.

Bjerkedal, T., Kristensen, P., Skjeret, G. A., & Brevik, J. I. (2007). Intelligence test scores and birth order among young Norwegian men (conscripts) analyzed within and between families. *Intelligence, 35*, 503–514.

Bjorklund, D. F. (2005). *Children's thinking: Cognitive development and individual differences* (4th ed.). Belmont, CA: Wadsworth.

Bjorklund, D. F., & Pellegrini, A. D. (2000). Child development and evolutionary psychology. *Child Development, 71*, 1687–1708.

Bjorklund, D. F., & Rosenblum, K. E. (2002). Context effects in children's selection and use of simple arithmetic strategies. *Journal of Cognition & Development, 3*, 225–242.

Bjorklund, D. F., Yunger, J. L., & Pellegrini, A. D. (2002). The evolution of parenting and evolutionary approaches to childrearing. In M. H. Bornstein (Ed.), *Handbook of parenting. Vol. 2: Biology and ecology of parenting* (pp. 3–30). Mahwah, NJ: Erlbaum.

Black, J. E. (2003). Environment and development of the nervous system. In I. B. Weiner, M. Gallagher, & R. J. Nelson (Eds.), *Handbook of psychology, Vol. 3: Biological psychology* (pp. 655–668). Hoboken, NJ: Wiley.

Black-Gutman, D., & Hickson, F. (1996). The relationship between racial attitudes and social-cognitive development in children: An Australian study. *Developmental Psychology, 32*, 448–456.

Blakemore, J. E. O. (2003). Children's beliefs about violating gender norms: Boys shouldn't look like girls, and girls shouldn't act like boys. *Sex Roles, 48*, 411–419.

Blatt-Eisengart, I., Drabick, D. A. G., Monahan, K. C., & Steinberg, L. (2009). Sex differences in the longitudinal relations among family risk factors and childhood externalizing symptoms. *Developmental Psychology, 45*, 491–502.

Block, J. H. (1978). Another look at sex differentiation in the socialization behavior of mothers and fathers. In J. Sherman & F. L. Denmark (Eds.), *Psychology of women: Future directions for research* (pp. 29–87). New York, NY: Psychological Dimensions.

Bloom, L. (1998). Language acquisition in its developmental context. In D. Kuhn & R. S. Siegler (Eds.), *Handbook of child psychology: Vol. 2. Cognition, perception, and language* (5th ed., pp. 309–370). New York, NY: Wiley.

Bloom, L., & Tinker, E. (2001). The intentionality model and language acquisition. *Monographs of the Society for Research in Child Development, 66* (Serial No. 267).

Bloom, L., Margulis, C., Tinker, E., & Fujita, N. (1996). Early conversations and word learning: Contributions from child and adult. *Child Development, 67*, 3154–3175.

Bloom, L., Rocissano, L., & Hood, L. (1976). Adult-child discourse: Developmental interaction between information processing and linguistic knowledge. *Cognitive Psychology, 8*, 521–552.

Boden, J. M., Fergusson, D. M., & Horwood, L. J. (2008). Does adolescent self-esteem predict later life outcomes? A test of the causal role of self-esteem. *Development & Psychopathology, 20*, 319–339.

Booth, J. L., & Siegler, R. S. (2006). Development and individual differences in pure numerical estimation. *Developmental Psychology, 42*, 189–201.

Bornstein, M. H. (1981). Psychological studies of color perception in human infants: Habituation, discrimination and categorization, recognition, and conceptualization. *Advances in Infancy Research, 1*, 1–40.

Bornstein, M. H. (1997). Stability in mental development from early life: Methods, measures, models, meaning, and myths. In G. E. Butterworth & F. Simon (Eds.), *The development of sensory, motor, and cognitive capacities in early infancy: From sensation to perception.* Hove, UK: Psychology Press.

Bornstein, M. H., & Arterberry, M. E. (2003). Recognition, discrimination, and categorization of smiling by 5-month-old infants. *Developmental Science, 6*, 585–599.

Bornstein, M. H., Putnick, D. L., Suwalsky, J. T., & Gini, M. (2006). Maternal chronological age, prenatal and perinatal history, social support, and parenting of infants. *Child Development, 77*, 875–892.

Bortfeld, H., & Morgan, J. L. (2010). Is early word-form processing stress-full? How natural variability supports recognition. *Cognitive Psychology, 60*, 241–266.

Bosco, F. M., Friedman, O., & Leslie, A. M. (2006). Recognition of pretend and real actions in play by 1- and 2-year-olds: Early success and why they fail. *Cognitive Development, 21*, 3–10.

Boseovski, J. J. (2010). Evidence for "rose-colored glasses": An examination of the positivity bias in young children's personality judgments. *Child Development Perspectives, 4*, 212–218.

Bosma, H. A., & Kunnen, E. S. (2001). Determinants and mechanisms in ego identity development: A review and synthesis. *Developmental Review, 21*, 39–66.

Bot, S. M., Engels, R. C. M. E., Knibbe, R. A., & Meeus, W. H. J. (2005). Friend's drinking behavior and adolescent alcohol consumption: The moderating role of friendship characteristics. *Addictive Behaviors, 30*, 929–947.

Bouchard, T. J. (2004). Genetic influence on human psychological traits. *Current Directions in Psychological Science, 13*, 148–151.

Bouchard, T. J. (2009). Genetic influence on human intelligence (Spearman's g): How much? *Annals of Human Biology, 36*, 527–544.

Bowker, A. (2006). The relationship between sports participation and self-esteem during early adolescence. *Canadian Journal of Behavioral Science, 38*, 214–229.

Bowlby, J. (1953). *Child care and the growth of love.* London, UK: Penguin.

Bowlby, J. (1969). *Attachment and loss* (Vol. 1). New York, NY: Basic Books.

Bowlby, J. (1991). Ethological light on psychoanalytical problems. In P. Bateson (Ed.), *The development and integration of behaviour: Essays in honour of Robert Hinde* (pp. 301–313). New York, NY: Cambridge University Press.

Bradley, L., & Bryant, P. E. (1983). Categorising sounds and learning to read—a causal connection. *Nature, 301*, 419–421.

Bradley, R. H., & Corwyn, R. F. (2002). Socioeconomic status and child development. *Annual Review of Psychology, 53*, 371–399.

Bradley, R. H., Corwyn, R. F., Burchinal, M., McAdoo, H. P., & Coll, C. G. (2001). The home environment of children in the United States—Part II: Relations with behavioral development through age thirteen. *Child Development, 72*, 1868–1886.

Braine, M. D. S. (1992). What sort of innate structure is needed to "bootstrap" into syntax? *Cognition, 45*, 77–100.

Brainerd, C. J. (1996). Piaget: A centennial celebration. *Psychological Science, 7*, 191–203.

Brainerd, C. J., & Reyna, V. (2007). Explaining developmental reversals in false memory. *Psychological Science, 18*, 442–448.

Brainerd, C. J., & Reyna, V. F. (2004). Fuzzy-trace theory and memory development. *Developmental Review, 24*, 396–439.

Brainerd, C. J., & Reyna, V. F. (2005). *The science of false memory.* New York, NY: Oxford University Press.

Brainerd, C. J., Reyna, V. F., & Ceci, S. J. (2008). Developmental reversals in false memory: A review of data and theory. *Psychological Bulletin, 134*, 343–382.

Brandone, A. C., & Wellman, H. M. (2009). You can't always get what you want: Infants understand failed goal-directed actions. *Psychological Science, 20*, 85–91.

Braungart-Rieker, J. M., Hill-Soderlund, A. L., & Karrass, J. (2010). Fear and anger reactivity trajectories from 4 to 16 months: The roles of temperament, regulation, and maternal sensitivity. *Developmental Psychology, 46*, 791–804.

Brazelton, T. B., & Nugent, J. K. (1995). *Neonatal behavioral assessment scale* (3rd ed). London: MacKeith.

Brazelton, T. B., Nugent, J. K., & Lester, B. M. (1987). Neonatal behavioral assessment scale. In J. D. Osofsky (Ed.), *Handbook of infant development.* New York: Wiley.

Brechwald, W. A., & Prinstein, M. J. (2011). Beyond homophily: A decade of advances in understanding peer influence processes. *Journal of Research on Adolescence, 21*, 166–179.

Brendgen, M., Boivin, M., Vitaro, F., Bukowski, W. M., Dionne, G., Tremblay, R. E., et al. (2008). Linkages between chidren's and their friends' social and physical aggression: Evidence for a gene-environment interaction? *Child Development, 79*, 13–29.

Brendgen, M., Lamarche, V., Wanner, B., & Vitaro, F. (2010). Links between friendship relations and early adolescents' trajectories of depressed mood. *Developmental Psychology, 46*, 491–501.

Brendgen, M., Vitaro, F., Boivin, M., Dionea, G., & Perusse, D. (2006). Examining genetic and environmental effects on reactive versus proactive aggression. *Developmental Psychology, 42*, 1299–1312.

Brennan, P. A., Grekin, E. R., Mortensen, E. L., & Mednick, S. A. (2002). Relationship of maternal smoking during pregnancy with criminal arrest and hospitalization for substance abuse in male and female adult offspring. *American Journal of Psychiatry, 159*, 48–54.

Brockington, I. (1996). *Motherhood and mental health.* Oxford, UK: Oxford University Press.

Brody, G. H. (1998). Sibling relationship quality: Its causes and consequences. *Annual Review of Psychology, 49*, 1–24.

Brody, G. H. (2004). Siblings' direct and indirect contributions to child development. *Current Directions in Psychological Science, 13*, 124–126.

Brody, G. H., & Ge, X. (2001). Linking parenting processes and self-regulation to psychological functioning and alcohol use during early adolescence. *Journal of Family Psychology, 15*, 82–94.

Brody, G. H., Kim, S., Murry, V. M., & Brown, A. C. (2003). Longitudinal direct and indirect pathways linking older sibling competence to the development of younger sibling competence. *Developmental Psychology, 39*, 618–628.

Brody, G. H., Stoneman, A., & McCoy, J. K. (1994). Forecasting sibling relationships in early adolescence from child temperament and family processes in middle childhood. *Child Development, 65*, 771–784.

Brody, N. (1992). *Intelligence* (2nd ed.). San Diego, CA: Academic Press.

Brodzinsky, D. M., & Pinderhughes, E. (2002). Parenting and child development in adoptive families. In M. H. Bornstein (Ed), *Handbook of parenting: Vol. 1: Children and parenting* (2nd ed., pp. 279–311). Mahwah, NJ: Lawrence Erlbaum.

Bronfenbrenner, U. (1995). Developmental ecology through space and time: A future perspective. In P. Moen, G. H. Elder, Jr., & K. Luscher (Eds.), *Examining lives in context: Perspectives on the ecology of human development.* Washington, DC: American Psychological Association.

Bronfenbrenner, U., & Morris, P. (2006). The ecology of developmental processes. In W. Damon & R. M. Lerner (Eds.), *Handbook of child psychology* (6th ed., Vol. 1, pp. 793–829). New York, NY: Wiley.

Brown, B. B., Herman, M., Hamm, J. V., & Heck, D. J. (2008). Ethnicity and image: Correlates of crowd affiliation among ethnic minority youth. *Child Development, 79*, 529–546.

Brown, B. B., Mounts, N., Lamborn, S. D., & Steinberg, L. (1993). Parenting practices and peer group affiliation in adolescence. *Developmental Psychology, 64*, 467–482.

Brown, J. R., & Dunn, J. (1996). Continuities in emotion understanding from three to six years. *Child Development, 67*, 789–802.

Brown, J. V., Bakeman, R., Coles, C. D., Platzman, K. A., & Lynch, M. E. (2004). Prenatal cocaine exposure: A comparison of 2-year-old children in parental and nonparental care. *Child Development, 75*, 1282–1295.

Brown, J., & Dunn, J. (1992). Talk with your mother or your sibling? Developmental changes in early family conversations about feelings. *Child Development, 63*, 336–349.

Brown, J., Meadows, S. O., & Elder, G. H., Jr. (2007). Race-ethnic inequality and psychological distress: Depressive symptoms from adolescence to young adulthood. *Developmental Psychology, 43*, 1295–1311.

Brown, R. (1973). *A first language: The early stages.* Cambridge, MA: Harvard University Press.

Brown, R. P., Osterman, L. L., & Barnes, C. D. (2009). School violence and the culture of honor. *Psychological Science, 20*, 1400–1405.

Brown, R., Pressley, M., Van Meter, P., & Schuder, T. (1996). A quasi-experimental validation of transactional strategies instruction with low-achieving second-grade readers. *Journal of Educational Psychology, 88*, 18–37.

Browne, K. D., & Hamilton-Giachritsis, C. (2005). The influence of violent media on children and adolescents: A public-health approach. *Lancet, 365*, 702–710.

Bruck, M., & Ceci, S. J. (1995). Amicus brief for the case of *State of New Jersey vs Michaels* presented by Committee of Concerned Social Scientists. *Psychology, Public Policy, & Law, 1*, 272–322.

Bruno, J. L., Manis, F. R., Keating, P., Sperling, A. J., Nakamoto, J., & Seidenberg, M. S. (2007). Auditory word identification in dyslexic and normally achieving readers. *Journal of Experimental Child Psychology, 97,* 183–204.

Buchanan, C. M., & Heiges, K. L. (2001). When conflict continues after the marriage ends: Effects of postdivorce conflict on children. In J. Grych & F. D. Fincham (Eds.), *Interparental conflict and child development* (pp. 337–362). New York, NY: Cambridge University Press.

Buchanan, C. M., Eccles, J. S., & Becker, J. B. (1992). Are adolescents victims of raging hormones? Evidence for activational effects of hormones on moods and behavior at adolescence. *Psychological Bulletin, 111,* 62–107.

Buckhalt, J. A. (2011). Insufficient sleep and the socioeconomic status achievement gap. *Child Development Perspectives, 5,* 59–65.

Buckhalt, J. A., El-Sheikh, M., & Keller, P. (2007). Children's sleep and cognitive functioning: Race and socioeconomic status as moderators of effects. *Child Development, 78,* 213–231.

Buckhalt, J. A., El-Sheikh, M., Keller, P. S, & Kelly, R. J. (2009). Concurrent and longitudinal relations between children's sleep and cognitive functioning: The moderating role of parent education. *Child Development, 80,* 875–892.

Bugental, D. B., & Happaney, K. (2004). Predicting infant maltreatment in low-income families: The interactive effects of maternal attributions and child status at birth. *Developmental Psychology, 40,* 234–243.

Bugental, D. B., & Schwartz, A. (2009). A cognitive approach to child maltreatment prevention among medically at-risk infants. *Developmental Psychology, 45,* 284–288.

Buhrmester, D., & Furman, W. (1990). Perceptions of sibling relationships during middle childhood and adolescence. *Child Development, 61,* 1387–1398.

Buhs, E. S., & Ladd, G. W. (2001). Peer rejection as antecedent of young children's school adjustment: An examination of mediating processes. *Developmental Psychology, 37,* 550–560.

Buijzen, M., Schuurman, J., & Bomhof, E. (2008). Associations between children's television advertising exposure and their food consumption patterns: A household diary-survey study. *Appetite, 50,* 231–239.

Bukowski, W. M., Sippola, L. K., & Hoza, B. (1999). Same and other: Interdependency between participation in same- and other-sex friendships. *Journal of Youth & Adolescence, 28,* 439–459.

Bullard, L., Wachlarowicz, M., DeLeeuw, J., Snyder, J., Low, S., Forgatch, M., et al. (2010). Effects of the Oregon model of Parent Management Training (PMTO) on marital adjustment in new stepfamilies: A randomized trial. *Journal of Family Psychology, 24,* 485–496.

Bullock, M., & Lütkenhaus, P. (1990). Who am I? The development of self-understanding in toddlers. *Merrill-Palmer Quarterly, 36,* 217–238.

Burack, J. A., Flanagan, T., Peled, T., Sutton, H. M., Zygmuntowicz, C., & Manly, J. T. (2006). Social perspective-taking skills in maltreated children and adolescents. *Developmental Psychology, 42,* 207–217.

Burk, W. J., & Laursen, B. (2005). Adolescent perceptions of friendship and their associations with individual adjustment. *International Journal of Behavioral Development, 29,* 156–164.

Burnham, D., & Dodd, B. (2004). Auditory-visual speech integration by prelinguistic infants: Perception of an emergent consonant in the McGurk effect. *Developmental Psychobiology, 45,* 204–220.

Buss, K. A., & Goldsmith, H. H. (1998). Fear and anger regulation in infancy: Effects on the temporal dynamics of affective expression. *Child Development, 69,* 359–374.

Buss, K. A., & Kiel, E. J. (2004). Comparison of sadness, anger, and fear facial expressions when toddlers look at their mothers. *Child Development, 75,* 1761–1773.

Busseri, M. A., Rose-Krasnor, L., Willoughby, T., & Chalmers, H. (2006). A longitudinal examination of breadth and intensity of youth activity involvement and successful development. *Developmental Psychology, 42,* 1313–1326.

Byrnes, J. P., Miller, D. C., & Schafer, W. D. (1999). Gender differences in risk taking: A meta-analysis. *Psychological Bulletin, 125,* 367–383.

Côté, S., Vaillancourt, T., Barker, E. D., Nagin, D., & Tremblay, R. E. (2007). The joint development of physical and indirect aggression: Predictors of continuity and change during childhood. *Development & Psychopathology, 19,* 37–55.

Côté, S., Zoccolillo, M., Tremblay, R. E., Nagin, D., & Vitaro, F. (2001). Predicting girls' conduct disorder in adolescence from childhood trajectories of disruptive behaviors. *Journal of the American Academy of Child & Adolescent Psychiatry, 40,* 678–684.

Cai, H., Brown, J. D., Deng, C., & Oakes, M. A. (2007). Self-esteem and culture: Differences in cognitive self-evaluations or affective self-regard? *Asian Journal of Social Psychology, 10,* 162–170.

Cain, K. (1999). Ways of reading: How knowledge and use of strategies are related to reading comprehension. *British Journal of Developmental Psychology, 17,* 293–312.

Caldwell, M. S., Rudolph, K. D., Troop-Gordon, W., & Kim, D-Y. (2004). Reciprocal influences among relational self-views, social disengagement, and peer stress during early adolescence. *Child Development, 75,* 1140–1154.

Callaghan, R., Rochat, P., Lillard, A., Claux, M. L., Odden, H., Itakura, S., et al. (2005). Synchrony in the onset of mental-state reasoning: Evidence from five cultures. *Psychological Science, 16,* 378–384.

Callahan, C. M. (2000). Intelligence and giftedness. In R. J. Sternberg (Ed.), *Handbook of intelligence* (pp. 159–175). Cambridge, UK: Cambridge University Press.

Callanan, M. A., & Sabbagh, M. A. (2004). Multiple labels for objects in conversations with young children: Parents' language and children's developing expectations about word meanings. *Developmental Psychology, 40,* 746–763.

Calvert, S. L., Rideout, V. J., Woolard, J. L., Barr, R. F., & Strouse, G. (2005). Age, ethnicity, and socioeconomic patterns in early computer use: A national survey. *American Behavioral Scientist, 48,* 590–607.

Cameron, C. A., Edmunds, G., Wigmore, B., Hunt, A. K., & Linton, M. J. (1997). Children's revision of textual flaws. *International Journal of Behavioral Development, 20,* 667–680.

Cameron, L., Rutland, A., Brown, R., & Douch, R. (2006). Changing children's intergroup attitudes toward refugees: Testing different models of extended contact. *Child Development, 77,* 1208–1219.

Campbell, F. A., Pungello, E. P., Miller-Johnson, S., Burchinal, M., & Ramey, C. T. (2001). The development of cognitive and academic abilities: Growth curves from an early childhood educational experiment. *Developmental Psychology, 37,* 231–242.

Campbell, R., & Sais, E. (1995). Accelerated metalinguistic (phonological) awareness in bilingual children. *British Journal of Developmental Psychology, 13,* 61–68.

Campos, J. J., Anderson, D. I., Barbu-Roth, M. A., Hubbard, E. M., Hertenstein, M. J., & Witherington, D. (2000). Travel broadens the mind. *Infancy, 1,* 149–219.

Campos, J. J., Hiatt, S., Ramsay, D., Henderson, C., & Svedja, M. (1978). The emergency of fear on the visual cliff. In M. Lewis & L. Rosenblum (Eds.), *The origins of affect.* New York, NY: Plenum.

Camras, L. A., Chen, Y., Bakeman, R., Norris, K., & Cain, R. T. (2006). Culture, ethnicity, and children's facial expressions: A study of European American, Mainland Chinese, Chinese American, and adopted Chinese girls. *Emotion, 6,* 103–114.

Camras, L. A., Ester, H., Campos, J., Campos, R., Ujiie, T., Miyake, K., et al. (1998). Production of emotional facial expressions in European, American, Japanese, and Chinese infants. *Developmental Psychology, 34,* 616–628.

Candel, I., Hayne, H., Strange, D., & Prevoo, E. (2009). The effect of suggestion on children's recognition memory for seen and unseen details. *Psychology, Crime, & Law, 15,* 29–39.

Cannon, T. D., Rosso, I. M., Hollister, J. M., Bearden, C. E., Sanchez, L. E., & Hadley, T. (2000). A prospective cohort study of genetic and perinatal influences in the etiology of schizophrenia. *Schizophrenia Bulletin, 26,* 351–366.

Canobi, K. H., Reeve, R. A., & Pattison, P. E. (2002). Young children's understanding of addition. *Educational Psychology, 22,* 513–532.

Capelli, C. A., Nakagawa, N., & Madden, C. M. (1990). How children understand sarcasm: The role of context of information. *Child Development, 61,* 1824–1841.

Card, N. A. (2010). Antipathetic relationships in child and adolescent development: A meta-analytic review and recommendations for an emerging area of study. *Developmental Psychology, 46,* 516–529.

Card, N. A., & Hodges, E. V. (2006). Shared targets for aggression by early adolescent friends. *Developmental Psychology, 42,* 1327–1338.

Card, N. A., Stucky, B. D., Sawalani, G. M., & Little, T. D. (2008). Direct and indirect aggression during adolescence: A meta-analytic review of gender differences, intercorrelations, and relations to maladjustment. *Child Development, 79,* 1185–1229.

Carlson, S. M., & Meltzoff, A. N. (2008). Bilingual experience and executive functioning in young children. *Developmental Science, 11,* 282–298.

Carpenter, P. A., & Daneman, M. (1981). Lexical retrieval and error recovery in reading: A model based on eye fixations. *Journal of Verbal Learning & Verbal Behavior, 20,* 137–160.

Carrere, S., & Gottman, J. M. (1999). Predicting the future of marriages. In E. M. Hetherington (Ed.), *Coping with divorce, single parenting, and remarriage: A risk and resiliency perspective.* Mahwah, NJ: Erlbaum.

Carroll, J. B. (1993). *Human cognitive abilities: A survey of factor-analytic studies.* New York, NY: Cambridge University Press.

Carroll, J. B. (1996). A three-stratum theory of intelligence: Spearman's contribution. In I. Dennis & P. Tapsfield (Eds.), *Human abilities: Their nature and measurement.* Mahwah, NJ: Erlbaum.

Carroll, J. L., & Loughlin, G. M. (1994). Sudden infant death syndrome. In F. A. Oski, C. D. DeAngelis, R. D. Feigin, J. A. McMillan, & J. B. Warshaw (Eds.), *Principles and practice of pediatrics.* Philadelphia, PA: Lippincott.

Carskadon, M. A. (2002). Factors influencing sleep patterns of adolescents. In M. A. Carskadon (Ed.), *Adolescent sleep patterns: Biological, social, and psychological influences* (pp. 4–26). New York, NY: Cambridge University Press.

Carver, K., Joyner, K., & Udry, J. R. (2003). National estimates of adolescent romantic relationships. In P. Florsheim (Ed.), *Adolescent romantic relations and sexual behavior: Theory, research, and practical implications* (pp. 23–56). Mahwah, NJ: Erlbaum.

Carver, P. R., Egan, S. K., & Perry, D. G. (2004). Children who question their heterosexuality. *Developmental Psychology, 40,* 43–53.

Case, R. (1992). *The mind's staircase: Exploring the conceptual underpinnings of children's thought and knowledge.* Hillsdale, NJ: Erlbaum.

Casey, B. J., Tottenham, N., Liston, C., & Durston, S. (2005). Imaging the developing brain: What have we learned about cognitive development? *Trends in Cognitive Neuroscience, 9,* 104–110.

Casiglia, A. C., Coco, A. L., & Zappulla, C. (1998). Aspects of social reputation and peer relationships in Italian children: A cross-cultural perspective. *Developmental Psychology, 34,* 723–730.

Casper, D. M., & Card, N. A. (2010). "We were best friends, But...": Two studies of antipathetic relationships emerging from broken friendships. *Journal of Adolescent Research, 25,* 499–526.

Caspi, A., Roberts, B. W., & Shiner, R. L. (2005). Personality development: Stability and change. *Annual Review of Psychology, 56,* 453–484.

Cassidy, J. (1994). Emotion regulation: Influences of attachment relationships. *Monographs of the Society for Research in Child Development, 59* (Serial No. 240), 228–283.

Castelli, L., Zogmaister, C., & Tomelleri, S. (2009). The transmission of racial attitudes within the family. *Developmental Psychology, 45,* 586–591.

Cattell, R. B. (1965). *The scientific analysis of personality.* Baltimore, MD: Penguin.

Cavanagh, S. E. (2004). The sexual debut of girls in early adolescence: The intersection of race, pubertal timing, and friendship group characteristics. *Journal of Research on Adolescence, 14,* 285–312.

Ceci, S. J., & Bruck, M. (1995). *Jeopardy in the courtroom: A scientific analysis of children's testimony.* Washington, DC: American Psychological Association.

Ceci, S. J., & Bruck, M. (1998). Children's testimony: Applied and basic issues. In W. Damon (Ed.), *Handbook of child psychology* (Vol. 4). New York, NY: Wiley.

Centers for Disease Control and Prevention. (2007). *2005 assisted reproductive technology success rates.* Atlanta, GA: Author.

Cerella, J., & Hale, S. (1994). The rise and fall in information-processing rates over the life span. *Acta Psychologica, 86,* 109–197.

Cervantes, C. A., & Callanan, M. A. (1998). Labels and explanations in mother-child emotions talk: Age and gender differentiation. *Developmental Psychology, 34,* 88–98.

Champion, T. B. (2003). A "matter of vocabulary": Performance of low-income African-American Head Start children on the Peabody Picture Vocabulary Test. *Communication Disorders Quarterly, 24,* 121–127.

Chandler, M. J., & Carpendale, J. I. M. (1998). Inching toward a mature theory of mind. In M. D. Ferrari & R. J. Sternberg (Eds.), *Self-awareness: Its nature and development* (pp. 148–190). New York, NY: Guilford Press.

Chanquoy, L. (2001). How to make it easier for children to revise their writing: A study of text revision from 3rd to 5th grades. *British Journal of Educational Psychology, 71,* 15–41.

Chao, R. K. (2001). Extending research on the consequences of parenting style for Chinese Americans and European Americans. *Child Development, 72,* 1832–1843.

Chapman, P. D. (1988). *Schools as sorters: Lewis M. Terman, applied psychology, and the intelligence testing movement, 1890–1930.* New York, NY: New York University Press.

Chase-Lansdale, P. L., Brooks-Gunn, J., & Zamsky, E. S. (1994). Young African-American multigenerational families in poverty: Quality of mothering and grandmothering. *Child Development, 65,* 373–393.

Chavajay, P. (2008). Organizational patterns in problem solving among Mayan fathers and children. *Developmental Psychology, 44,* 882–888.

Chavous, T. M., Bernat, D. H., Schmeelk-Cone, K., Caldwell, C. H., Kohn-Wood, L., & Zimmerman, M. A. (2003). Racial identity and academic attainment among African American adolescents. *Child Development, 74,* 1076–1090.

Chen, E., Cohen, S., & Miller, G. E. (2010). How low socioeconomic status affects 2-year-hormonal trajectories in children. *Psychological Science, 21,* 31–37.

Chen, J., & Gardner, H. (2005). Assessment based on multiple intelligences theory. In D. P. Flanagan & P. L. Harrison (Eds.), *Contemporary intellectual assessment: Theories, tests, and issues* (pp. 77–102). New York, NY: Guilford Press.

Chen, X., Chen, H., Li, D., & Wang, L. (2009). Early childhood behavioral inhibition and social and school adjustment in Chinese children: A 5-year longitudinal study. *Child Development, 80,* 1692–1704.

Chi, M. T. H. (1978). Knowledge structures and memory development. In R. Siegler (Ed.), *Children's thinking: What develops?* Hillsdale, NJ: Erlbaum.

Children's Defense Fund. (2010). *State of America's children: 2010.* Washington, DC: Author.

Chilman, C. S. (1983). *Adolescent sexuality in a changing American society* (2nd ed.). New York, NY: Wiley.

Chomitz, V. R., Cheung, L. W. Y., & Lieberman, E. (1995). The role of lifestyle in preventing low birth weight. *The Future of Children, 5,* 121–138.

Chomsky, N. (1957). *Syntactic structure.* The Hague, The Netherlands: Mouton.

Chomsky, N. (1995). *The minimalist program.* Cambridge, MA: MIT Press.

Chorpita, B. F., & Barlow, D. H. (1998). The development of anxiety: The role of control in the early environment. *Psychological Bulletin, 124,* 3–21.

Chou, R. J. A. (2011). Filial piety by contract? The emergence, implementation, and implications of the "Family Support Agreement" in China. *Gerontologist, 51,* 3–16.

Chow, B. W., McBride-Chang, C., Cheung, H., & Chow, C. S. (2008). Dialogic reading and morphology training in Chinese children: Effects on language and literacy. *Developmental Psychology, 44,* 233–244.

Christensen, A., & Heavey, C. L. (1999). Intervention for couples. *Annual Review of Psychology, 50,* 165–190.

Chung, H. L., & Steinberg, L. (2006). Relations between neighborhood factors, parenting behaviors, peer deviance, and delinquency among serious juvenile offenders. *Developmental Psychology, 42,* 319–331.

Cicchetti, D., & Toth, S. L. (2006). Developmental psychopathology and preventive intervention. In W. Damon & R. M. Lerner (Eds.), *Handbook of child psychology* (Vol. 4.) New York, NY: Wiley.

Cillessen, A. H. N., & Rose, A. (2005). Understanding popularity in the peer system. *Current Directions in Psychological Science, 14,* 102–105.

Clark, K. B. (1945). A brown girl in a speckled world. *Journal of Social Issues, 1,* 10–15.

Clark, K. B., & Clark, M. K. (1940). Skin color as a factor in racial identification of Negro preschool children. *Journal of Social Psychology, 11,* 159–169.

Clarke, P. J., Snowling, M. J., Truelove, E., & Hulme, C. (2010). Ameliorating children's reading-comprehension difficulties: A randomized controlled trial. *Psychological Science, 21,* 1106–1116.

Clarke-Stewart, K. A., & Bretano, C. (2005). *Till divorce do us part.* New Haven, CT: Yale University Press.

Clements, D. H. (1995). Teaching creativity with computers. *Educational Psychology Review, 7,* 141–161.

Cnattingius, S. (2004). The epidemiology of smoking during pregnancy: Smoking prevalence, maternal characteristics, and pregnancy outcomes. *Nicotine & Tobacco Research, 6,* S125–S140.

Coall, D. A., & Hartwig, R. (2010). Grandparental investment: Past, present, and future. *Behavioral & Brain Sciences, 33,* 1–19.

Coatsworth, J. D., & Conroy, D. E. (2009). The effects of autonomy-supporting coaching, need satisfaction, and self-perceptions on initiative and identity in youth swimmers. *Developmental Psychology, 45,* 320–328.

Coelho, J. S., Jansen, A., Roefs, A., & Nederkoorn, C. (2009). Eating behavior in response to food-cue exposure: Examining the cue-reactivity and counteractive-control models. *Psychology of Addictive Behaviors, 23,* 131–139.

Coffman, J. L., Ornstein, P. A., McCall, L. E., & Curran, P. J. (2008). Linking teachers' memory-relevant language and the development of children's memory skills. *Developmental Psychology, 44,* 1640–1654.

Cohen, G. L., Garcia, J., Apfel, N., & Master, A. (2006). Reducing the racial achievement gap: A social-psychological intervention. *Science, 313,* 1307–1310.

Cohen, L. B., & Cashon, C. H. (2003). Infant perception and cognition. In R. M. Lerner, D. K. Freedheim, I. B. Weiner, M. A. Easterbrooks, & J. Mistry (Eds.), *Handbook of psychology: Developmental psychology.* Hoboken, NJ: Wiley.

Cohen, M., & Piquero, A. R. (2009). New evidence on the monetary value of saving a high risk youth. *Journal of Quantitative Criminology, 25,* 25–49.

Cohen, R. W., Martinez, M. E., & Ward, B. W. (2010). *Health insurance coverage: Early release of estimates from the National Health Interview Survey, 2009.* Hyattsville MD: National Center for Health Statistics.

Cohen, S., & Williamson, G. M. (1991). Stress and infectious disease in humans. *Psychological Bulletin, 109,* 5–24.

Coie, J. D., Dodge, K. A., Terry, R., & Wright, V. (1991). The role of aggression in peer relations: An analysis of aggression episodes in boys' play groups. *Child Development, 62,* 812–826.

Colby, A., Kohlberg, L., Gibbs, J. C., & Lieberman, M. (1983). A longitudinal study of moral development. *Monographs of the Society for Research in Child Development, 48* (Serial No. 200).

Cole, C. A. (1991). Change in self-perceived competence as a function of peer and teacher evaluation. *Developmental Psychology, 27,* 682–688.

Cole, M. (2006). Culture and cognitive development in phylogenetic, historical and ontogenetic perspective. In W. Damon & R. M. Lerner (Eds.), *Handbook of child psychology* (6th ed., Vol. 2). New York, NY: Wiley.

Cole, P. M., Tamang, B. L., & Shrestha, S. (2006). Cultural variations in the socialization of young children's anger and shame. *Child Development, 77,* 1237–1251.

Collins, W. A. (2003). More than myth: The developmental significance of romantic relationships during adolescence. *Journal of Research on Adolescence, 13,* 1–24.

Collins, W. A., Welsh, D. P., & Furman, W. (2009). Adolescent romantic relationships. *Annual Review of Psychology, 60,* 631–652.

Committee on Genetics. (1996). Newborn screening fact sheet. *Pediatrics, 98,* 473–501.

Conboy, B. T., & Thal, D. J. (2006). Ties between the lexicon and grammar: Cross-sectional and longitudinal studies of bilingual toddlers. *Child Development, 77,* 712–735.

Conboy, B. T., Sommerville, J. A., & Kuhl, P. (2008). Cognitive control factors in speech perception at 11 months. *Developmental Psychology, 44,* 1505–1512.

Condry, J. C., & Ross, D. F. (1985). Sex and aggression: The influence of gender label on the perception of aggression in children. *Child Development, 56,* 225–233.

Conduct Problems Prevention Research Group. (2011). The effects of the Fast Track preventive intervention on the development of conduct disorder across childhood. *Child Development, 82,* 331–345.

Conger, R. D., & Elder, G. H. (1994). *Families in troubled times: Adapting to change in rural America.* New York, NY: Aldine de Gruyter.

Connecticut Department of Children and Families. (2003). *Leaving your child home alone.* Retrieved October 7, 2005, from http://www.state.ct.us/def/

Connor, C. M., Morrison, F. J., Fishman, B. J., Schatschneider, C., & Underwood, P. (2007). Algorithm-guided individualized reading instruction. *Science, 315,* 464–465.

Cook, E. C., Buehler, C., & Henson, R. (2009). Parents and peers as social influences to deter antisocial behavior. *Journal of Youth & Adolescence, 38,* 1204–1252.

Cooper, H., Hedges, L. V., & Valentine, J. C. (Eds.). *The handbook of research synthesis and meta-analysis* (2nd ed.). New York, NY: Russell Sage Foundation.

Coplan, R. J., & Armer, M. (2007). A "multitude" of solitude: A closer look at social withdrawal and nonsocial play in early childhood. *Child Development Perspectives, 1,* 26–32.

Coplan, R. J., Gavinski-Molina, M. H., Lagace-Seguin, D. G., & Wichman, C. (2001). When girls versus boys play alone: Nonsocial play and adjustment in kindergarten. *Developmental Psychology, 37,* 464–474.

Copper, R. L., Goldberg, R. L., Das, A., Elder, N., et al. (1996). The preterm prediction study: Maternal stress is associated with spontaneous preterm birth at less than thirty-five weeks' gestation. *American Journal of Obstetrics & Gynecology, 175,* 1286–1292.

Cordes, S., & Brannon, E. M. (2009). The relative salience of discrete and continuous quantity in young infants. *Developmental Science, 12,* 453–463.

Cornelius, M., Taylor, P., Geva, D., & Day, N. (1995). Prenatal tobacco exposure and marijuana use among adolescents: Effects on offspring gestational age, growth, and morphology. *Pediatrics, 95,* 738–743.

Cortesi, F., Giannotti, F., Sebastiani, T., & Vagnoni, C. (2004). Cosleeping and sleep behavior in Italian school-aged children. *Journal of Developmental & Behavioral Pediatrics, 25,* 28–33.

Cosmides, L., & Tooby, J. (2000). Evolutionary psychology and the emotions. In M. Lewis & J. Haviland-Jones (Eds.), *Handbook of emotions* (2nd ed., pp. 91–115). New York, NY: Guilford.

Costa, P. T., & McRae, R. R. (2001). A theoretical context for adult temperament. In T. D. Wachs & G. A. Kohnstamm (Eds.), *Temperament in context* (pp. 1–21). Mahwah, NJ: Erlbaum.

Costigan, C. L., & Dokis, D. P. (2006). Relations between parent–child acculturation differences and adjustment within immigrant Chinese families. *Child Development, 77,* 1252–1267.

Costin, S. E., & Jones, D. C. (1992). Friendship as a facilitator of emotional responsiveness and prosocial interventions among young children. *Developmental Psychology, 28,* 941–947.

Coulton, C. J., Crampton, D. S., Irwin, M., Spilsbury, J. C., & Korbin, J. E. (2007). How neighborhoods influence child maltreatment: A review of the literature and alternative pathways. *Child Abuse & Neglect, 31,* 1117–1142.

Coutelle, C. Themis, M., Waddington, S. N., Buckley, S. M., Gregory, L. G., Nivsarkar, M. S. et al. (2005). Gene therapy progress and prospects: Fetal gene therapy—first proofs of concept—some adverse effects. *Gene Therapy, 12,* 1601–1607.

Cox, M. J., & Paley, B. (2003). Understanding families as systems. *Current Directions in Psychological Science, 12,* 193–196.

Cox, M. J., Paley, B., & Harter, K. (2001). Interparental conflict and parent–child relationships. In J. H. Grych & F. D. Fincham (Eds.), *Interparental conflict and child development* (pp. 249–272). New York, NY: Cambridge University Press.

Cox, S. J., Mezulis, A. H., & Hyde, J. S. (2010). The influence of child gender role and maternal feedback to child stress on the emergence of the gender difference in depressive rumination in adolescence. *Developmental Psychology, 46,* 842–852.

Cragg, L., & Nation, K. (2008). Go or no-go? Developmental improvements in the efficiency of response inhibition in mid-childhood. *Developmental Science, 11,* 819–827.

Craig, K. D., Whitfield, M. F., Grunau, R. V. E., Linton, J., & Hadjistavropoulos, H. D. (1993). Pain in the preterm neonate: Behavioral and physiological indices. *Pain, 52,* 238–299.

Creusere, M. A. (1999). Theories of adults' understanding and use of irony and sarcasm: Applications to and evidence from research with children. *Developmental Review, 19,* 213–262.

Crick, N. R., & Dodge, K. A. (1994). A review and reformulation of social-information processing mechanisms in children's social adjustment. *Psychological Bulletin, 115,* 74–101.

Crick, N. R., & Grotpeter, J. K. (1995). Relational aggression, gender, and social-psychological adjustment. *Child Development, 66,* 710–722.

Crick, N. R., & Werner, N. E. (1998). Response decision processes in relational and overt aggression. *Child Development, 69,* 1630–1639.

Crick, N. R., Casas, J. F., & Nelson, D. A. (2002). Toward a more comprehensive understanding of peer maltreatment: Studies of relational victimization. *Current Directions in Psychological Science, 11,* 98–101.

Cristia, A. (2010). Phonetic enhancement of sibilants in infant-directed speech. *Journal of the Acoustical Society of America, 128,* 424–434.

Crocetti, E., Rubini, M., Luyckx, K., & Meeus, W. (2008). Identity formation in early and middle adolescence from various ethnic groups: From three dimensions to five statuses. *Journal of Youth & Adolescence, 37,* 983–996.

Crone, E A. (2009). Executive functions in adolescence: Inferences from brain and behavior. *Developmental Science, 12,* 825–830.

Crouter, A. C., & Bumpus, M. F. (2001). Linking parents' work stress to children's and adolescents' psychological adjustment. *Current Directions in Psychological Science, 10,* 156–159.

Crouter, A. C., Whiteman, S. D., McHale, S. M., & Osgood, D. (2007). Development of gender attitude traditionality across middle childhood and adolescence. *Child Development, 78,* 911–926.

Cuellar, I., Nyberg, B., Maldonado, R. E., & Roberts, R. E. (1997). Ethnic identity and acculturation in a young adult Mexican-origin population. *Journal of Community Psychology, 25,* 535–549.

Cullerton-Sen, C., Cassidy, A. R., Murray-Close, D., Cicchetti, D., Crick, N. R., & Rogosch, F. A. (2008). Child maltreatment and the development of relational and physical aggression: The importance of a gender-informed approach. *Child Development, 79,* 1736–1751.

Cummings, E. M., Merrilees, C. E., Schermerhorn, A. C., Goeke-Morey, M. C., Shirlow, P., & Cairns, E. (2011). Longitudinal pathways between political violence and child adjustment: The role of emotional security about the community in Northern Ireland. *Journal of Abnormal Child Psychology, 39,* 213–224.

Cummings, E., Schermerhorn, A. C., Davies, P. T., Goeke-Morey, M. C., & Cummings, J. S. (2006). Interparental discord and child adjustment: Prospective investigations of emotional security as an explanatory mechanism. *Child Development, 77,* 132–152.

Cunningham, A. E., Perry, K. E., Stanovich, K. E., & Share, D. L. (2002). Orthographic learning during reading: Examining the role of self-teaching. *Journal of Experimental Child Psychology, 82,* 185–199.

Curtiss, S. (1989). The independence and task-specificity of language. In M. H. Bornstein & J. S. Bruner (Eds.), *Interaction in human development* (pp. 105–137). Hillsdale, NJ: Erlbaum.

Cutuli, J. J., Wiik, K. L., Herbers, J. E., Gunnar, M. R., & Masten, A. S. (2010). Cortisol function among early school-aged homeless children. *Psychoneuroendocrinology, 35,* 833–845.

D'Onofrio, B. M., Goodnight, J. A., Van Hulle, C. A., Rodgers, J. L., Rathouz, P. J., Waldman, I. D., & Lahey, B. B. (2009). Maternal age at childbirth and offspring disruptive behaviors: Testing the causal hypothesis. *Journal of Child Psychology & Psychiatry, 50,* 1018–1028.

D'Onofrio, B. M., Singh, A. L., Iliadou, A., Lambe, M., Hultman, C. M., Neiderhiser, J. M., Långström, N., & Lichtenstein, P. (2010). A quasi-experimental study of maternal smoking during pregnancy and offspring academic achievement. *Child Development, 81,* 80–100.

Dale, P. S., Harlaar, N., Haworth, M. A., & Plomin, R. (2010). Two by two: A twin study of second-language acquisition. *Psychological Science, 21,* 635–640.

Daley, T. C., Whaley, S. E., Sigman, M. D., Espinosa, M. P., & Neumann, C. (2003). IQ on the rise: The Flynn effect in rural Kenyan children. *Psychological Science, 14,* 215–219.

Daly, M., & Wilson, M. (1996). Violence against stepchildren. *Current Directions in Psychological Science, 5,* 77–81.

Daniels, H. (2011). Vygotsky and psychology In U. Goswami (Ed.), *The Wiley-Blackwell handbook of childhood cognitive development* (2nd ed., pp. 673–696). West Sussex, UK: Wiley-Blackwell.

Dannemiller, J. L. (1998). Color constancy and color vision during infancy: Methodological and empirical issues. In V. Walsh & J. Kulikowski (Eds.), *Perceptual constancy: Why things look as they do.* New York, NY: Cambridge University Press.

Darling, H., Reeder, A. I., McGee, T., & Williams, S. (2006). Brief report: Disposable income, and spending on fast food, alcohol, cigarettes, and gambling by New Zealand secondary school students. *Journal of Adolescence, 29,* 837–843.

Darling, N., Cumsille, P., & Martínez, M. L. (2008). Individual differences in adolescents' beliefs about the legitimacy of parental authority and their own obligation to obey: A longitudinal investigation. *Child Development, 79,* 1103–1118.

David, A., & Rodeck, C. H. (2009). Fetal gene therapy. In C. H. Rodeck & M. J. Whittle (Eds.), *Fetal medicine: Basic science and clinical practice.* London: Churchill Livingstone.

Davidson, F. H., & Davidson, M. M. (1994). *Changing childhood prejudice: The caring work of the schools.* Westport, CT: Bergin & Garvey/Greenwood.

Davidson, M. C., Amso, D., Anderson, L. C., & Diamond, A. (2006). Development of cognitive control and executive functions from 4 to 13 years: Evidence from manipulations of memory, inhibition, and task switching. *Neuropsychologia, 44,* 2037–2078.

Davies, P. T., & Cummings, E. M. (1998). Exploring children's emotional security as a mediator of the link between marital relations and child adjustment. *Child Development, 69,* 124–139.

Davis, E. P., & Sandman, C. A. (2010). The timing of prenatal exposure to maternal cortisol and psychosocial stress is associated with human cognitive development. *Child Development, 81,* 131–148.

Day, J. D., Engelhardt, S. E., Maxwell, S. E., & Bolig, E. E. (1997). Comparison of static and dynamic assessment procedures and their relation to independent performance. *Journal of Educational Psychology, 89,* 358–368.

De Beni, R., & Palladino, P. (2000). Intrusion errors in working memory tasks: Are they related to reading comprension ability? *Learning & Individual Differences, 12,* 131–143.

De Brauwer, J., & Fias, W. (2009). A longitudinal study of children's performance on simple multiplication and division problems. *Developmental Psychology, 45,* 1480–1496.

de Haan, M., Wyatt, J. S., Roth, S., Vargha-Khadem, F., Gadian, D., & Mishkin, M. (2006). Brain and cognitive-behavioral development after asphyxia at term birth. *Developmental Science, 9,* 441–442.

de Schipper, E. J., Riksen-Walraven, J., & Geurts, S. A. (2006). Effects of child–caregiver ratio on the interactions between caregivers and children in childcare centers: An experimental study. *Child Development, 77,* 861–874.

De Wolff, M. S., & van IJzendoorn, M. H. (1997). Sensitivity and attachment: A meta-analysis on parental antecedents of infant attachment. *Child Development, 68,* 571–591.

Dearing, E., McCartney, K., & Taylor, B. A. (2009). Does higher quality early child care promote low-income children's math and reading achievement in middle childhood? *Child Development, 80,* 1329–1349.

Deary, I. J., Batty, G. D., & Gale, C. R. (2008). Bright children become enlightened adults. *Psychological Science, 19,* 1–6.

DeCasper, A. J., & Spence, M. J. (1986). Prenatal maternal speech influences newborns' perception of speech sounds. *Infant Behavior & Development, 9,* 133–150.

Dehaene, S., Izard, V., Pica, P., & Spelke, E. (2006). Core knowledge of geometry in an Amazonian indigene group. *Science, 311,* 381–384.

Dekker, M. C., Ferdinand, R. F., van Lang, D. J., Bongers, I. L., van der Ende, J., & Verhulst, F. C. (2007). Developmental trajectories of depressive symptoms from early childhood to late adolescence: Gender differences and adult outcome. *Journal of Child Psychology & Psychiatry, 48,* 657–666.

Dekovic, M., & Janssens, J. M. (1992). Parents' child-rearing style and child's sociometric status. *Developmental Psychology, 28,* 925–932.

Del Giudice, M., & Colle, L. (2007). Differences between children and adults in the recognition of enjoyment smiles. *Developmental Psychology, 43,* 796–803.

del Valle, J. F., Bravo, A., & Lopez, M. (2010). Parents and peers as providers of support in adolescents' social network: A developmental perspective. *Journal of Community Psychology, 38,* 16–27.

Delaney, C. (2000). Making babies in a Turkish village. In J. S. DeLoache & A. Gottlieb (Eds.), *A world of babies: Imagined child care guides for seven societies.* New York, NY: Cambridge University Press.

DeLoache, J. S. (1984). Oh where, oh where: Memory-based searching by very young children. In C. Sophian (Ed.), *Origins of cognitive skills.* Hillsdale, NJ: Erlbaum.

DeLoache, J. S. (1995). Early understanding and use of models: The modal model. *Current Directions in Psychological Science, 4,* 109–113.

DeLoache, J. S., Chiong, C., Sherman, K., Islam, N., Vanderborght, M., Troseth, G. L., Strouse, G. A., & O'Doherty, K. (2010). Do babies learn from baby media? *Psychological Science, 21,* in press.

DeLoache, J. S., Miller, K. F., & Pierroutsakos, S. L. (1998). Reasoning and problem solving. In W. Damon (Ed.), *Handbook of child psychology* (5th ed., Vol. 2, pp. 801–850). New York, NY: Wiley.

DeLoache, J. S., Miller, K. F., & Rosengren, K. S. (1997). The incredible shrinking room: Very young children's performance with symbolic and nonsymbolic relations. *Psychological Science, 8,* 308–313.

Demir, A., Levine, S. C., & Goldin-Meadow, S. (2010). Narrative skill in children with unilateral brain injury: A possible limit to functional plasticity. *Developmental Science, 13,* 636–647.

Denissen, J. J., Zarrett, N. R., & Eccles, J. S. (2007). I like to do it, I'm able, and I know I am: Longitudinal couplings between domain-specific achievement, self-concept, and interest. *Child Development, 78,* 430–447.

Dennis, T., Bendersky, M., Ramsay, D., & Lewis, M. (2006). Reactivity and regulation in children prenatally exposed to cocaine. *Developmental Psychology, 42,* 84–97.

deVilliers, J. G., & deVilliers, P. A. (1985). The acquisition of English. In D. I. Slobin (Ed.), *The cross-linguistic study of language acquisition.* Hillsdale, NJ: Erlbaum.

Dewey, C., Fleming, P., Golding, J., & the ALSPAC Study Team. (1998). Does the supine sleeping position have any adverse effects on the child? II. Development in the first 18 months. *Pediatrics, 101,* e5.

Dewey, K. G. (2001). Nutrition, growth, and complementary feeding of the breastfed infant. *Pediatric Clinics of North America, 48,* 87–104.

Dews, S., Winner, E., Kaplan, J., Rosenblatt, E., Hunt, M., Lim, K., et al. (1996). Children's understanding of the meaning and functions of verbal irony. *Child Development, 67,* 3071–3085.

Diamond, A. (2006). The early development of executive functions. In E. Bialystok & F. Craik (Eds.), *Lifespan cognition: Mechanisms of change* (pp. 70–95). New York, NY: Oxford University Press.

Diamond, A. (2007). Interrelated and interdependent. *Developmental Science, 10,* 152–158.

Diamond, A. (2009). The interplay of biology and the environment broadly. *Developmental Psychology, 45,* 1–8.

Diamond, M., Johnson, R., Young, D., & Singh, S. (1983). Age-related morphologic differences in the rat cerebral cortex and hippocampus: Male-female; right-left. *Experimental Neurology, 81,* 1–13.

Dick, D. M., & Rose, R. J. (2002). Behavior genetics: What's new? What's next? *Current Directions in Psychological Science, 11,* 70–74.

Dick-Read, G. (1959). *Childbirth without fear.* New York, NY: Harper & Brothers.

Dickens, S. T., & Flynn, J. R. (2001). Heritability estimates versus large environmental effects: The IQ paradox resolved. *Psychological Review, 108,* 346–369.

Dionne, G., Dale, P.S., Boivin, M., & Plomin, R. (2003). Genetic evidence for bidirectional effects of early lexical and grammatical development. *Child Development, 74,* 394–412.

DiPietro, J. A. (2004). The role of prenatal maternal stress in Psychological Science. *Current Directions in Child Development, 13,* 71–74.

DiPietro, J. A., Bornstein, M. H., Hahn, C. S., Costigan, K., & Achy-Brou, A. (2007). Fetal heart rate and variability: Stability and prediction to developmental outcomes in early childhood. *Child Development, 78,* 1788–1798.

DiPietro, J. A., Caulfield, L., Costigan, K. A., Merialdi, M., Nguyen, R. H. N., Zavaleta, N. et al. (2004). Fetal neurobehavioral development: A tale of two cities. *Developmental Psychology, 40,* 445-456.

DiPietro, J. A., Hodgson, D. M., Costigan, K. A., & Milton, S. C. (1996). Fetal neurobehavioral development. *Child Development, 67,* 2553–2567.

DiPietro, J. A., Novak, M. F., Costigan, K. A., Atella, L. D., & Reusing, S. P. (2006). Maternal psychological distress during pregnancy in relation to child development at age two. *Child Development, 77,* 573–587.

Dirix, C. E. H., Nijhuis, J. G., Jongsma, H. W., & Hornstra, G. (2009). Aspects of fetal learning and memory. *Child Development, 80,* 1251–1258.

Dishion, T. J. (1990). The family ecology of boys' peer relations in middle childhood. *Child Development, 61,* 874–892.

Dishion, T. J., Poulin, F., & Burraston, B. (2001). Peer group dynamics associated with iatrogenic effects in group interventions with high-risk young adolescents. In D. W. Nangle & C. A. Erdley (Eds.), *The role of friendship in psychological adjustment* (pp. 79–92). San Francisco, CA: Jossey-Bass.

Divan, H. A., Kheifets, L., Obel, C., & Olsen, J. (2008). Prenatal and postnatal exposure to cell phone use and behavioral problems in children. *Epidemiology, 2008*(19), 523–529.

Dixon, J. A., & Marchman, V. A. (2007). Grammar and the lexicon: Developmental ordering in language acquisition. *Child Development, 78,* 190–212.

Dodge, K. A., & Crick, N. R. (1990). Social information-processing bases of aggressive behavior in children. *Personality & Social Psychology Bulletin, 16,* 8–22.

Dodge, K. A., Bates, J. E., & Pettit, G. S. (1990). Mechanisms in the cycle of violence. *Science, 250,* 1678–1683.

Dodge, K. A., Coie, J. D., & Lynam, D. (2006). Aggression and antisocial behavior in youth. In N. Eisenberg (Ed.), *Handbook of child psychology: Vol. 3. Social, emotional, and personality development* (6th ed., pp. 719–788). New York, NY: Wiley.

Dodge, K. A., Coie, J. D., & Tremblay, R. E. (2006). Aggression. In W. Damon & R. M. Lerner (Eds.), *Handbook of child psychology, Vol. 3* (6th ed.). New York, NY: Wiley.

Dodge, K. A., Greenberg, M. T., & Malone, P. S. (2008). Testing an idealized dynamic cascade model of the development of serious violence in adolescence. *Child Development, 79,* 1907-1927.

Donaldson, S. J., & Ronan, K. R. (2006). The effects of sports participation on young adolescents' emotional well-being. *Adolescence, 41,* 369–389.

Donnellan, M. B., Trzesniewski, K. H., Robins, R. W., Moffitt, T. E., & Caspi, A. (2005). Low self-esteem is related to aggression, antisocial behavior, and delinquency. *Psychological Science, 16,* 328–335.

Donovan, W. L., Leavitt, L. A., & Walsh, R. O. (2000). Maternal illusory control predicts socialization strategies and toddler compliance. *Developmental Psychology, 36,* 402–411.

Doyle, J. M., & Kao, G. (2007). Are racial identities of multiracials stable? Change self-identification among single and multiple race individuals. *Social Psychology Quarterly, 70,* 405–423.

Draghi-Lorenz, R., Reddy, V., & Costall, A. (2001). Rethinking the development of "nonbasic" emotions: A critical review of existing theories. *Developmental Review, 21,* 263–304.

Driscoll, A. K., Russell, S. T., & Crockett, L. J. (2008). Parenting styles and youth well-being across immigrant generations. *Journal of Family Issues, 29,* 185–209.

Duckworth, A. L., & Seligman, M. E. (2005). Self-discipline outdoes IQ in predicting academic performance of adolescents. *Psychological Science, 16,* 939–944.

Duncan, G. J., & Brooks-Gunn, J. (2000). Family poverty, welfare reform, and child development. *Child Development, 71,* 188–196.

Duncan, G. J., Dowsett, C. J., Claessens, A., Magnuson, K., Huston, A. C., Klebanov, P., et al. (2007). School readiness and later achievement. *Developmental Psychology, 43,* 1428–1446.

Dunham, P. J., Dunham, F., & Curwin, A. (1993). Joint-attentional states and lexical acquisition at 18 months. *Developmental Psychology, 29,* 827–831.

Dunn, J., & Brophy, M. (2005). Communication, relationships, and individual differences in children's understanding of mind. In J. W. Astington & J. A. Baird (Eds.), *Why language matters for theory of mind* (pp. 50–69). New York, NY: Oxford.

Dunn, J., & Davies, L. (2001). Sibling relationships and interpersonal conflict. In J. Grych & F. D. Fincham (Eds.), *Interparental conflict and child development* (pp. 273–290). New York, NY: Cambridge University Press.

Dunn, J., & Kendrick, C. (1981). Social behavior of young siblings in the family context: Differences between same-sex and different-sex dyads. *Child Development, 52,* 1265–1273.

Dunn, J., O'Connor, T. G., & Cheng, H. (2005). Children's responses to conflict between their different parents: Mothers, stepfathers, nonresident fathers, and nonresident stepmothers. *Journal of Clinical Child & Adolescent Psychology, 34,* 223–234.

Dunson, D. B., Colombo, B., & Baird, D. D. (2002). Changes in age in the level and duration of fertility in the menstrual cycle. *Human Reproduction, 17,* 1399–1403.

Durik, A. M., Hyde, J. S., & Clark, R. (2000). Sequelae of cesarean and vaginal deliveries: Psychosocial outcomes for mothers and infants. *Developmental Psychology, 36,* 251–260.

Durston, S., Davidson, M. C., Tottenham, N., Galvan, A., Spicer, J., Fossella, J. A., et al. (2006). A shift from diffuse to focal cortical activity with development. *Developmental Science, 9,* 1–8.

Dwyer, T., & Ponsonby, A. L. (2009). Sudden Infant Death Syndrome and prone sleeping position. *Annals of Epidemiology, 19,* 245–249.

Eagly, A. H. (1995). The science and politics of comparing women and men. *American Psychologist, 50,* 145–158.

Eagly, A. H., Karau, S. J., & Makhijani, M. G. (1995). Gender and the effectiveness of leaders: A meta-analysis. *Psychological Bulletin, 117,* 125–145.

Eaton, D. K., Kann, L., Kinchen, S., Shanklin, S., Ross, J., Hawkins, J. et al. (2008). Youth risk behavior surveillance—United States, 2007. *Morbidity & Mortality Weekly Report, 57,* 1–131.

Eccles, J. S., & Harold, R. D. (1991). Gender differences in sport involvement: Applying the Eccles expectancy-value model. *Journal of Applied Sports Psychology, 3,* 7–35.

Edwards, C. A. (1994). Leadership in groups of school-age girls. *Developmental Psychology, 30,* 920–927.

Egan, S. K., Monson, T. C., & Perry, D. G. (1998). Social-cognitive influences on change in aggression over time. *Developmental Psychology, 34,* 996–1006.

Ehri, L., Nunes, S., Willows, D., Schuster, B., Yaghoub-Zadeh, Z., & Shanahan, T. (2001). Phonemic awareness instruction helps children learn to read: Evidence from the National Reading Panel's meta-analysis. *Reading Research Quarterly, 36,* 250–287.

Eigsti, I. M., Zayas, V., Mischel, W., Shoda, Y., Ayduk, O., Dadlani, M. B., et al. (2006). Predicting cognitive control from preschool to late adolescence and young adulthood. *Psychological Science, 17,* 478–484.

Eisbach, A. O. (2004). Children's developing awareness of diversity in people's trains of thought. *Child Development, 75,* 1694–1707.

Eisenberg, N. (2000). Emotion, regulation, and moral development. *Annual Review of Psychology, 51,* 665–697.

Eisenberg, N., & Fabes, R. A. (1998). Prosocial development. In W. Damon (Ed.), *Handbook of child psychology* (Vol. 3, pp. 701–778). New York, NY: Wiley.

Eisenberg, N., & Morris, A. S. (2002). Children's emotion-related regulation. *Advances in Child Development & Behavior, 30,* 189–229.

Eisenberg, N., & Shell, R. (1986). Prosocial moral judgment and behavior in children: The mediating role of cost. *Personality & Social Psychology Bulletin, 12,* 426–433.

Eisenberg, N., Cumberland, A., Spinrad, T. L., Fabes, R. A., Shepard, S. A., Reiser, M., et al. (2001). The relations of regulation and emotionality to children's externalizing and internalizing problem behavior. *Child Development, 72,* 1112–1134.

Eisenberg, N., Fabes, R. A., & Spinrad, T. (2006). Prosocial development. In W. Damon & R. M. Lerner (Eds.), *Handbook of child psychology, Vol. 3* (6th ed.). New York, NY: Wiley.

Eisenberg, N., Hofer, C., Spinrad, T., Gershoff, E., Valiente, C., Losoya, S. L., et al. (2008). Understanding parent-adolescent conflict discussions: Concurrent and across-time prediction from youths' dispositions and parenting. *Monographs of the Society for Research in Child Development, 73,* Serial No. 290.

Eisenberg, N., Michalik, N., Spinrad, T. L., Hofer, C., Kupfer, A., Valiente, C., et al. (2007). The relations of effortful control and impulsivity to children's symptoms: A longitudinal study. *Cognitive Development, 22,* 544–567.

Eisenberg, N., Sadovsky, A., Spinrad, T. L., Fabes, R. A., Losoya, S. H., Valienta, C., et al. (2005). The relations of problem behavior status to children's negative emotionality, effortful control, and impulsivity: Concurrent relations and predictions of change. *Developmental Psychology, 41,* 193–211.

Eisenberg, N., Shepard, S. A., Fabes, R. A., Murphy, B. C., & Guthrie, I. K. (1998). Shyness and children's emotionality, regulation, and coping: Contemporaneous, longitudinal, and across-context relations. *Child Development, 69,* 767–790.

Eisenberg, N., Zhou, Q., & Koller, S. (2001). Brazilian adolescents' prosocial moral judgment and behavior: Relations to sympathy, perspective taking, gender-role orientation, and demographic characteristics. *Child Development, 72,* 518–534.

Eizenman, D. R., & Bertenthal, B. I. (1998). Infants' perception of object unity in translating and rotating displays. *Developmental Psychology, 34,* 426–434.

El Nokali, N. E., Bachman, H. J., & Votruba-Drzal, E. (2010). Parent involvement and children's academic and social development in elementary school. *Child Development, 81,* 988–1005.

El-Sheikh, M., Kelly, R. J., Buckhalt, J. A., & Hinnant, J. B. (2010). Children's sleep and adjustment over time: The role of socioeconomic context. *Child Development, 81,* 870–883.

Elbert, T., Pantev, C., Weinbruch, C., Rockstroh, B., & Taub, E. (1995). Increased cortical representation of the fingers of the left hand in strings players. *Science, 270,* 305–307.

Elkind, D. (1978). *The child's reality: Three developmental themes.* Hillsdale, NJ: Erlbaum.

Elkind, D., & Bowen, R. (1979). Imaginary audience behavior in children and adolescents. *Developmental Psychology, 15,* 38–44.

Ellis, B. J. (2004). Timing of pubertal maturation in girls: An integrated life history approach. *Psychological Bulletin, 130,* 920–958.

Ellis, B. J., & Essex, M. J. (2007). Family environments, adrenarche, and sexual maturation: A longitudinal test of a life history model. *Child Development, 78,* 1799–1817.

Ellis, B. J., & Garber, J. (2000). Psychosocial antecedents of variation in girls' pubertal timing: Maternal depression, stepfather presence, and marital family stress. *Child Development, 71,* 485–501.

Ellis, B. J., Bates, J. E., Dodge, K. A., Fergusson, D. M., Horwood, L. J., Pettit, G. S., et al. (2003). Does father absence place daughters at special risk for early sexual activity and teenage pregnancy? *Child Development, 74,* 801–821.

Ellis, S., & Siegler, R. S. (1997). Planning and strategy choice, or why don't children plan when they should? In S. L. Friedman & E. K. Scholnick (Eds.), *The developmental psychology of planning: Why, how, and when do we plan?* (pp. 183–208). Hillsdale, NJ: Erlbaum.

Ellis, W. E., & Zarbatany, L. (2007). Explaining friendship formation and friendship stability—the role of children's and friends' aggression and victimization. *Merrill-Palmer Quarterly, 53,* 79–104.

Ellis, W. K., & Rusch, F. R. (1991). Supported employment: Current practices and future directions. In J. L. Matson & J. A. Mulick (Eds.), *Handbook of mental retardation* (2nd ed.). New York, NY: Pergamon.

Else-Quest, N. M., Hyde, J. S., & Linn, M. C. (2010). Cross-national patterns of gender differences in mathematics: A meta-analysis. *Psychological Bulletin, 136,* 103–127.

Else-Quest, N. M., Hyde, J. S., Goldsmith, H., & Van Hulle, C. A. (2006). Gender differences in temperament: A meta-analysis. *Psychological Bulletin, 132,* 33–72.

Engel, S. M., Berkowitz, G. S., Wolff, M. S., & Yehuda, R. (2005). Psychological trauma associated with the World Trade Center attacks and its effect on pregnancy outcome. *Paediatric & Perinatal Epidemiology, 19,* 334–341.

Engel, S. M., Zhu, C., Berkowitz, G. S., Calafat, A. M., Silva, M. J., Miodovnik, A. et al. (2009). Prenatal phthalate exposure and performance on the Neonatal Behavioral Assessment Scale in a multiethnic birth cohort. *Neurotoxicology, 30,* 522–528.

Engle, P., & Huffman, S. L. (2010). Growing children's bodies and minds: Maximizing child nutrition and development. *Food & Nutrition Bulletin, 31,* S186–S197.

Ennemoser, M., & Schneider, W. (2007). Relations of television viewing and reading: Findings from a 4-year longitudinal study. *Journal of Educational Psychology, 99,* 349–368.

Ensor, R., & Hughes, C. (2008). Content or connectedness? Early family talk and theory of mind in the toddler and preschool years. *Child Development, 79,* 201–216.

Epstein, L. H., & Cluss, P. A. (1986). Behavioral genetics of childhood obesity. *Behavior Therapy, 17,* 324–334.

Epstein, L. H., Leddy, J. J., Temple, J. L., & Faith, M. S. (2007). Food reinforcement and eating: A multilevel analysis. *Psychological Bulletin, 133,* 884–906.

Erel, O., & Burman, B. (1995). Interrelatedness of marital relations and parent–child relations: A meta-analytic review. *Psychological Bulletin, 118,* 108–132.

Erel, O., Margolin, G., & John, R. S. (1998). Observed sibling interaction: Links with the marital and mother–child relationship. *Developmental Psychology, 34,* 288–298.

Erikson, E. H. (1968). *Identity: Youth and crisis.* New York, NY: Norton.

Eskritt, M., & Lee, K. (2002). Remember when you last saw that card?: Children's production of external symbols as a memory aid. *Developmental Psychology, 38,* 254–266.

Eskritt, M., & McLeod, K. (2008). Children's note taking as a mnemonic tool. *Journal of Experimental Child Psychology, 101,* 52–74.

Espy, K. A., Fang, H., Johnson, C., Stopp, C., Wiebe, S. A., & Respass, J. (2011). Prenatal tobacco exposure: Developmental outcomes in the neonatal period. *Developmental Psychology, 47,* 153–169.

Evans, G. W., Gonnella, C., Marcynyszyn, L. A., Gentile, L., & Salpekar, N. (2005). The role of chaos in poverty and children's socioemotional adjustment. *Psychological Science, 16,* 560–565.

Evans, M., Platt, L., & De La Cruz, F. (Eds.). (2001). *Fetal therapy.* New York, NY: Parthenon.

Eyer, D. E. (1992). *Mother–infant bonding: A scientific fiction.* New Haven, CT: Yale University Press.

Fabes, R. A., Eisenberg, N., Jones, S., Smith, M., Guthrie, I., Poulin, R., et al. (1999). Regulation, emotionality, and preschoolers' socially competent peer interactions. *Child Development, 70,* 432–442.

Fabes, R. A., Eisenberg, N., Smith, M. C., & Murphy, B. C. (1996). Getting angry at peers: Associations with liking of the provocateur. *Child Development, 67,* 942–956.

Fabricius, W. V., & Luecken, L. J. (2007). Postdivorce living arrangements, parent conflict, and long-term physical health correlates for children of divorce. *Journal of Family Psychology, 21,* 195–205.

Fagan, J. F., Holland, C. R., & Wheeler, K. (2007). The prediction, from infancy, of adult IQ and achievement. *Intelligence, 35,* 225–231.

Fagot, B. I. (1985). Changes in thinking about early sex role development. *Developmental Review, 5,* 83–98.

Faith, M. S., Fontaine, K. R., Baskin, M. L., & Allison, D. B. (2007). Toward the reduction of population obesity: Macrolevel environmental approaches to the problems of food, eating, and obesity. *Psychological Bulletin, 133,* 205–226.

Falbo, T., & Polit, E. F. (1986). Quantitative review of the only child literature: Research evidence and theory development. *Psychological Bulletin, 100,* 176–186.

Falbo, T., Poston, D. L., Triscari, R. S., & Zhang, X. (1997). Self-enhancing illusions among Chinese schoolchildren. *Journal of Cross-Cultural Psychology, 28,* 172–191.

Falk, D., & Bornstein, M. H. (2005). Infant reflexes. In C. B. Fisher & R. M. Lerner (Eds.), *Encyclopedia of applied developmental science* (Vol. 1, pp. 581–582). Thousand Oaks, CA: Sage.

Farrar, M. J., & Boyer-Pennington, M. (1999). Remembering specific episodes of a scripted event. *Journal of Experimental Child Psychology, 73,* 266–288.

Farver, J. M., & Shin, Y. L. (1997). Social pretend play in Korean- and Anglo-American preschoolers. *Child Development, 68,* 544–556.

Farver, J. M., Lonigan, C. J., & Eppe, S. (2009). Effective early literacy skill development for young Spanish-speaking English language learners: An experimental study of two methods. *Child Development, 80,* 703–719.

Fasig, L. (2002). Calling all researchers. *SRCD Developments, 45,* 3–5.

Fasig, L. G. (2000). Toddlers' understanding of ownership: Implications for self-concept development. *Social Development, 9,* 370–382.

Fauth, R. C., Roth, J. L., & Brooks-Gunn, J. (2007). Does the neighborhood context alter the link between youth's after-school time activities and developmental outcomes? A multilevel analysis. *Developmental Psychology, 43,* 760–777.

Fearon, R. P., Bakermans-Kranenburg, M. J., van IJzendoorn, M. H., Lapsley, A., & Roisman, G. I. (2010). The significance of insecure attachment and disorganization in the development of children's externalizing behavior: A meta-analytic study. *Child Development, 81,* 435–456.

Feddes, A. R., Noack, P., & Rutland, A. (2009). Direct and extended friendship effects on minority and majority children's interethnic attitudes: A longitudinal study. *Child Development, 80,* 377–390.

Federal Interagency Forum on Child and Family Statistics. (2007). *America's children: Key national indicators of well-being, 2007.* Washington, DC: U.S. Government Printing Office.

Feigenson, L., Carey, S., & Hauser, M. (2002). The representations underlying infants' choice of more: Object files versus analog magnitudes. *Psychological Science, 13,* 150–156.

Feinberg, M. E., McHale, S. M., Crouter, A. C., & Cumsille, P. (2003). Sibling differentiation: Sibling and parental relationships trajectories in adolescence. *Child Development, 74,* 1261–1274.

Feldhusen, J. F. (1996). Motivating academically able youth with enriched and accelerated learning experiments. In C. P. Benbow & D. J. Lubinski (Eds.), *Intellectual talent: Psychometric and social issues.* Baltimore, MD: Johns Hopkins Press.

Feldman, H. M., Dollaghan, C. A., Campbell, T. F., Kurs-Lasky, M., Janosky, J. E., & Paradise, J. L. (2000). Measurement properties of the MacArthur Communicative Development Inventories at one and two years. *Child Development, 71,* 310–322.

Feldman, R., & Klein, P. S. (2003). Toddler's self-regulated compliance to mothers, caregivers, and fathers: Implications for theories of socialization. *Developmental Psychology, 39,* 680–692.

Feldman, R., Masalha, S., & Derdikman-Eiron, R. (2010). Conflict resolution in the parent-child, martial, and peer context and children's aggression in the peer group: A process-oriented cultural perspective. *Developmental Psychology, 46,* 310–325.

Feldman, S. S., & Wentzel, K. R. (1990). The relationships between parental styles, sons' self-restraint, and peer relations in early adolescence. *Journal of Early Adolescence, 10,* 439–454.

Feng, X., Keenan, K., Hipwell, A. E., Henneberger, A. K., Rischall, M. S., Butch, J. et al. (2009). Longitudinal associations between emotion regulation and depression in preadolescent girls: Moderation by the caregiving environment. *Developmental Psychology, 45,* 798–808.

Fennell, C. T., Byers-Heinlein, K., & Werker, J. F. (2007). Using speech sounds to guide word learning: The case of bilingual infants. *Child Development, 78,* 1510–1525.

Fenson, L., Dale, P. S., Reznick, J. S., Bates, E., et al. (1994). Variability in early communicative development. *Monographs of the Society for Research in Child Development, 59* (Whole No. 173).

Fergusson, D. M., & Woodward, L. J. (2000). Teenage pregnancy and female educational underachievement: A prospective study of a New Zealand birth cohort. *Journal of Marriage & the Family, 62,* 147–161.

Fernyhough, C. (2010). Inner speech. In H. Pashler (Ed.), *Encyclopaedia of the mind.* Thousand Oaks, CA: Sage.

Ferreol-Barbey, M., Piolat, A., & Roussey, J. (2000). Text recomposition by eleven-year-old children: Effects of text length, level of reading comprehension, and mastery of prototypical schema. *Archives de Psychologie, 68,* 213–232.

Field, T. (2010). Postpartum depression effects on early interactions, parenting, and safety practices: A review. *Infant Behavior & Development, 33,* 1–6.

Field, T. M. (1990). *Infancy.* Cambridge, MA: Harvard University Press.

Field, T. M., & Widmayer, S. M. (1982). Motherhood. In B. J. Wolman (Ed.), *Handbook of developmental psychology.* Englewood Cliffs, NJ: Prentice Hall.

Field, T., & Diego, M. (2010). Preterm infant massage therapy research: A review. *Infant Behavior & Development, 33,* 115–124.

Finley, G. E. (1999). Children of adoptive families. In W. K. Silverman & T. H. Ollendick (Eds.), *Developmental issues in the clinical treatment of children* (pp. 358–370). Boston, MA: Allyn & Bacon.

Fischer, K. W., & Immordino-Yang, M. H. (2008). The fundamental importance of the brain and learning for education. In *The Jossey-Bass reader on the brain and learning.* San Francisco, CA: Jossey-Bass.

Fisher, C. (1996). Structural limits on verb mapping: The role of analogy in children's interpretations of sentences. *Cognitive Psychology, 31,* 41–81.

FitzGerald, D. P., & White, K. J. (2003). Linking children's social worlds: Perspective-taking in parent-child and peer contexts. *Social Behavior & Personality, 31,* 509–522.

Fitzgerald, J. (1987). Research on revision in writing. *Review of Educational Research, 57,* 481–506.

Fivush, R., Brotman, M. A., Buckner, J. P., & Goodman, S. H. (2000). Gender differences in parent-child emotion narratives. *Sex Roles, 42,* 233–253.

Fivush, R., Reese, E., & Haden, C. A. (2006). Elaborating on elaborations: Role of maternal reminiscing style in cognitive and socioemotional development. *Child Development, 77,* 1568–1588.

Flavell, J. H. (1985). *Cognitive development* (2nd ed.). Englewood Cliffs, NJ: Prentice Hall.

Flavell, J. H. (1996). Piaget's legacy. *Psychological Science, 7,* 200–203.

Flavell, J. H. (1999). Cognitive development: Children's knowledge about the mind. *Annual Review of Psychology, 50,* 21–45.

Flavell, J. H. (2000). Development of children's knowledge about the mental world. *International Journal of Behavioral Development, 24,* 15–23.

Flavell, J. H., Flavell, E. R., & Green, F. L. (2001). Development of children's understanding of connections between thinking and feeling. *Psychological Science, 12,* 430–432.

Flom, R., & Bahrick, L. E. (2007). The development of infant discrimination of affect in multimodal and unimodal stimulation: The role of intersensory redundancy. *Developmental Psychology, 43,* 238–252.

Flores, E., Cicchetti, D., & Rogosch, F. A. (2005). Predictors of resilience in maltreated and nonmaltreated Latino children. *Developmental Psychology, 41,* 338–351.

Flynn, J. R. (1999). Searching for justice: The discovery of IQ gains over time. *American Psychologist, 54,* 5–20.

Flynn, J. R., & Weiss, L. G. (2007). American IQ gains from 1932 to 2002: The WISC subtests and educational progress. *International Journal of Testing, 7,* 209–224.

Fontaine, R. G. & Dodge, K. A. (2006). Real-time decision making and aggressive behavior in youth: A heuristic model of response evaluation and decision (RED). *Aggressive Behavior, 32,* 604–624.

Fontaine, R. G., Yang, C., Dodge, K. A., Pettit, G. S., & Bates, J. E. (2009). Development of response evaluation and decision (RED) and antisocial behavior in childhood and adolescence. *Developmental Psychology, 45,* 447–459.

Fonzi, A., Schneider, B. H., Tani, F., & Tomada, G. (1997). Predicting children's friendship status from their dynamic interaction in structured situations of potential conflict. *Child Development, 68,* 496–506.

Foreyt, J. P., & Goodrick, G. K. (1995). Obesity. In R. T. Ammerman & M. Hersen (Eds.), *Handbook of child behavior therapy in psychiatric setting* (pp. 409–425). New York, NY: Wiley.

Foster, E. M., & Watkins, S. (2010). The value of reanalysis: TV viewing and attention problems. *Child Development, 81,* 368–375.

Foster, S. H. (1986). Learning discourse topic management in the preschool years. *Journal of Child Language, 13,* 231–250.

Fox, S. E., Levitt, P., & Nelson, C. A. (2010). How the timing and quality of early experiences influence the development of brain architecture. *Child Development, 81,* 28–40.

Frank, D. A., Augustyn, M., Knight, W. G., Pell, T., & Zuckerman, B. (2001). Growth, development, and behavior in early childhood following prenatal cocaine

exposure: A systematic review. *Journal of the American Medical Association, 285,* 1613–1625.

Franklin, A., Pilling, M., & Davies, I. (2005). The nature of infant color categorization: Evidence from eye movements on a target detection task. *Journal of Experimental Child Psychology, 91,* 227–248.

Franquart-Declercq, C., & Gineste, M. (2001). Metaphor comprehension in children. *Annee Psychologique, 101,* 723–752.

Fredricks, J. A., & Eccles, J. S. (2006). Is extracurricular participation associated with beneficial outcomes? Concurrent and longitudinal relations. *Developmental Psychology, 42,* 698–713.

Fredriksen, K., Rhodes, J., Reddy, R., & Way, N. (2004). Sleepless in Chicago: Tracking the effects of adolescent sleep loss during the middle school years. *Child Development, 75,* 84–95.

French, S. E., Seidman, E., Allen, L., & Aber, J. (2006). The development of ethnic identity during adolescence. *Developmental Psychology, 42,* 1–10.

Fried, A. (2005). Depression in adolescence. In C. B. Fisher & R. M. Lerner (Eds.), *Encyclopedia of applied developmental science* (Vol. 1, pp. 332–334). Thousand Oaks, CA: Sage.

Friend, A., DeFries, J., & Olson, R. (2008). Parental education moderates genetic and environmental influences on reading disability. *Psychological Science, 19,* 1123–1129.

Frye, D. (1993). Causes and precursors of children's theories of mind. In D. F. Hay & A. Angold (Eds.), *Precursors and causes in development and psychopathology.* Chichester, UK: Wiley.

Fu, G., Xu, F., Cameron, C. A., Heyman, G., & Lee, K. (2007). Cross-cultural differences in children's choices, categorizations, and evaluations of truths and lies. *Developmental Psychology, 43,* 278–293.

Fuld, G. L., Mulligan, D. A., Altmann, T. R., Brown, A., Christakis, D. A., Clarke-Pearson, K., et al. (2009). Policy statement—media violence. *Pediatrics, 124,* 1495–1503.

Fuligni, A. J., Kiang, L., Witkow, M. R., & Baldelomar, O. (2008). Stability and change in ethnic labeling among adolescents from Asian and Latin American immigrant families. *Child Development, 79,* 944–956.

Gagliardi, A. (2005). Postpartum depression. In C. B. Fisher & R. M. Lerner (Eds.), *Encyclopedia of applied developmental science* (Vol. 2, pp. 867–870). Thousand Oaks, CA: Sage.

Gagne, J. R., & Saudino, K. J. (2010). Wait for it! A twin study of inhibitory control in early childhood. *Behavior Genetics, 40,* 327–337.

Garcia, M. M., Shaw, D. S., Winslow, E. G., & Yaggi, K. E. (2000). Destructive sibling conflict and the development of conduct problems in young boys. *Developmental Psychology, 36,* 44–53.

Garciaguirre, J. S., Adolph, K. E., & Shrout, P. E. (2007). Baby carriage: Infants walking with loads. *Child Development, 78,* 664–680.

Gardner, H. (1983). *Frames of mind: The theory of multiple intelligences.* New York, NY: Basic Books.

Gardner, H. (1993). *Multiple intelligences: The theory in practice.* New York, NY: Basic Books.

Gardner, H. (1995). Reflections on multiple intelligences: Myths and messages. *Phi Delta Kappan, 77,* 200–203, 206–209.

Gardner, H. (1999). *Intelligence reframed: Multiple intelligences for the 21st century.* New York, NY: Basic Books.

Gardner, H. (2002). *MI millennium: Multiple intelligences for the new millennium* [video recording]. Los Angeles, CA: Into the Classroom Media.

Gardner, H. (2006). *Multiple intelligences: New horizons.* New York, NY: Basic Books.

Gardner, M., Roth, J., & Brooks-Gunn, J. (2009). Sports participation and juvenile delinquency: The role of the peer context among adolescent boys and girls with varied histories of problem behavior. *Developmental Psychology, 45,* 341–353.

Gardner, W., & Rogoff, B. (1990). Children's deliberateness of planning according to task circumstances. *Developmental Psychology, 26*, 480–487.

Gartstein, M. A., Bridgett, D., Rothbart, M. K., Robertson, C., Iddins, E., Ramsay, K. et al. (2010). A latent growth examination of fear development in infancy: Contributions of maternal depression and the risk for toddler anxiety. *Developmental Psychology, 46*, 651–668.

Gartstein, M. A., Knyazev, G. G., & Slobodskaya, H. R. (2005). Cross-cultural differences in the structure of infant temperament: United States of America and Russia. *Infant Behavior and Development, 28*, 54–61.

Garvey, C., & Beringer, G. (1981). Timing and turn taking in children's conversations. *Discourse Processes, 4*, 27–59.

Gash, H., & Morgan, M. (1993). School-based modifications of children's gender-related beliefs. *Journal of Applied Developmental Psychology, 14*, 277–287.

Gass, K., Jenkins, J., & Dunn, J. (2007). Are sibling relationships protective? A longitudinal study. *Journal of Child Psychology & Psychiatry, 48*, 167–175.

Gathercole, S. E, Willis, C. S., Emslie, H., & Baddeley, A. D. (1992). Phonological memory and vocabulary development during the early school years: A longitudinal study. *Developmental Psychology, 28*, 887–898.

Gaulin, S. J. C., & McBurney, D. H. (2001). *Psychology: An evolutionary approach.* Upper Saddle River, NJ: Prentice-Hall.

Gauvain, M. (1998). Cognitive development in social and cultural context. *Current Directions in Psychological Science, 7*, 188–192.

Gauvain, M. (2001). *The social context of cognitive development.* New York, NY: Guilford.

Gauvain, M., & Munroe, R. L. (2009). Contributions of social modernity to cognitive development: A comparison of four cultures. *Child Development, 80*, 1628–1642.

Ge, X., Brody, G. H., Conger, R. D., Simons, R. L., & Murphy, V. M. (2002). Contextual amplification of pubertal transition effects on deviant peer affiliation and externalizing behavior among African American children. *Developmental Psychology, 38*, 45–54.

Ge, X., Conger, R. D., & Elder, G. H. (2001). Pubertal transition, stressful life events, and the emergency of gender differences in adolescent depressive symptoms. *Developmental Psychology, 37*, 404–417.

Ge, X., Kim, I. J., Brody, G. H., Conger, R. D., Simons, R. L., Gibbons, F. X., et al. (2003). It's about timing and change: Pubertal transition effects on symptoms of major depression among African American youths. *Developmental Psychology, 39*, 430–439.

Geary, D. C. (2002). Sexual selection and human life history. In R. V. Kail (Ed.), *Advances in child development and behavior* (Vol. 30, pp. 41–102). San Diego, CA: Academic Press.

Geary, D. C. (2005). *The origin of mind: Evolution of brain, cognition, and general intelligence.* Washington, DC: American Psychological Association.

Geary, D. C. (2010) Mathematical learning disabilities. In P. Bauer (Ed.), *Advances in Child Development and Behavior* (Vol. 38, pp. 45-77). San Diego CA: Academic Press.

Geary, D. C., Byrd-Craven, J., Hoard, M. K., Vigil, J., & Numtee, C. (2003). Evolution and development of boys' social behavior. *Developmental Review, 23*, 444–470.

Geary, D. C., Hoard, M. K., Byrd-Craven, J., Nugent, L., & Numtee, C. (2007). Cognitive mechanisms underlying achievement deficits in children with mathematical learning disability. *Child Development, 78*, 1343–1359.

Geisel, T. (1960). *Green eggs and ham, by Dr. Seuss.* New York, NY: Beginner.

Gelman, R., & Meck, E. (1986). The notion of principle: The case of counting. In J. Hiebert (Ed.), *Conceptual and procedural knowledge: The case of mathematics.* Hillsdale, NJ: Erlbaum.

Gelman, S. A. (2003). *The essential child.* New York: Oxford.

Gelman, S. A., & Gottfried, G. M. (1996). Children's causal explanations of animate and inanimate motion. *Child Development, 67*, 1970–1987.

Gelman, S. A., & Wellman, H. M. (1991). Insides and essences: Early understandings of the non-obvious. *Cognition, 38*, 213–244.

Gelman, S. A., Coley, J. D., Rosengren, K. S., Hartman, E., & Pappas, A. (1998). Beyond labeling: The role of maternal input in the acquisition of richly structured categories. *Monographs of the Society for Research in Child Development, 63*, Serial No. 253.

Gelman, S. A., Taylor, M. G., & Nguyen, S. P. (2004). Mother-child conversations about gender. *Monographs of the Society for Research in Child Development, 69* (Serial No. 275).

Gentile, D. (2009). Pathological video-game use among youth ages 8 to 18: A national study. *Psychological Science, 20*, 594–602.

George, C., Kaplan, N., & Main, M. (1985). *The adult attachment interview.* Unpublished manuscript, Department of Psychology, University of California, Berkeley.

George, J. B. F., & Franko, D. L. (2010). Cultural issues in eating pathology and body image among children and adolescents. *Journal of Pediatric Psychology, 35*, 231–242.

Gerken, L. (2006). Decision, decisions: Infant language learning when multiple generalizations are possible. *Cognition, 98*, 1–8.

Gerry, D. W., Faux, A. L., & Trainor, L. J. (2010). Effects of Kindermusik training on infants' rhythmic enculturation. *Developmental Science, 13*, 545–551.

Gershkoff-Stowe, L., & Smith, L. B. (2004). Shape and the first hundred nouns. *Child Development, 75*, 1098–1114.

Gershoff, E. T., & Bitensky, S. H. (2007). The case against corporal punishment of children: Converging evidence from social science research and international human rights law and implications for U.S. public policy. *Psychology, Public Policy, & the Law, 13*, 231–272.

Gershoff, E. T., Grogan-Kaylor, A., Lansford, J. E., Chang, L., Zelli, A., Deater-Deckard, K., et al. (2010). Parent discipline practices in an international sample: Associations with child behavior and moderation by perceived normativeness. *Child Development, 81*, 487–502.

Gertner, Y., Fisher, C., & Eisengart, J. (2006). Learning words and rules: Abstract knowledge of word order in early sentence comprehension. *Psychological Science, 17*, 684–691.

Ghetti, S. (2008). Rejection of false events in childhood: A metamemory account. *Current Directions in Psychological Science, 17*, 16–20.

Gibbs, D. A., Martin, S. L., Kupper, L. L., & Johnson, R. E. (2007). Child maltreatment in enlisted soldiers' families during combat-related deployments. *Journal of the American Medical Association, 298*, 528–535.

Gibbs, J. C., Clark, P. M., Joseph, J. A., Green, J. L., Goodrick, T. S., & Makowski, D. (1986). Relations between moral judgment, moral courage, and field independence. *Child Development, 57*, 185–193.

Gibson, E. J., & Walk, R. D. (1960). The "visual cliff." *Scientific American, 202*, 64–71.

Giles, J. W., & Heyman, G. D. (2005). Reconceptualizing children's suggestibility: Bidirectional and temporal properties. *Child Development, 76*, 40–53.

Gill, S. V., Adolph, K. E., & Vereijken, B. (2009). Change in action: How infants learn to walk down slopes. *Developmental Science, 12*, 888–902.

Gilligan, C. (1982). *In a different voice: Psychological theory and women's development.* Cambridge, MA: Harvard University Press.

Gilligan, C., & Attanucci, J. (1988). Two moral orientations: Gender differences and similarities. *Merrill-Palmer Quarterly, 34*, 223–237.

Ginsburg-Block, M. D., Rohrbeck, C. A., & Fantuzzo, J. W. (2006). A meta-analytic review of social, self-concept, and behavioral outcomes of peer-assisted learning. *Journal of Educational Psychology, 98*, 732–749.

Giordano, G. (2005). *How testing came to dominate American schools: The history of educational assessment.* New York, NY: Peter Lang.

Gleason, T. R., & Hohmann, L. M. (2006). Concepts of real and imaginary friendships in early childhood. *Social Development, 15*, 128–144.

Global Initiative to End All Corporal Punishment of Children. (2011). *States with full prohibition.* Retrieved March 26, 2011, from http://www.endcorporalpunishment.org

Goeke-Morey, M. C., Cummings, E. M., Harold, G. T., & Shelton, K. H. (2003). Categories and continua of destructive and constructive conflict tactics from the perspective of U.S. and Welsh children. *Journal of Family Psychology, 17*, 327–338.

Goldenberg, R. L., & Klerman, L. V. (1995). Adolescent pregnancy—another look. *New England Journal of Medicine, 332*, 1161–1162.

Goldfield, B. A., & Reznick, J. S. (1990). Early lexical acquisition: Rate, content, and the vocabulary spurt. *Journal of Child Language, 17*, 171–184.

Goldin-Meadow, S., Mylander, C., & Franklin, A. (2007). How children make language out of gesture: Morphological structure in gesture systems developed by American and Chinese deaf children. *Cognitive Psychology, 55*, 87–135.

Goldman, L. S., Genel, M., Bezman, R. J., & Slanetz, P. J. (1998). Diagnosis and treatment of attention-deficit/hyperactivity disorder in children and adolescents. *Journal of the American Medical Association, 279*, 1100–1107.

Goldsmith, H. H., Buss, K. A., & Lemery, K. S. (1997). Toddler and childhood temperament: Expanded content, stronger genetic evidence, new evidence for the importance of environment. *Developmental Psychology, 33*, 891–905.

Goldsmith, H. H., Pollak, S. D., & Davidson, R. J. (2008). Developmental neuroscience perspectives on emotion regulation. *Child Development Perspectives, 2*, 132–140.

Goldstein, M. H., & Schwade, J. A. (2008). Social feedback to infants' babbling facilitates rapid phonological learning. *Psychological Science, 19*, 515–523.

Goleman, D. (1995). *Emotional intelligence: Why it can matter more than IQ.* New York, NY: Bantam.

Goleman, D. (1998). *Working with emotional intelligence.* New York, NY: Bantam.

Goleman, D., Boyatzis, R., & McKee, A. (2002). *Primal leadership: Realizing the power of emotional intelligence.* Boston, MA: Harvard University Press.

Golinkoff, R. M. (1993). When is communication a "meeting of minds"? *Journal of Child Language, 20*, 199–207.

Golombok, S., & Tasker, F. (1996). Do parents influence the sexual orientation of their children? Findings from a longitudinal study of lesbian families. *Developmental Psychology, 32*, 3–11.

Golombok, S., MacCallum, F., Murray, C., Lycett, E., & Jadva, V. (2006). Surrogacy families: Parental functioning, parent-child relationships and children's psychological development at age 2. *Journal of Child Psychology & Psychiatry, 47*, 213–222.

Golombok, S., Perry, B., Burston, A., Murray, C., Mooney-Somers, J., Stevens, M., & Golding, J. (2003). Children with lesbian parents: A community study. *Developmental Psychology, 39*, 20–33.

Gonzales, P., Williams, T., Jocelyn, L., Roey, S., Kastberg, D., & Brenwald, S. (2008). *Highlights from TIMSS 2007: Mathematics and science achievement of U.S. fourth- and eighth-grade students in an international context.* Washington, DC: U.S. Department of Education.

Good, T. L., & Brophy, J. E. (1996). *Looking classrooms* (9th ed.). Boston, MA: Allyn & Bacon.

Good, T. L., & Brophy, J. E. (2008). Looking classroom Boston, MA: Pearson/Allyn & Bacon.

Goodnow, J. J. (1992). *Parental belief systems: The psychological consequences for children.* Hillsdale, NJ: Erlbaum.

Goodwyn, S. W., & Acredolo, L. P. (1993). Symbolic gesture versus word: Is there a modality advantage for onset of symbol use? *Child Development, 64,* 688–701.

Goossens, L. (2001). Global versus domain-specific statuses in identity research: A comparison of two self-report measures. *Journal of Adolescence, 24,* 681–699.

Gordon, B. N., Baker-Ward, L., & Ornstein, P. A. (2001). Children's testimony: A review of research on memory for past experiences. *Clinical Child & Family Psychology Review, 4,* 157–181.

Gordon, C. P. (1996). Adolescent decision making: A broadly based theory and its application to the prevention of early pregnancy. *Adolescence, 31,* 561–584.

Gordon, R. A., Chase-Lansdale, P. L., & Brooks-Gunn, J. (2004). Extended households and the life course of young mothers: Understanding the associations using a sample of mothers with premature, low birth weight babies. *Child Development, 75,* 1013–1038.

Gosso, Y., Morais, M. L. S., & Otta, E. (2007). Pretend play of Brazilian children: A window into different cultural worlds. *Journal of Cross-Cultural Psychology, 38,* 539–558.

Gottlieb, L. N., & Mendelson, M. J. (1990). Parental support and firstborn girls' adaptation to the birth of a sibling. *Journal of Applied Developmental Psychology, 11,* 29–48.

Gottman, J. M. (1986). The world of coordinated play: Same- and cross-sex friendships in children. In J. M. Gottman & J. G. Parker (Eds.), *Conversations of friends.* New York, NY: Cambridge University Press.

Gottman, J. M., Katz, L. F., & Hooven, C. (1996). Parental meta-emotion philosophy and the emotional life of families: Theoretical models and preliminary data. *Journal of Family Psychology, 10,* 243–268.

Goubet, N., Clifton, R. K., & Shah, B. (2001). Learning about pain in preterm newborns. *Journal of Developmental & Behavioral Pediatrics, 22,* 418–424.

Gough, P. B., & Tunmer, W. E. (1986). Decoding, reading and reading disability. *Remedial & Special Education, 7,* 6–10.

Governor's Task Force on Children's Justice. (1998). *Forensic interviewing protocol.* Lansing, MI: Author.

Govier, E., & Salisbury, G. (2000). Age-related sex differences in performance on a side-naming spatial task. *Psychology, Evolution, & Gender, 2,* 209–222.

Govindshenoy, M., & Spencer, N. (2007). Abuse of the disabled child: A systematic review of population-based studies. *Child Care, Health, & Development, 33,* 552–558.

Grabe, S., Hyde, J. S., Ward, L. M. (2008). The role of the media in body image concerns among women: A meta-analysis of experimental and correlational studies. *Psychological Bulletin, 134,* 460–476.

Graesser, A. C., Singer, M., & Trabasso, T. (1994). Constructing inferences during narrative text comprehension. *Psychological Review, 101,* 371–395.

Graham, S., & Perin, D. (2007). A meta-analysis of writing instruction for adolescent students. *Journal of Educational Psychology, 99,* 445–476.

Graham, S., Berninger, V. W., Abbott, R. D., Abbott, S. P., & Whitaker, D. (1997). Role of mechanics in composing of elementary school students: A new methodological approach. *Journal of Educational Psychology, 89,* 170–182.

Graham, S., Harris, K. R., & Fink, B. (2000). Is handwriting causally related to learning to write? Treatment of handwriting problems in beginning writers. *Journal of Educational Psychology, 92,* 620–633.

Granie, M. A. (2009). Effects of gender, sex-stereotype conformity, age and internalization on risk-taking among adolescent pedestrians. *Safety Science, 47,* 1277–1283.

Granrud, C. E. (1986). Binocular vision and spatial perception in 4- and 5-month-old infants. *Journal of Experimental Psychology: Human Perception & Performance, 12,* 36–49.

Grantham-McGregor, S., Ani, C., & Gernald, L. (2001). The role of nutrition in intellectual development. In R. J. Sternberg & E. L. Grigorenko (Eds.), *Environmental effects on cognitive abilities* (pp. 119–155). Mahwah, NJ: Erlbaum.

Graves, R., & Landis, T. (1990). Asymmetry in mouth opening during different speech tasks. *International Journal of Psychology, 25,* 179–189.

Gray, S. W., & Klaus, R. A. (1965). An experimental preschool program for culturally deprived children. *Child Development, 36,* 887–898.

Gray-Little, B., & Hafdahl, A. R. (2000). Factors influencing racial comparisons of self-esteem: A quantitative review. *Psychological Bulletin, 126,* 26–54.

Graziano, P. A., Keane, S. P., & Calkins, S. D. (2007). Cardiac vagal regulation and early peer status. *Child Development, 78,* 264–278.

Greenberg, M. T., & Crnic, K. A. (1988). Longitudinal predictors of developmental status and social interaction in premature and full-term infants at age two. *Child Development, 59,* 554–570.

Greenberg, M. T., Lengua, L. J., Coie, J. D., Pinderhughes, E. E. & the Conduct Problems Prevention Research Group. (1999). Predicting developmental outcomes at school entry using a multiple-risk model: Four American communities. *Developmental Psychology, 35,* 403–417.

Greene, J. (2007). The secret joke of Kant's soul. In W. Sinnott-Armstrong (Ed.), *Moral psychology: The neuroscience of morality, emotion, brain disorders, and development* (pp. 35–80). Cambridge, MA: MIT.

Greenfield, P. M. (1998). The cultural evolution of IQ. In U. Neisser (Ed.), *The rising curve: Long-term gains in IQ and related measures* (pp. 81–123). Washington, DC: American Psychological Association.

Greenough, W. T., & Black, J. E. (1992). Induction of brain structure by experience: Substrates for cognitive development. In M. Gunnar & C. Nelson (Eds.), *Minnesota symposia on child psychology: Vol. 24: Developmental behavioral neuroscience* (pp. 155–200). Hillsdale, NJ: Erlbaum.

Gregory, A. M., Light-Häusermann, J. H., Rijsdijk, F., & Eley, T. C. (2009). Behavioral genetic analyses of prosocial behavior in adolescents. *Developmental Science, 12,* 165–174.

Gregory, A. M., Rijsdijk, F., Lau, J. Y. F., Napolitano, M., McGuffin, P., & Eley, T. C. (2007). Genetic and environmental influences on interpersonal cognitions and associations with depressive symptoms in 8-year-old twins. *Journal of Abnormal Psychology, 116,* 762–775.

Grigorenko, E. L., & Sternberg, R. J. (1998). Dynamic testing. *Psychological Bulletin, 124,* 75–111.

Grigorenko, E. L., Jarvin, L., & Sternberg, R. J. (2002). School-based tests of the triarchic theory of intelligence: Three settings, three samples, three syllabi. *Contemporary Educational Psychology, 27,* 167–208.

Grigorenko, E. L., Sternberg, R. J., Jukes, M., Alcock, K., Lambo, J., Ngorosho, D., et al., (2006). Effects of antiparasitic treatment on dynamically and statically tested cognitive skills over time. *Journal of Applied Developmental Psychology, 27,* 499–526.

Groen, G. J., & Resnick, L. B. (1977). Can preschool children invent addition algorithms? *Journal of Educational Psychology, 69,* 645–652.

Grusec, J. E., Goodnow, J. J., & Cohen, L. (1996). Household work and the development of concern for others. *Developmental Psychology, 32,* 999–1007.

Guerra, N. G., & Slaby, R. G. (1990). Cognitive mediators of aggression in adolescent offenders: 2. Intervention. *Developmental Psychology, 26,* 269–277.

Guerra, N. G., Williams, K. R., & Sadek, S. (2011). Understanding bullying and victimization during childhood and adolescence: A mixed methods study. *Child Development, 82,* 295–310.

Guillemin, J. (1993). Cesarean birth: Social and political aspects. In B. K. Rothman (Ed.), *Encyclopedia of childbearing.* Phoenix, AZ: Oryx Press.

Güngör, D., & Bornstein, M. H. (2010). Culture-general and -specific associations of attachment avoidance and anxiety with perceived parental warmth and psychological control among Turk and Belgian adolescents. *Journal of Adolescence, 33,* 593–602.

Gunnar, M. R., Bruce, J., & Grotevant, H. D. (2000). International adoption of institutionally reared children: Research and policy. *Development & Psychopathology, 12,* 677–693.

Gurucharri, C., & Selman, R. L. (1982). The development of interpersonal understanding during childhood, preadolescence, and adolescence: A longitudinal follow-up study. *Child Development, 53,* 924–927.

Guttentag, R., & Ferrell, J. (2004). Reality compared with its alternatives: Age differences in judgments of regret and relief. *Developmental Psychology, 40,* 765–775.

Haeffel, G. J., Getchell, M., Koposov, R. A., Yrigollen, C. M., DeYoung, C. G., af Klinteberg, B., et al. (2008). Associations between polymorphisms in the dopamine transporter gene and depression: Evidence for a gene-environment interaction in a sample of juvenile detainees. *Psychological Science, 19,* 62–69.

Halford, G. S. (1993). *Children's understanding: The development of mental models.* Hillsdale, NJ: Erlbaum.

Halford, G. S., & Andrews, G. (2011). Information-processing models of cognitive development. In U. Goswami (Ed.), *The Wiley-Blackwell handbook of childhood cognitive development* (2nd ed., pp. 697–722). West Sussex, UK: Wiley-Blackwell.

Halgunseth, L. C., Ispa, J. M., & Rudy, D. (2006). Parental control in Latino families: An integrated review of the literature. *Child Development, 77,* 1282–1297.

Hall, D. G., Lee, S. C., & Belanger, J. (2001). Young children's use of syntactic cues to learn proper names and count nouns. *Developmental Psychology, 37,* 298–307.

Hall, G. S. (1904). *Adolescence, 1.* New York, NY: Appleton.

Hall, J. A., & Halberstadt, A. G. (1981). Sex roles and nonverbal communication skills. *Sex Roles, 7,* 273–287.

Hallinan, M. T., & Teixeira, R. A. (1987). Opportunities and constraints: Black-white differences in the formation of interracial friendships. *Child Development, 58,* 1358–1371.

Halpern, D. F., Benbow, C. P., Geary, D. C., Gur, R. C., Hyde, J. S., & Gernsbacher, M. A. (2007). The science of sex differences in science and mathematics. *Psychological Science in the Public Interest, 8,* 1–51.

Halpern, L. F., MacLean, W. E., & Baumeister, A. A. (1995). Infant sleep-wake characteristics: Relation to neurological status and the prediction of developmental outcome. *Developmental Review, 15,* 255–291.

Halpern-Meekin, S., & Tach, L. (2008). Heterogeneity in two-parent families and adolescent well-being. *Journal of Marriage & Family, 70,* 435–451.

Hamamura, T., Heine, S. J., & Paulhus, D. L. (2008). Cultural differences in response styles: The role of dialectical thinking. *Personality and Individual Differences, 44,* 932–942.

Hamilton, B. E., Martin, J. A., & Ventura, S. J. (2010). Births: Preliminary data for 2008. *National Vital Statistics Reports,* Vol. 58. Hyattsville, MD: National Center for Health Statistics.

Hamm, J. V. (2000). Do birds of a feather flock together? The variable bases for African American, Asian American, and European American adolescents' selection of similar friends. *Developmental Psychology, 36,* 209–219.

Hammen, C., & Rudolph, K. D. (2003). Childhood mood disorders. In E. J. Mash & R. A. Barkley (Eds.), *Child psychopathology* (2nd ed., pp. 233–278). New York, NY: Guilford.

Hane, A. A., & Fox, N. W. (2006). Ordinary variations in maternal caregiving influence human infants' stress reactivity. *Psychological Science, 17,* 550–556.

Hankin, B. L., & Abramson, L. Y. (2001). Development of gender differences in depression: An elaborated cognitive vulnerability-transactional stress theory. *Psychological Bulletin, 127,* 773–796.

Hankin, B. L., Mermelstein, R., & Roesch, L. (2007). Sex differences in adolescent depression: Stress exposure and reactivity models. *Child Development, 78,* 279–295.

Hannon, E. E., & Trehub, S. E. (2005). Metrical categories in infancy and adulthood. *Psychological Science, 16,* 48–55.

Harkness, K. L., Lumley, M. N., & Truss, A. E. (2008). Stress generation in adolescent depression: The moderating role of child abuse and neglect. *Journal of Abnormal Child Psychology, 36,* 421–432.

Harley, K., & Reese, E. (1999). Origins of autobiographical memory. *Developmental Psychology, 35,* 1338–1348.

Harlow, H. F., & Harlow, M. K. (1965). The affectional systems. In A. M. Schier, H. F. Harlow, & F. Stollnitz (Eds.), *Behavior of nonhuman primates* (Vol. 2.). New York, NY: Academic Press.

Harre, N. (2007). Community service or activism as an identity project for youth. *Journal of Community Psychology, 35,* 711–724.

Harris, B., Lovett, L., Newcombe, R. G., Read, G. F., Walker, R., & Riad-Fahmy, D. (1994). Maternity blues and major endocrine changes: Cardiff puerperal mood and hormone study II. *British Medical Journal, 308,* 949–953.

Harris, K. R., Graham, S., Mason, L., & Friedlander, B. (2008). *Powerful writing strategies for all students.* Baltimore, MD: Brookes.

Harris, P. L., Brown, E., Marriot, C., Whithall, S., & Harmer, S. (1991). Monsters, ghosts, and witches: Testing the limits of the fantasy-reality distinction in young children. *British Journal of Developmental Psychology, 9,* 105–123.

Harrist, A. W., Zaia, A. F., Bates, J. E., Dodge, K. A., & Pettit, G. S. (1997). Subtypes of social withdrawal in early childhood: Sociometric status and social-cognitive differences across four years. *Child Development, 68,* 278–294.

Harter, S. (1990). Self and identity development. In S. S. Feldman & G. R. Elliot (Eds.), *At the threshold: The developing adolescent.* Cambridge, MA: Harvard University Press.

Harter, S. (2005). Self-concepts and self-esteem, children and adolescents. In C. B. Fisher & R. M. Lerner (Eds.), *Encyclopedia of applied developmental science* (Vol. 2, pp. 972–977). Thousand Oaks, CA: Sage.

Harter, S. (2006). The self. In W. Damon & R. M. Lerner (Eds.), *Handbook of child psychology* (6th ed., Vol. 3). New York, NY: Wiley.

Harter, S., Waters, P., & Whitesell, N. R. (1998). Relational self-worth: Differences in perceived worth as a person across interpersonal contexts among adolescents. *Child Development, 69,* 756–766.

Harter, S., Whitesell, N. R., & Kowalski, P. S. (1992). Individual differences in the effects of educational transitions on young adolescents' perceptions of competence and motivational orientation. *American Educational Research Journal, 29,* 777–807.

Hartup, W. W. (1983). Peer relations. In P. H. Mussen (Ed.), *Handbook of child psychology* (Vol. 4). New York, NY: Wiley.

Hartup, W. W. (1992). Friendships and their developmental significance. In H. McGurk (Ed.), *Contemporary issues in childhood social development.* London: Routledge.

Hartup, W. W., & Stevens, N. (1999). Friendships and adaptation across the life span. *Current Directions in Psychological Science, 8,* 76–79.

Haslam, C., & Lawrence, W. (2004). Health-related behavior and beliefs of pregnant smokers. *Health Psychology, 23,* 486–491.

Hastings, P. D., & Rubin, K. H. (1999). Predicting mothers' beliefs about preschool-aged children's social behavior: Evidence for maternal attitudes moderating child effects. *Child Development, 70,* 722–741.

Hastings, P. D., Zahn-Waxler, C., & McShane, K. (2006). We are, by nature, moral creatures: Biological bases of concern for others. In M. Killen & J. G. Smetana (2006), *Handbook of moral development* (pp. 483–516). Mahwah, NJ: Erlbaum.

Hatania, R., & Smith, L. B. (2010). Selective attention and attention switching: Toward a unified developmental approach. *Developmental Science, 13,* 622–635.

Haviland, J. M., & Lelwica, M. (1987). The induced affect response: 10-week-old infants' responses to three emotion expression. *Developmental Psychology, 23,* 97–104.

Hawley, P. H. (1999). The ontogenesis of social dominance: A strategy-based evolutionary perspective. *Developmental Review, 19,* 7–132.

Hay, D., Pawlby, S. Waters, C. S., Perra, O., & Sharp, D. (2010). Mothers' antenatal depression and their children's antisocial outcomes. *Child Development, 81,* 149–165.

Hayes, D. P. (1988). Speaking and writing: Distinct patterns of word choice. *Journal of Memory & Language, 27,* 572–585.

Hayes, T. C., & Lee, M. R. (2005). The Southern culture of honor and violent attitudes. *Sociological Spectrum, 25,* 593–617.

Hazell, P. L. (2009). 8-year follow-up of the MTA sample. *Journal of the American Academy of Child & Adolescent Psychiatry, 48,* 461–462.

Hellekson, K. L. (2001). NIH consensus statement on phenylketonuria. *American Family Physician, 63,* 1430–1432.

Hellerstedt, W. L., Madsen, N. J., Gunnar, M. R., Grotevant, H. D., Lee, R. M., & Johnson, D. E. (2008). The International Adoption Project: Population-based surveillance of Minnesota parents who adopted children internationally. *Maternal & Child Health Journal, 12,* 162–171.

Hemker, L., Granrud, C. E., Yonas, A., & Kavsek, M. (2010). Infant perception of surface texture and relative height as distance information: A preferential-reaching study. *Infancy, 15,* 6–27.

Henderson, C. E., Hayslip, B., Sanders, L. M., & Louden, L. (2009). Grandmother-grandchild relationship quality predicts psychological adjustment among youth from divorced families. *Journal of Family Issues, 30,* 1245–1264.

Henderson, H. A., & Wachs, T. D. (2007). Temperament theory and the study of cognition-emotion interactions across development. *Developmental Review, 27,* 396–427.

Henderson, N. D. (2010). Predicting long-term firefighter performance from cognitive and physical ability measures. *Personnel Psychology, 63,* 999–1039.

Henry, D. B., Schoeny, M. E., Deptula, D. P., & Slavick, J. T. (2007). Peer selection and socialization effects on adolescent intercourse without a condom and attitudes about the costs of sex. *Child Development, 78,* 825–838.

Herman, M. (2004). Forced to choose: Some determinants of racial identification in multiracial adolescents. *Child Development, 75,* 730–748.

Hernandez, D. J. (2004). Demographic change and the life circumstances of families. *Future of Children, 14,* 17–47.

Herrnstein, R. J., & Murray, C. (1994). *The bell curve: Intelligence and class structure in American life.* New York, NY: Free Press.

Hertenstein, M. J., & Campos, J. J. (2004). The retention effects of an adult's emotional displays on infant behavior. *Child Development, 75,* 595–613.

Hespos, S. J., Ferry, A. L., & Rips, L. J. (2009). Five-month-old infants have different expectations for solids and liquids. *Psychological Science, 20,* 603–611.

Hess, U., & Kirouac, G. (2000). Emotion expression in groups. In M. Lewis & J. Haviland-Jones (Eds.), *Handbook of emotions* (2nd ed., pp. 368–381). New York, NY: Guilford.

Hetherington, E. M., & Kelly, J. (2002). *For better or for worse: Divorce reconsidered.* New York, NY: W. W. Norton.

Heyman, G. D. (2009). Children's reasoning about traits. In P. Bauer (Ed.), *Advances in child development and behavior* (Vol. 37, pp. 105–143). London, UK: Elsevier.

Heyman, G. D., & Legare, C. H. (2004). Children's beliefs about gender differences in the academic and social domains. *Sex Roles, 50,* 227–239.

Hill, J. L., Brooks-Gunn, J., & Waldfogel, J. (2003). Sustained effects of high participation in an early intervention for low-birth-weight premature infants. *Developmental Psychology, 39,* 730–744.

Hillman, C. H., Buck, S. M., Themanson, J. R., Pontifex, M. B., & Castelli, D. M. (2009). Aerobic fitness and cognitive development: Event-related brain potential and task performance indices of executive control in preadolescent children. *Developmental Psychology, 45,* 114–129.

Hipwell, A. E., Keenan, K., Loeber, R., & Battista, D. (2010). Early predictors of sexually intimate behaviors in an urban sample of young girls. *Developmental Psychology, 46,* 366–378.

Hirsh-Pasek, K., & Golinkoff, R. M. (2008). King Solomon's take on word learning: An integrative account from the radical middle. In R. V. Kail (Ed.), *Advances in child development and behavior* (Vol. 36, pp. 1–29). San Diego, CA: Elsevier.

Hitlin, S., Brown, J., & Elder, G. H., Jr. (2006). Racial self-categorization in adolescence: Multiracial development and social pathways. *Child Development, 77,* 1298–1308.

Ho, C. S., & Fuson, K. C. (1998). Children's knowledge of teen quantities as tens and ones: Comparisons of Chinese, British, and American kindergartners. *Journal of Educational Psychology, 90,* 536–544.

Hofer, M. A. (2006). Psychobiological roots of early attachment. *Current Directions in Psychological Science, 15,* 84–88.

Hoff, E. (2003). The specificity of environmental influence: Socioeconomic status affects early vocabulary development via maternal speech. *Child Development, 74,* 1368–1378.

Hoff, E. (2009). *Language development* (2nd ed). Belmont, CA: Wadsworth Cengage Learning.

Hoff, E., & Naigles, L. (2002). How children use input to acquire a lexicon. *Child Development, 73,* 418–433.

Hoff-Ginsburg, E., & Tardif, T. (1995). Socioeconomic status and parenting. In M. H. Bornstein (Ed.), *Handbook of parenting* (Vol. 2, pp. 161–188). Mahwah, NJ: Erlbaum.

Hogan, A. M., de Haan, M., Datta, A., & Kirkham, F. J. (2006). Hypoxia: An acute, intermittent and chronic challenge to cognitive development. *Developmental Science, 9,* 335–337.

Hogge, W. A. (1990). Teratology. In I. R. Merkatz & J. E. Thompson (Eds.), *New perspectives on prenatal care.* New York, NY: Elsevier.

Holden, G. W., & Miller, P. C. (1999). Enduring and different: A meta-analysis of the similarity in parents' child rearing. *Psychological Bulletin, 125,* 223–254.

Hollich, G. J., Golinkoff, R. M., & Hirsh-Pasek, K. (2007). Young children associate novel words with complex objects rather than salient parts. *Developmental Psychology, 43,* 1051–1061.

Hollich, G. J., Hirsh-Pasek, K., & Golinkoff, R. M. (2000). Breaking the language barrier: An emergentist coalition model for the origins of word learning. *Monographs of the Society for Research in Child Development, 65* (Serial No. 262).

Holowka, S., & Petitto, L. A. (2002). Left hemisphere cerebral specialization for babies while babbling. *Science, 297*, 1515.

Hood, B., Carey, S., & Prasada, S. (2000). Predicting the outcomes of physical events: Two-year-olds fail to reveal knowledge of solidarity and support. *Child Development, 71*, 1540–1554.

Hopkins, B., & Westra, T. (1988). Maternal handling and motor development: An intercultural study. *Genetic, Social, & General Psychology Monographs, 14*, 377–420.

Horowitz, F. D., & O'Brien, M. (1986). Gifted and talented children: State of knowledge and directions for research. *American Psychologist, 41*, 1147–1152.

Horst, J. S., Oakes, L. M., & Madole, K. L. (2005). What does it look like and what can it do? Category structure influences how infants categorize. *Child Development, 76*, 614–631.

Hotz, G., Kennedy, A., Lutfi, K., & Cohn, S. M. (2009). Preventing pediatric pedestrian injuries. *Journal of Trauma: Injury, Infection, & Critical Care, 66*, 1492–1499.

Houston, D. M., & Jusczyk, P. W. (2003). Infants' long-term memory for the sound patterns of words and voices. *Journal of Experimental Psychology: Human Perception & Performance, 29*, 1143–1154.

Howe, M. L., & Courage, M. L. (1997). The emergence and early development of autobiographical memory. *Psychological Review, 104*, 499–523.

Howe, N., & Ross, H. S. (1990). Socialization, perspective taking and the sibling relationship. *Developmental Psychology, 26*, 160–165.

Howell, K. K., Lynch, M. E., Platzman, K. A., Smith, G. H., & Coles, C. D. (2006). Prenatal alcohol exposure and ability, academic achievement, and school functioning in adolescence: A longitudinal follow-up. *Journal of Pediatric Psychology, 31*, 116–126.

Howes, C., & Matheson, C. C. (1992). Sequences in the development of competent play with peers: Social and social pretend play. *Developmental Psychology, 28*, 961–974.

Howes, C., Unger, O., & Seidner, L. B. (1990). Social pretend play in toddlers: Parallels with social play and with solitary pretend. *Child Development, 60*, 77–84.

Hubbard, F. O. A., & van IJzendoorn, M. H. (1991). Maternal unresponsiveness and infant crying across the first 9 months: A naturalistic longitudinal study. *Infant Behavior & Development, 14*, 299–312.

Hudson, J. A., Shapiro, L. R., & Sosa, B. B. (1995). Planning in the real world: Preschool children's scripts and plans for familiar events. *Child Development, 66*, 984–998.

Huesmann, L. R. (2007). The impact of electronic media violence: Scientific theory and research. *Journal of Adolescent Health Care, 41*, S6–S13.

Hughes, C., & Ensor, R. (2007). Executive functions and theory of mind: Predictive relations from 2 to 4. *Developmental Psychology, 43*, 1447–1459.

Hughes, J. M., Bigler, R. S., & Levy, S. R. (2007). Consequences of learning about historical racism among European American and African American children. *Child Development, 78*, 1689–1705.

Huizink, A., Robles de Medina, P., Mulder, E., Visser, G., & Buitelaar, J. (2002). Psychological measures of prenatal stress as predictors of infant temperament. *Journal of the American Academy of Child & Adolescent Psychiatry, 41*, 1078–1085.

Hulit, L. M., & Howard, M. R. (2002). *Born to talk: An introduction to speech and language development* (3rd ed.). Boston, MA: Allyn & Bacon.

Hulme, C., & Snowling, M. J. (2009). *Developmental disorders of language learning and cognition.* Chichester, West Sussex, UK: Wiley-Blackwell.

Human Genome Project. (2003). *Genomics and its impact on science and society: A 2003 primer.* Washington, DC: U.S. Department of Energy.

Hunt, E., & Carlson, J. (2007). Considerations relating to the study of group differences in intelligence. *Perspective on Psychological Science, 2*, 194–213.

Hurtado, N., Marchman, V. A., & Fernald, A. (2008). Does input influence uptake? Links between maternal talk, processing speed, and vocabulary size in Spanish-learning children. *Developmental Science, 11*, F31–F39.

Hurts, K. (2008). Building cognitive support for the learning of long division skills using progressive schematization: Design and empirical validation. *Computers & Education, 50*, 1141–1156.

Huston, A. C. (1983). Sex typing. In P. H. Mussen (Ed.), *Handbook of child psychology* (Vol. 4). New York, NY: Wiley.

Huston, A. C., & Wright, J. C. (1998). Mass media and children's development. In W. Damon (Ed.), *Handbook of child psychology* (Vol. 4). New York, NY: Wiley.

Huston, A. C., Duncan, G. J., McLoyd, V. C., Crosby, D. A., Ripke, M. N., Weisner, T. S., et al. (2005). Impacts on children of a policy to promote employment and reduce poverty for low-income parents: New hope after 5 years. *Developmental Psychology, 41*, 902–918.

Huston, A. C., Watkins, B. A., & Kunkel, D. (1989). Public policy and children's television. *American Psychologist, 44*, 424–433.

Huston, A. C. (2008). From research to policy and back. *Child Development, 79*, 1–12.

Hutchins, E. (1983). Understanding Micronesian navigation. In D. A. Gentner & A. Stevens (Eds.), *Mental models.* Hillsdale, NJ: Erlbaum.

Hutchinson, D. M., Rapee, R. M., & Taylor, A. (2010). Body dissatisfaction and eating disturbances in early adolescence: A structural modeling investigation examining negative affect and peer factors. *Journal of Early Adolescence, 30*, 489–517.

Huth-Bocks, A. C., Levendosky, A. A., Bogat, G. A., & von Eye, A. (2004). The impact of maternal characteristics and contextual variables on infant–mother attachment. *Child Development, 75*, 480–496.

Huttenlocher, J., Haight, W., Bryk, A., Seltzer, M., & Lyons, T. (1991). Early vocabulary growth: Relation to language input and gender. *Developmental Psychology, 27*, 236–248.

Huttenlocher, J., Waterfall, H., Vasilyeva, M., Vevea, J., & Hedges, L. V. (2010). Sources of variability in children's language growth. *Cognitive Psychology, 61*, 343–365.

Hyde, J. S. (2007). New directions in the study of gender similarities and differences. *Current Directions in Psychological Science, 16*, 259–263.

Hymel, S., Vaillancourt, T., McDougall, P., & Renshaw, P. D. (2004). Peer acceptance and rejection in childhood. In P. K. Smith & C. H. Hart (Eds.), *Blackwell handbook of childhood social development* (pp. 265–284). Malden, MA: Blackwell.

Iervolino, A. C., Hines, M., Golombok, S. E., Rust, J., & Plomin, R. (2005). Genetic and environmental influences on sex-typed behavior during the preschool years. *Child Development, 76*, 826–840.

Inhelder, B., & Piaget, J. (1958). *The growth of logical thinking from childhood to adolescence.* New York, NY: Basic Books.

Institute of Medicine. (1990). *Nutrition during pregnancy.* Washington, DC: National Academy Press.

International Food Information Council Foundation. (2000). *Starting solids: A guide for parents and child care providers.* Washington, DC: Author.

Israel, A. C., Guile, C. A., Baker, J. E., & Silverman, W. K. (1994). An evaluation of enhanced self-regulation training in the treatment of childhood obesity. *Journal of Pediatric Psychology, 19*, 737–749.

Iverson, J. M., & Goldin-Meadow, S. (2005). Gesture paves the way for language development. *Psychological Science, 16*, 367–371.

Izard, C. E. (2007). Basic emotions, natural kinds, emotion schemas, and a new paradigm. *Perspectives on Psychological Science, 2*, 260–280.

Izard, C. E., & Ackerman, B. P. (2000). Motivational, organizational, and regulatory functions of discrete emotions. In M. Lewis & J. Haviland-Jones (Eds.), *Handbook of emotions* (2nd ed., pp. 253–264). New York, NY: Guilford.

Jaccard, J., Blanton, H., & Dodge, T. (2005). Peer influences on risk behavior: An analysis of the effects of a close friend. *Developmental Psychology, 41*, 135–147.

Jack, F., MacDonald, S., Reese, E., & Hayne, H. (2009). Maternal reminiscing style during early childhood predicts the age of adolescents' earliest memories. *Child Development, 80*, 496–505.

Jacklin, C. N. (1989). Female and male: Issues of gender. *American Psychologist, 44*, 127–133.

Jacklin, C. N., & Maccoby, E. E. (1978). Social behavior at thirty-three months in same-sex and mixed-sex dyads. *Child Development, 49*, 557–569.

Jacobi, C., Hayward, C., de Zwaan, M., Kraemer, H. C., & Agras, W. S. (2004). Coming to terms with risk factors for eating disorders: Application of risk terminology and suggestions for a general taxonomy. *Psychological Bulletin, 130*, 19–65.

Jacobs, J. E., & Klaczynski, P. A. (2002). The development of judgment and decision making during childhood and adolescence. *Current Directions in Psychological Science, 11*, 145–149.

Jacobson, J. L., & Jacobson, S. W. (1996). Intellectual impairment in children exposed to polychlorinated biphenyls in utero. *New England Journal of Medicine, 335*, 783–789.

Jacobson, S. W., & Jacobson, J. L. (2000). Teratogenic insult and neurobehavioral function in infancy and childhood. In C. A. Nelson (Ed.), *The Minnesota Symposium on Child Psychology: Vol. 31. The effects of early adversity on neurobehavioral development* (pp. 61–112). Mahwah, NJ: Erlbaum.

Jaffe, S. R. (2003). Pathways to adversity in young adulthood among early childbearers. *Journal of Family Psychology, 16*, 38–49.

Jaffee, S., & Hyde, J. S. (2000). Gender differences in moral orientation: A meta-analysis. *Psychological Bulletin, 126*, 703–726.

Jahromi, L. B., Putnam, S. P., & Stifter, C. A. (2004). Maternal regulation of infant reactivity from 2 to 6 months. *Developmental Psychology, 40*, 477–487.

Jansen, J., de Weerth, C., & Riksen-Walraven, J. M. (2008). Breastfeeding and the mother-infant relationship—A review. *Developmental Review, 28*, 503–521.

Janson, H., & Mathiesen, K. S. (2008). Temperament profiles from infancy to middle childhood: Development and associations with behavioral problems. *Developmental Psychology, 44*, 1314–1328.

Jiao, S., Ji, G., & Jing, Q. (1996). Cognitive development of Chinese urban only children and children with siblings. *Child Development, 67*, 387–395.

Jiao, Z. (1999, April). *Which students keep old friends and which become new friends across a school transition?* Paper presented at the 1999 meeting of the Society for Research in Child Development, Albuquerque, New Mexico.

Jipson, J. L., & Gelman, S. A. (2007). Robots and rodents: Children's inferences about living and nonliving kinds. *Child Development, 78*, 1675–1688.

Johanson, R. B., Rice, C., Coyle, M., Arthur, J., Anyanwu, L., Ibrahim, I., et al. (1993). A randomized prospective study comparing the new vacuum extractor policy with forceps delivery. *British Journal of Obstetrics & Gynecology, 100*, 524–530.

John, O. P., & Gross, J. J. (2007). Individual differences in emotion regulation. In J. J. Gross (Ed.), *Handbook of emotion regulation* (pp. 351–372). New York, NY: Guilford.

Johnson, M. H., Grossman, T., & Cohen Kadosh, K. (2009). Mapping functional brain development: Building a social brain through interactive specialization. *Developmental Psychology, 45*, 151–159.

Johnson, M. J., Grossman, T., & Farroni, T. (2008). The social cognitive neuroscience of infancy: Illuminating the early development of social brain functions. In R. V. Kail (Ed.), *Advances in child development and behavior* (Vol. 36, pp. 331–372). San Diego, CA: Academic Press.

Johnson, S. C., Dweck, C. S., & Chen, F. S. (2007). Evidence for infants' internal working models of attachment. *Psychological Science, 18,* 501–502.

Johnson, S. P. (2001). Visual development in human infants: Binding features, surfaces, and objects. *Visual Cognition, 8,* 565–578.

Johnston, L. D., Delva, J., & O'Malley, P. M. (2007). Sports participation and physical education in American secondary schools: Current levels and racial/ethnic and socioeconomic disparities. *American Journal of Preventive Medicine, 33,* S195–S208.

Jokela, M. (2010). Characteristics of the first child predict the parents' probability of having another child. *Developmental Psychology, 46,* 915–926.

Jones, D. C. (2004). Body image among adolescent girls and boys: A longitudinal study. *Developmental Psychology, 40,* 823–835.

Jones, H. E. (2006). Drug addiction during pregnancy: Advances in maternal treatment and understanding child outcomes. *Current Directions in Psychological Science, 15,* 126–130.

Jones, N. A., & Smith, A. S. (2001). *Census 2000 brief: Two or more races.* Washington, DC: U.S. Census Bureau.

Jordan, N. C. (2007). The need for number sense. *Educational Leadership, 65,* 63–64.

Jordan, N. C., Kaplan, D., Ramineni, C., & Locuniak, M. N. (2008). Development of number combination skill in the early school years: When do fingers help? *Developmental Science, 11,* 662–668.

Jordan, N. C., Kaplan, D., Ramineni, C., & Locuniak, M. N. (2009). Early math matters: Kindergarten number competence and later mathematics outcomes. *Developmental Psychology, 45,* 850–867.

Joseph, D. L., & Newman, D. A. (2010). Emotional intelligence: An integrative meta-analysis and cascading model. *Journal of Applied Psychology, 95,* 54–78.

Joseph, R. (2000). Fetal brain behavior and cognitive development. *Developmental Review, 20,* 81–98.

Joseph, R. M., Keehn, B., Connolly, C., Wolfe, J. M., & Horowitz, T. S. (2009). Why is visual search superior in autism spectrum disorder? *Developmental Science, 12,* 1083–1096.

Joussemet, M., Vitaro, F., Barker, E. D., Côté, S., Zoccolillo, M., Nagin, D. S., et al. (2008). Controlling parenting and physical aggression during elementary school. *Child Development, 79,* 411–425.

Joyner, K., & Udry, J. R. (2000). You don't bring me anything but down: Adolescent romance and depression. *Journal of Health & Social Behavior, 41,* 369–391.

Juffer, F., & van IJzendoorn, M. H. (2007). Adoptees do not lack self-esteem: A meta-analysis of studies on self-esteem of transracial, international, and domestic adoptees. *Psychological Bulletin, 133,* 1067–1083.

Jusczyk, P. W. (1995). Language acquisition: Speech sounds and phonological development. In J. L. Miller & P. D. Eimas (Eds.), *Handbook of perception and cognition: Vol. 11. Speech, language, and communication* (pp. 263–301). Orlando, FL: Academic Press.

Jusczyk, P. W. (2002). How infants adapt speech-processing capacities to native-language structure. *Current Directions in Psychological Science, 11,* 15–18.

Justice, L. M., Pullen, P. C., & Pence, K. (2008). Influence of verbal and nonverbal references to print on preschoolers' visual attention to print during storybook reading. *Developmental Psychology, 44,* 855–866.

Kagan, J., Arcus, D., Snidman, N., Feng, W. Y., Hendler, J., & Greene, S. (1994). Reactivity in infants: A cross-national comparison. *Developmental Psychology, 30,* 342–345.

Kaijura, H., Cowart, B. J., & Beauchamp, G. K. (1992). Early developmental change in bitter taste responses

in human infants. *Developmental Psychobiology, 25,* 375–386.

Kail, R. (2002). Developmental change in proactive interference. *Child Development, 73,* 1703–1714.

Kail, R. (2008). Speed of processing in childhood and adolescence: Nature, consequences, and implications for understanding atypical development. In J. DeLuca & J. H. Kalmar (Eds.), *Information processing speed in clinical populations* (pp. 101–123). New York, NY: Taylor and Francis.

Kail, R., & Hall, L. K. (1999). Sources of developmental change in children's word-problem performance. *Journal of Educational Psychology, 91,* 660–668.

Kako, E. (1999). Elements of syntax in the systems of three language-trained animals. *Animal Learning & Behavior, 27,* 1–14.

Kalil, A., & Ziol-Guest, K. M. (2005). Single mothers' employment dynamics and adolescent well-being. *Child Development, 76,* 196–211.

Kanwisher, N., & Yovel, G. (2009). Cortical specialization for face perception in humans. In J. T. Cacioppo & G. G. Berntson (Eds.), *Handbook of neuroscience for the behavioral sciences.* Hoboken, NJ: John Wiley & Sons.

Kaplan, H., & Dove, H. (1987). Infant development among the Ache of eastern Paraguay. *Developmental Psychology, 23,* 190–198.

Karevold, E., Røysamb, E., Ystrom, E., & Mathiesen, K. S. (2009). Predictors and pathways from infancy to symptoms of anxiety and depression in early adolescence. *Developmental Psychology, 45,* 1051–1060.

Kärnä, A., Voeten, M., Little, T. D., Poskiparta, E., Kaljonen, A., & Salmivalli, C. (2011). A large-scale evaluation of the KiVa antibullying program: Grades 4-6. *Child Development, 82,* 311-330.

Karniol, R. (1989). The role of manual manipulative states in the infant's acquisition of perceived control over objects. *Developmental Review, 9,* 205–233.

Karraker, K. H., Vogel, D. A., & Lake, M. A. (1995). Parents' gender-stereotyped perceptions of newborns: The eye of the beholder revisited. *Sex Roles, 33,* 687–701.

Katz, L. F., & Woodin, E. M. (2002). Hostility, hostile detachment, and conflict engagement in marriages: Effects on child and family functioning. *Child Development, 73,* 636–652.

Katz-Wise, S. L., Priess, H. A., & Hyde, J. S. (2010). Gender-role attitudes and behavior across the transition to parenthood. *Developmental Psychology, 46,* 18–28.

Kaufman, J., & Charney, D. (2003). The neurobiology of child and adolescent depression: Current knowledge and future directions. In D. Cicchetti & E. Walker (Eds.), *Neurodevelopmental mechanisms in psychopathology* (pp. 461–490). New York, NY: Cambridge University Press.

Kaufman, J., & Lichtenberger, E. O. (2002). *Assessing adolescent and adult intelligence* (2nd ed.). Boston, MA: Allyn & Bacon.

Kavsek, M., & Bornstein, M. H. (2010). Visual habituation and dishabituation in preterm infants: A review and meta-analysis. *Research in Developmental Disabilities, 31,* 951–975.

Keane, S. P., Brown, K. P., & Crenshaw, T. M. (1990). Children's intention-cue detection as a function of maternal social behavior: Pathways to social rejection. *Developmental Psychology, 26,* 1004–1009.

Kearney, C. A. (2007). Forms and functions of school refusal behavior in youth: Am empirical analysis of absenteeism severity. *Journal of Child Psychology & Psychiatry, 48,* 53–61.

Kelemen, D. (2003). British and American children's preferences for teleo-functional explanations of the natural world. *Cognition, 88,* 201–221.

Kelemen, D., & DiYanni, C. (2005). Intuitions about origins: Purpose and intelligent design in children's reasoning about nature. *Journal of Cognition & Development, 6,* 3–31.

Keller, H., Yovsil, R., Borke, J., Kartner, J., Jensen, H., & Papaligoura, Z. (2004). Developmental consequences of early parenting experiences: Self-recognition and self-regulation in three cultural communities. *Child Development, 75,* 1745–1760.

Kellman, P. J., & Arterberry, M. E. (2006). Infant visual perception. In W. Damon & R. M. Lerner (Eds.), *Handbook of child psychology: Vol. 2. Cognition, perception, and language* (6th ed., pp. 109–160). Hoboken, NJ: Wiley.

Kellman, P. J., & Banks, M. S. (1998). Infant visual perception. In W. Damon (Ed.), *Handbook of child psychology* (Vol. 2). New York, NY: Wiley.

Kelly, D. J., Liu, S., Lee, K., Quinn, P., Pascalis, O., Slater, A., & Ge, L. (2009). Development of the other-race effect during infancy: Evidence toward universality? *Journal of Experimental Child Psychology, 104,* 105–114.

Kelly, P. (2011). Corporal punishment and child maltreatment in New Zealand. *Acta Paediatrica, 100,* 14–20.

Kendall, J., & Hatton, D. (2002). Racism as a source of health disparity in families with children with attention deficit hyperactivity disorder. *Advances in Nursing Science, 25,* 22–39.

Kiang, L., Yip, T., Gonzales-Backen, M., Witkow, M., & Fuligni, A. J. (2006). Ethnic identity and the daily psychological well-being of adolescents from Mexican and Chinese backgrounds. *Child Development, 77,* 1338–1350.

Kidd, E., & Holler, J. (2009). Children's use of gesture to resolve lexical ambiguity. *Developmental Science, 12,* 903–913.

Kilgore, K., Snyder, J., & Lentz, C. (2000). The contribution of parental discipline, parental monitoring, and school risk to early-onset conduct problems in African American boys and girls. *Developmental Psychology, 36,* 835–845.

Killen, M., & McGlothlin, H. (2005). Prejudice in children. In C. B. Fisher & R. M. Lerner (Eds.), *Encyclopedia of applied developmental science* (Vol. 2, pp. 870–872). Thousand Oaks, CA: Sage.

Killen, M., & Turiel, E. (1998). Adolescents' and young adults' evaluations of helping and sacrificing for others. *Journal of Research on Adolescence, 8,* 355–375.

Kim, J., & Cicchetti, D. (2006). Longitudinal trajectories of self-system processes and depressive symptoms among maltreated and nonmaltreated children. *Child Development, 77,* 624–639.

Kim, J.-Y., McHale, S. M., Crouter, A. C., & Osgood, D. (2007). Longitudinal linkages between sibling relationships and adjustment from middle childhood through adolescence. *Developmental Psychology, 43,* 960–973.

Kim, Y. H., & Goetz, E. T. (1994). Context effects on word recognition and reading comprehension of good and poor readers: A test of the interactive compensatory hypothesis. *Reading Research Quarterly, 29,* 178–188.

Kindermann, T. A. (2007). Effects of naturally existing peer groups on changes in academic engagement in a cohort of sixth graders. *Child Development, 78,* 1186–1203.

King, P. E., & Furrow, J. L. (2004). Religion as a resource for positive youth development: Religion, social capital, and moral outcomes. *Developmental Psychology, 40,* 703–713.

King, V. (2006). The antecedents and consequences of adolescents' relationships with stepfathers and nonresident fathers. *Journal of Marriage & the Family, 68,* 910–928.

King, V., Elder, G. H., & Whitbeck, L. B. (1997). Religious involvement among rural youth: An ecological and life-course perspective. *Journal of Research on Adolescence, 7,* 431–456.

Kirby, D., & Laris, B. A. (2009). Effective curriculum-based sex and STD/HIV education programs for adolescents. *Child Development Perspectives, 3,* 21–29.

Kirkorian, H. L., Pempek, T. A., Murphy, L. A., Schmidt, M. E., & Anderson, D. R. (2009). The impact of background television on parent-child interaction. *Child Development, 80,* 1350–1359.

Kithakye, M., Morris, A. S., Terranova, A. M., & Myers, S. (2010). The Kenyan political conflict and children's adjustment. *Child Development, 81,* 1114–1128.

Klaczynski, P. A. (2000). Motivated scientific reasoning biases, epistemological beliefs, and theory polarization. *Child Development, 71,* 1347–1366.

Klaczynski, P. A. (2004). A dual-process model of adolescent development: Implications for decision making, reasoning, and identity. In R. Kail (Ed.), *Advances in child development and behavior* (Vol. 32, pp. 73–123). San Diego, CA: Elsevier.

Klahr, D. (1985). Solving problems with ambiguous subgoal ordering: Preschoolers' performance. *Child Development, 56,* 940–952.

Klaus, M., & Kennell, H. H. (1976). *Mother-infant bonding.* St. Louis: Mosby.

Klump, K. L., & Culbert, K. M. (2007). Molecular genetic studies of eating disorders: Current status and future directions. *Current Directions in Psychological Science, 16,* 37–41.

Kochanska, G., & Aksan, N. (2006). Children's conscience and self-regulation. *Journal of Personality, 74,* 1587–1617.

Kochanska, G., Aksan, N., & Joy, M. E. (2007). Children's fearfulness as a moderator of parenting in early socialization: Two longitudinal studies. *Developmental Psychology, 43,* 222–237.

Kochanska, G., Coy, K. C., & Murray, K. T. (2001). The development of self-regulation in the first four years of life. *Child Development, 72,* 1091–1111.

Kochanska, G., DeVet, K., Goldman, M., Murray, K., & Putnam, S. P. (1994). Maternal reports of conscience development and temperament in young children. *Child Development, 65,* 852–868.

Kochanska, G., Gross, J. N., Lin, M., & Nichols, K. E. (2002). Guilt in young children: Development, determinants, and relations with a broader system of standards. *Child Development, 73,* 461–482.

Kochenderfer-Ladd, B., & Skinner, K. (2002). Children's coping strategies: Moderators of the effects of peer victimization? *Developmental Psychology, 38,* 267–278.

Kochenderfer-Ladd, B., & Waldrop, J. L. (2001). Chronicity and instability of children's peer victimization experiences as predictors of loneliness and social satisfaction trajectories. *Child Development, 72,* 134–151.

Koenig, M. A., & Woodward, A. L. (2010). Sensitivity of 24-month-olds to the prior inaccuracy of the source: Possible mechanisms. *Developmental Psychology, 46,* 815–826.

Kogan, N. (1983). Stylistic variation in childhood and adolescence: Creativity, metaphor, and cognitive style. In P. H. Mussen (Ed.), *Handbook of child psychology* (Vol. 3). New York: Wiley.

Kohlberg, L. (1966). A cognitive-developmental analysis of children's sex-role concepts and attitudes. In E. E. Maccoby (Ed.), *The development of sex differences.* Stanford, CA: Stanford University Press.

Kohlberg, L. (1969). Stage and sequence: The cognitive-developmental approach to socialization. In D. Goslin (Ed.), *Handbook of socialization theory and research* (pp. 347–480). Chicago, IL: Rand McNally.

Kohlberg, L., & Ullian, D. Z. (1974). Stages in the development of psychosexual concepts and attitudes. In R. C. Friedman, R. M. Richart, & R. L. Van Wiele (Eds.), *Sex differences in behavior* (New York, NY: Wiley.

Kojima, Y. (2000). Maternal regulation of sibling interactions in the preschool years: Observational

study in Japanese families. *Child Development, 71,* 1640–1647.

Kokis, J. V., Macpherson, R., Toplak, M. E., West, R. F., & Stanovich, K. E. (2002). Heuristic and analytic processing: Age trends and associations with cognitive ability and cognitive styles. *Journal of Experimental Child Psychology, 83,* 26–52.

Kokko, K., & Pulkkinen, L. (2000). Aggression in childhood and long-term unemployment in adulthood: A cycle of maladaptation and some protective factors. *Developmental Psychology, 36,* 463–472.

Kolb, B. (1989). Brain development, plasticity, and behavior. *American Psychologist, 44,* 1203–1212.

Kolberg, K. J. S. (1999). Environmental influences on prenatal development and health. In T. L. Whitman & T. V. Merluzzi (Eds.), *Life-span perspectives on health and illness* (pp. 87–103). Mahwah, NJ: Erlbaum.

Konijn, E. A., Nije Bijvank, M., & Bushman, B. J. (2007). I wish I were a warrior: The role of wishful identification in the effects of violent video games on aggression in adolescent boys. *Developmental Psychology, 43,* 1038–1044.

Kopp, C. B. (1997). Young children: Emotion management, instrumental control, and plans. In S. L. Friedman & E. K. Scholnick (Eds.), *The developmental psychology of planning: Why, how, and when do we plan?* (pp. 103–124). Mahwah, NJ: Erlbaum.

Kopp, C. B., & McCall, R. B. (1982). Predicting later mental performances for normal, at-risk, and handicapped infants. In P. B. Bates & O. G. Brim (Eds.), *Life-span development and behavior* (Vol. 4). New York Academic Press.

Kornhaber, M., Fierros, E., & Veenema, S. (2004). *Multiple intelligences: Best ideas from research and practice.* Boston, MA: Allyn & Bacon.

Kowal, A., & Kramer, L. (1997). Children's understanding of parental differential treatment. *Child Development, 68,* 113–126.

Kramer, L. (2010). The essential ingredients of successful sibling relationships: An emerging framework for advancing theory and practice. *Child Development Perspectives, 4,* 80–86.

Krebs, D. L., & Denton, K. (2005). Toward a more pragmatic approach to morality: A critical evaluation of Kohlberg's model. *Psychological Review, 113,* 672–675.

Krebs, D., & Gillmore, J. (1982). The relationships among the first stages of cognitive development, role-taking abilities, and moral development. *Child Development, 53,* 877–886.

Kreppner, J. M., Rutter, M., Beckett, C., Castle, J., Colvert, E., Groothues, C., et al. (2007). Normality and impairment following profound early institutional deprivation: A longitudinal follow-up into early adolescence. *Developmental Psychology, 43,* 931–946.

Krishnakumar, A., & Black, M. M. (2003). Family processes within three-generation households and adolescents mothers' satisfaction with father involvement. *Journal of Family Psychology, 17,* 488–498.

Krispin, O., Sternberg, K. J., & Lamb, M. E. (1992). The dimensions of peer evaluation in Israel: A cross-cultural perspective. *International Journal of Behavioral Development, 15,* 299–314.

Kroger, J., & Greene, K. E. (1996). Events associated with identity status change. *Journal of Adolescence, 19,* 477–490.

Kronenberg, M. E., Hansel, T. C., Brennan, A. M., Osofsky, H. J., Osofsky, J. D., & Lawrason, B. (2010). Children of Katrina: Lessons learned about postdisaster symptoms and recovery patterns. *Child Development, 81,* 1241–1259.

Kuebli, J., Butler, S., & Fivush, R. (1995). Mother-child talk about past emotions: Relations of maternal language and child gender over time. *Cognition & Emotion, 9,* 265–283.

Kuhl, P. K., Andruski, J. E., Chistovich, I. A., Chistovich, L. A., Kozhevnikova, E. V., Ryskina, V. L., et al. (1997). Cross-language analysis of phonetic units in language addressed to infants. *Science, 277,* 684–686.

Kuhl, P. K., Stevens, E., Hayashi, A., Deguchi, T., Kiritani, S., & Iverson, P. (2006). Infants show a facilitation effect for native language phonetic perception between 6 and 12 months. *Developmental Science, 9,* F13–F21.

Kuhn, D. (2011). What is scientific thinking and how does it develop? In U. Goswami (Ed.), *The Wiley-Blackwell handbook of cognitive development* (2nd ed., pp. 497–523). West Sussex UK: Wiley-Blackwell.

Kuhn, D., Garcia-Mila, M., Zohar, A., & Andersen, C. (1995). Strategies of knowledge acquisition. *Monographs of the Society for Research in Child Development, 60* (Serial No. 245).

Kulkofsky, S., Wang, Q., & Koh, J. B. K. (2009). Functions of memory sharing and mother-child reminiscing behaviors: Individual and cultural variations. *Journal of Cognition & Development, 10,* 92–114.

Ladd, G. W. (1998). Peer relationships and social competence during early and middle childhood. *Annual Review of Psychology, 50,* 333–359.

Ladd, G. W. (2003). Probing the adaptive significance of children's behavior and relationships in the school context: A child by environment perspective. In R. V. Kail (Ed.), *Advances in child development and behavior* (Vol. 31, p. 43-104). San Diego, CA: Academic Press.

Ladd, G. W. (2006). Peer rejection, aggressive or withdrawn behavior, and psychological maladjustment from ages 5 to 12: An examination of four predictive models. *Child Development, 77,* 822–846.

Ladd, G. W., & Ladd, B. K. (1998). Parenting behaviors and parent–child relationships: Correlates of peer victimization in kindergarten? *Developmental Psychology, 34,* 1450–1458.

Ladd, G. W., & Pettit, G. S. (2002). Parents and children's peer relationships. In M. Bornstein (Ed.), *Handbook of parenting: Vol. 4* (2nd ed., pp. 377–409). Hillsdale, NJ: Erlbaum.

Ladd, G. W., Herald-Brown, S. L., & Reiser, M. (2008). Does chronic classroom peer rejection predict the development of children's classroom participation during the grade school years? *Child Development, 79,* 1001–1015.

LaFreniere, P., Strayer, F. F., & Gauthier, R. (1984). The emergence of same-sex affiliative preferences among preschool peers: A developmental/ethnological perspective. *Child Development, 55,* 1958–1965.

Lagattuta, K. H. (2007). Thinking about the future because of the past: Young children's knowledge about the causes of worry and preventative decisions. *Child Development, 78,* 1492–1509.

Lagattuta, K. H., & Wellman, H. M. (2002). Differences in early parent–child conversations about negative versus positive emotions: Implications for the development of psychological understanding. *Developmental Psychology, 38,* 564–580.

Lagattuta, K. N., Nucci, L., & Bosacki, S. L. (2010). Bridging theory of mind and the personal domain: Children's reasoning about resistance to parental control. *Child Development, 81,* 616–635.

LaGreca, A. M. (1993). Social skills training with children: Where do we go from here? *Journal of Clinical Child Psychology, 22,* 288–298.

LaGreca, A. M., & Silverman, W. K. (2009). Treatment and prevention of posttraumatic stress reactions in children and adolescents to disasters and terrorism: What is the evidence? *Child Development Perspectives, 3,* 4–10.

Laible, D. J., & Carlo, G. (2004). The differential relations of maternal and paternal support and control to adolescent social competence, self-worth, and sympathy. *Journal of Adolescent Research, 19,* 759–782.

Laird, R. D., Pettit, G. S., Dodge, K. A., & Bates, J. E. (2003). Changes in parents' monitoring knowledge: Links with parenting, relationships quality, adolescent beliefs and antisocial behavior. *Social Development, 12,* 401–419.

Lamaze, F. (1958). *Painless childbirth.* London: Burke.

Lamb, M. E. (1999). Nonparental child care. In M. E. Lamb (Ed.), *Parenting and child development in "nontraditional" families.* Mahwah, NJ: Erlbaum.

Lamb, M. E., Orbach, Y., Hershkowitz, I., Esplin, P. W., & Horowitz, D. (2007). A structured forensic interview protocol improves the quality and informativeness of investigative interviews with children: A review of research using the NICHD Investigative Interview Protocol. *Child Abuse & Neglect, 31*, 1201–1231.

Lamb, M. E., Thompson, R. A., Gardner, W., Charnov, E. L., & Connell, J. P. (1985). *Infant-mother attachment: The origins and developmental significance of individual differences in Strange Situation behavior.* Hillsdale, NJ: Erlbaum.

Landerl, K., Fussenegger, B., Moll, K., & Willburger, E. (2009). Dyslexia and dyscalculia: Two learning disorders with different cognitive profiles. *Journal of Experimental Child Psychology, 103*, 309–324.

Lansford, J. E. (2009). Parental divorce and children's adjustment. *Perspectives on Psychological Science, 4*, 140–152.

Lansford, J. E., Malone, P. S., Castellino, D. R., Dodge, K. A., Pettit, G. S., & Bates, J. E. (2006). Trajectories of internalizing, externalizing, and grades for children who have and have not experienced their parents' divorce or separation. *Journal of Family Psychology, 20*, 292–301.

Laplante, D. P., Barr, R. G., Brunet, A., Du Fort, G. G., Meaney, M. L., Saucier, J., Zelazo, P. R., & King, S. (2004). Stress during pregnancy affects general intellectual and language functioning in human toddlers. *Pediatric Research, 56*, 400–410.

Larsen, J. T., To, R. M., & Fireman, G. (2007). Children's understanding and experience of mixed emotions. *Psychological Science, 18*, 186–191.

Larson, R. W., Hansen, D. M., & Moneta, G. (2006). Differing profiles of developmental experiences across types of organized youth activities. *Developmental Psychology, 42*, 849–863.

Lau, J. Y., Rijsdijk, F., Gregory, A. M., McGuffin, P., & Eley, T. C. (2007). Pathways to childhood depressive symptoms: The role of social, cognitive, and genetic risk factors. *Developmental Psychology, 43*, 1402–1414.

Laursen, B., & Collins, W. A. (1994). Interpersonal conflict during adolescence. *Psychological Bulletin, 115*, 197–209.

Laursen, B., Bukowski, W. M., Nurmi, J. E., Marion, D., Salmela-Aro, K., & Kiuru, N. (2010). Opposites detract: Middle school peer group antipathies. *Journal of Experimental Child Psychology, 106*, 240–256.

Laursen, B., Finkelstein, B. D., & Betts, N. T. (2001). A developmental meta-analysis of peer conflict resolution. *Developmental Review, 21*, 423–449.

Leaper, C., & Smith, T. E. (2004). A meta-analytic review of gender variations in children's language use: Talkativeness, affiliative speech, and assertive speech. *Developmental Psychology, 40*, 993–1027.

Lecanuet, J. P., Granier-Deferre, C., & Busnel, M. C. (1995). Human fetal auditory perception. In J. P. Lecanuet, W. P. Fifer, N. A. Krasnegor, & W. P. Smotherman (Eds.), *Fetal development: A psychobiological perspective.* Hillsdale, NJ: Erlbaum.

Leclercq, A-L., & Majerus, S. (2010). Serial-order short-term memory predicts vocabulary development: Evidence from a longitudinal study. *Developmental Psychology, 46*, 417–427.

Ledebt, A. (2000). Changes in arm posture during the early acquisition of walking. *Infant Behavior & Development, 23*, 79–89.

Ledebt, A., van Wieringen, P. C. W., & Saveslsbergh, G. J. P. (2004). Functional significance of foot rotation in early walking. *Infant Behavior & Development, 27*, 163–172.

Lee, K. T., Mattson, S. N., & Riley, E. P. (2004). Classifying children with heavy prenatal alcohol exposure using measures of attention. *Journal of the International Neuropsychological Society, 10*, 271–277.

Lee, R. M., Seol, K. O., Miyoung, M., Miller, M. J., & the Minnesota International Adoption Project Team. (2010). The behavioral development of Korean children in institutional care and international adoptive families. *Developmental Psychology, 46*, 468–478.

Leerkes, E. M., Blankson, A. M., & O'Brien, M. (2009). Differential effects of maternal sensitivity to infant distress and nondistress on social-emotional functioning. *Child Development, 80*, 762–775.

Legare, C. H., Gelman, S. A., & Wellman, H. M. (2010). Inconsistency with prior knowledge triggers children's causal explanatory reasoning. *Child Development, 81*, 929–944.

Legare, C. H., Wellman, H. M., & Gelman, S. A. (2009). Evidence for an explanation advantage in naïve biological reasoning. *Cognitive Psychology, 58*, 177–194.

LeMare, L. J., & Rubin, K. H. (1987). Perspective taking and peer interaction: Structural and developmental analyses. *Child Development, 58*, 306–315.

Lemmon, K., & Moore, C. (2007). The development of prudence in the face of varying future rewards. *Developmental Science, 10*, 502–511.

Lengua, L. J. (2006). Growth in temperament and parenting as predictors of adjustment during children's transition to adolescence. *Developmental Psychology, 42*, 819–832.

Lengua, L. J., Sandler, I. N., West, S. G., Wolchik, S. A., & Curran, P. J. (1999). Emotionality and self-regulation, threat appraisal, and coping in children of divorce. *Development & Psychopathology, 11*, 15–37.

Leon, K. (2003). Risk and protective factors in young children's adjustment to parental divorce: A review of the research. *Family Relations, 52*, 258–270.

Leppanen, J. M., Moulson, M. C., Vogel-Farley, V. K., & Nelson, C. A. (2007). An ERP study of emotional face processing in the adult and infant brain. *Child Development, 78*, 232–245.

Lerner, R. M., Fisher, C. B., & Giannino, L. (2006). Editorial: Constancy and change in the development of applied developmental science. *Applied Developmental Science, 10*, 172–173.

Lervåg, A., Bråten, I., & Hulme, C. (2009). The cognitive and linguistic foundations of early reading development: A Norwegian latent variable longitudinal study. *Developmental Psychology, 45*, 764–781.

Leventhal, T., & Brooks-Gunn, J. (2000). The neighborhood they live in: The effects of neighborhood residence on child and adolescent outcomes. *Psychological Bulletin, 126*, 309–337.

Levine, L. E. (1983). Mine: Self-definition in 2-year-old boys. *Developmental Psychology, 19*, 544–549.

Levine, L. E., Waite, B. M., & Bowman, L. L. (2007). Electronic media use, reading, and academic distractibility in college youth. *Cyberpsychology and Behavior, 10*, 560–566.

Levine, L. J. (1995). Young children's understanding of the causes of anger and sadness. *Child Development, 66*, 697–709.

Levine, S. C., Vasilyeva, M., Lourenco, S. F., Newcombe, N. S., & Huttenlocher, J. (2005). Socioeconomic status modifies the sex difference in spatial skill. *Psychological Science, 16*, 841–845.

Levitt, A. G., & Utman, J. A. (1992). From babbling towards the sound systems of English and French: A longitudinal two-case study. *Journal of Child Language, 19*, 19–49.

Levitt, M. J., Guacci-Franco, N., & Levitt, J. L. (1993). Convoys of social support in childhood and early adolescence: Structure and function. *Developmental Psychology, 29*, 811–818.

Levy, B. A., Gong, Z., Hessels, S., Evans, M. A., & Jared, D. (2006). Understanding print: Early reading development and the contributions of home literacy experiences. *Journal of Experimental Child Psychology, 93*, 63–93.

Levy, G. D., & Boston, M. B. (1994). Preschoolers' recall of own-sex and other-sex gender scripts. *Journal of Genetic Psychology, 155*, 367–371.

Levy, G. D., Taylor, M. G., & Gelman, S. A. (1995). Traditional and evaluative aspects of flexibility in gender roles, social conventions, moral rules, and physical laws. *Child Development, 66*, 515–531.

Levy, J. (1976). A review of evidence for a genetic component in the determination of handedness. *Behavior Genetics, 6*, 429–453.

Lewis, M. (1997). The self in self-conscious emotions. In J. G. Snodgrass & R. L. Thompson (Eds.), *The self across psychology: Self-awareness, self-recognition, and the self-concept* (pp. 119–142). New York, NY: New York Academy of Science.

Lewis, M. (2000). The emergence of human emotions. In M. Lewis & J. Haviland-Jones (Eds.), *Handbook of emotions* (2nd ed., pp. 265–280). New York, NY: Guilford.

Lewis, M., & Ramsay, D. (2004). Development of self-recognition, personal pronoun use, and pretend play during the second year. *Child Development, 75*, 1821–1831.

Lewis, M., Ramsay, D. S., & Kawakami, K. (1993). Differences between Japanese infants and Caucasian American infants in behavioral and cortisol response to inoculation. *Child Development, 64*, 1722–1731.

Lewis, M., Takai-Kawakami, K., Kawakami, K., & Sullivan, M. W. (2010). Cultural differences in emotional responses to success and failure. *International Journal of Behavioral Development, 34*, 53–61.

Lewkowicz, D. J. (2000). Infants' perception of the audible, visible, and bimodal attributes of multimodal syllables. *Child Development, 71*, 1241–1257.

Lewontin, R. C. (1976). Race and intelligence. In N. J. Block & G. Dworkin (Eds.), *The IQ controversy* (pp. 78–92). New York: Pantheon Books.

Li, Y., Anderson, R. C., Nguyen-Jahiel, K., Dong, T., Archodidou, A., Kim, I.-H., et al. (2007). Emergent leadership in children's discussion groups. *Cognition & Instruction, 25*, 75–111.

Liang, H., & Eley, T. C. (2005). A monozygotic twin differences study of nonshared environmental influence on adolescent depressive symptoms. *Child Development, 76*, 1247–1260.

Liben, L. S., & Bigler, R. S. (2002). The developmental course of gender differentiation. *Monographs of the Society for Research in Child Development, 67* (Serial No. 269).

Liben, L. S., Bigler, R. S., & Krogh, H. R. (2001). Pink and blue collar jobs: Children's judgments of job status and job aspirations in relation to sex of worker. *Journal of Experimental Child Psychology, 79*, 346–363.

Liebal, K., Behne, T., Carpenter, M., & Tomasello, M. (2009). Infants use shared experience to interpret pointing gestures. *Developmental Science, 12*, 264–271.

Li-Grining, C. P. (2007). Effortful control among low-income preschoolers in three cities: Stability, change, and individual differences. *Developmental Psychology, 43*, 208–221.

Lin, C. C., & Fu, V. R. (1990). A comparison of childrearing practices among Chinese, immigrant Chinese, and Caucasian-American parents. *Child Development, 61*, 429–433.

Lindberg, S. M., Hyde, J. S., Petersen, J. L., & Linn, M. C. (2010). New trends in gender and mathematics performance: A meta-analysis. *Psychological Bulletin, 136*, 1123–1135.

Lindsey, E. W., & Colwell, M. J. (2003). Preschoolers' emotional competence: Links to pretend and physical play. *Child Study Journal, 33*, 39–52.

Lindsey, E. W., & Mize, J. (2000). Parent–child physical and pretense play: Links to children's social competence. *Merrill-Palmer Quarterly, 46*, 565–591.

Linebarger, D. L., & Vaala, S. E. (2010). Screen media and language development in infants and toddlers: An ecological perspective. *Developmental Review, 30*, 176–202.

Linn, S. (2004). *Consuming kids: The hostile takeover of childhood.* New York, NY: New Press.

Linn, S. (2005). The commercialization of childhood. In S. Oldman (Ed.), *Childhood lost: How American culture is failing our kids* (pp. 107–122). Westport, CT: Praeger.

Lins-Dyer, M. T., & Nucci, L. (2007). The impact of social classes and social cognitive domain on northeastern Brazilian mothers' and daughters' conceptions of parental control. *International Journal of Behavioral Development, 31,* 105–114.

Linver, M. R., Roth, J. L., & Brooks-Gunn, J. (2009). Patterns of adolescents' participation in organized activities: Are sports best when combined with other activities? *Developmental Psychology, 45,* 354–367.

Lipsitt, L. P. (2003). Crib death: A biobehavioral phenomenon. *Psychological Science, 12,* 164–170.

Liu, D., Gelman, S. A., & Wellman, H. M. (2007). Components of young children's trait understanding: Behavior-to-trait and trait-to-behavior predictions. *Child Development, 78,* 1543–1558.

Liu, D., Wellman, H. M., Tardif, T., & Sabbagh, M. A. (2008). Theory of mind development in Chinese children: A meta-analysis of false-belief understanding across cultures and languages. *Developmental Psychology, 44,* 523–531.

Liu, H.-M., Kuhl, P. K., & Tsao, F.-M. (2003). An association between mothers' speech clarity and infants' speech discrimination skills. *Developmental Science, 6,* F1–F10.

Liu, H.-M., Tsao, F.-M., & Kuhl, P. K. (2007). Acoustic analysis of lexical tone in Mandarin infant-directed speech. *Developmental Psychology, 43,* 912–917.

Liu, R. X., Lin, W., & Chen, Z. Y. (2010). School performance, peer association, psychological and behavioral adjustments: A comparison between Chinese adolescents with and without siblings. *Journal of Adolescence, 33,* 411–417.

Livesley, W. J., & Bromley, D. B. (1973). *Person perception in childhood and adolescence.* New York, NY: Wiley.

Lobelo, F., Dowda, M., Pfeiffer, K. A., & Pate, R. R. (2009). Electronic media exposure and its association with activity-related outcomes in female adolescents: Cross-sectional and longitudinal analyses. *Journal of Physical Activity & Health, 6,* 137–143.

LoBue, V., & DeLoache, J. S. (2010). Superior detection of threat-relevant stimuli in infancy. *Developmental Science, 13,* 221–228.

Lockl, K., & Schneider, W. (2007). Knowledge about the mind: Links between theory of mind and later metamemory. *Child Development, 78,* 148–167.

Loock, C., Conry, J., Cook, J. L., Chudley, A. E., & Rosales, T. (2005). Identifying fetal alcohol spectrum disorder in primary care. *Canadian Medical Association Journal, 172,* 628–630.

Lorch, R. F., Lorch, E. P., Calderhead, W. J., Dunlap, E. E., Hodell, E. C., & Freer, B. D. (2010). Learning the control of variables strategy in higher and lower achieving classrooms: Contributions of explicit instruction and experimentation. *Journal of Educational Psychology, 102,* 90–101.

Lord, S. E., Eccles, J. S., & McCarthy, K. A. (1994). Surviving the junior high transition: Family processes and self-perception as protective and risk factors. *Journal of Early Adolescence, 14,* 162–199.

Low, J. (2010). Preschoolers' implicit and explicit false-belief understanding: Relations with complex syntactical mastery. *Child Development, 81,* 597–615.

Lowry, R., Wechsler, H., Kann, L., & Collins, J. L. (2001). Recent trends in participation in physical education among U.S. high school students. *Journal of School Health, 71,* 145–152.

Lubinski, D., Benbow, C. P, Webb, R. M., & Bleske-Rechek, A. (2006). Tracking exceptional human capital over two decades. *Psychological Science, 17,* 194–199.

Ludwig, J., & Phillips, D. (2007). The benefits and costs of Head Start. *SRCD Social Policy Report, 21,* 3–11, 16–18.

Luecke-Aleksa, D., Anderson, D. R., Collins, P. A., & Schmitt, K. L. (1995). Gender constancy and television viewing. *Developmental Psychology, 31,* 773–780.

Luo, Y., Kaufman, L., & Baillargeon, R. (2009). Young infants' reasoning about physical events involving inert and self-propelled objects. *Cognitive Psychology, 58,* 441–486.

Luthar, S. S., Shoum, K. A., & Brown, P. J. (2006). Extracurricular involvement among affluent youth: A scapegoat for "ubiquitous achievement pressures"? *Developmental Psychology, 42,* 583–597.

Luthar, S. S., Zigler, E., & Goldstein, D. (1992). Psychosocial adjustment among intellectually gifted adolescents: The role of cognitive-developmental and experiential factors. *Journal of Child Psychology & Psychiatry & Allied Disciplines, 33,* 361–373.

Luyckx, K., Soenens, B., Vansteeenkiste, M., Goossens, L., & Berzonsky, M. D. (2007). Parental psychological control and dimensions of identity formation in emerging adulthood. *Journal of Family Psychology, 21,* 546–550.

Lynne-Landsman, S. D., Graber, J. A., & Andrews, J. A. (2010). Do trajectories of household risk in childhood moderate pubertal timing effects on substance initiation in middle school? *Developmental Psychology, 46,* 853–868.

Lytton, H., & Romney, D. M. (1991). Parents' differential socialization of boys and girls: A meta-analysis. *Psychological Bulletin, 109,* 267–296.

MacCallum, F., Golombok, S., & Brinsden, P. (2007). Parenting and child development in families with a child conceived through embryo donation. *Journal of Family Psychology, 21,* 278–287.

Maccoby, E. E. (1984). Socialization and developmental change. *Child Development, 55,* 317–328.

Maccoby, E. E. (1990). Gender and relationships: A developmental account. *American Psychologist, 45,* 513–520.

Maccoby, E. E. (1998). *The two sexes: Growing up apart, coming together.* Cambridge, MA: Belknap Press.

Maccoby, E. E., & Jacklin, C. N. (1974). *The psychology of sex differences.* Stanford, CA: Stanford University Press.

Maccoby, E. E., & Jacklin, C. N. (1980). Sex differences in aggression: A rejoinder and reprise. *Child Development, 51,* 964–980.

Machatkova, M., Brouckova, M., Matejckova, M., Krebsova, A., Sperling, K., Vorsanova, S., Kutsev, S., Zerova, T., Arbuzova, S., Krejci, R., Petersen, M., & Macek, M. (2005). QF-PCR examination of parental and meiotic origin of trisomy 21 in central and eastern Europe. *Journal of Histochemistry & Cytochemistry, 53,* 371–373.

Mackey, A. P., Hill, S. S., Stone, S. I., & Bunge, S. A. (2011). Differential effects of reasoning and speed training in children. *Developmental Science, 14,* 582–590.

MacWhinney, B. (1998). Models of the emergence of language. *Annual Review of Psychology, 49,* 199–227.

Maggi, S., Ostry, A., Tansey, J., Dunn, J., Hershler, R., Chen, L., & Hertzman, C. (2008). Paternal psychosocial work conditions and mental health outcomes: A case-control study. *BMC Public Health, 8,* 104.

Magnuson, K., & Duncan, G. (2006). The role of family socioeconomic resources in black and white test score gaps among young children. *Developmental Review, 26,* 365–399.

Maguire, A. M., High, K. A., Auricchio, A., Wright, J. F., Pierce, E. A., Testa, F. et al. (2009). Age-dependent effects of RPE65 gene therapy for Leber's congenital amaurosis: A phase 1 dose-escalation trial. *Lancet, 374,* 1597–1605.

Maguire, E. A., Woollett, K., & Spiers, H. J. (2006). London taxi drivers and bus drivers: A structural MRI and neuropsychological analysis. *Hippocampus, 16,* 1091–1101.

Mahoney, J. L., & Parente, M. E. (2009). Should we care about adolescents who care for themselves? What we have learned and what we need to know about youth in self-care. *Child Development Perspectives, 3,* 189–195.

Maimburg, R. D., Vaeth, M., Durr, J., Hvidman, L., & Olsen, J. (2010). Randomised trial of structured antenatal training sessions to improve the birth process. *BJOG—An International Journal of Obstetrics & Gynaecology, 117,* 921–927.

Malinosky-Rummell, R., & Hansen, D. J. (1993). Long-term consequences of childhood physical abuse. *Psychological Bulletin, 114,* 68–79.

Malti, T., Gummerum, M., Keller, M., & Buchmann, M. (2009). Children's moral motivation, sympathy, and prosocial behavior. *Child Development, 80,* 442–460.

Mandara, J., Gaylord-Harden, N. K., Richard, M. H., & Ragsdale, B. L. (2009). The effects of changes in racial identity and self-esteem on changes in African American adolescents' mental health. *Child Development, 80,* 1660–1675.

Mandel, D. R., Jusczyk, P. W., & Pisoni, D. B. (1995). Infants' recognition of the sound patterns of their own names. *Psychological Science, 6,* 314–317.

Mangelsdorf, S. C. (1992). Developmental changes in infant–stranger interaction. *Infant Behavior & Development, 15,* 191–208.

Mangelsdorf, S. C., Gunnar, M., Kestenbaum, R., Lang, S., & Andreas, D. (1990). Infant proneness-to-distress temperament, maternal personality, and mother–infant attachment: Associations and goodness of fit. *Child Development, 61,* 820–831.

Mangelsdorf, S. C., Shapiro, J. R., & Marzolf, D. (1995). Developmental and temperamental differences in emotional regulation in infancy. *Child Development, 66,* 1817–1828.

Maratsos, M. (1998). The acquisition of grammar. In W. Damon (Ed.), *Handbook of child psychology.* New York, NY: Wiley.

Maratsos, M. (2000). More overregularizations after all: New data and discussion on Marcus, Pinker, Ullman, Hollander, Rosen, and Xu. *Journal of Child Language, 27,* 183–212.

Marcia, J. E. (1980). Identity in adolescence. In J. Adelson (Ed.), *Handbook of adolescent psychology.* New York, NY: Wiley.

Marcia, J. E. (1991). Identity and self-development. In R. M. Lerner, A. C. Petersen, & J. Brooks-Gunn (Eds.), *Encyclopedia of adolescence* (Vol. 1). New York, NY: Garland.

Marcus, G. F., Pinker, S., Ullman, M., Hollander, M., Rosen, T. J., & Xu, F. (1992). Overregularization in language acquisition. *Monographs of the Society for Research in Child Development, 58* (Serial No. 228).

Marcus, J., Maccoby, E. E., Jacklin, C. N., & Doering, C. H. (1985). Individual differences in mood in early childhood: Their relation to gender and neonatal sex steroids. *Developmental Psychology, 18,* 327–340.

Mareschal, D., & Tan, S. H. (2007). Flexible and context-dependent categorization by eighteen-month-olds. *Child Development, 78,* 19–37.

Markovits, H., Benenson, J., & Dolenszky, E. (2001). Evidence that children and adolescents have internal models of peer interactions that are gender differentiated. *Child Development, 72,* 879–886.

Marks, A. K., & Garcia Coll, C. (2007). Psychological and demographic correlates of early academic skill development among American Indian and Alaska Native youth: A growth modeling study. *Developmental Psychology, 43,* 663–674.

Marks, A. K., Patton, F., & García Coll, C. (2011). Being bicultural: A mixed-methods study of adolescents' implicitly and explicitly measured multiethnic identities. *Developmental Psychology, 47,* 270–288.

Marschik, P. B., Einspieler, C., Strohmeier, A., Plienegger, J., Garzarolli, B., & Prechtl, H. F. R. (2008). From the reaching behavior at 5 months of age to hand preference at preschool age. *Developmental Psychobiology, 50,* 511–518.

Marsh, H. W. (1991). Employment during high school: Character building or a subversion of academic goals? *Sociology of Education, 64,* 172–189.

Marsh, H. W., & Craven, R. G. (2006). Reciprocal effects of self-concept and performance from a multidimensional perspective: Beyond seductive pleasure and unidimensional perspectives. *Perspectives on Psychological Science, 1*, 133–163.

Marsh, H. W., & Kleitman, S. (2005). Consequences of employment during high school: Character building, subversion of academic goals, or a threshold? *American Educational Research Journal, 42*, 331–369.

Marsh, H. W., & Yeung, A. S. (1997). Causal effects of academic self-concept on academic achievement: Structural equation models of longitudinal data. *Journal of Educational Psychology, 89*, 41–54.

Marsh, H. W., Chessor, D., Craven, R., & Roche, L. (1995). The effects of gifted and talented programs on academic self-concept: The big fish strikes again. *American Educational Research Journal, 32*, 285–319.

Marsh, H. W., Ellis, L. A., & Craven, R. G. (2002). How do preschool children feel about themselves? Unraveling measurement and multidimensional self-concept structure. *Developmental Psychology, 38*, 376–393.

Marsh, H. W., Trautwein, U., Ludtke, O., Killer, O., & Baumert, J. (2005). Academic self-concept, interest, grades, and standardized test scores: Reciprocal effects models of causal ordering. *Child Development, 76*, 397–416.

Marshall, N. L. (2004). The quality of early child care and children's development. *Current Directions in Psychological Science, 13*, 165–168.

Martel, M. M., & Nigg, J. T. (2006). Child ADHD and personality/temperament traits of reactive and effortful control, resiliency, and emotionality. *Journal of Child Psychology, 47*, 1175–1183.

Martin, C. L., & Fabes, R. A. (2001). The stability and consequences of young children's same-sex peer interactions. *Developmental Psychology, 37*, 431–446.

Martin, C. L., & Halverson, C. F. (1987). The roles of cognition in sex role acquisition. In D. B. Carter (Ed.), *Current conceptions of sex roles and sex typing: Theory and research* (pp. 123–137). New York, NY: Praeger.

Martin, C. L., & Ruble, D. (2004). Children's search for gender cues: Cognitive perspectives on gender development. *Current Directions in Psychological Science, 13*, 67–70.

Martin, C. L., Fabes, R. A., Evans, S. M., & Wyman, H. (1999). Social cognition on the playground: Children's beliefs about playing with girls versus boys and their relationships to sex-segregated play. *Journal of Social & Personal Relationships, 16*, 751–772.

Martin, C. L., Ruble, D. N., & Szkrybalo, J. (2002). Cognitive theories of early gender development. *Psychological Bulletin, 128*, 903–933.

Martin, J. L., & Ross, H. S. (2005). Sibling aggression: Sex differences and parents' reactions. *International Journal of Behavioral Development, 29*, 129–138.

Martin, R. P., Olejnik, S., & Gaddis, L. (1994). Is temperament an important contributor to schooling outcomes in elementary school? Modeling effects of temperament and scholastic ability on academic achievement. In W. B. Casey & S. C. McDevitt (Eds.), *Prevention and early intervention*. New York, NY: Brunner/Mazel.

Mash, E. J., & Wolfe, D. A. (2010). *Abnormal child psychology* (4th ed). Belmont, CA: Cengage.

Masnick, A. M., & Morris, B. J. (2008). Investigating the development of data evaluation: The role of data characteristics. *Child Development, 79*, 1032–1048.

Masten, A. S., & Osofsky, J. D. (2010). Diasters and their impact on child development: Introduction to the special section. *Child Development, 81*, 1029–1039.

Masten, A. S., Roisman, G. I., Long, J. D., Burt, K. B., Obradovic, J., Riley, J. R., et al. (2005). Developmental cascades: Linking academic achievement and externalizing and internalizing symptoms over 20 years. *Developmental Psychology, 41*, 733–746.

Mastorakos, G., & Illias, I. (2003). Maternal and fetal hypothalamic-pituitary-adrenal axes during pregnancy and postpartum. *Women's Health & Disease: Gynecologic & Reproductive Issues, 997*, 136–149.

Masur, E. F. (1995). Infants' early verbal imitation and their later lexical development. *Merrill-Palmer Quarterly, 41*, 286–306.

Mattys, S. L., & Jusczyk, P. W. (2001). Phonotactic cues for segmentation of fluent speech by infants. *Cognition, 78*, 91–121.

Matusov, E., Bell, N., & Rogoff, B. (2002). Schooling as cultural process: Working together and guidance by children from schools differing in collaborative practices. In R. V. Kail & H. W. Reese (Eds.), *Advances in child development and behavior* (Vol. 29, pp. 129–160). San Diego, CA: Academic Press.

Maughan, A., & Cicchetti, D. (2002). Impact of child maltreatment and interadult violence on children's emotion regulation abilities and socioemotional adjustment. *Child Development, 73*, 1525–1542.

Maye, J., Weiss, D. J., & Aslin, R. N. (2008). Statistical phonetic learning in infants: Facilitation and feature generalization. *Developmental Science, 11*, 122–134.

Mayer, J. D., Roberts, R. D., & Barsade, S. G. (2008). Human abilities: Emotional intelligence. *Annual Review of Psychology, 59*, 507–536.

Mayer, J. D., Salovey, P., & Caruso, D. R. (2008). Emotional intelligence: New ability or eclectic traits? *American Psychologist, 63*, 503–517.

Maynard, A. E. (2002). Cultural teaching: The development of teaching skills in Maya sibling interactions. *Child Development, 73*, 969–982.

Mazur, E., Wolchik, S. A., Virdin, L., Sandler, I. N., & West, S. G. (1999). Cognitive moderators of children's adjustment to stressful divorce events: The role of negative cognitive errors and positive illusions. *Child Development, 70*, 231–245.

McCall, R. B. (1993). Developmental functions for general mental performance. In D. K. Detterman (Ed.), *Current topics in human intelligence* (Vol. 3, pp. 3–29). Norwood, NJ: Ablex.

McCandless, B. D. (2003). Brain based education. In J. Guthrie (Ed.), *Encyclopedia of education, Vol. 1* (2nd ed.). New York, NY: Macmillan Reference.

McCarty, M. E., & Ashmead, D. H. (1999). Visual control of reaching and grasping in infants. *Developmental Psychology, 35*, 620–631.

McCarty, M. E., Clifton, R. K., Ashmead, D. H., Lee, P., & Goubet, N. (2001). How infants use vision for grasping objects. *Child Development, 72*, 973–987.

McClure, E. B. (2000). A meta-analytic review of sex differences in facial expression processing and their development in infants, children, and adolescents. *Psychological Bulletin, 126*, 424–453.

McCormick, C. B. (2003). Metacognition and learning. In I. B. Weiner (Editor-in-Chief) and W. M. Reynolds & G. E. Miller (Eds.), *Handbook of psychology: Vol. 7. Educational psychology* (pp. 79–102). New York, NY: Wiley.

McCrink, K., & Wynn, K. (2007). Ratio abstraction by 6-month-old infants. *Psychological Science, 18*, 740–745.

McCutchen, D., Covill, A., Hoyne, S. H., & Mildes, K. (1994). Individual differences in writing: Implications of translating fluency. *Journal of Educational Psychology, 86*, 256–266.

McCutchen, D., Francis, M., & Kerr, S. (1997). Revising for meaning: Effects of knowledge and strategy. *Journal of Educational Psychology, 89*, 667–676.

McDonald, E. J., McCable, K., Yeh, M., Lau, A., Garland, A., & Hough, R. L. (2005). Cultural affiliation and self-esteem as predictors of internalizing problems among Mexican American adolescents. *Journal of Clinical Child & Adolescent Psychology, 34*, 163–171.

McDonald, K. L., Bowker, J. C., Rubin, K. H., Laursen, B., & Duchene, M. S. (2010). Interactions between rejection sensitivity and supportive relationships in the prediction of adolescents' internalizing difficulties. *Journal of Youth & Adolescence, 39*, 563–574.

McElwain, N. L., Booth-LaForce, C., Lansford, J. E., Wu, X., & Justin Dyer, W. (2008). A process model of attachment-friend linkages: Hostile attribution biases,

language ability and mother-child affective mutuality as intervening mechanisms. *Child Development, 79*, 1891–1906.

McGee, L. M., & Richgels, D. J. (2004). *Literacy's beginnings* (4th ed.). Boston, MA: Allyn & Bacon.

McGraw, M. B. (1935). *Growth: A study of Johnny and Jimmy*. East Norwalk, CT: Appleton-Century-Crofts.

McGuire, S., & Shanahan, L. (2010). Sibling experiences in diverse family contexts. *Child Development Perspectives, 4*, 72–79.

McHale, J. P., Laurette, A., Talbot, J., & Pourquette, C. (2002). Retrospect and prospect in the psychological study of coparenting and family group process. In J. P. McHale & W. Grolnick (Eds.), *Retrospect and prospect in the psychological study of families* (pp. 127–165). Mahwah, NJ: Erlbaum.

McHale, S. M., Crouter, A. C., Kim, J.-Y., Burton, L. M., Davis, K. D., Dotterer, A. M., et al. (2006). Mothers' and fathers' racial socialization in African American families: Implications for youth. *Child Development, 77*, 1387–1402.

McHale, S. M., Kim, J. Y., Whiteman, S. D., & Crouter, A. C. (2004). Links between sex-typed activities in middle childhood and gender development in early adolescence. *Developmental Psychology, 40*, 868–881.

McHale, S. M., Whiteman, S. D., Kim, J.-Y., & Crouter, A. C. (2007). Characteristics and correlates of sibling relationships in two-parent African American families. *Journal of Family Psychology, 21*, 227–235.

McKusick, V. A. (1995). *Mendelian inheritance in man: Catalogs of autosomal dominant, automosal recessive, and X-linked phenotypes* (10th ed.). Baltimore: Johns Hopkins University Press.

McLanahan, S. (1999). Father absence and the welfare of children. In E. M. Hetherington (Ed.), *Coping with divorce, single parenting, and remarriage: A risk and resiliency perspective* (pp. 117–145). Mahwah, NJ: Erlbaum.

McLellan, J. A., & Youniss, J. (2003). Two systems of youth service: Determinants of voluntary and required youth community service. *Journal of Youth & Adolescence, 32*, 47–58.

McMurray, B. (2007). Defusing the childhood vocabulary explosion. *Science, 317*, 631.

Meaney, M. J. (2010). Epigenetics and the biological definition of gene x environment interactions. *Child Development, 81*, 41–79.

Meeus, W., Oosterwegel, A., & Vollebergh, W. (2002). Parental and peer attachment and identity development in adolescence. *Journal of Adolescence, 25*, 93–106.

Meeus, W., van de Schoot, R., Keijsers, L., Schwartz, S. J., & Branje, S. (2010). On the progression and stability of adolescent identity formation: A five-wave longitudinal study in early-to-middle and middle-to-late adolescence. *Child Development, 81*, 1565–1581.

Mehta, C. M., & Strough, J. (2009). Sex segregation in friendships and normative contexts across the life span. *Developmental Review, 29*, 201–220.

Melby, J. N., Conger, R. D., Fang, S., Wickrama, K. A. S., & Conger, K. J. (2008). Adolescent family experiences and educational attainment during early adulthood. *Developmental Psychology, 44*, 1519–1536.

Mendle, J., Turkheimer, E., & Emery, R. E. (2007). Detrimental psychological outcomes associated with early pubertal timing in adolescent girls. *Developmental Review, 27*, 151–171.

Mennella, J. A., Jagnow, C. P., & Beauchamp, G. K. (2001). Prenatal and postnatal flavor learning by human infants. *Pediatrics, 107*, e88.

Mennella, J., & Beauchamp, G. K. (1997). The ontogeny of human flavor perception. In G. K. Beauchamp & L. Bartoshuk (Eds.), *Tasting and smelling: Handbook of perception and cognition*. San Diego, CA: Academic Press.

Menon, M., Tobin, D. D., Corby, B. C., Menon, M., Hodges, E. V., & Perry, D. G. (2007). The developmental costs of high self-esteem for antisocial children. *Child Development, 78,* 1627–1639.

Metcalfe, J. S., McDowell, K., Chang, T.-Y., Chen, L.-C., Jeka, J. J., & Clark, J. E. (2005). Development of somatosensory-motor integration: An event-related analysis of infant posture in the first year of independent walking. *Developmental Psychobiology, 46,* 19–35.

Metzger, A., Dawes, N., Mermelstein, R., & Wakschlag, L. (2011). Longitudinal modeling of adolescents' activity involvement, problem peer associations, and youth smoking. *Journal of Applied Developmental Psychology, 32,* 1–9.

Miceli, P. J., Whitman, T. L., Borkowsky, J. G., Braungart-Riekder, J., & Mitchell, D. W. (1998). Individual differences in infant information processing: The role of temperament and maternal factors. *Infant Behavior & Development, 21,* 119–136.

Midgette, E., Haria, P., & MacArthur, C. (2008). The effects of content and audience awareness goals for revision on the persuasive essays of fifth- and eight-grade students. *Reading & Writing, 21,* 131–151.

Milberger, S., Biederman, J., Faraone, S. V., Guite, J., & Tsuang, M. T. (1997). Pregnancy, delivery and infancy complications, and attention deficit hyperactivity disorder: Issues of gene-environment interaction. *Biological Psychiatry, 41,* 65–75.

Miles, S. B., & Stipek, D. (2006). Contemporaneous and longitudinal associations between social behavior and literacy achievement in a sample of low-income elementary school children. *Child Development, 77,* 103–117.

Miller, B. C., Fan, X., Christensen, M., Grotevant, H. D., & van Dulmen, M. (2000). Comparisons of adopted and nonadopted adolescents in a large, nationally representative sample. *Child Development, 71,* 1458–1473.

Miller, G. E., & Chen, E. (2010). Harsh family climate in early life presages the emergence of proinflammatory phenotype in adolescence. *Psychological Science, 21,* 848–856.

Miller, J. G., & Bersoff, D. M. (1992). Culture and moral judgment: How are conflicts between justice and interpersonal responsibilities resolved? *Journal of Personality & Social Psychology, 62,* 541–554.

Miller, K. F., Smith, C. M., Zhu, J., & Zhang, H. (1995). Preschool origins of cross-national differences in mathematical competence: The role of number-naming systems. *Psychological Science, 6,* 56–60.

Miller, P. H. (2011). Piaget's theory: Past, present, and future. In U. Goswami (Ed.), *The Wiley-Blackwell handbook of childhood cognitive development* (2nd ed., pp. 649–672). West Sussex, UK: Wiley-Blackwell.

Miller, P. M., Danaher, D. L., & Forbes, D. (1986). Sex-related strategies of coping with interpersonal conflict in children aged five to seven. *Developmental Psychology, 22,* 543–548.

Miller, S. A. (2009). Children's understanding of second-order mental states. *Psychological Bulletin, 135,* 749–773.

Miller, T. W., Nigg, J. T., & Miller, R. L. (2009). Attention deficit hyperactivity disorder in African American children: What can be learned from the past ten years? *Clinical Psychology Review, 29,* 77–86.

Mills, C. M., & Keil, F. C. (2005). The development of cynicism. *Psychological Science, 16,* 385–390.

Milunsky, A. (2002). *Your genetic destiny: Know your genes, secure your health, and save your life.* Cambridge, MA: Perseus Publishing.

Mingroni, M. A. (2007). Resolving the IQ paradox: Heterosis as a cause of the Flynn effect and other trends. *Psychological Review, 114,* 806–829.

Minkler, M., & Fuller-Thomson, E. (2005). African American grandparents raising grandchildren: A national study using the Census 2000 American Community Survey. *Journals of Gerontology: Psychological Sciences & Social Sciences, 60B,* S82–S92.

Mischel, W. (1970). Sex-typing and socialization. In P. H. Mussen (Ed.), *Carmichael's manual of child psychology* (Vol. 2). New York, NY: Wiley.

Mischel, W., & Ayduk, O. (2004). Willpower in a cognitive-affective processing system: The dynamics of delay of gratification. In R. F. Baumeister & K. D. Vohs (Eds.), *Handbook of self-regulation* (pp. 99–129). New York, NY: Guilford.

Mischel, W., & Ebbesen, E. (1970). Attention in delay of gratification. *Journal of Personality & Social Psychology, 16,* 329–337.

Mix, K. S., Huttenlocher, J., & Levine, S. C. (2002). Multiple cues for quantification in infancy: Is number one of them? *Psychological Bulletin, 128,* 278–294.

Mize, J., & Ladd, G. W. (1990). A cognitive social-learning approach to social skill training with low-status preschool children. *Developmental Psychology, 26,* 388–397.

Mize, J., & Pettit, G. S. (1997). Mothers' social coaching, mother–child relationship style, and children's peer competence: Is the medium the message? *Child Development, 68,* 312–332.

Mize, J., Pettit, G. S., & Brown, E. G. (1995). Mothers' supervision of their children's peer play: Relations with beliefs, perceptions, and knowledge. *Developmental Psychology, 31,* 311–321.

Mizes, J., Scott, P., & Tonya, M. (1995). Eating disorders. In M. Hersen & R. T. Ammerman (Eds.), *Handbook of prevention and treatment with children and adolescents: Intervention in the real world context* (pp. 441–465). New York, NY: Wiley.

Moerk, E. L. (2000). *The guided acquisition of first language skills.* Westport, CT: Ablex.

Moffitt, T. E. (2005). The new look of behavioral genetics in developmental psychopathology: Gene-environment interplay in antisocial behaviors. *Psychological Bulletin, 131,* 533–554.

Moffitt, T. E., Caspi, A., Belsky, J., & Silva, P. (1992). Childhood experience and the onset of menarche: A test of a sociobiological model. *Child Development, 63,* 47–58.

Molfese, D. L., & Burger-Judisch, L. M. (1991). Dynamic temporal-spatial allocation of resources in the human brain: An alternative to the static view of hemisphere differences. In F. L. Ketterle (Ed.), *Cerebral laterality: Theory and research. The Toledo symposium.* Hillsdale, NJ: Erlbaum.

Molina, B. S. G., Hinshaw, S. P., Swanson, J. M., Arnold, L. E., Vitiello, B., Jensen, P. S., et al. (2009). The MTA at 8 years: Prospective follow-up of children treated for combined-type ADHD in a multisite study. *Journal of the American Academy of Child & Adolescent Psychiatry, 48,* 484–500.

Molloy, L. E., Gest, S. D., & Rulison, K. L. (2011). Peer influences on academic motivation: Exploring multiple methods of assessing youths' most "influential" peer relationships. *Journal of Early Adolescence, 31,* 13–40.

Monahan, K. C., Lee, J. M., & Steinberg, L. (2011). Revisiting the impact of part-time work on adolescent adjustment: Distinguishing between selection and socialization using propensity score matching. *Child Development, 82,* 96–112.

Monahan, K. C., Steinberg, L., & Cauffman, E. (2009). Affiliation with antisocial peers, susceptibility to peer influence, and antisocial behavior during the transition to adulthood. *Developmental Psychology, 45,* 1520–1530.

Monk, C., Fifer, W. P., Myers, M. M., Sloan, R. P., Trien, L., & Hurtado, A. (2000). Maternal stress responses and anxiety during pregnancy: Effects on fetal heart rate. *Developmental Psychology, 36,* 67–77.

Montague, D. P., & Walker-Andrews, A. S. (2001). Peekaboo: A new look at infants' perception of emotion expressions. *Developmental Psychology, 37,* 826–838.

Moore, C. (2007). Understanding self and others in the second year. In C. A. Brownell & C. B. Kopp (Eds.), *Socioemotional development in the toddler years* New York, NY: Guilford.

Moore, C. F. (2003). *Silent scourge: Children, pollution, and why scientists disagree.* New York, NY: Oxford University Press.

Moore, D., & Johnson, S. (2008). Mental rotation in human infants: A sex difference. *Psychological Science, 19,* 1063–1065.

Moore, K. L., & Persaud, T. V. N. (1993). *Before we are born* (4th ed.). Philadelphia: W. B. Saunders.

Moore, M. R., & Brooks-Gunn, J. (2002). Adolescent parenthood. In M. H. Bornstein (Ed.), *Handbook of parenting: Vol. 3: Being and becoming a parent* (2nd ed., pp. 173–214). Mahwah, NJ: Erlbaum.

Moreno, A. J., Klute, M. M., & Robinson, J. L. (2008). Relational and individual resources as predictors of empathy in early childhood. *Social Development, 17,* 613–637.

Morgan, B., & Gibson, K. R. (1991). Nutritional and environmental interactions in brain development. In K. R. Gibson & A. C. Peterson (Eds.), *Brain maturation and cognitive development: Comparative and cross-cultural perspectives* (pp. 91–106). New York, NY: Aldine de Gruyter.

Morgane, P. J., Austin-LaFrance, R., Bronzino, J. D., Tonkiss, J., Diaz-Cintra, S., et al. (1993). Prenatal malnutrition and development of the brain. *Neuroscience & Biobehavioral Reviews, 17,* 91–128.

Morrissey, T. W. (2009). Multiple child-care arrangements and young children's behavioral outcomes. *Child Development, 80,* 59–76.

Morrongiello, B. A., Klemencic, N., & Corbett, M. (2008). Interactions between child behavior patterns and parent supervision: Implications for children's risk of unintentional injury. *Child Development, 79,* 627–638.

Morrow, J. R. (2005). Are American children and youth fit? It's time we learned. *Research Quarterly for Exercise & Sport, 76,* 377–388.

Mortimer, J. T., & Staff, J. (2004). Early work as a source of developmental discontinuity during the transition to adulthood. *Development & Psychopathology, 16,* 1047–1070.

Morton, J., & Johnson, M. H. (1991). CONSPEC and CONLERN: A two-process theory of infant face recognition. *Psychological Review, 98,* 164–181.

Moses, L. J., Baldwin, D. A., Rosicky, J. G., & Tidball, G. (2001). Evidence for referential understanding in the emotions domain at twelve and eighteen months. *Child Development, 72,* 718–735.

Moss, E., Cyr, C., Bureau, J.-F., Tarabulsy, G. M., & Dubois-Comtois, K. (2005). Stability of attachment during the preschool period. *Developmental Psychology, 41,* 773–783.

Moss, E., Smolla, N., Guerra, I., Mazzarello, T., Chayer, D., & Berthiaume, C. (2006). Attachement et problèmes de comportements intériorisés et extériorisés auto-rapportés á la période scolaire [Attachment and self-reported internalizing and externalizing behavior problems in school-age children]. *Canadian Journal of Behavioural Science, 38,* 142–157.

Mueller, M. M., & Elder, G. H. (2003). Family contingencies across the generations: Grandparents–grandchild relationships in holistic perspective. *Journal of Marriage & the Family, 65,* 404–417.

Mumme, D. L., Fernald, A., & Herrera, C. (1996). Infants' responses to facial and vocal emotional signals in a social referencing paradigm. *Child Development, 67,* 3219–3237.

Murphy, K. R., Barkley, R. A., & Bush, T. (2002). Young adults with attention deficit hyperactivity disorder: Subtype differences in comorbidity, educational, and clinical history. *Journal of Nervous & Mental Disease, 190,* 147–157.

Murphy, N., & Messer, D. (2000). Differential benefits from scaffolding and children working alone. *Educational Psychology, 20,* 17–31.

Murray, V. M., Berkely, C., Gaylord-Harden, N. K., Copeland-Linder, N., & Nation, M. (2011).

Neighborhood poverty and adolescent development. *Journal of Research on Adolescence, 21,* 114–128.

Murray-Close, D., Hoza, B., Hinshaw, S. P., Arnold, L. E., Swanson, J., Jensen, P. S., et al. (2010). Developmental processes in peer problems of children with attention-deficit/hyperactivity disorder in the Multimodal Treatment Study of Children with ADHD: Developmental cascades and vicious cycles. *Development & Psychopathology, 22,* 785–802.

Mustanski, B. S., Viken, R. J., Kaprio, J., Pulkkinen, L., & Rose, R. J. (2004). Genetic and environmental influences on pubertal development: Longitudinal data from Finnish twins at ages 11 and 14. *Developmental Psychology, 40,* 1188–1198.

Muter, V., Hulme, C., Snowling, M. J., & Stevenson, J. (2004). Phonemes, rimes, vocabulary, and grammatical skills as foundations of early reading development: Evidence from a longitudinal study. *Developmental Psychology, 40,* 663–681.

Nadig, A. S., & Sedivy, J. C. (2002). Evidence of perspective-taking constraints in children's online reference resolution. *Psychological Science, 13,* 329–336.

Naigles, L. G., & Gelman, S. A. (1995). Overextensions in comprehension and production revisited: Preferential-looking in a study of dog, cat, and cow. *Journal of Child Language, 22,* 19–46.

Nánez, J., Sr., & Yonas, A. (1994). Effects of luminance and texture motion on infants' defensive reactions to optical collision. *Infant Behavior & Development, 17,* 165–174.

Nangle, D. W., Erdley, C. A., Zeff, K. R., Staunchfield, L. L., & Gold, J. A. (2004). Opposites do not attract: Social status and behavioral-style concordances and discordances among children and peers who like or dislike them. *Journal of Abnormal Child Psychology, 32,* 425–434.

Nansel, T. R., Overpeck, M., Pilla, R. S., Ruan, W. J., Simons-Morton, B., & Scheidt, P. (2001). Bullying behaviors among U.S. youth: Prevalence and association with psychosocial adjustment. *Journal of the American Medical Association, 285,* 2094–2100.

Nation, K., Adams, J. W., Bowyer-Crane, C. A., & Snowling, M. J. (1999). Working memory deficits in poor comprehenders reflect underlying language impairments. *Journal of Experimental Child Psychology, 73,* 139–158.

Nation, K., Clark, P., Marshall, C., & Durand, M. (2004). Hidden language impairments in children: Parallels between poor reading comprehension and specific language impairment? *Journal of Speech, Language & Hearing Research, 47,* 199–211.

National Association for Sport and Physical Education. (2004). *Appropriate practices for high school physical education.* Reston, VA: Author.

National Cancer Institute. (2006). *DES: Questions and Answers.* Washington DC: Author.

National Center for Health Statistics. (2007). *Health, United States, 2007, with chartbook on trends in the health of Americans.* Atlanta, GA: Author.

National High Blood Pressure Education Program Working Group on Hypertension Control in Children and Adolescents. (1996). Update on the 1987 task force report on high blood pressure in children and adolescents: A working group report from the National High Blood Pressure Education Program. *Pediatrics, 98,* 649–658.

National Radiological Protection Board. (2004). Review of the scientific evidence for limiting exposure to electromagnetic fields (0-300 GHz). *Documents of the NRPB, 15*(3).

National Science Foundation. (2008). *Science and engineering indicators 2008.* Retrieved from http://www.nsf.gov/statistics/seind08

Natsuaki, M. N., Biehl, M. C., & Ge, X. (2009). Trajectories of depressed mood from early adolescence to young adulthood: The effects of pubertal timing and adolescent dating. *Journal of Research on Adolescence, 19,* 47–74.

Neisser, U., Boodoo, G., Bouchard, T. J., Boykin, A. W., Brody, N., Ceci, S. J., et al. (1996). Intelligence: Knowns and unknowns. *American Psychologist, 51,* 77–101.

Nelson, D. G., & O'Neil, K. (2005). How do parents respond to children's questions about the identity of artifacts? *Developmental Science, 8,* 519–524.

Nelson, E. A. S., Schiefenhoevel, W., & Haimerl, F. (2000). Child care practices in nonindustrialized societies. *Pediatrics, 105,* e75.

Nelson, I. A., & Gastic, B. (2009). Street ball, swim team and the sour cream machine: A cluster analysis of out of school time participation portfolios. *Journal of Youth & Adolescence, 38,* 1172–1186.

Nelson, K. (1973). Structure and strategy in learning to talk. *Monographs of the Society for Research in Child Development, 38* (Serial No. 149).

Nelson, K. (1993). Explaining the emergence of autobiographical memory in early childhood. In A. F. Collins & S. E. Gathercole (Eds.), *Theories of memory.* Hove, UK: Erlbaum.

Nelson, K. (2001). Language and the self: From the "Experiencing I" to the "Continuing Me." In C. Moore & K. Lemmon (Eds.), *The self in time: Developmental perspectives* (pp. 15–33). Mahwah, NJ: Erlbaum.

Nelson, K., & Fivush, R. (2004). The emergence of autobiographical memory: A social cultural developmental theory. *Psychological Review, 111,* 486–511.

Nesdale, D. (2001). The development of prejudice in children. In M. A. Augoustinos & K J. Reynolds (Eds.), *Understanding prejudice, racism, and social conflict* (pp. 57–73). London, UK: Sage.

Nesdale, D., Maass, A., Durkin, K., & Griffiths, J. (2005). Group norms, threat, and children's racial prejudice. *Child Development, 76,* 652–663.

Nevid, J. S., Rathus, S. A., & Greene, B. (2003). *Abnormal psychology in a changing world* (5th ed.). Upper Saddle River, NJ: Prentice-Hall.

Newcomb, A. F., & Bagwell, C. L. (1995). Children's friendship relations: A meta-analytic review. *Psychological Bulletin, 117,* 306–347.

Newcombe, N. S. (2002). The nativist-empiricist controversy in the context of recent research on spatial and quantitative development. *Psychological Science, 13,* 395–401.

Newman, G. E., & Keil, F. C. (2008). Where is the essence? Developmental shifts in children's beliefs about internal features. *Child Development, 79,* 1344–1356.

Newman, R., Ratner, N. B., Jusczyk, A. M., Jusczyk, P. W., & Dow, K. A. (2006). Infants' early ability to segment the conversational speech signal predicts later language development: A retrospective analysis. *Developmental Psychology, 42,* 643–655.

Newport, E. L. (1991). Contrasting conceptions of the critical period for language. In S. Carey & R. Gelman (Eds.), *The epigenesis of mind: Essays on biology and cognition* (pp. 111–130). Hillsdale, NJ: Erlbaum.

NICHD Early Child Care Research Network. (1997). The effects of infant child care on infant–mother attachment security: Results of the NICHD Study of Early Child Care. *Child Development, 68,* 860–879.

NICHD Early Child Care Research Network. (2001). Child-care and family predictors of preschool attachment and stability from infancy. *Developmental Psychology, 37,* 847–862.

NICHD. (2004). *The NICHD community connection.* Washington DC: Author.

NINDS. (2009). *Autism fact sheet* (NIH Publication No. 09-1877). Washington DC: Author.

Nishida, T. K., & Lillard, A. S. (2007). The informative value of emotional expressions: "Social referencing"

in mother–child pretense. *Developmental Science, 10,* 205–212.

Nishina, A., & Juvonen, J. (2005). Daily reports of witnessing and experiencing peer harassment in middle school. *Child Development, 76,* 435–450.

Nord, M., Andrews, M., & Carlson, S. (2007). *Household food security in the United States, 2006.* Washington, DC: U.S. Department of Agriculture.

Norlander, T., Erixon, A., & Archer, T. (2000). Psychological androgyny and creativity: Dynamics of gender-role and personality trait. *Social Behavior & Personality, 28,* 423–435.

Notaro, P. C., Gelman, S. A., & Zimmerman, M. A. (2001). Children's understanding of psychogenic bodily reactions. *Child Development, 72,* 444–459.

Nucci, L., & Gingo, M. (2011). The development of moral reasoning. In U. Goswami (Ed.), *The Wiley-Blackwell handbook of childhood cognitive development* (2nd ed., pp. 420–445). West Sussex, UK: Wiley.

Nucci, L., & Weber, E. (1995). Social interactions in the home and the development of young children's conception of the personal. *Child Development, 66,* 1438–1452.

Nurmsoo, E., & Bloom, P. (2008). Preschoolers' perspective taking in word learning: Do they blindly follow eye gaze? *Psychological Science, 19,* 211–215.

O'Connor, T., Heron, J., Golding, J., Beveridge, M., & Glover, V. (2002). Maternal antenatal anxiety and children's behavioral/emotional problems at 4 years. *British Journal of Psychiatry, 180,* 502–508.

O'Hara, M. W. (2009). Postpartum depression: What we know. *Journal of Clinical Psychology, 65,* 1258–1269.

O'Neill, D. K. (1996). Two-year-old children's sensitivity to a parent's knowledge state when making requests. *Child Development, 67,* 659–677.

Oakhill, J. V., & Cain, K. E. (2004). The development of comprehension skills. In T. Nunes & P. E. Bryant (Eds.), *Handbook of children's literacy* (pp. 155–180). Dordrecht: Kluwer Academic Publishers.

Oaten, M., Stevenson, R. J., & Case, T. I. (2009). Disgust as a disease-avoidance mechanism. *Psychological Bulletin, 135,* 303–321.

Oates, C., Blades, M., & Gunter, B. (2002). Children and television advertising: When do they understand persuasive intent? *Journal of Consumer Behavior, 1,* 238–245.

Oberlander, S. E., Black, M. M., & Starr, R. H., Jr. (2007). African American adolescent mothers and grandmothers: A multigenerational approach to parenting. *American Journal of Community Psychology, 39,* 37–46.

Odegard, T. N., Holliday, R. E., Brainerd, C. J., & Reyna, V. F. (2008). Attention to global gist processing eliminates age effects in false memories. *Journal of Experimental Child Psychology, 99,* 96–113.

Odgers, C. L., Moffitt, T. E., Tach, L. M., Sampson, R. J., Taylor, A., Matthews, C. L., et al. (2009). The protective effects of neighborhood collective efficacy on British children growing up in deprivation: A developmental analysis. *Developmental Psychology, 45,* 942–957.

OECD. (2006). *Starting strong II: Early childhood education and care.* Paris: OECD Publishing.

Offer, D., Ostrov, E., Howard, K. I., & Atkinson, R. (1988). *The teenage world: Adolescents' self-image in ten countries.* New York, NY: Plenum.

Ojanen, T., & Perry, D. G. (2007). Relational schemas and the developing self: Perceptions of mother and of self as joint predictors of early adolescents' self-esteem. *Developmental Psychology, 43,* 1474–1483.

Okagaki, L., & Frensch, P. A. (1994). Effects of video game playing on measures of spatial performance: Gender effects in late adolescence. *Journal of Applied Developmental Psychology, 15,* 33–58.

Okagaki, L., & Sternberg, R. J. (1993). Parental beliefs and children's school performance. *Child Development, 64,* 36–56.

Okami, P., Weisner, T., & Olmstead, R. (2002). Outcome correlates of parent–child bedsharing: An eighteen-year longitudinal study. *Developmental & Behavioral Pediatrics, 23,* 244–253.

Oliner, S. P., & Oliner, P. M. (1988). *The altruistic personality: Rescuers of Jews in Nazi Europe.* New York, NY: Free Press.

Olinghouse, N. G. (2008). Student- and instruction-level predictors of narrative writing in third-grade students. *Reading & Writing, 21,* 3–26.

Olson, S. L., Sameroff, A. J., Kerr, D. C. R., Lopez, N. L., & Wellman, H. M. (2005). Developmental foundations of externalizing problems in young children: The role of effortful control. *Development & Psychopathology, 17,* 25–45.

Olweus, D., Mattson, A., Schalling, D., & Low, H. (1988). Circulating testosterone levels and aggression in adolescent males: A causal analysis. *Psychosomatic Medicine, 50,* 261–272.

Opfer, J. E., & Gelman, S. A. (2011). Development of the animate-inanimate distinction. In U. Goswami (Ed.), *The Wiley-Blackwell handbook of childhood cognitive development* (2nd ed., pp. 213–238). West Sussex, UK: Wiley-Blackwell.

Opfer, J. E., & Siegler, R. S. (2004). Revisiting preschoolers' living things concept: A microgenetic analysis of conceptual change in basic biology. *Cognitive Psychology, 49,* 301–332.

Opfer, J. E., & Siegler, R. S. (2007). Representational change and children's numerical estimation. *Cognitive Psychology, 55,* 169–195.

Organisation for Economic Co-operation and Development. (2010). *PISA 2009 assessment framework—Key competencies in reading, mathematics and science.* Paris: Author.

Ostrov, J. M., & Godleski, S. A. (2010). Toward an integrated gender-linked model of aggression subtypes in early and middle childhood. *Psychological Review, 117,* 233–242.

Over, H., & Carpenter, M. (2009). Eighteen-month-old infants show increased helping following priming with affiliation. *Psychological Science, 20,* 1189–1193.

Padilla, A. M., Lindholm, K. J., Chen, A., Duran, R., Hakuta, K., Lambert, W., et al. (1991). The English-only movement: Myths, reality, and implications for psychology. *American Psychologist, 46,* 120–130.

Paquette, D. (2004). Theorizing the father-child relationship: Mechanisms and developmental outcomes. *Human Development, 47,* 193–219.

Parault, S. J., & Schwanenflugel, P. J. (2000). The development of conceptual categories of attention during the elementary school years. *Journal of Experimental Child Psychology, 75,* 245–262.

Parcel, G. S., Simons-Morton, B. G., O'Hara, N. M., Baranowksi, T., Kilbe, L. J., & Bee, D. E. (1989). School promotion of healthful diet and exercise behavior: An integration of organizational change and social learning theory interventions. *Journal of School Health, 57,* 150–156.

Park, G., Lubinski, D., & Benbow, C. P. (2008). Ability differences among people who have commensurate degrees matter for scientific creativity. *Psychological Science, 19,* 957–961.

Parke, R. D. (2002). Fathers and families. In M. H. Bornstein (Ed.), *Handbook of parenting: Vol. 3. Being and becoming a parent* (pp. 27–73). Mahwah, NJ: Erlbaum.

Parke, R. D., & Buriel, R. (1998). Socialization in the family: Ethnic and ecological perspectives. In W. Damon (Ed.), *Handbook of child psychology* (Vol. 3). New York, NY: Wiley.

Parke, R. D., & O'Neil, R. (2000). The influence of significant others on learning about relationships: From family to friends. In R. S. L. Mills & S. Duck (Eds.), *The developmental psychology of personal relationships* (pp. 15–47). New York, NY: Wiley.

Parke, R. D., Coltrane, S., Duffy, S., Buriel, R., Dennis, J., Powers, J., et al. (2004). Economic stress, parenting, and child adjustment in Mexican American and European American families. *Child Development, 75,* 1632–1656.

Parker, J. G., & Seal, J. (1996). Forming, losing, renewing, and replacing friendships: Applying temporal parameters to the assessment of children's friendship experiences. *Child Development, 67,* 2248–2268.

Parker, J. G., Low, C. M., Walker, A. R., & Gamm, B. K. (2005). Friendship jealousy in young adolescents: Individual differences and links to sex, self-esteem, aggression, and social adjustment. *Developmental Psychology, 41,* 235–250.

Parritz, R. H. (1996). A descriptive analysis of toddler coping in challenging circumstances. *Infant Behavior & Development, 19,* 171–180.

Parten, M. (1932). Social participation among preschool children. *Journal of Abnormal & Social Psychology, 27,* 243–269.

Pascalis, O., de Haan, M., & Nelson, C. A. (2002). Is face processing species-specific during the first year of life? *Science, 296,* 1321–1323.

Pascual, B., Aguardo, G., Sotillo, M., & Masdeu, J. C. (2008). Acquisition of mental state language in Spanish children: A longitudinal study of the relationship between the production of mental verbs and linguistic development. *Developmental Science, 11,* 454–466.

Pasterski, V. L., Geffner, M. E., Brain, C., Hindmarsh, P., Brook, C., & Hines, M. (2005). Prenatal hormones and postnatal socialization by parents as determinants of male-typical toy play in girls with congenital adrenal hyperplasia. *Child Development, 76,* 264–278.

Patterson, C. J. (1992). Children of lesbian and gay parents. *Child Development, 63,* 1025–1042.

Patterson, C. J. (2002). Lesbian and gay parenthood. In M. H. Bornstein (Ed.), *Handbook of parenting: Vol. 3. Status and social conditions of parenting* (2nd ed., pp. 317–338). Mahwah, NJ: Erlbaum.

Patterson, C. J. (2004). Gay fathers. In M. E. Lamb (Ed.), *The role of the father in child development* (pp. 397–416). New York, NY: Wiley.

Patterson, C. J. (2006). Children of lesbian and gay parents. *Current Directions in Psychological Science, 15,* 241–244.

Patterson, G. R. (1980). Mothers: The unacknowledged victims. *Monographs of the Society for Research in Child Development, 45* (Serial No. 186).

Patterson, G. R. (2008). A comparison of models for interstate wars and for individual violence. *Perspectives on Psychological Science, 3,* 203–223.

Patterson, M. M., & Bigler, R. S. (2006). Preschool children's attention to environmental messages about groups: Social categorization and the origins of intergroup bias. *Child Development, 77,* 847–860.

Pauker, K., Ambady, N., & Apfelbaum, E. P. (2010). Race salience and essentialist thinking in racial stereotype development. *Child Development, 81,* 1799–1813.

Paulussen-Hoogeboom, M. C., Stams, G. J. J., Hermanns, J. M., & Peetsma, T. T. (2007). Child negative emotionality and parenting from infancy to preschool: A meta-analytic review. *Developmental Psychology, 43,* 438–453.

Paus, T. (2010). Growth of white matter in the adolescent brain: Myelin or axon? *Brain & Cognition, 72,* 26–35.

Paxton, S. J., Eisenberg, M. E., & Neumark-Sztainer, D. (2006). Prospective predictors of body dissatisfaction in adolescent girls and boys: A five-year longitudinal study. *Developmental Psychology, 42,* 888–899.

Peake, P. K., Hebl, M., & Mischel, W. (2002). Strategic attention deployment for delay gratification in working and waiting situations. *Developmental Psychology, 38,* 313–326.

Pearlman, M., & Ross, H. S. (1997). The benefits of parent intervention in children's disputes: An examination of concurrent changes in children's fighting styles. *Child Development, 68,* 690–700.

Pederson, D. R., Gleason, K. E., Moran, G., & Bento, S. (1998). Maternal attachment representations, maternal sensitivity, and the infant–mother attachment relationship. *Developmental Psychology, 34,* 925–933.

Pellicano, E. (2010). Individual differences in executive function and central coherence predict developmental changes in theory of mind in autism. *Developmental Psychology, 46,* 530–544.

Pellis, S. M., & Pellis, V. C. (2007). Rough-and-tumble play and the development of the social brain. *Current Directions in Psychological Science, 16,* 95–98.

Pelphrey, K. A., Reznick, J. S., Davis Goldman, B., Sasson, N., Morrow, J., Donahoe, A., et al. (2004). Development of visuospatial memory in the second half of the first year. *Developmental Psychology, 40,* 836–851.

Peltola, M. J., Leppänen, J. M., Palokangas, T., & Hietanen, J. K. (2008). Fearful faces modulate looking duration and attention disengagement in 7-month-old infants. *Developmental Science, 11,* 60–68.

Pelucci, B., Hay, J. F., & Saffran, J. R. (2009). Statistical learning in a natural language by 8-month-old infants. *Child Development, 80,* 674–685.

Pennington, B. F., Willcutt, E., & Rhee, S. H. (2005). Analyzing comorbidity. In R. V. Kail (Ed.), *Advances in child development and behavior* (Vol. 22, pp. 263–304). San Diego, CA: Elsevier.

Perfetti, C. A., & Curtis, M. E. (1986). Reading. In R. F. Dillon & R. J. Sternberg (Eds.), *Cognition and instruction.* Orlando, FL: Academic Press.

Perkins, D. F., Jacobs, J. E., Barber, B. L., & Eccles, J. S. (2004). Childhood and adolescent sports participation as predictors of participation in sports and physical fitness activities during young adulthood. *Youth & Society, 35,* 495–520.

Perkins, S. A., & Turiel, E. (2007). To lie or not to lie: To whom and under what circumstances. *Child Development, 78,* 1255–1264.

Perone, S., Madole, K. L., Ross-Sheehy, S., Carey, M., & Oakes, L. (2008). The relation between infants' activity with objects and attention to object appearance. *Developmental Psychology, 44,* 1242–1248.

Perry, M. (2000). Explanations of mathematical concepts in Japanese, Chinese, and U.S. first- and fifth-grade classrooms. *Cognition & Instruction, 18,* 181–207.

Peterson, C. C., Wellman, H. M., & Liu, D. (2005). Steps in theory-of-mind development for children. *Developmental Psychology, 43,* 496–507.

Peterson, C., & Rideout, R. (1998). Memory for medical emergencies experienced by 1- and 2-year-olds. *Developmental Psychology, 34,* 1059–1072.

Peterson, C., & Slaughter, V. (2003). Opening windows into the mind: Mothers' preferences for mental state explanations and children's theory of mind. *Cognitive Development, 18,* 399–429.

Peterson, C., Wang, Q., & Hou, Y. (2009). When I was little: Childhood recollections in Chinese and European Canadian school children. *Child Development, 80,* 506–518.

Peterson, L. (1983). Role of donor competence, donor age, and peer presence on helping in an emergency. *Developmental Psychology, 19,* 873–880.

Pettit, G. S., Bates, J. E., & Dodge, K. A. (1997). Supportive parenting, ecological context, and children's adjustment: A seven-year longitudinal study. *Child Development, 68,* 908–923.

Pettito, L. A., Katerelos, M., Levy, B. G., Gauna, K., Tetreault, K., et al. (2001). Bilingual signed and spoken language acquisition from birth: Implications for the mechanisms underlying early bilingual language acquisition. *Journal of Child Language, 28,* 453–496.

Phinney, J. (1989). Stage of ethnic identity in minority group adolescents. *Journal of Early Adolescence, 9,* 34–49.

Phinney, J. S. (1990). Ethnic identity in adolescents and adults: Review of research. *Psychological Bulletin, 108,* 499–514.

Phinney, J. S. (2005). Ethnic identity development in minority adolescents. In C. B. Fisher & R. M. Lerner (Eds.), *Encyclopedia of applied developmental science* (Vol. 1, pp. 420–423). Thousand Oaks, CA: Sage.

Phipps, M. G., Rosengard, C., Weitzen, S., Meers, A., & Billinkoff, Z. (2008). Age group differences among pregnant adolescents: Sexual behavior, health habits, and contraceptive use. *Journal of Pediatric & Adolescent Gynecology, 21,* 9–15.

Piaget, J. (1929). *The child's conception of the world.* New York, NY: Harcourt, Brace.

Piaget, J., & Inhelder, B. (1956). *The child's conception of space.* Boston, MA: Routledge & Kegan Paul.

Pianta, R. C. (2007). Developmental science and education: The NICHD Study of Early Child Care and Youth Development findings from elementary school. In R. V. Kail (Ed.), *Advances in child development and behavior, Vol. 35* (pp. 254–296). Amsterdam: Elsevier.

Piehler, T. F., & Dishion, T. J. (2007). Interpersonal dynamics within adolescent friendships: Dyadic mutuality, deviant talk, and patterns of antisocial behavior. *Child Development, 78,* 1611–1624.

Pina, A. A., Zerr, A. A., Gonzales, N. A., & Ortiz, C. D. (2009). Psychosocial interventions for school refusal behavior in children and adolescents. *Child Development Perspectives, 3,* 11–20.

Pleck, J. H., & Masciadrelli, B. P. (2004). Paternal involvement by U.S. residential fathers: Levels, sources, and consequences. In M. E. Lamb (Ed.), *The role of the father in child development* (4th ed.). Hoboken, NJ: Wiley.

Plomin, R., & Crabbe, J. (2000). DNA. *Psychological Bulletin, 126,* 806–828.

Plomin, R., & Petrill, S. A. (1997). Genetics and intelligence: What's new? *Intelligence, 24,* 53–77.

Plomin, R., & Spinath, F. (2004). Intelligence: Genes, genetics, and genomics. *Journal of Personality & Social Psychology, 86,* 112–129.

Plomin, R., DeFries, J. C., McClearn, G. E., & McGuffin, P. (2001). *Behavioral genetics* (4th ed.). New York: Freeman.

Plomin, R., Fulker, D. W., Corley, R., & DeFries, J. C. (1997). Nature, nurture, and cognitive development from 1 to 16 years: A parent-offspring adoption study. *Psychological Science, 8,* 442–447.

Plumert, J. M., Kearney, J. K., & Cremer, J. F. (2007). Children's road crossing: A window into perceptual-motor development. *Current Directions in Psychological Science, 16,* 255–258.

Poehlmann, J., Schwichtenberg, A. J., Bolt, D. M., Hane, A., Burnson, C., & Winters, J. (2011). Infant physiological regulation and maternal risks as predictors of dyadic interaction trajectories in families with a preterm infant. *Developmental Psychology, 47,* 91–105.

Pollett, T. V., Nettle, D., & Nelissen, M. (2007). Maternal grandmothers do go the extra mile: Factoring distance and lineage into differential contact with grandchildren. *Evolutionary Psychology, 5,* 832–843.

Pollitt, E. (1994). Poverty and child development: Relevance of research in developing countries to the United States. *Child Development, 65,* 283–295.

Polman, J. L. (2004). Dialogic activity structures for project-based learning environment. *Cognition & Instruction, 22,* 431–466.

Poole, D. A., & Lamb, M. E. (1998). *Investigative interviews of children: A guide for helping professionals.* Washington, DC: American Psychological Association.

Poole, D. A., & Lindsay, D. S. (1995). Interviewing preschoolers: Effects of nonsuggestive techniques, parental coaching, and leading questions on reports of nonexperienced events. *Journal of Experimental Child Psychology, 60,* 129–154.

Popp, D., Laursen, B., Kerr, M., Stattin, H., & Burk, W. K. (2008). Modeling homophily over time with an actor-partner interdependence model. *Developmental Psychology, 44,* 1028–1039.

Porter, R. H., & Winburg, J. (1999). Unique salience of maternal breast odors for newborn infants. *Neuroscience & Biobehavioral Reviews, 23,* 439–449.

Poulin, F., & Boivin, M. (2000). The role of proactive and reactive aggression in the formation and development of boys' friendships. *Developmental Psychology, 36,* 233–240.

Poulin, F., & Chan, A. (2010). Friendship stability and change in childhood and adolescence. *Developmental Review, 30,* 257–272.

Poulin, F., & Pedersen, S. (2007). Developmental changes in gender composition of friendship networks in adolescent girls and boys. *Developmental Psychology, 43,* 1484–1496.

Poulson, C. L., Kymissis, E., Reeve, K. F., Andreatos, M., & Reeve, L. (1991). Generalized vocal imitation in infants. *Journal of Experimental Child Psychology, 51,* 267–279.

Pressley, M. (2002). *Reading instruction that works: The case for balanced teaching* (2nd ed). New York, NY: Guilford Press.

Pressley, M., & Hilden, K. (2006). Cognitive strategies. In D. Kuhn & R. S. Siegler (Eds.), *Handbook of child psychology* (6th ed., Vol. 2., pp. 511–556). Hoboken, NJ: Wiley.

Price, T. S., Grosser, T., Plomin, R., & Jaffee, S. R. (2010). Fetal genotype for the xenobiotic metabolizing enzyme NQO1 influences intrauterine growth among infants whose mothers smoked during pregnancy. *Child Development, 81,* 101–114.

Priel, B., & deSchonen, S. (1986). Self-recognition: A study of a population without mirrors. *Journal of Experimental Child Psychology, 41,* 237–250.

Principe, G. F., & Ceci, S. J. (2002). I saw it with my own ears: The effects of peer conversations on preschoolers' reports of nonexperienced events. *Journal of Experimental Child Psychology, 83,* 1–25.

Principe, G. F., Kanaya, T., Ceci, S. J., & Singh, M. (2006). Believing in seeing: How rumors can engender false memories in preschoolers. *Psychological Science, 17,* 243–248.

Prinstein, M. J., & Cillessen, A. H. N. (2003). Forms and functions of adolescent peer aggression associated with high levels of peer status. *Merrill Palmer Quarterly, 49,* 310–342.

Prinstein, M. J., & LaGreca, A. M. (2004). Childhood peer rejection and aggression as predictors of adolescent girls' externalizing and health risk behaviors: A 6-year longitudinal study. *Journal of Consulting & Clinical Psychology, 72,* 103–112.

Puhl, R. M., & Brownell, K. D. (2005). Bulimia nervosa. In C. B. Fisher & R. M. Lerner (Eds.), *Encyclopedia of applied developmental science* (Vol. 1, pp. 192–195). Thousand Oaks, CA: Sage.

Puhl, R. M., & Latner, J. D. (2007). Stigma, obesity, and the health of the nation's children. *Psychological Bulletin, 133,* 557–580.

Pungello, E. P., Kainz, K., Burchinal, M. R., Wasik, B. H., Sparling, J. J., Ramey, C. T., et al. (2010). Early educational intervention, early cumulative risk, and the early home environment as predictors of young adult outcomes within a high-risk sample. *Child Development, 81,* 410–426.

Qin, L., Pomerantz, E. M., & Wang, Q. (2009). Are gains in decision-making autonomy during early adolescence beneficial for emotional functioning? The case of the United States and China. *Child Development, 80,* 1705–1721.

Quas, J. A., Goodman, G. S., Bidrose, S., Pipe, M., Craw, S., & Ablin, D. S. (1999). Emotion and memory: Children's long-term remembering, forgetting, and suggestibility. *Journal of Experimental Child Psychology, 71,* 235–270.

Quillian, L., & Campbell, M. E. (2003). Beyond black and white: The present and future of multiracial friendship segregation. *American Sociological Review, 68,* 540–566.

Quinn, P. C., & Liben, L. S. (2008). A sex difference in mental rotation in young infants. *Psychological Science, 19,* 1067–1070.

Quinn, P. H. (2004). Development of subordinate-level categorization in 3- to 7-month-old infants. *Child Development, 75,* 886–899.

Quinn, P. H. (2011). Born to categorize. In U. Goswami (Ed.), *The Wiley-Blackwell handbook of childhood cognitive development* (2nd ed., pp. 129–152). West Sussex, UK: Wiley-Blackwell.

Raedeke, T. D., & Smith, A. L. (2004). Coping resources and athlete burnout: An examination of stress mediated and moderation hypotheses. *Journal of Sport & Exercise Psychology, 26,* 525–541.

Raikes, H., Luze, G., Brooks-Gunn, J., Raikes, H., Pan, B. A., Tamis-LeMonda, C. S., et al. (2006). Mother–child bookreading in low-income families: Correlates and outcomes during the first three years of life. *Child Development, 77,* 924–953.

Raine, A., Moffitt, T. E., Caspi, A., Loeber, R., Stouthamer-Loeber, M., & Lynam, D. (2005). Neurocognitive impairments in boys on the life-course persistent antisocial path. *Journal of Abnormal Psychology, 114,* 38–49.

Rakic, P. (1995). Corticogenesis in humans and nonhuman primates. In M. S. Gazzaniga (Ed.), *The cognitive neurosciences.* Cambridge, MA: MIT Press.

Rakison, D. H., & Hahn, E. R. (2004). The mechanisms of early categorization and induction: Smart or dumb infants? *Advances in Child Development & Behavior, 32,* 281–322.

Rakoczy, H. (2008). Taking fiction seriously: Young children understand the normative structure of joint pretence games. *Developmental Psychology, 44,* 1195–1201.

Ralph, L. J., & Brindis, C. D. (2010). Access to reproductive healthcare for adolescents: Establishing healthy behaviors at a critical juncture in the lifecourse. *Current Opinion in Obstetrics & Gynecology, 22,* 369–374.

Raman, L., & Gelman, S. A. (2005). Children's understanding of the transmission of genetic disorders and contagious illnesses. *Developmental Psychology, 41,* 171–182.

Ramani, G. B., & Siegler, R. S. (2008). Promoting broad and stable improvements in low-income children's numerical knowledge through playing board games. *Child Development, 79,* 375–394.

Ramey, C. T., & Campbell, F. A. (1991). Poverty, early childhood education, and academic competence: The Abecedarian experiment. In A. Huston (Ed.), *Children reared in poverty.* New York, NY: Cambridge University Press.

Ramey, S. L., & Ramey, C. T. (2006). Early educational interventions: Principles of effective and sustained benefits from targeted early education programs. In S. B. Neuman & D. K. Dickinson (Eds.), *Handbook of early literacy research* (Vol. 2, pp. 445–459). New York, NY: Guilford.

Ransjoe-Arvidson, A. B., Matthiesen, A. S., Lilja, G., Nissen, E., Widstroem, A. M., & Uvnaes-Moberg, K. (2001). Maternal analgesia during labor disturbs newborn behavior: Effects on breastfeeding, temperature, and crying. *Birth—Issues in Perinatal Care, 28,* 5–12.

Raskauskas, J., & Stoltz, A. D. (2007). Involvement in traditional and electronic bullying among adolescents. *Developmental Psychology, 43,* 564–575.

Rathunde, K. R., & Czikszentmihalyi, M. (1993). Undivided interest and the growth of talent: Longitudinal study of adolescents. *Journal of Youth & Adolescence, 22,* 385–405.

Rayner, K., Foorman, B. R., Perfetti, C. A., Pesetsky, D., & Seidenberg, M. S. (2001). How psychological science informs the teaching of reading. *Psychological Science in the Public Interest, 2,* 31–75.

Rayner, K., Foorman, B. R., Perfetti, C. A., Pesetsky, D., & Seidenberg, M. S. (2002). How should reading be taught? *Scientific American, 286,* 85–91.

Reese, E., & Cox, A. (1999). Quality of adult book reading affects children's emergent literacy. *Developmental Psychology, 35,* 20–28.

Reich, P. A. (1986). *Language development.* Englewood Cliffs, NJ: Prentice-Hall.

Reid, D. H., Wilson, P. G., & Faw, G. D. (1991). Teaching self-help skills. In J. L. Matson & J. A. Mulick (Eds.), *Handbook of mental retardation* (2nd ed.). New York, NY: Pergamon.

Reimer, M. S. (1996). "Sinking into the ground": The development and consequences of shame in adolescence. *Developmental Review, 16,* 321–363.

Repacholi, B. M. (1998). Infants' use of attentional cues to identify the referent of another person's emotional expression. *Developmental Psychology, 34,* 1017–1025.

Repacholi, B. M., & Meltzoff, A. N. (2007). Emotional eavesdropping: Infants selectively respond to indirect emotional signals. *Child Development, 78,* 503–521.

Repacholi, B. M., Meltzoff, A. N., & Olsen, B. (2008). Infants' understanding of the link between visual perception and emotion: "If she can't see me doing it, she won't get angry." *Developmental Psychology, 44,* 561–574.

Reynolds, A. J., & Robertson, D. L. (2003). School-based early intervention and later child maltreatment in the Chicago Longitudinal Study. *Child Development, 74,* 3–26.

Reynolds, A. J., Temple, J. A., White, B. A. B., Ou, S., & Robertson, D. L. (2011). Age 26 cost-benefit analysis of the child-parent center early education program. *Child Development, 82,* 379–404.

Rhoades, K. A. (2008). Children's responses to interparental conflict: A meta-analysis of their associations with child adjustment. *Child Development, 79,* 1942–1956.

Ricciardelli, L. A., & McCabe, M. P. (2004). A biopsychosocial model of disordered eating and the pursuit of muscularity in adolescent boys. *Psychological Bulletin, 130,* 179–205.

Richards, J. E., & Anderson, D. R. (2004). Attentional inertia in children's extended looking at television. In R. V. Kail (Ed.), *Advances in child development and behavior* (Vol. 32, pp. 163–212). San Diego, CA: Elsevier.

Richmond, J., & Nelson, C. A. (2007). Accounting for change in declarative memory: A cognitive neuroscience perspective. *Developmental Review, 27,* 349–373.

Richters, J. E., Arnold, L. E., Jensen, P. S., Abikoff, H., Conners, C. K., Greenhill, L. L., et al. (1995). NIMH collaborative multisite multimodal treatment study of children with ADHD: I. Background and rationale. *Journal of the American Academy of Child & Adolescent Psychiatry, 34,* 987–1000.

Rilea, S. L., Roskos-Ewoldsen, B., & Boles, D. (2004). Sex differences in spatial ability: A lateralization of function approach. *Brain & Cognition, 56,* 332–343.

Roberts, D. F., Foehr, U. G., & Rideout, V. (2005). *Generation M: Media in the lives of 8–18 year olds.* Menlo Park, CA: Henry J. Kaiser Family Foundation.

Roberts, J. E., Burchinal, M., & Durham, M. (1999). Parents' report of vocabulary and grammatical development of African American preschoolers: Child and environmental associations. *Child Development, 70,* 91–106.

Roberts, J. E., Burchinal, M., & Durham, M. (1999). Parents' report of vocabulary and grammatical development of African American preschoolers: Child and environmental associations. *Child Development, 70,* 91–106.

Robinson, A., & Clinkenbeard, P. R. (1998). Giftedness: An exceptionality examined. *Annual Review of Psychology, 49,* 117–139.

Robinson, E. J., Champion, H., & Mitchell, P. (1999). Children's ability to infer utterance veracity from speaker informedness. *Developmental Psychology, 35,* 535–546.

Roby, A. C., & Kidd, E. (2008). The referential communication skills of children with imaginary companions. *Developmental Science, 11,* 531–540.

Rochat, P. (2001). Origins of self-concept. In G. Bremmer & A. Fogel (Eds.), *Blackwell handbook of infant development* (pp. 191–212). Malden, MA: Blackwell.

Rodeck, C. H., & Whittle, M. J. (Eds.). (2009). *Fetal medicine: Basic science and clinical practice.* London: Churchill Livingstone.

Rodkin, P. C., & Roisman, G. I. (2010). Antecedents and correlates of the popular-aggressive phenomenon in elementary school. *Child Development, 81,* 837–850.

Roffwarg, H. P., Muzio, J. N., & Dement, W. C. (1966). Ontogenetic development of the human sleep-dream cycle. *Science, 152,* 604–619.

Rogers, L. A., & Graham, S. (2008). A meta-analysis of single subject design writing intervention research. *Journal of Educational Psychology, 100,* 879–906.

Rogoff, B. (1998). Cognition as a collaborative process. In W. Damon (Ed.), *Handbook of child psychology* (5th ed., Vol. 2, pp. 679–744). New York, NY: Wiley.

Rogoff, B. (2003). *The cultural nature of human development.* New York, NY: Oxford University Press.

Rogoff, B., Mistry, J., Goncu, A., & Mosier, C. (1993). Guided participation in cultural activity by toddlers and caregivers. *Monographs of the Society for Research in Child Development, 58,* Serial No. 236.

Rohrbeck, C. A., Ginsburg-Block, M. D., Fantuzzo, J. W., & Miller, T. R. (2003). Peer-assisted learning interventions with elementary school students: A meta-analytic review. *Journal of Educational Psychology, 95,* 240–257.

Rönnqvist, L., & Domellöff, E. (2006). Quantitative assessment of right and left reaching movements in infants: A longitudinal study from 6 to 36 months. *Developmental Psychobiology, 48,* 444–459.

Roschelle, J. M., Pea, R. D., Hoadley, C. M., Gordin, D. M., & Means, B. M. (2000). Changing how and what children learn in school with computer-based technologies. *Future of Children, 10,* 76–101.

Roschelle, J. M., Schechtman, N., Tatar, D., Hegedus, S., Hopkins, B., Empson, S., et al. (2010). Integration of technology, curriculum, and professional development for advancing middle school mathematics: Three large-scale studies. *American Educational Research Journal, 47,* 833–878.

Rose, A. J., & Asher, S. R. (1999). Children's goals and strategies in response to conflicts within a friendship. *Developmental Psychology, 35,* 69–79.

Rose, A. J., & Rudolph, K. D. (2006). A review of sex differences in peer relationship processes: Potential trade-offs for the emotional and behavioral development of girls and boys. *Psychological Bulletin, 132,* 98–131.

Rose, A. J., Carlson, W., & Waller, E. M. (2007). Prospective associations of co-rumination with friendship and emotional adjustment: Considering the socioemotional trade-offs of co-rumination. *Developmental Psychology, 43,* 1019–1031.

Rose, S. A., Feldman, J. F., & Jankowski, J. J. (2009). Information processing in toddlers: Continuity from infancy and persistence of preterm deficits. *Intelligence, 37,* 311–320.

Rose, S. A., Feldman, J. F., Futterweit, L. R., & Jankowski, J. J. (1997). Continuity in visual recognition memory: Infancy to 11 years. *Intelligence, 24,* 381–392.

Rosengren, K. S., Gelman, S. A., Kalish, C., & McCormick, M. (1991). As time goes by: Children's early understanding of growth in animals. *Child Development, 62,* 1302–1320.

Rosenstein, D., & Oster, H. (1997). Differential facial responses to four basic tastes in newborns. In P. Ekman & E. L. Rosenberg (Eds.), *What the face reveals: Basic and applied studies of spontaneous expression using the Facial Action Coding System (FACS).* New York, NY: Oxford University Press.

Rotenberg, K. J., & Mayer, E. V. (1990). Delay gratification in native and white children: A cross-cultural comparison. *International Journal of Behavioral Development, 13,* 23–30.

Rothbart, M. K. (2007). Temperament, development, and personality. *Current Directions in Psychological Science, 16,* 207–212.

Rothbart, M. K., & Rueda, M. R. (2005). The development of effortful control. In U. Mayr, E. Awh, & S. W. Keele (Eds.), *Developing individuality in the human brain: A tribute to Michael I. Posner* (pp. 167–188). Washington, DC: American Psychological Association.

Rothbart, M. K., & Sheese, B. E. (2007). Temperament and emotion regulation. In J. J. Gross (Ed.), *Handbook of emotion regulation* (pp. 331–350). New York, NY: Guilford.

Rothbaum, F., Weisz, J., Pott, M., Miyake, K., & Morelli, G. (2000). Attachment and culture: Security in the United States and Japan. *American Psychologist, 55,* 1093–1104.

Rotherman-Borus, M. J., & Langabeer, K. A. (2001). Developmental trajectories of gay, lesbian, and bisexual youth. In A. R. D'Augelli & C. Patterson (Eds.), *Lesbian, gay, and bisexual identities among youth: Psychological perspectives* (pp. 97–128). New York, NY: Oxford University Press.

Rovee-Collier, C. (1987). Learning and memory in infancy. In J. D. Osofsky (Ed.), *Handbook of infant development* (2nd ed.). New York, NY: Wiley.

Rovee-Collier, C. (1997). Dissociation in infant memory: Rethinking the development of implicit and explicit memory. *Psychological Review, 104,* 467–498.

Rovee-Collier, C. (1999). The development of infant memory. *Current Directions in Psychological Science, 8,* 80–85.

Rovee-Collier, C., & Barr, R. (2010). Infant learning and memory. In T. D. Wachs & G. Bremner (Eds.), *Blackwell handbook of infant development,* 2nd ed. Oxford, UK: Blackwell.

Rowe, M. L., & Goldin-Meadow, S. (2009). Early gesture selectively predicts later language learning. *Developmental Science, 12,* 182–187.

Rowland, C. F., Pine, J. M., Lieven, E. V. M., & Theakston, A. L. (2005). The incidence of error in young children's wh-questions. *Journal of Speech, Language, & Hearing Research, 48,* 384–404.

Rubin, K. H., Coplan, R. J., & Bowker, J. C. (2009). Social withdrawal in childhood. *Annual Review of Psychology, 60,* 141–171.

Rubin, K., Bukowski, W., & Parker, J. (2006). Peer interaction and social competence. In W. Damon & R. M. Lerner (Eds.), *Handbook of child psychology* (6th ed., Vol. 3). New York, NY: Wiley.

Rubinstein, O., Henrik, A., Berger, A., & Shahar-Shalev, S. (2002). The development of internal representations of magnitude and their association with Arabic numerals. *Journal of Experimental Child Psychology, 81,* 74–92.

Ruble, D. N., Boggiano, A. D., Feldman, N. S., & Loebl, N. H. (1980). Developmental analysis of the role of social comparison in self-evaluation. *Developmental Psychology, 16,* 105–115.

Ruble, D. N., Martin, C. L., & Berenbaum, S. A. (2006). Gender development. In N. Eisenberg, W. Damon, & R. M. Lerner (Eds.), *Handbook of child psychology: Vol. 3, Social, emotional, and personality development* (6th ed., pp. 858–932). Hoboken, NJ: John Wiley & Sons.

Ruble, D. N., Taylor, L. J., Cyphers, L., Greulich, F. K., Lurye, L. E., & Shrout, P. E. (2007). The role of gender constancy in early gender development. *Child Development, 78,* 1121–1136.

Rudolph, K. D., & Troop-Gordon, W. (2010). Personal-accentuation and contextual-amplification models of pubertal timing: Predicting youth depression. *Development & Psychopathology, 22,* 433–451.

Rudolph, K. D., Ladd, G., & Dinella, L. (2007). Gender differences in the interpersonal consequences of early-onset depressive symptoms. *Merrill-Palmer Quarterly, 53,* 461–488.

Rudolph, K. D., Troop-Gordon, W., & Flynn, M. (2009). Relational victimization predicts children's social-cognitive and self-regulatory responses in a challenging peer context. *Developmental Psychology, 45,* 1444-1454.

Ruff, H. A., & Capozzoli, M. C. (2003). Development of attention and distractibility in the first 4 years of life. *Developmental Psychology, 39,* 877–890.

Rushton, J. P., & Bonds, T. A. (2005). Mate choice and friendship in twins. *Psychological Science, 16,* 555–559.

Russell, A., & Finnie, V. (1990). Preschool children's social status and maternal instructions to assist group entry. *Developmental Psychology, 26,* 603–611.

Rutland, A., Killen, M., & Abrams, D. (2010). A new social-cognitive developmental perspective on prejudice: The interplay between morality and group identity. *Perspectives on Psychological Science, 5,* 279–291.

Rutter, M. (2007). Gene-environment interdependence. *Developmental Science, 10,* 12–18.

Rutter, M., Sonuga-Barke, E. J., Beckett, C., Castle, J., Kreppner, J., Kumsta, R. et al. (2010). Deprivation-specific psychological patterns: Effects of institutional deprivation. *Monographs of the Society for Research in Child Development, Serial No. 295, 75*(1).

Rymer, R. (1993). *Genie.* New York, NY: Harper Collins.

Saarni, C., Campos, J. J., Carmas, L. A., & Witherington, D. (2006). Emotional development: Action, communication, and understanding. In N. Eisenberg (Ed.), *Handbook of child psychology: Vol. 3. Social, emotional, and personality development.* Hoboken, NJ: Wiley.

Saffran, J. R., Aslin, R. N., & Newport, E. L. (1996). Statistical learning by 8-month-old infants. *Science, 274,* 1926–1928.

Saffran, J. R., Werker, J. F., & Werner, L. A. (2006). The infant's auditory world: Hearing, speech, and the beginnings of language. In W. Damon & R. M. Lerner (Eds.), *Handbook of child psychology: Vol. 2. Cognition, perception, and language* (6th ed., pp. 58–108). Hoboken, NJ: Wiley.

Sagi, A., Koren-Karie, N., Gini, M., Ziv, Y., & Joels, T. (2002). Shedding further light on the effects of various types and quality of early child care on infant–mother attachment relationship: The Haifa study of early child care. *Child Development, 73,* 1166–1186.

Sagi, A., van IJzendoorn, M. H., Aviezer, O., Donnell, F., Koren-Karie, N., Joels, T. et al. (1995). Attachments in a multiple-caregiver and multiple-infant environment: The case of the Israeli kibbutzim. In E. Waters et al. (Eds.), *Caregiving, cultural, and cognitive perspectives on secure-base behavior and working models: New growing points in attachment theory and research. Monographs of the Society for Research in Child Development, 60,* Serial No. 244.

Sahni, R., Fifer, W. P., & Myers, M. M. (2007). Identifying infants at risk for sudden infant death syndrome. *Current Opinion in Pediatrics, 19,* 145–149.

Salmivalli, C., & Isaacs, J. (2005). Prospective relations among victimization, rejection, friendlessness, and children's self- and peer-perceptions. *Child Development, 76,* 1161–1171.

Salovey, P., & Grewal, D. (2005). The science of emotional intelligence. *Current Directions in Psychological Science, 14,* 281–285.

Sandler, I. N., Tein, J.-Y., Mehta, P., Wolchik, S., & Ayers, T. (2000). Coping efficacy and psychological problems of children of divorce. *Child Development, 71,* 1099–1118.

Sangrigoli, S., Pallier, C., Argenti, A.-M., Ventureyra, V. A. G., & de Schonen, S. (2005). Reversibility of the other-race effect in face recognition during childhood. *Psychological Science, 16,* 440–444.

Sann, C., & Streri, A. (2007). Perception of object shape and texture in human newborns: Evidence from cross-modal transfer tasks. *Developmental Science, 10,* 399–410.

Saudino, K. J. (2009). Do different measures tap the same genetic influences? A multi-method study of activity level in young twins. *Developmental Science, 12,* 626–633.

Saudino, K. J., & Plomin, R. (2007). Why are hyperactivity and academic achievement related? *Child Development, 78,* 972–986.

Savage-Rumbaugh, E. S. (2001). *Apes, language, and the human mind.* New York, NY: Oxford University Press.

Saxe, G. B. (1988). Candy selling and math learning. *Educational Researcher, 17,* 14–21.

Scarr, S. (1992). Developmental theories for the 1990s: Development and individual differences. *Child Development, 63,* 1–19.

Scarr, S., & McCartney, K. (1983). How people make their own environments: A theory of genotype-environment effects. *Child Development, 54,* 424–435.

Schaal, B., Soussignan, R., & Marlier, L. (2002). Olfactory cognition at the start of life: The perinatal shaping of selective odor responsiveness. In C. Rouby et al. (Eds.), *Olfaction, taste, and cognition* (pp. 421–440). Cambridge, UK: Cambridge University Press.

Schauble, L. (1996). The development of scientific reasoning in knowledge-rich contexts. *Developmental Psychology, 32,* 102–119.

Schneider, W. (2011). Memory development in childhood. In U. Goswami (Ed.), *The Wiley-Blackwell handbook of cognitive development* (2nd ed., pp. 347–376). West Sussex UK: Wiley-Blackwell.

Scherf, K. S., Behrmann, M., Humphreys, K., & Luna, B. (2007). Visual category-selectivity for faces, places and objects emerges along different developmental trajectories. *Developmental Science, 10,* F15–F30.

Schermerhorn, A. C., & Cummings, E. M. (2008). Transactional family dynamics: A new framework for conceptualizing family influence processes. In R. V. Kail (Ed.), *Advances in child development and behavior* (Vol. 36, pp. 187–250). Amsterdam: Academic Press.

Schermerhorn, A. C., Chow, S., & Cummings, E. M. (2010). Developmental family processes and interparental conflict: Patterns of microlevel influences. *Developmental Psychology, 46,* 869–885.

Schinka, J. A., Letsch, E. A., & Crawford, F. C. (2002). DRD4 and novelty seeking: Results of meta-analyses. *American Journal of Medical Genetics, 114,* 643–648.

Schmale, R., & Seidl, A. (2009). Accommodating variability in voice and foreign accent: Flexibility of early word representations. *Developmental Science, 12,* 583–601.

Schmidt, F. L., & Hunter, J. (2004). General mental ability in the world of work: Occupational attainment and job performance. *Journal of Personality & Social Psychology, 86,* 162–173.

Schmidt, M. E., & Vandewater, E. A. (2008). Media and attention, cognition, and school achievement. *Future of Children, 18,* 63–85.

Schmidt, M. E., Pempek, T. A., Kirkorian, H. L., Lund, A. F., & Anderson, D. R. (2008). The effects of background television on the toy play behavior of very young children. *Child Development, 79,* 1137–1151.

Schneider, W., & Bjorklund, D. F. (1998). Memory. In W. Damon (Ed.), *Handbook of child psychology* (Vol. 2). New York, NY: Wiley.

Schneiders, J., Nicolson, N. A., Berkhof, J., Feron, F. J., van Os., J., & deVries, M. W. (2006). Mood reactivity to daily negative events in early adolescence: Relationship to risk for psychopathology. *Developmental Psychology, 42,* 543–554.

Schofield, T. J., Parke, R. D., Kim, Y., & Coltrane, S. (2008). Bridging the acculturation gap: Parent-child relationship quality as a moderator in Mexican American families. *Developmental Psychology, 44,* 1190–1194.

Schouten, A. P., Valkenburg, P. M., & Peter, J. (2007). Precursors and underlying processes of adolescents' online self-disclosure: Developing and testing an "Internet-attribute-perception" model. *Media Psychology, 10,* 292–314.

Schwartz, C. E., Wright, C. I., Shin, L. M., Kagan, J., & Rauch, S. L. (2003). Inhibited and uninhibited infants "grow up": Adult amygdalar response to novelty. *Science, 300,* 1952–1953.

Schwartz, D., Chang, L., & Farver, J. M. (2001). Correlates of victimization in Chinese children's peer groups. *Developmental Psychology, 37,* 520–532.

Schwartz, D., Dodge, K. A., Pettit, G. S., & Bates, J. E. (1997). The early socialization of aggressive victims of bullying. *Child Development, 68,* 665–675.

Schwartz, D., Dodge, K. A., Pettit, G. S., Bates, J. E., & The Conduct Problems Prevention Research Group. (2000). Friendship as a moderating factor in the pathway between early harsh home environment and later victimization in the peer group. *Developmental Psychology, 36,* 646–662.

Schwartz, P. D., Maynard, A. M., & Uzelac, S. M. (2008). Adolescent egocentrism: A contemporary view. *Adolescence, 43,* 441–448.

Schwarzer, G., Zauner, N., & Jovanovic, B. (2007). Evidence of a shift from featural to configural face processing in infancy. *Developmental Science, 10,* 452–463.

Schwenck, C., Bjorklund, D. F., & Schneider, W. (2009). Developmental and individual differences in young children's use and maintenance of a selective memory strategy. *Developmental Psychology, 45,* 1034–1050.

Scott, L. S., Pascalis, O., & Nelson, C. A. (2007). A domain-general theory of the development of perceptual discrimination. *Current Directions in Psychological Science, 16,* 197–201.

Scott, W. A., Scott, R., & McCabe, M. (1991). Family relationships and children's personality: A cross-cultural, cross-source comparison. *British Journal of Social Psychology, 30,* 1–20.

Scrimsher, S., & Tudge, J. (2003). The teaching/learning relationship in the first years of school: School revolutionary implications of Vygotsky's theory. *Early Education & Development, 14,* 293–312.

Sears, H. A., Graham, J., & Campbell, A. (2009). Adolescent boys' intentions of seeking help from male friends and female friends. *Journal of Applied Developmental Psychology, 30,* 738–748.

Sears, R. R. (1975). Your ancients revisited: A history of child development. In E. M. Hetherington (Ed.), *Review of child development research* (Vol. 5, pp. 1–73). Chicago: University of Chicago Press.

Segrin, C., Taylor, M. E., & Altman, J. (2005). Social cognitive mediators and relational outcomes associated with parental divorce. *Journal of Social & Personal Relationships, 22,* 361–377.

Seidl, A., & Johnson, E. L. (2006). Infants' word segmentation revisited: Edge alignment facilitates target extraction. *Developmental Science, 9,* 565–573.

Selman, R. L. (1980). *The growth of interpersonal understanding: Development and clinical analyses.* New York, NY: Academic Press.

Selman, R. L. (1981). The child as a friendship philosopher: A case study in the growth of interpersonal understanding. In S. R. Asher & J. M. Gottman (Eds.), *The development of children's friendships.* Cambridge, UK: Cambridge University Press.

Sénéchal, M., & LeFevre, J. (2002). Parental involvement in the development of children's reading skill: A five-year longitudinal study. *Child Development, 73,* 445–460.

Sénéchal, M., Thomas, E., & Monker, J. (1995). Individual differences in 4-year-old children's acquisition of vocabulary during storybook reading. *Journal of Educational Psychology, 87,* 218–229.

Serbin, L. A., Poulin-Dubois, D., Colburne, K. A., Sen, M. G., & Eichstedt, J. A. (2001). Gender stereotyping in infancy: Visual preferences for and knowledge of gender-stereotyped toys in the second year. *International Journal of Behavioral Development, 25,* 7–15.

Serbin, L. A., Powlishta, K. K., & Gulko, J. (1993). The development of sex typing in middle childhood. *Monographs of the Society for Research in Child Development, 58* (Serial No. 232).

Serbin, L., & Karp, J. (2003). Intergenerational studies of parenting and the transfer of risk from parent to child. *Current Directions in Psychological Science, 12,* 138–142.

Servin, A., Nordenstrom, A., Larsson, A., & Bohlin, G. (2003). Prenatal androgens and gender-typed behavior: A study of girls with mild and severe forms of congenital adrenal hyperplasia. *Developmental Psychology, 39,* 440–450.

Seyfarth, R., & Cheney, D. (1996). Inside the mind of a monkey. In M. Bekoff & D. Jamieson (Eds.), *Readings in animal cognition.* Cambridge, MA: MIT Press.

Shanahan, L., McHale, S. M., Crouter, A. C., & Osgood, D. (2007). Warmth with mothers and father from middle childhood to late adolescence: Within- and between-families comparisons. *Developmental Psychology, 43,* 551–563.

Shanahan, L., McHale, S. M., Crouter, A. C., & Osgood, D. W. (2007). Warmth with mothers and fathers from middle childhood to late adolescence: Within- and between-family comparisons. *Developmental Psychology, 43,* 551–563.

Shanahan, M. J., Elder, G. H., Burchinal, M., & Conger, R. D. (1996a). Adolescent earnings and relationships with parents: The work-family nexus in urban and rural ecologies. In J. T. Mortimer & M. D. Finch (Eds.), *Adolescents, work, and family: An intergenerational developmental analysis.* Thousand Oaks, CA: Sage.

Shanahan, M. J., Elder, G. H., Burchinal, M., & Conger, R. D. (1996b). Adolescent paid labor and relationships with parents: Early work-family linkages. *Child Development, 67,* 2183–2200.

Shapka, J. D., & Keating, D. P. (2005). Structure and change in self-concept during adolescence. *Canadian Journal of Behavioural Sciences, 37,* 83–96.

Share, D. L. (2008). Orthographic learning, phonological recoding, and self-teaching. In R. V. Kail (Ed.), *Advances in child development and behavior* (Vol. 36, pp. 31–84). San Diego, CA: Elsevier.

Shatz, M. (1983). Communication. In P. H. Mussen (Ed.), *Handbook of child psychology* (Vol. 3). New York, NY: Wiley.

Shatz, M., & Gelman, R. (1973). The development of communication skills: Modifications in the speech of young children as a function of listener. *Monographs of the Society for Research in Child Development, 38* (5, Serial No. 152).

Shaw, D. S., Winslow, E. B., & Flanagan, C. (1999). A prospective study of the effects of marital status and family relations on young children's adjustment among African American and European American families. *Child Development, 70,* 742–755.

Shaw, G. M., Schaffer, D., Velie, E. M., Morland, K., & Harris, J. A. (1995). Periconceptional vitamin use, dietary folate, and the occurrence of neural tube defects. *Epidemiology, 6,* 219–226.

Sherrod, K. B., O'Connor, S., Vietze, P. M., & Altemeier, W. A., III (1984). Child health and maltreatment. *Child Development, 55,* 1174–1183.

Shi, R., & Lepage, M. (2008). The effect of functional morphemes on word segmentation in preverbal infants. *Developmental Science, 11,* 407–413.

Shi, R., & Werker, J. F. (2001). Six-month old infants' preference for lexical words. *Psychological Science, 12,* 70–75.

Shin, H. B., & Kominski, R. A. (2010). *Language use in the United States: 2007.* (American Community Survey Reports, ACS-12). Washington, DC: U.S. Census Bureau.

Shoda, Y., Mischel, W., & Peake, P. K. (1990). Predicting adolescent cognitive and self-regulatory competencies from preschool delay gratification: Identifying diagnostic conditions. *Developmental Psychology, 26,* 978–986.

Shoemaker, L. B., & Furman, W. (2009). Interpersonal influences on late adolescent girls' and boys' disordered eating. *Eating Behaviors, 10,* 97–106.

Shonkoff, J. P. & Bales, S. N. (2011). Science does not speak for itself: Translating child development research for the public and its policymakers. *Child Development, 82,* 17–32.

Shulman, S., & Kipnis, O. (2001). Adolescent romantic relationships: A look from the future. *Journal of Adolescence, 24,* 337–351.

Shusterman, A., Lee, S. A., & Spelke, E. W. (2008). Young children's spontaneous use of geometry in maps. *Developmental Science, 11,* F1–F7.

Shutts, K., Banaji, M. R., & Spelke, E. S. (2010). Social categories guide young children's preferences for novel objects. *Developmental Science, 13,* 599–610.

Sicotte, N. L., Woods, R. P., & Mazziotta, J. C. (1999). Handedness in twins: A meta-analysis. *Laterality: Asymmetries of Body, Brain, & Cognition, 4,* 265–286.

Siddiqui, A. (1995). Object size as a determinant of grasping in infancy. *Journal of Genetic Psychology, 156,* 345–358.

Sidebotham, P., Heron, J., & the ALSPAC Study Team. (2003). Child maltreatment in the "children of the nineties": The role of the child. *Child Abuse & Neglect, 27,* 337–352.

Siegler, R. S. (1981). Developmental sequences within and between concepts. *Monographs of the Society for Research on Child Development, 46,* Serial No. 189.

Siegler, R. S. (1986). Unities in strategy choices across domains. In M. Perlmutter (Ed.), *Minnesota symposia on child development* (Vol. 19). Hillsdale, NJ: Erlbaum.

Siegler, R. S. (1996). *Emerging minds: The process of change in children's thinking.* New York, NY: Oxford University Press.

Siegler, R. S. (2000). The rebirth of children's learning. *Child Development, 71,* 26–35.

Siegler, R. S. (2007). Cognitive variability. *Developmental Science, 18,* 303–307.

Siegler, R. S., & Alibali, M. W. (2004). *Children's thinking* (4th ed.). Upper Saddle River, NJ: Prentice Hall.

Siegler, R. S., & Ellis, S. (1996). Piaget on childhood. *Psychological Science, 7,* 211–215.

Siegler, R. S., & Jenkins, E. (1989). *How children discover new strategies.* Hillsdale, NJ: Erlbaum.

Siegler, R. S., & Mu, Y. (2008). Chinese children excel on novel mathematics problems even before elementary school. *Psychological Science, 19,* 759–763.

Siegler, R. S., & Robinson, M. (1982). The development of numerical understanding. In H. W. Reese & L. P. Lipsitt (Eds.), *Advances in child development and behavior* (Vol. 16). New York, NY: Academic Press.

Siegler, R. S., & Shrager, J. (1984). Strategy choices in addition and subtraction: How do children know what to do? In C. Sophian (Ed.), *Origins of cognitive skills.* Hillsdale, NJ: Erlbaum.

Signorielli, N., & Lears, M. (1992). Children, television, and conceptions about chores: Attitudes and behaviors. *Sex Roles, 27,* 157–170.

Silk, J. S., Morris, A. S., Kanaya, T., & Steinberg, L. D. (2003). Psychological control and autonomy granting: Opposite ends of a continuum or distinct constructs? *Journal of Research on Adolescence, 13,* 113–128.

Silva, K. G., Correa-Chávez, M., & Rogoff, B. (2010). Mexican-heritage children's attention and learning from interactions directed to others. *Child Development, 81,* 898–912.

Silverman, W. K., La Greca, A. M., & Wasserstein, S. (1995). What do children worry about? Worries and their relations to anxiety. *Child Development, 66,* 671–686.

Simcock, G., & Hayne, H. (2002). Breaking the barrier? Children fail to translate their preverbal memories into language. *Psychological Science, 13,* 225–231.

Simmons, R., & Blyth, D. (1987). *Moving into adolescence.* New York, NY: Aldine de Gruyter.

Simons, D. J., & Keil, F. C. (1995). An abstract to concrete shift in the development of biological thought: The insides story. *Cognition, 56,* 129–163.

Simons, L. G., & Conger, R. D. (2007). Linking mother-father differences in parenting to a typology of family parenting styles and adolescent outcomes. *Journal of Family Issues, 28,* 212–241.

Simonton, D. K., & Song, A. V. (2009). Eminence, IQ, physical and mental health, and achievement domain: Cox's 282 geniuses revisited. *Psychological Science, 20,* 429–434.

Simpson, E. L. (1974). Moral development research: A case study of scientific cultural bias. *Human Development, 17,* 81–106.

Simpson, J. M. (2001). Infant stress and sleep deprivation as an aetiological basis for the sudden infant death syndrome. *Early Human Development, 61,* 1–43.

Singer, J. D., Fuller, B., Keiley, M. L., & Wolf, A. (1998). Early child-care selection: Variation by geographic location, maternal characteristics, and family structure. *Developmental Psychology, 34,* 1129–1144.

Skinner, B. F. (1957). *Verbal behavior.* New York, NY: Appleton-Century-Crofts.

Skinner, E. A. (1985). Determinants of mother-sensitive and contingent-responsive behavior: The role of childbearing beliefs and socioeconomic status. In I. E. Sigel (Ed.), *Parental belief systems: The psychological consequences for children* (pp. 51–82). Hillsdale, NJ: Erlbaum.

Skolnick Weisberg, D., & Bloom, P. (2009). Young children separate multiple pretend worlds. *Developmental Science, 12,* 699–705.

Slater, A. M., Riddell, P., Quinn, P. C., Pascalis, O., Lee, K., & Kelly, D. J. (2010). Visual perception. In T. D. Wachs & G. Bremner (Eds.), *Blackwell handbook of infant development,* 2nd ed. Oxford, UK: Blackwell.

Slobin, D. I. (1985). Cross-linguistic evidence for the language-making capacity. In D. I. Slobin (Ed.), *The cross-linguistic study of language acquisition: Vol. 2. Theoretical issues.* Hillsdale, NJ: Erlbaum.

Smetana, J. G. (2002). Culture, autonomy, and personal jurisdiction in adolescent-parent relationships. *Advances in Child Development & Behavior, 29,* 52–87.

Smetana, J. G. (2006). Social-cognitive domain theory: Consistencies and variations in children's moral and social judgments. In M. Killen & J. G. Smetana (2006). *Handbook of moral development* (pp. 119–153). Mahwah, NJ: Erlbaum.

Smith, E. R., & Mackie, D. M. (2000). *Social psychology* (2nd ed.). Philadelphia, PA: Psychology Press.

Smith, J., & Ross, H. (2007). Training parents to mediate sibling disputes affects children's negotiation and conflict understanding. *Child Development, 78,* 790–805.

Smith, L. B. (2000). How to learn words: An associative crane. In R. Golinkoff & K. Hirsch-Pasek (Eds.), *Breaking the word learning barrier* (pp. 51–80). Oxford, UK: Oxford University Press.

Smith, L. B. (2009). From fragments to geometric shape: Changes in visual object recognition between 18 and 24 months. *Current Directions in Psychological Science, 18,* 290–294.

Smith, L. B., Jones, S. S., Landau, B., Gershkoff-Stowe, L., & Samuelson, L. (2002). Object name learning provides on-the-job training for attention. *Psychological Science, 13,* 13–19.

Smith, P. K., & Drew, L. M. (2002). Grandparenthood. In M. H. Bornstein (Ed.), *Handbook of parenting: Vol. 3. Status and social conditions of parenting* (2nd ed., pp. 141–172). Mahwah, NJ: Erlbaum.

Smith, S. L., & Atkin, C. (2003). Television advertising and children: Examining the intended and unintended effects. In E. L. Palmer & B. M. Young (Eds.), *The faces of televisual media: Teaching, violence, selling to children* (pp. 301–326). Mahwah, NJ: Erlbaum.

Smits, I., Soenens, B., Vansteenkiste, M., Luyckx, K., & Goossens, L. (2010). Why do adolescents gather information or stick to parental norms? Examining autonomous and controlled motives behind adolescents' identity style. *Journal of Youth & Adolescence, 39,* 1343–1356.

Smock, T. K. (1998). *Physiological psychology: A neuroscience approach.* Upper Saddle River, NJ: Prentice-Hall.

Smoll, F. L., & Schutz, R. W. (1990). Quantifying gender differences in physical performance: A developmental perspective. *Developmental Psychology, 26,* 360–369.

Snedeker, B. (1982). *Hard knocks: Preparing youth for work.* Baltimore, MD: Johns Hopkins University Press.

Snedeker, J., Geren, J., & Shafto, C. L. (2007). Starting over: International adoption as a natural experiment in language development. *Psychological Science, 18,* 79–87.

Snell, E. K., Adam, E. K., & Duncan, G. J. (2007). Sleep and the body mass index and overweight status of children and adolescents. *Child Development, 78,* 309–323.

Snow, C. W. (1998). *Infant development* (2nd ed.). Upper Saddle River, NJ: Prentice Hall.

Snow, D. (2006). Regression and reorganization of intonation between 6 and 23 months. *Child Development, 77,* 281–296.

Snow, M. E., Jacklin, C. N., & Maccoby, E. E. (1983). Sex-of-child differences in father–child interaction at one year of age. *Child Development, 54,* 227–232.

Sodian, B., Zaitchik, D., & Carey, S. (1991). Young children's differentiation of hypothetical beliefs from evidence. *Child Development, 62,* 753–766.

Sokol, R. J., Delaney-Black, V., & Nordstrom, B. (2003). Fetal alcohol spectrum disorder. *Journal of the American Medical Association, 290,* 2996–2999.

Solantaus, T., Leinonen, J., & Punamäki, R.-L. (2004). Children's mental health in times of economic recession: Replication and extension of the family economic stress model in Finland. *Developmental Psychology, 40,* 412–429.

Somerville, L. H., & Casey, B. J. (2010). Developmental neurobiology of cognitive control and motivational systems. *Current Opinion in Neurobiology 20,* 236–241.

Sommerville, J. A., & Woodward, A. L. (2005). Pulling out the intentional structure of action: The relation between action processing and action production in infancy. *Cognition, 95,* 1–30.

Soska, K. C., Adolph, K. E., & Johnson, S. P. (2010). Systems in development: Motor skill acquisition facilitates three-dimensional object completion. *Developmental Psychology, 46,* 129–138.

Sousa, P., Altran, S., & Medin, D. (2002). Essentialism and folkbiology: Further evidence from Brazil. *Journal of Cognition & Culture, 2,* 195–223.

Southgate, V., & Csibra, G. (2009). Inferring the outcome of an ongoing novel action at 13 months. *Developmental Psychology, 45,* 1794–1798.

Southgate, V., Johnson, M. H., El Karoui, I., & Csibra, G. (2010). Motor system activation reveals infants' on-line prediction of others' goals. *Psychological Science, 21,* 355–359.

Spearman, C. (1904). "General intelligence" objectively determined and measured. *American Journal of Psychology, 15,* 201–293.

Spector, F., & Maurer, D. (2009). Synesthesia: A new approach to understanding the development of perception. *Developmental Psychology, 45,* 175–189.

Spelke, E. S. (1994). Initial knowledge: Six suggestions. *Cognition, 50,* 431–445.

Spelke, E. S., & Kinzler, K. D. (2007). Core knowledge. *Developmental Science, 10,* 89–96.

Spinks, A., Turner, C., McClure, R., & Nixon, J. (2004). Community based prevention programs targeting all injuries for children. *Injury Prevention, 10,* 180–185.

Spitz, R. A. (1965). *The first year of life.* New York, NY: International Universities Press.

Springer, K., & Keil, F. C. (1991). Early differentiation of causal mechanisms appropriate to biological and nonbiological kinds. *Child Development, 62,* 767–781.

St. George, I. M., Williams, S., & Silva, P. A. (1994). Body size and menarche: The Dunedin study. *Journal of Adolescent Health, 15,* 573–576.

St. James-Roberts, I., & Plewis, I. (1996). Individual differences, daily fluctuations, and developmental changes in amounts of infant waking, fussing, crying, feeding, and sleeping. *Child Development, 67,* 2527–2540.

Stacy, A. W., Zoog, J. B., Unger, J. B., & Dent, C. W. (2004). Exposure to televised alcohol ads and subsequent alcohol use. *American Journal of Health Behavior, 28,* 498–509.

Staff, J., & Schulenberg, J. E. (2010). Millenials and the world of work: Experiences in paid work during adolescence. *Journal of Business & Psychology, 25,* 247–255.

Stanovich, K. E., Toplak, M. E., & West, R. F. (2008). The development of rational thought: A taxonomy of heuristics and biases. In R. V. Kail (Ed.), *Advances in child development and behavior* (Vol. 36, pp. 251–285). San Diego, CA: Elsevier.

Steele, C. M. (1997). A threat in the air: How stereotypes shape intellectual identity and performance. *American Psychologist, 52,* 613–629.

Steele, C. M., & Aronson, J. (1995). Stereotype threat and the intellectual test performance of African Americans. *Journal of Personality & Social Psychology, 69,* 797–811.

Steelman, J. D. (1994). Revision strategies employed by middle level students using computers. *Journal of Educational Computing Research, 11,* 141–152.

Steinberg, L. (2001). We know some things: Parent-adolescent relationships in retrospect and prospect. *Journal of Research on Adolescence, 11,* 1–19.

Steinberg, L. D. (1999). *Adolescence* (5th ed.). Boston, MA: McGraw-Hill.

Steinberg, L., & Dornbusch, S. M. (1991). Negative correlates of part-time employment during adolescence: Replication and elaboration. *Developmental Psychology, 27,* 304–313.

Steinberg, L., & Monahan, K. C. (2007). Age differences in resistance to peer influence. *Developmental Psychology, 43,* 1531–1543.

Steinberg, L., & Silk, J. (2002). Parenting adolescents. In M. Bornstein (Ed.), *Handbook of parenting: Vol. 1* (2nd ed., pp. 103–133). Hillsdale, NJ: Erlbaum.

Steinberg, L., Graham, S., O'Brien, L., Woolard, J., Cauffman, E., & Banich, M. (2009). Age differences in future orientation and delay discounting. *Child Development, 80,* 28–44.

Steiner, J. E., Glasser, D., Hawilo, M. E., & Berridge, K. C. (2001). Comparative expression of hedonic impact: Affective reactions to taste by human infants and other primates. *Neuroscience & Biobehavioral Reviews, 25,* 53–74.

Sternberg, R. J. (1999). The theory of successful intelligence. *Review of General Psychology, 3,* 292–316.

Sternberg, R. J., & Grigorenko, E. L. (2002). *Dynamic testing: The nature and measurement of learning potential.* New York, NY: Cambridge University Press.

Sternberg, R. J., & Kaufman, J. C. (1998). Human abilities. *Annual Review of Psychology, 49,* 479–502.

Sternberg, R. J., & the Rainbow Project Collaborators. (2006). The Rainbow Project: Enhancing the SAT through assessments of analytical, practical, and creative skills. *Intelligence, 34,* 321–350.

Sternberg, R. J., Grigorenko, E. L., & Kidd, K. K. (2005). Intelligence, race, and genetics. *American Psychologist, 60,* 46–59.

Stevens, J., & Ward-Estes, J. (2006). Attention-deficit/hyperactivity disorder. In M. Hersen & J. C. Thomas (Series Eds.), & R. T. Ammerman (Vol. Ed.), *Comprehensive handbook of personality and psychopathology, Vol. 3: Child psychopathology* (pp. 316–329). Hoboken, NJ: Wiley.

Stevens, J., Harman, J. S., & Kelleher, K. J. (2005). Race/ethnicity and insurance status as factors associated with ADHD treatment patterns. *Journal of Child & Adolescent Psychopharmacology, 15,* 88–96.

Stevenson, H. W., & Lee, S. (1990). Contexts of achievement. *Monographs of the Society for Research in Child Development, 55* (Serial No. 221).

Stevenson, H. W., & Stigler, J. W. (1992). *The learning gap.* New York, NY: Summit Books.

Stevenson, R. J., Oaten, M. J., Case, T. I., Repacholi, B. M., & Wagland, P. (2010). Children's response to adult disgust elicitors: Development and acquisition. *Developmental Psychology, 46,* 165–177.

Stewart, L., & Pascual-Leone, J. (1992). Mental capacity constraints and the development of moral reasoning. *Journal of Experimental Child Psychology, 54,* 251–287.

Stewart, R. B., Mobley, L. A., Van Tuyl, S. S., & Salvador, W. A. (1987). The firstborn's adjustment to the birth of a sibling: A longitudinal assessment. *Child Development, 58,* 341–355.

Stice, E., & Shaw, H. (2004). Eating disorder prevention programs: A meta-analytic review. *Psychological Bulletin, 130,* 206–227.

Stice, E., Shaw, H., & Marti, C. (2006). A meta-analytic review of obesity prevention programs for children and adolescents: The skinny on interventions that work. *Psychological Bulletin, 132,* 667–691.

Stice, E., Shaw, H., Bohon, C., Martin, C. N., & Rohde, P. (2009). A meta-analytic review of depression prevention programs for children and adolescents: Factors that predict magnitude of intervention effects. *Journal of Consulting & Clinical Psychology, 77,* 486–503.

Stifter, C. A., & Fox, N. A. (1990). Infant reactivity: Physiological correlates of newborn and 5-month temperament. *Developmental Psychology, 26,* 582–588.

Stifter, C. A., Cipriano, E., Conway, A., & Kelleher, R. (2009). Temperament and the development of conscience: The moderating role of effortful control. *Social Development, 18,* 353–374.

Stigler, J. W., Gallimore, R., & Hiebert, J. (2000). Using video surveys to compare classrooms and teaching across cultures: Examples and lessons from the TIMSS video studies. *Educational Psychologists, 35,* 87–100.

Stiles, J., Reilly, J., Paul, B., & Moses, P. (2005). Cognitive development following early brain injury: Evidence for neural adaptation. *Trends in Cognitive Sciences, 9,* 136–143.

Stipek, D., & Miles, S. (2008). Effects of aggression on achievement: Does conflict with the teacher make it worse? *Child Development, 79,* 1721–1735.

Stjernqvist, K. (2009). Predicting development for extremely low birthweight infants: Sweden. In K. Nugent, B. J. Petrauskas, & T. B. Brazelton (Eds.), *The newborn as a person: Enabling healthy infant development worldwide.* Hoboken, NJ: Wiley.

Strauss, M. S., & Curtis, L. E. (1984). Development of numerical concepts in infancy. In C. Sophian (Ed.), *Origins of cognitive skills.* Hillsdale, NJ: Erlbaum.

Strayer, D. L., Drews, F. A., & Crouch, D. J. (2006). A comparison of the cell phone driver and the drunk driver. *Human Factors, 48,* 381–391.

Strayer, J., & Roberts, W. (2004). Children's anger, emotional expressiveness, and empathy: Relations with parents' empathy, emotional expressiveness, and parenting practices. *Social Development, 13,* 229–254.

Strenze, T. (2007). Intelligence and socioeconomic success: A meta-analytic review of longitudinal research. *Intelligence, 35,* 401–426.

Striano, T., Tomasello, M., & Rochat, P. (2001). Social and object support for early symbolic play. *Developmental Science, 4,* 442–455.

Stright, A. D., Gallagher, K. C., & Kelley, K. (2008). Infant temperament moderates relations between maternal parenting in early childhood and children's adjustment in first grade. *Child Development, 79,* 186–200.

Strough, J., & Berg, C. A. (2000). Goals as a mediator of gender differences in high-affiliation dyadic conversations. *Developmental Psychology, 36,* 117–125.

Studelska, J. V. (2006, Spring). At home in birth. *Midwifery Today,* 32–33.

Stunkard, A. J., Sorensen, T. I. A., Hanis, C., Teasdale, T. W., Chakraborty, R., Schull, W. J., et al. (1986). An adoption study of human obesity. *New England Journal of Medicine, 314,* 193–198.

Sturge-Apple, M. L., Davies, P. T., & Cummings, E. M. (2010). Typologies of family functioning and children's adjustment during the early school years. *Child Development, 81,* 1320–1335.

Sturge-Apple, M. L., Davies, P. T., Winter, M. A., Cummings, E. M., & Schermerhorn, A. (2008). Interparental conflict and children's school adjustment: The explanatory role of children's internal representations of interparental and parent-child relationships. *Developmental Psychology, 44,* 1678–1690.

Subrahmanyam, K., Greenfield, P., Kraut, R., & Gross, E. (2001). The impact of computer use on children's and adolescents' development. *Journal of Applied Developmental Psychology, 22,* 7–30.

Sullivan, L. W. (1987). The risks of the sickle-cell trait: Caution and common sense. *New England Journal of Medicine, 317,* 830–831.

Sullivan, M. W., & Lewis, M. (2003). Contextual determinants of anger and other negative expressions in young infants. *Developmental Psychology, 39,* 693–705.

Super, C. M. (1981). Cross-cultural research on infancy. In H. C. Triandis & A. Heron (Eds.), *Handbook of cross-cultural psychology: Vol. 4. Developmental psychology.* Boston, MA: Allyn & Bacon.

Super, C. M., Herrera, M. G., & Mora, J. O. (1990). Long-term effects of food supplementation and psychosocial intervention on the physical growth of Colombian infants at risk of malnutrition. *Child Development, 61,* 29–49.

Sussman, S., Pokhrel, P., Ashmore, R. D., & Brown, B. B. (2007). Adolescent peer group identification and characteristics: A review of the literature. *Addictive Behaviors, 32,* 1602–1627.

Suzuki, L., & Aronson, J. (2005). The cultural malleability of intelligence and its impact on the racial/ethnic hierarchy. *Psychology, Public Policy, & Law, 11,* 320–327.

Svirsky, M. A., Chin, S. B., & Jester, A. (2007). The effects of age at implantation on speech intelligibility in pediatric cochlear implant users: Clinical outcomes and sensitive periods. *Audiological Medicine, 5,* 293–306.

Svirsky, M. A., Robbins, A. M., Kirk, K. I., Pisoni, D. B., & Miyamoto, R. T. (2000). Language development in profoundly deaf children with cochlear implants. *Psychological Science, 11,* 153–158.

Sweeney, M. M. (2010). Remarriage and stepfamilies: Strategic sites for family scholarship in the 21st century. *Journal of Marriage & Family, 72,* 667–684.

Szücks, D., & Goswami, U. (2007). Educational neuroscience: Defining a new discipline for the study of mental representations. *Mind, Brain, & Education, 1,* 114–127.

Tager-Flusberg, H. (1993). Putting words together: Morphology and syntax in the preschool years. In J. Berko Gleason (Ed.), *The development of language* (3rd ed.). New York, NY: Macmillan.

Tager-Flusberg, H. (2007). Evaluating the theory-of-mind hypothesis of autism. *Current Directions in Psychological Science, 16,* 311–315.

Tamis-LeMonda, C. S., & Bornstein, M. H. (1996). Variation in children's exploratory, nonsymbolic, and symbolic play: An explanatory multidimensional

framework. In C. Rovee-Collier & L. P. Lipsitt (Eds.), *Advances in infancy research* (Vol. 10). Norwood, NJ: Ablex.

Tamis-LeMonda, C. S., & Bornstein, M. H. (2002). Maternal responsiveness and early language acquisition. In R. V. Kail & H. W. Reese (Eds.), *Advances in child development and behavior* (Vol. 29, pp. 90–127). San Diego, CA: Academic Press.

Tamis-Lemonda, C. S., Adolph, K. E., Lobo, S. A., Karasik, L. B., Ishak, S., & Dimitropoulou, K. A. (2008). When infants take mothers' advice: 18-month-olds integrate perceptual and social information to guide motor action. *Developmental Psychology, 44,* 734–746.

Tamis-LeMonda, C. S., Shannon, J. D., Cabrera, N., & Lamb, M. E. (2004). Father and mothers at play with their 2- and 3-year-olds: Contributions to language and cognitive development. *Child Development, 75,* 1806–1820.

Tan, K. L. (2009). Bed sharing among mother-infant pairs in Kiang District, Peninsular Malaysia, and its relationship to breast-feeding. *Journal of Developmental & Behavioral Pediatrics, 30,* 420–425.

Tanner, J. M. (1970). Physical growth. In P. H. Mussen (Ed.), *Carmichael's manual of child psychology* (3rd ed., pp. 77–135.). New York, NY: Wiley.

Tanner, J. M. (1990). *Fetus into man: Physical growth from conception to maturity* (2nd ed.). Cambridge, MA: Harvard University Press.

Tarabulsy, G. M., Bernier, A., Provost, M. A., Maranda, J., Larose, S., Moss, E., et al. (2005). Another look inside the gap: Ecological contributions to the transmission of attachment in a sample of adolescent mother–infant dyads. *Developmental Psychology, 41,* 212–224.

Tardif, T., Fletcher, P., Liang, W., Zhang, Z., Kaciroti, N., & Marchman, V. A. (2008). Baby's first 10 words. *Developmental Psychology, 44,* 929–938.

Taumoepeau, M., & Ruffman, T. (2008). Stepping stones to others' minds: Maternal talk relates to child mental state language and emotion understanding at 15, 24, and 33 months. *Child Development, 79,* 284–302.

Taylor, J., & Schatschneider, C. (2010). Genetic influence on literacy constructs in kindergarten and first grade: Evidence from a diverse twin sample. *Behavior Genetics, 40,* 591–602.

Taylor, M. G., Rhodes, M., & Gelman, S. A. (2009). Boys will be boys; cows will be cows: Children's essentialist reasoning about gender categories and animal species. *Child Development, 80,* 461–481.

Taylor, M., Carlson, S. M., Maring, B. L., Gerow, L., & Charley, C. M. (2004). The characteristics of fantasy in school-age children: Imaginary companions, impersonation, and social understanding. *Developmental Psychology, 40,* 1173–1187.

Taylor, M., Hulette, A. C., & Dishion, T. J. (2010). Longitudinal outcomes of young high-risk adolescents with imaginary companions. *Developmental Psychology, 46,* 632–1636.

Taylor, R. D., & Roberts, D. (1995). Kinship support and maternal and adolescent well-being in economically disadvantaged African-American families. *Child Development, 66,* 1585–1597.

Teachman, J. (2008). Complex life course patterns and the risk of divorce in second marriages. *Journal of Marriage & Family, 70,* 294–305.

Tegethoff, M., Greene, N., Olsen, J., Meyer, A. H., & Meinlschmidt, G. (2010). Maternal psychosocial adversity is associated with length of gestation and offspring size at birth: Evidence from a population-based cohort study. *Psychosomatic Medicine, 72,* 419–426.

Teichman, Y. (2001). The development of Israeli children's images of Jews and Arabs and their expression in human figure drawings. *Developmental Psychology, 37,* 749–761.

Teilmann, G., Pedersen, C. B., Skakkeback, N. E., & Jensen, T. K. (2006). Increased risk of precocious puberty in internationally adopted children in Denmark. *Pediatrics, 118,* 391–399.

Tenenbaum, H. R., & Leaper, C. (2002). Are parents' gender schemas related to their children's gender-related cognitions? A meta-analysis. *Developmental Psychology, 38,* 615–630.

Terlecki, M. S., & Newcombe, N. S. (2005). How important is the digital divide? The relations of computer and videogame usage to gender differences in mental rotation ability. *Sex Roles, 53,* 433–441.

The MTA Cooperative Group. (1999). Moderators and mediators of treatment response for children with attention-deficit/hyperactivity disorder. *Archives of General Psychiatry, 56,* 1088–1096.

Thelen, E., & Smith, L. B. (1998). Dynamic systems theories. In W. Damon (Ed.), *Handbook of child psychology* (Vol. 1). New York, NY: Wiley.

Thelen, E., & Ulrich, B. D. (1991). Hidden skills. *Monographs for the Society for Research in Child Development, 56,* Serial No. 223.

Thelen, E., Ulrich, B. D., & Jensen, J. L. (1989). The developmental origins of locomotion. In M. H. Woollacott & A. Chumway-Cook (Eds.), *Development of posture and gait across the life span.* Columbia: University of South Carolina Press.

Thiessen, E. D., & Saffran, J. R. (2003). When cues collide: Use of stress and statistical cues to word boundaries by 7- to 9-month-old infants. *Developmental Psychology, 39,* 706–716.

Thiessen, E. D., Hill, E., & Saffran, J. R. (2005). Infant-directed speech facilitates word segmentation. *Infancy, 7,* 53–71.

Thomas, A., & Chess, S. (1977). *Temperament and development.* New York, NY: Brunner/Mazel.

Thomas, A., Chess, S., & Birch, H. G. (1968). *Temperament and behavior disorders in children.* New York, NY: New York University Press.

Thomas, J. R., & French, K. E. (1985). Gender differences across age in motor performance: A meta-analysis. *Psychological Bulletin, 98,* 260–282.

Thomas, J. R., Alderson, J. A., Thomas, K. T., Campbell, A. C., & Elliot, B. C. (2010). Developmental gender differences for overhand throwing in Aboriginal Australian children. *Research Quarterly for Exercise & Sport, 81,* 432–441.

Thomas, L. A., De Bellis, M. D., Graham, R., & LaBar, K. S. (2007). Development of emotional facial recognition in late childhood and adolescence. *Developmental Science, 10,* 547–558.

Thomas, R., & Zimmer-Gembeck, M. J. (2011). Accumulating evidence for parent-child interaction therapy in the prevention of child maltreatment. *Child Development, 82,* 177–192.

Thomas, S., Reijntjes, A., Orobio de Castro, B., Bushman, B. J., Poorthuis, A., & Telch, M. J. (2010). I like me if you like me: On the interpersonal modulation and regulation of preadolescents' state self-esteem. *Child Development, 81,* 811–825.

Thompson, G. G. (1952). *Child psychology.* Boston, MA: Houghton Mifflin.

Thompson, R. (2007). *What is albinism?* East Hampstead, NH: National Organization for Albinism and Hypopigmentation.

Thompson, R. A. (2000). The legacy of early attachments. *Child Development, 71,* 145–152.

Thompson, R. A. (2006). The development of the person: Social understanding, relationships, conscience, self. In N. Eisenberg (Ed.), *Handbook of child psychology: Vol. 3. Social, emotional, and personality development* (6th ed). Hoboken, NJ: Wiley.

Thompson, R. A., & Limber, S. (1991). "Social anxiety" in infancy: Stranger wariness and separation distress. In H. Leitenberg (Ed.), *Handbook of social and evaluation anxiety.* New York, NY: Plenum.

Thompson, R. A., Laible, D. J., & Ontai, L. L. (2003). Early understandings of emotion, morality, and self: Developing a working model. *Advances in Child Development & Behavior, 31,* 137–172.

Thompson, R. A., Lewis, M. D., & Calkins, S. D. (2008). Reassessing emotion regulation. *Child Development Perspectives, 2,* 124–131.

Thornberry, T. P., Krohn, M. D., Lizotte, A. J., Smith, C. A., & Tobin, K. (2003). *Gangs and delinquency in developmental perspective.* New York, NY: Cambridge University Press.

Thorne, B. (1993). *Gender play: Girls and boys in school.* New Brunswick, NJ: Rutgers University Press.

Thurstone, L. L., & Thurstone, T. G. (1941). Factorial studies of intelligence. *Psychometric Monograph, No. 2.*

Tincoff, R., & Jusczyk, P. W. (1999). Some beginnings of word comprehension in 6-month-olds. *Psychological Science, 10,* 172–175.

Tisak, M. (1993). Preschool children's judgments of moral and personal events involving physical harm and property damage. *Merrill-Palmer Quarterly, 39,* 375–390.

Tither, J. M., & Ellis, B. J. (2008). Impact of fathers on daughters' age at menarche: A genetically and environmentally controlled sibling study. *Developmental Psychology, 44,* 1409–420.

Tolan, P. H., Gorman-Smith, D., & Henry, D. B. (2003). The developmental ecology of urban males' youth violence. *Developmental Psychology, 39,* 274–291.

Tomasello, M., Carpenter, M., & Liszkowski, U. (2007). A new look at infant pointing. *Child Development, 78,* 705–722.

Tomlinson, M., Cooper, P., & Murray, L. (2005). The mother–infant relationship and infant attachment in a South African peri-urban settlement. *Child Development, 76,* 1044–1054.

Tomson, L. M., Pangrazi, R. P., Friedman, G., & Hutchison, H. (2003). Childhood depressive symptoms, physical activity and health related fitness. *Journal of Sport Psychology, 25,* 419–439.

Toomey, R. B., Ryan, C., Diaz, R. M., Card, N. A., & Russell, S. T. (2010). Gender-noncomforming lesbian, gay, bisexual, and transgender youth: School victimization and young adult psychosocial adjustment. *Developmental Psychology, 46,* 1589–1589.

Torgesen, J. K. (2004). Learning disabilities: An historical and conceptual overview. In B. Y. L. Wong (Ed.), *Learning about learning disabilities* (3rd ed., pp. 3–40). San Diego, CA: Elsevier.

Tracy, B., Reid, R., & Graham, S. (2009). Teaching young students strategies for planning and drafting stories. The impact of self-regulated strategy development. *Journal of Educational Research, 102,* 323–331.

Trainor, L. J., & Heinmiller, B. M. (1998). The development of evaluative responses to music: Infants prefer to listen to consonance over dissonance. *Infant Behavior & Development, 21,* 77–88.

Trainor, L. J., Austin, C. M., & Desjardins, R. N. (2000). Is infant-directed speech prosody a result of vocal expression of emotion? *Psychological Science, 11,* 188–195.

Tran, H., & Weinraub, M. (2006). Child care effects in context: Quality, stability, and multiplicity in nonmaternal child care arrangements during the first 15 months of life. *Developmental Psychology, 42,* 566–582.

Treiman, R., & Kessler, B. (2003). The role of letter names in acquisition of literacy. *Advances in Child Development & Behavior, 31,* 105–135.

Tremblay, R. E., Schaal, B., Boulerice, B., Arsonault, L., Soussignan, R. G., & Paquette, D. (1998). Testosterone, physical aggression, and dominance and physical development in adolescence. *International Journal of Behavioral Development, 22,* 753–777.

Troseth, G. L., Pierroutsakos, S. L., & DeLoache, J. S. (2004). From the innocent to the intelligent eye: The early development of pictorial competence. In R. V. Kail (Ed.), *Advances in child development and behavior* (Vol. 32, pp. 1–35). San Diego, CA: Elsevier.

Trzesniewski, K. H., Donnellan, M. B., Caspi, A., Moffitt, T. E., Robins, R. W., & Poultin, R. (2006). Adolescent low self-esteem is a risk factor for adult poor health, criminal behavior, and limited economic prospects. *Developmental Psychology, 42,* 381–390.

Tudge, J. R. H., Winterhoff, P. A., & Hogan, D. M. (1996). The cognitive consequences of collaborative problem solving with and without feedback. *Child Development, 67,* 2892–2909.

Turiel, E. (1998). The development of morality. In W. Damon (Ed.), *Handbook of child psychology, Vol. 3: Social, emotional, and personality development* (pp. 863–932). New York, NY: Wiley.

Turiel, E. (2006). The development of morality. In W. Damon & R. M. Lerner (Eds.), *Handbook of child psychology* (6th ed., Vol. 3, pp. 789–857). Hoboken, NJ: Wiley.

Turiel, E., & Neff, K. (2000). Religion, culture, and beliefs about reality in moral reasoning. In K. S. Rosengren, C. N. Johnson, & P. L. Harris (Eds.), *Imagining the impossible: Magical, scientific, and religious thinking in children* (pp. 269–304). New York, NY: Cambridge University Press.

Turley, R. N. L. (2003). Are children of young mothers disadvantaged because of their mother's age or family background? *Child Development, 74,* 465–474.

Twenge, J. M., & Campbell, W. K. (2001). Age and birth cohort differences in self-esteem: A cross-temporal meta-analysis. *Personality & Social Psychology Review, 5,* 321–344.

Twenge, J. M., & Crocker, J. (2002). Race and self-esteem: Meta-analysis comparing Whites, Blacks, Hispanics, and American Indians and comment on Gray-Little and Hafdan (2000). *Psychological Bulletin, 128,* 371–408.

Tynes, B. M. (2007). Role taking in online "classrooms": What adolescents are learning about race and ethnicity. *Developmental Psychology, 43,* 1312–1320.

U.S. Census Bureau. (2008). *Who's minding the kids? Child care arrangements: Spring 2005.* Washington, DC: Author.

U.S. Census Bureau. (2011). America's Families and Living Arrangements: 2010. Retrieved March 31, 2011 from www.census.gov/population/www/socdemo/hh-fam/cps2010.html

U.S. Department of Health and Human Services. (2001). *The Surgeon General's call to action to prevent and decrease overweight and obesity.* Rockville, MD: Author.

U.S. Department of Health and Human Services. (2004). Youth risk behavior surveillance. *Morbidity and Mortality Weekly Report, 53* (No. SS-2). Atlanta, GA: Centers for Disease Control and Prevention.

U.S. Department of Health and Human Services. (2010). *Child Maltreatment 2009.* Available from http://www.acf.hhs.gov/programs/cb/stats_research/index.htm#can

U.S. Department of Health and Human Services. (2010). *The Surgeon General's vision for a healthy and fit nation.* Rockville, MD: Author.

U.S. Department of Labor. (2000). *Report on the youth labor force.* Washington, DC: Author.

Uchiyama, I., Anderson, D. I., Campos, J. J., Witherington, D., Frankel, C. B., Lejeune, L. et al. (2008). Locomotor experience affects self and emotion. *Developmental Psychology, 44,* 1225–1231.

Umaña-Taylor, A. J., & Guimond, A. B. (2010). A longitudinal examination of parenting behaviors and perceived discrimination predicting Latino adolescents' ethnic identity. *Developmental Psychology, 46,* 636–650.

Umaña-Taylor, A., Diversi, M., & Fine, M. (2002). Ethnic identity and self-esteem among Latino adolescents: Distinctions among Latino populations. *Journal of Adolescent Research, 17,* 303–327.

Umbel, V. M., Pearson, B. Z., Fernandez, M. C., & Oller, D. K. (1992). Measuring bilingual children's receptive vocabularies. *Child Development, 63,* 1012–1020.

UNICEF. (2006). *Progress for children: A report card on nutrition, 2000–2006.* New York, NY: Author.

UNICEF. (2007). *The state of the world's children, 2008.* New York: Author.

UNICEF. (2008). *The state of the world's children, 2008.* New York, NY: Author.

UNICEF. (2008). *The state of the world's children, 2009: Maternal and newborn health.* New York: Author.

Updegraff, K. A., McHale, S. M., Whiteman, S. D., Thayer, S. M., & Delgado, M. Y. (2005). Adolescent sibling relationships in Mexican American families: Exploring the role of familism. *Journal of Family Psychology, 19,* 512–522.

Updegraff, K. A., Thayer, S. M., Whiteman, S. D., Denning, D. J., & McHale, S. M. (2005). Aggression in adolescents' sibling relationships: Links to sibling and parent–adolescents relationship quality. *Family Relations: Interdisciplinary Journal of Applied Family Studies, 54,* 373–385.

Usher, E. L., & Pajares, F. (2009). Sources of self-efficacy in mathematics: A validation study. *Contemporary Educational Psychology, 34,* 89–101.

Vélez, C. E., Wolchik, S. A., Tein, J., & Sandler, I. (2011). Protecting children from the consequences of divorce: A longitudinal study of the effects of parenting on children's coping processes. *Child Development, 82,* 244–257.

Véronneau, M.-H., Vitaro, F., Brendgen, M., Dishion, T. J., & Tremblay, R. E. (2010). Transactional analysis of the reciprocal linkages between peer relationships and academic achievement from middle childhood to early adolescence. *Developmental Psychology, 46,* 773–790.

Vaish, A., Carpenter, M., & Tomasello, M. (2009). Sympathy through affective perspective taking and its relation to prosocial behavior in toddlers. *Developmental Psychology, 45,* 534–543.

Vaish, A., Woodward, A., & Grossmann, T. (2008). Not all emotions are created equal: The negativity bias in social-emotional development. *Psychological Bulletin, 134,* 383–403.

Valentino, K., Ciccetti, D., Rogosch, F. A., & Toth, S. L. (2008). Memory, maternal representations, and internalizing symptomatology among abused, neglected, and nonmaltreated children. *Child Development, 79,* 705–719.

Valkenburg, P. M., & Jochen, P. (2009). Social consequences of the Internet for adolescents: A decade of research. *Current Directions in Psychological Science, 18,* 1–5.

Valkenburg, P. M., & van der Voort, T. H. A. (1994). Influence of TV on daydreaming and creative imagination: A review of research. *Psychological Bulletin, 116,* 316–339.

Valkenburg, P. M., & van der Voort, T. H. A. (1995). The influence of television on children's daydreaming styles: A 1-year-panel study. *Communication Research, 22,* 267–287.

van den Boom, D. C. (1994). The influence of temperament and mothering on attachment and exploration: An experimental manipulation of sensitive responsiveness among lower-class mothers with irritable infants. *Child Development, 65,* 1457–1477.

van den Boom, D. C. (1995). Do first-year intervention effects endure? Follow-up during toddlerhood of a sample of Dutch irritable infants. *Child Development, 66,* 1798–1816.

van der Mark, I. L., van IJzendoorn, M. H., & Bakermans-Kranenburg, M. J. (2002). Development of empathy in girls during the second year of life: Associations with parenting, attachment, and temperament. *Social Development, 11,* 451–468.

van Doesum, K. T. M., Riksen-Walraven, J.M., Hosman, C. M. H., & Hoefnagels, C. (2008). A randomized control trial of a home-visiting intervention aimed at preventing relationship problems in depressed mothers and their infants. *Child Development, 79,* 547-561.

van Doorn, M. D., Branje, S. J. T., & Meeus, W. H. J. (2008). Conflict resolution in parent-adolescent relationships and adolescent delinquency. *Journal of Early Adolescence, 28,* 503–527.

van Goozen, S. H. M., Fairchild G., & Harold, G. T. (2008). The role of neurobiological deficits in childhood antisocial behavior. *Current Directions in Psychological Science, 17,* 224–228.

van Goozen, S. H., Fairchild, G., Snoek, H., & Harold, G. T. (2007). The evidence for a neurobiological model of childhood antisocial behavior. *Psychological Bulletin, 133,* 149–182.

van Hof, P., van der Kamp, J., & Savelsbergh, G. J. P. (2002). The relation of unimanual and bimanual reaching to crossing the midline. *Child Development, 73,* 1352–1362.

Van Hulle, C. A., Lemery-Chalfant, K., & Goldsmith, H. H. (2007). Genetic and environmental influences on socio-emotional behavior in toddlers: An initial twin study of the infant–toddler social and emotional assessment. *Journal of Child Psychology & Psychiatry, 48,* 1014–1024.

van IJzendoorn, M. (1995). Adult attachment representations, parental responsiveness, and infant attachment: A meta-analysis on the predictive validity of the Adult Attachment Interview. *Psychological Bulletin, 117,* 387–403.

van IJzendoorn, M. H., & Juffer, F. (2005). Adoption is a successful natural intervention enhancing adopted children's IQ and school performance. *Current Directions in Psychological Science, 14,* 326–330.

van IJzendoorn, M. H., Schuengel, C., & Bakermans-Kranenburg, M. J. (1999). Disorganized attachment in early childhood: Meta-analysis of precursors, concomitants, and sequelae. *Development & Psychopathology, 11,* 225–249.

van IJzendoorn, M. H., Vereijken, C. M. J. L., Bakermans-Kranenburg, M. J., & Riksen-Walraven, J. M. (2004). Assessing attachment security with the Attachment Q-Sort: Meta-analytic evidence for the validity of the observer AQS. *Child Development, 75,* 1188–1213.

Van Zalk, N., Herman, W., Kerr, M., Branje, S. J. T., Stattin, H., & Meeus, W. H. J. (2010). It takes three: Selection, influence, and de-selection processes of depression in adolescent friendship networks. *Developmental Psychology, 46,* 927–938.

Vandell, D. L., Belsky, J., Burchinal, M., Steinberg, L., Vandergrift, N., & The NICHD Early Child Care Research Network. (2010). Do effects of early child care extend to age 15 years? Results from the NICHD study of early child care and youth development. *Child Development, 81,* 737–756.

Vandell, D. L., Pierce, K. M., & Dadisman, K. (2005). Out-of-school settings as a developmental context for children and youth. In R. V. Kail (Ed.), *Advances in child development and behavior* (Vol. 33, pp. 43–77). Amsterdam: Elsevier Academic Press.

Vander Wal, J. S., & Thelen, M. H. (2000). Eating and body image concerns among obese and average-weight children. *Addictive Behaviors, 25,* 775–778.

Vazsonyi, A. T., & Huang, L. (2010). Where self-control comes from: On the development of self-control and its relationship to deviance over time. *Developmental Psychology, 46,* 245–257.

Vazsonyi, A. T., & Snider, J. B. (2008). Mentoring, competencies, and adjustment in adolescents: American part-time employment and European apprenticeships. *International Journal of Behavioral Development, 32,* 46–55.

Vazsonyi, A. T., Hibbert, J. R., & Snider, J. B. (2003). Exotic enterprise no more? Adolescent reports of family and parenting practices from youth in four countries. *Journal of Research on Adolescence, 13,* 129–160.

Veenstra, R., Lindberg, S., Oldenhinkel, A. J., De Winter, A. F., Verhulst, F. C., & Ormel, J. (2005). Bullying and victimization in elementary schools: A comparison of bullies, victims, bully/victims, and uninvolved preadolescents. *Developmental Psychology, 41,* 672–682.

Veenstra, R., Lindenberg, S., Munniksma, A., & Dijkstra, J. K. (2010). The complex relation between bullying, victimization, acceptance, and rejection: Giving special attention to status, affection, and sex differences. *Child Development, 81,* 480-486.

Ventura, S. J., Abma, J. C., Mosher, W. D., & Henshaw, S. K. (2008). Estimated pregnancy rates by outcome for the United States, 1990–2004. *National Vital Statistics Reports, 56,* 1–26.

Verkuyten, M., & De Wolf, A. (2007). The development of in-group favoritism: Between social reality and group identity. *Developmental Psychology, 43,* 901–911.

Verschaeve, L. (2009). Genetic damage in subjects exposed to radiofrequency radiation. *Mutation Research—Reviews in Mutation Research, 681,* 259–270.

Victora, C. G., Adam, T., Bruce, J., & Evans, D. B. (2006). Integrated management of the sick child. In D. T. Jamison et al. (Eds.), *Disease control priorities in developing countries* (2nd ed., pp. 1172–1192). New York, NY: Oxford University Press.

Vieno, A., Nation, M., Pastore, M., & Santinello, M. (2009). Parenting and antisocial behavior: A model of the relationship between adolescent self-discosure, parental closeness, parental control, and adolescent antisocial behavior. *Developmental Psychology, 45,* 1509–1519.

Visher, E. G., Visher, J. S., & Pasley, K. (2003). Remarriage families and stepparenting. In F. Walsh (Ed.), *Normal family processes* (pp. 153–175). New York, NY: Guilford.

Vitiello, B., & Swedo, S. (2004). Antidepressant medications in children. *New England Journal of Medicine, 350,* 1489–1491.

Volling, B. L., & Belsky, J. (1992). The contribution of mother–child and father–child relationships to the quality of sibling interaction: A longitudinal study. *Child Development, 63,* 1209–1222.

Vorhees, C. V., & Mollnow, E. (1987). Behavior teratogenesis: Long-term influences on behavior. In J. D. Osofsky (Ed.), *Handbook of infant development* (2nd ed.). New York, NY: Wiley.

Vouloumanos, A., Hauser, M. D., Werker, J. F., & Martin, A. (2010). The tuning of human neonates' preference for speech. *Child Development, 81,* 517–527.

Voyer, D., Voyer, S., & Bryden, M. P. (1995). Magnitude of sex differences in spatial abilities: A meta-analysis and consideration of critical variables. *Psychological Bulletin, 117,* 250–270.

Vrijheid, M., Martinez, D., Forns, J., Guxens, M., Julvez, J., Ferrer, M. et al. (2010). Prenatal exposure to cell phone use and neurodevelopment at 14 months. *Epidemiology, 21,* 259–262.

Vygotsky, L. S. (1978). *Mind in society: The development of higher psychological processes* (M. Cole, V. John-Steiner, S. Scribner, & E. Soubermen, Eds.). Cambridge, MA: Harvard University Press.

Waber, D. P. (1977). Sex differences in mental abilities, hemispheric lateralization, and rate of physical growth at adolescence. *Developmental Psychology, 13,* 29–38.

Wachs, T. D., & Bates, J. E. (2001). Temperament. In G. Bremner & A. Fogel (Eds.), *Blackwell handbook of infant development* (pp. 465–501). Malden, MA: Blackwell.

Wachs, T. D., Black, M. M., & Engle, P. L. (2009). Maternal depression: A global threat to children's health, development, and behavior and to human rights. *Child Development Perspectives, 3,* 51–59.

Wainryb, C. (2006). Moral development in culture: Diversity, tolerance, and justice. In M. Killen & J. G. Smetana (Eds.), *Handbook of moral development* (pp. 211–240). Mahwah, NJ: Erlbaum.

Wainwright, J. L., & Patterson, C. J. (2008). Peer relations among adolescents with female same-sex parents. *Developmental Psychology, 44,* 117–126.

Wainwright, J. L., Russell, S. T., & Patterson, C. J. (2004). Psychosocial adjustment, school outcomes, and romantic relationships of adolescents with same-sex parents. *Child Development, 75,* 1886–1898.

Wakschlag, L. S., Leventhal, B. L., Pine, D. S., Pickett, K. E., & Carter, A. S. (2006). Elucidating early mechanisms of developmental psychopathology: The case of prenatal smoking and disruptive behavior. *Child Development, 77,* 893–906.

Walberg, H. J. (1995). General practices. In G. Cawelti (Ed.), *Handbook of research on improvising student achievement.* Arlington, VA: Educational Research Service.

Walden, T., Kim, G., McCoy, C., & Karrass, J. (2007). Do you believe in magic? Infants' social looking during violation of expectations. *Developmental Science, 10,* 654–663.

Walker, L. J. (1980). Cognitive and perspective-taking prerequisites for moral development. *Child Development, 51,* 131–139.

Walker, L. J., Hennig, K. H., & Krettenauer, T. (2000). Parent and peer contexts for children's moral reasoning development. *Child Development, 71,* 1033–1048.

Walker, P., Bremner, J. G., Mason, U., Spring, J., Mattock, K., Slater, A., et al. (2010). Preverbal infants' sensitivity to synaesthetic cross-modality correspondences. *Psychological Science, 21,* 21–25.

Wang, Q. (2006). Culture and the development of self-knowledge. *Current Directions in Psychological Science, 15,* 182–187.

Wang, Q. (2007). "Remember when you got the big, big bulldozer?" Mother–child reminiscing over time and across cultures. *Social Cognition, 25,* 455–471.

Wang, Q., Pomerantz, E. M., & Chen, H. (2007). The role of parents' control in early adolescents' psychological functioning: A longitudinal investigation in the United States and China. *Child Development, 78,* 1592–1610.

Wang, S. S., & Brownell, K. D. (2005). Anorexia nervosa. In C. B. Fisher & R. M. Lerner (Eds.), *Encyclopedia of applied developmental science* (Vol. 1, pp. 83–85). Thousand Oaks, CA: Sage.

Wang, S.-H., & Baillargeon, R. (2005). Inducing infants to detect a physical violation in a single trial. *Psychological Science, 16,* 542–549.

Wansink, B., & Sobal, J. (2007). Mindless eating: The 200 daily food decisions we overlook. *Environment & Behavior, 39,* 106–123.

Warneken, F., & Tomasello, M. (2006). Altruistic helping in human infants and young chimpanzees. *Science, 311,* 1301–1303.

Warner, B., Altimier, L., & Crombleholme, T. M. (2007). Fetal surgery. *Newborn & Infant Nursing Reviews, 7,* 181–188.

Warnock, F., & Sandrin, D. (2004). Comprehensive description of newborn distress behavior in response to acute pain (newborn male circumcision). *Pain, 107,* 242–255.

Warren, A. R., & McCloskey, L. A. (1993). Pragmatics: Language in social contexts. In J. Berko Gleason (Ed.), *The development of language* (3rd ed., pp. 195–238). New York, NY: Macmillan.

Warren-Leubecker, A., & Bohannon, J. N. (1989). Pragmatics: Language in social contexts. In J. Berko Gleason (Ed.), *The development of language* (2nd ed., pp. 327–368). Columbus, OH: Merrill.

Waterhouse, L. (2006). Multiple intelligences, the Mozart effect, and emotional intelligence: A critical review. *Educational Psychologist, 41,* 207–225.

Waters, E., & Cummings, E. M. (2000). A secure base from which to explore close relationships. *Child Development, 71,* 164–172.

Waters, E., Merrick, S., Treboux, D., Crowell, J., & Albersheim, L. (2000). Attachment security in infancy and early adulthood: A twenty-year longitudinal study. *Child Development, 71,* 684–689.

Waters, H. F. (1993, July 12). Networks under the gun. *Newsweek,* 64–66.

Waters, H. S. (1980). "Class news": A single-subject longitudinal study of prose production and schema formation during childhood. *Journal of Verbal Learning & Verbal Behavior, 19,* 152–167.

Watson, J. B. (1925). *Behaviorism.* New York, NY: Norton.

Wax, J. R., Pinette, M. G., & Cartin, A. (2010). Home versus hospital birth: Process and outcome. *Obstetrical & Gynecological Survey, 65,* 132–140.

Waxman, S., Medin, D., & Ross, N. (2007). Folkbiological reasoning from a cross-cultural developmental perspective: Early essentialist notions are shaped by cultural beliefs. *Developmental Psychology, 43*, 294–308.

Webb, S. J., Monk, C. S., & Nelson, C. A. (2001). Mechanisms of postnatal neurobiological development: Implications for human development. *Developmental Neuropsychology, 19*, 147–171.

Weichold, K., & Silbereisen, R. K. (2005). Puberty. In C. B. Fisher & R. M. Lerner (Eds.), *Encyclopedia of applied developmental science* (Vol. 2, pp. 893–898). Thousand Oaks, CA: Sage.

Weinberg, M. K., Tronick, E. Z., Cohn, J. F., & Olson, K. L. (1999). Gender differences in emotional expressivity and self-regulation during early infancy. *Developmental Psychology, 35*, 175–188.

Weinert, F. E., & Haney, E. A. (2003). The stability of individual differences in intellectual development: Empirical evidence, theoretical problems, and new research questions. In R. J. Sternberg, J. Lautrey, & T. I. Lubart (Eds.), *Models of intelligence: International perspectives* (pp. 169–181). Washington, DC: American Psychological Association.

Weis, R., & Cerankosky, B. C. (2010). Effects of video-game ownership on young boys' academic and behavioral functioning: A randomized, controlled study. *Psychological Science, 21*, 463–470.

Weisgram, E. S., Bigler, R. S., & Liben, L. S. (2010). Gender, values, and occupational interests among children, adolescents, and adults. *Child Development, 81*, 778–796.

Weisner, T. S., & Wilson-Mitchell, J. E. (1990). Nonconventional family lifestyles and sex typing in six-year-olds. *Child Development, 61*, 1915–1933.

Weissman, M. D., & Kalish, C. W. (1999). The inheritance of desired characteristics: Children's view of the role of intention in parent-offspring resemblance. *Journal of Experimental Child Psychology, 73*, 245–265.

Weisz, J. R., McCarty, C. A., & Valeri, S. M. (2006). Effects of psychotherapy for depression in children and adolescents: A meta-analysis. *Psychological Bulletin, 132*, 132–149.

Weizman, Z. O., & Snow, C. E. (2001). Lexical output as related to children's vocabulary acquisition: Effects of sophisticated exposure and support for meaning. *Developmental Psychology, 37*, 265–279.

Wellman, H. M. (1992). *The child's theory of mind.* Cambridge, MA: MIT Press.

Wellman, H. M. (1993). Early understanding of mind: The normal case. In S. Baron-Cohen, H. Tager-Flusberg, & D. J. Cohen (Eds.), *Understanding other minds: Perspectives from autism.* Oxford, UK: Oxford University Press.

Wellman, H. M. (2002). Understanding the psychological world: Developing a theory of mind. In U. Goswami (Ed.), *Blackwell handbook of childhood cognitive development* (pp. 167–187). Malden, MA: Blackwell.

Wellman, H. M. (2011). Developing a theory of mind. In U. Goswami (Ed.), *The Wiley-Blackwell handbook of childhood cognitive development* (2nd ed., pp. 258–284). West Sussex, UK: Wiley-Blackwell.

Wellman, H. M., & Gelman, S. A. (1998). Knowledge acquisition in foundational domains. In W. Damon (Ed.), *Handbook of child psychology* (Vol. 2, pp. _523–573). New York: Wiley.

Wellman, H. M., Cross, D., & Watson, J. (2001). Meta-analysis of theory-of-mind development: The truth about false belief. *Child Development, 72*, 655–684.

Wentworth, N., Benson, J. B., & Haith, M. M. (2000). The development of infants' reaches for stationary and moving targets. *Child Development, 71*, 576–601.

Wentzel, K. R., Filisetti, L., & Looney, L. (2007). Adolescent prosocial behavior: The role of self-processes and contextual cues. *Child Development, 78*, 895–910.

Werner, E. E. (1995). Resilience in development. *Current Directions in Psychological Science, 4*, 81–85.

Werner, H. (1948). *Comparative psychology of mental development.* Chicago, IL: Follet.

Wertsch, J. V., & Tulviste, P. (1992). L. S. Vygotsky and contemporary developmental psychology. *Developmental Psychology, 28*, 548–557.

Whitaker, R. C., Wright, J. A., Pepe, M. S., Seidel, K. D., & Dietz, W. H. (1997). Predicting obesity in young adulthood from childhood and parental obesity. *New England Journal of Medicine, 337*, 869–873.

White, L., & Gilbreth, J. G. (2001). When children have two fathers: Effects of relationships with stepfathers and noncustodial fathers on adolescent outcomes. *Journal of Marriage & the Family, 63*, 155–167.

Whitehurst, G. J., & Vasta, R. (1975). Is language acquired through imitation? *Journal of Psycholinguistic Research, 4*, 37–59.

Whiting, J. W. M., & Child, I. L. (1953). *Child training and personality: A cross-cultural study.* New Haven, CT: Yale University Press.

Whitney, E. N., & Hamilton, E. M. N. (1987). *Understanding nutrition* (4th ed.). St. Paul: West.

Wicks-Nelson, R., & Israel, A. C. (2006). *Behavior disorders of childhood* (6th ed.). Upper Saddle River, NJ: Pearson Education.

Wie, O. B., Falkenberg, E.-S., Tvete, O., & Tomblin, B. (2007). Children with a cochlear implant: Characteristics and determinants of speech recognition, speech-recognition growth rate, and speech production. *International Journal of Audiology, 46*, 232–243.

Willatts, P. (1999). Development of means-end behavior in young infants: Pulling a support to retrieve a distant object? *Developmental Psychology, 35*, 651–667.

Williams, J. E., & Best, D. L. (1990). *Measuring sex stereotypes: A thirty-nation study* (rev. ed.). Newbury Park, CA: Sage.

Williams, J. M. (1997). *Style: Ten lessons in clarity and grace* (5th ed.). New York, NY: Longman.

Williams, S. T., Conger, K. J., & Blozis, S. A. (2007). The development of interpersonal aggression during adolescence: The importance of parents, siblings, and family economics. *Child Development, 78*, 1526–1542.

Wills, T. A., Sandy, J. M., Yaeger, A., & Shinar, O. (2001). Family risk factors and adolescent substance use: Moderation effects for temperament dimensions. *Developmental Psychology, 37*, 283–297.

Wilson, B. J. (2008). Media and children's aggression, fear, and altruism. *Future of Children, 18*, 87–118.

Wilson, B. J., Smith, S. L., Potter, W. J., Kunkel, D., Linz, D., Colvin, C. M., & Donnerstein, E. (2002). Violence in children's television programming: Assessing the risks. *Journal of Communication, 52*, 5–35.

Wilson, D. M., Gottfredson, D. C., Cross, A. B., Rorie, M., & Connell, N. (2010). Youth development in after-school leisure activities. *Journal of Early Adolescence, 30*, 668–690.

Wilson, G. T., Heffernan, K., & Black, C. M. D. (1996). Eating disorders. In E. J. Marsh & R. A. Barkley (Eds.), *Child psychopathology.* New York, NY: Guilford.

Wilson, M. (1989). Child development in the context of the black extended family. *American Psychologist, 44*, 380–383.

Wilson, R. D. (2000). Amniocentesis and chorionic villus sampling. *Current Opinion in Obstetrics & Gynecology, 12*, 81–86.

Winner, E. (2000). Giftedness: Current theory and research. *Current Directions in Psychological Science, 9*, 153–156.

Wolfe, C. D., & Bell, M. A. (2007). Sources of variability in working memory in early childhood: A consideration of age, temperament, language, and brain electrical activity. *Cognitive Development, 22*, 431–455.

Wolfe, D. A. (1985). Child-abusive parents: An empirical review and analysis. *Psychological Bulletin, 97*, 462–482.

Wolff, P. H. (1987). *The development of behavioral states and the expression of emotions in early infancy.* Chicago, IL: University of Chicago Press.

Wolraich, M. L., Lindgren, S. D., Stumbo, P. J., Stegink, L. D., Appelbaum, M. I., & Kiritsy, M. C. (1994). Effects of diets high in sucrose or aspartame on the behavior and cognitive performance of children. *New England Journal of Medicine, 330*, 301–307.

Wong-Fillmore, L., Ammon, P., McLaughlin, B., & Ammon, M. S. (1985). *Learning English through bilingual instruction.* Rosslyn, VA: National Clearinghouse for Bilingual Education.

Wood, J. J., Emmerson, N. A., & Cowan, P. A. (2004). Is early attachment security carried forward into relationships with preschool peers? *British Journal of Developmental Psychology, 22*, 245–253.

Woodward, A. L. (2009). Infants' grasp of others' intention. *Current Directions in Psychological Science, 18*, 53–57.

Woodward, A. L., & Markman, E. M. (1998). Early word learning. In W. Damon (Ed.), *Handbook of child psychology* (Vol. 2). New York, NY: Wiley.

Woollacott, M. H., Shumway-Cook, A., & Williams, H. (1989). The development of balance and locomotion in children. In M. H. Woollacott & A. Shumway-Cook (Eds.), *Development of posture and gait across the life span.* Columbia: University of South Carolina Press.

World Health Organization. (1997). Integrated management of childhood illness: A WHO/UNICEF initiative. *Bulletin of the World Health Organization, 75*, Supplement 1.

World Health Organization. (2005). *The World Health Report—2005: Making every mother and child count.* Geneva, Switzerland: Author.

Worobey, J. (2005). Effects of malnutrition. In C. B. Fisher & R. M. Lerner (Eds.), *Encyclopedia of applied developmental science* (Vol. 2, pp. 673–676). Thousand Oaks, CA: Sage.

Worthman, C. M., & Brown, R. A. (2007). Companionable sleep: Social regulation of sleep and cosleeping in Egyptian families. *Journal of Family Psychology, 21*, 124–135.

Wray-Lake, L., Crouter, A. C., & McHale, S. M. (2010). Developmental patterns in decision-making autonomy across middle childhood and adolescence: European American parents' perspectives. *Child Development, 81*, 636–651.

Wright, J. C., Huston, A. C., Murphy, K. C., St. Peters, M., Piñon, M., Scantlin, R. et al. (2001). The relations of early television viewing to school readiness and vocabulary of children from low-income families: The Early Window Project. *Child Development, 72*, 1347–1366.

Wynn, K. (1992). Addition and subtraction by human infants. *Nature, 358*, 749–750.

Wynn, K. (1996). Infants' individuation and enumeration of actions. *Psychological Science, 7*, 164–169.

Xie, H., Li, Y., Boucher, S. M., Hutchins, B. C., & Cairns, B. D. (2006). What makes a girl (or a boy) popular (or unpopular)? African American children's perceptions and developmental differences. *Developmental Psychology, 42*, 599–612.

Xu, F., Bao, X., Fu, G., Talwar, V., & Lee, K. (2010). Lying and truth-telling in children: From concept to action. *Child Development, 81*, 581–596.

Xu, Y., Farver, J. A., & Zhang, Z. (2009). Temperament, harsh and indulgent parenting, and Chinese children's proactive and reactive aggression. *Child Development, 80*, 244–258.

Yang, Q., Rasmussen, S. A., & Friedman, J. M. (2002). Mortality associated with Down's syndrome in the USA from 1983–1997: A population-based study. *The Lancet, 359*, 1019–1025.

Yap, M. B. H., Allen, N. B., & Ladouceur, C. D. (2008). Maternal socialization of positive affect: The impact of invalidation on adolescent emotion regulation and depressive symptomatology. *Child Development, 79,* 1415–1431.

Yau, J., Smetana, J. G., & Metzger, A. (2009). Young Chinese children's authority concepts. *Social Development, 18,* 210–229.

Yip, T., Seaton, E. K., & Sellers, R. M. (2010). Interracial contact and intraracial contact, school-level diversity, and change in racial identity status among African American adolescents. *Child Development, 81,* 1431–1444.

Young, S. K., Fox, N. A., & Zahn-Waxler, C. (1999). The relations between temperament and empathy in 2-year-olds. *Developmental Psychology, 35,* 1189–1197.

Young, S. K., Fox, N. A., & Zahn-Waxler, C. (1999). The relations between temperament and empathy in 2-year-olds. *Developmental Psychology, 35,* 1189–1197.

Youniss, J., McLellan, J. A., & Yates, M. (1999). Religion, community service, and identity in American youth. *Journal of Adolescence, 22,* 243–253.

Yuan, S., & Fisher, C. (2009). "Really? She blicked the baby?": Two-year-olds learn combinatorial facts about verbs by listening. *Psychological Science, 20,* 619–626.

Yumoto, C., Jacobson, S. W., & Jacobson, J. L. (2008). Fetal substance exposure and cumulative environmental risk in an African American cohort. *Child Development, 79,* 1761–1776.

Zaal, F. T. J., & Thelen, E. (2005). The developmental roots of the speed-accuracy trade-off. *Journal of Experimental Psychology: Human Perception & Performance, 31,* 1266–1273.

Zahn-Waxler, C., Cole, P. M., & Barrett, K. C. (1991). Guilt and empathy: Sex differences and implications for the development of depression. In J. Garber & K. Dodge (Eds.), *The development of emotion regulation and dysregulation* (pp. 243–272). Cambridge, UK: Cambridge University Press.

Zahn-Waxler, C., Radke-Yarrow, M., Wagner, E., & Chapman, M. (1992). Development of concern for others. *Developmental Psychology, 28,* 126–136.

Zarbatany, L., Hartmann, D. P., & Rankin, D. B. (1990). The psychological functions of preadolescent peer activities. *Child Development, 61,* 1067–1080.

Zarrett, N., Fay, K., Li, Y., Carrano, J., Phelps, E., & Lerner, R. M. (2009). More than child's play: Variable- and pattern-centered approaches for examining effects of sports participation on youth development. *Developmental Psychology, 45,* 368–382.

Zeanah, C. H., Smyke, A. T., Koga, S. F., & Carlson, E. (2005). Attachment in institutionalized and community children in Romania. *Child Development, 76,* 1015–1028.

Zelazo, P. D., & Cunningham, W. A. (2007). Executive function: Mechanisms underlying emotion regulation. In J. J. Gross (Ed.), *Handbook of emotion regulation* (pp. 135–158). New York, NY: Guilford.

Zelazo, P. D., Muller, U., Frye, D., & Marcovitch, S. (2003). The development of executive function: Cognitive complexity and control—revised. *Monographs of the Society for Research on Child Development, 68,* 93–119.

Zelazo, P. R., Weiss, M. J., Papageorgiou, A. N., & Laplante, D. P. (1989). Recovery and dishabituation of sound localization among normal-, moderate-, and high-risk newborns: Discriminant validity. *Infant Behavior & Development, 12,* 321–340.

Zeman, J., & Garber, J. (1996). Display rules for anger, sadness, and pain: It depends on who is watching. *Child Development, 67,* 957–973.

Zeman, J., & Shipman, K. (1997). Social-contextual influences on experiences for managing anger and sadness: The transition from middle childhood to adolescence. *Developmental Psychology, 33,* 917–924.

Zhang, B., Cartmill, C., & Ferrence, R. (2008). The role of spending money and drinking alcohol in adolescent smoking. *Addiction, 103,* 310–319.

Zhou, Q., Eisenberg, N., Losoya, S. H., Fabes, R. A., Reiser, M., Guthrie, I. K., et al. (2002). The relations of parental warmth and positive expressiveness to children's empathy-related responding and social functioning: A longitudinal study. *Child Development, 73,* 893–915.

Zhou, Q., Lengua, L., & Wang, Y. (2009). The relations of temperament reactivity and effortful control to children's adjustment problems in China and the United States. *Developmental Psychology, 45,* 724–739.

Zhou, Q., Wang, Y., Eisenberg, N., Wolchik, S., Tein, J-W., & Deng, X. (2008). Relations of parenting and temperament to Chinese children's experience of negative life events, coping efficacy, and externalizing problems. *Child Development, 79,* 493–513.

Ziegler, J. C., et al. (2010). Orthographic depth and its impact on universal predictors of reading: A cross-language investigation. *Psychological Science, 21,* 551–559.

Ziegler, J. C., Pech-Georgel, C., Dufau, S., & Grainger, J. (2010). Rapid processing of letters, digits, and symbols:

What purely visual-attentional deficit in developmental dyslexia? *Developmental Science, 13,* F8–F14.

Zigler, E. F., & Muenchow, S. (1992). *Head Start: Inside story of America's most successful educational experiment.* New York, NY: Basic Books.

Zigler, E., & Finn-Stevenson, M. (1992). Applied developmental psychology. In M. H. Bornstein & M. E. Lamb (Eds.), *Developmental psychology: An advanced textbook.* Hillsdale, NJ: Erlbaum.

Zigler, E., & Styfco, S. J. (1994). Head Start: Criticisms in a constructive context. *American Psychologist, 49,* 127–132.

Zimiles, H., & Lee, V. E. (1991). Adolescent family structure and educational progress. *Developmental Psychology, 27,* 314–320.

Zimmer-Gembeck, M. J., & Helfand, M. (2008). Ten years of longitudinal research on U.S. adolescent sexual behavior: Developmental correlates of sexual intercourse, and the importance of age, gender and ethnic background. *Developmental Review, 28,* 153–224.

Zimmerman, B. J. (2001). Theories of self-regulated learning and academic adjustment: An overview and analysis. In B. J. Zimmerman & D. H. Schunk (Eds.), *Self-regulated learning and academic achievement: Theoretical perspectives* (2nd ed., pp. 1–37). Mahwah, NJ: Erlbaum.

Zimmerman, C. (2007). The development of scientific thinking skills in elementary and middle school. *Developmental Review, 27,* 172–223.

Zinar, S. (2000). The relative contributions of word identification skill and comprehension-monitoring behavior to reading comprehension ability. *Contemporary Educational Psychology, 25,* 363–377.

Zmyj, N., Buttelman, D., Carpenter, M., & Daum, M. D. (2010). The reliability of a model influences 14-month-olds' imitation. *Journal of Experimental Child Psychology, 106,* 208–220.

Zosuls, K. M., Ruble, D. N., Tamis-LeMonda, C. S., Shrout, P. E., Bornstein, M. H., & Greulich, F. K. (2009). The acquisition of gender labels in infancy: Implications for gender-typed play. *Developmental Psychology, 45,* 688–701.

Zukow-Goldring, P. (2002). Sibling caregiving. In M. H. Bornstein (Ed.), *Handbook of parenting: Vol. 3. Status and social conditions of parenting* (2nd ed., pp. 253–286). Mahwah, NJ: Erlbaum.

Credits

PHOTOGRAPHS

CHAPTER 1 Page 2 Blend Images/SuperStock. Page 8 Nina Leen/Time Life Pictures/Getty Images. Page 9 Sonya Etchison/Shutterstock. Page 11 (top) Andy Sacks/Getty Images. Page 11 (bottom) AP Images/Koji Sasahara. Page 12 Elizabeth Crews Photography. Page 13 Peter Arnold Inc./Alamy. Page 16 HI & LOIS © 1993 King Features Syndicate. Page 17 Image Source/Alamy. Page 20 Charles Gupton Photography. Page 21 Steve Gorton/Dorling Kindersley. Page 23 Tony Freeman/PhotoEdit. Page 24 Pamela Johnson Meyer/Photo Researchers, Inc. Page 29 (top left) Sherry Lewis. Page 29 (top center) Sherry Lewis. Page 29 (top right) Sherry Lewis. Page 29 (bottom left) Courtesy of Sherry Lewis. Page 29 (bottom center) Courtesy of Sherry Lewis. Page 29 (bottom right) Courtesy of Sherry Lewis. Page 31 (top left) Jaimie Duplass/Shutterstock. Page 31 (top center) Joe Belanger/Alamy. Page 31 (top right) David Young-Wolff/Alamy. Page 31 (bottom left) Monkey Business Images/Shutterstock. Page 31 (bottom center) Monkey Business Images/Shutterstock. Page 31 (bottom right) Morgan Lane Photography/Shutterstock. Page 32 (top left) Sherry Lewis. Page 32 (top center) Sherry Lewis. Page 32 (top right) Sherry Lewis. Page 32 (bottom left) Courtesy of Sherry Lewis. Page 32 (bottom center) Courtesy of Sherry Lewis. Page 32 (bottom right) Courtesy of Sherry Lewis. Page 34 David Young-Wolff/PhotoEdit.

CHAPTER 2 Page 40 MBI/Alamy. Page 41 SPL/Custom Medical Stock Photo Inc. Page 42 (top) SPL M108/078/Photo Researchers, Inc. Page 42 (centre) David Phillips/Photo Researchers Inc. Page 42 (bottom) Alexander Tsiaras/Photo Researchers, Inc. Page 43 Biophoto Associates/Photo Researchers, Inc. Page 48 SPL M140/369/Photo Researchers, Inc. Page 52 Blaine Harrington III/Alamy. Page 59 Michael Newman/PhotoEdit

CHAPTER 3 Page 64 Picture Partners/Alamy. Page 66 (bottom) Scanpix Sweden AB/Lennart Nilsson. Page 67 (top right) Scanpix Sweden/Lennart Nilsson. Page 67 (bottom) Petit Format/Photo Researchers Inc. Page 69 (bottom) Scanpix Sweden AB. Page 71 (first) Scanpix Sweden AB/Lennart Nilsson. Page 71 (second from top) Scanpix Sweden/Lennart Nilsson. Page 71 (second from bottom) Petit Format/Photo Researchers Inc. (bottom) Scanpix Sweden AB. Page 77 BSIP SA/Alamy. Page 78 Ellen Senisi/The Image Works. Page 83 (top) Keith Brofsky/Photodisc/Thinkstock. Page 83 (bottom) SPL P680/354/Photo Researchers, Inc. Page 74 Dennis MacDonald/PhotoEdit. Page 89 (top) Purestock/Alamy. Page 89 (bottom) Sheila McKinnon/Mira.com. Page 92 Bernardo Gimenez/Alamy. Page 96 Dr. Robert Kail. Page 99 Dean Conger/National Geographic/Getty Images. Page 100 Stever Raymer/National Geographic Stock.

CHAPTER 4 Page 106 Rene Jansa/Shutterstock. Page 112 Ian O'Leary/Getty Images. Page 113 (top) Deanpictures/The Image Works. Page 113 (bottom) Blue Jean Images/Alamy. Page 114 Andy Reynolds/Getty Images. Page 116 Joanna B. Pinneo/Aurora Photos. Page 117 Anders Ryman/Alamy. Page 120 (top) Flirt/SuperStock. Page 120 (bottom) Dr. Robert Kail. Page 122 Kilkullen/Trobaire/Corbis. Page 123 Peter Banos/Alamy. Page 124 Imagestate Media Partners Limited-Impact Photos/Alamy. Page 126 (top) Earl & Nazima Kowall/Corbis. Page 126 (bottom) Purestock/Alamy. Page 127 IndexStock/SuperStock. Page 128 (top) Geostock/Getty Images. Page 128 (center) Ed Reschke. Page 128 (bottom) Don W. Fawcett/Photo Researchers, Inc. Page 130 CBCD, Birkbeck, University of London. Page 131 Richard T. Nowitz/Corbis. Page 133 Emmanuel Faure/Getty Images.

CHAPTER 5 Page 138 Gorilla/Shutterstock. Page 140 Dion Ogust/The Image Works. Page 141 John T. Fowler/Alamy. Page 142 AP Images/Gene J. Puskar. Page 144 Jose Luis Pelaez, Inc/Corbis. Page 147 (top) Michael Agliolo/Imagestate. Page 147 (bottom) Jan Mueller. Page 149 (top) Innervisions. Page 149 (bottom) Vasyl Dudenko/Shutterstock. Page 150 (top left) Alexandr Vlassyuk/Shutterstock. Page 150 (top middle) ChromoSohm Media/The Image Works. Page 150 (Top right) PCN Photography/

Alamy. Page 154 Laima Druskis/Pearson Education/PH College. Page 155 David Young-Wolff/PhotoEdit. Page 158 Kevin R. Morris/Corbis. Page 159 Images-USA/Alamy. Page 161 Dexter Gormley. Page 162 Mitch Reardon/Photo Researchers, Inc. Page 163 (top) Corbis RF/Alamy. Page 164 (top) Michael Newman/PhotoEdit. Page (bottom) Petro Feketa/Shutterstock. Page 166 (top) Dr. Robert Kail. Page 166 (bottom) Jose Carillo/PhotoEdit.

CHAPTER 6 Page 170 Morgan Lane Photography/Shutterstock. Page 172 Lynne Harty Photography/Alamy. Page 174 (top) Ruth Jenkinson/Dorling Kindersley Media Library. Page 174 (bottom) Jan Mueller Images. Page 175 Richard Mittleman/Alamy. Page 176 (bottom left) Laura Dwight Photography. Page 176 (bottom center) Laura Dwight Photography. Page 176 (bottom right) Laura Dwight Photography. Page 178 Richard Hutchings/Photo Researchers Inc.. Page 182 Cindy Charles/PhotoEdit. Page 184 Elizabeth Crews Photography. Page 185 JDC/Bridge/Corbis. Page 189 Blend Images/Alamy. Page 199 Elena Yakusheva/Shutterstock.

CHAPTER 7 Page 208 Ian Shaw/Alamy. Page 210 Courtesy of Carolyn Rovee-Collier. Page 211 Dr. Robert Kail. Page 213 DonSmith/Alamy. Page 214 Corbis Super RF/Alamy. Page 217 Dr. Robert Kail. Page 218 Ted Foxx/Alamy. Page 221 Steve Shott/Dorling Kindersley. Page 225 Elizabeth Crews/The Image Works. Page 230 Wavebreakmedia Ltd/Shutterstock. Page 235 Jennie Woodcock; Reflections Photolibrary/Corbis. Page 240 Alan Oddie/PhotoEdit. Page 242 Gary Conner / PhotoLibrary.

CHAPTER 8 Page 246 Jupiterimages/BananaStock/Thinkstock. Page 253 (top) David R. Frazier Photolibrary, Inc./Alamy. Page 253 (bottom) Anna E. Zuckerman/PhotoEdit. Page 256 Bob Daemmrich/ The Image Works. Page 260 Corbis RF/Alamy. Page 262 Bob Ebbesen/Alamy. Page 265 Stockbyte/Getty Images. Page 268 Britt Erlanson/Getty Images.

CHAPTER 9 Page 276 Grublee/Shutterstock. Page 280 Bob Daemmrich/Bob Daemmrich Photography, Inc. Page 285 (top) Paul Springett 02/Alamy. Page 285 (bottom) David Young-Wolff/PhotoEdit. Page 287 Topham/The Image Works. Page 291 Pictorium/Alamy. Page 293 A. Ramey/PhotoEdit. Page 295 Judy DeLoache. Page 300 Vic Cox/PhotoLibrary. Page 302 Jan Mueller. Page 305 (top) Laura Dwight/PhotoEdit. Page 305 (bottom) Cathy Datwani.

CHAPTER 10 Page 312 Mandy Godbehear/Shutterstock. Page 314 Science Photo Library/Alamy. Page 315 Dr. Robert Kail. Page 316 Myrleen Fergueson Cate/PhotoEdit. Page 318 Tetra Images/Alamy.Page 320 Jeff Greenberg/PhotoEdit. Page 325 Big Cheese Photo/SuperStock. Page 327 Innervisions. Page 332 Mary Kate Denny/PhotoEdit. Page 333 (bottom left) Everett Waters. Page 333 (bottom center) Everett Waters. Page 333 (bottom right) Everett Waters. Page 334 Michael Newman /PhotoEdit. Page 336 Harriet Gans/The Image Works.

CHAPTER 11 Page 342 Andresr/Shutterstock. Page 344 PT Santana/Getty Images. Page 345 Comstock Images. Page 347 (top) Juice Images/Alamy. Page 347 (bottom) Cathy Datwani. Page 349 Radius Images/Alamy. Page 355 Theodore Liasi/Alamy. Page 367 Big Cheese Photo LLC/Alamy. Page 368 Robert Maass/Corbis.

CHAPTER 12 Page 372 Myrleen Ferguson Cate/PhotoEdit. Page 374 Petr Bonek/Alamy. Page 376 Laura Dwight Photography. Page 380 Tony Freeman/PhotoEdit. Page 382 Jim West/Alamy. Page 383 Myrleen Ferguson Cate/PhotoEdit. Page 388 David Young-Wolff/PhotoEdit. Page 389 AP Images/Al Behrman. Page 391 Myrleen Ferguson Cate/PhotoEdit. Page 394 Bob Ebbesen/Alamy. Page 395 Dennis MacDonald/PhotoEdit. Page 401 Jennie Woodcock; Reflections Photolibrary/Corbis.

CHAPTER 13 Page 406 Lisa F. Young/Shutterstock. Page 409 David Young-Wolff/PhotoEdit. Page 414 (top left) Radius Images/Alamy. Page 414 (top right) Laima Druskis/Pearson Education/PH. Page 416 Peter Usbeck / Alamy. Page 417 WoodyStock/Alamy. Page 419 Janine Wiedel Photolibrary/Alamy. Page 422 Annika Erickson/Blend Images/Alamy. Page 423 Sally and Richard Greenhill/Alamy. Page 429 (top) Loisjoy Thurstun/Bubbles Photolibrary/Alamy. College. Page 429 (bottom) Tony Freeman/PhotoEdit

CHAPTER 14 Page 434 Oliveromg/Shutterstock. Page 437 Ablestock/Hemera Technologies/Alamy. Page 440 Michael Newman/PhotoEdit. Page 442 James Shaffer/PhotoEdit. Page 443 Catchlight Visual Services/Alamy. Page 444 Robert Brenner/PhotoEdit. Page 450 Michael Newman/PhotoEdit. Page 452 Richard Mittleman/Alamy. Page 455 (top) Corbis Flirt/Alamy. Page 455 (bottom) Gao Feng/Imaginechina/ZUMA Press/Newscom. Page 456 Pascal Le Segretain/Getty Images. Page 457 Cindy Charles/PhotoEdit. Page 458 Cathy Melloan.

CHAPTER 15 Page 468 Yuri Arcurs/Shutterstock. Page 470 Radius/SuperStock. Page 471 Urban Zone/Alamy. Page 473 Myrleen Ferguson Cate/PhotoEdit. Page 475 Thomas Cockrem/Alamy. Page 479 Mary Kate Denny/PhotoEdit. Page 480 Jan Greune/Getty Images. Page 484 Manfred Baumann/Westend61 GmbH/Alamy. Page 487 © CTW. Courtesy: Everett Collection. Page 490 Bill Aron/PhotoEdit. Page 492 Phyllis Picardi/Photo Network/Alamy. Page 493 (top) Boulton-Wilson/Jeroboam. Page 493 (bottom) Sally and Richard Greenhill/Alamy. Page 496 Catherine Ursillo/Photo Researchers, Inc. Page 498 Alison Wright/Danita Delimont/Alamy. Page 499 Inti St. Clair/Getty Images.

CARTOONS, FIGURES AND TABLES

CHAPTER 1 Page 16 HI & LOIS © 1993 King Features Syndicate.

CHAPTER 2 Fig 2.5 Reprinted figure 1 in Plomin, R. et al. Nature, Nurture, and cognitive development from 1 to 16 years: A parent-offspring adoption study. Psychological Science, 8, 442-447. Reprinted by permission of SAGE Publications. Table 2.1 McKusick, V.A. Mendelian inheritance in man. A catalog of human genes and genetic disorders, Volume 3, 1995. The Johns Hopkins University Press. Reprinted by permission. Table 2.3 Based on Milunsky, A. (2002). Your genetic destiny: Know your genes, secure your health, and save your life. Cambridge, MA: Perseus Publishing.

CHAPTER 3 Fig 3.4 Reprinted figures 7-1 and 9-12 from Moore and Persaud: Before We Are Born (1993). Reprinted with permission from Elsevier Science. Fig 3.5 Reprinted figures 7-1 and 9-12 from Moore and Persaud: Before We Are Born (1993). Reprinted with permission from Elsevier Science.

CHAPTER 4 Fig 4.5 From J.M. Tanner (1989). Fetus into Man. Cambridge, MA: Harvard University Press. Reprinted by permission of the publisher. © 1978, 1989 by J.M. Tanner

CHAPTER 6 Fig 6.3 COOK, JOAN LITTLEFIELD; COOK, GREG. CHILD DEVELOPMENT: PRINCIPLES AND PERSPECTIVES, 2nd Edition. © 2009. Reprinted by permission of Pearson Education, Upper Saddle River, NJ.

CHAPTER 8 Fig 8.1 Carroll, J. B. (1993). Human cognitive abilities: A survey of factor-analytic studies. New York: Cambridge University Press.

CHAPTER 9 Page 283 Johnny Hart/Creators Syndicate, Inc. Table 9.1 Based on Brown, R. (1973). A first language: The early stages. Cambridge, MA: Harvard University Press.

CHAPTER 11 Fig 11.1 Offer, D., Ostrov, E., Howard, K. I., & Atkinson, R. (1988). The teenage world: Adolescents' self-image in ten countries. New York: Plenum. With kind permission from Springer Science+Business Media B.V.

CHAPTER 12 Page 374 Calvin and Hobbes © 1993 Watterson. Dist. By Universal UClick. Reprinted with permission. All rights reserved.

Name Index

Subject Index